LESS	EQUALS	LESS: PERSONAL OUTLAYS			EQUALS	PERCENT OF DISPOSABLE PERSONAL INCOME			Gross national product		Disposable personal income		
						Personal outlays			Current prices	1958 prices	Current prices	1958 prices	
Personal tax and nontax payments	Disposable personal income	Total	Personal consumption expenditures	Interest paid by consumers	Personal saving	Total	Personal consumption expenditures	Personal saving					
Billions of dollars						Percent			Per capita dollars	Billions of dollars	Per capita dollars	Billions of dollars	Year
2.6	83.3	79.1	77.2	1.5	4.2	95.0	92.7	5.0	846	204	683	150	1929
2.5	74.5	71.1	69.9	.9	3.4	95.4	93.8	4.6	734	184	605	138	1930
1.9	64.0	61.4	60.5	.7	2.6	95.9	94.4	4.1	610	169	516	134	1931
1.5	48.7	49.3	48.6	.5	-.6	101.3	99.8	-1.3	464	144	390	114	1932
1.5	45.5	46.5	45.8	.5	-.9	102.0	100.6	-2.0	442	142	362	112	1933
1.6	52.4	52.0	51.3	.5	.4	99.3	98.0	.7	514	154	414	120	1934
1.9	58.5	56.4	55.7	.5	2.1	96.3	95.2	3.7	566	170	459	132	1935
2.3	66.3	62.7	61.9	.6	3.6	94.6	93.3	5.4	644	193	518	148	1936
2.9	71.2	67.4	66.5	.7	3.8	94.7	93.4	5.3	700	203	552	153	1937
2.9	65.5	64.8	63.9	.7	.7	98.9	97.6	1.1	652	192	504	144	1938
2.4	70.3	67.7	66.8	.7	2.6	96.3	95.0	3.7	690	209	537	156	1939
2.6	75.7	71.8	70.8	.8	3.8	94.9	93.6	5.1	754	227	573	166	1940
3.3	92.7	81.7	80.6	.9	11.0	88.2	86.9	11.8	933	264	695	190	1941
6.0	116.9	89.3	88.5	.7	27.6	76.4	75.7	23.6	1,170	298	867	213	1942
17.8	133.5	100.1	99.3	.5	33.4	75.0	74.4	25.0	1,402	337	976	223	1943
18.9	146.3	109.1	108.3	.5	37.3	74.5	74.0	25.5	1,518	361	1,057	232	1944
20.9	150.2	120.7	119.7	.5	29.6	80.3	79.7	19.7	1,514	355	1,074	230	1945
18.7	160.0	144.8	143.4	.8	15.2	90.5	89.6	9.5	1,474	312	1,132	227	1946
21.4	169.8	162.5	160.7	1.1	7.3	95.7	94.6	4.3	1,605	310	1,178	218	1947
21.1	189.1	175.8	173.6	1.5	13.4	92.9	91.8	7.1	1,757	324	1,290	230	1948
18.6	188.6	179.2	176.8	1.9	9.4	95.0	93.8	5.0	1,719	324	1,264	231	1949
20.7	206.9	193.9	191.0	2.4	13.1	93.7	92.3	6.3	1,877	355	1,364	250	1950
29.0	226.6	209.3	206.3	2.7	17.3	92.4	91.0	7.6	2,128	383	1,469	256	1951
34.1	238.3	220.2	216.7	3.0	18.1	92.4	90.9	7.6	2,200	395	1,518	263	1952
35.6	252.6	234.3	230.0	3.8	18.3	92.8	91.1	7.2	2,284	413	1,583	275	1953
32.7	257.4	241.0	236.5	4.0	16.4	93.6	91.9	6.4	2,246	407	1,585	278	1954
35.5	275.3	259.5	254.4	4.7	15.8	94.3	92.4	5.7	2,408	438	1,666	297	1955
39.8	293.2	272.6	266.7	5.4	20.6	93.0	91.0	7.0	2,492	446	1,743	309	1956
42.6	308.5	287.8	281.4	5.8	20.7	93.3	91.2	6.7	2,575	452	1,801	316	1957
42.3	318.8	296.6	290.1	5.9	22.3	93.0	91.0	7.0	2,569	447	1,831	319	1958
46.2	337.3	318.3	311.2	6.5	19.1	94.4	92.3	5.6	2,731	476	1,905	333	1959
50.9	350.0	333.0	325.2	7.3	17.0	95.1	92.9	4.9	2,788	488	1,937	340	1960
52.4	364.4	343.3	335.2	7.6	21.2	94.2	92.0	5.8	2,830	497	1,984	351	1961
57.4	385.3	363.7	355.1	8.1	21.6	94.4	92.2	5.6	3,001	530	2,066	367	1962
60.9	404.6	384.7	375.0	9.1	19.9	95.1	92.7	4.9	3,118	551	2,139	381	1963
59.4	438.1	411.9	401.2	10.1	26.2	94.0	91.6	6.0	3,292	581	2,284	408	1964
65.7	473.2	444.8	432.8	11.3	28.4	94.0	91.5	6.0	3,520	618	2,436	435	1965
75.4	511.9	479.3	466.3	12.4	32.5	93.6	91.1	6.4	3,806	658	2,605	459	1966
83.0	546.3	506.0	492.1	13.2	40.4	92.6	90.1	7.4	3,985	675	2,751	478	1967
97.9	591.0	551.2	536.2	14.3	39.8	93.3	90.7	6.7	4,295	707	2,946	499	1968
116.2	634.2	596.3	579.6	15.8	37.9	94.0	91.4	6.0	4,572	725	3,130	514	1969
115.9	687.8	633.7	615.8	16.9	54.1	92.1	89.5	7.9	4,756	720	3,358	532	1970
115.8	741.2	680.8	662.2	17.7	60.4	91.9	89.3	8.1	5,057	740	3,581	551	1971

CONTEMPORARY ECONOMICS

Contemporary Economics

MILTON H. SPENCER

Professor of Economics and
Director of the Center for
Business and Economic Education,
Wayne State University

WORTH PUBLISHERS, INC.

Contemporary Economics

Copyright © 1971 by Worth Publishers, Inc.

All rights reserved. No part of this publication
may be reproduced, stored in a retrieval system,
or transmitted in any form or by any means,
electronic, mechanical, photocopying, recording,
or otherwise, without the prior written
permission of the publisher.

Printed in the United States of America

Library of Congress Catalog Card No. 74–143551

Designed by Malcolm Grear Designers, Inc.

Fifth printing June 1972

Worth Publishers, Inc.

70 Fifth Avenue

New York, New York 10011

To Roz

Preface

Economics is exciting and important. Anyone who thinks otherwise has failed to realize that economic ideas and practices have moved men to rebellion, and nations to war. All the great issues that confront us today—among them recessions, inflation, poverty, racial discrimination, urban blight, and ecological decay—have economic roots. In order to diagnose and cure these ailments, we must first understand their complex nature.

Distinguishing Features

In this book I have tried to convey a vivid sense of the pertinence and importance of economics by presenting a balanced treatment of theory, problems, and policies. A list of special features will best convey the ways in which this balance is achieved.

ORGANIZATION

The sequence of topics, from macro to micro, accords with the preferences of the great majority of instructors. Although the coverage is comprehensive, I have tried throughout to be concise. I believe that most instructors will find the book comfortable to teach from and easily adaptable to both long and short courses.

EXHIBITS AND BOXED ESSAYS

A great many charts, tables, and illustrations are employed—more than twice the number found in any other text. In addition, short boxed essays are used to highlight important ideas and provide pleasant but pertinent diversions.

PHOTOGRAPHIC ESSAYS AND HISTORICAL PICTURES

Photographic essays are presented to help drive home some of the key social issues of our time: poverty, pollution, and urban transportation. In addition, historical pictures have been included where they are particularly useful in providing an appreciation of institutions and events which have helped to shape economic history.

LEADERS IN ECONOMICS

Brief sketches of many of the great economists of the past are introduced at appropriate places (topically, not chronologically) throughout the book. This illustrated series, ranging from Aristotle to Schumpeter, helps meet the demand for materials on intellectual history at the elementary level—something long recommended by national education committees.

VIEWPOINTS

Sixteen independent essays on topics of current interest complement the chapters in which they appear. They are written to stir debate and lead students to think in fresh ways about familiar problems.

RELEVANT TOPICS

Many interesting and important topics are given

extended and simplified treatment. For example, large sections and entire chapters deal with such *macroeconomic* topics as:

inflation—cost-push, demand-pull, profit-push, wage-push, and structural

Phillips curves—theoretical and empirical, and the racial implications of anti-inflationary policy

money-supply controversy—the Monetarists versus the New Economists

ecology and pollution—facts, fallacies, and alternative solutions

military-industrial complex—its scope and power

urban problems—education, housing, transportation, black capitalism, and local finance

socialism and communism—their development and current states

Marxian economics—theory and critique

Russia and China—their achievements and failures

Similarly, some of the important *microeconomic* topics that are given more than usual coverage are:

elasticity—an extended visual (graphic) treatment

supply and demand models—numerous graphic applications to commodity taxes, subsidies, black markets, tariffs, cobweb cycles, pollution control, minimum wages, agricultural price schemes, etc.

indifference curves—an optional supplement covering elementary concepts and their uses in demand theory

market structures—emphasizing different forms, characteristics, and consequences

price discrimination—types and strategies, with illustrations and applications

welfare criteria—their implications for evaluating market structures

duopoly models—applications of oligopoly pricing

input markets—complete graphic models of how the firm buys its resources

COMPREHENSIVE CASE PROBLEMS

Optional case problems are presented covering topics of current interest. They require students to integrate several chapters, thus providing excellent vehicles for oral or written analysis and discussion.

DICTIONARY

All technical terms and concepts are defined when they are first introduced. These expressions are catalogued for ready reference in a complete dictionary of over 400 entries at the back of the book.

Supplements and Teaching Aids

Instructors will be interested to know of additional materials available with the text.

SELF-CORRECTING STUDENT'S WORKBOOK AND STUDY GUIDE—containing chapter orientations, fill-in questions, problems, practice tests, and discussion questions. Answers are included so that the student can correct his own work.

TEACHER'S MANUAL—consisting of brief pedagogical comments, suggested answers to end-of-chapter problems and cases, and answers to the Model Examinations (described below).

TEST BANK—containing 1,200 five-choice multiple-choice questions on perforated strips. The questions can be removed and rearranged in any combination, thereby permitting photo or ditto masters to be constructed for inexpensive duplication without proofreading.

MODEL EXAMINATIONS—complete master sets of attractively printed multiple-choice tests, suitable for quizzes, midterms and finals, are available. The examinations, which can be reproduced by any photo or duplicating process, consist of the most comprehensive questions selected from the *Test Bank*, thus making it unnecessary for instructors to prepare their own examinations.

Acknowledgments

It is a pleasure to acknowledge the extraordinary help and cooperation I have received from the staff of Worth Publishers. This young and vigorous firm, with its eminently successful books in several fields outside economics, is setting a new standard in textbook publishing. Economists and other social scientists will be hearing a great deal about this organization in the near future.

Special thanks go to Roger Beardwood, a distinguished economic commentator and correspondent for *Time* magazine (formerly with the London *Financial Times* and *Fortune* magazine). He edited the entire manuscript, made many suggestions for improvement, and wrote the fascinating "Viewpoint" essays, which bear his initials.

The magnificent pictures in the photographic essays are the work of Magnum, a prominent organization of some of the world's leading photographers. Magnum's archivists spent a great many hours sifting literally thousands of photographs in order to select the most appropriate ones.

Lori Patterson and Karen Oleksiak typed the many versions of the manuscript and were helpful throughout its preparation.

At various stages in the development of the manuscript a number of dedicated teachers and scholars provided their advice and criticism. Most of their opinions were synthesized for me by Ted Behr, a graduate student at the Massachusetts Institute of Technology, who also provided many thoughtful criticisms of his own. It is a privilege to mention the names of the reviewers, thank them for their comments, and absolve them of any blame for shortcomings in the final product.

JOHN R. AIDEM, Miami-Dade Junior College
CARL J. ARNOLD, Rollins College
ROBERT E. ARNOLD, JR., Henry Ford Community College
DANIEL BAILEY, University of Texas
JOE S. BAIN, University of California
HAROLD BARNETT, University of Rhode Island
PHILLIS B. BASILE, Orange Coast College
ROBERT C. BUSHNELL, Ohio State University
ELIZABETH CLAYTON, University of Missouri, St. Louis
NORISS E. CLEMENT, San Diego State College
CHARLES H. CLINE, University of Minnesota
EDWARD COEN, University of Minnesota
LEWIS A. COSER, State University of New York, Stony Brook
HELEN CRAFTON, University of Michigan
DONALD C. DARNTON, Virginia Polytechnic Institute
KENNETH DEITCH, Harvard University
LOUIS A. DOW, University of Houston
MATTHEW EDEL, Massachusetts Institute of Technology
ALFRED S. EICHNER, Columbia University
HENRY E. FINLEY, Florida A & M University
MELVIN FREDLUND, Wayne State University
JOHN KENNETH GALBRAITH, Harvard University
HERBERT GINTIS, Harvard University
CLIFTON GRUBBS, University of Texas
JOHN HARDESTY, San Diego State College
ROBERT HORTON, Purdue University
LOVELL JARVIS, University of California

Wylie Logan Jones, Bakersfield College
Richard J. Kiesewetter, American River College
William P. Kinney, Foothill College
Sylvia Lane, University of California, Davis
Lawrence F. Mansfield, University of Miami
Jesse W. Markham, Harvard University
E. Scott McCuskey, St. Petersburg Junior College
Lee J. Melton, Jr., Louisiana State University
Don Morehead, Henry Ford Community College
Daniel G. Morgan, University of Texas
S. Floyd Mori, Chabot College
Dean Morse, Columbia University
Ernest Nadel, University of California
Angela Nation, Santa Fe Junior College (Florida)
Harvey Nussbaum, Wayne State University
Richard E. Pasternak, University of South Florida

Nicholas S. Perna, Williams College
Elizabeth H. Piersol, St. Petersburg Junior College
Stuart Schweitzer, Wayne State University
Howard Sherman, University of California, Riverside
Gerald Sirkin, City College of New York
Anthony H. Stocks, Youngstown State University
Myra H. Strober, University of Maryland
Arthur A. Thompson, University of Alabama
Norman Townshend-Zellner, Cal. St. College, Fullerton
Harold Watts, University of Wisconsin
Ralph E. Worthington, St. Petersburg Junior College

MILTON H. SPENCER
Detroit, Michigan
January 1971

CONTENTS IN BRIEF

Contents

Suggested Outlines for One Semester Courses

These recommendations are flexible. Many other chapter combinations are possible.

Chapter Topic	Macro-economic Emphasis	Micro-economic Emphasis	Balanced Macro/Micro Emphasis	Problems and Policy Emphasis
1. What Is Economics?	○	○	○	○
2. Resources & Goals	○	○	○	○
3. Capitalism & The Price System	○	○	○	○
4. "Laws" Of Supply & Demand	○	○	○	○
5. Private Sector: Households, Businesses	○	○	○	
Supplement: Financial Statements *(Optional)*				
6. Public Sector: Government				
7. National Income & Product	○	○	○	○
8. Business Cycles, Unemployment, Inflation	○	○	○	○
9. Consumption, Saving, Investment	○	○	○	○
10. Income & Employment Determination	○	○	○	○
11. Business Cycle Analysis: Multiplier-Accelerator				
12. Fiscal Policy	○	○	○	○
13. Money & Credit	○	○	○	○
14. Banking, Federal Reserve, Monetary Policy	○	○	○	○
15. Synthesis Of Fiscal & Monetary Policy	○	○	○	
16. The Monetarists versus The New Economists	□			
17. Explanations Of Economic Growth	□			
18. Problems Of Economic Growth	□		□	□
19. Ecology & The Economics of Pollution	○	○	○	○
Comprehensive Case Problems *(Optional)*				
20. Supply & Demand: Applications	○	○	○	○
(can follow ch. 4 if desired)				
21. Further Applications: Supply & Demand				
Supplement: Indifference Curves *(Optional)*				
22. Costs Of Production		□	□	
23. Perfect Competition		□	□	
24. Monopoly Behavior		□	□	
25. Imperfect Competition		□	□	
26. Factor Markets: Marginal Productivity				
27. Determination Of Factor Prices				
28. Business & Government				
29. Labor Unions & Industrial Relations				
30. Social Welfare: Insecurity, Poverty				□
31. Agricultural Decline				
32. Urban Crises	□			□
33. International Trade				
34. International Finance				□
35. International Policies				
36. Less Developed Countries				
37. Socialism And Communism				
38. Russia And China				
Comprehensive Case Problems *(Optional)*				

○ = Common core of chapters
□ = Chapters for kinds of emphasis desired

CHAPTER 1

What Is Economics?
What Do Economists Do?

CHAPTER PREVIEW

What is economics, and why should you study it?

How does economics relate to other social sciences?

Is economics theoretical? Is it practical?

What are the pitfalls to straight thinking in economics?

This is a book about a subject that has a long and curious history. It deals with ideas that have swayed the minds of kings and presidents, statesmen and politicians, philosophers and laymen. It surveys principles and practices that have shaped the domestic and foreign policies of nations as well as the everyday working lives of their citizens. It explores the main features of a discipline which over its hundreds of years of existence has attracted its fair share of brilliant minds, but has also experienced no shortage of crackpots and cranks. Perhaps most significant, it concerns an activity in which nearly everyone is engaged but about which relatively few have any knowledge.

You can master a new subject more readily once you have some notion of what it is about. The above Preview suggests the framework of ideas to be found in this chapter.

What Is Economics About?

Man's survival has always been hazardous. From the beginning he has faced the natural dangers of disease, rival animals, and the challenge of producing enough food and shelter to maintain the growing human population. Those hazards still endanger survival in the poor nations—and threaten the poor inhabitants of rich countries.

The rich nations—the United States, most European countries, and Japan—are oases of plenty in a world of want. But they face dangers created by their wealth. Their well-being, and perhaps their survival, is challenged by air and water pollution, ecological decay, and the overcrowding of major cities.

Everyone is affected by those problems; every day we are asked to express an opinion on them, sometimes by demonstrating and sometimes by voting. We are flooded with information and advice; some of it right and much of it wrong.

Economics helps us to form valid opinions. It is both a body of knowledge and a method of reasoning. It will not provide many ready-made answers, but it will give us the tools we need to reach the answers we seek.

THE MEANING OF ECONOMICS

Experts in any area, from anthropology to zoology, are usually reluctant to define their field for fear of what their definition might omit. Nevertheless, students beginning the study of a subject like to have a concise description of its nature and content. The following is a modern definition of economics:

Economics is a social science concerned chiefly with the way society chooses to employ its limited resources, which have alternative uses, to produce goods and services for present and future consumption.

More specifically, economics describes and analyzes the nature and behavior of an economy. It explores the ways in which economic systems of different types—whether capitalistic, communistic or socialistic—organize their limited human and material resources to meet people's individual wants for such things as food, clothing, shelter, and recreation, and society's collective wants for such things as education, transportation, and sanitation. To put it in a nutshell, *economics is broadly concerned with the production and delivery of a rising standard of living.*

The word "economy" comes from the Greek *oikonomia*, which means the management of a household or state. We say that someone is economical when he is frugal in the expenditure of money or

FOR CLASS DISCUSSION

(*a*) According to your understanding of the term "standard of living," is it a spiritual and cultural as well as material concept? (*b*) Do you think economics has anything to say about spiritual and cultural values? Explain your answer.

in the utilization of materials. When we speak of an economy (whether it be the American or the Russian economy, the economy of New England or of Chicago) we are referring to the ways in which a community manages its limited resources.

To say that resources are limited means simply this: people want more goods and services than there are means to produce them—human labor, machines, natural resources. An economy's resources are therefore *scarce* relative to society's demands, and hence people must make *choices* involving the most effective ways of utilizing those limited resources.

Who declares what, how much, and for whom society's human and material resources should be used to produce the goods that are wanted? We shall see in later chapters that in some economic systems, like those of Russia and Mainland China, these choices are made by government decree or command; in others, such as the United States and Canada, they are made primarily through the interaction of buyers and sellers in the marketplace; and in still others, like England and Sweden, they are made by substantial mixtures of both.

In view of this, you can think of the different economic systems in the world as being distributed along a horizontal line ranging from what might be called predominantly centralized or *command economies* at one extreme to predominantly decentralized or *market economies* at the other, with various shades of *mixed economies* in between. This is illustrated by the diagram in Exhibit 1, representing most of the major nations and regions of the world. The ideas underlying this diagram will be more fully developed in later chapters. In the meantime, from what you already know about history and world affairs, and on the basis of what was said

Exhibit 1

Market Economies versus Command Economies (by countries and regions)

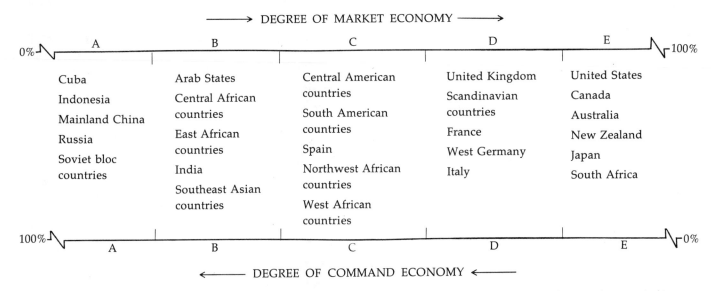

→ DEGREE OF MARKET ECONOMY →

	A	B	C	D	E	
0%	Cuba	Arab States	Central American countries	United Kingdom	United States	100%
	Indonesia	Central African countries	South American countries	Scandinavian countries	Canada	
	Mainland China	East African countries	Spain	France	Australia	
	Russia	India	Northwest African countries	West Germany	New Zealand	
	Soviet bloc countries	Southeast Asian countries	West African countries	Italy	Japan	
					South Africa	

| 100% | A | B | C | D | E | 0% |

← DEGREE OF COMMAND ECONOMY ←

Note the scale breaks on the upper and lower lines. This is to emphasize the fact that countries cannot be graded precisely by placing them at some particular point on the scale. At best we can try to rank them by groups, thus permitting us to say: Group A countries are more command-oriented or less market-oriented than Group B countries; Group B countries are more command-oriented or less market-oriented than Group C countries; and so on.

Of course, the countries within each group also vary. And in many of these countries and regions there are still large pockets of "traditional" economies—that is, primitive areas where economic activity is extremely simple and exchange is carried on by barter. This is especially true in some of the areas that comprise Groups A, B and C. But it is also found in certain countries in Group E, such as parts of Australia and South Africa.

above, can you make a stab at answering the questions at right about Exhibit 1?

Every economy operates within a framework of rules and regulations. Public utilities must establish their rates with the approval of governmental agencies; restaurants have to be licensed in order to sell food; doctors must be graduates of approved medical schools if they are to practice medicine; sellers of commodities are legally forbidden to engage in false advertising. These are only a few of the many rules that exist in our economy. All of the laws, regulations, customs, and practices taken together, and their relationships to the components of an economy such as its firms, households, and government, constitute an *economic system*. Thus capitalism, socialism, and communism are economic systems.

SOMETHING TO THINK ABOUT

On the basis of Exhibit 1, above:

1. Are there any "pure" command economies or market economies?

2. From your knowledge of history, how would you classify a slave economy? Can you describe the nature of the American economy during most of the nineteenth century?

3. Would you say that there may be a connection between economic freedom and political freedom (i.e., can a command economy be a political democracy? Can a market economy be a political dictatorship)?

ARISTOTLE

384–322 B.C.

The "First" Economist

The greatest scholar of antiquity was the Greek philosopher Aristotle. At the age of seventeen he went to Athens to study under Plato, and remained until the great teacher's death about twenty years later. He was then invited by Philip of Macedonia to serve as tutor for his son—who later became Alexander the Great. Aristotle subsequently returned to Athens and founded a school in the Lyceum which he conducted for twelve years. During the anti-Macedonian reaction in 323 B.C., he was forced into exile in Chalcis by a prosecution for impiety; he died the following year.

Aristotle is regarded as the first analytical economist, although he also made major contributions to ethics, logic, metaphysics, politics, rhetoric, history, psychology, and the natural sciences. Indeed, he is the founder of many sciences. His philosophy was later adopted by both Islamic and Catholic scholars. During the Middle Ages it was considered heretical to question Aristotelian doctrines.

Most of Aristotle's views on economic issues are in two of his books, Politics *and the* Nicomachean Ethics. *Among the topics he discussed are the principles of value and exchange, the division of labor, and the theory of money, interest, and usury. Since he was a product of the small Greek city-state, and was concerned with the economic problems he saw about him, he was sometimes led to oversimplification and generalization. Nevertheless, he understood the nature and importance of trade and commerce, and the necessity for money as a "sort of medium or mean" of exchange, and a "standard [of measurement and value] upon which the world agrees." As we shall see, these and certain other of Aristotle's explanations are as modern and relevant as if they had been written today.*

One of his major contributions was to the economic theory of value. "Of everything we possess," he wrote, "there are two uses: both belonging to the thing as such, but not in the same manner: one is the proper and the other the improper or secondary use of it. For example, a shoe is used for wear and for exchange: both are uses of the shoe." Aristotle thus recognized that a commodity may have both use value and exchange value, or subjective and objective value, as we say today.

In contrast, Aristotle's views on retail trade and on usury are of interest. He opposed both because they permit the accu-

mulation of unlimited wealth by "unnatural" means. The "natural" way to gain wealth, according to Aristotle, is by skillful management of the house and land. This limits the amount of wealth that can be gained. As for usury (which, like other scholars of antiquity, he defined as the charging of any interest on loans), it "makes a gain out of money itself, and not from the natural objects of it. Money was intended to be used in exchange, not to increase at interest . . . Of all modes of getting wealth this is the most unnatural."

Some of Aristotle's beliefs, especially on usury, appeared in biblical teachings. His ideas greatly influenced Arabian and Jewish philosophers after the 9th century, and his writings became the basis of Christian philosophical thought during the Middle Ages.

We shall be studying these systems in later chapters, but at the present time you might want to look up their definitions in the dictionary at the back of this book.

WHY STUDY ECONOMICS?

Economics is for people who like to climb "mountains." This book will guide you to the foothills, but the climb will be up to you. When you reach the peak and look back, you will see many intriguing and challenging questions. Here are a few examples:

Why is the American standard of living among the highest in the world, while poverty exists in many areas of the country?

What will business conditions be like next year, and what should the government do—if anything—to alter the situation?

How do changes in tax rates, the supply of money in the economy, or the level of interest rates affect businessmen's decisions to produce commodities or to build new factories? Do these decisions also affect consumers? Lenders? Workers?

Do capitalistic countries have to experience sharp changes in their levels of income and employment? Do socialistic countries avoid these problems and thereby experience greater stability in their economies?

Is it possible for our economy to have the best of all possible economic worlds: a healthy rate of economic growth with continuous full employment, stable prices, and an equitable distribution of income, all within a framework of democratic free enterprise?

In economics, asking good questions rates almost as high as answering them. This brief list suggests the questions you will encounter. Some of them may not mean too much to you at this time. However, the purpose of this book is to help you discuss these problems intelligently.

Some people think economics is a study of how to make money, or a guide for becoming a success in business. This is false. Economics usually examines problems from society's point of view—not from that of a particular individual or businessman. Of course, at some later date you may end up in the business world, or in government, or in one of the professions, and then you may feel that a familiarity with basic economics has made you better at your job than you would otherwise have been. However, regardless of the career you pursue, a knowledge of economics will make you a far more effective citizen, and this alone justifies the time devoted to its study.

ECONOMICS IS A SOCIAL SCIENCE

Is economics a science or an art? A dictionary will tell you that "science" involves the accumulation, classification, and systematization of knowledge for the purpose of discovering fundamental principles or the operation of general laws. "Art," in the sense used here, pertains to the skillful execution of a task or the application of a procedure. In the final analysis, economics is concerned with both the scientific development of economic principles and their artful application to the solution of real-world problems. Hence an important conclusion:

Economics is both a science and an art; it is a science in its methodology and an art in its application.

Since economics deals with the activities of society, it is a *social* science intimately related to other social or behaviorial sciences—history, political science, psychology, and sociology. We shall discover many examples of this in future chapters.

PRINCIPLES = LAWS; THEORIES = MODELS

Every science seeks to describe reality by simplifying it. Economics is no exception. When you simplify something you draw out its essential qualities or characteristics.

For example, suppose you wanted to study the economic factors that affect the spending patterns of students at your school. You would not merely list all the students along with their expenditures and leave it at that, because then you would have nothing more than a detailed description. Instead, you would try to single out the main features common to all, and thus draw an economic picture of the student body as a whole. This picture probably would not be a perfect representation of any particular student; but it would presumably be representative of all. You might then formulate some generalizations in the form of *principles* or *laws* that would help to explain, or perhaps even predict, students' spending patterns.

This method is known as *induction*—a process of reasoning from particular observations to general conclusions. The result is a simplified picture of reality, and may be called a *theory*.

A theory may be expressed in various ways—by words, graphs, diagrams, mathematical equations, or by combinations of these. Very often a theory may be referred to as a *model*. Regardless of what they are called, all economic principles, laws, theories, and models have this much in common: they are generalizations or idealizations about economic behavior, and they are derived by a process of abstracting from reality.

Good representations of real-world phenomena may be used to explain occurrences or perhaps even to make predictions. This is the method known as *deduction*—a process of reasoning from general assumptions or statements to particular conclusions. Of course, a scientist will then *verify* his conclusions by returning to his original facts and seeing whether the occurrences and predictions are correct. This entire cycle of induction, deduction, and verification constitutes the framework of the *scientific method.* The process characterizes sound thinking in all fields of knowledge.

The possibility that economic principles may be used for making predictions deserves some explanation. In economics, as in all social and physical sciences, the relationship between variables may not always be perfect. For one thing the scientist is likely to make some errors in his observation of phenomena; for another he will almost always leave out (inadvertently or otherwise) some information or data that exert an influence—though it may be slight—on the events being studied. Therefore, a scientist tries to develop principles that can be used to make predictions "on the average," and which will hold with some known *margin of error* based on statistical probabilities.

THE ELEGANCE OF THEORY

One of the highest compliments you can pay an economist (or any scholar for that matter) is to say that his theory is "elegant" or "beautiful." The notion of what constitutes beauty may be as hard to define in a theory as it is in a pretty girl. All it really means is that the ideas which make up the theory are interesting, and they are woven together in a harmonious way.

However, the elegance of a theory is also affected by the quality of its structure—that is, the elements of which it is composed. Basically, every theory consists of three sets of elements:

1. *Definitions,* which state clearly the meaning of the various terms in the theory.

2. *Assumptions,* which define the conditions under which the theory holds.

3. *Hypotheses,* which serve as working guesses about the way things actually behave, or about relationships between things in the real world. (In economics, the "things" about which hypotheses might be formulated include consumers, workers, businessmen, investors, government, households, business firms, and other economic organisms).

The quality and usefulness of a theory depend on the way these elements are put together. The construction of useful theories or their representation by meaningful models is one of the chief goals of all scientists.

A theory or model, since it is a simplification of reality, usually fits the observed facts approximately rather than exactly. Hence the theory may fail to incorporate newly discovered facts, in which case it may have to be revised or perhaps discarded. In physics, Einstein's theory of relativity is an example of a model which has revised and partly replaced the model of Newton. Similarly, in economics there are new theories which have revised and replaced older ones.

If economic theories or models are simplifications, does this mean they are unrealistic and impractical? Most emphatically not! Whenever a scientist in any field observes a segment of the real world, he must impose order on his observations; otherwise they will be hardly more than a confusing jumble of facts and ideas. Theories are the means by which these facts and ideas are brought together and related in a meaningful way. A theory can thus be likened in certain respects to a road map. A valid theory, like a valid road map, must be up to date, and must be based on facts in order to be realistic and useful. However, if it is too detailed it will be confusing; if it is insufficiently detailed it will be inadequate as a guide.

WHAT DO ECONOMISTS DO?

What will happen if Congress approves a 5 percent increase in personal income taxes? Will the increase in taxes take purchasing power out of the hands of consumers and thus cause them to reduce their spending? If consumers spend less, will prices fall? Will a decrease in production cause greater unemployment?

These questions—and many others in such areas as national defense, health, crime, the arts, poverty, transportation, etc.—are typical of the problems economists try to solve. Of course, in finding solutions, they become involved in formulating economic principles or theories which may then serve as a means for prediction and, hopefully, for control. For example, if economists can predict future changes of such variables as prices, employment, and spending, they can make recommendations to government officials, who in turn may use these suggestions as a basis for economic policies. Can you suggest some ways in which economists can be of use not only to the federal government, but also to state and local governments? To industry? To trade unions?

The questions that interest economists and the viewpoints they adopt are of great importance for society. Of course, economists do not always agree on the best way to implement policy decisions, and in this respect they are no different from most other experts. Engineers, for example, do not always agree on the best way to build a bridge; doctors are not always unanimous on the best way to treat a patient; and even in mathematics and physics, which students often think of as the most "exact" of all the sciences, the experts often disagree on the answers to advanced questions. But most economists, like scientists in other fields, are in remarkably close agreement on fundamental principles. [*Question:* Much of economics can be expressed in mathematical form. Does this make it more scientific?]

VALUE JUDGMENTS

When an economist steps out of the realm of economic facts and theories, he enters the world of economic policy. This does not mean his role as a scientist ceases to exist; he simply shifts his emphasis from "positive" economics, which concerns what *is*, to "normative" economics, which concerns what *ought to be*.

If you and I disagree over positive statements in economics, we should be able to settle our controversy by logical thinking and an appeal to the facts. But if we disagree over normative statements, we are disagreeing over value judgments—statements about what is "good" and what is "bad," what is "right" and what is "wrong"—and we may not be able to reach an agreement because our views are based on a complex mixture of philosophical, social, and cultural factors.

A few examples illustrate this point. The statement, "A 10 percent tax increase on individuals and corporations will reduce the rate of increase in consumer prices to 1.5 percent a year," is a positive statement because it can be tested by empirical research. Likewise the question, "How much should the government spend, holding tax rates constant, in order to keep unemployment from rising to more than 3.5 percent of the labor force?" is a positive question. However, the statement that "unemployment should be a problem of greater concern than inflation" is a normative statement, and the question, "Should we have more economic freedom or more government regulation?" is a normative question.

Most of the questions and problems in economics deal with positive rather than normative matters. But many normative questions pertaining to economic policy are of enormous significance. Indeed, the normative issues are sometimes the most interesting and exciting parts of the subject.

Hard Truths, Soggy Facts

One night recently several American and English economists were lingering over brandy at a London club. Agreeing that the world was in a bad way, they started trying to find collective nouns to describe the people responsible. They agreed on a "broadside" of admirals, a "brass" of generals, an "hypocrisy" of politicians, and a "grasp" of businessmen. "But how do we describe ourselves?" asked one of the economists. "Ah," said another, "that's easy. We are a *confusion* of economists."

The story points to an ironic truth. Economists are able to influence and sometimes to make policy; but too often events stubbornly refuse to confirm their judgments. In the late 1960s, for example, the United States government clamped down on credit, held back its own spending, and confidently forecast that the result would be a fall in the rate of inflation. As it turned out, the measures taken—all recommended by some of the most influential and reputable economists—helped to force the economy into a recession, while merely denting the rate of inflation.

Perceiving Patterns

How could reputable professional economists be so confounded? The answer is that economics is still an imprecise discipline. Different economists, observing the same data, will perceive different patterns, and therefore recommend different policies. Out of those differences, and the clash of ideas, intellectual progress is born. Unfortunately, the debate is public, and is to laymen an astonishing spectacle. After all, biochemists do not disagree on the front pages, and the medical profession usually maintains a monolithic unanimity in public.

Part of the problem is that economics claims to be a science. The claim is somewhat misleading: Economists use the scientific method, but cannot test their hypotheses against reality in the laboratory, as practitioners of the physical sciences can. Furthermore, they can never isolate two or more sets of identical phenomena, subject them to varying stimuli, and then compare the results. No two people are identical, no two groups of people are identical, and no two economies are identical.

Ultimately, much of the social sciences rests on a series of value judgments. We should not shy away from that realization. Value judgments are not intrinsically bad—they are your views and everybody else's. They become bad, in the sense of being misleading, when they masquerade as objective fact. And masquerade they sometimes do. In determining the health of the economy, for example, experts rely heavily on the unemployment rate. This is published monthly, and shows the percentage of the total labor force that was jobless in the preceding month. But does it really report the actual number of jobless people? It does not. The rate is the result of sample interviews conducted in households and a study of labor statistics reported by the Federal–State Unemployment Services.

An Aid In Policy Making

Two things need to be said here. First, only 20 percent of the work force is eligible to register as unemployed in some states. Second, the choice of households in which interviews are conducted is clearly the result of a value judgment—a judgment that the sample used is an accurate cross-section of America.

The point is far from academic. The rate of unemployment is widely used as an aid in economic forecasting, and thus in the formulation of policy.

Because it relies in part on methods and terminology inherited from the physical sciences, economics is replete with laws. Conventionally, economists describe these laws as positive or behavioristic: they describe what happens, not what ought to happen, which is the province of normative statements. In fact, the distinction is more semantic than real. For example, the proposition that "removal of import restrictions increases total economic welfare in a nation" is clearly normative: the connotations of the term "welfare" cannot be denied, even though the term is technical. Of course, one could rewrite the proposition to read: "The removal of import restrictions will tend to increase total real national output." But even in that form the proposition is normative because it implies that free trade is more beneficial than restricted trade.

If economic data are sometimes unreliable, and economic laws operate erratically, of what value is economics? Paradoxically, its usefulness is great: Whatever its shortcomings, it is the only analytical method that enables us to understand and control economic phenomena. The great economist must be a skeptic as well as a visionary; be a master of detail as well as a painter of the broad canvas; and a shrewd analyst of human behavior as well as of economic phenomena.

R. B.

Even if economic theory were devoid of value judgments, could economic policy ever be?

Six Common Fallacies in Economic Thinking

"He who enlists a man's mind wields a power even greater than the sword." This familiar quotation, although centuries old, is particularly pertinent to economics. For the ideas of economists, whether they are right or wrong, can sometimes shape and sway the world. Indeed, there have been some economic philosophers whose extraordinary ideas have helped to undermine governments and to inspire revolutions—both intellectual and bloody. It follows that if the pen can in fact be mightier than the sword, the ability to reason correctly is necessary to avoid pitfalls in economic thinking.

You will encounter the word "fallacy" in at least two different ways. In everyday conversation, it designates any mistaken idea or false belief, like the "fallacy" of believing that all people are honorable. But in a stricter sense "fallacy" means an error in reasoning or argument. Of course, an argument may be so incorrect that it deceives no one. But for our purposes it seems more useful to reserve the term "fallacy" for certain types of arguments which, although incorrect, are nevertheless persuasive. By familiarizing yourself with the following typical fallacies in economic thinking you will be able to pinpoint the errors in other people's reasoning as well as your own.

1. Fallacy of Criticizing the Man (*ad Hominem* Fallacy)

This fallacy is committed when, instead of trying to disprove the truth of an assertion, one attacks the person who made the assertion. This amounts to criticizing the individual instead of his ideas. Hence the full Latin name of this fallacy is *argumentum ad hominem,* the literal translation of which is "argument directed to the man."

The use of this argument is fallacious because a man's personal character or circumstances are logically irrelevant to the truth or falsehood of his statements or the correctness or incorrectness of his views. Of course, such arguments may often per-

suade, but they will do so for emotional rather than logical reasons.

Thus, to argue that an economic policy is bad or wrong *solely* because it was proposed by a "liberal" or by a "conservative," by a union leader or by a manager, by a white or by a black, by a Democrat or by a Republican, is to commit the *ad hominem* fallacy. A man's proposals should be judged on their own merits, independent of his political or social beliefs or his economic circumstances.

2. Fallacy of Appeal to the People (*ad Populum* Fallacy)

This fallacy, the complete Latin name of which is *argumentum ad populum,* is frequently employed as an emotional appeal "to the people" or "to the gallery" for the purpose of arousing the feelings and enthusiasm of the multitude. It is widely used by propagandists, demagogues, editorialists, and politicians to mobilize public sentiment for or against a particular measure—without presenting reliable evidence upon which to base a rational argument.

Advertising is one of the fields in which the *ad populum* fallacy is often encountered. If consumers buy a product because the maker advertises "10 million housewives can't be wrong," they are succumbing to the *ad populum* fallacy. General acceptance of an idea or widespread assent to a claim does not prove it to be true.

3. Fallacy of Appeal to Authority (*ad Verecundiam* Fallacy)

The fallacy of appeal to authority occurs when one attempts to support a conclusion by seeking the endorsement of a person who is *not* an authority on the subject. If a friend of yours supports his views on economics solely by saying that his uncle, a prominent businessman, agrees with them, he may be committing the fallacy of *argumentum ad verecundiam.* However, if your friend's uncle, aside from being a successful businessman, has investigated the issue carefully and objectively before coming to a conclusion, the argument may be correct.

The basic question, of course, is what makes a person an "authority" in a particular field. His education and experience are factors to consider; recognition and acceptance by other professionals in the field is another test. Despite these tangible criteria, students sometimes accept an economic conclusion simply because they "read it in the paper" or because some self-proclaimed "expert" said it was true.

The most valuable lesson you can learn from your first course in economics is the habit of thinking for yourself, analytically and critically, about economic issues.

4. Fallacy of False Cause (*Post Hoc Ergo Propter Hoc Fallacy*)

Every science tries to establish cause-and-effect relationships. The fallacy of false cause, or the *post hoc ergo propter hoc* fallacy, is committed when a person mistakenly attributes the wrong cause to an effect, or when he assumes that one event is the cause of another solely because the first event occurred before the second.

The fallacy of false cause may be illustrated by the following "if-then" form of argument, or variation of it:

If *A* occurs, then *B* occurs.
Therefore *A* causes *B*.

Is this good grounds for concluding that *A* causes *B*? Not necessarily. There are other possible explanations:

B may occur by chance.
B may be caused by factors other than *A* (or by a third factor *C* which is a common cause of both *A* and *B*.)
B may cause *A*.

Some possibilities are illustrated in the following examples:

EXAMPLE 1. Wisconsin has a higher per capita consumption of milk and a higher incidence of death from cancer than any other state.
Therefore, milk is a cause of cancer.

This argument is obviously a "false cause" or *post hoc* fallacy. It fails to point out that longevity in Wisconsin is relatively high compared with other states, and cancer is a cause of death in later years.

EXAMPLE 2. The severity of hay fever varies inversely with the price of corn. That is, the lower the price of corn, the greater the severity of hay fever and vice versa.
Therefore, the price of corn is the cause of hay fever.

It is indeed true that the price of corn and the severity of hay fever are inversely related. However, the fact is that ragweed is a cause of hay fever, and the summer conditions that will produce a bumper crop of ragweed—namely high temperatures and adequate rainfall—will also produce a bumper crop of corn and hence usually a lower price of corn. Thus it may *seem* as if corn prices affect hay fever; in reality these factors are independent of each other and there is a third factor which is a common cause of both.

Many cause-and-effect relationships in economics are subtle and by no means self-evident. By studying the subject you will learn to recognize these relationships and to avoid the fallacy of "false cause."

5. Fallacy of Special Pleading

When someone gives only the reasons which support his views, he is committing the fallacy of special pleading. This fallacy is illustrated by the following paragraph from a newspaper editorial:

> Gambling should be legalized in our state just as it is in Nevada. This would encourage more tourists to visit and spend their money here, and the state would benefit from a rich source of new revenue. Further, these increased revenues could be used to finance the construction of new schools and hospitals, thus providing some relief for citizens who are now paying for these items through various local and state taxes.

This argument fails to take into account the economic reasons for *not* legalizing gambling. For example, law-enforcement agencies might have to be expanded, and new administrative facilities established to supervise gambling. Further, undesirable moral implications might be attached to legalized gambling. These are called *social* costs because of their adverse effect on society as a whole. Thus there are usually many sides to an argument, and all should be evaluated before a judgment is made.

6. Fallacies of Composition and Division

Two fallacies are involved here. The *fallacy of composition* is committed when one reasons that what is true of the parts of a whole is also true of the whole. An example would be to argue that since individuals A, B, C, D . . . are excellent ball players, a team composed of these individuals is sure to win the season's championship. The error in this reasoning, of course, is based on the fact that a successful team requires its members to be not only good players, but also able to work well together as a group.

The converse of the fallacy of composition is the fallacy of division. The *fallacy of division* is committed when one contends that something which is true only of the whole is also true of its parts taken separately. Thus you would be committing the fallacy of division if you inferred that because a certain book is difficult to understand, every paragraph or page is difficult to understand. The following true statements provide illustrations from economics:

1. If prices in one industry were to increase tomorrow by X percent, the firms in that industry might find themselves better off. However, if prices of *everything throughout the economy* were to increase tomorrow by X percent, no one would be better off.

2. There are periods when a *general* increase in taxes is beneficial for the economy as a whole. Yet an increase in taxes may at times be damaging to particular persons and businesses.

3. A man who is unemployed but wants to work may be able to find a job by looking hard or by offering his services for less. However, *all* unemployed people who want to work cannot find jobs in this way.

4. Economic policies that may be wise for a *nation* are not necessarily wise for an *individual,* and vice versa.

To repeat: Each of the above statements is true, despite the possibility that each may seem to be contradictory. One of the main objectives of this book is to clear up these and many other paradoxes by learning how to think straight about economic problems and issues.

Microeconomics and Macroeconomics

The fallacies of composition and division suggest that the subject of economics might be "sliced" into two parts: one of these is called *microeconomics;* the other, *macroeconomics.*

1. *Microeconomics* studies and theorizes about the specific economic units or parts that make up an economic system, and the relationships between these parts. Thus, microeconomics examines the individual and interrelated behavior of particular firms, industries, and households. In analyzing microeconomic problems, economists are concerned with such things as consumer demand for a *specific* product, the cost to a business firm of a *particular* volume of production, the price per unit that a firm charges for a *specific* volume of its output, and so on.

2. *Macroeconomics* studies and theorizes about the economy as a whole, or large subdivisions of it. Hence macroeconomics analyzes data and behavior at a total or aggregate level as distinct from an individual level. In discussing macroeconomic problems, economists talk about such things as the *total* volume of output, the *general* level of prices, the *total* level of income, the *total* level of expenditure, and so on.

In short, microeconomics examines the trees, whereas macroeconomics studies the forest. The differences between the two are related to the fallacies of composition and division in the following way:

The *fallacy of composition* warns us that what is true of the parts is not necessarily true of the whole; hence generalizations made at the microeconomic level may not always be true at the macroeconomic level. The *fallacy of division* warns us that what is true of the whole is not necessarily true of the parts; hence generalizations made at the macroeconomic level may not always be true at the microeconomic level.

These fallacies may seem "obvious" when they appear in a textbook; but they can be remarkably subtle in many real-world discussions of economic problems.

SUMMARY OF IMPORTANT IDEAS

1. There are many definitions of economics, but the most common one today would define it in terms of a question: How does society utilize its scarce human and material resources, which have alternative uses, to produce goods and services for present and future consumption? Economics is thus seen to be concerned in a broad sense with the production and delivery of a rising standard of living.

2. Economics is both a science and an art, and is studied for several reasons:

a. It provides us with a better knowledge of society and its behavior.

b. It helps us to render intelligent decisions about economic issues and policies.

c. A knowledge of basic economics is not a guarantee of success in business, but it familiarizes us with the economic environment within which business operates.

3. Economic activity consists of people and institutions carrying on the processes of production, exchange, distribution, and consumption of goods and services. In economics we study these processes by induction, deduction, and verification.

a. The *inductive* method carries us from actual observations of the real world to the formation of general principles based on this factual knowledge.

b. The *deductive* method proceeds by logical analysis of what these general principles indicate about the occurrences or predictions of particular events.

c. The *verification* process consists of returning to the facts and, through experiment and observation, checking both the occurrences and the accuracy of the predictions.

This cycle is known as the "scientific method." The general principles derived are known as "laws," and they are closely related to "models," or "theories." These form the skeleton of economics.

4. Economic principles have several important characteristics:

a. They are not always as exact as certain elementary laws of physics, chemistry, or engineering. That is, economic predictions often tend to hold only "on the average," with many cases occurring within a given margin of error above and below the average. Thus you can almost always find some exceptions to a prediction based on an economic law.

b. Economic laws are good approximations, and there are many important principles and regularities in economics. This is why various social scientists in other fields have often said that economics is the "most scientific" of the social sciences.

c. Economic principles are simplified models of reality. They are particularly useful as a guide to the prediction and control of economic events; and they serve as a basis for formulating and evaluating economic policies.

FOR HOMEWORK AND DISCUSSION

1. *Terms and concepts to review:*

economics	induction
command economy	deduction
mixed economy	verification
market economy	scientific method
economic system	hypothesis
theory	positive economics
model	normative economics
principle	microeconomics
law	macroeconomics

2. "Everyone knows that the United States is the richest country in the world. Therefore, the definition of economics given in the chapter may be correct for poor countries, but certainly not for America where the problem is one of abundance, not scarcity." True or false? Explain.

3. How would you evaluate the following statements?

a. "The American economic system is the best in the world."

b. "America is great because it is good, and when it ceases to be good it will cease to be great."

4. "One of the most fundamental requirements of a science is that it contain principles or laws which can serve as a basis for prediction. Therefore, economics (as opposed to physics) is not a science because you can find exceptions and even contradictions to virtually every economic principle." Evaluate.

5. Senator Jason is campaigning for a tax reduction. He argues that tax cuts in other major industrial nations have stimulated their rapid economic growth. Senator Blaine replies that what happens in nations thousands of miles away is no guide to what will happen here. Do you agree with Senator Blaine? Explain.

6. Economics, like all social sciences, deals with human behavior. Since human behavior is not predictable, economic principles cannot be used for making predictions. True or false? Explain.

7. Distinguish between descriptive economics, economic theory, and economic policy, and explain the relationships between the three. Is economics "theoretical and impractical"? Explain.

8. (a) Are scientific laws created by man or are they discovered? (b) Why do we seek scientific laws? Explain.

9. What is "unscientific" about each of the following? (*Suggestion:* look up the meanings of such words as "analogy" and "extrapolate" in a good dictionary. Do you think that economists sometimes reason by analogy? Do they extrapolate? What about scholars in other sciences? Explain.)

EXAMPLES OF UNSCIENTIFIC METHOD

The male has more teeth than the female in mankind, and sheep, and goats, and swine. This has not been observed in other animals. Those persons which have the greatest number of teeth are the longest lived; those which have them widely separated, smaller, and more scattered, are generally more short lived.

Aristotle
History of Animals (4th Century B.C.)

There are seven windows in the head: two nostrils, two eyes, two ears, and a mouth; so in the heavens there are two favorable stars, two unpropitious, two luminaries, and Mercury alone, undecided and indifferent. From which and many other similar phenomena of nature, such as the seven metals, etc., which it were tedious to enumerate, we gather that the number of planets is necessarily seven.

Francesco Sizzi

In the space of one hundred and seventy-six years the Lower Mississippi has shortened itself two hundred and forty-two miles. That is an average of a trifle over one mile and a third per year. Therefore, any calm person, who is not blind or idiotic, can see that in the old Oolitic Silurian Period, just a million years ago next November, the Lower Mississippi River was upward of one million three hundred thousand miles long, and stuck out over the Gulf of Mexico like a fishing-rod. And by the same token any person can see that seven hundred and forty-two years from now the Lower Mississippi will be only a mile and three-quarters long, and Cairo and New Orleans will have joined their streets together, and be plodding comfortably along under a single mayor and a mutual board of aldermen. There is something fascinating about science. One gets such wholesale returns of conjecture out of such trifling investment of fact.

Mark Twain, *Life on the Mississippi* (1875)

Identify the fallacy in each of the following:

10. All rich nations have steel industries, so the surest way for a poor nation to become rich is to develop its own steel industry.

11. "Last week Mr. George Jackson, president of American Steel Corp., made a strong plea before a Congressional committee for a tariff on steel. Since a tariff is a tax on imports, his arguments should be considered with suspicion. After all, his company has everything to gain from a tariff that would protect the nation's steel industry from foreign competition."

Detroit *Daily Tribune*

12. "Both the U.S. Department of Justice and the Federal Trade Commission are government agencies which enforce the antitrust laws. As such, their purpose is to prevent the monopolization of industry by encouraging free competition. Unfortunately, these agencies sometimes become overly zealous; they forget that America's greatness was built by enterprise, ingenuity, and hard work. Hence if they are not careful in their enforcement activities, they

will change us from a vigorous nation into one which lacks the drive and imagination that are needed for progress and growth."

St. Louis Sentinel

13. The students who do best in economics have some working experience, so the surest way to receive a good grade in this course is to go out and get a job.

14. Democratic socialism must indeed be better than capitalism, for even a great mathematician and physicist like the late Dr. Albert Einstein once said: "I am convinced there is only *one* way to eliminate these grave evils of capitalism, namely through the establishment of a socialist economy, accompanied by an educational system which would be oriented toward social goals."

Albert Einstein, "Why Socialism?"
Monthly Review, May, 1949

15. "To press forward with a properly ordered wage structure in each industry is the first condition for curbing competitive bargaining; but there is no reason why the process should stop there. What is good for each industry can hardly be bad for the economy as a whole."

Twentieth Century Socialism,
Penguin Books, 1956, p. 74.

16. "Each person's happiness is a good to that person, and the general happiness, therefore, a good to the aggregate of all persons."

John Stuart Mill, Utilitarianism

17. In a capitalist system, each manufacturer is free to set his own price on the product he produces, so there can't be anything wrong with all manufacturers getting together to agree on the prices of the products they produce.

18. All economics textbooks are long and dull, so we can't expect this one to be short and interesting.

REFERENCES AND READING SUGGESTIONS

BOULDING, KENNETH E., *Economic Analysis: Microeconomics,* 4th ed., Harper & Row, New York, 1966, chap. 1.

BOULDING, KENNETH E., *Economics As A Science,* McGraw-Hill, New York, 1970, chap. 1.

BROWN, ROBERT, *Explanations in Social Science,* Aldine, Chicago, 1963, chaps. I, X, XI.

KEMENY, JOHN G., *A Philosopher Looks at Science,* Van Nostrand, New York, 1959, chaps. 6, 9, 10.

STIGLER, GEORGE J., *The Theory of Price,* 3rd ed., Macmillan, New York, 1966, chap. 1.

PART 1

American Capitalism:
An Overview

CHAPTER 2

Resources and Goals of Our Economic System

CHAPTER PREVIEW

What are the human and nonhuman resources of our economy?

What are the goals of our economic system? What do we want it to accomplish?

Are our resources scarce or plentiful? Should they be used economically or lavishly?

What goods should society produce—and how much of each? How should these goods be produced? For whom should they be produced?

This evening it would be nice if you could: (1) read this chapter, (2) do all your homework, (3) earn some money, (4) engage in pleasant recreational activity, and (5) relax and enjoy a leisurely dinner at the best restaurant in town. But you cannot do all these things. You will have to give up one or more because you are faced with limitations of time, and possibly of money.

Our economic system also faces limitations—limitations of human and nonhuman resources needed to produce the goods and services that society wants. This chapter describes the nature of those limitations and how the economy adjusts to them in the light of the objectives it tries to attain.

Resources of Our Economic System: What Do We Have?

Every economic system, whether American, Chinese, Russian, or Congolese, has various resources at its disposal to produce the goods and services society wants. These resources are of two broad types:

1. *Property resources*—including such things as natural resources, raw material, machinery and equipment, buildings, transportation and communication facilities.

2. *Human resources*—consisting of all physical and mental talents used by those who are engaged in productive activity.

This classification of resources is often adequate for informal discussion, but is too general for most practical problems. Economists therefore divide property resources into two subcategories called "land" and "capital," and human resources into two subcategories called "labor" and "entrepreneurship." These four types of resources are known as the *factors of production.*

FACTORS OF PRODUCTION

The four factors of production—land, capital, labor, and entrepreneurship—are the basic ingredients or "inputs" which any society must use to obtain the "outputs" that it desires. Let us see what these factors are.

1. The use of *land* in production includes all non-human or "natural" resources such as land itself, mineral deposits, timber, and water. In short, it includes all the basic and natural physical stuff on which any civilization must be built.

2. As a factor of production, *capital* may be defined as a produced means of further production. In this sense, capital means *capital goods* or *investment goods,* the things that are used by business. Examples are raw materials, tools, machinery and equipment, factory buildings, freight cars, and office furniture. Capital is thus an economic resource which is used to facilitate the production of consumer goods and services. *Consumer goods* are those bought and used by households—food, cars, appliances, clothing, health services, and so on.

An important distinction must be kept in mind—namely, the difference between *physical* capital (goods used in production) and *finance* capital (money). The term "capital" is frequently employed by businessmen to mean money—that is, the funds invested in a business or the money available to purchase capital goods. But since money itself is not a productive resource, it is not the same as a factor of production.

3. Land and capital are of no use unless they can be worked. That requires *labor*. This factor of production describes those hired workers whose efforts or activities are directed toward production.

In a broader sense, "labor" includes everyone who works for a living, and refers to the labor force of a nation, i.e., all the employable population above a certain age. The meaning of "labor force" and the notion of labor as a factor of production are different concepts in economics. Although they are sometimes related in economic discussions, the distinction between the two is always clear from the context in which the terms are used.

4. The other three factors of production must be organized and combined in order to produce. In other words, labor must be given a purpose if it is to work with land and capital to turn out goods and services. This is where the *entrepreneur* enters. He recognizes a need, and hence the opportunities to be gained from production. Accordingly, he generates new ideas and puts them into effect: he assembles the factors of production, raises the necessary money, organizes the management, makes the basic business policy decisions, and reaps the gains of success or the losses of failure. In some businesses the entrepreneur may double as a manager; in others he may not. But in any case, the *entrepreneurial function* must be performed in the economy.

FOR CLASS DISCUSSION

Is there such a thing as "human" capital? For instance, are scientists, engineers, teachers, doctors, lawyers, skilled workers, etc., part of our nation's capital? What criteria would you suggest in order to decide whether something is qualified to be called capital?

RETURNS TO RESOURCE OWNERS

In a capitalistic system the factors of production are privately owned—as opposed to other types of economic systems where one or more of the productive resources might be collectively owned. Can you think of some examples?

Since there are not enough of these resources to satisfy everyone, their owners can command a price for them in the market. Those who supply the factor of production known as "land" receive a payment called *rent*. The suppliers of "capital"—that is, the suppliers of the money which businessmen borrow in order to purchase capital goods—receive a return called *interest*. Workers who sell their "labor" receive a payment called *wages*, which includes salaries, commissions, and the like. Finally, those who perform the entrepreneurial function receive *profits* (or losses).

This grouping of the factors of production into four broad categories sometimes raises a question about the way in which a special type of resource or payment should be classified. Usually, the factor of production which causes the greatest confusion is entrepreneurship.

For instance, you might pose an example where an individual runs his own business—in which case he is both an entrepreneur and worker, and the payment he receives includes both profits and wages. Or you might argue that in a large corporation like General Motors or AT&T, there is a *separation of ownership and control* in the sense that the entrepreneurial function is performed largely by the salaried executives of the firm, whereas the typical stockholder shares in the profits by receiving dividends, but contributes little or nothing in the way of "entrepreneurship." How are these and similar situations classified?

A general answer is that some arbitrariness is necessary. Thus a certain resource and its payments may have to be spread among several categories. Usually, there is no particular difficulty in allocating wages, rent, and interest to the resource owners who supply the labor, land, and capital. Profit, on the other hand, is a reward to those who perform the *entrepreneurial function* within the economy; hence it may go partly to stockholders in the form of dividends and partly to executives in the form of bonuses and other benefits. Any income, therefore, can be grouped under one or more of the classifications of wages, rent, interest, and profits.

Goals of Our Economic System: What Do We Want to Accomplish?

When we refer to the American economy as a "system," we imply there is purpose or order in its structure. It is appropriate to examine the nature of this order and to explore its objectives. What do we want our economic system to do? What do we want it to be?

Most economists agree in principle that the following six objectives characterize the United States economic system—but many economists disagree over the interpretations and compromises that these goals entail.

1. Strong and sustained economic growth. The United States has accepted that it must grow. As long as population continues to increase, economic growth must at least keep pace if living standards are not to decline.

2. Continuous full employment. Everyone who wants a job should be able to find one without unreasonable difficulty and at prevailing rates of pay. This is the meaning of full employment. Of course, some unemployment will always exist because some people are temporarily out of work and others are unable to find a job in their line of work or in their community. As a general rule, a range of 3 to $3\frac{1}{2}$ percent might be taken as the maximum unemployment level compatible with what we call a "full employment" economy. A range of $3\frac{1}{2}$ to 4 percent would be characteristic of a so-called "high employment" economy.

3. Price stability. Purchasing power of the dollar should be maintained at a level that encourages investment, production, and employment of the economy's resources. This means that inflationary and deflationary price movements should be avoided, because they disrupt the smooth flow of economic activity.

4. Equitable distribution of income. Wide differences among income groups are due to both controllable and uncontrollable factors, such as native ability and intelligence, education and training, the extent of property ownership, and market power. Since equitable means "fair" or "just" (*not* "equal"), this goal requires that society seek reasonable methods of altering the controllable factors that cause wide disparities in income.

5. *Economic security.* Society should make reasonable provisions for those who cannot care for themselves—such as the aged, the disabled, the handicapped, and the chronically ill. This is a humanitarian goal which involves significant economic decisions.

6. *Democratic free enterprise.* America has developed an economic system characterized by private ownership of the means of production. This condition is basic to the concept of so-called "free enterprise." In addition, political democracy allows the American citizen to vote for legislators who influence government policy on taxes, foreign aid, regulation of utilities, protection of consumers, and other economic issues. The preservation of a predominantly capitalistic economy is a primary objective of the United States political system, which supports so-called "democratic free enterprise."

INTERPRETATIONS AND COMPROMISES VARY

Tremendous practical difficulties arise in the interpretation and implementation of these six objectives. For example, what rate of growth qualifies as "strong and sustained"? Would 3 percent a year be adequate? 4 percent? 5 percent? When does full employment cease to be "continuous"? In other words, for how long should society tolerate significant unemployment before it insists action be taken to correct the situation? Does price stability mean there should be little or no change in prices, or does it mean only moderate change—and if so, how much? What pattern of income distribution would be considered "equitable"? How can society distinguish between economic security and "big brother" paternalism? And finally, to what extent is government participation in the economy desirable, and does such participation dampen or stimulate economic initiative?

These are problems of definition and measurement. Further difficulties arise because some of the goals are at least partially conflicting if not mutually exclusive. For instance, economic growth and full employment also bring with them inflation and environmental decay. Government efforts through legislation or regulation to promote full employment may impinge on the economic freedoms of consumers, workers, and businessmen, and hence impede the attainment of another goal—that of democratic free enterprise.

Whenever fundamental goals are in conflict, a system of priorities must be established. This will permit compromises or tradeoffs between competing objectives. Thus, what target rate of economic growth should society choose as compatible with full employment and minimal inflation? To what extent can this compromise goal be achieved without sacrificing any of our existing economic freedoms?

A Fundamental Economic Challenge

In economics, *scarcity* is the name of the game and *economizing* is the way it is played. Every society is faced with the basic reality that people cannot have all they want. The things they want and the resources that produce them are not provided free by nature. Therefore every society has to cope with a fundamental economic challenge: how can it best use its *limited* resources to satisfy its *unlimited wants?*

THE LAW OF SCARCITY

Some people think it paradoxical to be told that resources in the United States are scarce. After all, the country covers several million square miles and embraces untold billions of dollars' worth of real and untapped natural resources. The population is expanding rapidly, and with it the civilian labor force. Science and technology are continually providing new and better types of capital equipment. Colleges and universities are turning out millions of educated men and women. In the face of these developments, can it be true that our resources are scarce?

Compared with many nations, our modern industrial society seems wealthy indeed. We have a substantially higher standard of living than our great-grandparents had. Yet most of us are conditioned to want more and better things—larger homes, nicer furniture, stylish clothes, electronic gadgets, improved education, longer vacations, and so on.

Today's Principle—Tomorrow's Fallacy

England in the middle of the nineteenth century was a disturbing place for anyone with a social conscience. The rich lived serenely, pampered by servants. Those who thought about poverty usually accepted it as inevitable; many blamed the poor themselves for their own plight. That plight was terrible indeed. Children worked—and died—in mines and factories. The sick, the old, and the unemployed depended on the charity of relatives, neighbors, and the few rich people who were ready to help.

The late-nineteenth-century British economist Alfred Marshall (see page 394), though he was born to privilege, did not like what he saw. He became determined to develop the human mind; but older friends warned him that Britain's resources would not allow to the mass of people the leisure and wealth necessary for study. That rebuttal helped to turn Marshall to the study of economics. His was a powerful voice in the rising chorus of economists who warned complacent England that the study of man must take place in the context of human institutions; when those institutions change, so does man's behavior. Marshall's message rings clear today. Economists should avoid the danger of presenting their interpretations as theorems with universal, timeless validity.

The Womb of Time

All thinkers and scholars are the creatures of their time. They may try to transcend it, to learn from the past and to divine the future; but they are molded by the present, and their thoughts are the products of its womb. Adam Smith, a late-eighteenth-century Scottish professor who was the founder of modern economics (see page 32), wrote at a time when the old, agrarian societies of England and Scotland were being replaced by the industrial revolution. The word "revolution" is not too strong. Hundreds of thousands of former countrymen had become townsmen. They lived poorly, and died obscurely; their employers made fortunes, and some were ennobled. How could this harsh, inhuman process be justified? Smith, a moral philosopher, enthroned individual self-interest. If men understood where their self-interest lay, and followed it, social harmony would be achieved. To tamper with the "invisible hand" of self-interest was to tamper with the best interests of society.

Not surprisingly, Smith's ideas appealed to the capitalists of his day. They were not insincere, merely misguided. Even today there are those who believe that unemployment benefits and welfare payments sap individual initiative. As a contemporary wrote, Smith "persuaded his own generation and governed the next."

Nearly a hundred years after Smith, Karl Marx, a prophet of socialism and communism (see page 646), evolved an economic theory that purported to show that the capitalist class was doomed to extinction. Marx's ideas are still potent: their supporters claim for Marxian economics a timeless and universal quality. But Marx's writings owe much to his experiences in that brutal, careless, and unabashedly unjust England in which he made his home. Even if he had lived in luxury, his powerfully analytical brain would almost certainly have discerned the weaknesses of capitalism. But would his visions of capitalism's downfall have been quite so violent?

Money Mellows

Some fifty years after Marx, John Maynard Keynes, a British economist (see page 144), came into prominence. Keynes was rich, witty, and popular; the capitalist system worked well for him. Yet, like Marx, he foresaw its breakdown. Unlike Marx, however, he determined to repair the mechanism. He succeeded brilliantly. Before Keynes, most economists believed that business cycles were self-correcting. It took Keynes to show they were not, and that determined government action might be needed to end recessions. Again, it is clear that Keynes thought and wrote within the context of his times; the dominant economic problem was one of decline, not growth. And in his writings he warned that his theories were directed toward specific ailments. Later economists, however, claim to have found within the body of his work principles that they have elevated to eternal truths.

This brief historical sketch contains at least one lesson. It is to realize that economics studies a constantly shifting, dynamic, and complex phenomenon. It is tempting to reach into this flux of events and extract timeless principles. But the temptation needs to be resisted. Today's principles can turn out to be tomorrow's fallacies.

R. B.

What do you think are some of the problems that economists today are concentrating on? Will their studies be at all relevant fifty years from now?

For a highly paid business executive who has everything he wishes, scarcity of material things is no problem—although he might find his time is too scarce for him to accomplish everything he wants to do. But for the majority of people scarcity is a fact of life because most goods are not *free goods* like fresh air and sunshine. And even so-called "free goods" may be scarce in some circumstances. Sunshine and surf are free for residents of Hawaii, but not for tourists who must expend time, effort, and money to get there. Trout in a mountain stream are free goods, but in a city they are scarce. In general, goods which are not free goods are called *economic goods*.

Since scarcity pervades the economic life of all societies, we may formulate an important "law":

Law of Scarcity. Economic resources are scarce. There are never enough at any given time to produce all the things that people want. Scarce resources can be increased, if at all, only through effort or sacrifice.

Thus, despite the fact that America is a so-called "affluent society," the law of scarcity still prevails. Our economic system does not satisfy everyone's wants.

ECONOMIZING—THE ANSWER TO SCARCITY

Scarcity creates the need to economize. What does it mean to "economize"? To tighten one's belt or to be stingy? These interpretations are correct in the narrow sense of the word, but for an economist the term has a broader meaning—*to do the most with what is available from society's viewpoint.*

To do the most it can with limited resources, society must make choices. A decision to produce something frequently implies a decision to produce less of other things. Therefore society often faces the basic problem of deciding what it is willing to *sacrifice* in order to get the things it wants. Sacrificing and economizing are thus closely related concepts.

Economizing is somewhat similar to the engineering concept of efficiency—"getting the most out for what is put in," or "putting the least in for what is gotten out." A mechanical engineer, for example, determines the efficiency of a machine by measuring the extent to which it transforms inputs of fuel into outputs of horsepower.

Economics also has its *inputs* and *outputs*. Inputs are the human and material resources that go into an economic activity (e.g., a production process); outputs are the goods and services that the activity turns out. *Economizing*, therefore, means attaining efficiency in economic activity—attaining the most favorable ratio of outputs to inputs. This is an important objective of economics.

THE BIG QUESTIONS: WHAT? HOW? FOR WHOM?

The need for economizing boils down to the fact that any society must answer several fundamental and interdependent questions if it is to use scarce resources efficiently.

1. WHAT Goods and Services Should Society Produce— and How Many?

Since resources are limited, how should society apportion them? Countless choices are possible, but they really amount to two classes of decisions.

First, how should society allocate its scarce resources between the production of consumer goods and of capital goods? Should society employ its scarce resources for the production of food? Automobiles? Apartment houses? Factory buildings? Or what? In other words, what items should society include in—as well as exclude from—its list of things to be produced?

Second, how much of each good should society produce? How many loaves of bread? How many Fords and Chevrolets, how many apartment houses, factory buildings, and so on?

In answering these questions, society is judging the merits of present versus future satisfactions. If more resources are devoted now to the production of capital goods, fewer can be devoted to the production of consumer goods. However, as more and better capital goods become available, they can produce more and better consumer goods. Therefore, the question of how society should allocate its resources between consumer goods and capital goods is really part of a more fundamental issue: How much current consumption should society sacrifice in order to provide the capital goods needed for increasing future consumption?

2. HOW Should Resources Be Organized for Production?

Most goods can be produced in more than one way by using resources in different quantities and combinations. In the early days of American history, for example, agricultural commodities were produced by farming larger quantities of land extensively, while using only small quantities of labor, because labor was relatively more scarce than land. In parts of the Far East, on the other hand, land is farmed intensively because it is relatively more scarce than labor. Similarly, in manufacturing it is often possible to vary the combinations of resources.

Any society must decide how it will *organize* its scarce resources in order to use them efficiently. How are resources to be increased in the industries that are producing desired goods, and how are they to be decreased in those that are not? Which are the most efficient combinations of resources in production processes, and which are the most suitable technologies to employ? These are the kinds of problems raised by the great HOW question.

3. FOR WHOM Shall the Goods be Produced?

How is the total output to be divided among the members of society? What proportions should go to households? Industries? Government? To put it in a nutshell—who is to get what share of the pie? Political and moral considerations are involved in these decisions.

The three big questions—WHAT, HOW, and FOR WHOM—are fundamental economic challenges. In the United States we seek to answer them so as to achieve the goals set forth earlier: *full employment, steady economic growth, price stability, and economic equity and security*—all within a framework of *democratic free enterprise*. In other economic systems, such as Mainland China or Soviet Russia, the same three basic questions must be answered; however, some of the goals of these societies differ, as do the means they use to achieve these goals.

Society's Production Possibilities

For every society, the answers to the questions of WHAT, HOW, and FOR WHOM are intimately related to the need for economizing. But in reality the problem of economizing is a complex one, so we must simplify in order to focus on the basic concepts involved.

We may begin by constructing a model of the economizing process for a hypothetical society. The model is based on three assumptions:

1. *A choice is to be made between producing two goods: agricultural, such as crops, livestock, etc., and capital, like machines and factories.* This situation is typical in many developing nations that are predominantly agricultural and seeking to industrialize.

2. *Resources or factors of production are fully employed in the most efficient way.* This means there is both full employment and full production—or, as some economists would say, there is no unemployment or underemployment of resources. A distinction between the two terms is important. *Unemployment* exists when men who want jobs cannot find them at going wage rates for the skills and experiences they have to offer. *Underemployment*, on the other hand, exists whenever employed resources are not used with maximum efficiency.

3. *The supply of resources and the state of technological knowledge are fixed.* This is equivalent to assuming a short-run state of affairs, because in the long run the supply of resources and the level of technological knowledge would be expansible rather than constant.

Our model teaches us this fundamental point: Since resources are fully employed in the most efficient way, any increase in the production of capital goods will require the shifting of resources out of agriculture; conversely, any increase in the production of agricultural goods will require resources to be shifted out of the manufacture of capital goods.

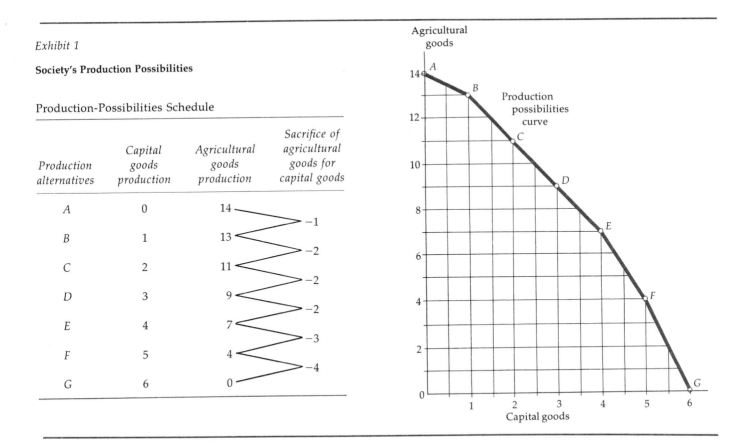

Exhibit 1

Society's Production Possibilities

Production-Possibilities Schedule

Production alternatives	Capital goods production	Agricultural goods production	Sacrifice of agricultural goods for capital goods
A	0	14	−1
B	1	13	−2
C	2	11	−2
D	3	9	−2
E	4	7	−3
F	5	4	−4
G	6	0	

This is illustrated by the model in Exhibit 1. The table is called a *production-possibilities schedule*. Referring to this table, we observe that if society chooses production alternative A, it will be devoting all of its resources to the production of agricultural goods and none of its resources to the production of capital goods; it will thus be producing 14 units of agricultural goods and zero units of capital goods. At the other extreme, if society chooses alternative G, it will be putting all its resources into the production of capital goods; it will thus be producing 6 units of capital goods and zero units of agricultural goods.

These two alternatives are extremes; realistically the society must seek some balance in between. However, as it tries to increase its capital goods production by choosing any of the alternatives, B, C, D, etc., it finds that it must *sacrifice* or give up some agricultural goods. The amount of sacrifice for

each production alternative is shown in the fourth column of the table.

All the information in the production-possibilities schedule can be transferred directly to the accompanying chart. Note that the units of capital goods are scaled on the horizontal axis and those for agricultural goods on the vertical. The line which connects the various production alternatives A through G may be called a *production-possibilities curve* because it reveals all possible combinations of total output for the society it represents.

LAW OF INCREASING COSTS

The production-possibilities curve raises two challenging questions: (1) What is the *optimum* or best combination of agricultural and capital goods? (2)

Why does the sacrifice of agricultural products *increase* as society gets more capital goods?

The optimum combination depends upon the goals of the society. In command economies such as those of Mainland China and the Soviet Union, concerted efforts toward rapid industrialization have been made, and more emphasis put on capital than agricultural goods. On the other hand, in more agrarian nations like New Zealand, Uruguay, and Cuba, larger proportions of resources are allocated to agricultural than to capital goods production. Thus, whether B or D or any other point on the curve is "best" or "worst" depends on the values and the goals of the particular society, and is not a question that economics per se can answer.

Concerning the second question, greater and greater sacrifices of agricultural output must be made to get more capital goods because *economic resources differ in quality and hence are not perfectly adaptable to alternative uses.* Fertile land, for example, is more suitable for crops than for factories, and unskilled farm workers are more adaptable to agriculture than to manufacturing.

For this reason, society finds that as it tries to increase its production of capital goods, it must take increasing amounts of resources out of agriculture, where they are relatively more productive, and "push" them into the manufacture of capital goods, where they are relatively less productive. From the viewpoint of the economy as a whole, therefore, the *real costs* of acquiring more capital goods are not the dollars spent for them, but the sacrifices of agricultural goods that society must "give up" or do without. Since these sacrifices tend to increase as the production alternatives move down the curve, the phenomenon may be called the *law of increasing costs.*

Thus, referring back to the fourth column of the table, note that the sacrifices are shown with negative numbers because they represent the amount of agricultural goods that society must *give up* to acquire one more unit of capital goods. For example, if society is at point D and wants to go to point E, it must give up 2 units of agricultural goods to get 1 more unit of capital goods. Similarly, if it is at point E and wants to get to point F, it must give up 3 units of agricultural goods to get 1 more unit of capital goods.

AN INTERESTING PROBLEM

You should be able to verify that the law of increasing costs also applies in going from G to A on the chart. That is, society must give up increasing amounts of capital goods to get successive one-unit increases in agricultural goods. The curve is "bowed out" or concave to the origin because of the law of increasing cost. What would it mean if the curve were "bowed in" or convex to the origin? Would such a curve make economic sense in this case? Illustrate your answer graphically.

SOME USES OF THE PRODUCTION-POSSIBILITIES CURVE

What happens when some of the assumptions underlying a society's production possibilities model are relaxed? Three sets of interesting examples may be analyzed.

Example 1. Resource Underutilization

If we discard the second assumption of full employment and full production—that is, if we allow some unemployment or underemployment to exist—the society will not be producing at full capacity as defined by its production-possibilities curve. Instead, some smaller level of output will be produced, and the output will be indicated by a point *inside* the curve. An example occurs at the point U in Exhibit 2: you can readily infer that the economy is not fully utilizing its available resources.

How can society utilize its resources more fully? The arrows show the paths that society may follow to get back on the curve. Thus, it may increase agricultural goods production without increasing capital goods production, as indicated by the vertical arrow. It may increase capital goods production without increasing agricultural goods production, as shown by the horizontal arrow. Or it may increase both agricultural and capital goods production in any one of various combinations, as suggested by the diagonal arrow.

Exhibit 2

Effect of Resource Underutilization

At any point inside the production-possibilities curve, there is some unemployment or underemployment of resources. Society can correct the situation by producing more of either or both of the two classes of products, as the arrows indicate.

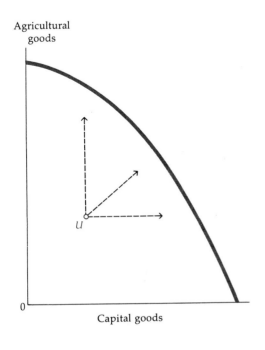

Exhibit 3

Economic Growth

Increases in resources or improvements in technology will tend to shift the curve outward to the right. The new curve permits a growing economy to enjoy larger quantities of both types of goods.

As shown in charts (a) and (b), the new curve need not necessarily be "parallel" to the old one. Changes in resources or technology may be such as to bring about a relatively greater shift in favor of one type of output as compared to the other.

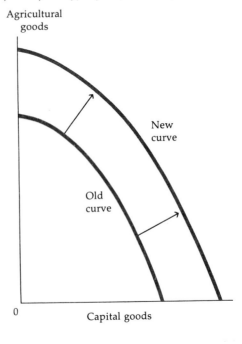

Example 2. Economic Growth

Suppose we drop one or both parts of the third assumption, and allow the supply of resources or the level of technology, or both, to be expansible rather than fixed. This situation would undoubtedly occur over the long run as the supply of the factors of production increased with a growing population, and more efficient machinery and equipment increased productivity. One or both of these possibilities would increase the economy's potential output.

In Exhibit 3, this increase is indicated by the fact that the production-possibilities curve has shifted outward to the right. At any point on the new curve,

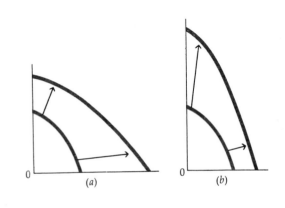

the economy would enjoy a larger total output than it would at any point on the old curve. But of course there is no assurance that society will know how to make full enough utilization of its available resources to get itself onto the new curve. Consequently, we shall have occasion in later chapters to explore possible solutions to this basic problem.

Example 3. Present Goods vs. Future Goods

As a final illustration of the many uses of production-possibilities curves, we might consider what would happen if, in the first assumption, the choice of producing agricultural goods were broadened to include a larger category which we call "consumption goods." In other words, society must now choose between current consumption goods (i.e., not just food but also automobiles, color TV, and the like) and current capital goods (such as machines, education, research, etc.)—but the choice of capital goods will make it possible to have more of *both* classes of goods in the future.

The results are demonstrated in Exhibit 4. Chart (*a*) shows what would happen if society chose to live "high off the hog" by producing relatively more consumer goods than capital goods, as indicated by point *A* on the curve. Chart (*b*) shows what would happen if society chose to produce relatively more capital goods than consumer goods, as indicated by *A'*. The outcome is that, in chart (*b*), the future production possibilities curve will be farther to the right than in chart (*a*). This evidences the fact that by doing with fewer consumer goods now and producing more capital goods instead, society will have the means of producing more consumer goods and capital goods in the future. Thus, a society's present choice of position on its production possibilities curve will tend to influence the future location of that curve.

These examples have a number of real-world applications. Russia, for instance, has been allocating relatively more of its resources to the production of capital goods than to consumer goods, and hence its economy has at times grown faster than America's. The *real cost* of this policy to the Russian people, however, must be measured in terms of the quantity, quality, and variety of consumer goods that they are

Exhibit 4

Present Goods vs. Future Goods

A society's present choice of position on its production-possibilities curve will affect the future location of the curve. By doing with fewer consumer goods in the present and producing more capital goods instead, it will have the means of providing more of both types of goods in the future.

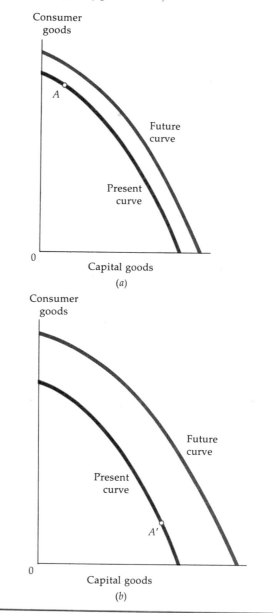

sacrificing in the present—goods such as automobiles and decent housing, to mention only two, which are much scarcer in the Soviet Union than in the United States.

SUMMARY OF IMPORTANT IDEAS

1. The American economic system seeks to attain certain objectives. These are: strong and sustained economic growth; continuous full employment of economic resources; price stability; an equitable distribution of income; and economic security—all within a framework of democratic free enterprise. Most Americans support these goals, but many differ about the ways in which they may be interpreted and about their order of importance.

2. The American economic system has both property resources and human resources at its disposal. The property resources are its land and capital; the human resources are its labor and entrepreneurship. These four classes of economic resources—land capital, labor, and entrepreneurship—are the necessary ingredients of production and hence are known as the "factors of production." The returns received by the owners of these resources are rent, interest, wages, and profits, the total of which make up the income of our society.

3. All societies are faced with the problem of scarcity because they have limited resources and apparently unlimited wants. Therefore, economizing is necessary if these scarce resources are to be used efficiently.

4. Most economic problems are aspects of the three big questions that every society must answer: WHAT to produce—and how much? HOW to produce? FOR WHOM to produce? In the United States these questions are answered within the framework of the goals summarized in the first paragraph above. In other economic systems, where the goals are different, the answers will also be different.

5. In an economy characterized by full employment and full production, any increases in the output of goods and services must cause a reduction of output elsewhere in the economy. With given resources and technology, the production choices open to an economy can be summarized by its production-possibilities curve.

6. A society's production-possibilities curve illustrates many basic economic processes: any point inside the curve indicates some unemployment or underemployment of resources; an outward shift of the curve to the right represents an increase in the supply of resources or in technological capability; a choice between the proportions of "present goods" and "future goods" in an economy's total output will affect the future location of the curve.

FOR HOMEWORK AND DISCUSSION

1. *Terms and concepts to review:*

full employment	interest
property resources	profit
human resources	free goods
factors of production	economic goods
land	law of scarcity
labor	production-possibilities curve
capital	
entrepreneurship	unemployment
rent	underemployment
wages	law of increasing costs

2. Is it possible for an economy to have strong economic growth full employment, price stability, an equitable distribution of income, and economic security—*without* having democratic free enterprise? Explain.

3. Is it possible to maximize all of the six objectives of our economic system? Explain.

4. Which factor of production is relatively most important in each of the following lines of activity: (*a*) iron mining, (*b*) radio and TV repair, (*c*) electric power generation, (*d*) toys and games.

5. "No one in the United States has to starve or go naked. Therefore, it is incorrect to say that scarcity pervades our economy. Food and clothing are available to all and hence are not scarce." True or false? Explain.

6. Economics has sometimes been defined as the

science of allocating scarce resources among competing uses. Do you agree with this definition?

7. a. Construct *your own* production-possibilities schedule for an economy that must choose between producing civilian and war goods.

   b. From your schedule, draw the corresponding production-possibilities graph.

   c. Label a point inside the graph. What does it mean?

   d. What would happen on the production-possibilities curve if a new "ultimate weapon" were invented as a result of which many resources were released from the production of war goods and became available for the production of civilian goods?

   e. Show the effect on the production-possibilities curve of general technological improvements in the production of both civilian goods and war goods.

8. Is technology or technological know-how a factor of production? Explain.

REFERENCES AND READING SUGGESTIONS

GALBRAITH, JOHN K., *American Capitalism*, rev. ed., Houghton Mifflin, Boston, 1956, chap. 2.

STIGLER, GEORGE J., *The Theory of Price*, 3d ed., Macmillan, New York, 1966, chap. 2.

WEISS, ROGER, *The Economic System*, Random House, New York, 1969, chap. 1.

CHAPTER 3

Capitalism and the Price System: Our Modified Market Economy

What is the nature of capitalism and what are its fundamental economic institutions?

How does a capitalistic system answer the three big questions, WHAT, HOW, and FOR WHOM?

Can we construct a model which provides a broad overview of a capitalistic system?

"Capitalism," it has been said,

> has created more massive and more colossal forces than have all preceding generations together. . . . It has accomplished wonders far surpassing Egyptian pyramids, Roman aqueducts, and gothic cathedrals; it has conducted expeditions that put in the shade all former migrations of nations and crusades.

These words were not taken from a recent speech by the head of the National Association of Manufacturers or the United States Chamber of Commerce. They were written by none other than history's greatest enemy of capitalism and the founder of modern socialism—Karl Marx—in a pamphlet entitled *The Communist Manifesto* published in 1848.

Modern capitalism had its origin in eighteenth-century Britain, and was later transplanted to northwestern Europe and North America. Scholars now agree that capitalism was a "revolution"—not always bloody as the American, French, and Russian Revolutions, but certainly more fundamental in the shaping of modern society. Today capitalism is more than an economic process; it is a *civilization* rooted in an ideology that reflects a way of life. This chapter examines some of the essential economic features of this remarkable system.

What Is Capitalism?

The economic system of the United States and most other countries of the Western world is commonly known as "capitalism," "free enterprise," or "private enterprise." These terms are generally regarded as synonymous. What do they mean?

Capitalism is a system of economic organization characterized by private ownership of the means of production and distribution (such as land, factories, railroads, etc.) and their operation for profit under predominantly competitive conditions.

But there is more to capitalism than is stated in this definition. On what foundations does a *pure* capitalistic system rest? Is the American system a model or prototype of pure capitalism?

PILLARS OF CAPITALISM

Certain elements are basic in a capitalistic system. They consist of rights and traditions that serve as cornerstones of capitalism. Five of these in particular may be noted

1. Private Property

The institution of private property is the most basic of all. It allows each person to control the things he owns, enjoy their benefits, enter into contracts involving their use, and dispose of them or bequeath them to others. In a capitalistic society, the things owned may include most types of goods as well as economic resources.

Government plays a dual role in capitalism. It protects private property, but it also limits the ownership and disposition of goods and resources that affect the health, safety, human rights, or welfare of the people. Thus, in the United States we have pure food and drug laws, utility and railroad regulations, zoning ordinances, open-housing legislation, fair-labor-practices acts, and so forth. But these laws are intended only to define the rules of the game. Most economic activities are carried on without direct government intervention or control.

2. Self-interest—The "Invisible Hand"

In 1776, a Scottish professor, Adam Smith, published *The Wealth of Nations.* This book earned him the title "founder of modern economics," because in it he clearly enunciated his principle of the "Invisible Hand"—the idea that each individual, if left to pursue his self-interest without interference by government, would be led as if by an invisible hand to achieve the best good for society. In Smith's words:

> An individual neither intends to promote the public interest, nor knows he is promoting it. . . . He intends only his own gain, and he is led by an invisible hand to promote an end which was no part of his intention. . . . It is not from the benevolence of the butcher, the brewer, or the baker that we expect our dinner, but from their regard to their self-interest. We address ourselves not to their humanity, but to their self-love, and never talk to them of our necessities, but of their advantages.

Self-interest drives men to action, but alone it is not enough. Men must also think rationally if they are to make the right decisions. This requirement ultimately led economists to introduce the concept of *economic man*—the notion that each individual in a capitalistic society, whether worker, businessman, consumer, or investor, is motivated by economic forces, and hence will always act in such a way as to obtain the greatest amount of satisfaction for the least amount of sacrifice or cost. To a businessman these satisfactions may take the form of profits; to a worker they may be leisure; to a consumer they may be the pleasure he gets from the goods he buys.

The modern economist knows these assumptions are not always realistic. People may be motivated by forces other than self-interest. The assumption of economic man, if pushed to its logical extreme, would require each individual to have the mind of a computer in order to solve the myriad of problems that he encounters in his economic activities. But the assumption does serve as a reasonable approximation of the way people tend to pattern their economic behavior in a capitalistic society. And in economics, just as in the other social sciences, reasonable approximations are often the most that can be made.

ADAM SMITH

1723–1790

Founder of Modern Economics

The year 1776 was marked by two great events in man's struggle for emancipation.

In North America, representatives of the British colonies adopted the Declaration of Independence—*an eloquent statement setting forth a doctrine of political freedom. In Europe, a former Scottish professor of philosophy at the University of Glasgow published a monumental book entitled* An Inquiry into the Nature and Causes of the Wealth of Nations—*or simply* The Wealth of Nations *as it is usually called. This was an equally eloquent statement expounding a doctrine of economic freedom. Both events, despite the geographic chasm that separated them, stand as milestones in the Age of Enlightenment and Liberalism that blossomed during the eighteenth century.*

Born in Scotland and educated at Glasgow and Oxford, Adam Smith became a lecturer on literature and philosophy in his mid-twenties, and at twenty-eight was appointed professor of logic and moral philosophy at the University of Glasgow. His great book, The Wealth of Nations, *took him ten years to write, and earned for him the title of "founder of economics" because it was the first complete and systematic study of the subject.*

It is a masterful synthesis of centuries of accumulated but separate economic ideas. The book argues that labor, rather than land or money, is the basic source of a nation's wealth; that individuals know best what is good for them, and if unrestricted by government controls or private monopolies will be motivated by the quest for profit to turn out the goods and services that society wants most. Therefore, through free trade and free markets, self-interest will be harnessed to the common good.

Many of the topics Smith discussed in The Wealth of Nations—*labor; value and price determination; the theory of income distribution involving wages, rent, and profit; the accumulation of capital; and the principles of public finance—appear today in economics textbooks. However, Smith's view of "the economic problem" was somewhat narrower than the modern one.*

Historical Pictures Service, Chicago

Smith conceived the central task of economics as man's struggle to conquer nature in the production of material wealth. Hence his concern was with increasing the productivity of labor and expanding the size of the market. Today, on the other hand, the basic problem of economics is seen to be a broader one of allocating scarce resources among different uses so as to maximize consumers' satisfactions, and to achieve full employment and stable economic growth without inflation.

3. Economic Individualism—Laissez-faire

In the late seventeenth century, when Louis XIV reigned as King of France, his finance minister Jean Baptiste Colbert asked a manufacturer by the name of Legendre how the government might help business. Legendre's reply was *"laissez nous faire"* (leave us alone). The expression became a watchword and motto of capitalism.

Today we interpret laissez-faire to mean that absence of government intervention leads to economic individualism and economic freedom. These terms mean that an individual's economic activities are his private affair. As a consumer he is free to spend his income as he chooses. As a producer he is free to purchase the economic resources he desires and to organize them as he wishes for the purpose of producing the things that society wants. But in reality we know that this concept of laissez-faire is significantly limited, because economic freedom is subject to restraints imposed by society for its protection and general welfare. Can you give some examples? Do you think laissez-faire leads naturally to economic individualism?

4. Competition or Free Markets

Capitalism, according to our definition, operates under conditions of *competition:* rivalry among sellers of similar goods to attract customers; among buyers to secure the goods that they want; among workers to obtain jobs; among employers to obtain workers; among buyers and sellers of resources to transact their business on the best terms that each can get from the other.

To an economist the degree of competition is gauged by two interrelated factors: one is the diffusion (as opposed to the concentration) of market power; the other is the freedom with which buyers and sellers can enter or leave particular markets.

Competition tends to be most intense when the diffusion of market power is greatest. This occurs, for example, when a businessman or farmer is not a big enough part of the total market to exert a personal influence on the price of the goods he is selling. He then finds himself at the "mercy of the market": he must accept the price that the market dictates; he cannot get more than this price, and he need not take less because he can sell all that he has at the going price.

Competition also tends to be most intense when markets are openly available to all buyers and sellers, so that each is free to make whatever buying and selling offers he wishes. Such open markets are called "free" markets; capitalism is often described as a "free market" system.

As we shall learn, a free market (1) establishes competitive prices for both consumer goods and the factors of production, and (2) encourages the efficient use of economic resources. It follows that since free markets are at least partially destroyed by the growth of monopolistic practices, society will frequently regulate such practices.

5. The Price System

Who tells the millions of workers in our economy where to work or what occupations to choose? Who decides that automobiles should be made in Detroit and steel in Pittsburgh? Who declares how many cars should be produced this year and how many homes should be built? Who specifies what will be the predominant style of women's fall dresses or the color of men's suits?

You will be able to derive some precise answers to these questions in later chapters. At present it will be enough to say that the greater the degree of competition in our economy, the more these matters will be decided not by some individual or group of individuals, but impersonally and automatically by a remarkable mechanism called the *price system* or the *market system*. This essentially is a system of rewards and penalties—rewards in the form of profits for firms and individuals that are able to survive, and penalties in the form of losses or possibly bankruptcy for those who are not.

How does the system work? Basically, it operates on the principle that everything that is exchanged—every good, every service, and every resource—has its price. In a free market characterized by a great many buyers and sellers the prices of these things will reflect the quantities that sellers make available and the quantities that buyers wish to purchase.

Thus if buyers want to purchase more of a certain good, their orders for it will increase. This will cause the price of the good to rise which in turn will encourage suppliers to produce and sell more of it. On the other hand, if buyers want to purchase less of a certain good, their orders for it will decrease. This will bring about a fall in the price of the good, and suppliers will thereby find it to their advantage to produce and sell less of it.

This type of interaction between sellers and buyers in a competitive market, and the resulting changes in prices of the commodities in which they deal, are what most people refer to by the familiar phrase "supply and demand."

Capitalism and the "Three Questions"

You will see later that there is considerably more to the workings of supply and demand than is indicated by the above description. However, enough has been said to sketch a brief answer to a central problem of economics: How does the price system guide a competitive market in its decisions about the three big questions, WHAT, HOW, and FOR WHOM?

REMARK. It is essential to keep in mind that we are talking here about a *competitive* economic system in which there are many buyers and sellers in each industry of the economy, and in which there are no "hot" or "cold" wars to influence the use of the nation's resources for military purposes. This is admittedly a hypothetical situation, but we have a specific reason for making these assumptions: we want to set up an "ideal" kind of economic model that will serve as a guide for evaluating the real-world economy which will be the subject of our interest in later chapters.

1. WHAT shall be produced? The question of WHAT to produce is answered by consumers. They are the ones who cast their dollar votes in the marketplace for the things they want, and thereby register their preferences through the price system. In competing for consumers' dollars, each producer finds he must either make the goods buyers want available or go out of business.

The price or market system also regulates the amount of each good that will be produced. For example, if buyers prefer more beef and less pork, they will bid up the price of beef relative to pork. Producers will then find it profitable to shift resources out of the production of pork and into the production of beef. Of course, as more beef is produced and less pork, the price of beef will tend to decrease somewhat and the price of pork will increase. This tendency will continue until the prices of beef and pork stand in an "equilibrium" or balanced relationship with one another—a relationship in which producers no longer find it profitable to shift their resources out of the production of one of the products and into the production of the other.

2. HOW shall goods be produced? Producers, of course, must buy their resources in the open market. Competition will force them to seek the least costly methods of production. If machines are cheap relative to labor, producers will tend to make relatively more use of machines and less of labor in a particular production process. Thus, at any particular time, physical efficiency and cost efficiency determine the production methods that are cheapest. The market system registers the differences in the prices of factors of production and guides businessmen in choosing the combinations of resources they need.

3. FOR WHOM shall goods be produced? Who gets how much? The price system also determines the payments received by the owners of the factors of production: wage rates, land rents, interest rates, and profits. These payments go to make up income, and are used by the owners of the resources to buy the goods and services that they helped to produce. The relative sizes of these incomes are determined in part by the supply and demand for the particular resources as reflected by their prices in the market. Thus if labor becomes more scarce relative to land, wages will tend to rise relative to rents, and the pattern of income distribution will thereby change. The way in which the total economic "pie" is distributed among the owners of the factors of production will be altered, giving a greater share to labor and a smaller share to landowners.

ST. THOMAS AQUINAS

1225–1274

The Great Scholastic of Early Capitalism

Bettmann Archive

Most historians would agree that the Middle Ages is a period in world history which covers approximately one thousand years—from the fall of the Roman Empire in A.D. *476 to about 1500.*

In the last three of these ten centuries modern capitalism took root, as money and credit instruments gained wider acceptance in trade among European towns and cities, the ownership of the tools of production became separated from their use, and a wage system emerged with the growth of urbanization and more centralized production.

The outstanding intellectual achievement of the late Middle Ages was the system of thought known as Scholasticism; the participants in this system are referred to as Scholastics or Schoolmen. Essentially, Scholasticism was an attempt to harmonize reason with faith by integrating philosophy and theology primarily on the basis of rationalism or logic rather than science and experience.

The greatest of the Scholastic philosophers was Thomas Aquinas, and his most famous work was the **Summa Theologica.** *The English translation runs to some twenty volumes. In his writings on economic problems, he applied the principles of Aristotelian philosophy and logic to biblical teaching and canonical dogma. He held that: private property accords with natural law; production under private ownership is preferred to production under communal ownership; trade is to be condoned to the extent that it maintains the household and benefits the country; a seller is bound to be truthful with his buyers; fairness exists when goods are exchanged at equal values and at a "just" price which reflects the customary price; wealth is good if it leads to a virtuous life; among the most vulgar of trade practices is "usury."*

Aquinas and the Schoolmen were not in sympathy with many of the economic practices of their time, but could do little to change them and hence proceeded to make them as respectable as possible by establishing moral and ethical rules of economic behavior. Many of these rules are now an integral part of American capitalistic philosophy.

For example, Aquinas decried usury, which he defined as a return for the use of a loan. But he permitted it if a lender had

to forego an alternative investment that would have yielded him an income. This was the principle of lucrum cessans—*a concept similar to that of "opportunity cost" in modern economics. Similarly, he justified the idea that buyers on credit could pay more than the cash price, that discounts were allowed on promissory notes, and that many business transactions could involve special charges and payments.*

Aquinas was canonized in 1323 and his teachings are held in the highest esteem by most Catholic as well as by many non-Catholic educators. He is perhaps the highest authority among Catholics on social subjects, especially since his views were endorsed by Pope Leo XIII in an 1879 encyclical.

It might seem that capitalism in its pure form gives rise to a strongly competitive economy and a high degree of economic efficiency in the use and allocation of its resources. Hence there would appear to be relatively little need for government regulation, except to protect personal freedoms.

Does this situation actually exist? Is the doctrine of laissez-faire—the notion that the government should limit itself to the preservation of law and order and not interfere with the operation of the economy—observed today? Does the "Invisible Hand" perform as smoothly as Adam Smith said it would, thereby resulting in the best of all possible economic worlds?

The answers to these questions are neither completely positive nor completely negative. Over the years our economy has become increasingly complicated, and the role of government has expanded in various ways.

Thus, through the use of special devices such as protective tariffs to curb imports, subsidies to stimulate production, and legislation of one type or another, government has come to play a significant role as a protector and regulator of certain groups, industries, and sectors within the economy. To cite a few examples, it has promoted particular interest groups as represented by agriculture, labor, and the consumer. It has controlled competition among the regulated industries, such as domestic transportation, communication, and power. It has sought to maintain effective competition in the unregulated industries that comprise the bulk of our business sector. It has assumed the responsibility of keeping the economy's total production and spending in balance in order to achieve the long-run objectives of economic growth and full employment. And it has become a large provider of many goods and services, among them education, highways, and national defense.

These long-run historical trends suggest the following conclusion:

The American economy is neither a pure market economy nor a pure command economy; it is a mixed economy in which both private individuals and government exercise their economic influence in the marketplace.

One of the most exciting and challenging tasks that you face in your study of economics is to evaluate the activities of government in our mixed economy.

Three Further Characteristics: Capital, Specialization, and Money

If all capitalistic economies have essentially the same institutions, why are some more productive and efficient than others? The answers depend largely on the existence of three further conditions that characterize all modern economies:

1. An advanced state of technology and an adequate supply of capital goods

2. A high degree of specialization and division of labor

3. The availability of a suitable form of money

An advanced degree of technology and specialization help make for efficient production, while the use of money permits the members of society to engage more easily in trade and exchange.

TECHNOLOGY AND CAPITAL

We live in an age of technology. Basically, technology is a part of applied science; it refers to the technical and scientific advances that enable man to increase the efficiency of production. Thus capital goods such as modern machines and factories are the products of technology. Evidently the growth of technology makes possible the production of greater amounts of capital goods, and this in turn permits a much larger output of consumer goods than would be possible otherwise.

This process—the route by which an economy first uses its limited resources to produce capital goods in order that it may have more consumer goods in the future—has long been described by economists as "roundabout production." Obviously, a nation with a high level of technology and a large supply of capital goods is in a much better position to increase its productivity and raise its standard of living than a nation which lacks these things.

SPECIALIZATION AND DIVISION OF LABOR

The birds do it. The bees do it. In most societies nearly everyone does it. What do they do? They *specialize*.

Specialization is the division of productive activities among individuals and regions so that no one person or area is self-sufficient. The result of specialization is an enormous gain in productivity that springs from a minute *division of labor*, because each individual and region is able to use to its best advantage any natural or acquired differences in abilities and resources. And even if there are no peculiar differences in a given situation, specialization may still pay because it is often the only way of getting a significant increase in total output. Adam Smith pointed this out in a classic quotation. (See Box 1.)

Why do specialization and division of labor increase production? To generalize from Smith:

1. They permit the development and refinement of skills.

2. They avoid the time that is wasted in going from one job to another.

3. They allow the employment of persons best suited to particular types of work.

Specialization also has its shortcomings. It leads to *interdependence*—indeed, specialization and interdependence go hand in hand. And it alienates workers because many never see the product to which they contribute only one small part. Their jobs then become naked means of subsistence, offering little personal satisfaction. This poses such interesting questions as whether specialization is "good" or "bad"; whether it is worth paying the price of specialization; and whether society as a whole would be "better off" if each of us were self-sufficient. These are normative questions which economics is not equipped to answer, because there is no universal agreement on the precise meanings of the words in quotation marks.

FROM BARTER TO MONEY

It has been said that man's three greatest inventions are fire, the wheel, and money.

What is money? Is it gold, silver, or paper currency? Is it fishhooks, whale teeth, elephant-tail bristles, or wampum? The answer is yes. All of these things and many others have served as money in various societies.

We use money because it is indispensable in a highly organized economy. Robinson Crusoe had no need for money when he was alone on a deserted island; he provided his own food, clothing, and shelter. Even in a small community it would be possible to get along without money if one family made clothes, another raised sheep for wool and meat, another baked bread, etc., and they all traded with each other for the things they needed. This swapping of one kind of good for another is called *barter*.

Viewpoint

The Necessary Nexus

Division of labor has conferred great benefits on society. In business, it has increased the productivity of labor and capital to levels that could not otherwise have been achieved. In the sciences, it has helped to extend the frontiers of knowledge by encouraging men to specialize. But whereas in manufacturing the components made by different specialists are eventually brought together to be assembled into a whole, in the sciences the different disciplines tend to stay separate. As a result there is fragmentation of knowledge. The tendency is particularly disturbing in the social sciences.

Speaking different jargons, and holding different views of society, sociologists, anthropologists, political scientists, psychologists, and economists find communication difficult—and sometimes downright impossible. Clearly, a synthesis of their disciplines is needed. But what university has a department of synthesis? What charitable foundation has paid for research into the methods of synthesis?

A Call for Communication

Fortunately, social scientists are increasingly aware of their need to speak to each other—to bring together into a meaningful whole the results of their research. The National Bureau of Economic Research, a prestigious nonprofit group, has recently called for more communication between economists and other social scientists. Without that communication, the Bureau fears, economists may be hampered in their attempts to see their discipline in its social perspective.

The need for synthesis is urgent. As society becomes more complex, and its balance more delicate, social scientists of every variety are in greater demand as advisers to government and business. Furthermore, each discipline increasingly relies on mathematical formulations—and often ignores what it cannot measure. As management consultant Peter R. Drucker puts it: "We cannot put into the computer what we cannot quantify—and we cannot quantify what we cannot define."

Ignoring the Unmeasurable

In economics, as in other social sciences, there is a temptation to discount or even ignore what cannot be measured. Examine what happens, for example, when a study is made of alternative sites for an airport. The study will usually include a cost-benefit analysis—in plain English, a study of how much the builders and users will get for their money. That can be measured; and into the computer it will go. The study will also include estimates of future needs, based on projections of area population and patterns of air travel. They can be quantified; and into the computer they will go.

But how can the objectors to an airport measure the loss of quiet that nearby residents will suffer? How can they measure the loss of green fields and wildlife? They cannot. All they can use to oppose the airport's supporters is their own common sense, and outrage at the proposed despoliation of the countryside. Those feelings might, to be sure, find their way into the computer in the form of opinion research studies; but they are pitifully weak barriers against the flood of apparently objective economic data.

In one sense at least, economics has not progressed. The great economists of the past were primarily social theorists; they were more concerned with people than with things. Furthermore, most of them made no false distinctions between economy and society, which were correctly perceived as two aspects of the same phenomenon. Most of the classical economists saw very clearly indeed that a change in the mode of production and distribution implied changes in the structure and nature of society.

In those days—the eighteenth and nineteenth centuries—economists were known as political economists. The term expressed a truth frequently overlooked today: there is a vital nexus between politics and economics. Political and economic decisions are inextricably intertwined; together, those decisions shape the future of society. Thus, in most economic studies due attention must be paid to social results. As the late John Maynard Keynes, a noted economist (see page 144), reminds us, the master economist "must study the present in the light of the past for the purposes of the future. No part of man's nature or his institutions must lie entirely outside his regard."

R. B.

1. *How might economists be aided by other social scientists in studying the economic problems of the inner city?*

2. *"There are no 'principles' of economics, sociology, or political science. There are only principles of science which we may hope to discover and apply to social behavior." Do you agree?*

Barter is obviously a cumbersome way of doing business. If you wanted to trade cows for a plow, you would have to find a person who had a plow and was willing to exchange it for some cows. This basic principle of barter is sometimes called the "double coincidence of wants" because it correctly implies that in order for barter to occur, each party must have what the other desires, and be willing to make an exchange on terms that are suitable to both.

MONEY ENTERS THE PICTURE

When an economy grows beyond the simplest stage, barter is no longer feasible. Money is developed because it is more convenient to exchange labor or goods for money, rather than try to find the person who has what is wanted and is willing to trade for what is offered. Money is a *medium of exchange* because it is widely accepted and generally used in payment for goods and services. This means that people do not ordinarily want money for its own sake; they want it for what it will buy.

Money serves other functions too—as a *measure of value* by enabling us to keep business records and to express the prices of things that people and business firms buy and sell; as a *standard of deferred payment* by allowing us to borrow or lend money for future repayment with interest; and as a *store of value* by permitting us to save some of our money so that it can be spent in the future. These four functions of money have long been epitomized by a popular rhyme:

> Money is a matter of functioning four,
> A medium, a measure, a standard, a store.

Money, therefore, may be broadly described as a social convention. It is anything that the members of a society will accept as money—cattle, shells, stones, or what have you. (See Box 2.) Its effectiveness is directly dependent on the extent to which it fulfills its four functions. In our modern society not only coins and currency, but also checks and credit cards serve as money. In fact, most students are usually surprised to learn that over ninety percent of the *value* (not number) of all transactions in our economy is conducted by checks.

Box 2

Odd and Curious Money

Unusual forms of money (lower left and going clockwise): A whale's tooth from the Fiji Islands; stone money of Yap which varied in size and could be as big as three feet in diameter; elephant tail bristles which were a popular medium of exchange in Portuguese West Africa until the early decades of this century (one tail was equal in value to two slaves and 50 bristles were worth 1,000 reis or $1.50 at that time); canine tooth money from the Solomon Islands; a copper cross from the Belgian Congo; Aztec money; tree money used in the Orient.

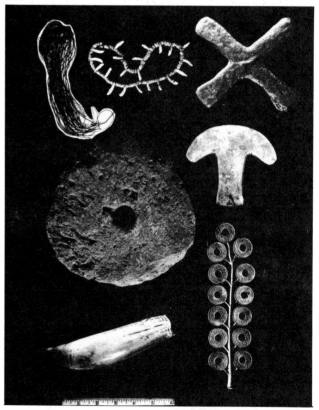

Chase Manhattan Bank Museum of Moneys of the World, New York.

The Circular Flow of Economic Activity

Some of the important features of a capitalistic system are illustrated by the diagram in Exhibit 1. This model assumes that the total economy is divided into two sectors: households and businesses; it also shows how these sectors meet one another in two sets of markets: the product markets and the resource markets.

In the *product markets,* households buy the goods and services that businesses sell, and their payments for these are represented by consumption expenditures which become the receipts of businesses. In the *resource markets,* businesses buy the factors of production that households sell, and their payments for these are costs which become the money incomes of households.

All these transactions are accomplished in free markets by a price system that registers the wishes of buyers and sellers. Through the price system, therefore, the product markets are the places where businesses decide WHAT to produce, whereas the resource markets are the places where they decide HOW to produce. (Can you explain why?)

One other feature of the diagram should be noted: the outer loop portrays the physical flow of goods and resources in one direction, while the inner loop

---

Exhibit 1

The Circular Flow of Economic Activity
or How Millions of Businesses and Households Take in Each Other's Washing

The prices of goods and services are determined in the product markets where households are **demanders** *and businesses are* **suppliers**. *The prices of the factors of production are determined in the resource markets where businesses are* **demanders** *and households are* **suppliers**. *The outer loop shows physical flows in one direction, while the inner loop shows dollar flows in the opposite direction. Can you suggest how the diagram can be made more detailed?*

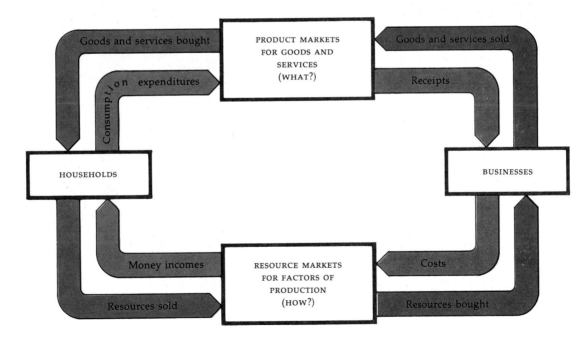

Goods and services bought — PRODUCT MARKETS FOR GOODS AND SERVICES (WHAT?) — Goods and services sold

Consumption expenditures — Receipts

HOUSEHOLDS — BUSINESSES

Money incomes — Costs

Resources sold — RESOURCE MARKETS FOR FACTORS OF PRODUCTION (HOW?) — Resources bought

---

shows the corresponding dollar flow in the opposite direction. In a barter economy, of course, only goods and resources would be exchanged and hence there would be no dollar flows.

SOME COMMENTS ABOUT THE MODEL

The circular flow model represents a broad overview of an economic system. Since it describes the "forest" rather than the "trees," some of its underlying omissions and limitations are worth noting.

1. The model is *macroeconomic* rather than microeconomic. If focuses on the overall linkages between sectors and markets and not on their internal workings. Thus it does not disclose anything about the relationships between households or between businesses, or about the ways in which these economic organisms react to one another. These considerations are taken up in subsequent chapters.

2. The model says nothing about government or its role in the total economy, because it represents a pure capitalistic system in which the economic functions of government are relatively minor.

3. The model assumes that the physical and dollar flows of goods, resources, incomes, and expenditures continue at a constant rate, and that resources and product prices are already determined and given. In reality, these flows and prices are the results of many complex forces as our later study will show. The circular flow model should be regarded as nothing more than a very simplified picture of the overall structure of a capitalistic system.

SUMMARY OF IMPORTANT IDEAS

1. The economic system of the United States and most other countries of the Western world is capitalistic. Capitalism is a type of economic organization in which the means of production and distribution are privately owned and used for private gain.

2. Pure capitalism rests on certain pillars: private property, self-interest, economic individualism or laissez-faire, competition, and the price system. The economic role of government in a pure capitalistic system is relatively minor. Since the nineteenth century, however, as capitalistic or market economies

have become increasingly complex, the economic functions of government have gained in importance. The American economy is neither a pure market economy nor a pure command economy; it is a "mixed" economy in which both private individuals and government exercise their economic influence in the marketplace.

3. There are at least three basic features that characterize all developed economies: (1) an advanced technology and adequate capital, (2) a high degree of specialization and division of labor, and (3) a suitable form of money. The ways in which these conditions interrelate with one another will affect an economy's productivity and efficiency.

4. The circular flow model represents a broad overview of the operation of a capitalistic system. It is a simplified model in which the two sectors of the economy, businesses and households, buy and sell goods and resources in two sets of markets, the product markets and the resource markets.

FOR HOMEWORK AND DISCUSSION

1. *Terms and concepts to review:*

capitalism	money
private property	barter
"invisible hand"	double coincidence of wants
economic man	
laissez-faire	circular flow of economic activity
competition	
price system	product markets
specialization	resource markets
division of labor	

2. Distinguish between the concepts of *capital* and *capitalism.*

3. The "profit motive" is sometimes said to be the most fundamental feature of capitalism. (*a*) What do you suppose is meant by the "profit motive"? (*b*) Why wasn't it explicitly listed in this chapter as one of the pillars of capitalism?

4. Do the self-interests of individuals and businesses interact to produce the best overall outcome in a freely competitive market? Explain your answer.

5. (*a*) "In a free competitive economy, the consumer is king." What does this mean? (*b*) "The producer, *not* the consumer, is king. After all, the producer is the one who advertises; hence he is the one who creates wants and thereby influences what consumers will purchase." True or false? Explain.

6. Does the price system settle the three questions of WHAT, HOW, and FOR WHOM in some particular order? Explain. Can you give an illustration or example?

7. It is often said that the beauty of the price system is to be found in its self-regulating nature. As a result, the market is its own guardian—provided it is left alone to function without outside interference. Can you explain this?

REFERENCES AND READING SUGGESTIONS

EBENSTEIN, WILLIAM, *Today's Isms*, 6th ed., Prentice-Hall, Englewood Cliffs, N.J., 1970, chap. 3.

LOUCKS, WILLIAM N., and WILLIAM G. WHITNEY, *Comparative Economic Systems*, 8th ed., Harper & Row, New York, 1969, chap. 2.

MONSEN, R. JOSEPH, JR., *Modern American Capitalism: Ideologies and Issues*, Houghton Mifflin, Boston, 1963, chaps. 1–3.

CHAPTER 4

The "Laws" of Supply and Demand: The Price System in a Pure Market Economy

CHAPTER PREVIEW

What are the "laws" of supply and demand? How do they determine prices?

What is a market economy? A price system?

What can be said about the "pros" and "cons" of a market economy? How well does it answer the three fundamental questions, WHAT, HOW, and FOR WHOM?

One unusual thing about economics is the fact that even a parrot can answer many of its questions with just three simple words, *supply and demand.* Here are a few examples:

QUESTION: Why are Rembrandts expensive while water is cheap—especially since everyone needs water more than he needs Rembrandts?
Answer: Supply and demand.

QUESTION: Why is the cost of medical care rising faster than prices generally?
Answer: Supply and demand.

QUESTION: Why are some luxurious apartments vacant, while there is a shortage of low-cost housing?
Answer: Supply and demand.

QUESTION: Why do the prices of some commodities fluctuate while the prices of others remain the same?
Answer: Supply and demand.

Most instructors would not appreciate such simplistic answers to complex problems. Nevertheless, much of economics is concerned with supply and demand—and in this chapter you discover more about this apparently simple but actually complicated subject.

What Do We Mean by Demand?

If pizzas were $4 each, how many would you buy per month? What if the price were $3? $2? Would you buy twice as many at $1 as at $2?

These are typical of the questions that arise in the study of demand. What is demand? In economics it has a special meaning:

Demand is a relation showing the various amounts of a commodity that buyers would be willing and able to purchase at possible alternative prices during a given period of time, all other things remaining the same.

The product can be anything—pizzas, shoes, transistor radios, TV sets, haircuts, books, houses, labor time, bulldozers, ICBMs, or any other good or service bought by consumers, businesses, or government agencies. Further, the definition assumes that demand means both desire and ability to pay, and that either of these taken separately is of no economic significance in the marketplace.

Thus if you want a steak but cannot pay for it— or if you can pay but prefer hamburger—you exercise no economic influence in the market for steaks. But if you have both the desire and the ability to pay, these together will affect your demand for the product—that is, the number of pounds of steak you would be willing to purchase at various prices during a period of time. These ideas are further illustrated below.

THE DEMAND SCHEDULE

Suppose you were a grain merchant dealing in wheat, corn, barley, oats, etc. What is your demand for a specific commodity such as wheat?

According to the above definition of demand, you must first ask, "At what prices and for how long?" It seems likely that within a given period you would buy more wheat at a lower price than at a higher one, and at a given price you would probably buy more in a longer period than in a shorter one. In view of this, you might prepare a hypothetical list of the number of bushels of wheat you would buy at different prices during a particular time interval,

Exhibit 1

An Individual's Demand Schedule for Wheat

A demand schedule is a list showing the number of units of a product that would be purchased at various possible prices during a given period of time.

	Price per bushel	Quantity demanded per day
A	$5	5
B	4	10
C	3	20
D	2	35
E	1	60

such as a day, *assuming that your income and the prices of other commodities remain the same.*

Such a list is what economists call a *demand schedule,* as shown in Exhibit 1. This schedule represents your individual demand for wheat over the price range shown. The schedule tells you that at $5 per bushel you would buy 5 bushels a day. At a price of $4 per bushel you would buy 10 bushels a day, and so on. Of course, you can make the schedule more detailed by extending the price scale from zero to "infinity" and by quoting the prices in dollars and cents instead of just dollars alone. But such detail is not necessary. As you will see, the schedule already gives you the highlights of your demand for wheat, which is all you need to draw a graph. (See also Box 1, on page 46.)

SKETCHING A DEMAND CURVE

Most people prefer to look at a chart instead of a table of figures. This is easily done by converting the information in Exhibit 1 to the diagram in Exhibit 2. The graphing process is done in three easy steps.

Step 1. Draw the vertical and horizontal axes of the chart and put the titles on them as shown. It is customary in economics to label the vertical axis P for price, and the horizontal axis Q for quantity. The

Exhibit 2

An Individual's Demand Curve for Wheat

A demand curve is the graph of a demand schedule. Each point along the curve represents a different price-quantity combination. A demand curve slopes downward from left to right, reflecting the fact that the quantity demanded of a product varies inversely with the price. This is called the law of demand.

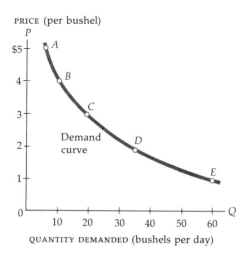

PRICE (per bushel)

QUANTITY DEMANDED (bushels per day)

price and quantity demanded, and to read off the values at a glance, much as you would use a map to locate a ship at sea by its latitude and longitude.

For instance, point *C* represents 20 bushels of wheat demanded per day at a price of $3 per bushel. Would you agree that at $1.50 per bushel the quantity demanded is 45 bushels per day? Can you verify from the chart that at a quantity demanded of 35 bushels per day, the *highest price* (called the *demand price*) you would be willing to pay is $2 per bushel?

THE LAW OF DEMAND

A look at the demand curve in Exhibit 2 reveals its most fundamental property: *the curve slopes downward from left to right*—from northwest to southeast. This characteristic is called the "law of demand." It applies to virtually all commodities: wheat, books, houses, automobiles, hi-fi records, clothing, or practically anything else you care to name. Here is a definition which will be elaborated in the following pages.

Law of Demand. The quantity demanded of a good varies inversely with its price, assuming that all other things which may affect demand—especially the buyer's income, tastes, and the prices of other commodities—remain the same. (By "inversely" is meant that as the price of a good decreases, the corresponding quantity demanded increases; as the price of a good increases, the corresponding quantity demanded decreases.)

Why does the law of demand operate as it does? This question can be answered in several ways. The following are among the most important of them:

1. If the price of a good decreases, you can *afford* to buy more of it if your income, tastes, and the prices of other goods remain the same. For instance, if you like pizza with all the trimmings, but find it too expensive to buy frequently, a lower price might induce you to purchase it more often.

2. When the price of a product is reduced, you may buy more of it because it becomes a better bargain than other goods are—assuming as before that your income, tastes, and the prices of other goods remain constant. Thus if the price of steak falls, you might

starting point or origin of the chart is always at the lower left-hand corner labeled *O*.

Step 2. Plot the corresponding prices and quantities as shown by the large dots, and label them with the appropriate letters *A, B, C, D, E* from the demand schedule in Exhibit 1. These letters help you to identify the points, as you will see below. After you gain some experience in graphing, the emphasized points and letters will no longer be necessary.

Step 3. Connect the points with a smooth curve.

The curve you now have is called a *demand curve*. It represents the graphic equivalent of the demand schedule in Exhibit 1. The advantage of the curve is that it enables you to "see" the relationship between

Box 1

Why Wheat?

You have probably wondered why we are using wheat as an example. Why not use a more familiar product like cars or television sets?

The answer, as you will see later in this chapter, is that we want to demonstrate how the price is established for a uniform or standardized product in a highly competitive market characterized by a great many buyers and sellers, each acting independently according to his best interests. This type of situation or model will result in a single market price *for the product at any given time. Clearly, autos and TV sets do not meet these requirements for several reasons: each is produced by a relatively small number of sellers; each is nonstandardized or differentiated by brand name, model year, style, color, etc.; and each is characterized by different prices rather than by single prices. These conditions are true in varying degrees for nearly all the other products we buy every day.*

On the other hand, products like wheat as well as the other commodities shown in the accompanying list approximate these requirements rather closely. Hence any one of them may be used in a model to illustrate the "pure" operation of supply and demand, which is our concern in this chapter. In later chapters you will see how this model may be modified in order to reflect the ways in which prices are determined in other industries of our mixed capitalistic system—including industries that produce products like automobiles and television sets.

Commodities

Cash Prices

(quotations as of 4 P.M. Eastern time)

	Tues.	Mon.	Yr. Ago
FOODS			
Flour, hard winter NY cwt......	$6.25	$6.25	$6.95
Coffee, Santos 4s NY lb	.37¾	.37¾	.39¼
Cocoa, Accra NY lb	.29⅝	.29⅜	.27½
Sugar, Raw NY lb	.0748	.0748	.0722
Butter, Fresh A-92 sc NY lb.....	.67¼–.67½	.67–.67½	.67
Eggs, lge ext. whites, Chgo., doz	.27	.27	.27
Broilers, 3 lb & under DelMV lb.	.16½	.16⅝	.14⅜
GRAINS AND FEEDS			
Pepper, black NY lb	.29¾	.29¾	.33¾
Wheat, No 2 ord hard KC bu...	1.51¾	1.53⅛	1.74⅞
Oats, No. 1 wh. heavy, Chgo., bu	.80	.78½	.73¾
Rye, No. 2 Minneapolis bu	1.14½	1.14½	1.22½
Barley, malting NY bu	1.66	1.66	1.78
MISCELLANEOUS			
Cottonseed Oil, crd Miss Vly lb.	.14½	.14	.12
Soybean Oil, crd Decatur, Ill. lb.	.0882	.0884	.1022
Peanut Oil, crd Southeast lb....	.13¾	.13½	.12¼
Cotton, one in. mid Memphis lb	.2550	.2550	.2250
Print Cloth, 64 × 60 38½ in. NY yd	.15¼	.15¼	.14¼
Steel Scrap, 1 hvy mlt Chg. ton .	26.00	26.00	27.50
Lead, NY lb..................	.13	.13	.14
Zinc, East St. Lous lb	.13½	.13½	.13½

SOURCE: Adapted from *The Wall Street Journal.*

buy more steak and fewer "substitutes" like hamburger or hot dogs. On the other hand, if the price of steak rises, you would tend to buy less steak and more substitutes.

3. Finally the downward-sloping demand curve tells you that you would be willing to pay a relatively high price for a small amount of something; but the more you have of it the less you would care to pay for one more unit. Why? Because *each extra unit gives you less additional satisfaction or "utility" than the previous unit.*

For example, however crazy you are about ice-cream sundaes there is a limit to the number you can eat in any given period: after the first few you would probably get sick. It follows, therefore, that no matter how much you like a product your demand curve will slope downward because of the three sets of reasons given above. And businessmen, of course, often operate as if they believe a law of (downward-sloping) demand exists, for why else would they advertise bargains that encourage people to buy more goods at lower prices?

MARKET DEMAND IS THE SUM OF INDIVIDUAL DEMANDS

If you were the only buyer of wheat in the market, your individual demand schedule would also be the total market demand schedule. In reality, of course, there are many other buyers besides yourself. Hence the total market demand schedule is obtained by simply adding up the quantities demanded by all buyers at each possible price.

Exhibit 3 shows how this is done. This assumes there are only three buyers in the market, Mr. *X*, Mr. *Y*, and Mr. *Z*—but you can easily extend the example to include as many buyers as you wish. Note that the demand curves have all been labeled so that they can be referred to as needed.

TWO KINDS OF CHANGES INVOLVING DEMAND

Once you understand the notion of a demand curve, you can use it to distinguish between two basic types of variation: One of these is called a "change in the quantity demanded"; the other is a "change in demand."

1. Changes in the Quantity Demanded

Let us look again at Exhibit 2. According to the law of demand, a downhill movement along the same curve in the general direction *A, B, C,* etc., signifies an increase in the quantity demanded as the price is reduced; on the other hand, an uphill movement along the curve in the general direction *E, D, C,* etc., signifies a decrease in the quantity demanded as the price is raised. We call any such movement along the same curve, whether downward or upward, a *change in the quantity demanded.* Note that this expression refers to changes in the quantities purchased by buyers.

2. Changes in Demand

The law of demand tells you that the quantity demanded of a good varies inversely with its price, assuming that all other things remain the same. What are these "all other" things? What happens if they do not remain the same?

Exhibit 3

Market Demand for Wheat, Three Buyers

The total market demand for wheat is obtained by summing all of the individual quantities demanded at each price.

(1) Price per bushel	(2) Quantity demanded by Mr. X		(3) Quantity demanded by Mr. Y		(4) Quantity demanded by Mr. Z		(5) Total market demand per day
$5	0	+	15	+	20	=	35
4	9	+	20	+	26	=	55
3	22	+	27	+	33	=	82
2	42	+	38	+	43	=	123
1	80	+	65	+	60	=	205

PRICE (per bushel)

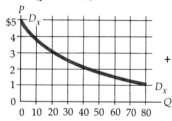 + 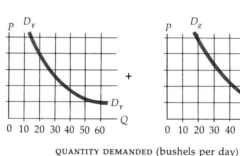 + 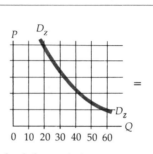 =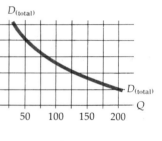

QUANTITY DEMANDED (bushels per day)

In addition to price, there are usually other factors that will influence the demand for a product: (1) consumers' money incomes, (2) the prices of related goods, (3) consumers' tastes or preferences, (4) the number of consumers in the market, (5) consumers' expectations of future prices and incomes. Since these five conditions are assumed to be constant when you draw a demand curve, a change in any one of them will cause a shift of the demand curve to a new position. When this happens, we say that there has been a *change in demand.* Two types of changes may occur.

INCREASE IN DEMAND. An increase in demand can be visualized on a chart as a shift of the demand curve to the right as shown in Exhibit 4. The shift takes place from the old demand curve D_1 to the new demand curve D_2, with the arrow serving to emphasize the direction of change.

What does this increase in demand tell you? It shows that, *at any given price, buyers are now willing to purchase more than they were willing to purchase before.* For example, the dashed lines on the chart indicate that at a price of $30 per unit, buyers were previously willing to purchase 300 units per week. After the increase in demand, they are willing to buy 400 units a week at the same price of $30 per unit.

DECREASE IN DEMAND. A decrease in demand, shown in Exhibit 5, can be visualized as a shift of the demand curve to the left. This time the chart illustrates that, *at any given price, buyers are now willing to purchase less than they were willing to purchase before.* Thus at $30 per unit, people were willing to buy 300 units a week. Now, after the decrease in demand, they are willing to buy only 200 units per week at the same price of $30 per unit.

Exhibit 4

Increase in Demand

An increase in demand can be represented by a shift of the demand curve to the right. At any given price, people are now willing to buy more than they were willing to buy before.

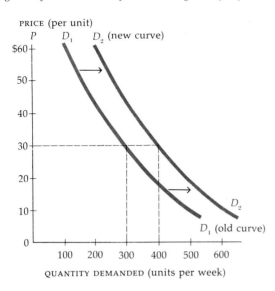

Exhibit 5

Decrease in Demand

A decrease in demand can be represented by a shift of the demand curve to the left. At any given price, people are now willing to buy less than they were willing to buy before.

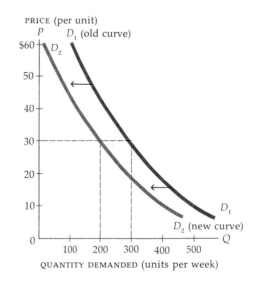

An increase in demand also means that for any given quantity demanded, buyers are now willing to pay a *higher price* per unit than they were willing to pay before.

1. Can you define a decrease in demand in a parallel way?

2. In Exhibit 4, what is your estimate of the highest price per unit that buyers were willing to pay for 300 units per week, before and after the increase in demand?

3. In Exhibit 5, what is your estimate of the highest price per unit that buyers were willing to pay for 200 units per week, before and after the decrease in demand?

How do changes in any of the five demand determinants listed above bring about a change in demand—that is, a shift of the demand curve either to the right or to the left?

1. Consumers' money incomes. For the majority of consumers' goods, changes in demand vary directly with changes in buyers' incomes. This means that the demand curves for these goods will shift to the right when incomes rise and to the left when incomes fall. Goods whose demand curves behave in this way are called *normal* goods. Examples include most food, clothing, appliances, and the other nondurable and durable items that people typically buy.

However, there are a few goods for which changes in demand may, under special conditions, vary inversely with changes in incomes. Such goods are called *inferior* goods—or sometimes "poor man's" goods, although this title is not entirely accurate. Some typical examples of inferior goods are bread and potatoes. Thus many poor families buy fewer cheap filling foods like bread and potatoes when their incomes rise, and demand instead more nutritious foods like dairy products, fresh fruits, and meats.

2. Prices of related goods. How is a change in the demand for a particular product affected by a change in the price of another product? The answer depends on the type of relationship that exists between the products involved.

Some products are *substitutes*; the more that people consume of one, the less they consume of the other. Thus if the price of Coke rose, people would probably buy less Coke and more Pepsi instead. The market demand curve for Pepsi would therefore shift to the right. Can you think of some other substitute products? What would happen to the demand for margarine if the price of butter were increased? What would happen to the demand for Fords if the price of Chevrolets were reduced?

Some products are *complements*; the more that people consume of one, the more they consume of the other. Thus if the price of hi-fi's is reduced, people will buy more hi-fi's—and more records. The market demand curve for records will then shift to the right. What would happen to the demand for bacon if the price of eggs were increased? What would happen to the demand for film if the price of cameras were reduced?

Some products are *independent*; the market demand for one bears no immediate relationship to the market demand for the other. Therefore a change in the price of one of them is not expected to cause a change in the demand for the other. Some examples are pencils and milk, wristwatches and tires, typewriters and blankets. You should have no difficulty thinking of others.

The three remaining factors that may cause a change in demand are:

3. Consumers' tastes. Consumers are capricious; advertising or even fashion may cause some to change their preferences for goods. Others alter their habits to gain status. Some change their preferences as new or better products come along. Any of these factors can increase demand for some products or decrease demand for others.

4. The number of consumers. Changes in the size or composition of the population can either increase or decrease the number of consumers. Shifts in population can increase markets in some regions and decrease them in others. In any case, an increase in the number of consumers will ordinarily shift the demand curve to the right; a decrease will shift it to the left.

5. *Consumer expectations.* If consumers expect higher prices or higher incomes in the future, they may be encouraged to buy now, thereby increasing their demand for goods. On the other hand, if they expect lower prices or lower incomes, they may refrain from buying now, thereby decreasing their demand for goods.

To Summarize

"Demand" can be represented by a schedule or curve which reflects buyers' attitudes at the time. If the demand curve does not shift, a change in price leads to a *change in the quantity demanded,* not to a change in demand. This means that there has been either an increase in the quantity demanded, as represented by a movement downward along the curve, or a decrease in the quantity demanded, as represented by a movement upward along the curve. The change is due either to a decrease or increase in the price of the product (while all other demand determinants remain the same).

A *change in demand* means that the schedule itself has changed, and hence that the demand curve has either shifted to the right if there has been an increase in demand, or to the left if there has been a decrease in demand. The shift is due to a change in one or more of the five demand determinants listed above.

Exhibit 6

An Individual's Supply Schedule for Wheat

A supply schedule is a list showing the number of units of a product that sellers would be willing and able to make available for sale at various prices during a given period of time.

	Price per bushel	Quantity supplied per day
A'	$5	50
B'	4	42
C'	3	33
D'	2	21
E'	1	0

Which of the following involve a change in the quantity demanded and which involve a change in demand:

1. People buy more bathing suits in the summer than in the winter.

2. Consumer incomes fall and the number of automobiles purchased declines.

3. RCA reduces the price of its TV sets by 10 percent and its sales increase.

4. State College raises its tuition and student enrollments fall off.

It is easy to commit many errors in economic reasoning by failing to understand the important distinctions between a change in the quantity demanded and a change in demand.

Exhibit 7

An Individual's Supply Curve for Wheat

A supply curve is the graph of a supply schedule. Each point along the curve represents a different price-quantity combination. A supply curve slopes upward from left to right, reflecting the fact that the quantity supplied of a product varies directly with the price. This is called the law of supply.

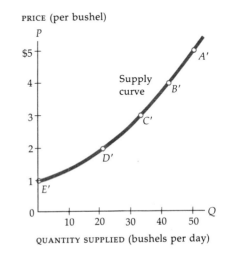

What Is Supply?

You now have a basic knowledge of demand. The other half of the picture involves supply. What do we mean by supply? Is there a law of supply?

Supply is a relation showing the various amounts of a commodity that sellers would be willing and able to make available for sale at possible alternative prices during a given period of time, all other things remaining the same.

How does this definition of supply compare with the definition of demand given near the beginning of this chapter? Are there any similarities? Any differences?

SUPPLY SCHEDULES AND SUPPLY CURVES

According to the definition of supply, each seller in the market has his own supply schedule for a product, just as each buyer has his own demand schedule. Thus if you were a wheat farmer, Exhibit 6 might represent your individual supply schedule for wheat. This schedule indicates that at a price of $1 per bushel you would not be willing to supply any wheat at all. At a price of $2 per bushel you would be willing to supply 21 bushels of wheat per day, and so on. When you plot these data on a chart, you get the supply curve shown in Exhibit 7. What is your estimate of the quantity supplied at a price of $2.50 per unit? What is the *least price*, approximately, that will persuade you to supply 40 bushels per day?

REMARK. The "least price" is more often called the *supply price*, which is the price necessary to call forth a given quantity. What do you estimate the supply price to be for 25 bushels per day?

An example of the supply schedules for three individual producers, Mr. *A*, Mr. *B*, and Mr. *C* is presented in Exhibit 8. When you plot the data,

---

Exhibit 8

Market Supply of Wheat, Three Sellers

The total market supply of wheat is obtained by summing all of the individual quantities supplied at each price.

(1) Price per bushel	(2) Quantity supplied by Mr. A		(3) Quantity supplied by Mr. B		(4) Quantity supplied by Mr. C		(5) Total market supply per day
$5	52	+	56	+	60	=	168
4	46	+	49	+	50	=	145
3	36	+	42	+	40	=	118
2	26	+	28	+	26	=	80
1	0	+	15	+	10	=	25

you get the corresponding supply curves shown on the charts. Note that the total market supply schedule is obtained by adding up the quantities supplied by all sellers at each market price. How does this compare with the way in which the total market demand schedule was derived earlier?

THE LAW OF SUPPLY

It does not take long to realize that the supply curve as drawn has a distinguishing feature: *the curve slopes upward from left to right*—from southwest to northeast. This feature reflects the "law of supply," which may be stated briefly here, and then elaborated upon in the following paragraphs.

Law of Supply. The quantity supplied of a commodity usually varies *directly* with its price, assuming that all other factors that may determine supply remain the same. By "directly" is meant that the quantity of a product produced and offered for sale will increase as the price of the product rises, and decrease as the price falls.

Note that the direct relation between quantity and price is "usually" true, but not always. There can be some supply curves where larger quantities are sold at the *same* price or even at *lower* prices. You will learn more about this in later chapters.

How would you behave according to the law of supply if you were a producer—say a farmer cultivating both wheat and corn? The law would prompt you to act in the following way: If the price of wheat in the market rose relative to the price of corn, you would make greater profits by shifting your limited resources—fertilizer, land, labor, machinery, etc.—out of corn and into wheat production. If the price of wheat rose high enough, you would even find it worth your while to grow wheat on land where you previously grew nothing. Thus it seems that the law of supply does indeed make sense.

TWO KINDS OF CHANGES INVOLVING SUPPLY

Two types of changes may arise in the study of supply: one is called a "change in the quantity supplied"; the other is known as a "change in supply."

On the basis of what you now know about the theory of demand, can you guess the meanings of these two concepts before we proceed to explain them?

1. Changes in the Quantity Supplied

Look again at Exhibit 7. According to the law of supply, an uphill movement along the same curve signifies an increase in the quantity supplied as the price is raised; on the other hand, a downhill movement along the curve signifies a decrease in the quantity supplied as the price is reduced. Any such movement along the same curve, whether upward or downward, is called a *change in the quantity supplied.*

2. Changes in Supply

The law of supply says that the quantity supplied of a product usually varies directly with its price, assuming that all other things remain the same. The "other things" that may have an influence in determining supply are primarily: (a) the state of technology, (b) resource prices or the costs of the factors of production, (c) prices of other goods, (d) the number of sellers in the market, and (e) sellers' expectations regarding future prices. A change in any one of these can cause a shift of the supply curve to a new position. In that case we get what is called a *change in supply.* Two such types of changes may occur:

INCREASE IN SUPPLY. This is a shift of the supply curve to the right, as shown in Exhibit 9. *At any given price sellers are now willing to supply more than they were willing to supply before.* For example, the dashed lines indicate that at a price of $30 per unit sellers were previously willing to supply a total of 300 units per week. Now, after the increase in supply, they are willing to sell a total of 400 units per week at the same price of $30 per unit.

DECREASE IN SUPPLY. This is represented by a shift of the supply curve to the left. *At any given price, sellers are now willing to supply less than they were willing to supply before.* Thus in Exhibit 10, they were previously willing to supply a total of 300 units per week at a price of $30 per unit. Now, after the

Exhibit 9

Increase in Supply

An increase in supply can be represented by a shift of the supply curve to the right. At any given price, sellers are now willing to supply more than they were willing to supply before.

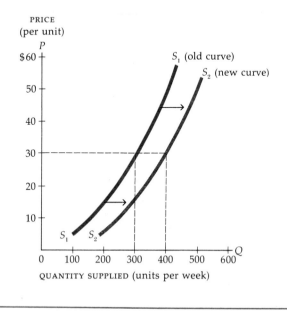

PRICE (per unit)

QUANTITY SUPPLIED (units per week)

Exhibit 10

Decrease in Supply

A decrease in supply can be represented by a shift of the supply curve to the left. At any given price, sellers are now willing to supply less than they were willing to supply before.

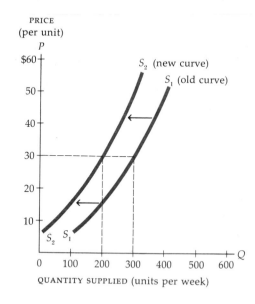

PRICE (per unit)

QUANTITY SUPPLIED (units per week)

TEST YOURSELF

An increase in supply also means that for any given quantity supplied sellers are now willing to accept a *lower price* per unit than they were willing to accept before.

1. Can you define a decrease in supply in a parallel way?

2. In Exhibit 9, what is your estimate of the lowest price per unit that sellers were willing to accept for a supply of 300 units per week, before and after the increase in supply?

3. In Exhibit 10, what is your estimate of the lowest price per unit that sellers were willing to accept for a supply of 200 units per week, before and after the decrease in supply?

decrease in supply, they are willing to sell a total of 200 units per week at the same price of $30 per unit.

How will a change in any of the five supply determinants listed above bring about a change in supply —that is, a shift of the supply curve either to the right or to the left?

1. The state of technology. Adoption of a new invention or a new production technique may decrease production costs and increase supply. Every child who studies American history in elementary school learns about the expansion in agricultural efficiency and production that resulted from the adoption of Eli Whitney's cotton gin (1794) and Cyrus McCormick's reaper (1834). In the history of nations, the great increases in output that have taken place can often be accounted for by *innovations*—that is, the adoption of new methods and ways of producing things.

2. *Resource prices.* Ordinarily, a decrease in resource prices in a particular industry will reduce production costs and thus broaden the profit potentials. However, if there is vigorous competition among businessmen within the industry they will be prompted to increase their output at each possible price in order to capture some of these profits. This action will shift the total market supply curve to the right. Conversely, an increase in resource prices in a given industry would tend to have the opposite effect, since it raises production costs and decreases profits, thereby encouraging businessmen in that industry to reduce their output at each possible price. This action shifts the market supply curve to the left.

3. *Prices of other goods.* Businessmen produce goods to make profits. Changes in the relative prices of goods may change their relative profitabilities and thereby bring about changes in their respective supply curves. For instance, if the price of wheat increases relative to the price of corn, farmers may find it more profitable to transfer resources out of corn and into wheat, thereby shifting the market supply curve of corn to the left and the market supply curve of wheat to the right.

4. *The number of sellers.* Given the size of each seller in a particular industry, the number of sellers will affect the market supply curve. If sellers enter the industry the curve will shift to the right; if sellers leave the industry the curve will shift to the left.

5. *Sellers' price expectations.* Sellers' beliefs about future prices will probably influence their supply decisions. Thus some producers may decide to hold back on their current output because they anticipate higher prices for their goods—and therefore higher profits; other producers may decide to increase their current output because they anticipate lower prices for their goods—and therefore lower profits or possibly losses.

To Summarize

"Supply" can be represented by a schedule or curve which reflects sellers' attitudes at the time. If the supply curve does not shift, a change in price leads to a *change in the quantity supplied,* not to a change in supply. This means that there has either been a movement upward along the curve in the case of an increase in the quantity supplied, or a movement downward along the curve in the case of a decrease in the quantity supplied.

A *change in supply* means that the schedule itself has changed—that is, the curve has shifted to the right if there has been an increase in supply, or to the left if there has been a decrease in supply. The shift is usually caused by a change in one or more of the five supply determinants listed above.

TEST YOURSELF

Which of the following involve a change in the quantity supplied and which involve a change in supply:

1. The market price of oats rises and the quantity supplied of oats increases.

2. The price of oranges decreases and the annual production of grapefruits increases.

3. Automobile workers get a 5 percent wage increase and the production of automobiles decreases.

4. The price of corn falls and the production of corn decreases.

Supply and Demand Together Make a Market

The time has now come to join together our theories of demand and supply. Once this union is effected, we will have the basis of a theory which explains how prices are determined in *competitive markets*—that is, markets composed of buyers and sellers so numerous that no single one can influence the market price by deciding to buy or not to buy, to sell or not to sell.

What is a market? A market exists whenever and wherever one or more buyers and sellers can negotiate for goods or services and thereby participate in determining their prices. A market, therefore, can be anywhere—on a street corner, on the other side of the world, or as close as the nearest telephone.

BUYERS AND SELLERS IN THE MARKETPLACE

How do buyers and sellers determine the market price of a product and the quantity of it that will be bought and sold? We can answer this question in terms of the wheat data used earlier.

Referring back to Exhibits 3 and 8, we take the *total* market demand and supply schedules and reproduce them in Exhibit 11, along with the corresponding market demand and supply curves abbreviated *D* and *S*. These curves are identical with the total market curves that were graphed earlier in Exhibits 3 and 8, but now they are both graphed on the same chart so that their interactions can be observed more easily.

The most important thing to observe is that the supply and demand curves intersect at a place called the *equilibrium point*. A dictionary will tell you that "equilibrium" refers to a state of balance between opposing forces. Let us see what this means in terms of Exhibit 11.

At any price above $2.50 per bushel, the quantity supplied exceeds the quantity demanded. For example, at a price of $5 per bushel, the quantity supplied is 168 bushels per day and the quantity demanded is 35 bushels per day. This means there is a *surplus* of 168 − 35 = 133 bushels per day. Since sellers thus have more wheat available than buyers want, sellers will compete with one another to dispose of their product and thereby drive the price down.

At any price below $2.50 per bushel, the quantity demanded exceeds the quantity supplied. Thus at $1 a bushel, for example, the quantity demanded is 205 bushels per day and the quantity supplied is 25 bushels per day. There is then a *shortage* at this price of 205 − 25 = 180 bushels per day. Since buyers want more wheat than sellers have available at this price, buyers will compete with one another to acquire the product and thereby drive the price up.

Exhibit 11

The Equilibrium Price and Quantity for Wheat

The intersection of the supply and demand curves determines the equilibrium price and the equilibrium quantity. At any price above the equilibrium price, the quantity supplied exceeds the quantity demanded and the price tends to fall. At any price below the equilibrium price, the quantity demanded exceeds the quantity supplied and the price tends to rise. At the equilibrium price, the quantity supplied precisely equals the quantity demanded and hence there is no tendency for the price to change.

Price per bushel	Total market supply per day	Total market demand per day
$5	168	35
4	145	55
3	118	82
2	80	123
1	25	205

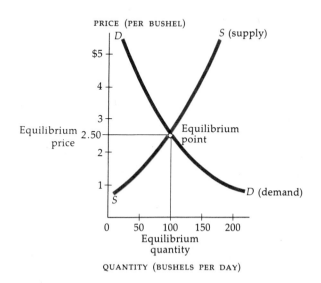

ARRIVING AT MARKET EQUILIBRIUM

At a price of $2.50 per bushel, the quantity demanded just equals the quantity supplied, namely 100 bushels per day. At this price there will be no surpluses or shortages. Hence we refer to this price as the *equilibrium price* and to the corresponding quantity as the *equilibrium quantity.*

Thus when the quantity demanded equals the quantity supplied, there is a state of *market equilibrium* because the price of the product and the corresponding quantities bought and sold are "in balance"—they have no tendency to change as a result of the opposing forces of demand and supply. On the other hand, when the quantities demanded and supplied at a given price are unequal or "out of balance," prices and quantities will be changing so that the market is then in a state of *disequilibrium.*

CHANGES IN DEMAND AND SUPPLY

Demand and supply curves do not usually remain fixed for long. You saw earlier, for example, that a demand curve can shift either to the right or to the left as a result of a change in such factors as consumers' incomes, prices of related goods like substitutes or complements, consumers' tastes, the number of consumers in the market, or consumers' expectations about future prices and incomes. Similarly, you learned that a supply curve may shift in either direction because of changes in technology, resource prices, prices of other goods, the number of sellers in an industry, or sellers' expectations about future prices.

What happens when a demand or supply curve moves to a new position? The answer is that there may also be a change in the equilibrium price, the equilibrium quantity, or both. Some examples are presented in Exhibit 12 with the arrows indicating the directions of change.

REMARK. Supply and demand curves may be drawn as straight lines rather than curved lines, because straight lines are often simpler to work with and are usually just as informative for most practical purposes. However, even when they are drawn as straight lines, we still refer to them as supply and demand *curves.*

What can you say about Exhibit 12?

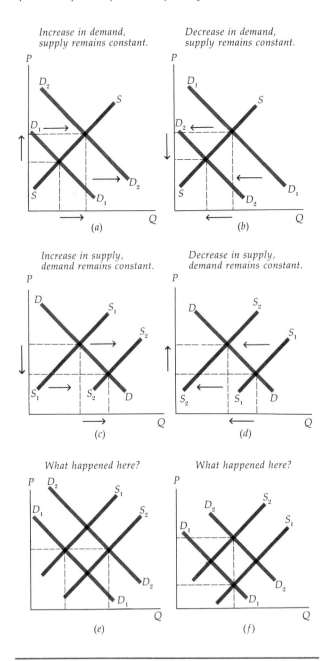

Exhibit 12

Changes in Demand and Supply

Shifts in the demand or supply curves will cause changes in equilibrium price, equilibrium quantity, or both.

Increase in demand, supply remains constant.

(a)

Decrease in demand, supply remains constant.

(b)

Increase in supply, demand remains constant.

(c)

Decrease in supply, demand remains constant.

(d)

What happened here?

(e)

What happened here?

(f)

In chart (a), an increase in demand with supply remaining constant has resulted in an increase in the equilibrium price and an increase in the equilibrium quantity. The opposite situation occurs in chart (b).

In chart (c), an increase in supply with demand remaining constant has resulted in a lower equilibrium price and a larger equilibrium quantity. The opposite situation occurs in chart (d).

Can you explain what happened in charts (e) and (f)?

The Market Economy: Is It "Good" or "Bad"?

This chapter has depicted the operation of a competitive market—a market in which prices are determined solely by the free play of supply and demand. An economy characterized entirely by such markets would be a *pure market economy*, sometimes called a "competitive economy." The two expressions are often used interchangeably.

What are the desirable features of such an economy? Does it have shortcomings? Is it realistic as a description of the capitalistic system?

THE "PROS" OF A PURE MARKET ECONOMY

Most economists agree that a pure market economy has three major points in its favor.

1. It establishes the consumer as king. A competitive economy is one in which *consumer sovereignty* prevails. This means that consumers "vote" by offering relatively more dollars for products that are in greater demand and relatively fewer dollars for products in lesser demand. In this way they bring about a relative shift in their demand curves as already illustrated in the simple case involving two commodities in Exhibit 12, charts (a) and (b). Hence, in competing with one another for consumers' dollars, producers find it profitable to produce more of the product at the higher price as represented by chart (a), and less of the product at the lower price as denoted by chart (b).

2. It allocates resources efficiently. The struggle for survival forces producers to be efficient by offering their goods at prevailing market prices. Any producer who is unable to offer his product at the "going" market price within his industry will eventually be driven out of business. In the long run, therefore, the sellers who survive will be those who —as if guided by Adam Smith's "Invisible Hand"— allocate their resources in the most efficient manner as they seek to respond to the dollar "votes" of consumers.

3. It assures substantial economic freedom. A pure market economy requires a relatively high degree of individual freedom of enterprise and economic choice. That is, unlike a command economy, there is no central authority that decides WHAT, HOW, and FOR WHOM economic resources should be used. In a competitive economy these decisions are made individually by producers as they seek to earn profits by allocating their resources according to the ways in which consumers freely register their preferences through the price system.

SOME "CONS"

Despite its blessings, critics of the pure market economy offer their own arguments:

1. It encourages a breakdown of competition. Competition strains the abilities of businessmen. Consequently, it encourages them to avoid competition either by conspiring among themselves to monopolize markets and fix prices, or by engaging in various unhealthy forms of deceptive, dishonest, or injurious methods of unfair competition such as "cutthroat" (below-cost) pricing, false advertising, bribery, and similar practices.

2. It fails to accord with modern technology. The model of a pure market economy makes the unrealistic assumption that industries are composed of large numbers of small firms as envisaged by Adam Smith. Yet modern technology requires that in many industries like automobiles, steel, cement, etc., a few large firms are dominant, and small firms just cannot survive. In fact, the large-scale operations

Box 2

Smokers of Marijuana Now Find Cost Can Be Higher Than Effect

Crackdown on Mexican 'Grass' Cuts Supply, Raises Price; Riskier Substitutes Feared

By Peggy J. Murrell
Staff Reporter of The Wall Street Journal

American college students and others who like to blow away their troubles in pungent clouds of smoky euphoria are in for still more trouble. Their grass is drying up.

Grass is marijuana. Pot began to be scarce in [1969] when Mexico started cracking down on shipments of the weed smuggled into the U.S. Now the U.S. and Mexico have agreed to greatly increase surveillance along their border. [Most] of the marijuana smoked in the U.S. is picked in Mexican fields and transported across the border.

"Nobody can get any grass," says Frank, a college sophomore spending his summer vacation in New York's East Village. "After all this damned LSD, speed (an amphetamine) and mescaline that's going around, it sure would be great to get back to some nice, soft pot." Frank had intended to stock up on marijuana in New York and take it to his friends at college, but the "pot drought" has left him empty-handed. "It's really awful," he complains. "What will I tell the kids?"

Frank can still buy weak grass, particularly the American-grown variety, but at as much as $30 an ounce, or about twice as much as he would have paid previously for the more potent Mexican variety.

The grass shortage has spawned do-it-yourself marijuana farmers. "There's a lot of the home-grown variety around," says a Washington, D.C., resident. "Here, you'll see it growing in window boxes, flower pots and backyard gardens. People are really desperate."

Far from rejoicing at the marijuana shortage, some narcotics officials are now afraid that pot smokers may switch to other, more dangerous routes to euphoria. Marijuana has so far been judged non-habit-forming by medical researchers.

SOURCE: Adapted from *The Wall Street Journal,* September 11, 1969.

The High Price of Pot?

Even the price of "grass" obeys the laws of supply and demand.

When the government clamped down on marijuana shipments, it restricted the supply and caused the price to rise. Some people fear that this has caused a greater use of substitutes, most of which are more damaging than pot.

Can economics help solve this problem? For example, since pot is believed by medical researchers to be non-habit forming (although its long-term effects are not yet known) would it be better to legalize it so as to increase the supply and lower the price, in the hope that this would discourage users from switching to more dangerous drugs?

Economists like to say that they are scientists, not moralists. In many real-world problems, however, science and morality are inseparable. Many physical scientists, for example, have refused to work on war-related research.

---

dictated by modern technology provide one of the chief explanations of why major industries in the United States economy as well as in all advanced industrial nations are dominated by small numbers of large firms.

3. It operates imperfectly. Last but not least, a pure market economy does not always work as smoothly in the real world as the theoretical supply and demand model suggests. One of the chief reasons for this can be summed up under the general heading of *resource immobility.* Thus, the factors of production do not usually shift rapidly from declining industries into expanding ones according to changes in demand. Workers may have to be retrained before they can do new jobs. New machines may have to be designed and new plant facilities may have to be constructed before production can be carried on efficiently. These processes may take months or years to complete. In the meantime, the declining industry can suffer from unemployment or underemployment because of the failure of its resources to adjust to basic structural changes in the economy.

American agriculture provides an outstanding example of this situation. The agricultural sector of the United States economy has been in a relatively declining trend for a number of decades. Yet it continues as a "sick" industry, largely because it has

The Consumer: Sovereign or Sucker?

The belief in consumer sovereignty is surprisingly durable. There is the marketplace, with a great many buyers milling around. At the end of the day some booths are empty of goods; their owners go home with bulging pocketbooks. But some booths are still stacked with goods; the consumer has used his royal right to reject them. It is an appealing picture, and still useful as a simplified explanation of what happens in a free market.

But we don't happen to live in one. The bulk of private sector economic activity in the United States is conducted by corporations. The 500 largest account for most of the goods produced in the United States. And whatever their other virtues, the giant corporations cannot be counted among supporters of a free market system.

Managing Demand

Whereas the man selling wicker baskets from his booth in that hypothetical free market has invested a few hours of his time and a little money in raw materials, the giant corporation has spent several years and millions of dollars on designing, tooling-up for, and launching its product—a plastic basket perhaps. With all that and a reputation at stake, the large corporation seeks to turn a gamble into a sure thing by *managing demand.* It will advertise the plastic basket on television and in magazines; retailers may turn it into a special promotional item; it may even be offered as a gift in return for two cornflake box-tops.

The plastic basket may still fail; business history is littered with the corpses of failed products. Supporters of the consumer-sovereignty theory are fond of pointing to them. But they do not prove that demand cannot be managed. *They only prove it cannot be managed all the time.*

Although manufacturers of similar products are clearly in competition for shares of the market, they are also in alliance. By their ceaseless promotion of a *class* of product—self-cleaning ovens, let us say—they are helping to create overall demand for it. The alternative would be to lose dollars to another class of product.

Because manufacturers of a class of product have a shared interest in promoting it, their products tend to be similar. The man who goes shopping for a car made in the United States is faced with a limited choice. In each price range the rival products are priced within a few dollars; their motors are of comparable size; and they feature similar gadgets.

Threat from Foreigners

Detroit explains its lack of innovation by saying it provides what people want. But how can the consumer demand a car that is not offered?

The size of the four big automobile manufacturers makes the entry of a new competitor impractical; the only real competition Detroit faces is from foreign cars. But the range of foreign cars is also limited.

Much of the similarity of technology, models and prices is inevitable: like most consumer durables, the car is mass-produced. Certainly, mass production has benefited most consumers; goods are more readily available and cheaper than they would be under any other production system. But mass production is precisely what its name implies; it is incapable of meeting a small demand. The person unfortunate enough to have a taste shared by relatively few people is doomed either never to satisfy it or pay a very high price indeed for his eccentricity.

The Price of Size

The basic cause of sluggish response to changing consumer demands may be technological. But the very large corporations have sometimes abused their power. As consumer crusader Ralph Nader has shown, some manufacturers have deliberately designed their products to cease functioning after a certain time, have wilfully disregarded warnings that their products are dangerous, and turned with fury on their critics. The major corporations have a more powerful voice in government than any consumer or group of consumers. Even the federal agencies that are supposed to regulate business frequently do not.

Fortunately, consumers are becoming aware of the pressures. To be sure, they are still diffused and weak in comparison with the industries they confront; but legislation to protect consumers shows that important changes are taking place.

Unfortunately, it is unlikely that even in the long run the consumer will ever be sovereign in life as he is in theory. But at least consumers, organized into groups and willing to use their political power, will be able to prevent manufacturers from abusing their privileged position as the few suppliers of many customers.

R. B.

1. *Does advertising create* new *demands or does it merely shift existing demands?*

2. *Why is it often assumed that creation of demand is bad? What is "bad" about it?*

more resources than it needs in order to function efficiently, and because government subsidies hold many relatively inefficient producers in the industry who would ordinarily have left it long ago.

IS IT REALISTIC?

These are the main arguments advanced against the model of a pure market economy. The question remains: Is the model realistic? Does it represent a true picture of the way in which the price system operates in a modern capitalistic economy?

As mentioned earlier, the "pure" model described in this chapter is that of a system in which large numbers of buyers and sellers are in rivalry with one another. Adam Smith envisioned this kind of model in the late eighteenth century. Today its most refined version is to be found in organized commodity markets, such as the Chicago Board of Trade and the New York and Liverpool Cotton Exchanges. There, staple commodities like wheat, corn, oats, barley, and cotton are traded by a remarkable and fascinating auction system involving numerous buyers and sellers.

Elsewhere, the price system of American capitalism departs in varying degrees from that of a competitive market economy. Nowadays, we live in an age of big business, big unions, and big government. This is hardly the type of economy that Adam Smith had in mind. In spite of this, we will see later that our pure market model nevertheless provides a useful framework for explaining the way in which a capitalistic system operates.

SUMMARY OF IMPORTANT IDEAS

1. The mechanism of supply and demand explains the ways in which a market economy answers the three big questions: WHAT, HOW, and FOR WHOM.

2. A demand schedule lists the quantities of a commodity that buyers are willing and able to purchase at various possible prices during a given period of time. The graphic equivalent of a demand schedule is a demand curve.

3. The law of demand tells you that demand curves are downward-sloping: that is, the quantity de-

manded of a good varies inversely with its price—all other things remaining the same.

4. A change in the quantity demanded is a movement along the same demand curve, either up or down, due to a change in price. A change in demand is a shift of the demand curve to a new position, due to a change in one or more of the "all other things" that are assumed to remain constant when a demand curve is being drawn. These may include:

a. Consumers' money incomes

b. The prices of related goods

c. Consumers' tastes or preferences

d. The number of consumers in the market

e. Consumers' expectations about future prices and incomes

5. "Supply" is defined as a relation between prices and quantity supplied per unit of time. The law of supply says that the quantity supplied of a commodity usually varies directly with its price, and hence supply curves are ordinarily upward-sloping. A "change in the quantity supplied" is a movement along the same supply curve due to a change in price, whereas a "change in supply" is a shift of the curve to a new position due to a change in one or more of the "all other" factors that are assumed to be constant when the curve is drawn. These may include:

a. The state of technology

b. Resource prices or the costs of the factors of production

c. The prices of other goods

d. The number of sellers in the market

e. Sellers' expectations regarding future prices

6. Equilibrium prices and quantities are determined in the market through the free play of supply and demand forces. Changes in supply or in demand may cause changes in these equilibrium prices or quantities, or perhaps changes in both, depending on where the curves intersect.

7. A market economy is highly competitive. Prices and quantities are determined by numerous buyers and sellers through the free operation of supply and demand. Organized trading markets, such as the

commodity exchanges in Chicago and some other cities, typify this situation, but most of the markets in our economy differ from this competitive type by varying degrees.

FOR HOMEWORK AND DISCUSSION

1. *Terms and concepts to review:*

demand	supply
demand schedule	supply schedule
demand curve	supply curve
demand price	supply price
law of demand	law of supply
normal goods	change in supply
inferior goods	equilibrium
change in quantity demanded	equilibrium price
change in demand	surplus
substitute goods	shortage
complementary goods	equilibrium quantity
change in quantity supplied	disequilibrium
	pure market economy
	consumer sovereignty

In the following problems, use graphs whenever possible to verify your answer.

2. Do the numerical quantities of a demand schedule characterize buyers' behavior? If not, what is the fundamental property of a demand schedule?

3. Evaluate the following editorial comments on the basis of what you know about the meaning of demand and scarcity in economics (HINT: How meaningful are the italicized words?)

"Our community *needs* more schools and better teachers; after all, what could be more critical than the education of our children as future citizens?"

Lynwood *Times*

"The health of our citizens is uppermost in our minds. Ever since the rate of garbage pick-up in our northwest suburbs deteriorated to its present deplorable levels, it has been evident that our shortage of collection facilities has reached *emergency* proportions."

Lexington *Daily Explicit*

4. Some people would buy more of a good (such as jewelry or furs) at a high price than at a low price. This results in an upward-sloping "demand curve." Would such a curve be an exception to the law of demand? Explain.

5. What would happen to the market demand curve for steak as a result of each of the following:

   a. An increase in the average level of income

   b. An increase in the number of families

   c. An increased advertising campaign for veal and pork

   d. An increase in the prices of veal and pork

   e. A decrease in the prices of veal and pork

6. What would happen to the demand for Pepsi-Cola if the price of Coca-Cola were doubled? Why would it happen?

7. What would be the effect on the supply of office buildings if each of the following things happened:

   a. The price of land rose.

   b. The price of steel fell.

   c. The price of cement fell.

   d. A new and faster method of construction were adopted.

   e. The number of firms building offices declined.

   f. Rents for office buildings were expected to decline.

8. Analyze the following:

   a. What would happen to the equilibrium price and quantity of butter if the price of margarine rose?

   b. What would happen if there were an increase in the cost of producing butter?

REFERENCES AND READING SUGGESTIONS

BOULDING, KENNETH E., *Economic Analysis: Microeconomics,* 4th ed., Harper & Row, New York, 1966, chaps. 8, 10, 11.

DOOLEY, PETER C., *Elementary Price Theory,* Appleton-Century-Crofts, New York, 1967, chap. 1.

WARD, BENJAMIN, *Elementary Price Theory,* The Free Press, New York, 1967, chap. 3.

CHAPTER 5

The Private Sector of the Economy: Households and Businesses

CHAPTER PREVIEW

How are incomes distributed among resource owners? Why are some people rich and some poor? What can be done about it?

How are businesses organized? What are the major types of business organizations, their advantages and disadvantages? Is there a trend toward "big business" in America—and if so, is this a curse or a blessing?

A mixed capitalistic economy is like a three-legged stool—one leg representing "households," the second "businesses," and the third "government." The first two comprise the *private sector* of the economy and are explored in this chapter; the last is the *public sector,* and is the subject of the next chapter.

You and your family are part of the household segment of the private sector—along with more than 60 million other families. This group is the ultimate supplier of the economy's inputs of human resources and the major purchaser of its outputs of goods and services. Businesses, of which there are over 11 million including farmers and professional people, are the second major group within the system. They are chiefly responsible for producing the things society wants.

These are just a few of the basic facts concerning the private sector. Some of the fundamental questions that can be asked about it are in the above Preview.

Households: The Haves and the Have Nots; Who Gets How Much?

How is the nation's total economic "pie" distributed among individuals and groups? This question concerns the economic problem of income distribution,

Exhibit 1

National Income by Type of Income

Functional Distribution of Income in the United States (in billions of dollars and percent of national income)

Item	1950		1955		1960		1965		1970	
National income:	$241	*100%*	$331	*100%*	$415	*100%*	$564	*100%*	$801	*100%*
Compensation of employees	155	*65*	225	*68*	294	*71*	394	*71*	600	*75*
Proprietors' income	38	*16*	42	*13*	46	*11*	58	*10*	68	*8*
Rental income of persons	9	*4*	14	*4*	16	*4*	19	*3*	23	*3*
Corporate profits and inventory valuation adjustment	38	*16*	47	*14*	50	*12*	74	*13*	77	*10*
Net interest	2	*1*	4	*1*	8	*2*	18	*3*	34	*4*

SOURCE: *Statistical Abstract of the United States,* annual.

Who Receives How Much?

In nineteenth-century England, economic resources or factors of production were divided by economists into three parts: labor, land, and capital, according to the way in which people earned their income. Owners of land and capital were regarded as a social class different from those who worked for wages. Today this particular distinction, with the addition of "entrepreneurship," is of greater economic than social significance because it enables us to analyze the way in which the nation's income is divided among the four major classes of resource owners.

What determines which factor of production will receive how much? In general, there are two kinds of forces that are at work in a predominantly market economy:

1. Economic or market forces represented by demand and supply conditions for the human and material resources used in production. (Can you illustrate with some supply and demand diagrams?)

2. Noneconomic or nonmarket forces such as laws, customs, union agreements, etc., which modify the income that a resource owner would have received from market forces alone. (What are some specific examples?)

the study of which customarily proceeds along two related lines. One is called *functional* income distribution and the other *personal* income distribution.

FUNCTIONAL INCOME DISTRIBUTION

The functional approach concerns the income payments made to owners of productive factors in return for their supplying the human and material resources that contribute to the production of the nation's output. The payments thus include wages and salaries, rents, interest, and profits.

Exhibit 1 shows the functional distribution of income in terms of amounts and percentages over several five-year intervals. Compensation of employees, i.e., wages and salaries, represent the largest portion of national income—approximately 75 percent. Since 1930 (not shown in the table) this share has been remarkably stable, averaging about two-thirds of the total. The long-run trend, however, has been steadily increasing.

What about the remaining income shares? Do they exhibit relative stability or instability? You will find it instructive to check the source of this table in your campus library. By filling in some of the "in between" amounts and calculating your own percentages, you can get a better idea of how to judge the relative trends.

Exhibit 2

Money Income—Percent Distribution of Familes, by Income Level and by Color of Head

Income level (percent distribution)

Color of head and year	Under $1,000	$1,000– $1,999	$2,000– $2,999	$3,000– $3,999	$4,000– $4,999	$5,000– $5,999	$6,000– $6,999	$7,000– $9,999	$10,000– $14,999	$15,000 and over	Median Income
All families											
1947	10.8	16.6	22.0	19.7	11.6	7.7	8.9		2.7		$3,031
1950	11.5	13.2	17.8	20.7	13.6	9.0	5.2	5.8	3.3		3,319
1955	7.7	9.9	11.0	14.6	15.4	12.7	9.5	12.9	4.8	1.4	4,421
1960	5.0	8.0	8.7	9.8	10.5	12.9	10.8	20.0	10.6	3.7	5,620
1965	2.9	6.0	7.2	7.7	7.9	9.3	9.5	24.2	17.7	7.6	6,957
1966	2.2	5.2	6.6	6.8	7.0	8.4	9.3	24.6	20.8	9.3	7,500
1967	2.1	4.4	6.0	6.3	6.5	7.8	8.3	24.3	22.4	12.0	7,974
1968	1.8	3.4	5.1	6.1	6.0	6.9	7.6	23.4	25.0	14.7	8,632
1970	1.5	3.0	4.2	5.5	5.2	6.3	6.0	23.0	29.2	16.1	9,600
White families											
1947	9.0	14.9	22.3	20.8	12.4	8.1	9.5		3.0		3,157
1950	10.0	12.2	17.3	21.3	14.4	9.6	5.5	6.1	3.5		3,445
1955	6.6	8.7	10.4	14.3	16.0	13.4	9.9	13.9	5.3	1.5	4,605
1960	4.1	6.9	8.1	9.4	10.5	13.3	11.2	21.3	11.2	4.1	5,835
1965	2.5	5.2	6.3	6.9	7.6	9.3	9.8	25.5	18.8	8.3	7,251
1966	1.9	4.4	5.9	6.1	6.5	8.2	9.5	25.4	22.0	10.1	7,792
1967	1.8	3.8	5.2	5.8	6.1	7.6	8.4	25.1	23.6	12.9	8,274
1968	1.5	2.9	4.5	5.4	5.6	6.7	7.6	24.0	26.2	15.7	8,937
1970	1.0	2.1	3.5	4.8	4.8	5.7	6.7	23.2	30.2	18.0	9,912
Nonwhite families											
1947	28.8	33.5	18.8	8.4	4.4	3.1	3.0		0.1		1,614
1950	28.1	25.3	23.5	13.5	4.3	1.9	1.5	1.7	0.3		1,869
1955	19.0	20.7	17.6	17.2	11.1	5.8	4.8	3.1	0.6	(Z)	2,549
1960	13.4	18.3	14.8	14.0	10.4	8.7	6.7	8.7	4.3	0.6	3,233
1965	7.1	13.6	14.6	14.8	10.8	9.5	6.8	13.7	7.6	1.4	3,994
1966	5.0	12.4	12.8	12.5	10.8	9.5	8.3	16.5	10.0	2.3	4,674
1967	4.9	9.4	12.8	11.5	10.0	9.7	8.0	16.9	11.7	5.0	5,141
1968	4.1	8.5	10.2	12.0	10.0	8.8	7.7	17.6	14.7	6.3	5,590
1970	3.5	7.0	9.2	11.5	9.8	8.0	7.0	20.0	16.0	8.0	6,510

Z Less than 0.05 percent.
SOURCE: U.S. Department of Commerce.

Can you suggest some possible reasons for the changing trends in the shares of national income—especially the rising trend in compensation of employees, and the declining trend in proprietors' income? These questions are examined later in the book, but you may already have some beliefs of your own.

PERSONAL INCOME DISTRIBUTION

The problems of personal income distribution are increasingly urgent. The American poor—black and white, Indian and Mexican—are no longer content merely to complain about their small slice of the economic pie. With growing militance, organized groups of poor people are challenging existing distributions of income by demonstrating, by taking their case to Congress—and sometimes by rioting.

Poor Americans are in the mainstream of history when they demand a more equitable distribution of income. That issue has moved men and nations for centuries, bringing revolution and war in its wake. Some sociologists think that the disparity of incomes in the United States is a primary cause of social unrest. The lesson of history is that society disregards at its peril the plight of the poor.

How are incomes distributed in the United States—in other words, who is rich and who is poor, and what is the gap between them? Exhibit 2 shows that the percentage of all families in the lower-income groups—i.e., below the $6,000 level—has been declining since World War II, while the percentage of families in the upper-income groups has been rising. Note too that the median income has been rising. (A *median* is a type of average that divides a distribution of numbers into two equal parts—one-half of the cases being equal to or less than this value and one-half being equal to or greater.) Can you interpret the median income for the most recent year? What important differences does the table reveal between white and nonwhite families?

INCOME INEQUALITY: WHY ARE SOME PEOPLE RICH? SOME POOR?

A different type of income classification is illustrated in Exhibit 3. Both the table and chart answer the question: What percentage of people, ranked from the poorest to the richest, received what percentage of the nation's total income in a given year? Study the description of the diagram carefully and note that, in the chart, the area between the diagonal line of equal income distribution and the curved line of actual income distribution reflects the degree of income inequality. Thus the more that the curved line is "bowed downward" in a southeasterly direction, the greater is the inequality of income distribution.

What causes disparities in incomes? Why do some people make more money than others? There are three major reasons.

1. Differences in wealth. The distribution of wealth, i.e., income-producing assets like stocks, bonds, land, etc., is even more unequal than the distribution of incomes. Indeed it has been estimated that over 70 percent of such wealth is concentrated among the top fifth of the population. Since wealth is a significant source of income, it appears obvious that a widely distorted distribution of wealth is perhaps the most important cause of income inequality.

FOR CLASS DISCUSSION

1. How would you distinguish between *income* and *wealth*?

2. Can a person have a high income without being wealthy?

3. Can a person be wealthy and have a low income?

4. Which is more likely—(2) or (3)?

2. Differences in earning ability and opportunity. People differ widely in education, intelligence, skill, motivation, and talent. In looking for jobs they face barriers because of their age, sex, race, religion,

Exhibit 3

**Percent of Aggregate Income Received by
Each Fifth and Top 5 Percent of Families**

Income rank of families:	1950	1955	1960	1965	1970
Lowest fifth	4	5	5	5	6
Second fifth	12	12	12	12	12
Middle fifth	17	18	18	18	18
Fourth fifth	24	23	23	24	24
Highest fifth	43	42	42	41	41
Top 5 percent	17	17	17	15	15

SOURCE: U.S. Department of Commerce.

You can use the data from the table to construct a Lorenz
curve. *This curve shows the extent of departure between an
equal distribution of income and the actual distribution of
income.*

*Thus, along the diagonal line representing equal distribu-
tion, the lowest 20 percent of the families received 20 percent
of total income, the lowest 40 percent of the families received
40 percent of total income, and so on. Can you estimate from
the curved line showing actual distribution the percent of
income received by the lowest 20 percent of families? The
lowest 40 percent? 60 percent? 80 percent? 100 percent?
Check your estimates against the results in the table to see if
you are correct.*

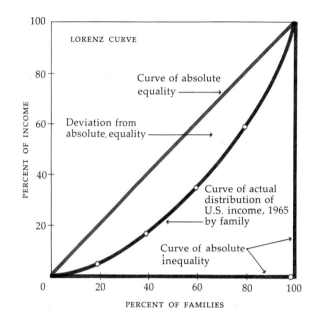

*The axes in the lower half of the diagram represent the curve
of absolute inequality. Thus, on the horizontal axis, a point
near the right end of the scale can be designated, showing
where 99 percent of the families receive no income, and the
remaining 1 percent receive it all.*

Can you sketch in the curve for 1970?

and nationality. Legislation has made some of these
barriers less formidable, but they are still responsible
for many of the inequalities in income distribution.

3. Differences in resource mobility. Adam Smith said,
"Of all baggage, man is the most difficult to transport." This dictum helps account for a good deal of
income inequality, because the factors responsible
for differences in earning ability and opportunity
also make for differences in resource mobility. Many
people, for example, are prevented by lack of information or resources from moving into higher-paying
occupations or locations. Consequently low incomes
and even poverty may exist for many years in various
regions of the country, as in parts of the South where
sharecroppers, migratory farm workers, and in some

cases factory laborers eke out a substandard living.
Exhibit 4 reveals the geographical distribution of
income very clearly.

REDUCING INCOME INEQUALITY

From the mid-thirties to the present, the distribution
of incomes in the United States has become somewhat more even—the "inequality gap" on the
Lorenz chart has narrowed. Most of the shift toward
greater income equality occurred between 1935 and
1945 as the economy—especially its laborers and
farmers—advanced from a depressed to a considerably more prosperous state. Since 1945 the shift
toward greater income equality has been less pronounced. This long-range leveling process, which

Exhibit 4

Per Capita Personal Income, 1970

Since World War II, aggregate personal income has been increasing fastest in the Southeast, Southwest, and Far West. In the South, historically an area with low per capita income, marginal (low wage) agriculture has been on the decline while job growth in nonfarm sectors has been strong. Continuing migration to the Far West, historically a high-income region, has stimulated—and has been stimulated —by expansion in economic activity there. In addition, the weight of defense spending has shifted from the Mideast and

Great Lakes areas to the South, and West.

Per capita incomes differ by region, in part, because of regional differences in the mix of industries and in the prevalence of large cities—where wage levels tend to be higher than in small towns and rural areas.

A small but significant share of personal income (as measured by the Department of Commerce) comprises items that are not cash flows or are not direct payments to consumers.

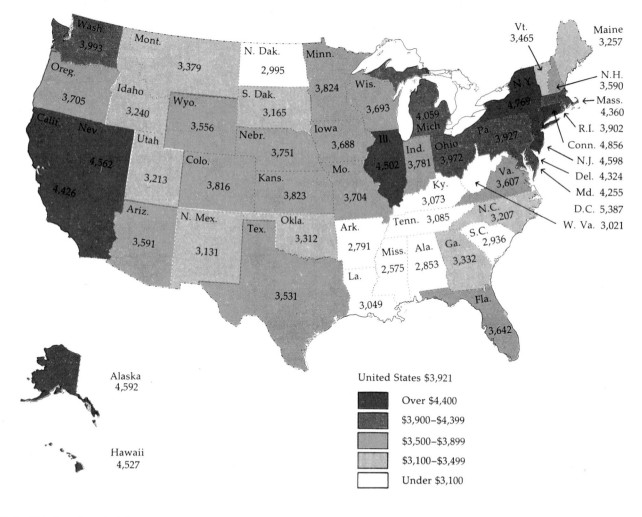

Vt. 3,465
Maine 3,257
N.H. 3,590
← Mass. 4,360
R.I. 3,902
Conn. 4,856
N.J. 4,598
Del. 4,324
Md. 4,255
D.C. 5,387
W. Va. 3,021

Wash. 3,993
Mont. 3,379
N. Dak. 2,995
Minn.
Oreg. 3,705
Idaho 3,240
Wyo. 3,556
S. Dak. 3,165
Wis. 3,693
N.Y. 4,768
Calif. 4,562
Nev. 4,426
Utah 3,213
Colo. 3,816
Nebr. 3,751
Iowa 3,688
Ill. 4,502
Mich 4,059
Ind. 3,781
Ohio 3,972
Pa. 3,927
Kans. 3,823
Mo. 3,704
Ky. 3,073
Va. 3,607
Ariz. 3,591
N. Mex. 3,131
Okla. 3,312
Ark. 2,791
Tenn. 3,085
N.C. 3,207
S.C. 2,936
Tex. 3,531
Miss. 2,575
Ala. 2,853
Ga. 3,332
La. 3,049
Fla. 3,642

Alaska 4,592

Hawaii 4,527

United States $3,921

Over $4,400
$3,900–$4,399
$3,500–$3,899
$3,100–$3,499
Under $3,100

SOURCE: U.S. Department of Commerce.

will probably continue at a gradual rate for many years to come, is due to a number of factors:

1. Reduction of the low-income farm population

2. Greater opportunities for working women and racial minority groups

3. Decline of earnings differentials between white-collar workers and manual workers

4. Larger income provisions for the unemployed

In addition, the federal income tax takes a larger percentage of higher incomes than of lower ones. Although the income redistribution effects of this tax are questionable, it nevertheless helps to keep incomes from becoming more unequal than they already are.

Thus the old saying that "the rich get richer and the poor get poorer" is not borne out by the facts. Although the rich are not significantly worse off then they were before, they are certainly not getting any richer.

How does the United States compare with other nations? According to the evidence, America's upper-income groups do not receive a larger share of income than the richer classes in other countries. The distribution of income in the United States is about the same as in Denmark, Sweden, and England, and considerably more equal than in most of the other countries for which data are available.

Businesses—Their Organization and Income

Between 80 and 90 percent of all productive activity in the American economy is carried on by 11 million firms, of which 5 million are manufacturers and retailers, $3\frac{1}{2}$ million are farms, and $2\frac{1}{2}$ million are professional firms in accounting, law, and the like. The remaining 10 to 20 percent of productive activity is accounted for by government.

Productive activity may be carried on in factory buildings, mines, mills, warehouses, stores, and so forth. Any such establishment is called a *plant*. A business organization which owns a plant is called a *firm*. Most firms own only one plant, but some firms, such as large steel or chemical companies, may own hundreds of plants.

One way in which firms may be classified is by the products they make. Firms that produce similar or identical products are said to be in the same *industry*. Thus General Motors and Ford are in the automobile industry. But General Motors also produces trucks, buses, and diesel locomotives among other things, so it would be correct to say that it is also in the truck industry, the bus industry, and the diesel locomotive industry. What about a company like General Electric? Can you name at least five industries in which GE is an important producer?

Another method of classifying firms is by their legal form of organization. Three types are particularly common: the individual proprietorship, the partnership, and the corporation. Let us see what these involve.

THE INDIVIDUAL PROPRIETORSHIP

If you wanted to own a business for which you were solely responsible, you would choose the simplest, oldest, and most common form: the individual or sole *proprietorship*. This is a "one-man" type of organization in which the owner or proprietor alone is responsible for the activities and liabilities of the business. There are over 9 million of these in the United States. Most of the businesses you see about you each day—restaurants, drugstores, barbershops, gas stations, radio and TV repair shops, etc.—are likely to be individual proprietorships.

To become an individual proprietor you just decide you want to be one, and if you have enough money you are in business. You may hire whomever you wish and borrow whatever money you can. You do not have to pay special taxes to the state in order to get started or to remain in business, nor are you ordinarily subject to special government controls or regulations (except in a few businesses like restaurants, pharmacies, and liquor stores, where a license is necessary and may ordinarily be acquired provided that certain standards of health or safety are met).

Since you are the sole owner, the general credit of the business will be limited to your personal resources. Thus in the eyes of creditors, there will be a danger of your business lacking stability and continuity. They will regard you as a substantial risk, and you will find yourself unable to borrow funds for long periods in order to finance expansion. Consequently the growth of the enterprise will rest largely on your ability to reinvest its earnings. If the business fails, you may find yourself with debts greater than your assets. You will be held personally liable for those debts, and creditors will be able to take your savings, your house, your car, and most of your other property in order to help satisfy their claims.

The chief advantages of the individual proprietorship are:

1. Ease of formation and simplicity of control

2. Presence of a strong personal element in the business

3. Freedom from organizational taxes and government regulation

The main disadvantages are:

1. Difficulty of raising funds for expansion

2. Lack of stability or permanence

3. Unlimited liability of the owner for all unpaid debts of the business

THE PARTNERSHIP

Suppose you decide that your business needs more money—perhaps to expand or to move into a new and better location. In that case you may take in a partner. He puts up an agreed amount of money, and you now have a partnership in which the profits and responsibilities of the business are shared by both of you. Thus a *partnership* is an association of two or more individuals to carry on, as co-owners, a business for profit. There are about 1 million partnerships in the United States.

Strictly speaking, of course, a partnership agreement should be in writing and should stipulate such things as the number of partners, the amounts contributed by each, the salaries of each, and the percentage of each partner's share in the profits or losses of the business.

A partnership is similar in many ways to an individual proprietorship except that it has two or more co-owners. This added condition makes for certain advantages as well as disadvantages.

The advantages of a partnership are:

1. Ease and inexpensiveness of organization

2. Sharing of managerial talents and responsibilities among the partners

3. Freedom from organization taxes and from government regulation

4. Ability of the partners to combine their financial resources

The disadvantages are:

1. Division of authority among partners may lead to disagreements

2. Financial resources for expansion are limited (although possibly less limited than for the individual proprietorship)

3. Lack of stability or permanence (since the withdrawal or death of a partner terminates the partnership)

4. Unlimited liability of the partners for all debts of the business

THE CORPORATION

By this time your business may have grown to a point where a partnership is no longer suitable. In that case you will want to consider forming a corporation.

What is a corporation? The most common definition was given by Chief Justice John Marshall of the United States Supreme Court in the famous Dartmouth College case of 1819:

A corporation is an artificial being, invisible, intangible, and existing only in the contemplation of the law. Being the mere creature of law, it possesses only those properties which the charter of its creation confers upon it, either expressly or as incidental to its very existence. . . . Among the most important are immortality, and, if the expression may be allowed, individuality: properties by which a perpetual succession of many persons are considered as the same, and may act as a single individual.

This means, in short, that a *corporation* is an anonymous entity in which the identity of its owners is irrelevant for the purpose of conducting business.

How does your corporation get started? Basically, it comes into existence when you and the other interested parties file a certificate of incorporation with the state, authorizing your group to act as a legal entity for the purpose of carrying on a specific activity or business. Unlike an individual proprietorship or partnership, your corporation will have to pay an initial organizational tax and an annual franchise tax to the state, as well as the federal income tax.

MANAGERIAL AND FINANCIAL FEATURES OF THE CORPORATION

The ownership of a corporation is divided into units represented by shares of *stock*. These are certificates issued in various denominations. A stockholder who owns 100 shares of stock in a corporation has twice as much "ownership" as a stockholder with only 50 shares. Each stockholder may participate in the profits of the corporation by receiving *dividends* in the form of a certain amount of dollars or cents per share, according to the number of shares he owns. If there are no profits, there may be no dividends declared.

One of the distinguishing features of a corporation is the *limited liability* of its stockholders. Unlike the individual proprietorship or the partnership, where the owners can be held personally liable for the debts of the business, stockholders in corporations cannot be held liable for any of the firm's debts. For almost all practical purposes, the most that stockholders can lose if the business goes bankrupt is the money they paid for stock.

Under the law stockholders elect a board of directors which is responsible for the management of the corporation. Each stockholder gets one vote for each share of stock he owns. A stockholder may thus elect himself to the board if he owns enough shares, or if he can get enough of the other stockholders to vote their shares for him. In large corporations, the board will often employ officers—a president and vice-presidents—to manage day-to-day operations and report back to it the results of these operations periodically. In smaller corporations it is common to find one or more members of the board serving as officers as well. (See Box 1.)

The corporation has durability. Its stockholders may come and go, but the corporation itself lives on. Indeed, some corporations in existence today were originally chartered hundreds of years ago. This stability and permanence makes the corporation highly flexible. It can raise large amounts of capital by selling stocks and *bonds* (promises to pay money plus interest in future years) to the public, and it can adapt itself to changing market needs and conditions.

The principal advantages of the corporation are:

1. Limited liability of stockholders

2. Ability to raise large amounts of funds for expansion through the sale of stocks and bonds

3. Stability and permanence

4. Flexibility in organization and management

The chief disadvantages are:

1. Formation may be complicated, depending on the nature of the business.

2. Taxation is burdensome, since there are not only organizational and franchise taxes, but also "double" income taxes including: (*a*) the income tax paid by the corporation on its profits, and (*b*) the income tax paid by the stockholder on the dividends he receives out of the corporation's profits.

3. Some difficulties may arise because of the non-uniformity of corporation laws among the states

4. Accounting methods and various financial practices are subject to strict government regulations.

BIG BUSINESS IN AMERICA

There are over 1 million corporations in the United States. More than half of them are "small," with assets (cash, buildings, equipment, inventories, etc.) totaling less than $100,000 each. At the other extreme are more than 100 giants in the "billion-dollar club" —companies whose total assets exceed $1 billion.

Box 1

A Typical Corporation's Organization Chart

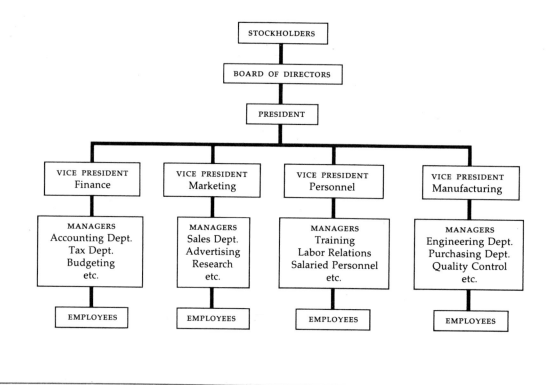

The names of the five largest United States companies in each of six fields are presented in Exhibit 5, along with some measures of size. Most of these companies are familiar to all of us. Not only their total assets, but also their annual sales and annual net profits after taxes are in excess of a billion dollars. Each employs hundreds of thousands of workers and distributes profits in the form of dividends to hundreds of thousands or even millions of stockholders. Together they control a large share of the nation's income-producing wealth.

How big is big? In 1969 General Motors had the seventeenth largest volume of output in the world: the value of its total production exceeded the gross national product of Argentina, Belgium, and fourteen other countries. Several United States corporations have a total output larger than that of some nations.

These facts raise issues that are among the most fundamental of our time: why do firms become big? Is bigness "good" or "bad"?

How and Why do Firms Become Big?

A business firm may grow in two distinct ways. First, it may expand through internal growth by reinvestment of its earnings—that is, by plowing most of its profits back into the business to pay for new equipment, research, and product development. The most notable examples of this type of growth have been the Aluminum Company of America and the Ford Motor Company. Second, a firm may expand by a process of combination—that is, through mergers or consolidation with other companies. This has been the most prevalent method of growth in American industry.

Exhibit 5

Who's Who Among the Giants? America's Largest Corporations in 1970

Five Largest Industrial Corporations (ranked by sales)

	Sales (billions)	Assets (billions)
General Motors	$18.8	$14.2
Standard Oil (New Jersey)	16.6	19.2
Ford Motor	15.0	10.0
General Electric	8.7	6.3
International Business Machines	7.5	8.5

Five Largest Commercial Banks (ranked by assets)

	Assets (billions)	Deposits (billions)
Bank America (San Francisco)	$29.7	$25.6
First National City Corp. (N.Y.)	25.8	21.0
Chase Manhattan Corp. (N.Y.)	24.5	21.2
Manufacturers Hanover Corp. (N.Y.)	12.7	11.1
J. P. Morgan (N.Y.)	12.1	9.6

Five Largest Life-Insurance Companies (ranked by assets)

	Assets (billions)	Life Insurance in force (billions)
Prudential	$29.1	$156.8
Metropolitan	27.9	167.3
Equitable Life Assurance	14.4	76.9
New York Life	10.7	50.3
John Hancock Mutual	10.0	60.9

Five Largest Retailing Companies (ranked by sales)

	Sales (billions)	Assets (billions)
Sears, Roebuck	$9.3	$7.6
Great Atlantic & Pacific Tea	5.6	1.0
Safeway Stores	4.9	0.9
J. C. Penney	4.2	1.6
Kroger	3.7	0.8

Five Largest Transportation Companies (ranked by operating revenues)

	Operating Revenues (billions)	Assets (billions)
Penn Central	$2.3	$6.8
UAL*	1.6	2.2
Southern Pacific	1.3	3.1
Trans World Airlines	1.2	1.4
American Airlines	1.1	1.5

* Holding company: includes United Air Lines

Five Largest Utilities (ranked by assets)

	Assets (billions)	Operating Revenues (billions)
American Tel. & Tel.	$49.6	$17.0
Consolidated Edison	4.5	1.3
Pacific Gas & Electric	4.3	1.1
Commonwealth Edison	3.8	0.9
American Electric Power	3.2	0.7

SOURCE: *Fortune Directory*, 1971.

Why do some firms become large? Their ultimate objective is usually to strengthen their financial position. For instance, a firm may combine with other firms in the same or in related types of activity in order to gain economies in production or distribution, or to regularize its supplies, or to round out its product line. Thus some container manufacturers also make tin cans, glass jars, and plastics. Some automobile producers own rubber companies, iron mines, and steel mills. Many companies have also chosen to grow by combining with firms in totally unrelated activities. This may reflect a desire on the part of the acquiring company to spread risks, find investments for idle capital funds, add products which can be sold with the firm's merchandising knowledge and skills, or simply to gain greater economic power on a broader front.

Is Bigness a Curse or a Blessing?

Is it "good" or "bad" to have an economy whose major industries are dominated by a few giant corporations—by companies like U.S. Steel in the steel industry, General Motors in the automobile industry, Standard Oil (New Jersey) in the petroleum industry, AT&T in the electronic communications industry, and so on? Would we be better or worse off if we had an economy whose industries were composed of many small firms in active competition?

There is no simple answer. The best we can do is sketch the main aspects of the problem, and leave you to think out some tentative conclusions. As you study later chapters, you may very well come to see some of these conclusions in a different light.

1. A striking feature of the modern corporation is its *separation of ownership and control.* Some of the largest corporations like General Motors and AT&T have millions of stockholders, and quite a few others have hundreds of thousands. Most of these stockholders, however, own relatively few shares—much less than even 100 shares each—but small minorities own enough shares to gain working control of their corporations.

Because stockholders are not usually sufficiently organized to do anything about correcting certain misuses and abuses of corporate powers, several undesirable consequences arise from the separation of ownership and management. The insiders of a corporation (the board of directors and officers) may be able to keep themselves in control even if they do not perform particularly well; they may also vote themselves high salaries, bonuses, pensions, and benefits at the stockholders' expense. To some extent these problems have been mitigated over the years— thanks to government regulations and laws to protect the interests of stockholders. But the difficulties continue to exist in varying degrees, and will probably never be completely eliminated.

2. Many important industries are dominated by a few large companies. Examples include aluminum, automobiles, telephone equipment, steel, cigarettes, and breakfast foods—plus many others. The giants in these industries exercise varying degrees of monopoly power over the markets in which they deal. This means, among other things, that: (a) they may charge prices higher than would occur if the industries were very competitive; (b) they may not improve their efficiency and productivity as much as they would do if they were subject to greater competition; and (c) they may have the power to influence the very legislators and federal agencies responsible for regulating them.

However, many of these giants—like General Electric, Boeing, IBM, General Motors, etc.—are the same companies whose massive productive resources and scientific know-how are vital to the country for peace as well as war. And as some qualified observers have contended, they are also firms which have been instrumental in no small way in providing us with the standard of living that we now possess.

Perhaps the problem for American capitalism, therefore, is not one of choosing between large firms and small ones, but of finding improved ways of encouraging big business to employ more of its resources for the betterment of society. We will have more to say about this at a later point.

Business and Social Progress

We live in an age when every major institution is under attack, when the leaders of those institutions are beset by the twin forces of external change and internal doubt, and when traditional roles are being either justified anew or wrenched into fresh directions. No institution has felt the shock of change more keenly than business. Its recruiters have been booed and even manhandled on some campuses. Antiwar protesters have turned up at corporate annual meetings. Some corporate headquarters have been bombed. Others have been besieged by groups for engaging in unfair hiring practices. In Congress Senators have denounced business for polluting, for making shoddy goods, for inflating profits on defense contracts, and for flouting the public interest in pursuit of private profit. At the heart of the attack on business is a growing doubt over its proper role in society. Increasingly, the questions are being asked: for whom is business run? For whom *should* it be run? Do the interests of business run counter to those of society? If there is a conflict, how can it be resolved?

False Alternatives?

On the spectrum of views about business and its place in society, theories run all the way from belief in nationalization to belief in an untrammeled free enterprise system. At one end we thus encounter supporters of socialism and communism, and at the other such apostles of free market virtues as Dr. Milton Friedman of the University of Chicago.

Advocates of nationalization contend there is an inherent and insoluble conflict between privately owned business and the needs of society: the key to that conflict is the need of business to make profit and to regard profit as paramount to all other considerations. Advocates of free enterprise, in contrast, regard the profit motive as being not only respectable, but also vital. They contend that in a truly competitive, market-oriented economy profits result from businesses providing consumers with what they want. Friedman, in particular, believes that market forces can be used to solve virtually all social and economic problems. He sees competition among firms as the mainspring of economic progress. To Friedman and his followers, the question whether business should make profits or serve social objectives is based on false alternatives: there is no conflict between private profit and public interest.

Somewhere between those two extremes—state ownership and more freedom for business—are those people who think there is a conflict between the goals of business and the needs of society, but do not support or want radical solutions. Alfred C. Neal, president of the business-backed Committee for Economic Development, and former first vice-president of the Federal Reserve Bank of Boston, believes we must recognize the modern corporation for what it is, "a form of government which happens to be devoted to pursuing some goals that are different from those of political government, but also some that are the same."

Pressures from Youth

Other executives point out that the pressures on businessmen to be good citizens are so great that they cannot be ignored. The result will be a growing effort to adopt pluralistic goals—those that offer opportunities for business profit as well as opportunities for service to society. What will force the pace of change is the growing influence of younger managers who are themselves part of what one social commentator calls "the critical generation."

In the ultimate analysis, business will have to reform itself, to become more responsive to public needs, if the corporation is to survive and prosper as the dominant form of organization in the United States economy. In recent years, attitude-research studies have shown that the business image is tarnished. The manager who tries to improve both the reality and the image of the corporation thus acts out of enlightened self-interest: if consumers dislike the corporation, they will dislike its products, and may buy those of rival manufacturers who show more "social awareness."

It is thus possible that competition will accomplish what exhortation cannot: the reform of corporate policies and the establishment of a new, socially oriented philosophy in executive suites across the nation.

R. B.

The restructuring of corporate goals clearly would affect not only the activities of firms but also the economy as a whole.

1. Give some examples of new goals that business might pursue.

2. Explain what effects these changes might have on the firm and on the economy —specifically on the level and composition of the nation's output and employment, and on its rate of economic growth.

SUMMARY OF IMPORTANT IDEAS

1. The private sector of the economy consists of households and businesses.

2. Wages and salaries constitute the highest share of national income—about 75 percent. The next two largest classes are corporate profits and proprietors' incomes, which together have averaged about 20 percent of the total. The balance consists of interest, less than 5 percent, and rental income, less than 4 percent.

3. The personal distribution of incomes has become less unequal since the 1930s, but there are still significant disparities. These are primarily due to differences among people with respect to (a) the distribution of wealth or income-producing assets, (b) their earning ability and opportunity, and (c) their mobility.

4. The business segment of the private sector consists primarily of proprietorships, partnerships, and corporations. Proprietorships are largest in number, but corporations produce by far the greatest proportion of the nation's total output. Among the chief advantages of the corporate form of organization are: (a) limited liability of its owners, and (b) the ability to raise large amounts of money for purposes of expansion.

5. There is a trend toward "big business" resulting primarily from firms' merging with other firms, and to a lesser extent from internal reinvestment of earnings. Firms seek to become large for various reasons. The chief one is perhaps to improve efficiency and financial strength through growth or expansion along different lines.

6. The consequences of bigness are mixed. On the one hand, it has created separation of ownership and control in the large corporation, and in many industries resulted in increased monopoly power for the largest firms. On the other hand, the largest firms have also been significantly responsible for some of the major advances in our standard of living and in our military preparedness. Hence there are fundamental issues concerning the role of big business in our society.

FOR HOMEWORK AND DISCUSSION

1. *Terms and concepts to review:*

private sector	industry
functional income distribution	proprietorship
personal income distribution	partnership
	corporation
median	stock
Lorenz curve	bond
income	dividend
wealth	limited liability
plant	separation of ownership and control
firm	

2. What factor of production receives the largest share of national income? Has this share tended to be stable or unstable over the long run? Why?

3. What are the chief causes of income inequality among households? Would it be better if all incomes were equal? Explain.

4. Is it a necessary condition of capitalism that some people be rich and some poor? Is it morally right for the government to tax the incomes of the rich and redistribute them to the poor? Defend your answer.

5. What are the two most important economic features of the corporate form of organization, as distinguished from the proprietorship or partnership form?

6. How and why do firms become big?

7. Is big business "good" or "bad"? Give some "pros" and "cons" of big business.

Supplement

The Financial Statements of Businesses: What They Tell You and How to Read Them

Business finance and accounting, like all other professions, have their own specialized vocabulary and ideas. After mastering a few technical terms and concepts, you will be in a good position to understand the two principal financial statements of businesses—the balance sheet and the income (or profit-and-loss) statement.

THE BALANCE SHEET

A *balance sheet* represents the financial position of a firm on a particular day of the year. It shows what the firm owns (its assets), what it owes (its liabilities) and the residual or equity of the owners (net worth). Thus a balance sheet reveals three broad classes of items:

Assets: the resources or things of value that a business firm or an individual owns, such as cash, property, and the rights to property.

Liabilities: the monetary debts that a business firm or an individual owes, as represented by the claims of creditors.

Net worth: the difference between the total assets and the total liabilities of a business or of an individual.

These definitions can be expressed by the following equation:

$$\text{Assets} - \text{Liabilities} = \text{Net Worth}$$

If the total assets of a business are $100,000 and the total liabilities or claims by creditors are $80,000, the net worth

---

Exhibit 6

XYZ Corporation, Balance Sheet, December 31, 19--

Assets			Liabilities and Net Worth		
			Liabilities		
Current assets			Current liabilities		
Cash		$ 475,000	Accounts payable		$ 500,000
Marketable securities, at cost					
(market value: $800,000)		775,000	Notes payable	425,000	
Accounts receivable	$1,050,000		Accrued expenses payable	165,000	
Less: provision for bad debts	50,000	1,000,000	Federal and state taxes	270,000	
Inventories		750,000	Total current liabilities		$1,360,000
Total current assets		$3,000,000	Long-term liabilities		
			Bonds payable		1,350,000
Noncurrent assets			TOTAL LIABILITIES		$2,710,000
Investments (long-term)		150,000			
Fixed assets			**Net Worth**		
Land	$ 75,000		Capital stock:		
Buildings	1,900,000		Preferred stock	$ 200,000	
Machinery	475,000		Common stock	300,000	
Office equipment	50,000				
	$2,500,000		Accumulated retained earnings	1,640,000	
Less: accumulated depreciation	900,000				
Total fixed assets		1,600,000	TOTAL NET WORTH		2,140,000
Prepayments and deferred charges		50,000			
Goodwill, patents, trademarks		50,000			
TOTAL ASSETS		$4,850,000	TOTAL LIABILITIES AND NET WORTH		$4,850,000

---

is $100,000 − $80,000 = $20,000. This $20,000 represents the owner's equity or extent of ownership in the business. The owner may have legal title to all of the assets but he owns only $20,000 of them.

The above equation may be transposed to the form in which it is more commonly written:

$$\text{Assets} = \text{Liabilities} + \text{Net Worth}$$

This equation is a fundamental identity that underlies every balance sheet. It tells you that everything a business owns (its total assets) is precisely equal to or *balanced* by everything that it owes (its total liabilities and net worth). To illustrate this, look at the balance sheet of the XYZ Corporation in Exhibit 6. Note that the assets are recorded on the left, the liabilities and net worth on the right. Let us see how this statement is interpreted.

Current assets. These include cash and those other assets that will be turned into cash in the near future, usually within the coming year.

Cash is what you would expect—bills and silver on hand and money in the bank.

Marketable securities are stocks and bonds of other corporations, and government securities. The XYZ Corporation earns dividends and interest on these investments. However, they are only temporary investments, the intention being to sell them for cash if the need arises. Hence both their cost and market value are shown for information purposes, but only the lower of the two is customarily used in the calculation of assets.

Accounts receivable represents amounts due from XYZ's customers who purchased goods on 30, 60, or 90 days' credit. XYZ's experience has been that some of these customers will fail to pay their debts. Hence the company deducts what it believes is a typical percentage of accounts receivable that will not be paid, and calls this a provision for bad debts.

Inventories include raw materials to be used in production, goods that are in process of manufacture, and finished goods ready for shipment to customers. The accountant normally values inventories conservatively—at their cost or market value, whichever is lower.

Noncurrent assets. These are the more permanent assets of the business—those that will still be in use beyond the coming year.

Investments consist of stocks and bonds of other corporations which the XYZ Corporation intends to keep for a long time and, if necessary, use as collateral to borrow cash for current needs.

Fixed assets are the durable assets used to help carry on the business. They may include land, buildings, machinery, equipment, office furniture, automobiles, and trucks.

Depreciation is the decline in useful value of a fixed asset due to wear and tear. (A fixed asset may also decline in value due to obsolescence as new and better techniques are developed.) If a fixed asset is expected to last for more than a year, its cost should be spread over its anticipated useful life. The balance sheet will then record each year that portion of the asset's original value which still remains.

Thus, suppose the company buys a machine for $1,000 which it expects to use for five years, after which time it will be discarded. One way to take depreciation is to assume the machine depreciates by an equal amount each year, in this case $200. At the end of the first year the balance sheet would show:

Machine (cost)	$1,000
Less: accumulated depreciation	200
Net depreciated value for balance sheet	$ 800

At the end of the second year the balance sheet would show:

Machine (cost)	$1,000
Less: accumulated depreciation	400
Net depreciated value for balance sheet	$ 600

Depreciation is thus a method of allocating the cost of a fixed asset by charging a portion of its cost to each year of its expected life. In Exhibit 6, the figure shown for accumulated depreciation represents buildings, machinery, and office furniture. Land is not subject to depreciation and is always shown on a balance sheet at its original cost.

Prepayments and deferred charges represent expenditures made in advance for items that will yield portions of their benefits in this and in future years. Examples include the advance premium paid on a three-year fire insurance policy, expenses incurred in developing and marketing a new product, costs of moving to a new location, etc. The benefits from these expenditures will be received over a period, and hence their costs will be amortized (prorated) over that period instead of writing them off entirely in the year that they were incurred.

Goodwill, patents, trademarks are "intangible" assets: they exist and they have considerable value to the company that owns them, but no one really knows how much. (What value can you place on the reputation of a company? How much is the name "Coke" worth to Coca-Cola? The symbol ◀■▶ to Chevrolet?) The value of these intangibles is decided almost arbitrarily by different companies. Many list them at the nominal value of $1. Other firms (e.g., General Motors) value them at millions of dollars.

Liabilities and net worth. These are, respectively, the claims of the creditors against the company and the equity of the owners. Creditors always have a prior claim over owners. Hence the net worth may also be regarded as a "residual" claim. What do you suppose this means?

Current liabilities. These include all debts due within the coming year. Generally speaking, the Current Assets classification is the counterpart to the Current Liabilities classification because current assets are the source from which current liabilities are paid.

Accounts payable are debts that the company owes to creditors from whom it has bought goods, supplies, or services, usually on a payment basis of 30 to 90 days.

Notes payable are promises to pay the holder, such as a bank, a sum of money at a certain time within a year at a stated rate of interest.

Accrued expenses payable are items like salaries and wages to employees, interest on borrowed funds, pensions, and similar obligations which accrue from day to day. The portions of these that are unpaid on the day the balance sheet is drawn up are included here.

Federal and state taxes include income taxes, social security taxes, and property taxes due to the federal, state, and local governments.

Long-term liabilities are obligations to creditors which will not be paid within one year, such as mortgages, long-term notes, and bonds.

Bonds payable are promises to pay the holder a sum of money at a certain time beyond one year at a stated rate of interest.

Net worth. This is the difference between the total assets and the total liabilities. It represents the financial investment or equity of the owners.

Capital stock represents units of ownership in a corporation. Each owner of a share is called a stockholder. Capital stock thus represents the stockholders' proprietary interest in the company. Two typical classes of capital stock are preferred stock and common stock.

Preferred stock gets preference over common stock in the distribution of dividends, or in the distribution of assets if the company is liquidated, or both. If it is preferred as to dividends, the holders receive dividends at a certain rate or amount per share before dividends may be declared on the common stock. If it is preferred as to assets, the holders receive their capital contributions before the common stockholders in the event that the corporation is dissolved.

Common stock shares have no fixed rate of dividends. Hence they can receive better dividends than the fixed dividend rate that may exist on preferred stock if the corporation's earnings are high.

Accumulated retained earnings represent net profits earned since the company was organized, after deducting losses sustained and dividends paid to stockholders. In some balance sheets the terms "surplus" or "earned surplus" are used instead of accumulated retained earnings.

This completes the explanation of the balance sheet. Two important points to keep in mind are:

1. The values of some of the assets shown on a balance sheet—especially the fixed assets—are *estimates;* they do not represent what the firm could actually get for them if they were sold. In fact most of the fixed assets would probably bring in much less than the values estimated for them. Their value to the company is a "going concern" value, since the firm ordinarily expects to remain in business and use these assets, not sell them.

2. There is *no specific correspondence* between individual items on the two sides of a balance sheet. Therefore any attempt to link pairs of items will lead to confusion and error. Generally speaking, only the totals have meaning.

THE INCOME STATEMENT

Whereas a balance sheet reflects the financial position of a company as of a given date, an income (or profit-and-loss) statement shows the company's operating activities over a period, usually a year. A balance sheet is thus somewhat akin to a financial "snapshot" of the company, whereas an income statement is more like a financial "motion picture."

An *income statement* compares the revenues of a firm during a period with its costs during that period in order to arrive at a measure of profit for the period as a whole. An equation underlies every income statement, namely:

Total Profits = Total Revenue − Total Costs

This equation is a fundamental identity of the income statement. An illustration of such a statement for the XYZ Corporation appears in Exhibit 7. Can you find the items that comprise the terms in the above equation?

Note that this statement includes both income and expenses resulting directly from the operations of the business, as well as income and expenses from other sources. Can you tell which is which?

RELATIONSHIPS BETWEEN THE BALANCE SHEET
AND THE INCOME STATEMENT

The two types of financial statements supplement and complement one another. For instance, income tends to increase net worth, while expenses and losses tend to decrease it. At the beginning of each period, the net profit from the income statement after dividends are paid to stockholders will be brought over to the balance sheet as

Exhibit 7

XYZ Corporation, Income Statement for the Year 19--

Net sales		$3,250,000
Cost of sales and operating expenses		
Cost of goods sold	$2,000,000	
Depreciation	450,000	
Selling and administratieve expenses	250,000	2,700,000
Operating profit		$ 550,000
Other income		
Dividends and interest		50,000
Total income		$ 600,000
Less: interest paid out on bonds		50,000
Profit before provision for federal and state taxes		$ 550,000
Provision for federal and state taxes		270,000
Net profit after taxes		$ 280,000

part of "accumulated retained earnings." The net profit is also reflected in the increases or decreases of various assets and liabilities when compared to those at the beginning of the period. Thus the two statements should usually be examined and interpreted together, not separately.

SOME IMPORTANT RATIOS

A fundamental economic question that is sometimes asked is: What is the earning power of a company, and how does its profitability compare with other firms in the same industry? The managers, stockholders, and creditors of an enterprise are obviously interested in this question because they are all involved in one way or another with its future success. Labor unions and government agencies are also concerned—the former when they seek wage increases for their members; the latter when they investigate a particular firm's degree of monopoly power in an industry.

There are four measures (or formulas) of profitability that are typically used to evaluate a firm's performance. Here is what they look like when the data are taken from the balance sheet and income statement of the XYZ Corporation.

1. *Operating Profit Ratio.* This is the ratio of the firm's operating profit to net sales, and tells you the profit per dollar of sales. In other words, it indicates how well the company is performing on its selling operations.

$$\text{Operating profit ratio} = \frac{\text{operating profit}}{\text{net sales}}$$

$$= \frac{\$550,000}{\$3,250,000} = 0.169 = 16.9\%$$

2. *Net Profit Ratio.* This is the ratio of net profit after taxes to net sales, thus providing a more general performance picture of the year's activities.

$$\text{Net profit ratio} = \frac{\text{net profit after taxes}}{\text{net sales}}$$

$$= \frac{\$280,000}{\$3,250,000} = 0.087 = 8.7\%$$

3. *Return on Total Assets.* This is the ratio of net profits after taxes to total assets. It measures the rate of return on the total asset investment in the firm—that is, the productivity of the total assets.

$$\text{Return on total assets} = \frac{\text{net profit after taxes}}{\text{total assets}}$$

$$= \frac{\$280,000}{\$4,850,000} = 0.058 = 5.8\%$$

4. *Return on Net Worth.* This is the ratio of net profit after taxes to net worth. It measures the rate of return on stockholders' investment, thus telling you how well the owners' funds are being utilized.

$$\text{Return on net worth} = \frac{\text{net profit after taxes}}{\text{net worth}}$$

$$= \frac{\$280,000}{\$2,140,000} = 0.131 = 13.1\%$$

To be useful, these percentages must be compared with those of other firms in the same industry groups. Fortunately, such comparisons are readily available. One of the chief publishers of this information is Dun and Bradstreet whose periodic reports on the subject can be found in the business and economics section of many university and public libraries.

SUMMARY OF IMPORTANT IDEAS

1. The balance sheet and the income statement are the two most important financial statements of businesses.

The Truth is in the Footnotes

To the innocent eye, a corporation's annual financial statement appears to be indisputably factual. There, in lavish and frequently tedious detail, are summaries of the company's transactions during the year, its profits, its assets and liabilities, and its obligations in the future. To the shrewd and skeptical eye, however, none of these figures is necessarily what it seems to be.

As the 1970s opened, a rash of financial scandals and near-scandals made it all too obvious that company officers could delude themselves and almost everyone else with ingenious accounting methods.

Some examples drawn from real life will show how companies can use cosmetic accounting without being dishonest. The companies in these examples have been disguised, because all have now mended their ways.

What is an Asset?

Rinky-Dink Resources Corporation explores for oil, gas, coal and ores. Within five years its assets rose from $15 million to almost $200 million—and the price of its stock rose from $5 to $76. Then the company admitted it was insolvent. How could it happen? Answer: The assets were not what they seemed to be. Instead of deducting from income the costs of exploring and developing potentially productive land, the company had added these costs to its assets. To justify that method, the company explained that its *total* expenditures on exploration and development improved the *total* value of its oil, gas, and ore leases. The method is legal; but it has three drawbacks. First, it inflates assets by adding to them expenditures on unproductive as well as productive exploration and develop-

ment. Second, it inflates profits by freeing them of the burden of exploration costs. Third, it gives investors no guide to the company's skills in prospecting and developing revenue-producing land.

Omniwhere Airlines showed long-term debt of $500 million, with an annual obligation of $73 million in payment of interest and retirement of debt. Along came the jumbo jets, and the airline wanted to borrow more money. The financial community turned it down. The reason: The company was committed to pay far more than the $73 million each year for jets bought with borrowed money. It had also signed rental agreements that required it to pay $40 million for the leasing of aircraft. But that transaction did not show up in the balance sheet; technically, leasing is an "off-balance-sheet transaction," recorded only in the footnotes. Stockholders were astonished when their company teetered on the brink of bankruptcy. They should not have been; "off balance sheet" or not, the rental agreement was a real commitment, and just as much a drain on the company's income as its debt obligations.

Counting its Chickens

Zilchburger Inc. franchises its name and its product, a hamburger, to investors. To obtain a franchise, the investor must agree to pay up to $100,000 for Zilchburger's name, food-processing equipment, and a building of approved design—a particularly nasty confection with a plastic roof shaped to look like a cheeseburger. The investor can pay as little as 10 percent down, and the rest over 10 years. But Zilchburger showed the whole $100,000 as a sale in

the year in which the deal was signed. The method was legal, and indeed common among companies in the franchise business. All went well until the number of new investors declined, and some earlier investors reneged because they were losing money. Zilchburger's revenues slipped, and with them earnings per share; the chairman resigned, and the company brought reality to its accounting methods.

Complexity is the Culprit

Who is guilty? Corporate officers, accountants, or auditors? In fact, the culprit is not so much the officers of a company or its auditors as the bewildering complexity of modern business. A large corporation's income comes from such diverse sources, and is of such a complicated nature, that no single rule will account for all of it adequately.

Most corporations do, however, observe with notable scrupulousness the legal obligation to spell out in footnotes to their annual financial statements the accounting methods they use. Unfortunately, many investors and creditors have until recently been too lazy or hasty to read those footnotes, or think of their implications.

R. B.

1. *If you were considering buying stock in a corporation, how would you protect yourself from being misled by rather "peculiar" accounting methods used in preparing the financial statements?*

2. *Explain how these examples prove that both the income statement and the balance sheet are needed if a truer picture of a company's financial condition is to be obtained.*

3. *If balance sheets and income statements are open to question, of what use are they?*

2. For purposes of financial evaluation and control, four convenient ratios are: operating profit ratio, net profit ratio, return on total assets, return on net worth. The last two in particular are often used in labor-management wage negotiations, economic studies of monopoly power within an industry, pricing practices of business firms, and so on.

FOR HOMEWORK AND DISCUSSION

1. *Terms and concepts to review:*

balance sheet	accounts payable
assets	notes payable
liabilities	accrued expenses
net worth	capital stock
current assets	preferred stock
accounts receivable	common stock
inventories	income statement
fixed assets	operating profit ratio
depreciation	net profit ratio
prepayments	return on total assets
goodwill	return on net worth
current liabilities	

2. Draw up a list of items that accountants would classify as assets. Do the same with liabilities.

3. How much would you pay for a business which yields a net profit of $20,000 a year after taxes? Assume that the business is secure, with little or no risk. (NOTE: Explain how you arrived at your answer.)

REFERENCES AND READING SUGGESTIONS

BONNEVILLE, JOSEPH H., LLOYD E. DEWEY, HARRY M. KELLEY, *Organizing and Financing Business,* 6th ed., Prentice-Hall, Englewood Cliffs, N.J., 1959, chaps. 3, 4, 5.

GILBEY, ELIZABETH W., *A Primer on Economics of Consumption,* Random House, New York, 1968.

MCGUIRE, JOSEPH W., *Business and Society,* McGraw-Hill, New York, 1963.

U.S. DEPARTMENT OF COMMERCE, *Survey of Current Business,* published monthly. Contains data and articles relevant to households and income.

CHAPTER 6

The Public Sector: Government

CHAPTER PREVIEW

How does the influence of government make itself felt through taxation and expenditure?

What is the nature or structure of the American tax system? What do we get for the taxes we pay?

Is there a theory of taxation that can serve as a guide for evaluating taxes?

Any serious discussion of government is bound to raise questions of taxes. Yet taxes, as everyone knows, have also been the subject of many witticisms.

Benjamin Franklin is reputed to have said, "Only two things in life are certain—death and taxes—and I resent that they don't come in that order." But we shall see that things have changed somewhat since Franklin's time: Certain taxes today do indeed come in that order. Similarly, Lewis Carroll, author of *Alice's Adventures in Wonderland,* once remarked that the things he hated most were spiders, ghosts, gout, an umbrella for three—and the income tax. Today there are probably few who would disagree.

The list of adages and aphorisms could go on. But taxes, for those who recall their study of history, have also been the cause of wars and revolutions. Obviously, anything that can have such widespread influences ought to be worth knowing something about.

When we speak of government, we ordinarily mean the federal government. But in this chapter we will also have occasion to say some things about lower orders of government, not only at the state but also at the local level—the latter including counties, cities, villages, townships, school districts, and so on.

Government's Soaring Expenditures

In the past few decades the public sector has been characterized by a remarkable growth of expenditures at all levels of government—federal, state, and local. The historical record is shown in Exhibit 1. What are the chief reasons for these steep increases in government spending?

War and National Defense. Most of the increase in federal spending can be attributed to expenditures on wars, national defense, and defense-related activities including international military assistance, space research and technology, veteran's services, and interest on the federal debt resulting mainly from the financing of our most recent major wars. Taken together these items constitute well over half —and in some years more than two-thirds—of all federal expenditures.

Increased Demand for Collective Goods and Services. The American people have come to expect more in the way of collective goods and services provided by federal, state, and local governments. As a result there have been increased expenditures by the public sector in numerous areas not shown in the chart. These include education, public assistance and welfare, agriculture, transportation, housing, sanitation, water supply, public safety, consumer protection, and so forth.

Inflation and Lagging Productivity. The costs of these collective benefits provided by government have been increasing for at least two reasons. First, inflation (i.e., rising prices) has been a long-run trend in our economy. This has made it necessary for government to pay larger amounts of money for the goods and services it provides. Second, most of the civilian benefits provided by government consist of services such as education, public safety, and health. Productivity in these fields has not risen as fast as in the economy as a whole, whereas public employees' wages have risen at roughly the same pace as wages in the private sector. Hence, government finds that the salaries it pays out are growing faster than the volume or efficiency of the services it performs.

Government revenues for the most part have increased concurrently with government expenditures over the years, although in any particular year one is usually greater or less than the other. You can get an indication of this by looking at the chart in Exhibit 2 showing the federal government's budget. As the chart suggests, the government's total revenues and expenditures for any given year are rarely equal. When they are, the budget is said to be *balanced.* On the other hand, when total revenues exceed total expenditures in any given year, the budget is said to have a *surplus;* when total revenues are less than total expenditures, the budget has a *deficit.*

Budgeting: Where Does the Money Come From? Where Does It Go?

The budget of the United States, like the budget of a family, is a curious document—a study in hopes, daydreams, and hard facts. A *budget* is an itemized

---

Exhibit 1

Growth of Government Expenditure

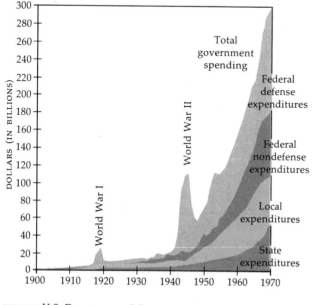

SOURCE: U.S. Department of Commerce.

Exhibit 2

Federal Budget Receipts and Outlays: 1954 to 1971*

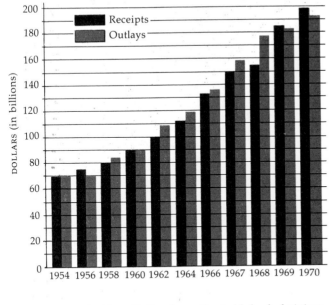

* For years ending June 30. Based on estimated federal administrative budget and trust fund receipts and expenditures.
SOURCE: U.S. Department of Commerce.

Exhibit 3

The Federal Government Dollar: 1968 to 1971*

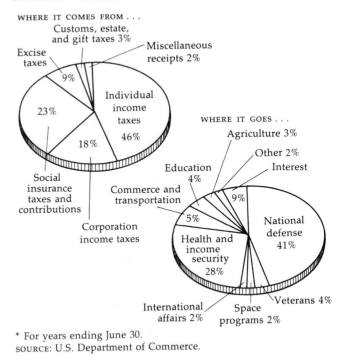

* For years ending June 30.
SOURCE: U.S. Department of Commerce.

estimate of expected revenues and expenditures for a given period in the future. The federal budget covers a fiscal year beginning July 1 and ending the following June 30.

THE FEDERAL BUDGET

Like every budget, the one given for the federal government in Exhibit 3 consists of two parts—one showing where the money comes from, the other showing where it goes.

On the revenue side income, employment, and excise taxes are the most important categories. *Income taxes*, both individual and corporate, make up the largest source of revenue. The base of these taxes is net income, which is the difference between gross income for a given year and certain specific items that are subtracted from it. The great bulk of personal income tax revenues comes from people in the middle- and lower-income groups. *Employment taxes*,

which are the next major source of revenue, are compulsory social security payments made by employers and employees as part of the nation's social security program. *Excise taxes*, which are levies imposed on the sales of goods like tobacco and alcohol products, and *"Other"* income consisting of customs duties and interest on trust fund investments provide most of the remaining revenue.

On the expenditure side the chief categories are national defense and "transfer payments." *National defense* and defense-related activities include expenditures for the United States armed forces and those of America's allies, atomic energy programs, and space research. Most of the other expenditures can be classified under a general heading not shown in the chart—*transfer payments*. These are expenditures made by government for which it receives no current goods or services in return. Examples of transfer payments are veterans' benefits, social welfare types of expenditures like social security payments, unemployment compensation, and relief payments, and certain government subsidies such as agricultural price supports. Transfer payments redistribute income from one group to another—from employed to unemployed or from city worker to farmer—and thus tend to modify the composition of goods and services produced by the private sector in favor of the recipients of the payments. Can you explain why?

STATE AND LOCAL BUDGETS

Where do the numerous state and local governments get their money? How do they spend it? The answers to these questions are given by the revenue and expenditure information in Exhibit 4A.

Revenues in the form of property taxes and sales taxes are most important. *Property taxes* are the principal source of income, and consist mainly of taxes on real property such as land and buildings. In some states they also include taxes on personal property like furniture, clothing, and jewelry, and on "intangibles" such as savings accounts and securities. *Sales taxes,* the second major source of revenue, consist of retail sales taxes, gross receipts taxes, processing taxes, etc. They have been gaining in relative importance over the years as state and local governments continue to seek new ways of obtaining the income they need to meet their mounting expenses.

The remaining major sources of revenue which fall into one or more of the general categories shown on the chart include: highway-user taxes such as

---

Exhibit 4

A. The State and Local Government Dollar: 1966 to 1970

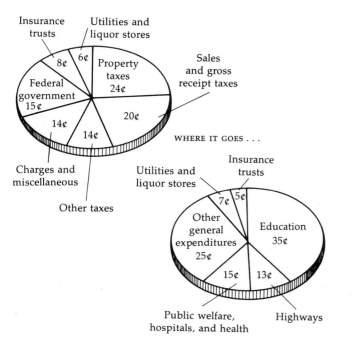

SOURCE: U.S. Department of Commerce.

B. Per Capita Tax Revenue by Level of Government: 1950 to 1970

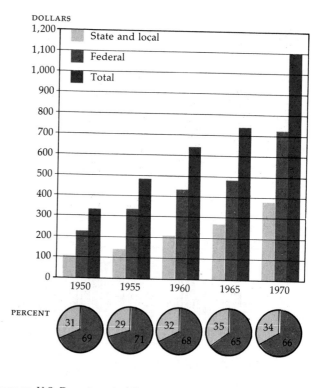

SOURCE: U.S. Department of Commerce.

vehicle license fees and gasoline taxes; income taxes on individuals and corporations; income from employee retirement and unemployment compensation trust funds; payments from the federal government to help meet the expenses of public welfare, education, highways, and social insurance; and income from the operation of gas, electricity, and water utilities, and from liquor stores.

Expenditures include education—mainly schools —which represents the largest single item. The remaining expenditures are self-explanatory. Some of the specific items under the category of "Other General Expenditures" include payments made for police and fire protection, the development and maintenance of natural resources and recreation facilities, and the administration of legislative and judicial functions.

Exhibit 4B shows the receipt of tax revenues by the federal government and by state and local governments. Can you interpret this chart? Does there seem to be a trend? If so, what does it suggest? See also Exhibit 4C.

INTERGOVERNMENTAL GRANTS-IN-AID

Certain types of financial aids that are becoming increasingly important are so-called intergovernmental *grants-in-aid*. They consist of (1) revenues received by local governments from their states and from the federal government, and (2) revenues received by state governments from the federal government.

These revenues are used primarily to pay for public welfare assistance, highways, and education, and thus tend to reduce the effects of—but by no means eliminate—the great differences in income that exist between rich states and poor states, high-income regions and low-income regions. Thus, if you live in a wealthy state like California or New York,

Exhibit 4 (continued)

C. State and Local Taxes

Per $1,000 of personal income, 1969 rates.

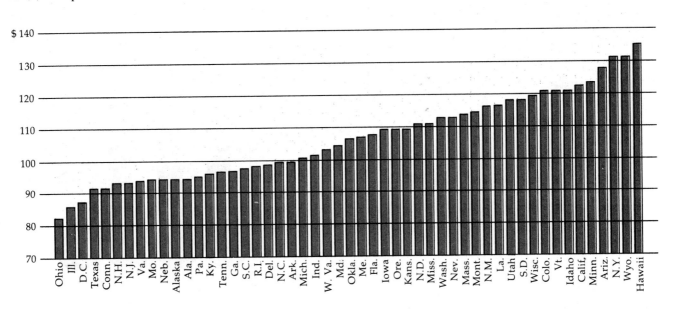

some of your federal income tax payments will go to poorer states like Alabama and Mississippi. If you live in a well-to-do suburb, some of your state income taxes will help to build schools and pave roads in rural areas and in the large cities. A portion of corporation income taxes is also used for these purposes.

In this way the federal and state governments serve as "transfer" agents, shifting some tax revenues from high-income areas to low-income areas according to social needs. This practice will become increasingly significant as states and localities find themselves faced with the growing financial strains imposed by an expanding population. See Box 1, page 88.

Various Kinds of Taxes: The American Tax System

A *tax* is a compulsory payment to the government to help meet its costs of operation. Taxes can be levied and classified in many ways. In the United States the main types are:

1. Taxes on income
   a. Personal income taxes
   b. Corporation income taxes

2. Taxes on wealth (including its ownership and transfer)
   a. Property taxes
   b. Death (estate and inheritance) and gift taxes

3. Taxes on activities (consumption, production, employment, etc.)
   a. Sales and excise taxes
   b. Social security taxes

Dozens of other less important kinds of taxes exist, but nearly all can be placed in one of these three main categories. Let us see what the above taxes involve.

TAXES ON INCOME

Income taxes are based on net income—that is, what remains after certain items are subtracted from gross income. The items that can be subtracted and the tax rates that are applied are specified by law, and differ between (1) the personal income tax, and (2) the corporation income tax.

Personal Income Tax

In the spring a young man's fancy turns to thoughts of love. But for millions of American taxpayers, spring is the season when their thoughts turn to much more mundane and certainly less romantic activities as they begin to sort their previous year's income and expense records. As you can see from Exhibit 5, this is the first step that must be completed in order to determine the personal income tax.

Exhibit 5

Logical Structure of the Federal Personal Income Tax

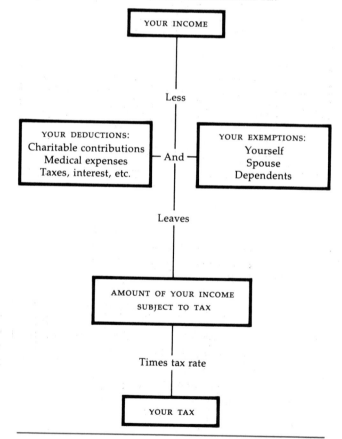

Trends in State and Local Finance

Since 1965, state and local government expenditures have accelerated from the already rapid rate of increase of the previous years (as is shown in the accompanying chart). Particularly marked were percentage increases in outlays for public welfare and higher education. Spending for health and hospitals also rose sharply.

Publicly provided services are essentially similar to most privately financed services in the sense that as incomes increase, people allocate increasing amounts of their incomes to consumption of government services. At the same time, the social unrest within our cities has been accelerating the pressure for increases in both the scope and quality of public services.

There can be little doubt that the accelerated pace of state and local government spending has also been stimulated by the proliferation of federal grant-in-aid programs. Federal expenditures under these programs rose at an annual rate of nearly 16 percent between 1965 and 1968. Federal funds support over 50 percent of welfare outlays. The medicaid program has provided a major boost to public welfare outlays. Federal support of higher education is becoming increasingly important.

The chart shows a projection of the state and local spending out to fiscal 1975 that would be required to maintain the same improvement in the scope and quality of government services that, it has been estimated, was maintained between 1963 and 1968 plus the growth in spending required to keep up with

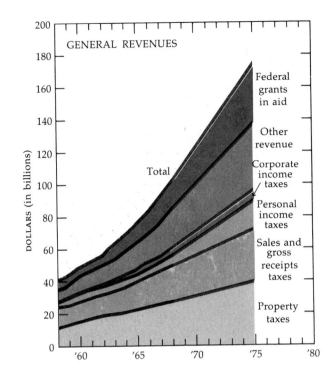

Thus, if you were calculating this tax yourself, you would be allowed to make specific types of deductions and exemptions. For instance, some deductions that may be made (within certain limits) from your income are: donations to the Red Cross, to your alma mater, and to various other nonprofit organizations; payments for doctor bills, X-rays, and medicines; sales and other taxes paid to state and local governments; interest paid on loans; and various other outlays. In addition, tax allowances or exemptions are permitted for support of yourself, your family and your dependents. In this way the government acknowledges the fact that larger families require more funds than smaller ones to meet their living costs.

THE RATE STRUCTURE. The amount of income tax you would have to pay at a given income level depends on several things. They include whether you are single or married and what the particular tax rates happen to be at the time. These rates usually change every few years. A hypothetical but fairly realistic tax rate schedule is illustrated in Exhibit 6, page 90.

Column (1) shows the different income levels, and column (2) tells you the amount of tax to be paid at each of these income levels. Note that the tax starts with $0 at the low income end and rises to $680,000 for an income of $1 million.

Column (3) reveals the percentage of tax at each income level. Since these percentages increase as

population expansion. The projections also reflect the impact of rising prices in the years ahead.

The projection of tax receipts shows the increase in revenues that would be generated by the current revenue structure in a growing economy with moderate inflation. Federal aid and local fees are projected as financing the same share of total spending (for the programs they help support) as they do today.

The projections yield a revenue-expenditure gap in the general fund budgets of state and local governments of around $15 billion by fiscal 1975. If long-term borrowing continues to grow at the recent pace, a net deficit of $5–10 billion is suggested for fiscal 1975.

Since they generally are required to match income with outgo, the payment-receipts gap projected for 1975 implies that state and local governments will have to make painful adjustments in expenditure goals and/or tax rates, unless additional revenue is forthcoming from federal aid programs.

There can be little question that state and local governments can raise tax rates or levy new taxes required to fill the gap. Many students of public finance argue, however, that if they try to obtain additional revenues by boosting property or sales tax rates, the inefficiency and inequity of many state and local tax systems will be compounded. On the other hand, if states and localities increase their reliance on income taxes, the payment-receipts gap might be bridged more easily.

SOURCE: First National City Bank of New York, October, 1969.

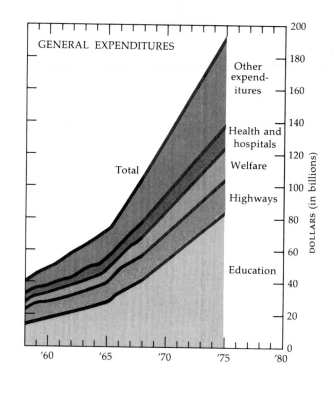

income rises, the tax rate is said to be "graduated" or *progressive:* it takes a larger share of higher incomes than of lower ones.

Columns (4) and (5) are shown in order to calculate column (6). What does column (6) tell you? It reveals the *extra* tax rate on additional dollars of income earned. This rate starts at 10 percent for incomes over $1,000 and increases—at first slowly and then steeply —until it levels off at 70 percent for incomes over $100,000. The distinction between the *average tax rate* in column (3) and the *marginal tax rate* in column (6) is shown by the formulas beneath the table.

In comparing columns (3) and (6), note that the marginal tax rate is always higher than the average

tax rate in going from one income level to the next. Observe also that you can never find yourself worse off by making an extra dollar. According to the marginal tax rate schedule, if your total taxable income were $1 million, you would still be able to keep 30 cents of every additional dollar you earned.

Two controversial aspects of the personal income tax should be noted.

1. Through legal methods of *tax avoidance,* taxpayers in the higher-income brackets often pay average rates of only 40 to 50 percent. This is because our tax system contains certain legal "loopholes" which permit relative tax advantages for the rich. Some millionaires pay no federal income taxes at all. (In contrast, illegal methods of escaping taxes, such as lying or cheating about income or expenses, come under the general heading of *tax evasion*.) Most economists agree that if the legal loopholes were closed the government could raise the same amount of revenue at significantly lower tax rates for every-one. As it is, the great bulk of tax revenues comes from the lower and "average" income groups.

2. The steepness of the marginal tax rate schedule may have serious economic consequences. It must be high enough at all income levels to yield the desired amounts of revenues. However, rates that are too high at the upper-income levels may discourage investment and risk taking, whereas rates that are too high at the lower levels may reduce the incentive for taking on overtime work or second jobs. Is there a "best" or optimum schedule for the economy as a whole? There probably is, but it changes with different needs and conditions, reflecting political as well as economic circumstances. Some of the historical rates for the United States are shown in Exhibit 7. (See also Box 2.)

Exhibit 6

Personal Income Tax Schedule
(Based on hypothetical data)

(1)	(2)	(3)	(4)	(5)	(6)
Total taxable income	Total personal income tax	Average tax rate† (2) ÷ (1) (percent)	Change in column (1)	Change in column (2)	Marginal tax rate‡ (5) ÷ (4) (percent)
Less than:					
$ 1,000	$ 0	0			
			$ 1,000	$ 100	10
2,000	100	5			
			1,000	110	11
3,000	210	7			
			1,000	130	13
4,000	340	8.5			
			1,000	160	16
5,000	500	10			
			5,000	1,000	20
10,000	1,500	15			
			10,000	3,500	35
20,000	5,000	25			
			30,000	15,000	50
50,000	20,000	40			
			50,000	30,000	60
100,000	50,000	50			
			100,000	70,000	70
200,000	120,000	60			
			200,000	140,000	70
400,000	260,000	65			
			600,000	420,000	70
1,000,000	680,000	68			

† Average tax rate = $\dfrac{\text{total personal income tax}}{\text{total taxable income}}$.

‡ Marginal tax rate = $\dfrac{\text{change in total personal income tax}}{\text{change in total taxable income}}$.

Exhibit 7

Taxation of One Additional Dollar of Income As Related to Net Income of an Individual

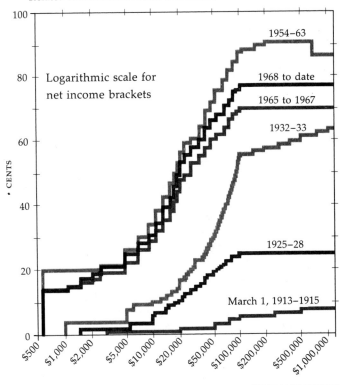

Corporation Income Tax

The second largest source of revenue to the federal government is the corporate income tax. (Many states also tax corporate incomes, but at lower rates.) The corporation income tax is simple to calculate since it is based on the difference between a company's total income and its total expenses—its net profit. Historically, the tax rate has varied over the years, as illustrated in Exhibit 8. Since 1950 it has averaged over 50 percent. Some international comparisons are shown in Box 3, on the next page.

The corporation income tax raises two major issues:

1. Some experts argue that the rates should be lower. This would leave corporations with more profits to use for expanding their operations, thereby creating more jobs. Other authorities, however, contend that the rates should be higher so that the government could then reduce the rates on other taxes, especially personal income taxes.

2. The claim is widely made that the tax is actually an unfair form of *double taxation:* the corporation

---

Box 2

Personal Income Taxes Around the World

The rates shown are those applicable on personal income by central governments. Local governments—cantons in Switzerland, states in the United States, municipalities in Norway, United States, etc.—also levy income taxes at rates that add considerably to the maximum marginal rates of central governments. The United States rate includes a 10 percent surtax which prevailed from 1968 to 1970. A surtax is an additional tax levied on a tax base after a normal tax has been applied.

Maximum marginal tax rates by central governments on personal income, 1968 (latest comparative data)

Country	Marginal rates (percent)	Point of application*
Italy	94.50	$800,000
United Kingdom	91.25	36,000
Canada	82.40	370,000
United States	77	100,000
France	76	15,000
Japan	75	167,000
Netherlands	70.50	46,000
Austria	69	206,000
Australia	68.34	36,000
Belgium	66	80,000
Sweden	65	29,000
Germany (F.R.)	54.59	28,000
Denmark	52.38	53,000
Norway	50	13,000
Switzerland	8	31,000

* Converted into United States dollars at official rates of exchange and rounded to the nearest $1,000.

NOTE: These are not necessarily the *effective* rates in the countries shown. Various loopholes exist which permit taxpayers to reduce the tax rates on their incomes.

SOURCE: First National City Bank of New York.

Exhibit 8

United States Corporate Income Tax Rates

The rates shown are the standard rates on taxable corporate income over $25,000 imposed by the federal government. The tax rates as a whole are often changed by Congress every few years. Through most of the 1960s, for example, the rate was 22 percent on the first $25,000 of taxable income, plus 48 percent on income over the $25,000 level. No account is taken in this chart of excess profits taxes. The 1909–12 levy on income was called an excise tax. The United States tax rate includes a 10 percent surtax imposed in 1968 and removed in 1970.

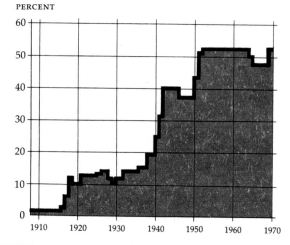

Corporation Income Taxes Around the World

In addition to corporate income taxation by the central government shown, there are other taxes on business imposed by central and local authorities. The United States rate includes a 10 percent surtax imposed in 1968 and removed in 1970. Some other nations also have surtaxes.

Maximum tax rates by central governments on corporate profits, 1968 (latest comparative data)

Country	Rates (percent)
Austria	58
United States	52.8
Germany (F.R.)	52.53
Canada	51.41
France	50.98
Netherlands	46
United Kingdom	42.50
Australia	42.50
Sweden	40
Belgium	35
Japan	35
Norway	30
Italy	27.50
Switzerland	7.2

SOURCE: First National City Bank of New York.

pays a tax on its profits, and the stockholder pays a personal income tax on the dividends he receives from those profits.

There are no completely right or wrong answers to either argument. Each has valid aspects which are discussed in subsequent chapters.

The remaining two categories which make up the structure of the American tax system—taxes on wealth and taxes on activities—can be sketched briefly.

TAXES ON WEALTH

Property taxes, which are levied primarily on land and buildings, vary from low rates in some rural areas where services are minor to high rates in localities with good streets, schools, and public safety facilities.

Death taxes are levied on estates and inheritances. They are imposed by the federal government and by all states except Nevada. Like income taxes, they exempt small estates and inheritances but tax the unexempt portions at progressive rates. Since many wealthy people would try to avoid these taxes by distributing most of their property before death, *gift taxes* are imposed on the transfer of assets beyond certain values. However, various legal devices such as trust funds and family foundations still enable many wealthy individuals to lighten the weight of these taxes.

TAXES ON ACTIVITIES

Sales taxes are flat percentage levies on the retail prices of items. In some states or cities certain things like food, medicine, and services are exempt, and in other places they are not. The federal government imposes no "general" sales tax, but it does impose special sales taxes called *excise taxes* on the manufacture, sale, or consumption of liquor, gasoline, and certain other products.

Social security taxes are payroll taxes which finance our compulsory social insurance program covering old-age and unemployment benefits. The contributions come from both employees and employers and are based on the incomes of the former. These taxes are actually a "reverse" form of income tax, since they exempt incomes above a certain level but not below it. This assures every income earner of being covered.

Some Theories of Taxation— Some Issues of Fairness

In his *Wealth of Nations*, Adam Smith advises governments to follow four guiding rules of taxation:

1. *Equality.* Each individual should pay taxes in proportion to his income.

2. *Certainty.* Every taxpayer should know precisely what his taxes are and when they should be paid.

3. *Convenience.* Taxes should be levied in a manner that is of greatest convenience to the taxpayer.

4. *Economy.* The cost of collecting a tax should be small in proportion to its yield.

These rules are simple and persuasive, but their implementation—especially the first—has been the subject of a good deal of economic controversy. Let us see why.

TWO PRINCIPLES OF TAXATION

A good tax system should be fair. If people generally believe it is unfair—that too many loopholes benefit some individuals and not others—taxpayers' morale and the effectiveness of the tax system itself will deteriorate. Hence, two fundamental principles have evolved over the years.

Benefit Principle

The so-called *benefit principle* holds that people should be taxed according to the benefits they receive. For example, the tax you pay on gasoline reflects the benefit you receive from driving on public roads. The more you drive, the more gasoline you use and the more taxes you pay. These tax revenues are typically earmarked (set aside) for financing highway construction and maintenance.

What is wrong with the benefit principle as a general guide for taxation? There are two major difficulties:

1. There are relatively few goods and services for which benefits can be readily determined—and for most goods and services they would be impossible to determine. Thus, the entire nation benefits from public education, health and sanitation facilities, police and fire protection, and national defense. How can we decide which groups should pay the taxes for these things and which should not?

2. Those who receive certain benefits may not be able to pay for them. For instance, it would be impossible to finance public welfare assistance or unemployment compensation by taxing the recipients.

Ability-to-Pay Principle

About 2,400 years ago, in his classic work *The Republic*, the philosopher Plato remarked: "When there is an income tax, the just man will pay more and the unjust less on the same amount of income."

Plato was speaking of an ideal world—a utopia in which all men strive to do what will be best for society. Unfortunately, with human nature as it is, most people are not inclined to pay any more taxes than the law requires of them.

However, the *ability-to-pay principle* is actually a modern and realistic restatement of Plato's ancient dictum, for it states that the fairest tax a government can impose is one that is based on the financial ability of the taxpayer—regardless of any benefit he may derive from the tax. This means that the more wealth a man has or the higher his income, the greater his taxes should be—on the assumption that each dollar of taxes paid by a rich man "hurts" less than each dollar paid by a poor man. The personal income tax in the United States is based on this principle.

There are two major difficulties in the use of this principle as a general guide for taxation. First, ability to pay is a debatable concept—difficult to determine and impossible to measure. How can we really know that a dollar of taxes always means less to a rich man than to a poor man? Although we ordinarily *assume* that such is the case, the entire notion of ability to pay involves deep psychological and philosophical issues that economics is not equipped to explore. Second, even if we could really be clear about what we mean by ability to pay, how could we distinguish between *degrees* of ability among different individuals? As with the benefit principle, the hardest problem is to develop a way of measuring the right concepts.

SOME PRACTICAL COMPROMISES

As a result of these philosophical difficulties, it has become necessary to adopt convenient methods of implementing the benefit and ability principles—even though the methods may not always be ideal. Accordingly, three major classes of tax rates have evolved over the years: proportional, progressive, and regressive. They differ from each other according to the way in which the tax is applied to the *tax base,* i.e., the object being taxed such as income (in the case of an income tax), the value of a taxpayer's property (in the case of a property tax), or the value of goods sold (in the case of a sales tax).

Proportional Tax. This is a tax whose percentage rate remains *constant* as the tax base increases. Hence the amount of the tax paid is proportional to the tax base. The property tax is an example. If the tax rate is constant at 5 percent, a man who owns property valued at $10,000 pays $500 in taxes; a man who owns property valued at $100,000 pays $5,000 in taxes. Similarly, an income tax would be a proportional tax if it were applied at the same percentage rate to all people regardless of their level of income.

Progressive Tax. This type of tax is one whose percentage rate *increases* as the tax base increases. In the United States, the federal personal income tax is the best example. The tax is graduated so that theoretically a man with a higher income pays a greater percentage in tax than a man with a lower income. We say "theoretically" because in reality, large loopholes in the tax structure distort and sometimes even prevent the progressive principle from operating over the full range of income—especially for those in the high-income brackets.

Regressive Tax. This is a tax whose percentage rate *decreases* as the tax base increases. In this strict sense there is no regressive tax in the United States. However, if we compare the rate structure of the tax with the taxpayer's net income rather than with its actual base, the term "regressive" applies to any tax which takes a larger share of income from the low-income taxpayer than from the high-income taxpayer. Most proportional taxes, such as consumption taxes of various kinds, are thus seen to have regressive effects. For instance, a 4 percent sales tax is the same rate for everyone, rich and poor alike. But people with smaller incomes spend a larger percentage of their incomes and hence the sales taxes they pay are a greater proportion of their incomes.

How do the foregoing principles and compromises apply to the American tax system? Generally speaking, our taxes tend to lean less toward the benefit principle and more toward ability to pay. Social security, license, and gasoline taxes are some typical examples of the former, whereas income, business, consumption, and death (estate and inheritance) taxes are more illustrative of the latter.

We can also find examples of progressive, regressive, and proportional taxes. Income and death taxes are progressive because their percentage rates increase with the tax base. Property taxes, general sales taxes, and excise taxes are proportional since their rates are a constant percentage of the tax base; however, they tend to have regressive effects when related to the *incomes* of the taxpayers. (See also Box 4.)

TAX SHIFTING AND INCIDENCE: DIRECT OR INDIRECT TAXES?

Surprisingly enough, the person or business firm upon whom a tax is initially imposed does not always bear its burden. For instance, a company may be able to *shift* all or part of a tax "forward" to its customers by charging them higher prices for its goods, or "backward" to the owners of its factors of production by paying them less for their materials and services. When a tax has been shifted, its burden or *incidence* is on someone else. It thus proves convenient to classify taxes into two categories: direct and indirect.

Direct Taxes. These are taxes that are not shifted; their burden is borne by the persons or firms originally taxed. Typical examples are personal income taxes, social security taxes paid by employees, most property taxes (excluding rental and business property), and death taxes. Certain taxes, notably those on corporate income, are sometimes only partially direct.

Indirect Taxes. These include all taxes that can be shifted either partially or entirely to someone other than the individual or firm originally taxed. Examples are sales taxes, excise taxes, taxes on business and rental property, social security taxes paid by employers, and most corporation income taxes.

In what direction will a tax be shifted—assuming it is shifted at all? This is a thorny problem in

Is Our "Progressive" Income Tax Regressive?

The personal income tax is presumably based on "ability to pay." This means it is supposed to allow for each individual's special circumstances and to tax the rich more heavily than the poor. There is widespread agreement, however, that the tax falls far short of this goal. Although the rates are graduated on paper, the tax laws contain so many loopholes and special provisions that the rates are hardly more than elaborate window dressing.

Many economists are strongly critical of the personal income tax, but none of them is more censorious than the University of Chicago's Professor Milton Friedman. This renowned economist points out that the tax would come closer to achieving its professed objectives if, simultaneously, it: (1) substituted a flat rate above personal exemptions for the present graduated rates; (2) eliminated present loopholes; and (3) disallowed all deductions except those related to occupational expenses strictly interpreted.

In Friedman's view, a revision of the personal income tax along these lines would yield several major benefits. It would permit the present exemptions—which are disgracefully low— to be greatly increased without the government's losing any revenue. It would provide a more equitable, vastly simpler, and much more efficient tax system. And it would eliminate the untold man-hours spent by accountants and lawyers advising their clients how to avoid taxes under the present law.

Even if it accomplished none of these things, however, it would at least release most people from the drudgery of unpaid bookkeeping they must now engage in to satisfy the Internal Revenue Service. That alone would make it a welcome blessing.

economic theory, and the experts do not always agree. In general, most taxes are like an increased cost to the taxpayer, and hence he will try to pass them on to someone else. As a result, once a tax is imposed, it tends—like lightning or water—to follow the path of "least resistance" through the markets in which the taxpayer deals, altering his prices, inputs, or outputs according to the least degree of opposition encountered. We shall examine this process more closely in a later chapter. Meanwhile, some interesting international comparisons are described in Box 5.

The United States Still Clings to the Income Tax

Foreign countries tend to rely on indirect taxes (such as taxes on spending) for most of their revenue; the United States, on the other hand, relies most heavily on direct taxes (namely taxes on income and wealth).

The chief argument against the predominance of indirect taxes has always been that they are by nature regressive: they fall harder on people with low incomes who spend most of their incomes. Some studies dispute this, however. For instance, a sales tax that exempts food and medicine turns out to be approximately proportional—taking nearly the same share from all income groups. On the other hand, a general sales tax which allows for no exceptions is clearly regressive. However, a sales tax can be made more progressive by graduating the rate—charging one rate on purchases under, say $100, and a higher rate on more expensive items.

Beyond the progressivity issue, the other major argument against primary reliance on indirect taxes has been that income tax receipts have a stabilizing effect on the economy: in recession, receipts shrink and taxes are not as much of a drag on the economy; in booms, they expand.

Even critics of the present system agree that indirect taxes come out second on this score, but they question whether a partial reduction in income taxes would seriously jeopardize the economy's stability.

Taxes on income and wealth as percent of total tax burden,* 1971.

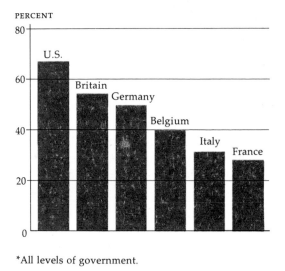

*All levels of government.

SUMMARY OF IMPORTANT IDEAS

1. The last several decades have witnessed a remarkable growth of expenditures at all levels of government. This has been due primarily to

a. War and national defense

b. Increased demand for collective goods and services

c. Inflation and lagging productivity

Government revenues have also increased with government expenditures at roughly the same rate over a period of years, but not usually within any one year.

2. In the federal budget, the chief sources of revenue are personal and corporate income taxes, and employment and excise taxes. The main expenditure items are national defense and transfer payments (such as veterans' benefits, social security, etc.).

3. In state and local budgets, the chief sources of revenue are property taxes and sales taxes, whereas the main expenditure items are education (especially schools), public welfare and health, and highways. Intergovernmental grants-in-aid to state and local governments are becoming increasingly important.

4. The American tax structure consists of taxes on income, taxes on wealth, and taxes on activities. Taxes on income, both personal and corporate, are graduated or progressive.

5. A chief requirement of a good tax system is that it be fair. The benefit principle and the ability-to-pay principle are the two major criteria for judging the fairness of a tax. These principles are often difficult to determine and measure. Hence they are usually implemented in practice by the use of proportional, progressive, and regressive taxes.

6. Those upon whom a tax is levied may sometimes be able to shift it forward or backward through changes in prices, inputs, or outputs so that its burden or incidence is on someone else. Such taxes are therefore indirect, as contrasted with direct taxes which cannot be shifted.

FOR HOMEWORK AND DISCUSSION

1. *Terms and concepts to review:*

budget	death tax
balanced budget	gift tax
budget surplus	sales tax
budget deficit	excise tax
grants-in-aid	social security tax
tax	benefit principle
income tax	ability-to-pay principle
average tax rate	tax base
marginal tax rate	proportional tax
tax avoidance	progressive tax
tax evasion	regressive tax
corporate income tax	tax shifting
double taxation	tax incidence
surtax	direct tax
property tax	indirect tax

2. What has been the long-run trend of expenditures and revenues at all levels of government? What are the main reasons for this trend?

3. (*a*) What are the major items of revenue and expenditure at the federal level? At the state and local levels? (*b*) Should New Yorkers be taxed to help Mississippians? Should Americans be taxed to help Latin Americans? Asians? Explain.

4. Outline the structure of the American tax system. Can you suggest some alternative bases for classifying taxes? Which classification basis is best?

5. "I can't afford to work overtime or to take on another job because it would just put me into a higher tax bracket." Is this a valid statement? Explain.

6. If you were considering taking on an extra part-time job, would you base the decision on your average tax rate or on your marginal tax rate? Why?

7. Evaluate the benefit and ability-to-pay principles of taxation.

8. Proportional taxes are frequently regressive taxes. Is this true? Explain.

9. The fairest personal income tax is one that leaves all taxpayers in the same relative position after the tax as before the tax? Do you agree? Explain.

REFERENCES AND READING SUGGESTIONS

COMMITTEE FOR ECONOMIC DEVELOPMENT, *A Fiscal Program for a Balanced Federalism*, 1967.

DUE, JOHN F., *Government Finance,* 4th ed., Irwin, Homewood, Ill., 1968, chaps. 1, 2.

ECKSTEIN, OTTO, *Public Finance,* 2d ed., Prentice-Hall, New York, 1967, chaps. 1, 3, 5.

PART 2

National Income, Employment, and Fiscal Policy

CHAPTER 7

National Income and Product: How Do We Measure the Economy's Performance?

CHAPTER PREVIEW

What are the basic measures of a nation's economic performance? What do these measures tell us? What do they fail to tell us?

How are the basic measures related to one another? What has been the nature of their historical pattern?

Americans like to take their own pulse; ours is probably the most self-analytical society in history, tirelessly searching for signs of normality, abnormality, and other statistical measurements of health —or illness.

Economic diagnoses and prognoses are as much a part of the daily news as football and baseball scores, and arouse similarly partisan feelings. That is unfortunate. The economic system is highly complicated, and more a subject for cool, rational analysis than hot, emotional debate.

The tools for analyzing the economy's performance, strengths, and weaknesses are the tables, charts, and data published by the federal government and some other public and private agencies. Since the early 1930s the U.S. Department of Commerce has been the nation's bookkeeper; its methods, terms, and concepts are the foundation on which economists have built what they call "National Income Accounting."

This chapter will familiarize you with National Income Accounting, and explain its advantages and shortcomings.

Gross National Product—The Basic Measure of a Nation's Output

The most comprehensive measure of a nation's economic activity, and the one quoted most frequently in newspapers and magazines, is *gross national product*, abbreviated GNP. This is always stated in money terms, representing the total value of a nation's annual output. More precisely:

GNP is the total market value of all final goods and services produced by an economy during a year.

The items that comprise GNP range from apples and automobiles to zinc and zippers. However, since you cannot add these different things, you must first express these diverse items in terms of their monetary values. Then, when you add X dollars' worth of automobiles to Y dollars' worth of oranges, Z dollars' worth of doctors' services, etc., you arrive at a total dollar figure. If you do this for all goods and services produced in the economy during any given year, the result is GNP. And if you repeat this process for a period of several years, the different GNPs can be compared to tell whether there has been a long-run growth or decline.

However, there are several pitfalls to avoid.

1. Watch Out for Price Changes

If the prices of goods and services change from one year to the next, the GNP may also change—even if there has been no change in physical output. For instance, if apples cost 10 cents each this year, five apples will have a market value of 50 cents. But

---

Exhibit 1

Gross National Product (in current and in constant dollars)

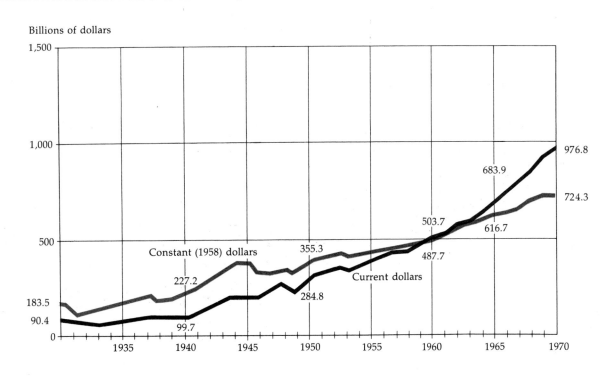

Exhibit 2

Deflating with a Price Index

How a value series in *current dollars* is converted into a value series in *constant dollars* of another year.

Column (4) expresses the prices of column (3) in the form of index numbers—*that is, percentages of a previous base period. Index numbers are widely used by government and private sources in reporting business and economic data. Ordinarily, the base period chosen is assumed to be fairly "normal." In this illustration, since the data are hypothetical, Year 2 has been arbitrarily selected as the base.*

When the value series in current dollars [*column (5)*] *is divided by these index numbers, the result is a new value series in* constant dollars *of the base year as shown in column (6). The two value series are plotted for comparison in the accompanying chart.*

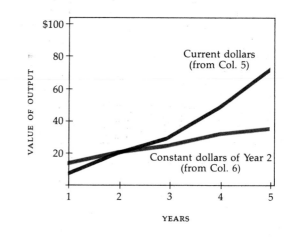

(1)	(2)	(3)	(4)	(5)	(6)
Year	Units of output	Price per unit of output	Price index; data in Col. (3) as percent of price in Year 2	Value of output in current dollars of each year (2) × (3)	Value of output in constant dollars of Year 2 (5) ÷ (4)
1	3	$2	2/4 = .50 or 50%	$ 6	6/ .50 = $12
2	5	4	4/4 = 1.00 or 100%	20	20/1.00 = 20
3	6	5	5/4 = 1.25 or 125%	30	30/1.25 = 24
4	8	6	6/4 = 1.50 or 150%	48	48/1.50 = 32
5	9	8	8/4 = 2.00 or 200%	72	72/2.00 = 36

next year if the price goes up to 15 cents each, the production of five apples will have a market value of 75 cents.

How can we tell whether the variations in GNP are due to differences in prices or to differences in *real* output—that is, output unaffected by price changes? The answer is shown in Exhibit 1, where GNP is expressed in two ways: (*a*) in *current dollars*, reflecting actual prices as they existed each year; (*b*) in *constant dollars*, reflecting the actual prices of a previous year, or the average of actual prices in a previous period.

The use of constant dollars is thus a way of compensating for the distorting effects of inflation—the

long-run upward trend of prices—by a reversing process of *deflation*. You can get an idea of how this is done by studying Exhibit 2.

2. Avoid Double Counting of Intermediate Goods

The above definition of GNP covers only *final goods and services* purchased for last use—as opposed to *intermediate goods and services* such as raw materials and goods in process which are purchased for further processing or resale. Since the values of final goods include the values of all intermediate goods, only final goods may be included in calculating GNP. If you allow intermediate goods to enter the picture you will commit the cardinal sin of *double counting* —or even triple and quadruple counting.

Exhibit 3 shows why, in terms of producing a loaf of bread. As you can see, the total sales value includes all the intermediate stages, and hence is an incorrect statement of the actual value of the product. However, the final sales value or the total *value added* for all the stages of production gives the true value of the total output as well as the total income—the sum of wages, rent, interest, and profit—derived from the production process.

We can summarize with an important principle:

GNP may be calculated either by totaling: (*a*) the final market values of all goods and services, or (*b*) the values added at all stages of production, which is equal to the sum of all incomes—wages, rent, interest, and profit—generated from production.

Exhibit 3

Sales Values and Value Added at Each Stage of Producing a Loaf of Bread

Stages of production	(1)	(2) Sales values, cents per loaf	(3) Value added (income payments: wages, rent, interest, profit) cents per loaf
			1¢
Stage 1: Fertilizer, seed, etc.		1¢	
			6¢
Stage 2: Wheat growing		7¢	
			5¢
Stage 3: Flour milling		12¢	
			10¢
Stage 4: Bread baking, final		22¢	
			8¢
Stage 5: Bread retailer, value		30¢	—
Total sales values		72¢	
Total value added (= total income)			(30¢)

Stage 1: A farmer purchases 1¢ worth of seed and fertilizer which he applies to his land.

Stage 2: The farmer grows wheat, harvests it, and sells it to a miller for 7¢. The farmer has thereby added 6¢ worth of value. His factors of production receive this 6¢ in the form of income: wages, rent, interest, and profit.

Stage 3: The miller, after purchasing the wheat for 7¢, adds 5¢ worth of value by milling it into flour. The miller's factors of production receive this 5¢ as income: wages, rent, interest, and profit.

Stage 4: The baking company buys the flour from the miller for 12¢, then adds 10¢ worth of value to it by baking it into bread. This 10¢ becomes factor incomes in the form of wages, rent, interest, and profit.

Stage 5: The retailer buys the bread from the baker for 22¢ and sells it to you, the final user, for 30¢. The retailer has thus added 8¢ in value, which shows up as factor incomes in the form of wages, rent, interest, and profit.

Note that the value of the final product, 30¢, equals the sum of the values added.

Obviously, it is considerably easier to employ the "final value" approach than the "value-added" approach in calculating GNP, although either method is logically correct.

3. Include Productive Transactions; Exclude Nonproductive Ones

The purpose of deriving GNP is to develop a measure of the economy's total output, based on the final market values of goods and services produced. However, even if all the final market values are estimated there are still some *productive* transactions that do not show up in the market but should nevertheless be included in GNP, and there are other *nonproductive* transactions which do appear in the market but should be excluded from GNP.

Productive nonmarket transactions include:

Rent of Owner-Occupied Homes. The rent which people pay to landlords enters into GNP. However, more than half the dwellings in the United States are owner-occupied. Therefore the rental value of this housing—the rent which people "save" by living in their own homes—may be thought of as the value of "shelter" produced. This value is assumed to be the same amount that homeowners would receive if they became landlords and rented out their homes to others. Hence this amount is included in GNP.

Farm Consumption of Home-Grown Food. The value of food which people buy is included in GNP. But what about the value of food that farmers grow and consume themselves? This too is a part of the nation's productive output, and is therefore included in GNP.

Some productive nonmarket activities never enter into GNP because their values are either too difficult to estimate, or involve complex definitional issues. Examples include the labor time of a do-it-yourselfer who performs his own repairs and maintenance around the house, and the productive services of a housewife in her capacity as a cook, housekeeper, governess, etc., for which she does not receive a salary. No wonder a famous British economist once remarked that a man who marries his housekeeper reduces the nation's output and income. Can you see why?

Nonproductive market transactions include:

Financial Transactions. These are mainly: (*a*) *transfer payments* such as social security benefits, veterans' bonuses, etc., which are merely shifts in funds from the government sector to the private (household) sector with no corresponding contribution to current production, and (*b*) securities transactions such as the buying and selling of stocks and bonds on the organized exchanges throughout the country. Neither of these activities adds anything to current production, and hence is excluded from GNP. (However, broker commissions on security transactions are included in GNP, since brokers perform a service by bringing buyers and sellers together.)

Used-goods sales. Billions of dollars are paid each year for used automobiles, houses, machines, factory buildings, and so on. But these goods are omitted from the calculation of current GNP. For instance, the used car you sell in any given year was already counted in GNP in the year it was made. Hence you would not count it again in the year you sell it. (As with brokers, however, the value added by dealers in used-merchandise transactions is included in current GNP.)

IS GNP A MEASURE OF SOCIETY'S WELL-BEING?

GNP is a comprehensive indicator of the economy's total output. However, it is an imperfect measure of society's "well-being" because it fails to tell us anything about:

1. The growth of leisure time, i.e., the substantial reduction in the workweek—by as much as 50 percent or more in some industries—that has taken place since the 1930s.

2. The composition of the nation's total output in terms of the improved quality and variety of goods and services.

3. The growth of total output among the members of society.

On the basis of the first two factors, the long-run trend of our economy is better than the GNP figures indicate. As for the third, you will often see GNP quoted on a per capita basis over the years, thereby reflecting the share that each person would have in the nation's total output if it were distributed equally to every man, woman, and child. What does it mean in terms of the economy's growth if the trend of GNP per capita is increasing over the years? Decreasing? Remaining the same?

WHAT ABOUT GROSS NATIONAL "DISPRODUCT"?

The gross national product—our standard index of economic growth—measures everything from the cost of hospital care to the wages of belly dancers. But it is only an index of dollar—not social—benefits.

In other words, there is no distinction in GNP between the useful and frivolous—regardless of the price that has been paid. For example, GNP includes cloth coats for people as well as mink coats for dogs, life-saving antibiotics as well as useless patent medicines. Further, there is no measure of the amount of "disproduct" or *social cost* that results from producing the "regular" GNP. Thus, to society:

☐ The cost of air and water pollution is the disproduct of the nation's factories.

☐ The cost of treating lung cancer victims is the disproduct of cigarette production.

☐ The cost of geriatric medicine is the disproduct of good medical care in the earlier years which results in increased longevity.

☐ The cost of commuter transportation is the disproduct of suburbia.

☐ The cost of aspirin for headaches resulting from TV commercials is the disproduct of advertising.

Can you suggest some more examples?

If we were to carry this process through our whole product list, the aggregate would be called *Gross National Disproduct*. And if the total were then set against the aggregate of production as measured by GNP, it would indicate our degree of progress toward (or departure from) social welfare. In fact, if we could discover a true "net" between disproduct and product, we would have our first great "social" indicator of what the country has accomplished.

The results would be disillusioning. We would find that while satisfying human wants from today's productivity, we were simultaneously generating present and future wants and needs to repair the damage and waste created by current production.

FOR CLASS DISCUSSION

1. Would it be better to produce wool suits and vaccines instead of mink coats and patent medicines, so that the nation moves closer to "worthwhile" national goals?

2. Does the GNP of an advanced, interdependent economy necessarily contain a considerable amount of disproduct in comparison to a relatively simple type of economic system?

3. Are the costs of the disproducts of our economy borne in the present or in the future?

Two Ways of Looking at GNP

Since GNP is the market value of the nation's output of final goods and services, we can express it conceptually by the simple diagram in Exhibit 4, or equivalently by the following fundamental identity which says that the *total amount spent equals the total amount received.*

$$\begin{Bmatrix} \text{Total flow of} \\ \text{expenditures} \\ \text{on final output} \end{Bmatrix} = \text{GNP} = \begin{Bmatrix} \text{Total flow of} \\ \text{income from} \\ \text{final output} \end{Bmatrix}$$

The left side of the identity or upper pipeline of the diagram views GNP as a sum of expenditures or flow of product; the right side or lower pipeline views it as a sum of incomes or values added at each stage of production. This lower pipeline thus represents *Gross National Income (GNI)*, which is the sum of wages, rent, interest, and profit earned in the production of GNP, and is always equal to GNP. It is to be emphasized that this diagram illustrates a *simple circular flow* model. Some complex considerations will be introduced later which will yield a more detailed model.

GNP FROM THE EXPENDITURE VIEWPOINT: A FLOW-OF-PRODUCT APPROACH

Four main sources of expenditures compose GNP. The data are shown in actual amounts in Exhibit 5, along with each item's corresponding percentage of

Exhibit 4

Gross National Product = Gross National Income

A simplified circular flow model can be used to illustrate the fundamental principle that gross national product and gross national income are actually two sides of the same coin. The nation's flow of output in the upper pipeline equals the nation's *flow of income in the lower pipeline. Profit is the residual or "balancing item" that brings this equality about. Can you explain why? How is the model affected if profits are positive? Zero? Negative (i.e., losses)?*

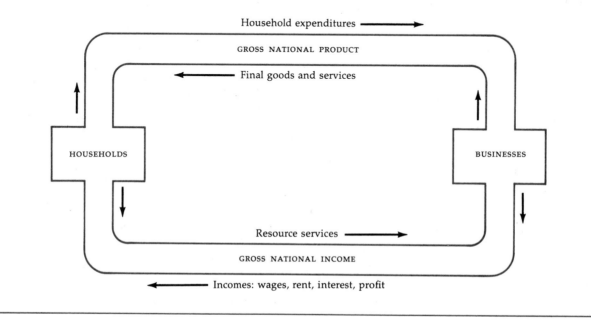

GNP. These percentages indicate the relative stability of each source of expenditure over the years. What can be said about the nature of these four categories?

Personal Consumption Expenditures. Frequently referred to as "consumption expenditures" or simply "consumption," this category includes household expenditures by households on such consumer nondurable goods as food and clothing, consumer durable goods such as automobiles and major appliances, and services like those of doctors, lawyers, and repairmen.

Government Purchases of Goods and Services. The items in this category are purchased by all levels of

government. They include guided missiles, school buildings, fire engines, pencils, paper clips, and the services of accountants, economists, statisticians, and all other government employees. However, a significant part of government expenditures—transfer payments—are omitted because they do not represent current output or purchases of goods and services.

Gross Private Domestic Investment. This category includes total investment spending by business firms. What do we mean by investment? The term has two interpretations. (1) In everyday language, a person makes an investment when he buys stocks, bonds, or other properties with the intention of receiving an income, or making a profit. (2) In economics,

Exhibit 5

Gross National Product from the Expenditure Viewpoint
(in billions of dollars and in percent* of gross national product)

	1950 Amount	1950 Percent of GNP	1955 Amount	1955 Percent of GNP	1960 Amount	1960 Percent of GNP	1965 Amount	1965 Percent of GNP	1970 Amount	1970 Percent of GNP
Gross national product or expenditure	$285	100%	$398	100%	$504	100%	$685	100%	$974	100%
Households: 1. Personal consumption expenditures	191	67	254	64	325	65	433	63	616	63
Government (federal, state, local): 2. Purchases of goods and services	38	13	74	19	100	20	137	19	219	23
Businesses: 3. Gross private domestic investment	54	19	67	17	75	15	108	16	135	14
International: 4. Net exports of goods and services	2	**	2	**	4	**	7	**	4	**

* Percentages may not add to 100 because of rounding.
** Less than 1%.

investment means spending by business firms on new job-creating and income-producing goods which thereby add to GNP. This concept of investment is the one that concerns us in this book.

Investment goods fall into two broad classes:

a. New capital goods, such as new machines, factories, offices, and residences. (Residential buildings include apartment houses and owner-occupied homes—the last on the assumption that they could just as well be rented out and thereby yield incomes to their owners, as do apartment houses.) Thus when a firm buys a used machine or existing factory, it merely exchanges money assets for physical assets; the purchase itself creates no additional GNP. But when it buys *new* machines or *new* buildings the firm creates jobs

and incomes for steelworkers, carpenters, bricklayers, etc., and thereby contributes to the nation's GNP.

b. Increases in *inventories* (including raw materials, supplies, and finished goods on hand) are as much a part of business firms' physical capital as are plant and equipment. Therefore, the market values of any additions to inventories are part of the current flow-of-product that makes up GNP; conversely, any declines in inventories are reductions from the flow-of-product that makes up GNP.

In the process of producing goods during any given year some existing plant and equipment is used up or *depreciated*. Therefore, a part of the year's gross private domestic investment goes to replace it.

Any amount over this is called *net private domestic investment* because it represents a net addition to the total stock of capital. For example,

If in a certain nation:

Gross private domestic investment	= $50 billion
and replacement for depreciation	= 30 billion
then net private domestic investment	= $20 billion

You might correctly infer from this that an economy will tend to grow, remain static, or decline according to whether:

1. Gross investment exceeds depreciation, in which case net investment is positive. The economy is thus adding to its capital stock and is thereby expanding its productive base.

2. Gross investment equals depreciation, in which case net investment is zero. The economy is merely replacing its capital stock and is neither expanding nor contracting its productive base.

3. Gross investment is less than depreciation, in which case net investment is negative. The economy is diminishing or *disinvesting* its capital stock and is thereby contracting its productive base.

To Summarize

Investment is spending by business firms on job-creating and income-producing goods. It consists of replacements or additions to the nation's stock of capital including its plant, equipment, and inventories, i.e., its nonhuman productive assets.

Net Exports. Some American expenditures purchase foreign goods—imports. Some foreign expenditures purchase American goods—exports. Therefore, to measure GNP in terms of total expenditures we have to: (1) add the value of *exported goods and services* to our total expenditures, since this represents the amount that foreigners spent on purchasing some of our total output; and (2) subtract the value of *imported goods and services* from our total expenditures, since we are interested only in measuring the value of domestic output. In performing these adjustments it is simpler to combine the separate figures for exports and imports into a single figure called net exports, according to the formula:

Net exports = total exports − total imports

Thus, if a nation's total exports in any given year amount to $20 billion, and its total imports are $15 billion, its net exports of $5 billion are part of that year's GNP. Of course, its imports may exceed its exports in any particular year, in which case its net exports will be a negative number and hence serve to reduce its GNP. If you have any doubts about this, just look back at Exhibit 5 and note what the effect would be on GNP if net exports were negative.

As a result of the breakdown shown in Exhibit 5, economists sometimes use the term *gross national expenditures* (GNE) to represent the total amount spent by the four sector accounts of the economy (i.e., household, government, business, and international) on the nation's output of goods and services. Evidently, GNE = GNP = GNI.

GNP FROM THE INCOME VIEWPOINT

Before we introduced changes in business inventories and imports, we said that the *total amount spent equals the total amount received*, i.e., GNP = GNI, and hence the following fundamental identity prevailed *conceptually*:

$$\begin{Bmatrix} \text{Total flow of} \\ \text{expenditures} \\ \text{on final output} \end{Bmatrix} = \text{GNP} = \begin{Bmatrix} \text{Total flow of} \\ \text{income from} \\ \text{final output} \end{Bmatrix}$$

We also emphasized that this *simple* model was devoid of any realistic complexities. Let us now see what these complexities involve.

Once we introduce changes in business inventories and imports on the left side of the identity, is the identity still true? Obviously not. Although the left side after the adjustment does equal GNP, we must also make adjustments on the right side in order to reestablish the identity. As you recall, the right side in our simple model is the sum of wages, rent, interest, and profit (or the sum of the values added at all stages of production).

The necessary adjustments are shown in Exhibit 6. It is apparent that GNP consists of the four major income payments—wages, rent, interest, and profit—*plus* two types of nonincome items: "indirect business taxes" and "capital consumption allowance" or depreciation. These last two concepts require some explanation.

Exhibit 6

Gross National Product from the Income Viewpoint

(in billions of dollars)

	1950	1955	1960	1965	1970
Income payments					
Wages:					
Compensation of employees	154.6	224.5	294.2	393.8	601.9
Wages and supplements					
Rent:					
Rental incomes of persons	9.4	13.9	15.8	19.0	23.3
Interest:					
Net interest	2.0	4.1	8.4	18.2	33.0
Profit:					
Proprietors' income	37.5	41.7	46.2	57.2	66.9
Business, professional, farm					
Corporate profits before taxes (adjusted)	37.7	46.9	49.9	76.1	70.8
	241.2	331.1	414.5	564.3	795.9
Plus **nonincome (expense) items**					
Indirect business taxes	25.3	33.1	45.5	62.5	92.9
Capital consumption allowance (depreciation)*	18.3	33.8	43.7	59.8	85.3
= Gross national product	284.8	398.0	503.7	684.9	974.1

* Capital consumption allowance is used here synonymously with depreciation, although it includes a few relatively minor items in addition to depreciation such as accidental damage to goods.

Indirect Business Taxes

These taxes are passed on or shifted forward by business firms to buyers. Sales taxes are typical. If you live in a state or city that has a 4 percent general sales tax and you buy a product whose price is $1, your total *expenditure* is actually $1.04. Of this, $1 goes to pay incomes—the wages, rent, interest, and profit—earned for making the product, and 4 cents goes to city hall, which has not contributed directly to production. It follows, therefore, that indirect business taxes cause the expenditure side of GNP to be greater than the income side. In view of this, indirect business taxes must be added to total incomes (or subtracted from GNP) if the two sides are to be brought closer together.

Capital Consumption Allowance (Depreciation)

This represents that portion of GNP set aside to replace the machinery and equipment that was "consumed" or used up in the process of production. It is thus the difference between "gross" and "net" private domestic investment, as already explained. From the standpoint of national income accounting, if there were no such thing as depreciation resulting from wear and tear, and if the government returned all indirect business taxes to households, the nation's income and output would be identical *in fact* as well as conceptually. However, since depreciation does exist in reality, it becomes a factor which causes the income side of GNP to be less than the expenditure side, and hence it must be added to total incomes (or

Leaders in Economics

FRANÇOIS QUESNAY

1694–1774

Founder of the Physiocrats

François Quesnay was the founder of the physiocratic school—the first "school" or group of people in economics to be held together by a common body of opinions and teachings. He was the court physician to Louis XV and Mme. de Pompadour, and is best known for his Tableau Economique (Economic Table) *written for the King of France in 1758. This table, shown below, purports to depict the flow of goods and money in a nation, and is thus the first attempt to describe the circular flow of wealth on a macroeconomic basis.*

The entire plan of the physiocrats was based on a concept of "natural order" consisting of duties and rights of all mankind and of all social classes. The physiocrats regarded land as the most important agent of production, and the landlord class, rather than farmers, as "productive." The other two groups of society were a proprietary class to whom the surplus or net product of the economy is paid, and a sterile or unproductive class composed of manufacturers, merchants, and artisans. (A fourth class consisting of wage earners was hardly recognized.)

The Tableau *is based on the assumption that each class will spend one-half of what it receives on the other two classes. If they spend less than half, society's income and the wealth of the state will decrease; if they spend more than half, the proper income shares of society will not be returned to the circular flow. An exact balance of expenditures is therefore necessary.*

Bettmann Archive

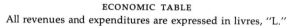

ECONOMIC TABLE
All revenues and expenditures are expressed in livres, "L."

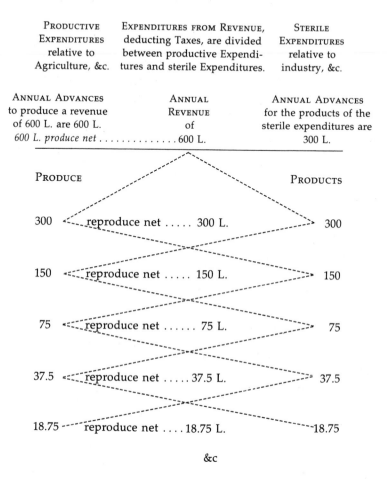

PRODUCTIVE EXPENDITURES relative to Agriculture, &c.	EXPENDITURES FROM REVENUE, deducting Taxes, are divided between productive Expenditures and sterile Expenditures.	STERILE EXPENDITURES relative to industry, &c.
ANNUAL ADVANCES to produce a revenue of 600 L. are 600 L. 600 L. produce net	ANNUAL REVENUE of . . . . . 600 L.	ANNUAL ADVANCES for the products of the sterile expenditures are 300 L.

PRODUCE   PRODUCTS

300 ⤎ reproduce net ..... 300 L. ⤏ 300

150 ⤎ reproduce net ..... 150 L. ⤏ 150

75 ⤎ reproduce net ...... 75 L. ⤏ 75

37.5 ⤎ reproduce net ..... 37.5 L. ⤏ 37.5

18.75 reproduce net .... 18.75 L. 18.75

&c

TOTAL REPRODUCTION. . . . . 600 L. of revenue; besides the annual expenditures of 600 L. and the interest on the original advances of the Husbandman, amounting to 300 L., which the land restores. Thus the reproduction is 1500 L., including the revenue of 600 L. which is the basis of the calculation, apart from taxes deducted, and the advances required for its annual reproduction, &c.

SOURCE: The economic table, translated from the French, is reprinted by permission of the publishers from Arthur Eli Monroe, *Early Economic Thought*, Cambridge, Mass.: Harvard University Press, 1924.

subtracted from GNP) in order to bring the two sides closer together.

To put it somewhat differently, business firms view indirect business taxes and depreciation as part of their *costs,* and hence charge higher prices for their goods in order to cover these costs. Therefore, these nonincome expense items must be added to the other income payments or expense items (wages, rent, interest, and profit) in order for the total expenditures on GNP to equal the total payments or expenses incurred in producing it.

Four Other Concepts—All Related

What relationship exists between the value of the nation's output and the money that households actually have available for spending? As we will see later on, it is important for us to know the answer to this question. Therefore we may proceed by tracing through the items listed in the national income accounts of Exhibit 7.

1. From Gross National Product to Net National Product

GNP is the total market value of the nation's annual output of final goods and services. But, as you know, this figure does not equal the actual dollar incomes available to households. To arrive at a closer measure of the dollars received by society we must subtract the proportion that was spent to replace used up capital goods—the so-called "capital consumption allowance" or depreciation figure. The new number that results is called net national product or simply NNP.

2. From Net National Product to National Income

Net national product measures the total sales value of goods and services available for society's consumption and for adding to its stock of capital equipment. Hence it may be thought of as "national income at market prices." But it still does not represent the dollars people actually had available to spend because NNP is overstated by the amount of indirect business taxes—such as sales taxes—which are shifted forward by sellers to consumers in the form of higher prices. These indirect business taxes must be deducted from NNP in order to arrive at a closer estimate of the dollars available to people for actual spending. This deduction yields a figure called National Income at factor cost, usually abbreviated simply as NI.

3. From National Income to Personal Income

National income (at factor cost) is the total of all incomes earned by the factors of production—the sum of wages, rent, interest, and profit earned by the suppliers of labor, land, capital, and entrepreneurship. Does NI represent the dollars that people actually had available for spending? Once again the answer is *no.* Some people earned income they did not receive; others received income they did not earn.

Thus the stockholders in a corporation are its owners and hence receive its profits. However, they do not receive all its profits, for two reasons. Some of the profits are paid to the government in the form of corporation income taxes, and some are plowed back into the business for future expansion instead of being distributed to stockholders as dividends. Likewise, social security contributions are taken out of workers' current earnings, and hence are also part of income earned but not received.

As for income received but not earned, the major items are transfer payments, which have already been defined. These are merely shifts of funds from the government sector to households—for reasons other than current production.

To measure the dollars people actually had available for spending, we therefore adjust the NI by *subtracting* income earned but not received, and *adding* income received but not earned. This results in a figure called personal income, or PI.

4. From Personal Income to Disposable Personal Income

Personal income is the total received by persons from all sources—the dollars that you and I receive for performing our jobs and thereby contributing to GNP. Does it measure the dollars actually available to people for spending? The answer is still *no,* because out of personal income people must first pay

Exhibit 7

Gross National Product and Related Concepts*
(In billions of dollars)

	1955	1960	1965	1970
Gross National Product, GNP	$398	$504	$685	$974
Minus:				
Capital consumption allowance (depreciation)	32	43	60	85
Equals: **Net National Product,** NNP	367	460	625	887
Minus:				
Indirect business taxes	32	45	63	93
Equals: **National Income,** NI	331	415	564	796
Minus: Income earned but not received				
Corporate income taxes	22	23	31	34
Undistributed corporate profits	17	13	27	16
Social security contributions	11	21	30	58
Plus: Income received but not earned				
Transfer payments (including interest)	26	42	58	111
Equals: **Personal Income,** PI	311	401	539	804
Minus:				
Personal taxes	36	51	66	116
Equals: **Disposable Personal Income,** DPI	275	350	473	688
Of which:				
Personal consumption expenditures	260	333	445	616
Personal saving	15	17	28	54

* Discrepancies in totals are due to the omission of minor items.

their personal taxes. This amount must therefore be deducted from PI, leaving a figure called *disposable personal income,* or DPI. It is this amount that people actually had available for spending. As you can see in Exhibit 7, the great bulk of it (between 90 and 95 percent) went for personal consumption, while the rest of it was saved.

There are thus five measures of income and output for the economy:

a. Gross national product
b. Net national product
c. National income
d. Personal income
e. Disposable personal income—or simply disposable income

All five measures are closely interrelated, can be derived from one another, and tend approximately to parallel one another over the years. (See Exhibit 8.) In many economic discussions (except those involving specific accounting practices as described in this chapter) *economists frequently use the term "national income" or simply "income" to represent all five terms.* A complete circular flow model is shown in Exhibit 9 on page 116

Measuring "Gross National Pleasure"

Americans are great scorekeepers. Batting averages and stock market averages, hot dog consumption and steel production—almost everything that can be measured is. And because most people associate growth with goodness, spirits rise when the figures do. The gross national product, in particular, is widely accepted as a measure of social progress. But a growing number of critics charge that the American preoccupation with quantity has led to a neglect of quality. What the critics would like to see—among them are many leading economists—is development of a system of social indicators that would measure national well-being, the bads as well as the goods.

Needed: A Social Index

President Nixon put the challenge cogently. "In the next ten years we shall increase our wealth by 50 percent," he said in 1970. "The profound question is: Does this mean we will be 50 percent richer in a real sense, 50 percent better off, 50 percent happier?" The plain answer is that we do not know. The GNP measures output. It does not measure satisfaction. The consequent need for social indicators has long been recognized by scholars. Jeremy Bentham, the eighteenth-century English philosopher and economist, believed that society should provide "the greatest happiness of the greatest number." He tried to construct what he called a "moral thermometer" to measure human pleasures, but was not successful.

Formidable theoretical and practical difficulties must be overcome before we can measure national happiness. In economics, physical units and money values are used as common measures.

In social accounting, there are no common measures, because there is little general agreement over the "values" to be put on different activities and phenomena. Social scientists are only beginning to grapple with that and associated problems. One approach was suggested in a report published by the Department of Health, Education and Welfare. By combining statistics on mortality with those on lengths of period of bed-disability, HEW was able to develop an index of "expectancy of healthy life." For some purposes, it is much more illuminating than a simple "expectation of life" statistic, which tells us about the length of time the average American will live.

One of the most ambitious attempts to assess the quality of life has been undertaken at the University of Michigan Survey Research Center. Using opinion survey techniques, researchers will discover people's views of their own health, marriage, family, job, housing, financial situation, and education. One possible result of the study will be an index showing how highly the average American rates those and other priorities for himself and his family. "We will never develop a single 'satisfaction index' to match the economists' figure for the gross national product, but we think we can develop genuinely reliable guides that will be extremely useful in forming public policy," said one researcher.

Declining Health, Poor Diet

Until that and other studies are completed, we must continue to rely on the qualitative and quantitative statistics that are available. For example, national expenditures on medical care are compiled annually; and if they were ac-

cepted as a measure of health, they would show that the average American is in fine shape. More useful are the statistics on infant mortality. These show that the United States has been falling behind the rest of the world. In 1950, the United States ranked fifth for infant mortality rates; twenty years later it ranked eighteenth. Such figures should act as an "early warning" device for government.

Similarly, the statistics showing the average American's expenditure on food make him seem the best-fed man in the world. But another set of statistics, compiled by the Department of Agriculture, show that in fact the average American's diet has been declining in quality. Some social scientists believe that by looking at diet, health, and even the incidence of divorce, a composite social indicator can be developed. It might not be conclusive evidence of happiness, or lack of it; but it would serve as a rough guide to the quality of life the average American leads.

The development of social indicators has been neglected too long. But now there is real hope that Americans will in the future not only follow their traditional pursuit of happiness, but also be able to define and measure it. An index of "gross national pleasure" might then replace in popularity and importance the gross national product.

R. B.

1. *If you were to construct an index to measure well-being, what factors would you include?*

2. *How would you put together such an index for the economy as a whole, given the fact that people place different subjective valuations on different things?*

Exhibit 8

Five Measures of Income and Output

GNP and its components tend roughly to parallel one another, but the differences between them have widened, due primarily to increased taxation.

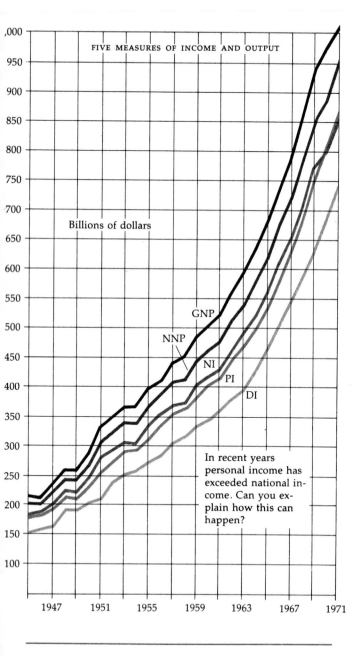

FIVE MEASURES OF INCOME AND OUTPUT

Billions of dollars

GNP
NNP
NI
PI
DI

,000
950
900
850
800
750
700
650
600
550
500
450
400
350
300
250
200
150
100

1947   1951   1955   1959   1963   1967   1971

In recent years personal income has exceeded national income. Can you explain how this can happen?

SUMMARY OF IMPORTANT IDEAS

1. GNP is the basic and most comprehensive measure of a nation's output, since it represents the total market value of all final goods and services produced during a year.

Three pitfalls to avoid in calculating GNP include: (*a*) the effects of price changes; (*b*) the possibility of double (actually multiple) counting; (*c*) the inclusion of nonproductive transactions.

2. GNP can be viewed from the expenditure standpoint as the sum of personal consumption expenditures, government purchases of goods and services, investment, and net exports. GNP can be viewed from the income standpoint as the sum of wages, rent, interest, and profit, plus two nonincome business expense items: indirect business taxes and depreciation.

3. The items which make up the nation's income accounts are: GNP, NNP, NI, PI, and DPI. All five measures are closely related and can be derived from one another. They are among the most important measures of our economy's performance. In economic discussions (except those involving actual accounting practices) we generally refer to all five measures as "national income" or simply "income."

FOR HOMEWORK AND DISCUSSION

1. *Terms and concepts to review:*

gross national product

gross national disproduct

gross national income

social cost

real output

current dollars

constant dollars

index numbers

deflation

value added

transfer payments

investment

disinvestment

inventory

depreciation

gross national expenditure ·

capital consumption allowance

net national product

national income (at factor cost)

personal income

disposable personal income

Exhibit 9

The Flow of National Income and Related Concepts

Can you fill in the data for the most recent year? See front endpaper.

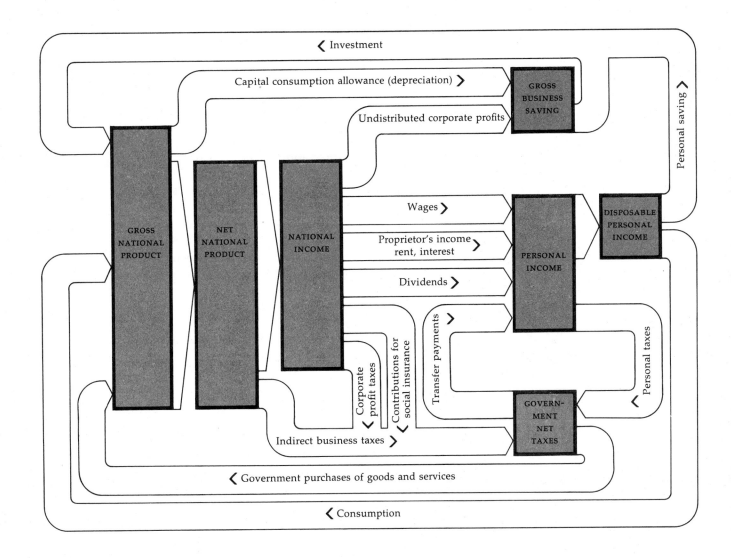

2. Suppose a nation's GNP increased from $100 billion to $200 billion. What has happened to its *real* GNP during that period if:

a. Prices remained the same

b. Prices doubled

c. Prices tripled from their constant level in (*a*)

d. Prices fell by 50 percent of their constant level in (*a*)

3. When you "deflate" a *rising* current dollar series, as in Exhibit 1, the constant dollar series lies below the current dollar series for all years after the base year, and above it for all years prior to the base year. What would happen if you deflated a current dollar series that was *declining* rather than rising? Explain.

4. Explain why "value added" is a logically correct method of measuring the nation's output.

5. Suppose that inventories decline by $1 billion next year. How will this affect next year's GNP? What if inventories increase by $1 billion?

6. How is the growth or decline of an economy related to its net investment? Do you think an economy's percentage growth or decline is related to its percentage change in net investment? Explain.

7. Does a man decrease the national income if he marries his housekeeper? Explain.

8. Which of the following is included, and which is not included, in calculating GNP:

a. One hundred shares of General Motors stock purchased this week on the New York Stock Exchange

b. Wages paid to teachers

c. A student's income from a part-time job

d. A student's income from a full-time summer job.

e. Value of a bookcase built by a do-it-yourselfer

f. Purchase of a used car

g. A monthly rent of $250 which a homeowner "saves" by living in his own home instead of renting it out to a tenant

9. Each year the total amount of dollar payments by checks and cash far exceeds—by many billions of dollars—the GNP. If GNP is the market value of the economy's final output, how can this huge difference exist?

REFERENCES AND READING SUGGESTIONS

SCHULTZE, CHARLES L., *National Income Analysis,* 2d ed., Prentice-Hall, Englewood Cliffs, N.J., 1967, chap. 2.

SHAPIRO, EDWARD, *Macroeconomic Analysis,* 2d ed. Harcourt, Brace & World, New York, 1970, chaps. 2–5.

U.S. DEPARTMENT OF COMMERCE, *Survey of Current Business* (July issues on national income).

CHAPTER 8

Business Cycles, Unemployment, and Inflation: What Does the Record Show?

CHAPTER PREVIEW

What are business cycles? What causes them? Can they be predicted and controlled?

How significant is unemployment in our economy? What are the "costs" of unemployment? Who pays these costs?

What is inflation? Who benefits from it? Who suffers from it? Can inflation be avoided?

Business cycles and unemployment have been an unending plague for capitalistic nations. Inflation—or rising prices—is a cost we pay to abate that plague, as we have done since World War II.

This chapter examines the nature of business cycles, unemployment, and inflation, and their interrelationship. Once we understand their characteristics we can start to do something about the problems themselves, which are among the most potent challenges confronting affluent Western nations.

Essentially, as you will learn, the United States government tries to keep all three ailments at bay simultaneously; but it is not consistently successful because both the ailments themselves and their cure are still subjects of debate and experiment.

Business Cycles—The "Dance of the Dollar"

Although we no longer have the extreme booms and busts that characterized the economy in the decades up to World War II, we nevertheless have fluctuations in business activity. Hence the following modern definition of business cycles is appropriate:

Business cycles are recurrent but nonperiodic fluctuations in general business and economic activity that take place over a period of years. These fluctuations occur in aggregate variables like income, output, employment, and prices, most of which move at about the same time in the same direction, but at different rates.

The meaning and implications of this definition will be explained as we go along. Meanwhile, note that the definition is as important for what it excludes as for what it includes:

1. Business cycles are not *seasonal fluctuations,* such as the upswing in retail sales that occurs each year during the Christmas and Easter periods.

2. Business cycles are not secular *trends,* such as the long-run growth or decline—or the sweeping upward or downward "drift"—that characterizes practically all economic data over a long period of years.

Since business cycles are not these things, we may turn our attention to explaining them in closer detail.

HOW DO BUSINESS CYCLES LOOK?

For our purposes at this time, we can visualize business cycles as deviations around a long-term trend, like the deviations of GNP around its trend as shown in Exhibit 1. In this and all other instances when data such as GNP, sales, prices, employment, or any other figures are arranged chronologically as in this chart or in a table, they are referred to as *time series.* The measurement of "time" may be in years, months, weeks, days, etc., and is usually scaled on the horizontal axis when depicted graphically.

According to the definition of business cycles given above, the fluctuations may occur in production, prices, income, employment, or in any other time series of economic data. In order to measure business cycles for the economy as a whole, therefore, it becomes necessary to combine many different time series into a single index of business activity covering a number of years. Then, if the value of the index for each year is expressed as a percentage of the long-term trend, the resulting data when graphed might look like the fluctuations in Exhibit 2. No wonder a famous American economist by the name of Irving Fisher (1867–1947) once described business cycles as the "dance of the dollar."

Exhibit 1

Gross National Product—Actual and Trend

The vertical axis of this chart is a "ratio" or logarithmic scale on which equal distances are represented by equal percentage changes. For example, the changes from 100 to 200, 200 to 400, 300 to 600, etc., all equal 100 percent, and hence are represented by equal distances on the chart.

This type of scale permits the trend of GNP to be plotted as a straight line; otherwise, it would have plotted as a line curving upward if an ordinary (nonratio) scale had been used.

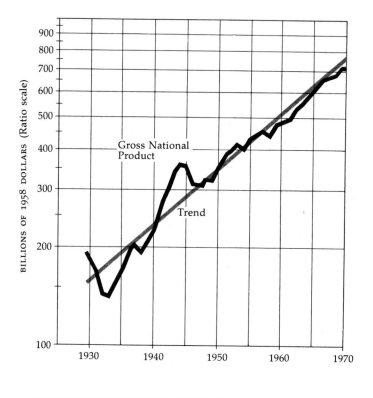

PHASES OF THE CYCLE

The ups and downs you see in Exhibit 2 prompted some writers on business cycles to speculate before World War II whether these fluctuations were actually "cycles"—that is, whether the peaks and troughs occurred at regular time intervals as shown by the idealized cycle in Exhibit 3. If this were actually the case, the cycle would resemble a sine or cosine curve in trigonometry, or perhaps an alternating electric current, and would therefore be highly predictable.

However, as more data and improved methods of measurement became available, it was found that business cycles are *recurrent but not periodic*. Hence the terms "business cycles" and "business fluctuations" are used synonomously in economics, with the understanding that the word "cycles" in no sense implies periodicity.

The names of the four phases of the business cycle shown in Exhibit 3 are probably familiar to you since you often encounter them in the news media. But since they may mean different things to different people, the following brief explanations will help avoid ambiguity:

Prosperity: the upper phase of a business cycle in which the economy is operating at or near full employment, and a high degree of business and consumer optimism is reflected by a vigorous rate of capital investment and consumption.

Recession: the downward phase, in which the economy's income, output, and employment are decreasing, and declining business and consumer optimism is reflected by a falling rate of capital investment and consumption.

Depression: the lower phase, in which the economy is operating with substantial unemployment of its resources, and there is very little business and consumer optimism as reflected by a sluggish rate of capital investment and consumption.

Recovery: the upward phase, in which the economy's

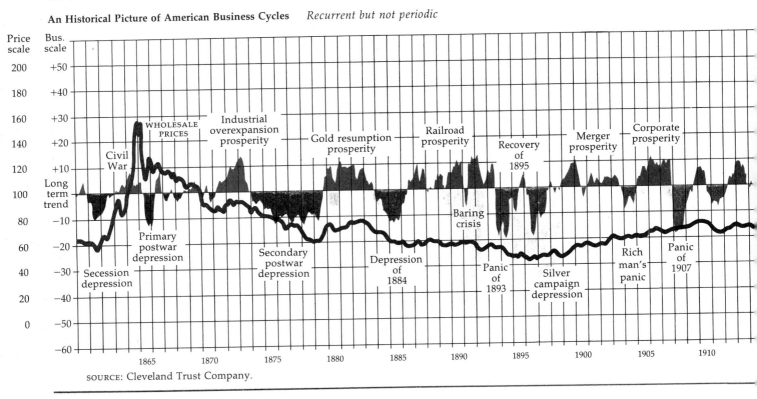

Exhibit 2

An Historical Picture of American Business Cycles   *Recurrent but not periodic*

SOURCE: Cleveland Trust Company.

income, output, and employment are rising, and there is a growing degree of business and consumer optimism as reflected by an expanding rate of capital investment and consumption.

In reality, the four phases of the cycle are by no means equal in scope or intensity, and do not always come in the order shown. For example, an economy may fluctuate between contractions and expansions for many years without experiencing either high prosperity or deep depression. Further, the transition from one phase of a cycle into the next is occasionally imperceptible; it may be almost impossible at times to distinguish between the end of one phase and the beginning of another. For these reasons, the names of the four phases should be viewed only as convenient descriptions, and the diagram in Exhibit 3 as an oversimplified picture.

Exhibit 3

Idealized Business Cycles

Recurrent and periodic . . . like a sine or cosine curve in trigonometry, or an alternating electric current.

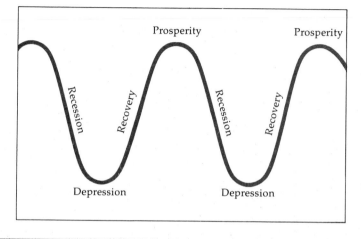

Exhibit 2 (continued)

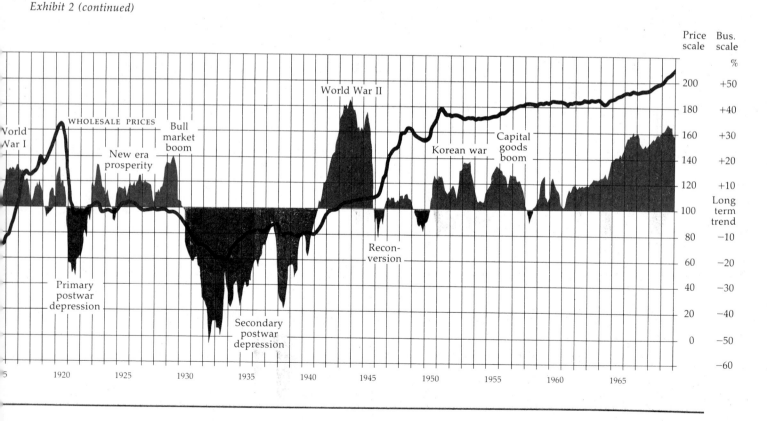

SOME FACTS ABOUT BUSINESS CYCLES

Economists who specialize in business cycles have learned a great deal about them, based on studies going back as far as the early nineteenth century. Exhibit 4 summarizes some of their more important statistical findings. But business cycles also have

---

Exhibit 4

How Much Do We Know About Business Cycles?

The study of business cycles since the early nineteenth century has revealed certain things that are known—and some that are not—about their behavior:

SOME THINGS THAT ARE KNOWN . . .

1. Peacetime business cycles—depending upon how far back you go—have averaged from three to five years, with recoveries averaging somewhat less than three years and recessions less than two years.

2. Usually, the greater the decline in production and employment during the first few months of a recession, the greater the severity of the recession as a whole; conversely, the smaller the initial decline, the milder the recession as a whole.

3. The recovery phases of business cycles are usually more uniform, and their rates of advance more predictable, than the recession phases.

4. The rate of expansion is usually more rapid: (a) in the early months of an upswing as compared to the later months, and (b) after a severe contraction as compared to a mild one.

AND NOT KNOWN . . .

1. The factors that determine the duration of different recoveries and recessions are still obscure; as a result these cyclical phases are very difficult to forecast.

2. There is no historical basis for predicting the amplitudes of recoveries and recessions.

3. Present statistical methods of calculation are inadequate for disentangling the more meaningful cyclical fluctuations from the seasonal and other forces that influence the data.

4. Little is known about the quantitative effects which national and international policies have at different stages of the cycle.

---

certain economic characteristics which must be understood. For instance:

Over the course of a business cycle, the durable goods industries tend to experience relatively wide fluctuations in output and employment and relatively small fluctuations in prices; the nondurable goods industries tend to experience relatively wide fluctuations in prices and relatively small fluctuations in output and employment.

The reasons for this are based primarily on two sets of factors: durability and competition.

Durability

Durable goods—precisely because they are durable —do not have to be replaced at a particular time; they can be repaired and thereby made to last longer if necessary. What effects does this have on businessmen who buy capital goods like iron and steel, cement, machine tools, etc., and consumers who purchase durable goods like automobiles, refrigerators, and television sets?

In a recession or depression, when aggregate demand is low, businessmen find themselves with excess production capacity, and therefore see little prospect of profiting from investment in capital goods. Likewise, consumers find they can get along with their existing cars and other durable goods rather than purchase new ones. Hence the "hard goods" industries experience sharp decreases in demand.

During recovery and prosperity, on the other hand, the reverse situation occurs. Aggregate demand is high, and businessmen and consumers are ready to replace as well as add to their existing stocks of capital and durable goods. The hard goods industries therefore experience sharp increases in demand.

Capital goods and consumer durables are thus goods whose purchase can be postponed to a later date. The contrary, however, is true of nondurables and semidurables—the so-called "soft goods" like food, clothing, and some services. Their purchase is not readily postponable, and hence the change in demand for them over the course of a business cycle is much less pronounced.

WESLEY CLAIR MITCHELL

1874–1948

Wesley C. Mitchell was born in Illinois, educated at the University of Chicago, and served for many years as a professor of economics at Columbia University in New York. He was a founder of the National Bureau of Economic Research, which is one of the world's major centers for quantitative research in aggregate economic activity, and a recipient of honorary degrees for distinguished research and scholarship from the Universities of Paris, Chicago, California, Columbia, Harvard, Pennsylvania, and Princeton, and the New School for Social Research. In 1947 the American Economic Association—the major organization of economists in the United States—bestowed upon him its highest honor, the Francis A. Walker medal (named after the Association's first president, 1885–1892), which is awarded once every five years to an American who "in the course of his life made a contribution of the highest distinction to economics."

Although many of Mitchell's writings were broadly in the history of money and prices, his lifework and greatest research appeared in several editions of his book **Business Cycles,** *first published in 1913. This was a monumental work. Mitchell studied, sifted, and analyzed data on commodity prices, wages, bond yields, bond prices, and money for the United States, Great Britain, Germany, and France, covering the period of 1890 to 1911. He then presented, as he said, "an analytic description of the complicated process by which seasons of business prosperity, crisis, depression, and revival come about in the modern world."*

In later years, as research director of the National Bureau of Economic Research, Mitchell inspired original investigations into many aspects of capitalism. In 1927 he published **Business Cycles, The Problem and Its Setting,** *a revised edition of his earlier book. This served as a standard textbook in economics courses for many years. Finally, in 1946 he coauthored his last volume on the subject,* **Measuring Business Cycles,** *in which his thesis was carried to its conclusion.*

Broadly, Mitchell viewed business cycles as self-generating processes based on mutual interdependencies of causes and effects. Perhaps his greatest contribution was the impetus he gave to the use of empirical data and quantitative model-building, which have characterized much of macroeconomics and business cycle research since the early 1950s.

Culver Pictures

Modern business cycle models are not intended to give detailed accounts of economic phenomena. However, if we make meaningful assumptions about the data and about the relationships between such variables as income, consumption, saving, and investment, we can construct models that convey many of the essential workings of an economy. Such models help to explain past economic changes, to predict future changes, and to serve as guides for policy makers. But they can never give results with certainty because they represent the "highlights" of reality rather than the complete picture.

Competition

The degree of competition (i.e., number of sellers) in an industry usually has a bearing on the way in which the industry adjusts its prices and outputs to changes in demand. In view of this, how does a fall in aggregate demand affect hard goods producers as compared to soft goods producers?

Most industries that manufacture capital and consumer durable goods are characterized by fewness of sellers. The "big three" or the "big four" producers in each of these industries typically account for the great majority of the industry's sales. Hence if aggre-

gate demand falls, these firms possess sufficient monopoly power in the marketplace to resist making substantial price decreases; instead, they seek to cut their costs, mainly by reducing output and employment.

In the nondurable and semidurable goods industries, the reverse is true. These industries are characterized by relatively larger numbers of sellers. Being more competitive, they tend to counter a decrease in demand by reducing their prices while holding their output and employment relatively steady.

These factors explain why, whenever there is a

Exhibit 5

A Guide to the Main Business Cycle Theories of the Past

EXTERNAL THEORIES

These theories (usually called exogenous *theories), assume that business cycles are caused by factors "outside" the economic system.*

1. **The sunspot theory** *of business cycles was proposed in England during the late nineteenth century. It was found that during the third quarter of the nineteenth century a remarkably high correlation existed between sunspot cycles (disturbances on the surface of the sun) and agricultural cycles. This led to the hypothesis that sunspots affect the weather, the weather influences agricultural crops, and the crops affect business conditions. The correlation subsequently fell apart because it was the result of accidental rather than causal factors. Nevertheless, the theory created a sensation throughout the world when it was first introduced.*

2. **The innovation theory** *contends that business cycles result from innovations (new inventions, new methods, and new ways of doing things) which forward-looking businessmen adopt in order to reduce costs and increase profits. Once an innovation proves successful, other businessmen jump on the bandwagon by adopting the same or similar techniques. Innovations thus cause flucutations in investment which result in business cycles.*

INTERNAL THEORIES

These theories (also known as endogenous *theories) accept the fact that certain types of external forces influence the economy, but assume the main causes of business cycles are based on factors "inside" the economic system.*

1. **The psychological theory** *holds that people respond to political, social, and economic events with waves of optimism and pessimism, and these responses set off cycles in economic activity. The psychological reactions of businessmen to changes in: (a) prospects for peace or war; (b) rates of return on investment, (c) new discoveries of natural resources, (d) labor-management attitudes, and (e) consumer tastes, are among the chief underlying factors causing business change.*

2. **The monetary theory** *attributes business cycles to factors such as changes in the quantity of money, credit and interest rates. The upswing occurs when credit conditions become favorable enough for businessmen to borrow; the downswing takes place when banks begin to restrict their expansion of credit because their reserves are being depleted and the central banks are unwilling to supply additional credit.*

3. **The underconsumption theory** *claims that recessions result from consumption lagging behind output, and from too much income getting into the hands of the wealthy and thrifty compared to what can be invested. Underconsumption may thus result from either; (a) too large a proportion of society's income not being spent on consumption, or (b) the economic system distributing income too inequitably to enable enough people to purchase all the goods produced.*

4. **The overinvestment theory** *holds that business cycles result from too much investment in the economy as businessmen try to anticipate rising demands, and from sharp cutbacks in investment when businessmen realize that their expansion was excessive. These fluctuations in investment cause the entire economy to react in a cyclical manner.*

---

recession, we first hear about production cutbacks and layoffs in industries like automobiles and steel—not in food processing or textiles. These latter industries may also reduce their output and employment, but for them the percentage decreases are usually much smaller.

THEORIES OF THE BUSINESS CYCLE

Why do business cycles occur? Many theories have been proposed since the nineteenth century. The more famous are identified briefly in Exhibit 5.

The external theories assume that business cycles are largely unpredictable and uncontrollable because they result from forces "outside" the economic system. The internal theories, on the other hand, assume that some degree of prediction and control is possible, but they differ as to the means and methods of accomplishment.

Which of the theories is correct? The sunspot theory excepted, there is some truth in all, but complete truth in none. In other words, there is no single cause of business cycles; instead many causes are at work, some of which are more important than others in any given phase of the cycle.

Since World War II, economists have increasingly explained business cycles through the *interaction* of changes in consumption and investment expenditures. As we shall see in later chapters, these variables are related to national income. As a result, a change in one variable, such as investment, can induce changes in income and consumption, and the interaction of these changes can generate different patterns of fluctuation in economic activity depending on the *rates* of change in consumption and investment. Various interesting patterns of fluctuation are shown in Exhibit 6.

CAN WE FORECAST BUSINESS CYCLES?

If we could first know where we are and whither we are tending, we could better judge what to do and how to do it.
Abraham Lincoln

These words are more than a century old, but they explain as well as any the necessity of forecasting. As long as we live in a world in which no one can

---

Exhibit 6

Different Patterns of Business Cycles

Modern business cycle theory emphasizes the interaction between changes in consumption and changes in investment. These interactions may produce different types of cyclical patterns depending on the rates *at which the changes in consumption and investment occur. Each pattern may represent a different "model."*

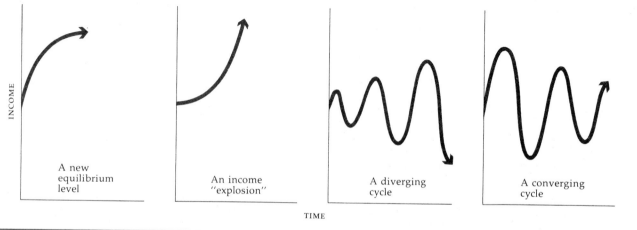

A new equilibrium level

An income "explosion"

A diverging cycle

A converging cycle

INCOME

TIME

---

predict the future with certainty, virtually all business and economic decisions rest upon forecasts. For instance, if you were a businessman, would you invest without knowing something about future economic conditions in your industry or in the economy? As a consumer, would you delay buying a house or a car if you thought the price was going to drop in the near future? If you were a speculator in commodities or in common stocks, would you buy and sell if you did not expect to make a profit? If you were a congressman, would you vote for a tax increase to help curb inflation if you thought that prices throughout the economy were going to leap upward next year?

Each of these questions involves a prediction of the future. Forecasting is a means of reducing uncertainty that surrounds the making of business and economic decisions.

How are the forecasts made? There is no single method that everyone uses, but there are several that are employed by economic forecasters working in industry, government, and universities:

1. *Mechanical extrapolations.* These are straightforward projections of statistical data, such as the projection of time series trends, moving averages, or other statistical relations. They are called "mechanical" because little or no attention is paid to analysis of the underlying economic relationships that determine the data or the trends that are being projected—usually because very little is known about them.

2. *Opinion polling.* Several privately and publicly sponsored organizations conduct periodic surveys of: (a) businessmen's intentions to invest in plant, equipment, and inventories, and (b) consumers' finances and plans to purchase automobiles, houses, and major appliances. These surveys, covering thousands of respondents, are used as bases for predictions about the economy as a whole.

3. *Econometric models.* These are economic relationships expressed in mathematical terms and verified by statistical methods. They may be constructed for firms, industries, regions, or the entire economy, and may serve not only as a basis for prediction, but also as a guide for policymaking. A large-scale econometric model may contain hundreds of equations

and require a staff of economists and statisticians to keep it up to date.

4. *Economic indicators.* There are literally thousands of time series covering economic and business activity. Many of them may be classified into one of three categories:

a. *Coincident indicators.* Those time series that move approximately "in phase" with the aggregate economy, and hence are measures of current economic activity.

b. *Leading indicators.* Those time series that tend to move ahead of aggregate economic activity, thus reaching peaks and troughs before the economy as a whole.

c. *Lagging indicators.* Those time series that follow or trail behind aggregate economic activity.

Which forecasting method is best? There is no simple answer, because all four have been used with varying success. However, the last three are the more satisfying because they incorporate the most scientific and reliable means we have for predicting future economic activity.

Unemployment

You will often hear it said that one of our primary national objectives is to maintain the economy's resources at a "full" or "high" level of employment. What do these terms mean?

First, examine the interesting charts in Exhibit 7. Can you conclude from these charts that since there always seems to be some unemployment there can be no such thing as "full" employment? Would you consider 3 percent a "normal" rate of unemployment? 4 percent? 5 percent?

Before these questions can be answered, it is necessary to understand some basic terms and concepts that are part of the modern language of economics. The first notion to be clarified is that of the *labor force.* It may be defined as all people sixteen years of age or older who are employed, plus all those unemployed who are actively seeking work. The total labor force includes those in the armed services plus the civilian labor force. However, only

Exhibit 7

Trends in the Labor Force: 1956 to 1970

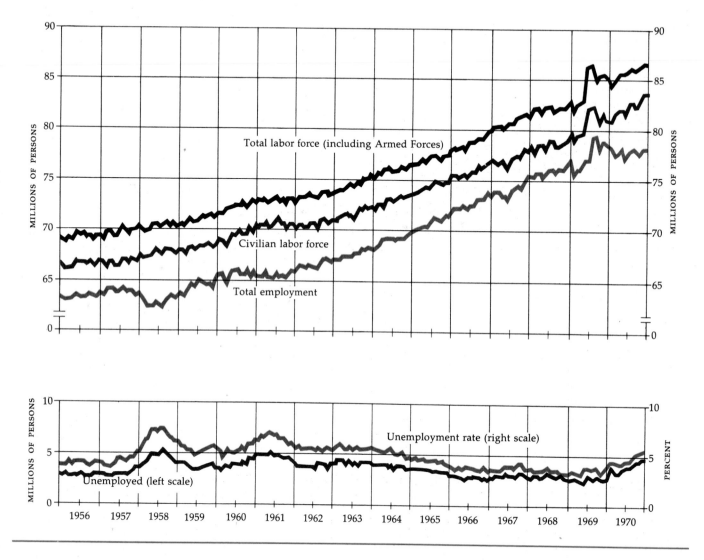

the *civilian labor force* is of interest to us here, since this is the segment that experiences unemployment.

TYPES OF UNEMPLOYMENT

The Census Bureau of the Commerce Department encounters certain difficulties when it tries to measure unemployment. Basically, it finds that the circumstances and conditions of unemployment vary widely among individuals. Accordingly, economists have chosen to distinguish three different kinds of unemployment: frictional, cyclical, and structural.

Frictional unemployment. A certain amount of unemployment, which is of a short-run nature and is characteristic of our dynamic economy, may be called *frictional unemployment*. It exists because of "frictions" in the economic system resulting from imperfect labor mobility, imperfect knowledge of job opportunities, and the economy's inability to match people with jobs instantly and smoothly. Typically, it consists of people temporarily out of work because they are "between" jobs or in the process of changing jobs. Frictional unemployment can be reduced by improving labor mobility and knowledge, but cannot—and in a democratic society should not—be completely eliminated. In view of its nature, an equally suitable and more descriptive name for it might be *transitional unemployment*.

Cyclical unemployment. Over the history of American business cycles, the major kind of unemployment has been *cyclical*—resulting from business recessions and depressions when aggregate demand is too far below the full employment level of aggregate output and income. Obviously, our society would like to reduce cyclical unemployment as much as possible, but the only way this can be done is to conquer the business cycle itself by eliminating depressions and minimizing recessions. This is a subject about which more will be said later on.

Structural unemployment. In the 1950s, a particularly disturbing phenomenon called *structural unemployment* became increasingly apparent. It arose because of certain basic or "structural" changes that occurred and are still occurring in the economy—changes which prevent some people from getting jobs because of their race, age, lack of education or training, or geographic location. These *hard core unemployed* are mainly members of minority groups: blacks, Puerto Ricans, and Mexicans, the "too young," the "too old," the high-school dropouts, and the permanently displaced victims of technological change. Many of them lack the skills needed in today's scientific and technological economy. Some are victims of racial prejudice. Some also lack the means to move to areas where jobs might be available. As a group they constitute one of America's major economic problems and challenges.

FULL EMPLOYMENT AND THE COST OF UNEMPLOYMENT

Ideally we want the economy to maintain *full employment*—a situation in which the entire civilian labor force is working, except for those few who are victims of frictional unemployment. This is equivalent to saying there should be no *involuntary unemployment*: every person who wants to work should be able to find a job at going wage rates for the skills and experiences he has to offer, so that there is no cyclical or structural unemployment.

It would be convenient if we could express this goal in terms of percentages of the labor force. Unfortunately, economists are not in complete agreement on this point. Some have argued that full employment exists when the unemployment rate is no more than 3 percent of the labor force. Others have said that an unemployment rate of 4 percent might be more realistic. This latter figure reflects the growing significance of the "hard core" unemployment problem. If you think that a controversy over 1 percent is needless hairsplitting, remember that it can involve the employment or unemployment of hundreds of thousands of people —depending on the size of the labor force. Take another look at Exhibit 7 and estimate the consequences for yourself.

What are the costs to society of unemployment? There are two—an economic cost and a social cost. (1) the economic cost is the output that society foregoes and never gets back. It consists of all the consumer goods and capital goods that would be produced if there were full employment of all resources, and the deterioration of human capital resulting from loss of skills. Even for an unemployment figure as low as 3 percent, the value of foregone output may amount to many billions of dollars. (2) The social cost is the human misery, deprivation, and social and political unrest brought on by large-scale unemployment. Social cost is usually more difficult to measure than economic cost, but is nevertheless a matter of deep and general concern. Further, it is a cost which is higher for some groups than for others —see Exhibit 8.

Exhibit 8

Unemployment Rates—Do they tell the whole story?

How meaningful is it to talk about an "average" unemployment rate? Equally important is the distribution of unemployment rates by age, sex, race, time, and occupational categories. A desirable "average" of 3 to 4 percent for all workers may actually be hiding much higher rates among some groups.

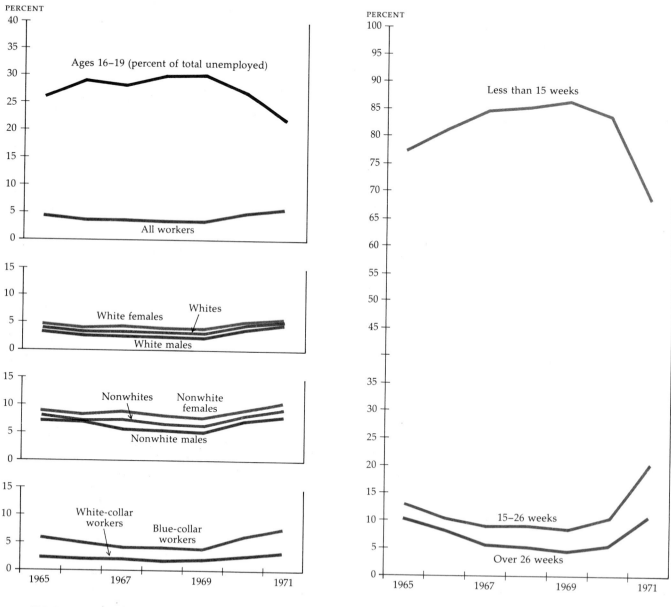

SOURCE: U.S. Department of Labor.

Exhibit 9

Inflation Around the World (latest comparative data)

Inflation is a reduction in the purchasing power of money—a shrinkage or depreciation of a nation's currency. This reduction is typically measured by increases in official cost-of-living or consumer price indexes.

Industrialized Countries	Indexes of Value of Money (1959=100)		Annual Rates of Depreciation		
	1964	1969	'59–'69*	'68–'69	'69–'70†
Greece	93	83	1.9%	2.3%	2.3%
Finland	79	61	4.8	2.2	2.5
Switzerland	87	74	3.0	2.5	2.5
Australia	92	78	2.4	2.8	3.1
Germany (F.R.)	89	78	2.4	2.6	3.6
Italy	80	70	3.6	2.5	3.7
Austria	85	72	3.2	3.0	3.8
Spain	79	58	5.3	2.2	3.9
Belgium	91	77	2.6	3.6	4.0
Canada	93	78	2.4	4.3	4.0
Luxembourg	93	81	2.1	2.2	4.1
Netherlands	86	67	3.8	6.9	4.1
South Africa	92	79	2.3	2.8	4.4
New Zealand	90	73	3.1	4.7	4.9
Denmark	81	59	5.1	3.2	5.2
United Kingdom	87	71	3.4	5.1	5.3
France	82	69	3.7	5.7	5.4
United States	94	79	2.2	5.1	5.7
Sweden	84	69	3.7	2.6	5.8
Turkey	82	57	5.5	4.8	6.3
Portugal	88	67	3.9	8.1	6.4
Ireland	85	68	3.8	6.9	6.6
Japan	77	60	5.0	4.9	7.5
Norway	85	71	3.3	3.0	8.6
Iceland	63	37	9.5	16.2	11.8

Less-Developed Countries	Indexes of Value of Money (1959=100)		Annual Rates of Depreciation		
	1964	1969	'59–'69*	'68–'69	'69–'70†
Honduras	92	81	2.1%	2.3%	−0.4%
Thailand	94	83	1.9	2.1	1.5
Morocco	80	77	2.6	2.8	1.5
Venezuela	98	90	1.1	2.3	1.7
Dominican Rep.	86	85	1.6	1.0	1.9
El Salvador	100	96	0.4	−0.3	2.9
Guatemala	100	96	0.5	2.2	3.1
Israel	75	60	4.9	2.4	3.3
Iran	84	78	2.4	3.0	3.3
Bolivia	72	55	5.8	3.1	3.4
Ecuador	83	67	3.8	6.0	3.9
Peru	69	39	9.0	5.9	4.0
Mexico	90	77	2.5	2.8	4.0
Pakistan	87	70	3.6	3.1	4.5
China (Taiwan)	75	63	4.6	4.8	4.6
India	80	56	5.6	0.8	4.8
Colombia	56	36	9.8	9.2	8.1
Argentina	36	13	18.4	7.1	8.8
Jamaica	86	71	3.4	5.8	9.3
Philippines	67	56	5.7	2.8	10.7
Indonesia	5	‡	58.2	5.8	12.0
Korea	51	29	11.5	11.0	14.5
Brazil	11	2	31.4	18.8	17.9
Chile	35	11	19.7	23.4	23.8
Vietnam	84	20	14.9	18.0	27.2

* Compounded annually.
† Based on average of monthly data available for 1970 compared with corresponding period of 1969.
‡ Less than one.
NOTE: Depreciation computed from unrounded data. Value of money is measured by reciprocals of official cost-of-living or consumer price indexes.
SOURCE: First National City Bank.

Exhibit 9 (continued)

Cost-of-Living Trends for Selected Countries, 1958–1971.

NOTE: Ratio scale to show proportionate changes; index, 1959 = 100.

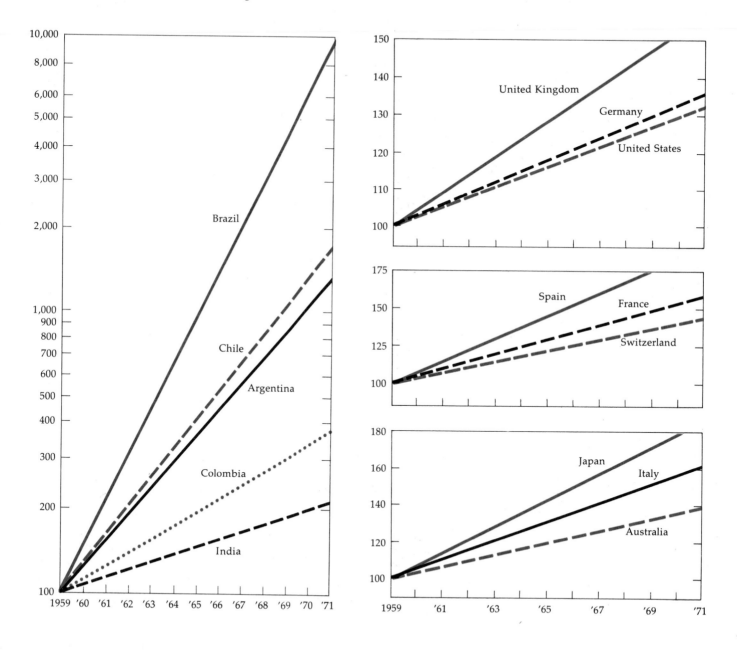

Inflation

A famous comedian once said that inflation means "your money won't buy as much as it would during a depression when you don't have any." This suggests the following general definition of inflation:

Inflation is a rise in the general price level (or average level of prices) of all goods and services. The general price level thus varies inversely with the purchasing power of money. For example, if prices double, purchasing power decreases by one-half; if prices halve, purchasing power doubles. Therefore, inflation is also a reduction in the purchasing power of money. (See Exhibit 9.)

The opposite of inflation is *deflation*. Can you formulate your own definition? (Be careful not to confuse its meaning here with that of "deflating" a time series, as described in a previous chapter.)

Does inflation mean that all prices rise? Clearly not. In almost any inflation some prices rise, some are fairly constant, and some even fall. However, the "average" level of prices—the so-called *general price level*—rises.

This is the meaning behind Exhibit 10. As total demand rises from depression levels, there are at first sufficient unemployed resources to keep the average level of prices steady. But as full employment is approached, shortages of specific resources begin to appear, the bargaining position of labor unions improves, and some producers find themselves able to increase prices as their unit costs of production rise. Thereafter, further increases in demand are associated with more than proportional increases in the general price level.

TYPES OF INFLATION: IS THE UNITED STATES INFLATION-PRONE?

Inflation always means rising prices, but a number of different explanations for inflation have been given from time to time—both in this country and abroad. Here are six common types you are likely to encounter in the news media, and should know something about. Note that some of them may be overlapping in their causes and effects.

Exhibit 10

The General Price Level and Inflation

Increases in aggregate demand or total spending may result in moderate increases in the general price level as full employment is approached. Thereafter further increases in total spending result in pure or hyperinflation as the general price level rises without any increases in output.

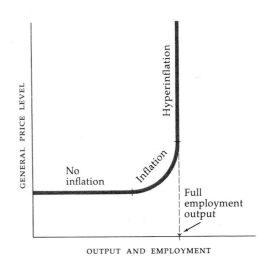

1. *Cost-push inflation* exists when prices rise because production costs are increasing faster than productivity or efficiency. One of the chief reasons advanced in support of this explanation is that sellers' prices are determined by their costs, and wages are the primary element of total costs. When strong labor unions manage to push wage costs up, they may cause sellers to raise their prices and thereby bring about inflation. Hence, a cost-push inflation is frequently called a "*wage-push*" inflation.

2. *Demand-pull inflation* takes place when consumers' and investors' aggregate demand is rising while the available supply of goods is becoming increasingly

limited. Goods may be in short supply because re-sources are fully utilized or because production can-not be increased rapidly enough to meet the growing demand.

3. *Profit-push inflation* occurs when corporate prices and profits rise before any increase in wages takes place. Profits may climb for two reasons: first, be-cause of improved production and work methods which reduce unit labor costs; second, because of higher prices. Rising profits prompt labor to "catch up" by seeking sharply higher pay. Ultimately, unit labor costs rise, too, giving inflation a further push. Considerable evidence supports this view. There have been several prolonged periods since World War II in which United States factory prices and profits climbed substantially, while unit labor costs were constant or even declining.

4. *Structural inflation* may result from uneven up-ward demand or cost pressures in specific industries even though aggregate demand is in balance with aggregate supply for the economy as a whole. For instance, wage increases in basic industries like steel or cement can cause cost and price increases in the automobile and construction industries. These increases can then spread throughout the economy. Likewise, increases in aggregate demand may cause shortages and pull up prices in some industries faster than in others. In either case, an upward cost-price spiral can result as workers try to match rising prices with further wage gains.

5. *Hyperinflation* occurs when prices are rising with little or no increases in output; hence it is sometimes called "runaway" or "galloping" inflation. The most extreme examples occurred in Germany after World War I and in China, Greece, and Hungary after World War II. The governments of these countries, in order to pay their mounting postwar bills or reparations obligations, simply ran the printing presses and turned out paper money instead of drastically raising taxes. In 1923, the peak year of Germany's inflation, a cup of coffee cost 6 billion German marks—as much money as was in circulation in all of Germany ten years earlier; a pair of shoelaces cost 11 billion marks; and in New York City souvenir packages containing 3 trillion genuine marks were sold for 5 cents. Prices in these countries rose several thou-sand percent a month, and workers were literally carrying their wages home in wheelbarrows and bushel baskets.

6. *Creeping inflation* occurs when there is a slow but persistent upward movement in the general price level over many years, typically at an average annual rate of up to 3 percent. You will often hear terms like "walking" inflation or "trotting" inflation for price increases that are somewhat higher than this.

The trend of inflation in the United States has varied between "creeping" and "trotting," due at one time or another to cost-push, demand-pull, profit-push, and structural factors. All of these forces have been at work in different degrees—especially in a high-employment economy—thus suggesting that the United States is "inflation-prone" or that it has a built-in "inflationary bias." Some of the im-plications of this will be examined shortly.

WHO SUFFERS FROM INFLATION? WHO BENEFITS?

Are the consequences of inflation good or bad? Be-fore answering this question, it helps to distinguish between two kinds of income: *money income*, which is the amount of money received for work done, and *real income*, representing the purchasing power of money income or the quantity of goods and services that can be bought with money income. Clearly, your money income may be quite different from your real income, since the latter depends not only on your money income, but also on the prices you pay for the things you buy. A short history of prices is illustrated in Exhibit 11.

Against this background we may identify three major classes in society whose economic well-being tends to be impaired by inflation: (1) Fixed money-income groups, and those whose money incomes lag behind increases in prices—like teachers, civil ser-vice employees, pensioners, and most white-collar workers—are penalized by inflation because their real incomes or standards of living decline when the prices of the things they buy increase faster than their money incomes. (2) Creditors, or those who lend money, suffer from inflation because they are repaid in the future with dollars that buy less than the dollars they originally lent. Promissory notes,

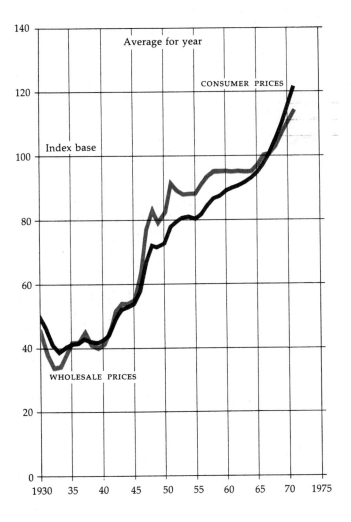

Exhibit 11

Price Indexes

1967 = 100

The Consumer Price Index and the Wholesale Price Index are the most widely used measures of inflationary price trends in our economy.

bonds, and mortgages are examples of credit instruments which depreciate in real value as a result of inflation. (3) Savers, or those who hold assets in such forms as savings accounts, insurance policies, bonds, mortgages, and other fixed-value paper claims, are harmed by inflation for much the same reasons as creditors: the dollars they originally put away as savings were "dearer" in terms of purchasing power than those dollars are worth now.

In contrast, three classes in society tend to benefit from inflation: (1) Flexible money-income groups, and those whose money incomes rise faster than prices will ordinarily fare well. Most business firms fall into this category, since there is substantial evidence that manufacturers' selling prices (and profits) often tend to rise faster than costs. Stockholders in such companies may therefore benefit from these increasing profits. (2) Debtors benefit from inflation for the same reason that creditors suffer: the dollars that are paid back are "cheaper" than the ones that were initially borrowed. (3) *Speculators*, who buy and sell goods or securities with the hope of profiting on the basis of price movements, may do well in inflation if they operate with borrowed funds. For instance, people who spend all their income (in contrast to those who save some of it) will avoid the losses of inflation by converting their income into goods, thereby at most increasing their *money* wealth but not their *real* wealth as the dollar values of their assets rise in line with the general price level. But those individuals who can do this with borrowed money will increase their real wealth as well.

Some General Effects of Inflation

From the economy's point of view, inflation has a number of adverse consequences. Among them:

☐ It redistributes income and wealth haphazardly and inequitably.

☐ It unjustly penalizes those groups most vulnerable to it, which is why inflation has been called the "cruelest tax."

☐ It raises costs and prices, thereby impairing the nation's productive efficiency and its competitiveness in world markets.

Box 1

A Guide to U.S. Living Costs, 1970

Inflation affects us all. But the cost of living may vary widely in different parts of the country.

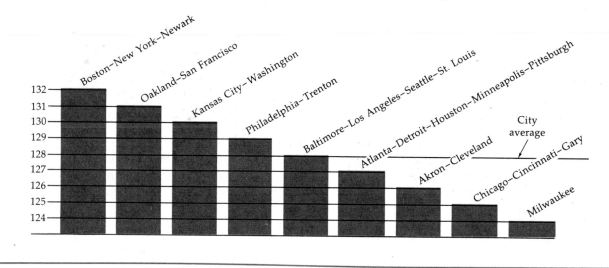

Inflationary pressures, of course, are not uniform throughout the economy. They bear down differently in various parts of the country, making living costs in some areas more expensive than others. (See Box 1.)

THE GOAL OF PRICE STABILITY

Since the consequences of inflation are serious and pervasive, price stability becomes an important goal. But neither the United States nor any other major industrial nation has yet succeeded in combining price stability with a high level of employment. In view of this, what do we mean by price stability?

Perhaps the most realistic way of answering this question is to state what price stability does *not* mean:

1. Price stability does not mean there will be no average changes in prices. In a free economy, average changes in consumer prices are certain to occur, and they will usually be upward in a high-employment economy because the various demand-pull, cost-push, profit-push, and structural forces create an "inflationary bias." Many economists believe, how-

ever, that the average annual increase in consumer prices should be no more than 1 to 1½ percent. This, they say, would even be economically healthy from a social point of view because it would yield overall benefits which far outweigh the overall costs. Thus:

a. If such a mild inflation results in selling prices rising faster than costs, as has usually but not always been the case, profits will increase; this will stimulate further investment and encourage the introduction of new and better consumer goods without significantly eroding the purchasing power of the dollar.

b. Such mild inflation will have only moderately adverse effects on savers as long as the interest rate on savings—typically around 5 percent— continues to exceed the desired inflationary rate of 1 or 1½ percent.

For these reasons, therefore, a slight inflation, according to the economists who take this position, is a cheap price to pay for the associated benefits of continuous high employment, output, and economic growth.

2. Price stability does not mean that any specific prices must be held constant. Within a moderately stable average price level, there can and must be constant price adjustments to changing levels and patterns of demand, to diverse movements of cost, and to technological change.

3. Price stability does not mean that wages must remain constant. Labor compensation can move up in line with the average growth of labor productivity without adding to the labor costs of output.

Conclusion: How Much Inflation? How Much Unemployment?

Economists generally believe we are faced with a "tradeoff" between inflation and unemployment. We can probably reduce or even avoid unemployment through increased government spending, if necessary, as will be shown in later chapters. But the consequences of such actions are likely to be inflationary, as evidenced by most Western European countries that have maintained lower rates of unemployment—but higher long-run rates of inflation—than we have. In view of this, what is the best course of action for the United States?

The answer is by no means simple. However, if we assume that our economy is indeed "inflation-prone"—that it has a built-in "inflationary bias" because of various cost-push, demand-pull, and structural forces mentioned above that are *inherent* in the economic system—then our problem is to face the fact that we must live with inflation and do our best to hold it back. In that case, the correct view to adopt is that we should strive to maintain full employment with an average annual inflationary rate of not more than about $1\frac{1}{2}$ percent.

This is an objective which most economists would favor. But the difficulties of achieving this objective are considerable, as the next several chapters will show.

SUMMARY OF IMPORTANT IDEAS

1. Capitalistic economies suffer from recurrent but nonperiodic fluctuations in economic activity known as business cycles. The four phases of cycles are termed prosperity, recession, depression, and recovery.

2. Industries in the economy react to business cycles in different ways. Durable goods industries tend to be less competitive than nondurable goods industries, and therefore experience relatively wide fluctuations in output. The opposite situation tends to occur in nondurable goods industries: prices fluctuate relatively more than output and employment.

3. There are many business cycle theories, each of which attributes fluctuations in economic activity to innovative, psychological, monetary, underconsumption, and overinvestment factors. All of these undoubtedly play a role in varying degrees, but modern business cycle theory holds that economic fluctuations are best explained by interactions between changes in consumption and changes in investment. The rates at which these variables change determine the type of cyclical pattern that results.

4. If economists can learn how to forecast business cycles, they will be in a better position to recommend government policies for avoiding downturns in economic activity. Today the most scientific methods of business cycle forecasting involve the use of surveys and opinion polling, econometric models, and economic indicators.

5. The level of unemployment is measured as a percentage of the labor force. Most economists define frictional unemployment as no more than 3 percent of the labor force, and hence involuntary unemployment (consisting of cyclical and structural unemployment) as anything over 3 percent. Some economists prefer a figure of 4 percent. Any disagreement between these two percentages is due primarily to the growing problem of "hard-core" unemployment. In any case, society pays both an economic and social cost of unemployment.

6. Inflation is a rise in the general price level or a reduction in the purchasing power of money. Since World War II inflationary trends have been attributed to cost-push, demand-pull, profit-push, and structural factors. In general, inflation tends to redistribute income and wealth unjustly and to increase inefficiency. A growing number of economists believe that there is an "inflationary bias" in our economy, and that it is a realistic and sensible objec-

tive to hold inflation to an average annual rate of no more than 1½ percent while striving to maintain full employment of economic resources.

FOR HOMEWORK AND DISCUSSION

1. *Terms and concepts to review:*

business cycles	leading indicators
seasonal fluctuations	lagging indicators
trend	labor force
time series	frictional unemployment
ratio (logarithmic) scale	cyclical unemployment
	structural unemployment
prosperity	hard-core unemployed
recession	involuntary unemployment
depression	inflation
recovery	deflation
sunspot theory	general price level
innovation theory	cost-push inflation
psychological theory	wage-push inflation
monetary theory	demand-pull inflation
underconsumption theory	profit-push inflation
	structural inflation
overinvestment theory	hyperinflation
	creeping inflation
econometrics	speculation
economic indicators	
coincident indicators	

2. If business cycles were recurrent and periodic, would they be easily predictable? Why? What, precisely, would you be able to predict about them?

3. If you were to compare two industries, automobiles and agricultural products, over the course of a business cycle, which would be more stable with respect to: (*a*) output and employment; (*b*) prices? Explain why.

4. (*a*) How do seasonal variations and secular trends complicate the measurement of business cycles? (*b*) What has been the approximate average length of business cycles?

5. Can you suggest how the interaction of changes in consumption and investment may cause business cycles?

6. What do you suppose are some of the chief difficulties in using leading indicators for forecasting purposes?

7. Is an increasing level of aggregate demand likely to cure the problems of cyclical unemployment and structural unemployment—without inflation? Explain.

8. Is it better to have full employment with mild inflation or moderate unemployment with no inflation? Explain.

REFERENCES AND READING SUGGESTIONS

DAUTEN, CARL A., and LLOYD M. VALENTINE, *Business Cycles and Forecasting,* 3d ed., South-Western, Cincinnati, 1968, chaps. 1, 4, 14, 15.

LEE, MAURICE W., *Macroeconomics: Fluctuations, Growth, and Stability,* 4th ed., Irwin, Homewood, Ill., 1967.

LEWIS, JOHN P., and ROBERT C. TURNER, *Business Conditions Analysis,* 2d ed., McGraw-Hill, New York, 1967, chaps. 14, 15.

SPENCER, MILTON H., *Managerial Economics,* 3d ed., Irwin, Homewood, Ill., 1968, chap. 3.

SPENCER, MILTON H., COLIN CLARK, and PETER HOGUET, *Business and Economic Forecasting,* Irwin, Homewood, Ill., 1961, chaps. 1–4.

U.S. DEPARTMENT OF COMMERCE, *Survey of Current Business,* (January issues report on previous year's economic conditions).

CHAPTER 9

Consumption, Saving, and Investment: Elements of the Theory of Income and Employment

CHAPTER PREVIEW

Can a predominantly market or capitalistic economy such as ours achieve and maintain *full employment* of its resources?

How did the classical theory of the pre-1930s answer this question?

The modern theory of income and employment is built on such fundamental concepts as consumption, saving, and investment. What do these terms mean? What relationships do they involve?

In every era there is often a tendency for one economic question to dominate all others. In the 1930s it was the overcoming of depression. In the late 1940s and early 1950s it was the prevention of a new depression as the economy converted from wartime to peacetime. Since the mid 1950s the dominant question has been whether America's mixed economy can achieve and maintain full employment of all its resources without suffering inflation.

Now that we have examined the record of business cycles in the United States, and the associated problems of unemployment and inflation, we must turn to a body of principles known as "the theory of income and employment." This theory is built on the associated phenomena of consumption, saving, and investment. Each plays a distinctive role in the economy; acting in combination they help to determine the social and economic course of history.

In this and following chapters we shall examine each phenomenon separately, and then show how they interact, how they can be controlled—and how economists rightly identify them as the foundations on which much of modern economic policy is built.

The Classical Theory of Income and Employment

You have probably heard about the "old" mathematics and the "new" mathematics, but did you know that there is an "old" economics and a "new" economics?

The "old" economics—or *classical economics*—started mainly with Adam Smith and grew until by the 1930s it was the predominant body of economic theory in the non-Communist world. The "New" Economics—or modern economics—started with a British scholar named John Maynard Keynes (pronounced "canes") in the late 1930s. It has since undergone various refinements and modifications, and its basic analytical tools and methods are now widely used by practically all economists.

But in the social sciences, great theories, like the phenomena they try to describe, rarely remain constant for all time. Today's modern economic ideas represent a broad synthesis of the best thinking from the "old" and the "new" economics, as the following pages and chapters will point out.

SAY'S LAW: "SUPPLY CREATES ITS OWN DEMAND"

In the early nineteenth century, a French economist by the name of Jean Baptiste Say wrote:

> . . . a product is no sooner created than it, from that instant, offers a market for other products to the full extent of its own value. . . . Thus, the mere circumstance of the creation of one product immediately opens a market for other products.

This conclusion has come to be known as *Say's Law*. But the idea has been expressed more pointedly by David Ricardo, a British contemporary of Say and one of the great pioneers in economic thought:

> No man produces but with a view to consume or sell, and he never sells but with an intention to purchase some other commodity which may be immediately useful to him or which may contribute to future production. By producing, then, he necessarily becomes either the consumer of his own goods, or the purchaser and consumer of the goods of some other person.

Say's Law—whether expressed in its original form by Say or in its more precise form by Ricardo—amounts to saying that *supply creates its own demand.* This viewpoint was central to classical economic thought of the nineteenth and early twentieth centuries, and is still held with varying degrees of conviction by some people today. In view of this, what does the classical model really tell us? What are its implications for our economic system?

ESSENTIALS OF THE CLASSICAL THEORY

The classical model assumes the operation of a free enterprise, highly competitive economic system in which there are many buyers and sellers in both the product and resource markets, and in which all prices are flexible so that they can quickly adjust upward or downward to changing supplies and demands in the marketplace. In this type of economic system output and resource markets will *automatically* adjust to full employment levels as if guided by an "invisible hand" because:

1. Aggregate Demand = Aggregate Income

We have learned that an economy's aggregate output equals its aggregate income. But Ricardo argued that the purpose of earning income is to spend it on output. Hence the level of *aggregate demand*—which is the total value of output that all sectors of the economy are willing to purchase—will *automatically* tend to equal the level of aggregate income.

But what if households choose to *save*—i.e., not spend—a certain proportion of their income on goods and services? Will these savings represent a withdrawal or "leakage" of funds from the income stream? Will aggregate demand then fall below aggregate output or supply, resulting in excess production, increasing unemployment, and decreasing incomes? The classical economists' answer is no because:

2. All Savings Are Invested

If some people save, there will always be other people—namely businessmen—who will want to borrow these savings and pay a price for them called *interest.* They then invest this borrowed money in

JEAN BAPTISTE SAY

1767–1832

"Law of Markets"

Say's major work, entitled Treatise on Political Economy, *was the first popular book on economics published on the European continent. But Say was more than a popularizer of other men's ideas. The terminology he developed and the approach he employed in dividing economic activity into the production, distribution, and consumption of wealth have become classic. Indeed, the definition of economics found in virtually all dictionaries today is basically a description of this division first evolved by Say.*

In his own time, Say was probably best known as the man who systematized the concepts formulated by Adam Smith and introduced them to French readers. His success at this task was evidenced by the influence he had among other scholars of his time: he became the founder of his own school of thought— the so-called "liberal optimistic school"—which dominated economic thinking in France for most of the nineteenth century.

Say regarded economics as a natural science and assumed that wealth is created, distributed, and consumed in accordance with the laws of nature and without the necessity for any government interference. His famous Law of Markets (loi des débouchés) reflected the fact that he was seeking "natural" equilibrium forces in economics along the lines of those that are encountered in physics. He thought of economics as a positive science yielding no ethical evaluations or empirical directions to legislators, and went far beyond Adam Smith in his aversion to government control, claiming that it was objectionable even when it was indispensable.

Say's Law of Markets, asserting the impossibility of general overproduction, dominated nineteenth-century economic thought. Although he expressed the Law under simplified assumptions of a barter economy engaged in free competition, Say's Law was usually interpreted literally as a description of the actual operation of the economy. Consequently, business cycles came to be regarded as short-run deviations from the long-run tendencies toward general stability.

It is important to understand that Say did not regard temporary overproduction of a particular commodity as impossible. It was the notion of general overproduction that he denied. In his words, ". . . the glut of a particular commodity arises from its having outrun the total demand for it." Such temporary gluts can be corrected if government interference ceases: "No sooner is the cause of this political disease removed, than the means of production feel a natural impulse

Radio Times Hulton Picture Library

towards the vacant channels, the replenishment of which restores activity to all others." It then becomes clear that "the total supply of products and the total demand for them must of necessity be equal, for the total demand is nothing but the whole mass of commodities which have been produced; a general congestion would consequently be an absurdity."

Say's Law did not go unchallenged by a few nineteenth-century dissenters, but it was not until 1936, more than one hundred years later, that the Law of Markets was given its final quietus by John Maynard Keynes in his General Theory of Employment, Interest and Money.

DAVID RICARDO

1772–1823

David Ricardo was born in England, the son of a broker on the London Stock Exchange. He received an early training in finance and prospered rapidly after going into business as a loan broker. While in his late twenties, Smith's book **The Wealth of Nations** stimulated his interest in economics and led him to become one of the great pioneers in economic thought.

In 1814 he retired from active business and turned his attention to research and scholarly contemplation. The result of this effort was the publication in 1817 of his famous **Principles of Political Economy and Taxation.** The book was an immediate success, and a school of Ricardian disciples formed within a few years. Ricardo's influence was pervasive and lasting: Ricardian economics became a synonym for classical political economy (or "classical economics" as we call it today). Fifty years were to pass before that influence waned.

Ricardo, like most other economists, was mainly concerned with the central problem of economics: the forces that determine the production of an economy's wealth and its distribution among the various classes of society. But he was not only a "pure" theorist, as were some of the other classical economists; he also made major policy recommendations concerning the dominant social and economic problems of his day.

For instance, in his writings on international trade, he demonstrated how England would be better off to import the food it needs from foreign countries and pay for those imports by exporting its manufactured goods. This provided the supporters of free trade with an admirable rationale for arguing in favor of repealing the English Corn Laws (tariffs) in order to lower the price of corn.

To Ricardo's analytical mind, the economy was like an elaborate watch with many interrelated parts. His task was to study this mechanism and to lay bare the laws that determine its behavior. Thus he formulated theories of value, rent, and wages which, though not entirely original, were for the first time stated completely, authoritatively, and systematically. Portions of these theories became the bases of many subsequent writings by later scholars, including Marx and Keynes.

Ricardo's scientific view of economics—or political economy as it was known until the late nineteenth century—was expressed on October 9, 1820, in a letter addressed to his friend and colleague, the Reverend Thomas R. Malthus:

Historical Pictures Service, Chicago

Political Economy you think is an enquiry into the nature and causes of wealth—I think it should be called an enquiry into the laws which determine the division of the produce of industry amongst the classes which occur in its formation. No law can be laid down respecting quantity, but a tolerably correct one can be laid down respecting proportions. Every day I am more satisfied that the former enquiry is vain and delusive, but the latter only the true objects of the science.

In the opinion of most scholars, David Ricardo ranks not only as the greatest of the classical economists, but also as one of the most distinguished economists of all time.

capital goods in order to carry on profitable production. In other words, no income receiver will save (and thereby forego the pleasure of spending) unless he is offered interest in return, and no businessman will borrow unless he plans to invest. Therefore every dollar saved by households will be borrowed and invested by businesses, thereby *automatically* assuring an uninterrupted flow of the income-expenditure stream.

3. Prices and Wages Are Flexible

Since prices in all markets—the product markets, the resource markets, and the money market—are assumed to be flexible, they *automatically* adjust to their individual full employment equilibrium levels, as shown in Exhibit 1. Thus if the price in any market is below its particular equilibrium level, the quantity demanded will exceed the quantity supplied. Competition among buyers (demanders) in that market will therefore drive the price up. If the price in any market is above its equilibrium level, the

quantity supplied will exceed the quantity demanded. Competition between sellers (suppliers) in that market will therefore drive the price down. At the equilibrium price in each market, the quantity that sellers want to sell is equal to the quantity that buyers want to buy. At these prices there are *no shortages* and *no surpluses* in any of the product, resource, or money markets; hence there must be full employment and full production throughout the economy.

4. Therefore, Capitalism Is a "Natural" Process

In the classical economists' view it follows that a capitalistic economic system will *automatically* adjust to full employment through the free operation of the price system. Clearly, since the system is self-regulating, the obvious conclusion is that it should be left alone to "run itself." Laissez-faire should therefore be the watchword of capitalism, because government interference in the operation of the economy is not only unnecessary, but probably even harmful.

Exhibit 1

Markets in the Classical Theory of Income and Employment

In the classical model, all markets are assumed to be competitive and all resources mobile. Hence, prices and quantities
are flexible and adjust automatically to their full employment equilibrium levels through the free play of market forces.

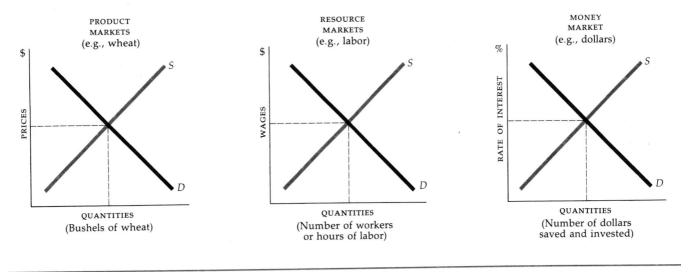

The Modern Theory of Income and Employment

The Great Depression of the 1930s was long and painful; it found approximately 13 million persons (one-fourth of the entire labor force) out of work. Since this situation was largely contrary to the classical model, many economists were inclined to explain the situation away by saying that it was the "world" and not the theory that was at fault. The depression would be terminated, they said, if only unions and business monopolies would accept wage and price cuts, and the government would stop interfering with the free operation of the markets through its New Deal legislation and activities.

But for some economists, including the eminent British scholar John Maynard Keynes, the depression was too prolonged and too deep to be brushed away as a "temporary" phenomenon that would automatically correct itself—as many loyal classicists were arguing at the time. When Keynes published his monumental treatise, *The General Theory of Employment, Interest, and Money* in 1936, he undermined the classical theory and founded the "new" economics.

KEYNES AND THE MODERN THEORY

The modern theory of income and employment (i.e., modern macroeconomic theory) is rooted in the work done by Keynes—but the theory has been greatly refined and extended since then. Today most of the major controversial economic issues you read and hear about—taxes, inflation, national debt, employment, balance of payments, interest rates, and so on—are analyzed within the framework of modern income and employment theory. The remainder of this chapter will deal with the elements of this topic; subsequent chapters will build upon it.

We begin by answering a basic question: How does the modern theory of income and employment contrast with the classical theory?

1. Aggregate Demand May Not Equal Aggregate Income

The modern theory rejects the notion that aggregate demand always equals aggregate income, and that the economic system automatically tends toward its full employment equilibrium level. The modern theory demonstrates that the economic system may be in equilibrium at less than full employment, and may remain in this state for an indefinite period.

Changes in aggregate demand play a critical role in the modern theory. Thus an economy may be operating at a level equal to or below full employment, and may experience a drop in aggregate demand and a consequent decline in real output and resource use. On the other hand, an economy may be operating at a level below full employment and may experience an increase in aggregate demand and a consequent rise in real output and resource use. Further, if aggregate demand continues to increase above full employment levels the result will be rising prices and inflation—a situation sometimes described as "too many dollars chasing too few goods."

In any case, prolonged periods of unemployment, full employment, or inflation may occur because of the failure of two adjustment mechanisms in the classical theory—interest rates and prices.

2. Savers and Investors Are Different People with Different Motivations

In a primitive economy saving and investing are undertaken largely by the same groups for the same reasons. But in an advanced economy saving and investing are undertaken by different groups for different reasons. In the United States, for example, households like yours and mine may save for several reasons: to purchase a new car, make a down payment on a house, or pay for a vacation; to provide for future security and loss of income resulting from illness, old age, or retirement; to amass an estate which can be passed on to future generations; to buy stocks and bonds for income or future profit; or simply to accumulate funds without any specific purposes in mind.

Business firms save when they retain some of their profits instead of distributing them to stockholders. Their reasons for saving, however, are different from those of households. Businesses usually save in order to invest in plant, equipment, and inventories, and they may also borrow for this purpose too. In any

JOHN MAYNARD KEYNES

1883–1946

Founder of the "New Economics"

John Maynard Keynes was among the most brilliant and influential economists of all time. As one who helped shape the thinking of future generations of scholars he ranks with Adam Smith and Karl Marx.

Keynes was born in Cambridge, England, the son of a noted economist, John Neville Keynes. He was educated at Eton and Cambridge, where he first majored in mathematics but later turned his attention to philosophy and economics. After college he took a civil service post in the India Office. Later, he returned to England and served as a teaching fellow at Cambridge, where his talents were quickly recognized. He became editor of the Economic Journal, *Britain's most distinguished economic publication—a position which he held for thirty-three years.*

To say that Keynes was brilliant is an understatement; he was a genius with diverse talents who combined teaching at Cambridge with an active and highly successful business life in the fields of insurance, investments, and publishing. In addition to his many publications in economics, he wrote a remarkable book on the philosophical foundations of probability which is required reading by graduate students in mathematical logic and philosophy; and he amassed a fortune of over $2 million by speculating in the international currency and commodity markets. Perhaps most impressive, however, is the fact that he accomplished these feats in his "spare time"; he wrote his mathematics book while employed in government service, and accumulated his fortune by analyzing financial reports and phoning orders to his broker for a half-hour each morning before breakfast.

Keynes's most celebrated work, The General Theory of Employment, Interest, and Money *(1936), was one of the most influential books ever written in economics. Here he made it clear that he was departing significantly from traditional economic theory which held that there is a natural tendency for the economy to reach equilibrium at full employment. Indeed, Keynes showed that equilibrium can be reached and maintained at a level of output less than full employment. He thus advocated reduction in the bank interest rate in order to stimulate investment, progressive income taxation in order to make incomes more equal and thereby increase the percentage of aggregate income that people spend on consumption, and government investment through public works and other means as*

Leo Rosenthal—PIX

a "pump-priming" process when private investment expenditures fall off. Today, these and related policy suggestions are part of a larger family of concepts which make up what we call the "New Economics."

Nowadays, practically all economists are "Keynesians." That is, they use the fundamental theoretical tools and concepts which Keynes developed. However, they may not always agree on the ways in which those ideas should be implemented in matters of public policy.

case, they invest primarily on the basis of the rate of profit they anticipate, rather than the interest rate they must pay for the money they use. Thus:

Saving and investing are done by different people for different reasons. While much of the economy's saving is done by households, its investing and net capital formation is done mainly by businesses on the basis of their profit expectations. The amount of investment from year to year is therefore highly variable and not likely to equal the amount of saving. Consequently, fluctuations in income, output, and employment may be characteristic of a capitalistic economy.

3. Prices and Wages Are Not Flexible

Do prices and wages exhibit the flexibility the classicists assumed? The answer is no. Our economy is characterized by big unions and big businesses, and there is great resistance to reductions in prices and wages. We almost always hear of prices and wages going up, but we rarely hear of them going down. Moreover, even if prices and wages were flexible on the downside, it seems doubtful that declines would help restore a depressed economy to full employment, as the classicists assumed. Lower prices and wages throughout the economy would instead bring with them lower money incomes, and a consequent reduction in total spending. This would perpetuate if not worsen an already depressed situation.

Hence, although a *single* firm may find itself better off with lower prices and wages during a recession, *all* firms may not. The classical economists failed to recognize this distinction, and thereby committed a logical fallacy in their reasoning. Can you name the fallacy?

4. Therefore . . .

The modern theory concludes there is *no automatic tendency* toward full employment in a capitalistic economy. The levels of aggregate output and employment are determined by the level of aggregate demand, and there is no assurance that aggregate demand will always equal full-employment aggregate income. As aggregate demand increases, so do aggregate output and employment—up to the level of full employment. Therefore, businessmen's decisions to produce goods or not to produce them—to employ resources or not to employ them—are based on whether they think their output can be sold at a profit. In view of this, let us see what modern theory says about the concept of *aggregate demand* which consists of consumption demand, private investment demand, government demand for goods and services, and net export demand.

Consumption Demand

Which factors determine *consumption* demand or personal expenditures on goods and services in our economy?

Take your own case. What determines the amount spent by *your* family on goods and services? You can probably think of several factors, but first and foremost is your family's disposable income—the amount it has left after paying personal taxes.

The situation is much the same with other families. *Disposable income is usually the single most important factor affecting a family's consumption expenditures,* while other conditions such as the size of the family, the ages of its members, its past income, and its expectations of future income, etc., will also have a bearing.

Of course, no two families spend their incomes in the same way. However, some generalizations about family expenditure patterns can be made. These generalizations are known as *Engel's Laws,* derived from the work of a German statistician, Ernst Engel, who first conducted such research in 1857. Here is a modernized version of Engel's Laws, based on budgetary studies of family expenditures.

As a family's income increases:

1. The percentage spent on food decreases.

2. The percentage spent on housing and household operations remains approximately constant (except for fuel, light, and refrigeration, which decrease).

3. The percentage spent on all other categories and the amount saved increases (except for medical care and personal care items, which remain fairly constant).

Note that the *total amount spent increases as a family's income increases*. The decreases occur only as a percentage of the total.

THE PROPENSITY TO CONSUME

The relationship between a family's income and its consumption expenditures is illustrated by the schedule in the first two columns of Exhibit 2. The difference between income and consumption is saving, shown in column (3). The first thing to notice is that as income increases consumption increases and so does saving.

The consumption and savings data are graphed in Exhibit 3. Let us consider the upper chart first.

Note that consumption expenditures are measured on the vertical axis and disposable income on the horizontal, and that both axes are drawn to the same scale. Therefore, the 45-degree diagonal is a line along which consumption, C, is 100 percent of disposable income, DI—that is, the ratio C/DI = 1.

The consumption curve, C, is the graph of the data in columns (1) and (2) of the table. The intersection of this curve with the diagonal line is the family's "break-even point"—the point where consumption is exactly equal to income. At this level the family is just getting by, neither borrowing nor saving.

To the right of the break-even point the vertical distance representing consumption is less than the horizontal distance denoting income. The difference, saving, is represented by the vertical distance between the consumption line and the diagonal.

To the left of the break-even point the family is consuming more than its income. The difference is called *dissaving*. How does a family dissave or live beyond its means? Either by spending its previous savings or by borrowing.

Here are some important ideas to remember:

The level of consumption depends on the level of income in a manner such that as income increases, consumption increases, but not as fast as income. This relation between consumption and income is

---

Exhibit 2

A Family's Consumption and Saving Schedule (hypothetical data)

How do consumption and saving relate to income?

(1) Disposable Income (DI)	(2) Consumption (C)	(3) Saving (S) (1) − (2)	(4) Average Propensity to Consume (APC) (2) ÷ (1)	(5) Average Propensity to Save (APS) (3) ÷ (1)	(6) Marginal Propensity to Consume (MPC) change in (2) / change in (1)	(7) Marginal Propensity to Save (MPS) change in (3) / change in (1)
$ 4,000	$ 4,600	$−600	1.15	−.15		
					0.70	0.30
5,000	5,300	−300	1.06	−.06		
					0.70	0.30
6,000	6,000	0	1.00	0.00		
					0.70	0.30
7,000	6,700	300	0.96	0.04		
					0.70	0.30
8,000	7,400	600	0.93	0.07		
					0.70	0.30
9,000	8,100	900	0.90	0.10		
					0.70	0.30
10,000	8,800	1,200	0.88	0.12		
					0.70	0.30
11,000	9,500	1,500	0.86	0.14		
					0.70	0.30
12,000	10,200	1,800	0.85	0.15		

Exhibit 3

A Family's Consumption and Saving in Relation to Its Income

The C curve denotes the propensity to consume, and . . .

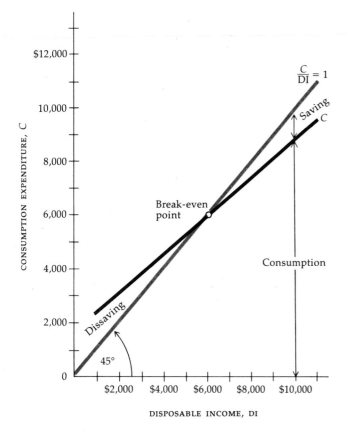

. . . the S curve denotes the propensity to save.

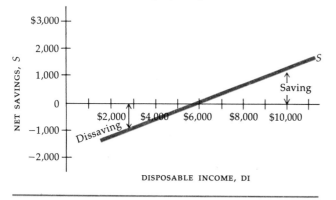

called the *propensity to consume* or the *consumption function*. The word "function" is thus used here in its mathematical sense to mean a quantity whose value depends on the value of another quantity, e.g., the value of consumption *depends on* the value of income.

You will find it helpful to look up the different meanings of "function" in a good dictionary. Meanwhile, note that the consumption curve C is the family's propensity-to-consume curve, with all other things held constant.

THE PROPENSITY TO SAVE

Since saving is the difference between income and consumption, and since consumption depends on income, it follows that saving also depends on income.

The graph of the savings data in the third column of the table, taken together with the first column, is shown in the lower panel of Exhibit 3. This time, disposable income is again measured on the horizontal axis, but savings are now scaled vertically. Graphically, the saving curve S depicts the vertical differences between the diagonal line and the consumption curve in the upper chart.

The level of saving depends on the level of income. This relation between saving and income is called the *propensity to save* or the *saving function*.

Thus the saving curve S is the family's propensity-to-save curve.

AVERAGE PROPENSITIES TO CONSUME AND TO SAVE

What will the family's *average* consumption be in relation to its income? What will be its *average* amount of saving? The answers are given in columns (4) and (5) of Exhibit 2.

The *average propensity to consume, APC,* is simply the ratio of consumption to income. It tells you the proportion of each income level that the family will spend on consumption. Similarly, the *average propensity to save, APS,* is the ratio of saving to income, and tells you the proportion of each income level that the family will save—i.e., not spend on consumption. For example, at an income level of $10,000, the family will spend 88 cents of each dollar or a total of $8,800, and it will save 12 cents of each dollar or a total of $1,200. In other words, it will spend 88 percent of its income, and save 12 percent.

Note that as income increases, *APC* decreases; therefore *APS* increases since both must total to 1 (or 100 percent) at each income level. What can you learn from the fact that *APC* declines with rising incomes? Basically, this tendency confirms the everyday observation that the rich save a larger proportion of their incomes than the poor. You probably would have guessed this without looking at the figures in the table; but they help to fix this important notion more firmly in your mind.

MARGINAL PROPENSITIES TO CONSUME AND TO SAVE

It is important to know the amount of each *extra* dollar of income that the family will spend on consumption, and the amount it will save. These amounts are shown in the remaining two columns of Exhibit 2.

The *marginal propensity to consume, MPC,* is the change in total consumption resulting from a unit change in income. As you can see from the table, the formula for calculating *MPC* is

$$MPC = \frac{\text{change in total consumption}}{\text{change in income}}$$

The *MPC* tells you *the fraction of each extra dollar of income that goes into consumption.* An *MPC* of 0.70, for instance, means that 70 percent of any increase in income will be spent on consumption.

The *marginal propensity to save, MPS,* is the change in total saving resulting from a unit change in income. Its formula is:

$$MPS = \frac{\text{change in total saving}}{\text{change in income}}$$

The *MPS* thus tells you *the fraction of each extra dollar of income that goes into saving.* An *MPS* of 0.30, for example, means that 30 percent of any increase in income will be saved.

What is the difference between *APC* and *MPC*? Between *APS* and *MPS*? At any given level of income, the *APC* relates total consumption to income, whereas the *MPC* relates a *change* in total consumption to a *change* in income. The "average" may thus be quite different from the "marginal," as you can see from the table. The same kind of reasoning applies to *APS* and *MPS*. The "average" and the "marginal" tell you two distinctly different things. Note from the table, however, that just as *APC* and *APS* must always total 1 (or 100 percent) at any income *level, MPC* and *MPS* must always total 1 (or 100 percent) for each *change* in income.

By now you have probably recognized an important idea:

Since the *MPC* is the change in total consumption resulting from a unit change in income, it measures the *slope* (steepness) of the consumption function or line. The slope of any straight line is always measured by the change in its vertical distance resulting from (divided by) the change in its horizontal distance. Thus for the accompanying line:

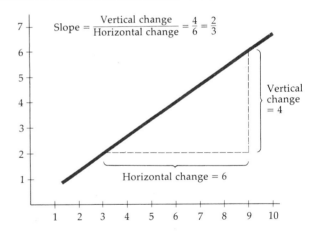

Similarly, the *MPS* measures the slope of the saving line. You should be able to verify that the slope of a straight line is the same at every point. This is why the table shows all values of *MPC* as equal and all values of *MPS* as equal: the consumption curve and the saving curve in this example are each straight lines.

NATIONAL CONSUMPTION FUNCTIONS

What would a consumption function for the nation as a whole look like? One possibility is illustrated in Exhibit 4.

The dots in the diagram represent the coordinates of income and consumption, but each dot has been labeled with its corresponding year. Thus the dot identified as "65" enables you to estimate from the chart the level of income and consumption for the year 1965—and similarly with every other dot. The consumption line is then drawn in to represent a kind of "average" of all of the dots.

This diagram illustrates a long-run *empirical* consumption function based on actual data covering a *period*. It thus differs from the short-run *theoretical* type of consumption function that we studied previously, which represented an assumed relationship between consumption expenditures and income at a given *moment*.

TWO KINDS OF CHANGES

There are some important theoretical implications of the diagram in Exhibit 4. For instance, the upward

chronological trend of the dots tells you there has been a *change in the amount consumed*—specifically, an increase in the amount consumed as income has risen over the years. If the chronological trend of the dots had been downward, the chart would have portrayed a decrease in the amount consumed as income declines. Thus, whether upward or downward, a change in the amount consumed always refers to a movement along the same consumption curve resulting from a change in the level of income while all other factors remain the same.

A second type of movement not shown in Exhibit 4 is a *change in consumption*—specifically, an increase in consumption, whereby the curve shifts to a higher level, or a decrease in consumption, shown by a shift of the curve to a lower level. This is illustrated by the curves in Exhibit 5. An increase in consumption from curve C_0 to curve C_1 means that at any given level of income people are now willing to consume more and save less than they were willing to consume and save before. What does a decrease from curve C_0 to curve C_2 mean?

The consumption curve—i.e., the consumption function or propensity to consume—may shift as a result of a change in any one of the "all other" things that were assumed to remain constant when the curve was initially drawn. What are these factors? Some of the more important ones are:

1. The volume of liquid assets (e.g., currency, stocks, bonds, etc.) owned by households

2. Expectations of future prices and incomes

3. Anticipations of product shortages (resulting, for example, from wars, strikes, etc.)

4. Credit conditions

An increase in any one of these factors (as well as several others you may be able to think of) can result in an increase in consumption by shifting the curve upward; a decrease in any one can result in a decrease in consumption by shifting the curve downward. Since all four of these factors have changed significantly during the past several decades we cannot be sure of the *true* consumption function for the economy at any given time—or even over the long run. At best, any consumption function based on actual data is a *working assumption* that

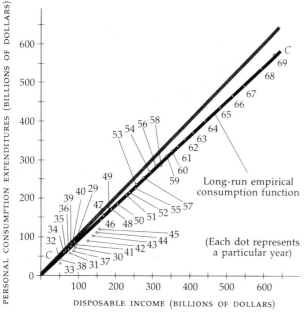

Exhibit 4

Consumer Expenditures and Disposable Personal Income

Long-run empirical consumption function

(Each dot represents a particular year)

Exhibit 5

Changes in Consumption and Saving

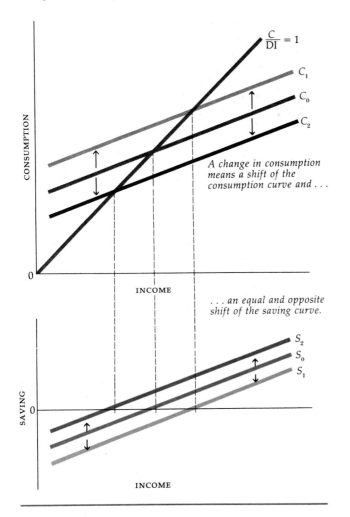

$$\frac{C}{DI} = 1$$

A change in consumption
means a shift of the
consumption curve and . . .

. . . an equal and opposite
shift of the saving curve.

helps to explain the real relationships between consumption and income. We can use it as long as it serves this purpose, or until we learn enough to be able to formulate a better hypothesis. This is the nature of science.

Private Investment Demand

The second component of aggregate demand is investment. Private *investment* demand consists of planned or desired additions to plant, equipment, inventories, etc.

If you were a businessman, what would determine your decision to invest? The fundamental answer, of course, is your profit expectation. If you think a new machine would add to your profit, you will try to purchase it; if you believe that an additional wing on your factory would yield greater profits, you will try to build it.

The profit from an addition to capital is usually expressed as a percent or rate of return on the investment. Economists call the expected rate of return on an investment the *marginal efficiency of investment, MEI.* Thus you might have an *MEI* of 15 percent for one type of investment, 25 percent for another, and so on. The *MEI* will be influenced by many factors, but at least four are particularly important:

1. Expected product demand. To an individual businessman, the *expected* net return on his investment will depend to a large extent on the demand that he anticipates for his product. For the economy as a whole, the expected return on new investment will be influenced by total consumer spending on the products of businesses.

2. Technology and innovation. The development of improved new products and better ways of doing things will tend to reduce businessmen's costs and hence raise their profit expectations and *MEI.*

3. Production costs. If businessmen expect increases in their production costs, this may tend to reduce their *MEI.* Conversely, if they expect reductions in their production costs, this may tend to increase their *MEI.* Some of the factors that will have an influence on production costs are union wage policies, taxes (which businessmen often view as "costs" of doing business), and the prices of raw materials.

4. Stock of capital. The greater the quantity of capital in the form of productive facilities and inventories that exist in a given industry, the greater the industry's capacity—perhaps even excess capacity—to meet future market demands at modest levels of profit, and hence the lower its *MEI.* If this notion is extended to a national scale, it provides a partial explanation of why the long-run trend of private investment has sometimes been a declining percentage of GNP for many years at a time.

THE "MEI" AND THE INTEREST RATE

What does a business firm's *MEI* curve look like? At any given time a firm is faced with alternative investment outlets—such as renovating its existing plant, adding a wing to a factory, replacing existing machines, purchasing a fleet of trucks, and so on. Each of these projects compete for a firm's limited funds, but some are expected to be more profitable than others. Hence we may imagine that the managers of a firm *rank* alternative investment projects in decreasing order of their *MEIs* as shown in the upper panel of Exhibit 6. The downward-sloping direction of the curve can be attributed to the fact that for a given degree of risk, there are fewer investment opportunities available to a firm at relatively higher, as compared to lower, rates of return. This means that the volume of investment a firm can undertake varies inversely with its expected rate of return.

At the same time there is also an interest rate in the market which represents the current cost of borrowed funds. If the interest rate is the *cost of (money) capital* to a firm, then a higher interest cost will mean a smaller expected return after allowance for interest cost, and hence a lower volume of investment. Conversely a lower interest cost will mean a greater expected return after allowance for interest cost, and therefore a higher level of investment. We may conclude that in general terms:

Investment by a firm occurs when the *MEI* or expected rate of return on an addition to investment exceeds the rate of interest or cost of capital that is incurred in making the investment.

For example, look again at the upper panel of Exhibit 6. The graph shows that at an interest cost of 20 percent, this particular firm would demand $1 million for investment, because each of the dollars that it spent on its investment projects *up to* $1 million has an *MEI* greater than 20 percent as shown by the portion of the curve above the 20 percent level. Similarly, at an interest cost of 10 percent the firm

Exhibit 6

Private Investment

At any given time, the MEI curve shows the amount of investment that a firm will undertake at various interest costs. Hence the MEI is the firm's demand curve for investment.

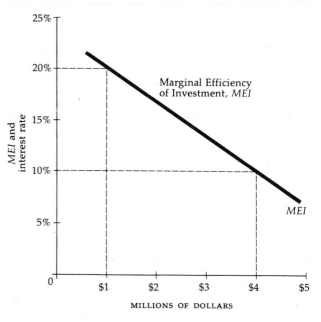

Over a period of years, private investment spending fluctuates widely.

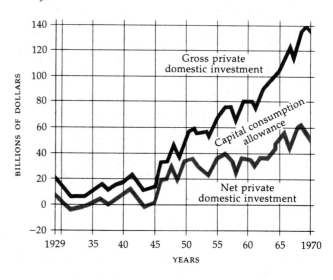

would demand $4 million for investment, while each of its dollars *up to* that amount yields an *MEI* greater than 10 percent.

This analysis leads to two important principles. *At any given time:*

1. A demand curve relates the quantities of a commodity that buyers would be willing and able to purchase at various prices. In this case the prices are interest rates. Hence the *MEI* curve shows the amounts of investment that a firm would be willing and able to undertake at various interest rates. It follows that *a firm's MEI curve is its demand curve for investment.*

2. Each firm will have its own *MEI* curve based on its particular investment needs and expectations. If we aggregate all of the individual *MEI* curves, we get the *MEI* curve for the economy as a whole. This represents the total demand for private investment at different rates of interest.

What about the level of private investment over a *period of time?* Here we arrive at another important principle. Since private investment is affected by expected rates of return, and since the factors determining it obviously do not remain constant, the economy's level of private investment is highly unstable from year to year as can be seen from the lower panel of Exhibit 6. Indeed, *fluctuation in private investment over the years is the single most important cause of fluctuations in income and employment—i.e., the major reason for prosperities and recessions.*

Government Demand and Net Foreign Demand

The remaining components of aggregate demand stem from government and from international sources. Government demand depends to a large extent on public needs (such as highways, schools, and welfare) and on defense requirements. The volume of government demand is independent of profit expectations and, beyond the minimum levels required by society, is determined at will by government. There is no scientific law or guiding set of principles which we can use to determine changes in

the level of public investment. Nevertheless, we shall have more to say about it in later chapters.

Net foreign demand plays a relatively passive and fortuitous role in our economy. Since it represents the difference between our exports and our imports, it will depend on such things as tariff and quota policies, relative prices and incomes between nations, foreign exchange rates and restrictions, the level of economic activity here and abroad, and so on. As with public investment, there are no guiding principles for predicting foreign investment. Moreover, it constitutes for the United States a very small proportion of expenditure on GNP (typically much less than 1 percent) and hence we may neglect it for purposes of income and employment analysis.

Reviewing the Basic Relationships

We now have the basic building blocks that are needed for understanding the elementary theory of income and employment. The further development of this theory awaits us in the next chapter. In the meantime, you can test your understanding of the basic relationships learned thus far by verifying the truth of the equations presented in Exhibit 7.

SUMMARY OF IMPORTANT IDEAS

1. The *classical theory* of income and employment holds that in a competitive capitalistic system, supply creates its own demand: aggregate demand equals aggregate income or output. Hence the economy automatically tends toward full employment through the free operation of the market system in which prices, wages, and interest rates are free to adjust to their full employment levels.

2. The *modern theory* of income and employment argues that aggregate demand may be greater than, equal to, or less than aggregate income; that the interest rate need not equate intended saving and intended investment because these are done by different people for different purposes; and that

Exhibit 7

Some Key Relationships in the Theory of Income and Employment

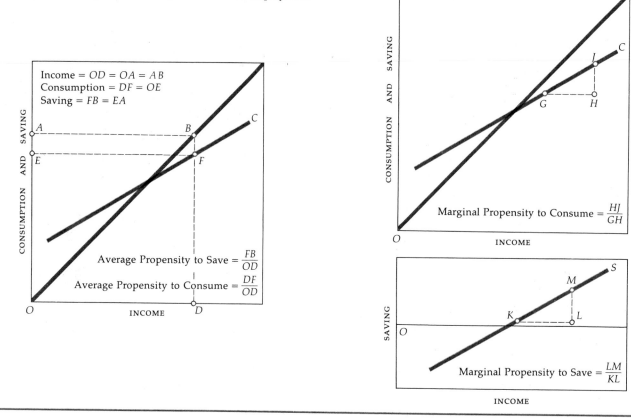

Income = $OD = OA = AB$
Consumption = $DF = OE$
Saving = $FB = EA$

Average Propensity to Save = $\dfrac{FB}{OD}$

Average Propensity to Consume = $\dfrac{DF}{OD}$

Marginal Propensity to Consume = $\dfrac{HJ}{GH}$

Marginal Propensity to Save = $\dfrac{LM}{KL}$

prices and wages are not flexible—especially on the downside—due to resistance by business monopolies, unions, minimum wage legislation, and other institutional forces. Hence the economy may not necessarily adjust itself to full employment equilibrium.

3. Some of the key variables of modern income and employment theory are consumption C and saving S. The propensity to consume (or the consumption function) and the propensity to save express the relationship of consumption to income and of saving to income. The average propensity to consume, *APC*, and to save, *APS*, tell you the fraction of any level of *total* income that is consumed and saved. Thus: $C + S =$ income, and $APC + APS = 1$ (or 100 percent).

The marginal propensity to consume, *MPC*, and to save, *MPS*, tell you the fraction (slope) of any *change* in income that is consumed and saved. Thus $MPC + MPS = 1$ (or 100 percent).

4. A *change in the amount consumed* means a movement along the consumption curve due to a change in income. A *change in consumption* means a shift of the entire consumption curve to a new level, due to a change in one or more of the "all other" things that are assumed to be constant when the curve is initially drawn. These factors include: the volume of liquid assets owned by households; expectations of future prices and income; anticipations of product shortages; and credit conditions.

5. Investment demand is another major variable in income and employment theory. The expected rate of return on an investment is called the marginal efficiency of investment, *MEI,* and is determined by such factors as expected product demand, the rate of technology and innovation, production costs, and the stock of capital. Investment occurs when the *MEI* exceeds the rate of interest or cost of (money) capital that is incurred in making the investment. In general, therefore, since private investment spending depends on profit expectations of businessmen, it tends to be highly volatile over the years.

FOR HOMEWORK AND DISCUSSION

1. *Terms and concepts to review:*

classical economics	propensity to save
New Economics	average propensity to consume
Say's Law	
aggregate demand	average propensity to save
aggregate supply	
saving	marginal propensity to consume
interest	
consumption	marginal propensity to save
investment	slope
Engel's Laws	change in amount consumed
dissaving	
propensity to consume	change in consumption
consumption function	marginal efficiency of investment

2. Of what significance are interest rates and prices in the classical model?

3. Does Say's Law apply to *individual* goods? Explain.

4. Why do people save? Why do businessmen invest?

5. During a recession, a firm will probably increase its sales if it cuts its prices, and it will reduce its costs if it cuts its wages. It follows that the whole economy will be better off if all firms do this. True or false? Comment.

6. Express Engel's Laws in terms of the average propensity to consume, *APC.*

7. Why does the *APC* differ from the *MPC? APS* from *MPS?*

8. What factors other then income are likely to be most important in determining consumption?

9. What factors determine investment? Why is investment more unstable than consumption?

REFERENCES AND READING SUGGESTIONS

HEILBRONER, ROBERT L., *The Worldly Philosophers,* 3d ed., Prentice-Hall, Englewood Cliffs, N.J., 1969.

SCHULTZE, CHARLES L., *National Income Analysis,* 2d ed., Prentice-Hall, Englewood Cliffs, N.J., 1967, chaps. 3, 4.

SHAPIRO, EDWARD, *Macroeconomic Analysis,* 2d ed., Harcourt-Brace & World, New York, 1970, chaps. 6, 7.

STEWART, MICHAEL, *Keynes and After,* Penguin, Baltimore, 1967.

CHAPTER 10

Income and Employment Determination

CHAPTER PREVIEW

How do consumption and investment combine to determine an equilibrium level of income and employment?

What influences do changes in net investment have on the level of income? Is it possible for income to change by some multiple of the change in investment?

How do changes in saving, when not offset by changes in investment, affect the level of income and output?

What pressures, either inflationary or deflationary, are created in the economy when total spending on consumption and investment fails to correspond with full employment levels?

The crucial factor in determining whether we live in a state of full employment or unemployment is the level of investment. However, the level of investment must be discussed in conjunction with the levels of consumption and saving in order to understand how the three variables interact to bring about equilibrium in the economy as a whole.

After completing this chapter we shall be able better to analyze the way in which economic fluctuations arise, and to propose government policies designed to minimize them. Those policies are of great importance; upon their success depends the achievement of stable economic growth, and full employment without inflation.

The Simple Theory of Income and Employment Determination

The time has come to join together the concepts of consumption, saving, and investment into a meaningful whole. We then build an exciting model which helps to explain how income and employment are determined in an economic system.

Examine carefully the hypothetical model illustrated in Exhibit 1. This model shows how an equilibrium level of income and employment is established. The table and charts provide three different ways of viewing the same basic ideas, while the following comments will add to your understanding.

Exhibit 1

Determination of Income and Employment Equilibrium

(hypothetical economy—all dollars in billions)

Two different views of the same idea:

1. By a table

(1) Aggregate supply (output = income)* NNP = DI	(2) Level of employment (millions)	(3) Consumption C	(4) Saving S (1) − (3)	(5) Private investment I	(6) Aggregate demand C + I (3) + (5)	(7) Tendency of income and employment
$400	40	$430	$ −30	$30	$460	increase
450	50	450	0	30	480	increase
500	60	470	30	30	500	equilibrium
550	70	490	60	30	520	decrease
600	80	510	90	30	540	decrease
650	90	530	120	30	560	decrease

* Includes only the private sector (households and firms), not the public sector (government) or the international sector. Also, households are assumed to be the sole source of savings. Therefore, NNP as a measure of aggregate supply equals NI, PI, and DI because there are no taxes, transfer payments, etc., since there is no presence of government. Thus, the total income received by households (DI) equals the net value of the economy's output (NNP).

STRUCTURE OF THE MODEL

Columns (1) and (2) tell you that for every level of income and output there is a corresponding level of employment. Thus increases in output bring with them increases in employment.

Columns (3) and (4) say that consumption and saving also increase as income in column (1) increases. This is what you would expect from your knowledge of the propensities to consume and to save. Graphically, the consumption schedule *C* is shown in chart A, and the saving schedule *S* in chart B.

Now look at column (5) of the table. Why is investment the same at all levels of aggregate supply?

As pointed out in the previous chapter, businessmen's investment plans are largely independent of current income and output levels. They depend instead on the marginal efficiency of investment relative to the interest rate—the former determined by such factors as expected product demand, the rate of technology and innovation, the level of production costs, and the stock of capital. Thus the investment schedule *I* can be drawn as a horizontal line in chart B, because we *assume* that it remains fairly stable in relation to output (although it varies widely over time as we have already seen). This assumption, which is convenient for our simple theoretical model, will be relaxed later on as more complex considerations are introduced.

2. By a graph

Chart A.   By intersection of $C + I$ curve with 45° line

Chart B.   By intersection of S and I curves

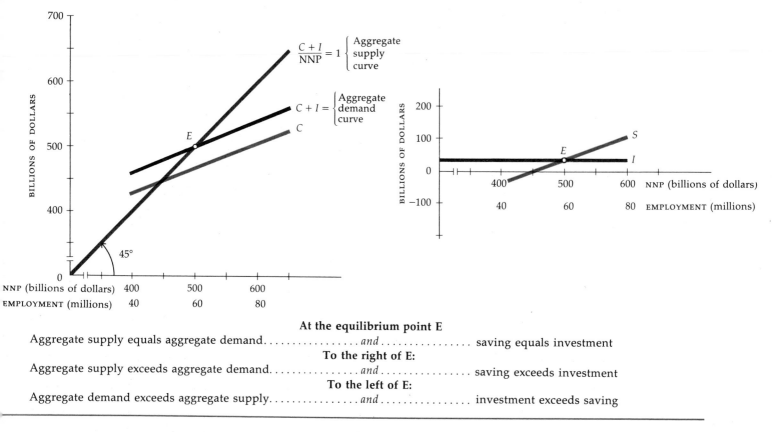

At the equilibrium point E
Aggregate supply equals aggregate demand. . . . . *and* . . . . saving equals investment
To the right of E:
Aggregate supply exceeds aggregate demand. . . . . *and* . . . . saving exceeds investment
To the left of E:
Aggregate demand exceeds aggregate supply. . . . . *and* . . . . investment exceeds saving

In column (6) of the table, aggregate demand is simply the sum of consumption and investment at each income or output level. This is represented by the $C + I$ curve in chart A.

HOW ARE INCOME AND EMPLOYMENT DETERMINED? THE EQUILIBRIUM LEVEL

What will be the level of income and employment? In other words, since NNP = NI = DI in this model, where will the level of output and the corresponding level of employment finally settle? In order to find out, we may look to the table as well as the two charts.

Column (7) points out that, at the *equilibrium* level of output, aggregate supply creates a level of aggre-

gate demand which is exactly equal to that level of output. This is also the level of income, output, and employment at which saving equals investment. The equilibrium point E in the charts depicts these notions graphically.

Thus, what happens to the right of E in chart A when aggregate supply exceeds aggregate demand, or in chart B when the amount that households intend to save exceeds the amount that businessmen intend to invest? The answer is that businessmen find their sales to be less than they anticipated and their inventories pile up, so they cut back on production and lay off workers. This reduces NNP, income, and the level of employment, thereby moving the system westward toward E.

Conversely, suppose the system is to the left of E. Then, in Chart A, aggregate demand exceeds aggregate supply, and in Chart B, businessmen's intended investment exceeds households' intended saving. Households are consuming goods at a faster rate than firms are producing them, and business inventories are being depleted. Businessmen will thus seek to expand their production and to hire more workers, thereby increasing both NNP and the level of employment. In this way the system moves eastward toward E.

To Summarize

The equilibrium level of output does not necessarily occur at the full employment level of output. A capitalistic economic system may be in equilibrium at a level of income and output which is less than full employment, and the system will have no tendency to change from its equilibrium position.

These ideas can also be illustrated pictorially by the "bathtub theorem" in Exhibit 2.

Exhibit 2

The "Bathtub Theorem"

The water in the bathtub can be in equilibrium at any level as long as the inflow equals the outflow. If the inflow exceeds the outflow, the level in the tub will rise. If the outflow exceeds the inflow, the level in the tub will fall.

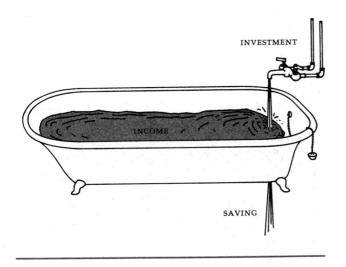

The Multiplier Principle

You already know that an increase in net investment will cause an increase in income; a decrease in net investment will cause a decrease in income. But what you may not know is that:

An increase in net investment will cause a magnified increase in income and output, and a decrease in net investment will cause a magnified decrease in income and output. Investment spending thus has an amplifying effect on economic activity. The amount by which a change in investment is multiplied to produce a change in income and output is called *the multiplier.*

For instance, if an increase in investment of $5 billion causes an increase in income and output of $10 billion, the multiplier is 2. If instead the increase in income and output is $15 billion, the multiplier is 3. How does the multiplier work? It can be illustrated in three ways: numerically by a table, graphically by a chart, and algebraically by a formula.

NUMERICAL ILLUSTRATION

Suppose the management of a company decides to build a $1,000,000 addition to its factory. If the owners of the factors of production hired to do the job—the bricklayers, materials suppliers, etc.—all have an MPC of $\frac{4}{5}$ and hence an MPS of $\frac{1}{5}$, they will tend to spend four-fifths and save one-fifth of any additional income they receive.

Let us assume for simplicity that the company pays out the entire $1,000,000 at one time, as shown in Exhibit 3. In Round 1, therefore, the total income of the resource owners increases by $1,000,000. Out of this, the income recipients increase their consumption by four-fifths or $800,000 and their savings by one-fifth or $200,000.

In Round 2, when this four-fifths is spent, firms find their sales increasing and their inventories decreasing; they therefore hire more resources in order to increase their production, thereby creating $800,000 of income for the owners of these resources. These income recipients then increase their consumption by four-fifths or $640,000, and their saving by one-fifth or $160,000. In Round 3 and in all subsequent rounds, the process is repeated as $\frac{4}{5}$ of each increase in income is spent and is thereby added to the income stream.

Thus, from an original investment of $1,000,000, the company has brought about an ultimate increase in income of $5,000,000. The multiplier is therefore 5. This overall increase in income consists of a $4,000,000 increase in consumption plus a $1,000,000 increase in saving. The latter is always the amount of the original investment, as you can verify by tracing the steps through the table.

Note from the table that the greatest increases in income occur during the first few rounds. After that the income effects tend to fade away—much like the ripples caused by a stone dropped into a pond.

GRAPHICAL ILLUSTRATION

Exhibit 4 presents a different example, showing graphically the multiplier effect of an increase in

---

Exhibit 3

The Multiplier Illustrated Numerically

$MPC = \frac{4}{5}$
$MPS = \frac{1}{5}$
Multiplier = 5

Round	Increase in income	Increase in consumption $MPC = \frac{4}{5}$	Increase in saving $MPS = \frac{1}{5}$
1.*	$1,000,000 →	$ 800,000	$ 200,000
2.	800,000 →	640,000	160,000
3.	640,000 →	512,000	128,000
4.	512,000 →	409,600	102,400
5.	409,600 →	327,680	81,920
6.	327,680 →	262,144	65,536
All other rounds	1,310,720	1,048,576	262,144
Totals	$5,000,000	$4,000,000	$1,000,000

* Original investment = $1,000,000

Exhibit 4

The Multiplier Effect Shown Graphically

$MPC = \frac{1}{2}$
$MPS = \frac{1}{2}$
Multiplier = 2

An increase in the level of investment by $50 billion causes an increase in the level of income by $100 billion. Hence the multiplier is 2.

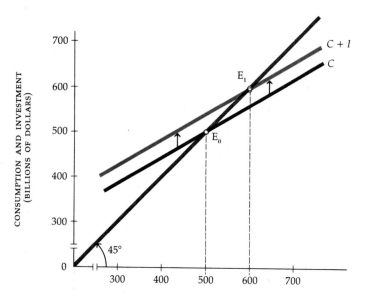

What happens to income if investment falls back to zero? To a negative number such as −$50 billion?

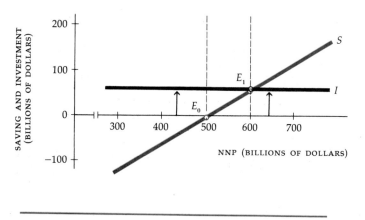

investment. This time the *MPC* and *MPS* are each equal to $\frac{1}{2}$. The point E_0 in both charts represents an equilibrium level at which all income is being spent on consumption and there is no saving or investment. The point E_1 defines a new equilibrium resulting from an increase in investment. Note from the description accompanying the charts that the increase in income is a *multiple* of the increase in investment.

Can you see that the multiplier also works in reverse? What happens to income if investment falls back to its initial level?

FORMULA ILLUSTRATION

The tabular and graphical illustrations of the multiplier demonstrate that the increase in income is related to the marginal propensities to consume and to save. For example, it has already been established in the previous chapter that

$$MPC + MPS = 1$$

Therefore by "transposing":

$$MPS = 1 - MPC$$

Further, you can readily verify from the information given in Exhibits 3 and 4 that

$$\text{Multiplier} = \frac{1}{MPS} = \frac{1}{1 - MPC}$$

This means that if you know either the *MPC* or the *MPS*, you can determine the multiplier immediately. Do this for the *MPC* and *MPS* figures given in Exhibits 3 and 4. Then, once you know the value of the multiplier, you can predict the ultimate change in income resulting from a change in investment by the formula:

Multiplier × change in investment = change in income

The same formula applies to a decrease as well as an increase in investment. Go back and check it out in Exhibits 3 and 4, just to make sure that you see how it works.

Notice that *the multiplier is the reciprocal of the* MPS. (The reciprocal of a number is 1 divided by that number.) Thus the lower the *MPS*, the less "leakage" into extra saving that occurs at each round of income, and hence the greater the *MPC*; therefore the greater the value of the multiplier. Conversely, the greater the *MPS*, the lower the *MPC*, and hence the lower the value of the multiplier.

To Summarize

The *multiplier* principle states that changes in investment bring about magnified changes in income, as expressed by the equation: multiplier × change in investment = change in income. The formula for the multiplier coefficient is thus:

$$\text{Multiplier} = \frac{\text{change in income}}{\text{change in investment}}$$
$$= \frac{1}{MPS} = \frac{1}{1 - MPC}$$

where *MPS* stands for the marginal propensity to save, and *MPC* the marginal propensity to consume. (NOTE: This multiplier is also sometimes called the *investment multiplier* in order to distinguish it from other types of multipliers in economics.)

The Paradox of Thrift

The multiplier principle states that any increase (or decrease) in investment sets in motion a multiple expansion (or contraction) of income. But do changes in saving or consumption also bring about a multiplied effect on income? The answer is yes—as your intuition would probably lead you to believe. But you can sharpen that intuition with some diagrams.

Take a look at the upper chart in Exhibit 5. It illustrates the effect of an increase in saving (or equivalently, the effect of a decrease in consumption) on income and output. An increase in saving, such as from S_0 to S_1 means that at any given level of income households now plan to save more than they planned to save before. This might occur if they expect a recession and hence want to be better prepared for future contingencies.

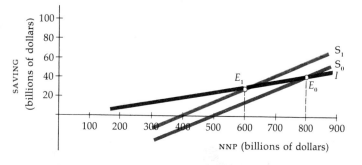

Exhibit 5

Effect of an Increase in Saving

An increase in saving causes a multiplied decrease in NNP, but at the new equilibrium point E_1, saving is the same as it was previously at E_0.

If investment depends on income so that the I curve slopes upward, the shift from S_0 to S_1 reduces income and therefore causes investment to fall. Note that at E_1, saving is less than it was at E_0.

Can you estimate the changes involved in each diagram?

The lower chart in Exhibit 5 reflects the same idea as the upper one, but now the investment curve is drawn with a moderate upward tilt. This indicates the more realistic fact that investment is not completely *autonomous*—i.e., independent of income, output, and general economic activity as we have assumed until now for the sake of simplicity. More likely, investment in the economy will tend to grow somewhat with expanding income and output, because businessmen become more optimistic and are willing to spend more on investment goods as economic activity increases. We are thus relaxing the assumption of a horizontal investment curve, as was promised earlier.

This tendency of rising economic activity to stimulate higher levels of investment is called *induced investment*. Note that as a result of a rising *I* curve, the multiplier effect on output resulting from an increase in saving is even greater than in the upper chart.

What does the new equilibrium at E_1 as compared to E_0 tell us? As Exhibit 5 illustrates: *A small upward shift of the saving curve (or downward shift of the consumption curve) when not offset by an upward shift of the investment curve will cause a multiplied decrease in income and output.* This results in an interesting paradox:

An increase in thrift may be desirable for an individual family because it can lead to greater saving and wealth. However, it may be undesirable for all of society because it leads to reductions in income, output, and employment, and under certain circumstances will lead to a reduction in society's rate of saving. This is the *paradox of thrift*. Thus what is good for an individual is not necessarily good for everyone. (What logical fallacy is demonstrated by this paradox?)

The paradox of thrift leads to a remarkable economic implication. If in a recession there is an upward shift of the savings curve because households in general save more (consume less), they should be doing exactly the opposite if they want to improve their own and society's economic well-being—unless their actions can be offset by an upward shift in the investment curve. We shall learn more about this implication in a later chapter.

Inflationary and Deflationary Gaps

The modern theory of income and employment demonstrates that the level of aggregate demand may be greater than, equal to, or less than the level

Chapter 10 Income and Employment 161

of aggregate supply. These three possibilities are shown in Exhibit 6.

The amount by which aggregate demand (equal to $C + I$) exceeds aggregate supply at full employment is called the *inflationary gap*, because the excess volume of total spending when resources are already fully employed creates inflationary pressures that pull up prices and hence the *money* rather than the *real* value of NNP. Conversely, the amount by which aggregate demand falls short of aggregate supply is called the *deflationary gap*, because the deficiency of total spending pulls down the *real* value of NNP.

Obviously, therefore,

In order to close an inflationary gap, we have to find ways of reducing aggregate demand; in order to close a deflationary gap, we have to find ways of increasing aggregate demand.

In general, the economy does not move automatically toward full employment equilibrium. Indeed, an inflationary gap, for instance, could create an upward spiral of further price inflation as businessmen grant union demands for wage increases, and then proceed to compensate for these demands with price increases.

As you will soon see, although the modern theory of income and employment was born in the depression of the thirties, it can be used to study "inflation economics" as well as "recession economics."

Exhibit 6

Inflationary and Deflationary Gaps

Inflationary and deflationary gaps are always measured at the full employment level, and are shown by the vertical distances.

This model assumes for simplicity that prices are constant up to the level of full employment, and thereafter turn up sharply. In reality, they would tend to turn up as the economy approached full employment, and continue to rise at steeper and steeper rates.

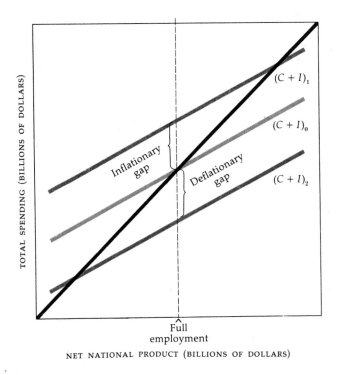

NET NATIONAL PRODUCT (BILLIONS OF DOLLARS)

SUMMARY OF IMPORTANT IDEAS

1. The equilibrium level of NNP occurs where aggregate supply = aggregate demand, which is also where saving = investment. If aggregate supply exceeds aggregate demand, or planned saving exceeds planned investment, output, income, and employment fall. If aggregate supply is less than aggregate demand, or planned saving is less than planned investment, output, income, and employment rise.

2. Any increase (or decrease) in investment causes a multiple expansion (or contraction) of income. Any changes in consumption, or saving, similarly produce multiple effects on income. All such effects are called *multiplier effects*. The investment multiplier, which shows how changes in investment cause magnified changes in income, is equal to the reciprocal of the marginal propensity to save.

3. The *paradox of thrift* tells us that although an increase in saving may be desirable for an individual, a general increase in saving by society can actually reduce income and employment. Therefore, what is good for an individual is not necessarily good for society.

4. The amount by which aggregate demand exceeds the full employment aggregate supply is called the inflationary gap; the amount by which it falls short is called the deflationary gap. There is no automatic tendency for the two to be equal. Hence methods must be found to close these gaps if a capitalistic economy is to maintain full employment without inflation.

FOR HOMEWORK AND DISCUSSION

1. *Terms and concepts to review:*

multiplier	induced investment
paradox of thrift	inflationary gap
autonomous investment	deflationary gap

2. Complete the following table for a hypothetical economy. (All figures are in billions of dollars.) Assume that the propensity to consume is linear and that investment is constant at all levels of income.

NNP = DI	C	S	I	APC	APS	MPC	MPS
$100	$125		$25				
200	200						
300							
400							
500							

a. From the data in the table, draw a graph of the consumption function and of the consumption -plus-investment function. Underneath your chart, draw a graph of the saving and investment curves and connect the two sets of break-even points with vertical dashed lines.

b. Has there been a multiplier effect as a result of the increase in investment? If yes, by how much? What is the numerical value of the multiplier?

c. What is the equilibrium level of income and output before and after the increase in investment?

d. What will income be if investment increases by $10 billion?

3. How does the size of the multiplier vary with MPC? MPS? Explain why, without using any equations.

4. Distinguish between the individual and community viewpoints concerning the desirability of thrift.

5. Can you suggest at least one method of closing inflationary or deflationary gaps?

REFERENCES AND READING SUGGESTIONS

DILLARD, DUDLEY, *The Economics of John Maynard Keynes*, Prentice-Hall, Englewood Cliffs, N.J., 1948.

MCKENNA, JOSEPH P., *Aggregate Economic Analysis*, 3d ed., Holt, Rinehart & Winston, New York, 1969, chap. 4.

PETERSON, WALLACE C., *Income, Employment, and Economic Growth*, rev. ed., Norton, New York, 1967, chaps. 5–9.

SHAPIRO, EDWARD, *Macroeconomic Analysis*, 2d ed., Harcourt, Brace & World, New York, 1970, chaps. 7–12.

CHAPTER 11

Modern Business Cycle Analysis: The Multiplier and the Accelerator

What happens to the "multiplier effect" if there is a succession of investment expenditures instead of a single investment expenditure? Are any forces at work which reduce the effectiveness of the multiplier?

The multiplier principle shows how changes in investment work through consumption to cause changes in income. But there is a "reverse" principle which shows how changes in consumption may cause changes in investment. How does this principle operate?

What happens when these two principles are combined so that they work simultaneously? Can they generate business cycles? Can they provide us with a better understanding of such cycles?

We have learned that business cycles are recurrent but nonperiodic fluctuations in economic activity, and that such cycles have existed in the United States as far back as the records go. We have also learned about the basic concepts entering into the modern theory of income and employment—concepts like consumption, saving, and investment—and have studied some of the important relationships that tie these concepts together.

Our task now is to extend the theory of income and employment so that it can be used to analyze business cycles. The theory will then provide a much better explanation of why and how economic fluctuations occur.

Further Aspects of the Multiplier Principle

There is considerably more to the theory of the multiplier than our simple treatment of it thus far. In view of its importance in modern business cycle analysis, it should be examined more closely.

The multiplier, as we already know, is related to the marginal propensities to consume and to save by the formula:

$$\text{Multiplier} = \frac{1}{1 - MPC} = \frac{1}{MPS}$$

Thus if the *MPC* is $\frac{1}{2}$, the multiplier is 2; if the *MPC* is $\frac{2}{3}$, the multiplier is 3; if the *MPC* is $\frac{3}{4}$, the multiplier is 4; and so on. In general, the multiplier increases as the *MPC* rises, and decreases as the *MPC* falls.

EFFECTS OF A SUSTAINED INJECTION

Let us assume that the *MPC* is $\frac{3}{4}$, and hence the multiplier is 4. Recalling from the previous chapter that

Multiplier × change in investment = change in income

it follows that a sustained increase in investment of, say, $1,000 should eventually increase income by four times that amount or $4,000. This is because three-quarters of each addition to income is spent on consumption in the next round, thus becoming new income which in turn is spent again.

Exhibit 1

The Multiplier Effects of a Sustained Injection

The successive increases in income will decline as a result of a sustained increase in investment. In this illustration, the MPC is $\frac{3}{4}$ and the multiplier is 4. Hence an injection of $1,000 into the income stream results in a cumulative increase in income of $4,000.

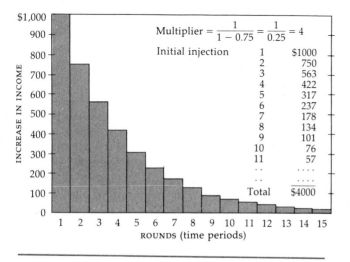

$$\text{Multiplier} = \frac{1}{1 - 0.75} = \frac{1}{0.25} = 4$$

Initial injection	1	$1000
	2	750
	3	563
	4	422
	5	317
	6	237
	7	178
	8	134
	9	101
	10	76
	11	57
	..	....
	..	....
Total		$4000

The process is illustrated by the chart in Exhibit 1. In Round 1, an injection of $1,000 of investment is made into the income stream. We already know that the recipients of this $1,000 will spend three-fourths and save one-fourth; hence $750 appears as added income in Round 2, as shown by the vertical bar. Of this, three-fourths, or $563, will be spent on consumption, thus adding to the economy's income in Round 3. The process continues in this way, with the *cumulation* of successive rounds of spending approaching a limit of $4,000, as shown in the chart.

EFFECTS OF MULTIPLE INJECTIONS

The multiplier principle was first introduced in 1931, and was amplified in subsequent years. In early expressions of the concept, a sustained injection was assumed, with the effects traced over a number of successive periods, as described above. However, when looked at as a cumulative process which undergoes expansions and contractions, the multiplier can produce wavelike movements in income that help to explain business cycles.

This viewpoint is illustrated in Exhibit 2. The *MPC* in this model is the same as before, namely $\frac{3}{4}$, and hence the multiplier is 4. If we assume that increases in spending represent government expenditure or some other source of increased money flow (the particular source of new spending is of no importance at this time), the chart is interpreted in the following manner:

1. The bottom bars are the same as in the previous chart; they show the successive increases in income resulting from an initial injection of $1,000.

2. In Round 2, an *additional injection* of $1,000 of investment is made, as shown by the upper bar. Income is then increased by this $1,000 *plus* $750 in the lower bar which resulted from the $1,000 of new investment that was injected in the previous round. The total increase in income is thus $1,750, as shown at the top of the upper bar.

3. In each of Rounds 3 through 6, there is an additional injection of $1,000, with the results tracing out the same successive sequence as before. The total increase in income thus rises to a peak of $3,289 in Round 6.

Exhibit 2

Multiplier Effects of Multiple Injections

(figures are rounded to nearest dollar)

$MPC = \frac{3}{4}$; $MPS = \frac{1}{4}$; Multiplier $= 4$

A new injection of $1,000 in each period adds to the total creation of income in that period. When no new injections are made after the sixth period, the increments in income fall off rapidly.

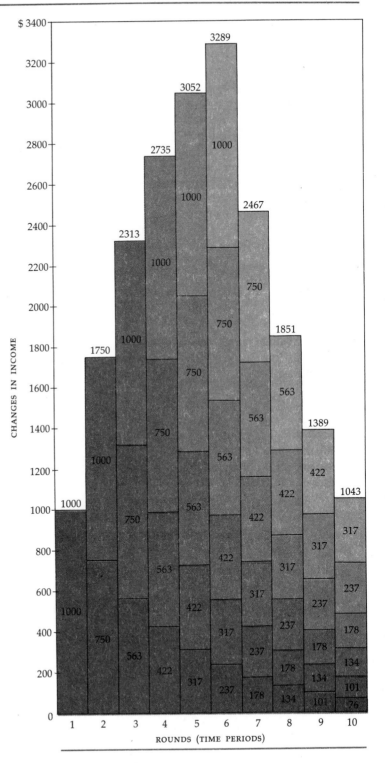

4. Beginning with Round 7, no additional injections are made; as a result, the total increments in income drop off rapidly to $2,467, then to $1,851 and so on.

This model assumes for simplicity that the *MPC* remains constant through all periods of changing investment and income, and hence that the multiplier is stable. In reality this is not likely to be so. We learned in an earlier chapter that changes in consumption and saving will be caused by a number of factors over the course of a business cycle, and hence the multiplier will also change since it varies directly with the *MPC* and inversely with the *MPS*.

SOME MODIFYING FACTORS

These illustrations of the multiplier principle suggest that the process operates in an exact way, and that it leads to precisely predictable results. Unfortunately, this is not the way it works in the real world. Certain difficulties exist which tend to modify the size of the multiplier, transforming it into a useful but blunt tool for predicting changes in total income resulting from changes in net investment. Among the more important ones:

1. The conventional multiplier model as developed above fails to distinguish between the effect of new investment on gross national income (which by definition equals gross national product) and on disposable personal income. Yet the difference is important because the marginal propensity to consume,

which is the factor that determines the size of the multiplier, will be influenced by the amount of change in disposable personal income.

Thus when a firm undertakes new investment, most of its expenditure, at least on the first round, becomes the gross income of its supplying firms such as steel mills, cement plants, and machinery producers. The latter organizations, as was learned in the study of national income accounting, retain part of their gross income for depreciation reserves and undistributed profits, pay part of it out in the form of taxes, and disburse part of it to those who supply them with productive services. Hence only a portion of the initial increase in gross income ends up in the pockets of consumers as disposable personal income. However, it is only the increase in the DPI portion that can induce an increase in consumption. Therefore, the actual size of the multiplier will be smaller than the "theoretical" size as calculated from the formula.

2. The conventional multiplier model does not recognize that different kinds of new investment may have different multiplier effects. For example, new spending for construction will not necessarily produce the same magnified increase in total income as new spending for defense goods—for two reasons: (a) the particular groups who receive the first increase in income resulting from a specific type of spending may have marginal propensities to consume that are higher or lower than the average of all consumers; and (b) some types of autonomous spending may create a more favorable business climate, thereby not only inducing increases in consumption, but also increases in investment which would not otherwise have occurred. For these reasons, it may be unrealistic to assume that the same total outcome will result from *different kinds* of new investment.

3. The conventional model is unable to predict the time required—the number of "rounds" in terms of weeks or months—for the full impact of the multiplier to be realized. The problem arises because it takes time for a portion of the increase in gross national income to filter down and become an increase in disposable personal income. This filtering process may take place rapidly or slowly. The rate at which it occurs will help determine how fast disposable personal income builds up within the economy, and hence the time it takes for the complete multiplier process to work itself out.

These are among the more important factors that impede the use of the conventional multiplier principle as a predictive device. Despite these limiting conditions, however, it is a powerful tool of economic theory. When used in conjunction with the accelerator principle described next, it provides the basis for understanding modern business cycle analysis.

The Accelerator Principle

In the multiplier theory, the path of interdependence runs from investment to consumption expenditure. But what about the reverse? Is it possible to have an interaction which runs from consumption to investment? Such a possibility does indeed exist, and the relationship this involves is known as the "accelerator principle."

The *accelerator principle* states that small changes in the demand for consumer goods can generate magnified changes in the subsequent demand for investment goods (including inventory holdings) needed for their production. This relationship is expressed by the "accelerator coefficient" which is defined as the volume of net investment (or change in capital) resulting from a preceding change in consumption. Hence it may be measured by the formula:

$$\text{Accelerator} = \frac{\text{net investment or change in capital}}{\text{change in consumption from preceding period}}$$

The accelerator principle thus links net investment to changes in consumption. The reasoning that underlies this link is fundamentally one of technology. If technology within the economy remains the same, an increase in demand for consumer goods from one period to the next may prompt firms to increase their capital equipment in order to satisfy the larger demand. Therefore, the economy's net investment or demand for new capital will bear some relation to the increase in its output. This relation can be expressed by a formula based on the above equation for the accelerator. By "transposing" and by shortening the language a bit, we can rewrite the above equation simply as:

Net investment = accelerator × change in consumption

keeping in mind that net investment is still assumed to be due to a change in consumption from the preceding period. This means that the accelerator is some constant figure, and hence the amount of net investment will be some multiple of the change in consumption, depending on the value of the accelerator.

A CAPITAL EQUIPMENT ILLUSTRATION

We may illustrate the operation of the accelerator principle in numerical terms. Let us assume that for some hypothetical industry there is a capital/output ratio of about 3 to 1, which means that approximately three additional units of capital are needed to produce one additional unit of output for consumption. We can think of the accelerator coefficient, therefore, as being equal to 3; that is, $3 more of capital is needed in this industry to produce $1 more of output for consumption.

An example of the accelerator principle is presented in Exhibit 3. The first three columns of the table show that for each period a given level of output for consumption is "supported" by three times as much capital equipment. The fourth column

---

Exhibit 3

Illustrative Application of the Accelerator Principle for a Hypothetical Industry

(Accelerator coefficient = 3, i.e., $3 of additional capital is needed to produce $1 of additional output for consumption.)

(1)	(2)	(3)	(4)	(5)
Time period	Output for consumption	Capital equipment 3 × col. (2)	Change in consumption*	Change in capital (net investment)† 3 × col. (4)
1	$ 95	$285		
2	100	300	$ 5 → $15	+100%
3	110	330	10 → 30	
4	115	345	5 → 15	− 50%
5	115	345	0 → 0	−100%
6	100	300	−15 → −45	

(Column (2) notations: between 2 and 3: +10 %; between 3 and 4: +4.5%; between 4 and 5: 0 %)

* Each change in consumption is assumed to occur *between* the beginning of one period and the beginning of the next, such as from Jan. 1 of one year to Jan. 1 of the next year.

† Each change in capital (or net investment) is assumed to occur *during* a period, such as from Jan. 1 to Dec. 31 of any given year.

---

merely lists arbitrary changes in consumption from one period to the next, and the fifth column demonstrates how the change in capital or net investment *within* any given period responds by a multiple of 3 to the change in consumption from the previous period, as emphasized by the arrows.

Thus from Period 1 to Period 2 a $5 increase in consumption results in a $15 increase in capital equipment during the second period. From Period 2 to Period 3, a rise in consumption by $10 or 10 percent requires net investment of $30 which is an increase of 100 percent in the third period. During the next time interval, consumption increases by only $5 or about 4.5 percent and net investment then must be $15, but this amounts to a *decrease* of 50 percent from the previous increase. From Period 4 to Period 5, consumption does not change, and as a result new investment falls to zero in the fifth period, a drop of 100 percent. Finally, from Period 5 to 6, consumption decreases, and this in turn causes a liquidation of some capital; hence net investment is negative.

In general, the accelerator principle demonstrates that small changes in consumption may result in large changes in net investment. When expressed in relative terms, the accelerator principle illustrates the fact that a mere slowing down of the percentage rate of growth in demand is capable of producing an actual decline in net investment. These changes in investment, of course, will also affect income.

What is the implication for business cycle analysis? It means that if consumption increases at a decreasing rate from one period to the next (such as 10 percent, 9 percent, 8 percent, etc., in each successive calendar quarter) businessmen striving to maintain their normal capital/output ratio will cause investment to taper off or at best to remain the same. If consumption remains constant or if it decreases, businessmen will *disinvest* or reduce their total stock of capital goods by not replacing all their factories and machines as they wear out. These actions, of course, will have significant effects on income.

AN INVENTORY ILLUSTRATION

The accelerator principle can also be explained in terms of inventory. This is realistic in today's econ-

omy, because recessions in the United States since World War II have been caused largely by reductions in the stocks businessmen keep on hand to meet unexpected increases in customers' demands.

Suppose a department store sells an average of 100 shirts a month, and keeps an inventory equal to two months' sales. The inventory/sales ratio is therefore 2 to 1. If the demand for shirts increases permanently to 110 shirts a month, the store will have to increase its inventory to 220 shirts in order to maintain its desired inventory/sales ratio. The increase in inventory demand will thus be twice the increase in consumer demand.

It follows that changes in inventory demand will exhibit wider swings than changes in consumer demand, just as happened in the previous example pertaining to capital equipment. And these swings may occur on the downturn as well as on the upturn of a business cycle.

SOME QUALIFICATIONS OF THE ACCELERATOR PRINCIPLE

What are the main qualifications that should be kept in mind if the accelerator principle is to be used as a partial explanation of business cycles? For the most part, the conditions involve the assumed stability of the accelerator coefficient. Thus:

1. The assumption of a stable capital/output ratio is too rigid to be valid for all phases of the business cycle. When there is less than high employment, many firms have excess capacity, and can meet increases in demand without acquiring additional plant and equipment. As demand continues to expand, it is often possible to increase output still further by putting on additional shifts of workers rather than purchasing additional capital. Beyond some point, however, it becomes necessary to acquire new equipment, and it is then that the accelerator principle begins to take effect.

2. Similarly, the assumption of a stable inventory/sales ratio is questionable. As shown in Exhibit 4, such ratios vary widely over the business cycle, mainly because they are more dependent on managerial beliefs, customs, and practices than on economic factors. There is nothing to indicate that a

Exhibit 4

Manufacturing and Trade Inventories Compared with Monthly Sales*

The inventory-sales ratio fluctuates widely from year to year.
This helps reduce the effectiveness of the accelerator as a force

contributing to business cycles.
* Ratios based on seasonally adjusted data.

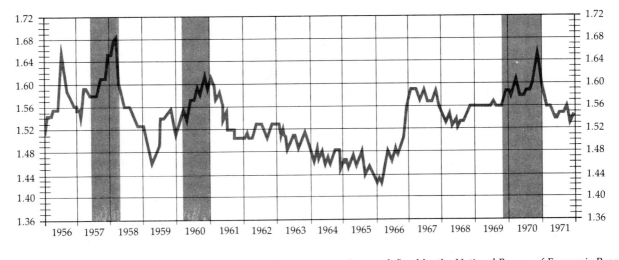

SOURCE: U.S. Department of Commerce. Shaded areas represent business recessions as defined by the National Bureau of Economic Research.

relatively fixed ratio is maintained at all times, especially in the short run when dealers will often "speculate" in inventories by increasing or decreasing their stocks in anticipation of changes in the prices of materials.

Some evidence suggests that although the accelerator principle does not operate automatically within most individual industries, it is nevertheless a fundamental force within the economic system. The principle illustrates the distinct tendency within the economy to build new capital goods in order to meet increased demands, and to reduce the production of capital goods when demand falls.

Interactions of the Multiplier and the Accelerator

The multiplier principle explains how autonomous changes in investment can operate through con-

sumption to cause changes in income. The accelerator principle explains how autonomous changes in consumption can cause changes in investment which in turn bring about changes in income. What happens to income when the multiplier and accelerator join forces?

A few of the possibilities are illustrated in Exhibit 5, and may be described briefly.

BUMPING ALONG THE CEILING

Chart A helps to explain how a downturn may happen. Suppose the economy is in recession, and that income manages to start rising again (due perhaps to increased government spending or other factors that we will be considering in later chapters). As income rises, so does consumption, and this induces—via the multiplier—further increases in income. The economic system may thus experience a self-reinforcing expansion at a rate of, say, 6 or 7 percent annually.

But the economy cannot continue indefinitely at this rate when its labor force and productivity have an annual growth of less than 2 or 3 percent. At most the system may bump along the "full employment ceiling" for a short time until the slowing down of the economy's growth brings the accelerator into play. With the sharp drop-off in investment, the economic system plummets downward into a recession just as a balloon falls when it is punctured.

BOUNCING ALONG THE FLOOR

When the economy is in recession, do forces come into play that help bring about an upswing?

To answer this question, we turn to chart B. With the fall in output from the previous prosperity, the accelerator principle causes businessmen to reduce their total stock of capital goods by *disinvesting*—that is, by not replacing used factories and machines as they wear out. However, the rate at which these capital goods wear out puts a lower limit on how fast disinvestment can take place. This might be called a "disinvestment floor."

The economy may bounce along this floor until firms reduce their stock of capital goods to the level warranted by the recession level of income. When this adjustment is completed, disinvestment ceases and a new cycle can start all over again.

Exhibit 5

Interactions of the Multiplier and the Accelerator

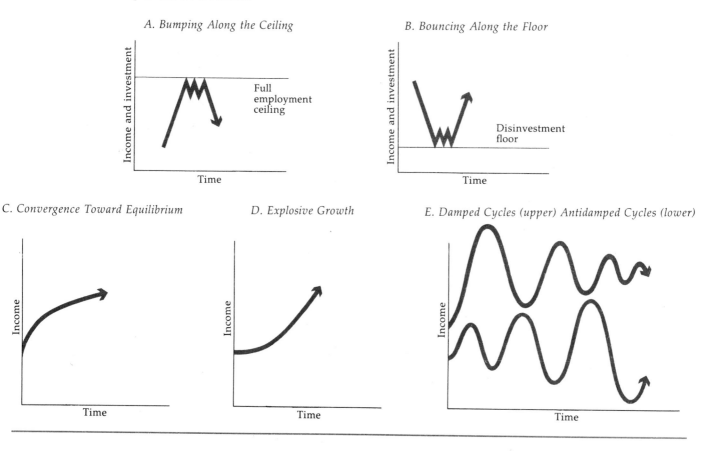

A. Bumping Along the Ceiling

B. Bouncing Along the Floor

C. Convergence Toward Equilibrium

D. Explosive Growth

E. Damped Cycles (upper) Antidamped Cycles (lower)

CONCLUSION

Various cyclical patterns may be generated by the interaction of the multiplier and the accelerator, depending on the values of their coefficients at any particular time.

Thus in chart C, income converges steadily to an equilibrium level; in chart D, income explodes upward at an increasing rate; and in chart E, income fluctuates in cycles that may be either of two types: (1) damped, in which case the amplitudes become smaller as the cycle converges upon a central equilibrium level, or (2) antidamped, in which case the amplitudes increase as the cycle diverges from a central equilibrium level. Of course, none of these patterns will continue indefinitely, because the multiplier and accelerator coefficients themselves will change due to changes in the factors that determine them. This is to be expected in a dynamic economy.

Thus we see that the multiplier and accelerator, through their interaction, can produce a stable equilibrium level of income, but can also reinforce each other and thereby generate a cumulative inflationary or deflationary spiral.

Today economists attribute business cycles largely to these types of interactions between the multiplier and the accelerator.

SUMMARY OF IMPORTANT IDEAS

1. The increases in income resulting from a sustained injection of new investment into the economy tend to taper off, whereas the increases in income resulting from a series of successive injections are cumulative as long as the injections are continued. Leakages, however, tend to reduce the effectiveness of the multiplier.

2. The accelerator principle shows how small changes in the demand for consumer goods may generate magnified changes in the demand for capital goods, including capital equipment and inventories. Although the principle does not always operate automatically because firms do not usually maintain rigid capital/output or inventory/sales ratios through all phases of a business cycle, it nevertheless tends to be a force within the economy.

3. The interactions of the multiplier and the accelerator can generate different types of cyclical patterns in income and investment, depending on the values of the coefficients. This is the approach used by most economists today in analyzing and interpreting business cycles.

FOR HOMEWORK AND DISCUSSION

1. *Terms and concepts to review:*

    accelerator principle

    disinvestment

2. On the basis of this chapter, which would you expect to rise first during the upswing of a business cycle—consumption or investment? Which would decline first near the peak of the cycle? Can you explain why?

3. What must happen to such basic variables as population and technology in order for the accelerator to stimulate economic growth and development? Explain your answer.

4. If the interaction of the multiplier and the accelerator can produce various kinds of "odd" cycles, why have we not usually experienced such cycles?

REFERENCES AND READING SUGGESTIONS

DAUTEN, CARL A., and LLOYD M. VALENTINE, *Business Cycles and Forecasting*, 3d ed., South-Western, Cincinnati, 1968, chap. 6.

DOW, LOUIS A., *Business Fluctuations in a Dynamic Economy*, Merrill, Columbus, Ohio, 1968, chap. 12.

LEWIS, JOHN P., and ROBERT C. TURNER, *Business Conditions Analysis*, 2d ed., McGraw-Hill, New York, 1967, Part II.

MATTHEWS, R. C. O., *The Business Cycle*, University of Chicago Press, Chicago, 1959, chaps. 2, 3.

SHAPIRO, EDWARD, *Macroeconomic Analysis*, 2d ed., Harcourt, Brace & World, New York, 1970, chaps. 7, 8.

CHAPTER 12

Fiscal Policy and Full Employment Without Inflation

CHAPTER PREVIEW

How do changes in government spending and taxes affect aggregate demand and hence the level of income and employment?

What are the basic principles of fiscal policy? How can they be made to work in order to achieve the goals of continuous full employment without inflation?

Is our public debt too large? What are the real burdens of the debt? How large should the debt be?

At the end of World War II, it was widely predicted that the United States would be faced with a serious problem of unemployment as servicemen returned to civilian life and many industries converted from wartime to peacetime production. Accordingly, Congress, with the approval of the President, passed the *Employment Act of 1946* in which it said:

> The Congress hereby declares that it is the continuing policy and responsiblity of the Federal Government to . . . create and maintain, in a manner calculated to foster and promote free competitive enterprise and the general welfare . . . maximum employment, production, and purchasing power.

This law is interpreted to mean that the government should use its fiscal powers of taxing and spending to stimulate full employment and economic growth. Since the early 1960s, increasing emphasis has been placed on achieving these objectives without causing inflationary pressures.

The noun "fisc" (from Latin *fiscus,* translated as basket, money basket, treasury) means a state or royal treasury. But instead of the noun, we use the adjective "fiscal" to refer to all matters pertaining to the public treasury, particularly its revenues and expenditures. Thus modern fiscal policy deals with the deliberate exercise of the government's power to tax and spend for the purpose of bringing the nation's output and employment to desired levels.

Introducing Government

In our previous treatment of the theory of income and employment we assumed that net national product consists of two components, consumption expenditures C, and private net investment I. We concluded that in order to close an inflationary or deflationary gap, methods must be found to alter aggregate demand. Our objective now is to show how government fiscal policy can do this.

The proper economic role of government is always controversial. Should taxes be raised or lowered? Should government spending be increased or reduced? These are among the fundamental issues of fiscal policy. They are also typical of the questions you read and hear about almost every day in the news media.

GOVERNMENT EXPENDITURES INCREASE AGGREGATE DEMAND

How does government fiscal policy affect our previous model of income and employment? The two major variables of fiscal policy are taxes and spending. Let us assume for the moment that *taxes are held constant;* then government spending on goods and services G becomes a net addition to total spending or aggregate demand—that is, a net addition to household consumption expenditures C, and business investment expenditures I, as illustrated in the hypothetical case of Exhibit 1.

The C + I + G curve shows total spending at each level of national income. The new equilibrium point at which aggregate demand equals aggregate supply occurs at E.

Exhibit 1

Effect of Increased Government Spending on National Income

Increased government spending raises aggregate demand and produces a multiplier effect on national income. (Note the scale break on the vertical axis. This enables us to compare the increase in government spending of $20 billion with the increase in consumption expenditures of $80 billion, without crowding the curves.)

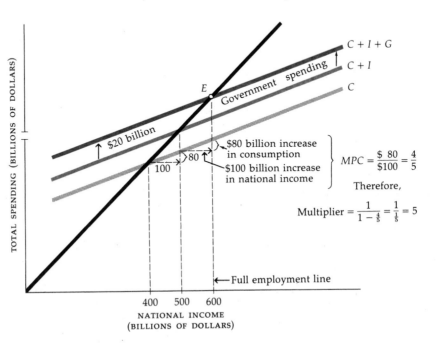

$$MPC = \frac{\$\,80}{\$100} = \frac{4}{5}$$

Therefore,

$$\text{Multiplier} = \frac{1}{1 - \frac{4}{5}} = \frac{1}{\frac{1}{5}} = 5$$

Note that an increase in government expenditure, with taxes held constant, has a multiplier effect on national income just like an increase in private investment expenditure. In the diagram, an increase in aggregate demand of $20 billion, from $C + I$ to $C + I + G$, increases national income by $100 billion. We can infer from this that a rise in government demand has the same multiplier effect on national income as a rise in consumer demand and in business demand; it increases the sales and profits of firms that sell to the government, and in turn causes further increases in income and output throughout the economy. Thus:

Increased government spending may be used to raise the level of aggregate demand from an unemployment to a full employment level. However, any additional spending which raises aggregate demand above full employment levels will be inflationary.

Observe how the multiplier principle actually comes into play. In Exhibit 1 we know from the constant slope of the consumption curve that MPC is $\frac{4}{5}$ at every point, and hence the multiplier is 5. Given this information, and knowing that the increase in national income must be $100 billion in order to reach full employment, we can deduce that the increase in government spending must be $20 billion in order to achieve the desired goal, since $5 \times \$20$ billion = $100 billion.

INCREASED TAXES REDUCE AGGREGATE DEMAND

What happens to the equilibrium level of national income when *government spending is constant* and taxes vary? Your intuition tells you that an increase in taxes will reduce income and hence consumption expenditures, and this in turn will decrease output and employment. Of course, there are many different kinds of taxes: direct or indirect, progressive or regressive, personal or business. Further they may all have different effects on income and employment. For simplicity, however, let us assume that an increase in personal income taxes of $20 billion is imposed on consumers in our hypothetical economy.

In Exhibit 2, the consumption schedule C_0, whose MPC is $\frac{4}{5}$, is shifted downward and parallel until it

becomes C_1 as a result of the tax T. But has the consumption curve shifted downward by the exact amount of the tax? The answer is no because:

After the tax the decrease in consumption, as represented by the drop in the curve, means that at any given level of income people will now consume less than they consumed before; or equivalently, for any given level of consumption people now need a larger income than they needed before. For example, the chart shows that a consumption level of $490 billion now requires an income of $520 billion instead of $500 billion, with the additonal $20 billion of income representing the amount of the tax.

Thus the consumption curve has shifted horizontally rightward according to the amount of the tax, in this case $20 billion. But since the two curves

---

Exhibit 2

Effect of Increased Taxes on Consumption and National Income

The C curve will shift downward by an amount equal to MPC × T. Thus since MPC = $\frac{4}{5}$ and the tax is $20 billion, the C curve will shift downward by $\frac{4}{5}$ × $20 billion = $16 billion. (The scale break on the horizontal axis between $400 and $500 billion permits different scales to be used on each side of the break in order to emphasize different features of the chart.)

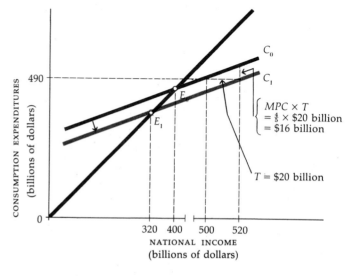

---

are parallel, both must have the same slopes or MPCs, namely $\frac{4}{5}$. Therefore, the consumption curve must shift vertically downward by \$16 billion in order to retain its MPC of $\frac{\$16}{\$20} = \frac{4}{5}$.

To conclude, the tax causes a rightward shift of the curve by the amount of the tax, but this also involves a simultaneous downward shift according to the value of the MPC. What will be the effect of T on national income? Since we know from Exhibit 1 that the multiplier is 5, it follows that a decrease in consumption expenditures of \$16 billion will reduce national income by $5 \times \$16$ billion = \$80 billion. This is shown in Exhibit 2, where the equilibrium income changes from E_0 at \$400 billion to E_1 at \$320 billion.

VARYING "G" AND "T" TOGETHER: THE BALANCED-BUDGET MULTIPLIER

Suppose that we now allow G and T to vary simultaneously. As you saw in Exhibit 1, the effect of a \$20 billion increase in G is a \$100 billion increase in national income, because the added expenditure goes through the rounds of consumption and saving according to the multiplier principle. In Exhibit 2, on the other hand, the effect of a \$20 billion increase in T is an \$80 billion decrease in national income, because the multiplier operates in reverse to contract income as consumption and saving are reduced.

It follows, therefore, that if G and T are both increased simultaneously by the same amount—in our example by \$20 billion—the effect of the increase in G is to raise national income by 5 times that amount, or \$100 billion, while the effect of the increase in T is to lower national income by 4 times that amount, or \$80 billion. Therefore, the *net* effect of equal increases in G and T together is to increase national income by 1 times that amount or \$20 billion—the amount of the initial increment. The reason is that the effects of balanced increases in G and T are precisely equal but opposite, and hence the two multiplier processes cancel each other out—except on the very first round when the full amount of G (\$20 billion) is added to national income. Therefore, the net multiplier effect of equal increases in G and T is 1.

We can generalize the foregoing ideas in this way:

Balanced-Budget Multiplier Principle: If G and T are increased or decreased simultaneously by an equal or *balanced* amount, national income will be increased or decreased by the same amount. For example, a balanced increase of G and T by \$1 will raise national income by \$1, and a balanced decrease by \$1 will lower national income by \$1.

The balanced-budget multipler principle has two intensely practical implications. First, in a full-employment economy an increase in government spending for any purpose (e.g., defense spending) will cause an inflationary gap unless taxes are increased by *more than the increase in spending*—that is, by *more than enough to balance the budget*. Second, in an economy operating at less than full employment a general tax reduction will result in an increase in consumption and aggregate demand. This may be almost as effective in raising the equilibrium level of national income as an increase in government spending, but it might have the further advantage of expanding the private (business) sector of the economy rather than the public (government) sector.

Several countries including the United States and Japan have successfully applied this tax-cutting concept in order to increase their levels of income and employment. Hence it is possible that these modern notions of fiscal policy may gain increasing use as time goes on.

Essentials of Fiscal Policy

The foregoing analysis suggests some guides for discretionary *fiscal policy*—that is, deliberate actions by the government in its spending and taxing activities to help dampen the swings of business cycles and to bring the nation's output and employment to desired levels.

During recession when it is desired to raise aggregate demand to a full employment noninflationary level, an *expansionary* fiscal policy is needed in order to close the deflationary gap. This may involve either an increase in G, a decrease in T, or some combination of both. If the federal budget is balanced to begin with, an expansionary fiscal policy of this type will require a budget *deficit,* since the government's expenditures will exceed its revenues.

During inflation when aggregate demand must be reduced, a *contractionary* fiscal policy is needed in order to close the inflationary gap. This may entail either a decrease in G, an increase in T, or some combination of both. If the federal budget is already in balance, a contractionary fiscal policy would require a budget *surplus,* since the government's revenues will exceed its expenditures.

REMARK. Strictly speaking, since a balanced increase in the budget is actually inflationary due to the balanced-budget multiplier principle, an increased budget that results in a relatively small surplus might also be slightly inflationary rather than deflationary. Therefore the budget surplus must be large enough to induce deflationary effects if a contractionary fiscal policy is to operate effectively.

Not all fiscal activity is discretionary. Much is *nondiscretionary,* reflecting the fact that significant changes in government spending and taxes occur automatically over the business cycle without any explicit decisions by the President or Congress. Let us examine these changes.

OUR AUTOMATIC OR "BUILT-IN" FISCAL STABILIZERS

Our economy has certain "built-in" fiscal stabilizers which go to work automatically, cushioning a recession by creating a budget deficit and curbing an inflation by creating a budget surplus. They thus help to keep the economic system in balance without human intervention or control, much as a thermostat balances the temperature in a house.

Four of these stabilizers are particularly important:

1. Tax receipts. The federal government's chief sources of revenue are the personal and corporation income taxes. Since the rates on these taxes—expecially the former—are progressive, rising national income results in more than proportional increases in government tax receipts, thereby tending to dampen an economic boom; declining national income results in more than proportional decreases in government tax receipts, thereby tending to soften an economic recession. This "automatic" tendency for tax receipts to rise or fall with inflation or defla-

tion creates a powerful stabilizing effect on the business cycle.

2. Unemployment taxes and benefits. Unemployment insurance also has automatic stabilizing tendencies. During prosperity and high employment total tax receipts to finance the program exceed total benefits paid out, thus creating a surplus; during recession and unemployment, the reverse occurs, thereby creating a deficit.

3. Agricultural price supports. "Parity prices" for farmers have automatic stabilizing effects on agricultural prices. The Agriculture Department buys and stores farm surpluses in order to put a "floor" under falling agricultural prices, and releases these goods to impose a "ceiling" on rising agricultural prices.

4. Corporate dividend policy. Corporations maintain fairly stable dividends in the short run; that is, their dividend payouts to stockholders do not fluctuate with each reported increase or decrease in profits. As a result, corporate retained earnings or undistributed profits, to the extent that they are saved and not invested, tend to have a stabilizing influence in both inflationary and deflationary times.

On the whole, these automatic stabilizers tend to reduce the severity of business cycles. Some studies suggest that all of the automatic stabilizers acting together may reduce the amplitudes of cyclical swings by about one-third. But if we want to control the spread of economic booms or declines rather than merely reduce their highs and lows, we must turn to discretionary methods of fiscal policy.

DISCRETIONARY FISCAL POLICY IN ACTION

The prescriptions of discretionary fiscal policy seem to be simple and straightforward: to expand the economy, cut taxes and raise government expenditures; to contract the economy, raise taxes and cut government expenditures. The principal concerns of discretionary fiscal policy thus involve ways in which the federal government (represented by the Treasury) raises and spends money, and the economic consequences of these actions. Let us examine these activities carefully.

First, there is the problem of how the government chooses to raise money. Basically, it has three sources of revenue: taxation, borrowing, and printing.

TAXATION. All increases in taxes tend to be contractionary because they take some purchasing power from those who are taxed. However, certain taxes such as the personal and corporation income taxes are progressive, while others like the sales and excise taxes are regressive. Some economists believe that regressive taxes tend to be more contractionary because they depress total consumer spending; others think that progressive taxes may be more contractionary because they cause a decline in both consumption and corporate investment. Similar difficulties arise in assessing the results of tax decreases. Economists are not always sure whether reductions in progressive or regressive taxes have the greater expansionary effects in terms of production and employment.

However, the level of taxes is not the only factor to consider. Changes in the composition and rate structure may also affect government revenues and the pace of economic activity, *depending on the MPCs of the income groups involved.* For instance, a change in tax rates which puts a greater burden on higher income groups, and a lesser burden on lower income groups, may have the net effect of stimulating total consumer demand and raising the general level of economic activity. (Can you explain why?) It may also reduce government tax revenues in the short run since the great bulk of such revenues comes from the lower- and middle-income groups, but raise it in the long run as national income rises.

BORROWING. The government can also raise money by borrowing—that is, by selling Treasury bonds to the public, namely households and businesses. (It can also borrow from commercial banks, but we shall neglect the effects of such actions at this time.) If the public buys the bonds with income that it would otherwise have spent on consumption or investment, then the overall economic effect will be at least neutral. But experience indicates that except in periods of full-scale war when patriotism runs high, neither households nor businesses are inclined to reduce significantly their consumption or investment in order to buy government bonds. Therefore this

form of borrowing will often have expansionary effects. Can you suggest conditions under which the effects will be contractionary?

PRINTING NEW MONEY. Instead of taxing or borrowing, the government may simply decide to print money. It can then pay for the resources it wants without depressing private consumption and investment spending. This seems like a delightful and painless way to finance public expenditures. In fact, a number of governments—some Latin American countries are notable—turn frequently to the printing presses to pay for armies, build highways, and meet other obligations and expenses. But the results are not always painless—for two related reasons: (1) during high employment the effects will be inflationary unless private spending is reduced by raising taxes enough to offset the increase in government spending; (2) if private spending is not reduced, the resulting inflation will act as a "tax" by raising prices throughout the economy and thereby shrinking real incomes. These effects, however, would not necessarily occur during recession. That is, printing money to pay for public goods may not be inflationary if the increased government spending raises aggregate demand, thereby expanding real incomes as output and employment rise.

The second aspect of discretionary fiscal policy concerns the ways in which the government spends money. Two types of government spending are of chief concern: transfer payments and public works expenditures. How does each affect income and employment?

TRANSFER PAYMENTS. As pointed out earlier, certain types of transfer expenditures such as unemployment compensation and old-age retirement benefits act as automatic stabilizers, rising and falling in a somewhat inverse relationship with national income. On the other hand, certain transfer expenditures such as veterans' bonuses and interest payments on the public debt are independent of national income and do not have this automatic stabilizing characteristic. But the *net* effect of transfer payments is expansionary to the extent that people spend them for goods and services instead of withholding them from the income-expenditure stream; otherwise, they tend to be neutral.

PUBLIC WORKS EXPENDITURES. Highways, parks, public buildings, rural electrification, slum clearance, and regional development are examples of *public works*—that is, government-sponsored construction or development projects which would not ordinarily be undertaken by the private sector of the economy. Hence, as an instrument of fiscal policy, public works have at least three desirable features: (1) they stimulate the capital goods and construction industries, in which unemployment is usually greatest during a recession; (2) they provide society with socially useful goods like schools, parks, and highways; and (3) they provide jobs which help to maintain workers' morale and self-respect.

But public works also have certain fundamental disadvantages—mainly with respect to timing and classification. (1) They pose a difficult timing problem because they are hard to start when the need for them is greatest, and hard to stop when the need for them is past. For example, it takes several years for the design, engineering, and legal work to be approved before construction of a major bridge or freeway can begin. By that time the economy may be well on its way to prosperity. (2) Certain types of investment cannot be classified as either strictly public or strictly private. As a result, some public works such as low-cost housing and perhaps power and reclamation projects may compete with private investment and thereby discourage the development and expansion of the economy's private (business) sector.

DOES DISCRETIONARY FISCAL POLICY REALLY WORK?

How well do these principles of discretionary fiscal policy actually operate? Since they require implementation by Washington, many knotty economic and political issues arise. Nevertheless, four broad classes of difficulties may be identified.

First, there is the technical problem of cyclical forecasting and fiscal timing. Substantial advances have taken place in economic model building over the years. However, business-cycle forecasting is still far from being an "exact" science. Hence the proper timing of appropriate fiscal measures to ward off an inflation or recession is extremely difficult. In fact the fiscal measures are often applied after the inflation or recession has already occurred, instead of before.

A second problem is to gain political and public acceptance of fiscal measures. Even if business-cycle turning points are reasonably predictable, there is still the need to persuade a President or Congress to risk—and the public to accept—unpopular fiscal measures. Among these are increased taxes and reduced government spending. Further, there is the apparently insurmountable problem of overcoming the inherent sluggishness of the democratic process itself: it may take a year or more for Congress to hammer out a budget that incorporates the desired expenditures and taxes. By that time the fiscal needs themselves may have changed fundamentally, or no longer exist.

Third, there is a problem of federal vs. state and local fiscal policies. Ideally, federal fiscal policies should mesh with those of state and local governments, so that all three levels of government may launch a unified countercyclical attack against inflations and recessions. In reality, however, the reverse frequently happens. Thus during prosperity, state and local governments often run deficits in their budgets in order to build highways, schools, and public libraries; in recession they frequently reduce expenditures so as to balance their budgets or even incur surpluses. The reasons for this are due largely to the fact that state and local governments are much more restricted than the federal government in their sources of funds: they cannot print money, and their opportunities for taxing and borrowing, which are considerably more limited, tend to vary directly with general economic conditions. In view of this, it becomes necessary to rely much more heavily on federal fiscal policy as compared to state and local fiscal policies in order to achieve and maintain economic stability.

A fourth problem is to dovetail government and private investment. It was pointed out earlier that government investment should hopefully supplement private investment and even stimulate it, but certainly not depress it. Yet government investment may clearly have depressive effects if it is competitive with private investment. To avoid this, public expenditures should be concentrated on projects that are clearly noncompetitive with private enterprise. Highway construction, slum clearance, and urban redevelopment are several possible examples.

In view of these problem areas, can it be said that fiscal policy actually works in practice? Experiences since the 1930s indicate that it does. And, in the Kennedy and Johnson administrations of the 1960s we learned from actual experience that:

1. A tax cut may stimulate business activity so that in the long run, as national income rises, the government through our progressive tax system will collect larger revenues.

2. A cut in taxes will tend to stimulate both consumption and investment spending so as to produce a gradual rise in consumption and a magnified increase in income—just as the theories of the consumption function and the multiplier predict.

3. Too high a level of government spending, without any offsetting tax increases, will cause a demand-pull inflationary gap. This was demonstrated in the latter part of the 1960s as a result of heavy military expenditures in the Vietnam War.

THE HIGH-EMPLOYMENT BUDGET; FISCAL DRAG AND FISCAL DIVIDENDS

The surpluses and deficits which occur from year to year in the federal budget are not entirely *discretionary;* to some extent they are *automatic* as a result of our progressive tax structure. Thus, as national income increases, the rising tax revenues of the federal government automatically push the budget toward a surplus; as national income decreases, the falling tax revenues automatically push the budget toward a deficit.

Therefore, given the government's existing tax rates and spending policies, the actual budget surplus or deficit that occurs in any particular year is not necessarily the same as the surplus or deficit that would occur in a year of full employment. For instance, in a specific year when the economy is operating at less than full employment the government may incur a budgetary deficit of several billion dollars. Yet with the same tax rates and the same amount of federal spending the government might instead have incurred a budgetary surplus of several billion dollars if the economy had been operating at

full or close to full employment. Why? Because the greater level of national income during a period of high employment would have produced a larger volume of tax revenues for the government.

This prompts us to introduce a new concept called the *high-employment budget*. It may be defined as an estimate of annual government expenditures and revenues that would occur if the economy were operating at a high level of employment—that is, at an unemployment rate of not more than 4 percent. Any resulting surplus (or deficit) in this budget is called a *high-employment surplus* (or *deficit*). The calculation of the government's high-employment budget is usually based on the national income accounts, and hence reflects more accurately the impact of budget surpluses and deficits on the economy's current levels of output and employment. (NOTE: A high-employment budget is also sometimes called a *full-employment budget*. In that case the underlying principles and concepts are the same, except that the unemployment rate is usually set at a lower level—say 3 percent.)

Like any other surplus, the effect of a high-employment surplus is deflationary: the government has taken more purchasing power out of the income stream through taxes than it has put back through spending. Under inflationary conditions this situation serves to dampen price increases; under normal expansionary conditions it tends to retard the economy's growth. In view of this, how can we assure a proper utilization of our high-employment surpluses? Two points should be noted:

1. The automatic and more rapid increases in tax revenues relative to expenditures which a growing economy experiences at high employment will produce revenue surpluses that tend to impede the economy's growth. This phenomenon is called *fiscal drag*.

2. The federal government can offset the effect of fiscal drag by declaring a *fiscal dividend*—that is, by disbursing the accumulated surpluses to society so that people can share in the benefits of these surpluses in any one or combination of several ways:

a. Increased federal spending on important public goods like education, regional development, and health

b. Reduced taxes on the private sector in order to increase consumption and investment

c. Larger unrestricted revenue grants to the state and local governments which they can use to meet their expenditure needs

Thus over the long run the high-employment budget may gain increasing use by economic policy makers in Washington, because it combines the principles of discretionary fiscal policy with the concept of fiscal dividends.

Budget Policies and the Public Debt

Modern fiscal theory calls for budget deficits to ward off recessions and budget surpluses to combat inflations. This is the essence of countercyclical fiscal policy. What does it mean as far as balancing the budget is concerned? How does the government debt, resulting from unbalanced budgets, affect our economy?

FOUR BUDGET POLICIES

Since the early 1930s, the question has often arisen whether the federal budget should be balanced frequently, occasionally, or not at all. Four distinctly different policies have been proposed: an annually balanced budget; a cyclically balanced budget; "functional finance"; and a high-employment balanced budget. Let us see what these policies involve.

ANNUALLY BALANCED BUDGET. Those who argue that the budget should be balanced every twelve months claim that this policy would place the government in an economically "neutral" position by providing a constraint on runaway spending and fiscal disorder, and by assuring that annual revenues and expenditures are equal. Political leaders and businessmen often make such statements. Are they true?

If the federal government balanced the budget each year without regard to fluctuations in the private sector the effects would not be neutral; in fact, they would be procyclical. The reasons for this are clear. In recession periods, when tax revenues

are falling, tax rates would have to be increased and spending would have to be reduced in order to balance the budget. Conversely, in inflation periods, when tax revenues are rising, tax rates would have to be reduced and spending would have to be increased in order to achieve budgetary balance.

Obviously, therefore, if the budget is to be used as a tool for countercyclical fiscal policy, adherence to annually balanced budgets is impossible.

CYCLICALLY BALANCED BUDGET. The growing influence of Keynesian economics in the 1930s and '40s led to the proposal that the budget should be balanced over the course of the business cycle. This means that the government should incur budget deficits during depression in order to stimulate the economy, but should offset those deficits with budget surpluses during prosperity in order to curb inflationary pressures and help pay off the public debt. Some economists have argued that such a policy would turn the budget into a countercyclical fiscal tool, while still preserving the long-term objective of budgetary balance.

In practice, unfortunately, business cycles are regular but not periodic, and their peaks and troughs are not ordinarily equal. Hence it would be virtually impossible for the government to forecast its revenues and expenditures over the length of a business cycle, and it would be very unlikely for the surplus in any given prosperity to equal or even approximate the deficit of a previous recession.

"FUNCTIONAL FINANCE." This is a philosophy which holds that the government should pursue whatever fiscal measures are needed to achieve noninflationary full employment and economic growth—without regard to budget balancing per se. The federal budget is thus viewed functionally as a flexible fiscal tool for achieving economic objectives, rather than as an accounting statement to be balanced periodically.

Functional finance is the logical consequence of the New Economics. However, it has not gone without criticism—especially by conservative economists and political leaders. In their opinion, a balanced budget serves as a rough fiscal guide that should be applied with discretion. They argue that by accepting functional finance as a budget policy the long-run goal of a balanced budget is consigned to oblivion, and with it go both the means and criteria for preventing runaway spending and inflation.

HIGH-EMPLOYMENT BALANCED BUDGET. Can a budget policy incorporate the best features of the foregoing proposals? The Committee for Economic Development, an organization composed of some of the nation's most prominent business leaders, thinks that it can. Its plan is simple. First, determine a level of expenditures based on long-term merits without regard to stabilization considerations. Then, set tax rates to cover those expenditures at high employment, and yield a moderate surplus besides.

This plan, in the opinion of the CED, has two major advantages: (1) it produces a balanced budget over the full course of a business cycle; and (2) it rejects the use of discretionary fiscal policy, which is often difficult to apply for both political and economic reasons, and relies instead on the use of automatic stabilizers to keep the economy at a high level of employment. The result is a long-run cyclically balanced budget with automatic built-in flexibility.

Unfortunately, however, the plan has some disadvantages. For example: Reliance on automatic stabilizers may not be enough to keep small swings from developing into big ones; and there are times when the private sector is either too weak or too strong, so that stabilization may require more substantial and intentional federal deficits or surpluses than this plan would permit.

As a general rule, therefore, a high-employment balanced budget would not necessarily assure high employment. Nevertheless, many economists believe that this plan would have worked quite well for the years since World War II—probably better than actual budget policies for most of those years. That alone is a major factor in its behalf.

THE PUBLIC DEBT: IS IT TOO LARGE?

Since the start of World War II, the number of general budget deficits has far exceeded the number of surpluses. As a result, the government has accumulated a substantial public debt, the size of which has been the subject of a good deal of controversy and criticism. Before exploring the issues that are involved, you should examine the facts by studying the charts and statements in Exhibit 3.

Is our present public debt "too large"? Many people think it is, and they fear that the debt will (1) endanger the nation's credit standing and possibly lead to bankruptcy, or (2) burden future generations unfairly. Are these dire predictions justified? Let us examine them and see.

1. Endangers National Credit and May Lead to Bankruptcy

The credit standing of the United States government is determined as it is for any borrower, by those who lend it money—the banks, insurance companies, corporations, and households that buy the bonds and other securities sold by the Treasury. Despite its large debt, the government is able to borrow (i.e., sell securities) in competitive markets at the lowest interest rates.

As for bankruptcy, this term applies to a borrower who is unable to pay his debts. But the federal government need never go bankrupt, for even if it is unable to borrow new funds to pay off old debts, it can always raise taxes or even print money if it wishes. In the final analysis, *the economic consequences of these actions will depend on the nation's productive output, such as its real GNP, and not on the size of the public debt per se.*

Thus the objections that a large public debt may endanger the nation's credit rating, or lead to bankruptcy, do not stand up. They should be recognized for what they are: criticisms based on the speaker's psychological fears rather than on economic facts.

2. Burdens Future Generations

Many people argue that when the government incurs long-term debt it burdens future generations with the cost of today's policies. There is some merit to this argument; but several aspects of it need to be examined. First, keep in mind that the basic idea of cost involves sacrifice; the real cost of anything is not the dollars you spend for it, but the value of the alternative to it that you renounce. In view of this, what are the real costs of public debt? The answer depends on the circumstances under which it is incurred.

Exhibit 3

The Public Debt Exceeds a Third of a Trillion Dollars

Most of our public debt was not incurred as a result of counter-cyclical fiscal policy, but to help pay for World War II.

The growth of a nation's income, such as its real GNP, is the best measure of its ability to carry a large public debt.

The chief burdens of a public debt are the annual interest payments. Although these payments have increased over the years, they have remained at a relatively stable proportion of about 2 percent or less of GNP since the late forties.

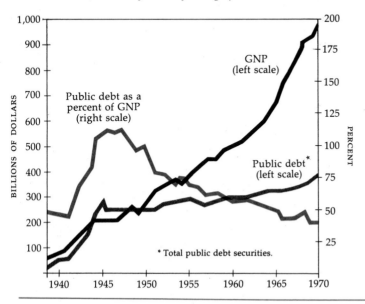

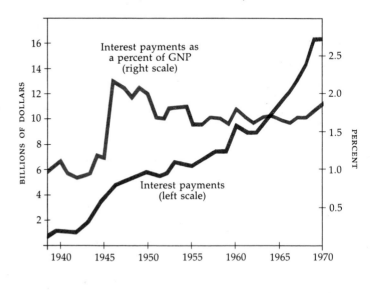

a. If the debt is increased by deficit spending during a period of unemployment, resources are put to work that would otherwise have remained idle. Hence the increase in debt levies no real cost on either the generation that incurs it, or on future generations. Society has benefited from the greater output, and some of it has added to the nation's capital stock inherited by later generations.

b. The case is somewhat different if debt is increased by war. Although that generation bears the heaviest sacrifice, because it has gone without civilian goods in order to buy military ones, several succeeding generations can also feel the burden. Almost inevitably, spending on war starves the nation of capital goods which are not replaced as fast as they are used up. That burden, more than the debt itself, may be the one borne by later generations.

Turning to the debt itself, we find that, first, most of it is owed to American bondholders rather than to foreign ones; and that, second, the payment of interest and repayment of capital must therefore be classified as transfer payments. Of course, like all transfer payments these are made by one group to another; the taxpayers who finance them are not identical with the bondholders who receive them. The result is a tendency to make the rich richer, because most bondholders are in the middle- and upper-income groups.

However, in charging past generations with burdening the future, we must remember that *every* economic decision helps to determine the course of history. The world we live in was largely fashioned by people now dead; the decisions we make today will affect people not yet born. Society thus has an awesome responsibility, and should not be too quick to incur large debts before considering both the burdens and the benefits.

WHAT ARE THE REAL BURDENS AND BENEFITS?

To conclude, these are the main burdens:

1. External-debt burden. A debt which is owed to foreigners does impose a burden on future generations, for it means they must pay interest and principal without necessarily receiving corresponding benefits in return. The foreign bondholders may well spend their incomes in their own country, rather than in the United States. However, an exception occurs to the extent that the original borrowing was spent in the United States to buy capital goods and create jobs, so that the resulting current output is at least large enough to cover the interest and principal payments on the debt.

2. Capital-consumption burden. As we learned earlier, any increase in public debt which uses up some of the nation's capital goods without replacing them imposes a burden on future generations. This happens typically during wars, when the government shifts resources out of civilian and into military production.

3. Inflationary burden. An increase in the public debt will impose inflationary burdens on the economy if, barring any offsetting measures, it is incurred during full employment, or if it makes bondholders feel wealthier and thereby raises their propensity-to-consume curve above the level that would otherwise exist.

4. Transfer payments burden. Although each generation as a whole both bears the monetary costs and receives the benefits of the public debt, transfer payments will be a burden on it and on future generations to the extent that the taxpayers are not the same people as the bondholders. As we have seen, bondholders are predominantly in the middle- and upper-income groups, whereas total tax revenues are drawn from all income groups.

5. Debt management burden. A large public debt may pose a conflict between fiscal and monetary policy. For example, the Treasury will normally desire low interest rates in the economy in order to keep down the costs of refunding or selling new bonds, whereas

there are times when the monetary (i.e., Federal Reserve) authorities will desire high interest rates in order to help choke off inflationary tendencies. The task of debt management raises significant problems that you will be reading more about in later chapters.

In contrast, the chief benefits of a public debt are these:

1. Negotiable treasury bonds and other securities are a desirable investment for many families and large institutions, because they provide assured safety of principal, interest payments, and a high degree of liquidity.

2. Changes in the public debt, as already pointed out, can have desirable effects when used as a tool for discretionary fiscal policy. Indeed modern countercyclical fiscal theory relies heavily on debt manipulation to achieve and maintain full employment without inflation.

HOW LARGE SHOULD THE DEBT BE?

Do these arguments imply that the public debt should be allowed to grow without limit? There is no simple answer. However, certain principles of debt management are illustrated by the facts presented earlier in Exhibit 3. They suggest that the government's ability to pay its debt interest and refundings is determined by the taxable capacity of the nation, and this in turn depends on the growth of its real GNP. Therefore, there need be no adverse consequences of an indefinitely large public debt—even a debt running into the trillions of dollars—provided that:

☐ The public debt does not grow faster than real GNP

☐ Taxes are used to curb inflationary pressures resulting from increases in debt

☐ Interest payments on the debt are a relatively small and stable percentage of real GNP

The fact that some countries are always suffering from serious inflation due to an expanding public debt is often a result of their government's failure to adhere to these basic principles of debt management.

The Real Costs of War

War lays a burden on the state,
And peace does nothing to relieve the weight.
   William Cowper (1731–1800)

As the 1960s drew to a close, a majority of United States politicians, bankers, businessmen, and economists finally came to accept Cowper's viewpoint; they laid to rest the hoary old myth that capitalism thrives on war.

The new consensus was a long time in the making. Until the Vietnam War and its economic consequences forced them to change their minds, "capitalist" and "socialist" economists usually agreed that defense spending kept the United States economy buoyant. They had precedent for their beliefs. The end of World War I brought a slump. True, the economy recovered again in the early 1920s; but the depression that started in 1929 did not end until spending on World War II stimulated economic activity.

Hidden Penalties

World War II started when the nation had idle resources waiting to be put to work. The Vietnam War started when the economy was already running close to capacity. By the late 1960s, it became clear that America could have guns or butter, but not both. Corporate profitability stabilized, inflation became endemic, and the civilian economy was starved of funds. Many of the businessmen who had once supported the Vietnam War became its opponents. And the belief began to grow that once the war was ended government would have funds available for the cities and desperately needed social services. Unfortunately for those hopes, it also became clear that defense spending carries hidden penalties that continue

after the shooting has stopped. Some of these costs do not even appear in the official defense budget.

In fiscal 1971 the defense budget was $71.8 billion—some $5 billion less than in the year before. But the federal budget included at least another $20 billion of expenditures that were defense-related, though labeled as civilian.

One large but little-noted item is the cost of payments to veterans and their dependents. In fiscal 1971, it totaled about $8.9 billion. Since 1965, the annual cost of veterans' medical care has risen by $500 million; the Vietnam War is responsible for virtually all the rise. Future payments to veterans represent a considerable mortgage on the future: some experts estimate that the total cost of pensions for Vietnam veterans alone will eventually reach $220 billion.

A second major item is war-related public debt. Interest payments in fiscal 1971 totaled $19 billion; of that amount, at least $11 billion was accounted for by past wars (the interest paid on the debt from World War II has amounted to some $200 billion so far).

Mislabeled Spending

At least half the $3.6 billion allocated for space programs in 1971 can be considered defense-related. The Agency for International Development spent about $1 billion of its $1.9 billion 1971 budget on helping the United States meet military commitments overseas; $474 million in AID funds went to Vietnam alone.

But the dollar figures, large as they are, do not tell the whole story. The real

cost of war is the lost opportunities it represents: the production foregone, the future incomes unearned by the dead and maimed, and their unborn children; and the distortion of the economy's investments and goals. Robert Eisner, a distinguished economist at Northwestern University, calculates that by 1970 the Vietnam conflict had already cost $219 billion. Direct expenditures accounted for $113 billion; the remaining $106 billion was the cost of production and demand foregone for one reason or another.

Hopes of a substantial "peace dividend" are thus remote. Even if America cut its defense spending in half, the cost of past belligerence would continue to be felt, in the form of interest on war-related debt, foregone investment and production, malformation of the economy, and payments to veterans and their dependents. Those costs are built into the economy, and will affect generations yet unborn.

Peace indeed does nothing to relieve the burden that war lays upon the state, but at least it prevents the burden from increasing.   *R. B.*

When the United States entered World War II, there was substantial unemployment. When we entered the Vietnam War, there was relatively little unemployment. Would the real economic costs of both wars be the same per dollar of military expenditures?

SUMMARY OF IMPORTANT IDEAS

1. The Employment Act of 1946 requires the government to strive for the achievement of continuous full employment. Modern fiscal policy would add to this the further objective of price stability.

2. Through government spending and tax policies, aggregate demand can be altered to close inflationary or deflationary gaps. For example, an increase in government spending, with taxes held constant, will raise aggregate demand; an increase in taxes, with government spending held constant, will reduce aggregate demand. A simultaneous and equal change in government spending and taxes will alter national income by the amount of the change because of the operation of the balanced-budget multiplier principle.

3. Fiscal policy may be discretionary or nondiscretionary. The former is "active" in that it involves conscious changes in government spending and taxation to create expansionary or contractionary effects; the latter is "passive" in that it relies on automatic or built-in stabilizers to keep the economy on course. Modern fiscal policy embraces some degree of both, but there are differences of opinion as to the proper combination. The controversy among economists hinges on the extent to which government should be involved in economic activity.

4. In carrying out its discretionary fiscal activities, the government's sources of funds may include taxation, borrowing, or printing of money, and its spending may include transfer and public works expenditures. In brief and general terms, taxation tends to be more contractionary than borrowing, whereas printing is ordinarily expansionary; transfer payments are expansionary if they are spent, but public works expenditures are even more expansionary because they stimulate the capital goods and construction industries directly.

5. The administration of fiscal policy must grapple with problems of business cycle forecasting and timing, political and public acceptance of fiscal measures, the meshing of federal with state and local fiscal policies, and the avoidance of government investment which may interfere with or discourage private investment.

6. The high-employment budget is usually based on the national income accounts, and hence reflects the impact of budget surpluses and deficits on the economy's current levels of income and employment. The high-employment budget permits integration of the principles of discretionary fiscal policy with the concept of "fiscal dividends" in order to overcome the undesirable effects of "fiscal drag."

7. There is an erroneous tendency to associate some of the dangers of private debt with those of public debt. Thus it is often mistakenly argued that a large public debt can endanger the nation's credit standing, lead to bankruptcy, and inevitably shift a burden of principal and interest payments to future generations. In reality, the real burdens of a debt depend on whether it (1) is externally held, (2) results in using up capital which is unreplaced, (3) induces inflationary effects, (4) imposes a transfer-payments burden due to its distribution among bondholders, and (5) creates a debt management conflict between the fiscal and monetary authorities.

8. Although a large public debt may have adverse psychological consequences, its principal and interest must be assessed in relation to real GNP and to the growth of the economy as a whole before a meaningful evaluation can be made.

FOR HOMEWORK AND DISCUSSION

1. *Terms and concepts to review:*

Employment Act of 1946	high-employment budget
balanced-budget multiplier	full-employment budget
fiscal policy	annually balanced budget
automatic fiscal stabilizers	cyclically balanced budget
public works	"functional finance"
fiscal drag	refunding
fiscal dividend	

2. Assume the economy is in recession, that the MPC is $\frac{1}{2}$, and that an increase of $100 billion in national income is needed in order to reach full employment. Then, using diagrams if necessary, and assuming that private investment is constant:

a. How much should government spending be increased in order to achieve full employment?

b. What would happen if taxes were reduced by $10 billion? Is this enough to restore full employment? If not, how much of a tax reduction is needed? (HINT: refer back to Exhibit 2.)

c. What would be the effect of a simultaneous increase in government spending and taxes of $50 billion? A simultaneous decrease of $50 billion? Explain why. Would the situation be different in the case of a simultaneous increase in G and T under full employment? Explain.

3. What are our chief automatic stabilizers, and how do they operate?

4. What are the government's sources of revenue and its outlets for expenditures? Which are expansionary? Contractionary?

5. In view of the difficulties of applying fiscal policies, it has been suggested that a law involving an automatic tax rate formula be enacted. In this way tax rates could be tied to GNP and perhaps other measures, and would vary automatically when these other measures changed by given percentages. What are some of the chief advantages of such a proposal?

6. What fiscal-policy advantages do you see in the concept of a high-employment budget?

7. Evaluate the following argument about the public debt:

No individual or family would be wise to continue accumulating indebtedness indefinitely, for eventually all debts must either be paid or repudiated. It follows that this fundamental principle applies equally well to nations, for as Adam Smith himself said, *"What is prudence in the conduct of every private family can scarce be folly in that of a great kingdom."*

8. Prepare a "checklist" of questions covering the chief factors to be considered in evaluating the consequences of a public debt.

REFERENCES AND READING SUGGESTIONS

DOW, LOUIS A., *Business Fluctuations in a Dynamic Economy,* Merrill, Indianapolis, 1968, chap. 24.

ECKSTEIN, OTTO, *Public Finance,* 2d ed., Prentice-Hall, Englewood Cliffs, N.J., 1967, chap. 8.

Economic Report of the President, Government Printing Office, annual.

HEILBRONER, ROBERT L., and PETER L. BERNSTEIN, *A Primer on Government Spending,* Random House, New York, 1963.

THUROW, LESTER C. (ed.), *American Fiscal Policy,* Prentice-Hall, Englewood Cliffs, N.J., 1967.

TOBIN, JAMES, *National Economic Policy,* Yale University Press, New Haven, 1966, Part 2.

PART 3

Money, Banking, and
Monetary Policy: The
Fiscal-Monetary Mix

CHAPTER 13

Money and Credit in Our Economy

CHAPTER PREVIEW

What is the nature of money and of our monetary system?

Is credit the same as money? How important is credit in our economy?

Does money affect output and prices? Can we predict price-level changes in the economy on the basis of changes in the money supply?

Most people want money. Few can define it. Ask the average man, and he will probably say: "It's cash, and whatever you've got in the bank." Ask an economist, and he will probably answer by defining the four functions of money you learned about in an earlier chapter:

1. A *medium of exchange:* money used to conduct transactions.

2. A *measure of value:* money used to express the prices of current and future transactions.

3. A *standard of deferred payments:* money borrowed or loaned, earning interest until it is repaid.

4. A *store of value:* money saved so that it can be spent in the future.

But money and credit—which is an "extension" of money—are even more important than these functions indicate. For money and credit have a direct influence on the level of economic activity, and some economists argue that the supply of money is the chief determinant of the economy's health or sickness.

Money and Our Monetary System

A monetary system's primary task is to provide society with money that is widely acceptable and flexible enough in supply to meet the needs of economic activity.

The long history of money shows this is no easy task. As a result there has been a continuous evolution of monetary systems designed to achieve these two objectives.

What does it mean to say that the supply of money must be flexible? Interestingly enough, this question can only be answered in terms of the demand for money. Indeed, the demand for money, as this and the following chapters will show, poses the most fundamental problem faced by our monetary and banking system.

MONEY AND NEAR-MONIES

In the United States three main types of money are in use—coins, paper money, and demand deposits or checking-account money.

Coins comprise about 1 percent of the total money supply. Coins are *token money*, which means that their value as money is significantly greater than the market value of the metals from which they are made. If this were not so, it would pay for individuals to melt the coins down for their metallic content.

Paper money, such as one-dollar bills, five-dollar bills, and so on, makes up roughly 20 percent of the money supply. Any paper money you have will almost certainly say "Federal Reserve Note" across the top, signifying that it is issued by the Federal Reserve Banks, about which you will read more later. Federal Reserve Notes represent more than 98 percent of the total value of paper money in circulation. The rest consists of certain other types of paper money—some dating back to Civil War days—which are being retired by the Treasury. Coins and paper money together are called *currency*.

Demand deposits constitute the largest proportion of the money supply—almost 80 percent. Why are demand deposits regarded as money? Because a *demand deposit* is a promise on the part of a bank to pay immediately an amount of money specified by the customer who owns the deposit. Thus a demand deposit is sometimes called "checkbook money" because it permits transactions to be paid for by check rather than with currency. In contrast, money which is held in a bank account of an individual or firm for which the bank can require advance notice of withdrawal is called a *time deposit*. Such deposits,

for example, are held in commercial banks and savings banks.

Since currency and demand deposits are freely convertible into one another, economists ordinarily regard money as consisting of both currency and demand deposits; that is, *money = currency + demand deposits*. But a broader definition which includes time deposits might be preferable for certain purposes. See Exhibit 1.

Some other assets are almost, but not quite, money. These are called *near-monies* because their values are known in terms of money and they can easily be converted into money if desired. The most important examples are: (1) time or savings deposits, for which banks can require advance notice of withdrawal; (2) United States government bonds held by individuals and businesses; and (3) cash values of insurance policies. The concept of near-monies is important, because people who possess near-monies may feel wealthier than those who do not, and hence will have a higher propensity-to-consume curve.

MONETARY STANDARDS

Every nation has a *monetary standard*—a set of laws and practices which determines the quantity and quality of its money, and establishes the conditions, if any, under which currency is ultimately redeemable. For instance, if a nation's money supply is based on the quantity of gold that it has, and if its currency is redeemable in gold, the country is said to be on a gold standard.

Historically, certain metals have usually been used as monetary bases by most nations, but gold and silver—especially the former—have been preferred above all others since the early Christian era. In principle, platinum, copper, diamonds, or any commodity could be used as a monetary base—even skunks or pigs—if the public were willing to accept it. Gold and silver are used because they are widely accepted, limited in supply, durable, and easily divided into monetary units. Diamonds and skunks, in contrast, do not meet all these qualifications. Historically, five major monetary standards have been used in various countries at one time or another.

Exhibit 1

Trying to Define Money

If you think you know exactly what money is, you are way ahead of most economists. For economists now are in the midst of a painstaking search for M_x—an ideal measure of the quantity of money available to the United States public.

Right now, two basic definitions of the quantity of money are in use:

1. M_1—demand deposits plus currency in circulation. This is the narrowest definition of the money supply, covering only portions of the liquid wealth that are instantly acceptable in exchange. Most economists would select this definition if forced to choose.

2. M_2—this includes not only demand deposits and currency, but also time deposits in the commercial banks. This definition is preferred by some economists who believe that changes in the nation's total money stock are the most crucial factor in shaping the course of the economy.

The answer to the money enigma apparently lies somewhere between these two definitions. Some monetary economists are working to develop a more precise definition—one which can be used to determine the influence of money on the levels of income, employment, and prices.

THE NATION'S MONEY SUPPLY

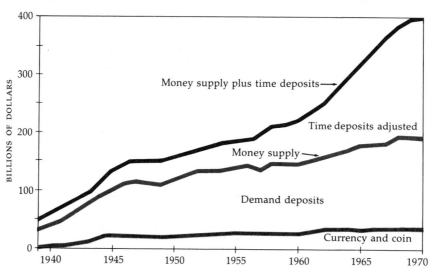

SOURCE: Board of Governors of the Federal Reserve System.

Gold (Coin) Standard

The essentials of a *gold coin standard,* or simply a gold standard, are that: (1) the national unit of currency (such as the dollar, pound, franc, mark, etc.) is defined by law in terms of a fixed weight of gold; (2) there is a free and unrestricted legal flow of the metal in any form into and out of the country; (3) gold coins are full legal tender for all debts; (4) there is free convertibility between the national currency and gold coins at the defined rate; and (5) there are no restrictions on the coinage of gold. This standard reigned supreme for the United States and about fifty other countries from the late 1800s to 1914, and then prevailed on a somewhat modified basis from 1914 to the early 1930s. Since then, no country has been on the gold standard.

Gold is said to be the disciplinarian *par excellence,* because under a gold standard the domestic money supply is regulated by, and tied directly to, the amount of gold that a country has. When a nation adhered to this standard, it found that an outflow of gold for business or speculative reasons would reduce the domestic money supply, and this in turn could induce contractions in investment, income, and employment within the economy; an inflow of gold, on the other hand, would increase the domestic money supply and this could have expansionary or even inflationary effects at home. Thus the gold coin standard assured automatic contractions and expansions of the money supply but did not always provide such changes at the most appropriate times or in the most desirable ways. Indeed, in the early 1930s those changes were strongly adverse, prompting nations to abandon the gold coin standard during the Great Depression.

Gold Bullion Standard

A *gold bullion standard* defines the national unit of currency in terms of a fixed weight of gold, but the gold is held in bars rather than coin. Gold does not circulate within the economy, and is available solely to meet the needs of industry (e.g., jewelers and dentists) and to settle international transactions. The United States and most of the other advanced nations adopted this monetary standard when they went off the gold coin standard in the 1930s. By switching from a gold coin to a gold bullion standard these countries felt that they would be able to "manage" their money rather than be subservient to it, while continuing to preserve confidence in their currencies both at home and abroad.

Gold Exchange Standard

A *gold exchange standard* provides gold exchange (a demand draft on a bank in a country which is on the gold coin standard) as redemption for its legal tender money. The gold exchange standard was particularly popular among nations which lacked gold or were politically dependent on other nations after World War I. But with the worldwide abandonment of the gold coin standard in the early thirties, this standard ceased to exist.

Bimetallic Standard

Under a *bimetallic standard,* the national currency is defined in terms of a fixed weight of two metals, usually gold and silver. The results, for the most part, have been unsatisfactory, largely because of the operation of an interesting phenomenon first described by Sir Thomas Gresham, a sixteenth-century financier and Master of the Mint under Queen Elizabeth I:

Gresham's Law. When two kinds of metals of differing market values circulate with equal legal tender powers, the cheaper metal will become the chief circulating medium while the more costly metal is hoarded, melted down, or exported, thereby disappearing from circulation. Thus, cheap money tends to drive out dear money.

Gresham's Law operates in the following way. Suppose the government fixes the official *mint ratio* of two metals, say silver and gold, at 15:1. This means that $1 can be converted into 15 grains of silver or 1 grain of gold—a situation that actually existed in the United States during part of the nineteenth century. It follows that any change in the world market value (as distinguished from the fixed official mint value) of one metal in relation to the other will cause the metal with the higher value to disappear from circulation. This is because the metal which is relatively cheaper in the market will be taken to the mint, coined, and put into circulation, while coins made of the metal that is relatively dearer in the market will be taken out of circulation and hoarded, or else melted down and sold as bullion. In other words, a fixed mint ratio and a variable market ratio allow people to hold the more valuable money and pass on the less valuable.

This happened when the United States was on a bimetallic standard during the nineteenth century. Either gold or silver was always disappearing from circulation. Thus, during the first period of bimetallism, from 1792 to 1834, gold went out of circulation; during the second period, from 1834 to 1873, silver went out. After 1873, the political power of the silver producers was strong enough to persuade Congress to overvalue silver at the mint (thereby benefiting the western silver mining states). As a result gold disappeared from circulation.

Inconvertible Paper Standard

Under an *inconvertible paper standard,* the nation's unit of money cannot be freely converted into precious metals, although its value may be expressed in metallic terms. This standard has typically arisen during wars or economic emergencies when governments needed more freedom to control their money supplies than metallic standards would permit.

During the 1930s inconvertible paper standards became widespread as nations such as ours sought to manage their currencies in order to hasten economic recovery. In other words, an inconvertible paper standard may be quite compatible with a gold bullion standard. Thus, for international purposes, the United States and other advanced nations are on a gold bullion standard in that they may use gold to settle international claims; but for domestic purposes, all countries are on an inconvertible paper standard in that their currencies cannot be officially converted into gold, and gold is not available for domestic monetary use (although it can be bought and sold in some countries by private citizens).

WHAT IS THE VALUE OF MONEY?

If you cannot get gold for your money, what good is it? The answer is that the real value of money depends on its purchasing power—the quantity of goods or services that can be bought with a dollar.

You have probably heard it said that the dollar today is worth only 60 cents, or 50 cents—or perhaps even less. Such statements try to convey the idea that today's dollar buys only a fraction of what a dollar bought during some period in the past. Which period? It depends on the one you choose. The decline in the purchasing power of the dollar was much greater in the inflated 1960s than it was in the depressed 1930s.

In general, the value of money is defined in terms of its purchasing power, and is measured as the reciprocal or inverse of the general price level. Thus the higher the level of prices, the lower the value or purchasing power of money, and vice versa. These ideas are illustrated in Exhibit 2.

Exhibit 2

The Value of Money and Consumer Prices

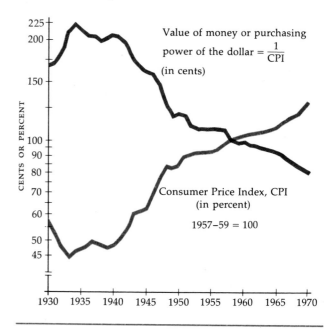

Box 1

Paper Money—A Long and Interesting History

The oldest known paper money dates from China, Ming Dynasty, between the years 1368 to 1399. This piece bears a stern warning to counterfeiters.

A 24-shilling note, Massachusetts, 1775, engraved by Paul Revere.

Obverse and reverse of three-pence note, Pennsylvania, 1764.

A $55 Continental Congress currency note, 1779, typical of issues to finance the Revolution. After 1781, the currency depreciated and was "Not worth a Continental."

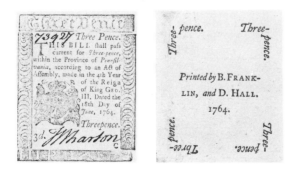

Obverse and reverse of penny note issued by first United States chartered bank, 1789.

Dix or $10 note, Louisiana, 1856.

United States fractional currency note worth 50 cents, 1875.

A 1,000 franc assignat note of the French Revolution. The republic issued these bills for a time, on the security of appropriated lands.

Hungarian inflation currency, a 100 quintillion pengo note, 1946, highest denomination note issued in the history of currency. (100,000,000,000,000,000,000)

SOURCE: The Chase National Bank Museum of Moneys of the World, New York. Published by special permission of the United States Secret Service. Further reproduction, in whole or in part, is strictly prohibited.

The Role of Credit

In the business world, the term *credit* always implies a promise by one party to pay another for money borrowed or for goods or services received. Credit may therefore be regarded as an extension of money.

From the viewpoint of the economy as a whole, credit and debt are the same thing looked at from two different sides. If a friend lends you some money, his credit to you is the same as your debt to him. The functions of credit and debt are intricately intertwined with those of money, since credit replaces money, supplements money, and in the final analysis serves as the base of our money supply.

WHAT ARE THE FUNCTIONS OF CREDIT?

Credit, like money, serves at least two major functions:

1. It *facilitates trade* by eliminating the necessity for barter. The production and distribution of goods is a complex process of many diverse activities involving exchanges of property and property rights on a credit basis. Imagine the effect on business if all credit were suddenly eliminated—if everyone in the economy had to pay cash for everything purchased.

2. It *channels savings* into productive investment, thereby encouraging technological progress and economic growth. A credit system means that businessmen can borrow savings and return them to the income stream through investment in plant, equipment, and research.

You may be able to think of other functions of credit. For example, how might credit affect the time distribution of consumption expenditures? Can you see how, if no lending were possible, a person with a large income today might have to hoard part of it for consumption later, while a person with a low income would have to do without some possible present consumption?

CREDIT INSTRUMENTS

Some credit is negotiated informally by verbal agreement between the borrower and lender, and some is handled on an open-book-account basis between business firms. For our purposes, however, the most significant part is credit represented by *credit instruments*—that is, written or printed financial documents serving as either promises to pay or orders to pay by means of which funds are transferred from one person to another.

The principal classes of credit instruments are notes, drafts, and bonds. A *promissory note,* or simply *note,* is one person's promise to pay another a specified sum of money by a given date, usually within a year. Such notes are issued by individuals, corporations, and government agencies. Firms make heavy use of notes in order to borrow working capital from banks at certain busy times of the year. The interest (or discount) on such loans is the commercial banks' chief source of income.

A *bond* is an agreement to pay a specified sum of money (called the *principal*) either at a future date or periodically over the course of a loan, during which time a fixed rate of interest may be paid on certain dates. Bonds are issued by corporations (corporate bonds), state and local governments (municipal bonds), and the federal government (government bonds). Bonds are used for long-term financing.

A *draft* is an unconditional written order by one party (the creditor or drawer) on a second party (the debtor or drawee) directing him to pay a third party (the bearer or payee) a specified sum of money. An ordinary check is an example. When you write a check, you are drawing a draft against your bank, ordering it to pay someone a certain amount of money.

The above definition of a draft applies equally well to a *bill of exchange,* which is used in international trade. An exporter, for instance, draws up a bill of exchange against his customer, an importer, and discounts it—i.e., sells it to his local bank at a little less than its face value. The bank then sends the bill to its correspondent bank in the city of the importer, which presents it to the importer for collection or acceptance at face value. If the bill of exchange were drawn on or accepted by a bank instead of an individual or firm, it would be called a *banker's acceptance.* This is a promise by a bank to pay specific bills for one of its customers.

THE MONEY MARKET

Markets exist for many types of credit instruments, just as they do for commodities. A *money market* is a center where short-term credit instruments are bought and sold. It is thus distinguished from the *capital market,* which deals with long-term instruments such as bonds, stocks, and mortgages. However, it is closely related to the capital market and to the foreign exchange, commodity, insurance, and bullion markets, all of which rely on the money market for credit.

The money market is actually a number of diverse markets, each involved in different types of credit. For instance, in the New York money market the principal subdivisions include: (1) the short-term government securities market, which trades in Treasury bills and certificates; (2) the commercial paper market, which handles short-term promissory notes of businesses; and (3) the acceptance market, which trades in bankers' acceptances.

In the money market the supply of short-term funds made available by lenders meets the demand for funds from borrowers. It is here that holders of short-term credit instruments convert these assets into cash. Lenders consist mainly of the Federal Reserve Banks which are the primary source of credit for most other banks; large commercial banks which place their funds in various kinds of credit instruments; and financial institutions like insurance and trust companies which invest in short-term "paper." Borrowers are chiefly the United States government, which sells 90-day Treasury bills and other short term certificates in order to meet its current expenses; brokerage houses and dealers in government securities, which borrow chiefly for the accounts of their customers; and investment banking houses, commodity dealers, importers, exporters, and business firms, all of whom sell future claims against money in order to obtain cash for current operations.

The New York money market is the largest in the United States. It attracts funds from the entire country and performs a vital function in financing the short-term needs of the federal government as well as the requirements of the business community.

Money Affects Output and Prices

How much money do people want to hold? How quickly do people spend money after they receive it? Both questions are obviously related, and both are important, but the second in particular has an interesting history dating back at least as far as the mid-eighteenth century.

You may not be able to see how fast individual dollars are spent, but you can measure the average speed of money movements as a whole rather easily. Let V stand for the *income velocity of money,* that is, the average number of times per year a dollar is spent on purchasing the economy's annual flow of final goods and services—its GNP. Then, if M denotes the nation's money supply as measured by the amount of money including currency and demand deposits in the hands of the public, the income velocity of money is defined as:

$$V = \frac{\text{GNP}}{M}$$

For example, if in a certain year the GNP was $800 billion and the stock of money was $200 billion, $V = (\$800/\$200) = 4$ per year for that year. In other words, each dollar must have been used an average of four times to purchase the economy's GNP. The income velocity of money is thus a measure of the economy's "output per dollar."

THE EQUATION OF EXCHANGE

The letter M in the above equation, of course, can be "transposed" to the left side so that the equation becomes:

$$MV = \text{GNP}$$

Suppose, however, that we make the equation more refined by expressing GNP in terms of its components—prices and quantities. Thus, let P stand for the average price of final goods and services produced during the year and let Q represent the physical quantity of those goods and services. The *value* of total output is then price times quantity; that is,

GNP = $P \times Q$, since, for example, GNP = price of apples times number of apples, plus price of haircuts times number of haircuts, plus . . . and so on for all final goods and services produced. The above equation can therefore be written:

$$MV = PQ$$

This is known as the *equation of exchange*. To illustrate it, consider a highly simplified case in which the students in your class compose an economy whose total supply of money M is $80; the class produces a quantity of output Q, equal to 60 units of a good; and the average price P of this output is $4 per unit. Then the equation of exchange tells us that V must equal 3, since

$$MV = PQ$$

or

$$(\$80)(3) = (\$4)(60)$$

In other words, each dollar is spent an average of 3 times per year on the class's output.

Thus the equation of exchange is actually an identity because it states that the total amount of money *spent* on goods and services, MV, is equal to the total amount of money *received* for goods and services, PQ.

THE QUANTITY THEORY OF MONEY

To understand what the equation of exchange tells us about the role of money in influencing national income and expenditure we have to examine some of its components.

1. Suppose we assume that V *remains constant*. This means that by controlling M we could control GNP. For instance, what happens if M is increased? In that case either P, or Q, or both will have to increase in order to maintain equality between the right and left side of the equation. The changes in P or Q will depend on the state of the economy. In a period of recession, Q will tend to rise relatively more than P as unemployed resources are put to work; in a period of high employment, P will tend to rise relatively more than Q as full utilization of resources is ap-

proached. What do you suppose would happen in a period of full employment?

2. Suppose we assume that *both V and Q remain constant*. This, in fact, is what the classical economists believed. They assumed that V was constant because it was determined by the long-run money-holding habits of households and business firms which, they argued, were fairly stable; and they assumed that Q was constant because the economy always tended toward full employment. In view of this they concluded that P depends directly on M. As a result, their theory has come to be known as the *quantity theory of money*.

Quantity Theory of Money. The level of prices in the economy is directly proportional to the quantity of money in circulation, such that a given percentage change in the stock of money will cause an equal percentage change in the price level.

The quantity theory thus states, for example, that a 10 percent increase in M will cause a 10 percent increase in P; a 5 percent decrease in M will cause a 5 percent decrease in P; and so on.

WHAT DOES THE EVIDENCE SHOW?

How well does the theory correspond with the facts? Can changes in M be used to predict changes in P?

In evaluating the quantity theory of money, it is necessary to distinguish between very long-term changes covering two or more decades, and short-term changes covering several years (or perhaps many quarters) up to as much as a decade. On this basis, the historical evidence suggests two major classes of findings.

1. During a number of long-run periods changes in P have appeared to be closely tied to changes in M. For example, the Spanish importation of gold and silver from the New World caused major price increases in Spain and Europe; the discovery of gold in the United States, Canada, and South Africa during the latter half of the nineteenth century brought sudden expansions in the money supply and rapidly rising prices; and the excessive borrowing and printing of money by certain countries during and after World Wars I and II resulted in a continuous upward spiraling of prices. In these and various other cases

prices rose with increases in the quantity of money and without corresponding increases in output, while the long-run income velocity of money was fairly stable.

2. In the short run, V varies a good deal, as can be seen in Exhibit 3. But if we omit the exceptional years, like those of the Great Depression, World Wars I and II, and Vietnam, we find that V has usually stayed in the 3 to 4 range. But this is still a fairly wide range: an increase from 3 to 4 is 33⅓ percent; a decrease from 4 to 3 is 25 percent. And output, of course, may also fluctuate substantially from year to year. As a result of complexities such as these, the quantity theory of money has not yet proved very suitable for predicting short-run changes in P on the basis of changes in M.

Exhibit 3

The Income Velocity of Money

The income velocity of money has usually ranged between 3 and 4—except during extreme periods of war or depression.

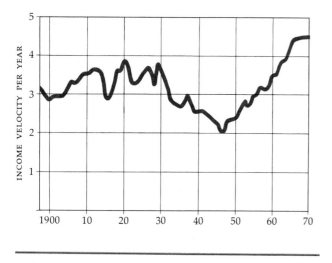

THE REBIRTH OF THE QUANTITY THEORY

After lying relatively dormant for several decades, the quantity theory of money has, since the 1960s, been revived by some economists, notably Professor Milton Friedman of the University of Chicago. The so-called Friedmanites are largely concerned with developing a theory of how V changes in the short run. For example, it is already known that at least two major sets of factors that affect V are:

1. The frequency with which people are paid. Money moves more quickly if payments are made weekly instead of monthly because people then need to hold less money for their day-to-day transactions.

2. Public confidence in the economy. If people fear unemployment or are pessimistic about the future, they will tend to refrain from spending by increasing their percentage of income saved. The larger the proportion of saving that occurs without a corresponding increase in investment, the more slowly money turns over and hence the lower its velocity.

It follows that if economists can learn more about the factors affecting short-run fluctuations in V, and if these factors can be predicted or controlled with sufficient reliability, the quantity theory of money may become the basis of a general theory of price-level changes within the economy.

SUMMARY OF IMPORTANT IDEAS

1. Money is a medium of exchange, a measure of value, a standard of deferred payments, and a store of value. The demand for money is the most fundamental problem of our monetary and banking system.

2. The supply of money consists of both currency and demand deposits. Near-monies consist of highly liquid assets like time and savings deposits, United States government bonds, and the cash value of insurance policies.

3. Historically, the chief monetary standards of nations have been the gold (coin) standard, gold bullion standard, gold exchange standard, bimetallic standard, and inconvertible paper standard. Most advanced nations today are on a gold bullion standard for international settlement of claims, and an inconvertible paper standard for domestic purposes.

4. Credit serves the same functions as money in varying degrees. The chief instruments of credit are notes, drafts, and bonds. Various types of short-term credit instruments are bought and sold in the money market.

5. The equation of exchange describes a useful relationship between money, its velocity of circulation, the price level, and the volume of output. But it must be interpreted with care. Research indicates that among these four variables velocity in particular varies widely in the short run, thereby limiting predictions of the price level on the basis of changes in the supply of money.

FOR HOMEWORK AND DISCUSSION

1. *Terms and concepts to review:*

money	inconvertible paper
token money	standard
currency	promissory note
demand deposit	draft
time deposit	bill of exchange
near-monies	banker's acceptance
monetary standard	bond
gold (coin) standard	money market
gold bullion standard	capital market
gold exchange standard	income velocity of
bimetallic standard	money
Gresham's Law	equation of exchange
mint ratio	quantity theory of
credit instrument	money

2. What are the basic functions of money? How might a severe inflation affect these functions?

3. On what kind of monetary standard are the United States and most other advanced nations? Why?

4. An increase in the general price level means that goods cost more in terms of money. This obviously makes money more valuable. True or false? Explain.

5. (*a*) Credit is said to be an "extension" of money. Why? (*b*) Where is the largest volume of short-term credit bought and sold? Explain.

6. (*a*) What would happen to the price level if the supply of money in the economy were doubled within the next few weeks? The next few years? Explain. (*b*) What causes the income velocity of circulation to change?

REFERENCES AND READING SUGGESTIONS

ANGELL, N., *The Story of Money*, Stokes, Philadelphia, 1929. A classic history of money.

BOARD OF GOVERNORS OF THE FEDERAL RESERVE SYSTEM, *The Federal Reserve System: Purposes and Functions*, 5th ed., Washington, D.C., 1963, chaps. 1, 4.

CHANDLER, LESTER V., *The Economics of Money and Banking*, 5th ed., Harper & Row, New York, 1969, chaps. 1–4.

ROBERTSON, ROSS M., *History of the American Economy*, 2d ed., Harcourt, Brace & World, New York, 1964, chaps. 7, 13, 20.

CHAPTER 14

Deposit Banking, the Federal Reserve System, and Monetary Policy

CHAPTER PREVIEW

How do banks create money?

What is the Federal Reserve System? How did it come about? What are its objectives, organization, and functions?

How does the Federal Reserve System establish monetary policy? What instruments of monetary policy are available to it?

The average person probably thinks of a bank as a place in which to deposit money on payday against which he can write checks as the need arises. But banks are much more than mere depositories for people's funds. They are institutions which play a fundamental role in the financial and monetary structure of our economy.

In a more specific sense, banks deal in money and credit instruments. A *commercial bank* is a financial institution chartered by federal or state governments, and is primarily engaged in making short-term commercial and industrial loans by creating demand or checking deposits, and retiring loans by canceling demand deposits. In addition, it may or may not carry on functions performed by other financial institutions (e.g., insurance companies, savings-and-loan associations, etc.), such as providing life insurance, holding time or savings deposits, making long-term mortgage loans, renting safe-deposit boxes, operating a trust department, and so on.

Against this background, the present chapter is concerned with answering the basic questions about our banking system in the above Preview.

How Commercial Banks Create Deposits

We have already learned that:

Money = currency + demand deposits

This formula states at a glance what economists ordinarily mean by money. But most of us are more familiar with currency than with demand deposits. In view of this it seems appropriate to ask: Who determines the amount of currency in circulation?

The answer is "the public"—you and I and everyone else. Since currency and demand deposits are interchangeable, you will generally "cash" a check when you need currency, and deposit currency in your checking account when you have more cash than you need.

Everyone else behaves in much the same way. As a result, the public always holds the exact amount of cash that it wants, shifting its holdings back and forth between currency and demand deposits. On an average for the year as a whole, the economy holds about 20 percent of its money in currency and 80 percent in demand deposits. But at certain times of the year, such as Christmas and Easter, the proportion of currency in circulation increases because people desire more cash for spending; after the holidays, the proportion of currency in circulation decreases as businessmen deposit their cash receipts in their checking accounts.

THE FUNDAMENTAL PRINCIPLE OF DEPOSIT BANKING

Since demand deposits are by far the largest part of our money supply, it is important for us to know how they come into existence and the role they play.

The credit creation process of deposit banking is based on the following fundamental principle:

The customers of a bank will not withdraw their funds at once. On any given day, some customers will decrease their deposits by withdrawing funds in the form of cash and checks drawn on the bank, while others will increase their deposits by bringing in funds in the form of cash and checks drawn on other banks. Under normal conditions, the volume of deposits and withdrawals will tend to be equal over a period of time.

This principle was discovered centuries ago by the English goldsmiths. They found that when people deposited gold with them for safekeeping, it was not usually necessary to store all of the gold away; a portion of it could be kept on reserve in the event that some individuals might want to withdraw their gold, and the rest could be "put to work" earning interest by lending it out to others with the promise of repayment.

In a bank, of course, there is always the possibility that withdrawals will exceed deposits during some periods. Experience suggests that reserves equal to less than 5 percent of deposits are usually more than adequate to meet such contingencies. However, the percentage of reserves which banks actually keep on hand is considerably higher than this, for reasons of monetary control which will be explained subsequently.

CREATING BANK DEPOSITS

Suppose you received $1,000 in the mail this morning—perhaps as an inheritance from a deceased rich relative whom you never knew you had, or as a bonus from your boss, or as a reward for returning a rich lady's lost poodle.

Let us assume that you deposit the money in a commercial bank. This means the bank now owes you $1,000 because the bank has legally obligated itself to honor checks drawn by you upon it up to that amount.

After your check has "cleared," what the bank does with the money depends on the *legal reserve* requirement, that is, the minimum proportion of its demand deposits that a bank is required by law to keep on hand in the form of vault cash or as a deposit at the central bank (the Federal Reserve Bank). (In contrast, any amount over and above the legal reserve is called an *excess reserve*, since it represents the surplus of vault cash or deposits with other banks which a bank has available for loans and investments).

For instance, suppose the legal reserve requirement is 20 percent. Then your $1,000 will have the following effects when you take it to the bank:

STAGE 1.   You deposit $1,000 in the bank. The bank will set aside 20 percent or $200 as legal reserves, and

---

Exhibit 1

Multiple Expansion of Bank Deposits through the Banking System
(data are rounded to nearest dollar)

Cumulative expansion in deposits by the banking system as a whole, assuming a $1,000 initial deposit and a legal reserve requirement of 20 percent.

Banks	New deposits	Legal reserves	New loans (excess reserves)	Cumulative deposits
Stage 1	$1,000	$ 200	$ 800	$1,000
Stage 2	800	160	640	1,800
Stage 3	640	128	512	2,440
Stage 4	512	102	410	2,952
Stage 5	410	82	328	3,362
Stage 6	328	66	262	3,690
Stage 7	262	52	210	3,952
Stage 8	210	42	168	4,162
Stage 9	168	34	134	4,330
Stage 10	134	27	107	4,464
All other stages	536	107	429	5,000
Totals	$5,000	$1,000	$4,000	

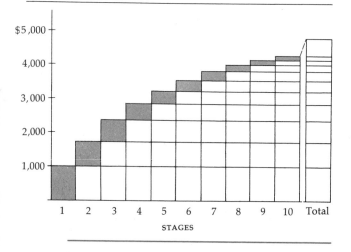

try to put the remaining 80 percent or $800 "to work" by acquiring such income-earning assets as bonds, mortgages, or loans. Suppose that the bank lends the $800 to a businessman who needs the money to buy raw materials. In return, the businessman gives the bank his promissory note for the amount of the loan.

What does the businessman do with the $800? Although he could take it out in cash, he will probably find it more convenient to write checks against it in order to pay his bills. When his suppliers receive the checks totaling $800, they deposit them in their own banks which in turn present them to your bank for payment. Thus, your bank, which may be called a "Stage 1" bank, loses $800 in cash reserves to some other banks in the system which we shall call "Stage 2" banks.

STAGE 2.   What do the Stage 2 banks do with the $800 in new deposits that they now have? They simply follow the same lending procedure as the Stage 1 bank: first they set aside 20 percent of $800 or $160 as legal reserve, and then lend the remaining 80 percent or $640. The money soon ends up in other banks which we may call "Stage 3" banks.

The deposit creation process thus goes on and on until all excess reserves in the system are "used up" —that is, loaned out—or, equivalently, until no bank in the system has reserves greater than its legal reserve.

The entire process is illustrated in Exhibit 1. Note that the *total* expansion of deposits created by the banking system as a whole is a multiple of the initial deposit—in this case $5,000 for $1,000, or a ratio of 5:1.

TEST YOURSELF

Does the multiple expansion of bank deposits work in reverse? If you make a $1,000 withdrawal from the bank, will this result in a 5:1 multiple contraction of deposits for the banking system as a whole? The answer is yes. However, you might try to prove it to yourself by reversing the process in Exhibit 1 and explaining your reasoning.

The same process is described in Exhibit 2 in terms of changes in the banks' balance sheets. Either approach can be used to illustrate what may be called the principle of *multiple expansion of bank deposits*. Can you express this principle in your own words?

THE DEPOSIT EXPANSION MULTIPLIER

You may have noticed that the expansion in deposits of the banking system as a whole is related to the legal reserve ratio. This is indeed the case. You can check for yourself in Exhibit 1 that

$$\text{Deposit expansion multiplier} = \frac{1}{\text{legal reserve ratio}}$$

Hence if you know the legal reserve ratio, you can determine the deposit expansion multiplier immediately. For instance, the legal reserve ratio is 20 percent, or $\frac{1}{5}$. Therefore:

$$\text{Deposit expansion multiplier} = \frac{1}{\frac{1}{5}} = 5$$

This means that an increase in a bank's deposits of $1,000 may result in as much as a $5 \times \$1,000 = \$5,000$ total expansion in deposits for the banking system as a whole (including the initial deposit). The same formula also applies to a decrease in bank deposits. Go back and check this for yourself in Exhibit 1, just to make sure you see how it works.

Deposit Expansion Multiplier. An increase in a bank's deposits may (because of an increase in its excess reserves) cause a larger or magnified increase in the total deposits of the banking system as a whole; similarly, a decrease in a bank's deposits may cause a larger or magnified decrease in the total deposits of the banking system as a whole. The total cumulative expansion (or contraction) will at most be some multiple of the initial deposit, as determined by the reciprocal of the legal reserve ratio.

How does this multiplier principle compare with the one you studied earlier pertaining to investment and income? Do you see any analogy between the legal reserve ratio and the marginal propensity to save? Now is a good time to turn back and refresh your knowledge of the investment multiplier, but keep in mind as you compare the two multiplier concepts that income and money are not the same thing. One is a "flow"; the other is a "stock."

A "MONOPOLY BANK" AND THE BANKING SYSTEM

It is interesting to observe how the principle of multiple expansion of bank deposits would operate if there were just one bank—a "monopoly" bank—instead of many independently owned banks.

Exhibit 2

Multiple Expansion of Bank Deposits through the Banking System, Expressed in Terms of Balance Sheet Changes

1. You deposit $1,000. The bank sets aside 20 percent or $200 in legal reserves, and hence has 80 percent or $800 in excess reserves available for lending.

STAGE 1 BANK

Assets (what the bank owns)		Liabilities (what the bank owes)	
Reserves	+$1,000	Deposits	+$1,000
Legal reserves	+$200		
Excess reserves	+ 800		

2. Businessmen borrow the $800 from a Stage 1 bank, and write checks for this amount which recipients then deposit to their own accounts in Stage 2 banks. The Stage 2 banks set aside 20 percent or $160 as legal reserves, and hence have 80 percent or $640 in excess reserves available for lending.

STAGE 2 BANKS

Assets (what the banks own)		Liabilities (what the banks owe)	
Reserves	+$800	Deposits	+$800
Legal reserves	+$160		
Excess reserves	+ 640		

3. Businessmen then borrow the $640 from Stage 2 banks, and write checks for this amount, which soon ends up as deposits in Stage 3 banks. What would the balance sheet look like for Stage 3 banks?

This process continues as the banking system's new deposits approach a total of $5,000.

A monopoly bank would behave exactly as the banking system as a whole behaves. It would receive all deposits and grant all loans, and since it would be the only bank in the system, there would be no other banks to which it could lose reserves when checks that were drawn upon it were presented for payment. Thus, assuming a legal reserve requirement of 20 percent, the monopoly bank would simply continue to lend its excess reserves until it produced a 5:1 expansion of bank deposits.

Could one bank in a system of many banks expand its loan-created deposits at a faster rate than the rest? Clearly not, for as the borrowers wrote checks against their new deposits, those checks would be deposited by their recipients in other banks, which would in turn present them to the individual bank for payment. This individual bank, therefore, would soon find itself losing its cash reserves to other banks in the system. On the other hand, if all banks in the system expanded their loan-created deposits simultaneously by about the same amounts, the new checks deposited and paid out by the various banks would tend to cancel each other and hence no individual bank would need to lose its cash reserves.

THREE QUALIFICATIONS

The principle of multiple expansion of bank deposits assumes that the banking system will produce a magnified expansion in deposits, such as 5:1 or some other ratio, depending on the legal reserve requirement and the assumption that banks always lend out their full amount of new excess reserves. Actually, this principle is modified in practice by at least three factors.

1. *Leakage of Cash into Circulation.* A businessman borrowing money from a bank may take part of it in cash. Or, someone who is paid a debt by check may "cash" some or all of it, rather than deposit the entire amount. For these reasons, some money that would otherwise serve as excess reserves will tend to leak out of the banking system, thereby leaving fewer new reserves available for banks to lend.

2. *Additional Excess Reserves.* Banks do not always lend out every dollar of their excess reserves. They may desire a "safety margin," or be unable to find good investments. Thus, if the legal reserve requirement were 20 precent, banks might have available an average reserve of 25 percent. This, of course, would reduce the deposit-creating ability of the banking system from 5:1 to 4:1.

3. *Willingness to Borrow and Lend.* The principle of multiple expansion of bank deposits assumes, of course, that businessmen are willing to borrow and banks are willing to lend. This may not always be so. During a recession or depression, for example, when businessmen are gloomy about the future, they may not borrow all that banks have available for lending; and banks, on the other hand, may prefer the safety of liquidity and hence decide to maintain a higher level of excess reserves rather than risk heavy withdrawals by the public or possible default on loans. Under most circumstances, however, bankers' decisions as to the levels of excess reserves that they want to keep on hand are likely to be more influenced by the interest rates that they can earn on the investment of these reserves, and less by other factors.

The Federal Reserve System

On December 23, 1913, President Woodrow Wilson signed the Federal Reserve Act establishing the Federal Reserve System. It was, according to its preamble, "An Act to provide for the establishment of Federal Reserve Banks, to furnish an elastic currency, to afford means of rediscounting commercial paper, to establish a more effective supervision of banking in the United States, and for other purposes." Section 4 of the new statute charged the Federal Reserve Banks with making ". . . such discounts, advancements, and accommodations as may be safely and reasonably made with due regard for . . . the maintenance of sound credit conditions, and the accommodations of commerce, industry, and agriculture."

The Act marked a new era in American banking. Periodic money panics, highlighted by the Panic of 1907, had plagued the country for many years. Basically, the Act was designed to end extreme variations in the money supply and to end panics, and thus to contribute to economic stability.

MONEY PANICS AND THE BANKING SYSTEM

American banking history records a series of attempts to provide a currency which could expand or contract according to the demands of business. Theoretically, the ability of commercial banks, through the lending process, to expand or contract the amount of money available should have provided for the demands occasioned by changes in business activity.

Commercial banks, however, while they could expand credit, could not add to the amount of available currency. Inasmuch as bank depositors had a legal right to withdraw their money in the form of currency or coin, banks provided for ordinary withdrawals by retaining a part of their total deposits in the form of reserves. These reserves usually consisted of currency, coin, and deposits in other banks.

A general demand by depositors for their money, therefore, at a time when the deposits created by loans were high could create a situation where the available amount of currency and coin might not cover the percentage of reserves which the banks had set up. An unusual demand by depositors forced banks to exchange their assets for currency. An attempt by one bank to supply itself with currency by withdrawing its reserve balance from another all too frequently set up a "chain reaction" which resulted in a widespread shortage of currency among many banks.

Some banks were forced to close, although their assets could have been converted into currency if sufficient time had been allowed. A widespread closing of banks resulting from unusual demands by depositors invariably brought on a period of economic depression. These unusual demands were called "money panics," and one which occurred in 1907 set into motion a thorough study of the money system.

The Congressional commission charged with this study found that almost all countries which had a money supply that could be expanded or contracted to meet the needs of the depositors also had some form of central bank. This bank had the power to issue a currency which depositors would accept. As a result of this and other studies, Congress in 1913 passed a law which created the Federal Reserve System.

OBJECTIVES, ORGANIZATION, AND FUNCTIONS OF THE FEDERAL RESERVE SYSTEM

The *Federal Reserve System* is the nation's central bank. Like other central banks throughout the world, its chief responsibility is to regulate the flow of money and credit in order to promote economic stability and growth. It also performs many service functions for commercial banks, the Treasury, and the public. In specific terms, the Federal Reserve System seeks to provide monetary conditions favorable to the realization of four national objectives: high employment, stable prices, economic growth, and a sound international financial position.

The Federal Reserve System is organized essentially as a pyramid, as illustrated in Exhibit 3. It is composed of several parts:

1. Member banks
2. Federal Reserve Banks
3. Board of Governors
4. Federal Open Market Committee
5. Other committees

Member Banks. At the base of the Federal Reserve pyramid are the System's member banks. All national banks (chartered by the federal government) must be members, and state banks may join if they meet certain requirements. Of about 14,000 commercial banks, rather less than half are members. However these member banks are for the most part the larger banks in the country, holding about 85 percent of all commercial bank deposits.

There are two classes of member banks: *reserve city banks,* located in any of about four dozen major centers of the nation, and *country banks.*

Each member bank has both obligations and privileges. The obligations include holding specified reserves at its district Federal Reserve Bank against the demand deposits of its depositors, subscribing to the capital stock (and thus being a part owner) of its district Federal Reserve Bank, and complying with the laws and regulations of membership. The privileges include prestige of membership, ability to borrow under certain conditions from its district Federal Reserve Bank, and the opportunity to use the many facilities and services provided by the System.

Exhibit 3

Organization of the Federal Reserve System

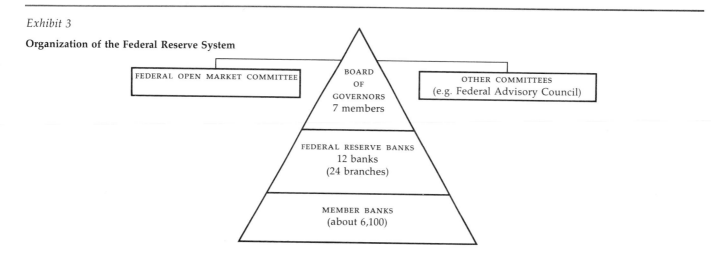

Exhibit 4

Federal Reserve Map of the United States

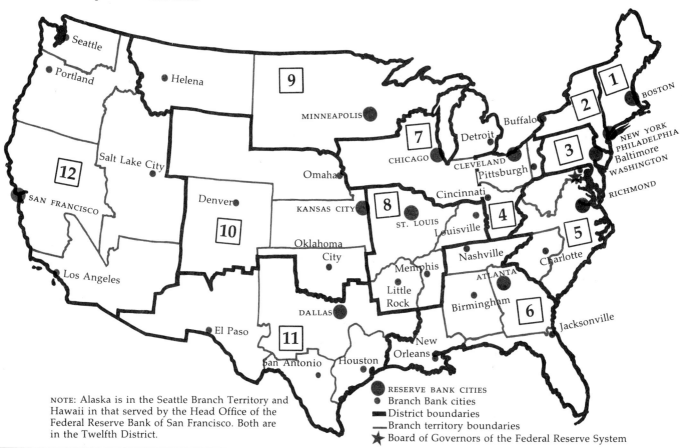

NOTE: Alaska is in the Seattle Branch Territory and Hawaii in that served by the Head Office of the Federal Reserve Bank of San Francisco. Both are in the Twelfth District.

● RESERVE BANK CITIES
• Branch Bank cities
▬ District boundaries
— Branch territory boundaries
★ Board of Governors of the Federal Reserve System

Federal Reserve Banks. The country is divided into 12 Federal Reserve districts, each with a Federal Reserve Bank. There are also 24 Federal Reserve Bank branches serving areas within the districts. As shown in Exhibit 4, the 12 cities with Federal Reserve head offices are Boston, New York, Philadelphia, Cleveland, Richmond, Atlanta, Chicago, St. Louis, Minneapolis, Kansas City, Dallas, and San Francisco.

Technically, each Federal Reserve Bank is owned by its member banks, which are the stockholders. However, unlike most private institutions, the Reserve Banks are operated in the public interest rather than for profit—even though they are in fact highly profitable. Thus, after meeting their expenses, they pay a relatively small part of their earnings to the member banks as dividends, and the major portion goes to the United States Treasury as "interest" on Federal Reserve Notes issued by the Reserve Banks. Note that the district Federal Reserve Banks (and branches) constitute the second level of the pyramid.

Board of Governors. At the peak of the pyramid is the Board of Governors in Washington. It consists of seven members appointed by the President and confirmed by the Senate. Members are appointed for 14 years, one term expiring every 2 years, thereby minimizing the influence of political pressure groups.

The Board supervises the System, and sees that it performs effectively. But its prime function is to influence the role of money and credit within the economy by altering the reserve requirements of member banks, changing discount (or interest) rates which member banks incur when they borrow from their Reserve Banks, authorizing the purchase or sale of government securities by the Federal Reserve Banks, setting margin (or down payment) requirements on the purchases of securities by the public, and establishing maximum interest rates payable on member banks' time deposits.

Federal Open Market Committee. The most important policy-making body within the System, this committee consists of 12 members—the 7 Governors plus 5 Presidents of the Federal Reserve Banks. Its chief function is to make policy for the System's purchase and sale of government and other securities in the open market in New York. Actual transactions are carried on by the so-called "Trading Desk" of the Federal Reserve Bank of New York. Government securities bought outright are then prorated among the 12 Reserve Banks according to a formula based upon the reserve ratios of the various Reserve Banks.

Other Committees. Several other committees play a significant role in the System's operations. One of these is the Federal Advisory Council, which advises the Board on important current developments.

Like the central banks of many other countries, the Federal Reserve System also provides a number of important services to the Treasury, the public, and commercial banks. These are described briefly in Exhibit 5.

The Federal Reserve Banks and Monetary Policy

"Federal Reserve Raises Reserve Requirements"
"Discount Rate Increased by Fed"
"Fed Enters Market to Sell U.S. Securities"

Headlines like these often appear in the financial news. They raise a number of questions: How effectively does the Federal Reserve perform? How does it influence money? Credit? Interest rates? Spending? Prices?

The Federal Reserve System is the nation's central bank—a "banker's bank" which performs much the same role for its member banks that the member banks perform for the public. But the System also possesses certain important instruments of control which are used to implement the nation's monetary policy, and thereby modify or even reverse the direction of the economy. There are basically five such instruments:

1. Reserve requirements
2. Open market operations
3. Discount rate
4. Margin regulations
5. Moral suasion

The first three are general controls because they influence the nation's money supply and the availability of credit. The fourth is a selective tool aimed specifically at the stock market. The fifth is a psychological device which relies on personal talk and public opinion.

Exhibit 5

Service Functions of the Federal Reserve System

1. Fiscal agency functions. The Reserve Banks service the Treasury's checking accounts; assist in the sale, transfer, and redemption of government securities; pay interest coupons; and assist the Treasury and other government agencies in many other ways.

2. Collection of checks and noncash items. The System operates a nationwide "clearing house" for checks, drafts, and similar items. Member banks route these items to Reserve Banks, which in turn send them to the proper places for collection. Settlement is accomplished by means of entries to the accounts which member banks maintain with the Reserve Banks.

3. Wire transfer of funds. The System transfers funds by wire from one part of the country to another. For example, if a national concern headquartered in New York wishes to transfer funds to its Chicago office it can have its bank request the transfer through the System's wire transfer facilities. The New York Reserve Bank will deduct the funds from the balance of the New York commercial bank, and the Chicago Reserve Bank will add the funds to the reserve balance of the firm's bank in Chicago, which will credit the account of the firm. The Reserve Banks will then settle by means of an entry on the books of the Interdistrict Settlement Fund—a System clearing agency in Washington.

4. Supplying coin and currency. The Federal Reserve Banks provide a vital part of the machinery through which most coin and currency moves into and out of circulation. As the public demands more cash from commercial banks, the banks draw down their balances at the Federal Reserve in exchange for additional cash. Similarly, when cash flows in from the public, the banks deposit the funds in their accounts with the Reserve Banks.

5. Note issue. Look in your billfold and chances are that you will find a bill bearing a green seal. This is a Federal Reserve Note—the most common type of currency in circulation today. These notes, which are issued by the 12 Reserve Banks, are fully collateralized by government securities and certain other types of assets. When a Reserve Bank needs more currency to meet the demands of commercial banks, it can easily obtain the additional Federal Reserve Notes by pledging the proper collateral.

SOURCE: Adapted from the Federal Reserve Bank of Richmond.

Let us see how each of these instruments helps to shape the nation's monetary policy.

CHANGING RESERVE REQUIREMENTS

Commercial banks are required by law to maintain a reserve equal to a minimum percentage of their deposits. Members of the Federal Reserve System may hold this minimum reserve as a deposit in a Reserve Bank and as cash in their own vaults. The Board of Governors may change these legal reserve requirements within the following limits:

Reserve city banks:	10 to 22 percent
Country banks:	7 to 14 percent

Changes in reserve requirements affect the actions of member banks in two ways:

1. A decrease in the legal reserve ratio makes available more excess reserves for lending, and this tends to bring about an expansion in the privately held money supply. An increase in the legal reserve ratio has the opposite effect.

2. Changes in the reserve requirement alter the amount of deposits that a given volume of reserves can support. For example, if the legal reserve ratio is 10 percent, $1 million in additional reserves can support up to $10 million of new deposits. But if the reserve requirement is 20 percent, the additional reserves can only support up to $5 million of new deposits.

Thus, changes in the legal reserve requirement affect the economy as a whole in the following way:

A *decrease* in legal reserve requirements tends to be expansionary because it enlarges the money supply. An *increase* is contractionary because it reduces the money supply. The System can thus affect the supply of money, interest rates, and the availability of bank credit through its control over the legal reserve requirements and the volume of bank reserves.

The ability to alter the legal reserve ratio is the System's most powerful monetary tool. But it is a somewhat blunt tool, and is employed relatively seldom because other instruments of control are applied with greater flexibility and more refinement.

CHANGING THE DISCOUNT RATE

Federal Reserve Banks lend money at interest to their member banks just as the member banks lend money at interest to the public. Thus it may be said that the Federal Reserve Banks are wholesalers of credit, while the member banks are retailers. No Federal Reserve policy tool is as well known or as poorly understood as the *discount rate*—the interest rate charged member banks on their loans from the Reserve Banks. (It is called a "discount rate" because the interest on the loans is discounted when the loan is made, rather than collected when the loan is repaid.)

Member banks can borrow from the Federal Reserve Banks in two ways: by giving their own secured promissory notes or by "rediscounting" drafts, bills of exchange, or notes which they have already discounted for their customers. Since the late 1930s, it has been the typical practice of borrowing banks to use their own notes secured by government obligations rather than their customers' promissory notes. Hence we use the expression "discount rate" rather than "rediscount rate," the latter being an old-fashioned term which continues to hang on.

When a member bank borrows, the Federal Reserve Bank simply increases the member bank's reserves, thus permitting the member bank to increase its loans. Why would a member bank want to borrow from the Fed? Usually, it wants to replenish its reserves which may have "run down" for one or more of the reasons given in Exhibit 6. It follows that the Federal Reserve's policy at the "discount window" (an expression widely used in banking circles) can be quite significant for the economy as a whole.

Changes in the discount rate may be a significant tool for fighting inflationary and recessionary tendencies because (1) they directly affect the cost of borrowing by member banks, and (2) they indirectly affect interest rates and credit conditions in the economy.

Thus the direct effect of changes in the discount rate is to raise or lower the price of admission to the discount window. An increase in the discount rate makes it more expensive for member banks to borrow; a reduction has the opposite effect. Indirectly, increases in the discount rate exert pressure to bring about a rise in interest rates and a general tightening of credit; decreases in the discount rate tend to reduce the level of interest rates and encourage an easing of credit. See also the effects described in Exhibit 7.

The discount rate, although not the preeminent tool of monetary policy that it was during the early years of the Federal Reserve System, is nevertheless an important instrument. It is usually coordinated with open market operations because each helps to make the other more effective.

OPEN MARKET OPERATIONS: "THE FED IS IN THE MARKET"

"The Fed is in." This expression is heard frequently on Wall Street when the Federal Reserve Bank of New York buys or sells government securities such

---

Exhibit 6

Why Do Bank Reserves Fluctuate?

1. Seasonal (or short-term) forces may increase reserves in one season and be a persistent drain on them in another. In agricultural areas, banks tend to experience an inflow of funds during the crop-marketing season, when farmers deposit the checks they receive from the sale of their crops, and an outflow of funds during the rest of the year, when farmers draw on their deposit balances to meet living expenses and the cost of producing next year's crop. In resort areas, banks gain funds during the vacation season and lose funds during the off season.

2. Trend (or long-term) forces due to a bank's own policies may cause it to gain or lose reserves. If a bank is expanding its loans and investments less rapidly than other banks in its market area, it will find its reserves increasing; if it is expanding more rapidly, it will suffer a persistent loss of reserves.

3. Irregular forces of one or a few days' duration may cause a bank to have a reserve deficiency one day, an excess the next. There are many possible reasons for this. For example, a corporation may authorize its bank to transfer a large portion of its deposit to a bank in another city where additional funds are needed to meet expenses; or a crop failure, flood, or similar disaster may put local banks under severe reserve pressure. Obviously, it is impossible for banks to anticipate these and other sudden changes with reasonable accuracy.

as Treasury bills and Treasury bonds—sometimes as agent for the Federal Open Market Committee and sometimes as agent for the United States Treasury, foreign central banks, and some of the member banks

---

Exhibit 7

Bond Prices and Bond Yields Vary Inversely

If you buy a debt security such as a bond, the effective *or* going market rate of interest *on it is called the* yield to maturity, *or simply the* yield.

The accompanying chart shows the relationship between the market price and effective yield of a $100 bond maturing one year hence with a nominal interest rate of 3.5 percent (paying its holder an interest of $3.50 per annum). The chart shows that if you could buy the bond in the market today for around $99, you would receive $100 upon maturity plus $3.50 in interest, which is an effective yield of about 4.5 percent. On the other hand, if you bought the bond today at a market price of $101, you would still get $100 back at maturity (thereby losing $1 from your purchase price) plus $3.50 in interest, making an effective yield of about 2.5 percent. Thus:

The price of a bond varies inversely with its yield.

What bearing does this inverse relationship have on the discount rate?

1. When the discount rate is increased, banks find it more costly to borrow from the Federal Reserve, and hence prefer to replenish their reserves by selling some of their debt securities instead. The increased sale of securities tends to lower security prices and raise their yields. These higher market yields in turn tend to push up longer-term interest rates.

2. On the other hand when the discount rate is lowered, banks are likely to maintain their borrowings at the Federal Reserve's discount window at a higher level than would otherwise be the case. This tends to push interest rates down by encouraging banks to hold larger quantities of government securities.

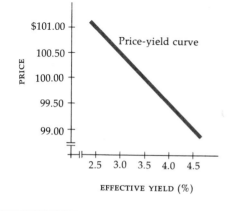

(as part of the services rendered by the Federal Reserve System).

Such transactions are commonly referred to as *open market operations.* They directly affect the volume of member bank reserves and hence the overall cost and availability of credit. They are the Fed's most important monetary tool for economic stabilization.

Here, essentially, is the way open market operations work.

When the Fed *buys* government securities in the open market, commercial banks' reserves are increased because:

1. If the Fed buys securities from member banks, it pays by increasing their reserves with the Federal Reserve Banks by the amount of the purchase.

2. If the Fed buys securities from nonbanks (such as individuals or corporations), it pays with checks drawn on itself. The sellers then deposit these checks in their own commercial banks, which in turn send the checks to the Federal Reserve Banks for collection. The Reserve Banks pay by increasing the reserves of the commercial banks.

When the Fed *sells* government securities in the open market, commercial banks' reserves are thereby decreased because:

1. If the Fed sells securities to member banks, they pay by reducing their reserves with the Federal Reserve Banks by the amount of the purchase.

2. If the Fed sells securities to nonbanks, they pay with checks drawn on commercial banks. The Federal Reserve Banks collect on these checks by reducing the reserves of the commercial banks. The commercial banks return the canceled checks to their depositors and reduce their deposit accounts accordingly.

The overall economic effects of these transactions can be summarized briefly:

Open market purchases of government securities are expansionary because they increase bank reserves and therefore permit a multiple growth of deposits; conversely, open market sales of government securities are contractionary because they reduce bank reserves and hence force a multiple decline of deposits.

MARGIN REGULATIONS

The Federal Reserve Board is also empowered to set *margin requirements*: the percentage down payment required when borrowing to finance purchases of stock. This power was granted by Congress because the excessive use of credit was a significant factor that led to the stock market crash of 1929. The higher the margin requirement, the larger the proportion of a stock purchase that must be paid for in cash. Therefore:

An increase in margin requirements discourages speculation on borrowed credit; a decrease may encourage security purchases.

The margin requirement is thus a device for dampening or stimulating activity in the securities market.

MORAL SUASION

Of course, Reserve officials can always exert pressure on bankers by using oral and written appeals to expand or restrict credit without compelling compliance. This process, called *moral suasion,* has been successful on a number of occasions: in recessions, to stimulate the expansion of credit by encouraging banks to lend more; in inflations, to discourage lending and to restrict the expansion of credit. In a more general sense, the Federal Reserve exercises moral suasion every day when it advises individual member banks on ordinary loan policy.

The Board also has the power to establish interest ceilings on member-bank time and savings deposits. In the past, it has also exercised control over installment terms for the purchase of consumer goods, and mortgage terms for the purchase of houses.

Of course, all the above instruments of monetary control are coordinated by the Federal Reserve in order to achieve its overall objective of promoting economic growth and stability through the money supply.

Is Monetary Policy Really Useful?

How effective is monetary policy in influencing economic activity? As with all policy areas of economics, these questions are the subject of continuous debate. However, the chief "pros" and "cons" can be outlined briefly.

ADVANTAGES OF MONETARY POLICY

In evaluating the usefulness of monetary policy, it is often instructive to compare it with fiscal policy as an alternative approach to fighting inflation and unemployment.

NONDISCRIMINATORY. Monetary controls are ordinarily employed in a general way to influence the total volume of credit. The Fed is nondiscriminatory with respect to the borrowers or activities that are to be encouraged or curtailed, and leaves it to the market to be "discriminatory" instead. Thus the home construction industry, for example, feels the effects of tight credit more quickly than most other industries because of its dependence on the mortgage market. Fiscal policy, on the other hand, involves changes in taxation and government spending, and these changes can alter the composition of total production as well as its overall level.

FLEXIBLE. Since control over monetary policy is centered in the Board of Governors, changes in policy can be made quickly and smoothly without getting snarled in administrative red tape. In contrast, fiscal policy involves budgetary considerations of taxation and spending, and Congress deliberates for many months before arriving at a decision.

NONPOLITICAL. In establishing the Federal Reserve System, Congress gave it political independence to assure its effective performance. Thus, it provided 14-year terms of office for appointed Board members, made them ineligible for reappointment, staggered their terms of office, and provided for the election of Reserve Bank presidents by their own boards of directors subject to the approval of the Federal Reserve Board. As a result, the institution can base its day-to-day decisions on economic grounds without political interference. In contrast, fiscal policy is always partly influenced by politics.

LIMITATIONS OF MONETARY POLICY

Whereas the advantages of monetary policy are fairly general, most of its limitations arise out of specific situations and circumstances.

INCOMPLETE COUNTERCYCLICAL EFFECTIVENESS. During an inflation the Federal Reserve can use its instruments of control to choke off borrowing and to establish an effective tight money policy. But during a recession, even the easiest money policy provides no assurance that businessmen will want to borrow. If they regard the business outlook as poor, the desired increase in loans and spending will not be realized. Further, there is the possibility that commercial bankers may be unwilling to lend out their excess reserves. For these reasons, monetary policy is far more effective as an anti-inflationary, rather than an anti-recessionary, device.

COST-PUSH AND PROFIT-PUSH INFLATION. Monetary policy is more effective in curbing excessive demand, or in coping with demand-pull inflationary forces rather than cost-push or profit-push forces. The last two result from upward pressures on wages and prices—pressures which monetary policy can at most hope to dampen but not eliminate.

CONFLICT WITH TREASURY OBJECTIVES. Every debtor likes low interest rates, especially the United States Treasury, which is the biggest debtor of all. Since the Treasury is continually refunding or selling new bonds, it wants to keep the interest cost as low as possible. Indeed, a difference of 1 percent in the interest rate on government securities can cost the Treasury several billion dollars. Reserve officials, on the other hand, regard high interest rates as an important anti-inflationary weapon. These two distinctly different goals have at times resulted in a policy conflict between the Treasury and the Federal Reserve. Although compromises or "accords" were eventually worked out, they tended to reduce somewhat the full effectiveness of anti-inflationary monetary policies.

LACK OF COMPLETE CONTROL. During the past several decades, two types of situations have made it more difficult for the Reserve authorities to exercise as high a degree of control over the total volume of lending as they would like. First, there has been a substantial growth of *financial intermediaries*, that is, nonbank lenders such as savings and loan associations, insurance companies, personal finance companies, and credit unions. These institutions do not create demand deposits, but they hold large volumes of savings which they are continually trying to "put to work" by investing or lending to the public. This will help to offset any restrictive monetary policies that the Reserve officials may be trying to pursue. Second, large holdings of government securities are in the hands of commercial banks and business corporations, which can sell them off as needed. Thus a bank which is short of reserves can sell some of its government securities to replenish its reserves, and a company which is unable to obtain additional bank credit can sell its securities in order to get the cash that it needs. Both these situations have weakened the effectiveness of monetary policies because they are outside the Fed's control.

CHANGES IN THE VELOCITY OF MONEY. An increase in the velocity of money ordinarily accompanies a restriction in its quantity, and vice versa. As you will recall, the reasons are understandable since changes in the velocity of money are affected by the public's confidence in the future course of the economy. The inverse relationship, of course, means that changes in velocity may tend to offset somewhat the efforts of the monetary authorities to reduce the money supply in inflationary periods and to expand it during recessions.

FORECASTING AND TIMING. Although monetary policies may be implemented more quickly than fiscal policies, they nevertheless suffer from similar kinds of forecasting and timing problems. As a result, the Federal Reserve has sometimes applied the brakes "too soon," thereby stopping economic expansions short of full employment.

The fact that there are more limitations than advantages should not lead you to believe that monetary policy is useless. It is a powerful force for stabilization, and will continue to play an important role in the economy.

SUMMARY OF IMPORTANT IDEAS

1. The public ultimately decides how much currency should be in circulation by interchanging currency and demand deposits as it wishes.

2. Deposit banking is based on the fundamental principle that all the customers of a bank will not withdraw their funds at the same time. On any given day, some people increase their demand deposits while others decrease them, so that the volume of deposits and withdrawals tends to be equal over a period of time.

3. A commercial bank creates money in the form of demand deposits when it makes loans. The amount of money that an individual bank can create depends on the size of its excess reserves.

4. Although an individual bank can lend no more than its excess reserves, the banking system as a whole can lend an amount which is a multiple of any initial deposit. This multiple expansion of bank deposits can be expressed concisely by the deposit creation multiplier, which is equal to the reciprocal of the legal reserve ratio. The multiplier process works both ways—for a deposit expansion as well as for a deposit contraction.

5. A "monopoly bank" would have the same multiple-deposit expansion ability as the banking system as a whole. But in a system of many independently owned competitive banks, a bank that tried to expand its loan-created deposits at a faster rate than other banks would find itself losing cash reserves to other banks as its checks were presented for payment. The opposite situation would occur for a bank that contracted its loan-created deposits at a faster rate than other banks. It would find itself gaining cash reserves in relation to them.

6. The potential expansion of bank credit by the banking system may in reality be limited, depending on the leakage of cash into circulation, the additional excess reserves which banks choose to hold, and the willingness of banks to lend and the public to borrow. These factors tend to reduce the deposit creation multiplier effect.

7. The Federal Reserve System is the nation's central bank—a banker's bank which emerged in the early part of this century after a long history of money

panics. Its chief responsibility is to regulate the supply of money and credit in order to promote economic stability and growth. It also performs many service functions for its member banks, the United States Treasury, and the public.

8. The chief instruments of monetary policy available to the Federal Reserve System are reserve requirements, the discount rate, open market operations, margin regulations, and moral suasion. These tools are usually coordinated by the Reserve officials in order to achieve the System's overall objectives of promoting stable economic growth through the money supply.

9. Monetary policy has advantages and limitations as a method of economic stabilization. Its chief advantages are that it is:

    a. Nondiscriminatory
    b. Flexible
    c. Nonpolitical

Its main limitations are that it:

    a. May serve as an incomplete countercyclical weapon
    b. Is relatively ineffective in combating inflationary forces caused by cost-push pressures
    c. Sometimes conflicts with Treasury goals
    d. Lacks control of nonbank lending and credit operations
    e. May be offset by changes in the velocity of circulation of money
    f. Suffers from precision due to imperfect forecasting and timing

Despite these shortcomings, monetary control will probably continue to play an integral role in our general stabilization policy.

FOR HOMEWORK AND DISCUSSION

1. *Terms and concepts to review:*

commercial bank	Board of Governors
legal reserve	Federal Open Market
excess reserve	Committee
multiple expansion of bank deposits	Federal Advisory Council
	discount rate

deposit expansion
multiplier

yield

Federal Reserve
System

open market operations

margin regulations

moral suasion

member bank

financial intermediaries

Federal Reserve Bank

2. Construct a stair-step chart showing the potential cumulative expansion of deposits at each "round," on the basis of an initial deposit of $1,000 and a legal reserve of 15 percent. On your chart, show the initial deposit, then show the results of 10 complete rounds and the total as suggested by the following axes.

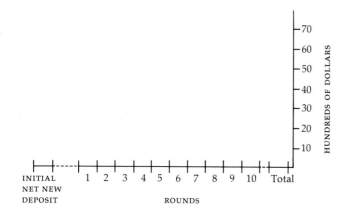

3. If banks are required to hold $12 out of every hundred dollars they receive, what is the total potential expansion of new deposits by the banking system resulting from an initial deposit of $5,000?

4. Does the deposit creation multiplier state the *actual* coefficient of deposit expansion for the banking system? Explain.

5. Since no bank holds enough reserves to honor all possible withdrawals simultaneously, what is the purpose of having a legal reserve requirement?

6. How do changes in reserve requirements, the discount rate, and margin requirements affect economic activity?

7. How do open market operations work? When might they tend to be expansionary? Contractionary?

REFERENCES AND READING SUGGESTIONS

BERNSTEIN, PETER L., *A Primer on Money, Banking, and Gold*, Random House, New York, 1965.

DOW, LOUIS A., *Business Fluctuations in a Dynamic Economy*, Merrill, Indianapolis, 1968, chaps. 21–23.

DUESENBERRY, JAMES S., *Money and Credit: Impact and Control*, 2d ed., Prentice-Hall, New York, 1967.

SUBCOMMITTEE ON DOMESTIC FINANCE, Committee on Banking and Currency, House of Representatives, *A Primer on Money* (88th Congress, 2d Session, August 5, 1964), and *Money Facts* (88th Congress, 2d Session, September 21, 1964).

CHAPTER 15

Synthesis of Fiscal and Monetary Policy: Problems of Coordination and Conflict

CHAPTER PREVIEW

What is the nature of the conflict between full employment and inflation? Are there practical guidelines which policy makers can use to minimize the conflict?

Is there a conflict between economic growth and inflation? Can we select a "best" combination of fiscal and monetary policies—one which provides sustained economic growth without significant inflation?

How do fiscal and monetary policies affect our position in the world economy? Is one combination of policies desirable for domestic purposes and another for international purposes?

How can monetary and fiscal policy be used to bring about a high level of employment and steady economic growth without inflation? Responsibility for achieving these goals of economic stabilization has been given to various policy-making authorities.

Thus, the major responsibility for monetary management rests with the Federal Reserve System. Fiscal actions, on the other hand, consist of spending and taxing by the federal government, for which the Congress and the Administration—including the Treasury, the Bureau of the Budget, and the President—are responsible.

The purpose of this chapter is to synthesize the two policy approaches by pointing out the need for their coordination and by illustrating the types of conflicts that arise in attempting to use monetary and fiscal tools for achieving the goals stated above.

Conflicts Between Full Employment and Inflation

The preceding chapters emphasized fiscal and monetary policy as means of maintaining the level of spending needed to assure full employment. To review briefly: in Exhibit 1, the line $(C + I + G)_0$ represents the objective of a well-coordinated fiscal

Exhibit 1

**Full Employment and Price Stability
Through Fiscal and Monetary Policy**

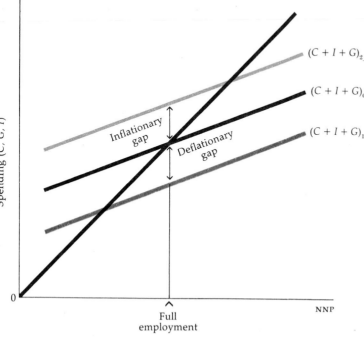

and monetary policy. It expresses the full employment level of *total* spending by households, businesses, and government. A lower level of total spending such as $(C + I + G)_1$ will produce a deflationary gap; a higher level will produce an inflationary gap.

GUIDELINES FOR POLICY COORDINATION

What kinds of fiscal and monetary policies should be employed to close a deflationary or an inflationary gap?

Since fiscal policy alters government spending, its direct impact is felt through changes in G. And since it also varies taxes on both consumers and businesses, it may well have a direct impact on C and I. On the other hand, since monetary policy involves changes in demand deposits and the money supply,

its direct impact is on businessmen and hence is first felt through modifications in I. Therefore, we can suggest several guidelines for coordinating fiscal and monetary policies.

If a deflationary gap exists, as represented by the aggregate demand schedule $(C + I + G)_1$, then:

1. An appropriate fiscal policy would increase government expenditures and reduce taxes, thereby increasing G and probably C and I as well. (Why do we say "probably" C and I? Why not "surely"?)

2. An appropriate monetary policy would increase the money supply by easing credit, thereby further encouraging businessmen to increase I.

The result of these combined policies would be to shift the aggregate demand schedule back up toward the full-employment level represented by the $(C + I + G)_0$ line.

On the other hand, an inflationary gap as represented by the aggregate demand schedule $(C + I + G)_2$ requires a different approach to fiscal and monetary policy. Can you suggest the proper guidelines?

This analysis emphasizes that different combinations of fiscal and monetary policy can be used to bring about full employment. In the real world, of course, political and administrative factors will also play a powerful part in determining the proper mix, and so the final choice may not always be the one suggested by economic considerations alone.

OBJECTIVES TEND TO CONFLICT

Unfortunately, the situation is not as simple as the above guidelines suggest. We have learned since the 1950s that *there is a conflict between maintaining price stability and achieving full employment; the general price level begins to rise before full employment is reached.*

This situation occurs for several reasons. As the economy approaches full employment:

1. Shortages of specific resources develop in some markets even though there are surpluses in others, thereby tending to raise production costs.

2. The overall reduction in unemployment strengthens the bargaining position of unions, enabling them to press more effectively for wage increases. Non-

union wages also tend to rise, sometimes more rapidly than union wages.

3. Rising profit margins and fuller utilization of capacity make it easier for businessmen to grant wage increases and to "pass on" part or all of these increases by raising prices.

Prices will remain stable only if aggregate spending is sufficiently below the full employment level. What should fiscal and monetary policy do—feed inflation by raising aggregate demand to the full employment level, or permit price stability with excess unemployment?

USING PHILLIPS CURVES

You can express the relation between inflation and unemployment by a so-called *Phillips curve* (named after Australian economist A. W. Phillips). The concept is illustrated in Exhibit 2. Each point along a particular curve designates a specific combination of unemployment and inflation. The point labeled *A*, for instance, represents a 3 percent unemployment rate and a zero percent inflationary rate. What happens to the combinations of unemployment and inflation as you move upward or downward along the curve?

On any higher curve—that is, on any curve located in a more northeasterly direction—a given point denotes at least as much of one variable plus more of the other, when compared to a point directly below or to the left on the lower curve. Thus point *B* represents the same 3 percent unemployment rate as point *A*, but denotes a 4 percent inflationary rate; point *C*, on the other hand, denotes the same zero percent inflationary rate as point *A*, but a 6 percent unemployment rate. The same idea applies to any other point you may choose. Any point on the curve between *B* and *C*, however, represents a higher rate of both unemployment and inflation as compared to point *A*.

At any given time an economy can be represented by only one Phillips curve. Since the diagram suggests that lower curves are "good" and higher curves are "bad," what conditions will determine the height of a particular curve? The chief factors are those affecting the *overall competitive structure of*

the economy, such as the state of technology and efficiency in various industries, the effectiveness of competition through imports from foreign countries, and the ability of quasi-monopolistic business firms and labor unions to press for inflationary price and wage increases. These factors are assumed to be constant when drawing a particular Phillips curve. Changes in one or more of them, therefore, will shift the curve to a new position.

Two challenging tasks confront policy makers and legislators: (1) attaining a better (lower) Phillips curve, and (2) selecting a particular point on the

---

Exhibit 2

Phillips Curves Showing the Tradeoff Between Inflation and Unemployment

On any given curve, a movement from one point to the other measures the change in inflation corresponding to a change in unemployment. The lower the curve, the "better" it is for the economy as a whole.

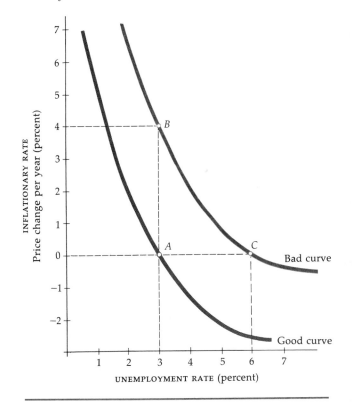

---

economy's existing Phillips curve. The first objective can be achieved mainly by long-run measures; the second involves primarily short-run considerations.

Lowering the Phillips Curve: Long-Run Measures

Both legislative and fiscal actions can shift a Phillips curve in a southwesterly direction over the long run. In the legislative area, antitrust laws should be extended and vigorously enforced so as to make both the product and resource markets more competitive. In the fiscal area, government expenditures on agriculture, housing, medical care, etc., should supplement competition rather than replace it. Government investment in manpower development and training should seek to reduce structural unemployment by providing the "hard-core" unemployed with marketable skills. Government tax policies, on the other hand, should stimulate industrial growth and capacity so as to minimize upward pressures on prices.

Choosing a Point: Short-Run Changes

In the short run our economy has a given Phillips curve; hence, changes in fiscal or monetary policies can be used to select a particular point on that curve. But each point represents a different combination of unemployment and inflation, and value judgments must be used to decide which combination or trade-off rate is best for the economy. No precise point may be "right" in any absolute sense, although most of us would probably agree on a fairly well-defined range within which the point should fall.

Conflicts Between Economic Growth and Inflation

Suppose we want the economy to grow fast enough to raise real output per capita. To accomplish this, the rate of investment must be increased. What role should fiscal and monetary policy play?

Easy Money—Tight Fiscal Policy. Easy money with low interest rates encourages maximum investment. To achieve the desired level of investment without causing inflation, a tight fiscal policy consisting of higher taxes or lower government spending is needed to generate a full-employment level of saving equal to the full-employment level of investment induced by monetary policy.

Thus, if we want economic growth without inflation through easy money, we have to pay the price by refraining from consumption—that is, we have to save enough to provide the investment needed.

Conflicts Between Full Employment and the Balance of Payments

We have learned how fiscal and monetary policies affect full employment and price stability in our own country. But since the United States is a major trading nation, what international repercussions do our domestic fiscal and monetary policies have?

To answer this question, we must first explain the meaning of an important economic term that is often encountered in the news media—the *balance of payments.* This expression refers to the money value of all transactions that take place between a nation and the rest of the world during a year. The transactions consist of imports and exports of goods and services as well as the movements of short- and long-term investments, gifts, currency, and gold. Some transactions result in an inflow of funds to a country, while others result in an outflow. In general, a nation is said to have a balance-of-payments deficit when its payments to foreigners for the year exceed its receipts. Conversely, a nation has a balance-of-payments surplus when its annual receipts from foreigners exceed its payments.

THE AMERICAN EXPERIENCE

The United States has had a balance-of-payments deficit in most years since World War II. Among the reasons are:

1. Although the value of merchandise exports has, over the long run, tended to exceed the value of merchandise imports, our percentage share of world exports of manufactured goods has declined. This is particularly true of products like cars, steel, and machinery, in which there is growing competition

from Western Europe and Japan. Hence our relative share of incoming receipts is not as large as we would like.

2. United States military and foreign-aid expenditures in other countries have been large, resulting in a heavy outflow of payments.

3. American business firms have built plants abroad; American citizens have invested in (purchased securities of) foreign corporations; and American lenders, during long periods of relatively lower interest rates in the United States, have tended to become a significant source of credit for foreign borrowers.

One of the approaches that may be taken to cut the deficit is to impose a tight monetary policy. This helps to reduce the United States' outflow of funds relative to its inflows in three ways. First, it exerts an overall contractionary effect, thereby tending to dampen not only domestic demand for goods, but also import demand. Second, it reduces inflationary price pressures, thus making the prices of our goods relatively more attractive to foreigners and the prices of their goods relatively less attractive to us. Third, it raises our interest rates, thereby making it less advantageous for foreigners to borrow from us and more advantageous for them to invest here; in addition, it makes the yields on our own securities relatively more attractive than those of foreign securities.

THE CONFLICT AND SOME PROPOSED SOLUTIONS

Is there a connection between our country's level of employment and its balance of payments? If so, what role, if any, should monetary and fiscal policy play in influencing this relationship?

Some evidence suggests that a rise in our national income tends to worsen our balance-of-payments situation. As our income and employment increase, we tend to import more goods from foreign countries; American tourists take more trips abroad; American corporations open more subsidiaries around the world. These conditions cause an outflow of dollars from the United States which may not be compensated by the inflow of dollars resulting from other offsetting factors such as higher returns on investment for American firms, increased exports to

the countries from which we import, and so on.

In view of this apparent conflict between full employment and the balance of payments, should we always seek to attain a high level of employment through an expansionary fiscal and monetary policy? Perhaps not. Some people have suggested the following approach instead.

Tight Money—Easy Fiscal Policy. A restrictive monetary policy drives up interest rates, making it less attractive for foreigners to borrow here and making foreign securities less attractive to Americans. However, since a restrictive monetary policy tends to dampen national income and employment, its effects in this area could be offset by an easy fiscal policy consisting of lower taxes or increased government spending.

Do you agree with this policy? If so, keep in mind the price to be paid: a restrictive monetary policy with high interest rates tends to discourage investment and thus reduce the long-term expansion of output. This is in direct opposition to the previous objective of achieving long-run economic growth. Note, too, that this policy is inherently in conflict with the previous one, namely "easy money—tight fiscal policy," for achieving economic growth.

In view of the difficulty of reconciling these differences, an alternative approach to solving the conflict between domestic and foreign objectives has in fact been adopted—one which employs "selective" measures rather than the more general tools of fiscal and monetary policy. Some of these selective measures which the government has used with limited success at one time or another include efforts to: attract tourists from abroad, increase exports to foreign countries, require that American loans and grants to foreign countries be spent on American goods, raise short-term interest rates to discourage American lending abroad while keeping down the lid on long-term interest rates in order to stimulate domestic capital investment, encourage voluntary restraint on investment overseas by American corporations, and in other ways to curb if not reduce the deficit in our balance of payments. In the meantime, fiscal and monetary policies have been used to cope mainly with domestic rather than international problems.

Nixon's "Domestic" N.E.P.: Snake in the Bottle*

In his 1968 election campaign Richard Nixon promised to cure two ailments that were inflaming the minds and thinning the pocketbooks of ordinary Americans: inflation and unemployment. Once elected, President Nixon found that the promises he had made as Candidate Nixon were hard to keep. For the first two and a half years of his presidency he pushed and pulled the levers of conventional fiscal and monetary policy tirelessly. Unfortunately, economic victory at home was as elusive as success in Vietnam.

Convictions Contradicted

Meanwhile, the President and his spokesmen said that government control of prices and incomes was not only undesirable, but also unnecessary—everything would come right eventually.

But on August 15, 1971, the President reversed himself, making a nationwide television broadcast in which he announced the imposition of price and wage controls. For ninety days there was an absolute freeze on increases. When Phase I expired, Phase II took over, with a cluster of government bodies to ensure that approved increases in wages and prices were not "inflationary"—a definition that varied from industry to industry and from time to time.

In one sense the announcement was a shattering defeat for economists around the President. Probably no group of economists anywhere was more dedicated to the virtues of a market-oriented economy, and more hostile to the concept of a command economy—one in which the forces of demand and supply are distorted by and subordinated to government policies. Ironically, Nixon is a conservative who furthered his early career by speaking and acting against Communism—the archetypal command economy. Even more ironically, Nixon called his August 15 measures a New Economic Policy—the very name chosen by Lenin for his Soviet economic program exactly fifty years earlier.

Storming Out?

Undoubtedly, Nixon's N.E.P. was brave, and in some ways necessary. But it raises grave issues for the future. Perhaps the most important is what some observers dub the "snake in the bottle" effect. They argue that legal controls over wages and prices merely confine inflationary pressures. Like a snake trapped in a bottle, workers and employers will storm out once the cork is pulled. Then they may demand not only all the increases denied them while the bottle was corked, but also something extra in case the government decides to replace the cork.

The snake in the bottle phenomenon has plagued other countries that have experimented with wage and price controls, notably Britain. There, inflation zoomed to a 10 percent annual rate in 1971 after being considerably less while the government held down price increases. It is too early to say whether the British experience will be repeated in the U.S. But one thing is certain: Nixon's experiment means that future Washington Administrations will be faced with hard choices. Essentially, Washington will have to choose between renouncing controls, thereby demonstrating its faith in a market economy's ability to grow healthily; or Washington will have to keep controls, either in use or in reserve, thereby turning a temporary expedient into a durable feature of the economic landscape.

Fruits of Impatience

Was the August 15 program really necessary? Many reputable economists argue, perhaps self-servingly, that the Administration was too impatient—that before August it was on the right course, but refused for political reasons to follow it to the end. In that view, the N.E.P. was more concerned with the President's worries about the 1972 election than the state of the economy.

That view is probably correct. It illustrates a fact which economists must consider when they foresake the groves of academe for the precincts of the White House: there are times when economic policies must yield to political necessity.   R. B.

The Administration's New Economic Policy was a tradeoff between maintenance of a market-oriented economy and a restoration of economic health. Was the President right to put practice before principle?

Is the N.E.P. really a signal that the United States is heading in a new direction? Or do government controls of wages and prices merely recognize and emphasize what has been true for a long time—that the interplay of market forces is distorted by big corporations, big labor unions, and big government?

* International aspects of Nixon's N.E.P. are discussed on page 615.

A Look at Some Long-Run Phillips Curves

The notion that a Phillips curve expresses a "trade-off" between unemployment and inflation has been of great interest—not only to economists, but also to editorialists and political leaders. Indeed, articles, comments, and editorials on the problems of unemployment versus inflation appear almost continually in leading newspapers and news magazines.

THE ORIGIN OF PHILLIPS CURVES

How do Phillips curves come about?

In 1958 an English-born Australian economist named A. W. Phillips reported in a professional economic journal the results of a study he had made of the relation between wages and unemployment in England. His approach was to construct for Great Britain a "tradeoff" curve between the unemployment rate and wage changes, similar to the curve shown in Exhibit 3a for the United States. Professor Phillips argued on the basis of this relationship that *wages tend to rise rapidly when unemployment is declining and slowly when unemployment is rising.*

Since Phillips published his article, other economists have contended that a similar relationship exists between prices and unemployment, giving rise to a similar type of Phillips curve. They base their belief on observations such as those illustrated in Exhibit 3b and on the assumption that wages are a principal determinant of prices, or that the same factors which influence wages also influence prices. Thus:

A *Phillips curve* expresses a relationship between percentage changes in wages (or prices) and the rate of unemployment. It suggests that slowly changing wages and prices tend to be associated with high rates of unemployment, while rapidly rising wages and prices are usually accompanied by low rates of unemployment. Hence it measures the tradeoff between these two variables—that is, the extent of wage-price change resulting from a unit change in the unemployment rate.

Phillips curves are drawn on the assumption that if *all other things remain constant,* wage-price changes

Exhibit 3

Long-Run Phillips Curves for the United States, 1961–1968

These Phillips curves have been drawn (i.e., "fitted") so that they best represent the years 1961–1968. They may thus be thought of as a kind of "average" for those years. If they had been drawn so as to represent all of the years from 1953 to 1968, they would be shifted a bit farther to the right.

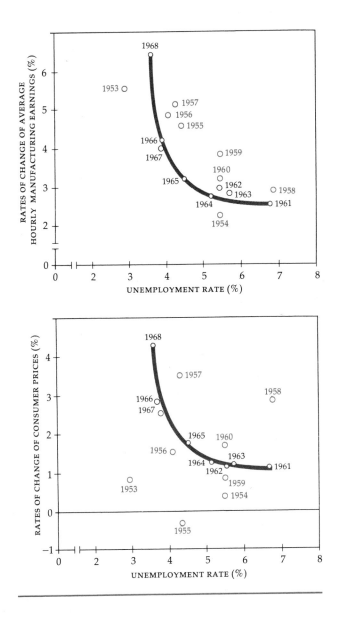

are determined by the unemployment rate. As always, therefore, we must ask: What are these "all other things," and what happens if they fail to remain constant?

FACTORS DETERMINING WAGE-PRICE CHANGES

Earlier in this chapter we said that three conditions affecting the overall competitive structure of the economy are assumed to remain constant when drawing Phillips curves:

1. The state of technology and efficiency in various industries

2. The effectiveness of competition through imports from foreign countries

3. The ability of quasi-monopolistic business firms and labor unions to press for inflationary wage and price increases

The first two of these factors are somewhat general and difficult to isolate, whereas the third is more precise and capable of being identified. Hence economists who have constructed long-run Phillips curves from actual data have tended to focus on the last item, while assuming that for purposes of short-run analysis it is reasonable to expect the first two to remain fairly constant.

What are the components of this last item? In other words, which elements determine the ability of firms and unions to raise wages and prices? Three variables are believed to be of primary importance: (1) changes in profits from their previous levels; (2) changes in prices from their previous levels; and (3) the rate of labor productivity.

The significance of the first two variables arises from the fact that many wage contracts in manufacturing are written annually. When unions seek to renegotiate these contracts, they base their new wage demands more on economic changes in the past year or so, and less on what they think will happen in the coming year. Hence they use the most recent corporate earnings reports and the latest government cost-of-living (or consumer price) indexes covering the past several quarters as a basis for negotiation. Further, some unions have cost-of-living escalator clauses written into their contracts, thereby assuring that wage increases automatically *follow* cost-of-living increases.

Therefore, when constructing long-run Phillips curves from actual data, these factors must be held "constant" by the use of certain statistical methods in order to express a relationship between wages (or prices) and unemployment as was done in Exhibit 3.

What about the third variable—labor productivity? This factor undoubtedly influences wage changes in the long run. But studies have yielded no consistent conclusions about the influence of productivity on wages in the *short run*. As a result, it is customary when constructing long-run Phillips curves to assume simply that the economy is experiencing a steady increase in productivity at some constant rate. This "eliminates" the effect of productivity as yet another factor that may influence wage-price changes.

CONCLUSION: WHAT DO THE CURVES MEAN?

In view of the various assumptions and statistical adjustments that must be made when constructing long-run Phillips curves from actual data, there is a question of just how meaningful such curves really are.

For example, there is no doubt that the "good" and "bad" Phillips curves presented earlier in Exhibit 2 are useful analytical devices for interpreting tradeoff problems involving inflation and unemployment, because they are *theoretical* curves which are assumed to portray a particular situation at a given moment of time. But the long-run Phillips curves in Exhibit 3 are a different matter, since they are *statistical* or *empirical* curves representing what is believed to be an "average" relationship among the observed variables over a period of time. It follows from the foregoing explanation of how such curves are derived that they are not the only Phillips curves which are possible; other curves can also be derived from the same set of data, depending on the underlying assumptions and statistical adjustments that are made.

As a result, it is necessary to interpret long-run or statistical Phillips curves with great care. We can look back at Exhibit 3*b*, for instance, and conclude that for the period represented by the curve, a 4 percent rate of unemployment is consistent with a $2\frac{1}{2}$ percent rate of inflation. However, the usefulness of

Exhibit 4

The Phillips Curve and Qualitative Considerations: A Dilemma for Public Policy

Selected Unemployment Rates in Prosperities and Recessions

The concept of the Phillips curve is helpful for expressing the quantitative *terms of the tradeoff between inflation and unemployment, but it normally says nothing about the quali-*tative *considerations. Nowadays, there is concern not only with* how many *people are unemployed, but also with* who *are unemployed.*

*As the accompanying chart shows, those groups con-*sisting *of teenagers, nonwhites, and blue-collar workers (especially the unskilled and semiskilled) have historically benefited least or not at all from sustained prosperity. These disadvantaged workers are the last to be hired when demand is strong, and the first to be let go when demand weakens. Consequently, the burden of any tradeoff involving higher unemployment will fall heaviest on these groups.*

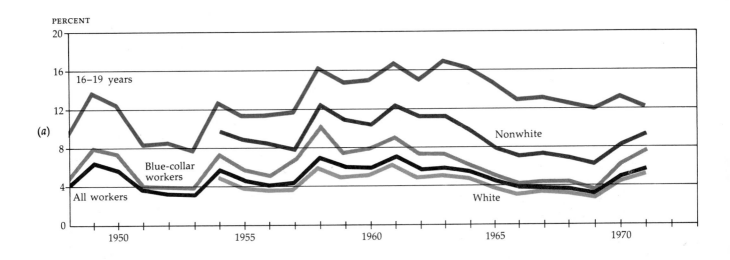

The Phillips Curve and the "Black Tradeoff"

Unemployment hits Negroes much harder than whites. In 1962, for example, the black unemployment rate was 11 percent while the white jobless rate was 5 percent. At the same time, the rate of price increase was only 1.2 percent. As the economy began to overheat during the remainder of the decade, unemployment rates for both black and white fell sharply. By 1968, black unemployment stood at 6.3 percent, and white unemployment at 3.7 percent. But the relatively tight labor market had boosted the annual inflationary rate to 4.5 percent.

The Phillips curve raises some controversial questions among economists. But practically all of them would agree that if the inflationary rate were cut back to about 1 percent, the black unemployment rate could easily soar to more than 12 percent.

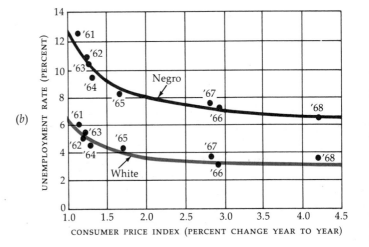

this conclusion is no better than the validity of the assumptions on which the model rests.

Finally, it should be noted that although Phillips curves may be useful for what they include, they neglect completely certain important aspects of the tradeoff problem. Two different views of this are described in Exhibit 4, charts (*a*) and (*b*).

SUMMARY OF IMPORTANT IDEAS

1. A conflict between unemployment and inflation exists primarily because increases in the general price level occur before full employment is reached. Since there is a competitive relation between unemployment and inflation, the tradeoff between them can be represented by a Phillips curve.

2. A conflict between economic growth and inflation may occur if an easy-money policy which stimulates too rapid a rate of investment is not offset by a tight fiscal policy consisting of higher taxes and lower government spending.

3. A conflict between full employment and the balance of payments exists because as our level of national income and employment increase, we tend to import more goods from abroad, open more branch companies and subsidiaries in foreign countries, and send more capital and tourists overseas. A tight money and easy fiscal policy might offer an appropriate solution, but it would be in direct opposition to the type of easy money and tight fiscal policy advocated for economic growth.

4. Long-run or statistical Phillips curves are often derived from historical data. However, such curves must be interpreted with great care, since the methods of deriving them vary according to the underlying assumptions and statistical adjustments that are made.

FOR HOMEWORK AND DISCUSSION

1. *Terms and concepts to review:*
   Phillips curve
   balance of payments

2. What are the underlying reasons for the conflict between full employment and inflation?

3. (*a*) What is the difference between "good" and "bad" Phillips curves? Explain. (*b*) Explain the factors determining the height of a particular Phillips curve. (*c*) What actions would you recommend in order to improve an economy's Phillips curve?

4. Distinguish between (*a*) the conflict between economic growth and inflation, and (*b*) the conflict between full employment and the balance of payments. That is, explain how monetary and fiscal policies may conflict in trying to achieve the three goals of full employment, economic growth, and balance-of-payments equilibrium without significant inflation.

5. Are theoretical Phillips curves the same as statistical Phillips curves? Explain your answer.

REFERENCES AND READING SUGGESTIONS

BOARD OF GOVERNORS OF THE FEDERAL RESERVE SYSTEM, *The Federal Reserve System: Purposes and Functions*, 5th ed., Washington, D.C., 1963, chaps. 3–7

JACOBY, NEIL H. (ed.), *United States Monetary Policy*, rev. ed., Praeger, New York, 1964.

MAYER, THOMAS, *Elements of Monetary Policy*, Random House, New York, 1968.

RITTER, LAWRENCE S., and WILLIAM L. SILBER, *Money*, Basic Books, New York, 1970.

CHAPTER 16

Today's Great Debate: How Important Is Money? The Monetarists Versus the New Economists

CHAPTER PREVIEW

What is the historical background of the money-supply controversy?

How does the Keynesian or New Economist view differ from the Monetarist view?

What sorts of problems and difficulties are posed by the Monetarist viewpoint?

Will a synthesis of fiscal and monetary views emerge which is capable of promoting full employment, orderly economic growth, stable prices, and long-run balances in our international payments?

During most of the 1960s, when the New Economists were riding high in Washington under Presidents Kennedy and Johnson, certain so-called "Monetary" economists were looked upon as highly eccentric. That day has gone. Under the leadership of Professor Milton Friedman of the University of Chicago, the Monetarists have become what a leading New Economist has called "that small, but influential, brilliant, and growing circle of true believers."

True believers in what? The answer to this question opens the door to a great controversy that continues to rage among many economists and political leaders:

Is it the rate at which the Federal Reserve adds to the nations' money supply that chiefly determines the levels of output, employment, and prices, as the Monetarists hold? Or is it mainly changes in the federal budget that make the difference, as the New Economists of the fiscal school contend? Or, as a third possibility, does the answer lie somewhere in between?

These are the fundamental issues in today's great economic debate—a debate which may appropriately be called the "money-supply controversy."

History of the Money-Supply Controversy

Today's great debate over the importance of money and the money supply has had a long and interesting history. Although it is rooted in some of the monetary debates that took place in Congress prior to the establishment of the Federal Reserve System, it is sufficient for our purposes to go back to the period just before the Great Depression.

THE CLASSICAL OR PRE-KEYNESIAN VIEW

If you had studied economics before the 1930s, you probably would have been taught that the quantity of money (currency plus private demand deposits) had a strong influence on prices, but very little if any influence on jobs, production, or general economic activity. This, in essence, was the crude *quantity theory of money* and prices that we studied in an earlier chapter. You will recall that it was expressed by the equation of exchange:

$$MV = PQ$$

where M stands for the quantity of money, V for its velocity of circulation, P for the average price of goods and services, and Q for the quantity of goods and services.

According to this theory—both in its simple and more refined versions—the quantity of goods and the velocity of circulation of money were important determinants of the price level. But they were believed to be stable and independent of changes in the quantity of money; hence, increases or decreases in prices within the economy as a whole were attributed primarily to increases or decreases in the quantity of money, and little else.

Thus, a simple version of the quantity theory would predict that a 10 percent increase in the money supply would bring about a 10 percent increase in the price level, assuming there was no increase in the quantity of goods and services. This assumption of a stable quantity of output (and hence a stable volume of employment) accords with the classical theory of income and employment, because the classical model assumes that all production and all productive resources are guided to their full-employment levels by the "invisible hand" of market forces—independently of changes in the quantity of money.

Of course, not every economist saw the world in precisely this way. But these generalizations provide a reasonably accurate description of typical pre-Depression views—views which assumed an automatic tendency toward full employment, together with a price level determined by the quantity of money.

THE BEGINNINGS OF A NEW VIEW

With the coming of the Great Depression, the validity of prevailing economic doctrines was questioned long and seriously. With millions of people out of work and the economy stagnating at levels far below its capacity, how could it be argued that the economic system "automatically" tends toward full employment? Something obviously was wrong, and classical theory was unable to explain what it was.

The British economist J. M. Keynes offered an answer. According to Keynes, the level of aggregate demand—or the amount of goods demanded by consumers, businessmen, and the government—was not high enough to keep the economy operating at full employment. After all, how could businessmen be expected to produce what they did not expect to sell? The Keynesian prescription was clear and straightforward: If private demand proved insufficient to pull the economy out of depression, then Washington should stimulate enough spending to provide buyers for the nation's full-capacity output. This prescription, as we have seen, later came to mean that the federal government was responsible for maintaining full employment. This responsibility was subsequently expressed in the form of the Employment Act of 1946.

FISCAL POLICY AND THE NEW ECONOMICS

With the groundwork laid, the next question was how Washington could best fulfill its responsibility.

It soon became clear to most Keynesians that fiscal policy—the use of the government's taxing and spending powers—offered the logical means of filling the gap between insufficient aggregate demand and the level needed to achieve and maintain full employment. The federal government could, for example, reduce taxes, thereby leaving the private sector with more disposable income to spend, or it could increase its own spending and thereby add directly to the total demand for goods and services. Although Keynesian economists did not always agree on the exact amount of change needed in taxation or spending, they agreed remarkably closely on the use of fiscal policy to achieve full employment.

"You Can't Push on a String"

This did not mean that Keynesians neglected the use of monetary policy. To them, however, monetary policy had a secondary and relatively passive role to play in most instances.

Thus, Keynesian economists tended to believe that monetary policy could ordinarily do little by itself to stimulate economic activity. In their view, the Federal Reserve System could adopt an easy-money policy which would result in lower interest rates, and this *might* induce businessmen to borrow funds for the purpose of spending on plant and equipment. However, low interest rates by themselves provided no assurance that businessmen would borrow, and hence the unused funds would simply pile up in the banks as excess reserves.

"You can't push on a string" was therefore a favorite homily of the 1940s and 1950s; it meant the same thing as the older and more familiar saying, "You can lead a horse to water but you can't make him drink." This attitude reflected the prevailing skepticism about the effectiveness of monetary policy.

When President Kennedy took office in 1961, he made a significant attempt to implement the "New Economics" propounded by the Keynesians. Through his efforts, Congress in 1964 enacted a tax cut for the express purpose of stimulating the economy, and in 1968, under similar economic policies pursued by President Johnson, Congress passed a tax increase designed to curb economic activity. There has been much dispute over whether these fiscal actions accomplished what they set out to do, but they nevertheless demonstrate that the philosophy of the New Economists was widely accepted—a philosophy which held that the economy could be "fine-tuned" through fiscal and monetary action.

MONETARY POLICY CATCHES ON

Although fiscal policy reigned supreme during most of the 1960s, two occurrences prompted economists to reconsider the supposed superiority of fiscal over monetary policy as a tool for economic stabilization:

1. *Time Lag in Fiscal Legislation.* Fiscal actions take much longer to implement than monetary actions, because the former require Congressional approval whereas the latter are decided at frequent periodic meetings of the Federal Reserve System's Board of Governors. This fact was driven home in 1967–68, when it took Congress 18 months to enact a tax increase for the purpose of curbing inflationary pressures. Monetary policy decisions, of course, could have been implemented much more quickly.

2. *Changed Economic Environment.* In the 1930s and 1940s, the main challenge (except during World War II) was to keep the economy buoyed up, and attention tended to center on methods of economic stimulation. During the 1950s, a new problem—inflation—came to the forefront, and in the 1960s the United States experienced unprecedented difficulties with its balance of payments, as we learned in a previous chapter.

"You Can Pull on a String"

These problems called for restrictive rather than expansionary policies. Consequently, many New Economists began to take the position that if "you can't push on a string," then perhaps "you can pull on a string." In other words, even if monetary policy cannot *push* total spending up, there is a good chance that it can *pull* it down. They have come to believe, therefore, that monetary policy is flexible and easy to implement, even if it happens to be more effective in restricting total spending than in stimulating it.

THE NEW ECONOMICS: A "POLICY MIX"

As a result of these and other developments, most New Economists today believe that an appropriate "mix" of fiscal and monetary actions should be undertaken to achieve a stable rate of economic growth. They do not all agree on the proportions of the mix, but they generally agree on the relative emphasis. In general, the New Economists tend to prefer a policy mix which combines occasional shifts in fiscal policy with flexible and frequent monetary actions by the Federal Reserve.

The New Economics thus provides political leaders with a clear guide for action: if unemployment rises, Washington should cut taxes in order to stimulate spending; if prices rise, Washington should "temporarily" raise taxes in order to soak up purchasing power. Monetary policy should be used also to supplement and complement the major shifts in economic activity brought about by changes in fiscal policy. By thus adhering to an appropriate blend of fiscal and monetary policy, it is not only possible, but also feasible, in the opinion of the New Economists, to "fine-tune" the economy.

A modern definition of the "New Economics" helps tie the foregoing ideas together:

The *New Economics* is an economic philosophy which emerged in the 1930s from the ideas of John Maynard Keynes. In contrast with classical economic theory, it holds that a capitalistic economy does not tend automatically toward full employment. Therefore, the government should pursue active fiscal policies, supported by appropriate monetary policies, to achieve and maintain full employment and steady economic growth.

The Monetarist View

Unlike the New Economists, who acknowledge the importance of both fiscal and monetary policy, the Monetarists argue that changes in the money supply are the chief determinants not only of prices, but also of production, employment, and spending. They do not believe that fiscal policy is an effective stabilizing device, and they object to the whole concept of fine-tuning the economy.

Who are the Monetarists? Just as the New Economists (or Keynesians) are linked with the late J. M. Keynes, the Monetarists are associated with Professor Milton Friedman of the University of Chicago— one of America's most distinguished economists. The money-supply controversy which you can read about in prominent newspapers such as the *New York Times* and the *Wall Street Journal,* and in leading news and business magazines like *Time, Newsweek, Business Week,* and *Fortune,* is fundamentally a debate between the New Economists and the Monetarists.

THE MONETARIST THEORY

Monetarists do not always agree on all points, but they are unanimous in their belief that money exercises a major influence on economic activity.

According to Monetarist theory, the amount of money people wish to hold is closely related to their level of income. Hence if the supply of money increases faster than income—that is, faster than the amount people want to have on hand—they will spend away the unwanted portion, thereby causing inflation. On the other hand, if the supply of money increases more slowly than income—that is, not fast enough to provide people with the amount of money they want to have on hand—the opposite effect will occur: people will try to build up their money balances by cutting back on their spending, thereby causing unemployment. Therefore, Monetarists conclude, there is a cause-and-effect relationship between the supply of money and the changes that occur in income, economic activity, and prices. They believe that changes in the money supply *cause* swings in the business cycle.

However, Monetarists do not claim that business cycles result exclusively from changes in the money supply. Like the New Economists, they recognize that the economy is always in the process of adjusting to the varying expectations of businessmen and to underlying structural changes in population, consumer habits, competition within industries, etc. But they believe that changes in the supply of money are the dominant cause of business cycles.

Monetarists contend that the economy is inherently stable and tends toward full employment and sustained growth. They cite detailed studies analyzing the behavior of money and prices going as far back as the Civil War. These apparently show that changes in the money supply have larger, more predictable, and quicker effects on GNP than fiscal-policy changes in tax rates, government expenditures, and the federal deficit. In the monetarists' opinion, therefore, the government should help the economy achieve its full employment potential by adhering to a simple and well-defined guide:

The Federal Reserve should expand the nation's money supply at the economy's growth rate or capacity to produce, namely about 3 to 5 percent a year. More than this would lead to strong inflationary pressures; less would tend to be stagnating if not deflationary. This guide for economic expansion advanced by Monetarists is often called the *money-supply rule.*

Monetarists, in other words, believe that the Federal Reserve has the power to stabilize the economy —or at least to permit the economy to stabilize itself —through its ability to control bank reserves and therefore the supply of money. Monetarists contend that the New Economists—in their well-meant efforts to employ fiscal policy for purposes of economic stabilization—have misused monetary policy, and thereby magnified rather than mitigated business cycles. Thus the Monetarists show that the growth of the money supply, as a result of discretionary efforts by the New Economists to "manage" the economy, has fluctuated; with the help of various charts and models, they allege that increases in the money supply have resulted in economic expansions while decreases have caused economic contractions. This is illustrated in Exhibit 1, page 234.

Monetarists conclude, therefore, that even though the Federal Reserve's influence over the money supply may not be perfect, adherence to the money-supply rule would nevertheless produce better results for economic stabilization and growth than the flexible policy mix followed by the New Economists.

What about interest rates? Do they influence total spending and business activity as the New Economists contend? Monetarists think not. In line with the rest of their theory, they believe that spending and interest rates are a *result* of changes in the money supply.

Some Unresolved Considerations

The Monetarists' views are strong and persuasive. They have been the subject of Congressional hearings and are among the most hotly debated economic topics of our time. Yet many economists are skeptical about the Monetarist position. Their doubts are summarized in the following unanswered questions:

1. Is money all-important, or do other factors play a role in affecting economic activity?

2. Do changes in the supply of money *cause* changes in economic activity, or vice versa?

3. Of what significance is the velocity of circulation of money?

4. What do we mean by "money," and what is the importance of other financial assets which possess varying degrees of "moneyness"?

5. Is the Monetarist view too aggregated, thereby tending to see only the economic "forest" as a whole and not the "trees" that make it up?

These questions pose many deep problems in economic theory, but we can point out some of the main implications of the issues rather briefly.

IS MONEY ALL-IMPORTANT?

The Monetarists, as we have seen, believe that the money supply is the dominant influence on economic activity and that other considerations may be neglected.

Many economists, however, feel that to neglect other factors would be a serious mistake. They argue that significant changes in total spending may result from a number of causes. For example: Businessmen may alter their expenditure decisions on plant and equipment because their expectation of profits changes; consumers may buy less for reasons unrelated to the money supply—such as an increase in taxes; the government may alter its spending policy; strikes in important industries may reduce business activity. Any of these factors, they point out, can influence total spending and economic activity just as much as a change in the money supply.

IS MONEY A CAUSE OR AN EFFECT?

Monetarists believe that changes in the money supply *cause* changes in income and production. Is this contention correct? The answer is probably yes. But a reverse type of relation may also be true.

Thus, if spending and production increase, the expansion in business may increase the demand for money. If the Federal Reserve then enlarges the supply of money the increase in spending will be the cause of bringing more money into circulation. In such a case, the change in the money supply is an effect rather than a cause of total spending.

IS VELOCITY SIGNIFICANT?

It may be recalled that according to the familiar equation of exchange:

$$MV = PQ \quad \text{and hence} \quad V = \frac{PQ}{M}$$

The equation thus tells us that velocity is the ratio of income (or output) to money; that is, velocity measures the speed at which money changes hands within the economy.

The Monetarists believe that V tends to remain relatively stable. Whether they are correct in this belief, however, is still an unsettled question. If V does not remain stable, a decrease in M will not reduce total spending as the Monetarists contend; instead it may increase total spending if people decide to spend the smaller supply of money more quickly—that is, if the decrease in M is substantially offset by an increase in V. Some economists are investigating the possibility of this happening, and the conditions that may lead to it.

WHAT IS MONEY?

We saw in a previous chapter that it is hard to define money precisely. The Monetarists prefer to include not only currency and private demand deposits in their definition, but also time deposits in savings accounts.

But what about the growing importance of other types of interest-bearing financial assets that have become increasingly important since the 1950s and which possess varying degrees of "moneyness"? Should these be included in a definition of money? The Monetarists agree that perhaps some of them should, for they recognize that their own measure of money is not an ideal one. However, they are not sure of just what to put into their definition and what to leave out. There is an entire spectrum of financial assets differing as to liquidity, dates of maturity, degrees of risk, and other considerations, all of which may serve as "money" for certain purposes.

For example, if time deposits which are an interest-bearing asset are included in a definition of money, why not also include Treasury bills or other highly marketable securities which investors often substitute for time deposits? The answer to this question, which is a definitional one, is as yet unresolved.

IS THE MONETARIST VIEW TOO AGGREGATED?

A final difficulty to be considered is the "aggregation" problem.

The Monetarist position is one which takes an aggregate view of the economy and of the impact of changes in the money supply, while neglecting the disproportionate effects which monetary actions may have on certain segments of the economy. As pointed out in an earlier chapter, for example, the home-building industry is heavily dependent on the availability of mortgage money, and hence is among the first to feel the effects of changes in the flow of funds through savings institutions.

Monetarists, because of their aggregate outlook, prefer to let the distribution of money and income— that is, the impact of monetary changes—be determined by competitive forces in the market. Many other economists, however, feel that the market operates too imperfectly and too inequitably to be relied upon completely as a mechanism for allocating funds, and that a sound monetary policy is one which recognizes and adapts to special situations.

Exhibit 1

Changes in Money Supply Plus Time Deposits

This chart shows monthly percentage changes in the money supply on a seasonally adjusted daily average basis over a period of 20 years. (Money is defined here as currency in the hands of the public plus private demand and time deposits.) The shaded areas represent recessions. The highly erratic nature of month-to-month movements in the money supply makes it extremely difficult to see any clear-cut cyclical pattern in the chart. Nevertheless, the letters P and T denote cyclical peaks and troughs in the money supply series, based on one of Professor Friedman's studies. (See Milton Friedman and Anna J. Schwartz, "Money and Business Cycles," Review of Economics and Statistics, *Supplement,* February, 1963, *pp. 34–38.)*

As can be seen, each monetary peak occurred somewhere outside a recession—that is, during the expansion phase of a business cycle—and thus led the peak in business. Similarly, a monetary trough occurred during the first three recessions, whereas the fourth trough in the first quarter of 1960 occurred a few months before the onset of recession.

Do the peaks and troughs in the money series lead the subsequent peaks and troughs in business activity? Perhaps they do, but the leads are extremely variable, ranging from a few months to several years. As a result, it becomes highly problematical whether cycles in money cause cycles in business.

This suggests that factors in addition to money influence business peaks and troughs, or that the business cycle exerts an important **reverse** *influence on the monetary cycle.*

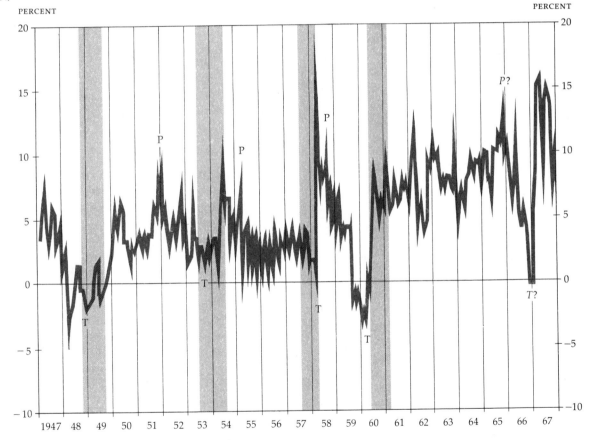

Month-to-month percentage changes; compound annual rates.
Note: Percentage changes are based on seasonally adjusted data. Shaded areas represent recession periods, according to National Bureau of Economic Research chronology.
SOURCE: Board of Governors of the Federal Reserve System.

Exhibit 2

Changes in Gross National Product and in Money Supply
Plus Time Deposits

How do we measure "the lag" between monetary cycles and business cycles?

This is a somewhat technical question, but it makes a great deal of difference which measure is used. For example, instead of comparing quarterly levels *of the money supply with quarterly* levels *of some measure of business activity such as GNP, we might compare quarterly* changes *in each as measured perhaps by the amounts of changes or by percentage changes.*

In this chart, percentage changes have been used. The lead of peaks P and troughs T in the rate of change of money over peaks and troughs in the rate of change of GNP appears to average about one-quarter or less.

On the other hand, when amounts of change are used rather than percentage changes, a different pattern of lead-lag relationship is obtained. It is thus difficult to prove that monetary cycles cause business cycles, or that the relationships are consistent.

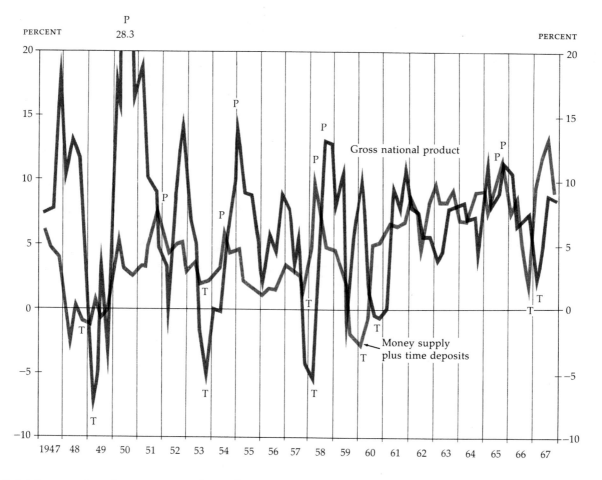

Quarter-to-quarter percentage changes; compound annual rates
Note: Percentage changes are based on seasonally adjusted data.

SOURCE: Board of Governors of the Federal Reserve System; United States Department of Commerce.

Exhibit 3

**Changes in Money Supply and Government Expenditures
in Relation to Changes in Economic Activity**

*The most interesting comparisons are to be found where the
monetary and fiscal influences (lower chart) are operating in
opposite directions. In those periods the movement in economic
activity (upper chart) will indicate which influence is dom-*
*inant. The monetary and fiscal variables move in opposite
directions in the periods 1919–21, 1931–32, 1939, 1948–50,
and 1966–67. In each of these years economic activity, after a
short lag, moved in the same direction as the monetary variable*

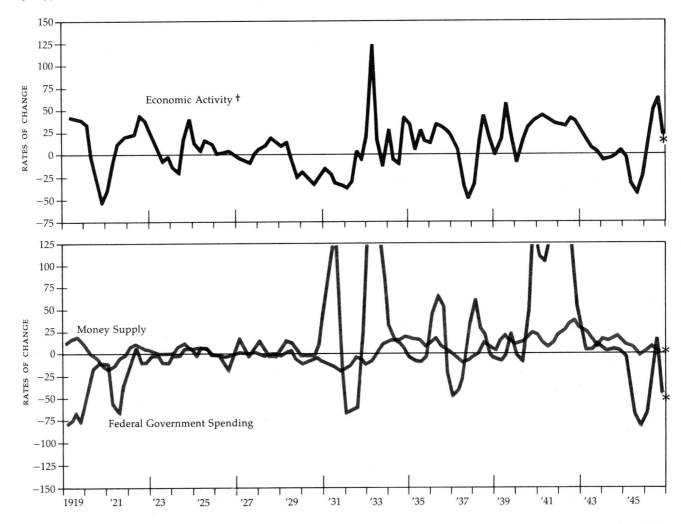

Quarterly data at annual rates.
* *Note:* The magnitude of fluctuations in the three series plotted
decreased considerably after World War II. The rate-of-change
scale for the years *beginning with 1947* consequently has been
enlarged to facilitate comparisons among the three series.

† Economic Activity is measured by the scaled product of the
Consumer Price Index (CPI) and the Industrial Production Index
(IPI) multiplied by Gross National Product (GNP) in the base years
1957–59:

$$\left(\frac{\text{CPI} \times \text{IPI}}{10{,}000}\right) \times \$457.4 \text{ billion} = \text{economic activity}$$

and in the opposite direction to the fiscal variable. As a matter of fact, all cyclical movements in the money stock were followed by proportional cyclical movements in economic ac- tivity. Of the **twelve** cyclical movements in economic activity from 1919 to 1969, **eleven** are preceded by corresponding movements in the money stock.

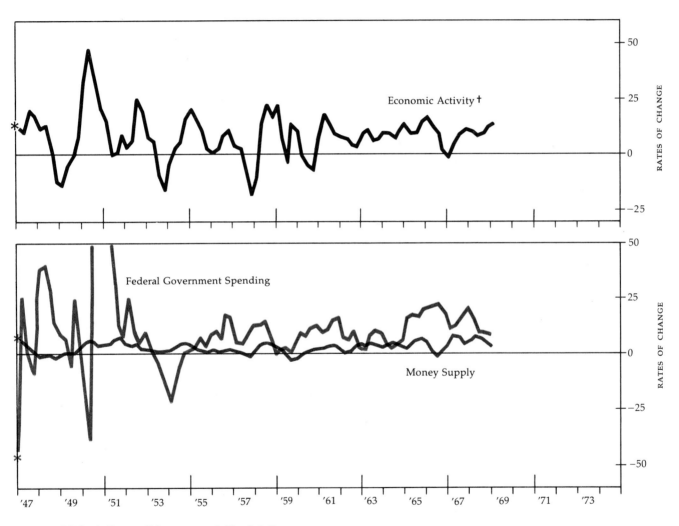

SOURCE: Michael Keran, "Monetary and Fiscal Influences on Economic Activity," *Review,* Federal Reserve Bank of St. Louis, November, 1969.

For these and other reasons—including some technical problems of measurement as suggested in Exhibit 2, page 235—many economists will continue to disagree with certain Monetarist views for some time to come. But study Exhibit 3, pages 236 and 237, and note how it compares with Exhibit 2.

Is There a Future for the New Economics?

The New Economist doctors have tended to practice curative medicine by prescribing a combined dose of fiscal and monetary remedies if the economy gets sick; the Monetarist doctors have opted for preventive medicine by prescribing steady growth in the money supply and the counsel of patience.

It remains for future research and experience to test the effectiveness of those two approaches. In the meantime, you can expect to read and hear a great deal about this issue in the news media.

But what will happen to the New Economics? Will our children read about it as a past event in their history books, or will it remain with us in varying degrees as a viable philosophy to be studied by present and future generations of students?

These are not idle questions. The American economy is one in which high employment, rising output of goods and services, stable prices, and a satisfactory balance of payments are among the accepted national economic goals. The voting population, like that in the other market economies of the world, will not tolerate for very long the adverse consequences of wide departures from these goals. It is appropriate to ask, therefore, what the New Economics achieved during its eight years under Presidents Kennedy and Johnson.

LET'S LOOK AT THE RECORD

The Bourbons, it has been said, never forgot anything because they never learned anything. The same may be said of those diehards who have never studied—or have refused to acknowledge—the economic accomplishments of the 1960s. During most of this period the fiscal policies of the New Economics—and the monetary policies of the Federal Reserve, which were often adapted to accommodate the immediate credit needs of the Treasury—produced high employment and unprecedented economic growth. True, the Vietnam war was responsible for a substantial rate of government spending, but this merely corroborates a fundamental lesson of the New Economics: If war can bring about high employment, so can peace; what war dollars can do, *any* dollars can do.

However, the economic achievements of the 1960s levied substantial costs. During the latter part of the decade—with the help of hot-war Vietnam spending—we did indeed bring unemployment down to a 15-year low of less than $3\frac{1}{2}$ percent, but inflationary price increases took their toll at a rate of over 5 percent per year. In addition, heavy deficits in the balance of payments reduced our gold stock from $18 billion to less than $11 billion, resulting in the imposition of direct controls on foreign lending and investment; the surplus in our balance of trade essentially disappeared for the first time in many years; and a 10 percent surtax coupled with expenditure reductions legislated by Congress failed to eliminate budget deficits.

What Conclusion?

These results, some favorable and some unfavorable, suggest that two extreme policy questions face any administration, Democratic or Republican:

Should we adopt positive fiscal and monetary action to assure high employment and a strong, steady rate of growth, while taking our chances on coping with inflations and balance-of-payments deficits as they arise?

OR

Should we accept less employment and slower rates of growth, while paying the price in terms of losses of potential output and possible social unrest?

Most people would prefer that the nation search for a position somewhere between these two limits. Thus there is a growing awareness among the New Economists and the Monetarists that a synthesis of views must emerge. Indeed, there are already some signs of such a synthesis, indicating that a proper combination of both fiscal and monetary policy is needed to keep the economy on a chosen path. The choice of the precise combination is one of the great issues in economics today.

SUMMARY OF IMPORTANT IDEAS

1. The classical or pre-Keynesian view held that the quantity of money exercises a direct influence on prices, but has little or no effect on general economic activity. This view can be expressed in terms of the quantity theory of money and the familiar equation of exchange: $PQ = MV$.

2. With the development of Keynesian or New Economics, fiscal policy came to play a dominant role in the theory of economic stabilization. Monetary policy, it was believed, was for the most part a less effective and therefore secondary device which may be used in conjunction with fiscal policy to provide an overall "policy mix."

3. The Monetarist view, which has been gaining increasing attention since the 1950s, holds that changes in the money supply *cause* swings in the business cycle. Monetarists advocate adherence to a money-supply rule, namely, that the Federal Reserve should increase the supply of money at the economy's growth rate or capacity to produce— about 3 to 5 percent a year. This, they believe, should be the guide for economic stabilization policy, rather than discretionary fiscal policies which, in their opinion, have magnified rather than mitigated business cycles.

4. The Monetarist view holds that money is all that matters in affecting economic activity, that the relationship between the money supply and total spending is of a one-way causal nature, that velocity of circulation is stable, that "money" includes time deposits as well as currency and private demand deposits, and that only the aggregate impact of changes in the money supply are important for stabilization policy. Many other economists contend that all these beliefs are open to serious question because they involve major issues which have yet to be resolved.

5. The New Economists argue that the budgetary deficits and other fiscal policies of the 1960s produced high employment and rapid economic growth, and there is no reason why the same fiscal policies could not be followed in peace as well as in war. Monetarists have replied that these policies also brought unprecedented inflation, a severe outflow of gold from the country, deficits in our international balance of payments, the imposition of controls on foreign lending and investing, and higher taxes.

6. A fundamental question that remains to be answered is the tradeoff between inflation and unemployment, and the role that fiscal and monetary policy should play in our economy. There is evidence that a synthesis of ideas is emerging, but the proper combination of fiscal and monetary policies continues to be one of the most hotly debated issues of our time.

FOR HOMEWORK AND DISCUSSION

1. *Terms and concepts to review:*

   quantity theory of money   New Economics
   equation of exchange   money-supply rule

2. Of what significance was monetary policy in the 1940s, 1950s, and 1960s? Explain.

3. Do you see any connection between the Monetarists and the classical economists as far as basic philosophy is concerned?

4. What sort of arguments have the New Economists offered to criticize the Monetarists?

5. What do you see as the central economic issues between the Monetarists and the New Economists? Can you suggest what the outcome will be?

REFERENCES AND READING SUGGESTIONS

CHANDLER, LESTER V., *The Economics of Money and Banking*, 5th ed., Harper & Row, New York, 1969, chaps. 25, 26.

FEDERAL RESERVE BANK OF ST. LOUIS, *Review* (monthly). Contains data and articles on money and the money supply.

MAYER, THOMAS, *Elements of Monetary Policy*, Random House, New York, 1968.

RITTER, LAWRENCE S., and WILLIAM L. SILBER, *Money*, Basic Books, New York, 1970.

PART 4

Economic Growth
and Ecology

CHAPTER 17

Explanations of Economic Growth

CHAPTER PREVIEW

How do we define economic growth? What is the basis of the definition? How is economic growth measured?

Did the classical economists have anything to say about economic growth? Is their theory of use to us in explaining modern economic growth?

What types of specific factors determine a nation's economic growth? How are these factors "measured"?

Can a simple model be constructed to illustrate some of the basic concepts of growth? What do we mean by a full employment growth rate? Can it be measured with a simple formula?

Since the late 1940s economic growth has been regarded as one of our fundamental economic problems. It has been a significant issue in presidential campaigns, and will undoubtedly remain a major national concern for a long time to come.

Why this interest in growth? The reasons will be spelled out in some detail in the following pages, but in general terms at least two are already somewhat obvious: Our population and labor force are expanding rapidly, making it necessary for the economy to take care of millions more people and to provide them with jobs; living standards must rise if social tensions are to be reduced without government intervention.

Our purpose in this chapter is to sketch the meaning and implications of economic growth, thus providing a theoretical basis for judging the actual growth of various economies. We shall find that there is no single "theory" of economic growth in the sense of a unified body of propositions. Instead, certain elements are common ingredients to almost all theories, and when taken together constitute the basis for most modern discussions of the subject.

What Is Economic Growth?

What do we mean by economic growth? There is often confusion about it, because politicians and economists are fond of hurling statistics at each other showing growth rates of various countries or regions over different periods of time. Hence an explanation is in order.

Economic Growth is the rate of increase in an economy's real output or income over time—that is, the rise in its full employment output in constant prices. Economic growth may be expressed in either of two ways: (1) as total real GNP or NNP over time; or (2) as per capita real GNP or NNP over time.

The first of these measures is usually employed to describe the expansion of a nation's economic output. The second is used to express the development of its material standard of living and to compare it with other nations.

This does not mean that economic growth deals only with dull facts and figures about a nation's output. In the most fundamental sense, economic growth is concerned with policy measures aimed at expanding a nation's *capacity* to produce. It thus contrasts with monetary and fiscal policies which seek to make full and efficient use of a nation's *existing* capacity.

The concept of economic growth can be illustrated in terms of the familiar production-possibilities curves in Exhibit 1. Since each curve represents an economy's capacity to produce, an outward shift of the curve is a measure of a nation's economic growth.

MEASURING ECONOMIC GROWTH

Is the United States economy growing, declining, or stagnating? How does its growth compare with the Russian economy? The Japanese economy? The answers are determined by the way in which we measure growth. Although the definition seems clear-cut, economists do not always agree on the results, because the methods of calculation can involve some slippery procedures.

Part of the trouble is that the concept of growth, like so many concepts in economics, is derived from the natural sciences—in this case from biology. The classic definition of growth was given by the biologist D'arcy Thompson. Growth, Thompson said, is "a process, indirectly resulting from chemical, osmotic, and other forces, by which material is introduced into the organism and transferred from one part of it to another." In general terms, therefore, *growth is an organic process.*

Exhibit 1

Economic Growth Can Be Seen as an Outward Shift of an Economy's Production-Possibilities Curve

Economic growth is not a movement along a given curve such as from S to T, since this is merely a change in the composition of total output, nor is it a movement from a point of unemployment such as U to the production possibilities curve.

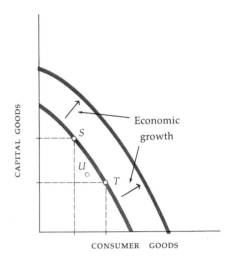

Conceptually, economic growth should involve similar processes in economic organisms—that is, in the firms, households, and governmental units that compose our economy. These organisms are responsible for producing and consuming the economy's stream of goods and services, and their complex interactions with one another determine the rate of economic growth.

In practice, the biological definition of growth makes it quite clear that we cannot measure the fundamental *organic* growth of an economy. Economists, therefore, have adopted an alternative approach: they use past measures of output or income, as suggested by the definition of economic growth given earlier, and they derive long-term growth trends from these historical records. Frequently, these trends are projected into the future at various assumed compound rates of growth—like money growing at compound interest in a savings account.

An example is shown in Exhibit 2. The growth rates are averages based on each country's historical experience for a selected period of years up to the terminal year 1965. If longer or shorter historical periods had been chosen, the averages would undoubtedly have been different. Quite clearly, a growth rate of 3 percent as compared to 4 percent is no minor matter. For a country with a GNP of say, $500 billion, the difference between 3 and 4 percent in a given year amounts to goods and services worth $5 billion. And of course, the relative economic significance is even greater for poor nations than for rich ones.

Exhibit 2

GNP Per Capita in 1965 for Selected Countries, with Projections to the Year 2000

Country	GNP per capita, 1965 U.S. dollars	Assumed average annual growth rate, %	Projected GNP per capita in 1965 U.S. dollars	
			1985	2000
United States	$3,557	3.0	$6,510	$10,160
Canada	2,464	3.0	4,550	7,070
France	1,924	3.7	3,920	6,830
West Germany	1,905	4.1	4,230	7,790
United Kingdom	1,804	3.7	3,750	6,530
U.S.S.R.	1,288	3.7	2,660	4,650
Italy	1,101	4.1	2,440	4,450
Japan	857	6.8	2,080	8,590
India	99	2.9	169	270
China	98	3.5	186	321

SOURCE: Projections are based on assumed medium growth rates of GNP and population, based on historical averages for varying periods of years up to 1965. Data are adapted from Herman Kahn and Anthony J. Wiener, *The Year 2000,* Macmillan, New York, 1967.

The "Classical" Theory of Growth

In the late eighteenth and early nineteenth centuries, certain classical British economists—notably Adam Smith, David Ricardo, and Thomas Malthus—formulated economic concepts and theories which dealt in large part with the problem of economic development. The conclusions of Ricardo and Malthus were basically pessimistic; they argued that a country's economic growth must end in decline and stagnation. The ideas of these men compose what may appropriately be called the "classical" theory of economic growth. Their views are interesting, and can help us to understand modern economic problems of growth.

THE SUBSISTENCE THEORY AND DIMINISHING RETURNS

The classical model of economic growth is fascinating, because it is based on a so-called *subsistence theory,* which gives rise to some interesting implications. In its simplest form the classical model can be expressed in terms of two basic propositions:

1. The population of a country tends to adjust to a subsistence level of living.

2. Increases in population, with techniques and natural resources (land) held constant, result in *eventually* decreasing per capita incomes due to the operation of the "law of diminishing returns."

These concepts are illustrated in Exhibit 3. In this chart the population of a country is scaled on the horizontal axis, and its material "standard of living" as measured by per capita real income is scaled on the vertical. The curve labeled *LL* shows the actual level of living that the society can maintain for each amount of population applied to the fixed quantity of other resources. It may therefore be thought of as an *average product curve* representing the average output per person (or per worker) which results from adding more and more people to a given amount of land while production techniques are held constant.

The average product or actual level-of-living curve, *LL,* rises to a maximum and then declines, thereby

Exhibit 3

The Subsistence Theory and Diminishing Returns

In the classical model of Ricardo and Malthus, the actual level of living LL depends on the size of the population (or number of workers) applied to a fixed amount of land. The population tends toward an equilibrium size of OM, corresponding to the subsistence level MR. Even an upward shift of the actual level- *of-living curve from LL to L'L', due to the development of new resources or new production techniques, is of short-run duration. The population simply expands to the size OK, leaving the average output per person KT at the same subsistence level as before.*

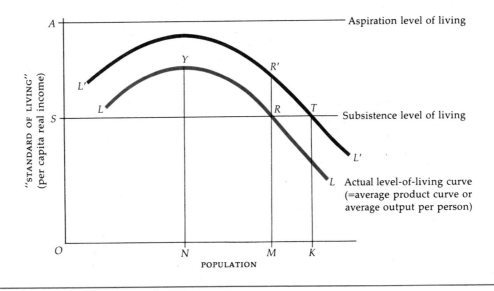

evidencing the eventual tendency for "diminishing returns" to set in as a growing population is applied to a fixed amount of resources. The ideal or *optimum population* is therefore *ON*, since this yields a level of living equal to *NY*, which is the highest level attainable on the curve. Any other combination of population and fixed resources is not optimal because it yields a lower output per person.

The classical economists contended that there was some standard of living at which the population—especially the working population—would just maintain itself with no tendency to increase or decrease. They called this the "subsistence level." Although primarily a physical or biological level, this level is also determined by social and customary needs which in turn influence the rearing of children. Thus the classicists argued that if wages per worker fell below the subsistence level, people would tend to stop having children and the population would

decline, thereby increasing per capita real incomes; conversely, if wages per worker rose above the subsistence level, people would tend to start having more children and the population would increase, thereby lowering per capita real incomes. This early-nineteenth-century classical theory is known as the *subsistence theory of wages* (also called the *iron* or *brazen law of wages*).

Although the early classical economists did not use graphs, these ideas can be expressed in the form of a model as shown on the chart. If *OS* represents the subsistence level of living, the equilibrium size of the population, according to the classicists, is *OM* (= *SR*). For if the population is larger than *OM*, the actual level of living will be below the subsistence level; hence the population will decline and per capita real incomes will therefore increase. On the other hand, if the population is less than *OM*, the actual level of living will be above the subsistence level; hence the population will rise and per capita real incomes will therefore decrease. Thus it is apparent that the "subsistence level" in the classical model is a long-run equilibrium level of living for the population as a whole.

ECONOMICS—THE "DISMAL SCIENCE"

Because of this pessimistic theory, economics (or political economy as it used to be called) came to be known as the "dismal science." For if the subsistence level of living is a long-run equilibrium toward which society is always tending, there is no hope of ever improving the lot of mankind. Even the discovery of new natural resources or the development of new techniques would at best provide only temporary benefits until the population had time to adjust to these new developments. Then a larger number of people would be left living in the same minimal circumstances as before.

For example, suppose that new natural resources are discovered, or more land becomes available, or new production techniques are developed. The effect is to raise the average product curve from LL to $L'L'$, for now the same population has more or better fixed resources with which to work. However, this increase in benefits per person from MR to MR' will be of limited duration. Since average product is now above the subsistence level, the population will increase until it reaches a new equilibrium, namely OK. At this point more people will be living at the same subsistence level OS ($= KT$) as before.

THE MALTHUSIAN SPECTER

Among the English classical economists of the late eighteenth and early nineteenth centuries, there was one whose theory of population as illustrated by the above model is especially well known. His name was Thomas R. Malthus, and his famous theory is often encountered by students in high school history courses.

The Malthusian Theory of Population (first published by Malthus in 1798 and revised in 1803) stated that population increases faster than the means of subsistence. That is, population tends to increase as a geometric progression (1, 2, 4, 8, 16, 32, etc.) while the means of subsistence increase at most only as an arithmetic progression (1, 2, 3, 4, 5, 6, etc.). This is because a growing population applied to a fixed amount of land results in eventually diminishing returns to workers. Human beings are therefore destined to misery and poverty unless the rate of population growth is retarded. This may be accomplished either by: (1) preventive checks such as moral restraint, late marriages, and celibacy, or if these fail then by (2) positive checks such as wars, famines, and disease.

Has the prediction of Malthus been realized? There is no doubt that it has, in certain crowded underdeveloped areas of Asia, Africa, and South America where the Malthusian specter hangs like a dark cloud. In these countries, industrialization and economic growth are impeded because agriculture is inefficient and unable to feed both the people on farms and those who live and work in the cities. In many of these countries wars, famines, and disease are the main curbs on population, although major efforts are now being made to use contraception.

Critics of colonialism point out, of course, that many of the poor countries' problems result from foreign interference. For example, foreign exploitation of their natural resources has drawn workers away from the farms, while doing little to raise agriculture above subsistence levels. Well-meaning medical missionaries have contributed to the shortage of food by reducing infant mortality and death rates, thereby increasing population. In short, the poor countries' economies have been distorted by the rich countries' use of them as sources of raw material and cheap labor. Furthermore, the critics add, the rich nations have usually propped up regimes that defend foreign interests at the expense of local well-being.

SOME PROPOSED SOLUTIONS

The overpopulated countries are thus caught in a "Malthusian trap," even though it may not be entirely of their own making. Is there any way of escape? Three possibilities may be suggested.

One solution would be to shift millions of people

THOMAS ROBERT MALTHUS

1766–1834

In the last third of the eighteenth century two great problems occupied the attention of most thinking people in England: one was widespread poverty; the other was how many Englishmen there were. Socialists called attention to the poverty problem with a promise of a Utopian world—a paradise—in which all would be well. The population problem had prompted Adam Smith to remark in his Wealth of Nations (1776) *that "No society can surely be flourishing and happy, of which the far greater part of the members are poor and miserable."*

Were England's resources adequate to bring about a fulfillment of the socialists' dreams? A hitherto unknown English clergyman, Thomas Robert Malthus, thought not. In 1798 he published a treatise of fifty thousand words entitled An Essay on the Principle of Population, as it Affects the Future Improvement of Society. *The essay was based on his observations and travels in various countries. From these he expounded his famous rule that "population, when unchecked, goes on doubling every twenty-five years or increases in a geometric ratio," but the means of subsistence can only increase in an arithmetic ratio.*

Malthus became a professor of history, and published a revision of his essay in 1803. In this he moderated his rigid "formula" and spoke more of a tendency of population to outrun the supply of food. Human beings, he concluded, were destined to misery and poverty unless the rate of population growth is retarded either by: (1) preventive checks such as moral restraint, late marriages, and celibacy, or if these fail then by (2) positive checks such as wars, famine, and disease.

Malthus and his population theory were severely criticized by people in nearly every walk of life—politicians, clergymen, philosophers, and journalists—all of whom raised cries of heresy. Some, like the Quarterly Review (July, 1817), *admitted that it was easier simply "to disbelieve Mr. Malthus than to refute him." And some, notably Ricardo and other classical economists, made Malthus's theory the basis of their own theories of wages and rent.*

The generalizations expressed by Malthus have been recognized by governments throughout the world, and by the United Nations in its efforts to assist the overpopulated, underdeveloped countries. Although there may be a tendency to dismiss the gloomy forebodings of the Malthusian theory, its

Bettmann Archive

warnings cannot be pushed aside. They are a stark reality for millions of people in many nations today.

In addition to his population theory, Malthus made outstanding contributions to economics, notably in his Principles of Political Economy (1820). *He was an intimate friend of David Ricardo, and it is impossible to disassociate their economic views, even though the two men were often in substantial disagreement. For one thing, Ricardo was as incapable of grasping the pragmatic and empirical approach of Malthus as Malthus was incapable of appreciating the rigor and subtle deductive reasoning of Ricardo.*

Among the notable contributions that Malthus made to economic thought was the concept of "effective demand," which he defined as the level of aggregate demand necessary to maintain continuous production. More than a century was to pass before the problem of effective demand would rise again to public notice: In his General Theory, *John Maynard Keynes paid tribute to the pioneering work of Malthus on this subject.*

from overpopulated to underpopulated regions—from the small farms in southeast Asia, for example, to the vast jungles of South America which await development. But there are many obvious political and social obstacles, and hence this is not a realistic policy for the foreseeable future.

A second possibility would be to develop new resources and production techniques at a sufficiently rapid rate so that the upward shifts of the average product curve more than offset the growth in population. In this way the population would never "catch up" with the rising level of output per person, and the level of living would continually increase.

A third approach would be to seek ways of raising the "subsistence level" to where it becomes an *aspiration level* or target for which to strive. Referring back to Exhibit 3, for example, the standard of living might be raised from *OS* to *OA*. Since this new level is above the maximum possible actual level of living that is attainable with any present combination of population and resources, there would be continual pressure to: (1) reduce the existing population in order to rise higher on the average product curve; or (2) discover and develop new resources and production techniques so as to shift the entire average product curve upward.

THE "HOT-BATHS" HYPOTHESIS

The second and third solutions, in varying degrees, have occurred and are continuing to occur in the economic development of some of today's advanced nations. The third approach, that of raising the subsistence level to an aspiration level, is based on a fascinating assumption—one which suggests a connection between population growth and living standards that may be applicable to the overpopulated, underdeveloped countries. It can be called—facetiously—the *hot-baths hypothesis:*

There may be a significant relationship between fecundity and "hot baths." That is, once a society reaches a certain minimum level of living at which it has reasonable creature comforts of life—i.e., adequate food, clothing, housing, sanitation, etc.—its desire for more and better material things as measured by its aspiration level continually rises. If this is true, the society's population will tend automatically to seek its economically optimum size, provided its living conditions can first be brought (probably with outside help from other nations) to this minimum threshhold level.

To repeat, this is only an hypothesis—a tentative proposition which has yet to be explored and tested in different nations under varying environmental (especially cultural and social) conditions. Nevertheless, it is an interesting and important concept. For as we shall see in a later chapter, American aid to poor, overpopulated nations since World War II has sought, at least in part, to raise living conditions in those countries to some minimum level at which their economies can break out of their stationary states and enter a new phase of more self-sustaining and self-propelling economic growth.

CAPITAL DEEPENING AND DIMINISHING RETURNS

The subsistence theory of wages in the classical model of a stationary state implies the existence of a *subsistence theory* of profits as well.

For example, the model of population growth which was developed in Exhibit 3 may be adapted to serve as a model of the growth of nonhuman capital including buildings, machines, inventories, etc. This can be done by measuring the rate of interest along the vertical axis and the total stock of capital along the horizontal. For simplicity, we may ignore the existence of risk, so that the rate of interest is the same as the rate of profit. (Can you explain why?) The curve *LL* is then the profit curve of capital which results from applying different amounts of capital to a fixed quantity of other resources.

When looked at in this way, the model indicates that capital is accumulated in anticipation of future interest returns or profits. Thus when the stock of capital in the economy is relatively low, the anticipated return on capital is high, thereby encouraging further accumulation. As capital is accumulated, however, the law of diminishing returns eventually sets in. If we suppose that *OS* represents the "subsistence rate" of profits, capital accumulation will proceed to *OM*. Improvements in any of the fixed resources or in production techniques will, of course,

JOHN STUART MILL

1806–1873

John Stuart Mill was an eminent philosopher and social scientist, and the leading economist of the mid-nineteenth century. In many ways, he was one of the most unusual men who ever lived.

Any discussion of Mill must make mention of his remarkable education, based on the experiences reported in his famous **Autobiography.** *He was the son of James Mill, a noted philosopher, historian, and economist. James Mill was also an intimate friend of David Ricardo and of the great utilitarian philosopher Jeremy Bentham. This intellectual background exercised a profound influence on the younger Mill, who was educated at home by his father.*

Thus, at the age of three, before most children can even recite the alphabet, John Stuart was reading English fluently and began the study of Greek. By the time he was seven, he had read the dialogues of Plato, the great books of the ancient Greek historians Herodotus and Xenophon, the philosophical writings of Diogenes, and most of the nearly eighty works of the second century Greek prose writer Lucian. At the age of eight he took up the study of Latin. Before he was twelve years old, he had already digested, among other things, the major writings of Aristotle, Aristophanes, Horace, Lucretius, Sallust, and Socrates; made a comprehensive survey of algebra, calculus, and geometry; embarked on a serious study of logic through the writings of the early seventeenth-century British philosopher Thomas Hobbes; and written, in addition to some verses, a "History of Rome," a "History of Holland," and the "Abridged Ancient Universal History."

At the age of thirteen, John Stuart was introduced by his father to the books of Smith, Ricardo, and Malthus. Thus began his education in political economy—an education that eventually established him as one of the abler critics of classical economic liberalism. For although Mill as an economist is considered a member of the classical school, he actually repudiated some of its most basic premises. In contrast to Smith, for example, he did not believe that laissez-faire led to the best of all possible worlds. Instead he advocated social reforms. These included the taxation and redistribution of wealth, a shorter working day, abolition of the wage system, and the establishment of democratic producers' cooperatives in which the workers would own the factories and elect the managers to run them. It should be emphasized, however, that Mill

Culver Pictures

believed too strongly in individual freedom ever to go far as a socialist. He distrusted the power of the state, and his reason for favoring producers' cooperatives was not to exalt the laboring class, but to assure the individual worker the fruits of his labor.

Mills' chief contribution to economics was his collection and systemization of its literature. His major two-volume work, the **Principles of Political Economy,** *published in 1848, was considered to be a masterful synthesis of post-Ricardian economic writings. The book offered a calm prescription for peaceful progress and served as a standard text in economics for several decades. It is a noteworthy coincidence that in the same year, an incendiary pamphlet entitled the* **Communist Manifesto** *was published by a then relatively unknown prophet of socialism, Karl Marx, whose ideas ultimately shook the world.*

As for Mill himself, few individuals were ever held in higher esteem. Like the great and beloved Greek philosopher Plato of some 2,200 years earlier, Mill was a selfless man with a gentle, kind, and reasonable manner that endeared him to everyone. He was regarded with the deepest affection and respect— indeed, he was almost worshiped—by his contemporaries throughout the world. And like Plato, when he died an entire nation mourned his passing.

shift the profit curve upward from *LL* to *L'L'*, thereby bringing about a further accumulation of capital to *OK*.

It is customary among economists to refer to an increase in the stock of capital relative to other resources, especially labor, as *capital deepening*. What are the effects of such a deepening, assuming that there are no changes in techniques? Clearly, with the operation of the inexorable law of diminishing returns, the interest or profit rate on capital must decline, while the real wages of labor must *rise* as this resource becomes more and more scarce relative to the growing stock of capital.

The Wages-Fund Theory

These ideas gradually led to a reformulation of the subsistence theory of wages in the classical model. The reformulation, known as the "wages-fund" theory, existed or was implied in the writings of Smith (1776) and Ricardo (1817), but it was best articulated several decades later in 1848 by John Stuart Mill—not only the greatest economist of his time, but also one of history's most distinguished intellectuals.

The *wages-fund theory* was a mid-nineteenth-century classical theory of wages which held that the producer sets aside, from his capital, funds from which to hire the workers needed for production. This is necessary because of the indirect or "roundabout" nature of the production process: it takes time for goods to be produced, sold, and paid for. Therefore, workers must be given advanced payments—out of the producer's "wages fund"—in order to meet their basic needs. The amount of the wages fund, and hence the real wage of labor, depends directly on the size of the capital stock relative to the number of workers. But in the long run, as we have seen in the classical model, the accumulation of capital tends to be determined by the minimum subsistence rate of profits. Hence the only effective way to raise real wages is to reduce the number of workers or size of the population.

CONCLUSION: THE CLASSICAL VIEW OF GROWTH

These ideas led the English classical economists—especially Ricardo—to the conclusion that the devel-

opment of an economy depends on the relative growth of two critical variables: *population* and *capital*. If population grows faster than capital, wages fall and profits rise; conversely, if capital grows faster than population, profits fall and wages rise. From time to time, one of these variables may grow faster than the other, thereby causing an upward shift in the level-of-living curve of population or in the profit curve of capital, but eventually both wages per worker and profits per unit of capital must tend toward a long-run level of subsistence. Land, on the other hand, remains fixed in supply; therefore, landlords stand to benefit over the long run as rents continue to rise with increases in population and in output per worker.

What Are the Long-Run Trends?

Have these predictions been vindicated by history? For most of the advanced or developed economies of the Western world the answer is no. In the United States, for example, three very long-run patterns since the nineteenth century have been evident:

First, the trends of real wages and of output per man-hour have been sharply upward, not downward. These have been due mainly to two factors: (1) rapid expansion in technology; and (2) growth of the capital stock at a faster rate than the population, thus resulting in a deepening of capital. Second, interest rates or profit have fluctuated in the business cycle with no particular upward or downward trend. Third, land rents have moved upward only slightly, while actually declining in relation to other factor prices.

What we are saying in general terms is that the average product curve of the economy has shifted upward over time at a pace rapid enough to more than offset the tendencies toward diminishing returns and Malthusian subsistence equilibrium. This upward shift can be attributed to changes in the conditions that are assumed to remain "fixed" when the curve is drawn. In broad terms these include: (1) improvements in the quality of labor; (2) discoveries of new and better natural resources; and (3) technological advances in production. We shall see shortly that these are actually the kinds of factors that determine a nation's economic growth. As a result, the classical or "Ricardian" model is useful not only for what it includes, but also for what it excludes in explaining many of the dynamic processes of economic history.

What Factors Determine Economic Growth?

The classical theory of economic growth presents only a partial explanation of economic development. As yet, no unified body of principles provides what might be called a *general theory* of economic growth. However, certain factors will undoubtedly play a significant role in the development of such a theory. Our purpose at this time is to see what they are.

Let us assume that aggregate demand is sufficient to maintain full employment, and that government will take the necessary monetary and fiscal measures to assure this. The growth of real GNP will then be determined by improvements in the nation's resources and the "environment" in which they are used. These major growth-determining factors include:

1. Quantity and quality of human resources
2. Quantity and quality of "natural" resources
3. Accumulation of capital
4. Specialization and scale of production
5. Rate of technological progress
6. Environmental factors

These are also the kinds of factors that influence an economy's production-possibilities curve. Hence we should examine the importance of each of them.

QUANTITY AND QUALITY OF HUMAN RESOURCES

On the basis of our earlier definition of economic growth, the following simple formula may be kept in mind as a convenient guide for discussion:

$$\text{Real GNP per capita} = \frac{\text{total real GNP}}{\text{population}}$$

The rate of economic growth is measured by the rate at which the left side of this equation increases over time. This in turn will depend, in terms of the right side of the equation, on the rate at which the numerator of the ratio increases relative to the denominator.

The faster the rate of increase in total real GNP as compared to the rate of increase in population, the greater the rise in real GNP per capita and hence in the rate of economic growth.

The above formula uses population only in quantitative terms. But there are quantitative and qualitative considerations that should be taken into account. For instance, increases in population will bring about increases in the size of the labor force—that is, in the number of people working or looking for work. The productivity of the labor force will influence the rate of economic growth. What are the chief factors determining labor productivity? They include among other things: (1) the time spent at work, such as the average length of the workweek; (2) the education, health, and skills of workers; and (3) the quantity and quality of the tools and capital equipment with which they work. Over the past several decades, modern industrial nations have experienced a steady decline in the first of these factors along with a continuous increase in the last two.

Thus it is not just the *quantity* of a country's human resources that has a bearing on its economic growth, but the *quality* of those resources as well.

QUANTITY AND QUALITY OF "NATURAL" RESOURCES

Human resources are only part of the picture. An economy's output and economic growth also depend on the quantity and quality of its soil, minerals, water, timber, etc.—its so-called natural resources.

Some economists contend that there is no such thing as a "natural" resource. They argue that resources provided by nature are of no value to society unless man is able to put them to use. When that happens, the resources are not natural but man-made. Thus a nation may be rich in resources, but its material well-being or rate of economic growth will not be influenced in the slightest if these resources remain "neutral" or untapped. Hence it follows that demand and cost conditions must be favorable in order for a resource to be converted from a neutral to a positive state. This means that there must be: (1) a high enough level of demand for the product which the resource will help to produce; and (2) an adequate supply of capital, labor, and technical skills to transform the resource to profitable use.

It should be recognized that the quantity and quality of a nation's natural resources are not necessarily fixed. By diverting some of its *existing* labor, capital, etc., into research, a society may be able to discover or develop *new* natural resources within its own borders which will enhance its future rate of economic growth. In terms of the production-possibilities curve, this means that some consumer goods must be sacrificed in the present to enable the economy to reach a higher curve in the future.

ACCUMULATION OF CAPITAL

A society must also forego some current consumption in order to build capital goods such as factories, machines, transportation facilities, dams, educational institutions, and so on. The rate at which a nation can add to its stock of capital will influence its economic growth.

What determines the rate of capital accumulation? Why is the rate greater in some countries than in others? We have already learned in the study of macroeconomic theory that many considerations may influence investment, but two fundamental factors are (1) profit expectations of businessmen, and (2) government policies toward investment. Of course, the influence of these conditions differs among nations. Nevertheless, one aspect of the process of capital accumulation is relevant to all economies—the necessity for sacrifice.

Thus, capital accumulation is closely related to the volume of savings—the proportion of a society's income that is not spent for consumption. In order to add to their long-run stock of capital goods, the people of a country must refrain from consuming a portion of their current output so that a part of the flow can be diverted into investment. This principle helps to explain why poor countries, like poor families, are ordinarily unable to save as much as rich ones, and hence experience little or no economic growth. In general:

The *cost* of economic growth to a society is the consumption it must sacrifice in order to save for the purpose of accumulating capital.

SPECIALIZATION AND SCALE OF PRODUCTION

Adam Smith observed in his *Wealth of Nations* that "The greatest improvement in the productive powers of labor and the greater part of the skill, dexterity, and judgment with which it is any where directed, or applied, seem to have been the effects of the division of labour." He then gave the celebrated example of a pin factory: "One man draws out the wire, another straights it, a third cuts it, a fourth points it, a fifth grinds it. . . ." and as a result there is a far greater output than if each man were to make the entire pin himself.

Smith also made the interesting point that the division of labor is limited by the "extent of the market." He pointed out that in a small isolated economy there will be less division of labor and a smaller scale of operations to satisfy local needs than in a large exchange economy like Glasgow or a still larger one like London.

These comments on specialization and scale of production provide significant insights into the process of economic growth. In the early stages of a nation's economic development, production is relatively nonspecialized and the scale of operations is small; "manufacturers" produce only to supply the needs of the surrounding community. In a number of localities more extensive industries grow up without advancing to the factory stage of production. This type of situation prevailed in the United States, for example, until the end of the eighteenth century. But with the expansion of the market and advances in the technology of production, greater specialization and scale of operations became possible, thereby bringing about larger volumes of output at the same if not lower unit costs. This is a continuing process in the economic growth of nations and regions.

Modern economic growth is not just an increase in the quantity of the factors of production; it involves fundamental changes in the organization and techniques of production—that is, changes in the *structure* of production as represented by the input-output relationships that characterize an economy's firms and industries.

A nation's economic growth, therefore, will be determined in part by the potential it has for increasing the specialization of its resources and the scale of its production.

RATE OF TECHNOLOGICAL PROGRESS

There are thus qualitative as well as quantitative considerations that determine economic growth. One of the most important of these qualitative factors is the rate of technological progress. This refers, in a broad sense, to the speed at which new knowledge is both developed and applied to raising the standard of living.

A brief look at a remarkable series of events that took place in the United States within the short space of 13 years, between 1790 and 1803, provides an interesting example of how the rate of technological progress can influence the evolution of a national economy.

In 1790, a brilliant young Englishman named Samuel Slater, employed by a merchant firm in Rhode Island, began spinning cotton thread by machine, thus marking the first effective introduction of the factory system in this country. In the same year, John Fitch constructed and operated successfully the world's first regularly scheduled steamboat, which, when later employed on western waters, cut the costs of transportation remarkably and enabled the West to become part of the national economy. In 1793, Eli Whitney invented the cotton gin, which made possible the extensive cultivation of cotton and subsequently transformed the economic structure of the South. In 1800 this same young graduate of Yale College contracted to manufacture 10,000 rifles for the government, and succeeded in producing them with precisely made interchangeable parts—the first step toward assembly-line production. By 1803, a Philadelphia inventor named Oliver Evans almost achieved complete automation in the milling of wheat into flour by an ingenious system of machines that weighed, cleaned, ground, and packed the flour with virtually no human assistance.

These technological advances were accompanied by legal and economic innovations which had important consequences for the nation's development. Two that were particularly spectacular were: (1) the sudden growth of banking, including the creation of the Bank of the United States as well as more than two dozen state-chartered banks, which provided new and important sources of credit for business transactions; and (2) the rapid adoption of the corporate form of business organization, which provided opportunities for accumulating large amounts of financial capital (i.e., money) with limited liability on the part of owners. In an expanding economy where risk taking was a vital element of growth, these features made possible the financing and adoption of the technical innovations mentioned above. Clearly, therefore:

Technological progress involves more than just invention; it embraces an effort on the part of society as a whole to get the most out of existing resources, and to discover new and better resources through continuous improvements in education, engineering, management, and marketing.

ENVIRONMENTAL FACTORS

What all this leads to is the fact that economic growth cannot take place in a vacuum. The political, social, cultural, and economic environment must be favorable if significant growth is to occur. This means, among other things, that there must be a banking and credit system capable of financing growth, a legal system that establishes the ground rules of business behavior, a tax system that does not discourage new investment and risk-taking, and a stable government that is sympathetic to economic expansion. It is no accident that countries like the United States, Canada, Great Britain, Japan, and the Soviet Union have experienced periods of rapid economic growth despite their different political systems, whereas some Latin American and Asian countries have had little or no significant economic growth for many years—and in some cases even for many decades.

CONCLUSION: THE PROBLEM OF MEASUREMENT

How important is each of the above factors in determining a country's economic growth? Can we measure their separate influences? These questions are extremely difficult to answer because some causes of growth are qualitative rather than quantitative. Consequently, there is a tendency among economists to reduce the determinants of growth to three sets of "measurable" factors:

1. Growth of the labor force

2. Growth of capital

3. Technical progress (including "all other things")

The first two factors can be measured quite precisely, whereas the third cannot. Therefore, in measuring the causes of an economy's growth, once the contributions of the first two factors to total economic growth have been quantitatively estimated, the contribution of the third factor may be viewed as a "residual" or catch-all for all determinants other than labor and capital.

As a simple example, if an economy grows at the rate of 6 percent annually over a period of time, and 4 percent of that growth is estimated to have been due to the growth of labor and capital combined, then the remaining 2 percent might be attributed to technical progress. For purposes of measurement, therefore, "technical progress" includes such things as better machinery and technology, better management, and greater skills on the part of workers. It has been estimated that in the United States more than 80 percent of the increase in output per capita since the early part of the century has been due to this "technical-progress" factor, leaving less than 20 percent to be explained by the other two factors. In terms of *total* output (as distinct from output per capita), technical progress has accounted for almost 50 percent of the growth of production in the United States and various other industrial nations. This suggests that economic growth is best envisioned as a continuous development and discovery of new and better ways of doing things, rather than just a quantitative expansion of existing inputs.

A Simple Growth Model

Modern approaches to the theory of economic growth are closely tied to analysis of business cycles. The reasons are obvious. When we studied business cycles in an earlier chapter, we learned that an economy's rate of growth will vary in different stages of the cycle. We also learned that if the consumption function is assumed to be stable, the level of income and employment is determined by net investment.

But in the study of economic growth net investment has yet another function: It *adds to the economy's capacity.* Therefore, the more net investment undertaken in any one period, the greater will be the productive capacity of the economy in the next period, and hence the higher the level of investment needed to sustain aggregate demand and full employment at capacity output.

THE CAPITAL-OUTPUT RATIO

This point is illustrated by the familiar consumption-function diagram in the upper chart of Exhibit 4. For simplicity, only the private sector is represented; the influence of the public sector (government) is excluded. Let us suppose that output ON_1 represents the economy's full employment NNP in Year 1. Hence the corresponding level of consumption is N_1C_1, and the corresponding level of saving is C_1S_1. We assume that this volume of saving flows into new investment, i.e., that planned saving equals planned investment, so that the output ON_1 is maintained.

As a result of this new investment, the economy's capacity to produce is enlarged in Year 2 to the output ON_2. In order to produce this output, the volume of planned saving C_2S_2 must flow into new investment. If it does, the capacity of the economy will be further enlarged in Year 3 to the output ON_3.

If this process continues, the economy's ability to produce will shift to the right by increasing amounts, requiring *increasing levels of investment* in order to sustain full employment of a *growing productive capacity.* This is further emphasized by the lower chart in Exhibit 4, where the level of investment each year shifts upward by larger and larger amounts.

Exhibit 4

Investment and the Growth of Capacity at Full Employment

In the upper chart, let ON₁ be the full employment NNP in Year 1. Then savings in that year will be C₁S₁, which, when invested in plant and equipment, will increase productive capacity in Year 2 by N₁N₂. Saving and investment must then rise to C₂S₂, and this in turn will increase productive capacity in Year 3 by N₂N₃. Investment must thus rise by increasing amounts, as emphasized in the lower chart, in order to sustain full employment of a growing productive capacity.

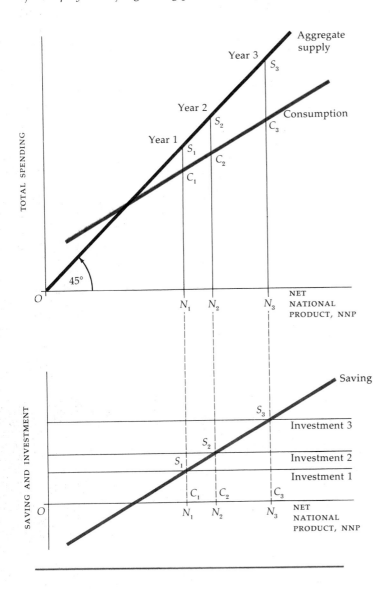

How much will the economy's productive capacity rise each year? The answer depends on what economists call the *capital-output ratio*, which is the relationship between the economy's stock of capital and the resulting change in its output or productive capacity. A ratio of 3:1, for instance, which has been the approximate long-run trend in the United States, means that 3 units of additional capital produce 1 unit of additional output.

FULL EMPLOYMENT GROWTH RATE

We can extend the foregoing ideas to develop an important formula that is widely used as an expression of economic growth at full employment.

Thus, in addition to assuming full employment, let us also assume that *saving* equals *investment* and that all investment results in an increase in *capital*. Therefore, if we know the *average propensity to save*, i.e., the proportion of the economy's income or output that is not spent on consumption, we can tell how much saving will flow into investment and hence into the creation of additional capital. Then, if we also know the capital-output ratio, we can calculate the expected full employment growth of NNP.

The procedure is illustrated in Exhibit 5. The first two columns show, for each year, the full employment output represented by NNP. For convenience in calculation, we begin with an arbitrary NNP of $100 in Year 1. In the third column of the table, saving equals investment or the increase in capital, and the average propensity to save, APS, is assumed to be 10 percent. This is equivalent, of course, to saying that the average propensity to consume is 90 percent. If we assume that the capital-output ratio is also 3:1, the resulting increase in output will be ⅓ of the increase in capital as shown in the fourth column. This increase in output then becomes the next year's addition to NNP in the second column, as emphasized by the arrows. The table can thus be extended very easily by simply continuing the pattern; that is, take 10 percent of NNP, then calculate ⅓ of that, and add the result to the current year's NNP to get next year's NNP.

You may be able to estimate from the table that the full employment output of NNP is growing at a rate

Exhibit 5

The Full Employment Rate of Economic Growth

What will be the full employment NNP for Year 5? To find out, take 10 percent of Year 4's NNP, then calculate $\frac{1}{3}$ of that, and add the result to the NNP for Year 4. The arrows illustrate the pattern to be followed.

(1) Year	(2) Full employment output of NNP	(3) Saving = investment = increase in capital (APS = 0.10) 10% of col. (2)	(4) Resulting increase in output (capital-output ratio = 3:1) $\frac{1}{3}$ of col. (3)
1	$100.00	$10.00	
			3.33
2	103.33	10.33	
			3.44
3	106.77	10.68	
			3.56
4	109.33		

of something over 3 percent per year. However, a closer estimate can be made in terms of the variables in the model by applying the simple formula:

Full employment growth rate

$$= \frac{\text{average propensity to save}}{\text{capital-output ratio}}$$

This basic formula is widely used in modern theories of economic growth. It can be applied for any average propensity to consume and for any capital-output ratio. In the above model, for example, we assumed a long-run APS of 0.10 and a capital-output ratio of 3; hence the full employment growth rate is 0.10/3 = 0.033 or 3.3 percent a year. Of course, a larger or smaller growth rate can be obtained, depending on the values of the APS and the capital-output ratio used in the formula.

The growth-rate formula and the simple model on which it is based are useful primarily because they illustrate important relationships. But it should be kept in mind that they assume a number of simplifying conditions, not the least of which are (1) a fixed capital-output ratio, (2) a fixed average propensity to save, and (3) a neglect of such real-world factors as business taxes, government monetary and fiscal policies, changes in technology, and other considerations. These assumptions have been the subject of much debate among economists engaged in the study of economic growth.

SUMMARY OF IMPORTANT IDEAS

1. The study of economic growth is concerned with the rate of increase in an economy's actual and potential real output or income over time. Economic growth may be viewed as an outward shift of an economy's production-possibilities curve.

2. The classical theory of economic growth, developed in the early nineteenth century, was a subsistence theory, based on the operation of the law of diminishing returns. It held that the development of an economy depended on the relative rates of growth of population and capital, but the returns to both in the form of wages and profit tended toward subsistence levels in the long run. Although the evidence has not borne this theory out for the advanced nations of the world, the classical model nevertheless is useful for explaining many of the dynamic processes of economic history.

3. The more important factors that determine a nation's economic growth include the quantity and quality of its human and natural resources, rate of capital accumulation, degree of specialization and scale of production, rate of technological progress, and the nature of its socioeconomic-political environment. For measurement purposes, however, these are usually reduced to three sets of factors: (1) growth of the labor force; (2) growth of capital; and (3) technical progress (or "all other things" not represented by the previous two measurable factors).

4. The full employment growth of an economy's productive capacity depends on its capital-output ratio which, for the United States, has had a long-run trend of about 3:1. A basic approach for measuring the full employment growth rate is to divide the average propensity to save by the capital-output

ratio. This formula is based, however, on a number of simplifying conditions, thus making it useful only for illustrating some important relationships.

FOR HOMEWORK AND DISCUSSION

1. *Terms and concepts to review:*

economic growth

subsistence theory of wages

Malthusian theory of population

capital deepening

wages-fund theory

capital-output ratio

2. Is our economic definition of growth "better" than the biological definition? Explain.

3. What are the shortcomings of the economic definition of growth? That is, what sort of "amenities" does the definition omit as far as the growth of a society is concerned?

4. If Ricardo and Malthus had been living in the United States rather than England during the early nineteenth century, do you think they would have developed the same theory of economic growth? Explain your answer. (HINT: Think in terms of the subsistence theory and the supply of scarce resources as compared to plentiful ones.)

5. What is meant by an "optimum population?" Do you believe there really is such a thing? Is it as applicable to the United States as it is to India? Why or why not?

6. The factors that determine an economy's growth are both quantitative and qualitative. The quantitative factors are susceptible to measurement and can be incorporated in a growth model. Does this mean that such models are incomplete to the extent that qualitative factors are omitted? What can be done about correcting the situation? Explain your answer.

7. How is the full employment growth rate of an economy influenced by the size of its APS relative to its capital-output ratio? Can you suggest some general policies that the government can adopt through the tax system for reducing the capital-output ratio and thus stimulating economic growth?

8. (*a*) It has been suggested that the income tax system, which provides equal deductions for each dependent, might be revised with the objective of regulating family size by taxation. How might this be done? Develop a specific example. (*b*) What do you think of a population control plan which parallels our agricultural policy, giving subsidies for "fallow acres" and penalties for "overcropping?"

REFERENCES AND READING SUGGESTIONS

BOULDING, KENNETH E., *Economic Analysis,* 3d ed., Harper, New York, 1955, chap. 33.

GILL, RICHARD T., *Economic Development: Past and Present,* 2d ed., Prentice-Hall, New York, 1967, chaps. 1–4.

MANSFIELD, EDWIN, *The Economics of Technological Change,* Norton, New York, 1968.

MORRIS, BRUCE R., *Economic Growth and Development,* Pitman, New York, 1967.

CHAPTER 18

Problems of Economic Growth

CHAPTER PREVIEW

What has been the record of American economic growth? How does it compare with that of other advanced nations? What are the sources of growth?

How fast should we grow? Are there some simple guides for understanding and measuring rates of growth?

Is economic growth "free," or must costs be paid for it?

What obstacles must be overcome if a given rate of growth is to be sustained?

How do problems of taxation and inflation affect the rate of growth?

The "goodness" of economic growth was for most people an article of faith until recently. After all, economic growth brings more goods, more services, and high employment. What could possibly be wrong with such objectives?

As it turns out, quite a lot. More goods include more chemicals, petroleum products, automobiles, etc., which defile the environment and upset the ecological balance. And, in an unplanned economy like America's, economic growth disrupts the lives of millions of people whose skills are made obsolete by changing technology—sometimes impoverishing whole regions of the country which lose their economic base when the demand for their traditional products or raw materials declines.

These problems are not new. But in the 1960s society's awareness of them increased. Some economists started to question the wisdom of growth for its own sake, and many began to ask what *kind* of growth was beneficial—in other words, which mix of goods and services would help to make America a better place.

We shall examine these issues in this and the following chapter. But first we must compare the historical record of growth in the United States with the experience of other advanced economies. Then we shall consider the costs of growth, both financial and social.

American Economic Growth: A Look at the Record

By summarizing some of the main trends, we shall understand better the pattern of economic growth in the United States. In the period prior to the Civil War "modern" America was being born. The country was developing a *national* economy marked by increased specialization, interdependence of regions, and growing economies in the scale of production. In regional terms, however, economic growth was not "balanced." The South, for example, changed less than any other section of the country as cotton remained "king" and slavery became its most important economic institution.

When the Civil War broke out, the United States was still primarily an agricultural country; its industrial output, though important and increasing, was nowhere near that of major European nations. But the wave of industrialization after the Civil War had a profound effect on America's economic development, and the nation entered a period of sustained growth that has lasted until the present time.

By 1900, the United States was the world's leading manufacturing nation, far ahead of such major producing countries as Great Britain and Germany. In 1859, the value of American manufactured goods stood at $1.8 billion; in 1869 it was $3.3 billion; and in 1899 it was over $13 billion. In terms of the rate of economic growth, the period from 1870 to 1900 was one in which total real GNP is estimated to have increased at an average annual compound rate of 5 percent, while per capita real GNP increased at about 3 percent.

MAJOR TRENDS SINCE 1900

For most of this century both total real GNP and per capita real GNP have grown steadily. In specific terms, the *long-run trend* of total real GNP has been continually upward at an average annual rate of more than 3 percent, while the trend of real GNP per capita has averaged a little less than 2 percent annually.

We may examine some of the underlying implica-

Exhibit 1 (at right)

The Anatomy of United States Economic Development

Since 1900, the country's net national product and net capital stock (upper chart) have grown faster than the population, while real hourly wages and per capita output (middle chart) have grown at about the same rate. The long-run trend of the interest rate (lower chart) has been flat and the long-run trend of the capital-output ratio (lower chart) has been stable at an average of about 3:1 or slightly less. This means that in general terms, the average product curves of capital and labor have shifted upward and to the right as a result of technological progress, at rates sufficient to offset any tendencies toward diminishing returns to either factor.

tions of these trends by looking at several of the variables that play a key role in the theory of economic growth. These variables are presented in Exhibit 1. The charts reveal three important sets of features:

1. The top chart shows that NNP increased at about the same rate as the net capital stock, but the latter increased much faster than the population (as well as the labor force). Hence there has been a substantial amount of capital deepening, i.e., more capital per worker.

2. The middle chart shows that the trend of real wages has been steadily upward and that its rate of growth has approximately equaled the increase in per capita output. The rise in the latter, of course, is a reflection of capital deepening and advancements in technology. Thus, labor has continued to earn approximately the same *proportion* of total output over the years.

3. The middle and lower charts show that along with the process of capital deepening, real wages have risen relative to the interest rate or return on capital. This is what the theory of economic growth would predict. The fact that the long-run trend of the interest rate is roughly flat, as is the trend of the capital-output ratio, can probably be accounted for by the tendency of diminishing returns to be approximately offset by advances in technology.

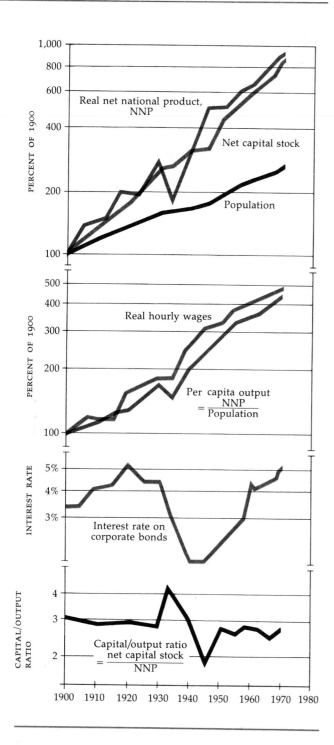

In general, therefore, it appears that the theory of economic growth, with the inclusion of technological advance, tends to be supported by the available evidence for the United States. Similar tendencies have also been found for other advanced Western nations.

SOME INTERNATIONAL COMPARISONS

How does America's growth rate compare with that of other relatively advanced nations? Some data for selected countries covering different periods of time are presented in Exhibit 2. Note that there are fewer differences in growth rates over longer periods than over shorter ones. (Can you suggest some reasons why?)

As the data indicate, some industrialized nations

Exhibit 2

Growth Rates of Selected Countries (latest comparative data)

Growth Rates of Real Gross National Product

Country	1870–1964	1929–1964	1950–1964	1960–1964
United States	3.6%	3.0%	3.6%	4.4%
Japan	3.8	4.2	9.9	11.4
Germany	2.8	3.9	7.0	4.8
United Kingdom	1.9	2.2	3.0	3.6
France	1.7	1.9	4.8	5.4
Italy	2.0	2.9	5.8	5.7
Canada	3.5	3.6	4.3	5.1

Growth Rates of Real Gross National Product Per Capita

Country	1870–1964	1929–1964	1950–1964	1960–1964
United States	1.9%	1.7%	1.8%	2.8%
Japan	—	—	8.7	10.3
Germany	1.7	2.8	5.9	3.5
United Kingdom	1.3	1.7	2.4	2.7
France	1.5	1.4	3.8	3.9
Italy	1.4	2.2	5.2	5.0
Canada	1.7	1.8	1.8	3.2

SOURCE: Department of Commerce, *Long-term Economic Growth, 1860–1965,* Washington, D.C., Government Printing Office, 1966.

have experienced faster rates of growth in recent decades than the United States. Japan and West Germany, in particular, had very high growth rates after World War II, thus prompting many economists to believe that this was a temporary phenomenon of postwar recovery. But the high rates have persisted, so that the phenomenon has long since been regarded as anything but "temporary."

Some interesting comparisons between the United States and the Soviet Union are shown in Exhibit 3. These are particularly important because they compare the rates of growth of the world's two major types of economic systems—America's predominantly market economy and Russia's predominantly command economy. Note that the Soviet economy's rate of growth was slower in the 1960s than in the 1950s, but its overall growth rate for both decades exceeded that of the United States.

THE SOURCES OF UNITED STATES GROWTH

In our discussion of the theory of growth we learned about the chief factors that determine a nation's economic development. For our present purposes, these may be summarized broadly in terms of the five factors listed in Exhibit 4.

The table in Exhibit 4 provides rough estimates of the contribution each of these five factors has made

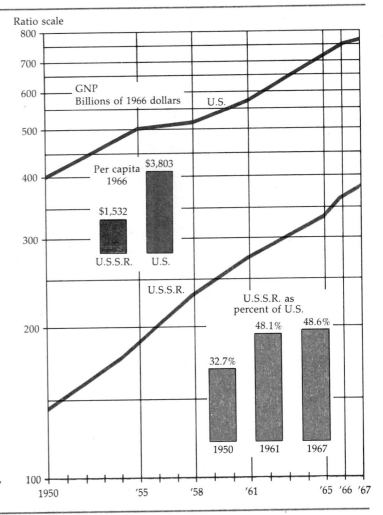

Exhibit 3

The United States and Soviet Economies

The rate of growth of the Soviet economy has been slowing, but year-to-year percent increases in output continue to exceed those of output in the United States. Hence, real GNP in the U.S.S.R. continues to increase relative to that in the United States, although less rapidly than in the 1950s.

There has been a relative decline, however, in the ability of the Soviet Union to utilize its resources efficiently. In the 1960s, the U.S.S.R. depended more than the United States on additions to its active labor force and to its plant and equipment to achieve increases in output. And agriculture continues to play a far larger and more critical role in the Soviet Union than in the United States; therefore, bad or good crop years affect U.S.S.R. economic growth much more.

In 1966 and 1967—good agricultural years in the Soviet Union—the rate of increase in output of consumer goods nearly equaled that of producer goods. Still, U.S.S.R. production of most items—capital or consumer—is well below that in the United States, though the population in the U.S.S.R. is almost one-fourth larger.

SOURCE: The Conference Board, *Road Maps of Industry*, Dec. 15, 1968.

Exhibit 4

Sources of United States Economic Growth

	Percent of total growth	
Source	1909–1929	1929–1957
Quantitative factors		
Increase in quantity of labor*	39	27
Increase in quantity of capital	26	15
Qualitative factors†		
Improved education and training	13	27
Improved technology	12	20
All other things‡	10	11
Total growth in real national income	*100*	*100*

* Adjusted for decreases in the work week.
† Some qualitative factors are at least partially quantitative. Improvements in education, for example, depend on the number of years of schooling as well as on the quality of schooling.
‡ Consists primarily of increased economies of large-scale production resulting from the expanding size of the market.
SOURCE: adapted from Edward Denison, *The Sources of Economic Growth in the United States,* Committee for Economic Development, New York, 1962.

to the nation's total economic growth. Note that in the pre-1929 period increases in the *quantitative* factors, namely the supplies of labor and capital, accounted for about two-thirds of the economy's expansion, while the remaining third was due to increases in such qualitative factors as improvements in education and training, technology, and "all other things." Since 1929, the situation has almost reversed itself, with the *qualitative* factors playing a major role in economic growth and the quantitative factors a minor one.

Investment in Human Capital

The trends in the table suggest that improvements in education and training have become the single most important factor contributing to economic growth. In other words, the scarcest resource for our society is not land or muscle power, but brainpower. The advances of modern science and technology are making this increasingly evident. Hence our invest-

Exhibit 5

Educational Attainment and Expenditures on Public Elementary and Secondary Education*

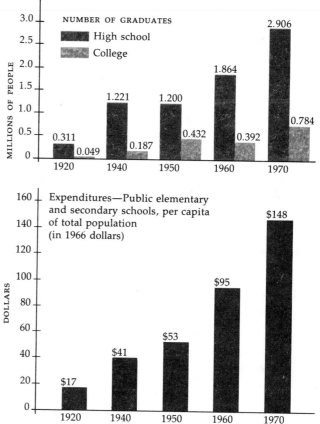

SOURCE: U.S. Department of Commerce; U.S. Department of Health, Education and Welfare.

ment in human capital, reflecting a rising long-run trend in the number of high school and college graduates and in expenditures on public elementary and secondary education, as shown in Exhibit 5, will continue to expand in the years to come. This is all the more likely in view of mounting evidence to suggest that society's returns from investment in human capital are probably much higher than its returns from investment in capital goods.

Can Students Find Happiness by Paying Their Own Way?

American colleges and universities are, to put it mildly, hotbeds of discontent and dissent. Much of that discontent is directed toward college itself—symbol and focus of a system that many students see as unduly restrictive, repressive, and irrelevant to real life, whatever that may be.

Paradoxically, there have never been more students. An estimated 8.2 million enrolled in colleges and universities at the start of the 1970 fall semester, almost three times as many as in 1955. In just ten years the cost of higher education has tripled—to some $26 billion. And that figure does not count either parental subsidy of students, or the earnings students lose by choosing to go to college instead of finding remunerated work. Indeed, if those *total* costs are counted, the average bachelor's degree at a four-year college carries a price-tag of $40,000.

Costly and Hasty Expansion

Until very recently, only unreconstructed conservatives of the late-eighteenth-century mold doubted that more education was synonymous with progress. But this uncritical acceptance of education as a desirable objective led to a huge, costly, unplanned, and hasty expansion of the higher educational system. Nobody asked the subjects of education, young people, for their opinion; most of them had no choice but to submit themselves to a prolonged period of dependency, financial and psychological, on adults. "I think it is unnatural to keep a young person in dependence for some twenty years of school attendance," writes Dr. Bruno Bettelheim, professor of psychology and psychiatry at the University of Chicago: "The tremendous push now on everyone to 'go to university' has brought incredibly large numbers to the student life who do *not* find their self-realization through study or the intellectual adventure—or not at that point in their lives. What they still want urgently, however, is to find their manhood."

Are There Any Solutions?

In a thoughtful article in *Fortune* in 1970, Edmund K. Faltermayer wrote: "One way to motivate students is to make them responsible for financing their own education. Society, of course, should continue to bear the full costs of elementary and secondary education for all. But once that basic social investment is made, society's commitment to pay the costs of education should largely come to an end." Faltermayer cited a study made in 1967 by a panel headed by physicist Jerrold R. Zacharias, which suggested that if students could borrow against future income to buy their education "both real and psychological dependence on adults could be appreciably reduced."

How would such a system work? First of all, a student's repayment would not be fixed, but would be a percentage of his earnings. Second, by *buying* his education instead of *receiving* it, the student would become a member of a group with considerable power in the marketplace. Colleges and universities that did not receive enough "dollar votes" would find themselves in financial trouble. Of course, some students might prefer to continue as dependents of their parents; but at least they would have a choice, which most do not have at present.

The Need For Choice

Why should so many high school students go automatically to college with hardly a break? There is no reason at all, except habit and custom. Indeed, there is much evidence to suggest that a large number of young people would enjoy—and would benefit from—a break of several years between high school and college. In that break they could do whatever fancy dictated: climb a mountain, sit and think, take a job, travel, or do nothing. The value of such a hiatus is obvious: it would give the student time to reflect about his values, his objectives, and his life-style.

Out of the student rebellion has come something very healthy: an unfreezing of society's attitudes toward education, which for centuries have been held in the glacial grip of superstition.

In the remaking of education economists have a vital role to play: they can show how the transformation of students from welfare recipients into buyers would unleash the market forces needed to compel change.

R. B.

1. *From the point of view of society as a whole, can you justify a scholarship or fellowship program that gives tax money to selected students who ultimately benefit through higher income yet never have to pay the money back?*

2. *Do you think that society has become so specialized that a "liberal education" is no longer of value?*

The Growth-Rate Problem: How Fast Should We Grow?

Now that we have looked at the background and history of economic growth, we may turn our attention to the future. What does it mean to talk about growth rates of 3, 4, 5 percent, or more? Should we try to set some desirable or "target" rate of growth?

GROWING AT COMPOUND INTEREST

First of all, we have to understand what is meant by the term *annual percentage rate of growth*. This expression is based on what is known as *compound interest*—that is, interest which is computed on a principal sum and also on all the interest earned by that principal sum as of a given date. A convenient table which conveys this type of information is presented in Exhibit 6. This table shows the future values of $1 compounded annually at various rates of interest, and can be employed to study several types of growth problems.

EXAMPLE 1.   If you deposit $1 in a savings account which pays 5 percent interest compounded annually, how much will your deposit be worth at the end of 1 year? 2 years? 10 years? 50 years?

Solution.   Looking at the table in the 5 percent column, we find that a deposit of $1 will be worth: $1.050 at the end of the first year; $1.103 at the end of the second year; $1.629 at the end of the tenth year; and $11.467 at the end of the fiftieth year. (For a deposit of $100, simply move the decimal point two places to the right; for a deposit of $1,000, three places to the right, and so on.)

EXAMPLE 2.   Real GNP (in 1958 prices) increased from $323.7 billion in 1948 to $487.7 billion in 1960. What was the rate of growth at compound interest?

Solution.   An increase from $323.7 billion to $487.7 billion is proportional to an increase from $1 to $1.507; thus:

$$\frac{\$487.7}{\$323.7} = \$1.507$$

Since this increase occurred over 12 years (from 1948 to 1960), we look at the 12-year horizontal line of the table and locate the closest number to $1.507; then read the interest-rate figure at the top of that column. Thus the growth rate was between 3 and 4 percent annually—apparently about 3.5 percent. (A closer estimate can be made by interpolation if desired, but this is not usually necessary.)

EXAMPLE 3.   (*a*) If an economy's real income as measured by its GNP per capita is $3,000, how long would it take to double that income if the economy grows at a compound annual rate of 6 percent? (*b*) If in fact the economy doubled its real income or GNP per capita in 18 years, what was its compound annual rate of growth?

Solution.   (*a*) Under the 6 percent column in the table, we note that $1 will double to $2 within 12 years (i.e., it will exactly double sometime during the twelfth year, and will be worth $2.012 at the end of the twelfth year). Hence, $3,000 will double to $6,000 in the same amount of time. (*b*) On the 18-year horizontal line, we find that $1 will double to $2 at an interest rate between 3 and 4 percent as shown at the top of the columns—but at a rate somewhat closer to 4 percent. We can thus conclude that the economy grew at a compound annual rate of about 4 percent— or actually a little less than that if we wish to interpolate for a closer estimate.

THE "RULE OF 72"

The third example above, which involves the general problem of how long it takes for a number to double when it grows at compound interest, is an extremely practical one. Businessmen who borrow money, bankers who lend it, and people who buy bonds or other fixed income-yielding securities are often concerned with this question. For convenience, when a table is not readily available we can employ a quick way of getting good approximate answers to the problem. It may be called the *Rule of 72*:

The *Rule of 72* is a simple growth formula which states: Given the annual rate of compound interest, divide this rate into 72 to obtain the approximate number of years it takes for a quantity to double; conversely, given the number of years it takes for a quantity to double, divide this amount into 72 to obtain the approximate annual rate of compound interest.

Exhibit 6

Growth-Rate Table

The growth of $1 compounded annually at various rates of interest

End of year	1%	2%	3%	4%	5%	6%	7%	8%	9%	10%	12%	15%
					Future value of $1 at							
1	1.010	1.020	1.030	1.040	1.050	1.060	1.070	1.080	1.090	1.100	1.120	1.150
2	1.020	1.040	1.061	1.082	1.103	1.124	1.145	1.166	1.188	1.210	1.254	1.322
3	1.030	1.061	1.093	1.125	1.158	1.191	1.225	1.260	1.295	1.331	1.405	1.521
4	1.041	1.082	1.126	1.170	1.216	1.262	1.311	1.360	1.412	1.464	1.574	1.749
5	1.051	1.104	1.159	1.217	1.276	1.338	1.403	1.469	1.539	1.611	1.762	2.011
6	1.062	1.126	1.194	1.265	1.340	1.419	1.501	1.587	1.677	1.772	1.974	2.313
7	1.072	1.149	1.230	1.316	1.407	1.504	1.606	1.714	1.828	1.949	2.211	2.660
8	1.083	1.172	1.267	1.369	1.477	1.594	1.718	1.851	1.993	2.144	2.476	3.059
9	1.094	1.195	1.305	1.423	1.551	1.689	1.838	1.999	2.172	2.358	2.773	3.518
10	1.105	1.219	1.344	1.480	1.629	1.791	1.967	2.159	2.367	2.594	3.106	4.046
11	1.116	1.243	1.384	1.539	1.710	1.898	2.105	2.332	2.580	2.853	3.479	4.652
12	1.127	1.268	1.426	1.601	1.796	2.012	2.252	2.518	2.813	3.138	3.896	5.350
13	1.138	1.294	1.469	1.665	1.886	2.133	2.410	2.720	3.066	3.452	4.363	6.153
14	1.149	1.319	1.513	1.732	1.980	2.261	2.579	2.937	3.342	3.797	4.887	7.076
15	1.161	1.346	1.558	1.801	2.079	2.397	2.759	3.172	3.642	4.177	5.474	8.137
16	1.173	1.373	1.605	1.873	2.183	2.540	2.952	3.426	3.970	4.595	6.130	9.358
17	1.184	1.400	1.653	1.948	2.292	2.693	3.159	3.700	4.328	5.054	6.866	10.761
18	1.196	1.428	1.702	2.026	2.407	2.854	3.380	3.996	4.717	5.560	7.690	12.375
19	1.208	1.457	1.754	2.107	2.527	3.026	3.617	4.316	5.142	6.116	8.613	14.232
20	1.220	1.486	1.806	2.191	2.653	3.207	3.870	4.661	5.604	6.727	9.646	16.367
21	1.232	1.516	1.860	2.279	2.786	3.400	4.141	5.034	6.109	7.400	10.804	18.821
22	1.245	1.546	1.916	2.370	2.925	3.604	4.430	5.437	6.659	8.140	12.100	21.645
23	1.257	1.577	1.974	2.465	3.072	3.820	4.741	5.781	7.258	8.954	13.552	24.891
24	1.270	1.608	2.033	2.563	3.225	4.049	5.072	6.341	7.911	9.850	15.179	28.625
25	1.282	1.641	2.094	2.666	3.386	4.292	5.427	6.848	8.623	10.835	17.000	32.919
26	1.295	1.673	2.157	2.772	3.556	4.549	5.807	7.396	9.399	11.918	19.040	37.857
27	1.308	1.707	2.221	2.883	3.733	4.822	6.214	7.988	10.245	13.110	21.325	43.535
28	1.321	1.741	2.288	2.999	3.920	5.112	6.649	8.627	11.167	14.421	23.884	50.066
29	1.335	1.776	2.357	3.119	4.116	5.418	7.114	9.317	12.172	15.863	26.750	57.575
30	1.348	1.811	2.427	3.243	4.322	5.743	7.612	10.063	13.268	17.449	29.960	66.212
31	1.361	1.848	2.500	3.373	4.538	6.088	8.145	10.868	14.462	19.194	33.555	76.143
32	1.375	1.885	2.575	3.508	4.765	6.453	8.715	11.737	15.763	21.114	37.582	87.565
33	1.391	1.922	2.652	3.648	5.003	6.841	9.325	12.676	17.182	23.225	42.091	100.700
34	1.403	1.961	2.732	3.794	5.253	7.251	9.978	13.690	18.728	25.548	47.142	115.805
35	1.417	2.000	2.814	3.946	5.516	7.686	10.677	14.785	20.414	28.102	52.800	133.176
40	1.489	2.208	3.262	4.801	7.040	10.286	14.974	21.725	31.409	45.259	93.051	267.863
45	1.565	2.438	3.782	5.841	8.985	13.765	21.002	31.920	48.327	72.890	163.988	538.769
50	1.645	2.692	4.384	7.107	11.467	18.420	29.457	46.902	74.358	117.391	289.002	1083.657
55	1.729	2.972	5.082	8.646	14.636	24.650	41.315	68.914	114.408	189.059		
60	1.817	3.281	5.892	10.520	18.679	32.988	57.946	101.257	176.031	304.482		
65	1.909	3.623	6.830	12.799	23.840	44.145	81.273	148.780	270.846	490.371		
70	2.007	4.000	7.918	15.572	30.426	59.076	113.989	218.606	416.730	789.747		
75	2.109	4.416	9.179	18.945	38.833	79.057	159.876	321.205	641.191	1271.895		
80	2.217	4.875	10.641	23.050	49.561	105.796	224.234	471.955	986.552	2048.400		
85	2.330	5.383	12.336	28.044	63.254	141.579	314.500	693.456	1517.948	3298.969		
90	2.449	5.943	14.300	34.119	80.730	189.465	441.103	1018.915	2335.501	5313.023		
95	2.574	6.562	16.578	41.511	103.035	253.546	618.670	1497.121	3593.513	8556.676		
100	2.705	7.245	19.219	50.505	131.501	339.302	867.716	2199.761	5529.089	13780.612		

EXAMPLE. If an economy's real GNP per capita grows at 6 percent, it will double its real income in 72/6 = 12 years; conversely, if it takes 12 years for an economy to double its real GNP per capita, its growth rate is 72/12 = 6 percent. The Rule of 72 as well as the principles underlying compound interest apply to any growing quantity, whether it be the growth of GNP, the growth of money in a savings account, or the growth of a tree.

IS THERE A TARGET RATE OF GROWTH?

Should we set a desired growth rate for the economy —a so-called target rate for which to shoot? If so, what should the rate be? The Japanese economy, for example, has gone through periods when its growth rate has been 10 percent or more. At this rate, an economy doubles its GNP in slightly more than seven years.

Consider what a 10 percent growth rate would mean over a period, say, of 30 years. If your income in 1970 was only $5,000 a year—which is approximately what the United States' GNP per capita was in 1970—it would expand to about $88,000 a year during the next 30 years. Can you imagine a per capita GNP of that amount by the year 2000? Even with our present rate of inflation it would be an astounding figure.

In real terms, our long-run growth record has been more like 3 percent rather than 10 percent. At this rate it takes about 24 years for per capita GNP to double. If we want to grow faster than this, we have to decide how much faster, and we have to know the costs that are involved. Keep in mind that an increase in growth from 3 to 4 percent amounts to a $33\frac{1}{3}$ percent increase in the annual rate. Looked at in this way, the difference is considerable. No wonder a country ordinarily finds it extremely difficult to raise its growth rate by an additional percentage point. Some of these difficulties are pointed out in further detail below.

The Costs of Economic Growth

What are the costs of increased growth? The answer should be thought of in terms of society's *sacrifices*— the pleasures it must postpone today for greater future satisfactions. From this standpoint, the basic costs of economic growth are five in number:

1. The sacrifice of leisure for employment
2. The sacrifice of consumption for investment
3. The sacrifice of the present for the future
4. The sacrifice of environmental quality for more goods
5. The sacrifice of security for progress

Let us see what each of these involves.

LEISURE VERSUS EMPLOYMENT

The rate of economic growth can be raised by using society's resources more fully. If this is done on a permanent rather than temporary basis (for example, by increasing the size of the labor force or the length of the workweek), it will result in a larger economic pie to be divided at any given time.

The cost of this increased growth, however, must be measured in terms of a sacrifice of leisure. What do we mean by leisure? Is it the same as idleness? Emphatically not! Leisure is a matter of choice. Some people may choose to use their leisure time by pursuing a hobby or by engaging in "civilized loafing." But in any case the value of leisure can be expressed in terms of (1) the income that can be obtained from alternative work-uses of time, and (2) the contribution to the supply of goods and services that some leisure activities produce and which the man of leisure would otherwise have purchased in the market. Some examples include the products of woodworking, photography, etc. Since these values are never actually recorded in the marketplace, they are omitted from estimates of GNP.

In contrast, idleness is not a matter of choice; it tends to have no uses and to yield no income. Consequently, if we consider leisure as one of the goals, or part of the real income for which we work, then who is to say that a 5 percent rate of growth in real GNP is better than a 3 percent rate of growth? Indeed, the latter rate of growth may include more leisure, and may in fact be preferable to the former. Hence the loss of value of leisure for the sake of more rapid growth must be recognized as one of the costs of growth, even though that cost can at best be only roughly estimated rather than precisely measured.

CONSUMPTION VERSUS INVESTMENT

What if an economy cannot use its resources more fully? Can it still increase its output per capita or rate of growth? It probably can, provided it is able to reduce its consumption in the present so as to achieve higher investment that will increase production in the future. The consumption that is foregone (or in fact postponed) becomes the measure of society's real cost of growth. It is somewhat easier to determine than the cost of leisure foregone, because the prices of consumer goods and services can be obtained from the market, whereas the price of leisure cannot be estimated as readily.

The amount of investment is not the only thing that matters in increasing a nation's production; the type of investment is also important. This point is significant because in most theoretical discussions it is convenient to assume a rigid relationship between investment in capital and the resulting rate of output or economic growth. This relationship is typically expressed in terms of the familiar capital-output ratio. Thus if the ratio equals 3, an investment of $300 should increase the output rate per period by $100. In reality, however, the relationship between investment and economic growth (i.e., the productivity of investment) is not rigid, for several reasons:

1. Investment is not restricted to the production of tangible assets such as plant and equipment; it also includes expenditures on the "production" of intangible assets such as human resources and new skills, and on research and development. The returns to society on the latter (intangible) types of investment are variable, and are extremely difficult to estimate with close accuracy.

2. It is not always sufficient to think only in terms of capital-output ratios. Some kinds of investment, such as investment in education, yield various cultural and social benefits to a nation which are not reflected by its measures of GNP.

3. Certain types of investment may contribute to GNP, but do not enhance society's material welfare if the resulting output is not wanted by consumers.

For example, investment that results in the creation of large agricultural surpluses for which there are no markets at existing prices detracts from society's welfare and even wastes resources that might better be used in other ways.

For these reasons, the nature and types of investment that an economy undertakes are at least as important as the amount of its investment as far as the costs to society are concerned.

PRESENT COSTS VERSUS FUTURE COSTS

The greater the rate of growth, the greater the sacrifice or postponement that must be made in leisure, in consumption, or in both. This does not necessarily mean, however, that *any* gain in economic growth (defined as an increase in real output per capita) is better than none. Future income or future consumption is never worth as much as present income or present consumption. Therefore, the value or cost of the sacrifices that must be made today and "tomorrow" in order to achieve a given rate of growth must be compared with the value of the benefits that will be received in the future.

In comparing these costs and benefits, three basic questions must be answered. First, what will be the increment in benefits as compared to the increment in costs? That is, how much will the economy's future income and consumption increase as a result of present and future sacrifices of consumption and leisure? Second, how long will it take before the increased benefits are realized? Third, is the increment in benefits and the time required to receive them worth the sacrifice? In other words, since present income and present consumption are worth more than the same amount of future income and future consumption, how does the *present value* of the future benefits compare with the *present value* of the costs involved?

The third question provides a guide for decision making and policy formulation as we shall see in the conclusion below. Actually, what this question is asking us to do is express the future values of costs and benefits in equivalent terms of *today's* dollars, so that a correct comparison can be made in the present between the costs and benefits involved. In more technical language, this entails a process in financial mathematics known as "discounting."

ENVIRONMENTAL QUALITY VERSUS MORE GOODS

Ill fares the land, to hast'ning ill a prey,
Where wealth accumulates, and men decay.

Oliver Goldsmith

Writers, poets, and artists have long warned against the headlong pursuit of riches. But their voices have seldom been heeded until recently. Now it is becoming uncomfortably clear that they may have been right all along.

In America, the richest nation in the world, wealth continuously accumulates while men, the environment, the cities, and the quality of life itself decay. Much of this decay must be counted as a cost of growth, even though precise measurement is difficult, if not impossible.

Does this mean that economic growth is necessarily bad? Not at all. But it does mean that the pursuit of growth for its own sake is bad. Indeed, the thought of a nation with a per capita gross income of $88,000—as envisioned earlier—is horrifying, if the $88,000 is to be made and spent as it would be today.

The result would inevitably be larger traffic jams, sprawling airports, air and water pollution at lethal levels, lakes, rivers and yacht marinas congested with pleasure craft—in short, a nation of rich people living in extreme discomfort, and almost certainly racked by associated mental ailments.

Clearly, the composition of GNP may be even more important than its rate of growth. Hence a primary task for a free society is to determine what that composition should be. (In an authoritarian society, the decision would be made by a central agency.) This and related problems pertaining to environmental quality are as much a part of ecology as of economics. In view of the growing significance today of ecological issues, we shall devote a later chapter to an analysis of their economic implications.

SECURITY VERSUS PROGRESS?

The above costs of growth are applicable to all types of economic systems. But in a capitalistic system there is still another cost which takes such forms as fluctuations in economic activity, frictional and technological unemployment, and obsolescence of capital and skills. This is because economic growth tends to occur in spurts rather than as a smooth and continuous process. As a result, the eminent economist Joseph Schumpeter (1853–1950) was led to conclude that a capitalistic economy by its very nature grows by replacing old methods of production, old sources of supply, and old skills and resources with new ones; to use his famous phrase, it grows by engaging in a continual *"process of creative destruction."*

The fundamental message in the above paragraph is that economic growth in a capitalistic economy entails a clash between security and progress. The basic question, therefore, is whether this clash is really necessary—that is, whether some economic insecurity is inevitable in a dynamic economy, or whether we must turn to some form of command economy in order to achieve maximum security (and probable loss of some personal freedoms). As with most issues in economics, the approach to a solution is a matter of degree—a problem of achieving what society regards as a desirable "trade-off" between the two extremes.

CONCLUSION

It is sometimes said that the best things in life are free, but economic growth certainly is not one of them. Costs must be paid, and sacrifices must be made, in order to sustain any rate of growth. It is not correct to say, therefore, as some writers in the popular press have said, that "the more we grow or the faster we grow, the better off we are."

It is necessary to balance the corresponding costs and benefits of alternative growth rates. In general, *the optimum rate of growth is determined where the increased costs of more growth are just offset by the increased benefits.* (It is assumed that these increased costs and benefits are expressed in terms of their present values.) The optimum rate may be "high" or "low," depending upon the value that society places on the advantages of growth.

Thus if an economy is growing, say, at 3 percent, it should compare the incremental or "marginal" costs and benefits involved if it wishes to increase its growth rate to 4 or 5 percent. Clearly, the optimum rate of growth need not be the maximum rate. An economy may increase its growth rate by putting its population on an austerity level of living and channeling all savings thus obtained into investment. This, in varying degrees, is a policy that has been followed at one time or another by the Soviet Union, China, and some other countries.

Barriers to Economic Growth

In any society there are obstacles to economic growth. These obstacles differ according to whether the particular society is "traditional" or "advanced."

In traditional societies, the obstacles to growth are primarily cultural, consisting of social and religious attitudes toward business practices, money and interest, new productive techniques, and new institutions. In such societies, the barriers to growth are mainly the result of conflicts of values rather than conflicts of interest.

In advanced societies such as our own, on the other hand, the obstacles to growth are chiefly economic. They take such forms as (1) labor immobility, (2) capital immobility, and (3) limitations on the proportion of resources that can be committed to capital goods production. As we examine these more closely, we find that the barriers to growth are primarily the result of conflicts of interest rather than conflicts of values.

LABOR IMMOBILITY

We have learned in a number of places in this book that labor immobility has been an important factor contributing to depressed conditions in certain industries and regions of the country. Two typical examples are agriculture and sawmilling in several low-income areas of the South. The fundamental causes of labor immobility are ignorance of alternative employment opportunities and the costs of movement. Although these obstacles to growth will never be entirely eliminated, their reduction helps

significantly to clear the path for sustained economic development.

Ignorance of employment opportunities has decreased substantially over the past several decades. This has been accomplished through the development of free government employment services, improved communication and information facilities pertaining to job openings—such as newspaper classified ads, trade publications, and school placement services—and a shift of population from rural to urban areas, where job opportunities and the knowledge of such opportunities are more readily available.

Reductions in the cost of movement, on the other hand, are more difficult to achieve. The cost of moving from one city to another, for example, has been greatly reduced over the years, at least in relation to income. But this is only one aspect of the problem. The cost of transferring from one occupation to another, or even from one job to another, may involve a temporary decline in income while new skills are being acquired, and a permanent loss of pension rights, seniority privileges, job security, and other fringe benefits. In addition, there may be costs of entry into new jobs in the form of high license fees or union initiation fees, long periods of apprenticeship at low pay, or restrictions on the number of people admitted to an occupation.

To some extent, the costs of movement have been absorbed by federal and state governments through the provision of training programs, unemployment benefits, and the like, thereby reducing the costs of labor mobility as an obstacle to growth. But care must be taken not to shift too much of the cost from workers to the government, for this could result in excessive labor mobility. The result might be a waste of resources as reflected in high transfer costs resulting from frequent retraining, breaking into new jobs, etc. These are activities which can be undertaken more productively if the workers who benefit from it are made to bear some of its costs.

CAPITAL IMMOBILITY

The factors that make for immobility of capital including money and capital goods are fundamentally the same as those that cause immobility of labor—namely, ignorance and the costs of movement.

Ignorance, where capital immobility is involved, may consist of inadequate information about new markets, changes in technology, or new methods of production, distribution, finance, etc. In general, the significance of such barriers to capital movement has been reduced in recent decades as a result of the growing amount of diversified information and services provided by both government and private agencies such as the Departments of Agriculture and Commerce, trade associations, business publishing houses, and consulting firms. On the other hand, it is readily apparent that specialized plants and equipment are not easily adaptable to alternative uses (which is one type of capital immobility), as a result of which there are significant cost barriers to the movement of capital. But cost barriers can also arise in less obvious ways, as when government policies are instituted which "protect" capital and thereby immobilize it. Examples of such policies are discriminatory taxes, tariffs, quotas, subsidies, price supports, etc., which are given to particular industries and sectors of the economy in order to shelter them from the adverse effects they would experience under unrestricted competition.

The reduced mobility of capital which results from such policies can be overcome—but only at a price. The problem is whether society, and its elected representatives in Washington, can be made sufficiently aware of the price to decide whether it is worth paying.

LIMITATIONS ON THE PROPORTION OF RESOURCES THAT CAN BE COMMITTED TO CAPITAL GOODS PRODUCTION

The United States economy is already so highly capitalized that a substantial share of present resources must be devoted merely to replacing existing plant and equipment as it wears out. A fundamental problem, therefore, is to find ways of increasing the proportion of resources that can be applied to the production of capital goods, over and above the proportion needed to keep the existing stock of capital intact.

The problem is further compounded by the fact that our "standard" or *goal* of living seems to increase about as fast as our actual level of living so that "the more we have, the more we want." As a result, the proportion of income saved does not appear to be rising over the long run, and may even be declining.

NOTE. Be careful to observe that this statement refers to a *long-run period* during which all factors in addition to income which may affect consumption and saving are allowed to vary. Hence it does not contradict the concept of the "consumption function," which is a principle that applies only at a *given* time when all factors other than income which may affect consumption and saving are assumed to remain constant.

Is the overall percentage of income saved likely to decline in the future? There is good reason to believe that it will. Reduced savings are encouraged by such factors as: (1) the increasing availability of easy credit and the growth in real assets per capita; (2) the expanding social welfare functions of government in providing for unemployment, old age, etc.; and (3) the possible shift in the economic attitudes of society toward a more high-consumption "live-it-up" philosophy. In addition, there is probably a greater chance that income and inheritance tax rates will be raised in future years rather than lowered. If this happens, it will tend to make the distribution of income less unequal, and thereby reduce still further the proportion that is saved.

For all of these reasons, therefore, the savings ratio of the economy, i.e., the average propensity to save, will probably decline gradually over the years. This means that corporate and government saving and investment will have to become increasingly important, as is already the trend, if a steady rate of economic growth is to be sustained.

Problems of Taxation, Inflation, and Economic Growth

In previous chapters dealing with fiscal and monetary policies we talked about the problems of taxation and inflation in affecting economic growth. A few additional comments are appropriate at this time. In general terms, the questions we want to answer are: What role might government tax policies play in contributing to the rate of economic growth? How does inflation, which we have seen is closely tied to the problems of full employment and economic growth, fit into the picture?

TAXATION AND THE INVESTMENT DECISION

We have learned that increases in investment bring about increases in productivity which help to sustain economic growth. We have also learned from macroeconomic theory that the *expectation of profit* is the most important factor motivating businessmen to invest. This means that the volume of investment can be assured by improving the expectation of profit, or by reducing the risk of loss, or both. Taxes can be a critical factor in this respect.

For instance, when the executives of a corporation contemplate making *any* investment, they consider, among other things, three important variables:

1. The corporation income tax rate

2. The minimum accepted rate of return on the investment after taxes

3. The expected rate of return on the investment before taxes

The first of these factors is written into law by Congress and is therefore known. The second is predetermined in each firm as a matter of top-level corporate financial policy; it is based on the different returns and risks that are available to a firm from its alternative investment opportunities. (If you should ever take a course in business or corporate finance, you will find that determining the minimum acceptable rate is the single most critical economic task facing the top management of a corporation.) The third factor, which the firm compares with other investment alternatives before deciding on the one it wants, is determined directly from the previous two by the simple formula:

Expected rate of return before taxes

$$= \frac{\text{minimum accepted rate of return after taxes}}{1 - \text{tax rate}}$$

Thus if the management of a corporation believes that a minimum accepted rate of return of 15 percent after taxes is necessary in order to persuade it to invest in a project (such as a machine or a plant), and if the corporation income tax rate is 48 percent, the denominator in the above formula will be $1 - 0.48 = 0.52$. Hence the expected rate of return before taxes must be *at least* $0.15/0.52 = 28.8$ percent in order for the investment to be considered. On the other hand, if the tax rate were, say, 55 percent, the expected rate of return before taxes would have to be at least $0.15/0.45 = 33.3$ percent in order for the investment to be eligible for consideration. Evidently, the higher the tax rate, the higher will be the expected rate of return before taxes, as is apparent from the above formula.

NOTE. The formula should not be taken as a rigid guide, since factors besides the tax rate influence investment and expected returns. It is merely intended to convey some basic tendencies within reasonable tax ranges.

TAX IMPLICATIONS

What does this imply as far as taxes are concerned?

We learned in macroeconomic theory that at a given level of risk there are fewer investment opportunities available at higher rates of return than at lower ones. Therefore, it follows from the above formula that the volume of investment in plant and equipment will be influenced by the steepness of the corporation income tax in the following way:

Other things being equal, higher corporation income tax rates tend to raise the expected rate of return before taxes, thereby closing out many investment opportunities and reducing the total volume of investment; conversely, lower corporation income tax rates tend to reduce the expected rate of return before taxes, thereby opening up many investment opportunities and increasing the total volume of investment.

Does this mean that corporation income taxes should be abolished? The answer is no, for considerations other than growth must be taken into account. What it does mean, however, is that in order to finance a given level of government expenditures, alternative methods of raising revenue should be considered. Other forms of taxes such as higher sales taxes or higher personal income taxes may be less injurious to investment and economic growth than the corporation income tax.

How much less injurious? The answer is not yet known. But we do know that the *marginal* tax rate on personal income plays a significant role. Thus if the marginal tax rate—that is, the tax paid on an additional dollar of income—is high, the rate of economic growth may be retarded. Why? Because, other things being equal, high marginal tax rates tend to reduce the amount of personal savings and the incentive to invest among people in the higher income brackets. To some extent, however, this tendency may be offset by the capital-gains provisions in our income tax laws, which permit long-term profits on investment to be taxed at special lower rates.

Income Taxes or Sales Taxes?

The possibility that steep income tax rates may stifle economic growth has prompted many economists to advocate higher sales taxes as a partial substitute for higher income taxes. Most foreign governments, in fact, obtain the bulk of their revenues from sales taxes, as contrasted with the United States, which derives most of its revenues from taxes on income and wealth. Various tax studies indicate that a sales tax which exempts food and medicine is approximately proportional—taking about the same share from all income groups. It may be, therefore, that a partial reduction in income taxes and an increase in sales taxes with selected exemptions would perhaps be a desirable step to take in seeking to sustain a target of economic growth.

INFLATION AND "FORCED" SAVING

The relation between inflation and economic growth has been the subject of much discussion. Too rapid a rate of inflation discourages savings and thereby sets a limit on the volume of investment. This, in turn, can inhibit economic growth.

It has long been known that one way in which an economy can finance its investment in order to encourage economic growth is by *forced savings*—a situation in which consumers are prevented from spending part of their income. Forced savings may take place in different situations, as when (1) prices rise faster than money wages, causing a decrease in real consumption and hence an increase in real (forced) saving; (2) a corporation plows back some or all of its profit for investment instead of distributing it as dividend income to stockholders, thereby keeping stockholders from spending part of this income on consumption; and (3) a government taxes its citizens and uses the funds for investment, thus preventing the public from utilizing a portion of its income for the purchase of consumer goods.

In the United States, all three forms of forced saving, especially the second, have helped to finance economic growth. Other nations, by contrast, have leaned more toward the first or the third. For example, most Latin American countries have depended heavily on the printing press to run off the money they need to pay for investment. The outcome has been prolonged and severe inflation, resulting in the first of the above forms of forced saving. At the other extreme, Russia and China have placed heavy reliance on taxation to accumulate the funds needed for capital formation, thus placing greater dependence on the third form of forced saving.

CONCLUSION: "BALANCED" GROWTH

There is general agreement that a certain amount of inflation is probably inevitable in a dynamic economy such as ours, given its institutions and rigidities, its tendency to generate obsolescence, and its citizens' desire to raise their general standard of living at a rate at least as fast as the system's productive capacity. The problem, of course, is to hold back inflation to a rate that is compatible with sound economic growth. Too much inflation will impede economic growth, while excessive unsound growth will tend to promote inflation.

Assuming, therefore, that we must live with inflation—and anyone who is naive enough to deny this is simply ignoring the facts of history—is there some rate of inflation that can be regarded as "proper"? From what we have learned in previous chapters, an average annual rate not exceeding 2 percent would be compatible with the maintenance of full employment and would permit our economy to maintain a long-run growth trend of 3 to 4 percent a year. If we allow inflation to proceed for a while at much higher rates than this, we run the risk of distorting the internal structure of the economy—that is, the relationships among firms, industries, and resources within the system. The result is that the economy achieves a type of unbalanced or disproportional growth—analagous, for example, to a biological situation in which a man's nose or ears grow too fast or too slow in relation to each other and to the rest of his head. What we seek, of course, is a healthy or "balanced" form of growth.

SUMMARY OF IMPORTANT IDEAS

1. For the United States, the long-run trend of total real GNP has been upward at an average annual rate of over 3 percent, while the growth trend of real GNP per capita has averaged a little less than 2 percent annually. In general, the theory of economic growth, with the inclusion of technological advance, tends to be supported by the available evidence for the United States and for other advanced Western nations.

2. International comparisons of long-term growth rates show that the United States has grown more slowly than a number of other advanced nations. Since 1929, the expansion of "qualitative" factors such as education and technology have been relatively more important in influencing United States economic growth than the increase in such "quantitative" factors as the amount of labor and capital; prior to 1929, the reverse was true.

3. "Growth" is a technical notion, which for measurement purposes involves the concept of compound interest. Compound interest tables can be used to estimate growth, and a simple growth formula like the "Rule of 72" can be employed when tables are not readily available.

4. The real costs of economic growth are expressed in terms of the sacrifices which society must bear in order to achieve growth. These include such sacrifices as: leisure for employment; consumption for investment; present for the future; environmental quality for more goods; and to some extent security

for progress. The optimum rate of growth equates the increased costs of more growth with the increased benefits.

5. The chief barriers to economic growth in advanced societies are conflicts of interest rather than conflicts of values. They consist of labor immobility, capital immobility, and limitations on the proportion of resources that can be committed to capital goods production.

6. In addition to the foregoing challenges to economic growth, there are problems of taxation and inflation. Increases in corporation income taxes tend to reduce the number of investment opportunities, while decreases in taxes tend to expand them. This and other considerations suggest that a partial substitution of increased sales taxes for increased income taxes, with special exemptions for food and medicine, would be more conducive to economic growth. As for inflation, it appears that an average annual rate of 2 percent or less would be compatible with full employment and with a sustained "balanced" growth of 3 to 4 percent annually.

FOR HOMEWORK AND DISCUSSION

1. *Terms and concepts to review:*

"process of creative destruction"   compound interest

forced saving   Rule of 72

2. Outline briefly the major features of United States economic growth from the pre-Civil War period to the present.

3. From the standpoint of economic growth, is it better for our economy to invest relatively more of its resources in machines and factories, or should it concentrate instead on education and training? What are the "costs" of choosing either one? Discuss.

4. Can you develop a rule, analogous to the "Rule of 72," which tells you how long it takes for an investment to increase by 50 percent? (SUGGESTION: Use the growth-rate table in this chapter as a guide, and some trial-and-error experiments.) Using your newly derived "rule," how much better off will your children (i.e., the next generation) be if we merely grow at 2 percent? In view of your answer, do you think

that an increase in growth is worth the extra costs and sacrifices that must be incurred to attain it?

5. Evaluate the statement: "The more we grow or the faster we grow, the better off we are."

6. Would industrial progress, or economic development in general, be faster or slower in a perfectly certain, as compared with an uncertain, economy? (NOTE: A perfectly certain economy is one in which the nature and time of occurrence of all future events can be predicted with certainty.) Of what significance is your answer to a welfare-oriented economy which seeks to eliminate the risks of unemployment, bankruptcy, etc.?

7. Evaluate the following suggestions that have been made by various people:

a. "Labor mobility, and therefore economic growth, would be increased if the government simply absorbed all costs of moving, retraining, and the like."

b. "The government should 'protect' important industries through tariffs, subsidies, price supports, etc., in order to encourage their development to the point where they can fend for themselves.

This sort of policy would also encourage general economic growth."

8. "The government should reduce income taxes, thereby leaving more savings available for investment and economic growth." If the government followed this suggestion, how would it get the revenues it needs to finance its expenditures?

REFERENCES AND READING SUGGESTIONS

BOWEN, HOWARD R., and GARTH L. MANGUM (eds.), *Automation and Economic Progress*, Prentice-Hall, New York, 1966.

CHAMBER OF COMMERCE OF THE UNITED STATES, *The Promise of Economic Growth*, Washington, D.C., 1963.

COLEMAN, JOHN R. (ed.), *The Changing American Economy*, Basic Books, New York, 1967.

GILL, RICHARD T., *Economic Development: Past and Present*, 2d ed., Prentice-Hall, New York, 1967, chap. 4.

PETERSON, JOHN M., and RALPH GRAY, *Economic Development of the United States*, Irwin, Chicago, 1969, chaps. 11, 12.

CHAPTER 19

Ecology and the Economics of Pollution

CHAPTER PREVIEW

What is ecology? How does it relate to economics?

How can we distinguish between the economic fallacies and realities of pollution?

Are there economic principles that can serve as guidelines for formulating policies pertaining to pollution control?

The Walrus and the Carpenter
Were walking close at hand;
They wept like anything to see
Such quantities of sand:
"If this were only cleared away,"
They said, "it would be grand!"

"If seven maids with seven mops
Swept it for half a year,
Do you suppose," the Walrus said,
"That they could get it clear?"
"I doubt it," said the Carpenter,
And shed a bitter tear.

Lewis Carroll, *Through the Looking Glass* (1872).

If the Carpenter were alive today, he would probably shed much more than a bitter tear. For while Americans are enjoying the benefits of the world's highest gross national product, their environment is seriously threatened by GNP's mirror image: gross national pollution. As the nation's production of goods has soared, so have dangerous doses of chemicals, garbage, sewage, fumes, and noise. Thus for each American, environmental decay is now a personal experience: the water he drinks may be bitter with impurities, the scenes he views may be obscured by haze, the air he breathes may be acrid with automobile exhaust and industrial smoke, and the piercing sounds he hears from trucks, jackhammers, and jets may cause permanent damage to his ears. This, in broad scope, is the problem of pollution. And, since it is an environmental problem, it involves ecological as well as economic considerations.

Economics and Ecology

The words "ecology" and "economics" stem from the same Greek root—*oikos,* meaning "house." Despite this common origin, these sciences had little contact with one another until the late 1960s. At that time, with concern mounting over problems of environmental quality, ecologists and economists began to recognize that they might have much to learn from one another, and that a new science of "econology" might someday be forged from a blending of their separate disciplines. To appreciate the implications of these possibilities, the answers to two fundamental questions must be explored: What is ecology? What basic similarities are there between ecology and economics?

WHAT IS ECOLOGY?

Ecology is a study of the relationships or interdependencies between living organisms and their environment, both at a micro and macro level, in order to see how they function together in their so-called "ecosystems." Ecology is thus a systems approach to nature—a science which attempts to describe and analyze the "web of life." Hence, according to its Greek root, ecology deals with the "household of nature," while economics deals with the "household of man."

An ecosystem, like any other system, is a collection of related elements. But in an ecosystem, as shown in Exhibit 1, the elements consist of four interdependent links, some living and some nonliving, which make up the chain of life:

1. *Nonliving or inorganic matter.* Sunlight, carbon dioxide, water, and minerals used by green plants for their growth.

2. *Producer plants.* Lower organisms, namely green plants, ranging from microscopic size through shrubs and trees, which convert sunlight, oxygen, water, and minerals into carbohydrates or food used by themselves and other organisms in the ecosystem.

3. *Animal consumers.* Higher organisms, namely

Exhibit 1

Elements of an Ecosystem: The Web of Life

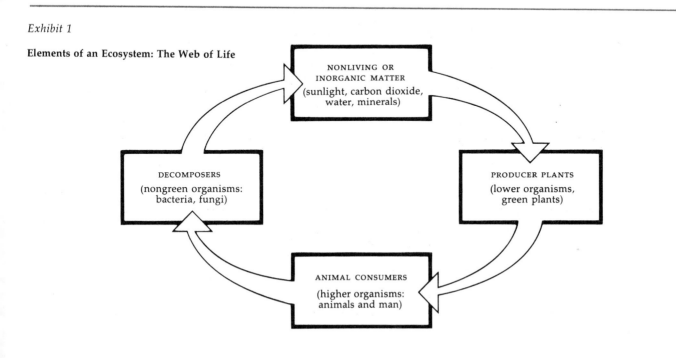

Complexity Promotes Stability

The food web of a Long Island estuary has been thoroughly investigated by biologists George Woodwell, Charles Wurster, and Peter Isaacson. The relationships they discovered are illustrated; their study shows several important characteristics of most food webs. One is complexity. Although only some of the kinds of plants and animals in this ecosystem are shown in this figure, it is evident that most of the consumers feed on several different organisms, and that most prey organisms are attacked by more than one predator. To put it another way, the food chains are interlinked. Ecologists believe that complexity is in part responsible for the stability of most ecosystems. Apparently, the more food chains there are in an ecosystem, and the more cross-connecting links there are among them, the more chances there are for the ecosystem to compensate for changes imposed upon it.

For example, suppose that the marsh plant-cricket-redwing blackbird section represented an isolated entire ecosystem. If that were the case, removing the blackbirds—say, by shooting—would lead to a cricket plague. This in turn would lead to the defoliation of the plants, and then to the starvation of the crickets. In short, a change in one link of such a simple chain would have disastrous consequences for the entire ecosystem. Suppose, however, that the cormorants were removed from the larger system. Populations of flukes and eels would probably increase, which in turn might reduce the population of green algae (Cladophora). But there would be more food for mergansers and ospreys, and their populations would probably enlarge, leading to a reduction of eels and flukes. In turn, the algae would recover.

Needless to say, things do not normally happen that simply and neatly in nature. But we have both observational and theoretical reasons to believe that the general principle holds: complexity is an important factor in producing stability. Complex communities, such as the deciduous forests that cover much of the eastern United States, persist year after year if man does not interfere with them. An oak-hickory forest is quite stable in comparison with an ultrasimplified community, such as a cornfield, which is a man-made stand of a single kind of grass. A cornfield has little natural stability and is subject to almost instant ruin if it is not constantly managed by man. Similarly, arctic and subarctic ecosystems, which are characterized by simplicity, tend to be less stable than complex tropical forest ecosystems. In arctic regions the instability is manifested in frequent, violent fluctuations in the populations of such northern animals as lemmings, hares, and foxes. In contrast, outbreaks of one species do not occur as often in complex tropical forests. . . . Although the bases of stability . . . appear somewhat . . . complicated, . . . the idea that complexity promotes stability still appears to be theoretically sound.[1]

[1] *Population, Resources, Environment,* by Paul R. Ehrlich and Anne H. Ehrlich, W. H. Freeman, and Company, San Francisco. Copyright 1970, pp. 158, 159.

---

animals, consisting of "primary" consumers, such as cows, pigs, and sheep that feed upon the plant producers, and "secondary" consumers, such as man, the lion, the tiger, and the wolf that feed upon the primary consumers.

4. *Decomposers.* Simple nongreen organisms such as bacteria and fungi that complete the circle of the ecosystem by breaking down the dead producers and consumers and returning their chemical compounds to the ecosystem for reuse by the producer plants.

An ecosystem is governed by distinct laws of growth and decay; these laws operate simultaneously, tending to move the system toward a state of balance or equilibrium. For example, there is a law of "adaptation" which permits each species to find its own place in the particular ecosystem that will provide it with the food, water, and shelter it needs for survival. There is a law of "balance" between predator and prey which enables the former to keep a hold on the population of the latter. Hence the spider that devours the fly, or the cheetah that preys upon the gazelle, is performing a needed function. Still another law is the law of "diversity" which permits many different species to live in an ecosystem, thereby reducing the chance of any particular species proliferating and dominating the community. In this sense, even the rarest species is part of nature's grand design for a stable and viable ecosystem. (See Box 1.)

Portion of a food web in a Long Island estuary. Arrows indicate flow of energy. Numbers are the parts per million of DDT found in each kind of organism.

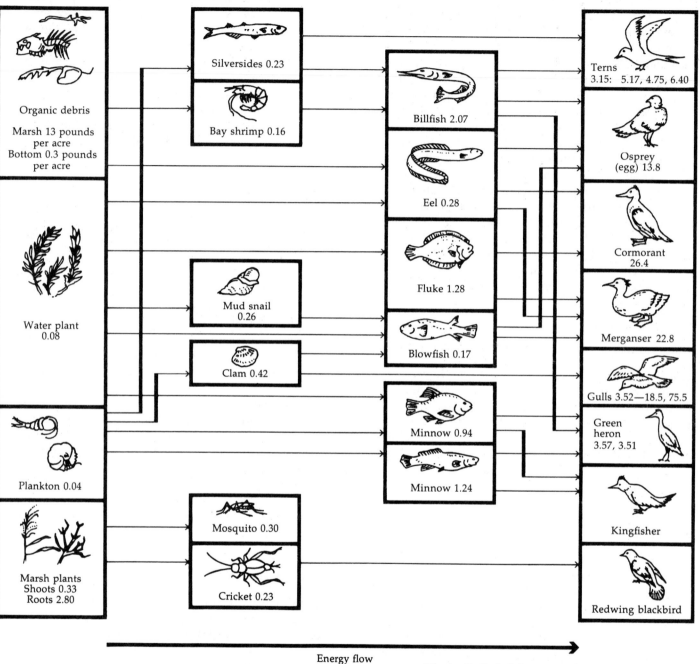

The problem is that man, as a result of careless efforts to raise his material level of living, has violated the laws of ecology—thereby endangering nature as well as himself. Ecologists have observed, for example, that many nonhuman species such as certain fish or rodent populations have remarkable resiliencies; as much as 50 percent or more of their populations in a particular ecosystem may be destroyed by disease or disaster, yet they will restore their original numbers within a year or two. But the automatic restoration of this equilibrium requires that there be no external interference with the ecosystem so that its natural laws of growth and decay can operate freely. It is man-made interference—in the form of pollution of the environment—that has profoundly disturbed the total ecosystem and its tendency toward equilibrium. Smog in the air, detergents, oil, and chemicals in the water, and garbage in the streets—all of these are altering the balance of life, with consequences that may very well be disastrous for all of civilization.

SIMILARITIES BETWEEN ECOLOGY AND ECONOMICS

Since economic motivations and attitudes have been partly responsible for this state of affairs, it is appropriate to examine some of the basic similarities between economics and ecology. We may then be able to recognize concepts and relationships which blend economic and ecological principles for the purpose of solving environmental problems.

At least five basic similarities may be identified:

1. Populations

Both ecology and economics are concerned with the study of "populations." In ecology the populations are classified by species, that is, groups of things which have certain common characteristics or qualities that distinguish them as a whole from all other organisms. In economics the populations may be living, nonliving, or social, and they may also be classified by species. For example, economic species of living populations include consumers, workers, and businessmen; economic species of nonliving populations consist of commodities such as automobiles, machine tools, and refrigerators; economic species of social populations include households, steel firms, and labor unions. Each of these economic species, like populations in ecology, are born, grow, and often die. It can therefore be said that commodities, firms, and even governments (which may be viewed as an economic species of social populations along with households, businesses, farms, etc.) are subject to their own laws of growth, survival, and decay according to the particular economic forces and environmental conditions that exist within the system.

2. Equilibrium

This suggests a second important feature which ecology and economics have in common—the tendency to move toward equilibrium. In ecology, as we have seen, the ecosystem will respond to its own natural laws to bring about a state of general balance between its four sets of elements: nonliving matter, producer plants, animal consumers, and decomposers. This requires that the birth and death rates of all species in the system be equated. In economics, the economic system is also conceived as having its own birth rates and death rates—the former being represented, for example, by the rate of production of commodities, and the latter by the rate of consumption of commodities. As we learned in earlier chapters, the stock of commodities in the economy (like the water in a bathtub) may be in equilibrium at any level, but the level itself will rise or fall according to the relative rates of production and consumption (or the rates of inflow and outflow) in the system as a whole.

3. Exchange

A third basic similarity between ecology and economics is the existence of a system of exchange. In ecology, exchange takes place between the four "sectors" or elements that comprise the ecosystem. For example, the nonliving sector gives up sunlight, water, carbon dioxide, organic compounds, and other nutrients to the producer plants sector, which in turn gives up carbohydrates to the animal consumers sector, and so on. Eventually the circle of exchange is completed within the ecosystem as a whole. In economics, similar and perhaps more complex circles of exchange occur. Thus we find that exchange takes place between economic organisms such as consumers and producers, between workers and employers, and between sectors of the economy such as households, businesses, and government.

4. Development

A fourth feature that is common to ecology and economics is development. Neither an ecosystem nor an economic system ordinarily desires to remain at the same level or stage of development. In ecology, the ecological process itself may bring about long-run growth or decline. Thus a lake may, through a gradual process of change among its four ecological sectors, eventually turn into a desert, a swamp, a prairie, or a forest. In economics, internal and external processes are at work which also make for changes in development. An economic system, for example, may experience growth or decline, depending on relative changes in its population, capital, technology, knowledge, and other fundamental variables.

5. Policy

A fifth similarity between ecology and economics concerns the role of man as an agent of change in the establishment of policy. In ecology, man intentionally adopts policies which change the natural processes of the ecosystem so that he can achieve particular objectives. A farmer, for example, applies seed, chemicals, machines, and human effort to his land in order to produce marketable commodities like corn and hogs. If the farmer left the land alone, the ecosystem would produce its own natural but unmarketable products consisting of prairie grass, trees, and gophers. In economics as well as in other social sciences, man establishes policies in the form of customs and laws for the purpose of adjusting the economic or social system in which he lives to his own values and ideals.

NEEDED: AN ECOLOGICAL OUTLOOK

Men in general, and economists in particular, have traditionally assumed that the reservoirs of land, air, and water provided by nature are infinite, that they can be drawn upon indefinitely, and that they can be polluted with impunity. This means, in effect, that the economy has been viewed as a closed system with respect to nature, drawing from it the inputs it needs and returning to it the effluent wastes of its expanding output. This attitude has been less pronounced in the case of land, where soil conservation policies have existed for decades in many countries, but it is clearly noticeable nevertheless in regions where timberlands have been stripped and where soil mining has been practiced.

In contrast, ecology looks upon the earth—and perhaps even the universe—as a total ecosystem of which man's activities are only a small part. From this viewpoint the resources of nature are not infinite reservoirs. Indeed, it may be possible for man, through imprudent actions, to deplete and to change the composition of these reservoirs in a manner that can prove fatal. With the growth of population, the likelihood of this happening becomes greater.

Clearly, therefore, there is a great need for serious thinking about the relationships between economics and ecology. For unless we can derive unifying principles from these disciplines, and unless we can adopt an ecological outlook which views society as a great interacting network of coexisting populations, many of our social and economic policies will be doomed to failure.

Environmental Destruction: Fallacies and Realities

Any discussion of economics and ecology must come to grips with the very real problems of pollution. Critics and social reformers have had much to say on this subject. As a result, there has emerged a widespread belief that pollution can be attributed to one or more of three fundamental causes:

1. Society's preoccupation with economic growth

2. The trend toward overpopulation

3. Too much private relative to public spending

All three explanations contain important elements of truth; hence it is useful to examine them in some detail.

"GROWTHMANIA"

Those who attribute environmental defilement to economic growth contend that there is a direct relationship between the level of pollution and GNP: as the latter increases, so does the former, and both of them grow at compound (although not necessarily equal) rates. This has led certain critics of our society —especially those among the college population— to contend that we should go back to a simpler life in which there is less concern with economic growth. Some have even argued that we should adopt measures which will cut our rate of economic growth from approximately 4 percent to about 1 or 2 percent—or perhaps even to zero—and that we should focus attention on improving the material well-being of society not by expanding total output but by redistributing output in a more equitable manner.

These critics, like Don Quixote, are seeking the impossible dream. The rising standard of living which Americans have experienced since the nineteenth century has been due to gains in productivity resulting from improved technology, better methods of management, and the development of a more skilled labor force. It is possible that further improvements would be realized through income redistribution, but it is folly to assume that this could be employed as a main solution. In 1970, for example, the top 20 percent of America's 60 million families received 41 percent of the nation's income, or $258 billion. Even if as much as one-fourth of this income were distributed equally to the remaining 80 percent of families, it would increase their incomes by less than $1,400 each.

It appears, therefore, that we must look to increases in productivity as the chief means of fulfilling society's economic desires. This is especially true as long as the population continues to grow. Further, there is every indication that the great majority of people want more material things rather than fewer.

Hence a return to a simpler life of the carriage and the spinning wheel would, *in a free society*, be impossible if not undesirable: it would not only be contrary to what most people want, it would also be a return to a life in which a much larger proportion of the population was poor. (On the other hand, a low or zero growth rate might stimulate significant debate and action with respect to income distribution—a sorely neglected topic in economics.)

Aside from this, it is most unlikely that any advanced economic system would eliminate economic growth entirely. This is as true in communistic and socialistic systems as in capitalistic ones. For as long as resources are scarce they must be used efficiently, and managers will seek to improve efficiency by introducing new and better methods of production. This can only result in greater productivity and hence a rising standard of living. It is no accident that the association between economic growth and pollution is as pronounced in Russia, for example, as in the United States. The desire for improved efficiency and for material advancement is not limited to particular political ideologies. See Box 2.

The "Iron" Law of Compound Interest

If the level of pollution is a consequence of economic growth, its rate of increase is a direct outcome of the law of compound interest. Pollution, to be sure, is not a new phenomenon; it existed in medieval and in ancient Europe. What is new, however, is its recognition as a critical problem of modern societies.

To be more specific, it was not until the late 1960s that the cry of pollution reached widespread proportions. For a decade or so before then, concerned citizens had voiced occasional warnings, but these were looked on as hardly more than admonitions.

Why was pollution such a minor consideration? Because, relatively speaking, it was of minor importance. In 1950 our GNP in constant dollars stood at $355 billion; corresponding to this was an inestimable but apparently tolerable level of smog, tin cans, and bottles. By 1968 our GNP practically doubled to $708 billion, which amounts to an average annual compound rate of growth of almost 4 percent.

Pollution: Is There Less Under Socialism?

Protesters against environmental havoc disrupted scores of corporate annual meetings as the decade of the 1970s started. Many of them argued that pollution is an integral part of the capitalist system, because its control adds to cost, but not to value, and is therefore unprofitable. Some of the protesters concluded that the only cure for pollution was a change in the system itself. Oscar Lange, a Polish economist, added weight to their argument by asserting that socialism is environmentally superior to capitalism because it encompasses social values and costs.

Certainly, the command economies of eastern Europe have the power to eliminate pollution. But do they have the will? It seems they do not. Pollution became a big, emotional issue in the Soviet Union at about the time it became a popular cause in the United States and other capitalist nations. Soviet newspapers carried reports of wildlife being destroyed by the thoughtless use of pesticides and insecticides; of smog blanketing industrial cities; and of other environmental ailments familiar in the West. At the turn of the decade the Soviet government passed legislation designed to reduce pollution— and was promptly accused by some critics of not doing enough (their criticism was indirect, and took the form of more prominent display of stories about pollution problems).

MASSIVE LURCHES. *Dr. Marshall I. Goldman, an associate of Harvard University's Russian Research Center, believes that communism's record is no better than capitalism's when it comes to controlling pollution. The Soviet economy "often lurches suddenly and massively into new and sometimes unexpected directions," without regard for environmental effects, he writes. The labor theory of value, which teaches that all value derives from the labor used to produce a good, until recently encouraged Soviet economists to regard natural resources as "free goods." Dr. Goldman concludes: "The Russians have been no more successful than the rest of us in making explicit the social costs arising from an enterprise's activities and including them in the cost of production."*

The lessons are clear. Whatever their underlying socioeconomic systems, all industrial countries are bound to pollute —unless the people in charge of their well-being have both the power and the will to enforce environmental standards. The American executive is under pressure to produce profits, and believes antipollution laws will reduce them. The Soviet executive is under pressure to produce as cheaply as possible, and believes that antipollution laws will add to costs. Each subscribes to what he thinks are the popular values of his society; and as it turns out each has a virtually identical allegiance to the cult of efficiency, narrowly defined as obtaining the maximum possible output from a given amount of input.

Pollution will continue without great check until industrial managers in both the socialist and capitalist countries are forced to redefine their objectives—and that redefinition will occur only when their respective governments give the lead.

SOURCE: Gladwin Hill, "Soviet Pollution Reaches Capitalistic Quantities," *The New York Times*, May 10, 1970.

Associated with this larger GNP was a correspondingly higher level of pollution—one which also grew at some compound rate—although the exact percentage is impossible to determine.

The frightening thing is this:

If our GNP continues to expand at a rate of 4 percent compounded annually, it will double in 18 years. If the level of pollution should grow at the same rate, we will then be inundated with twice as much rubbish and refuse as we are at present; and even if the level should rise at only half that rate— that is, at 2 percent rather than 4 percent—we would be 43 percent worse off in 18 years than we are now.

The Effluence of Affluence

There is no doubt that pollution is due in part to a rising GNP. Does this mean there is no escape from the inexorable law of growth at compound interest, and that Americans as well as other advanced societies are doomed to drown in the effluence of their affluence? At first blush it may seem so. But closer analysis indicates that to attack pollution in terms of this "iron law" is to wage a major part of the war on the wrong battlefield.

By focusing attention on economic growth, we are overlooking a critical consideration: *One of the fundamental causes of pollution is that society has made it profitable to pollute.* By not understanding that there is a "cost" of contaminating land, air, and water, governments at all levels (through market mechanisms) have failed to assess appropriate prices for the use of these natural resources, and hence have encouraged the development of industries whose production processes use relatively large amounts of these "free" inputs. Thus by not charging for the use of rivers and lakes, society has made it cheaper for individuals and manufacturing plants to discharge their residues in these waters than to develop more costly methods of waste disposal on land. And by not understanding the cost of utilizing air and land, society has given households and business firms an incentive to defile these environmental resources with smoke, smog, strip mines, and garbage dumps.

The problem of pollution, therefore, cannot be blamed entirely on economic growth. If an economic solution is to be found, it will have to be through an economic system which evaluates the costs to society of using air, land, and water, and assigns appropriate prices to these resources. Of course, this may well affect the rate of economic growth significantly. Nevertheless, since the physical and biological laws of the environment remain fixed, it is economics that must be adjusted to the needs of society. This helps to explain the growing interest which economists are showing in the field of ecology.

THE OVERPOPULATION ARGUMENT

A second factor that is frequently mentioned as a cause of pollution is overpopulation. The contention is made, for example, that since there are far fewer Americans than Asians, the former exert less of a drain on the earth's resources. Moreover, this difference is becoming increasingly pronounced as the gap between the United States' population and the rest of the world's rapidly accelerates, as shown in Exhibit 2. It follows that at these growth rates, the earth will not be able to support the billions of people that are projected for the coming decades. Therefore, either family planning practices must be adopted on a broad scale—especially in the poorer nations of Asia and Latin America where the pressures of overcrowding are severe—or else there will be war,

Exhibit 2

Population Growth Trends

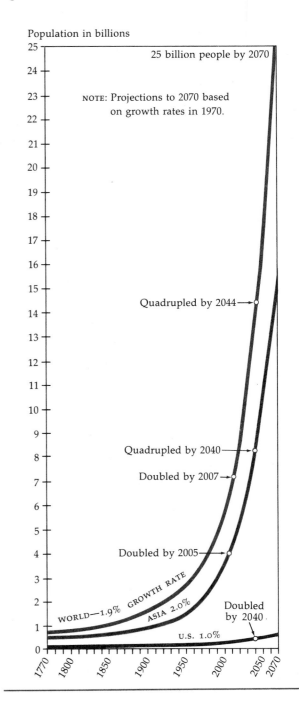

pestilence, and famine to reduce the swarm of humanity. This, of course, is the familiar neo-Malthusian thesis.

From an ecological standpoint, it is not enough to view the problem of population solely in terms of growth. The geographic distribution of population densities (such as population per square mile in specific regional areas) and the volume of pollution per person are far more critical variables. On these bases, the United States is one of the most *over-populated* countries of the world. More than half its people live in urban areas, and by the year 2000 over 80 percent of them will be living in cities occupying only 2 percent of the land.

The strains and massive filth that will be created within the urban ecosystem by this sheer density of people can only be imagined. Even now, the volume of pollution per person in the United States far surpasses anything found in the most crowded countries of Africa and Asia. For example, the average American uses more electric power (the generation of which is a prime cause of pollution) than 55 Africans and Asians; he disposes of more detergents, pesticides, fertilizers, etc., in water and on land than a thousand Indonesians; he is responsible for contaminating the air with more toxic gases such as carbon monoxide and sulphur dioxide than 200 Pakistanis or Indians; and he generates 2,500 pounds of waste a year—far more for the country as a whole than the rest of the world combined! In fact, the United States, with about 6 percent of the world's population, produces one-third of all of the poisons discharged in the skies and seas, and half the world's total industrial pollution.

There is no doubt that the growth of population adds to pollution. This can perhaps best be appreciated from an engineering standpoint: just as an engine is not 100 percent efficient and hence creates waste as it transforms fuel inputs into energy outputs, so too a population creates some waste as it transforms resource inputs into commodity outputs. The larger the population, the greater the volume of waste that it will create—all other things being equal.

However, in the real world all other things are not equal. Ecologists have estimated that a child born in the United States is 50 times more of a burden on the environment than a child born in India—even though India's population per square mile is almost ten times that of the United States. Therefore the contention that Americans are less of a drain on the Earth's resources than Asians or Africans, because Americans are fewer in number, is a fallacy. The problem is much more complex than population figures alone would indicate. The fact is that in the United States and other advanced countries where millions of cars and billions of bottles and cans are junked annually, effluence is rising with affluence and population. Hence the task, as we shall see later, is to suggest some economic measures to deal with this relationship.

PRIVATE VERSUS PUBLIC SPENDING

A third approach that has been widely proposed as a solution to the pollution problem—especially by many college students and by members of the New Left—is for society to utilize less of its resources for the production of consumer gadgetry with its resulting by-products of waste and filth, and more of its resources for the production of those goods that will improve the fundamental quality of life. This amounts to the contention that the composition of GNP should be changed so as to include a larger proportion of "public goods" and a smaller proportion of "private goods."

The argument sounds plausible but on closer examination is seen to be specious. This is because government spending is of three types:

1. Purchase of goods (military goods, school buildings, office equipment)

2. Transfer payments (social security payments, welfare, veterans' benefits)

3. Provision of services (police and fire protection, education, sanitation)

How would a shift from private to public spending affect the level of pollution? To the extent that the increase in public spending is funneled into the first two of the above categories, there would be just as much production of goods as before and therefore no improvement in environmental quality. On the other hand, to the extent that the higher level of public spending is directed into the third category, there would perhaps be some reduction in pollution levels because of the greater production of services as opposed to goods. But it is doubtful that very much could be accomplished by this approach because (1) the larger numbers of policemen, teachers, and other service workers on government payrolls would still want to spend their incomes on consumer goods just like everyone else, and (2) there are very real (but admittedly unknown) limits to the quantity of consumer goods that an advanced society would be willing to "trade off" in return for more services. Concerning the latter point, there is ample evidence that all advanced societies, capitalistic as well as socialistic, want more private as well as more public goods—not more of one type at the expense of less of the other.

CONCLUSION: ZERO POPULATION GROWTH OR ZERO ECONOMIC GROWTH?

United States population growth has been slowing down since about 1960. This has led many demographers to conclude that as birth control and abortion reform spread, America will reach a stage of zero population growth sometime in the 1970s. If this trend of population growth could be accompanied by a redistribution of people away from the overcrowded east and west coasts toward the more sparsely populated inner regions, it would help immeasurably to reduce the problems of congestion and ecological imbalance which are currently plaguing large sections of the country. Such a redistribution could be greatly encouraged through a new and enlarged type of "Homestead Act"—a comprehensive program providing tax incentives and subsidies to businesses and individuals as an inducement to relocate.

On the other hand, there are some zealots who are advocating zero economic growth. Their arguments seem to make no sense whatsoever. If the economy does not grow, the millions of people currently trapped in the quagmire of poverty will never earn enough to extricate themselves. Further, the nation will not be able to obtain the resources to solve its social ills—to provide the schools, medical care,

hospitals, and other things it needs. The results of a no-growth economy can only be lower per capita income and more unemployment. In 1969–70, for example, there was almost no real growth, and unemployment rose to over 5.5 percent; some 4-million people were out of work. With a larger population and labor force, even a relatively low rate of economic growth will cause considerably higher levels of unemployment.

Three conclusions seem apparent. First, a movement toward zero population growth is compatible with environmental improvement and the eventual solution to the problem of poverty. Second, a short-run prescription of zero economic growth may sometimes be a painful but necessary antidote to curb inflationary excesses, but it cannot be sustained as a long-run goal of economic or social policy. Third, some redistribution of both population and the composition of output would be desirable from an ecological standpoint, but in a free society every effort should first be made to attain these objectives by the use of economic incentives or market-oriented mechanisms before resorting to direct regulations. We shall have more to say about this at a later point in the chapter.

Economic Analysis for Environmental Improvement

One major challenge of pollution stems from the widespread difference between "private costs" and "social costs." According to classical economic theory, the operation of a free market assures that the price system will automatically allocate resources to their socially most efficient uses. But it appears that the price system is not always effective in dealing with environmental factors. For as firms seek to maximize profits, they generate adverse "side effects" in the form of polluted environments which become the real costs that are borne by society. The problem, therefore, is to develop modified market as well as nonmarket mechanisms for allocating resources when the internal or private costs of firms differ substantially from their social costs. Three analytical approaches are useful for this purpose:

1. Marginal or incremental analysis

2. Benefit-cost analysis

3. Cost-effectiveness analysis

As we shall see, the ideas underlying these methods of analysis are applicable not only to pollution control, but also to a wide variety of other socioeconomic problems as well.

MARGINAL OR INCREMENTAL ANALYSIS

One of the most fundamental rules of economics which serves as a guide for making rational decisions is the so-called "marginal" or "incremental" principle:

The net gain of any activity is maximized at the point where the incremental (added or "marginal") cost of that activity is equal to its incremental benefit. Thus, expenditures on pollution abatement will result in added costs as well as added benefits. But the degree of pollution will be at an optimum level from society's point of view when the incremental cost of reducing it further is equal to the incremental benefits derived therefrom.

This means that if an upstream steel mill discharges its wastes into a river, and if by spending a dollar it can save downstream fisheries at least a dollar, it should do so—from the standpoint of society's well-being.

As was pointed out above, a problem arises because of the fundamental distinction between private costs and social costs. The upstream steel mill, for example, disposes of its wastes in a manner that affects others, but does not pay for this disposal; it treats the stream as a free good, and hence its costs of production are artificially lower than they would otherwise be. The downstream fisheries, on the other hand, incur higher private costs because they must absorb the pollutants of the upstream mill. Therefore, to the extent that prices tend to reflect production costs, the upstream mill's prices are understated and the downstream fisheries' prices are overstated. The result is a net loss to society because of a failure of all firms concerned to equate their private and social costs. The general consequences are therefore undesirable: society gets too much steel and not enough fish; consumers of fish, by paying higher prices, sub-

sidize consumers of steel; and economic resources are not allocated in the most efficient way.

Most private decisions produce side effects of one type or another, some of which may be favorable and some unfavorable. Social scientists refer to such consequences as *externalities*. In the case of pollution, the undesirable externalities can be reduced by special taxes, charges, subsidies, or laws. A fundamental problem, of course, is to derive methods for evaluating each type of action.

BENEFIT-COST ANALYSIS

One method that has been developed for such purposes is known as *benefit-cost analysis*. It is a technique of evaluating alternative programs by comparing, for each program, the (discounted) present value of all expected benefits with all expected costs. The discount factor that is used to arrive at an estimate is a percentage figure representing the "opportunity cost" of capital—that is, a rate equal to what the funds would have earned in their best alternative use of equal risk.

EXAMPLE. Suppose the present value of expected benefits to be derived from a particular pollution-abatement program is estimated to be $1 million, and the present cost is $0.9 million. Then the ratio of benefit to cost is 1:11. This suggests that the program may be worth undertaking, depending on how it ranks with alternative investment projects, because the benefit/cost ratio is greater than 1; i.e., the incremental benefit exceeds the incremental cost, since each $1 of investment stands to return $1.11 in benefits. On the other hand, if the ratio turned out to be less than 1, the incremental cost would exceed the incremental benefit, and hence the program would not be warranted.

Benefit-cost analysis has been used since the 1930s, primarily in government investment projects for flood control and river valley development. It has also been employed to evaluate pollution-abatement projects as well as other socioeconomic programs such as manpower training, family planning, vocational rehabilitation, and disease control. Despite its extraordinary success in some of these areas, two major limitations prevent its widespread application:

1. *Benefits Are Difficult to Define and Measure.* In the case of a smog-abatement program, for instance,

there are certain benefits that are relatively easy to establish, such as the savings in painting and cleaning expenses that will result from purer air. But how do we define the effects on human life? If the program results in reducing the death rate from respiratory diseases, the benefit/cost ratio will rise. But if people live longer, the benefit/cost ratio will decline because older people become ill more often and require more medical care. Similarly, in a program to reduce the pollution of a lake or river, it may be possible to forecast the probable financial benefits to fisheries in terms of the higher earnings they are likely to receive, but how do we establish the nonmonetary benefits of the program to the community?

2. *Priorities May Conflict with Benefits.* Even if all the monetary benefits of a program could be established, the resulting benefit/cost ratio would not always reflect the relative need for the program from society's overall standpoint. Thus a particular pollution-abatement project may yield an expected benefit/cost ratio of 1.2 to 1, whereas a program for training the hard-core unemployed may produce an expected benefit/cost ratio of 1.1 to 1. Does this mean that society's limited supply of funds should be taken from the latter and put into the former? Not necessarily. An attack on hard-core unemployment may have nonmonetary but socially desirable consequences that simply cannot be precisely identified for purposes of benefit-cost analysis.

COST-EFFECTIVENESS ANALYSIS

The difficulty of defining and measuring benefits led to the introduction in 1961 of another method of efficiency planning known as *cost-effectiveness analysis.* This is a technique of selecting from alternative programs the one that will attain a given objective at the lowest cost. It is most useful where benefits cannot be measured in money. Thus, cost-effectiveness analysis is of no use in deciding whether it would be better to develop a program for abating pollution or for reducing the number of deaths from traffic accidents, but given the decision to spend on one of these, cost-effectiveness analysis may be used to select the alternative that will cost least.

As a *hypothetical* example, a cost-effectiveness analysis of deaths resulting from smog might conclude that on the average, a reduction of one death could be achieved for each expenditure of $90,000 on the development of clean-burning fuels, or $60,000 on the installation of furnace and engine filtering devices, or $45,000 on the provision of improved medical treatment, or $18,000 on the vigorous enforcement of existing smog-abatement laws, or $150 on the production of special "gas masks" or breathing devices for all citizens. If the only factor to be considered were the cost, it follows that the last choice is the one to be adopted since it achieves the given objective at the lowest cost.

Unfortunately, there are many types of environmental problems—as well as urban and social welfare problems—where cost-effectiveness analysis has not yet demonstrated its usefulness. For example, should the limited funds that are available for general pollution abatement be spent for smog control, water purification, or waste disposal? This question is critical. Yet it may not be specific enough for cost-effectiveness analysis to answer, unless a common objective can be defined and measured, and the costs of alternative actions for achieving that objective can be identified, as in the hypothetical example above. These, of course, are the fundamental difficulties. However, as more and better information becomes available, cost-effectiveness analysis will continue to gain in importance as a powerful tool for program evaluation.

Some Guidelines for Public Policy

How much will it cost to undertake antipollution programs? Who will pay the costs?

Historically, the federal government has dealt with the environment piecemeal and with comparatively paltry sums, as the chart in Exhibit 3 indicates. After the mid-fifties, the trends of federal expenditures for controlling water and air pollution rose steadily, and by the late sixties they were literally soaring. But the out-of-pocket costs for checking total pollution on a national scale, as shown in the table, must amount to at least $13.5 billion annually, while the annual

Exhibit 3

Pollution Control

The annual cost of pollution control [billions of dollars]

	Capital	Operating	Total
Air pollution:			
Automobile afterburners	$1.5	$1.0	$2.5
Sulfur dioxide removal from			
stack gases	0.3	1.0	1.3
Industrial control equipment	0.3	—	0.3
Total	2.1	2.0	4.1
Water pollution:			
Reservoirs for seasonal			
equalization of river flows			
for waste oxidation	0.4	—	0.4
Municipal sewage collection			
and treatment	0.9	0.6	1.5
Industrial effluent treatment	1.1	0.5	1.6
Separation of combined sewers			
and storage of storm waters	0.5	—	0.5
Electric utility cooling towers	0.1	0.6	0.7
Total	3.0	1.7	4.7
Solid waste disposal:			
Collection of municipal			
wastes	—	2.6	2.6
Incineration of municipal			
wastes	—	0.7	0.7
Land fill of municipal wastes	—	0.3	0.3
Junk auto disposal	—	0.2	0.2
Demolition waste disposal	—	0.9	0.9
Total	—	4.7	4.7
Total	**5.1**	**8.4**	**13.5**

SOURCE: Harvard Center for Population Studies. *Business Week.*

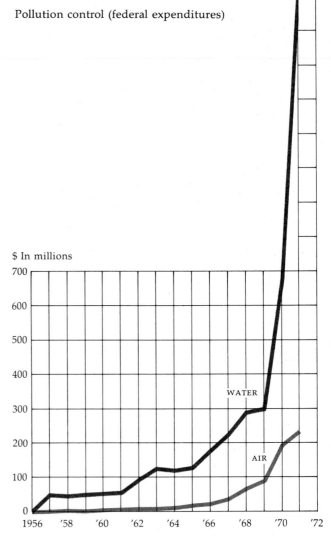

Pollution control (federal expenditures)

SOURCE: Bureau of the Budget. Department of Interior.

expenditure (not shown in the table) needed to reverse the course of pollution has been estimated by various sources as high as 20 percent of GNP.

The trouble with statements and figures such as these is that they reflect our ignorance of the facts that are really important. We do not know very much about the damages caused by pollution, nor do we always know the value of eliminating a particular waste. Hence we spend too much money reducing some wastes that are not very damaging, and not enough reducing those wastes that are. Clearly, some specific guidelines are needed for helping to formulate correct judgements. Four proposals may be considered:

1. Levy emission fees on polluters
2. Sell pollution "rights"
3. Subsidize pollution-abatement efforts
4. Impose direct regulations

An analysis of these alternatives will suggest some conclusions for public policy.

LEVY EMISSION FEES ON POLLUTERS

Many economists and legislators have increasingly emphasized the idea that the costs of pollution should be built into the price-profit system as an incentive feature. In simplest terms, this approach involves the use of metering devices to measure the amount of pollution emitted by factories, and then charging fees for every unit of pollutant discharged. A pollution-control board—a state or federal agency —could determine safe limits of emission, and the fees it charges could be varied not only by the amount of waste emitted, but by the hour of the day, by the day of the week, and by geographic location. By setting its own multiple fee schedules on these bases, the board could exert a strong influence on *how much, when,* and *where* pollutants are discharged. And since the emission fees would become part of a firm's costs of operation, the board would be using the price mechanism as a carrot as well as a stick.

There are several arguments in favor of this approach.

1. It would permit the imposition of variable charges on the generation of wastes. Historically, governmental systems for controlling waste have usually been on a yes-or-no basis. However, as indicated above, we do not yet know enough about the different kinds of waste to permit them in terms of "all or none." By levying emission fees, it would be possible to impose degrees of control as the needs arose.

2. It would enable government to distribute pollution more evenly throughout the country. By charg-

ing lower emission fees in sparsely populated areas and higher fees in the more densely populated regions, factories would be encouraged to locate away from the cities where they could pollute with less social damage.

3. It would cause firms to calculate the costs of waste, as well as the costs and benefits of abatement, and to consider these alternatives in their production and pricing decisions. They would thus be stimulated to seek methods of reducing waste—perhaps by "recycling" it into production, or by developing socially harmless methods of disposal.

The rebuttals to these arguments can be readily anticipated. Essentially, opponents of emission fees contend that: (1) only certain types of pollution can be measured with metering devices; (2) many factors other than emission fees, such as the availability of a suitable labor supply, access to raw materials and markets, etc., influence the geographic location of firms; and (3) benefits and costs are impossible to measure and use precisely. Therefore, those who object to the levying of emission fees argue that such a system would at best have only limited advantages.

SELL POLLUTION "RIGHTS"

A second proposal for dealing with the problem of pollution is to establish a system of marketable licenses. Each license would give its owner the "right" to pollute—up to a specified amount in a given place during a particular period of time. These licenses or rights could be bought and sold in an organized market—not unlike the stock market or the commodities market. Their prices would fluctuate according to the forces of supply and demand, reflecting the general desire of polluters to dispose of waste. The basic economic features of the proposal are explained in Exhibit 4.

At a very low price, those who wanted to pollute could do so at relatively little cost. If the price were very high, some form of supplementary rights would have to be issued to financially weaker firms in order to enable them to pollute, while limiting the opportunities for financially stronger firms through the market system. A similar type of scheme might also be developed for households.

Exhibit 4

A Market for Pollution "Rights"

One way to attack the pollution problem is through the price system.

The government would determine the maximum amount of a specific type of pollution that is within safe limits—such as the number of tons of raw sewage per year that can be dumped into a lake and would disintegrate by normal bacterial processes. It could then sell rights to pollution in a free market. Each "right" would permit the owner to dump a specified quantity of sewage per year into the lake.

The supply curve S in this case would be a vertical line, while the demand curve D_1 would be downward sloping. This indicates that some polluters would find it cheaper to buy the pollution rights than to invest in pollution-abatement equipment, while others would not. Hence the equilibrium price would settle at OP_1, and the equilibrium quantity at OQ_1. Note that this quantity is less than the amount OQ_2 which would prevail if the price of pollution were zero.

Over the years, the growth in income and population would cause the demand curve to rise—say to D_2, thus bringing about a higher equilibrium price OP_2.

Supply of, and demand for, pollution rights

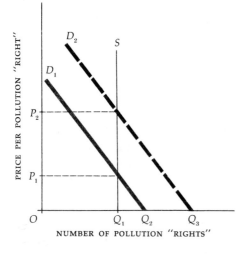

This approach to waste control would not be adaptable to all forms of pollution. But to those for which it was suited, its fundamental advantage would be its operation through the free market and use of the price system as a mechanism for coping with pollution problems.

SUBSIDIZE POLLUTION-ABATEMENT EFFORTS

A third approach to curbing pollution is through government subsidization schemes for firms. This could take various direct and indirect forms: outright payments for the reduction of pollution levels; subsidies for particular control devices; exemptions from local property taxes on pollution-abatement equipment; and special fast depreciation allowances and tax credits for the purchase of pollution-control equipment.

If subsidization of any type were to be employed in a pollution-control scheme, several considerations would have to be kept in mind:

1. It would be better to give firms outright payments for the reduction of pollution levels than to offer them tax credits for investing in abatement equipment. The former would leave them free to adopt the least costly means of reducing the discharge of pollutants; the latter would discourage them from seeking alternative methods of pollution abatement, including the possibility of burning nonpolluting fuels.

2. If firms are to be subsidized for investing in pollution controls, the subsidies should be given for equipment that is likely to enhance their net profits by either adding to revenues or reducing costs. A pollution-control device which was not expected to increase profits would leave firms with very little incentive to acquire it—even if the government offered to pay part of the cost.

3. Subsidy payments should be tied to the amounts by which pollutants were reduced below "normal"— that is, below the levels that would have prevailed without the payments. Such standards are extremely difficult if not impossible to estimate, especially for new firms. Yet, failure to establish guidelines of this type would make any subsidization scheme largely ineffective.

4. Subsidy payments would violate the "benefit principle" of equity if, as is most likely, the subsidies were financed out of general tax revenues. According to the benefit principle—which has strong support on moral and ethical grounds—pollution-control measures should be part of the costs of production, and the consumers who buy products ought to pay the antipollution costs just as they pay for labor, capital, and other inputs. In other words, even though all of society benefits from subsidies to control pollution, it can be argued that consumers who buy the products which are responsible for pollution should pay the costs of reducing it.

5. Moral and ethical principles of fairness would be violated if indirect subsidies were given in the form of tax credits to firms that invest in pollution-abatement equipment. Such credits would mean that some taxpayers would have to pay higher taxes than otherwise. This would introduce further biases into the tax system, resulting in resource misallocation.

These considerations make it clear that subsidy schemes, though frequently proposed, are not necessarily the best approach for public policy.

IMPOSE DIRECT REGULATIONS

A fourth method for pollution control is to invoke the legislative powers of government at all levels. This would involve the use of licenses, permits, zoning regulations, registration, the maintenance of compulsory standards, etc., with violations subject to civil and criminal procedings. Direct regulations such as these are wholly within the province of federal and state governments, which, under the "general welfare" and so-called "police power" clauses of the Constitution, have the authority to pass laws promoting the health and safety of citizens.

The general objection to direct regulation is the same for pollution abatement as for anything else. It leads to rigidities and, in many cases, unwieldy and inefficient forms of control. Thus a law which sets a limit on pollution levels will cause a greater misallocation of resources than, say, a system of emission fees, since the latter can accomplish the same overall reductions in pollution while leaving firms free to adjust to their own particular production

situations as they think best. This does not mean that direct regulations should be avoided at all costs. In a capitalistic economy they may very well be needed, but they should be adopted only after all other market-oriented mechanisms have been found unsuitable.

Which Policy?

It is impossible to say which of the four approaches to pollution control—emission fees, pollution "rights," subsidization, or direct regulations—would be best. There are different kinds and sources of pollution, many of which are not well understood. Hence a method of control that might work effectively for curbing air or water contamination might not be suitable for reducing noise levels or land exploitation. Each class of pollution problems must be analyzed separately and a specific control system designed for it. If such a procedure were followed, it might very well be found that different combinations of policies were needed for various kinds of pollution. In the meantime, almost all present pollution controls are in the form of direct regulation, leaving few or no bases for judging the effectiveness of alternative control schemes.

What about technology as a solution? To many environmentalists, including ecologists and economists, this is the culprit that has been responsible for the mess. Cans and bottles, though they broaden consumer satisfactions (by providing "time" and "place" utility in the consumption of food), accumulate because they cannot be burned. The automobile, though it overcomes the distance barrier between people, turns cities into parking lots and greeneries into paved highways, thereby eliminating over 1 million acres of oxygen-producing trees each year. Environmentalists now fear that people will again turn to technology—perhaps to the dream of building air-conditioned geodesic domes over the cities, or to visions of inhabiting outer space—as an answer. But these are as yet only fantasies. Although technology will no doubt play a vital short-run role in rescuing society from its own effluence, man's most fundamental need if he is to survive on this planet is to *create a value system that will enable him to assess the various parts of the environment.* As philosopher Lewis Mumford once stated: "Any square mile of inhabited earth has more significance for man's future than all of the planets in the solar system."

Economic policies, of course, are rarely indepen-dent of politics. At present the structure of govern-ment is too fragmented, and the responsibility among federal agencies is too scattered, to cope effectively with environmental problems. Funda-mental changes in administrative organization are sorely needed. Some interesting suggestions by two noted Stanford University ecologists are presented in Box 3.

Box 3

The Need for Political Change

The lack of overall control of environmental matters and the impossibility of dealing with problems in any coordinated way are illustrated by the fact that the area of urban affairs comes under the jurisdiction of the Department of Housing and Urban Development, the Department of Health, Education and Wel-fare, and the Departments of Labor, Commerce, Interior, Justice, and Transportation, to name just the main ones. It is clear that the Executive branch needs reorganizing, and that substantial changes in the Legislative branch are also called for.

Perhaps one of the most fundamental changes needed is that an upper age limit—of perhaps 65 years—be established for appointed and elected federal officials. The advice of older people who have experience and wisdom could still be sought, but the actual work of running the country in our complex world is simply too great a strain for most older men, es-pecially in an era when instant worldwide communications are capable of putting extraordinary loads of responsibility on individuals. A second reason for age limits is the principle that in a dangerous and rapidly changing world those responsible for making decisions should have a reasonable expectation of having to live with the consequences of those decisions. A 65-year old retirement age might mean the loss of some fine talent, but wise men can always be consulted, and it has be-come clear that some way must be found to keep the senile out of powerful positions.

The communications problem is especially severe for the President, who must now serve functions previously dele-gated to ambassadors and military commanders in the field. The time may have come to divide the Executive into two branches, one concerned with domestic matters, the other with international affairs. Each could be headed by a co-president assisted by an executive officer whose role would be an ex-panded version of that now played by the vice-president. This suggestion may be bad or impractical but it is high time our governmental system was modernized, and serious examination of such problems is urgently required.

It may well be necessary for a new political party to be formed, one founded on the principles of population control, environmental quality, and a stabilized economy. Such a party would be national and international in its orientation, rather than basing its power on parochial issues as our current parties do. In 1854 the Republican party was created de novo, founded on the platform of opposition to the extension of slavery. It seems probable that in the 1970s the environmental issue will become even more prominent than the slavery issue was in the 1850s, and the creation of a powerful new party might be possible.

Obviously such changes as those briefly proposed above will threaten not only numerous politicians of both major parties, but many economic institutions and practices. They are likely to be opposed by vast segments of the Industrial State; by much of the oil and petrochemical industry, the steel industry, the automobile industry, the nuclear power industry, the heavy construction industry, and by many subdividers, the Army Corps of Engineers, the USDA, the AEC, the Chamber of Commerce, to name only a few. Even a cursory knowledge of the pervasive nature and degree of control of these interests leads to the conclusion that the necessary change in attitudes and behavior is extremely unlikely among the individuals and organizations where it would be most helpful. But the name of the game is human survival, and each one of us is dealt in, whether we like it or not. These individuals and organizations have an unprecedented opportunity to help everyone win. Will they accept the challenge?

SOURCE: *Population, Resources, Environment,* by Paul R. Ehrlich and Anne H. Ehrlich, W. H. Freeman and Company, San Francisco. Copyright 1970, pp. 290, 291.

Pollution

The penultimate Western man, stalled in the ultimate traffic jam and slowly succumbing to carbon monoxide, will not be cheered to hear from the last survivor that the gross national product went up by a record amount.

This wry comment, by Harvard's noted economist John Kenneth Galbraith, reflects the deep concern many of us have about the future of our environment. Has the United States become "the Effluent Society"—a nation whose headlong drive for material wealth has caused it to defile its land, air, and water, and to create dangerous social tensions as well? Many would answer yes. British economist E. J. Mishan, for instance, expresses his apprehen-

Bruce Davidson

sion this way: "As the carpet of increased choice is being unrolled before us by the foot, it is simultaneously being rolled up behind us by the yard."

These are serious indictments, not only of our economy, but also of economics. It has always been part of the "conventional wisdom" of economics that a nation's output of goods and services is a measure of its material welfare. From the time of

Adam Smith it has been assumed that society is better off if it produces more rather than less.

This view is now being called into question. The issues revolve around such difficult problems as whether there is a "trade-off" between economic growth and environmental quality, whether we can reduce the rate of growth without creating unemployment, and whether it would be possible to redirect growth rather than repress it. These questions involve so many complex conceptual problems that no one has yet come up with satisfactory answers.

Among the fundamental obstacles to be overcome is the fact that clean air, fresh water, and unspoiled land are no longer essentially "free goods." The growth of population makes increasing demands on

Erich Hartmann

them, while pollution imposes heavy economic and social costs. We must learn to use these resources properly. Hopefully, this can be done by making the market work against pollution instead of for it. From an economic standpoint, the need is for "incentive" schemes combining legislation, taxation, and subsidization, designed to persuade firms to adopt pricing and costing methods that will enable society to improve its environment with the least sacrifice in terms of economic growth.

SUMMARY OF IMPORTANT IDEAS

1. Ecology is concerned with the management of the household of nature, whereas economics deals with the management of the household of man. Both disciplines have certain features in common including concepts of populations, equilibrium, exchange, development, and policy.

2. Economic growth has given us a rising standard of living, but it has also caused pollution. However, it is not likely that a planned reduction in the rate of growth would be an acceptable weapon in the war against pollution. A much more effective method would be for society to evaluate the costs of using various parts of the environment, and to assign appropriate prices for these resources instead of making them available "free."

3. The growth of population has also been a cause of pollution. However, the problem is much more complex than population figures alone would indicate. Many ecologists point out that the level and growth-rate of population in Asia and Latin America are far higher than in the United States, yet the average American as a consumer is a much greater burden on the total environment than the average Asian or Latin American.

4. Some people contend that the composition of GNP is a third cause of pollution because too few public goods and too many private goods are produced. It is doubtful, however, that very much can be accomplished by changing the composition, because: (a) a large proportion of public goods consists of material goods rather than just services; and (b) there is ample evidence that a free society is not willing to sacrifice very much in the way of consumer goods in order to get more services.

5. Marginal or incremental analysis forces us to recognize both the costs and benefits of pollution. Thus the optimum level of pollution occurs where the incremental cost of reducing it further is equal to the incremental benefits derived therefrom. Two rough but practical analytical tools which are gaining increasing use for implementing this concept are benefit-cost analysis and cost-effectiveness analysis.

6. Several approaches to pollution control are possible: (a) levy emission fees on polluters; (b) sell pollution "rights"; (c) subsidize pollution-abatement efforts; and (d) impose direct regulations. Since relatively little is known about the many causes and effects of pollution, it is virtually certain that no one of these policies would be suitable in all cases. Instead, various combinations would be desirable. At present, however, most policies are in the form of direct regulations.

FOR HOMEWORK AND DISCUSSION

1. *Terms and concepts to review:*

   benefit-cost analysis

   cost-effectiveness analysis

2. The four components of an ecosystem have been given in this chapter as: (a) nonliving or inorganic matter, (b) producer plants, (c) animal consumers, and (d) decomposers. Can you suggest four sets of counterparts to these that exist in an economic system? Explain your answer.

3. The dictionary defines a system as "an ordered assemblage or combination of parts forming a complex or unitary whole." Is this a suitable definition of an ecosystem? An economic system? Explain.

4. "There is a 'tradeoff' between pollution and poverty: if we reduce pollution, we must increase poverty." What is the basis of this statement? Do you agree? Explain.

5. "If all land and inland waters were privately owned, this would be a first step in controlling pollution." Can you explain the justification for this statement?

6. One way of reducing pollution is to charge higher taxes of all kinds in urban areas and lower taxes in rural areas. Do you agree? Explain.

7. Ecologists and economists have expressed an interest in developing an ideal "index of pollution" —a single number which measures the degree of pollution at a given time. What sort of difficulties exist in developing such a measure?

8. A state agency recently submitted to its legislature two alternative 25-year investment programs for the abatement of river pollution. The relevant economic

data for the two programs are as follows:

	Program A	Program B
a. Initial investment costs	$15,000,000	$16,000,000
b. Annual operating costs	5,000,000	8,000,000
c. Annual benefits	8,000,000	10,000,000
d. Present value of discounted total costs	54,200,000	63,040,000
e. Present value of discounted total benefits	62,720,000	78,400,000

Other things being equal, which program would you vote for if you were a member of the state legislature? What are some of the significant implications of this type of problem?

9. Of the various policy alternatives that have been suggested, which one would probably be the most practical and least costly to administer, other things being equal? Explain your answer.

REFERENCES AND READING SUGGESTIONS

BOULDING, KENNETH E., "Economics and Ecology," in F. F. Darling and J. P. Milton (eds.), *Future Environments of North America*, Natural History Press, New York, 1966.

DALE, EDWIN L., JR., "The Economics of Pollution," *New York Times Magazine*, April 19, 1970.

"Dawn for the Age of Ecology," *Newsweek*, Jan. 26, 1970.

EHRLICH, PAUL R., and EHRLICH, ANNE H., *Population, Resources, Environment*, Freeman, San Francisco, 1970.

"Fighting to Save the Earth from Man," *Time*, Feb. 2, 1970.

GOLDMAN, MARSHALL I. (ed.): *Controlling Pollution*, Prentice-Hall, New York, 1967. See especially the selection by Edwin S. Mills, pp. 100–106.

JARRET, HENRY (ed.), *Environmental Quality in a Growing Economy*, Hopkins, Baltimore, 1966.

KNEESE, ALLEN V., *Economics and the Quality of the Environment* (Resources for the Future, Washington, D.C., Reprint No. 71, April, 1968).

PERLOFF, HARVEY, *The Quality of the Urban Environment*, Hopkins, Baltimore, 1969.

REUFF, LARRY E., "The Economic Common Sense of Pollution," *The Public Interest*, Spring, 1970.

"The Environment: A National Mission for the Seventies," *Fortune*, February, 1970. See especially the article by Sanford Rose.

A. Wage-Price Inflation or Price-Wage Inflation?

Are inflations caused by rising wages or by rising profits? Adam Smith once remarked in the *Wealth of Nations:*

> Our merchants and master-manufacturers complain much of the bad effects of high wages in raising the price, and thereby lessening the sale of their goods both at home and abroad. They say nothing concerning the bad effects of high profits. They are silent with regard to the pernicious effects of their own gains. They complain only of those of other people.

Thus, Smith believed that an inflation could be as much *profit-push* as *wage-push*. However, during the 1950s and 1960s there were three distinct periods in which corporate profits began a sharp upturn *before* a rise in prices, while labor costs per unit were actually *declining* when the price increase began.

The accompanying charts (published by the United Automobile Workers in December, 1969) present a history of prices, profits, and labor costs for selected years covering three major periods of price inflation: (1) 1950–51; (2) 1955–57; and (3) 1965–69.

QUESTIONS

1. Describe what happened to (*a*) prices, (*b*) profits, and (*c*) wages, i.e., labor costs, during the first, second, and third major periods of price inflation.

2. Does it seem that labor costs have pushed prices up during these three periods? Explain.

3. If rising profits precede an initial inflationary push, does this mean that profits must level off before prices tend to stabilize?

4. Are we to conclude that the United States economy is faced with the choice of flat profits versus painful inflation? In other words, can profits rise without inducing inflationary price and wage increases? Explain.

Prices, Labor Costs, and Profits in Manufacturing, January 1949 to December 1951 (Indexes 1957–59 = 100)

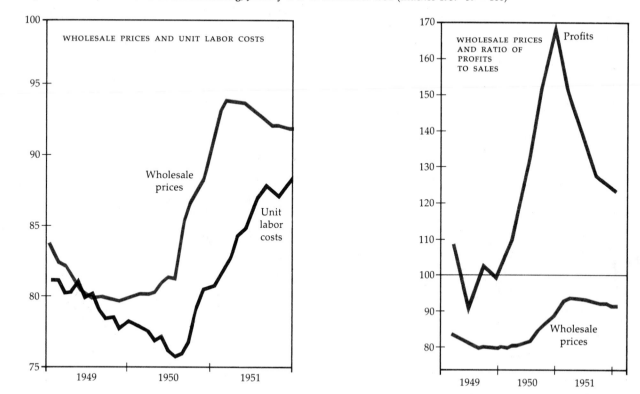

Prices, Labor Costs, and Profits in Manufacturing, January 1954 to December 1957 (Indexes 1957–59 = 100)

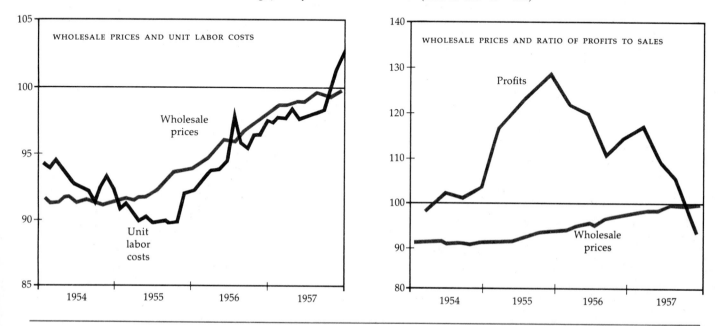

Prices, Labor Costs, and Profits in Manufacturing, July 1958 to June 1969 (Indexes 1957–59 = 100)

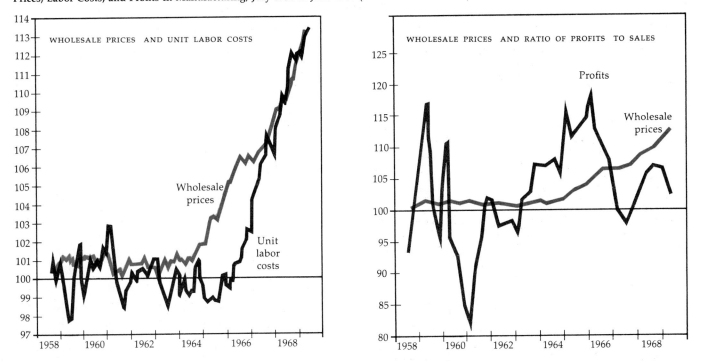

Prices, Labor Costs, and Profits, Nonfinancial Corporations, January 1949 to December 1951 (Indexes 1957–59 = 100)

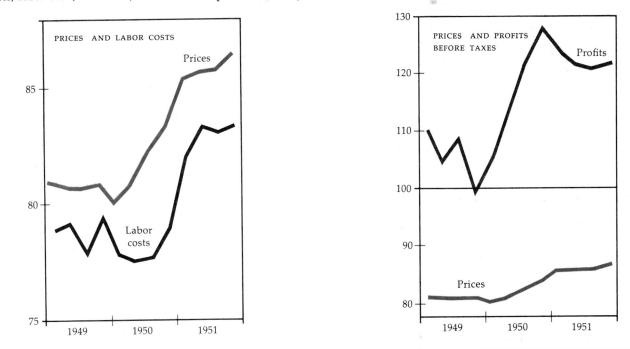

Prices, Labor Costs, and Profits, Nonfinancial Corporations, January 1954 to December 1957 (Indexes 1957–59 = 100)

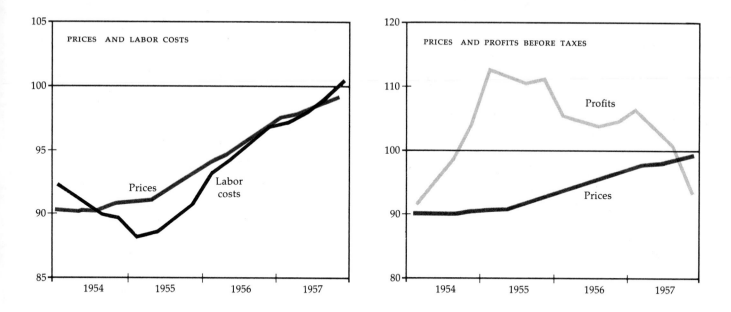

Prices, Labor Costs, and Profits, Nonfinancial Corporations, January 1958 to September 1969 (Indexes 1957–59 = 100)

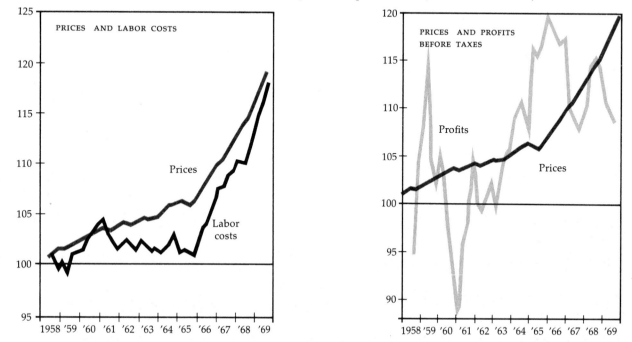

B. Is Defense Spending Needed to Maintain Prosperity?

War has been closely linked with prosperity and inflation in the United States. As the accompanying charts show, heavy defense spending and its aftermath have caused significant episodes of inflation.

During the Civil War, consumer prices rose at an average annual rate of 15 percent. In World War I, the existence of unused capacity in the early stages of the war helped keep consumer prices down, but from mid-1914 to mid-1920 they nevertheless rose at an average rate of 13 percent a year. During World War II, government controls helped retard the increase in prices, but consumers paid an average of 7 percent more each year from late 1939 to late 1948. In the Korean War (see page 302) which was relatively short, speculative forces pushed consumer prices up by a phenomenal 12 percent between June 1950 and February 1951. In the Vietnam War, consumer prices increased by an average of about 4 percent per year between 1965 and 1970.

War and inflation tend to go hand in hand for several reasons. The government sector bids away needed resources; the flow of consumer goods does not match the higher incomes generated by defense production; and fiscal or monetary policies are not usually restrictive enough to curb inflationary pressures.

Many people believe that *a buoyant and growing American economy is dependent on high and rising defense expenditures.* Indeed, most students of the Left—both the Old and the New—have adopted the dogma (which originated with V. I. Lenin, the founder of Soviet Russia) that the nature of capitalistic countries is to be aggressive and warlike in order to sustain economic expansion. Many other people of more moderate persuasion have also subscribed to this so-called "defense-economy thesis"—an hypothesis which holds that *heavy defense spending is vital to the growth of the economy.*

The Importance of Defense Expenditures

National defense expenditures as a per cent of the total federal budget reached 89.3 percent in 1951, remained at or near this level until 1957, and then declined to 74.8 percent in 1965. With the buildup in Vietnam, the defense portion of the budget reached 79.8 percent in 1967 and has declined moderately since.

Defense spending, as a percent of all government purchases, equaled 37.2 percent in 1950, and 61.4 percent in 1952, but in 1967 the percentage was only 40.1, and declining. With a leveling in defense outlays expected in 1970, the relative importance of this category should continue to decline.

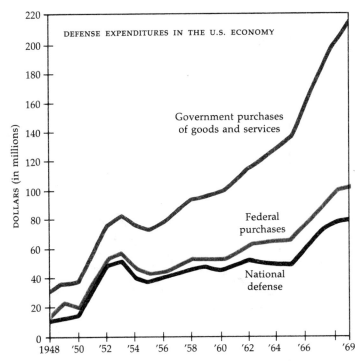

DEFENSE EXPENDITURES IN THE U.S. ECONOMY

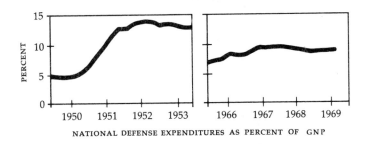

NATIONAL DEFENSE EXPENDITURES AS PERCENT OF GNP

SOURCE: The Conference Board, Inc.

QUESTIONS

1. From your previous study of America's business cycles and economic growth during peacetime periods since the Civil War, does the defense-economy thesis appear warranted? Explain your answer.

2. The defense-economy thesis first became popular at the beginning of World War I, and again during the early part of World War II. What economic conditions at the outset of these two wars prompted these views?

3. From your understanding of macroeconomic theory and policy, what basic assumptions underlie the defense-economy thesis?

4. Evaluate the assumptions given in your answer to Question 3.

War and Prices

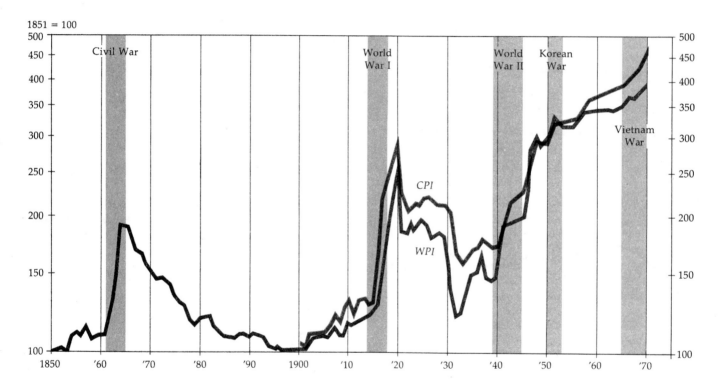

NOTE: *Ratio scale to show proportionate changes. Annual data. 1969 figure for consumer price index (CPI) based on a 10-month average; for wholesale price index (WPI) based on an 11-month average. Source: "Retail Prices After 1850," chapter by Ethel D. Hoover, in* Trends in the American Economy in the Nineteenth Century (*Princeton University Press for the National Bureau of Economic Research, 1960*); U.S. Bureau of Labor Statistics, adjusted to 1851 = 100 basis by FNCB.

SOURCE: First National City Bank of New York.

Economic Changes During Two Conflicts: Korea and Vietnam

Gross national product increased at a 9.1 percent rate annually during the Korean conflict versus an average 8.1 percent annual rate through the last four years of Vietnam. Personal income grew at almost identical rates of 8.6 percent per year and 8.7 percent per year, respectively, during the two periods. Corporate profits before taxes increased rapidly after hostilities commenced in Korea, quickly reached a peak, and then declined. They remained at a lower level, probably reflecting the imposition of price and wage controls.

Plant and equipment expenditures rose at a rate of 11.7 percent per year under the influence of Korea, and 8.0 percent per

year during the last four years of Vietnam. Outlays had increased substantially in 1964 and 1965 as a result of the 7 percent investment tax credit and the accelerated depreciation schedule.

Consumer prices increased more under the influence of Vietnam than under the impact of Korea. The reverse is true of the wholesale price index. The GNP implicit price deflator increased about the same in both periods. The industrial production index increased more under the impact of Korea, accounting for the higher rate of growth in GNP during that period.

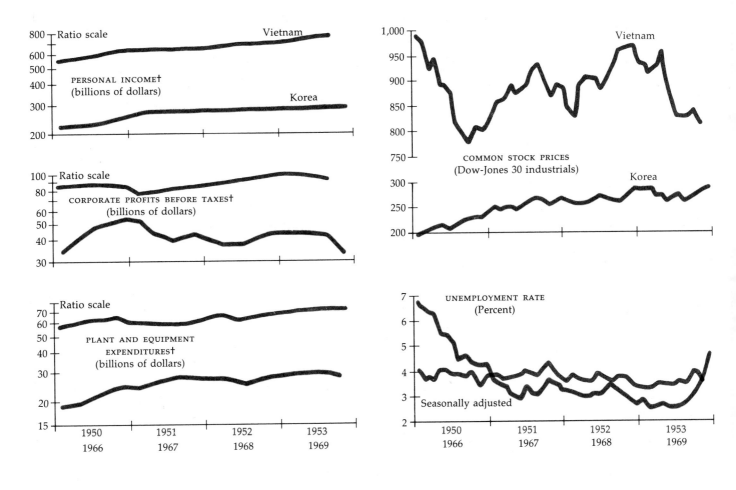

† Seasonally adjusted, annual rate.

SOURCE: The Conference Board Inc.

C. What is Inflation? Fiscal Versus Monetary Views and Policies

The following case is adapted from a study by the Federal Reserve Bank of St. Louis, "Inflation Continues," *Review*, August 1969. The accompanying charts should be studied carefully.

Inflation is a rise in the general level of prices, or stated differently, a decline in the overall purchasing power of the dollar. Inflation does not necessarily involve an increase in the price of every good or even of every group of goods. Increases and decreases in prices of particular goods or services, which reflect changes in supplies or demands, are essential for the smooth operation of an efficient economy. Rising prices in one sector may be accompanied by declining prices elsewhere, and the changes in relative prices give incentive for transferring resources to areas where demands are greatest. Frequently used measures of inflation include the Consumer Price Index and the Wholesale Price Index.

THE FISCAL VIEW

Some observers ascribe the inflation of 1965–70 chiefly to the course of federal spending and taxation. One analytical measure of the thrust of fiscal actions is an estimate of the national income accounts budget which would prevail at a constant rate of resource use, the so-called "high-employment" budget. By eliminating the effect of changing levels of economic activity on Government receipts and expenditures, the high-employment budget is believed to indicate the impact of changes in tax laws and in legal provisions for expenditures. A surplus of receipts over expenditures is presumed to be indicative of Governmental restraint on total spending, and, conversely, greater expenditures than receipts imply Governmental stimulus to total spending.

The high-employment budget surplus declined from an annual rate of $12 billion in 1960–63 to about balance in the last half of 1965, as taxes were reduced and Government spending rose rapidly. The high-employment budget then moved to a deficit of more than a $12 billion annual rate from early 1967 to mid-1968.

Government expenditures taken alone are another possible indicator of the fiscal impact on the economy, and have been used to explain the recent inflation. The expansion of the Vietnam conflict, together with rapid growth of non-defense expenditures, resulted in rapid acceleration of total Government outlays. Federal expenditures rose at a 15 percent annual rate from mid-1965 to mid-1968, after rising at a 6 percent rate from 1957 to 1965.

Fiscal views of the cause of inflation imply that if these expansionary developments had not taken place, the excessive growth of total spending might have been avoided, or at least limited. These views were the basis for the long-debated proposals for a tax increase and/or Government expenditures restraint, which culminated in the 10 percent surtax in mid-1968 and some cuts in proposed spending. Passage of the tax bill resulted in moving the high-employment budget to a surplus of about an $8 billion seasonally adjusted annual rate in the first half of 1969. Government expenditure growth also slowed. Expenditures increased 6 percent in the last twelve months, after growing at the 15 percent rate in the preceding three years.

THE MONETARY VIEW

Monetary developments provide an alternative or supplementary explanation of changes in total spending and of inflation. While specialists differ on how to measure monetary actions, we may roughly distinguish two main current views on how monetary developments are measured: money market conditions and monetary aggregates.

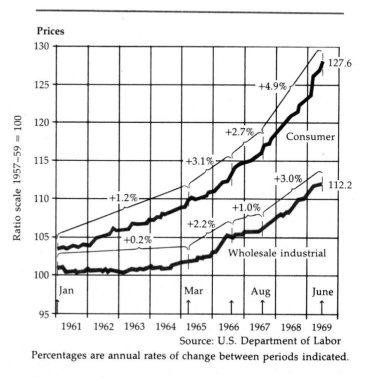

Source: U.S. Department of Labor
Percentages are annual rates of change between periods indicated.

General Price Index*

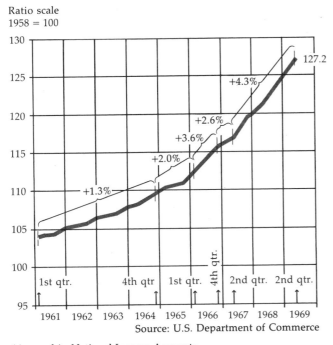

Ratio scale
1958 = 100

Source: U.S. Department of Commerce

*As used in National Income Accounts
Percentages are annual rates of change between periods indicated.

Demand and Production

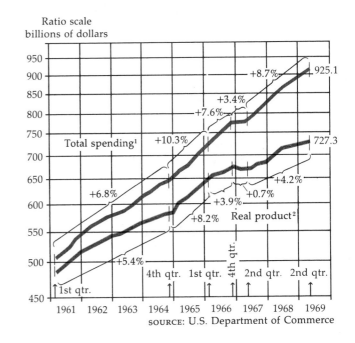

Ratio scale
billions of dollars

SOURCE: U.S. Department of Commerce

[1]GNP in current dollars.   [2]GNP in 1958 dollars.
Percentages are annual rates of change between periods indicated.

Money Stock

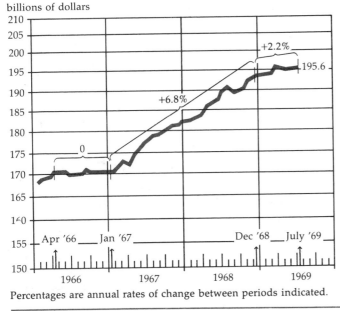

Ratio scale
billions of dollars

Percentages are annual rates of change between periods indicated.

Federal Budget Influence*

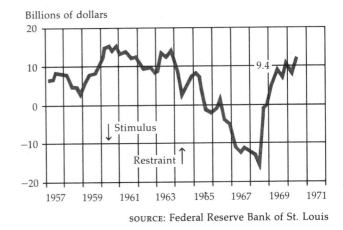

Billions of dollars

SOURCE: Federal Reserve Bank of St. Louis

*The High-Employment Budget, first published by the Council
of Economic Advisers.

Interest Rates

Ratio scale
of yields

SOURCE: Board of Governors of the Federal Reserve System

The course of the money stock, the most frequently used monetary aggregate, may be viewed as explaining in large measure the general course of total spending. The acceleration of money growth from the 1953–61 average annual rate of 1.4 percent to a 3 percent rate from 1961 to early 1965 was accompanied by recovery and expansion in the early Sixties. From the spring of 1965 to the spring of 1966 money rose 6 percent, and both spending and inflationary pressures accelerated. The nine-month pause of monetary growth in 1966 was followed by a deceleration of spending growth in early 1967. Resumption of rapid growth of money in early 1967 appears to be related to the acceleration of total spending growth and of inflation since mid-1967.

Many analysts feel that money market conditions, measured possibly by interest rates, are a more reliable indicator of the monetary authorities' impact on the economy. According to this view, monetary restraint is indicated by high or rising interest rates, and expansive policy is denoted by low or declining interest rates. However, the record offers little evidence of the reliability of interest rates as an indicator of monetary influences. Interest rates

are determined, as are other prices, by demand and supply. The Federal Reserve can influence the price charged and paid for loan funds in the short run by influencing the supply of credit, but it can do little, if anything, to influence the demand for credit within a short period. On the other hand, in the longer run the monetary authority affects interest rates importantly by its influence on the demand for credit.

QUESTIONS

1. How effectively did fiscal action during the 1960s influence total spending? Explain in detail.

2. Did the high interest rates of 1968 indicate restrictive monetary actions? How did these high interest rates come about? Did the supply of money appear to have an influence on inflationary pressures? Explain in detail.

3. What are the implications of a third view of inflation, such as "cost-push" or "demand-pull"? Would government price and wage controls be desirable to curb such inflations? Discuss.

D. Projecting Long-Term Economic Growth*

Total output of goods and services at any given time is determined by how many people are employed and how efficiently they work. Consequently, when economists project growth trends for the economy, their analysis usually proceeds within a framework of employment and productivity variables. How big will the labor force be, given indicated changes in the population and in rates of participation in the work force? How will changes in investment in plant and equipment and in the length of the work week affect output per worker? Those are the crucial issues the forecaster wrestles with. The following comments, and the accompanying chart, summarize what has been happening to the rate of growth in the key variables since 1948 and what is reasonable to expect in the 1970s.

LABOR FORCE

Trends in the work force are based on estimates of the actual labor force in 1948 and 1960, together with projec-

* Courtesy Morgan Guaranty Trust Company.

Factors in Potential Growth

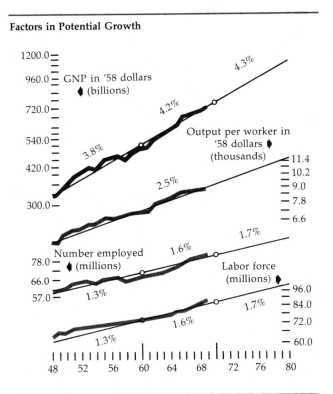

to continue its steady uptrend. If marriage and fertility rates continue at their present comparatively low levels, the participation rate for women will probably exceed the BLS projection. That distinct possibility suggests that 1.7 percent annually is a conservative assumption for labor-force growth in the 1970s.

EMPLOYMENT

The growth rates for employment, as depicted in the chart, are precisely the same as those for the labor force. This is simply the mechanical result of assuming a 4 percent unemployment rate as "normal." This, of course, is considerably less unemployment than the 4.7 percent actual average of the past twenty years, but the lower reading can be defended as a more realistic assumption in view of the increased political significance of the unemployment rate and the structural changes which have been, and are, taking place within U.S. society.

It is debatable whether, or to what degree, the growth rate of potential GNP is affected by different unemployment levels. It can be argued that a shortage of labor encourages research and capital investment and, thereby, increases the potential growth of output per worker. Since the projected trend of output per worker (discussed below) is based on the experience during the period 1948 to 1968 when the unemployment rate averaged 4.7 percent, it perhaps understates the growth rate in output per worker that could result from a lower level of unemployment during the next decade.

PRODUCTIVITY

The growth rate of output per worker, as shown in the chart, is held constant at 2.5 percent throughout the entire period 1948–80. Such a projection assumes that underlying trends of the past will continue, or that changes in trends will be offsetting. As an example, one trend that has put a drag on gains in output per worker as conventionally measured is the rapid rise (3.9 percent annual rate) in government employment since 1948. Real output per government worker is regarded, for purposes of national income accounting, as constant—that is, no allowance is made for any increase in productivity. The effect of this accounting treatment has been to reduce growth rates in per-worker output from 2.9 percent for the private sector alone to 2.5 percent for the total economy including government employment. Two other trends that have slowed growth in worker output—and which will act in the same fashion in the seventies—are the decline in average hours worked (0.5 percent per year since 1948 for the private sector) and the shift of demand away from the goods producing sec-

tions by the Bureau of Labor Statistics for the decade of the 1970s. A faster rate of labor-force growth in the seventies is expected to account for the faster rise in GNP. Between 1948–65, the labor-force growth held to a fairly constant 1.3 percent annual rate. It then accelerated markedly in the second half of the 1960s, reflecting the coming of age of the large number of babies born in the years immediately after World War II. Demographic factors point to continuing rapid growth in the 1970s—at a pace of 1.7 percent annually. This, if realized, will be slightly higher than the indicated growth rate of 1.6 percent for the decade now ending.

Certain assumptions need to be made in forecasting the probable labor-force participation of various population subgroups. The number of adults available for work can be forecast with great accuracy for the seventies. More difficult to project is the number who will actually choose to work. Nearly all adult men are in the labor force, but participation rates for women and young people are relatively much more volatile. The BLS has assumed that increases in high school and college enrollment will reduce the participation rate of those in the 16–24 age bracket. On the other hand, the participation rate for women is expected

tors and toward service sectors where productivity gains tend to be smaller.

Operating to increase the productivity gains of the private sector has been the movement of farm labor into nonagricultural pursuits. Since 1948, total farm employment has been cut in half. This shift of workers from the farm to the nonfarm sector was responsible for raising the annual growth rate of output per worker in the 1948–68 period from 2.6 percent for the nonfarm sector alone to 2.9 percent for the total private sector, including agriculture.

TOTAL OUTPUT

Taken together, a faster growing work force than in the sixties and a continuation of past gains in output per worker are expected to yield a growth rate in GNP of 4.3 percent a year in the 1970s, up from the estimated 4.2 percent rate of increase in potential output during the 1960s.

Such extrapolations, of course, could overstate—or understate—actual performance in the seventies. The growth rate in the future could well be, say, three tenths of a percentage point higher or lower, and the effect would not be inconsequential. The difference between a 4 percent rate of real growth and a 4.6 percent rate would equal $86 billion of output per year in 1980 at 1969's prices.

QUESTIONS

1. This is a typical long-term projection of GNP that economists often prepare. What are some of the key assumptions underlying this kind of growth model?

2. In general, what are some of the important limitations of this type of growth projection?

D–1. Projection for Disaster: Doomsyear 2075 ± 25.

When Thomas R. Malthus, the early nineteenth century economist, predicted eventual disaster because population would outrun the food supply, many people branded him a crackpot. More than a hundred years elapsed before the Malthusian specter was widely recognized as a grim reality in many parts of the world. And even then, it took several decades before some nations began to do anything about it.

Now, however, the deadline for making the necessary corrections is almost upon us—according to Dennis L. Meadows and his 16-member team of computer scientists at M.I.T.'s Sloan School of Industrial Management. In a recent book entitled *The Limits to Growth* (New York, Universe Books, 1972), the Meadows group uses "systems dynamics" to construct a computer model that simulates the conflict between economic growth and human survival. Their conclusion is that further progress must take man over the edge of the abyss and result in the end of civilization sometime during the last half of the next century.

The new study, which has aroused worldwide interest, rests on two basic propositions:

1. Five controlling variables—population, food production, industrialization, pollution, and consumption of nonrenewable natural resources—determine the course of economic growth. These variables are all interconnected; in the language of servomechanics, they interact on one another through "feedback loops."

2. The annual increase of the five controlling variables follows a pattern that mathematicians call exponential growth. This means they expand at an accelerating rate, sometimes even geometrically, thereby doubling within certain time intervals.

The M.I.T. researchers show that under different sets of assumptions, interactions among the five controlling variables trace out different growth paths; however, they always lead to the same end result: the eventual collapse of civilization around the year 2075, give or take as much as 25 years.

For example, what would happen if worldwide birth control measures were introduced? A lowered birth rate would effectively increase per capita food production and capital investment. According to the computer model, population would then expand to take advantage of the larger food supply, while increased industrialization would accelerate the pollution crisis. Even a cut in the birth rate by as much as one-third (which is highly improbable) would, according to the M.I.T. team, delay the impending disaster by only 20 years at best.

Similar dire results are projected when other conditions of the model are allowed to vary. For instance, if new natural resources are developed, capital investment and industrialization will be encouraged; this will stimulate population growth—and eventual collapse from pollution.

Alternatively, if pollution levels are reduced, population will grow and will absorb land that would otherwise be available for agriculture; hence if pollution doesn't put an end to civilization, starvation will.

And so it goes, with each possible scenario leading to eventual disaster as typified by Chart 1 showing what would happen if present trends continue. Chart 2, on the other hand, illustrates a stabilized world model approaching a "steady state" or "equilibrium" condition. This is possible, according to the M.I.T. team, *only* if: (1) average family size is limited to two children by 1975; (2) capital investment is limited to replacing worn-out equipment; and (3) technological innovations such as recycling and the development of longer-lasting machinery succeed in retarding the rate of resource depletion.

QUESTIONS

1. The solution to the problem, according to the M.I.T. group, is to achieve world equilibrium. Is this possible without a great deal of inequality?

2. A hundred years ago, a model such as this would quite literally have concluded that the cities of today would be asphyxiated beneath mountains of horse manure. (*a*) Why has this not happened? (*b*) What does your answer suggest about the shortcomings of the model?

3. Do you see any subtle assumptions in this model that are similar to the Malthusian model? Explain.

4. The M.I.T. model omits prices of resources. Of what significance is this?

Chart 1

Chart 2

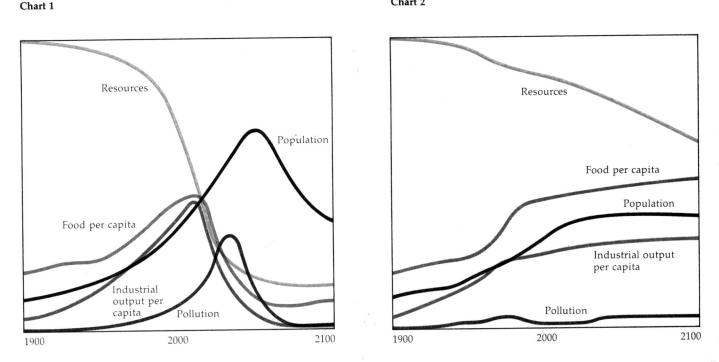

SOURCE: Potomac Associates.

PART 5

Using Supply and Demand. The Laws of Production and Cost

CHAPTER 20

Working with Supply, Demand, and Elasticity: Some Interesting Applications

CHAPTER PREVIEW

To what extent do changes in the price of a good affect changes in the quantities demanded or supplied? Can these changes be measured, compared, and interpreted?

The government has influenced market prices and quantities of certain commodities by imposing price controls, price supports, commodity taxes, and subsidies. How can supply and demand models analyze the effects of these actions?

What are some of the assumptions that underlie the use of supply and demand models?

How does the price system of a market economy "filter" out buyers and sellers in the marketplace?

Asked to defend the distinction between pure and applied science, the nineteenth-century French scientist Louis Pasteur replied, "No, a thousand times no; there does not exist a category of science to which one can give the name applied science. There are science and the applications of science, bound together as the fruit to the tree which bears it."

Supply and demand can be viewed in much the same way. You are already familiar with the "pure" side of the subject from an earlier chapter, and can brush up on the basic concepts very quickly by studying the brief review in Exhibit 1. In this chapter we explore the "applied" aspects of supply and demand by solving some interesting problems. When you complete this chapter you will probably agree with Pasteur that the principles and applications of supply and demand, like those of any science, are indeed "bound together as the fruit to the tree."

The Concept of Elasticity—A Measure of Responsiveness to Changes in Price

You already know from Exhibit 1 that the relationship between the price and quantity of a good is causal. For instance, a rise in price will cause a de-

Exhibit 1

Brief Review of Supply and Demand

(a) The law of demand *states that the quantity demanded of a good varies inversely with its price. This means that people will buy more of a good at a lower price than at a higher price.*

(b) The law of supply *states that the quantity supplied of a good usually varies directly with its price. Thus sellers are willing to supply larger quantities at higher prices than at lower prices.*

(c) When demand and supply curves are graphed on the same

coordinate axes, *their intersection determines the* equilibrium *market price and quantity. Any price above this equilibrium level results in the quantity supplied exceeding the quantity demanded, thereby driving the price down; any price below the equilibrium level results in the quantity demanded exceeding the quantity supplied, thereby driving the price up. At the equilibrium level there are no product surpluses or shortages; the market is precisely cleared.*

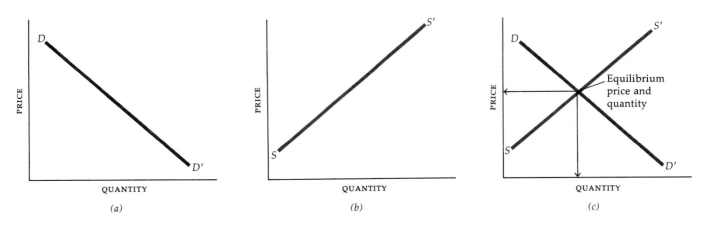

(a)   *(b)*   *(c)*

(d) and (e) A change in demand *or a* change in supply *is represented by a shift of the given curve to a new position. Such shifts may occur as a result of changes in any of the factors that are assumed to remain constant when the curves are drawn. In the case of demand these factors include buyer tastes, expectations, incomes, the prices of related goods, and the num-*

ber of buyers in the market. In the case of supply they are technology, resource costs, sellers' expectations, the prices of other goods, and the number of sellers in the market. Changes or shifts in demand or supply may bring about new equilibrium prices and quantities.

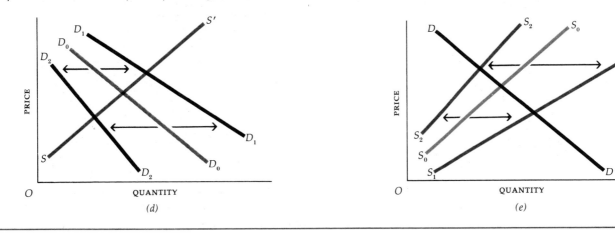

(d)   *(e)*

Exhibit 1 (continued)

(f) and (g) *If the demand curve remains fixed, a movement along the curve from one point to another denotes a change in the quantity demanded;* likewise, if the supply curve remains

fixed, a movement along the curve denotes a change in the quantity supplied. *Such changes are always associated with changes in price.*

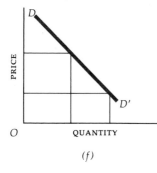

(f)

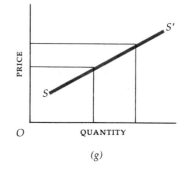

(g)

crease in the quantity demanded and an increase in the quantity supplied. A fall in price will produce the opposite effects—an increase in the quantity demanded and a decrease in the quantity supplied.

But by *how much* will a change in price affect the quantities supplied or demanded? There is a big difference, for example, between a commodity like salt for which the quantity demanded varies relatively little with changes in price, and a commodity like around-the-world vacation trips for which changes in price may cause relatively large changes in the quantity demanded.

How can we measure these changes? One way is to use a concept called "elasticity":

1. *Elasticity* is the percentage change in quantity (demanded or supplied) resulting from a 1 percent change in price. (This is an interpretative definition; you can use it to understand and explain the meaning of elasticity.)

2. *Elasticity* is the ratio of the percentage change in quantity (demanded or supplied) to the percentage change in price:

$$\text{Elasticity} = \frac{\text{percentage change in quantity}}{\text{percentage change in price}}$$

(This is a mathematical definition; you can use it to calculate elasticities of demand or supply as illustrated later.)

Since the law of supply expresses a *direct* relationship between price and quantity supplied, the coefficient you get when you calculate supply elasticity will be positive. On the other hand, since the law of demand expresses an *inverse* relationship between price and quantity demanded, the coefficient of demand elasticity will be negative. In practice, however, we often disregard the negative sign and express all elasticities as if they were either positive or zero, as you will see shortly.

TEST YOURSELF

1. If you calculate the elasticity of supply for a given commodity as 2.8, this means that a 1 percent increase in the price of the product will result in a 2.8 percent increase in the quantity supplied. (*a*) What would a 1 percent decrease in the price mean? (*b*) A 10 percent increase in the price? (*c*) A 10 percent decrease in the price?

2. If you estimate the elasticity of demand for a product as −0.5, this means that a 1 percent increase in the price of the commodity will result in a 0.5 of 1 percent *decrease* in the quantity demanded. (*a*) What would a 1 percent decrease in the price mean? (*b*) A 10 percent increase in the price? (*c*) A 10 percent decrease in the price?

3. Instead of measuring elasticity in terms of relative amounts or percentages, why not measure it in terms of actual amounts instead? For example, suppose you wanted to know which has the greater influence on quantity demanded—a $100 per carat reduction in the price of diamonds, or a $1 per bushel reduction in the price of wheat:

a. Would you express the price and quantity changes in terms of actual amounts or in terms of percentages?

b. If you chose to express the changes in terms of actual amounts, would you be able to compare carats and bushels in order to tell which was more affected by the changes in price?

VISUALIZING ELASTICITIES FROM GRAPHS

Since elasticity measures the responsiveness of changes in quantity to changes in price, it is helpful to distinguish among the different degrees of responsiveness. This is done in Exhibit 2, where five types of elasticity are defined and illustrated. Study these diagrams and definitions carefully, and notice from the statement near the top of the exhibit that the elasticity coefficients are expressed *numerically* without regard to algebraic sign. As mentioned above, this practice is common in economic discussions.

Here is an easy way to remember the charts in Exhibit 2: Think of them as the frames of a motion picture. The first "frames" start off with their curves in horizontal positions; in successive frames the demand curve gradually tilts downward while the supply curve tilts upward until both curves end up in a vertical position.

Do the five different definitions of elasticity in Exhibit 2 sound intuitively reasonable? They should.

After all, elasticity is nothing more than the "stretch" in quantity compared to the "stretch" in price, with both stretches measured in percentages.

MEASURING ELASTICITY

A hypothetical demand curve is shown in Exhibit 3. Our objective is to estimate the elasticity of demand for this curve. We may choose two points near the ends of the line, such as the points A and B because they are conveniently located on at least one of the grids, and calculate the elasticity for the segment AB.

How does the change in quantity demanded compare with the change in price over this segment? Disregarding for the time being the calculations shown beneath the chart, we observe from the chart alone that a movement along the curve from A to B is measured by two changes: an increase in quantity from 20 bushels to 80 bushels, and a corresponding decrease in price from about $52 to $17. A change or increase in quantity of 60 bushels is thus associated with an opposite change or decrease in price of $35. The change in quantity per unit change in price, therefore, is $60/-35 = -1.72$, or simply 1.72 if the sign is disregarded.

Is this the elasticity of demand? *The answer is no,* because the result is obviously affected by the units in which the quantities and prices are measured. The solution would have been different, for example, if quantities had been expressed in millions of bushels or if prices had been expressed in British pounds or in French francs. Since a chief purpose of calculating elasticity is to permit relative comparisons to be made between products, we need a measure of elasticity that is unaffected by the units in which the data are quoted—that is, we need a *coefficient of elasticity.*

The Coefficient of Elasticity

You will recall from the definition of elasticity that its measurement is simply the percentage change in quantity divided by the percentage change in price. The most common method of measuring these percentage changes is to divide the observed change in quantity by the average of the two quantities, and

Exhibit 2

Five Different Kinds of Elasticity

E = *numerical* elasticity (i.e., algebraic signs are disregarded). The symbol < means "less than"; the symbol > means "greater than."

Case (*a*): Perfectly elastic. *An infinitesimally small percentage change in price results in an infinitely large percentage change in the quantity demanded or supplied. The numerical elasticity is infinite. Thus a change in price from OP_1 to OP_2 produces a change in quantity demanded or supplied from zero to a positive amount. In terms of percentages, this is an infinite change.*

Case (*b*): Relatively elastic. *A given percentage change in price results in a larger percentage change in quantity. The numerical elasticity is greater than unity. For example, a change in price from OP_1 to OP_2 causes a more than proportionate change in quantity from OQ_1 to OQ_2.*

Case (*c*): Unit elastic. *A given percentage change in price results in an equal percentage change in quantity. The numer-*

ical elasticity is unity. Thus a change in price from OP_1 to OP_2 causes an equal proportionate change in quantity from OQ_1 to OQ_2.

Case (*d*): Relatively inelastic. *A given percentage change in price results in a smaller percentage change in quantity. The numerical elasticity is less than unity (but greater than zero). For example, a change in price from OP_1 to OP_2 causes a less than proportionate change in quantity from OQ_1 to OQ_2.*

Case (*e*): Perfectly inelastic. *A given percentage change in price results in no change in quantity. The numerical elasticity is zero. Thus a change in price from OP_1 to OP_2 causes a zero change in quantity.*

REMARK. The slope of a curve at any point is its steepness (or flatness) at that point. A straight line has the same slope at every point, but not necessarily the same elasticity. Therefore *you cannot always infer the elasticity of a curve from its slope alone.* These charts are designed to help you visualize the five different kinds of elasticity.

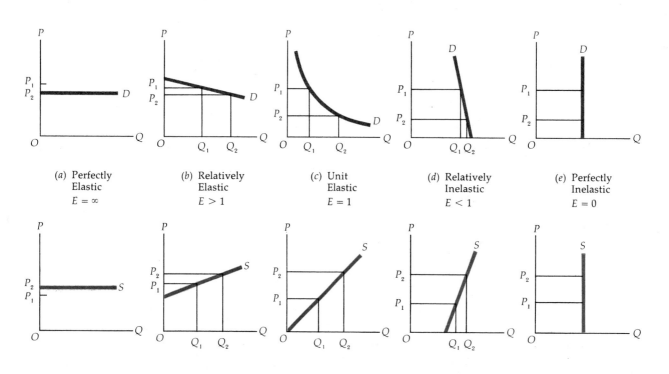

(*a*) Perfectly Elastic $E = \infty$	(*b*) Relatively Elastic $E > 1$	(*c*) Unit Elastic $E = 1$	(*d*) Relatively Inelastic $E < 1$	(*e*) Perfectly Inelastic $E = 0$

the observed change in price by the average of the two prices. This enables us to express the definition by the formula:

$$\text{Elasticity} = \frac{\text{percentage change in quantity}}{\text{percentage change in price}} = \frac{\dfrac{\text{change in quantity}}{\text{average quantity}}}{\dfrac{\text{change in price}}{\text{average price}}}$$

You can use this formula to calculate the elasticity of demand in Exhibit 3. In doing so, however, it is convenient to substitute the letters P for price and Q for quantity in the formula, and to attach subscripts to the letters so that you do not mix up your P's and Q's. Thus let:

Q_1 = old quantity, or quantity before change
Q_2 = new quantity, or quantity after change
P_1 = old price, or price before change
P_2 = new price, or price after change

The formula for elasticity of demand E_d is then

$$E_d = \frac{\dfrac{Q_2 - Q_1}{(Q_2 + Q_1)/2}}{\dfrac{P_2 - P_1}{(P_2 + P_1)/2}} = \frac{\dfrac{Q_2 - Q_1}{Q_2 + Q_1}}{\dfrac{P_2 - P_1}{P_2 + P_1}}$$

Notice from the middle part of the equation that the average quantity is the sum of the two quantities divided by 2, and the average price is the sum of the two prices divided by 2. These 2s then cancel out, leaving the complex fraction at the end.

An application of this formula is illustrated beneath the chart in Exhibit 3. Observe that the same result is obtained regardless of whether the change is from A to B or from B to A. This is an important advantage, since many practical situations arise in which we know only two prices and two quantities, and we wish to find the elasticity of demand.

EXAMPLE. The Savemore Paint Company sold an average of 300 gallons of paint per week at $5 per gallon, and 500 gallons of paint per week at $4 per gallon. What is the elasticity of demand?

The answer is −2.25, or 2.25 numerically, regardless of the values you choose for your initial price and quantity. Work it out both ways and see for yourself. How do you interpret this answer? What would you expect the percentage change in quantity to be if the price changed by 10 percent? (HINT: Refer back to Exhibit 3.)

Exhibit 3

Estimating the Elasticity of Demand for the Segment AB

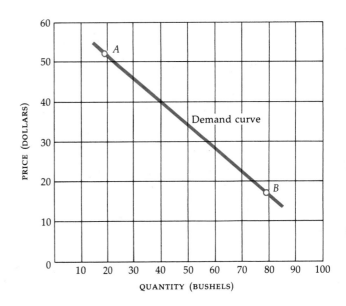

Change from A to B:
At A: $Q_1 = 20$, $P_1 = 52$
At B: $Q_2 = 80$, $P_2 = 17$

$$E_d = \frac{\dfrac{(Q_2 - Q_1)}{(Q_2 + Q_1)}}{\dfrac{(P_2 - P_1)}{(P_2 + P_1)}} = \frac{\dfrac{(80 - 20)}{(80 + 20)}}{\dfrac{(17 - 52)}{(17 + 52)}} = \frac{0.60}{-0.51} = -1.2, \text{ or } 1.2 \text{ numerically}$$

Change from B to A:
At B: $Q_1 = 80$, $P_1 = 17$
At A: $Q_2 = 20$, $P_2 = 52$

$$E_d = \frac{\dfrac{(Q_2 - Q_1)}{(Q_2 + Q_1)}}{\dfrac{(P_2 - P_1)}{(P_2 + P_1)}} = \frac{\dfrac{(20 - 80)}{(20 + 80)}}{\dfrac{(52 - 17)}{(52 + 17)}} = \frac{-0.60}{0.51} = -1.2, \text{ or } 1.2 \text{ numerically}$$

INTERPRETATION. A 1 percent change in price results in a 1.2 percent change in quantity demanded. (Similarly, a 10 percent change in price results in a 12 percent change in quantity demanded.) Demand is thus relatively elastic, since the change in quantity demanded is more than proportional to the change in price.

What about elasticity of supply E_s? Do we measure it in the same way? The answer is yes, and the formula is exactly the same, except that Q_1 and Q_2 stand for the quantities supplied before and after the change, and P_1 and P_2 are the corresponding prices.

ELASTICITY OF DEMAND AND TOTAL REVENUE

In many practical situations involving the study of demand, it is convenient to have a simple guide for judging whether demand is elastic or inelastic. An easy method that can be used for this purpose is to compare the change in the price of the commodity with the corresponding change in the seller's gross receipts or, as it is customarily called in economics, his total revenue. It is important to keep in mind that a seller's total revenue (abbreviated TR) is equal to his price (P) per unit times the quantity (Q) of units that he sells; that is: $TR = P \times Q$. Thus if a shirt manufacturer charges $6 per shirt and sells 50 shirts, his total revenue is $300.

A convenient visual illustration of the connection between demand elasticity and total revenue is presented in Exhibit 4. These charts are similar to three of the five types of demand elasticities described in Exhibit 2. We shall examine each separately.

Relatively Elastic Demand

Exhibit 4a illustrates a relatively elastic demand curve. If the price is assumed to be OP, the corresponding quantity demanded is OM and the seller's total revenue is simply price times quantity or $OP \times OM$. But this is also the area of the rectangle

---

Exhibit 4

Demand Elasticity and Total Revenue

A seller's total revenue is equal to his price per unit multiplied by the number of units that he sells, and therefore can be measured by the rectangular area under the demand curve. Thus at a price of OP, quantity demanded is OM, and total revenue is the area of the rectangle OPSM. At a price of OT, quantity demanded is ON, and total revenue is the area of the rectangle OTVN. Hence we see that:
Case (a): Relatively elastic. When demand is relatively elastic,
a decrease in price results in an increase in total revenue, and an increase in price results in a decrease in total revenue.
Case (b): Unit elastic. When demand is unit elastic, a decrease or increase in price results in the same total revenue.
Case (c): Relatively inelastic. When demand is relatively inelastic, a decrease in price results in a decrease in total revenue, and an increase in price results in an increase in total revenue.

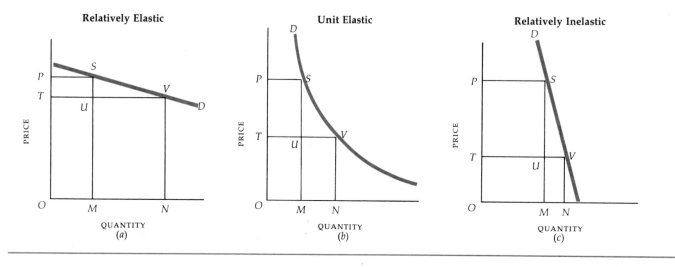

OPSM, since the area of *any* rectangle is the product of its base and height.

Suppose the seller lowers his price to *OT.* The quantity demanded then increases to *ON,* and the seller's new total revenue is again equal to price times quantity or the area of the rectangle *OTVN.* This new rectangle is larger in area than the old one; that is, as a result of a price reduction the seller has lost a relatively small amount of total revenue represented by the rectangle *TPSU,* but has gained a larger amount of total revenue represented by the rectangle *MUVN.* Since the gain more than offsets the loss, the seller's final total revenue is larger after the price reduction than before.

What happens if price increases, say from *OT* to *OP?* The result is exactly the opposite: total revenue declines from *OTVN* to *OPSM.* In other words, the large loss more than offsets the small gain.

This relationship between changes in price and changes in total revenue can be readily explained in terms of elasticity. When demand is relatively elastic, a given percentage decrease in price is more than offset by a corresponding percentage increase in quantity demanded, so total revenue rises; conversely, a given percentage increase in price is more than offset by a corresponding percentage decrease in quantity demanded, so total revenue falls.

Unit Elastic Demand

A second type of situation occurs in Exhibit 4*b,* where demand is unit elastic. At a price of *OP* the quantity demanded is *OM;* hence the seller's total revenue is the area of the rectangle *OPSM.* On the other hand, at a price of *OT* the quantity demanded is *ON;* therefore the seller's total revenue is the area of the rectangle *OTVN.* In both these cases—and in any others involving a unit elastic demand curve—the rectangular areas associated with each corresponding price and quantity are always equal. This means that a given percentage decrease (or increase) in price is exactly offset by an equal percentage increase (or decrease) in quantity demanded, so that the total revenues remain the same. These principles help to explain why a unit elastic demand curve has such a special shape. It is the only type of mathematical

curve (called a "rectangular hyperbola") that permits percentage changes in price to be exactly offset by equal percentage changes in quantity demanded so that the elasticity remains equal to 1 and hence the total revenue stays constant.

Relatively Inelastic Demand

What happens in the case of a relatively inelastic demand, as in Exhibit 4*c?* The relationships are obvious. When price is reduced from *OP* to *OT,* total revenue decreases from *OPSM* to *OTVN.* Clearly, the percentage decrease in price more than offsets the percentage increase in quantity demanded, causing total revenue to fall. The converse situation occurs in the case of a price increase, say from *OT* to *OP.* Total revenue rises because the percentage increase in price more than offsets the percentage decrease in quantity demanded.

The foregoing ideas are helpful for analyzing and predicting the effects of price changes on sellers' total revenues. We shall encounter many practical situations in later chapters where such predictions are a useful guide to policy formulation. A brief summary of these basic concepts is appropriate.

The relationship between price and total revenue depends on whether the elasticity of demand is greater than, equal to, or less than unity. Thus:

1. If demand is relatively elastic, a change in price causes a change in total revenue in the *opposite* direction.

2. If demand is unit elastic, a change in price causes *no* change in total revenue.

3. If demand is relatively inelastic, a change in price causes a change in total revenue in the *same* direction.

How well do you understand these basic ideas? You can judge for yourself by answering the following practical questions.

FOR CLASS DISCUSSION

1. Various public transit systems have often raised their rates to offset increased costs. Many of these systems found that their gross incomes declined in

the first few weeks or months after the rate increase, and then rose. What does this suggest about the elasticity of demand for their services?

2. When Britain devalued the pound in 1967 (i.e., made its currency cheaper for foreigners to buy), it soon experienced both:

a. A relatively modest increase in exports of Scotch whisky

b. A relatively large influx of American tourists

How would you interpret these occurrences?

3. If your college football stadium is drawing less than capacity crowds, under what conditions might a price increase be desirable? A price decrease? No change in price?

WHAT DETERMINES ELASTICITY?

Once you learn how to calculate elasticity, you have mastered only half the job; the other half is to understand the factors that determine elasticity so that this important concept can be put to use. For example, what makes some demand or supply curves elastic and others inelastic? The answers involve three key words—"substitutes," "inexpensiveness," and "time."

1. The most important determinant of both demand and supply elasticity is the number and closeness of available *substitutes.*

This means that the elasticity of demand for a product depends on the ease of substitution in consumption. If a commodity has good substitutes, and if the prices of these substitutes remain the same, a rise in the price of the commodity will divert consumer expenditures away from the product and over to the substitutes. A fall in the commodity's price will swing consumer expenditures away from the substitutes and back to the product. The demand therefore tends to be elastic. On the other hand, if a commodity has poor substitutes, consumers will not respond significantly to changes in its price and hence the demand for the product will tend to be inelastic.

The elasticity of supply depends on the ease of substitution in production. For example, suppose

the resources used in the production of a certain commodity can easily be supplemented by resources employed in other occupations. If the price of the commodity rises relative to its costs of production, while the prices of other products remain the same, many resources will tend to shift out of the other occupations and into the production of the higher-priced and more profitable product, thereby significantly increasing its output. Conversely, a fall in the price of the product relative to its costs will cause many resources engaged in the production of the less profitable commodity to shift into other occupations, thus significantly decreasing its output. In both instances, supply tends to be elastic. On the other hand, if it is difficult for resources to enter or leave a particular occupation the supply curve will tend to be inelastic.

2. The more *inexpensive* a good—that is, the smaller the fraction of their total expenditures that consumers allocate for a good—the more inelastic in demand it is likely to be.

Thus the demand for such commodities as salt, matches, toothpicks, soft drinks, etc., tends to be relatively inelastic; each is such a relatively small part of consumers' total expenditures that changes in their prices result in less than proportional changes in the quantities demanded.

3. Elasticities of demand and supply for a given product tend to increase over *time*—that is, to be greater in the long run than in the short run—because buyers and sellers have more time to adjust to changes in price.

This principle is based on the assumption that the longer the time that elapses after a change in price, the easier it may become for buyers and sellers to use substitutes. Demands for specific products may therefore tend to become more elastic as buyers develop new tastes and habits of consumption. Supplies of specific products may tend to become more elastic as sellers find alternative resources for production of their outputs.

You may think of exceptions to one or more of these principles—as you can with almost any principle in the social sciences. But there is ample evidence to indicate that the principles work in most cases.

Models of Supply and Demand

After studying supply and demand we can apply its principles to the solution of practical problems. Many people do not enjoy learning about a subject unless they can see how it "works" in the world around them. Fortunately, supply and demand analysis lends itself to a wide variety of concrete applications. Some are illustrated here in the form of real-world models.

PRICE FIXING BY LAW

A government may interfere with the normal operation of supply and demand because it wants to establish a price that is either lower or higher than that which would rule in an unregulated market. For example, price ceilings were placed on many consumer goods during World War II to keep their prices from going "too" high; today price floors keep the hourly wages of many workers from going "too" low. What are some of the economic effects of these legally established prices?

Price Ceilings Cause Shortages

The nature of a price ceiling is illustrated by the normal supply and demand curves in Exhibit 5. The equilibrium price that would be established in the market if there were no outside interference would be OP (= NP'), and the equilibrium quantity would be ON.

What happens if the government regards the equilibrium price as too high, and hence establishes a ceiling price making it illegal to sell the product at a price above OH? The result will be a *shortage* equal to the amount RL, since this represents the excess of quantity demanded over quantity supplied at the ceiling price.

When this situation occurs, the limited supplies of the commodity OR will be snatched up by the early buyers, leaving nothing for later customers who want the remaining RL units of the product at the ceiling price. The government, therefore, may introduce *rationing* as an equitable method of restricting purchases. This happened during World War II, for

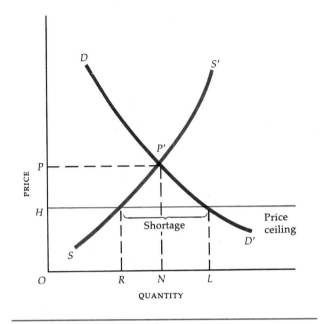

Exhibit 5

Price Ceilings Result in Product Shortages.

example, when there were shortages of such price-controlled items as sugar, butter, meat, and gasoline. The government distributed ration coupons to consumers permitting them to purchase limited quantities each week.

REMARK. The ration coupons were in the form of "points" which entitled consumers to purchase a wide variety of price-controlled commodities at "point prices." For example, a housewife buying hamburger might pay 25 cents per pound plus 3 points in ration coupons. The point prices were changed from time to time by the government in an attempt to minimize the imbalances between consumption and production. Thus the ration coupons became a supplementary form of money, and *the ration-coupon price rather than the dollar price performed the market function of adjusting consumption to available supplies!*

Price Floors Cause Surpluses

Price floors are the opposite of price ceilings; they are designed to prevent a price from falling below a specified level. Although price ceilings have typically but not exclusively been a wartime phenomenon in the United States (but not in some other countries), price floors play a continuing role in our daily lives. There are two types that are particularly common: agricultural price supports and minimum wage legislation.

In the general model of Exhibit 6 the equilibrium price and quantity that would emerge from an unregulated market are *OP* and *ON*, respectively. But now *OH* represents a government-imposed price floor. At this price the quantity supplied will exceed the quantity demanded, resulting in a surplus of the amount *RL*.

What can be done about this surplus? In agriculture, where surpluses have been a phenomenon for decades, the government has sought to cope with the situation in three major ways: (1) *restrict supply* by imposing acreage allotments on farmers, thereby limiting the amount of land they can use to grow certain agricultural commodities; (2) *stimulate demand* by encouraging research in order to find new uses for agricultural products; and (3) *buy up surpluses* of certain agricultural commodities and store them for future sale or disposal.

With respect to price floors, Exhibit 6 may be thought of as a model of the supply and demand for labor. The horizontal axis measures the quantity of labor in terms of hours of labor time; the vertical axis measures the price of labor in terms of wages per hour. The surplus is then the volume of unemployment *RL* occurring at the minimum wage level *OH*. Therefore, one way to reduce this labor surplus is to lower the hourly wage rate. What would this do to total payrolls if the demand for labor were relatively elastic? Relatively inelastic? Can you suggest other possible methods of reducing the unemployment surplus?

EFFECTS OF SPECIFIC TAXES AND SUBSIDIES

Supply and demand analysis can be helpful in solving problems involving certain kinds of commodity taxes and subsidies. Different degrees of elasticities affect in surprising ways the prices and quantities of some of the things we buy every day.

Exhibit 6

Price Floors Result in Product Surpluses.

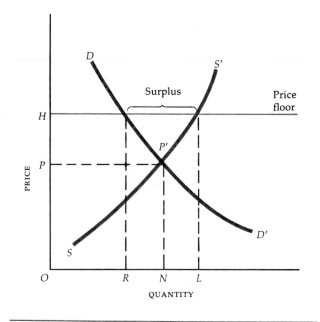

A Specific Tax

Suppose a *specific tax* is imposed on the sale of a commodity. That is, for each unit of a commodity sold a fixed amount of money must be paid to the government. A specific tax is thus a *per-unit* tax independent of the price of the product. Some of the taxes on cigarettes and gasoline are of this kind.

How does a specific tax on a product affect its market prices and quantities? Is the *incidence* or burden of such a tax borne by those upon whom the tax is initially imposed, or is it *shifted* to others? These are the practical questions which our analysis will answer.

We can proceed by examining the model in Exhibit 7a. The curves *DD'* and *SS'* are the market demand and supply curves before the tax is imposed. The equilibrium quantity is therefore *ON*; the equilibrium price is *NP*.

Exhibit 7

Effects of Specific Taxes and Subsidies

Taxes will affect the equilibrium prices and quantities of commodities, depending on the relative elasticities of demand and supply. Subsidies have the opposite effects of taxes, but their *influence is also determined by the relative elasticities of demand and supply.*

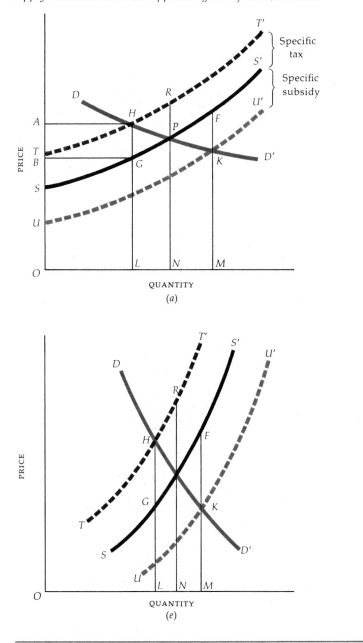

(a)

(e)

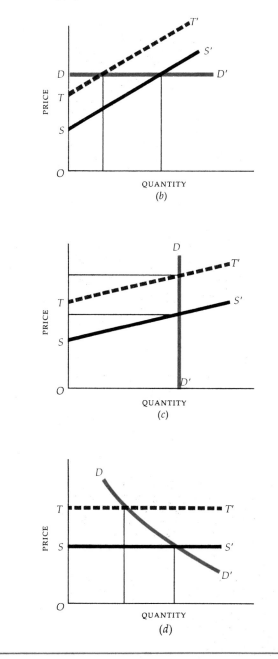

(b)

(c)

(d)

Suppose that sellers are required to pay a tax of ST per unit. The results of such a tax can be analyzed in two steps:

1. The supply curve shifts to the parallel position TT', showing that less will be supplied at any given price. This is because the tax is an added cost to the producer at all levels of output. Hence the *supply price*—the price necessary to call forth a given output—will be higher by the amount of the tax. For example, before the tax consumers paid a price of NP in order to obtain the quantity ON. After the tax they must pay a price of NR in order to call forth the same quantity ON. When the seller receives NR, he will pay a tax of $PR (= ST)$ to the government, leaving himself with a net price of NP.

2. The tax will therefore cause the equilibrium point to shift from P to H. This movement will be associated with a decrease in quantity from ON to OL and an increase in price from NP to LH, where GH is the amount of the tax.

Are there any general principles that can tell us the extent to which prices and quantities will be altered as a result of the tax? The next three charts in Exhibit 7 will help answer this question.

In Exhibit 7b, since demand is perfectly elastic, any increase in price will cause sales to drop to zero. Therefore the same price is maintained after the tax as before, but sellers compensate for the added cost of the tax by reducing their quantity. Consumers thus get fewer units of the good even though they continue to pay the same price per unit.

In Exhibit 7c the demand curve is perfectly inelastic. Therefore the entire burden of the tax is shifted forward from sellers to buyers in the form of a higher price, with no reduction in the equilibrium quantity.

In Exhibit 7d both price and quantity are affected as a result of a perfectly elastic supply curve: the burden of the tax is shifted entirely to buyers *and* the equilibrium quantity is reduced. Note how this compares with the case in Exhibit 7c, where only price is affected, and not quantity. What would have happened in 7d if the demand curve had been perfectly inelastic?

We can now establish two important principles:

1. The more *inelastic* the demand and the supply of a commodity the smaller will be the decline in output resulting from a given tax. This is illustrated in Exhibit 7e, where the letters have the same meaning as before.

2. The relative burden of a tax among buyers and sellers tends to follow the path of least resistance, being shifted in proportion to where the inelasticity is greatest.

The first principle leads to the conclusion that *if we want to minimize disruptions in production, industries whose commodities are inelastic in demand and supply are better suited to commodity taxation because they suffer smaller contractions in output and hence in employment.*

The second principle results in the conclusion that *in most supply and demand situations (except the extreme ones involving perfect elasticity or inelasticity) the tax will be shared by both consumers and producers according to the relative elasticities of demand and supply.* Thus the consumer's price will rise, but by less than the amount of the tax; the producer's net price will fall, but by less than the amount of the tax.

REMARK. Exhibit 7 does not demonstrate the effect of a tax in the case of a perfectly inelastic supply curve. Can you illustrate such a case and explain it? Be careful; this is a tricky question. (HINT: Since the supply curve is perfectly inelastic, can it shift as a result of the tax?) You will learn more about this problem in a later chapter when you encounter a concept known as the "single tax." In the meantime, see if you can deduce the answer yourself.

Subsidies

A *subsidy* is a payment a government makes to individuals or businesses so that they will continue to produce a product in larger quantities or at lower prices than they would otherwise. Federal subsidies are granted to agriculture, airlines, railroads, shipping and shipbuilding, and to certain other groups in the economy.

A *specific subsidy* is thus a per-unit bounty; it is the opposite of a specific tax—in fact, it can be thought of as a "negative" specific tax since the government is giving money to the seller rather than taking it away.

The effects are illustrated in Exhibit 7a. As a result

of a subsidy equal to the amount *US*, the supply curve shifts to the right from its normal position *SS'* to the new position *UU'*. This is because the subsidy is like a reduction in cost to the producer at all levels of output. Therefore his supply price will be lower by the amount of the subsidy.

For instance, the subsidy causes the equilibrium point to shift from *P* to *K*, and hence the equilibrium price to decrease from *NP* to *MK* and the equilibrium output to increase from *ON* to *OM*. At this new and larger output, buyers will pay the price *MK* but sellers will receive the additional amount *KF* (= *US*) which is the amount of the subsidy per unit of output.

This analysis enables us to generalize with an important principle.

The more elastic the supply and demand curves, the greater will be the expansion in output and the less will be the reduction in price resulting from a subsidy. This can be verified by comparing charts *(a)* and *(e)* in Exhibit 7.

Although the economic purposes of a subsidy are to reduce price or to increase output, the latter objective is usually the primary one when the product is to be used wholly for domestic consumption. The above principle thus leads to the conclusion that *if we want to increase production through the use of a subsidy, industries whose commodities are elastic in demand and supply are better suited to subsidies because they experience larger expansions in output and hence in employment.*

Subsidies are not only encountered in the domestic economy; they are also quite common in international trade as when a government subsidizes a firm or even an entire industry in order to help it penetrate foreign markets at lower prices. For example, Japan has subsidized at various times the production of automobiles, electronic products, and cameras in order to encourage their export to the United States and other countries.

AN AD VALOREM TAX OR SUBSIDY

The foregoing analyses can also be applied to ad valorem taxes and subsidies. An *ad valorem* (at value) tax is a fixed percentage of the price or value of a commodity. Therefore, unlike a specific tax, which yields eroding revenues to the government in times of inflation, an ad valorem tax is affected only by changes in the price of the product itself; hence it tends to yield tax revenues increasing at approximately the rate of inflation. Examples of ad valorem taxes are general sales taxes, property taxes, and most import duties.

A model of an ad valorem tax is presented in Exhibit 8. We can analyze its effect in four basic steps.

1. The original supply and demand curves are *SS'* and *DD'*. Their intersection at *P* determines the equilibrium output *ON* and the equilibrium price *NP*.

Exhibit 8

Effect of an Ad Valorem Tax or Subsidy

The vertical distance between the old and the new supply curve must get larger with increases in output and price, in order for the amount of the ad valorem tax (or subsidy) to remain a constant percentage of the selling price.

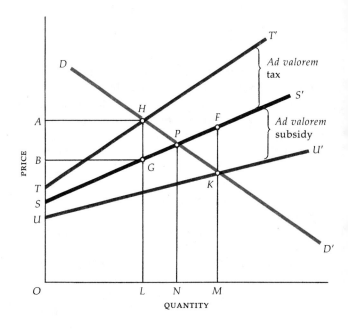

---

2. When an ad valorem tax is imposed, sellers' costs increase as a result of the tax, thereby shifting the supply curve to *TT'*. The equilibrium point thus changes from *P* to *H*, signifying a decrease in the equilibrium level of output from *ON* to *OL* and an increase in the equilibrium price from *NP* to *LH*. This means that in order to call forth the output *OL* consumers will pay and sellers will receive the price *LH*, but sellers will turn the tax *GH* over to the government, leaving them with a *net* price of *LG*.

So far the effects of an ad valorem tax do not seem to vary significantly from those of a specific tax as described previously. However, there is this essential difference:

3. Although an ad valorem tax is a *constant percentage* of the selling price, the *amount* of the tax, as measured by the vertical distance between the old supply curve *SS'* and the new supply curve *TT'*, becomes larger with increases in output and price. (Verify this analysis by substituting your own numbers for the letters in the diagram. Once this is done, you can analyze the effects of an *ad valorem subsidy* in the same way.)

4. How much total revenue does the government get from the tax? You can find out by drawing the rectangle *AHGB*. The area of the rectangle is the number of units sold *times* the amount of the tax per unit, and this equals the government's total revenue. Note that the same kind of rectangle has been drawn in Exhibit 7a.

Some Assumptions and Conclusions

Before concluding this elementary study of supply and demand, it is important to be made aware of certain key assumptions that underlie the previous models and some of the implications about the overall role of supply and demand in a market economy.

TWO UNDERLYING ASSUMPTIONS

In addition to the general assumptions about the law of supply and the law of demand, two special assumptions are relevant to the kinds of models developed in this chapter. These serve as warnings about the limitations of the analysis.

First, theoretical models of supply and demand assume that a particular economic action—such as the imposition of price ceilings, price floors, taxes, or subsidies—can be analyzed in terms of simple economic considerations alone, rather than in terms of multiple considerations involving both economic and noneconomic factors. In reality, of course, both forces are usually at work. For example, a tax on cigarettes may prompt some people to give up smoking for psychological reasons because they associate the unpleasant task of paying taxes with the act of smoking. This will cause the demand curve to shift to the left, resulting in a different equilibrium situation from the one in our model. Likewise, in analyzing the effects of taxes, subsidies, etc., it must be remembered that supply and demand curves are always changing over time due to changes in technology, tastes, and the other underlying economic as well as psychological factors that we ordinarily assume to be constant. Hence, although our models have purposely been kept simple, it should be apparent that complexities such as these must be introduced if the models are to be made more realistic.

Another limitation is that the models are *static* rather than *dynamic*. In a dynamic model, for instance, the influence of expectations by buyers or sellers would be recognized, because the process of moving toward an equilibrium position might itself cause changes in the supply and demand curves. As an example, a fall in price might prompt consumers to postpone their purchases in anticipation of further price decreases. This would cause a fall (shift to the left) of the demand curve. Similarly, the supply curve might rise (shift to the right) as suppliers sought to offset the future effects of the expected price drop by producing and selling more now at the higher price. Situations such as these continually occur in the stock and commodities markets.

Such limitations do not, however, make our models too simple to be useful. They merely remind us that any model is a simplification of reality, and we should be careful not to claim more for it than it really is.

MARKET PRICE AND NORMAL PRICE

Having learned how prices and quantities are determined under competitive market circumstances, it will be useful at this point to summarize what we already know:

1. The central idea behind supply and demand is the notion that competition among many buyers and sellers will cause market prices and quantities to move toward equilibrium.

2. Prices in a market reflect the *eagerness* of people to buy or sell. In competitive markets there will be a tendency for equilibrium prices to establish themselves automatically through the free operation of supply and demand.

3. Once equilibrium prices are established, they will have no tendency to change unless there are changes in the factors that determine supply and demand.

This third point requires some amplification. In reality, the equilibrium price is rarely if ever the actual price that exists at any given instant of time. The forces that are at work to determine an equilibrium price are always changing, thereby causing the equilibrium price to change. In view of this, it helps to distinguish between two kinds of price: *market price* and *normal price*.

The *market price* is the actual price that prevails in a market at any particular moment. The *normal price* is the equilibrium price toward which the market price is always tending but may never reach. (Normal price may thus be viewed as a dynamic equilibrium price.)

You can think of the market price as pursuing the normal price in much the same way as a missile pursues a moving target. The missile may never reach the target, just as the market price may never reach the dynamic equilibrium price. Yet the target is necessary in order to explain where the missile is heading, just as the concept of a normal price is necessary in order to explain where the market price is heading.

THE PRICE SYSTEM AS A RATIONING MECHANISM

We now come to one of the most significant conclusions in our study of economics—an explanation of the way in which the market system allocates scarce goods among competing buyers.

You already know that scarcity—the inability of limited resources to produce all the goods and services that people want—is an economic fact of life. In a command economy some central governmental authority—perhaps a king, a commissar, or a committee—decides the alternative uses to which these limited resources will be put, and to a large extent may also ration the fruits among the members of society. It is thus the central authority that answers the three big questions: *what* to produce, *how* to produce, and *for whom.*

In a pure market economy, on the other hand, these questions are decided by a competitive price system through the free operation of supply and demand. The concept is described in Exhibit 9. Thus for any given commodity or resource which may be represented by a pair of supply and demand curves, the equilibrium price automatically admits certain buyers and sellers to the marketplace while simultaneously excluding others. The cost of admission to the market is the *demand prices* of buyers and the *supply prices* of sellers—two terms that are already familiar to you. The diagram and its accompanying description thus lead to the following conclusion:

A *price system* is a mechanism that allocates scarce goods or resources among competing uses by rationing them among those buyers and sellers in the marketplace who are willing and able to deal at the going price.

A competitive price system, as we have seen, allocates and rations through the free play of supply and demand resulting from the interaction of many sellers and buyers. But what about "noncompetitive" price systems, where buyers or sellers are relatively few? This, as will be shown in later chapters, results in pricing situations quite different from the familiar supply and demand models we have studied thus far.

The Free Market: Myth or Goal?

Even the phrase itself has an appealing ring: the *free* market. How often newspapers publish editorials lauding the desirability of freedom and competition; how often politicians and speakers at Chamber of Commerce meetings hold forth on the evils of government intervention in the workings of the market. Yet the question has to be asked: How many of those who support the free market in theory would enjoy it in practice? Do they really understand what a free market would entail?

Shattering the Giants

There would, for a start, be no labor unions. In a free market, each worker would receive a wage determined by the impersonal play of supply and demand forces. When labor was scarce relative to demand, wages would rise. When the reverse was true, wages would fall. For employers, that situation might appear to be desirable; but they, too, would be the playthings of market forces. A government dedicated to the institution of a free market would have to break down corporate giants into smaller companies. The objective would be to ensure that in no industry could a handful of very large companies have sufficient power to interfere with the free market system—in which, by definition, neither buyers nor sellers have any individual influence over prices.

The government would also have to abandon some of its current activities. At present, for example, federal funds encourage farmers to reduce their output by offering them guaranteed prices for some of the commodities they produce. In a free market system, each farmer would have to decide for himself what and how much to grow. If his appraisal of market conditions were accurate, he would survive. If it were not, he would go bankrupt. Similarly, a government dedicated to the free market system would have to end subsidies to shipowners, aerospace companies, and scientific research organizations.

Paradoxically, some people in these groups inveigh against what they conceive to be government interference in their business. But they also resist vigorously any attempts to lessen the financial benefits they receive from government. Like most other supporters of the free market ideal, they recognize that an equitable economic system allows government to intervene when the alternative would be hardship for a group or sector.

Theory and Practice

When we strip the rhetoric from the speeches, we find that most people really want a mixture of competitive and regulated markets. Indeed, the person who believes that competition in consumer goods provides greater choice and keeps prices keen, will frequently support regulation of electricity supply, telephones, and transportation. In those activities, he believes, regulation keeps prices low.

In the theory of perfect competition, of course, regulation does not exist. But economic policy in the real world strays far from theory, impelled there by such noneconomic forces as popular pressures on politicians, the persuasive power of special-interest groups, and considerations of national security.

A Case for Freedom?

The result of such departures from economic theory is sometimes detrimental both to the consumer and to industry. One example is natural gas. At the start of the seventies there was a widely proclaimed shortage of natural gas. The producers argued that it was caused by regulation of prices, which had two harmful results: First, natural gas at the regulated price was cheap in relation to other fuels, and consequently rose in popularity. Second, the low price made natural gas an unattractive investment for producers in comparison with other investments available; the consequence was a failure to explore for and develop sufficient natural gas supplies. Some producers contend that natural gas should no longer be regulated, but should be allowed to find its own price in the marketplace.

There is certainly some merit in those (and similar) arguments for a free market in fuels. Unfortunately, the structure of the energy industry and the pattern of production and consumption have been formed by the mixture of freedom and regulation evolved over the years. It is always difficult to unscramble such a situation—and the task is always unwelcome to politicians.

R. B.

1. *Can you think of any industries for which free markets would not work at all or be inefficient?*

2. *Can you think of any publicly supplied services that could be supplied efficiently by free markets?*

Exhibit 9

**How a Market Economy Rations Goods or Resources Among
Buyers and Sellers**

The equilibrium price serves as a highly selective filter. It admits to the market only those buyers whose demand price is greater than or equal to the equilibrium price, and those sellers whose supply price is less than or equal to the equilibrium price. All other buyers and sellers who are not able and willing to deal at the going price are excluded.

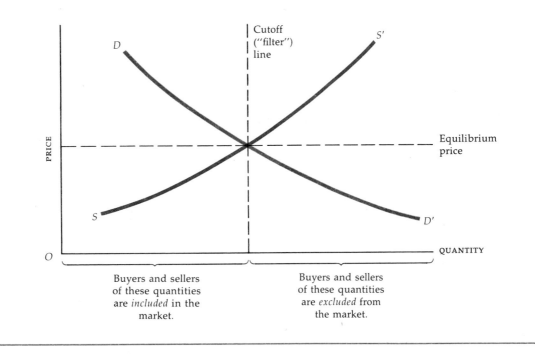

SUMMARY OF IMPORTANT IDEAS

1. Elasticity is a basic concept in supply and demand analysis. It may be defined interpretatively as the percentage change in quantity (demanded or supplied) resulting from a 1 percent change in price; or it may be defined mathematically by the ratio: Elasticity = (percentage change in quantity)/(percentage change in price).

2. The coefficient of elasticity is commonly expressed in its absolute-value or numerical form; in other words, the minus signs are disregarded. There are thus five types of elasticity ranging from zero to infinity:

perfect elasticity	$(E = \infty)$
relative elasticity	$(E > 1)$
unit elasticity	$(E = 1)$
relative inelasticity	$(E < 1)$
perfect inelasticity	$(E = 0)$

These five types apply both to supply and to demand.

3. Since elasticity is a measure of relative changes, it may vary for each segment along a curve. Our formula for elasticity gives a type of "average" elasticity over an entire segment.

4. Elasticity is *not* the same as slope. Therefore, the elasticity of a curve cannot always be judged from its slope alone. An exception occurs in the case of vertical and horizontal curves. In most other cases the exact elasticity must be calculated.

5. You can tell whether demand elasticity is greater or less than unity by observing the effect of a price change on total revenue. If price and total revenue change in opposite directions, demand elasticity is greater than unity. If price and total revenue change in the same direction, demand elasticity is less than unity.

6. The availability of good commodity substitutes tends to make demand more elastic; likewise, the availability of good resource substitutes tends to make supply more elastic. Goods which are relatively inexpensive tend to be more inelastic in demand because they are a small part of the consumer's total expenditures. Elasticities of both demand and supply tend to be greater over longer periods because buyers and sellers can adjust to the use of substitutes or to changes in price.

7. Price ceilings are imposed to keep the market price of a commodity below its normal (free market) equilibrium price. Price floors, on the other hand, are imposed to keep the market price of a commodity above its normal (free market) equilibrium price. Price ceilings cause product shortages and the need for rationing. Price floors cause product surpluses, which may require government action to absorb them.

8. Specific taxes tend to be shifted between buyers and sellers according to where the inelasticity is greatest. Industries whose commodities are inelastic in demand are better suited to commodity taxation because they suffer smaller contractions in output and hence in employment. On the other hand, industries whose commodities are elastic in demand are better suited to subsidies because they experience larger expansions in output and hence in employment.

9. Some important lessons are:

a. Our simple supply and demand models do not take into account complex economic and non-economic considerations, and are static rather than dynamic.

b. The competitive market is always tending toward the equilibrium price, but may never reach it because the underlying forces are always changing.

c. In a market economy, the price system allocates goods or resources by rationing them among those buyers and sellers whose demand and supply prices are sufficient to admit them to the market.

FOR HOMEWORK AND DISCUSSION

1. *Terms and concepts to review:*

elasticity	subsidy
shortage	specific subsidy
rationing	ad valorem tax
surplus	ad valorem subsidy
specific tax	market price
incidence	normal price
supply price	price system

2. Several studies have found that the overall demand for automobiles has an elasticity of about 1.3.

a. How do you interpret this coefficient?

b. After hearing about these studies, a Ford dealer in Chicago cut his prices by 10 percent and sold 22 percent more cars. What is the elasticity of demand in this case? Does it mean that the estimate of 1.3 is incorrect? Explain.

3. Suppose we are given the following demand schedule for a commodity.

	Price (cents)	Quantity demanded
A	20	50
B	15	100
C	10	200
D	5	400

a. Calculate the elasticity between points A and B, B and C, C and D. (SUGGESTION: Sketch the demand curve and label it with the points A, B, C, D in order to help you "see" what you are doing.)

b. How will your results compare if you calculate the elasticity in reverse directions, i.e., from *B* to *A*, *C* to *B*, and *D* to *C*? Explain.

4. Fill in the blank space in each of the following rows:

Price	Total revenue	Elasticity
increases		> 1
decreases	decreases	
decreases	no change	
	increases	< 1
	decreases	> 1
increases		1

5. How does elasticity of supply and demand affect shortages and surpluses resulting from price ceilings and price floors? Illustrate with diagrams.

6. Use a supply and demand diagram to answer the following questions about specific and ad valorem taxes:

a. Assuming that both types of taxes imposed on sellers are the same at zero output, which type will yield a higher revenue per unit to the govern-ment: a 10-cent specific tax or a 10 percent ad valorem tax? (HINT: Draw all the relevant supply curves on one diagram.)

b. Which will cause less disruption of output?

c. How would you compare the total revenues received by the government from the two types of taxes?

7. Many people criticize public transit systems (subways, buses, etc.) for being too crowded during rush hours. From what you know about the price system as a rationing mechanism, how would you correct the situation?

REFERENCES AND READING SUGGESTIONS

BOULDING, KENNETH E., *Economic Analysis*, vol. 1, *Microeconomics*, 4th ed., Harper & Row, New York, 1966, chaps. 7, 8, 10.

DOOLEY, PETER C., *Elementary Price Theory*, Appleton-Century-Crofts, New York, chaps. 1, 2.

WARD, BENJAMIN, *Elementary Price Theory*, The Free Press, New York, 1967, chap. 3.

WATSON, DONALD S., *Price Theory and Its Uses*, 2d ed., Houghton-Mifflin, Boston, 1968, chap. 3.

CHAPTER 21

Further Applications of Supply and Demand. Looking Behind the Demand Curve

What is a black market? How can supply and demand analysis illustrate its operation?

Who suffers and who benefits from a tarrif? Can supply and demand analysis help to evaluate tariffs?

How can we account for periodic fluctuations in the prices and production of certain agricultural commodities, notably hogs and cattle?

What is the basis for the law of (downward-sloping) demand? That is, what are the underlying assumptions and principles of consumer behavior on which the law rests?

We have already seen how supply and demand models can be applied to the analysis and interpretation of a wide range of interesting economic problems. In this chapter the applications will be extended to further areas. Once the study of these models is completed you will have a better background for probing more deeply into the theory of demand. This will be the function of later portions of the chapter, where we examine the underpinnings of the theory and some of the controversial questions raised by it.

Theory of a Black Market

The history of price control in the United States and in practically all other nations attests to the fact that whenever ceiling prices and rationing are introduced, whether in peace or in war, a black market is almost certain to emerge. What is a *black market*? It may be defined as an illegal market in which a good is sold at a price above its legal ceiling price.

In certain countries black markets exist for such commodities as sugar, meat, gasoline, gold, and American dollars. These are goods whose prices in those countries are subject to government control and for which there is a strong and widespread demand. It is interesting to see how supply and demand analysis can illustrate and evaluate the operation of a black market under such circumstances.

In Exhibit 1, curves S and D represent the normal supply and demand curves in a free or unregulated market. We now suppose that a ceiling price of OC is imposed by the government. At this price sellers will supply the amount CJ, whereas buyers will want to purchase the quantity CR. There will thus be an excess or unsatisfied demand equal to JR.

THE BLACK MARKET PRICE

Let us assume that as a result of this "shortage," a black market develops with its own supply and demand curves. The consequences may then be analyzed in the following way.

The black market supply curve is JS_B. This curve lies to the left of, and rises more steeply than, the normal supply curve JS because in a black market sellers incur greater costs and risks than in a free market. Hence at any given price above the legal ceiling sellers are willing to supply less in the black market than in the free market. In other words, because of the higher costs and risks the supply price—the price necessary to call forth a given output—is higher in the black market than in the free market. In fact, the greater the costs of operation in the black market, the steeper will be the supply curve JS_B.

Similarly, the black market demand curve is represented by LD_B. This curve's lower end point is at L rather than at R because even at the legal ceiling price of OC, some potential buyers will not buy in the black market. Hence the quantity demanded in the black market at the ceiling price OC is not the total unsatisfied demand JR, but a smaller quantity JL. The higher the price in the black market, the less the quantity demanded in it, until at some price such as OF the quantity demanded is zero.

The black market price is thus N_1P_1, as determined by the intersection of the black market supply and demand curves. The quantity traded in the black market is JK, and the quantity traded in the legal market is CJ; hence the total quantity traded in both the legal market and the black market is CK.

Exhibit 1

Theory of a Black Market

The intersection of the black market supply and demand curves, shown by the dashed lines, determines the price in the black market. The more elastic these curves, the lower will be the price. Also, the greater the penalties imposed on buyers rather than sellers, the lower the black market price is likely to be.

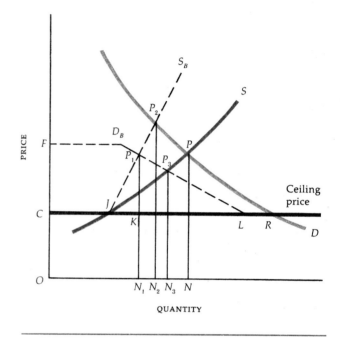

CONCLUSIONS

Three conclusions emerge from this analysis of a black market:

1. The black market price may be less than, equal to, or greater than the price (NP) that would have been established in an unregulated market. This is because the black market price is determined wherever the black market supply and demand curves—that is, the *dashed* curves—happen to intersect, and this is independent of where the free market curves intersect.

2. The more inelastic the dashed black market supply or demand curves, the greater will be the black

market price, since the intersection of the dashed curves will occur at a higher point. In most cases, however, the *average* of the ceiling price and the black market price will be lower than the free market price. This is apparent from the chart, since the black market price would have to be considerably higher than the free market price in order to pull the average of the black market price and the ceiling price above the free market price.

3. The greater the penalties imposed on *buyers* in the black market and the smaller the penalties imposed on *sellers*, the lower the black market price is likely to be. This can be explained in terms of the chart as follows:

First, if legal and moral penalties were imposed on *sellers* in a black market, but not on buyers, the supply curve in the black market would be the existing dashed curve, but the demand curve would become the normal free market demand curve DP_2. The result would be a relatively high black market price of N_2P_2.

Second, if legal and moral penalties were imposed on *buyers* instead of sellers, the demand curve in the black market would be the present dashed curve in the diagram, but the supply curve would become the normal free market supply curve JS. The result would be a relatively low black market price of N_3P_3.

This suggests that, other things being equal, it is better to penalize buyers rather than sellers—housewives rather than grocers—for dealing in a black market. However, all other things are not usually equal in black markets. It is the seller, not the buyer, who ordinarily does business at an established location and is required to keep accounting records; hence it is usually easier and more expedient to penalize the seller rather than the buyer for black market activities. In some communist countries, buyers and sellers are subject to the same penalties.

Effects of a Tariff

Another interesting type of problem that can be studied with supply and demand analysis is a *tariff*. This is a customs duty or tax imposed by a government on the importation (or exportation) of a good.

Tariffs may be: (1) specific, based on a tax per unit of the commodity, or (2) ad valorem, based on the value of the commodity. For our present purposes we shall concentrate on the somewhat simpler case of a specific tariff, although the underlying principles and effects are essentially the same for both types.

THE NATURE OF ARBITRAGE

Let us assume that the world is divided into two economies, the United States and the "rest" of the world. What will be the world equilibrium price of a commodity under such circumstances?

As a basis for answering this question, we may note that if there are no internal taxes on the good, and if international trade in the product is free and unrestricted, the difference in the price of the commodity between the United States and the rest of the world should differ essentially by transportation costs. The reason is not hard to see: If prices between the two markets differ by more than the cost of transporting the product from one to the other, businessmen will find it profitable to buy the commodity in the cheaper market and sell it in the dearer. This process will tend to raise the price in the cheaper market as the demand for the good increases relative to its supply, and lower the price in the dearer market as the supply of the good increases relative to its demand.

The act of buying a commodity in one market at a lower price and simultaneously selling it in another market at a higher price is known as *arbitrage*. Under competitive conditions, arbitrage will tend to bring about equal prices of a commodity between markets, except for differences in the costs of trading in the commodity, such as transportation, risk, etc. Arbitrage is always taking place—in domestic as well as in international markets—and it results in greater price stability and hence a smoother flow of goods.

EQUILIBRIUM IN WORLD TRADE

Against this background, we can analyze the effects of a tariff in terms of Exhibit 2. These charts show the supply and demand curves of a particular commodity under the assumptions made above—a set of two

Exhibit 2

Effect of a Tariff

In the absence of tariffs or transport costs, the world equilibrium price of the commodity will be OP (= O'P'). *At this price, imports into the United States of EF will just equal exports from the rest of the world of E'F'. If a tariff equal to LM' is now imposed, the price in the United States rises to OM and the price in the rest of the world falls to O'L, because these are the price levels at which the United States'* imports of TJ *will just equal the rest of the world's exports of T'J'. Equilibrium is thus restored.*

The results of a tariff are much the same as an increase in the cost of transportation between the two economies. Thus, both economies feel the effects of the tariff in different ways, according to the relative elasticities of demand and supply.

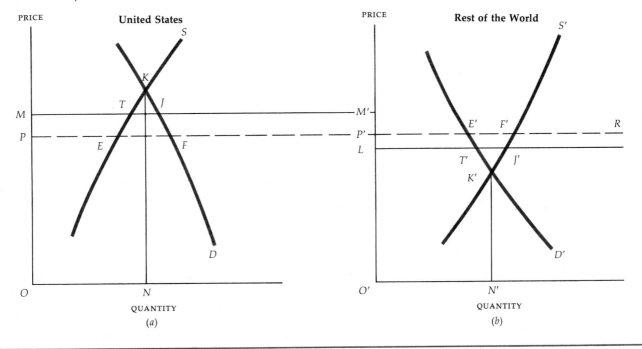

(a)

(b)

economies consisting of the United States and the rest of the world.

It is important that the meanings of the curves in the diagrams be understood. In Exhibit 2a curve D represents the demand for the commodity by American consumers, while curve S represents the supply of the commodity by American producers. Similarly, in Exhibit 2b, curve D' represents the demand for the commodity by foreign consumers, and curve S' represents the supply of the commodity by foreign producers.

The analysis can now be conveniently conducted in two steps.

1. No Tariff or Transport Costs

Let us assume there are no tariffs and no costs of transportation and that trade between the two economies is completely free and unrestricted. If such a situation exists, the world equilibrium price of the commodity will tend to settle at the level OP for the following reasons:

1. At the price OP the excess demand or "shortage" of EF in the United States is exactly equal to the excess supply or "surplus" of E'F' in the rest of the world. Hence this amount of the good will flow from the rest of the world to the United States, and there

will be no tendency for world stocks of the commodity to accumulate or diminish.

2. At any price other than OP there will be surpluses or shortages which will not offset one another, and hence world stocks of the commodity will either accumulate or diminish. This will cause the world price to fluctuate—that is, the horizontal dashed line PR to move up or down—until it reaches the equilibrium level at which $EF = E'F'$.

It is important to note that as a result of trade the price in the United States (OP) is less than it would be if there were no trade (NK), and the price in the rest of the world ($O'P'$) is greater than it would be if there were no trade ($N'K'$).

2. With Tariff or Transport Costs

Suppose that a tariff is now introduced which is equal to LM' per unit of commodity. This will have the same effect as imposing an added cost on the transportation of the good. Thus the price in the United States will rise to OM, and the price in the rest of the world will fall to $O'L'$, because at these levels the amount TJ, representing imports into the United States, exactly equals the amount $T'J'$, representing exports from the rest of the world. The two economies are therefore in equilibrium.

What are the economic consequences of the tariff? Some of the more important results may be noted:

1. The price effects of the tariff, LM', are shared by both economies. In the United States, the price rises by the amount PM (= $P'M'$ on the right-hand chart) and in the rest of the world the price falls by the amount $P'L$. Thus the equilibrium price in the importing economy is higher, and the equilibrium price in the exporting economy is lower, than the world equilibrium price that would result in the absence of tariffs.

2. Both economies experience a decline in the volume of trade—in the United States from EF to TJ, and equivalently in the rest of the world from $E'F'$ to $T'J'$.

3. Broadly speaking, the tariff benefits producers in the United States by permitting them to increase their production from PE to MT and it benefits consumers in the rest of the world by enabling them to increase their consumption from $P'E'$ to LT'. The converse of this—namely that the tariff penalizes consumers in the United States and producers abroad—is also true and can be verified in a similar way.

Of course, the extent of these effects—like those of commodity taxes which we studied earlier—will depend on other factors, including the relative elasticities of the supply and demand curves in both economies. Nevertheless, it should be noted that the above economic consequences of a tariff are to a large extent the same as those resulting from an increase in transport costs. In this sense, anyone who argues in favor of imposing or raising a tariff on a commodity in order to protect it from foreign competition should, in order to be logically consistent, also argue in favor of increasing the *cost of transporting* the commodity.

The Cobweb Theorem

One of the most interesting and famous models in supply and demand analysis is the *cobweb theorem*. This is a generic name for a theory which helps to explain patterns of cyclical fluctuations in the prices and quantities of various agricultural commodities. These fluctuations arise for certain agricultural products because the quantity demanded of the commodity at any given time depends on its price at that time, and the quantity supplied at any given time depends on its price at a *previous* time, i.e., when production plans were initially formulated. This is particularly true of such livestock products as hogs and beef cattle, for which fairly regular cycles in prices and production have long been observed.

In any one year the quantity supplied of the commodity may be small and the price high. This high price encourages farmers to plan an increase in output of the product—which, however, will mature and reach marketable age a year or two later. When the increased output is placed on the market, the price falls. Producers then move out of production of the commodity, and when the effects of their decisions are felt a year or two later, the reduced quantity

Exhibit 3

Three Patterns of Cobweb Cycles

Pattern (*a*): Converging cycles. *Prices and quantities con-*
verge toward a stable equilibrium level.

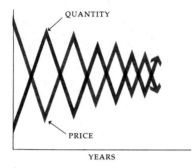

Pattern (*b*): Diverging cycles. *Prices and quantities diverge*
from a stable equilibrium level.

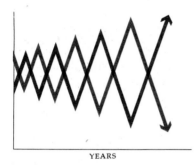

Pattern (*c*): Oscillating cycles. *Prices and quantities oscillate*
without relation to any stable equilibrium level.

supplied brings about an increase in price. The cycle thus goes on and on, with prices and quantities varying inversely with one another, as suggested by the simplified curves in Exhibit 3.

THREE COBWEB MODELS

These curves come into existence because of the interactions of supply and demand as shown by the three cobweb models in the left-hand charts of Exhibit 4. In each of these models the demand curve D expresses the relationship between quantity demanded and price in any one year, whereas the supply curve S represents the relationship between the price in any one year and the quantity which will be produced in the *following* year (or equivalently, the quantity which will be produced in any one year and the price in the *previous* year).

Suppose that in any one year the quantity produced equals OA. The highest price sellers will get for that quantity will be AB. But if the price is AB in any one year, sellers will produce the amount ZC in the following year, according to the meaning of the supply curve S given above. This will cause the price in the second year to fall to the level at E. Production in the third year will then drop to the level represented by the point F. These fluctuations will continue, following the arrowheads in the diagram, thereby tracing out the cobweb patterns as shown.

What determines these patterns? They are based on a fundamental principle:

Cobweb cycles will be stable, unstable, or neutral, depending on the relative numerical elasticities of supply E_s and of demand E_d. Thus the cycle will be stable if E_s is less than E_d, unstable if E_s is greater than E_d, and neutral if E_s is equal to E_d.

In the right-hand charts of Exhibit 4, the corresponding price fluctuations have been plotted over discrete time intervals, so that any given price level may be thought of as occurring during a period of time such as a year. (In contrast, the previous charts in Exhibit 3 were plotted on the assumption that changes in time were continuous rather than discrete.) The curves representing quantity were omitted from the right-hand charts in Exhibit 4 in order

Exhibit 4

The Cobweb Theorem: Three Models

(*a*): **Stable equilibrium model.** *Price and quantity converge toward the intersection of supply and demand. The elasticity of supply is less than the elasticity of demand:*

$$E_s < E_d$$

(*b*) **Unstable equilibrium model.** *Price and quantity diverge from the intersection of supply and demand. The elasticity of supply is greater than the elasticity of demand:*

$$E_s > E_d$$

(*c*): **Neutral equilibrium model.** *Price and quantity oscillate at a regular rate, neither converging nor diverging toward an equilibrium. The elasticities of supply and demand are equal:*

$$E_s = E_d$$

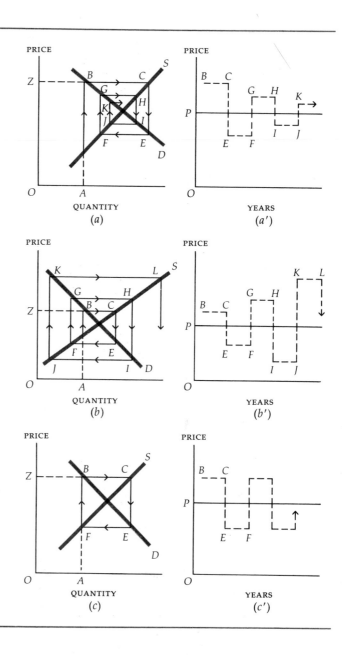

to avoid confusion. However, if they were shown they would follow a similar but *inverse* cycle with respect to the price.

Fluctuations such as these do not continue in the same pattern indefinitely. Why? Because in reality the supply and demand curves and their elasticities tend to change fairly frequently, so that different cyclical patterns are generated which at any given moment may be tending toward stable, unstable, or neutral equilibrium.

Lengths of Cycles

It is interesting to inquire about the length of cob-

Exhibit 5

The Hog Cycle

(a) *Cycles in hog prices are pronounced. Data going back to the mid-nineteenth century (not shown) indicate that the* *lengths of cycles, measured from peak to peak or from trough to trough, have averaged about four years.*

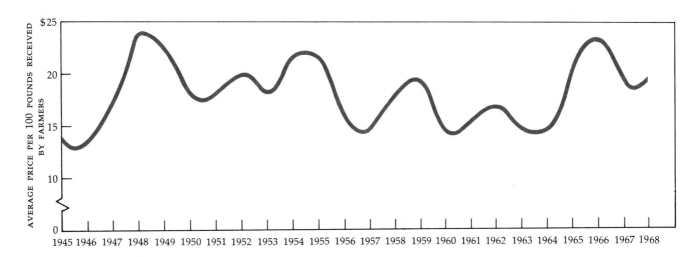

(b) *Cycles in hog prices and hog slaughter; there is a high inverse correlation between the two cycles.*

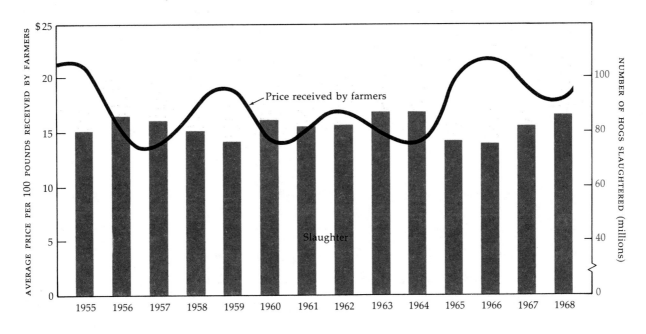

web cycles. Such cycles vary with different commodities. However, *the chief underlying factor determining the length of a particular cycle is the time required for a change in price to bring about a change in production.* This response of changes in production to changes in price is in turn influenced by two major conditions:

1. The time it takes farmers to produce surpluses and people to consume them. For example, hog cycles are shorter than cattle cycles because hog surpluses can be produced and consumed much faster than cattle surpluses.

2. The time it takes for the product to reach marketable weight. Hogs, for instance, reach their average slaughter weight in about one year, whereas cattle require approximately two years.

THE HOG CYCLE

Although cobweb cycles of different types have been observed in agriculture at various times, the most pronounced cycles in production and prices have occurred with hogs and beef cattle, and to a lesser extent with sheep. Coffee and pepper have also exhibited cyclical patterns.

The hog cycle, illustrated in Exhibit 5, is perhaps the most consistent and famous of all commodity cycles. Chart (*a*) shows that the price of hogs has been characterized by a cycle averaging about four years. Chart (*b*), based on a representative sample of years, suggests a fact confirmed in various studies: When the effects of changes in demand are taken into account, the cycles in hog prices are caused mainly by opposite cycles in hog slaughtering. Thus when hog slaughtering is high, hog prices are low, and vice versa.

The Hog-Corn Price Ratio

In view of this apparent inverse correlation between hog prices and hog slaughtering, what factors determine cycles in hog slaughter? The answer is found mainly in the so-called *hog-corn price ratio,* which has a major influence on hog production. The relation between these two factors is extremely important. Indeed, it affects the livelihood of many farmers in a number of states. The relation may be measured by the formula

$$\text{Hog-corn price ratio} = \frac{\begin{array}{c}\text{price of live hogs}\\ \text{per 100 pounds}\end{array}}{\text{price of corn per bushel}}$$

This formula is interpreted in the following way:

The *hog-corn price ratio* measures the number of bushels of corn required to *buy* 100 pounds of live pork (not the number of bushels needed to *produce* 100 pounds of pork). When the ratio is relatively low, hog production decreases because farmers find it more profitable to sell their corn in the market rather than use it for breeding and feeding hogs; conversely, when the ratio is relatively high, hog production increases because farmers use the corn to breed and feed more hogs, and to market them at heavier weights.

In Exhibit 6, chart (*a*) presents a graph of the hog-corn price ratio for a representative period of years, and chart (*b*) shows the definite effects of this ratio on the pig-crop cycle a year later.

It is interesting to note that even though it takes about 12 months to raise an average market hog from breeding to slaughter at 200 to 250 pounds, the hog cycle is not two years, as would be expected. Instead it averages approximately four years. This is because farmers do not respond immediately to a change in the hog-corn price ratio. If they did, they might find that the price change was only temporary, and any decision to adjust hog production to the new ratio might be unprofitable. Only after the ratio has departed significantly from its long-run average for about a year or more do farmers begin to "accept" the new price structure and arrange to alter their hog production plans. It may take another six months or more before the effects of these changes in plans are felt in the market.

Farmers thus appear to pay more attention to the span of time over which a price change persists than they do to the magnitude of the price change itself. As was stated above, therefore, *the length of the cycle depends primarily on the time it takes for a change in price to bring about a change in production.*

Exhibit 6

Effects of Hog-Corn Ratio on Pig-Crop Cycle

Chart (*a*) shows changes in the hog-corn ratio and chart (*b*) shows sows farrowed the following year. *The long-run average for the hog-corn ratio during the years shown was almost 15. (In earlier decades it was closer to 11.) When the* ratio rises significantly above this break-even level, farmers increase their hog litters in the following year. The opposite situation occurs when the ratio drops significantly below the break-even level.

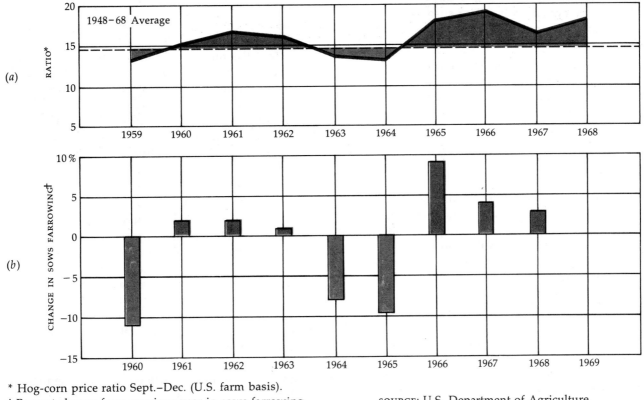

* Hog-corn price ratio Sept.–Dec. (U.S. farm basis).
† Percent change from previous year in sows farrowing.

source: U.S. Department of Agriculture.

Theory of Utility and Consumer Demand

Economists have long been interested in the factors that account for the shape of demand curves. Until now we have taken it pretty much for granted that such curves slope downward from left to right. Upon closer examination, however, we find several reasons for their negative inclination.

One explanation is simply "common sense"—by which we mean observation and intuition. On the basis of our experiences it seems reasonable to expect that a reduction in the price of a product will enable a buyer to purchase more of it; an increase in its price will reduce that ability.

A second and more formal explanation can be given in terms of what economists call "income effects" and "substitution effects." The income effect tells us that a decrease in the price of a product, while the prices of other goods and the consumer's income and tastes remain the same, enables the consumer to buy more of the commodity and perhaps more of other commodities as well; hence this results in an increase in the consumer's real income. The substitution effect says that a reduction in the price of a product, with the consumer's income, tastes, and other prices remaining constant, makes the cheaper good relatively more attractive and thus enables the consumer to substitute more of it for other products.

These concepts can be expressed in more general terms:

The effects of a price change may be divided into two parts—an income effect and a substitution effect:

1. The *income effect* measures the increase or decrease in a buyer's real income—that is, in goods purchased—resulting from a change in the price of a commodity while his money income, tastes, and the prices of all other goods remain the same.

2. The *substitution effect* measures the extent to which a buyer substitutes a cheaper commodity for other relatively more expensive goods as its price falls while his income, tastes, and other prices remain the same.

The concepts of income and substitution effects thus provide somewhat deeper insights into the shape of a consumer's demand curve. Taken together, they explain how a price increase or decrease affects a consumer's *willingness* and *ability* to buy—two terms which were emphasized when we first studied the nature of demand.

THE MEANING OF UTILITY

A third and in many ways much more fundamental explanation of the downward-sloping demand curve can be given in terms of utility. By *utility* is meant the ability or power of a good to satisfy a want as determined by the satisfaction that one receives from consuming something—whether it be pizzas, vacation trips, or textbooks.

The concept of utility was employed by the classical economists of the eighteenth and early nineteenth centuries, but the theory of utility as such did not come into full flower until the late nineteenth century, when it was crystallized by certain neoclassical economists. As you study the theory in the following paragraphs be careful not to confuse "utility" with "usefulness." At any given time, water may be much more useful than diamonds, but the utility for either one may be quite different to various individuals.

Total Utility and Marginal Utility

Although no one knows how to measure utility, it is interesting to *assume* that it can be measured. Suppose for example, that a "utility meter" could be strapped to your arm to measure the units of satisfaction, called *utils*, that you get from consuming a product—much as a doctor could strap a meter to your arm to measure your blood pressure. What would such a utility meter reveal?

The answer is suggested by the data and curves in Exhibit 7, showing the utils or units of satisfaction that you might experience from consuming a hypothetical product. This model assumes that your consumption is taking place at a *given period of time during which your tastes are constant*. Otherwise, it would make no sense to talk about the utility of different quantities of a product, as will become evident shortly.

The exhibit illustrates that one unit of the commodity yields a certain amount of total utility, two units yield a larger amount, three units still more, and so on. Eventually, a level of intake is reached at which total utility is a maximum; thereafter, the consumption of further units results in total utility declining. This is clearly seen from the graph of total utility in the exhibit.

Much more important than total utility is *marginal utility*, which is defined as the change in total utility resulting from a unit change in the quantity of the product consumed. As you can see from column (3) of the table, it may be measured by the formula

$$\text{Marginal utility} = \frac{\text{change in total utility}}{\text{change in quantity consumed}}$$

Marginal utility thus measures the *ratio of change* in the two variables. This is emphasized by the way its values are recorded in column (3) of the table—a half-space "between" those shown for columns (1) and (2).

Observe from the charts that the marginal utility curve reaches a maximum and begins to turn downward while the total utility curve is still rising. When the total utility curve reaches its maximum height the marginal utility curve is at zero height, i.e., intersects the horizontal axis, as emphasized by the vertical dashed line. The reason for this relationship will be explained in a later chapter when we encounter other types of "marginal" and "total" curves.

Exhibit 7

Total and Marginal Utility

The table and charts convey the same fundamental relations:

As consumption of the product is increased, both total utility and marginal utility rise to a maximum and then decline. The marginal utility curve is most important, for it reveals the operation of the law of diminishing marginal utility. *The vertical dashed line emphasizes the fact that marginal utility equals zero when total utility is at a maximum.*

(1) Units consumed of product	(2) Total Utility TU	(3) Marginal Utility $MU = \dfrac{\text{change in (2)}}{\text{change in (1)}}$
0	0	
		10
1	10	
		14
2	24	
		15
3	39	
		13
4	52	
		9
5	61	
		3
6	64	
		1
7	65	
		−1
8	64	

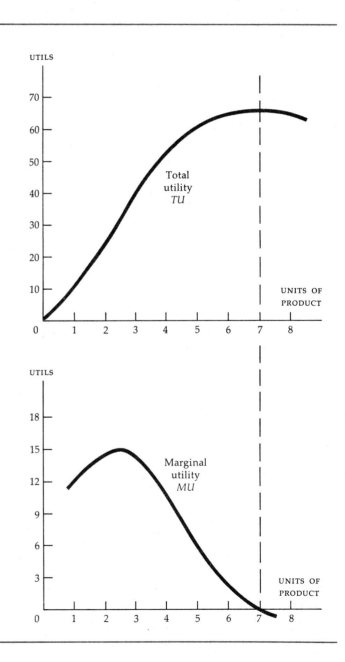

Law of (Eventually) Diminishing Marginal Utility

It is important to emphasize that although marginal utility may at first increase, it must *eventually* decrease as more units of the product are consumed. What this means, for example, is that you might very well enjoy the second unit of a commodity (e.g., a slice of pizza) more than the first, and the third perhaps even more than the second, but you must eventually reach a point where each successive unit gives you less satisfaction than the previous one. This idea can be expressed more formally by an important law:

Law of Diminishing Marginal Utility. In a given period of time, the consumption of a product while tastes remain constant may at first result in increasing marginal utilities per unit of the product consumed, but a point will be reached beyond which the consumption of further units of the product will result in decreasing marginal utilities per unit of the product consumed. This is the point of diminishing marginal utility.

As suggested by the word "diminishing" in this law, it is the *decreasing* part of the marginal utility curve that is relevant. The reason will be seen shortly. Thus the law means in effect that on the downward side of the curve, the more you have of something, the less important to you any one unit of it is.

CONSUMER EQUILIBRIUM

How can these concepts be used to describe the economic theory of consumer behavior and the existence of negatively inclined demand curves?

Consider the case of a consumer with a given amount of money to spend on two commodities, *A* and *B*. Let us designate his marginal utility for product *A* as MU_a, and the price of product *A* as P_a; similarly, let his marginal utility for product *B* be represented by MU_b, and the price of product *B* by P_b.

Now, keeping in mind that it is the *downward* side of a product's marginal utility curve that is relevant, how should the consumer distribute his expenditures on these two products so as to maximize his total satisfaction or utility? The answer is that he must allocate his expenditures so that the marginal utility *per dollar* spent on the two commodities is equal; that is,

$$\frac{MU_a}{P_a} = \frac{MU_b}{P_b}$$

In other words, the consumer will adjust the quantities he buys to achieve this result. If this is not the case—if, for example, he has a combination of *A* and *B* such that MU_a is greater than MU_b—he can increase his total utility by giving up some of product *B* (thereby moving up on his *MU* curve of *B*) and buying more of product *A* (thereby moving down on his *MU* curve of *A*). It can be demonstrated mathematically that the gain will more than offset the loss.

But what about *money* which is being exchanged for these products? We can think of money like any other commodity, with its marginal utility to the consumer represented by MU_m and its price by P_m. The above equation, in order to be complete, should then be extended to read:

$$\frac{MU_a}{P_a} = \frac{MU_b}{P_b} = \frac{MU_m}{P_m}$$

But since the price of a dollar is 1, the denominator in the last ratio may be omitted and the equation becomes

$$\frac{MU_a}{P_a} = \frac{MU_b}{P_b} = MU_m$$

This last equation expresses the consumer's equilibrium—the conditions which exist when he has allocated his money and commodities in the face of market prices in such a way as to maximize his total utility.

This equation is also equivalent to saying that for the consumer to be in equilibrium the last dollar spent on *A* must yield the same marginal utility (equal to the value of MU_m) as the last dollar spent on *B*.

This principle can be extended to any number of commodities. The point is that in order for the consumer to be in equilibrium his marginal utility per dollar of expenditure must be equal for all commodities, which in turn must equal his marginal utility for money. Otherwise he will be able to increase his total utility by reshuffling his expenditures.

MARGINAL UTILITY AND DEMAND CURVES

We now wish to derive the consumer's demand curve for a specific commodity based on his utility data. The above equation tells us that for any particular commodity, say commodity A,

$$\frac{MU_a}{P_a} = MU_m$$

If we "transpose" and solve for P_a, we get

$$P_a = \frac{MU_a}{MU_m}$$

Suppose we now simplify by assuming that at any given time the consumer's marginal utility for money is a constant positive amount. For example, let us assume that MU_m is any positive number, say 3. (The number itself makes no difference for our present purposes; any positive number can be chosen, as will be seen momentarily.) The consumer's individual demand curve for commodity A can then be derived if his marginal utility schedule is known.

This is illustrated in Exhibit 8, where the price data in column (4) are obtained from the given information in the other columns. As you can see from the explanation accompanying the diagram, the demand curve represents the demand schedule from columns (1) and (4) of the table. This curve is negatively sloped, a fact which is uninfluenced by the constant positive value chosen for MU_m.

Exhibit 8

Deriving a Consumer's Demand Curve for a Commodity, Based on Utility Data

The demand curve is graphed from columns (1) and (4) of the table. The curve will be negatively inclined regardless of the constant positive value chosen for MU_m.

(1) Units of product A	(2) Marginal Utility of money MU_m	(3) Marginal Utility of product MU_a	(4) Price of product P_a $\left(P_a = \frac{MU_a}{MU_m}\right)$
(given)	(given)	(given)	
1	3	15	5
2	3	12	4
3	3	9	3
4	3	6	2
5	3	3	1

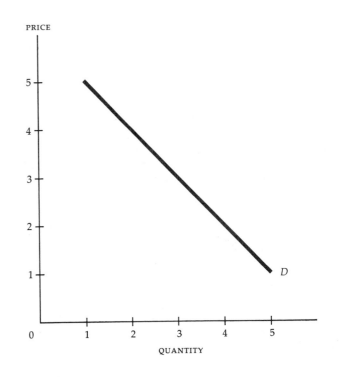

The development of utility theory in general, and the concept of marginal utility in particular, permit us to interpret more precisely problems that would otherwise be handled in relatively crude ways.

For example, a question asked earlier was: Why is the price of water low and the price of diamonds high, especially since everyone needs water but no one really needs diamonds? If we knew nothing about utility theory the answer would be given simply in terms of "supply and demand." But now we can go a step further. Thus, to most of us the marginal utility of water is ordinarily low because it is usually available in ample amounts, i.e., the more we have of something, the less we care about *one* unit of it; hence, we do not usually hesitate to use the extra water we need to sprinkle our lawns and wash our cars. The marginal utility of diamonds, on the other hand, is relatively high and their supply is scarce, so a single unit of it has considerable value. In a desert or on a battlefield, however, the circumstances might be quite reversed: we might be quite willing to trade a diamond for a pint of water, or perhaps a "kingdom" for a "horse."

This suggests an interesting point: For some products, total utility may be high while marginal utility is low or even zero. For example, an urban freeway during off-peak hours, a fire department when there is no fire, a doctor's service when there is no need for it. You can undoubtedly think of other illustrations.

CONSUMER'S SURPLUS

A concept directly relevant to utility theory is *consumer's surplus*. It may be defined as the value or utility that a buyer receives as a result of paying less than the maximum he would have been willing to pay for the quantity of the commodity he purchases; thus it is determined by the difference between the buyer's *demand price* and the price that he actually pays.

The concept of consumer's surplus is illustrated in Exhibit 9, where it is measured from a buyer's demand curve and from his marginal utility curve, both based on the data given previously in Exhibit 8. In both cases, however, the curves have been extended to touch the axes of the charts. Notice that although the curves seem to look alike, the scales on the vertical axes of the charts are measured in different units.

In chart (*a*), the demand curve tells us that the consumer would be just willing to pay $2 for the fourth unit of the commodity, and that he would have been willing to pay more, if necessary, for the first, second, and third units. He therefore gets a consumer's surplus—a net amount of "pure" satisfaction—by paying only $2 each for all four units. His total expenditure is therefore $8, which is the rectangular area (equal to base × height) shown in the diagram. His consumer's surplus, which is the right-triangular area (equal to $\frac{1}{2}$ base × height), also happens to be $8 in this case. These two amounts, of course, need not always be the same, depending on the slope of the demand curve.

In chart (*b*) we can calculate the same information in utils. Thus the total expenditure *in utils* equals $4 \times 6 = 24$ utils; likewise consumer's surplus *in utils* equals $(4 \times 12)/2 = 24$ utils. If we invoke our earlier assumption that the marginal utility of money is equal to 3 utils per dollar, the total expenditure in dollars comes to $8, and the consumer's surplus in dollars also comes to $8. These amounts, of course, are the same as those calculated previously from the demand curve in chart (*a*).

The concept of consumer's surplus has a long and interesting history. For our present purposes it poses two important questions:

1. Since consumer's surplus represents the "extra" value or satisfaction to a buyer, could the government tax it away without affecting either the quantity purchased or its price?

2. If a seller could measure a buyer's demand curve, would the seller be able to capture the consumer's surplus for himself by charging the highest price he can get for the first unit, the next highest price he can get for the second unit, and so on—instead of charging the *same* price per unit for *all* units?

The answer to both questions is yes, but there are limitations and conditions. Some of these are spelled out below; the rest must wait until we have covered more ground in a later chapter.

Exhibit 9

Measuring Consumer's Surplus from a Demand Curve and from a Marginal Utility Curve

The rectangular and triangular areas, respectively, measure total expenditure and consumer's surplus, whether in dollars as in chart (a) or in utils as in chart (b).

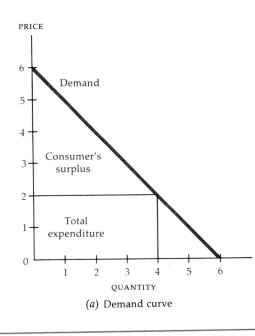

(a) Demand curve

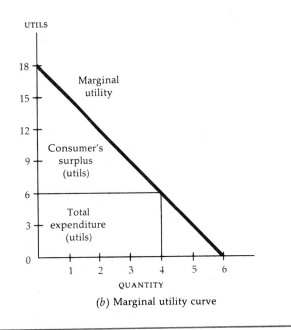

(b) Marginal utility curve

CONCLUSION: TWO MAJOR SHORTCOMINGS

As mentioned earlier, the theory of utility provides one of the more fundamental explanations of why a demand curve is downward-sloping. However, it suffers from several serious shortcomings, at least two of which are especially important.

1. Indivisibility of Products. The theory assumes that commodities are sufficiently divisible to be consumed in small units—like ice-cream cones, candy bars, or cups of coffee. To the ordinary consumer who may buy one house or one piano in a lifetime, or a new and different type of car every several years, the idea of marginal utility has little or no application, since it is a concept which by definition refers to the consumption of increasing units of the *same commodity within a given period of time while tastes remain constant.* The theory of utility is thus weakened by the fact that many products bought by consumers are indivisible and cannot be consumed in small, successive doses.

2. Immeasurability of Utility. A more fundamental difficulty is that no method has yet been devised for measuring a consumer's intensity of satisfaction (utility) in the same way as we might measure the weight of an object in ounces or pounds, or the distance between two points in inches, feet, or miles. In other words, we cannot measure utility in terms of *cardinal* numbers like 10, 23, 32.7, and so on, as the theory of utility assumes.

In view of the theory's rather tenuous assumptions, must we conclude that one of its most fundamental features—namely the law of diminishing marginal utility—is invalid? Most economists think not:

> Despite the shortcomings of utility theory, the law of diminishing marginal utility is valid because if the ratio of the marginal utility of commodity A to the price of A were greater than the ratios of the marginal utilities of all other commodities to their respective prices, and if the marginal utilities of all other commodities remained constant as the consumption of them increased, the consumer would spend his entire income on commodity A and nothing on the other commodities. In reality, of course, we know that consumers do not behave in this way.

In other words, if it were not for the law of diminishing marginal utility, we would spend all of our money on the one commodity that gave us the greatest gain in satisfaction. Since this does not happen in reality, the above argument suggests the conclusion that even though there is no absolute measure of utility, the theory nevertheless permits the development of meaningful principles pertaining to consumer demand and equilibrium.

SUMMARY OF IMPORTANT IDEAS

1. Black markets tend to emerge when ceiling prices and rationing are introduced. Analysis indicates that black market prices would be lower if buyers rather than sellers were penalized for dealing in it.

2. The economic consequences of a tariff are much like those resulting from an increase in transportation costs. In general, the effects of a tariff on prices and the volume of trade depend on the relative elasticities of demand and supply between the trading nations. On the whole, tariffs tend to benefit domestic producers and foreign consumers, while penalizing domestic consumers and foreign producers.

3. The cobweb theorem describes price and quantity fluctuations of certain agricultural commodities. These fluctuations occur because the quantity supplied depends on the price in a previous period when production plans were initially formulated.

Such fluctuations may result in diverging, converging, or "neutral" cycles, depending on the relative elasticities of demand and supply. The hog cycle, which is significantly influenced by the hog-corn price ratio, provides the most pronounced illustration of the cobweb theorem.

4. An explanation of the law of (downward-sloping) demand can be given on the bases of observation and experience, substitution and income effects, or the theory of utility. The last assumes that utility can be measured in cardinal numbers, thus giving rise to the law of diminishing marginal utility—one of the most famous laws in economics.

5. The theory of utility shows how consumer equilibrium is obtained when the marginal utility per dollar of expenditure is equal for all commodities including money. On the basis of this principle, a consumer's demand curve for a commodity can be derived and the concept of consumer's surplus can be demonstrated.

FOR HOMEWORK AND DISCUSSION

1. *Terms and concepts to review:*

black market	utility
tariff	marginal utility
arbitrage	law of diminishing
cobweb theorem	marginal utility
hog-corn price ratio	consumer's surplus
substitution effect	demand price
income effect	conspicuous consumption

2. Suppose there is a free and unregulated domestic market in gold, and the normal or equilibrium price is $40 an ounce. The government then decides to impose a ceiling price of $35 an ounce. What would be the effects of such an action in the market for gold? Explain and illustrate. What should the government do to minimize the undesirable consequences of its action?

3. Why do we find that wherever black markets arise, they almost always involve products like butter, gasoline, meat, foreign currencies, and gold, and not usually such products as machinery and equipment?

WILLIAM STANLEY JEVONS

1835–1882

Marginal Utility Theorist—Mathematical Economist

"Repeated reflections and inquiry have led me to the somewhat novel opinion that value *depends entirely upon utility. Prevailing opinions make labor rather than utility the origins of value; and there are even those who distinctly assert that labor is the* cause *of value. I show, on the contrary, that we have only to trace out carefully the natural laws of the variation of utility, as depending on the quantity of commodity in our possession, in order to arrive at a satisfactory theory of exchange, of which the ordinary laws of supply and demand are a necessary consequence."*

These were the words with which the great English economist Jevons introduced his major work in economics, a book entitled Theory of Political Economy *(first published in 1871, with three subsequent editions appearing in later years).*

Jevons is one of the towering figures in the development of economic thought. He made many significant contributions to value and distribution theory, capital theory, and to statistical research in economics. But he is perhaps best known as a leading contributor to marginal utility analysis. In one of the key passages of his book, he points out that exchange between two individuals will cease when "the ratio of exchange of any two commodities is . . . the reciprocal of the ratio of the final degrees of utility of the quantities of commodity available for consumption," which is just a clumsy way of saying that in equilibrium marginal utilities will be proportionate to prices.

Jevons was educated in England; he majored in chemistry and the natural sciences, but maintained a strong interest in philosophy, science, logic, mathematics, and political economy (i.e., economics). He served as Professor of Political Economy at Owens College, Manchester, and at University College, London. In addition to a famous study called The Coal Question *(1865), which gained him recognition as an economist, Jevons wrote a distinguished text entitled* Elementary Lessons in Logic and Principles of Science *(1870). His main work, however, was* Theory of Political Economy, *mentioned above, in which he made clear his desire to develop economics as a mathematical science. In his own words:*

"It is clear that Economics, if it is to be a science at all, must be a mathematical science. There exists much prejudice against attempts to introduce the methods and language of mathematics into any branch of the moral sciences. Many persons seem to

Radio Times Hulton Picture Library

think that the physical sciences form the proper sphere of mathematical method, and that the moral sciences demand some other method—I know not what. My theory of Economics, however, is purely mathematical in character. Nay, believing that the quantities with which we deal must be subject to continuous variation, I do not hesitate to use the appropriate branch of mathematical science, involving though it does the fearless consideration of infinitely small quantities. The theory consists in applying the differential calculus to the familiar notions of wealth, utility, value, demand, supply, capital, interest, labour, and all the other quantitative notions belonging to the daily operations of industry. As the complete theory of almost every other science involves the use of that calculus, so we cannot have a true theory of Economics without its aid."

Jevons also did pioneering work in statistics and business forecasting. He formulated statistical correlations and forecasts of business and economic data which he sold to businessmen—an idea that was at least 50 years ahead of its time.

Jevons's productive efforts were brought to an untimely end. In his late thirties he began to suffer ill health, and at the age of 47 he drowned while visiting a health resort.

THORSTEIN BUNDE VEBLEN

1857–1929

The Great Iconoclast—Institutionalist—"Antimarginalist"

Historical Pictures Service, Chicago

Theories in economics are not always accepted without reservation; throughout their development, economic doctrines have been challenged and criticized. But no one has ever been more challenging and more critical than Thorstein Veblen—philosopher, anthropologist, sociologist, economist, "compleat" social scientist, and prophet extraordinary. Indeed, Veblen ranks as one of the most creative and original thinkers in the history of economics, and he influenced an entire generation of brilliant economic scholars who succeeded him.

Veblen was born on a backwoods farm in Wisconsin, of Norwegian immigrant parents. His life was unusual; in fact, there is no question that in material terms he was a failure. After his undergraduate education at Carleton College, he spent a checkered career in which he pursued some graduate work at Johns Hopkins University and eventually ended up at Yale where he recieved a Ph.D. degree in philosophy in 1884.

Despite his brilliant mind, Veblen was quite eccentric, had difficulty getting along with people, and earned a reputation of being an extremely dull and uninterested teacher of undergraduate students. As a result he stumbled from one precarious teaching position to another, never reaching a rank higher than associate professor which he held at Stanford University from 1906 to 1909. In later years he taught at the University of Missouri and at the New School for Social Research in New York City.

Historically, Veblen was part of what is known as the "institutionalist" school of economic thought. He believed that human behavior could best be understood in terms of the practices and customs of society, its methods of doing things, and its ways of thinking about things, all of which compose "settled habits of thought common to the generality of men." These habits become institutions—deeply ingrained patterns of thought and action on which all material civilization is built.

Institutions, however, are not permanent. They unfold and grow into new patterns of change. In this sense, socioeconomic behavior is more evolutionary and dynamic than it is mechanisitic—more like biology than physics—because it is devoid of the "natural," "normal," "controlling principles" that are found in the writings of marginal utility theorists and other classical economists.

This is the type of argument that Veblen used in hammering away at the accepted economic doctrines of his time. He wrote more than a dozen books, all of them interesting and controversial. His first and most well-known book, The Theory of the Leisure Class (1899; new ed., 1918), is often required reading even today for students taking courses in sociology. In this book he coined a famous phrase, conspicuous consumption, by which he meant the tendency of those above the subsistence level, i.e., the "leisure class," to be mainly concerned with impressing others through standards of living, taste, and dress—that is, through what he called "pecuniary emulation"—which is the hallmark of society. This, Veblen argued, was a "commonly observed pattern of behavior" which was contrary to marginal utility theory, for it clearly could imply that people may sometimes buy more of a good at higher prices than at lower prices in order to impress others.

Thorstein Veblen, more perhaps than any other social scientist, criticized practically every phase of social life. Throughout his writings there are prophecies about the changing structure of society, many of which have materialized with astounding accuracy. History may someday record that Veblen was the greatest prophet of social and economic change who ever lived.

4. A protectionist (someone who favors tariffs) often contends that a tariff does not raise the price to the consumer in the importing country because the foreign seller must accept a lower price in order to sell the product abroad.

A free trader (someone who opposes tariffs) may argue that a tariff always raises the price to the consumer in the importing country by the amount of the tariff because the foreign seller must get his old price or else he will not produce.

Evaluate these arguments. What general principles can you suggest to cover all such arguments?

5. In terms of elasticities of demand and supply, which types of products will be least affected by a tariff as far as volume of trade is concerned? Illustrate with diagrams.

6. It has been suggested from time to time that the government should speculate in certain commodities in order to even out their price fluctuations. How would this proposal work in terms of the cobweb theorem? Explain and illustrate.

7. Assume that Mr. R is rich and Mr. P is poor, and that both have the same marginal utility of money curve (MU_m), as shown in Exhibit 10. Let Mr. R's income be OR and Mr. P's income be OP.

a. What is Mr. R's marginal utility for money? Mr. P's?

b. What is Mr. R's total utility for money? Mr. P's?

c. If you could reallocate the total incomes of these two individuals, how would you do it so as to maximize their *combined* total utility for money? Illustrate on the diagram.

d. Which individual would experience a loss in total utility for money as a result of this income reallocation? Which individual would experience a gain?

e. Is the *net* effect of income reallocation a gain or a loss in the total utility for money?

f. Does this problem suggest any implications for society as a whole? Discuss.

REFERENCES AND READING SUGGESTIONS

BOBER, M. M., *Intermediate Price and Income Theory,* rev. ed., Norton, New York, 1962, chap. 3.

BOULDING, KENNETH E., *Economic Analysis,* vol. 1, *Microeconomics,* 4th ed., Harper & Row, New York, 1966, chaps. 9, 11, 12.

DOOLEY, PETER C., *Elementary Price Theory,* Appleton-Century-Crofts, New York, 1967, chap. 2.

Exhibit 10

Marginal Utility of Money for Two Individuals

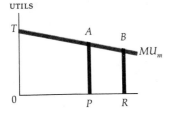

Supplement: Indifference Curves

The law of diminishing marginal utility has long been used to explain the existence of downward-sloping demand curves. The chief difficulty with this explanation, however, lies in our *inability to measure utility*. Unlike the weight of an object or the distance between two points, utility cannot be ascertained in terms of cardinal numbers. It was largely because of this shortcoming that economists devised an alternative approach for explaining demand phenomena— an approach that makes use of a concept known as *indifference curves*.

THE PRICE LINE OR BUDGET LINE

Imagine a consumer possessing, say, two dollars, entering the market to spend his money on goods. He is confronted with two commodities, X and Y. The price of X is $2; the price of Y is $1. In other words, the price of X is twice the price of Y. Algebraically, if P denotes price, then $P_x = 2P_y$.

Now the consumer could spend his entire two dollars on X, in which case he could buy only one unit and have nothing left to spend on Y; or he could spend his whole two dollars on Y and have nothing left to spend on X. The table in Exhibit 11 shows some of the combinations of X and Y that he could purchase with his two dollars. Thus, for $2, with P_x equal to $2 and P_y equal to $1, our individual can buy any of the combinations shown in the table as well as any other combinations that will total two dollars.

The diagram in Exhibit 11 illustrates the same situation graphically. In this chart, the vertical axis OY represents the different quantities of commodity Y that the consumer can purchase, whereas the horizontal axis OX shows the amounts of X that can be had.

Thus if our consumer spends his entire two dollars on Y, he can purchase two units or an amount equal to OM. If he spends his two dollars on X, he can purchase one unit or an amount equal to ON. If we connect these two points with a line, the resulting MN is called a "price line" or "budget line."

Just what does this price line tell us? It indicates all the possible combinations of X and Y that could be purchased for a total of $2, assuming that $P_x = $2 and $P_y = $1. Thus, point Q shows that the consumer could purchase one unit of Y and one-half unit of X for a total of $2. Likewise with any other point on MN. Notice, however, that as we move along the line from M to N, more of X can be purchased and less of Y. This is just as we should expect: out of any given money income, the more we spend on one commodity the less we have left to spend on other things.

By definition, therefore, a *price line* (or *budget line*)

Exhibit 11

A Consumer's Alternative Purchase Combinations

Assumptions: consumption budget = $2; price of X = $2; price of Y = $1.

Purchase combinations	Units of X	Units of Y	Total amount spent
N	1	0	$2 + $0 = $2
Q	½	1	$1 + $1 = $2
M	0	2	$0 + $2 = $2

The price line *represents all the possible combinations of commodities X and Y that the consumer can purchase at a particular time, given the market prices of the commodities and the consumer's budget.*

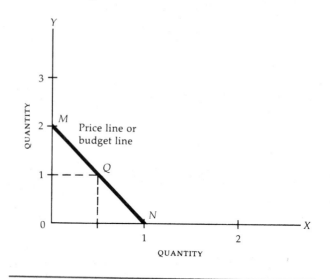

represents all the possible combinations of two commodities that a consumer can purchase at a particular time, given the market prices of the commodities and the consumer's money budget or income.

Many Possible Price Lines. Suppose now that our individual, instead of possessing only $2, had say, $4. Since he has twice as much money, he can buy twice as much of each commodity, provided that their prices do not change. Thus, for $2, he was able to buy as much as $2Y$ or $1X$, or any combination in between. Now he can buy as much as 4Y or 2X, or any combination in between. This fact is shown in Exhibit 12, where $M'N'$ represents the new price line at a higher income or budget of $4, and MN the old price line at a lower income or budget of $2. Obviously, for every level of income there will be a different price line corresponding to that income level. If income rises, so too does the price line; if income falls, the price line falls. Thus, since an infinite number of budgets or income levels are possible, so too an infinite number of price lines are possible.

THE NATURE OF INDIFFERENCE CURVES

When a consumer is confronted with two commodities, X and Y, he will probably not spend his entire income on only one of these commodities. Instead, he will probably purchase some combination of the two. Since there are many possible combinations of X and Y that can be bought, the question is: Just which combination of the many possible combinations will he purchase?

Let us disregard the price relationships that were made in the previous section and pay attention solely to the satisfaction our consumer would derive from possessing commodities X and Y. That is, let us forget for the moment that $P_x = \$2$ and $P_y = \$1$ and that the consumer has a given income.

We start by constructing what is called an *indifference schedule*. This is a list showing the various combinations of two commodities that would be equally satisfactory to the consumer at a given time. Column (*a*) of the table in Exhibit 13 is an example of a possible indifference schedule for two commodities X and Y.

In this column, each combination of X and Y is equally satisfactory to the consumer. Thus, the consumer would just as soon have combination 1, that is, 60Y and 1X, as he would combination 2, that is, 50Y and 2X, or combination 3, 41Y and 3X, and so on. This is true because each combination yields him the same total satisfaction or utility. Hence, he is completely *indifferent* as to which combination he prefers, for he prefers no one combination; they are all equally desirable because they *all yield the same total utility*.

Now there is this important thing to notice about an indifference schedule: Since each combination yields the same total utility, it follows that if the consumer were to increase his X intake by one unit at a time, he would have to decrease his Y holdings by some amount in order that each successive combination continue to yield the same total utility. For example, when he possesses combination 1 of 60Y and 1X, he derives a certain amount of total utility. If now he were to have 60Y and 2X, his total utility

Exhibit 12

An Increase in the Price Line

An increase in the consumer's income results in the price line being shifted outward, thus enabling him to buy more of X and Y at the given market prices.

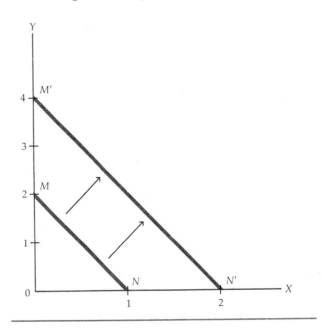

would be greater than the total utility of 60Y and 1X, for he would have the same amount of Y plus more of X. Therefore, in order to keep his total utility the same, he must give up a certain amount of Y for each unit increase in X. Column (*a*) shows this relationship.

Marginal Rate of Substitution. Next, we should notice that as the consumer increases his X intake, the amount of Y that he is willing to give up *decreases*. Thus, when he possesses combination 1 of 60Y and 1X, he is willing to give up 10 units of Y for 1 unit of X, leaving him with 50Y and 2X, or combination 2. At this point, he is willing to give up only 9 units of Y for 1 more unit of X, which would leave him at combination 3. Column (*b*) indicates this relationship. It shows us the amount of Y he is willing to surrender for every unit increase in his X holdings in order that the new combination yield him the same satisfaction as the previous one, i.e., the same total utility.

The rate at which the consumer is willing to substitute commodity X for commodity Y is called the *marginal rate of*

Exhibit 13

A Consumer's Indifference Schedule, Indifference Curve, and Marginal Rate of Substitution

Each combination in column (a) yields the consumer the same total utility. Hence he is indifferent as to which combination he prefers.

In column (b), the marginal rate of substitution measures the amount of commodity Y the consumer must give up to get one unit of commodity X, while maintaining the same total utility. The numerical value of this ratio decreases as additional units of X are acquired.

Combina-tions	(a) Indifference schedule	(b) Marginal rate of substitution of X for Y
1	60Y and 1X	
2	50Y and 2X	10/1
3	41Y and 3X	9/1
4	33Y and 4X	8/1
5	26Y and 5X	7/1
6	20Y and 6X	6/1
7	15Y and 7X	5/1
8	11Y and 8X	4/1
9	8Y and 9X	3/1
10	6Y and 10X	2/1
11	5Y and 11X	1/1

An indifference curve is a graph of an indifference schedule. Any point on the curve denotes a particular combination of commodities X and Y that yield the same total utility.

Note that as X increases one unit at a time, the amount of Y that the consumer is willing to give up decreases. This reflects a decreasing marginal rate of substitution of X for Y.

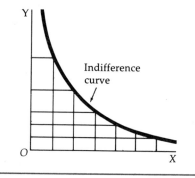

Indifference curve

substitution, often abbreviated *MRS.* It may be defined as the change in the amount of one commodity which will just offset a unit change in the holdings of another commodity so that the consumer's total utility remains the same. Since the ratio of the change in Y to the change in X is negative (because the amount of one commodity decreases when the other increases), we may express the marginal rate of substitution by the formula:

$$MRS = - \frac{\text{change in } Y}{\text{change in } X}$$

As a general rule the minus sign is understood; hence it may be omitted in written and oral discussions.

Why does the *MRS,* as shown in column (*b*) of the table, decrease? You will remember that the reason a demand curve sloped downward from left to right was that the marginal utility of the commodity decreased as more of the commodity was consumed. (The more we have of something, the less we want more of it.)

The concept of a decreasing *MRS* is similar to that of decreasing marginal utility. As *X increases* (one unit at a time), the marginal utility of X *decreases.* As *Y decreases,* the marginal utility of Y *increases.* Thus, the more we have of X, the less we want more of it, and the less we have of Y, the less we are willing to give up more of it. That is, as we give up Y for X, the less of Y we are willing to give up for further units of X.

For example, when the consumer possessed 60Y and 1X, he was willing to give up a relatively large amount of Y, namely 10Y, for 1 unit of X. After that, he was willing to give up only 9 units of Y, then 8Y, and so forth, for further units of X. This is because he cares less and less for additional units of X, and hence is willing to give up less and less of Y. (Or conversely, he cares more and more for his smaller holdings of Y and is willing to give them up at a slower and slower rate.)

Many Possible Indifference Curves. Suppose now that we were to extend our indifference schedule far enough and then plot the various combinations on a chart. We would get a curve similar to the one appearing earlier in Exhibit 13. This curve is called an *indifference curve* because every point on it represents a particular combination of the two commodities X and Y that is equally satisfactory to the consumer, i.e., yields him the same total utility.

Just as it is possible to have an infinite number of price lines, so too it is possible to have an infinite number of indifference curves. This is suggested in Exhibit 14, where point Q represents a combination of OM of X and ON of Y. This combination yields the same total utility as any other combination on the same curve. On the higher curve at

Exhibit 14

Two Indifference Curves

The higher a consumer's indifference curve, the greater his total utility. *The points S and R, in comparison with the point Q, represent at least as much of one commodity plus more of the other. Any point between S and R, such as T, represents more of both commodities. Although this chart depicts only two indifference curves, an infinite number of such curves exist.*

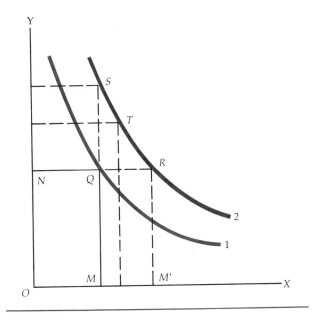

point *R*, however, the consumer possesses the same amount of *Y*, namely *ON*, plus more of *X*, namely *OM'*. Therefore, this combination must yield a higher total utility than any of the previous combinations to be found on curve 1.

In a similar fashion we note that at point *S* on the higher curve as compared to point *Q* on the lower one there is the same amount of *X* plus more of *Y*. Finally, at any point between *S* and *R* on the higher curve, say at *T*, there is more of *both X* and *Y* as compared to the combination denoted by point *Q* on the lower curve.

These ideas suggest three important conclusions about indifference curves:

1. The higher an indifference curve—that is, the farther it lies to the right—the greater the consumer's total utility, for any point on a higher curve will always denote *at least* the same amount of one commodity plus more of the other.

2. A consumer will always try to be on his highest possible indifference curve, since it is assumed that he will always try to maximize his total utility.

3. Each indifference curve represents a *different* level of total utility; therefore, indifference curves can never intersect at any point.

THE EQUILIBRIUM COMBINATION

Now let us combine the previous two sections dealing with price lines and indifference curves. Superimposing one diagram upon the other, we get a result such as that depicted in Exhibit 15.

The price line *MN* shows us the possible combinations of *X* and *Y* that could be purchased with given prices of *X* and *Y* at a given income. The indifference curves 1, 2,

Exhibit 15

The Equilibrium Purchase Combination.

The tangency of the price line with an indifference curve determines the equilibrium purchase combination. Thus, since the tangency is at point Q, the consumer will buy OP units of X and OL units of Y.

A given price line may intersect any number of indifference curves, but it can be tangent to only one indifference curve.

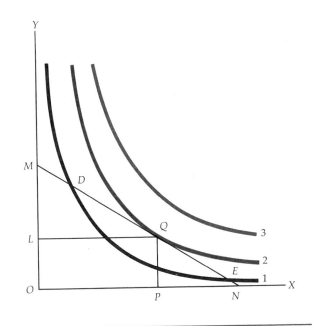

and 3 show various combinations of X and Y that yield the same total utility. The higher the indifference curve, the greater the total utility; therefore, the consumer will always try to be on the highest possible indifference curve.

Given these price lines and indifference curves, precisely what combination of X and Y will be purchased? The answer is based on the following fundamental notions:

The indifference curves represent the consumer's *subjective* valuations of X and Y and have no relationship to the *objective* facts that X and Y have certain prices and that the consumer has a certain money income to spend. These objective facts are shown by the price line.

Subjectively, the consumer will try to be on the highest possible indifference curve; objectively, he is limited in doing so by the price line. The problem, therefore, is to reconcile this difference.

Since the price line shows all the possible combinations of X and Y that can be purchased for a given money income, it follows that there will be only one point on the price line that will also be on the highest possible indifference curve. This is point Q, where the price line is tangent to curve 2. Point Q, therefore, shows the combination of X and Y that will be purchased, namely OL of Y and OP of X.

Thus the consumer would not want to be on curve 1, where he would purchase a combination determined by D or E, because his purchasing power as determined by the price line permits him to be on a higher indifference curve. The highest curve that he can be on and yet remain within his income as determined by the price line is curve 2, and the only place where the price line touches the highest indifference curve within the consumer's means is point Q. This point, therefore, indicates the combination of X and Y that will be purchased at the prevailing prices and income.

The consumer is thus in a position not unlike that of the legendary Buridan's ass. The ass, it will be remembered, stood equidistant between two equal bundles of hay, and starved to death because it could not choose between them. Likewise, all combinations on any one indifference curve are equally desirable; it is the point of tangency of an indifference curve with a price line that determines the equilibrium purchase combination.

WHAT HAPPENS WHEN INCOME CHANGES?

Suppose now that the consumer's income increases while the prices of X and Y remain the same. The consumer could now purchase more of both X and Y. This condition is shown in Exhibit 16, where the price line shifts to the right from MN to M'N' to M"N", indicating that a greater

Exhibit 16

Income-Consumption Curve

An increase in income may increase the consumer's purchases of both X and Y. *The line QRS connects the tangency points of price lines and indifference curves as the consumer's income increases. It is called an* income-consumption curve, *abbreviated ICC.*

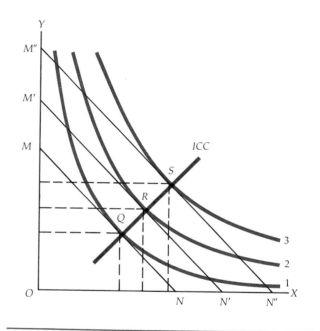

combination of both commodities can be purchased. At each new level of income there is a tangency with a new and higher indifference curve. Connecting these points of tangency, we get the line QRS, and dropping a perpendicular from each of these points to the X and Y axes shows us by how much the consumer increases his purchases of both X and Y as his income rises.

The line QRS may be called an *income-consumption curve,* abbreviated *ICC;* it connects the tangency points of price lines and indifference curves by showing the amounts of two commodities that a consumer will purchase if his income changes while their prices remain constant.

It is possible, however, that as income increases, the consumption of one commodity may increase while the consumption of the other commodity decreases. This is shown in Exhibit 17, charts (a) and (b). In chart (a), as income rises, the consumption of Y also rises, and though X at first increases, it gradually falls off. The opposite is

Exhibit 17

Superior and Inferior Goods

As a consumer's income increases, he may buy more of one commodity (superior good) and less of another commodity (inferior good).

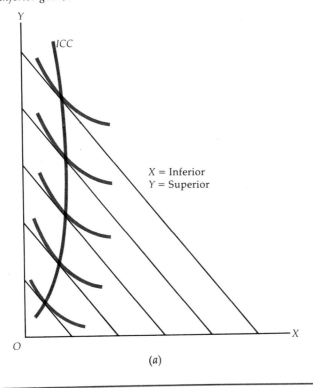

(a)

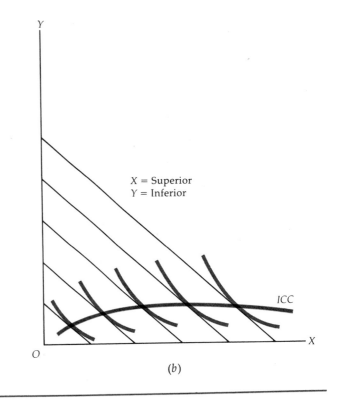

(b)

seen in chart (b); as income rises, the consumption of both X and Y increase, but Y soon decreases.

A good whose consumption is decreased relative to other goods as the consumer's income rises is called an *inferior good*. Some classic examples are potatoes, used clothing, and other so-called "poor man's goods" consumed mainly by low-income families. But in a larger sense there are goods that may be "inferior" at any income level. Thus when a family "steps up" from a Chevrolet to an Oldsmobile because of an increase in its income, the Chevrolet becomes an inferior good.

On the other hand, a good whose consumption is increased relative to other goods as the consumer's income rises is called a *superior good*. Illustrations of such goods are dairy products and beef. Can you think of other examples?

WHAT HAPPENS WHEN PRICE CHANGES?

The previous case assumed that the consumer's income increased while the prices of X and Y remained constant. Let us now allow both the consumer's income and the price of Y to remain constant, but the price of X to decrease. What happens?

The result is seen in Exhibit 18. The lower end of the price line shifts to the right from MN to MN' to MN", indicating that as P_x falls, more of it can be purchased. The price line thus fans outward as a result of decreases in P_x.

We can work the same idea in the other direction by permitting the lower end of the price line to shift left. For instance, let us assume that the price line to begin with is MN". Then suppose that the price of X gradually rises while the price of Y and the consumer's income remain the

Exhibit 18

Price-Consumption Curve

With the consumer's income and the price of Y constant, decreases in the price of X result in the consumer buying more of it. The line QRS connects the tangency points of price lines and indifference curves under these circumstances. It is called a price-consumption curve, abbreviated PCC.

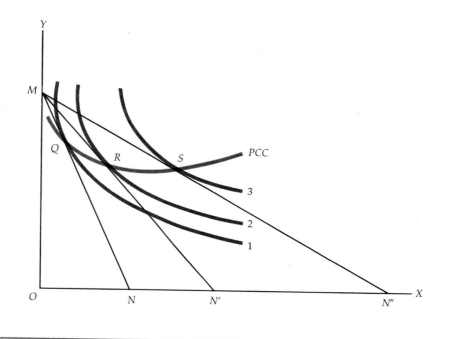

same. As P_x rises, less of X can be bought, until finally the price of X is so high that it is not purchased at all, and the price line becomes *MO*, indicating that the consumer spends his entire income on Y.

The line *QRS* in the diagram is thus a *price-consumption curve*, abbreviated PCC. It connects the tangency points of price lines and indifference curves by showing the amounts of two commodities that a consumer will purchase when his income and the price of one commodity remain constant while the price of the other commodity varies.

DERIVING A DEMAND CURVE

How do the principles of indifference curves and price lines relate to the law of demand? As you recall, this is the problem we started out to solve.

The answer is that we can now combine the foregoing concepts to derive a *demand curve*. This is illustrated in Exhibit 19, where numbers are used with letters so that the computations can be followed easily.

In chart (*a*), the price line *MN* signifies that with a consumer income of $10, and with $P_y = \$1$ and $P_x = \$2$, the buyer can purchase either 10 units of Y, or 5 units of X, or various combinations in between. The tangency of this price line with the consumer's indifference curve, however, shows that the buyer will maximize his total utility by purchasing 4 units of Y and 3 units of X.

Suppose now that the price of X falls to $1, while the consumer's income and the price of Y remain constant. The tangency of the new price line *MN'* with the higher indifference curve indicates that the consumer will be in equilibrium by purchasing 3 units of Y and 7 units of X.

Exhibit 19

Derivation of a Demand Curve from Indifference Curves

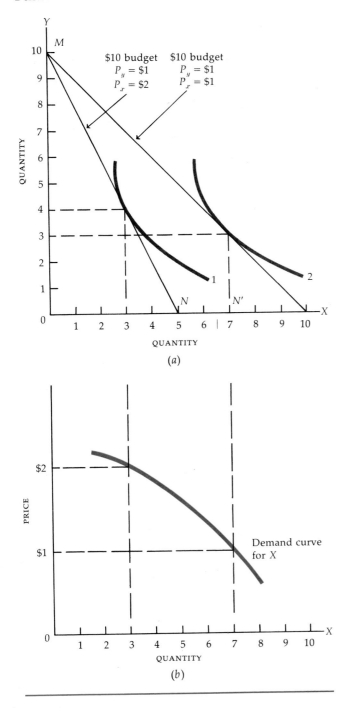

(a)

(b)

We need this kind of information to derive a demand curve. For example, in chart (b) we see the relationship between the price of X and the quantity demanded of X while all other things—namely the buyer's income and the price of Y—remain the same. Thus the dashed lines emphasize the fact that the buyer will purchase 3 units of X at a price of $2 per unit, and 7 units of X at a price of $1 per unit. Connecting these two points (as well as all the in-between points that may be similarly derived) we get the demand curve for X. As you can see, this curve obeys the law of demand: the lower the price, the greater the quantity demanded.

CONCLUSION

The theory of indifference curves had its origins in the late nineteenth century, and reached full flower in the 1930s. It marked a major advance in the history of economics, for it freed the concept of demand from a reliance on the older and controversial concept of utility.

You can easily see the reason for this. In the indifference curve approach, it need only be assumed that the consumer knows his preferences. He must know whether he prefers one combination of goods to another, or whether he regards them as equivalent. He does not have to know by *how much* he prefers one good to another. Hence the older approach to demand theory, which rested on the unrealistic assumption of a cardinal utility relationship (1, 2, 3, etc.), is replaced by the more realistic assumption of an ordinal preference relationship (first, second, third, etc.).

The significance is clear:

From the standpoint of indifference curve analysis, the inability to measure utility is no longer a problem, for such a measure is no longer needed: A downward-sloping demand curve can be derived directly from a consumer's indifference curves and price lines without using or even assuming a "law" of utility.

SUMMARY OF IMPORTANT IDEAS

1. The theory of indifference curves relates *objective* facts determined by market prices and the consumer's income to the consumer's *subjective* valuations of commodities. The key mechanisms employed in the theory are price lines and indifference curves.

2. Through indifference curve analysis, we can show how the consumption of goods changes when a buyer's income increases while prices are held constant; we can also illustrate how a buyer's consumption of a good changes when its price varies, while his income and all other prices remain the same.

3. A consumer's demand curve can be derived directly from the tangency points of indifference curves and price lines. The law of demand can thus be established without relying on the controversial theory of utility.

FOR HOMEWORK AND DISCUSSION

1. Terms and concepts to review:

price line (budget line)	income-consumption curve
indifference schedule	inferior good
marginal rate of substitution	superior good
indifference curve	price-consumption curve

2. We have drawn indifference curves so that they are *convex* to the origin. What would it mean to draw an indifference curve that is *concave* to the origin? Would it make sense? Explain. (HINT: Think in terms of the *MRS*.)

3. Draw a consumer's indifference curve which represents each of the following situations:

a. Two commodities that are perfect complements, i.e., used in 1:1 proportions, such as left shoes and right shoes

b. Two commodities that are perfect substitutes, such as nickels and dimes in the ratio of 2:1

4. Commodities such as diamonds and furs are sometimes cited as an exception to the law of demand because some people will buy more of these at a higher price than at a lower price. Does this mean that the "demand" curve for these products is upward-sloping? Explain. (Be careful in your thinking. This is a much deeper question than is immediately apparent.)

5. In terms of indifference curve analysis, what might be the effects of each of the following:

a. An increase in taxes

b. An increase in the cost of living

c. Expectation of inflation

REFERENCES AND READING SUGGESTIONS

BOBER, M. M., *Intermediate Price And Income Theory,* rev. ed., Norton, New York, 1962, chap. 4.

DOOLEY, PETER C., *Elementary Price Theory,* Appleton-Century-Crofts, New York, 1967, appendix to chap. 2.

WARD, BENJAMIN, *Elementary Price Theory,* The Free Press, New York, 1967, chap. 4.

Costs of Production

CHAPTER PREVIEW

What does the word "cost" mean? Is the term employed in different senses? Can we establish some useful definitions of costs that can be helpful in analyzing and interpreting production problems?

How are costs related to production? Can this information help us to understand the economic behavior of business firms?

According to a familiar saying, you have to spend money in order to make money. In the business world this can be translated to mean that a company must be willing to incur costs if it is to receive revenues.

What do we mean by costs? The term is by no means as simple as most people think. Engineers, accountants, and economists are each concerned with the nature and behavior of costs, but they often deal with different kinds of cost concepts for solving different problems.

For example, if you were the president of a corporation and you were interested in constructing a new manufacturing plant, you might employ an industrial engineer to study the cost of designing the plant, and a cost accountant to classify and analyze production costs after the plant was in operation. However, you might also hire an economist to advise you on the ways in which the plant's costs of production would be affected by changes in its volume of output, and how these costs could be used as a guide to helping you achieve the volume of production that would bring maximum profits.

Thus, the analysis of costs by engineers, accountants, and economists may be undertaken for quite different purposes. Our objective in this chapter is to discover those basic cost concepts and relationships that are of interest in economics.

What Do We Mean by "Cost"?

As long ago as 1923, a famous economist by the name of Professor J. M. Clark wrote, "A class in economics would be a success if the students gained from it an understanding of the meaning of cost in all its many aspects." Professor Clark was prompted to make this statement by the fact that although the general idea of cost can cover a wide variety of meanings, one meaning is common to all types of cost:

Cost is a sacrifice that must be made in order to do or to acquire something. The nature of the sacrifice— i.e., what is given up—may be tangible or intangible, objective or subjective, and may take one or more of many forms such as money, goods, leisure time, income, security, prestige, power, or pleasure.

Let us amplify this definition by describing and illustrating the notion of cost.

OUTLAY COSTS VERSUS OPPORTUNITY (ALTERNATIVE) COSTS

To most of us, the concept of cost that readily comes to mind is what we may call *outlay costs*. These are the moneys expended in order to carry on a particular activity. Some examples of outlay costs to a business are: wages and salaries of its employees; expenditures on plant and equipment; payments for raw materials, power, light, and transportation; disbursements for rents, advertising, and insurance; and taxes paid to the government. Such costs are also frequently called *explicit costs, historical costs,* or *accounting costs* because they are the objective and tangible expenses that an accountant records in the company's books.

There is a more basic concept of cost which economists call *opportunity cost*. This may be defined as the value of the benefit that is foregone by choosing one alternative rather than another. This is an extremely important concept because the "real" cost of any activity is measured by its opportunity cost, not by its outlay cost. How do you identify opportunity costs? By making a comparison between the alternative that was chosen and the one that was rejected. Here are some examples:

1. To a student, the cost of getting a full-time college education includes not only his outlay costs on tuition and books, but also the income he foregoes by not working full time.

2. To a business firm, the cost of allocating more money for advertising includes not only its outlay costs for magazine or TV time, but also the earnings it foregoes by not putting these funds to some other use—perhaps into the purchase of new equipment or the training of more salesmen.

3. To a city, the cost of a public park includes not only its outlay costs for construction and maintenance, but also the tax income that it foregoes by not zoning the land for residential, commercial, or industrial use.

You can probably think of other examples, and it should be evident why opportunity costs are often called "alternative costs."

The concept of opportunity cost arises whenever the inputs of any activity are scarce and have alternative uses. The real cost or sacrifice is then measured by the value of the foregone alternative. This principle applies at all levels of economic activity— macro as well as micro. Thus:

For any economic organism such as a society, a business, a household, or an individual, it is incorrect to confine the cost of an activity or a decision to what the organism is doing. *It is what the organism is not doing but could be doing that is the correct cost consideration.*

What About Nonmonetary Alternatives?

This principle raises an important question: Is it not true that the alternative cost of a given action may often involve nonmonetary considerations such as riskiness, working conditions, prestige, and similar factors? The answer is yes. This helps to explain why window washers in skyscrapers earn more than dishwashers in restaurants; why college professors on the average earn less—but probably have fewer headaches—than corporation executives; why the prices of "glamor" securities in the stock market fluctuate much more widely than the prices of public utility shares; and why a man may be willing to work for a smaller return in his own business where he can be his own boss, rather than for a higher return in someone else's.

Of course, the nonmonetary elements that help make for differences in resource allocation are often difficult to measure. But *in principle* the monetary returns plus or minus the various nonmonetary advantages and disadvantages determine the ways in which the owners of the factors of production put their human and material resources to use.

ECONOMIC COST INCLUDES NORMAL PROFIT

Once we recognize the existence of opportunity costs, it becomes apparent that there is a sharp distinction between costs in accounting and costs in economics. *Economic costs* are payments that must be made to persuade the owners of the factors of production to supply them for a particular activity. This definition emphasizes the fact that economic costs are supply prices or "bids" that buyers of resources must offer to attract the factor inputs they want.

Thus a firm buys its resources such as capital, land, and labor in the open market. Its expenditures for these resources are part of its economic costs, and these money outlays are the *explicit costs* that an accountant records in the company's books. But there are other types of economic costs, called *implicit costs* because they are the costs of self-owned or self-employed resources that are not entered in a company's books of account. For example, if an individual owns a business, including the building and its real estate, and if he manages this business himself, part of his cost includes:

1. The *interest* return on his investment that he is foregoing by not putting his money into an alternative investment of equal risk

2. The *rental* receipts that he is passing up by not renting the land and building to another firm

3. The *wages* (including the return for entrepreneurship) that he would earn if he could be hired to manage the same kind of business for someone else.

These implicit costs of ownership comprise what may be called *normal profit*—that is, the least payment the owner of an enterprise would be willing to accept for performing the entrepreneurial function, including risk taking, management, and the like.

Normal profit is thus part of a firm's total economic costs, since it is a payment which the owner must receive in order to keep him from withdrawing his capital and managerial effort and putting them into some other alternative. Further, since economic costs include both explicit costs and implicit costs, and since implicit costs include normal profit, any receipts which a firm may get over and above its economic costs represents *economic* or *pure profit*.

SHORT RUN AND LONG RUN

Any discussion of costs must include an explanation of two useful concepts—the short run and the long run. These do not refer to clock or calendar time, but to the time necessary for resources to adapt fully to new conditions—regardless of how many weeks, months, or even years this may take. At any given time a firm has available a certain *capacity* to produce as determined by the quantity or scale of its plant and equipment. If it experiences unexpected increases or decreases in the demand for its products, it can change its level of output by using existing plant and equipment either more or less intensively, but it cannot alter plant scale or production capacity with equal speed. Business firms do not put up new factories or discard old ones with every increase or decrease in demand, any more than colleges and universities erect new classroom buildings or abandon old ones with every rise or fall in enrollment.

This leads to an important distinction between the short run and the long run. The *short run* is a period in which a firm can vary its output through a more or less intensive use of its resources, but cannot vary its capacity because it has a fixed plant scale. The *long run* is a period long enough for a firm to enter or leave an industry, and to vary its output by varying all its factors of production, including plant scale.

These concepts of the short run and the long run suggest an appropriate passage from Henry Wadsworth Longfellow's famous poem, *The Old Clock on the Stairs*:

And the night shall be filled with music,
   And the cares that infest the day,
Shall fold their tents, like the Arabs,
   And as silently steal away.

Exhibit 1

Production Function

(1) Units of variable factor F	(2) Total Product TP	(3) Average Product AP $AP = \dfrac{TP}{F}$	(4) Marginal Product MP $MP = \dfrac{\text{change in } TP}{\text{change in } F}$
A 1	6	6	
			8
B 2	14	7	
			12
C 3	26	8.7	
			11
D 4	37	9.3	
			9
E 5	46	9.2	
			6
F 6	52	8.7	
			5
G 7	57	8.1	
			3
H 8	60	7.5	
			1
I 9	61	6.8	
			−3
J 10	58	5.8	

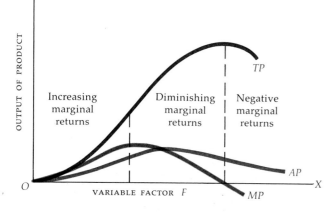

In economics as in poetry, business firms, like the Arabs to whom Longfellow referred, can also come and go by unfolding or folding their tents—but by our definition they can do this only in the long run, not in the short run.

The Production Function

Every businessman is well aware that his costs of production depend on two things: the prices he pays for his resources and the quantity of resources he buys. At this point our concern is with the latter. Therefore, it will be useful to analyze a concept known as the *production function*—a relationship between the number of units of output that a firm produces, and the number of units of various types of input that it employs.

THE LAW OF (EVENTUALLY) DIMINISHING RETURNS

You have probably heard of the *law of diminishing returns*—a law that is as famous in economics as the law of gravity in physics. But you are not likely to have a precise understanding of this law without a prior course in elementary economics, any more than you would have a clear understanding of the law of gravity if you never had a basic course in physics. Hence Exhibit 1, which displays a production function, enables you to "see" the operation of the law of diminishing returns as well as to understand it in terms of the following definition:

Law of (eventually) diminishing returns. In a given state of technology, the addition of a variable factor of production, keeping the other factors of production fixed, will yield increasing marginal returns per unit of the variable factor added until an input point is reached beyond which further additions of the variable factor will yield diminishing marginal returns per unit of the variable factor added. (NOTE: This law is also known by the more general name of the *law of variable proportions.*)

The law of diminishing returns was first discovered in agriculture in 1815, and marked an heroic advance in the history of economics. Indeed, it is one of the most widely held and best developed principles in all of economics, for it is a law that encompasses many kinds of production functions ranging from agriculture and automobiles through retailing and textiles to zinc and zippers. It thus has enormous significance as well as generality.

First, note that columns (1) and (2) of Exhibit 1 are in general terms. In order to put them into specific terms, the variable input in column (1) of the table might represent pounds of fertilizer applied to an acre of land, whereas the corresponding output in column (2) could be bushels or pounds of an agricultural product. Or the variable input might be the number of workers on an assembly line in a factory and the output could be the number of units of the finished good produced. Practically any simple type of "input-output" relation or production process could be used to illustrate the basic concepts that are involved.

Second, the curves in the chart are actually "idealized" or smoothed-out versions of the data given in the table. This enables us to focus most of our attention on the graphs rather than the numbers. Thus, the horizontal axis of the chart shows the variable factor from column (1) of the table, and the vertical axis represents the corresponding output from the remaining columns.

HOW IS THE LAW INTERPRETED?

The first thing you probably noticed in the chart is the shape of the total product or TP curve. As the variable input increases from zero, the TP curve goes through three phases—first rising rapidly, then tapering off until it reaches a maximum, and then declining. These three phases are reflected by the *marginal product, MP*, which is defined as the change in total product resulting from a unit change in a variable input. For measurement purposes, however, the expression "resulting from" in this definition means the same thing as "divided by"; hence marginal product is given by the formula:

$$MP = \frac{\text{change in total product}}{\text{change in variable input}}$$

You can verify these changes in MP from the table. *Average product, AP*, on the other hand, is simply the ratio of total product to the amount of variable input needed to produce that product:

$$AP = \frac{\text{total product}}{\text{variable input}}$$

For example, if Exhibit 1 is taken to represent the number of men working on a given parcel of land in order to produce tomatoes, the results could be interpreted in the following way.

When the first man, call him A, is applied to the fixed amount of land, he has to spread his efforts too thinly by covering all the land, and so the total output is only 6 boxes of tomatoes. If a second man, B, is added who is *equally as efficient* as A, they can work the same amount of land and thereby increase total output to 14 boxes of tomatoes. The average output is then 7 boxes of tomatoes per man, but the marginal product or gain in output is 8 boxes of tomatoes. Adding further men increases the total output, but a point is eventually reached where there are so many men that they get in each other's way and even trample the tomatoes—the TP curve passes its maximum point and turns downward. The gain in output or marginal product then becomes negative.

Note, therefore, that the MP curve at first rises and eventually begins to fall even though *all the men are equally efficient*. This is an extremely important point. The reason the MP curve declines is not that the last man hired is less efficient than the previous one. It declines solely for quantitative reasons; that is, it declines because of the changing proportions of variable to fixed factors employed, while all qualitative considerations are assumed to remain equal. This is why the term "law of variable proportions" is more often employed than "law of diminishing returns."

Mathematically, of course, the MP curve is derived from changes in the TP curve. Indeed, the MP curve represents the *slope* of the TP curve, since the slope of any curve is the change in its vertical distance per unit of change in its horizontal distance. Thus the fact that the TP curve first increases at an increasing rate and then at a decreasing rate is what causes the MP curve to rise to a maximum point and then fall.

The resulting three phases—*increasing marginal returns, diminishing marginal returns,* and *negative marginal returns*—are labeled on the chart. It is to these phases—especially the first two—that the definition of the law of diminishing returns refers.

Since all three curves rise to a maximum and then decline, it can be said that a law of diminishing returns applies to the total product, the average product, and the marginal product curves. Indeed, from the time the law was initially formulated in 1815 until the first third of this century, it was often stated in general terms without distinguishing between total, average, and marginal returns. But it then came to be realized that *marginal* returns are of key importance for decisions involving changes in either input or output, as will become increasingly apparent in subsequent chapters.

It is clear from Exhibit 1 that the point of diminishing marginal returns occurs at the input level where the *MP* curve is a maximum. Where is the point of diminishing average returns? Diminishing total returns?

Short-Run Costs

We have seen that in the short run some resource inputs for a firm are variable while others are fixed. This is because it may be possible in a given production process, for example, to vary the number of unskilled workers or to draw down larger or smaller quantities of raw materials available in inventory, but it may take considerable time to construct a new wing on a plant or have machines built to specification.

In view of this, what is the nature and behavior of a firm's costs in the short run? We shall answer this question by analyzing three families of cost concepts: *total cost, average cost,* and *marginal cost.*

COST SCHEDULES AND CURVES

The table in Exhibit 2 presents a company's cost schedule illustrating the relationship between quantities of output produced per day as shown in column (1), and the various costs per day of producing these

outputs, as shown in the remaining columns. The accompanying charts present the graphs of the various cost data in the table, thus conveying the fundamental relationships more clearly. Note that, as usual, output is measured on the horizontal axes of the charts, and dollars on the vertical axes.

Our objective is to see how the different costs in Exhibit 2 are related to output—how they do or do not vary with changes in output. Since the cost curves have a number of important properties, it is important to examine them closely. Remember that we are assuming that *a firm's total costs are its economic costs and hence include normal profit.*

The Family of Total Costs

The first class of costs to be considered is the "total" group shown in columns (2), (3), and (4) of the table.

Total Fixed Costs. TFC in column (2) represents those costs that do not vary with output. Examples are rental payments, interest payments on debt, property taxes, depreciation of plant and equipment, and the wages and salaries of a skeleton staff that the firm would employ as long as it stayed in business—even if it produced nothing. The TFC figure is $25 at all levels of output in the table and hence appears as a horizontal line on the chart.

Total Variable Costs. TVC in column (3) consists of those costs that vary directly with output, rising as output increases over the full range of production. Examples are payments for materials, labor, fuel, and power. Note from the chart that as output increases TVC increases first at a decreasing rate and then at an increasing rate, thus reflecting the operation of the law of diminishing (total) returns as explained earlier.

Total Costs. TC in column (4) represents the sum of total fixed cost and total variable cost. Thus we have the following equation:

$$TC = TFC + TVC$$

By "transposing," you can get for TFC

$$TFC = TC - TVC$$

Exhibit 2

Short-Run Cost Schedules and Curves for a Firm

(1) Quantity of output per day Q	(2) Total Fixed Cost TFC	(3) Total Variable Cost TVC	(4) Total Cost TC $TC = TFC + TVC$	(5) Average Fixed Cost AFC $AFC = \dfrac{TFC}{Q}$	(6) Average Variable Cost AVC $AVC = \dfrac{TVC}{Q}$	(7) Average Total Cost ATC $ATC = \dfrac{TC}{Q}$	(8) Marginal Cost MC $MC = \dfrac{\text{change in } TC}{\text{change in } Q}$
0	$25	$ 0	$ 25	$ —	$ —	$ —	
							$10
1	25	10	35	25.00	10.00	35.00	
							6
2	25	16	41	12.50	8.00	20.50	
							4
3	25	20	45	8.33	6.67	15.00	
							2
4	25	22	47	6.25	5.50	11.75	
							2
5	25	24	49	5.00	4.80	9.80	
							3
6	25	27	52	4.17	4.50	8.67	
							5
7	25	32	57	3.57	4.57	8.14	
							8
8	25	40	65	3.13	5.00	8.13	
							14
9	25	54	79	2.78	6.00	8.78	
							21
10	25	75	100	2.50	7.50	10.00	

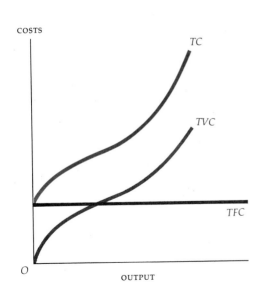

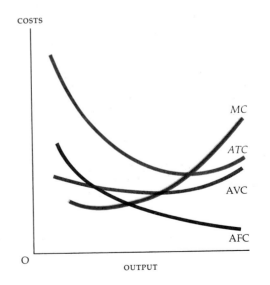

and for *TVC*

$$TVC = TC - TFC$$

You should also note from the table and chart that *TC* equals *TFC* at zero output; this is because there are no variable costs when there is no production. Observe too that the shape of the *TC* curve is the same as—or "parallel" to—the *TVC* curve, the only difference between them being the constant vertical distance represented by *TFC*. In other words, since total fixed cost is constant, changes in total cost are due to changes in total variable cost.

The Family of Average Costs

Columns (5), (6), and (7) give us three different types of average costs. These are also represented by the chart which accompanies the table.

Average Fixed Cost. *AFC* is the ratio of total fixed cost to quantity produced:

$$AFC = \frac{TFC}{Q}$$

Note from the chart that *AFC* continually decreases as output increases. This is because *TFC* in the above equation is constant; therefore increases in *Q* will always reduce the value of the ratio.

Average Variable Cost. *AVC* is the ratio of total variable cost to quantity produced:

$$AVC = \frac{TVC}{Q}$$

Notice that as output increases, the *AVC* curve falls to a minimum point and then rises. The *AVC* curve thus reflects the operation of the law of diminishing (average) returns described earlier.

Average Total Cost. *ATC* is the ratio of total cost to quantity:

$$ATC = \frac{TC}{Q}$$

Hence it is also equal to the sum of *AFC* and *AVC*:

$$ATC = AFC + AVC$$

Of course, you can also "transpose" either *AFC* or *AVC* in order to express the equation in terms of the other variables.

REMARK. Businessmen often use the terms "unit cost" or "cost per unit" when they mean average *variable* cost. If you were a shirt manufacturer, for example, you might figure your cost per shirt to be $3.50 based on the cost of labor, materials, and other variable resources used. You would then set a "markup" price of perhaps $6 per shirt to cover "overhead" or fixed costs. Economists, on the other hand, include fixed costs with total costs right from the outset, and hence use unit cost or cost per unit to mean average *total* cost.

Notice that the vertical distance between *ATC* and *AVC* diminishes as output increases; that is, *ATC* and *AVC* come progressively closer together. This is because the difference between them, *AFC*, continually decreases as output expands.

Marginal Cost

Before we conclude this analysis of costs, there is an important lesson to be learned from the table or graph: *Total cost always increases as output increases.* That is, the more a firm produces, the greater its total costs of production, since increased production always requires the use of more materials, labor, power, and other variable resources. Only average costs—both *ATC* and *AVC*—decrease as output increases until some "optimum" or best level of production is reached. Thus when you hear a businessman say that he needs to increase production in order to lower costs, he is talking about his unit costs—either his *ATC* or his *AVC*—not his *TC* or *TVC*.

The fact that total cost changes with variations in production gives rise to an important cost concept called *marginal cost, MC,* which is defined as the change in total cost resulting from a unit change in output. As you know from your previous acquaintance with marginal concepts in economics, the expression "resulting from" is used for interpretative purposes, and it means the same thing as "divided by" for mathematical purposes. Therefore, marginal cost may be measured by the formula:

$$MC = \frac{\text{change in } TC}{\text{change in } Q}$$

Of course, changes in *TC* are due to changes in *TVC*, since *TFC* remains constant as production varies; hence, marginal cost can also be measured by dividing the change in *TVC* by the change in *Q*.

What does marginal cost really mean? Mathematically, it represents the *slope* of the total cost curve (just as we saw earlier that marginal product represents the slope of the total product curve). Economically, it tells you, for any given output, the *additional* amount of cost a business firm would incur by increasing its output by one unit.

We shall see later that *for economic decisions involving changes in output, marginal cost is the single most important cost concept.*

THE AVERAGE-MARGINAL RELATIONSHIP

By this time you may have noticed an interesting geometric principle that characterizes all average and marginal curves. For convenience, Exhibit 3 groups the foregoing production curves and cost curves together so that they may be examined simultaneously. However, we are interested for the moment only in the average and marginal curves, so these curves are shown in separate charts below their corresponding total curves.

Referring to these lower charts, we note an important relationship:

When an average curve is rising, its corresponding marginal curve is above it; when an average curve is falling, its corresponding marginal curve is below it; and when an average curve is neither rising nor falling, i.e., is either at a maximum or at a minimum, its corresponding marginal curve intersects (is equal to) it. This may be called the *average-marginal relationship*.

Does this relationship hold true for the production-function curves as well as for the cost curves? The diagrams indicate that it does, but in the production diagram the marginal curve intersects the average curve at its maximum point, whereas in the cost diagram the marginal curve intersects the two average curves at their minimum points.

The sense behind the average-marginal relationship can be appreciated by a simple example. If to a class of students we add an extra or "marginal" student whose age is above the average age of the class, the average will increase; if we add a student whose age is below the average, the average will decrease; and if we add a student whose age is equal to the average, the average will remain the same.

In later chapters we will encounter other types of average and marginal curves, but the underlying principle stated above characterizes all of them.

THE TOTAL-MARGINAL RELATIONSHIP

There is also a geometric principle common to all total and marginal curves; hence it is generally called the "total-marginal relationship." It is based on the fact that every marginal curve is a graph of the *slope* of its corresponding total curve, as we have already seen.

Referring again to Exhibit 3, this time to both the upper and lower charts, we see an interesting relationship which is emphasized by the vertical dashed lines:

When a total curve is increasing at an increasing rate, its corresponding marginal curve is rising; when a total curve is increasing at a decreasing rate, its corresponding marginal curve is falling; and when a total curve is increasing at a zero rate, as occurs when it is at its maximum, its corresponding marginal curve is zero. This is the *total-marginal relationship*.

Observe from the diagrams that the point at which the rate of change of the total curves changes is called the *point of inflection* and that this point corresponds to either a peak or trough of the marginal curve as shown by the vertical dashed lines.

Note that in the above statement of the total-marginal relationship, it is not necessary to include the fact that when the total curve is falling—as in the case of the *TP* curve at its right end—the corresponding *MP* curve is negative. Although negative marginal curves may exist from a theoretical standpoint, they do not ordinarily have any economic significance. An employer, for example, will not knowingly hire so many units of an input as to yield him a negative marginal product. (Of course, an exception might occur if the input happens to be the boss's son-in-law.)

Exhibit 3

Illustration of the Average-Marginal Relationship (lower charts) and Total Marginal Relationship (upper and lower charts)

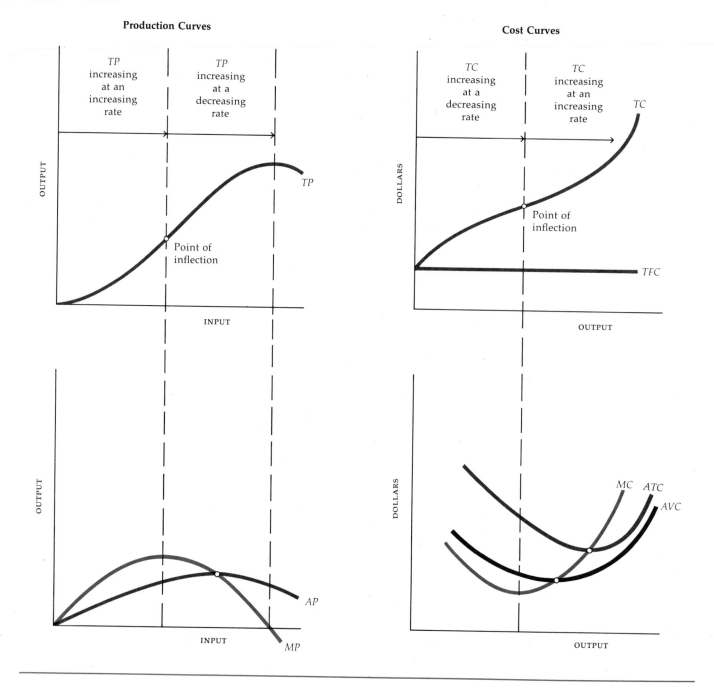

Production Curves

Cost Curves

As with the average-marginal relationship, there are several total-marginal relationships that we shall be encountering in later chapters, but the above statement of the principle characterizes all of them.

Long-Run Costs

It was emphasized earlier that a chief distinction between the short run and the long run is this: In the *short run* a firm can vary its output but not its plant capacity, and hence will have some variable costs and some fixed costs; in the *long run* a firm can vary not only its output but also its plant capacity, and therefore has no fixed costs. *In the long run all costs are variable.*

Of what practical value is this in the study of costs? We can answer this question by noting that the previous analysis of short-run costs reveals how a firm's costs will vary in response to output changes within a period short enough for the size of the plant to remain fixed. If we now extend the logic one step further, we can develop a firm's *long-run cost curve,* which, correspondingly, shows the variation of cost with output in a period long enough for all its resource inputs, including plant and equipment, to be freely variable in amount. Once this is done, a knowledge of such a long-run cost curve can be of use to businessmen in determining the most economical size of a plant and its general operational standards.

ALTERNATE PLANT SIZES

Let us look at the problem in this way. Suppose you were a manufacturer whose plant had gone through a series of additions and expansions over a period of years. For each plant size with its associated complement of equipment, there would be a different production function and hence a different cost structure. Each of these cost structures would be represented by a different set of short-run cost curves of the type we have already studied. To illustrate, Exhibit 4a presents five short-run average total cost curves labeled ATC_1, ATC_2, etc., for five different plant sizes. Theoretically, there could be infinitely many such curves, one for each possible plant size.

These short-run curves can be looked at from still another point of view. If you were a businessman thinking of entering into the production of a commodity and were planning to construct a plant and equip it, all your factors of production—and hence all of your costs—would be variable. Each possible plant size or "layout" would then be represented by a different cost structure, as illustrated by these short-run average cost curves. As before it should be borne in mind that from a theoretical standpoint there can be infinitely many such curves, one for each possible layout.

Some important lessons may be learned from this diagram. On the basis of the information presented it seems intuitively clear that the "optimum" output level is ON, and the lowest-cost plant for producing this output is represented by ATC_3. However, for all other levels of output two interesting principles exist—based on the assumption of infinitely many ATC curves:

1. At any output less than the optimum output ON, it pays better to "underuse" a larger plant than to "overuse" a smaller one. For example, in order to produce output ON_1, it is cheaper to use the larger-scale plant ATC_2 at an average production cost of N_1J per unit than to use the smaller-scale plant ATC_1 at an average cost of N_1K per unit.

2. At any output greater than the optimum output ON, it pays better to "overuse" a smaller plant than to "underuse" a larger one. Thus in order to produce output ON_2, it is cheaper to use the smaller-scale plant ATC_4 at an average cost of N_2G per unit than to use the larger-scale plant ATC_5 at an average cost of N_2H per unit.

It should be noted that these principles are true for *all* outputs—even for outputs like ON_4 and ON_5. Why? Because of the assumption that infinitely many ATC curves may be drawn. Hence you can sketch in the possible ATC curves for ON_4 and ON_5 to demonstrate the validity of these concepts.

THE PLANNING CURVE

These principles suggest that the lower portions of the short-run average total cost curves, shown by the heavy lines, are the only ones economically rel-

Exhibit 4

Short-Run Average Total Cost Curves and the Long-Run Average Cost or Planning Curve

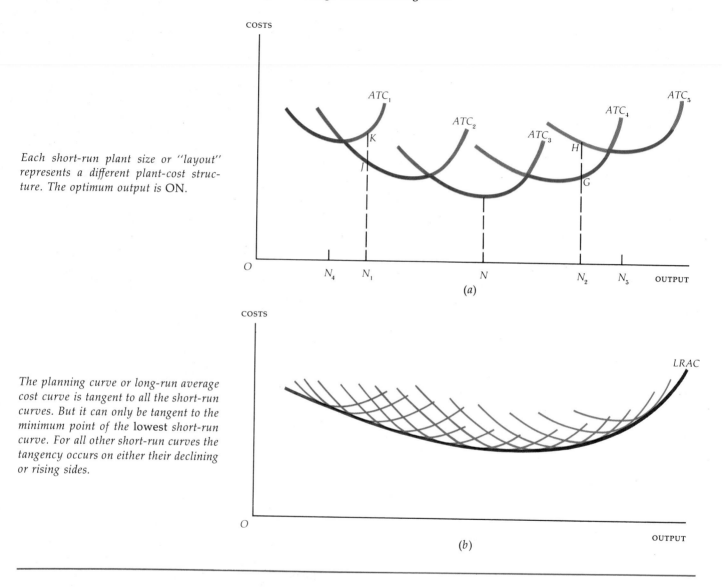

Each short-run plant size or "layout" represents a different plant-cost structure. The optimum output is ON.

(a)

The planning curve or long-run average cost curve is tangent to all the short-run curves. But it can only be tangent to the minimum point of the **lowest** short-run curve. For all other short-run curves the tangency occurs on either their declining or rising sides.

(b)

evant to the selection of a particular plant. What would happen to these heavy lines if, instead of having just five short-run curves, there were an infinitely large number of them, as we have theoretically assumed? To find out we may look to chart (b). The heavy line, which is called a *planning curve,* is a

long-run average cost curve (*LRAC*) that is tangent to each of the short-run average total cost curves from which it is derived. The reason for calling it a "planning curve" has already been indicated: When the plant is still in the blueprint stage and all costs are variable, it tells you the average total cost of producing a given level of output. Thus it can be thought of as a curve that shows what costs would be like at the present time for alternative outputs if different-sized plants were built.

THE BEHAVIOR OF LONG-RUN AVERAGE COST: ECONOMIES AND DISECONOMIES OF SCALE

We now come to an important question: What causes the LRAC curve (or the successive ATC curves of which it is composed) to decrease to a minimum and then rise? Or, to put the question in terms of real-world examples: Why are steel mills larger than machine shops? Why do some firms remain small while others become large?

The answers are based on what may be called *economies and diseconomies of scale*—the decreases or increases in a firm's long-run average costs as the size of its plant is increased.

Economies of Scale

Several factors may give rise to economies of scale—that is, to decreasing long-run average costs of production.

1. Greater Specialization of Resources. As a firm's scale of operation increases, its opportunities for specialization—whether performed by men or by machines—are greatly enhanced because a large-scale firm can often divide the tasks and work to be done more readily than a small-scale firm.

2. More Efficient Utilization of Equipment. In many industries, the technology of production is such that large units of expensive equipment must be used. The production of automobiles, steel, and refined petroleum are notable examples. In such industries, companies must be able to afford whatever equipment is necessary and must be able to use it efficiently by spreading the cost per unit over a sufficiently large volume of output. A small-scale firm cannot ordinarily do these things.

3. Reduced Unit Costs of Inputs. A large-scale firm can often buy its inputs—such as its raw materials—at a cheaper price per unit, thus incurring quantity discounts resulting from larger transactions. And for certain types of equipment, the price per unit of capacity is often much less when larger sizes are purchased. Thus, the construction cost per square foot for a large factory is usually less than for a small one. The price per horsepower of electric induction motors varies inversely with the amount of horsepower.

4. Utilization of By-Products. In certain industries, large-scale firms can make effective use of many by-products that would be wasted by a small firm. A typical example is in the meat-packing industry, where companies like Swift and Armour make glue from cattle hoofs, as well as pharmaceuticals, fertilizer, and other products from the remains of livestock.

5. Growth of Auxiliary Facilities. In some places, an expanding firm may often benefit from, or encourage other firms to develop, ancillary facilities such as warehousing, marketing, and transportation systems, thus saving the growing firm considerable costs. For example, urban colleges and universities benefit from nearby public libraries; individual farms benefit from common irrigation and drainage ditches; commercial and industrial establishments often encourage the development of, and receive the benefit from, improved transportation facilities.

Diseconomies of Scale

At the same time that economies of scale are being realized, a point may be reached where diseconomies of scale begin to exercise a more than offsetting effect. As a result, the long-run average cost curve starts to rise primarily for two reasons.

1. Decision-Making Role of Management. As a firm becomes larger, heavier burdens are placed on management so that eventually this resource input is overworked relative to others, and "diminishing returns" to management set in. Of course, management may be able to delegate authority to others, but ultimately decisions must emanate from a final center if there is to be uniformity in performance and policy. Even the modern principles of scientific management do not eliminate these diseconomies; at most they may only postpone them or perhaps lessen their seriousness.

2. Competition for Resources. Rising long-run average costs can occur as a growing firm increasingly bids labor or other resources away from other industries. This may raise the prices it pays for its factors and cause increases in its per-unit production costs.

A CLASSIFICATION OF ECONOMIES AND DISECONOMIES

These causes of increasing and decreasing returns to scale are often classified according to whether they are internal or external to the firm. The distinction is important, since the internal factors may be subject to a certain amount of managerial control, whereas the external factors are not.

Internal economies and diseconomies are those conditions that bring about decreases or increases in a firm's long-run average costs or scale of operations as a result of size adjustments within the firm as a producing unit. They occur regardless of adjustments within the industry and are due mainly to physical economies or diseconomies. Thus, reductions in long-run average costs occur largely because the indivisibility of productive factors is overcome when size and output are increased; on the other hand, increases in long-run average costs occur because of adverse "factor interaction" between management and other resources.

External economies and diseconomies are those conditions that bring about decreases or increases in a firm's long-run average costs or scale of operations as a result of factors that are entirely outside the firm as a producing unit. They depend on adjustments of the industry and are related to the firm only to the extent that it is part of the industry.

On the basis of this distinction, you should be able to classify each of the various economies and diseconomies given above as either internal or external.

CONCLUSION: WHAT DOES THE EVIDENCE SHOW?

How have business firms adjusted to the existence of economies of scale? Do the long-run average cost curves of firms actually look like the ones shown earlier or do their shapes vary according to the economics of the industry in which they operate?

Some firms—especially large ones—have chosen to decentralize their operations into autonomous divisions in order to avoid the rigidities of size. A typical illustration is General Motors, with its five separate divisions for Chevrolet, Pontiac, Buick, Oldsmobile, and Cadillac. However, when a firm decentralizes it sacrifices some of the gains of economies of scale. Thus by establishing a number of autonomous units, each with its own management group, the parent firm becomes hardly more than a business trust. It gains administrative flexibility, but it may lose some of the benefits of quantity purchases.

Relatively few studies have been done about the shape of a firm's long-run average costs, and no conclusive statements about this factor can be made. Nevertheless, the limited evidence that exists, coupled with what economists know about the theory of production and costs, suggest that there may be three basic variations of curves. These are illustrated and described in Exhibit 5 on page 374.

SUMMARY OF IMPORTANT IDEAS

1. Cost is a sacrifice that must be made in order to acquire something. The sacrifice may include monetary and nonmonetary elements.

2. Opportunity costs are critical in economics because they measure the value of a foregone alternative. Opportunity costs arise because resources are limited and have alternative uses.

3. Economic costs are payments that must be made to attract resources. Such costs include not only explicit costs or money expenditures for resources, but also the implicit costs of self-owned or self-employed resources.

4. The law of diminishing returns—a more general name is the law of variable proportions—states what happens to output when a variable input is combined with fixed inputs. Although the law covers total, average, and marginal returns, the last is most important where output changes are involved. Graphically, marginal product always intersects average product at its maximum point.

Exhibit 5

Three Typical Long-Run Average Cost Curves

The shapes of different firms' long-run average costs vary in different industries.

Chart (a) shows the situation in which economies of scale out-weigh the diseconomies over a wide range of output. Examples are the aluminum, automobile, and steel industries.

Chart (b) shows the situation in which diseconomies of scale set in quickly and many small firms exist side by side. Examples are the retailing, textiles, metal fabrication, and publishing industries.

Chart (c) shows where economies of scale are either quickly exhausted and diseconomies take a long time coming, or else the economies and diseconomies tend to cancel each other out. Examples are the chemicals, food processing, furniture, and appliance industries.

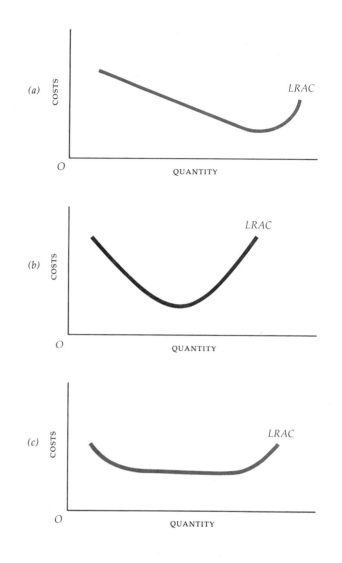

5. There are three families of costs: total, average, and marginal. The family of total costs consists of total fixed costs, which do not vary with output, and total variables costs, which increase as output increases. The family of average costs consists of average fixed costs, which is the ratio of total fixed cost to quantity, and average variable cost, which is the ratio of total variable cost to quantity. Marginal cost is a one-member family consisting of marginal cost alone: it is the change in total cost resulting from a unit change in output. Graphically, marginal cost always intersects average variable cost and average total cost at their minimum points.

6. The short run is a period long enough to vary output, but not plant capacity. The long run is a period long enough to vary plant capacity. Therefore, in the short run some of a firm's costs are fixed and some are variable, but in the long run all of a firm's costs

are variable because all of its factors of production are variable.

7. The long-run average cost curve or planning curve tends to be U-shaped, reflecting first economies and then diseconomies of scale. Economies of scale result from greater specialization of resources, more efficient utilization of equipment, reduced unit costs of inputs, and fuller utilization of by-products. Diseconomies of scale arise mainly from the increasing complexities of management as a firm grows larger.

8. The actual shape of a planning curve tends to vary within different industries. For example, in heavy industries like autos and steel, internal economies extend over a wide range of output; hence, such industries tend to have small numbers of large firms. In light industries like textiles and retailing, internal economies are exhausted rather quickly over a narrow range of output; hence such industries tend to have large numbers of small firms.

FOR HOMEWORK AND DISCUSSION

1. *Terms and concepts to review:*

cost
outlay costs
opportunity cost
economic costs
explicit costs
implicit costs
normal profit
economic (pure) profit
short run
long run
production function
law of diminishing
    returns (law of
    variable proportions)
marginal product
average product
total fixed costs

total variable costs
total cost
average fixed cost
average variable cost
average total cost
marginal cost
average-marginal
    relationship
total-marginal
    relationship
long-run average cost
    curve (planning curve)
economies and dis-
    economies of scale
internal economies and
    diseconomies of scale
external economies and
    diseconomies of scale

2. Complete the table on page 376, then graph the family of total costs on one chart and all of the remaining costs on another. (NOTE: When you graph the marginal cost curve, plot each MC figure to the midpoint between successive outputs. Thus on your chart, the first MC figure corresponds to an output of 0.5, the second to 1.5, the third to 2.5, and so on.)

a. Discuss the various curves in terms of their shape as influenced by the law of diminishing returns. (HINT: Sketch the family of total costs on one chart, and the family of average and marginal costs on another chart directly beneath it. Then see if you can draw a vertical dashed line through both charts such that the stage of increasing marginal returns is on the left side of the vertical line, and the stage of decreasing marginal returns is on the right.) In your answer, account for the relative distances between ATC and AVC at different levels of output, and the reason for the intersection of MC with ATC and AVC at their minimum points.

3. Are opportunity costs entered in the accounting records of a firm? If so, what are they used for? If not, what good are they?

4. In estimating the annual cost of owning a fully paid-up $3,000 automobile, you might show the following cost entry on your books: "Interest on investment at 5 percent: $150." What would this mean? Explain.

5. Why do you suppose that some of your teachers, who could earn considerably more by working in industry, continue to accept a lower salary by remaining in education?

6. Do you agree with the theory that as a firm becomes larger and decision making more complex, the long-run average cost curve turns upward because the burden of administration becomes disproportionately greater and "diminishing returns" to management set in? Would this be true of such well-managed firms as Proctor & Gamble or American Telephone and Telegraph? Of what significance is technology, organizational structure, managerial ability, etc.?

(1) Quantity of output	(2) Total fixed cost	(3) Total variable cost	(4) Total cost	(5) Average fixed cost	(6) Average variable cost	(7) Average total cost	(8) Marginal cost
0	$100	$ 0	$_____	$_____	$_____	$_____	
1	____	40	_____	_____	_____	_____	$_____
2	____	64	_____	_____	_____	_____	_____
3	____	80	_____	_____	_____	_____	_____
4	____	88	_____	_____	_____	_____	_____
5	____	96	_____	_____	_____	_____	_____
6	____	108	_____	_____	_____	_____	_____
7	____	128	_____	_____	_____	_____	_____
8	____	160	_____	_____	_____	_____	_____
9	____	216	_____	_____	_____	_____	_____
10	____	300	_____	_____	_____	_____	_____

REFERENCES AND READING SUGGESTIONS

BOBER, M. M., *Intermediate Price And Income Theory,* rev. ed., Norton, New York, 1962, chaps. 5, 6, 7.

BOULDING, KENNETH E., *Economic Analysis,* vol. 1, *Microeconomics,* 4th ed., Harper & Row, New York, 1966, chaps. 18, 19, 20.

DOOLEY, PETER C., *Elementary Price Theory,* Appleton-Century-Crofts, New York, 1967, chap. 3.

DUE, JOHN F., and ROBERT W. CLOWER, *Intermediate Economic Analysis,* 5th ed., Irwin, Homewood, Illinois, 1966, chaps. 6, 7.

SPENCER, MILTON H., *Managerial Economics,* 3d ed., Irwin, Homewood, Illinois, 1968, chaps. 6, 7.

WARD, BENJAMIN, *Elementary Price Theory,* The Free Press, New York, 1967, chaps. 5, 6.

PART 6

The Economics of the Firm: How Are Prices and Outputs Determined?

CHAPTER 23

The Imaginary World of Perfect Competition: Criteria for Evaluating Competitive Behavior

CHAPTER PREVIEW

What do we mean by perfect competition? Is it a fantasy or is it real?

How do business firms operate under perfect competition? Do they receive profits? Do they incur losses? How much do they produce?

What are the consequences of perfect competition? Does it have both favorable and unfavorable features? What would it be like to live in a world of perfect competition?

Early in this book we learned that economics is concerned with how society allocates its limited resources, which have alternative uses, to the production of goods and services. Of course, economists have always been interested in seeing this task accomplished with the least amount of waste. Hence they have developed a theory which yields certain "ideal" results as far as the attainment of economic efficiency is concerned.

This theory is known as "perfect competition" or "pure competition." (The two terms are used synonomously for most purposes, although a technical distinction that is sometimes made between them will be explained subsequently.) This theory underlies the operation of supply and demand that we studied in previous chapters. Hence it is a theory that attempts to explain how a "perfect" market economy or "pure" free-enterprise system tends to operate.

What Is Perfect Competition?

Whenever a scientist seeks to describe a complicated problem, he proceeds by constructing a simplified picture of the situation, or *model*. This is what we shall be doing in this chapter as we develop a model or theory of perfect competition.

Let us begin with a definition.

Perfect (or *pure*) *competition* is the name given to an industry or to a market characterized by a large number of buyers and sellers all engaged in the purchase and sale of a homogeneous commodity, with perfect knowledge of market prices and quantities, no discrimination, and perfect mobility of resources.

This definition contains five essential conditions which require further examination.

EXPLAINING THE DEFINITION

You will often hear and use the expression "perfect competition" when talking about an industry or a market. This should be no cause for ambiguity, however, since the distinction is always clear from the context in which the term is used, and the above definition is applicable to both categories—industries as well as markets. Now let us analyze the rest of the definition.

Large Number of Buyers and Sellers. What do we mean by a "large" number of buyers and sellers? Is 1,000 large and 999 small? To answer yes would be silly since the words "large" or "small" are relative rather than absolute terms. Hence our definition does not establish the size of a perfectly competitive market in terms of numbers. Instead, it uses the word "large" to mean *large enough so that no one buyer or seller can affect the market price by offering to buy or not to buy, to sell or not to sell.* Therefore, whether it takes 1,000 or 1 million buyers or sellers is of no relevance. The only requirement is that the market price for any buyer or seller is *given.* He can take it or leave it, but he cannot alter it by going into or out of the market.

Homogeneous Commodity. This means that all units which sellers make available must be identical in the minds of buyers. The reason for this requirement, as will be shown later, is that buyers must be indifferent as to which seller they deal with; they must be willing to purchase from the seller who offers the good at the lowest price.

Notice, therefore, that we are referring to *economic homogeneity*, not physical homogeneity. Two sellers may be selling the same physical product, but buyers may be willing to pay more to seller A than to seller B because seller A provides service with a smile, or a more attractive package, or perhaps a brand name. In that case the two products are *not* economically homogeneous.

We can illustrate this point with a concrete example. Beet sugar and cane sugar are physically the same for all practical purposes: they look and taste the same. Yet beet sugar in most regions of the country sells for less than cane. Why? Because buyers do not regard them as the same; instead, they believe that beet is somehow inferior to cane, and since a package of sugar must be labeled either "beet" or "cane," there tends to be a price difference between them. In this case the two products are physically homogeneous but *economically heterogeneous;* i.e., they are similar but not identical. How about butter and margarine? Two nickels and a dime? Are they homogeneous? Heterogeneous?

Perfect Knowledge of Market Prices and Quantities. The third condition—that of "perfect knowledge"—means that all buyers and sellers are completely aware of the prices and quantities at which transactions are taking place in the market and that all have the opportunity to participate in those transactions. For example, perfect knowledge does not exist if buyers do not know that sellers across the street are charging a lower price for a certain commodity. Likewise, perfect knowledge does not exist if sellers do not know that buyers across the street are offering a higher price for a certain product. In both instances the buyers and sellers on one side of the street are not competing with the buyers and sellers on the other side, and hence are not even in the same market.

No Discrimination. This fourth condition tells us that buyers and sellers must be willing to deal openly and aboveboard with one another—to buy and sell at the market price with any and all that may wish to do so —without offering any special deals, discounts, or favors to selected individuals. Discrimination thus has an economic meaning, not just a social one.

Perfect Mobility of Resources. The fifth condition of perfect resource mobility requires that there be no obstacles—economic, legal, technological, or otherwise—to prevent firms or resources from entering or leaving the particular market or industry, and there be no impediments to the purchase or sale of commodities. This means that firms, resources, and commodities can be shifted about swiftly and smoothly without friction. For example, the land, labor, capital, and entrepreneurship used in wheat production can be moved quickly into corn production if it is more profitable. Potatoes stored in Idaho can be sold instantly in New York or in San Francisco if the price is right. And, in general, owners of resources and commodities are free and able to take advantage of the best market opportunities as they arise.

IS IT REALISTIC?

Is the concept of perfect competition realistic or a fantasy? After all, there is not a market or an industry anywhere in the world that meets all five requirements described above exactly. Should you infer, therefore, that the notion of perfect competition is "theoretical and impractical"?

The answer is no. As we shall see shortly, the concept of perfect competition is a *theoretical extreme*—like the concept of a perfect vacuum or the assumption of a frictionless state in physics. If you take a course in elementary physics, you will actually study many problems of motion in which it is expressly assumed that there is *no friction,* although everyone knows that a certain amount of friction always exists in the real world. However, by assuming no friction, you create an "idealized" situation which permits simplification of a problem in order to analyze it. Similarly, when you read about the theory of perfect competition in this chapter, you will be studying a "frictionless" economic system in which the movement of goods and resources is unobstructed. In this way, as in physics, you are using an idealized model in order to simplify and analyze the problems involved.

But our model of perfect competition developed below will not be completely unreal. Some markets do approach the conditions of perfect competition at least roughly, although none meets all the con-

ditions precisely. The examples that come closest to the ideal are the organized commodity and stock exchanges in New York, Chicago, and many other cities, and to a lesser extent some industries producing standard raw materials. In these markets the approximation to perfect competition varies, but is close enough to make the theory and conclusions of this chapter both meaningful and useful.

REMARK. As you will see below, the conditions of perfect knowledge and perfect resource mobility are not absolutely essential to our theory. They are desirable, however, because they serve as "lubricating" features which tend to make a perfectly competitive system operate more quickly and smoothly than it would if these two conditions did not exist.

Costs, Revenues, and Profit Maximization in the Short Run

It follows from our explanation of perfect competition that the market price of a commodity under such circumstances would be established independently through the free operation of total supply and total demand. We have already seen in previous chapters how this happens: No individual buyer or seller can influence the price, yet the price emerges automatically as a reflection of the interaction of numerous buyers and sellers.

This leads us to ask a vital question: How does a firm in perfect competition, faced with a market price over which it has no influence, decide how much of a commodity it will produce? Our objective at this time is to answer this question, and in so doing we will develop one of the most fundamental principles of economics.

TOTAL COSTS AND TOTAL REVENUES

Let us begin by turning our attention to the table in Exhibit 1, showing the costs and revenues of a firm in perfect competition. The only costs shown are those needed for our analysis.

Columns (1) and (2) are already familiar concepts, since they represent quantities produced and the corresponding levels of total cost. As always, total cost increases as quantity increases.

Exhibit 1

Cost and Revenue Schedules of a Firm Under Perfect Competition

(1) Quantity per day Q	(2) Total Cost TC	(3) Price per unit or Average Revenue $P = AR$ $AR = \dfrac{TR}{Q}$	(4) Total Revenue TR $TR = P \times Q$	(5) Average Total Cost ATC $ATC = \dfrac{TC}{Q}$	(6) Marginal Cost MC $MC = \dfrac{\text{change in } TC}{\text{change in } Q}$	(7) Marginal Revenue MR $MR = \dfrac{\text{change in } TR}{\text{change in } Q}$	(8) Net Revenue NR $NR = TR - TC$
0	$ 25	$10	$ 0	$ —			$ −25
					$10	$10	
1	35	10	10	35.00			−25
					6	10	
2	41	10	20	20.50			−21
					4	10	
3	45	10	30	15.00			−15
					2	10	
4	47	10	40	11.75			− 7
					2	10	
5	49	10	50	9.80			1
					3	10	
6	52	10	60	8.67			8
					5	10	
7	57	10	70	8.14			13
					8	10	
8	65	10	80	8.13			15
					14	10	
9	79	10	90	8.78			11
					21	10	
10	100	10	100	10.00			0

Column (3) denotes what we call *average revenue* (*AR*). Average revenue is the price per unit of output or, as we shall see momentarily, the ratio of total revenue to quantity. In this case the average revenue is $10 per unit. Thus we are assuming that the price established in the market through the free interaction of supply and demand is $10, and hence this is the price with which the firm is faced and over which it has no control. Or, to put it somewhat differently, the firm finds that it can sell all the units it wants to at the market price, *P*, of $10.

Column (4), called *total revenue* (*TR*), is simply the price per unit times the number of units sold. Looking at the headings of columns (3) and (4) together, it takes only the simplest arithmetic to see the connection between average revenue, total revenue, and price:

$$AR = \frac{TR}{Q} = \frac{P \times \cancel{Q}}{\cancel{Q}} = P$$

Finally, we can skip temporarily to column (8) of the table and note that *net revenue* or net profit—the difference between total revenue and total cost—is at first negative, but it rises to a peak of $15 at 8 units of output and then falls.

Graphic Illustration

The *TC* and *TR* figures are graphed in the upper chart of Exhibit 2. The *TC* curve has a familiar shape, but note that the *TR* curve is a straight line. This reflects the fact, as stated above, that the firm receives the same price per unit for all the units it sells.

The points labeled B_1 and B_2 are called *break-even points* because they designate levels of output at which a firm's revenue equals its cost, and hence the firm is incurring neither an economic profit nor an economic loss. At any output between these two points, the firm's profit or net revenue is positive, and at any output beyond the break-even points it

Exhibit 2

Cost and Revenue Curves of a Firm Under Perfect Competition

Profit Maximization: Three Viewpoints

1. Total curves. *The most profitable level of output is determined where the curves TR − TC, as represented by the distance GH, is a maximum. This occurs at an output of 8 units. At this output, a tangent to the TC curve, such as the tangent at H, is parallel to the straight-line TR curve. At smaller or larger outputs such as 6, 7, or 9 units, a tangent to the TC curve would not be parallel to the TR curve.*

The break-even points are at B$_1$ and B$_2$, where TC = TR. The break-even outputs are thus 5 units and 10 units.

2. Marginal curves. *The most profitable level of output is determined where MC = MR, as explained in the text. This is also evident by following the vertical dashed line downward at 8 units of output.*

The break-even points are at B$_1$ and B$_2$, where ATC = AR.

3. Net revenue curve. *The most profitable level of output is determined where the net revenue curve NR (= TR − TC) is a maximum. The vertical dashed line at 8 units of output emphasizes these profit-maximizing principles in all three charts.*

TECHNICAL NOTE (OPTIONAL). If you are geometrically inclined, you may note that since parallel lines have equal slopes, the most profitable output in the top chart is the one at which the *slope* (steepness) of the *TC* curve equals the *slope* (steepness) of the *TR* curve. In the middle chart, marginal cost is the graph of the *slope* of total cost, and marginal revenue is the graph of the *slope* of total revenue. Hence at the level of maximum profit:

$$MC = MR$$

which is the same as saying that:

Slope of *TC* = slope of *TR*

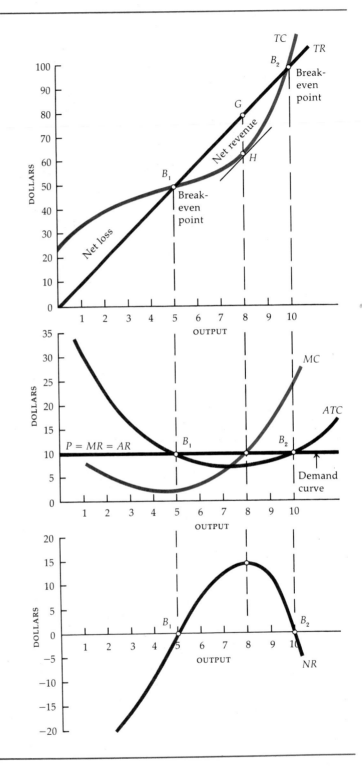

has a net loss (or negative net revenue) because its costs exceed its revenues.

Finally, it should be pointed out that net revenue, as represented by the vertical distance GH, is a maximum at 8 units of output. At this output the *slope* of the total cost curve as measured by the slope of the tangent at H is equal to the *slope* of the total revenue curve. This suggests an important fundamental concept:

The *slope* (steepness) of a line is the change in its vertical distance per unit of change in its horizontal distance. The slope of a straight line (such as the TR curve) is the same at every point, but the slope of a curved line (like the TC curve) differs at every point. Geometrically, you can find the slope of a curve at a point by drawing a straight-line tangent to the curve at that point. The slope of the tangent will then be the slope of the curve at the point of tangency. As you recall from high school geometry, parallel lines have equal slopes. Thus the tangent at H is parallel to the TR curve.

This important concept is amplified further in the paragraphs below and in the descriptions in Exhibit 2.

MARGINAL COST AND MARGINAL REVENUE

The use of total revenue and total cost is a valid method of determining the most profitable level of output for a firm, but it is not the method that economists usually employ. Instead, they prefer to use an approach which at first may seem a little more complicated, but is actually much more useful for understanding and interpreting changes in production and costs.

Referring back to the table in Exhibit 1, we note that column (5) contains average total cost, and column (6) presents marginal cost. Column (7), however, has a new term called *marginal revenue (MR)*, which is defined as the change in total revenue resulting from a unit change in output. As in previous cases, the expression "resulting from" in the definition is an interpretative term; for mathematical purposes it means the same thing as "divided by." Therefore, the formula we use for measuring marginal revenue is:

$$MR = \frac{\text{change in } TR}{\text{change in } Q}$$

Marginal revenue is thus a concept that is exactly analogous to marginal cost. And, since the slope of a curve is the change in its vertical distance resulting from a unit change in its horizontal distance, it should now be clear that *marginal cost measures the slope of a total cost curve, and marginal revenue measures the slope of a total revenue curve.*

Note that the marginal revenue figures in column (7), namely $10, are precisely the same as the average revenue or price figures in column (3). Thus, $MR = AR = P$. This is no accident. If price remains constant while quantity increases, total revenue (which equals $P \times Q$) will have to increase by the amount of the price, and this amount of change will also be the same as marginal revenue. You can verify this by experimenting with a few numbers yourself.

Finally, observe that columns (1) and (3) taken together constitute a *demand schedule*, since they disclose the price per unit that buyers will pay and the seller will receive for various quantities of the commodity.

Now let us see what these data look like on a chart.

Graphic Illustration

When we graph the ATC, MC, and the $MR = AR$ data, we get the results shown in the middle chart of Exhibit 2. The first thing to notice is that the horizontal revenue line at the price of $10 is a demand curve based on columns (1) and (3) of the table; indeed, it is a *perfectly elastic demand curve*. Hence the curve is labeled $P = MR = AR$ in order to emphasize the fact that it represents price, marginal revenue, and average revenue—all at the same time. However, this is a special property which exists only under perfect competition. As we shall see in subsequent chapters dealing with other types of competition, a different situation arises when the demand curve slopes downward instead of being horizontal.

What is the firm's most profitable level of output? We already know from before that the answer is 8. But we can verify it further by extending the vertical dashed line at 8 units of output from the top chart down to the middle chart, and then to the bottom chart which shows the graph of net revenue *NR* from column (8) of the table. When we do this, the middle chart, along with the other two supporting charts, reveals the operation of one of the most important principles in all of economics:

The most profitable level of output for a firm occurs where its MC = MR. This is a general principle which applies under all types of competition. But under the special case of perfect competition it is also true that the most profitable level of output occurs where MC = MR = P = AR, since the last three terms are one and the same. For it is only at this output that a firm's net revenue, as measured by the difference between its total revenue and total cost, is at a maximum.

This *MC = MR* rule is of such great importance that it may appropriately be called the *fundamental prin-*

ciple of profit maximization. You may also verify that in the table of Exhibit 1 the demarcated section at 8 units of output shows that when *NR* reaches a maximum of 15, *MC* rises from 8 to 14, while *MR* remains constant at 10. The charts, of course, reveal the relationships more clearly; hence you should study them and their accompanying explanations carefully.

INTERPRETING THE *MC = MR* RULE

The *MC = MR* rule must be elaborated more fully. In particular, we need to ask: Why does the rule "work" as a guide for profit maximization, and how does a firm react to the rule within the setting of a competitive market?

Part of the answer is given in Exhibit 3. In (*a*), the market price *OP* and market output *ON* are determined by the intersection of *total* demand and *total*

Exhibit 3

An Industry and Firm in a Perfectly Competitive Market

INDUSTRY
A perfectly competitive market with many buyers and sellers. *The market price* OP *and market output* ON *are determined by the intersection of the* total *market demand and supply curves. The total market demand curve is downward-sloping, because the quantity demanded will be greater at lower prices.*

FIRM
A typical firm in a perfectly competitive market. *Each seller is confronted with a perfectly elastic demand curve at the market price. By producing to where his* MC = MR, *his most profitable output* OJ *is an infinitesimal fraction of the industry's output* ON. *(The two charts have different horizontal scales.)*

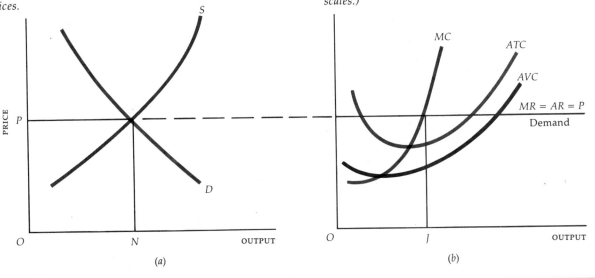

(*a*)   (*b*)

supply, representing the interactions of many buyers and many sellers. In (b) any individual seller finds that by producing to where his $MC = MR$ he maximizes his net revenue or profit, and his output OJ is an infinitesimal proportion of the industry's output ON. But note that there is also this important principle:

Under perfect competition, each seller faces a perfectly elastic demand curve at the market price—for two reasons:

1. Since the product is homogeneous, buyers will purchase the commodity from the seller who offers it at the lowest price.

2. Since each seller supplies only an infinitesimal part of the total market, he can sell *all* his output at the going market price. He cannot sell any of his output for more than that price, and he has no reason to sell any of it for less.

Thus at any output less than OJ, each one-unit increase in output adds more to total revenue than it adds to total cost—that is, MR exceeds MC—so it pays to expand production. Conversely at any output greater than OJ, each one-unit decrease in output reduces total cost more than it reduces total revenue—that is MC is greater than MR—so it pays to cut back production. Only at the point where $MC = MR$ do we find the most profitable output OJ; hence we call this $MC = MR$ point the seller's *equilibrium* position because it determines the profit-maximizing output that his firm will seek to achieve and maintain under the given market conditions and the company's existing cost curves.

We can illustrate this concept with a simple example. Suppose you were a manufacturer of some commodity, and you knew that by increasing your production by a specific amount you would raise your total revenue by $10 and your total cost by $8. In that case you would try to expand output and thereby increase net profit by $2. On the other hand, if you knew that by decreasing production by a given amount you would cut total cost by $15 and total revenue by $10, you would try to reduce output in order to increase net profit by $5. As a general rule, the only time you would not want to alter the production rate is when profits were already at a

maximum. In that case the *changes* in TC and TR would be the same—that is MC would equal MR.

ANALYZING SHORT-RUN EQUILIBRIUM

What is the nature of the profit-maximizing or equilibrium position which the firm is trying to attain? Some of its important properties are illustrated by the diagram in Exhibit 4.

First, note from the title that the diagram depicts the firm in short-run equilibrium. This means that under the existing market conditions for the inputs that the firm buys and the output that it sells, and the given set of cost curves with which it operates, the

---

Exhibit 4

Profit Maximization in the Short Run for a Perfectly Competitive Firm

At the output where a firm's MC = MR, *the area of its net revenue rectangle* TULK *is a maximum. This is the largest net profit rectangle that can be drawn.*

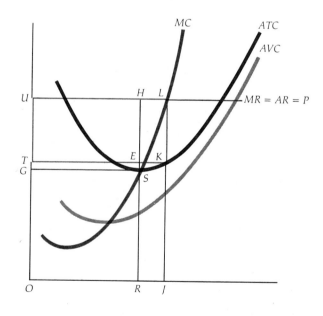

most profitable output is OJ because it is here that $MC = MR$ for this particular firm. We shall see later that in the long run certain market conditions, as well as the seller's cost curves, are likely to change, thereby resulting in a different equilibrium position for the firm.

Second, you should verify that at the most profitable level of output OJ, the following geometric cost and revenue conditions exist. Thus, the average total cost of producing output OJ is represented by the distance JK ($= OT$), and the average revenue received from the sale of this output is JL ($= OU$). The difference between these two amounts, of course, is the net revenue per unit—that is, average net revenue—as represented by KL ($= TU$). Therefore, the total net revenue can be found by multiplying the net revenue per unit by the number of units, thereby obtaining the area of the rectangle $TULK$.

The same result can also be arrived at in a different way. The average revenue per unit JL times the number of units OJ equals total revenue, which is the area of the large rectangle $OULJ$. Similarly, average total cost JK times the number of units OJ equals total cost or the area of the rectangle $OTKJ$. Therefore, when you subtract the total cost rectangle from the total revenue rectangle, the difference is the net revenue rectangle $TULK$.

Finally, it is important to observe that profits are maximized at the output where $MC = MR$, even though this output may be beyond the point of minimum average total cost. Profit, in other words, is *not* maximized at output OR, despite the lower average total cost of that output, namely RS. For by increasing his output from OR to OJ, the seller's net revenue rectangle increases from $GUHS$ to $TULK$. The rectangle thus gains the larger area $EHLK$ while losing the smaller area $GTES$. In general, the output at which the largest net profit rectangle can be drawn is determined by the point L where $MC = MR$ and by the corresponding point K on the ATC curve. Or, to put it differently, it can be proved mathematically that any other net profit rectangle must of necessity be smaller than the one determined by points K and L. But this is equivalent to saying that the net revenue curve reaches a maximum at the output where $MC = MR$, which is a fact you already know.

DERIVING SUPPLY CURVES FROM MARGINAL COST CURVES

When we first studied the operation of supply and demand we learned that a supply curve expresses a relation between the price of a product and the amount that sellers will be willing and able to produce at each price. We are now in a position to show how a perfectly competitive firm's supply curve is actually derived, based on what we know about the $MC = MR$ rule.

Suppose we represent a firm in perfect competition by the cost curves shown in Exhibit 5. If the market price of the product is OP_1, the firm will produce an output ON_1 since this is where its MC is equal to MR_1. If the price falls to OP_2, it will reduce its output to ON_2 following its marginal cost curve. At a price of OP_3 it will produce the amount ON_3, but since this price is tangent to its minimum average total cost, it will not be earning a positive net revenue; its net revenue will be zero. This means, as we learned earlier, that the firm is only normally profitable, since average total cost includes normal profit.

We conclude from this that a perfectly competitive firm maximizes its profit by always adjusting its output so as to follow its marginal cost curve.

MINIMIZING SHORT-RUN LOSSES

What will the firm do if the price falls below OP_3, say to OP_4? The answer is the same as before: It will decrease its output following its marginal cost curve, thus producing the amount ON_4. At this output the firm's net revenue will be negative, but it will be *minimizing its losses* for the following reason.

In the short run, the firm has certain fixed costs such as rent, property taxes, etc., which it must continue to pay as long as it remains in business, regardless of how much it produces. Therefore, as long as it can get a price that is at least high enough to cover its average variable (or "out-of-pocket") costs, anything that it earns over and above this amount will go toward paying its fixed costs, which it is "stuck" with in any case. Hence, even at a price of OP_4, the firm will lose less by operating and producing ON_4 than by temporarily shutting down. In the long run, on the other hand, it must receive a price at least high enough to cover all its costs including a normal profit if it is to stay in business, i.e., it must cover its ATC.

We can now summarize with an important principle:

A perfectly competitive firm will increase or decrease its output by following its marginal cost curve, thereby maximizing its profit or minimizing its losses. Therefore, *a perfectly competitive firm's supply curve is its marginal cost curve above its average variable cost.*

Exhibit 5

In Perfect Competition, a Firm's Supply Curve Is Its MC Curve Above Its AVC

The firm will always produce to where its MC = MR. Therefore, as the market price falls from OP_1 to OP_4, the firm reduces its output from ON_1 to ON_4 following its marginal cost curve. At OP_4 it is just covering its average variable (out-of-pocket) costs.

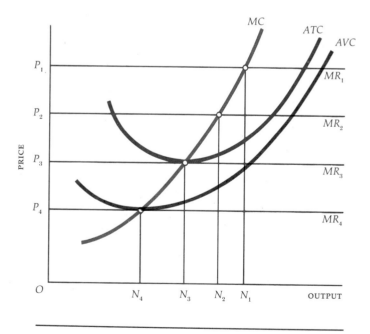

DERIVING THE INDUSTRY'S SHORT-RUN SUPPLY CURVE

This principle can easily be extended to include all firms in a perfectly competitive industry. The industry's supply curve is then derived from all of the firms' marginal cost curves.

The idea is illustrated in Exhibit 6. Although only four firms are included for illustrative purposes, it is a simple matter to generalize the conclusions to any number of firms.

Thus, at the market price of OP_1 Firm A produces the output OR_1. At the price of OP_2 it will produce the larger output OS_1, while Firm B will produce the output OS_2. Similarly, at higher and higher prices firms that are already in the market find it profitable to increase their production by following their marginal cost curve, while firms that were previously not in the market because their costs were too high now find it profitable to enter.

The overall effect on the industry supply curve is also shown in the diagram. As the market price rises because of a rightward shift of the total demand curve, the aggregate supply curve also rises, thereby reflecting the increasing outputs of the various firms. The industry's short-run supply curve is thus the sum of all the individual firms' marginal cost curves above their average variable costs.

Long-Run Equilibrium of a Firm and Industry

We have seen that in the short run a firm in a perfectly competitive industry may earn profits in excess of its normal profits. Can this also happen in the long run? The answer is no, because the conditions that are assumed in our definition of perfect competition prevent it from occurring. Let us see why.

THE ADJUSTMENT PROCESS

An industry is said to be in *equilibrium*—that is, in a state of "balance"—when there is no tendency for it to expand or to contract. This means that the least profitable or borderline firm in the industry—usu-

Exhibit 6

The Derivation of Supply Curves from Marginal Cost Curves

As the market price rises due to a rightward shift of the demand curve, each firm increases its output following its marginal cost curve. Each firm's supply curve is the same as its marginal cost curve above its average variable cost. The industry's short-run supply curve is the sum of these marginal

cost (supply) curves. Thus:
Industry's OR_1 = Firm A's OR_1
Industry's OS_1 = Firm A's OR_1 + R_1S_1
Industry's OS_2 = Firm A's OR_1 + R_1S_1 + Firm B's OS_2
and so on.

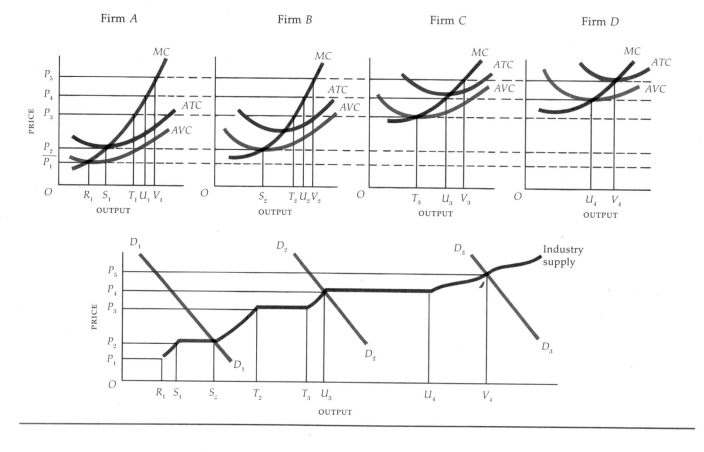

ally called the "marginal" firm—is only normally profitable.

For instance, if any firms in the industry are earning less than their normal profit in the long run, then by definition of normal profit their owners are receiving less than the least return they are willing to accept on the basis of their opportunity costs. They will therefore leave the industry, thereby causing the industry supply curve to shift to the left and the

market price to rise. The remaining firms will then become more profitable. This exodus of firms will continue until the least profitable firm is just normally profitable, at which point the industry will have no further tendency to contract.

The opposite situation occurs when the least profitable firm is earning more than normal profits. New firms will then be tempted to enter the industry in order to get a share of those profits. The industry will thus expand, its total output will increase as the industry supply curve shifts to the right, and the market price will fall, thereby making existing firms less profitable. This entry of new firms will continue until the least profitable firm is just normally profitable, at which point the industry will have no further tendency to expand.

GRAPHIC ILLUSTRATION OF LONG-RUN EQUILIBRIUM

This final adjustment to long-run equilibrium for a typical firm is illustrated in Exhibit 7. The firm will have an average total cost curve and a corresponding marginal cost curve for each possible scale of plant. It follows that if some firms in the industry operate with optimum-size plants when the price is higher than the long-run equilibrium level, they will earn above-normal profits, which in turn will attract new firms into the industry. Market supply will increase, market price will fall, and supernormal profits will disappear. Firms with plants that are larger or smaller than the optimum size will thus suffer losses, whereas those with optimum-size plants will earn normal profits. It follows that firms in perfectly competitive industries have no choice of whether they want to build large-scale or small-scale plants; they must eventually build optimum-size plants if they are to survive in the long run.

The firm's optimum-size plant is thus ATC_3, the long-run equilibrium price is OP, and the firm's rate of output is ON. Exhibit 7 represents a typical single firm, and a diagram similar to this could be made for each firm in the industry.

Exhibit 7

Long-Run Equilibrium for a Typical Firm in Perfect Competition

At any given time, a firm may be represented by an ATC curve and a corresponding MC curve.
In the long run, competition will force each firm in the industry to end up with an optimum-size plant such as ATC_3. At the optimum level of output for each firm, such as ON for this particular firm,

$$MC = MR = AR = ATC = LRAC$$

This equation defines the long-run conditions of equilibrium for the firm.

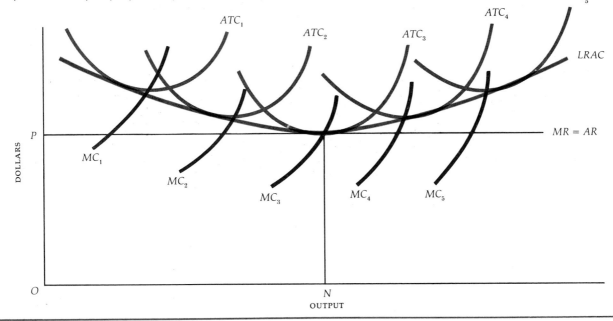

THE LONG-RUN INDUSTRY SUPPLY CURVE

We now know enough about the operation of supply and demand in competitive markets to introduce a new concept pertaining to the long-run supply price of an industry.

Each of the diagrams in Exhibit 8 represents the supply and demand situation for a different industry. We assume in each case that the industry is in equilibrium and that the point E_1, representing the intersection of the industry's supply and demand curves, defines its equilibrium price and output. Remember that an industry supply curve is made up of the individual supply curves of all of its sellers. Our present purpose is to examine the nature of each industry's long-run supply curve or supply price.

Suppose there is an increase (shift) in demand from D_1 to D_2. If the costs of the firms in the industry remain the same the equilibrium point shifts from E_1 to E_2, representing a higher market price and a larger market output than before. This expanded output occurs because firms that are already in the industry find it profitable to increase their production in response to the higher market price.

The equilibrium at E_2, however, is likely to be of relatively short duration because the higher and more profitable price will soon attract new firms into the industry. As this happens, the supply curve of the industry will shift to the right and the market price will be driven down along the D_2 curve until it is no longer profitable for new firms to enter the industry. The supply curve will ultimately settle at S_2, and the final equilibrium will be at E_3, where the new supply and demand curves intersect. The point

---

Exhibit 8

Long-Run Supply Curves for Constant-, Increasing-, and Decreasing-Cost Industries

The immediate effect of an increase in demand from D₁ to D₂ is to change the industry's equilibrium from the long-run point E₁ to the short-run point E₂. At this higher price, new firms will find it profitable to enter the industry, and the supply curve will shift to the right until it finally settles at S₂. The long-run industry supply curve S₁ is therefore defined as the locus or "path" of the industry's long-run equilibrium points.

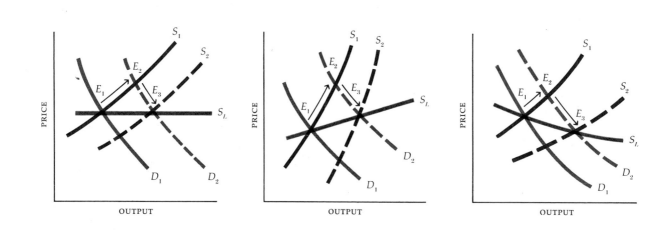

Constant cost   Increasing cost   Decreasing cost

E_3 represents the *long-run equilibrium* position of the industry.

This analysis suggests the following principle:

If we connect the industry's two long-run equilibrium points E_1 and E_3—that is, the equilibrium points that existed before and after the changes in both demand and supply—we get the *long-run industry supply curve* labeled S_L. This curve may be either horizontal, rising, or falling, depending on whether the industry is one of constant, increasing, or decreasing costs.

This principle requires an explanation of what is meant by constant-cost, increasing-cost, and decreasing-cost industries.

Constant-Cost Industries

A *constant-cost industry* is one which experiences no increases in resource prices or in its costs of production as new firms enter the industry. This tends to happen when an industry's demand for the resources it employs is an insignificant proportion of the total demand for those resources. In that case, new firms will be able to enter the industry and buy the labor, capital, and other inputs that they need without bidding up the prices of these factors of production. The long-run industry supply curve will thus be perfectly elastic. Unspecialized resources (such as unskilled workers) which are in wide use by many industries are examples of such inputs.

Increasing-Cost Industries

An *increasing-cost industry* is one which experiences rising resource prices and therefore increasing costs of production as new firms enter the industry. This happens because the industry's demand for resources is a significant enough proportion of the total demand so that any new firms must bid up the prices of these factors of production in order to acquire them from other firms. Specialized resources (such as skilled workers) whose supplies are not readily expanded as the demand for them increases provide examples of such inputs. In general, increasing-cost industries are more common than constant-cost industries. This is especially true in our expanding scientific and technological age, when firms must make growing use of highly specialized resources. The computer, electronic, and aircraft industries are a few prominent examples.

Decreasing-Cost Industries

A *decreasing-cost industry* is one which experiences declining resource prices and therefore falling costs of production as new firms enter the industry and the industry expands. This, of course, is not as common as the two previous cases, but it could arise for a while as a result of substantial external economies of scale as we have already learned. Can you give some examples?

Partial and General Equilibrium

What are the achievements of perfect competition? Are they "good" or "bad"? What would it be like to live in a world of perfectly competitive industries?

These questions require that we evaluate the social consequences of perfect competition—that is, its effects on society as a whole. We shall see that it has many favorable features, but also some unfavorable ones.

THE EQUILIBRIUM CONDITIONS

Let us look back at Exhibit 7 and note carefully the properties that characterize a perfectly competitive firm in long-run equilibrium. As you can see, these properties may be described succinctly by the equations:

$$MC = MR = AR = ATC = LRAC$$

These equations are called *equilibrium conditions.* They constitute a set of relationships that define the equilibrium position of an economic organism—in this case a firm in perfect competition. In certain advanced courses in economic theory, other sets of equilibrium conditions are studied—not only for firms but also for households, and even for entire economies.

Our purpose is to analyze and interpret the meaning of the above equations, and in so doing we will see what perfect competition actually accomplishes. You may find it helpful to refer back to Exhibit 7 while reading the following explanation. Keep in mind that these characteristics apply to *every* firm in the industry.

☐ $MC = MR$ means that the firm is maximizing its profits and there is no incentive for it to alter its output; the firm is thus in short-run (as well as long-run) equilibrium.

☐ $MR = AR$ (or price) means that the firm is selling in a perfectly competitive market, for as we shall see in the following chapters, any other type of market situation results in a firm's marginal revenue being always less than its average revenue or demand.

☐ $ATC = AR$ means that the firm is earning only normal profits and there is no incentive for other firms to enter or leave the industry.

☐ $MC = ATC$ means that the firm is operating at the lowest point on its average total cost curve and hence is making the most efficient use of the variable resources available to it with its given plant.

☐ $MC = ATC = LRAC$ means that the firm is producing the optimum output with the optimum-size plant, and hence is allocating *all* its resources in an optimum manner.

PARTIAL AND GENERAL EQUILIBRIUM THEORY

This set of properties, and the entire analysis on which it is based, prompts us to distinguish between two viewpoints of equilibrium theory, called "partial" and "general."

Partial equilibrium theory analyzes and develops an economic model of a particular market on the assumption that other markets are in balance. It thus ignores the mutual interrelationships of prices and outputs that may exist between markets. The familiar supply and demand analysis is a typical example of partial equilibrium theory. Although the supply and demand curves in previous chapters were extremely helpful in analyzing the economic effects of such things as price control, rationing, minimum wages, and commodity taxes, they always focused on a particular market, ignoring the ramifications and repercussions of price and output changes which may

have occurred in other markets and which could in turn affect the market we were studying.

General equilibrium theory analyzes the interrelations between prices and outputs of goods and resources in different markets and demonstrates the possibility of simultaneous equilibrium between all markets. It is based on the assumption that if, for each particular market, we are given such information as consumer demand schedules, resource supply schedules, production functions, and the demand for money, equilibrium forces will cause resource and commodity prices to adjust themselves in a mutually consistent manner. The entire system can then settle down in a stable equilibrium of supply and demand. Any change in the determinants affecting one good can, however, upset the entire system and have widespread repercussions on the equilibrium prices and outputs of all other goods. Although general equilibrium analysis is primarily of theoretical interest, it nevertheless forces us to keep in mind the fact that in the real world there is often a significant degree of interdependence among various markets.

FAVORABLE FEATURES OF A PERFECTLY COMPETITIVE PRICE SYSTEM

The equilibrium conditions listed above are useful because they can serve as a basis for describing the favorable features of a perfectly competitive price system—that is, an economic system composed entirely of perfectly competitive factors and firms. For example, such a system would yield certain beneficial consequences in long-run or general equilibrium:

1. Consumer preferences as reflected in the marketplace would be fulfilled with the largest amount of goods consistent with the minimum (average cost) prices and known production techniques of business firms.

2. Society's resources would be allocated in the most efficient way, both within and between industries.

3. Flexible factor and product prices would assure full employment of all resources.

4. Competition among employers for inputs and among factors for jobs would cause factor owners to be paid their opportunity costs; these would be de-

ALFRED MARSHALL

1842–1924

In the last quarter of the nineteenth century there arose in Europe and America a system of economic thought known to all economists as the neoclassical *school. One of the leaders of this school was Alfred Marshall, a British scholar whose landmark treatise, the* Principles of Economics *(1890), will forever be regarded as a masterwork.*

Marshall was born in London and educated at Cambridge University where he majored in the classics and mathematics. "My acquaintance with economics," he once wrote, started in 1867–68 and "commenced with reading [John Stuart Mill and David Ricardo] while I was still earning my living by teaching mathematics at Cambridge; and translating the doctrines into differential equations as far as they would go; and, as a rule, rejecting those which would not go."

Several decades later, John Maynard Keynes, himself a leading scholar and at one time a student of Marshall's at Cambridge, referred to his former teacher "as a scientist . . . who, within his own field, was the greatest in the world in a hundred years."

Alfred Marshall was, indeed, one of the great economic thinkers of all time. His Principles, *which went through eight editions, was a leading text in economics for several decades. Among the major contributions of this and other works by Marshall were the distinction between the short run and the long run, the extensive use of partial equilibrium models to describe economic behavior, the equilibrium of price and output resulting from the interaction of supply and demand, the concept of elasticity, the distinction between money cost and real cost, and many other ideas. In short, almost everything we read today pertaining to supply and demand analysis, equilibrium, and related notions were originally formulated precisely and definitively by Marshall. Few students today realize or appreciate the significant role that Marshallian ideas play in their economics education.*

Although he was acquainted with the general equilibrium theory of Continental economists and was an adept mathematician, Marshall chose the less vigorous method of partial equilibrium analysis because it served to make economic science a better "engine for discovery" in the investigation of specific problems. His approach to his predecessors was unusually conciliatory, and throughout his career, he tended to phrase his own doctrines so as to minimize the change from the classical tradition. In contrast to the earlier utility theorists,

he did not take supply for granted but considered it as "the other blade of a pair of scissors." Underlying demand was marginal utility as reflected in the price offers of buyers. Underlying supply was marginal effort, reflected in the supply prices of sellers.

Marshall's partial equilibrium method is illustrated in typical fashion by his discussion of demand. Since the demand schedule relates solely to the relationship between price and quantity demanded, other things must be held constant, or, as Marshall has it, "impounded in ceteris paribus.*" Thus, the taste of consumers, their money incomes, the number of buyers, and the prices of other commodities are held constant in the discussion of the equilibrium determination of supply and demand. This procedure is still the accepted method of analyzing changes in demand.*

By the time he retired from his professorship at Cambridge, Marshall had trained several generations of England's greatest economists, and these disciples went on to assume major positions in universities and government service. Although much has changed in economics since the eighth edition of Principles of Economics *was published in 1920, these changes have for the most part been gradual, and Marshall's neoclassical structure is still clearly identifiable today throughout the whole body of economic literature.*

termined by the respective contributions to total output of each factor, as measured by its marginal productivity.

5. With consumer incomes and tastes given, aggregate consumer satisfaction would be maximized because goods would be distributed among consumers in the most efficient way.

These desirable features of a perfectly competitive price system in long-run equilibrium, and other characteristics which we have not mentioned, can be formulated as theorems which are actually proved in more advanced theoretical discussions. For our purposes, it is sufficient that they be described as above so that they can be compared with the following shortcomings.

SOME UNFAVORABLE FEATURES

Several undesirable consequences of a perfectly competitive price system were pointed out when we first studied the laws of supply and demand earlier in the book. At that time we did not have a formal knowledge of the theory of perfect competition, nor did we know that it is the basis for supply and demand analysis. Now, however, we are in a better position to enrich our understanding of the various shortcomings and to learn a few additional ones as well. Since the paramount concern of economics is to study the way in which society allocates its scarce resources, we shall evaluate the shortcomings of a perfectly competitive price system against this objective.

1. Incomplete Reflection of Consumer Desires

In a perfectly competitive system, sellers react only to those preferences that consumers register through their "dollar votes" in the marketplace. Consequently, this type of system does not measure the desires of consumers for "collective" goods like national defense, highways, parks, and unpolluted air and water. Further, to the extent that incomes are unequally distributed, the competitive price system will reflect the dollar votes of the rich more than the poor. Hence as Charles Dickens might have portrayed it, Ebenezer Scrooge could buy the milk for his cat that poor Bob Cratchit could not afford for his frail, crippled son, Tiny Tim.

2. Inadequate Measure of Social Costs and Social Benefits

A chemical company disposes of its waste products in a nearby lake; a steel mill's smoke permeates the air of a neighboring city; a drive-in theater discharges its patrons onto a highway at the end of a movie. In each of these and many other situations, two types of costs are involved: *private costs,* which are the economic costs to a firm for performing a particular act, and *social costs,* which are the reductions in incomes or benefits that accrue to society as a result of a particular act. In the above examples, the social costs would include the displeasures suffered by the community due to water pollution, destruction of recreational areas, and congested highways.

A similar distinction can be made in terms of benefits. If you get a good education, this act will lead to *private benefits* for you in the form of higher income, but society will also incur *social benefits* because you will (hopefully) become a more enlightened and informed citizen. Likewise, if you maintain an attractive lawn, your neighbors will be pleased; bathing regularly will help keep you from becoming a social outcast.

The significance of these concepts is based on the argument frequently raised by economists that the competitive prices which are established in the market through the interaction of many sellers and buyers tend to reflect only private costs and private benefits while they largely exclude social costs and social benefits. Therefore, to the extent that marginal cost neglects the influence of social costs and to the extent that marginal revenue neglects the influence of social benefits, the $MC = MR$ (= price) rule will not allocate all of society's resources in the most efficient way.

This type of distinction between the private and social consequences of economic activities is important. It is discussed in a number of places in later chapters.

3. Insufficient Incentives for Progress

It has been argued by some that perfect competition would lead to economic stagnation. In a system where technological advances can be quickly duplicated by competing firms, there is little incentive to innovate with new production techniques and ideas. Further, it is doubtful whether the typically small firm in perfect competition could acquire the financial resources that are needed to undertake the kinds of substantial research and development projects that often lead to major innovations.

LIFE UNDER PERFECT COMPETITION— DISMAL AND DULL?

In view of the various desirable and undesirable features described above, what would it be like to live in a perfectly competitive world? Most of us might find it monotonous. Goods would be standardized in each industry and the range of consumer choices severely limited. At the grocery store, bread would be bread and ketchup would be ketchup, and the modern supermarket with its endless and colorful varieties of goods would cease to exist. The choice of an automobile, like some ladies' lingerie, might be confined to "small," "medium," and "large," but without the frills. There would clearly be no need for advertising (except perhaps for industry-wide or institutional advertising like "Eat more bread" or "Drink more milk") or even for trademarks or brand names, and the excitement of New York's Madison Avenue, where most of these creations are born, would—for good or evil—be lost. Hence there would be no commercial television as we now know it, and newspapers and magazines (could they possibly be homogeneous?) would cost more. For in a world of perfect competition, where it would be assumed that consumers knew their alternatives, the only type of advertising needed would inform rather than persuade. This means that there would be no need for anything other than, perhaps, classified advertising and the Sears, Roebuck catalog.

CONCLUSION—AND A LOOK FORWARD

Is this the kind of world we want? Each individual must answer for himself, for in economics the most we can do is identify the alternatives and their consequences, and leave it up to each person to make his choice. As we have already seen, although a perfectly competitive economy would have various

beneficial consequences, it would also have what many people would undoubtedly regard as undesirable features.

Since the imaginary world of perfect competition is so unreal, why do we study it? Does it have any practical value? The answer is simple: We do not necessarily learn about perfect competition in the vain hope of making it a reality; instead, we study it because it provides us with a guide for evaluating and improving the real world of imperfect competition, which we shall be analyzing later on.

REMARK. As mentioned earlier, the terms "perfect competition" and "pure competition" are ordinarily used synonymously for most purposes. However, when a distinction is made, pure competition is defined simply as a large number of buyers and sellers dealing in a homogeneous commodity, without discrimination. Pure competition thus tends to operate in essentially the same way and to attain the same long-run equilibrium conditions as perfect competition. However, it may not achieve these results as quickly or smoothly because the two "lubricating" features of perfect competition—namely perfect knowledge and perfect resource mobility, which eliminate any frictions in the system—are left out of the definition.

SUMMARY OF IMPORTANT IDEAS

1. A perfectly competitive industry or market is characterized by many buyers and sellers engaged in the purchase and sale of a homogeneous commodity, with perfect knowledge of market prices and quantities, no discrimination, and perfect mobility of resources. Perfect competition is thus a theoretical extreme rather than real-world phenomenon, although some of its features are roughly approximated in the organized commodity and stock markets.

2. In perfect competition, prices are established in the market through the interaction of many buyers and sellers. Each firm thus finds itself faced with a market price over which it has no influence. It cannot sell any of its output at a price which is the slightest bit above the market price; it can sell its entire output at the market price, and hence there is no inducement for it to sell at any lower price.

3. In terms of costs and revenues, each firm's most profitable level of output occurs where its marginal cost equals its marginal revenue. This is the output at which its total revenue minus total cost is a maximum.

4. In perfect competition, a firm's supply curve is its marginal cost curve above its average variable cost. The industry's short-run supply curve is thus derived by summing all the firms' marginal cost curves at each price above average variable cost. In the short run, a firm will operate as long as the market price is at least equal to its average variable (out-of-pocket) costs, since any price it gets over and above that will go to pay at least part of its fixed costs. In the long run, the firm will have to receive a price high enough to cover all costs, including a normal profit, if it is to remain in business.

5. In the long run, competition will force all firms to earn only normal profits and to operate with optimum-size plants. When this occurs, the industry as well as all firms in it will be in long-run equilibrium, with no tendency to expand or contract.

6. The industry's long-run supply curve connects all of its long-run supply-and-demand equilibrium points. The long-run supply curve may be constant (or perfectly elastic), increasing, or decreasing.

7. Partial equilibrium theory deals with prices and outputs in a particular market without regard to the influence of other markets, as in the familiar supply-and-demand analysis. General equilibrium theory deals with the interrelations of prices and outputs in all markets simultaneously. In view of its much greater complexity, general equilibrium analysis is primarily of theoretical interest.

8. In long-run equilibrium, a perfectly competitive economy will have allocated its resources in the most efficient way so as to maximize consumer satisfactions. This is assured by the equations

$$MC = MR = AR = ATC = LRAC$$

which if analyzed separately tell us that firms are maximizing their profits and making the most efficient use of society's resources, given the distribution of consumers' incomes and tastes.

9. Among the favorable features of a perfectly competitive price system are: (a) it fulfills consumer preferences with the largest amount of goods in the most efficient way; (b) it allocates society's resources optimally and, as a result of flexible product and factor prices, tends to encourage full employment of all resources; (c) it provides for factor payments at their opportunity costs as determined by their respective marginal productivities. Among the unfavorable features are: (a) it reflects consumer desires incompletely; (b) it does not always measure social costs and social benefits; (c) it provides insufficient incentives for economic progress.

FOR HOMEWORK AND DISCUSSION

1. *Terms and concepts to review:*

perfect competition	equilibrium conditions
average revenue	partial equilibrium
total revenue	theory
net revenue	general equilibrium
break-even point	theory
marginal revenue	neoclassical economics
long-run industry supply curve	private costs
	social costs
constant-cost industry	private benefits
increasing-cost industry	social benefits
	pure competition
decreasing-cost industry	

2. What is the "fundamental principle of profit maximization"? Explain. What special application of this rule applies to perfect competition? Why?

3. Is the price of a product determined by its cost of production, or is the cost of production determined by the price?

4. If new firms enter an industry, they will compete for factors of production and thereby raise the prices of those factors. How will this affect the cost curves of firms in the industry? Discuss.

5. "The farmer must receive a living price for milk." Discuss in terms of this chapter.

6. If you owned a shoe store and the shoes you carried cost you $10 a pair, would you stay in business if the highest price you could get for them was $10 a pair? Explain your answer in terms of this chapter.

7. The long-run history of the automobile industry reveals an enormous growth of output and a substantial reduction in prices. How do you account for this, since we have usually assumed that larger outputs come only from higher prices?

8. Insert words in the following sentences to make them true. Do not delete any words. Underline your inserted words.

a. A firm is in equilibrium when its costs and revenues are equal.

b. A perfectly competitive firm is in equilibrium when it is producing at its minimum average cost.

c. A perfectly competitive firm cannot earn supernormal profits.

d. A perfectly competitive firm's supply curve is its marginal cost curve.

9. What are the "equilibrium conditions" for a perfectly competitive industry in long-run equilibrium? Explain.

10. "It is an indictment of our price system that our country can spend more on such unimportant things as cosmetics or liquor than it spends on education." Evaluate this statement.

REFERENCES AND READING SUGGESTIONS

ALLEN, CLARK LEE, *The Framework of Price Theory*, Wadsworth, Belmont, Calif., 1967, chap. 9.

BOBER, M. M., *Intermediate Price and Income Theory*, rev. ed., Norton, New York, 1962, chap. 9.

BOULDING, KENNETH E., *Economic Analysis*, vol. 1, *Microeconomics*, 4th ed., Harper & Row, New York, 1966, chap. 19.

DOOLEY, PETER C., *Elementary Price Theory*, Appleton-Century-Crofts, New York, 1967, chap. 4.

DUE, JOHN F., and ROBERT W. CLOWER, *Intermediate Economic Analysis*, 5th ed., Irwin, Homewood, Illinois, 1966, chap. 8.

CHAPTER 24

Monopoly Behavior:
The Other End
of the Spectrum

The types of competitive systems that are of interest to economists are usually classified into several categories. Each of these categories may be regarded as occupying a position along a spectrum. Up to now we have studied only the system called "perfect competition," which may be visualized as lying at the left end of the competitive spectrum:

Perfect competition	?	Pure monopoly

In this chapter we turn our attention to the right end of the spectrum as we examine the extreme "opposite" of perfect competition—namely, pure monopoly. We shall find that this type of market structure is, like perfect competition, a theoretical limiting case, and that it is virtually nonexistent in its pure (unregulated) form.

Does this mean that the study of monopoly is "theoretical and impractical"? The answer is no. The theory of monopoly provides many useful tools and concepts for understanding the behavior of actual business firms. Against this background, the next chapter will combine the features of perfect competition and monopoly in order to help explain the competitive behavior of firms in the real world. For the time being, we will represent this "real" world by a question mark in the above spectrum.

The Meaning and Types
of Monopoly

What do we mean by monopoly? How do monopolies come into existence? What conditions must prevail in order for monopolies to survive? How does a monopolist determine his price and output? What is wrong with monopoly and what can be done about it?

The answers to these questions comprise the basic aspects of the theory of monopoly to which we now turn our attention.

WHAT IS A MONOPOLY?

A *monopoly* is defined as a single firm producing a product for which there are no close substitutes. This means that no other firms produce a similar product. Hence the monopoly firm constitutes the entire industry, and is thus a "pure" monopoly. A buyer who wants this particular product must either buy it from the monopolist or do without it.

REMARK. According to Webster, the derivation of the word "monopoly" is from the Greek *monopolion,* which means a right of exclusive sale. The dictionary, however, will also tell you that *mono* means "one" and *poly* means "many," which implies that a monopoly is one seller facing many buyers. This is the way in which we ordinarily think of monopoly. But in a later chapter relationships are studied in which one seller faces either one or several buyers. A number of interesting models will be constructed from such situations.

Pure monopolies are relatively rare, but they do exist. The electric, gas, and water companies in your locality are good examples, since they each produce a product for which there are no close substitutes. But notice that a firm's degree of monopoly may vary among markets. For instance, the electric company has a monopoly in the production of electricity for lighting purposes, but for heating purposes its electricity may compete with gas, coal, and fuel oil sold by other producers. An electric company may thus be a pure monopoly in the lighting market, but a "partial" monopoly in the heating market. Similarly, railroads, buses, taxis, and airlines are not pure monopolies, but they are certainly partial monopolies depending on the extent to which buyers can substitute the products of these industries in meeting their transportation needs.

Most firms in our economy may be characterized as "partial monopolies." In the following pages we will be developing a theory of pure monopoly, but we shall find that many of its principles and conclusions are applicable to partial monopolies as well.

SOURCES AND TYPES OF MONOPOLY

What are the origins of monopoly, and why do monopolies continue to exist? There are several possible explanations, all of which amount in one form or another to "obstacles to entry"—that is, legal, technical, or economic barriers that permit a firm to monopolize an industry and prevent new firms from entering. These obstacles give rise to several common types of monopolies.

Natural Monopoly

A *natural monopoly* is a "legal" monopoly established by a state or federal government, usually when either one or both of two conditions exist within an industry: (1) there are increasing economies of scale over a wide range of output so that one firm can supply the market more efficiently than two or more firms; (2) unrestricted competition among firms in the industry is deemed by society as undesirable. Hence the government grants such monopolies an exclusive right to operate, in return for which the government may also impose standards and requirements pertaining to the quantity and quality of output, geographic areas of operation, and the prices or rates that are charged. Public utilities are classic examples of natural monopolies (also sometimes called *legal monopolies* or *virtual monopolies*).

The first justification stated above for natural monopolies—that of increasing economies of scale—is largely a technological one. The technology of public utilities is such that once the heavy fixed-cost facilities are established (such as power generators, or gas transmission lines, or railroad tracks and terminals), additional customer service will reduce average total costs over a wide range of output and also permit the construction of more optimum-size plants so as to lower long-run average costs.

The second justification—that of social undesirability of unrestricted competition—is based on judicial opinions handed down for many decades by the courts that a "business affected with a public interest" may qualify as a public utility (or natural monopoly) because the welfare of the entire community is directly dependent on the manner in which the business is operated. This vague definition has resulted in some of our states establishing the following as public utilities: common carriers of all kinds, water, gas, electricity, telephones, telegraphs, bridges, warehouses, cemeteries, gristmills, sawmills, grain elevators, stockyards, hotels, docks, cotton gins, refrigeration plants, markets, and news services.

Whereas many natural monopolies are privately owned but governmentally regulated, there are some *government monopolies* which are both owned and regulated by a federal or local government. Examples are the U.S. Post Office, the water and sewer systems of almost all local municipalities, the electric power plants of many cities, and the central banks of most countries.

Strategic-Resource Monopoly

A firm might achieve a monopoly by gaining control of an essential input to a production process. The classic example of this is the Aluminum Company of America (ALCOA), which, prior to World War II, had a monopoly in aluminum production because it controlled all the bauxite-ore deposits from which aluminum is made. Similarly, International Nickel Company of Canada today owns almost the entire world's supply of nickel reserves, and the De Beers Company of South Africa owns most of the world's diamond mines.

Patent Monopoly

A *patent monopoly* is a firm upon which government has conferred the exclusive right—through issuance of a patent—to make, use, or vend its own invention or discovery. A patent therefore enables a firm to profit from its invention while preventing its adoption by competitors. Firms like the National Cash Register Company and the United Shoe Machinery Company each held a series of patents on their line of products which for many years enabled them to monopolize their respective industries. Today, firms like IBM, Xerox, Polaroid, and others have varying degrees of monopoly power through patent protection.

There are many instances in American history of firms that gained monopolistic positions in their industries through various types of "unfair"—and now largely illegal—methods of competition such as below-cost ("cutthroat") pricing, false and misleading advertising, intimidation of competitors, and other deceptive and injurious practices. We shall have more to say about this interesting area of economics in a later chapter dealing with the problems of government regulation of business.

Price and Output Determination

When we studied the theory of perfect competition, we learned that a perfectly competitive seller has no influence over the price at which he can sell his output; he is faced with a perfectly elastic demand curve at the market price, and he maximizes his profit by producing the output at which his $MC = MR (= P)$.

A pure monopolist is in a different situation. Since he *is* the industry, instead of just a small part of it, he can exercise complete control over the price at which he sells his output. He will thus find that the market demand curve for his product will be less than perfectly elastic: *it will slope downward instead of being horizontal*. On the other hand, we may *assume* that the shapes of his production function and cost curves are similar to those of a perfectly competitive seller's since he must purchase both his variable and fixed factors in the input markets and then combine these factors in order to produce a product. Later on we will note a significant exception to this assumption.

Exhibit 1

Cost and Revenue Schedules of a Monopolist

(1) Quantity per day Q	(2) Average Revenue or Price AR = P	(3) Total Revenue TR ($TR = P \times Q$)	(4) Total Cost TC	(5) Average Total Cost ATC ($ATC = \frac{TC}{Q}$)	(6) Marginal Cost MC ($MC = \frac{\text{change in TC}}{\text{change in Q}}$)	(7) Marginal Revenue MR ($MR = \frac{\text{change in TR}}{\text{change in Q}}$)	(8) Net Revenue NR ($TR - TC$)
0	$16	$ 0	$ 25	$ ∞			$ −25
					$10	$15	
1	15	15	35	35.00			−20
					6	13	
2	14	28	41	20.50			−13
					4	11	
3	13	39	45	15.00			−6
					2	9	
4	12	48	47	11.75			1
					2	7	
5	11	55	49	9.80			6
					3	5	
6	10	60	52	8.67			8
					5	3	
7	9	63	57	8.14			6
					8	1	
8	8	64	65	8.13			−1
					14	−1	
9	7	63	79	8.78			−16
					21	−3	
10	6	60	100	10.00			−40

COST AND REVENUE SCHEDULES

These ideas are illustrated by the cost and revenue data of a monopolist, shown in Exhibit 1. It should be apparent from this table that columns (1) and (2) actually compose the demand schedule facing the monopolist. Note that his average revenue (= price) is inversely related to the quantity. This means that *for the monopolist to sell more units of his product he must charge a lower price per unit for all units that he sells.*

Since the average revenue or price varies inversely with quantity, total revenue rises to a maximum and then begins to fall. The changes in total revenue, as always, are reflected by marginal revenue [column (7)], which now turns out to be different from average revenue because of the changes in price.

The cost schedules in the table are those we used in the previous chapter for a perfectly competitive firm, since as stated above we are assuming that the monopolist's cost structure is essentially similar to that of a seller's in perfect competition. Besides, by using the same cost data, we shall be able to see more clearly that the chief differences between the two firms originate in the output market where goods are sold, rather than in the input market where factors are bought.

A look at the table shows quite clearly that the fundamental principle of profit maximization still holds: the monopolist's most profitable level of output—the output at which his net revenue [column (8)] is a maximum—is at six units, which is also where his MC is equal to MR. Why is this so? Because as we learned in the previous chapter, at any output less than this the added cost of an additional unit is less than the added revenue, so it pays to increase production. At any output greater than this the opposite is true. Only where MC = MR is the firm's output at its most profitable level.

LOOKING AT THE GRAPHS

You can visualize these ideas more easily by examining the graphs of the cost and revenue schedules rather than the data. In Exhibit 2 the monopolist's total revenue and total cost curves are shown in the

Exhibit 2

Exhibit 2

Cost and Revenue Curves of a Monopolist

Profit Maximization: Three Viewpoints

1. Total curves. The most profitable level of output is determined where the curves TR − TC, as represented by the distance GH, is a maximum. This occurs at an output of 6 units. At this output, a tangent to the TR curve is parallel to a tangent to the TC curve, as at G and H. At smaller or larger outputs such as 5 or 7 units, the tangents would not be parallel.

2. Marginal curves. The most profitable level of output is determined where MC = MR, as explained in the text. You can verify this by simply following the vertical dashed line downward at 6 units of output.

3. Net revenue curve. The most profitable level of output is determined where the net revenue curve NR (= TR − TC) is a maximum. The vertical dashed line emphasizes these profit-maximizing principles in all three charts.

TECHNICAL NOTE (OPTIONAL). If you like to think in geometric terms, remember that parallel lines have equal slopes or steepness. Hence the most profitable output in the top chart is determined where the *slopes* of the *TC* and *TR* curves are equal, which is where the tangents are parallel. In the middle chart, since marginal cost is the graph of the *slope* of total cost, and marginal revenue is the graph of the *slope* of total revenue, it is true that at the level of maximum profit:

$$MC = MR$$

or, equivalently,

$$\text{Slope of } TC = \text{slope of } TR$$

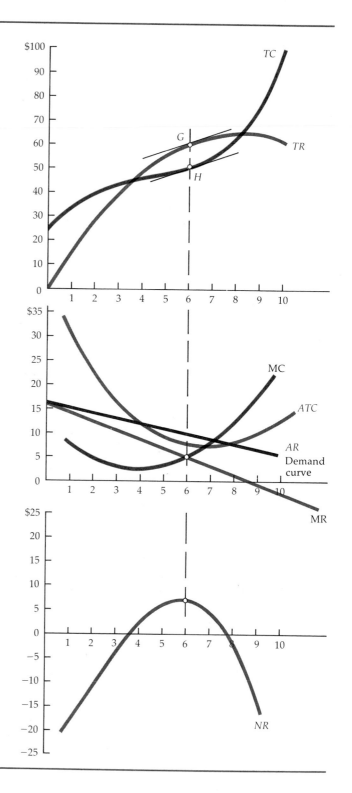

top chart, his appropriate average and marginal curves in the middle chart, and his net revenue curve in the bottom chart. The vertical dashed line that passes through all three charts emphasizes the fact that at the most profitable level of output:

1. $TR - TC$ is a maximum.

2. $MC = MR$, since the tangents to TC and TR are parallel.

3. NR is a maximum.

Note also in the middle chart that the average revenue or demand curve facing the monopolist slopes downward, which was not the case for a perfectly competitive seller. This means, as explained above, that for the monopolist to sell more units of his product he must charge a lower price per unit for *all* units that he sells. Since AR or price varies inversely with the quantity demanded, the MR curve lies below the AR curve. You can verify this for yourself by experimenting with a few prices and quantities on your own and then sketching their graphs.

USING THE $MC = MR$ PRINCIPLE

We must examine the profit-maximizing behavior of a monopolist more closely so that we are in a better position to evaluate the consequences of his actions. Let us therefore put him under a microscope, so to speak, by analyzing his performance in terms of the fundamental $MC = MR$ principle illustrated by the diagrams in Exhibit 3.

In Exhibit 3a, the monopolist finds that the $MC = MR$ rule leads him to produce the output ON. At this output, the demand curve facing him indicates that the highest price he can charge is NG ($= OP$). His total profit is thus the area of the rectangle shown in the chart, as explained in the accompanying description.

In Exhibit 3b, the monopolist's costs are relatively high. This is due either to an increase in the prices of his factors of production which causes his cost curves to shift upward, or a decrease in demand for his output which causes his revenue curves to shift downward, or both. He finds that at the $MC = MR$ output, namely ON, the corresponding price NG is just high enough to yield a normal profit. Since the ATC curve

is tangent to the AR curve at this output, he knows that any other level of production would yield losses because his ATC would be greater than his AR.

In Exhibit 3c, the monopolist's ATC curve is everywhere higher than his AR curve, which, as before, is the result of an increase in costs or a decrease in demand, or both. He finds that, at least for the short run, the $MC = MR$ rule still prevails because the output ON and the corresponding price NG will *minimize his loss;* that is, any other price and output will yield a larger loss area than the rectangle in the diagram.

Since it is often necessary to sketch both average revenue and marginal revenue curves, here is a convenient geometric rule to remember:

An MR *curve always bisects any horizontal line drawn from the vertical axis to the* AR *curve.* Thus in Exhibit 3a, the distance $PW = WG$, and similarly for any other horizontal line that may be drawn.

This rule is based on a theorem which we shall not prove here, but you can easily verify it for yourself by constructing your own tables and plotting the graphs. Actually, all that this rule means is that at any given price, an MR curve is twice as steep as (or has twice the slope of) its corresponding AR curve.

MARGINAL REVENUE IS NOT PRICE; MARGINAL COST IS NOT SUPPLY

These models illustrate an important distinction between a monopoly firm and a perfectly competitive firm. When we studied the theory of perfect competition, we learned that the seller's marginal revenue curve was the same as his average revenue (= price) or demand curve, and his marginal cost curve was his supply curve above the level of minimum average variable cost. Do these conditions also apply to a monopolist? The answer is *no*, for as you can verify from the cost and revenue schedules in Exhibit 1 and the charts in Exhibit 3:

1. Marginal revenue falls faster than average revenue or demand because the seller must charge a lower price per unit for all units in order to sell more output. Thus, *marginal revenue is not price.*

2. The most profitable level of output for the seller,

Exhibit 3

Three Possible Profit Positions for a Monopolist

At $MC = MR$, where output = ON and price = NG (= OP):

Total revenue = OPGN
Total cost = ODEN
Net revenue = DPGE

Total revenue = OPGN
Total cost = OPGN
Net revenue = zero

Total revenue = OPGN
Total cost = OKLN
Net loss = PKLG

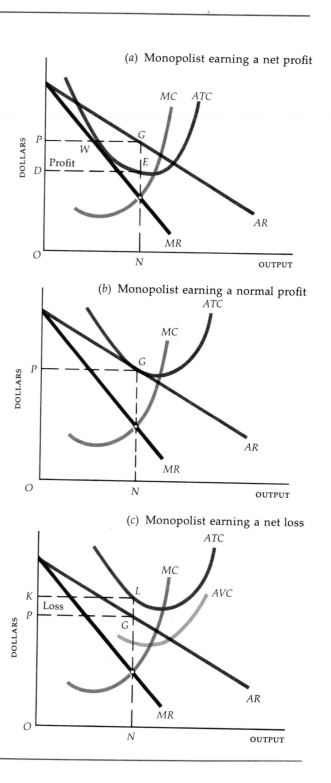

(a) Monopolist earning a net profit

(b) Monopolist earning a normal profit

(c) Monopolist earning a net loss

and the most profitable price that he can charge for that output, are determined by $MC = MR$, not by $MC = AR (= P)$. Thus, *marginal cost is not supply.*

The reasons for these differences between price and output determination by a monopolist as compared to a perfectly competitive seller are explained further in Exhibit 4. Each diagram compares a given

MC curve of a monopolist with two arbitrarily different demand or AR curves and their corresponding MR curves. A study of these diagrams and the accompanying analysis leads to the startling conclusion that *a less than perfectly competitive firm has no supply curve; therefore, only in perfect competition are prices determined by supply and demand.*

Exhibit 4

No Supply Curve for a Firm with a Downward-Sloping Demand Curve

For any given marginal cost curve, the most profitable price and output depend on the firm's particular average revenue curve and its corresponding marginal revenue curve. Thus in chart (a) the single output ON corresponds to the two prices OP and OS. In chart (b), the two outputs ON and OL correspond to the single price OK. This suggests the following principle:

A firm faced with a downward-sloping (or less than per-

fectly elastic) demand curve has no supply curve, since there is no single quantity that the firm will necessarily supply at a *given* price, and no single price at which the firm will necessarily supply a *given* quantity.

We thus come to the surprising conclusion that only under perfect competition are prices determined by supply and demand, since a less than perfectly competitive firm has no supply curve.

A single output at multiple prices

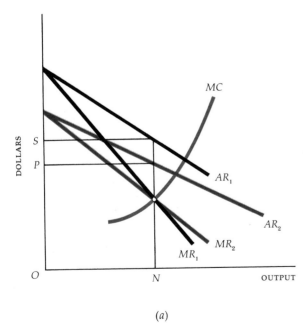

(a)

Multiple outputs at a single price

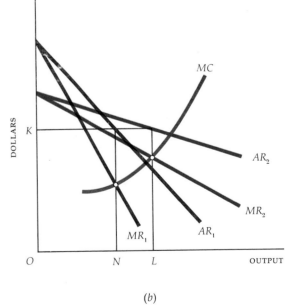

(b)

DO MONOPOLIES EARN "LARGE" PROFITS?

We now know enough about the behavior of a monopolist to draw three important conclusions about monopoly pricing:

1. An unregulated monopolist does not charge the "highest price that he can get"—a fact that may surprise many people. Instead he charges the highest price that is consistent with maximizing his profits. In Exhibit 3a, for instance, the monopolist could produce somewhat less than ON and charge a price higher than NG; then, as long as his ATC did not exceed his AR he would still make a profit, but he obviously would not make the maximum possible profit.

2. A pure monopolist does not necessarily receive "high" profits just because he is a monopolist. In fact, if his profits are relatively high, he may find that the owners of some of his factors of production, such as workers or landlords, will absorb part of the surplus by demanding larger payments. This will cause the monopolist's ATC curve to rise, possibly to the point where he is earning a "small" profit or perhaps only a normal profit, as in Exhibit 3b.

3. In the short run a monopolist may earn less than a normal profit and still remain in business, as in Exhibit 3c. But in the long run he would have to earn at least a normal profit to continue in operation.

Thus, being a pure monopoly does not in itself guarantee extraordinary profit, although a monopoly is likely to be more profitable than a perfectly competitive firm. For a monopolist is faced with certain market restraints that affect his price and output decisions, and his ability to cope with these restraints will affect the profitability of his firm. By adhering to the $MC = MR$ principle, the monopolist will always maximize his profits (or minimize his losses), but this principle in itself does not guarantee whether those profits will be "large" or "small."

Evaluating Monopoly: What's Wrong with It?

You have probably heard that monopolies are "bad," but may not know exactly why. Now, however, on the basis of what you have learned from economic theory, you can give three significant reasons:

1. It Misallocates Resources

The basic economic criticism of pure monopoly is this:

A monopoly misallocates society's resources by restricting output and charging a higher price than a similar firm in perfect competition. By "similar" is meant a firm with the same production function and cost structure.

This criticism of monopoly is illustrated in Exhibit 5. Given the firm's cost curves, a perfectly competitive seller will, in the long run, end up producing at his minimum ATC—that is, he will produce the

---

Exhibit 5

Monopolist Versus Competitive Seller

Given the firm's cost curves, a monopoly restricts output and charges a higher price than a similar firm in perfect competition.

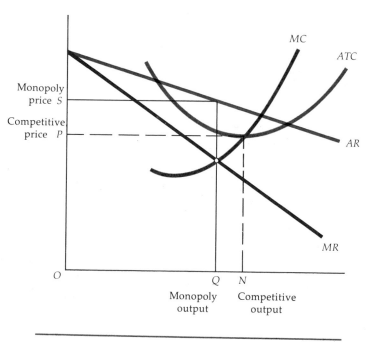

---

output *ON* and charge the going market price of *OP*. He will thereby earn a normal profit and he will be allocating society's resources "ideally" by making the most efficient use of all of his productive factors.

A monopolist, on the other hand, will produce the smaller output *OQ* and charge the higher price *OS*. Further, since there are obstacles to other firms' entry, the monopolist will not find himself under competitive pressure to reduce his price or increase his production, and he may continue to earn supernormal profits in the long run. In restricting his output, he will also restrict his input by hiring fewer factors of production. He will thereby misallocate society's resources by failing to make as full and efficient use of his inputs as he would if he were a perfectly competitive seller. (See also Box 1.)

REMARK. (1) The prices of the factors of production will affect the *height* of the cost curves but not their *shapes*, since the latter are determined by the underlying production function and technology. (2) The above criticism assumes the shape of the cost curves to be the same for a monopoly as for a competitive firm, which is not always the case in practice. In some industries, technology may influence the shape of the cost curves by bringing about increasing economies of scale over a wide range of output, so that one firm can supply the market more efficiently than several. This, as you recall, is one of the justifications of natural monopolies, e.g., public utilities, mentioned earlier.

2. It Contributes to Income Inequality

A second criticism is that monopoly tends to create greater income inequality than would exist in a perfectly competitive economy. By restricting output and charging a higher price, the monopoly makes supernormal profits. These go to its relatively few owners who, as corporation stockholders, are among the upper-income groups in our economy. This class thus benefits at the expense of the many consumers and resource owners who make up the rest of society.

3. It Lacks Incentives for Efficiency and Progress

A third major criticism of monopoly is that, unlike the perfectly competitive firm, it lacks the incentive to meet consumer needs and to make the most efficient use of *known* productive techniques. In addition, it need not be sufficiently inspired to develop

Box 1

Pricing Under Monopoly

"A monopoly granted either to an individual or to a trading company has the same effect as a secret in trade or manufactures. The monopolists, by keeping the market constantly understocked, by never fully supplying the effectual demand, sell their commodities much above the natural price, and raise their emoluments, whether they consist in wages or profit, greatly above their natural rate.

"The price of monopoly is upon every occasion the highest which can be got. The natural price, or the price of free competition, on the contrary, is the lowest which can be taken, not upon every occasion indeed, but for any considerable time together. The one is upon every occasion the highest which can be squeezed out of the buyers, or which, it is supposed, they will consent to give: the other is the lowest which the sellers can commonly afford to take, and at the same time continue their business.

"The exclusive privileges of corporations, statutes of apprenticeship, and all those laws which restrain, in particular employments, the competition to a smaller number than might otherwise go into them, have the same tendency, though in a less degree. They are a sort of enlarged monopolies, and may frequently, for ages together, and in whole classes of employments, keep up the market price of particular commodities above the natural price, and maintain both the wages of the labor and the profits of the stock employed about them somewhat above their natural rate."

Adam Smith, *Wealth of Nations*, 1776, Book I, Chap. 7.

The concept of a downward-sloping demand or *AR* curve did not exist in Smith's time. As a result, he made an error in his evaluation of monopoly. Can you find the error and correct it?

new productive techniques, and hence may retard economic progress. This is because the obstacles to entry make the monopolist relatively secure in his position; he does not face competitive pressures which would otherwise stimulate him to innovate. Public utilities—especially the railroads and telephone companies—are often used as illustrations of monopolies that have intentionally retarded the development of new and improved products so as not to increase the obsolescence rate of their existing equipment.

WHAT CAN BE DONE ABOUT MONOPOLY?

These general criticisms of monopoly are rooted in the fundamental notion of resource misallocation resulting from the restriction of output and higher prices. In view of this, what can be done about monopolies in our society? There are three major possibilities, all of which require government action:

1. Tax away all the profits of monopolies above their normal profits and distribute these revenues to the public through more or improved government services. This would not drive monopolies out of business, since they would still be normally profitable, but it would reduce the tendency for monopolies to contribute to income inequality.

2. Treat all monopolies as "public utilities" by regulating their outputs and prices, requiring them to produce more and charge less than they would if they were completely free and unregulated.

3. Break monopolies up into competing firms.

None of these approaches, or a combination of them, would overcome completely the fundamental problem of resource misallocation, but each would tend to reduce somewhat the adverse effects of misallocation. Some of the important problems that arise from these suggestions are discussed in a later chapter dealing with antitrust problems involving government regulation of business.

Price Discrimination

Until now we have assumed that when a monopolist decides on his most profitable volume of output, he sells the required number of units at the *same* price per unit. However, a monopolist may sometimes find it more profitable to charge different prices instead of a single price for the units he sells. He is then engaging in what is known as "price discrimination"—one of the most interesting problems in the theory of monopoly.

Price discrimination may be defined as the practice of charging different prices to the same or to different buyers for the same good. Hence it is also sometimes called *differential pricing*. In general terms, price discrimination or differential pricing is a method that some sellers may use to tailor their prices to the specific purchasing situations or circumstances of the buyer.

"TAPPING" THE DEMAND CURVE

An example of price discrimination occurs when a monopolist "taps" the demand curve of the buyer by charging lower prices for larger quantities instead of a single price per unit for all units purchased. This approach may also be combined with charging different prices to different classes of buyers.

For example, an electric company does not usually charge the same price per unit of electricity to all buyers for all units. Instead it *segments* the total market—that is, divides it into homogeneous submarkets consisting, say, of residential users, commercial users, and industrial users—and charges a different price to each class of user. In this way it earns more money than it would if all users paid the same price.

A simplified version of this concept is illustrated in Exhibit 6. Assuming the AR curve to be the demand curve of a single buyer or of a single homogeneous class of buyers, the seller may simply charge a price of OP_4 per unit and sell ON_4 units. In this case there is no discrimination, and the seller's total revenue is his price times quantity, or the area of the rectangle $OP_4M_4N_4$.

However, he can enlarge his total receipts considerably if he discriminates in price. Thus, he may charge a price of OP_1 for the first ON_1 units, giving him a total revenue of $OP_1M_1N_1$. Then he may lower his price to OP_2 per unit and sell an additional N_1N_2 units. After that, he can lower the price to OP_3 and sell an additional N_2N_3 units, and finally he can lower it to OP_4, where he sells a further N_3N_4 units. Although he still ends up selling the same total number of units, namely ON_4, his total revenue is now the entire shaded area instead of the area $OP_4M_4N_4$ when he charged a price of OP_4 per unit without discrimination. Evidently, the smaller the reductions in his

Exhibit 6

Price Discrimination Based on Quantity

By charging a different price to the same buyer (or to the same homogeneous class of buyers) according to the quantity purchased, the seller earns a larger total revenue (shown by the shaded areas) than if he charges the same price per unit for all units purchased.

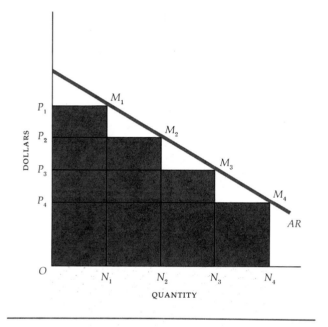

price, the narrower the steps under the demand curve become and hence the larger his total revenue. Theoretically, the limit would be a total revenue equal to the entire area under the curve, but this would require price reductions in infinitesimal amounts. In practice, the reductions are in finite amounts for blocks of units, and the sales are made simultaneously to different classes of buyers at different price scales.

DUMPING

Another form of price discrimination occurs when a monopolist sells the same product in different markets at different prices. This practice is known in international trade as *dumping*, but its underlying principles are equally applicable to domestic trade.

The basic concept is illustrated by the diagrams in Exhibit 7. A firm which has a monopoly in the domestic market, for example, will probably find that the demand for its product at home is more inelastic than the demand abroad because foreign buyers have more alternative sources from which to purchase the product, which makes their demand for the monopolist's product more elastic.

Exhibit 7, therefore, shows the demand curve in the domestic market to be more inelastic than that in the foreign market. The total demand in both markets may be obtained by simply summing the horizontal ordinates in the domestic and foreign markets—that is, the quantities demanded in those markets at each price—thus yielding the curve $AR_1 + AR_2$. The total marginal revenue of both markets, namely $MR_1 + MR_2$, is derived in a similar way by summing the horizontal ordinates to the MR_1 curve and the MR_2 curve in the domestic and foreign markets, or in other words the quantities in both markets at each marginal revenue.

The MC curve in the total market is the monopolist's marginal cost curve. His most profitable total output is thus O_3N_3 because this is where the marginal cost of his output equals the total marginal revenue. It should be emphasized that only one marginal cost curve is assumed to exist in this case, since it makes no difference to costs whether the product is sold at home or abroad; the product is still the same, and the marginal cost is determined by the total output. Hence at the output O_3N_3, the monopolist's marginal cost is N_3L_3, and this is equal to N_1L_1 in the domestic market and N_2L_2 in the foreign market.

Equilibrium in the Submarkets

How will the monopolist divide his total output among the two submarkets? What price will he charge in each market? The answers to these questions follow from the $MC = MR$ principle we have already learned. In order to maximize profit, the monopolist will sell O_1N_1 units in the domestic

Exhibit 7

Illustration of Dumping

By adhering to the MC = MR *principle, the monopolist maximizes profit by allocating his total equilibrium output* O_3N_3 *among the two submarkets, and charging a higher price in the submarket where the demand elasticity is less.*

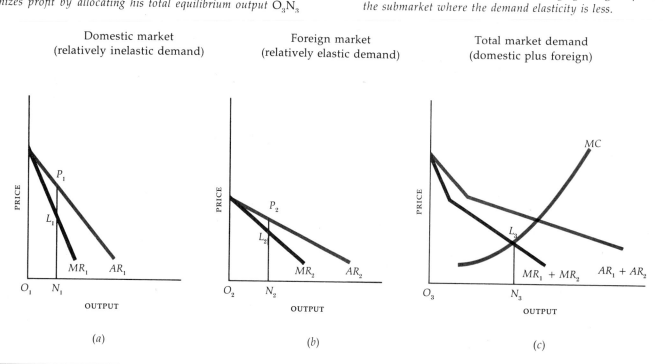

Domestic market
(relatively inelastic demand)

Foreign market
(relatively elastic demand)

Total market demand
(domestic plus foreign)

(a)

(b)

(c)

market because this is where the marginal revenue in that market is equal to his marginal cost of N_1L_1. Likewise, he will sell the remaining O_2N_2 units in the foreign market because this is where the marginal revenue in that market equals his marginal cost of N_2L_2.

There are many illustrations of dumping at both the domestic and international level. For example, some manufacturers of appliances and various other products sell part of their output to mail-order firms and department stores (e.g., Sears and Montgomery Ward) at lower prices under different brand names. Milk cooperatives frequently sell milk at a high price to consumers and at a low price to butter and cheese manufacturers. Tire manufacturers have sold under

their own brand names in the domestic market and under different brand names through other marketing channels in both domestic and foreign markets. In each case, the seller earns a higher profit by making fuller utilization of his excess capacity—provided that the extra or marginal cost of the additional output does not exceed the extra or marginal revenue.

THE CONDITIONS FOR PRICE DISCRIMINATION

Price discrimination is thus a practice of charging different prices to different *segments* of a market for the same good, where each segment defines a distinct market or submarket for the product. If you were a seller, what practical conditions would have to exist in order to enable you to practice price discrimination effectively? There are three: (1) multiple demand elasticities, (2) market segmentation, and (3) market sealing.

Multiple Demand Elasticities

There must be differences in demand elasticity among buyers due to differences in income, location, available alternatives, tastes, or other factors. If the underlying conditions that normally determine demand elasticity are the same for all purchasers, the separate demand elasticities for each buyer or group of buyers will be approximately equal, and a single rather than multiple price structure may be warranted.

Market Segmentation

The seller must be able to partition (segment) the total market by segregating buyers into groups or submarkets according to elasticity. Profits can then be enhanced by charging a different price in each submarket. There are many ways in which a total market can be effectively segmented into submarkets. For example:

□ *Segmentation by income*—as when a doctor charges a rich patient more than a poor patient for the same operation

□ *Segmentation by quantity of purchase*—as when a manufacturer offers quantity discounts to large buyers

□ *Segmentation by geographic location*—as when a state university charges out-of-state students a higher tuition than in-state residents

□ *Segmentation by time (including clock time and calendar time)*—as when a theater, night club, or telephone company charges more at certain hours than at others, or when a resort hotel, restaurant, or clothing store charges higher prices during certain seasons of the year

□ *Segmentation by brand name*—as when the same product is sold under different brand names at different prices

□ *Segmentation by age*—as when an airline charges less for children than for adults, despite equal time and space costs of serving them

Segmentation by race, religion, sex, and education provide still further opportunities for partitioning a market into relatively homogeneous subgroups. Can you suggest some examples?

Market Sealing

The seller must be able to prevent—or natural circumstances must exist which will prevent—any significant resale of goods from the lower- to the higher-priced submarket. Any leakage in the form of resale by buyers between submarkets will, beyond minimum critical levels, tend to neutralize the effect of differential prices and narrow the effective price structure to where it approaches that of a single price to all buyers. For example, a movie theater may use tickets of different color for matinees and for evenings, or for children and for adults. In this way it seals the segmented markets and prevents buyers from purchasing at the lower price and selling or using the product at the higher price. Similarly, some publishers of magazines, newspapers, and professional journals will sell subscriptions to students at special rates. Of course, market sealing cannot always be accomplished with one-hundred percent perfection. When it is not, a certain amount of "leakage" will occur between submarkets, thereby reducing the effectiveness of price discrimination.

Public Utility Rates

Public utilities provide an interesting application of monopoly pricing. As we have seen, these firms are industries characterized by substantial economies of scale, so that one large firm may be able to produce a given quantity more cheaply than several small firms could. Legislatures have therefore protected these firms from competition by granting them franchises to operate, in return for which utility rates are controlled by state or federal regulatory commissions.

THREE ALTERNATIVE PRICING POLICIES

Three types of pricing policies for public utilities may be identified: monopoly (or profit-maximizing) pricing; full-cost pricing; and marginal-cost pricing. Each of these is illustrated in Exhibit 8.

Monopoly (Profit-Maximizing) Pricing

The monopoly price N_1P_1 maximizes the firm's profit since it is determined by the intersection of marginal cost with marginal revenue. This $MC = MR$ price, if charged by a public utility, would probably not be socially acceptable. Why? Because as we have already learned, it results in a monopoly profit at society's expense. That is, it brings about output restriction and a misallocation of resources because the value to consumers of additional output exceeds the value of the resources used to produce that additional output. (Remember the criticisms of monopoly as compared to the long-run equilibrium conditions of perfect competition.)

Full-Cost Pricing

The price N_2P_2 represents what economists call *full-cost* (or *average-cost*) *pricing*. It is the price at which the firm covers all of its costs, both fixed and variable, and earns a normal profit. Regulatory commissions usually try to set this price because it provides a fair rate of return on investment in the utility.

Exhibit 8

Public Utility Rates: Three Alternatives

The monopoly price *maximizes profit, but is socially undesirable because it results in a misallocation of society's resources.*

The full-cost price *is the one regulatory commissions try to establish because it represents a "fair rate of return" on the* utility's investment.

The marginal-cost price *is the socially optimum price for the welfare of society, but in this particular case it leaves the utility suffering a loss because it results in a price below average total cost. This may not always happen, however.*

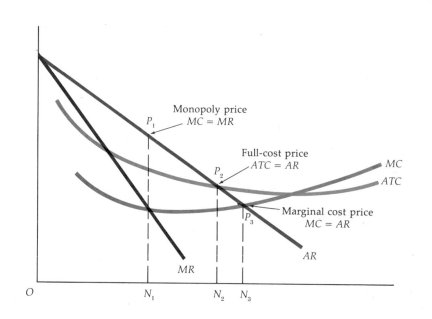

The history of utility rate making, however, is long and controversial, involving such questions as what to include in the "rate base" and what constitutes a "fair" return. For example, should the original cost of the utility's assets be used, or should the current replacement costs serve as a base? The choice is important because during periods of inflation the cost of replacing assets is usually greater than the original cost. Similarly, what rate of return does the utility need to earn in order to attract stockholder investments and yet not cause the price of its product to be so high as to exploit consumers? These are among the basic issues raised in the study of public utility rate regulation.

Marginal-Cost Pricing

The price N_3P_3 illustrates *marginal-cost pricing*—the price at which a firm's marginal cost equals its demand or average revenue. There is a branch of economic theory called "welfare economics" which has much to say about the importance of this price. Thus as we move down the demand curve toward the marginal-cost price, the welfare of society is increased because the added value of the extra output exceeds the added cost of providing it. Below this price, the welfare of society is decreased for the opposite reason. The marginal-cost price is therefore the socially optimum price—the price that maximizes society's welfare—because at this price the value of the last unit to the marginal user (measured by the price he pays for the last unit, which is equal to the price he pays for all units) is equivalent to the value of the resources used to produce that unit.

The marginal-cost price, however, has a disadvantage in this case: as you can see from Exhibit 8, it lies below the utility's ATC curve and hence if the regulatory commission required that the utility charge this price the result would be financial loss and eventual bankruptcy. In such cases, some economists who favor marginal-cost pricing have argued that the government should pay a subsidy to the utility so that it can cover all its costs, or that the government should simply own the utility itself, in which case it would not have to be concerned with covering all costs out of revenues. What do you think of these proposals?

PRICE DISCRIMINATION BY UTILITIES

All three of these alternative pricing possibilities have assumed, for simplicity, a single price policy. In reality, public utilities often segment their total market into homogeneous subgroups and set different price structures for each segment. This, as we know, results in multiple prices or *price discrimination*—the opposite of single prices. Thus telephone companies have different rates for different classes of users (such as residential and business), as well as different rates based on time and distance. Similarly, railroads, electric companies, gas companies, etc., also have complex rate structures.

In general, all regulatory commissions in the United States and in most European countries adhere to the full-cost approach for setting overall rate structures, but they allow modifications and exceptions for discriminating in special segments of the market. In France and Sweden, on the other hand, there has been a growing interest in applying marginal-cost pricing to public utilities—particularly in those cases where the firm's marginal cost is above its average total cost at the desired output.

SUMMARY OF IMPORTANT IDEAS

1. A monopoly is a single firm producing a product for which there are no close substitutes. Three major types are natural monopolies, strategic-resource monopolies, and patent monopolies.

2. The most profitable output of a monopoly is determined where its $MC = MR$. Unlike a firm in perfect competition, any firm faced with a downward-sloping demand curve is a partial monopoly. It thus finds that its marginal revenue curve is not a price curve, and its marginal-cost curve is not a supply curve.

3. The basic economic criticism of monopoly is that it misallocates resources by restricting output to a point which is short of its minimum average-cost output and charges a correspondingly higher price. In addition, monopolies contribute to income inequality and they lack incentives for efficiency and progress. Three possible "solutions" are to tax away their supernormal profits, regulate them as public utilities, or break them up into competing firms.

4. Price discrimination enlarges revenues by segmenting the market into submarkets and charging different prices in each according to relative demand elasticities. Markets may be segmented by income, brand names of products, location of buyer, and various other criteria. Dumping is a typical form of price discrimination.

5. Public utilities are regulated monopolies. Their rates tend to accord with principles of full-cost pricing, rather than monopoly pricing or marginal-cost pricing.

FOR HOMEWORK AND DISCUSSION

1. *Terms and concepts to review:*

monopoly	price discrimination
natural monopoly	dumping
government monopoly	full-cost (average-
strategic-resource	cost) pricing
monopoly	marginal-cost pricing
patent monopoly	monopoly pricing

2. Evaluate the judicial definition that a monopoly is "a business affected with a public interest."

3. Answer true or false, and explain why:

a. A monopolist is secure since, by controlling his price and output, he can guarantee himself a profit.

b. A perfect monopoly is almost as unlikely as perfect competition.

c. A monopolist's price is higher than a perfect competitor's price in the long run.

d. A monopolist maximizes his profit by charging the highest price he can get.

4. "A monopolist is most likely to be successful when the demand for his product is relatively inelastic." True or false? (HINT: Prove that a monopolist will never produce at an output at which the elas-

ticity of demand is numerically less than 1. You can do this by first proving that when marginal revenue is positive, the elasticity of demand is numerically greater than 1.)

5. What is the most profitable output for a monopolist who is faced with a unit elastic demand curve throughout its entire length? (HINT: What is marginal revenue when demand is unit elastic?) Explain.

6. If the government wanted to extract the maximum revenue from a monopolist without driving him out of business, should it tax his profits, or tax each unit of output? Explain.

7. "The prices of automobiles, TV sets, and cornflakes are each determined by supply and demand." Evaluate this statement. What do "supply" and "demand" actually mean in this case?

8. Complete the table showing cost and revenue data of a monopolist in Exhibit 9 (page 416) and sketch the following curves on three separate charts, one beneath the other, as was done in this chapter:

a. Total revenue and total cost

b. Marginal cost, average total cost, average revenue, and marginal revenue

c. Net revenue

Draw vertical dashed lines showing the most profitable level of output and the two break-even points. (NOTE: You will have to "project" the curves in order to obtain the second break-even point.) Label all the curves and explain their significance.

9. Suppose you were an economic advisor to a monopolist. Can you suggest ways in which he could engage in price discrimination by segmenting his market on the basis of: (*a*) quantity, (*b*) geographic location, and (*c*) "time"?

10. What do you think of the suggestion that public utilities should be subsidized, or even governmentally owned, in order to have them adhere to a socially desirable policy of marginal-cost pricing?

Exhibit 9

Cost and Revenue Schedules of a Monopolist

(1) Quantity per day Q	(2) Average Revenue or Price $AR = P$	(3) Total Revenue TR $TR = P \times Q$	(4) Marginal Revenue MR $MR = \dfrac{\text{change in } TR}{\text{change in } Q}$	(5) Total Cost TC	(6) Average Total Cost ATC $ATC = \dfrac{TC}{Q}$	(7) Marginal Cost MC $MC = \dfrac{\text{change in } TC}{\text{change in } Q}$	(8) Net Revenue NR $NR = TR - TC$
0	$21	$ 0		$22			
1	20	20		37			
2	19	38		42			
3	18	54		45			
4	17	68		47			
5	16	80		50			
6	15	90		54			
7	14	98		59			
8	13	104		65			
9	12	108		72			
10	11	110		80			
11	10	110		89			
12	9	108		99			

REFERENCES AND READING SUGGESTIONS

BOBER, M. M., *Intermediate Price and Income Theory*, rev. ed., Norton, New York, 1962, chap. 10, part 1.

BOULDING, KENNETH E., *Economic Analysis*, vol. 1, *Microeconomics*, 4th ed., Harper & Row, New York, 1966, chaps. 21, 23.

DOOLEY, PETER C., *Elementary Price Theory*, Appleton-Century-Crofts, New York, 1967, chap. 5.

DUE, JOHN F., and ROBERT W. CLOWER, *Intermediate Economic Analysis*, 5th ed., Irwin, Homewood, Illinois, 1966, chap. 9.

WARD, BENJAMIN, *Elementary Price Theory*, The Free Press, New York, 1967, chap. 7.

CHAPTER 25

The Real World of Imperfect Competition

CHAPTER PREVIEW

How does monopoly contrast with perfect competition? Is there a model of monopoly that can be used to describe and evaluate its behavior?

What is the theory of monopolistic competition? Of oligopoly? How well do these theories serve to describe the behavior of industries in our economy?

Do imperfectly competitive firms compete in the same way as competitive firms? What are the similarities? The differences?

If the world of perfect competition is largely imaginary, and the world of monopoly is relatively limited and regulated, what does the *real* world look like? In this chapter we answer that question by constructing models that come closer to approximating the kinds of markets in which most firms and industries in our economy tend to operate. We shall find that our knowledge of perfect competition and monopoly provides a basis for comparing and evaluating the consequences of these more realistic situations.

To give yourself a bird's-eye view of where you are at the present time and where you will be heading in this chapter, simply examine the following spectrum of market structures:

Perfect competition	Varying degrees of imperfect competition consisting of monopolistic competition and oligopoly	Pure monopoly

We have already analyzed the cases of perfect competition and monopoly at the extreme ends of the spectrum. Now we turn our attention to the broad middle range in order to examine situations encompassing what is known as "imperfect competition,"—that is, market structures which are classified as "monopolistic competition" and "oligopoly." These names arise from the fact that imperfect competition consists of various "mixtures" of perfect competition and pure monopoly. We shall find that these mixed structures characterize most of the markets in our economy.

Theory of Monopolistic Competition

We have seen that perfect competition consists of many firms producing a homogeneous product, and pure monopoly consists of one firm producing a unique product for which there are no close substitutes. Both types are important for economic analysis. Some industries, like the producers of standard raw materials, and the organized commodity and stock exchanges, operate under conditions that exhibit many characteristics of perfect competition. Other industries, such as the public utilities, have features similar to those of monopoly.

In reality, most of our economic activity is carried on under conditions of imperfect competition—that is, in industries and markets that fall between the two extremes of perfect competition and pure monopoly. One "in-between" case which exists in a large portion of the American economy is called *monopolistic competition;* it may be defined as an industry characterized by a large number of firms of different sizes producing heterogeneous (i.e., similar but not identical) products, with relatively easy entry into the industry. We will be studying this type of competition at the present time. The other subcategory of imperfect competition, known as "oligopoly," will be examined later.

PRODUCT DIFFERENTIATION IS A KEY FACTOR

Does the term "monopolistic competition" contradict itself? How can a market be both monopolistic and competitive at the same time?

The answer is based on the fact that in an industry characterized by monopolistic competition the products of the firms in the industry are *differentiated.* But product differentiation, like beauty, is in the eye of the beholder—and in economics the beholder is always the buyer. This means that products may be differentiated by brand name, color of package, location of the seller, customer service, credit conditions, or the smile of the salesman—even if the products themselves are physically the same. As a result, each firm has a "partial monopoly" of its own differentiated product.

Monopolistic competition is found in many industries. Retailing provides a good general illustration. Some more specific examples include: the manufacture of clothing, household goods, shoes, and furniture; and the services provided by most barbers, doctors, and dentists. In each of these industries the products sold are usually only moderately differentiated. This helps to explain why similar kinds of goods in monopolistic competition tend to have similar prices—as is usually the case with household detergents, appendectomies, and teeth fillings. The less the degree of product differentiation in the minds of buyers, the less the disparity in prices.

PRICE AND OUTPUT DETERMINATION

When we apply these ideas to the construction of a model, we find that the theory of monopolistic competition is as much a *theory of the firm* as it is of market or industry behavior. Thus:

1. Since each seller has a partial monopoly due to product differentiation, there will be a separate *AR* or demand curve for each firm. These curves will be downward-sloping, indicating that a seller can raise his prices to some degree without losing all of his sales.

2. We learned in the study of monopoly that a firm with a negatively inclined demand curve has no supply curve, since a given price may be associated with multiple outputs and a given output may be associated with multiple prices, depending on the position of the *AR* curve. Hence there can be no industry supply curve; indeed, the whole concept of an industry becomes somewhat cloudy and vague in monopolistic competition because of the existence of product differentiation.

3. Since the products of competitors are close but not perfect substitutes, we may assume that their elasticity of demand is relatively high. Indeed, the coefficient of elasticity will vary inversely with the degree of product differentiation. And of course, the less the degree of product differentiation and the greater the number of sellers, the closer the model will be to pure competition.

The $MC = MR$ Principle Again

As always, each firm will seek to produce to where its $MC = MR$ in order to maximize its profit. But since many firms are in the industry, and entry is relatively easy, some firms will, in the short run, earn modest supernormal profits. This is illustrated by the firms in Exhibit 1.

In the long run, there will be a *tendency* for surviving firms to be only normally profitable, but not necessarily precisely so, depending on the degree of product differentiation and the number of firms. For example, a small retail store might continue to be somewhat more than normally profitable because it happens to be in a particularly good location. On the other hand, a similar kind of store in a different location may continue to be less than normally profitable, because the seller would prefer to be his "own boss" —even if he has to incur an economic loss in doing so—rather than hire himself out to do the same job at a higher salary for someone else. Hence, although

most firms in a monopolistically competitive industry *tend* to earn normal profits in the long run, some firms do not.

THE IMPORTANCE OF SELLING COSTS

Since product differentiation plays such a key role in monopolistic competition, many firms will spend money on advertising, merchandising, sales promotion, public relations, and the like in order to increase their profits. Marketing expenditures of this type, which are aimed at adapting the buyer to the product, are termed *selling costs*. This distinguishes them from production costs, which are designed to adapt the product to the buyer. For purposes of analysis, economists generally view all sales outlays or selling costs as synonomous with advertising.

The seller in monopolistic competition who engages in advertising seeks to attain a delicate balance between commodity homogeneity and heterog-

---

Exhibit 1

Firms in Monopolistic Competition

Firm A is earning above-normal profits, Firm B is receiving only normal profits, and Firm C is earning below-normal profits. In the long run most firms in monopolistic com- *petition will* tend *to be normally profitable, but there may be some exceptions due to locational disadvantages or other special circumstances.*

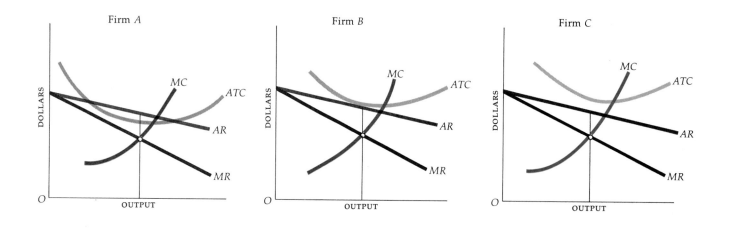

---

eneity. To attract customers away from his competitors he must convey two ideas:

1. His product is not sharply differentiated from the competing products, so that buyers will find it feasible to purchase his product instead of his competitors'.

2. His product is somehow superior to those of his competitors', so that buyers believe there is greater heterogeneity than exists in fact.

These objectives of advertising account for the erroneous statement sometimes made about it as explained in Exhibit 2. As you can see from the explanation accompanying the diagram, the purpose of advertising is to *shift* the demand curve to a higher position.

IS ADVERTISING "GOOD" OR "BAD"?

Advertising has been a subject of much debate among economists. The arguments have tended to revolve around three major issues:

Information Versus Persuasion. Those in favor of advertising argue that it educates and informs buyers about firms, products, and prices, and thereby tends to make markets more perfect than they otherwise would be. Those who oppose advertising reply that it seeks to persuade buyers rather than inform them, thereby creating wants that result in a distortion of "natural" preference patterns.

Efficiency Versus Waste. Proponents of advertising contend that it familiarizes consumers with products and thereby broadens the market for goods; this not only encourages further capital investment and employment, but also large-scale operations that result in low-cost mass production. Critics of advertising reply that it encourages artificial product differentiation among goods that are physically similar and that advertising among competing firms tends to have a canceling effect; this duplication of effort results in a waste of resources, higher product costs, and higher prices, so that any real economies of scale—even if they exist—are lost through inefficiencies. This argument of efficiency versus waste is amplified in Exhibit 3.

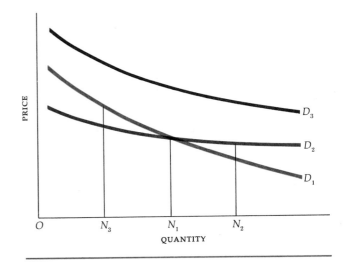
Competition Versus Concentration. Defenders of advertising argue that it encourages competition by exposing consumers to competing products, and enabling firms to gain market acceptance for new products more rapidly than they could without advertising. Critics of advertising contend that it facilitates the concentration of monopoly power because

Exhibit 3

Advertising and Economies of Scale

Chart (a). *In the short run, advertising raises a firm's average total cost curve by the advertising cost per unit. Thus, at output OM, if the advertising cost per unit is DC, total advertising expenditures are equal to the area of the rectangle ABCD.*

Chart (b). *Advertising may also shift a firm's demand curve to the right and raise its long-run average costs, thereby influencing its economies of scale. For example, suppose that without advertising the firm would have produced the output OJ at a unit cost of JE. Then, as a result of advertising, there may be several possible effects:*

1. *Advertising may give the firm economies of scale, enabling it to produce the larger output OK at the lower unit cost KG, even though point G is on a higher LRAC curve than point E.*

2. *Advertising may have a canceling effect, leaving output unchanged at OJ and simply increasing unit costs from JE to JF.*

3. *Advertising may cause diseconomies of scale, causing the firm to produce the output OL at unit costs of LH. This case is not very likely, however, since monopolistic competition results in firms of less than optimum size as will be pointed out below.*

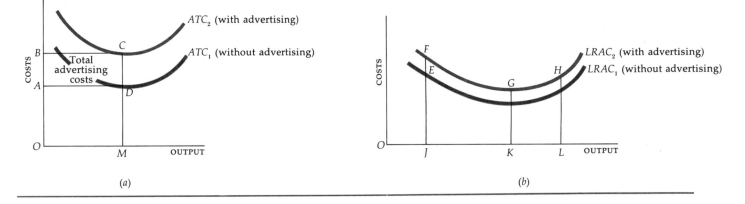

(a)   (b)

large firms can usually afford continuous heavy advertising, whereas new and small firms cannot.

These arguments indicate the fundamental nature of the controversy. Many students find the economics of advertising an interesting topic for a term paper. You can obtain a great deal of information on the subject in your college library, since numerous books and articles have been written about it.

EVALUATING MONOPOLISTIC COMPETITION

From what we already know about the results of perfect competition and monopoly, the more relevant social effects of monopolistic competition may be stated briefly.

First, monopolistically competitive firms misallocate resources by underutilizing their plants, thereby restricting outputs and charging higher prices than similar firms in perfect competition. Note that this is the same basic criticism that was given for monopoly. However, in the case of monopolistic competition, the extent of resource misallocation with its associated output restriction and higher prices will depend, in each industry, on the degree of product differentiation and the number of sellers.

Second, monopolistic competition encourages *nonprice competition*—that is, methods of competition that do not involve changes in selling price. Examples include advertising, sales promotion, customer services, and product differentiation. Nonprice activities that result in greater innovation and product improvement may be desirable; but to the extent that they result in higher production costs due to duplication of resources, excessive style changes, etc., they tend to be undesirable.

Third, monopolistically competitive firms create what economists have called the *"wastes" of monopolistic competition*—the existence of "sick" industries characterized by chronic excess capacity resulting from too many sellers of differentiated products dividing up markets, operating inefficiently at outputs less than their minimum average costs, and charging higher prices. Examples abound in the retail trades, such as grocery stores, clothing shops, restaurants, etc., as well as in the light manufacturing industries like textiles, shoes, and plastics.

Why do the chronically "sick" industries of monopolistic competition continue to exist? There are several reasons: low initial capital requirements, not much need for technical know-how, and the desire to own a business and "be your own boss." As a result, new firms enter the industry as fast or even faster than the unprofitable ones leave it.

Theory of Oligopoly

When you drive a car, open a can of tuna fish, replace a light bulb, buy cigarettes, wash your hands with soap, play a phonograph record, type a term paper, or talk on a telephone, you are using products manufactured by oligopolistic industries. An *oligopoly* is an industry composed of a few firms producing either: (1) a homogeneous product, in which case it is called *perfect oligopoly,* or (2) heterogeneous products, in which case it is called *imperfect oligopoly.* Oligopolistic industries are typically characterized by high obstacles to entry, usually in the form of substantial capital requirements, technical know-how, patent rights, and the like.

Examples of perfect oligopoly are found primarily among producers of industrial goods like aluminum, cement, copper, steel, and zinc. These goods are bought by other manufacturers who usually order them by specification—that is, in a particular form like sheet steel, structural steel, cold rolled steel, etc., of a specific temper (i.e., hardness and plasticity). A specified type of steel is virtually identical whether it is made by U.S. Steel, Bethlehem Steel, Republic Steel, or any other steel company. Examples of imperfect oligopoly are found among producers of consumer goods, such as automobiles, cigarettes,

gasoline, major appliances, soaps and detergents, television tubes, rubber tires, and typewriters.

In both perfect and imperfect oligopolies, the majority of sales goes to the "big three" or the "big four" companies in each industry—like ALCOA, Kaiser, and Reynolds in aluminum, and General Motors, Ford, and Chrysler in automobiles. Can you think of other leading firms in some of the oligopolistic industries mentioned above?

SOME CHARACTERISTICS OF OLIGOPOLIES

In addition to fewness of sellers, high obstacles to entry, and similar if not identical products, most oligopolistic industries tend to have several other characteristics in common.

Substantial Economies of Scale. Firms in oligopolies typically require large-scale production in order to obtain low unit costs. If total market demand is sufficient only to support a few large firms of optimum size, then competition will ensure that only a few such firms survive.

Growth Through Merger. Many of the oligopolies that exist today have resulted from mergers of competing firms—in some cases as long ago as the late nineteenth century. By combining two or more firms through merger, the resulting firm may gain a substantial increase in market share, greater economies of scale, larger buying power in the purchase of its inputs, and various other advantages which smaller firms do not possess to the same extent.

Mutual Dependence. The fewness of sellers in an oligopolistic industry makes it necessary for each seller to consider the reactions of his competitors when he sets his own price. In this sense the behavior of oligopolists in the marketplace may be somewhat similar to the behavior of players in games of skill like chess and bridge; in such games, the participants try to win by formulating strategies that recognize the possible counterreactions of their opponents.

Price Rigidity and Nonprice Competition. These features, and others that will be mentioned below, give rise to a "live and let live" policy in most oligopolistic industries. Firms find it more comfortable to maintain constant prices and to engage in various forms of nonprice competition such as advertising and customer service in order to hold if not increase their market shares. Price reductions, when they occur, tend to be sporadic, and ordinarily come about only under severe pressures resulting from weakened demands or excessive inventories.

PRICE AND OUTPUT DETERMINATION

With these characteristics as a background, how do oligopolistic firms determine their prices and outputs?

A number of different models may be used to portray various types of oligopoly situations. One of the more interesting possibilities is demonstrated in Exhibit 4. This model illustrates what is known as the *kinked demand curve*—i.e., a "bent" demand curve and a corresponding discontinuous marginal revenue curve, facing an oligopolistic seller.

Thus, suppose the oligopolist's current price is *OP* and his output is *ON*. When contemplating a change in price either up or down he must consider how his rivals will react. Hence, he might visualize his firm's demand curve by reasoning in the following way:

> If I reduce my price below *OP*, my competitors will lose some of their customers to me and this will probably prompt them to match my price cut. Therefore, my sales will increase relatively little following the curve *KD*. On the other hand, if I increase my price above *OP*, my competitors probably won't match the increase and I'll lose some of my customers to them. Therefore, my sales will fall off rapidly along the curve *KL*.

In other words, the kinked demand curve reflects the greater tendency of competitors to follow price reductions than price increases. Price reductions take sales away from other firms, and prompts them to cut prices in retaliation; price increases do not usually invite such responses because other firms will take sales from the firm that raises its price. It follows that the more homogeneous or standardized the product, the sharper the kink, since customers will shift more readily and sellers will therefore react more quickly to changes in prices.

As you can see, the large discontinuity in the *MR*

Exhibit 4

A Kinked Demand Curve Facing an Oligopolist

Given *the kink at K, any price reduction below* OP *will increase sales slowly along* KD *because other firms will probably match any price cuts. A price increase above* OP *will reduce sales rapidly along* LK *because other firms will probably not match the price rise. Since marginal cost can fluctuate widely between* G *and* H, *the equilibrium price* OP *and output* ON *tend to be stable. However, this model leaves some price uncertainty because it does not explain* why *the kink happens to occur at* K *rather than at some other point.*

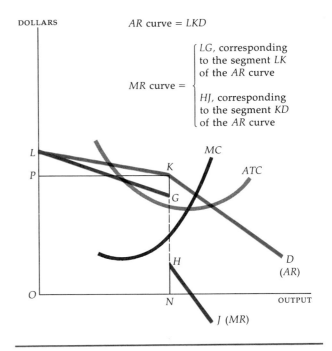

curve between *G* and *H* permits the *MC* curve to fluctuate widely within this range. This helps to explain why oligopolies exhibit a high degree of price stability. But there is also this seeming paradox:

The kinked demand curve model leaves oligopolists with a considerable degree of price uncertainty. The model demonstrates that once the kink is *given*, the price at that point will tend to be stable; however, it does not say anything about *why* the kink happens to occur where it does instead of at some other point.

Some oligopolies have tried in various ways to

reduce the state of uncertainty in which they operate. Two such methods have been collusion and price leadership.

OLIGOPOLIES IN COLLUSION

Oligopolists in some industries have occasionally colluded—"gotten together" and agreed on a single industry-wide price which they would all charge. This situation is most probable when the firms in the industry are faced with similar demands and either the same or different cost curves, as might occur in a case of perfect oligopoly. The result may then be much the same as in monopoly, except that there is more than one firm. Two interesting models can be employed to illustrate these possibilities.

Duopoly with Identical Costs

In Exhibit 5 we assume for simplicity a case of perfect oligopoly, in which the industry consists of only two firms producing a standardized product. An industry composed of two sellers is also called a *duopoly*. It may be either a perfect or imperfect duopoly, depending on whether the product is standardized or differentiated.

In Exhibit 5a, we further suppose that if the products and the prices of the two firms are identical, each firm will have a 50 percent chance of selling to any buyer, and hence the market will be divided equally between them. Therefore, the AR curve of the industry will be downward-sloping. At any given price such as OP, the quantity sold by each firm will be one-half the industry's, and similarly, as we learned

---

Exhibit 5

Price and Output Determination: Two Oligopolists

In chart (a) *each firm maximizes its profit by adhering to the* MC = MR *rule, thereby producing* ON *units and charging* OP *per unit. Both firms may also agree to stick to this rule at all times, thereby always charging a single, industry-wide price.*

In chart (b) *if each firm followed the* MC = MR *rule, Firm X*

represented by MC_x *would prefer price* OP, *whereas Firm Y represented by* MC_y *would prefer price* OP'. *By colluding, both firms might agree on a price within this range. But through price leadership by the larger firm, Firm Y may be willing to follow a price of* OP *established by Firm X.*

Identical demands and costs

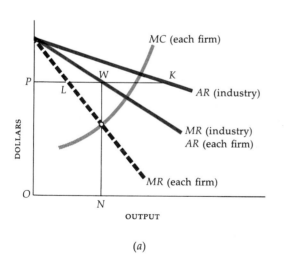

(a)

Identical demands and different costs

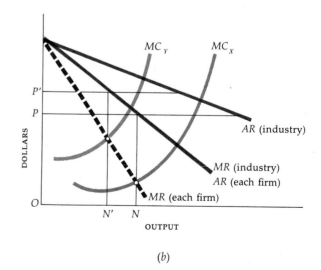

(b)

earlier in the study of monopoly, the *marginal revenue curve must bisect any horizontal line drawn from the vertical axis to the average revenue curve.* Hence the *AR* curve of each firm corresponds to the *MR* curve of the industry, and so the distance *PW* = *WK*. Similarly, the *MR* curve of each firm is such that *PL* = *LW*.

If we assume that the two firms have identical marginal-cost curves, it follows that each will maximize its profits by following the *MC* = *MR* rule, producing *ON* units of output and charging *OP* per unit. They might also collude by agreeing not to deviate from the *MC* = *MR* rule even temporarily and to maintain a single-price policy even in the face of changing business conditions.

Duopoly with Different Costs

The identical demand conditions exist in Exhibit 5b, but now we assume that the two duopolists *X* and *Y* have different costs. Thus duopolist *X* is a larger-capacity producer than duopolist *Y* because the marginal-cost curve of Firm *X* as represented by MC_X is farther to the right than the marginal-cost curve of Firm *Y* as represented by MC_Y. This means that for any given marginal cost, Firm *X* can produce more than Firm *Y*.

In this case, by following the *MC* = *MR* rule, Firm *X* will maximize its profit by producing *ON* units and charging *OP* per unit, whereas Firm *Y* will maximize its profit by producing *ON'* units and charging *OP'* per unit.

The two firms are thus in conflict. If Firm *X* charges its preferred lower price, Firm *Y* *must* charge the same price or else lose sales. If Firm *Y* charges its preferred higher price, Firm *X* need not do the same, in which case Firm *Y* will again suffer the consequences.

What will the two firms do? They might collude by agreeing on a single price for both. This price may be *OP*, or *OP'*, or some price in between, and it may be a price that is profitable for both firms as long as each is earning at least normal profits.

In practice, there are a number of real-world obstacles to collusion. They include: (1) the antitrust laws (to be studied in a later chapter) that make such behavior illegal; (2) the number of firms in the industry—since the larger the number, the harder it may be for sellers to "get together"; and (3) the degree of product differentiation—since greater differentiation makes collusion more difficult. Despite these obstacles, cases of collusion are sometimes uncovered by the government.

PRICE LEADERSHIP

Instead of formally agreeing on a mutually satisfactory price as in Exhibit 5b, it is possible that Firm *Y* would adhere to a policy of *price leadership*—a situation in which all firms in an oligopolistic industry adhere, often tacitly and without formal agreement, to the pricing policies of one of its members. Usually, but not always, the price leader will be the largest firm in the industry, and other firms in the industry will simply go along with the leader.

Thus in the diagram, Firm *X* is the largest, and would probably be the price leader; it could therefore set a price of *OP* to maximize its own profit, and Firm *Y* would follow the leader by charging the same price. This policy avoids uncomfortable price wars, it has not been regarded as illegal by the courts, and leaves the price followers earning at least normal, although not maximum, profits. This explains why price leadership has at one time or another been a widespread practice in most oligopolistic industries including cigarettes, steel, anthracite coal, farm equipment, newsprint, tin cans, lead, sulphur, sugar, and many others.

EVALUATING OLIGOPOLY

Oligopoly is a major form of market structure in our economy. What can be said about its social consequences? Unfortunately, the issues are extremely complex and the conclusions are by no means clear-cut. Nevertheless, three interesting aspects of oligopoly are worth noting.

First, the basic criticism of oligopoly is the same as that of monopoly and monopolistic competition: It misallocates resources by restricting output short of the point which corresponds to minimum average costs and charges correspondingly higher prices. But this criticism assumes that the shapes of the cost curves are the same under oligopoly as under perfect competition—an assumption which we have seen is questionable because in oligopolistic industries where technology is such that economies of scale are important (e.g., automobiles or steel), lower long-run unit costs may be achieved than if these industries were perfectly competitive. An automobile manufacturer, for example, could not gain significant reductions in unit costs without the technology and economies of assembly-line mass production.

Second, oligopolistic industries tend to be more progressive in research and development than perfectly competitive industries, but evidence suggests that they are considerably less progressive than has been generally believed—for reasons explained in Exhibit 6.

Third, the economic influence of oligopoly (and also monopoly) may be somewhat offset by the growth of *countervailing power*. This term means that the growth of market power by one group may stimulate the growth of a counterreaction and somewhat offsetting influence by another group on the other side of the market. For instance, powerful labor unions have grown up to face oligopolistic industries across the bargaining table; chain stores have emerged to deal with large processing and manufacturing firms; and even government has grown larger, partly in response to the growth of big business and big labor. Countervailing power therefore has some favorable competitive effects within the economy, but it does not exist with equal effectiveness in all oligopolistic industries.

Thus, although oligopolies are subject to the same basic criticism as monopoly and monopolistic competition—namely resource misallocation resulting from output restriction and higher prices—they may mitigate these shortcomings to the extent that they seek to (1) realize known economies of scale, and (2) develop and innovate with new products and techniques. Although there is no evidence on the first of these points one way or another, the findings that exist on the second are disappointing at best.

Do Firms Really Maximize Profits?

Now that we have completed our introduction to the theory of business behavior under imperfect competition, it is appropriate to ask: Do firms really strive to maximize profits as economic theory assumes? In other words, do businessmen actually behave the way we have said they do, equating their *MC* and *MR*?

Exhibit 6

Are Oligopolies Progressive in Research and Development?

Economists have long believed that since oligopolistic firms may earn substantial pure profits over the long run, it is to their advantage to use these profits for financing research on new and better products in order to ensure their market position. Indeed, this type of research and development is a significant and often necessary form of nonprice competition. Yet, various analyses of patent statistics as well as several studies of inventions and innovations have come up with the following interesting findings:

1. Approximately two-thirds of the major inventions since 1900, including air conditioning, automatic transmissions, power steering, cellophane, the cotton picker, the helicopter, the gyro-compass, the jet engine, quick-freezing, insulin, the continuous casting of steel, and the catalytic cracking of petroleum are the products of independent inventors working alone or in small research firms—rather than in the laboratories of large oligopolies. Only a relatively small proportion of the major inventions, including nylon, tetraethyl lead, the diesel electric locomotive, and transistors were developed by large private firms such as DuPont, General Motors, and Bell Telephone laboratories.

2. In some oligopolistic industries like aircraft, chemicals, electrical equipment, and petroleum, large sums were spent on research, but a substantial share was financed by the federal government for defense reasons.

3. In many oligopolstic industries such as agricultural machinery, basic metals, and food products, relatively little has been spent on research.

In contrast, research and development in agriculture, which serves as a rough approximation of perfect competition, has been accomplished mainly by government support in federal research laboratories, experiment stations, and land grant colleges and universities.

SOURCE: U.S. Congress, Hearings before the Joint Economic Committee, *Employment, Growth and Price Levels*, Washington, 1959, pp. 2337–57; Daniel Hamberg, "Invention in the Industrial Research Laboratory," *Journal of Political Economy*, April, 1963; John Jewkes, David Sawers, and Richard Stillerman, *The Sources of Invention*, St. Martin's Press, New York, 1958. Some recent unpublished studies have reached similar conclusions.

This problem often comes up in discussions of politics, labor-management relations, and other areas of current social and economic interest. Hence it is instructive for us to look into the matter more closely.

Basically, there are three dimensions of the profit-maximization problem that should be examined. We may refer to them as: (1) definitional, (2) mensurational, and (3) environmental.

"DEFINITIONAL" PROBLEMS: WHICH CONCEPT OF PROFIT?

It is easy to define profit as total revenue minus total cost. But is this all there is to the concept of profit? The answer is not as simple as it may seem because: (1) businessmen do not always know whether they are seeking to maximize short-run profit or long-run profit, and (2) they do not always view the approach to profit management in the same way. As a result of these *"definitional"* problems, it becomes extremely difficult to state unequivocally that firms in the real world either do or do not strive to maximize their profits.

For example, firms will often adopt policies which may reduce short-run profits but which are designed to establish a better long-run situation. Illustrations of such policies include: (1) costly research and development programs for creating new products and new markets, and (2) fringe benefits to employees aimed at developing long-run loyalties. At the same time, these firms may exploit short-run market situations to the fullest advantage at the risk of adversely affecting their long-run corporate image.

Likewise, firms often view the profit problem in discordant ways. Many studies conducted by business economists and management researchers have found that corporations tend to approach the formulation of profit policies differently. A policy that may seem wise to one firm may seem folly to another. A typical illustration of this is found in the field of employee relations. One firm may regard pension programs, health and accident plans, or even coffee breaks as means of raising labor morale and productivity. Another firm may consider them at best a necessary evil.

"MENSURATIONAL" PROBLEMS: WHICH INDICATOR OF PROFIT?

The problems of defining a concept of profit are closely tied to the problems of measuring it. Our elementary theory of the firm has assumed that businessmen know their marginal costs and marginal revenues and can simply adjust their outputs to the most profitable levels—the levels at which $MC = MR$.

But in a dynamic economic environment, where changes in technology, tastes, and other underlying forces constantly influence costs and demands, businessmen cannot possibly have a precise understanding of how changes in their output will affect their costs and revenues. At best they may be able to gain a rough idea of their costs at a few "typical" or standard volumes of output, but even this would be of relatively limited value as a guide for profit maximization in the manner described by economic theory.

As a result of these and other difficulties, business firms in imperfect competition do not set prices with full knowledge of their marginal costs and marginal revenues as economic theory assumes. Instead, they establish their prices on the basis of experience, trial-and-error, and the customs and practices of the industry of which they are a part. And their prices are not usually set with the direct objective of maximizing profits, but rather to achieve other objectives which may (or may not) indirectly maximize profits. These objectives include:

1. Pricing to achieve a certain target or percentage return on investment
2. Pricing to stabilize a firm's prices and outputs over the business cycle
3. Pricing to achieve a certain target or percentage share of the market
4. Pricing to meet or match the prices of competitors.

None of these measures is a substitute for profit maximization. All, however, influence a firm's net revenue and are usually easier for executives to use as a practical guide for profit management and control. Hence they serve as *indicators* of profit rather than measures of profit. In studies of pricing practices of large corporations, it has been found that the first of the above goals is dominant, but the others also play important roles.

EDWARD HASTINGS CHAMBERLIN

1899–1967

Harvard University News Office

The theory of monopolistic competition had its origin in the early 1930s. Prior to that time there was only a theory of perfect competition and a theory of monopoly.

In the United States, the person responsible for the development of the theory was a professor at Harvard University named Edward Chamberlin. His distinguished treatise, The Theory of Monopolistic Competition, *was published in 1933. As Chamberlin put it, the theory was needed because:*

". . . With differentiation appears monopoly, and as it proceeds further the element of monopoly becomes greater. Where there is any degree of differentiation whatever, each seller has an absolute monopoly of his own product, but is subject to the competition of more or less imperfect substitutes. Since each is a monopolist and yet has competitors, we may speak of them as 'competing monopolists,' and of the forces at work as those of 'monopolistic competition.'

"It is this latter problem which is of especial interest and importance. In all of the fields where individual products have even the slightest element of uniqueness, competition bears but faint resemblance to the pure competition of a highly organized market for a homogeneous product."

In the same year, quite independently (the two were unknown to each other), an eminent economist at Cambridge University in England, Mrs. Joan Robinson, published a volume entitled The Economics of Imperfect Competition. *These two books by Chamberlin and Robinson formed the basis of what we know today about economic behavior in monopolistically competitive markets.*

Both authors stressed the joint influence of competitive and monopolistic elements in the determination of equilibrium. They pointed out that the distinguishing characteristics in imperfect markets are product differentiation and consumer preferences, rather than the absence of a large number of sellers. This makes each seller a "partial" monopolist, regardless of

the number of competitors in his industry.

Although there were some differences in their views, both used the critical concepts of marginal cost and marginal revenue, and both showed how the firm maximizes profits by equating these two variables. They also discussed short- and long-run equilibrium, barriers to entry into an industry, and the role of normal profits. Chamberlin, in addition, provided a substantial analysis of the role of advertising.

One year later, in 1934, a German economist named Heinrich Von Stackelberg published a book entitled Marktform und Gleichgewicht (Market Structure and Equilibrium), *which emphasized the interdependence of firms and the problems of oligopoly. One of Stackelberg's chief conclusions was that a democratic state cannot eliminate market structures that fail to achieve a socially desirable equilibrium, whereas authoritarian states can. He thus developed a defense of government intervention in the economy in order to bring about the results deemed best by society.*

"ENVIRONMENTAL" CONDITIONS: PROFIT-LIMITING FACTORS

From a different point of view, conditions may exist in the economic environment which encourage a firm to avoid—purposely and consciously—the max-

imization of (short-run) profits, although the execution of these policies may be argued to be best in the long run. Four such motives for limiting profit may be noted.

1. Discourage Competitive Entry. If profits could be

large due to higher prices rather than lower costs and superior efficiency, or if the company has a weak monopoly position in the industry, management may prefer lower profits in order to discourage potential competitors from entering the industry. In this case a long-run price policy that is in line with the rest of the industry will be more advantageous to the firm than one which exploits current market conditions for immediate profit.

2. Discourage Antitrust Investigation. Certain monopolistic practices (which we will be reading about in a later chapter dealing with the antitrust laws) are illegal. Profits are one of a number of criteria used by the government as evidence of firms' monopolistic market control. This can seem somewhat of a paradox when contrasted with the previous consideration. On the one hand, management may maintain lower profits in order to exclude competitors and thereby strengthen its monopoly control. ´Yet the federal government's antitrusters may consider high profits, not low profits, as one of several indexes of monopoly power.

3. Restrain Union Demands. Reducing the possibility of having to pay higher wages is another factor prompting management to restrain profits. This is particularly applicable in industries with strong labor unions. As long as the economy is prosperous and profits are rising, unions can more easily demand higher wages without inflicting damage on the firm. But if, in a recession, prices are falling faster than wages, the profit margin is squeezed at both ends. Those companies that curbed wage increases in the beginning would then have a better opportunity to cope with changing market conditions.

4. Maintain Consumer Goodwill. Management may choose to limit profits in order to preserve good customer relations. Consumers frequently have their own ideas of a "fair" price, whether such ideas are based on "what used to be in the old days," or whether they are the results of "comparison shopping."

CONCLUSION: MAXIMIZE OR "SATISFICE"?

The "profit problem" is thus complex, making it extremely difficult to state unequivocally that firms in imperfect competition do or do not seek to maximize profits. Perhaps in reality they do not seek to "maximize" but to "*satisfice*"—that is, to attain targets of satisfactory performance such as a specific rate of return on investment, a particular share of the market, or a defined average annual growth of sales —as some scholars have suggested. In economic theory, however, we *assume* that the underlying objective is to maximize profit because, as already shown on previous occasions, this assumption enables us to evaluate the social performance of the firm as a "resource allocator."

SUMMARY OF IMPORTANT IDEAS

1. Monopolistic competition exists in industries characterized by many firms producing heterogeneous products. Product differentiation, which is a matter for buyers to decide, is thus a key factor among firms in such industries. Monopolistically competitive industries are a major segment of the United States economy.

2. The $MC = MR$ principle serves as a guide for profit maximization in monopolistic competition. Since there is reasonable freedom of entry, firms will *tend* to earn normal profits in the long run, but there may be exceptions.

3. Advertising plays a major role in monopolistic competition because of the importance of product differentiation. The "pros" and "cons" of advertising have centered around three major issues: information versus persuasion; efficiency versus waste; competition versus concentration.

4. Monopolistic competition is subject to the same basic criticism as monopoly—namely resource misallocation resulting from output restriction and higher prices as compared to perfect competition. In addition, it encourages nonprice competition which may or may not be undesirable, and it results in the "wastes" of monopolistic competition or the perpetuation of "sick" industries that are overcrowded and inefficient.

5. Oligopolistic industries consist of several firms producing either homogeneous products (perfect oligopoly) or heterogeneous products (imperfect

oligopoly). These industries play a major role in our economy. Oligopolistic firms usually tend to be characterized by substantial economies of scale, a history of growth through merger, mutual dependence, price rigidity, and nonprice competition.

6. The $MC = MR$ principle applies to oligopolistic firms that seek to maximize profit. In addition, each firm tends to see itself as being faced with a kinked demand curve, indicating that competitors will follow a price decrease by any one seller, but not a price increase.

7. The kinked demand curve results in a stable price, but it leaves the seller uncertain about the determination of the price itself. This has prompted oligopolists to reduce price uncertainty either by colluding with competitors or by accepting one of the competitors as a price leader and matching his price.

8. Oligopolies are subject to the same basic criticism as monopolies—namely resource misallocation resulting from output restriction and higher prices as compared to perfect competition. But this criticism is open to some question, since the cost structures of oligopolistic firms are subject to more substantial economies of scale than those of perfectly competitive firms. In addition, oligopolies have not exhibited as much progress in research and development as might be expected. On the other hand, their market power has in some cases been mitigated by the growth of countervailing power.

9. It is difficult to state unequivocally that firms in imperfect competition either do or do not seek to maximize profits. In reality, it is quite likely that they strive to "satisfice" rather than maximize. Nevertheless, the assumption of profit maximization is fundamental in microeconomic theory because it permits an evaluation of the social function of the firm as a resource allocator.

FOR HOMEWORK AND DISCUSSION

1. *Terms and concepts to review:*

imperfect competition	oligopoly
monopolistic competition	kinked demand curve
	duopoly
selling costs	price leadership
nonprice competition	countervailing power
"wastes" of monopolistic competition	"satisfice"

2. Firms in monopolistic competition tend to be only normally profitable in the long run. The same is true of firms in perfect competition. Therefore, why criticize monopolistic competition?

3. Why should firms in monopolistic competition spend so much money on advertising if much of it has canceling effects?

4. Is the kinked demand curve an objective fact of the marketplace, or is it a subjective phenomenon in the mind of each oligopolist? Explain.

5. Why is there a tendency toward some type of "externally" imposed price decision in oligopoly? What are some examples?

6. The need for "self-protection" is one reason often given for the rise of labor unions, consumer cooperatives, and agricultural cooperatives. Can you explain in the light of this chapter?

7. One could easily argue that it is more *ethical* for people to cooperate than to compete. Do you agree?

8. "Economic theory is unrealistic because it assumes that firms seek to maximize profits. Yet we know that in reality this assumption is not a valid one." Evaluate.

REFERENCES AND READING SUGGESTIONS

BOBER, M. M., *Intermediate Price and Income Theory*, rev. ed., Norton, New York, 1962, chaps. 11, 12.

BOULDING, KENNETH E., *Economic Analysis*, vol. 1, *Microeconomics*, 4th ed., Harper & Row, New York, 1966, chap. 22.

DOOLEY, PETER C., *Elementary Price Theory*, Appleton-Century-Crofts, New York, 1967, chaps. 6, 7.

DUE, JOHN F., and ROBERT W. CLOWER, *Intermediate Economic Analysis*, 5th ed., Irwin, Homewood, Illinois, 1966, chaps. 10, 11.

WATSON, DONALD S., *Price Theory and Its Uses*, 2d ed., Houghton-Mifflin, New York, 1968, chaps. 18–20.

CHAPTER 26

The Firm in the Factor Markets: Marginal Productivity and Income Distribution

CHAPTER PREVIEW

We have already learned that the $MC = MR$ rule determines the most profitable level of *output* for a firm. Can a similar rule be developed for determining the most profitable level of *input* for a firm?

What conditions determine a firm's demand for inputs?

Can any social implications be drawn from the principles pertaining to the hiring of factors of production?

Until now we have focused on the behavior of firms in the *output* markets by examining the principles of product pricing and production under the three classes of market conditions called perfect competition, monopoly, and imperfect competition.

But to manufacture products, firms have to buy factors of production. In this chapter we concentrate on the behavior of firms in the *input* markets in order to see how principles of resource employment can be developed. This chapter thus "counterbalances" some of the previous chapters by establishing microeconomic principles pertaining to the input rather than output side of the market. As you will soon see, the most interesting aspect of these principles is the way in which they parallel the ones that were learned earlier, so that the various pieces fit together like a large jigsaw puzzle.

The Marginal Productivity Theory: How the Firm Buys Factors of Production

If you were a businessman, what principles would guide you in deciding how much of a resource you should purchase? After all, buying too little can be just as unprofitable as buying too much. A major problem facing a firm that wishes to maximize its profits is to utilize precisely the right combination of inputs. In order to do this, it must understand the nature of its demand for resources.

The first thing to point out is that the demand for any resource should be thought of as a *derived demand*—a demand based on what a particular factor of production contributes to the product for which it is used. For example, the demand for steel is derived in part from the demand for automobiles; the demand for land in the heart of a city is derived from the demand for office space and stores that will be built upon it; the demand for college professors is derived mostly from the demand for education as measured by college enrollments. As a general rule, and as we shall see shortly, the concept of derived demand embraces the following principles:

Other things being equal, the quantity of a factor of production which a firm demands will depend on three things: (1) the productivity of the factor; (2) the value or price of the product which the factor is used to make; and (3) the price of the factor relative to the prices of other factors.

These principles make a good deal of practical sense. For instance, they tell us that, other things remaining constant:

1. An increase in the output of a factor of production relative to its input will result in a greater demand for that factor by the firms that use it.

2. If improvements in a product or reductions in its price create a greater demand for it, the need for the factors which produce or use that commodity will also increase (for example, electronic computers and computer programmers.

3. If the price of a factor of production becomes cheaper relative to other factors, the demand for it will increase if producers begin to substitute it for the more expensive inputs (for example, labor-saving machinery relative to high-cost labor).

PHYSICAL INPUTS, OUTPUTS, AND REVENUES

Exhibit 1 gives us a more precise understanding of a firm's demand for an input. The first three columns of the table convey the operation of the law of dimin-

---

Exhibit 1

The Demand for a Resource by a Firm

Perfect competition in the output market; perfect competition in the input market

(1) Units of Variable Factor F (labor)	(2) Total Physical Product TPP	(3) Marginal Physical Product MPP $MPP = \dfrac{change\ in\ TPP}{change\ in\ F}$	(4) Product Price P	(5) Total Revenue TR (2) × (4)	(6) Marginal Revenue Product MRP $MRP = \dfrac{change\ in\ TR}{change\ in\ F}$	(7) Average Revenue Product ARP $ARP = \dfrac{TR}{F}$
0	0		$10	$ 0		$?
		4			$40	
1	4		10	40		40.0
		8			80	
2	·12		10	120		60.0
		5			50 ·	
3	17		10	170		56.7
		3			30	
4	20		10	200		50.0
		1			10	
5	21		10	210		42.0
		−1			−10	
6	20		10	200		33.3

ishing returns, which we learned in an earlier chapter; they show how the total and marginal physical product change when a variable input such as labor is applied to fixed inputs like land and capital. The remaining columns of the table convert these physical data into revenues on the assumption that the firm (as stated in the first subtitle of the exhibit) is a perfect competitor in the sale of the product to which the variable factor is contributing. The price [column (4)], therefore, is assumed to be constant at $10 per unit.

After obtaining the total revenue figures [column (5)] by multiplying the price and the quantity produced, the last two columns of the table introduce

Exhibit 1 (continued)

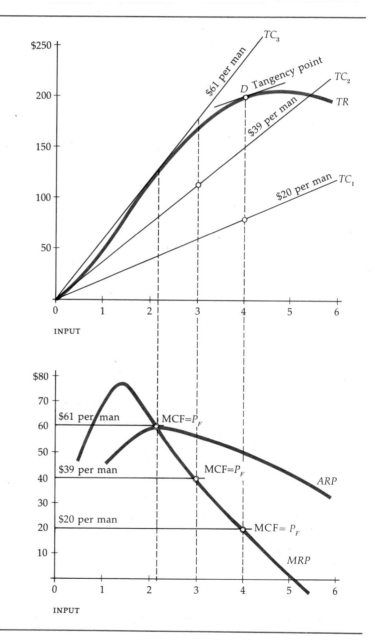

The most profitable input level occurs where the distance between the TR and TC curves is a maximum—that is, where a tangent to the TR curve is parallel to the TC curve. (For example, at $20 per man, the most profitable input is 4 men, because this is the input at which the tangent at D is parallel to the straight-line TC₁ curve.)

By following the vertical dashed lines downward, the most profitable input also occurs where the marginal cost of the factor (MCF) or its price (P_F) equals its marginal revenue product (MRP). Therefore, given the marginal costs or prices of the factors of production, the firm will maximize its profits by hiring each factor of production up to the point where its $MCF = P_F = MRP$. The firm's demand curve for an input is thus the MRP curve up to the maximum point on the ARP curve. As the price of the input falls, the firm hires more of it by following its MRP curve.

The principle which holds that the price paid to a factor of production will equal its marginal productivity, and hence that each factor will be paid the value of what it contributes, is called the *marginal productivity theory of income distribution.*

TECHNICAL NOTE (OPTIONAL). Here is a simple explanation in geometric terms. Each *MCF* curve in the lower chart is a graph of the *slope* of its corresponding *TC* curve in the upper chart. Likewise, the *MRP* curve in the lower chart is a graph of the *slope* of the *TR* curve in the upper chart. The input at which the slopes are equal (or at which a tangent in the upper chart is parallel to a *TC* curve) is the one at which net profit is maximized. You can verify these profit-maximizing principles by following the vertical dashed lines downward at each level of input.

two new terms: *marginal revenue product* (MRP), defined as the change in total revenue resulting from a unit change in input, and *average revenue product* (ARP), which is the ratio of total revenue to the quantity of the variable input employed.

The subtitle of the exhibit also tells us that the firm is operating under perfect competition in the input market. This means that the supply of labor resources is so large that the firm cannot influence the price by buying or not buying. It can purchase as many units as it wants at the given price. Hence the *marginal cost of the resource will be the same as its price.*

THE MOST PROFITABLE LEVEL OF INPUT

When the revenue data in Exhibit 1 are graphed, we get the curves shown in the charts accompanying the table. In this case, however, since we want to relate the firm's revenues to the labor that it hires, it is easier to plot the revenue curves against input rather than output on the horizontal axis. It also helps simplify matters a bit to assume that there are no fixed costs, i.e., that the firm's fixed factors of production are available free. This means that the firm's total variable costs are the same as its total costs; hence the TC curve retains its shape but emanates from the origin of the chart instead of from a point higher up on the vertical axis.

We now ask: What is the most profitable level of input for the firm? The answer depends on the *marginal cost of the input* as compared to its *marginal revenue product*—or in other words the amount that each additional unit of the input adds to the firm's total cost as compared to the amount that it adds to total revenue.

For example, when the marginal cost or price of labor is $20 per man, the upper chart shows that the most profitable input level is 4 men; at this input the TC_1 curve in the chart is parallel to a tangent drawn to the TR curve at D. At the same time, the lower chart shows that at this level of input the marginal cost of the factor MCF, which is the same as the price of the factor P_F, is equal to its marginal revenue product MRP. Similarly, at $39 per man, the firm's most profitable input is 3 men, which is again determined in the lower chart where $MCF = P_F = MRP$. On the

other hand, if the factor were available free, the most profitable input level would be 5 men because the TC curve in the upper chart would lie along the horizontal axis and would be parallel to a horizontal tangent drawn at the peak of the TR curve. Finally, at $61 per man the firm would just be covering its variable costs, since TC_3 is tangent to TR. Hence the most profitable input would, theoretically, be 2.2 men, which is again determined in the lower chart where $MCF = P_F = MRP$. (NOTE: If you dislike the idea of measuring "fractions of men," you can think of the horizontal axis as being scaled in terms of hours of labor time instead of numbers of men.)

Since the MCF or P_F line tells you the number of workers available to the firm at the particular wage, it is a *supply curve* of labor. The firm is thus faced with a horizontal supply curve of the factor in the input market just as it is faced with a horizontal demand curve for its product in the output market.

TWO IMPORTANT PRINCIPLES

Two important principles follow directly from our understanding of marginal concepts.

When there is perfect competition in the input market, the marginal cost of an input will be the same as its price, and therefore:

1. The firm's demand curve for an input will be its MRP curve below the maximum point of its ARP.

2. The firm will maximize its profits by purchasing factors of production up to the point where $MCF = P_F = MRP$.

By this time you may have noticed a certain symmetry between the theory of input and the theory of output. For example, these two principles are analogous to the notion that in the output market a perfectly competitive firm finds that: (1) its MC curve is its supply curve above the minimum point on its AVC; (2) it maximizes its profit by producing to where its $MC = P = MR$. In fact, if you flip the lower chart in Exhibit 1 upside down on its horizontal axis (or if you turn the book upside down and look through the back of the page while holding it up to the light), the ARP and MRP curves will resemble the AVC and MC curves of a firm in perfect competition.

This is evidence of the fact that there is indeed a symmetry between the theory of perfect competition in the input and output markets, in that the curves in one market are the reciprocals of the corresponding curves in the other market.

In economic terms, why does the firm maximize its profit at the input level where $MCF = P_F = MRP$? Because at any input less than this the added cost of an additional unit is less than the added revenue, so it pays to hire another unit. At any input greater than this the opposite is true. Hence the fundamental principle of profit maximization, i.e., the $MC = MR$ rule which we learned in previous chapters, applies here as well.

IMPERFECT COMPETITION IN THE OUTPUT MARKET

Of course, a firm may be an imperfect competitor in the output market and a perfect competitor in the input market. This situation is illustrated in Exhibit 2. Notice that the production function in the first three columns is the same as before; however, the price of the product [column (4)] decreases instead of remaining constant because the firm is now faced with a downward-sloping demand curve for its output: to increase sales, it must charge a lower price per unit for *all* units. As a result, the revenue data in the remaining columns are now different from what they were in Exhibit 1.

The revenue curves are graphed in the accompanying charts on page 436 as *solid* curves, along with the revenue curves which we studied previously in Exhibit 1 but which are now shown as *dashed* curves. This enables us to compare both situations in order to see what happens as the firm maximizes its profit by following the $MCF (= P) = MRP$ rule. For instance, at a price or MCF of $20 per man, the firm in imperfect competition will hire 2.5 men, whereas the same firm in perfect competition will hire 4 men. Similarly, if workers are available free, so that the price or MCF curve lies along the horizontal axis, the firm in imperfect competition will hire 3.5 men, whereas the same firm in perfect competition will hire 5 men.

This suggests the following basic criticism.

Exhibit 2 (see also page 436)

The Demand for a Resource by a Firm

Imperfect competition in the output market; perfect competition in the input market

(1) Units of Variable Factor F (labor)	(2) Total Physical Product TPP	(3) Marginal Physical Product MPP $MPP = \dfrac{change\ in\ TPP}{change\ in\ F}$	(4) Product Price P	(5) Total Revenue TR (2) × (4)	(6) Marginal Revenue MRP $MRP = \dfrac{change\ in\ TR}{change\ in\ F}$	(7) Average Revenue ARP $ARP = \dfrac{TR}{F}$
0	0		$10	$ 0		$?
		4			$36	
1	4		9	36		36.0
		8			60	
2	12		8	96		48.0
		5			23	
3	17		7	119		39.7
		3			1	
4	20		6	120		30.0
		1			−15	
5	21		5	105		21.0
		−1			−25	
6	20		4	80		18.3

Exhibit 2 (continued)

The revenue curves of a firm in imperfect competition are lower than they would be for the same firm in perfect competition. As a result, the imperfectly competitive firm tends to restrict its input at any given factor price.

Thus in the upper chart, the most profitable input level occurs where the distance between the TR and TC curves is a maximum—that is, where the tangents at D and E are parallel to the given straight-line TC curve. At any other level of input, a tangent to TR would not be parallel to TC.

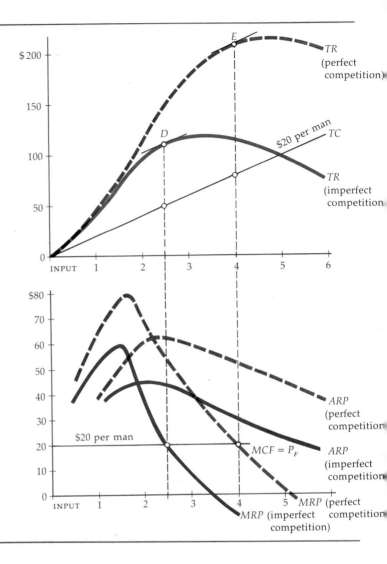

By following the vertical dashed lines, we observe that at a given cost of $20 per man the perfectly competitive firm maximizes its profit by hiring 4 men, whereas the imperfectly competitive firm maximizes its profit by hiring 2.5 men. The imperfectly competitive firm thus restricts its input as compared to the perfectly competitive firm.

TECHNICAL NOTE (OPTIONAL). In geometric terms, the *slopes* of the curves are equal in the upper chart when the tangents at *D* and *E* are parallel to the given *TC* curve. Since *MCF* and *MRP* in the lower charts are the graphs of the respective *slopes* of the *TC* and *TR* curves, profits are maximized at the input where the slopes are equal.

The imperfectly competitive firm restricts its input by purchasing fewer units of a factor at any given price than the same firm in perfect competition. This corresponds with the basic criticism, which we already know, that the imperfectly competitive firm restricts its output as compared to a firm in perfect competition.

The following point may also be noted: The *MRP* curve of the perfectly competitive firm is less steep than that of the imperfectly competitive firm. This is because the perfectly competitive firm's *MR* remains constant while its *MPP* declines; on the other hand,

for the imperfectly competitive firm both its *MR and MPP* decline. This adds to the basic criticism mentioned above, as will be seen later.

Demand for Inputs

When we studied the theory of supply and demand, we learned that the market demand curve for a product is derived by summing the individual demand curves of all buyers in the market. A parallel situation exists in the market for input: Other things remaining the same, the market demand curve for a factor is derived by summing the individual demands or *MRP* curves of all firms in the market. Like any other demand curve, this aggregate *MRP* curve for a factor of production will be subject to two kinds of changes: (1) changes in demand, and (2) changes in the quantity demanded.

CHANGES IN DEMAND

The market *MRP* curve for a given factor may shift from one position to another for several reasons:

1. A Change in Demand for the Final Product. For example, a change in demand for houses will affect the price of houses and may also change the demand for lumber, bricks, carpenters, and other resources.

2. A Change in Productivity. Improvements in the quantity and quality of the "fixed" factors of production will increase the productivity of the "variable" factor. Thus, workers who have more and better machines and land are more productive than those who do not.

3. A Change in the Prices of Substitute or Complementary Factors. Some resources may be substitutable, some may be complementary, and some may be neither. Labor and machines are a typical example; changes in the price of one relative to the other may encourage firms to use more or less of either or both, depending on the proportions in which they must be used—such as the number of workers needed to operate a machine.

CHANGES IN THE QUANTITY DEMANDED: ELASTICITY OF DEMAND FOR FACTOR SERVICES

There are also conditions that will determine changes in the quantity demanded for a given factor. As you recall, these changes represent movements along the curve due to a change in price. Hence these movements reflect the sensitivity or elasticity of demand for the resource. What determines this elasticity?

1. The Rate of Decline of Marginal Physical Product. The rate at which the *MPP* curve declines as the variable factor is added to the fixed factors depends on the technological nature of the production process.

The faster it declines, the more inelastic the resulting *MRP* curve will be and hence the less will be the change in the quantity of input demanded relative to a change in its price.

2. The Elasticity of Demand for the Final Product. The greater the elasticity of demand for the final product, the more elastic the demand for the factors used in making it. For instance, if the demand for a final product is relatively elastic, a small increase in its price will result in a more than proportional decrease in its output and hence a relatively large drop in the quantity demanded of the resources that are used to produce it.

3. The Proportion of the Factor's Cost to Total Production Cost. The larger the cost of a factor of production relative to the total cost of the product, the more elastic the demand for the factor. For example, if labor costs are only 10 percent of the cost of a product, a 10 percent wage increase will raise production costs by 1 percent; hence the effect on the final price of the product should be small, and the quantity demanded of the factor should be relatively little affected. On the other hand, if labor costs are 90 percent of production costs, a 10 percent wage increase will have a more substantial impact on production costs as well as on final prices and sales. Hence the decrease in the quantity demanded of the factor is likely to be relatively large.

4. The Ease of Factor Substitutability. The greater the number of different factors that can be substituted for one another in a given production process, the larger will be the elasticity of demand for any one of these factors. Thus if copper, aluminum, and other light metals had equal conductive properties, the demand for each of them by the electrical industry would be highly elastic; but the fact is that copper is a superior conductor and hence the demand for it is relatively inelastic within its typical price ranges.

DEMAND FOR SEVERAL FACTORS BY A FIRM

The $MCF = P_F = MRP$ rule applies to all factors of production that the firm may purchase. Let us assume, therefore, that the firm is buying two factors of production, labor L and capital C, and that these factors are perfectly substitutable for one another. We already know that the firm will maximize its profits by buying units of labor up to the point where the marginal revenue productivity of labor MRP_L equals the price of labor P_L:

$$MRP_L = P_L$$

Similarly it will buy units of capital up to the point where the marginal revenue productivity of capital MRP_C equals the price of capital P_C:

$$MRP_C = P_C$$

It is convenient to combine these two equations into a single profit-maximizing equation which describes the equilibrium conditions of a perfectly competitive firm. This can be done by dividing each side of one of the equations by the corresponding side of the other—which is a perfectly legitimate algebraic operation based on a famous axiom in mathematics that you probably recall from high school days: "When equal quantities are divided by the same or equal quantities, the results are equal." Thus:

$$\frac{MRP_L}{MRP_C} = \frac{P_L}{P_C} \qquad (1)$$

Interpreting equation (1): The most profitable level of input for a competitive firm occurs where the ratio of the marginal revenue products of the factors is equal to the corresponding ratio of their prices.

We can leave the equation in this form, but most students can "see" its implications more clearly by putting it into an equivalent but different form. This can be done in two steps:

First, we cross-multiply the terms and get:

$$(MRP_L)(P_C) = (P_L)(MRP_C)$$

Second, we "transpose" the P_L and P_C, thereby forming the final results:

$$\frac{MRP_L}{P_L} = \frac{MRP_C}{P_C} \qquad (2)$$

To repeat: Equation (2) is equivalent to equation (1); it defines the profit-maximizing or equilibrium conditions of a perfectly competitive firm in the input market.

Interpreting equation (2): The most profitable level of input for a competitive firm occurs where it earns the same increment in revenue *per dollar of outlay* from each of the factors that it hires.

If this equality did not occur—that is, if the first ratio in equation (2) were greater than the second and if the employment of capital were already in equilibrium at the point where $MRP_C = P_C$, the firm would be earning more of an increment in revenue on its labor relative to the price of labor than it would be earning on its capital relative to the price of capital; graphically, this means that it would be to the *left* of its optimum input point for labor. Hence it would pay for the firm to hire more workers, thereby reducing MRP_L, until the ratios were equal. Conversely, if the first ratio were less than the second, the firm would be to the *right* of its optimum input point for labor. Hence it would pay for the firm to reduce its number of workers, thereby raising MRP_L, until the ratios were again equal.

In a more general sense, neither factor need be in equilibrium to start. You can think of the firm as juggling all its factors of production simultaneously until it achieves the desired equilibrium ratio noted above. Thus the profit-maximizing equations (1) or (2) can be extended to include all the firm's factors of production, not just labor and capital.

Marginal Productivity, Income Distribution, and Social Justice

We have seen that when there is perfect competition in the input market, each firm will purchase factors of production up to the point where the price or marginal cost of the factor is equal to its marginal revenue productivity. Expressed in real terms, this means that each factor will be paid a value equal to what it contributes to the national output—that is, it will be paid what it is "worth." This concept is known as the *marginal productivity theory of income distribution*.

The theory itself was first introduced near the turn of the present century and was widely supported because it showed that a competitive (capitalistic) system distributed the national output in a socially "just" and "equitable" manner. But over the years economists and social critics have pointed out three fundamental criticisms of this interpretation.

1. A large part of the market for input is imperfect rather than perfect. Thus, certain factors of production tend to be relatively immobile, and in some markets there may be only one or a few firms buying inputs instead of a large number of firms. In addition, union restrictions, patent controls, tariff barriers, etc., will also create obstacles to a smoothly functioning market for inputs as envisioned in the competitive model.

2. Many production processes are complex. When a variety of factors are employed it is usually impossible to divide the total output into the amounts contributed by each class of factors such as labor and capital, much less by each "subfactor" such as each type of worker.

3. Terms like "just" and "equitable" involve normative rather than positive concepts, and their meanings may vary from time to time and from place to place according to the customs and beliefs of society. Thus, it is not necessarily "just" that a man who is twice as productive as another should be paid twice as much. It might equally well be argued, for example, that it is "just" for a family of six to receive twice as much as a family of three—regardless of their productivities. In other words, the normative question of what constitutes a just distribution of income is quite different from the positive question of what specific steps should be taken to alter the distribution of income. The former is a philosophical question; the latter is an economic one.

We can therefore conclude with an important generalization:

The central idea of the marginal productivity principle is that an employer will not pay more for a unit of input—whether it be a man, or an acre of land, or a dollar's worth of borrowed capital—than it is worth to him. He will continue to acquire an input as long as each unit he purchases adds more to his total revenue than it adds to his total cost. Since we assume in theory that the units can be infinitesimally small, the net result is that the employer's profit is maximized where the added (or marginal) cost of the input equals its added (or marginal) revenue product.

In short, although the marginal productivity principle is correct in the sense that it can be deduced logically from given assumptions, it should be understood for what it is: *a guide for maximizing a firm's profits in the input market under prescribed market conditions.*

SUMMARY OF IMPORTANT IDEAS

1. The marginal productivity theory explains how a firm purchases its inputs in the factor market. In general, a firm's demand for any factor of production is a derived demand based on the productivity of the factor, the price of the final product, and the price of the factor relative to the prices of other factors.

2. The most profitable level of input for a perfectly competitive firm in the resource market is where $MCF = P_F = MRP$. The firm's demand curve for an input will be its MRP curve below its maximum ARP. If the firm is a monopolist or imperfect competitor in the output market, it will restrict its input of a factor at any given price as compared to a similar competitive firm.

3. The aggregate MRP curve for a factor of production is determined by summing the individual MRP curves. Like any demand curve, the MRP curve is subject to changes in demand for a factor and to changes in the quantity demanded. The latter reflects the elasticity of demand for a factor.

4. A perfectly competitive firm in the input market will maximize its profits by purchasing factors of production up to the point where the ratio of their marginal revenue products equals the corresponding ratio of their prices. This is also the point where the firm earns the same incremental revenue per dollar of outlay from each factor that it hires.

5. The marginal productivity theory of income distribution is a guide for profit maximization in the input market. It does not purport to say what pattern of income distribution is "just" or "equitable," for this is a normative question based on philosophical rather than economic considerations.

JOHN BATES CLARK

1847–1938

Marginal Productivity Theory

"It is the purpose of this work to show that the distribution of the income of society is controlled by a natural law, and that this law, if it worked without friction, would give to every agent of production the amount of wealth which that agent creates."

In these words, J. B. Clark outlined the general plan for his book, The Distribution of Wealth, *which was published in 1899. This was the first American work in pure economic theory. Prior to that time, American economists were generally interested in the socioeconomic problems of their period and with the achievement of social reforms. Clark's book still stands as one of the greatest works in economic theory published in any language.*

Clark began by asking: "Is there a natural law according to which the income of society is divided. . . .? If so, what is that law? This is the problem which demands solution."

As he proceeded to answer this question, he developed a distinction between static and dynamic forces in the economy. The static forces, he said, are the result of "universal economic laws" which are always applicable to the economy, such as the law of diminishing returns, the law of diminishing utility, and so on. But the dynamic forces that exist in society, namely changes in population, capital, production techniques, and forms of industrial organization, are constantly causing fluctuations in production, prices, and the like. In Clark's words, "Static forces set the standards, dynamic forces produce the variations." He then went on to say:

"Each unit of labor . . . is worth to its employer what the last unit produces. When the force is complete, no one body of a thousand men can withdraw without lessening the product of the whole society by the same amount that we have attributed to the one that we last set working. The effective value of any unit of labor is always what the whole society with all its capital produces, minus what it would produce if that unit were to be taken away. This sets the universal standard of pay. A unit of labor consists, in the supposed case, of a thousand men, and the product of it is the natural pay of a thousand men. If the men are equal, a thousandth part of this amount is the natural pay of any one of them."

Actually, Clark had much in common with his great British contemporary, Alfred Marshall. Each used the so-called static analysis, but Marshall was more realistic and analyzed many problems of dynamics and change. Clark, however, raised marginal utility analysis to its highest standard of perfection, and in so doing he founded a "marginalist school" of thought which established a pattern for teaching and research in economics that exists to this day.

The modern version of the marginal productivity theory is essentially due to Clark's treatment. His theory of wages is a demand theory which assumes a given quantity of labor in its analysis of the marginal product of labor. It was this theory, with its impeccable logic, that was widely employed by others to support the contention that a (perfectly competitive) capitalistic system distributes incomes in a "just" manner according to what each factor contributes.

In later decades, the development of the theory of imperfect competition and the growing power of labor unions made some of the unreal assumptions of Clark's theory more apparent.

FOR HOMEWORK AND DISCUSSION

1. Terms and concepts to review:

   derived demand

   marginal revenue product

   average revenue product

   marginal productivity theory of income
      distribution

2. What analogies do you see between a firm in the output market and a firm in the input market with respect to each of the following:

a. The profit-maximizing rule

b. Under perfect competition: marginal cost and average variable cost; marginal revenue product and average revenue product

c. Basic criticism of monopoly and imperfect competition in the two markets as compared to perfect competition.

3. Distinguish between a change in demand for an input and a change in the quantity demanded. What are the causes of each?

4. Suppose that a perfectly competitive firm is maximizing its profit on the employment of capital and that the marginal revenue product of capital is 10 while its price is 2. If the firm's marginal revenue product of labor is 18 and the price of labor is 3, what should the firm do?

5. "The marginal productivity theory of income distribution is a *fair* theory because it demonstrates that each worker gets what he earns." Evaluate.

REFERENCES AND READING SUGGESTIONS

BOBER, M. M., *Intermediate Price and Income Theory*, rev. ed., Norton, New York, 1962, chap. 13.

DOOLEY, PETER C., *Elementary Price Theory*, Appleton-Century-Crofts, New York, 1967, chaps. 8–10.

DUE, JOHN F., and ROBERT W. CLOWER, *Intermediate Economic Analysis*, 5th ed., Irwin, Homewood, Illinois, 1966, chap. 12.

WARD, BENJAMIN, *Elementary Price Theory*, The Free Press, New York, 1967, chap. 8.

CHAPTER 27

Determination of Factor Prices

CHAPTER PREVIEW

Are there wage-determination models that can explain why workers in some occupations earn less than workers in others, and why some industries establish wage levels by collective bargaining between management and labor?

Is there any connection between the rent paid for land and the prices received for the products of land?

What is interest, and why does it exist?

How are profits determined, and what are the sources of profit?

Most of the national income consists of wages and salaries paid to workers. The rest of the economic "pie" is sliced into rent, interest, and profit. These incomes, we have learned, are the payments made to resource owners who sell their factors of production —labor, land, capital, and entrepreneurship—in the economy's markets.

What forces determine the levels of wages, rent, interest, and profit? In this chapter we seek answers to these questions by constructing models and deriving basic principles. We shall find that many of the ideas from previous chapters dealing with supply and demand, competition, market structures, cost and demand curves, and the like play an integral role in determining factor prices.

What will not be so apparent, however, is the fact that although the theory of wages, and to a somewhat lesser extent the theory of rent, are fairly well established in modern economics, the theories of interest and profit involve various unsettled questions that are the subject of more advanced discussions. We shall not delve into these issues in much detail, since our purpose at this time is to concentrate on the main features of the various theories rather than on the controversies which surround them.

Theory of Wages

Wages constitute about three fourths of the national income. But what determines their level? Let us begin with some definitions.

Wages are the price paid for the use of labor, and are usually expressed as time rates, such as so much per hour, day, or week, or less frequently as piece rates of so much per unit of work performed.

Labor, as used in economics, means all personal services including the activities of wageworkers, professional people, and independent businessmen. "Laborers" are thus workers who may receive not only compensation in the form of wages, but also in the form of salaries, bonuses, commissions, and the like. However, our interest in this chapter is with wages as defined above, especially wages expressed as time rates.

Finally, *money wages* are the amount of money received per unit of time, such as cash wages received on an hourly, weekly, or monthly basis. In contrast, *real wages* are the quantity of goods that can be bought with money wages; real wages thus depend on money wages and on the prices of the goods that are purchased with money wages. For instance, it is quite possible for your money wages to increase while your real wages rise, remain the same, or fall, depending on what happens to prices.

THE TRENDS OF WAGES AND PRODUCTIVITY

Most of us know that wages differ between occupations and individuals. Nevertheless, there tends to be a close long-run relationship between the wages of workers and their productivity. Both have increased over the years at roughly the same rate, although the former have tended to outstrip the latter since the mid-1960s, as shown in Exhibit 1. These gains in productivity are due partly to improvements in the quality of labor, which result from better education, training, and health, and partly to the remarkable growth in the quantity and quality of the other factors of production with which labor works. Since an economy's real income is the same as its real output, its income per worker is likely to keep pace with its output per worker over the long

Exhibit 1

Output and Earnings in the Private Sector

Wages and productivity have tended to increase at about the same rate over the years. But the gap has widened considerably since the late 1960s.

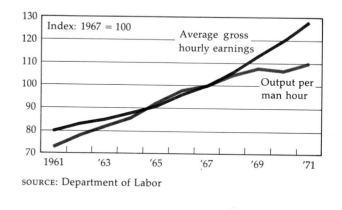

SOURCE: Department of Labor

run if its markets are reasonably free and competitive.

SOME WAGE-DETERMINATION MODELS

Against this background covering the long-run trend of wages, we must now ask: How are wages determined in the market at any given time? The answer depends on the type of market model that is assumed to exist in a particular situation. There are several interesting possibilities.

Competitive Model: Many Buyers, Many Sellers

Suppose there is such a large number of employers hiring a certain type of labor and such a large number of employees selling it that no single employer or employee can influence the wage rate. We would then have a competitive model of wages as illustrated in Exhibit 2.

In Exhibit 2*a,* the downward-sloping aggregate demand curve for this type of labor represents the sum of the individual *MRP*s of the buyers; the upward-sloping aggregate supply curve reflects the fact that if these workers are already employed, the firms buying labor will have to offer higher wages to attract workers from other occupations and localities. The equilibrium wage OW and equilibrium quantity OM are determined by the intersection of the labor supply and labor demand curves.

In 2b, the buying firm is faced with a perfectly elastic supply curve of labor at the market wage. The horizontal supply curve represents the marginal cost or price of the factor, as we learned earlier in the study of marginal productivity analysis. Since the firm's most profitable input is obtained by following the MCF = MRP rule, it will hire ON units of labor at the market wage of OW.

What analogies do you see between this model and that of a perfectly competitive seller in the output market?

Monopsony Model: One buyer, Many Sellers

A *monopsony* is a market structure consisting of a single buyer and many sellers of a good or service. Hence it may be thought of as a "buyer's monopoly." An example would be a firm which is the sole employer in a "company town," as has been the case in many mining communities. Similarly, in some farm areas we find a single food-processing plant dominating employment for many miles around.

A monopsony wage model is shown in Exhibit 3. As you can see from his cost schedule, the monopsonist must offer a higher wage rate or price per unit for *all* units in order to acquire more labor (just as a monopolist in the output market must charge a lower price per unit for *all* units in order to sell more products). The result is that the marginal cost of labor will be greater than its average cost at each input, as shown in the chart.

Exhibit 2

A Competitive Model of Wage Determination

In the competitive model, the wage OW and the quantity OM for a particular type of labor is determined in the market through the free interaction of supply and demand. Each firm can buy all the labor it wants at the market wage; hence the supply curve of this factor to any individual firm is perfectly elastic and is the same as the marginal cost of the factor. The firm's most profitable input ON at the wage OW is determined where its MCF = MRP.

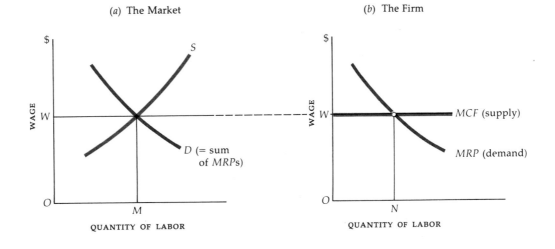

(a) The Market

(b) The Firm

Exhibit 3

A Monopsony Model of Wage Determination

In order to acquire more labor, the monopsonist must offer a higher price per unit for all *units that he wants to hire. His average cost of labor will thus rise, and his marginal cost of labor will be different from his average cost.*

Cost schedule of labor factor

Units of Labor Factor F	Average Cost of Labor Factor (= wage rate or price of labor) ACF or S	Total Cost of Labor Factor TCF	Marginal Cost of Labor Factor MCF
1	$5	5	
2	6	12	$ 7
3	7	21	9
4	8	32	11
5	9	45	13

The MCF curve lies above the average cost curve ACF, which is also the labor supply curve S. By hiring to the point where MCF = MRP, the monopsonist employs OL units and pays the lowest price per unit consistent with that volume of input, namely LT.

The monopsonist thus restricts his employment of resources and pays a lower price per unit of input than he would if he were a perfectly competitive buyer in the factor market

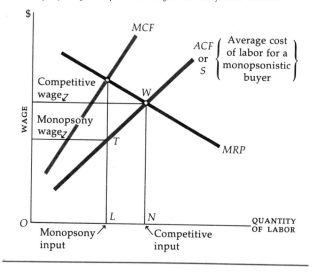

The monopsonist's most profitable input level is determined, as always, where his MCF = MRP. Thus he will employ OL units of labor and pay the lowest price he can for that quantity of labor, namely LT per unit. In so doing, he will restrict his input as compared to the amount ON and pay a lower price per unit as compared to the wage NW that he would have paid if he were a perfectly competitive buyer in the input market.

What analogies do you see between this model and that of a pure monopolist in the output market?

Monopoly Model: One Seller, Many Buyers

Suppose that a labor monopoly, such as a union whose members include all workers in a particular trade like printers or plumbers, faces a market composed of many buyers of that particular skill. What level of wages and what corresponding volume of labor output will result?

The model is illustrated in Exhibit 4, and is exactly the same as that of a pure monopolist. The AR curve represents the market's demand curve for this particular type of labor, and the MC curve (however it might be measured) represents the marginal cost to the union of supplying different quantities of this type of labor. As you already know from your study of monopoly, the union will follow the MC = MR rule, supplying OL units of labor at a wage rate of OU per unit. In so doing, it will restrict its output of labor and charge a higher wage rate than would occur in the competitive case.

This analysis helps to explain why some labor unions have established long apprenticeship requirements, high initiation fees, and similar obstacles to entry. Their motives, at least partly, have been to curb the supply of labor in the market and to boost wage rates. Of course, some unions do not seek to maximize "net" wages; they try to maximize membership instead so that they can wield more market power. In such cases, the model in Exhibit 4 must be modified to reflect these objectives.

Bilateral Monopoly Model: One Buyer, One Seller

A *bilateral monopoly* is a market structure in which a monopsonist buys from a monopolist. The simplest

Exhibit 4

A Monopoly Model of Wage Determination

The monopoly union will, like any monopolist, equate its MC *and* MR, *thus supplying the quantity* OL *at the wage* OU. *It will thereby restrict the supply of labor and command a higher rate as compared to the competitive case.*

If you sketch in an ATC *curve, you can then draw a rectangle representing maximum "net" wages (equivalent to a rectangle representing maximum net profits for a monopolist). It is this rectangle which, in this model, the union seeks to maximize.*

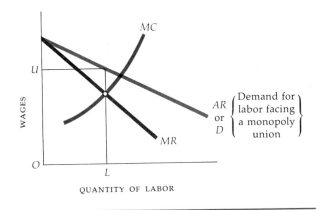

Exhibit 5

A Bilateral Monopoly Model

In a bilateral monopoly, both parties may agree on the quantity OL, *but the theory does not predict the exact price. At best, we can only say that the price of labor will be somewhere between the monopsonist's preferred wage of* OT *and the monopolist's preferred wage of* OU.

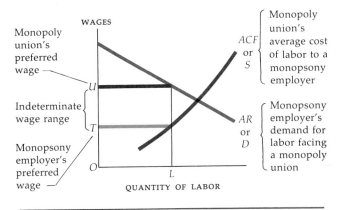

version, which merely combines the previous monopsony and monopoly models, is shown in Exhibit 5. Both the buyer and the seller are seeking to maximize their profits from the transaction. Therefore, if the two parties can agree on a given quantity to be exchanged, say OL, the monopsonist will wish to purchase that quantity at the lower price of OT, while the monopolist will want to sell that quantity at the higher price of OU. What will be the transaction price?

Economists have been trying to solve this problem for decades. Some years ago a remarkable series of controlled experiments was conducted by an economist and a psychologist at Pennsylvania State University, in which many pairs of students were involved in bargaining for real money Out of these and other studies, there has emerged a fair amount of agreement that although the quantity figure may be determinate in a bilateral monopoly model, the price

level is not. Thus, even if the two traders agree on a quantity that maximizes their *joint* profits, the highest price acceptable to the buyer will give the whole profit to the seller, and vice versa.

The solution, therefore, is logically indeterminate; the price will end up somewhere between the monopsony wage rate of *OT* and the monopoly wage rate of *OU*, but the theory does not predict the precise level within this range.

Which Model Exists Today?

All these models are applicable to the modern economy. In the input markets, just as in the output markets, there are *degrees* of competition and monopoly. Hence these models, or mixtures and modifications of them, can be useful in describing fundamental patterns of wage determination.

About three-fourths of the American labor force is not organized in any labor union. Among agricultural and white-collar workers, for example, union membership is relatively slight and the situation conforms roughly to the competitive model. On the other hand, in some of the service industries and in parts of the South and Midwest where significant segments of the labor force are unorganized and relatively immobile for long periods, the monopsony model provides a good approximation—with an allowance, of course, for the legal minimum wage (although it does not apply to many farmworkers).

Within the one-fourth of the labor force that is organized into unions there are some segments, such as those in the garment and building trades, coal mining, and stevedoring, where the balance of power is with the unions rather than the employers. The situation in those segments approximates that of monopoly. In most of manufacturing, transportation, and related sectors, strong unions face strong employers or employers' associations and the bilateral monopoly model applies. In these cases, collective bargaining between unions and management is the chief means of settling issues. Thus a wide variety of situations exists in American labor markets. These models or modifications of them can go a long way toward explaining and predicting the consequences of various outcomes.

Theory of Rent

In the early nineteenth century, a political controversy arose that was responsible for producing one of the great theoretical advances in the history of economics.

The place: England. The period: 1814–16.

For most of the previous century, from 1711 to 1794, the price of "corn" (the generic name for all grains) had been extremely stable. But between 1795 and 1800 the price tripled, and it continued to rise over most of the following two decades. Since grain was a primary source of food, the rise in price created considerable political unrest. Many workers starved, and employers reluctantly raised wages because of soaring food prices.

One group argued that the landlords were in a "conspiracy" to keep up corn prices by charging high rents to farmers. Another group, including the great English classical economist David Ricardo, argued exactly the opposite: Corn prices are high,

said the "Ricardians," because of shortages resulting from the Napoleonic Wars. The high price of corn makes corn cultivation more profitable; this increases the demand for land and hence the price paid for the use of the land—namely rent. If the price of corn fell, corn cultivation would become less profitable, and this would bring decreased rents. In Ricardo's own words:

"Corn is not high because a rent is paid, but a rent is paid because corn is high." Ricardo meant that the price of land is determined by demand and supply, and that *rent is price-determined, not price-determining.*

Ricardo and his followers carried on a vigorous battle for the repeal of the English Corn Laws (tariffs) of 1815 in order to bring more corn into the country, thereby increasing its supply and lowering its price.

ECONOMIC RENT IS A SURPLUS

Ricardo's argument was based on the assumptions that the amount of land available is unchangeable; that land used for growing corn has no alternative uses; and that a landlord would prefer to receive *any* payment for his land rather than leave it idle and receive nothing. In the language of modern economics, this is equivalent to saying that the *supply of land is perfectly inelastic,* as illustrated in Exhibit 6a.

The intersection of the supply curve with the demand curve D establishes the equilibrium quantity ON and the equilibrium price OP. It follows that this price (or rent) per unit of land must be a *surplus* to the landlord since he would be willing to supply the same amount of land at a lower price, even down to a price of zero, depending on where the demand curve intersects the supply curve. We call this surplus "economic rent" and define it as follows:

Economic rent is any payment made to a factor of production, in an industry in equilibrium, in excess of the factor's supply price or opportunity cost—that is, in excess of the minimum amount necessary to keep that factor in its present occupation.

Note that this definition restricts the concept of economic rent to an *equilibrium* surplus. This is be-

Exhibit 6

The Determination of Rent

The landlord's opportunity cost is zero. Hence the total amount he receives, namely the area OPRN, represents economic rent, since he would be willing to supply the same amount of land at zero rent.

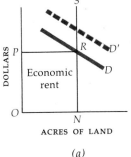

(a)

The total amount received by the bus drivers is the area OPRN.

However, only the Nth driver is getting his opportunity cost; those to the left of him are getting more than their opportunity costs as represented by their total economic rent, namely the area KPR.

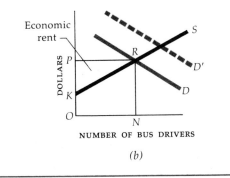

(b)

cause some factors may receive surpluses while they are in a transitory stage from one equilibrium position to another and because such surpluses may exist even in long-run equilibrium. It follows that the entire rectangular area in Exhibit 6a, namely OPRN, represents the total economic rent received by the landlord.

Originally, "rent" meant the payment made for the use of land. But economists eventually realized that any factor of production, not just land, may receive a surplus above its opportunity cost. Hence

they coined the expression "economic rent" to represent all such differentials.

Thus in Exhibit 6b, a hypothetical model of the supply and demand for bus drivers under perfect competition is shown. According to the chart, a quantity of bus drivers equal to ON would each receive a wage of OP. But only for the Nth bus driver is this wage his supply price or opportunity cost: each of the others that make up the amount ON would have been willing to work for less as determined by the height of the segment KR of the supply curve. Therefore all these other drivers are receiving a total economic rent equal to the area KPR. You should be able to see from the dashed lines in both diagrams that if the supply curve remains the same, an increase in demand will enlarge the amount of economic rent, whereas a decrease in demand will reduce it.

This leads to the important conclusion that economic rent arises because the owners of the various units of a particular factor of production differ in the eagerness with which they are willing to supply those units—i.e., in their supply price. If all had equal supply prices, the supply curve would be perfectly elastic and there would be no economic rent. Thus in Exhibit 6b, the area of economic rent would diminish to zero if the supply curve were to pivot on point R so as to approach the horizontal.

Economic rent is a concept similar to that of net revenue, since both represent surpluses. The difference between them is merely a matter of reference: When the surplus is received by a factor of production it is usually called economic rent; when the surplus is incurred by a firm it is typically referred to as net revenue.

IS RENT A COST OR A SURPLUS? WHICH VIEWPOINT?

Contrary to Ricardo's assumptions, units of land often have alternative uses and are of different quality. These factors explain why the demand for an acre of real estate in the heart of Chicago's business district may be quite different from the demand for an acre of farm land in Kansas or an acre of desert land in New Mexico. These differences in demand

HENRY GEORGE

1839–1897

The Single Tax

Henry George was born and raised in Philadelphia by middle-class, strongly devout parents. His religious background is reflected in the missionary tendency in all his writings. After quitting school at thirteen he worked as an errand boy and clerk, went to sea while in his teens, and then lived in stark poverty in San Francisco for a number of years.

He turned his attention to politics and ran for the state legislature, but was defeated by the opposition of the Central Pacific Railroad. George vehemently opposed the land subsidy the company was receiving from the state, and the speculation occasioned by the completion of the railroad between Sacramento and Oakland. At this time the seeds of his opposition to land monopoly and exploitation were sown. In 1871 he sketched the bare outlines of his later theory in a pamphlet entitled Our Land and Land Policy, *but did not elaborate the theme until 1879, when his famous book,* Progress and Poverty, *was published.*

Ironically, George had difficulty in finding a publisher. But it turned out to be a work that brought him great fame, for it was an immediate success both at home and abroad. Many millions of copies have been sold throughout the world, and it is undoubtedly the most successful popular economics book ever published.

The central concept in George's writing is that poverty is caused by the monopolization of land by the few, who deprive the rest of the people of their birthright. Since land is endowed by nature, all rent on land is unearned surplus, and the injustice to the landless grows when, as a result of natural progress, the value of land is augmented and rent increases correspondingly. The solution, therefore, is the confiscation of rent by the government through a single tax *on land. No other taxes would be necessary, according to George.*

Famous economists, including Alfred Marshall and J. B. Clark, debated with Henry George over the single-tax issue. Their conclusions, and those of later economists, suggested that a land tax would probably have fewer adverse effects on the allocation of society's resources than other taxes. However, it would have three major shortcomings: (1) a single tax on land alone would not produce enough revenue to meet governments' needs; (2) the tax would be unjust because surpluses or economic rent may accrue to other resource owners

Culver Pictures

besides landlords if the owners can gain monopolistic control over the sale of their resources in the marketplace; (3) the tax might be impossible to administer because it does not distinguish between land and capital—that is, between the proportion of rent that represents a surplus and the proportion that results from improvements made on the land.

George entered politics again in 1886 as a candidate of the Labor and Socialist parties for mayor of New York City. By this time he was enormously popular, and it took the maximum efforts of a coalition of parties to defeat him at the polls. He became a candidate again in 1897, but the strain was too much for him, and he died during the campaign at the age of 58.

also account for the differences in rent that are paid by their users.

Are these rents a cost or a surplus? The answer depends on the point of view you take. From the firm's viewpoint, rent is the price it must pay to attract land from its alternative uses. Hence rent is a *cost*. From the economy's viewpoint, rent is the value which society receives for making available the land provided free by nature, regardless of the alternative uses to which the land is put and the rents that are paid. Hence rent is a *surplus*. The fallacy of composition thus plays a role in the interpretation of rent from the individual versus social viewpoint.

Theory of Interest

If you borrow money to buy a car, a house, or a washing machine, you must pay interest to the lender for the money that you borrow. Hence *interest* is defined as the price paid for the use of money or loanable funds over a period of time. Several characteristics of interest must be understood:

1. Interest is stated as a rate—that is, as a percentage of the amount of money borrowed. Thus an interest rate of 5 percent means that the borrower pays 5 cents per $1 borrowed per year, or $5 per $100 borrowed per year, and so on.

2. Interest is paid for the use of money, and money in turn is employed to buy productive resources or capital goods. You will often hear reference made to the interest on capital, but what this really means is the interest on the money represented by capital invested.

3. In our economy there are hundreds of different interest rates on debt instruments of all types. These include government and corporation bonds, bank loans, mortgages, etc. The rates vary according to such factors as: (*a*) the length of time over which the money is borrowed; (*b*) the risk of the borrower's defaulting on the loan; and (*c*) the degree of competition among lenders in a particular money market. Other things being equal, interest rates will tend to vary directly with the first two factors and inversely with the third. If you are not sure of the reasons for

this, ask yourself how these factors would affect the interest rate that you would charge if you were a banker making loans.

As a result of the wide structure of interest rates, economists find it convenient to talk about "the" rate of interest. By this they mean the theoretical *pure interest rate* on a long-term, riskless loan, where the interest payments are made solely for the use of someone else's money over a period of time. This rate is often approximated by the interest on long-term negotiable United States Treasury bonds.

We have defined interest as the price paid for the use of money or loanable funds over a period of time. We shall see shortly that this price is determined by the interactions of demand and supply forces. What factors lie behind demand and supply?

DEMAND FOR LOANABLE FUNDS

You and I and everyone else want money, but from the economy's viewpoint we fall into three major groups: businesses, households, and governments.

Businesses. Businesses are the largest source of demand for loanable funds. Corporations borrow money because they want to invest the funds in capital goods such as new plants, new machines, new fleets of trucks, the renovation of existing plants, and the like. In Exhibit 7, therefore, the first two columns of the firm's investment schedule show the number of dollars that it could invest at various expected (predicted) rates of return. These investment dollars are cumulated in the third column of the table. For a firm with many such investment projects, or for an entire economy, these cumulated data would look like the graph in the accompanying chart, representing the marginal revenue productivity of capital expressed in percentages. Since the rate of interest on borrowed funds is also expressed in percentages, we again have a familiar marginal productivity principle:

Under competitive conditions, a firm will demand loanable funds up to the point where the capital purchased with those funds is such that its marginal revenue productivity is equal to the interest rate (or price) that must be paid for the loan. The *MRP*

Exhibit 7

Productivity of Capital for a Firm

The first two columns show the amount of money the firm can invest at different expected *or predicted rates of return. These amounts are cumulated in the third column to form the demand or marginal revenue productivity schedule of capital.*

Investment schedule for a firm

(1)	(2)	(3)
		Cumulative
	Number	*investment*
	of dollars	*(number of*
Expected	*that can*	*dollars that*
rate of	*earn this*	*can earn*
return on	*return on*	*this amount*
investments	*investment*	*and more)*
		MRP
30%	$ 5,000	$ 5,000
20	10,000	15,000
10	25,000	40,000
5	30,000	70,000
2	100,000	170,000

In a competitive market, the firm will demand loanable funds up to the point where the MRP *of capital equals the interest rate or price. Thus a decrease in the interest rate from 8 percent to 5 percent will increase the quantity of capital demanded from $50,000 to $70,000.*

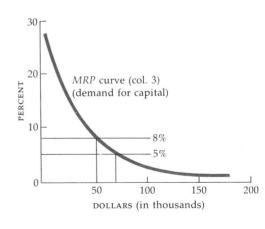

curve of capital is therefore the firm's demand curve for capital.

Thus in the chart, a reduction in the interest rate from 8 to 5 percent on borrowed funds would increase the amount of investment from approximately $50,000 to $70,000.

Households. Households are the second major source of demand for loanable funds. Households borrow to buy automobiles, washing machines, vacation trips, homes, and so forth. There is some limited evidence to suggest that the household demand curve for funds is downward-sloping, indicating that households will tend to borrow large amounts of money at lower interest rates.

Governments. Federal, state, and local governments —are the third major source of demand for loanable funds. Governments borrow money against future tax revenues in order to finance highways, education, welfare, national defense, and so forth. The federal government often borrows to finance a budget deficit, and hence we cannot assume that its demand curve for loanable funds is downward-sloping. However, there is ample evidence that this is not the case for state and local governments; they tend to borrow more when interest rates are low than when they are high, and hence their demand curves for funds slope downward.

Many studies indicate that for all three sources— businesses, households, and governments—taken together, the aggregate demand curve for loanable funds is downward-sloping. (An exception may occur in time of war when net borrowing by the federal government is sometimes enough to alter this tendency.) Economists also believe that the demand for loanable funds is relatively inelastic, thus reflecting the substantial insensitivity of borrowers to changes in interest rates.

Three Important Motives

In modern economic theory, the interest rate is viewed as the price paid to overcome *liquidity preference*—that is, the desire on the part of households and businesses to hold their money in the form of liquid assets such as cash or checking accounts. Why do they have this desire? There are three reasons or motives.

1. *Transactions Motive.* Most people receive incomes weekly or monthly, while making payments almost daily. Hence the transactions motive reflects the desire of households and businesses to hold a certain amount of cash on hand for the purpose of carrying on their day-to-day activities. Economists believe that the transactions motive is relatively insensitive to changes in the interest rate and that it is probably more influenced by the level of income.

2. *Precautionary Motive.* Life is full of unpredictable events. Cars break down, illness strikes, unemployment occurs, sales suddenly drop. The precautionary motive reflects the desire of households and businesses to hold cash for unexpected rainy-day needs. This motive, it is believed, is also affected mainly by income levels and relatively little by changes in the interest rate.

3. *Speculative Motive.* Some households and businesses, but not all, hold cash on hand in order to satisfy a speculative motive for financial investment. This motive is reflected by their tendency to hold more securities and less cash when the interest rate is high in order to take advantage of higher returns, and to hold more cash and less securities when the interest rate is low in anticipation of buying securities at a higher return in the future when the interest rate rises.

To summarize the foregoing points: The total demand for loanable funds is made up of the demands of businesses, households, and governments. The demands of businesses and households are determined by their transactions and precautionary motives, both of which are primarily influenced by income levels rather than by changes in the interest rate, and by their speculative motive, which is directly influenced by the interest rate.

SUPPLY OF LOANABLE FUNDS

Now that we know what underlies the demand side of the picture, we must turn our attention to the supply side and ask: What are the sources of loanable funds? There are two basic categories.

1. *The Federal Reserve System*—the central banking system of the country—exercises a great deal of influence over the supply of money and hence the supply of loanable funds. This influence is intertwined with government monetary and fiscal policies for combatting recessions and inflations.

2. *Households and Businesses* supply some loanable funds to the money market out of their past or present savings. Household savings are that part of household income not spent on consumption. Business savings are mainly undistributed (plowed back) profits and depreciation reserves. Most businesses reinvest their savings in new plant and equipment, but some find their way into the money market. In general, very little is known about the effects which interest rates have on household and business saving, but the influences are believed to be relatively slight.

DETERMINATION OF THE INTEREST RATE

These demand and supply forces combine to determine the equilibrium interest rate in the market, as shown by the familiar supply and demand diagram in Exhibit 8. As mentioned above, the downward-sloping aggregate demand curve at any *given level of income* reflects the willingness on the part of businessmen to desire more funds for investment at a low interest rate than at a high interest rate. The upward-sloping supply curve, though it is based on much more complex and uncertain factors, *assumes* that household and business savers will make available somewhat larger quantities of loanable funds at a high interest rate than at a low one.

Actually, the determination of the interest rate has much deeper implications than is apparent from this simple supply and demand diagram. Further, government monetary and fiscal policies, as learned in macroeconomics, exercise a powerful influence on the forces that help determine the interest rate. As a result, the interest rate tends to be more stable and does not fluctuate as freely as do the prices of commodities that are determined by supply and demand in perfectly competitive markets.

Exhibit 8

Determination of the Interest Rate

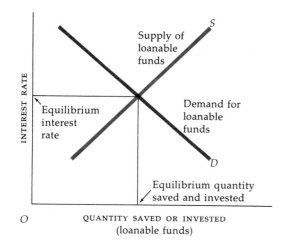

THE RATIONING OR ALLOCATING
FUNCTION OF INTEREST

Since the interest rate is a price, it performs the same rationing function as any other price by allocating the economy's scarce supply of funds among those who are willing to pay for them. Thus in a free market, only the most profitable investment projects— those projects whose expected return or productivity is equal to or greater than the rate of interest—are undertaken. Any project whose prospective yield is below the interest rate is dropped from consideration. In this way the interest rate decides the critical question of *who* shall participate in the limited supply of capital, and in so doing directs the growth of productive capacity in a capital-using economy such as ours.

Does the interest rate actually perform this function in the American economy? For the most part the answer is yes, but there are some qualifications:

The interest rate in our economy does not always perform perfectly as an allocative mechanism because:

1. The government allocates some of the available

capital to projects which it believes to be in the public interest, regardless of their financial profitability.

2. Large oligopolistic firms, by virtue of their prestige and market power, can usually acquire capital on more favorable terms (i.e., at lower interest rates) than many smaller and less well-known firms that have relatively greater prospects for growth and profit.

SUMMARY: LIQUIDITY PREFERENCE AND
LOANABLE FUNDS THEORIES

The theory of interest contains elements of two theories that have been an integral part of economics since the 1930s: the liquidity preference theory and the loanable funds theory.

The *liquidity preference theory of interest* (formulated by J. M. Keynes) contends that people would rather hold their assets or wealth in the most liquid form, namely cash, in order to satisfy three motives: the "transactions motive" to carry out everyday purchasing needs; the "precautionary motive" to meet possible unforeseen emergencies; and the "speculative motive" to take advantage of a rise in interest rates. Accordingly, interest is the price or reward that must be paid to overcome liquidity preference.

The *loanable funds theory of interest* holds that the interest rate is determined by the demand for, and supply of, loanable funds only, as distinguished from *all* money. The sources of demand for loanable funds are businesses that want to invest, households that want to finance consumer purchases, and government agencies that want to finance deficits. The sources of supply of loanable funds are the central banking system which influences the supply of money (and hence loanable funds) in the economy, and households and businesses that make loanable funds available out of their past or present savings.

These two approaches should not be regarded as "alternative" theories of interest. Although they involve many subtleties and complexities which are treated in greater detail in more advanced courses, they often tend to supplement and complement each other rather than compete.

Theory of Profit

We have learned that *profit* or net revenue represents the difference between total revenue and total cost. Profit is thus a *residual* or *surplus* over and above normal profit, and it accrues to the entrepreneur after all costs including explicit costs and implicit costs have been deducted from total revenue. What does economic theory tell us about the determinants of profit? What functions does profit perform?

The history of economics reveals a number of theories of how profits are derived. Three are generally recognized by economists today as being particularly relevant:

1. Friction and monopoly theory
2. Uncertainty theory
3. Innovation theory

This system of classification is not all-inclusive. Furthermore, any one of the theories may contain elements of the others. The system merely emphasizes the main lines that have been followed historically in the course of thinking on the subject.

FRICTION AND MONOPOLY THEORY

By the end of the nineteenth century, the theory of a perfectly competitive economy was well on its way toward becoming a unified body of thought. Against this setting the noted American economist J. B. Clark constructed a model of the economy that was intended to reconcile the static laws of theory with the dynamic world of fact.

According to Clark's "stationary" model (or the theory of perfect competition as it is commonly called today), the economy is characterized by a smooth and frictionless flow of resources, with the system automatically clicking into equilibrium through the free play of market forces. Changes may occur that cause a departure from equilibrium, but so long as resources are mobile and opportunities equally accessible to all economic organisms (i.e., knowledge is perfect), the adjustment to change and a new equilibrium will be accomplished quickly and smoothly. In this type of economic equilibrium all factors of production would receive their opportunity costs; the revenues of each enterprise would ex-actly equal its costs (including the implicit wages and interest of the owner), and hence no economic surplus or profit residual could result.

In the real world, however, surpluses do occur, and in accordance with the theory they can be attributed only to the frictions (or obstacles to resource mobility) and monopoly elements that actually characterize a dynamic economy. In the long run, according to theory, the forces of competition would eliminate any surpluses, but the surpluses in reality recur because new frictions and new monopoly elements continually arise. Therefore: <u>Profits are the result of institutional rigidities in the social and economic system that prevent the working-out of competitive forces, and are to the temporary advantage of the surplus recipient.</u>

Many illustrations from real life substantiate the existence of friction and monopoly as a cause of economic surplus. The construction of military posts during a war brings profit bonanzas to neighboring cities; cold-war crises have often rescued domestic industries from threatening oversupplies of their products; the existence of patents and franchises enables many firms to reap profits by legally excluding competitors from the field; a favorable location for a business may result in the value of the site exceeding the rental payment for it; or, in general, the control of any resource whose supply is scarce relative to its demand provides a basis for pure or windfall profits. A surplus would not arise if resources were sufficiently mobile to enter the market, or if the economy were frictionless (perfect) in its competitive structure. At best, any surpluses that did arise would be short-lived and vanish entirely when the adjustments had time to exert their full effect in the market. But social processes—customs, laws, traditions, etc.—make these rapid adjustments impossible.

UNCERTAINTY THEORY

The uncertainty theory of profit was introduced by Professor Frank Knight of the University of Chicago in a remarkable doctoral thesis entitled *Risk, Uncertainty, and Profit* published in 1921. The theory is rooted in a distinction between "risk" and "uncertainty."

The Meaning of Risk

Risk is defined as the quantitative measurement of an outcome, such as a gain or a loss, in a manner such that the mathematical probability (or "odds") of the outcome can be predicted. Since the distinguishing feature of risk is predictability, the firm can "insure" itself against expected losses by incorporating them in advance into its cost structure. This is true whether the risk is of an intrafirm or interfirm nature, as explained below.

Intrafirm risk occurs when management can establish the probability of loss because the number of occurrences within the firm is large enough to be predicted with known error. For example, a factory may experience a loss of about 2 machine-hours out of every 100 machine-hours due to equipment breakdown. In this case, the cost of the production lost can be added to the cost of the production resulting from the remaining 98 machine-hours, and the profit rate altered by the revision in the cost structure. In other words, where the average expected loss for the company can be predicted for the coming period, the loss can be "self-insured" by treating it as a cost of doing business, and hence no insurance from outside sources is necessary. Thus, small-loan companies expect a certain percentage of defaults; banks regularly charge off as "bad debts" a portion of their loans; and many companies institute self-insurance programs against risks for which they can prepare themselves through proper reserve accounting.

Interfirm risk occurs when the number of observations or experiences is not large enough within any one firm for management to feel that it can predict the loss with reasonable confidence. However, when many firms are considered, the observations become numerous enough to exhibit the necessary stability for prediction. Examples of such risks are losses caused by floods, storms, fires, deaths, etc. Since managers are unable to predict such losses for themselves, they are able to shift the burden of the risk to insurance companies whose function is to establish the probability of such losses based on a large number of cases. Although insurance companies cannot establish that a particular individual will die or that a particular building will burn, they can predict with small error how many people will die next year or how many buildings out of a given number will burn. It follows that since a firm pays a risk premium for insurance, it can and does treat this risk premium as a cost of doing business.

The Meaning of Uncertainty

Uncertainty is defined as a state of knowledge in which the probabilities of outcomes resulting from specific actions are not known and cannot be predicted. Unlike risk, therefore, uncertainty is a subjective (rather than objective) phenomenon: no two individuals will view an event and necessarily formulate the same quantitative opinion because there is not enough information on which to base a definite probability estimate.

Under uncertainty conditions, decision makers must make choices based on incomplete knowledge. They may do this by forming mental images of future outcomes that cannot be verified quantitatively. It follows from this that uncertainty is not insurable, and cannot be integrated within the firm's cost structure, as can risk. At best, each businessman may harbor his own "subjective" probability about a future outcome, but it is nothing more than a strong hunch.

According to this theory, the great majority of events in our society are unpredictable—that is, they are uncertainties. Hence, *profits are the rewards, and losses are the penalties, of bearing uncertainty.*

The uncertainty theory concludes that in a market economy entrepreneurs undertake an activity because they *expect* but do not necessarily *receive* profits. Like a dog chasing a rabbit, the expectation of profit is the incentive that keeps entrepreneurs running.

INNOVATION THEORY

In the 1930s, one of the most distinguished economists of this century, Joseph Schumpeter, introduced a theory of business cycles based on innovations. This theory has often been extended to include the notion of innovation as a cause of profits.

An *innovation*, as economists define it, is "the setting up of a new production function"—that is, a new relation between the output and the various inputs (capital, land, labor, etc.) in a production process. Innovations may thus embrace such wide varieties of activities as the discovery of new markets, differentiation of products, or, in short, new ways of doing old things or different combinations of existing methods to accomplish new things. There is an important distinction to be made between invention and innovation: Invention is the creation of something new; innovation is the adaptation of an invention to business use. Many inventions never become innovations.

Schumpeter's original purpose in propounding the innovation theory was to show how business cycles result from these "disturbances" and from successive adaptations to them by the business system. His procedure was to assume a stationary (perfectly competitive) system in equilibrium—in which all economic life is repetitive and goes on smoothly, without disturbance. Into this system a shock—an innovation—is introduced by an entrepreneur who foresees the possibility of extra profit. The quietude and intricate balance of the system is then shattered as if invaded by a Hollywood-staged cattle stampede. The successful innovation causes a herd of businessmen (followers rather than leaders) to plunge into the new field by adopting the innovation, and these mass rushes create and stir up secondary waves of business activity. When the disturbance has finally ironed itself out, the system settles into equilibrium once again, only to be disturbed later on by another innovation. Profits and economic activity are thus experienced as a series of fits and starts (cycles) rather than progressing smoothly and continuously.

FUNCTIONS OF PROFITS

As mentioned earlier, there is no single "correct" theory of profit; all three theories contribute significantly to explaining the causes of profit. They also help us to understand the functions of profits. Thus:

Profits perform two major functions in our economy:

1. They stimulate innovation by inducing businessmen to undertake new ventures and to improve production methods.

2. To the extent that markets are free and competitive, the desire for profits induces businessmen to allocate their resources efficiently in accordance with consumer preferences.

These functions are important because the role of profits and "the profit system" account for a fundamental distinction between our capitalistic system and the socialistic systems of other countries like the Soviet Union, which we will be reading about later on.

SUMMARY OF IMPORTANT IDEAS

1. The long-run trend of real wages in our economy has been upward, based fundamentally on the increased productivity of labor resulting from improvements in the quality and quantity of the factors of production.

2. Wages are determined in the market under different competitive conditions. Four models which explain most of the situations that exist in our economy are: competitive model, monopsony model, monopoly model, and bilateral monopoly model. The bilateral monopoly model may yield a determinate solution on quantity, but it yields an indeterminate solution on price.

3. Economic rent is a surplus which is price-determined, not price-determining. To an individual firm, rent is a cost of production just like any other cost; but to society rent is a surplus which it receives for making available nature's free land.

4. Interest is the price paid for the use of loanable funds—that is, the price necessary to overcome liquidity preference resulting primarily from the speculative motive for holding money. However, money is also held for transactions and precautionary motives. Although interest is determined by the supply of, and demand for, loanable funds, it is administered by the government and is not freely fluctuating. The chief function of the interest rate is to allocate scarce funds for alternative uses, thus directing the flow of capital.

5. Profit is a residual or surplus over and above all costs including normal profit. It may result from frictions and monopoly elements in our economy,

JOSEPH ALOIS SCHUMPETER

1883–1950

One of the most famous economists of the twentieth century was Joseph Schumpeter. Indeed, in the opinion of some scholars he was one of the great economic thinkers of all time. His claim to this rare title rests as much on his total achievements as a social scientist as on his contributions to the advancement of economics. For although many scholars have excelled in special fields, Schumpeter was one of the few who was extraordinarily well versed in many, including economics, mathematics, philosophy, sociology, and history.

Schumpeter was born in Moravia (now part of Czechoslovakia) and educated in law and economics at the University of Vienna. After a varied and successful career as a professor, cabinet minister, banker, and jurist, he accepted a teaching position at the University of Bonn in 1925. When Hitler came to power, he migrated to the United States, and was a professor of economics at Harvard University until his death.

Schumpeter's output of books, essays, articles, and monographs was enormous, but his most important works fell broadly in the field of business-cycle theory. Perhaps his greatest theoretical contribution was the model he developed to describe how business cycles result from innovations by a business system under capitalism. This innovation theory was subsequently adopted by many economists as a partial explanation of how profits (surpluses) arise in a capitalistic system.

In one of his classic works Schumpeter discussed the "crumbling walls" of capitalism—that is, the eventual decay of the system due to the obsolescence of the entrepreneurial function. In his own words:

"... the economic wants of humanity might some day be so completely satisfied that little motive would be left to push productive effort still further ahead. Such a state of satiety is no doubt very far off even if we keep within the present scheme of wants; and if we take account of the fact that, as higher standards of life are attained, these wants automatically expand and new wants emerge or are created, satiety becomes a flying goal, particularly if we include leisure among consumers' goods. However, let us glance at that possibility, assuming, still more unrealistically, that methods of production have reached a state of perfection which does not admit of further improvement.

"A more or less stationary state would ensue. Capitalism, being essentially an evolutionary process, would become atro-

Bettmann Archive

phic. There would be nothing left for entrepreneurs to do. They would find themselves in much the same situation as generals would in a society perfectly sure of permanent peace. Profits and along with profits the rate of interest would converge toward zero. The bourgeois strata that live on profits and interest would tend to disappear. The management of industry and trade would become a matter of current administration, and the personnel would unavoidably acquire the characteristics of a bureaucracy. Socialism of a very sober type would almost automatically come into being. Human energy would turn away from business. Other than economic pursuits would attract the brains and provide the adventure."

Although Schumpeter was widely respected, and his many pioneering works were studied by scholars throughout the world, he never founded a "school" of economic thought or gathered a following which could eventually assume the status of a school. In other words, no Schumpeterians ever emerged, as did, for example, Marshallians or Keynesians. Various reasons may be advanced for this. Perhaps the most significant is that his theory contained no cause célèbre—no fundamental challenge that could offer a rallying point. Although his innovation theory of business cycles was developed on a high theoretical plane, it offered no concrete solutions to the world's economic problems.

from uncertainty, and from innovations. The chief functions of profit are: (1) to stimulate economic progress by inducing businessmen to invest in plant and equipment, and (2) to the extent that markets are competitive, to allocate resources in accordance with consumer preferences.

FOR HOMEWORK AND DISCUSSION

1. *Terms and concepts to review:*

wages	transactions motive
labor	precautionary motive
money wages	speculative motive
real wages	liquidity preference theory of interest
monopsony	
bilateral monopoly	loanable funds theory of interest
economic rent	profit
single tax	risk
interest	uncertainty
pure interest rate	innovation
liquidity preference	

2. Why has the long-run trend of real wages been upward, especially since the supply of labor today is so much larger than it was years ago?

3. Which wage-determination model best explains each of the following? Illustrate and explain each with an actual model.

a. The wages of file clerks and secretaries

b. The wages of unskilled farm workers

c. The wages of typographers and longshoremen

4. A union official once advised the men in an industry to ask for a 10 percent wage cut. Was he crazy? What economic factors might have prompted him to offer such advice?

5. "Wages are determined by the marginal productivity of labor just as prices are determined by costs of production." True or false? Explain.

6. Do you see any similarity between the concept of economic rent received by a factor of production and net revenue received by a firm? Explain.

7. Henry George ran for mayor of New York in 1886. If you had been a voter at that time, how would you have reacted to his single-tax idea?

8. Money itself is not a resource and is unproductive. Why, then, should people be willing to pay a price in the form of interest in order to acquire it? What determines the interest rate that is paid? What functions does interest perform?

9. Classify each of the following as an interfirm or intrafirm risk:

a. Glassware and china breakage in a restaurant

b. Egg breakage on a dairy farm

c. Absenteeism in a factory

d. "Acts of God" (cite examples)

10. (*a*) From a dairy farmer's standpoint, is the price of eggs a risk or an uncertainty? (*b*) How about the sale of next year's Plymouths by Chrysler? Why?

11. "Economic profits should be taxed away since they result from frictions and monopolistic influences." Evaluate.

REFERENCES AND READING SUGGESTIONS

BOBER, M. M., *Intermediate Price and Income Theory,* rev. ed., Norton, New York, 1962, chaps. 14–17.

DOOLEY, PETER C., *Elementary Price Theory,* Appleton-Century-Crofts, New York, 1967, chaps. 8–10.

DUE, JOHN F., and ROBERT W. CLOWER, *Intermediate Economic Analysis,* 5th ed., Irwin, Homewood, Illinois, 1966, chaps. 14–17.

WARD, BENJAMIN, *Elementary Price Theory,* The Free Press, New York, 1967, chaps. 8, 9.

PART 7

Domestic Economic Problems

CHAPTER 28

Business and Government: Monopoly, Antitrust, the Military-Industrial Complex

CHAPTER PREVIEW

What is the nature of the "monopoly problem" in the United States?

What are the major laws that seek to prevent monopoly and to maintain competition in our economy? How are these laws enforced?

What methods have firms used to monopolize markets, and what have been the major court cases dealing with monopolization and related activities?

Is our economy "monopolized" at the present time? If so, what is the extent of monopolization, and what should be done about it?

What is the so-called "military-industrial complex"? Of what significance is it in our economy?

Adam Smith once remarked in a famous passage in the *Wealth of Nations*:

> People of the same trade seldom meet together, even for merriment and diversion, but the conversation ends in a conspiracy against the public, or in some contrivance to raise prices. It is impossible indeed to prevent such meetings, by any law which either could be executed, or would be consistent with liberty and justice. But though the law cannot hinder people of the same trade from sometimes assembling together, it ought to do nothing to facilitate such assemblies; much less to render them necessary.

According to Smith, competition among businessmen is not a "natural" form of behavior; given the opportunity, businessmen would prefer to seek ways of avoiding competition if they could strengthen their market positions by doing so.

The history of American business suggests that this is indeed the case. As a result, the American government has, since the late nineteenth century, been engaged in constructing a body of laws and policies to assure that competition in our economy is at least maintained if not enhanced. The purpose of this chapter is to sketch the main features of these laws, to see the interesting ways in which they have been applied in some exciting court cases, and to evaluate the chief economic issues pertaining to problems of competition and monopoly in our society.

Big Business and the Monopoly Problem

In economic theory, a market is said to be monopolized when it consists of a single firm producing a product for which there are no close substitutes. This narrow difinition is usually adequate for analyzing market structures, but when it comes to matters of public policy, economists, government officials, and judges in courts of law take a much broader view: They regard a market as being monopolized if it is dominated by one or a few firms—that is, if it is "oligopolized." The automobile, aluminum, chemical, and steel industries, as well as many others in the American economy, are notable examples. In each of these industries there are two, three, or four large firms whose sales are a major share of the total market, leaving a relatively minor share for smaller competitors to divide among themselves. According to this interpretation, big businesses like General Motors, Alcoa, du Pont, and U.S. Steel, as well as their chief competitors, qualify as "monopolies."

Some "Pros" and "Cons" of Monopoly

The charges against big-business monopolies and the arguments in defense of them have been debated for decades. Among the chief objections are that: (1) they maximize profit by restricting output and charging higher prices than competitive producers, thereby misallocating society's resources and contributing to inequality in income distribution; (2) they retard economic progress and technological advance because they are protected from the pressures of competition; and (3) they exert disproportionate influences at all levels of government, giving rise to an "industrial-political complex" which favors big business at the expense of the rest of society.

Arguments in defense of big-business monopolies assert that: (1) they are more effectively competitive than the numbers of firms alone indicate, since there is rivalry among particular products in specific markets (e.g., aluminum versus copper, steel, plastics, etc.), as well as countervailing power on the opposite side of the market exerted by monopolistic sellers of resources; (2) they permit mass-production econo-mies at lower unit costs and prices than would be possible with large numbers of small firms; and (3) they have the financial ability to support extensive research and development, as well as the ethical and moral sense not to exploit their monopoly power.

There are varying degrees of truth and falsity in all these statements, and it requires an analysis of the facts in each case before one can judge the relative merits of the arguments.

Reactions to Monopoly: The Antitrust Laws

The period 1879–1904 saw the first great *merger movement* in American history. During these years, an unprecedented number of firms expanded by combining or merging with others, thereby forming new single business units with huge investments, capacities, and outputs. These new business organizations were called "monopolies" or "trusts," and in reaction to them and to subsequent economic developments Congress passed a body of legislation that is commonly referred to as the "antitrust laws."

The *antitrust laws* are acts passed by Congress since 1890 which commit the United States government to preventing monopoly and maintaining competition in American industry. There are also antitrust laws in almost every state in the country, but these are largely ineffectual and spasmodically enforced, since they are powerless to control agreements or combinations in major industries whose activities extend into interstate commerce. This, coupled with inadequate funds, has left the task of maintaining competition via antitrust law enforcement almost entirely to the federal government. Thus it is the federal antitrust laws that will be of concern to us here. These laws include the Sherman Antitrust Act, the Clayton Antitrust Act, the Federal Trade Commission Act, the Robinson-Patman Act, the Wheeler-Lea Act, and the Celler Antimerger Act.

The substantive provisions of the antitrust laws may be outlined briefly.

THE SHERMAN ACT (1890)

The *Sherman Antitrust Act* was the first attempt by the federal government to regulate the growth of monopoly in the United States. The provisions of the law were concise (probably too concise) and to the point. The Act declared as illegal:

1. Every contract, combination, or conspiracy in restraint of trade which occurs in interstate or foreign commerce.

2. Any monopolization or attempts to monopolize, or conspiracy with others in an attempt to monopolize, any portion of trade in interstate or foreign commerce.

Violations of the Act were made punishable by fines and/or imprisonment, and persons injured by violators could sue for triple damages.

The Act was surrounded by a cloud of uncertainty by failing to state precisely which kinds of actions were prohibited. Also, no special agency existed to enforce the law until 1903, when the Antitrust Division of the U.S. Department of Justice was established under an Assistant Attorney General. In order to put some teeth into the Sherman Act, therefore, Congress passed the Clayton Act and the Federal Trade Commission Act.

THE CLAYTON AND FEDERAL TRADE COMMISSION ACTS (1914)

Aimed at practices of *unfair competition*—that is, deceptive, dishonest, and injurious methods of competition—the *Clayton Antitrust Act* was concerned with four specific areas: price discrimination, exclusive and tying contracts, intercorporate stockholdings, and interlocking directorates.

Price Discrimination. For sellers to discriminate in prices by charging different prices to different buyers for the same good is *illegal.* However, such discrimination is permissible where there are differences in the grade, quality, or quantity of the commodity sold; where the lower prices make due allowances for cost differences in selling or transportation; and where the lower prices are offered in good faith to meet competition. Illegality exists where the effect is

---

Box 1

"Colossus of Roads"

The post-Civil War era produced some of America's greatest tycoons. This 1879 illustration depicts W. H. Vanderbilt, son of "Commodore" Cornelius Vanderbilt ("The public be damned.") monopolizing the railroads leading into New York. Assisting him are Cyrus Field, of the city's transit system, and Jay Gould, one of the most audacious swindlers in American business history.

Culver Pictures, from *Puck*, 1879

"to substantially lessen competition or tend to create a monopoly."

Exclusive and Tying Contracts. For sellers to lease, sell, or contract for the sale of commodities on condition that the lessee or purchaser not use or deal in the commodity of a competitor is *illegal* if such exclusive or tying contracts "substantially lessen competition or tend to create a monopoly."

Intercorporate Stockholdings. For corporations engaged in commerce to acquire the shares of a competing corporation, or the stocks of two or more corporations competing with each other, is *illegal* if such intercorporate stockholdings "substantially lessen competition or tend to create a monopoly."

Interlocking Directorates. For corporations engaged in commerce to have the same individual on two or more boards of directors is an interlocking directorate, and such directorships are *illegal* if the corporations are competitive and if any one has capital, surplus, and undivided profits in excess of $1 million.

Thus, price discrimination, exclusive and tying contracts, and intercorporate stockholdings were not declared by the Clayton Act to be absolutely illegal, but rather, in the words of the law, only when their effects "may be to substantially lessen competition or tend to create a monopoly." On interlocking directorates, however, the law made no such qualification: The fact of the interlock itself is illegal, and the government need not find that the arrangement results in a reduction in competition.

Box 2

"When We All Get Wise": The Stock Market Titans

Before the establishment of the Federal Reserve System in 1913, the United States experienced a number of financial panics. Reckless speculation produced stock market booms and busts, *with consequent large-scale unemployment. Labor and agrarian interests attributed the cause directly to the giant Wall Street "manipulators," as this 1911 cartoon indicates.*

Library of Congress, from *Life*, Oct. 26, 1911

The *Federal Trade Commission Act* served primarily as a general supplement to the Clayton Act by stating broadly and simply that "unfair methods of competition in commerce are hereby declared unlawful." But what significant contribution to monopoly control was made by these laws?

Essentially, both the Clayton Act and the Federal Trade Commission Act were directed toward the prevention of abuses, whereas the Sherman Act emphasized the punishment of abusers. To be sure, the practices that were prohibited in the two later laws could well have been attacked under the Sherman Act as conspiracies in restraint of trade or as attempts to monopolize, but now the nature of the problem was brought more sharply into focus. Moreover, under the Federal Trade Commission Act, the FTC was established as a governmental antitrust agency with federal funds appropriated to it for the purpose of attacking unfair competitive practices in commerce.

The FTC is also authorized under the Act to safeguard the public by preventing the dissemination of false and misleading advertising of foods, drugs, cosmetics, and therapeutic devices used in the diagnosis, prevention, or treatment of disease. It thus supplements in many ways the activities of the Food and Drug Administration which, under the Food, Drug, and Cosmetic Act (1938), outlaws adulteration and misbranding of foods, drugs, devices, and cosmetics moving in interstate commerce.

Box 3

"The Bosses of the Senate"

This classic 1889 sketch by Joseph Keppler depicts the public's attitude toward the Senate on the trust problem. Shortly thereafter, as a result of mounting pressure, hearings began on the Sherman Antitrust Bill.

THE BOSSES OF THE SENATE.

THE ROBINSON-PATMAN ACT (1936)

Frequently referred to as the "Chain Store Act," the *Robinson-Patman Act* was passed for the purpose of providing economic protection to independent retailers and wholesalers, such as grocers and druggists, from "unfair discriminations" by large sellers attained "because of their tremendous purchasing power." The law was an outgrowth of the increasing competition faced by independents that came with the development of chain stores and mass distributors after World War I. Those who favored the bill contended that the lower prices charged by these large organizations were attributable only in part to their lower costs, and more so if not entirely to the sheer weight of their bargaining power which enabled them to obtain unfair and unjustified concessions from their suppliers. The Act was thus a response to the cries of independents who demanded that the freedom of suppliers to discriminate be more strictly limited.

The Act, which amended Section 2 of the Clayton Act relating to price discrimination, contained the following essential provisions:

1. The payment of brokerage fees where no independent broker is employed is *illegal*. This was intended to eliminate the practice of some chains of demanding the regular brokerage fee as a discount when they purchased direct from manufacturers. The argument posed was that such chains obtained the discount by their sheer bargaining power and thereby gained an unfair advantage over smaller independents that had to use and pay for brokerage services.

2. The making of concessions by sellers, such as manufacturers, to buyers, such as wholesalers and retailers, is *illegal* unless such concessions are made to all buyers on proportionally equal terms. This provision was aimed at preventing advertising and promotional allowances from being granted to large-scale buyers without allowances being made to small competing buyers on proportionally equal terms.

3. Other forms of discrimination, such as quantity discounts, are *illegal* where they substantially lessen competition or tend to create a monopoly, either among sellers or among buyers. However, price discrimination is not illegal if the differences in prices make "due allowances" for differences in cost or if offered "in good faith to meet an equally low price of a competitor." But even where discounts can be justified by lower costs, the FTC is empowered to fix quantity limits beyond which discounts may not be granted, if it believes that such discounts would be "unjustly discriminatory or promotive of monopoly in any line of commerce."

4. It is *illegal* to give or to receive a larger discount than that made available to competitors purchasing the same goods in equal quantities. Also, it is *illegal* to charge lower prices in one locality than in another for the same goods, or to sell at "unreasonably low prices," where either of these practices is aimed at "destroying competition or eliminating a competitor."

THE WHEELER-LEA ACT (1938)

An amendment to part of the Federal Trade Commission Act, the *Wheeler-Lea Act* was passed for the purpose of providing consumers, rather than just business competitors, with protection against unfair practices. The Act makes *illegal* "unfair or deceptive acts or practices" in interstate commerce. Thus, a consumer who may be injured by an unfair trade practice is, before the law, of equal concern with the merchant who may be injured by an unfair competitive practice. The Act also defines "false advertising" as "an advertisement other than labeling which is misleading in a material respect," and makes the definition applicable to advertisements of foods, drugs, curative devices, and cosmetics.

THE CELLER ANTIMERGER ACT (1950)

The *Celler Antimerger Act* is an extension of Section 7 of the Clayton Act relating to intercorporate stockholdings. The latter law, as stated earlier, made it illegal for corporations to acquire the stock of competing corporations. But that law, the FTC argued, left a loophole through which monopolistic mergers could be effected by a corporation acquiring the *assets* of a competing corporation, or by first acquiring the stock and, by voting or granting of proxies, acquiring the assets. Moreover, the Supreme Court in several cases held that such mergers were not illegal under the Clayton Act if a corporation used its stock purchases to acquire the assets before the FTC's complaint was issued or before the Commission had issued its final order banning the stock acquisition.

The Antimerger Act plugged the loophole in the Clayton Act by making it illegal for a corporation to acquire the stock *or assets* of a competing corporation where the effect may be "substantially to lessen competition, or to tend to create a monopoly." The Act thus bans all types of mergers—*horizontal* (similar plants under one ownership, such as steel mills), *vertical* (dissimilar plants in various stages of production, integrated under one ownership), and *conglomerate* or *circular* (dissimilar plants and unrelated product lines)—provided the Commission can show that the effects *may* substantially lessen competition or tend towards monopoly.

It should be noted, however, that the intent of Congress in passing the Act was that there be a maintenance of competition. Accordingly, the Act was intended to apply to mergers with large firms or large with small firms, but not to mergers among small firms which may be undertaken to strengthen their competitive position.

ENFORCEMENT OF THE LAWS

In general, the application of the antitrust laws is effected on a *case-by-case* basis. That is, an order or decision resulting from an action is not applicable to all of industry, but only to the defendants in the particular case. Cases may originate in the complaints of injured businessmen, suggestions made by other government agencies, or in the research of the Antitrust Division of the Department of Justice, since it is this organization which may bring into the federal courts criminal or civil suits against violators of the Act. About 90 percent of the cases, it has been estimated, arise from complaints issued by injured parties, and at present most of the ensuing investigations are conducted by the FBI. The Federal Trade Commission Act, on the other hand, is enforced by the FTC and, when their orders become final, through suits brought by the Department of Justice. Finally, with respect to the Clayton Act, both the FTC and the Justice Department have concurrent jurisdiction in its enforcement, and in practice it is usually a matter of which agency gets there first.

Section 14 of the Clayton Act fixes the responsibility for the behavior of a corporation on its officers and directors and makes them subject to the penalties of fine or imprisonment for violating the laws. Under the Sherman Act, the fine is limited to $50,000, but fines have actually been pyramided into several hundred thousand dollars in a single case by exacting the $50,000 on each count of an indictment (e.g., monopolizing, attempting to monopolize, conspiring, and restraining trade) and by imposing the fine on each of the defendants in a suit (e.g., a trade association, each member of the association, and each of the directors and officers of the member firms). Other penalties are also possible as provided in other acts.

Businessmen who want to avoid risking violation of the law may consult with the Justice Department by presenting their proposed plans for combination or other particular practices. If the plans appear to be legal, the Department may commit itself not to institute future criminal proceedings, but it will reserve the right to institute civil action if competition is later restrained. The purpose of a civil suit is not to punish, but to restore competition by providing remedies. Typically, three classes of remedies are employed:

1. *Dissolution, divestiture,* and *divorcement* provisions may be used. Examples include an order to dissolve a trade association or combination, to sell intercorporate stockholdings, or to dispose of ownership in other assets. The purpose of these actions is to break up a monopolistic organization into smaller but more competitors.

2. An *injunction* may be issued. This is a court order requiring that the defendant refrain from certain business practices, or perhaps take a particular action that will increase rather than reduce competition.

3. A *consent decree* may be employed. This is usually worked out between the defendant and the Justice

Department without a court trial. The defendant in this instance does not declare himself guilty, but agrees nevertheless to abide by the rules of business behavior set down in the decree. This device is now one of the chief instruments employed in the enforcement of the Sherman and Clayton Acts.

Finally, the laws are also enforced through private suits. Under the Sherman Act, injured parties (individuals, corporations, or states) may sue for treble damages including court costs, and under the Clayton Act, a private plaintiff may also sue for an injunction—a restraining order—whenever he is threatened by loss or damage resulting from some firm's violation of the antitrust laws. Under the Federal Trade Commission Act, the FTC is authorized to prevent unfair business practices as well as to exercise, concurrently with the Justice Department, enforcement of the prohibited provisions of the Clayton Act as amended by the Robinson-Patman Act. Accordingly, the FTC has taken action against agreements that have tended to curtail output, fix prices, and divide markets among firms, thereby striving to maintain competition as well as to prevent unfair methods.

EXEMPTIONS AND INTERPRETATIONS

A compact summary of the antitrust laws is presented in Exhibit 1. A few industries and economic groups are exempt from these laws. The most important ones are: (1) the transport industries, including railroads, trucks, ships, and barges, which are largely subject to the control of regulatory agencies such as the Interstate Commerce Commission, and (2) labor unions. The exemption of labor unions was originally justified on the basis that they do not normally seek to monopolize markets or engage in methods of unfair competition, but seek instead to protect and enhance the position of labor. However, they may be subjected to antitrust prosecution if they combine with management to violate the antitrust laws.

Thus as we have seen, the antitrust laws have various things to say about monopoly, competition, and related concepts. Specifically, the Sherman Act forbade restraints of trade, monopoly, and attempts to monopolize; the Clayton Act forbade certain practices where the effects may be to lessen substantially the degree of competition or tend to create a monopoly; and the Federal Trade Commission Act forbade unfair methods of competition. But though Congress succeeded in passing these laws, it failed to define, and left up to the courts to interpret in their own way, the meaning of such terms as "monopoly," "restraint of trade," "substantial lessening of competition," "unfair competition," and so on. As a result, a number of major controversies have arisen.

Exhibit 1

The Antitrust Laws in a Nutshell

1. It is flatly illegal, without any qualification, to:

a. *Enter a contract, combination, or conspiracy in restraint of trade (Sherman Act, Sec. 1)*

b. *Monopolize, attempt to monopolize, or combine or conspire to monopolize trade (Sherman Act, Sec. 3)*

2. When and if the effect may be substantially to lessen competition or tend to create a monopoly, it is illegal to:

a. *Acquire the stock of competing corporations (Clayton Act, Sec. 7)*

b. *Acquire the assets of competing corporations (Clayton Act, Sec. 7, as amended by the Antimerger Act in 1950)*

c. *Enter exclusive and tying contracts (Clayton Act, Sec. 3)*

d. *Discriminate unjustifiably among purchasers (Clayton Act, Sec. 2, as amended by Robinson-Patman Act, Sec. 1)*

3. In general, it is also illegal to:

a. *Engage in particular forms of price discrimination (Robinson-Patman Act, Sec. 1 and 3)*

b. *Serve as a director of competing corporations of a certain minimum size (Clayton Act, Sec. 8)*

c. *Use unfair methods of competition (Federal Trade Commission Act, Sec. 5)*

d. *Use unfair or deceptive acts or practices (Federal Trade Commission Act, Sec. 5, as amended by Wheeler-Lea Act, Sec. 3)*

Thus the laws taken as a whole are designed not only to prevent the growth of monopoly, but to maintain competition as well.

Box 4

The "Rule of Reason"

*The Sherman Act outlawed **every** contract, combination, and conspiracy in restraint of trade. In both the Standard Oil and the American Tobacco cases of 1911—which were among the most famous in the history of antitrust—the Supreme Court upheld the government. But it went on to write the "rule of reason" into law, contending that a distinction should be made between "good" trusts and "bad" trusts.*

Judicial interpretations have been crucial in determining the applications and effects of the antitrust laws. Hence, we shall attempt to sketch briefly some of the major issues, court decisions, and leading trends that have emerged in the past few decades—confining ourselves for the most part to the years since World War II.

Restrictive Agreements— Conspiracies

The state of the law as to restrictive agreements or conspiracies of virtually any type among competitors is reasonably clear, and the courts have almost always upheld the government in such cases. In general, a *restrictive agreement* is regarded by the government as a conspiracy of firms that results in a restraint of trade among separate companies. It is usually understood to involve a direct or indirect, overt or implied, form of price fixing, output control, market sharing, or exclusion of competitors by boycotts or other coercive practices. It makes no difference whether the agreement was accomplished through a formal organization such as a trade association, informally, or even by habitual identity of behavior frequently referred to as *conscious parallel action,* i.e., identical price behavior among competitors. It is the effect, more than the means, that is judged.

For instance, in a major case against the American Tobacco Company in 1946, it was charged that the "big three" cigarette producers exhibited striking uniformity in the prices they paid for tobacco and in the prices they charged for cigarettes, as well as in other practices. Despite the fact that not a shred of evidence was produced to indicate that a common plan had even so much as been proposed, the Court declared that conspiracy "may be found in a course of dealings or other circumstances as well as in an exchange of words"; hence the companies were held in violation of the law [328 U.S. 781, 810]. Thus:

No secret meetings in a smoke-filled room and no signatures in blood are needed to prove the conspiracy provisions of the Sherman Act. Any type of agreement, explicit or implicit, any practice, direct or indirect, or even any action with the knowledge that others will act likewise to their mutual self-interest, is likely to be interpreted as illegal if it results in exclusion of competitors from the market, restriction of output or of purchases, division of markets, price fixing, elimination of the opportunity or incentive to compete, or coercion.

The doctrine of conscious parallel action has been partially repudiated by judges in more recent cases. However, it still remains as a fairly significant antitrust barometer, although it has not often been employed since the American Tobacco case of 1946.

THE ELECTRICAL EQUIPMENT CASE

In February, 1961, one of the most significant antitrust cases in the history of the United States was concluded. Nearly $2 million in fines were levied on the electrical equipment industry, and seven executives were jailed for terms of 30 days. Several dozen companies, including General Electric and Westinghouse, and a number of corporate officials were charged with unlawful price-fixing and dividing the market.

Though the fines were huge, it was the jail sentences that were more remarkable. For, although sending men to jail is not unheard of in antitrust cases, it is unusual—especially when the individuals are "pillars of the community."

NOTE. From 1890 to 1959 a total of about 200 people had received prison sentences for violating the Sherman Act. Most of these were union members and petty racketeers, and a few were wartime spies. Only seven were businessmen, all of whom received suspended prison sentences. Thus, until 1959, no important businessman ever spent a day in jail for violating the Sherman Act.

In 1959, however, a Federal District Court in Columbus, Ohio, decided that four officials of garden tool companies who pleaded *nolo contendere* (no contest or no defense) to price-fixing charges should not, as was typically the case, get off merely with fines and lectures. Accordingly, even though the government (Department of Justice) had not sought jail terms, the judge nevertheless gave 90-day sentences to each of the four.

At this time, the government was also conducting its investigation of the electrical industry, and these jail sentences encouraged formerly reluctant witnesses to "volunteer" information to the grand jury in hopes of obtaining immunity from criminal prosecution.

As brought out in the electrical case, the various conspiracies were remarkably well organized, involving regular meetings of executives in resorts and hotel rooms, coded communications, and complicated formulas for rigging bids on government contracts. Although many newspapers and periodicals throughout the world carried editorials on the matter, one of the better and more comprehensive accounts is given in Exhibit 2.

Since the electrical equipment case, there have been further indications in other cases that the courts will continue to strike down all types of restrictive agreements with increasing vigor—even to the extent of imposing jail sentences if fines alone seem to be inadequate. If this seems to be too severe a punishment, the words spoken by Judge Ganey when he imposed sentence on the electrical company executives are worth thinking about:

> This is a shocking indictment of a vast section of our economy, for what is really at stake here is the survival of the kind of economy under which America has grown to greatness, the free enterprise system. The conduct of the corporate and individual defendants alike . . . flagrantly mocked the image of the economic system of free enterprise which we profess to the country and destroyed the model which we offer today as a free world alternative to state control and eventual dictatorship.

Exhibit 2

The Great Electrical Conspiracy

In a tense and packed Philadelphia courtroom a drama took place that U.S. business will long remember—to its shame. The cases before him, said Federal District Judge J. Cullen Ganey, were "a shocking indictment of a vast section of our economy." They were more than that. They showed clearly that the executives of a mighty industry, publicly devoted to the concept of competition, had privately conspired to rig prices to the detriment of their customers on a scale so vast that it embraced everything from the Tennessee Valley Authority to the private utilities that supply the nation's light and power.

Up for sentencing were 29 electrical equipment companies, headed by the industry's two "competitive" giants, General Electric and Westinghouse, and 44 of their executives. Earlier, faced with incontrovertible evidence gathered by the Eisenhower Administration's relentless trustbusters, the companies and individuals had pleaded guilty or nolo contendere *(no contest) to charges that they conspired over a period of seven years (1953–60) to fix prices and rig bids in the sale of some $7 billion worth of heavy electrical equipment.*

One by one, lawyers rose to describe their clients as pillars of the community. But despite pleas attesting to the public usefulness and position of the defendants, the federal judge handed out the greatest number of jail terms ever in an antitrust proceeding. He also fined the 29 electrical companies a total of $1,787,000, levied fines ranging from $1,000 to $12,500 on various executives and gave 21 other executives suspended 30-day jail sentences—advising some that they would also have gone to jail except for reasons of age and health.

IDENTICAL BIDS. *The government said that the conspiracy had been going on for nearly 25 years. The companies involved might have got away with it even longer had not TVA become aroused over a succession of almost identical bids for turbogenerators. It tipped off the Justice Department, which began digging into the conspiracy in 1959.*

The threads wove a fantastic pattern. Top electrical equipment executives, gathering together at conventions or in hotels, homes and resorts, worked out common prices, split up markets as if they were personal property, and devised ingenious systems for rigging bids on contracts, such as the "phase of the moon" system in which each firm knew when to bid low or high, taking its turn in rotation at the low bid. With most of the industry represented, the conspiracy directly or indirectly affected almost every dam built, every power generator installed and every electrical distribution system set up in the United States, even reached into the new and vital field of atomic energy.

Many of the executives complained that they had to go along with the conspiracy if they hoped to keep their jobs or have a chance for promotion. Some, even after indictment, openly defended what they had done. F. F. Loock, president and general sales manager of Milwaukee's Allen-Bradley Co., who was slapped with a $7,500 fine and whose company was fined $40,000, maintained that "no one attending the gatherings was so stupid he didn't know they were in violation of the law." Then he added, in a surprising non sequitur: "But it is the only way a business can be run. It is free enterprise."

SOURCE: Adapted with changes from *Time*, February 17, 1961.

Combination and Monopoly

Concerning monopoly, the state of the law is less certain and the position of the courts less consistent than in cases involving restrictive agreements. There are three aspects of the problem to be considered: monopoly per se; vertical and horizontal mergers; and conglomerate mergers.

MONOPOLY PER SE

There has been a fundamental change in the attitude of the courts since 1945. Before then the courts held that the mere size of a corporation, no matter how impressive, is no offense; it required "unreasonable" behavior in the form of actual exertion of monopoly power, as shown by unfair practices, for a firm to be in violation of the law. This has been called the *rule of reason* or, what is roughly equivalent, the "good trust versus bad trust" criterion.

But the decisions handed down in various antitrust cases since 1945 have reversed this outlook almost completely. In the case against the Aluminum Company of America in 1945, in which Judge Learned Hand turned the trend in judicial thinking on monopoly [148 F 2d 416], it was the Court's opinion that:

1. To gain monopolistic power even by growing with the market, i.e., by reinvesting earnings rather than by combining with others, is nevertheless illegal.

2. The mere size of a firm *is* an offense, for the power to abuse and the abuse of power are inextricably intertwined (pp. 427–28).

3. The Company's market share was 90 percent and that "is enough to constitute a monopoly; it is doubtful whether 60 or 64 percent would be enough; and certainly 33 percent is not" (p. 424).

4. The good behavior of the Company which, prior to 1945, would have been an acceptable defense to the Court, is no longer valid, for "Congress did not condone 'good' trusts and condemn 'bad' ones; it forbade all" (p. 427).

With this decision, Judge Learned Hand greatly tempered the "rule of reason" criterion that had been used since the Standard Oil case of 1911 (see Box 4 on page 469). Subsequent court decisions have not repudiated his doctrines, although they have softened them somewhat. At the present time, the judgment of monopoly is based on such factors as the number and strength of the firms in the market, their effective size from the standpoint of technological development and competition with substitutes and with foreign trade, national security interests in maintaining strong productive facilities and maximum scientific research, and the public's interest in lower costs and uninterrupted production.

The Aluminum Company case was a major milestone in the history of antitrust. It suggests that monopoly *may* be held illegal without requiring proof of intent and even if the power were lawfully acquired; and the power may be condemned even if never abused, especially if it tends to limit or bar market access to other firms.

MERGERS

A *merger* is an amalgamation of two or more firms under one ownership. It may result from one of three types of integration:

1. *Vertical mergers,* which unite, under one ownership, unlike plants engaged in various stages of production from raw materials to finished products. They may take the form of forward integration into buyer markets or backward integration into supplier markets. They may result in greater economies by combining different production stages and regularizing supplies, thereby increasing profit margins.

2. *Horizontal mergers,* which unite, under one ownership, like plants engaged in like products. The products may be close or moderate substitutes (e.g., cement plants; tin cans and jars). The objective is to round out a product line which is sold through the same distribution channels, thereby offering joint economies in selling and distribution efforts.

3. *Conglomerate mergers,* which unite, under one ownership, unlike plants producing unrelated products. They reflect a desire by the acquiring company to spread risks, find outlets for idle capital funds, add products which can be sold with the firm's merchandising knowledge and skills, or simply to gain greater economic power on a broader front.

Although the courts have often upheld the government by disapproving of mergers that resulted in a substantial lessening of competition or tendency toward monopoly—regardless of the type of merger involved—the changes in the law on corporate acquisition made in the Celler Antimerger Act of 1950 were given specific meaning in a landmark 1962 decision by the Supreme Court known as the Brown Shoe Case.

In this case, involving both horizontal and vertical merger, the Supreme Court ruled against the defendant. The Brown Shoe Co. was the nation's fourth-largest shoe manufacturer with 4 percent of the industry's total, and it also controlled a number of retail outlets. Seven years earlier in 1955, it had merged with the G. R. Kinney Corporation, which operates the nation's largest retail shoe chain, accounting for 1.2 percent of national shoe sales and also serving as the nation's twelfth-largest shoe manufacturer. Chief Justice Warren spoke for the Court in upholding a federal district court's decision ordering Brown to divest itself of Kinney. He pointed out that despite the relatively small market shares of the companies:

1. The vertical aspect of the merger of Brown's manufacturing facilities with Kinney's retail outlets would likely "foreclose competition from a substantial share of the markets for men's, women's, and children's shoes, without producing any countervailing competitive, economic, or social advantages."

2. The horizontal aspect of the merger—the marriage of Brown's retailing outlets with those of Kinney—involved a retail market that could be the entire nation, or a single metropolitan area. "The fact that two merging firms have competed directly on the horizontal level in but a fraction of the geographic markets in which either has operated does not, in itself, place their merger outside the scope of Section 7" of the Clayton Act. The Court must recognize "Congress' desire to promote competition through the protection of viable, small, locally owned businesses."

On the basis of this and other cases, the following conclusion seems plausible:

The government's policy is not to wage an all-out war on mergers in general. Instead, it applies its own judgement to the merits of each situation. However, both vertical and horizontal mergers are likely to be declared illegal unless the companies can clearly demonstrate that the mergers will tend to increase competition (as when a few small or weak firms in an oligopolistic industry merge in order to compete more effectively with the giants in the industry) and thus promote the public interest.

Conglomerate or "circular" mergers, where the merging firms are neither competitors nor have a supplier-customer relationship, have proved to be the most popular form of combination since the early 1950s. Some outstanding examples have been Ling-Temco-Vought, or LTV, which acquired airline, computer technology, basic steel, aerospace, electronics, car rental, meat-packing, and sporting-goods firms; and Boise Cascade, which owns lumber, mobile homes, plastics, computer services, and land-development companies. In addition, some other well-known conglomerates are International Telephone and Telegraph, Gulf and Western, Litton Industries, and Radio Corporation of America.

Conglomerate mergers raise many difficult antitrust issues. Some may be settled in the years to come as the government devotes increasing attention to the "conglomerate problem" posed in Exhibit 3. Until then the most that can be said is that according to the general trend of antitrust attitudes:

☐ Internal growth is preferable to growth by merger.

☐ Any merger, no matter how small, in a concentrated or oligopolistic industry like automobiles, chemicals, or steel, will be subjected to an evaluation.

☐ Any industry which has ever been charged with price-fixing will automatically draw attention on a matter of mergers.

☐ Mergers on the part of top companies within industries, as well as between industries, will be scrutinized.

☐ The larger a company, the more carefully it will be watched, especially if it seeks merger in an industry characterized by small companies.

In short, the antitrusters and the Supreme Court are likely to look with disfavor at a merger when the industry is concentrated, entry into the market is dif-

Exhibit 3

The Conglomerate Movement

In July, 1968, the Federal Trade Commission made the following announcement about the increasing number of conglomerate mergers:

There is growing concern on the part of the Commission, as well as congressional committees, as to the long-run dangers of the continuation of the conglomerate merger movement.

The Commission has already conducted investigations to cover not only the short-run anticompetitive aspects of such mergers, but also broader issues, including the relationship between conglomerate mergers and technical or business efficiencies, the economic performance of conglomerate firms in the marketplace, and the effect of conglomerate mergers on the competitive vigor of enterprises by their change in status from independent firms to subsidiaries or divisions of conglomerates, *and the impact of such structural changes on long-run competitive activity.*

A review will be made of recent merger developments in the light of the basic increases in the concentration of economic power, to encourage internal growth as a competition-promoting process, to preserve the competitive opportunities of medium-size and small businesses and to eliminate monopolistic tendencies in their incipient stages.

The study will also explore various causes of mergers and whether new legislation may be necessary to bring the conglomerate merger movement under control.

After the completion of the staff investigation, the Commission plans to hold a public hearing on this matter.

The Big Conglomerates
(Acquisitions of manufacturing and mining firms with assets of $10 million or more, by type of acquisition, 1948–1967)

The Tidal Wave of Mergers
(Number of manufacturing and mining concerns acquired, 1948–1968)

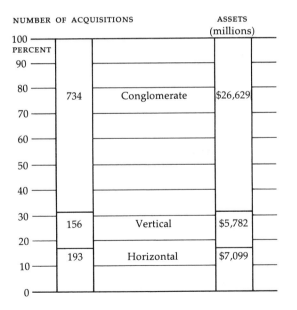

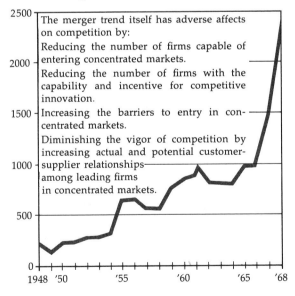

Exhibit 3 (continued)

The Stepup in Takeovers of Large Companies
(Acquisitions of manufacturing and mining firms with assets of $10 million or more, 1948–1968)

NUMBER OF ACQUISITIONS

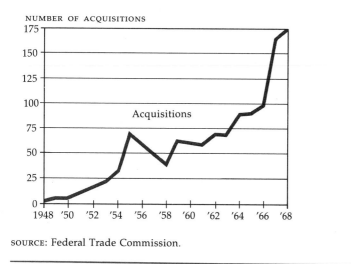

BILLIONS OF DOLLARS

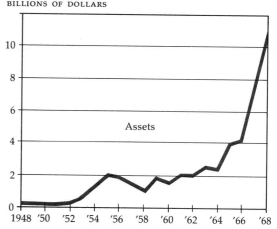

SOURCE: Federal Trade Commission.

ficult, the firm being eliminated is a particularly **vigorous** competitor, there is a merger trend in the industry, or one or both of the companies are large in relation to competitors.

Patents

The Constitution of the United States (Art. 1, Sec. 8, Par. 8) empowers Congress "To promote the progress of Science and useful Arts, by securing for limited Times to Authors and Inventors the exclusive Right to their respective Writings and Discoveries. . . ." Though this power was not denied to the states, it came in time to be exercised solely by the federal government, and upon this authority the American patent and copyright system is based.

What are the economic implications of patents?

A *patent* is an exclusive right conferred by a government on an inventor, for a limited time period. It authorizes the inventor to make, use, transfer, or withhold his invention, which he might do even without a patent, but it also gives him the right to exclude others or to admit them on his own terms, which he can do only with a patent.

Patents thus promote invention by granting temporary monopolies to inventors. But the patent system, it is held, has also been employed as a means of controlling output, dividing markets, and fixing prices of entire industries. Since these perversions of the patent law have a direct effect on competition, they have been criticized by the antitrusters, and the courts have increasingly limited the scope and abuses of patent monopoly. Among the chief issues have been the standard of patentability, the right of nonuse by the patentee, the use of tying contracts, the employment of restrictive licenses, and the practices of cross-licensing and patent pooling. The trends based on court decisions in each of these areas may be sketched briefly.

STANDARD OF PATENTABILITY

The chief standard employed by the courts is the so-called "flash of genius" test. Thus, in the Cuno Engineering Corporation case in 1941, involving the patentability of a wireless lighter, Justice Douglas, speaking for the Court, said that usefulness and novelty alone do "not necessarily make the device patentable. . . . The device must not only be 'new and useful,' it must also be an 'invention' or 'discovery.' . . . The new device, however useful it may be, must reveal the *flash of creative genius*, not merely the skill of the calling. If it fails, it has not established its right to a private grant on the public domain." (314 U.S. 84, 91; italics supplied.)

The flash of genius test has been criticized as resting on the subjective judgment of the Court, and as not taking sufficient recognition of inventions that are the product of teams rather than individuals, especially in large corporations. In response to these arguments, Congress passed the Patent Act of 1952 which provides that a formula, method, or device, in order to be patentable, must be "new" in that it must be unknown to the public prior to the patent application, or it must be "useful" in that it evidences a substantial degree of technical advance in the object invented or in the process of producing something. But the courts have not found in the Act an adequate definition of "invention" and continue to rely on case law and their own judgment in determining what constitutes an invention. It appears, therefore, that the flash of genius test, tempered perhaps by the political and economic attitudes of the courts with respect to the public interest, will be the chief criterion of patentability.

RIGHT OF NONUSE

The right of a patentee to withhold an invention from use has been upheld by the courts. In numerous cases tried since the turn of the century, the courts have viewed a patent as a form of private property and hence have upheld the patentee's right to refuse putting it to use. In response, it has been argued by some that a patent is a privilege and not a right, that the practice of nonuse may result in retarding technological progress and economic development, and hence that the courts should exercise more judgment and discretion in such cases. And even the courts in recent decades have spoken of patents as privileges contingent upon the enhancement of public welfare. But the right of nonuse appears nevertheless to be supported by the law, for as stated by the Supreme Court in the Hartford Empire case in 1945: "A patent owner is not . . . under any obligation to see that the public acquires the free right to use the invention.

He has no obligation either to use it or to grant its use to others." (323 U.S. 386.)

What do you think? Is a patent a privilege or a right? Would our economy be better off if the law were changed so that it specifically prohibited the right of nonuse?

TYING CONTRACTS

A seller uses a *tying contract* (or tie-in sale) to require the buyer to purchase one or more additional or "tied" products as a condition for purchasing the desired or "tying" product. For the tie-in sale to be effective, the major or tying product must be difficult to substitute, not easily dispensed with, and relatively more inelastic in demand than the subsidiary or tied item. A good example occurs in block-bookings of motion pictures in which movie theaters are required to take a certain number of grade B films as a condition for obtaining grade A films. Many other examples can be cited.

An ideal opportunity for tie-in sales exists when the seller possesses an exclusive and essential patent. A classic example is the United Shoe Machinery Co., which once compelled shoemakers to purchase other materials and intermediate products as a condition for purchasing shoe machinery. In the United case as well as in a number of subsequent cases involving such firms as Radio Corporation of America, International Business Machines, and International Harvester, the courts have struck down tying contracts that were found substantially to lessen competition within the meaning of the Clayton Act. On the whole, the trend of the courts is to disallow a tying contract of any kind, regardless of circumstances, when they believe its effect is to extend the scope of a patent monopoly, or cause substantial injury—or even the probability of such injury—to competition.

NOTE. An extreme example was Eastman Kodak prior to 1954. The company sold amateur color film at a price which included the charge for finishing, thereby tying the sale of the film itself to the provision of finishing services. In 1954 the company signed a decree, agreeing to sell the film alone and thus admit competitors to the finishing business.

RESTRICTIVE LICENSING

Under a *restrictive license*, a patentee sells a patented

product to a licensee on restricted conditions. Typically, the restrictions include the patentee's fixing the geographic area of the licensee, his level of output, or the price he may charge in selling the patented good. Usually such licensing is motivated by considerations of reciprocal favor (e.g., the exchange of patents among competitors) or perhaps performed for the purpose of minimizing the incentive of the licensee to develop an alternative process. In any case, three major trends based on various court cases may be noted:

1. The right of a patentee to fix the licensee's prices on patented products has been and still is upheld by the courts.

2. The right of the patentee to fix the prices charged for unpatented products made by patented processes (e.g., a patented machine) has been doubtful since the 1940s.

3. The use of restrictive licensing is illegal when employed for the purpose of eliminating competition among many licensees.

In general, the extent to which a patent owner may license his patent is limited quite strictly. When each of several licensees accepts restrictive terms on condition or with the knowledge that others will do likewise, they are committing a conspiracy in restraint of trade in the opinion of the Court and hence are guilty of violating the law.

CROSS-LICENSING AND PATENT POOLING

Various "sharing" devices such as the cross-licensing of patents or the pooling of patents for mutual benefit are not held to be illegal as such, but they generally are declared illegal when, in the eyes of the courts, they are used as a means of eliminating competition among patent owners and licensees. But what constitutes elimination of competition? In the Hartford Empire case, decided in 1945, it was held that Hartford employed the patents in its pool to dominate completely the glass container industry, curtail output, divide markets, and fix prices through restrictive licenses, and therefore this was unlawful conspiracy. In the National Lead case in 1947, a cross-licensing agreement that divided markets and fixed the prices of titanium pigment was also declared illegal. And in the Line Material case of 1948, the Court was most emphatic in its denunciation of a cross-licensing arrangement that fixed the price of fuse cutouts used in electric circuits.

On the whole, it appears that although patent pooling per se is not illegal (the automobile industry being frequently cited as an outstanding example of successful and desirable patent pooling), the courts will declare that abuse exists either when the pool is restricted to certain competitors or available only at excessive royalty payments, or when the pool is used as a device to cross-license competitors for the purpose of fixing prices and allocating markets.

CONCENTRATION OF PATENT OWNERSHIP

Patent concentration within a single firm has been frowned on increasingly since the late 1940s. Prior to that time, the ownership of many patents by a single firm was held to be legal. Since then, the courts have held that the concentration of patents by a dominant firm in an industry—regardless of whether the firm's patents were achieved by research, assignment, or purchase—may constitute monopolization and hence violate the antitrust laws *even if the firm did nothing illegal and did not use the patents to hinder or suppress competition.*

The courts have provided strong remedies in such cases. These include: compulsory licensing, sometimes on a royalty-free basis for a company's existing patents, and on a reasonable royalty basis for future patents; and the provision of necessary know-how in the form of detailed written manuals and even technical consultants, available at nominal charges, to licensees and competitors.

NOTE. Thus Eastman Kodak agreed to provide other color-film finishers with up-to-date manuals on its processing technology and to provide technical representatives to assist competitors in using the methods described. In a number of other cases involving Standard Oil of New Jersey, the Aluminum Company of America, Merck & Co., A. B. Dick, Libbey-Owens-Ford, Owens-Corning Fiberglas, American Can, and General Electric, as well as several dozen other firms, somewhat similar provisions have been arrived at since the forties.

Hundreds of patents involving a wide variety of manufacturing areas have thus been freed, and it is to be expected that the courts will continue to move in this direction in future years.

Trademarks

The purpose of a trademark, as originally conceived, was to identify the origin or ownership of a product. In an economic sense, however, managements have come to look upon trademarks as a strategic device for establishing product differentiation and, through advertising, strong consumer preference. In this way firms have sometimes been able to establish a degree of market entrenchment that has remained substantially unrivaled for as long as several decades. Moreover, by establishing product differentiation through trademarks, firms have exploited this advantage in various ways with the aim of enhancing long-run profits. Five examples may be noted in view of their antitrust significance.

Price Discrimination. This has been implemented by the use of trademarks. Rohm & Haas sold methyl methacrylate as Lucite and Crystalite to manufacturers at 85 cents per pound, and as Veronite and Crystalex to dentists at $45 per pound. A decision rendered in 1948 was made against the company for using trademarks in this discriminatory manner.

Output Control. Output control can be accomplished through the use of trademarks. United States Pipe and Foundry licensed companies to produce under its patents at graduated royalty rates on condition that they stamp their products with the trade name "de Lavaud." The decision, rendered in 1948, was against the company for using a trademark in controlling output.

Exclusive Markets. These can be attained through the use of trademarks. General Electric was able to persuade procurement agencies to establish specifications requiring the use of Mazda bulbs. It licensed Westinghouse to use the name but denied its other licensees the same right. A decision against General Electric was rendered in 1949 on the grounds that the company had used the trademark as a device for excluding competitors from markets.

Market Sharing. Market sharing cartels have been accomplished through the use of trademarks. A *cartel* (sometimes called an "international monopoly") is an international association of firms in the same industry, established for the purpose of allocating world markets among its members and regulating prices in those markets. Thus a cartel member may be granted the exclusive right to use a trademark in his own territory. If he oversteps his market boundary, he is driven back by an infringement suit. Trade names that have provided examples of such regional monopolies include Mazda, Mimeograph, Merck, and Timken, and the trademarks of General Storage Battery, New Jersey Zinc, American Bosch, and S.K.F. Industries.

Since the 1940s, the courts have found such arrangements to be in violation of the Sherman Act. In establishing remedies, they have sometimes forbidden cartel members to grant their foreign partners exclusive trademark rights abroad, to sell in American markets, and to interfere with American imports.

Resale Price Maintenance. This practice, popularly referred to as "fair trade," permits the manufacturer or distributor of a branded product to set the minimum retail price at which that product can be sold, thereby eliminating price competition for the good at the retail level. This practice, though no longer as significant as it was prior to the 1950s, has been implemented by the use of trademarks even where patents and copyrights have failed.

The Evidence on Concentration

We have examined the antitrust laws and their application. Some basic questions that remain to be answered are: (1) To what extent does monopoly power exist in the United States? (2) What should public policy be with respect to competition and monopoly?

HOW MUCH CONCENTRATION IS THERE?

The growth and importance of big business in the United States have resulted in charges, frequently made and widely believed, that: (1) economic power is concentrated in the hands of a few corporate giants, (2) this concentration has grown over the years, and therefore (3) there has been a general "decline of competition." Upon close examination the evidence shows the first to be only partially true, and the second and third to be highly debatable if not unfounded. Let us see why.

A measure which is extensively used by economists and the antitrust agencies to evaluate the extent of competition in an industry is the *concentration ratio;* this is simply the percentage of an industry's output accounted for by its four leading firms. An illustration of such ratios for a variety of different industries is presented in Exhibit 4.

Many studies of this kind have been done since the early thirties by economists working in universities and in research organizations like the Brookings Institution in Washington, D.C., and the National Industrial Conference Board in New York. Their purpose has been to discover the concentration of assets, employment, income, and sales in large firms. The groups studied have included nonbanking corporations, manufacturing as a whole, particular manufacturing industries, and the output of manufactured products.

Has the long-run trend of concentration been increasing, stable, or decreasing? A synthesis of various studies indicates that:

1. The trends of big business, both in number and in size, have grown at a rate proportional to the economy as a whole.

2. The 500 largest corporations in the economy (listed annually by *Fortune* magazine) are dynamic; many new firms are added each year and many old firms are dropped. However, in the more concentrated industries, the largest firms tend to remain.

3. The overall pattern of concentration ratios for manufacturing as a whole has exhibited two long-run trends: (*a*) a slight decrease for the period 1900 to 1946; (*b*) stability or possibly a slight increase from 1947 to 1960, and perhaps a moderate increase since then, although the evidence is extremely murky and is currently under analysis by many economists in and out of government.

4. Some manufacturing industries like transportation, communication, and finance have a moderate to high degree of concentration, while the trade and service industries are characterized by a low degree of concentration.

5. Over any long period of time, some concentration figures for individual industries, product groups, and product classes will rise while others fall; hence

---

Exhibit 4

Concentration Ratios: Percentages of Industry Output Produced by Firms In Ten Selected Low-Concentration and High-Concentration Industries

Output measured by value of shipments

Low-concentration industries	Percent of industry output produced by: four largest firms	twenty largest firms
Veneer and plywood	26	50
Jewelry, precious metal	23	38
Men's and boy's suits and coats	17	59
Metal furniture	14	40
Upholstered furniture	14	31
Setup paperboard boxes	12	32
Wood furniture	12	29
Millinery	12	27
Women's and misses suits, coats	12	22
Women's and misses dresses	7	14

High-concentration industries	Percent of industry output produced by four largest firms
Primary aluminum	100
Locomotives and parts	97
Motor vehicles	92
Telephone and telegraph equipment	92
Electric lamps	91
Steam engines and turbines	88
Synthetic fibers	86
Cigarettes	81
Sewing machines	81
Gypsum products	80

SOURCE: U.S. Bureau of Census, Census of Manufacturers, 1967, Special Report Series: *Concentration Ratios in Manufacturing,* M67(S)-2.1, Table 5.

it is extremely difficult if not impossible to say whether the trend of concentration in the economy as a whole has been increasing, stable, or decreasing.

What can be said about the validity of concentration figures in general? The problem is much more complicated than is readily apparent. The main difficulties are outlined in Exhibit 5.

WHICH FUTURE POLICY FOR ANTITRUST?

What policy should society adopt to encourage competition and discourage monopoly? Three major approaches that have been suggested are: (1) public regulation or ownership of large-scale firms; (2) vigorous enforcement of the antitrust laws; and (3) revision of the antitrust laws to make competition more "workable."

Public Regulation and Ownership

Some economic and political reformers have argued that the "engine of monopoly" has overtaken the American economy. As a result, American industry is dominated by large firms with strong monopoly powers, the consequence of which is serious misallocation of society's resources.

Some who take this position—especially those

Exhibit 5

What Do Concentration Ratios Really Tell You?

Do concentration ratios measure "monopoly power"? The answer is no, because the results can differ according to the way in which the calculations are made.

CHOICE OF BASE. *The degree of concentration will vary depending on the base chosen, such as all businesses, all manufacturing, all corporations, all nonfinancial corporations, all industries, and so on. The concentration figures for all nonbanking corporations include, for instance, railroads and utilities whose monopolistic powers are regulated by public agencies and whose assets amount to half the assets of the 200 largest corporations; they also include several firms operating in highly competitive industries (e.g., A&P; Macy's; Sears, Roebuck) as well as other firms that do not necessarily exercise significant control over their output and input markets. The figures, therefore, do not indicate the real degrees of unregulated monopoly.*

CHOICE OF UNIT. *The degree of concentration will vary depending on the unit of measurement chosen, such as a plant or a firm, or a single-product or multiple-product firm. The figures apply to a heterogeneous conglomeration of industries some of which are highly competitive, some that are moderately so, and some that are virtually monopolized. Further, the ratios are obscured because they pertain to the three, four, six, or eight largest firms in an industry, without revealing the degree of domination by a single firm. The ratios thus disclose little as to the extent of competition or monopoly.*

CHOICE OF INDEX. *Still another factor affecting the measure of concentration is the index of concentration used, such as assets, employment, output, income, or sales. The concentration ratios by industries are normally based on the Census of Manufacturers' classification, in which industries are defined, in part, by the materials and processes they employ. Accordingly, some firms producing noncompeting products are grouped in one industry, while others producing competing products are grouped in separate industries. Similarly, the ratios for particular goods are based upon a classification that defines products, in part, by the materials, fabrication processes, and degree of manufacturing integration involved in their production, so that the result may be multiple listings for a single commodity. In some cases, the concentration ratio is seriously understated because the output figures are national and markets are regional, or because heterogeneous goods are lumped together into a single category. In some cases the ratios are greatly overstated because the figures are limited to domestic production with competition from imports ignored, and because readily substitutable products are listed in unrelated categories. Thus the data on concentration reveal little either as to the structure of markets for particular goods or as to the index of concentrated power.*

CONCLUSION. *It is apparent, therefore, that measures of economic concentration are not measures of "monopoly power," as is often contended. At best, these measures may reveal the results of monopolistic restriction or collusion, or of innovation, market development, and lower costs and prices. But they may also conceal the influence of potential competition, and the existence—on the other side of the market—of countervailing power.*

---

with strong socialist leanings—argue in favor of greater public regulation or even public ownership of large-scale monopolies and oligopolies. (We will have more to say about this view in a later chapter dealing with the nature of socialism.)

Vigorous Enforcement of the Laws

A second group composed of many academic economists and political leaders argues that the growth of monopolies and oligopolies has resulted from inadequate application of the antitrust laws. They believe that much more competition will be encouraged if these laws are vigorously enforced. This requires, of course, that Congress appropriate larger budgets to the antitrust agencies so that they can engage in more extensive and intensive investigations.

Supporters of this view have suggested that vigorous enforcement of the laws can be implemented by the antitrust agencies, the courts, and Congress in at least three ways:

1. The government should be willing to ask for, and the courts should be willing to order, dissolution (i.e., the breaking up of large firms into smaller competing firms) on a much broader scale than hitherto, especially if such dissolution would not impair the efficiency or rate of technological progress of large-scale firms. For example, it has often been suggested that Chevrolet Division should be separated from General Motors and established as an independent corporation.

2. Congress should eliminate all exceptions to the antitrust laws so that labor unions, transport industries, etc., are no longer exempt.

3. Congress should consider revising the patent laws and other "protective" legislation (e.g., tariffs) which aid special-interest groups and strengthen their monopolistic position.

Revision of the Laws for More "Workable" Competition

Finally, another large group of economists and politicians denies that there is a significant absence of competition in big business. They argue that the antitrust laws were written too long ago to reflect the current structure of the economy, and hence may have to be revised to reflect the needs of our time.

Their position may be summarized briefly:

1. Numerous studies indicate that "effective" competition exists in large-scale enterprises and that the traditional assumptions of nineteenth-century (pure) competition are unrealistic and cannot be applied in our twentieth-century economy, characterized by rapid product development, market growth, and vast technological advancement. Firms compete with one another, and for the consumers' dollar, in many ways other than price—through service, convenience, quality, style, etc.—and so competition is of a "workable" form. It is only in the manufacturing sector of our economy that the problem of unregulated monopoly exists, and even here, as we have seen, the scope is narrowed down to a select group of industries where concentration is high.

2. The tendency of economic reformers to identify the major producers in these fields as monopolies merely because of their size only serves to distort the real nature of the problem. Production in these industries is characterized by a small number of large firms, so that the antitrust problem is one of *oligopoly*, not monopoly. And economic theory does not say that oligopoly is not fiercely competitive; it only states that there may be a stronger tendency to avoid price (as compared to nonprice) competition.

3. Therefore, if the antitrust laws are to preserve or even enhance the workability of competition in our economy, a fundamental revision of these laws is necessary. Moreover, the new or revised laws should be based on the competitive structure of today's oligopolistic economy. Thus, the various forms of nonprice competition should become relevant indicators of competitive behavior, rather than price competition alone, which is too often used by the antitrust agencies and the courts because it happens to be easier to observe and measure.

You may see some elements of truth in all these viewpoints. Of course, problems of enforcement and revision of the antitrust laws are decided in Washington by the administration and Congress. But as educated citizens who are concerned about the relations between business and government, it is our responsibility to be aware of the issues.

The Military-Industrial Complex

In his Farewell Address of January, 1961, President Dwight D. Eisenhower issued a grave warning to the American people:

> Until the latest of our world conflicts, the United States had no armaments industry. American makers of plowshares could, with time and as required, make swords as well.
>
> But we can no longer risk emergency improvisation of national defense. We have been compelled to create a permanent armaments industry of vast proportions. Added to this, three and a half million men and women are directly engaged in the defense establishment. We annually spend on military security alone more than the net income of all United States corporations.
>
> Now this conjunction of an immense military establishment and a large arms industry is new in the American experience. The total influence—economic, political, even spiritual—is felt in every city, every state house, every office of the Federal Government. We recognize the imperative need for this development. Yet we must not fail to comprehend its grave implications. Our toil, resources and livelihood are all involved; so is the very structure of our society.
>
> In the councils of Government, we must guard against the acquisition of unwarranted influence, whether sought or unsought, by the military-industrial complex. The potential for the disastrous rise of misplaced power exists and will persist.
>
> We must never let the weight of this combination endanger our liberties or democratic processes. We should take nothing for granted. Only an alert and knowledgeable citizenry can compel the proper meshing of the huge industrial and military machinery of defense with our peaceful methods and goals, so that security and liberty may prosper together.

At the time President Eisenhower spoke these words, no one in his wildest imagination foresaw that before the end of the decade the Pentagon would become what many conservative as well as liberal critics regard as one of the largest and most dangerous organizations ever created by man. For in spite of the fact that the nation's Founding Fathers clearly intended the military to be subservient to a civilian government, the Department of Defense has become almost the primary executive as well as legislative body of the federal government. With a staggering budget amounting to approximately half of every tax dollar (in 1969 it received $80 billion), the Department has built a defense establishment consisting of an elaborate network of friends and alliances that extends to every sector of society. Through congressmen and senators, colleges and universities, and corporate contractors and subcontractors, the Pentagon feeds money to military installations, finances research programs, and pays for the production of war goods. The recipients of these funds in turn lend their support to domestic and foreign military policies that are largely formulated by the Defense Department. In this way all the participants in the system feed upon each other.

This so-called *military-industrial complex* is by no means the product of evil minds. On the contrary, few critics would say that most of the individuals who make up the system are anything other than men of good will. The system has grown out of a combination of ignorance, a fear of military insecurity, an effort to get elected, and a desire to make money. All of these blended together have produced an elaborate defense establishment whose closest world rival is a similar and probably equally dangerous organism—the "Military-Presidium Complex" in the Soviet Union. For despite some opinions to the contrary, it is naive to believe that ignorance, fear, or the desire for personal aggrandizement and political patronage are less pronounced in Russia than in the United States.

NETWORKS OF PROBLEMS

The military-industrial complex has generated a variety of interrelated problems. Three of the key ones may be noted.

1. Disturbingly high overruns and waste frequently occur in defense spending—waste which Senator William Proxmire of Wisconsin documents in his well-known *Report From Wasteland* as amounting to over $10 billion annually. This arises, he says, from faulty military procurement policies, broad conflicts of interest, and a protective network of practices and traditions that have grown up between the Pentagon and Congress.

2. A "state management" system has emerged in the Department of Defense—a system which noted professor-critic Seymour Melman of Columbia University convincingly argues, in his *Pentagon Capitalism*, is much more than just an informal relation between high-ranking military officers, industrial executives, and congressmen. Instead it is one which has displaced the market with its own decision-making power on a scale so vast that it has become the single most powerful management in the United States. In this system, cost-minimization is of secondary importance, and there is ordinarily no market for testing the adequacy or price of key products.

3. Military work, instead of being widely dispersed, is concentrated by industry, geography, and occupation. Thus a half-dozen industries producing such goods as ordnance and accessories, machine shop products, electronic components, electrical machinery equipment, aircraft and parts, and transportation equipment have more than 25 percent of their labor force dependent on Pentagon orders; seven states—namely Massachusetts, Connecticut, New York, New Jersey, Texas, California, and Washington—account for more than half of all military industry; and 6 percent of the nation's workers (including 20 percent of its engineers) are engaged directly in defense work, while an additional 15 percent are indirectly dependent on Pentagon contracts. This high density of military effort means that any transfer of men and material from defense to civilian tasks is virtually impossible to accomplish without inflicting severe economic damage. Nor can fiscal and monetary policies be of much help in alleviating the situation, because they are *general* in their effects whereas the problems of conversion are localized.

These difficulties have many obvious ramifications, leading to what are more aptly described as entire networks of political and economic problems. Indeed, according to Senator Proxmire, the system's elements are so intermeshed that it should more appropriately be called a "military-industrial-bureaucratic-labor-intellectual-technical-academic-complex." And, because of its intricacy and vastness, he doubts that the complex can be changed without inflicting widespread pain and suffering.

Many views similar to Senator Proxmire's have been voiced by others. Perhaps most significant is the opinion expressed by Dr. Arthur Burns, a distinguished conservative economist and chairman of the Federal Reserve Board. The complex, he says (as reported in *Time,* June 1, 1970), "will remain a formidable factor in our economic and social life in the calculable future. It will continue to suggest to many foreign citizens, as it sometimes does even to our own, that our national prosperity is based on huge military spending, when, in fact, we could be much more prosperous without it."

WHAT CAN BE DONE ABOUT IT?

These pessimistic opinions—coming from respected liberals and conservatives alike—help to account for a growing uneasiness among many knowledgeable citizens. They view the present government decision-making process with alarm, and believe that the Department of Defense must be brought under control. There is already evidence to indicate that the nation is being hindered more than it is being helped in its efforts to improve the efficiency and effectiveness of its military policies. Although most critics have not clearly specified what should be done, a few steps which are feasible and would have broad economic as well as political implications may be suggested:

1. Foreign policy (which affects foreign economic aid) is strongly influenced by the Defense Department, and should be shifted entirely to the State Department and the President.

2. Authority for the procurement of military weapons and the granting of contracts for military research should be taken away from the Pentagon and placed in the hands of an independent civilian agency.

3. A system of "zero budgeting" should be introduced in the Budget Bureau, requiring all military programs to be reviewed annually from scratch.

4. Severe penalty systems should be instituted against military contractors who fail to meet contractual requirements and delivery dates, and against contractors as well as Pentagon officials who, according to Senator Proxmire, do not tell the complete

truth about the cost of weapons. In fact, says the Senator, "they deliberately lie about the cost."

Even these proposals, though relatively moderate, would require substantial Congressional reform. If adopted, they would save billions of dollars. It is unrealistic to assume that a day will come when there will be no defense establishment. However, if the establishment must exist, it can and should be made distinctly subservient *in fact* as well as in principle to the legislative and executive branches of our government.

SUMMARY OF IMPORTANT IDEAS

1. The antitrust laws are intended to curb monopoly and to maintain competition in the American economy. The chief antitrust laws are the Sherman Act, the Clayton Act, the Federal Trade Commission Act, the Robinson-Patman Act, the Wheeler-Lea Act, and the Celler Antimerger Act. Taken together and in a broad sense, they forbid restraint of trade, monopolization, price discrimination, and unfair competition. The major groups that are exempt from the antitrust laws are the transport industries and labor unions.

2. The courts have consistently struck down restrictive agreements or conspiracies in restraint of trade. With respect to combination and monopoly, however, the state of the law is less certain and the position of the courts less consistent. Various court decisions suggest that:

a. Monopoly *may* be held illegal, for the power to abuse, even if lawfully acquired and never exercised, is sufficient to rate condemnation.

b. Vertical and horizontal mergers will be disallowed unless they increase competition, as when the smaller or weaker firms in an oligopolistic industry merge so as to compete with the giants.

c. Conglomerate mergers may be held illegal, but the tests or standards of illegality remain to be established in future court cases.

3. Patent abuse and the power of patent monopoly have been significantly weakened in the past several decades. It appears that the courts will continue to move in the direction of preventing the abuses of the patent grant. Similarly, with respect to trademark abuse, the courts have acted increasingly to prevent the use of trademarks to promote price discrimination, market exclusion, and market sharing in the international sphere (i.e., cartel arrangements) among competitors.

4. Concentration ratios are typically used to evaluate the extent of "monopoly power." According to the available evidence, economic concentration in manufacturing may not be significantly greater today than it was in previous decades. In general, however, concentration ratios do not really measure monopoly power because the results can differ widely according to the way in which the calculations are made. The choice of base, unit, and index can all influence the outcome.

5. Three broad alternatives to antitrust policy consist of: (*a*) public regulation or ownership of large-scale monopolies and oligopolies; (*b*) more vigorous enforcement of the antitrust laws; (*c*) fundamental revisions of the antitrust laws to make competition more workable and to reflect the nature of oligopolistic competition in today's economy.

6. The military-industrial complex is a serious threat to our society. Many liberals and conservatives alike agree that the Defense Department exercises too strong an influence in business-government relations and that its power should be curbed by congressional action.

FOR HOMEWORK AND DISCUSSION

1. *Terms and concepts to review:*

antitrust laws	injunction
Sherman Antitrust Act (1890)	consent decree
	restrictive agreement
Clayton Antitrust Act (1914)	conscious parallel action
	rule of reason
unfair competition	merger
price discrimination	horizontal merger
interlocking directorate	vertical merger
Federal Trade Commission Act (1914)	conglomerate merger

Federal Trade Commission	patent
Robinson-Patman Act (1936)	tying contract
	restrictive license
Wheeler-Lea Act (1938)	cartel
Celler Antimerger Act (1950)	resale price maintenance
	concentration ratio

2. "The rationale underlying restrictive agreements among competitors is based on the potential danger arising from the existence of the power of sellers to manipulate prices. Where this power does not exist, the laws pertaining to restrictive agreements are practically meaningless. Thus, there is no point in holding unlawful an agreement among competitors to fix prices, allocate customers, or control production, when the competitors involved are so small that they lack significant power to affect market prices." Evaluate.

3. Suppose that tomorrow morning, all grocers in Chicago, without previous public notice, raised their prices for milk by 3 cents per quart. Does this action prove the existence of an agreement, or constitute an offense, on the part of the grocers? What would your answer be if the automobile manufacturers without notice announced a 5 percent price increase next year on all new model cars? Explain.

4. If all the companies in an oligopolistic industry quote identical prices without prior agreement by following the prices of the industry leader, is this evidence of a combination or conspiracy?

5. In an industry characterized by price leadership without prior arrangement, is there likely to be a charge of combination or conspiracy leveled against that industry if: (a) prevailing prices are announced by the industry's trade association rather than by a leading firm; (b) all firms in the industry report their prices to their industry trade association; (c) all firms in the industry quote prices on a basing point system, i.e., the delivered price is the leader's price plus rail freight from the leader's plant; (d) all firms follow the leader not only in price, but in product and sales policies as well? (These four questions should be answered as a group rather than individually.)

6. In the Columbia Steel case (1948), the Supreme Court said: "We do not undertake to prescribe any set of percentage figures by which to measure the reasonableness of a corporation's enlargement of its activities by the purchase of the assets of a competitor. The relative effect of percentage command of a market varies with the setting in which that factor is placed." Does this conflict with Judge Hand's statement in the ALCOA case? Explain.

7. "Since there are 'good' monopolies and 'bad' monopolies, a company should be judged by its total contribution to society—not by its market behavior alone." Do you agree? Explain.

8. "Many trustbusters and economists forget that *concentration is a function of consumer sovereignty,* and that the same consumers who make big businesses big can make them small or even wipe them out by simply refraining from the purchase of their products. This is a not-so-obvious principle of our free enterprise system which needs to be better understood." Do you agree? Explain.

9. "To say that the degree of competition depends on the number of sellers in the marketplace is like saying that football is more competitive than tennis." Do you agree? Explain: (HINT: Can you describe different forms of competition, in addition to price competition, that exist in American industry?)

10. Suppose that General Motors, the largest firm in the automobile industry, were to reduce prices on its automobiles to levels which yield only a "fair" profit for itself, but not for its competitors. As a result, consumer purchases shift to General Motors because of its lower prices, and the other automobile manufacturers subsequently find themselves driven out of business as a result of bankruptcy. In the light of the ALCOA case, would General Motors be guilty of monopolizing the market and hence violating the Sherman Act?

11. It is generally stated that growth, stability, and flexibility are three primary objectives of mergers.
a. With respect to growth, it has been said that "a firm, like a tree, must either grow or die." Evaluate this statement.

b. Why may instability be a motive for merger? Instability of what?

c. What is meant by flexibility as a motive for merger? (HINT: Compare flexibility vs. vulnerability.)

12. Section 7 of the Clayton Act of 1914 and its amendment, the Celler Antimerger Act of 1950, states:

> No corporation engaged in commerce shall acquire, directly or indirectly, the whole or any part of the stock or other share capital and no corporation subject to the jurisdiction of the Federal Trade Commission shall acquire the whole or any part of the assets of another corporation engaged also in commerce, where in any line of commerce in any section of the country, the affect of such acquisition may be substantially to lessen competition, or to tend to create a monopoly.

Assume that you are a business economist for a large corporation, and you are asked to prepare a report on why this legislation should be repealed. What main points would you bring out in your argument?

13. CASE PROBLEM: SHOULD MEDICAL DOCTORS BE LICENSED IN ORDER TO PRACTICE?

How about dentists, lawyers, and other professionals?

These questions usually take the great majority of people by surprise. After all, you ask, "Who in his right mind would want to allow unlicensed individuals to call themselves doctors and to practice medicine? That would be quackery, pure and simple!"

The fact is, however, that a number of distinguished scholars advocate precisely that, but they call it "free enterprise," not quackery. The question is really part of a larger issue dealing with the general purpose of licensing and the way it has been used as a device for restricting competition by keeping newcomers out of a field.

A summary of the subject as a whole makes for an interesting research project, or for a class report by an ambitious student. The following sources, and the references cited therein, may be used as a starter:

FARMER, RICHARD N., and KASSARJIAN, HAROLD H., "The Right to Compete," *California Management Review*, vol. VI, no. 1, Fall, 1963, pp. 61–68.

FRIEDMAN, MILTON, *Capitalism and Freedom*, University of Chicago Press, Chicago, 1962, chap. IX. Professor Friedman, one of America's foremost economists, opposes the licensing of doctors.

KESSEL, REUBEN A., "Price Discrimination in Medicine," *Journal of Law and Economics*, October, 1958, pp. 20–53.

MOORE, THOMAS G., "The Purpose of Licensing," *Journal of Law and Economics*, October, 1961, pp. 93–117.

REFERENCES AND READING SUGGESTIONS

BAUMGARTNER, JOHN STANLEY, *The Lonely Warriors*, Nash Publishing, Los Angeles, Calif., 1970. A defense of the military-industrial complex.

CAVES, RICHARD, *American Industry: Structure, Conduct, Performance*, 2d ed., Prentice-Hall, New York, 1967, chap. 4.

EINHORN, HENRY ADLER, and WILLIAM PAUL SMITH, *Economic Aspects of Antitrust: Readings and Cases*, Random House, New York, 1968.

LENS, SIDNEY, *The Military Industrial Complex*, Pilgrim Press, 1970.

MELMAN, SEYMOUR, *Pentagon Capitalism*, McGraw-Hill, New York, 1970.

MUND, VERNON, *Government and Business*, 4th ed., Harper & Row, New York, 1965.

PROXMIRE, WILLIAM, *Report From Wasteland*, Praeger, New York, 1970.

SICHEL, WERNER (ed.), *Industrial Organization and Public Policy: Selected Readings*, Houghton-Mifflin, Boston, 1967.

STELZER, IRWIN M., *Selected Antitrust Cases*, 3d ed., Irwin, Homewood, Illinois, 1966.

WILCOX, CLAIR, *Public Policies Toward Business*, 3d ed., Irwin, Homewood, Illinois, 1966.

CHAPTER 29

Labor Unions and Industrial Relations

CHAPTER PREVIEW

How did American labor unions evolve? What sorts of obstacles did they face, and what kinds of assistance did they receive in their long and turbulent history?

What is collective bargaining? How does it work?

How do unions seek to raise wages in the labor market? Are unions "good" or "bad"?

STRIKE THREATENS TO DISRUPT PRODUCTION
UNEMPLOYMENT HIGHER IN THE GHETTOS
UNION WAGE DEMANDS ARE TOP PRIORITY
EXTRA PAY FOR HOLIDAYS A NEW TARGET

These are the kinds of headlines we frequently encounter in the news media. They are labor problems that involve all of us, not only in our personal capacities as consumers, employees, or employers, but also as citizens who are concerned with significant economic issues.

We shall find in this chapter that a study of labor problems involves, in a very fundamental way, a study of unions—how they have evolved since the time of the Revolution, how they bargain with management, and how they may advance or impede the general welfare. These concepts are at best only vaguely sensed, and at worst are generally misunderstood by most people.

We shall also learn that *the primary and continuous objective of all unions is to improve the wages and working conditions of their members by bargaining with employers.* Through this negotiation process unions and management work out arrangements for higher wages and salaries, new and better pension plans, holidays and vacations with pay, health and welfare plans, shorter hours, and safer working conditions. This bargaining approach to the solution of labor problems is a characteristic feature of labor economics and industrial relations in the United States.

History of American Unionism: The Labor Movement

The development of labor unions in the United States during the nineteenth and twentieth centuries is often referred to as the *labor movement*. This fascinating story plays an integral role in the nation's political and economic history.

What is a *union*? We may define it as an organization of workers which seeks to gain a degree of monopoly power in the sale of its services so that it may be able to secure higher wages, better working conditions, and other economic improvements for its members.

Our purpose in studying the history of the labor movement is to discover the extent to which unions have succeeded in achieving these objectives. This can be done by viewing the development of unionism as spanning roughly four periods of time:

1. The local movement: Revolution to the Civil War

2. The national movement: post-Civil War to the Depression

3. The era of rapid growth: Depression to World War II

4. The age of maturity: post-World War II to the present

THE LOCAL MOVEMENT: REVOLUTION TO THE CIVIL WAR

Although labor organizations were started prior to the Revolutionary War, they were very short-lived and of no significant consequence. Not until the last quarter of the eighteenth century—and particularly in the last decade of that century—did some of the unions have sufficient durability to survive for a number of years. These were localized *craft unions* or "horizontal" unions composed of workers in a particular trade such as bakers, carpenters, longshoremen, printers, shoemakers, and teamsters. Throughout the history of unionism, the crafts have always been the first to organize, largely because their specialized skills or abilities put them in a relatively stronger position to gain monopolistic power in the marketplace.

In these early decades of the American labor movement, craft workers organized on a local basis not only to demand increased wages and shorter hours, but also to seek abolition of imprisonment for debt, the enactment of mechanics' lien laws to give them first call on the assets of bankrupt and defaulting employers, the establishment of free (rather than charitable) public schools for their children, the leasing of public lands to settlers, and similar types of "liberal" legislation.

Their efforts did not go unchallenged. Employers organized to meet the threat, and in Philadelphia, Pittsburgh, New York, and elsewhere union leaders were punished for organizing "labor combinations in restraint of trade" by judges who invoked the conspiracy provisions of English common law.

REMARK. The doctrine of *conspiracy*, defined as ". . . a confederacy of two or more, by indirect means to injure an individual or to do any act which is unlawful or prejudicial to the community," was developed in England during the late Middle Ages, and was applied in the United States some 500 years later to prevent the unionization of craftsmen.

It was not until 1842, in the landmark Massachusetts case of *Commonwealth vs. Hunt*, that a court held a trade union to be a lawful organization, and declared that workers could legally form a union for the purpose of bargaining collectively with employers over wages, working conditions, and related issues.

In the years that followed, the nation's industrial development continued apace as the railroads reached westward. Unionism spread to almost every craft and to most American cities. Several unions concluded trade agreements with their employers as they federated nationally along craft lines. The first of these permanent federations of labor were the National Typographic Union (1852), the United Hatters (1856), and the Iron Moulders' Union of North America (1859).

There were some mild improvements in working conditions during the two decades preceding the Civil War. The most significant developments were the gradual decline in the length of the average working day from about 13 hours to 10 or 11 hours in most factories, and the passage of 10-hour laws by many states. Laws were also passed to regulate child labor, but these were seldom enforced.

Leaders of the labor movement learned three major lessons during the pre-Civil War period:

1. Unions must seek the right to bargain collectively with management and to use such weapons as strikes and boycotts to achieve their aims.

2. The *closed shop,* whereby an employer makes union membership a condition of employment, is a powerful device for protecting the security of unions.

3. Federations of unions at the local and national level bring greater bargaining strength to labor.

The financial panic of 1857 and the ensuing depression of 1858 dealt the labor movement a severe blow. As a result, union organizing came to a virtual standstill on the eve of the Civil War.

THE NATIONAL MOVEMENT: POST-CIVIL WAR TO THE GREAT DEPRESSION

Unionism remained relatively dormant until the end of the Civil War. After the war, the growth of national craft unions quickened perceptibly with the spread of industrialism across the country and the expansion of the railroads into the West. As the sections of the nation were being welded together, goods produced in different geographic areas began to compete in the same markets, and workers began to find it feasible to move from one part of the country to another to take advantage of better job opportunities.

With these changing conditions of economic life, the 15 years following the Civil War were an important formative period for the American labor movement. Unions became increasingly "national" as they embraced formerly local unions which now became local branches of their national organization; the movement for an eight-hour working day was begun; and the first signs of the long, bitter, and almost unbelievable hostility toward labor's struggle for union recognition and survival started to take shape.

The following developments mark the highlights of union history from the end of the Civil War to the beginning of the depression.

The struggle for unionization was long and bitter in the late nineteenth century. Here, striking Pennsylvania coal miners and their wives taunt the "scabs" or nonstriking miners.

Culver Pictures, from *Harper's Weekly,* 1871.

Knights of Labor

In 1869, seven tailors met in Philadelphia and founded the Noble Order of the Knights of Labor—or simply the *Knights of Labor*—a national labor organization which attempted to unify all types of workers regardless of their craft, and without regard to race, sex, nationality, or creed. The organization was powerful and influential; it won several strikes against the railroads, and its membership rose rapidly to a peak of 730,000 in 1886. Its growth was so rapid, in fact, that at one point the central office had to suspend organizing to assure that no "lawyers, bankers, gamblers or liquor dealers, and Pinkerton detectives" could gain membership and possibly wreck the union.

The Knights' program called for various improvements and reforms including: establishment of the eight-hour day; equal pay for equal work by women; abolition of child and convict labor; public ownership of utilities; and the establishment of cooperatives. In a broader sense the organization championed the cause of workers in general; it sought the replacement of a competitive society with a socialist Utopia, mainly through educational and political methods or so-called "uplift" campaigns. Strikes were to be used as weapons only after all other means had failed.

The Knights were a curious group with one foot in the past, the other in the future. They rejected the traditional organizing of workers by crafts, preferring instead the mass unionization of both unskilled and skilled workers. This philosophy ultimately contributed to its decline. After 1886, membership in the Knights fell rapidly for three major reasons:

1. Opposition by craft leaders who saw no reason why the bargaining position of labor's elite—the skilled workers—should be wasted on efforts to secure benefits for the unskilled.

2. Dissension among leading members and groups over whether a more aggressive approach through strikes and collective bargaining should replace the slower evolutionary methods of political and social change.

3. Accusations (which were never proved) that the union was connected with anarchist activities such as the violence and bombing that occurred in Chicago's Haymarket riot in 1886—a famous incident in American political as well as labor history.

As a result of these conditions, the Knights of Labor steadily lost ground in the labor movement, and it finally ceased to exist in 1917.

American Federation of Labor

In the early 1880s, representatives of several craft unions became dissatisfied with the philosophy and policies of the Knights and formed their own group, which became known in 1886 as the American Federation of Labor. Under the leadership of Samuel Gompers, who served as its president from 1886 until his death in 1924 (except for one year when he was succeeded by William Green), the AFL led and dominated the labor movement. Its philosophy was based on three fundamental principles:

1. "Business unionism"—a practical policy of seek-

The Haymarket Riot: Haymarket Square, Chicago, May 4, 1886

By 1886 the movement for the eight-hour day had gained wide support by striking workers in many cities. In Chicago, about 80,000 workers were demonstrating when a group of anarchists took advantage of the excitement by throwing a bomb into the crowd in front of the McCormick Harvester Works at Haymarket Square. Seven policemen were killed and many people were injured. Although the anarchists bore the wrath of public indignation, organized labor in general, and especially the Knights of Labor, suffered heavily.

Harper's Weekly, May 15, 1886.

ing short-run "bread and butter" improvements in wages and working conditions and long-run improvements through evolution rather than revolution, without engaging in the class struggles of society.

2. "Federalism"—an organizational policy of maintaining autonomous national and international craft unions, each controlling its own trade specialty.

3. "Voluntarism"—a policy of opposition to government interference, either for or against labor, in all matters pertaining to labor organization, labor negotiations with management, and related activities.

The concept of unionism adopted by the AFL was thus largely the opposite of that held by the Knights of Labor. As the Knights declined in importance, the AFL grew, with its membership exceeding 1 million shortly after the turn of the century. By World War I, the AFL was clearly voicing the views of a majority of organized workers.

The achievements of unionism between the Civil War and World War I were not obtained without a struggle. Indeed, these were years of extraordinary hostility toward unions, resulting in much violence and bloodshed. State and federal governments firmly supported business opposition to unions, and it was considered a legitimate use of police power to call out federal troops in order to break strikes. These actions were also condoned by the courts, both state and federal, which were quick to grant injunctions to enjoin labor leaders from calling or continuing a strike. Yet, despite these odds, labor as a class made progress in achieving higher wages and a shorter workweek.

The years during and immediately after World War I constituted an "era of good feeling" toward labor. Under a favorable climate of federal protection to support the war effort, union-management cooperation was promoted and union organizing activity was expanded. By 1920, union membership had increased to over 5 million, and workers had earned substantial gains in wages and working conditions.

But then the growth of unionism started to take a turn for the worse. The government withdrew its limited protection of labor's right to organize, and employers refused to recognize labor unions in their plants. As a result, unions suffered lost membership. Lethargy and lack of aggressiveness engulfed American labor as technological changes, unfavorable court decisions, the growth of company unions, and a period of national prosperity all contributed to the dampening of union activity. By the early thirties, union membership had declined to less than 3 million.

THE ERA OF RAPID GROWTH: DEPRESSION TO WORLD WAR II

The fortunes of organized labor underwent a dramatic reversal during the Depression. The first piece of pro-labor legislation passed by Congress was the *Norris-LaGuardia Act* of 1932 which modified or eliminated the worst abuses against organized labor:

1. The hated *yellow-dog contract,* which required the employee to promise, as a condition of employment, that he would not belong to a labor union, was declared illegal.

2. The conditions under which court injunctions could be issued against unions were greatly restricted.

The stage was now set. Under President Roosevelt's New Deal administration of the 1930s, other favorable labor legislation was passed which created standards for minimum wages, maximum hours, and child labor, and provided for the formation of the United States Employment Service and the establishment of social security. But none of these was more important for the union movement than the National Labor Relations Act of 1935, which was hailed as Labor's Magna Carta.

Women and children constituted a significant portion of factory labor in the latter half of the nineteenth century, as this drawing by Winslow Homer suggests. Judging from the expressions on their faces, the prospect of going to work was by no means pleasant.

Library of Congress, from *Harper's Weekly,* 1868.

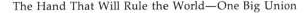

The Hand That Will Rule the World—One Big Union

Solidarity, June 30, 1917.

Industrial Workers of the World—The "Wobblies"

The early 1900s saw the formation of the Industrial Workers of the World (IWW), a labor union of immigrants who were mostly unskilled factory workers, miners, lumbermen, and dock workers. Popularly known as the "Wobblies," the organization's members had a militant style with the slogan: "Labor Produces All Wealth. All Wealth Must Go to Labor." Hence their goals were to unite all workers into "One Big Union," tear down capitalism by force, and replace it with socialism. The IWW reached a peak membership of about 100,000 by 1912, but declined thereafter due to internal dissension and the imprisonment of nearly 100 of its leaders on sedition charges.

During the next several decades the IWW faded steadily into obscurity, but it did not become extinct. In the late 1960s there were less than 300 Wobblies, most of them retaining membership in the IWW for philosophical or nostalgic reasons. Since then there has been a renewed interest in the organization—primarily by younger people of the radical left—as a result of which membership has risen considerably. Though still relatively small, the IWW has concentrated mainly on organizing workers in small plants that major unions have

skipped as too insignificant. According to its leaders, the Wobblies' bargaining demands today are "basically the normal types of demands for (better) working conditions and rates of pay, but flavored with a different perspective"; violence, they say, is avoided for the most practical of reasons: "The other side has more capacity."

The major publication of the IWW was a weekly magazine called **Solidarity.** The accompanying song, "Solidarity Forever," has long been the anthem of the entire American labor movement, and is by far the best-known union song in the United States. It was composed by Ralph Chaplin (1887–1961), an artist, poet, songwriter, pamphleteer, and one of the editors of **Solidarity.** In his autobiography Chaplin stated that the idea for "Solidarity Forever" came to him while he was editing a labor paper in West Virginia during the Kanawha Valley coal mining strike in January, 1915. "I wanted a song," he said, "to be full of revolutionary fervor and to have a chorus that was ringing and defiant."

"Solidarity Forever" appeared in **Solidarity,** January 9, 1915.

SOLIDARITY FOREVER!

By Ralph Chaplin

(Tune: "Battle Hymn of the Republic")

When the Union's inspiration through the workers' blood
   shall run,
There can be no power greater anywhere beneath the sun
Yet what force on earth is weaker than the feeble strength
   of one?
But the Union makes us strong.

Chorus:
Solidarity forever!
Solidarity forever!
Solidarity forever!
For the Union makes us strong.

Is there aught we hold in common with the greedy parasite
Who would lash us into serfdom and would crush us with
   his might?
Is there anything left for us but to organize and fight?
For the Union makes us strong.

It is we who plowed the prairies; built the cities where
   they trade;
Dug the mines and built the workshops; endless miles of
   railroad laid.
Now we stand, outcast and starving, mid the wonders we
   have made;
But the Union makes us strong.

All the world that's owned by idle drones, is ours and ours
   alone.
We have laid the wide foundations; built it skyward stone
   by stone.
It is ours, not to slave in, but to master and to own,
While the Union makes us strong.

They have taken untold millions that they never toiled
   to earn.
But without our brain and muscle not a single wheel can
   turn.
We can break their haughty power; gain our freedom when
   we learn
That the Union makes us strong.

In our hands is placed a power greater than their hoarded
   gold;
Greater than the might of armies, magnified a thousand-
   fold.
We can bring to birth the new world from the ashes of the
   old,
For the Union makes us strong.

The *National Labor Relations Act* (or *Wagner Act*) of 1935 is the basic labor relations law of the United States. It:

1. Guarantees the right of workers to organize and to bargain collectively through representatives of their own choosing

2. Forbids the employer from engaging in "unfair labor practices" such as: (*a*) interfering or discriminating against workers who form unions or engage in union activity; (*b*) establishing a *company union* or organization of workers that is limited to a particular firm; (*c*) refusing to bargain in good faith with a duly recognized union

3. Established the *National Labor Relations Board* (NLRB) to enforce the Act and to supervise free elections among a company's employees so as to determine which union, if any, is to represent the workers

With this firm legal umbrella provided by Congress—especially the right of labor to organize and bargain collectively—the labor movement embarked on the fastest and longest upward journey in its history. Thousands of workers went back into their old unions and thousands of others joined new ones. As shown in Exhibit 1, there was a total of 10 million union members by 1940.

Congress of Industrial Organizations

In the mid-1930s, several union leaders in the AFL, under the chairmanship of John L. Lewis, president of the United Mine Workers, launched an attack against the "craft bias" of the Federation. They argued that craft unions were "horizontal" unions which were not well adapted to the needs of workers in modern mass-production industries, and that *industrial unions* or "vertical" unions were needed which would organize all workers in a particular industry, e.g., automobile manufacturing, coal mining, etc. Although the Federation never refused to recognize industrial unions—indeed, Lewis and his group were all leaders of industrial unions that were affiliated with the AFL—the parent organization had been relatively unsuccessful in organizing workers in mass-production industries.

Exhibit 1

Union Membership since 1900

The union movement experienced its most rapid growth during the 1930s. Since the 1950s, union membership has averaged about 25 percent of the civilian labor force.

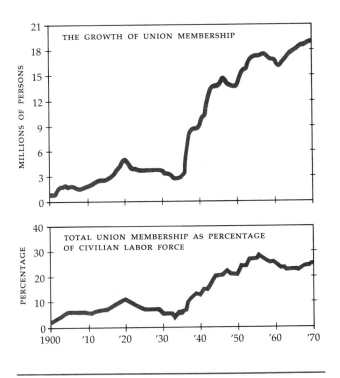

ma,or industries during 1945 and 1946. These strikes raised a great wave of antiunion sentiment both in and out of Congress, resulting in the passage of new restrictive labor legislation. Thus came the end of an era in the history of the union movement.

THE AGE OF MATURITY: POST-WORLD WAR II TO THE PRESENT

The public's outrage was brought to a head in November, 1946, when John L. Lewis's United Mine Workers defied a federal court injunction to cease striking and return to work. Although Lewis and the UMW were fined for contempt of court and the miners went back to their jobs, the wheels of antiunion legislation were already turning in Congress. In June, 1947, a coalition of Republicans and conservative Democrats passed, over President Truman's veto, a new Labor Management Relations Act commonly known as the Taft-Hartley Act. This provided the most detailed and extensive regulation of labor unions and industrial relations in the nation's history:

The *Labor-Management Relations Act (Taft-Hartley Act)* of 1947 amended the National Labor Relations Act (Wagner Act) of 1935. It retains the rights that had been given to labor by the latter Act, but it also:

1. Outlaws as "unfair labor practices" of unions: (*a*) coercion of workers to join a union; (*b*) failure of a union to bargain with an employer in good faith; and (*c*) *jurisdictional strikes* (or disagreements between two or more unions as to which shall perform a particular job), *secondary boycotts* (or attempts by a union through strikes, picketing, etc., to stop one employer from doing business with another employer), and *featherbedding* (or "make work" rules which are designed to increase the amount of labor or labor time on a particular job)

2. Outlaws the closed shop but permits the *union shop,* which allows a nonunion employee to be hired on condition that he join the union after he is employed

3. Requires unions to file financial reports with the NLRB, and union officials to sign non-Communist affadavits

A controversy thus arose within the AFL leadership that lasted for several years. Finally, in 1938, the insurgent unions were expelled from the Federation, and under the presidency of John L. Lewis formed an independent rival union called the *Congress of Industrial Organizations* (CIO).

The CIO was immediately successful in organizing millions of previously unorganized workers in the automobile, steel, and other mass-production industries. But the AFL also continued to make huge gains. Both the AFL and CIO emerged from World War II stronger than ever before. However, with the termination of wartime economic controls, prices rose faster than wages, and strikes broke out in many

4. Prohibits strikes called before the end of a 60-day notice period prior to the expiration of a collective bargaining agreement, in order to give conciliation agencies enough time to try to resolve disputes before a walkout occurs

5. Enables the President to obtain an 80-day court injunction in order to provide a "cooling-off" period in cases involving strikes which endanger the national health or safety

The Taft-Hartley Act also permitted state legislatures to pass *right-to-work laws*—that is, state laws which make it illegal to require membership in a union as a condition of employment. About 20 states, mostly in the South and Midwest, adopted such laws, the main effect of which was to outlaw the union shop. In practice, however, these laws have been relatively weak in many states.

The Taft-Hartley Act was strongly denounced by unions as a "slave labor law," and several unsuccessful attempts were made to repeal it or at least to soften it by amending some of its provisions. It became an issue in two presidential campaigns— 1948 and 1952—but within a few years the shouting died down and the Act was recognized by the unions as an established fact. On the whole, the law does not appear to have put the unions at a disadvantage in bargaining, nor is it likely to have been a significant obstacle in the path of union growth. Labor-management relations have been generally favorable since the Act was passed, and the nickname "slave labor" has been heard rarely since the mid-fifties.

The AFL–CIO

Most but not all labor organizations joined either the AFL or the CIO. Those unions not affiliated with any federation of labor organizations were (and are) called *independent unions;* they may be national or international, and are not limited to workers in any one firm.

For a number of years during and after World War II, labor leaders in both the AFL and CIO dreamed of merging the two federations into a single and powerful union. When Philip Murray died in 1952 after serving as president of the CIO for more than a decade, he was succeeded by Walter

P. Reuther, head of the United Automobile Workers. Two weeks after Murray's death, William Green, who was president of the AFL, died and was succeeded by George Meany.

The two new presidents began shortly thereafter to work for a merging of their federations. After several years of discussion the two groups combined in 1955 to form a single organization known as the *American Federation of Labor–Congress of Industrial Organizations* (AFL–CIO) under the presidency of George Meany. Stated briefly, the purposes of the organization as paraphrased from its Constitution are: to improve wages, hours, and working conditions for workers, to realize the benefits of free collective bargaining, and to strengthen America's democratic traditions by protecting the labor movement from Communists, Fascists, and other totalitarians.

The union movement thus entered an age of maturity and power. With this growth of power came a mounting political attack against organized labor. Some union leaders were charged with mismanagement and embezzlement of union funds, and others with extorting money from employers and employees under the threat of invoking "labor trouble." The AFL–CIO dealt with these problems by adopting Codes of Ethical Practices and by expelling several unions. In 1959, Congress passed a new law: the Labor-Management Reporting and Disclosure Act, which again indicated that the government would discipline labor as a whole in order to protect it from a few of its corrupt leaders.

The *Labor-Management Reporting and Disclosure Act* (or *Landrum-Griffin Act*) of 1959 amended the National Labor Relations Act by: (1) requiring detailed financial reports of all unions and union officers; (2) severely tightening restrictions on secondary boycotting and picketing; (3) requiring periodic secret-ballot elections of union officers; and (4) imposing restrictions on ex-convicts and Communists in holding positions as union officers.

Alliance for Labor Action

In the mid-sixties, a cold war developed between the AFL–CIO and Walter P. Reuther, president of the

Box 1

Long-Term Employment Trends in the United States

The United States has become increasingly a "service-oriented" economy as the proportion of employed persons engaged in agriculture has declined, the proportion in manu- *facturing has remained fairly stable since World War II, and the proportion in the service industries and in state and local governments has increased.*

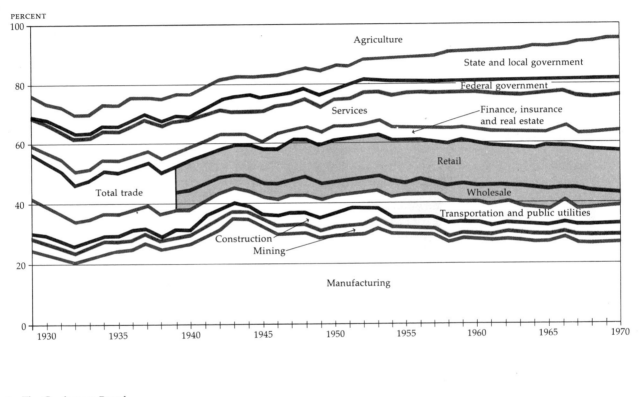

SOURCE: The Conference Board.

United Automobile Workers, which was perhaps the federation's most powerful affiliate. Among the fundamental disagreements between the two groups were: the organizing of farm workers and the working poor; national wage and collective bargaining policies; the improvement of public education, pension, and health benefits; labor disputes in public service industries; and methods of handling racial discrimination and civil rights.

As a result of this feud, Reuther disaffiliated the UAW from the AFL–CIO in 1968 and aligned his union with the International Brotherhood of Teamsters to form a new federation called the *Alliance for Labor Action.* The ALA has sought to expand by recruiting new member unions from the AFL–CIO. Its success remains to be seen, however, particularly since the untimely death of Reuther, its dynamic leader, in 1970.

Changing Occupational Needs
(Employment by broad occupational groups)

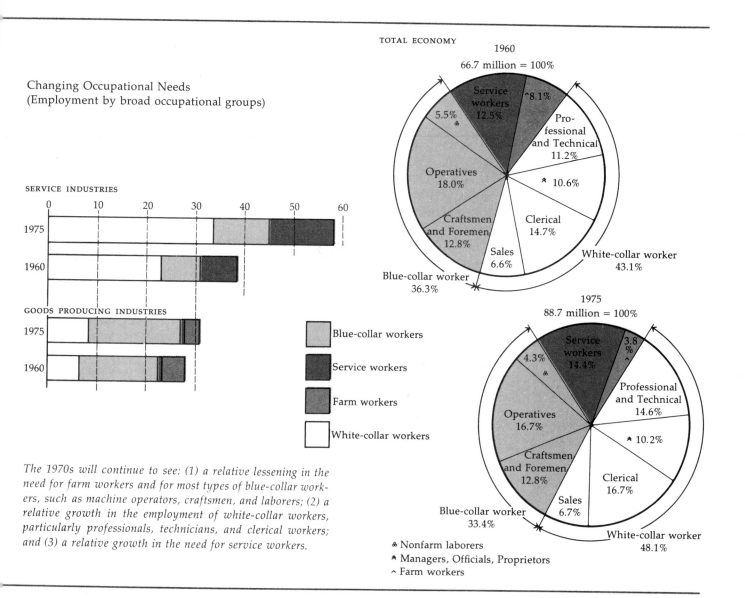

SERVICE INDUSTRIES

	0	10	20	30	40	50	60
1975							
1960							

GOODS PRODUCING INDUSTRIES

1975							
1960							

Blue-collar workers

Service workers

Farm workers

White-collar workers

The 1970s will continue to see: (1) a relative lessening in the need for farm workers and for most types of blue-collar workers, such as machine operators, craftsmen, and laborers; (2) a relative growth in the employment of white-collar workers, particularly professionals, technicians, and clerical workers; and (3) a relative growth in the need for service workers.

TOTAL ECONOMY

1960
66.7 million = 100%

Service workers 12.5%
8.1%
Professional and Technical 11.2%
5.5%
10.6%
Operatives 18.0%
Clerical 14.7%
Craftsmen and Foremen 12.8%
Sales 6.6%
White-collar worker 43.1%
Blue-collar worker 36.3%

1975
88.7 million = 100%

Service workers 14.4%
3.8%
Professional and Technical 14.6%
4.3%
10.2%
Operatives 16.7%
Clerical 16.7%
Craftsmen and Foremen 12.8%
Sales 6.7%
White-collar worker 48.1%
Blue-collar worker 33.4%

♣ Nonfarm laborers
♠ Managers, Officials, Proprietors
^ Farm workers

THE FUTURE: STABILIZATION OR EXPANSION?

What will be the future of the American labor movement? Many labor economists believe that union membership will stabilize at about 25 percent of the labor force—the average since the end of World War II. Their reasons for thinking this are:

1. *Changing composition of the labor force.* The proportion of blue-collar workers, which is the chief source from which unions draw their membership, has declined steadily from almost 50 percent of the civilian labor force after World War II to less than 30 percent today, while the proportion of white-collar workers has increased correspondingly. Of the blue-collar workers who remain, most are employed in small manufacturing plants and in the trade and service industries, all of which are more difficult to unionize. (See Box 1.)

Structural Organization of the American Federation of Labor and Congress of Industrial Organizations

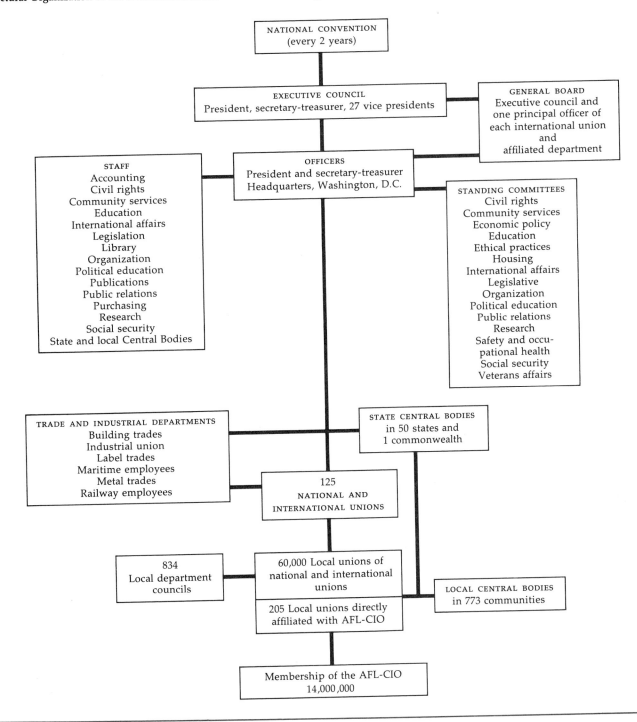

NATIONAL CONVENTION
(every 2 years)

EXECUTIVE COUNCIL
President, secretary-treasurer, 27 vice presidents

GENERAL BOARD
Executive council and
one principal officer of
each international union
and
affiliated department

STAFF
Accounting
Civil rights
Community services
Education
International affairs
Legislation
Library
Organization
Political education
Publications
Public relations
Purchasing
Research
Social security
State and local Central Bodies

OFFICERS
President and secretary-treasurer
Headquarters, Washington, D.C.

STANDING COMMITTEES
Civil rights
Community services
Economic policy
Education
Ethical practices
Housing
International affairs
Legislative
Organization
Political education
Public relations
Research
Safety and occu-
pational health
Social security
Veterans affairs

TRADE AND INDUSTRIAL DEPARTMENTS
Building trades
Industrial union
Label trades
Maritime employees
Metal trades
Railway employees

STATE CENTRAL BODIES
in 50 states and
1 commonwealth

125
NATIONAL AND
INTERNATIONAL UNIONS

834
Local department
councils

60,000 Local unions of
national and international
unions

LOCAL CENTRAL BODIES
in 773 communities

205 Local unions directly
affiliated with AFL-CIO

Membership of the AFL-CIO
14,000,000

2. *Changing attitudes toward unions.* The public as well as some political leaders in Congress have become less sympathetic toward unions as a result of what sometimes appear to be unreasonably prolonged strikes, the discovery of fraudulent practices among union officials, and the growing belief—whether true or not—that union pressures for wage increases are a chief cause of cost-push inflation.

3. *Changing type of union leadership.* Unions have become big businesses with millions of members and hundreds of millions of dollars in welfare funds. As a result, they have come increasingly to seek a new type of leadership—men who are professional *administrators* capable of dealing effectively with Congress, management, the public, and their own rising proportion of more educated members, rather than men who are merely militant organizers.

Other labor economists, as well as union leaders, contend that union membership will continue to expand since there is still a large pool of unorganized labor in agriculture, government, trade, and the service industries.

Collective Bargaining

The chief objective of unions has been to improve the status of workers. This goal is now achieved for the most part through the method of *collective bargaining*—a process of negotiation between representatives of a company's management and a union for the purpose of arriving at mutually acceptable wages and working conditions for employees.

If a union represents a majority of workers in a firm, it may be "certified" by the government's National Labor Relations Board and recognized by management as the collective bargaining agent for the employees. Representatives of the union and of management then meet together at the bargaining table to work out a *collective agreement* or contract. The two sides are rarely in accord when they begin, but the bargaining process is one of give and take by both parties until a contract is agreed upon. The union representatives then take the contract back to their members for a vote of acceptance or rejection. If the members reject it, they may send their union

representatives back to continue the bargaining process or they may decide to reinforce their demands by going on strike.

When a collective agreement is ratified both by union and management, it becomes a legally binding contract as well as guiding principle of labor-management relations for the period of time specified in the arrangement. More than 95 percent of all such agreements in existence today were successfully negotiated without any strikes or work stoppages.

Collective bargaining contracts differ greatly in their size and content; some are brief and cover only a few pages, while others are highly detailed and run to several hundred pages. The major issues with which such agreements deal may be divided into four broad groups:

1. Wages
2. Industrial relations
3. Multiunit bargaining
4. Settling labor-management disputes

WAGES

You may read in a newspaper that a labor-management negotiation has resulted in a 20-cent-per-hour "package," consisting of 12 cents in wages and 8 cents in other benefits. Such "packages" are composed of two parts:

1. *Basic wages:* payments received by workers for work performed, based on time or output
2. *Supplementary* or *fringe benefits:* compensation to workers other than basic wages, such as bonuses, pension benefits, holiday pay, vacation pay, and so on

The term "wages" is thus a complex one in many collective bargaining discussions, and may give rise to various issues and problems such as the following.

Basic Wages: Time or Incentive Payments?

If you were a worker, would you want to be paid on the basis of "time," or would you prefer some sort of incentive system which compensated you according to how much you produced? This issue arises in some collective bargaining negotiations.

The great majority of American workers in manufacturing—about 70 percent—are paid on the basis of time, i.e., by the hour, day, week, or month, with extra compensation for work done during nights, weekends, and holidays. The remaining 30 percent of manufacturing workers receive their basic compensation through some type of incentive payment that is related to output or profit. It may be in the form of wages, commissions, bonuses, and so on.

Many employers have criticized the time-payment concept by arguing that it provides no "incentive" for workers to produce, since it relates earnings received to "time" rather than output. Unions, on the other hand, have usually preferred time pay because it compensates workers on a uniform basis rather than penalizing the slower ones and rewarding the faster ones.

Time-payment systems tend to prevail in industries where an individual's production cannot be precisely measured and where his rate of output is largely controlled by established technology, as in automobiles, chemicals, and machine-tool production. On the other hand, incentive systems have been effective in competitive industries where labor costs are a high proportion of total costs and where workers' outputs are measurable, as in clothing and textile production.

The great majority of unions have not strongly opposed incentive systems as such. However, they have been very much concerned with the operation of such systems, and the problems that they pose. For example:

1. How should a worker be compensated if a machine breaks down or if there is a stoppage of material flow due to causes beyond his control?

2. Since it may be possible to measure the outputs of only certain types of workers in a plant (e.g., maintenance personnel or assembly-line operators) can an equitable incentive and time system be established for all workers in the plant?

3. Will management provide an adequate staff of accountants, time-study engineers, and personnel men to see that the incentive system continues to operate effectively and equitably?

Profit Sharing

Some companies have introduced a different type of incentive system known as profit sharing. These firms distribute to their workers a share of the profits after certain costs such as wages, materials, and overhead have been covered. Profit-sharing plans of various types (including bonuses) have existed since the early nineteenth century and are by no means uncommon in American industry. In general, profit-sharing is most widespread in firms and industries characterized by:

1. Consistent and relatively large profits, so that profit sharing becomes a worthwhile incentive

2. Year-round stability of the work force (as opposed to high seasonal instability), thus permitting a permanent body of employees to build up an interest and equity in the company

3. High turnover costs among key personnel, for whom profit sharing can have significant holding power

4. Relatively weak or no unionization

The first three characteristics are readily understandable, but why the fourth? The answer is that unions have traditionally opposed profit sharing for two major reasons. First, it establishes an employer-employee "partnership" in profits and thereby weakens the influence of unions. Second, it makes the employee's compensation dependent on profits, which in turn are due to managerial policies (such as pricing practices, product design, technology, etc.) over which the worker has no direct control.

For these reasons, unions have argued that workers should be paid for what they do, and should not be penalized when a company loses money or rewarded with a share of the profits when it makes money.

Wage Structure and Job Classification

Should all workers in a particular job classification, such as welders or assemblers, receive a single rate of pay, or should there be a range of wages for each job based on years of experience, merit, length of service, and other factors? Questions of this type are obviously important for many collective bargaining discussions.

Most manufacturing firms have adopted formal wage structures since World War II. This has been accomplished largely by the method of *job classification*—a process of describing the duties, responsibilities, and characteristics of jobs, point-rating them (perhaps by established formulas based on engineering studies of workers in such jobs), and then grouping the jobs into graduated classifications with corresponding wage rates and wage ranges. Thus, riveters, welders, painters, etc., may receive job classifications by this method. Employers prefer job classification since it systematizes the wage structure and facilitates the handling of problems dealing with wage administration.

Some of the chief problems of job classification plans revolve around the issue of single rates versus rate ranges for each job grouping. Unions have tended to favor the single-rate approach because it reduces friction and dissension among workers in each rank. Employers, on the other hand, have usually preferred the use of rate ranges because this permits them to grant rewards on the basis of merit within each rank.

Supplementary or Fringe Benefits

Wage supplements or fringe benefits such as pensions, insurance, and welfare plans have grown remarkably since the beginning of World War II. This trend is likely to endure as long as union negotiators continue to emphasize the need for worker "security" in their bargaining with employers. Moreover, the various plans are becoming increasingly liberal. Health plans, for example, once included only hospitalization, but now they often cover outpatient care, free eyeglasses, psychiatric and dental care, and so on. Similarly, sick leaves, time off with pay, vacation allowances, etc., have all expanded substantially.

Supplementary wages or fringe benefits raise at least two fundamental questions:

1. Whereas wages used to be paid exclusively for time worked, there is a significant trend in the payment of some wages for time *not worked*. If this trend continues with more and more labor costs going into fringe benefits, will payment for time worked decrease in importance and will our traditional mode of payment therefore become outdated?

2. To an employer, total fringe benefit payments vary largely with the number of employees rather than with the hours worked per employee, since a worker receives the same vacations, holidays, group insurance, etc., whether he puts in 30, 40, or 50 hours per week. It may be cheaper for an employer, therefore, to pay his existing workers at overtime rates than to hire new employees. Does this mean that the growth of fringe benefits in American industry will add so much to employers' costs that it will reduce their propensity to employ?

INDUSTRIAL RELATIONS

A second major area of collective bargaining pertains to *industrial relations*. This may be defined simply as the rules and regulations governing the relationship between union and management. Since the subject of industrial relations is quite broad, we will focus our attention on a few of the more important topics.

Union Security

"In unity there is strength." This is the fundamental principle upon which unionism is based. It follows that a primary objective of unions is "union security." What determines a union's ability to attain security? There are two major factors: the type of recognition that it is accorded, and its financial arrangement for collecting dues. Thus, the more common forms of union recognition are the "closed shop" and the "union shop," and the typical method of dues collection is the "checkoff." Let us see what these concepts involve.

Closed Shop. A plant or business establishment in which the employer agrees that all workers must belong to the union as a condition for employment is known as a *closed shop.* This arrangement may be advantageous to some of the parties and disadvantageous to others:

1. It enables the union to control entrance into the job or trade, and thereby strengthens its bargaining position.
2. It deprives the employer of his right to hire whom he wishes.

The Taft-Hartley Act of 1947 made the closed shop illegal for firms engaged in interstate commerce. It is generally agreed, however, that the Act only drove the closed shop underground. It does not exist in union-management contracts, but nevertheless exists in fact in certain skilled trades and industries such as printing, construction, and transportation.

Union Shop. A plant or business establishment in which the employer is free to hire whom he wants, but agrees to require that the employee must join the union within a specified time after hiring (usually 30 days) as a condition for continuing in employment, is called a *union shop.*

The union shop is the most common form of union recognition found in industry today. There are two major reasons for this: (1) the Taft-Hartley Act of 1947 made the closed shop illegal; and (2) the tendency of various industries to switch to the union shop from other less common types of union recognition arrangements.

Both the closed shop and the union shop have certain obvious disadvantages to employers—the major one being that they give the union greater bargaining strength. Hence management has often argued in favor of the *open shop*—that is, a plant or business establishment in which the employer is free to hire union or nonunion members as he wishes. Unions have always opposed the open shop on the grounds that it often results in a closed nonunion shop because of the antiunion hiring preferences of many employers.

Checkoff. If a union is to continue to function, it must have an efficient means of collecting dues from its members. In the old days, unions often stationed strongarm men at plant gates on paydays in order to enforce the payment of dues. Those workers who held back their union dues risked a bloody nose or even a fractured skull. But with the growth of unionism and union recognition, the *checkoff* system was introduced. The employer, with the written permission of the workers, withholds union dues and other assessments from paychecks and then transfers the funds to the union, thereby simplifying the dues collection process and assuring the prompt and regular payment of dues.

Restricting Membership and Output

Many unions seek to obtain higher incomes for their members by restricting membership; this creates a scarcity of their particular kind of labor. Membership may be controlled in various ways such as: (1) varying apprenticeship requirements; (2) sponsoring state licensing for those in the trade (e.g., barbers, electricians, plumbers, etc.); (3) varying initiation fees, and (4) establishing seniority agreements which provide for the order in which workers may be laid off and rehired.

Many unions also seek to restrict their members' output in order to increase the demand for labor and thereby secure higher wages. Output restriction may be accomplished by shortening the working day, limiting the output per worker, and opposing the introduction of labor-saving technology.

Thus, whereas management may seek to increase profits by raising productive efficiency, unions are primarily interested in improving earnings and working conditions for their members. Since these objectives often conflict, the means that are chosen to achieve them must be ironed out around the bargaining table.

MULTIUNIT BARGAINING

Perhaps the most controversial issue in the practice of collective bargaining involves multiunit agreements.

Multiunit bargaining (sometimes inaccurately called "industry-wide bargaining") is a collective bargaining arrangement covering more than one plant. It may occur between one or more firms in an industry and one or more unions, and it may take place on a national, regional, or local level. Although it can be national in scope and very inclusive, it is rarely completely industry-wide.

A number of examples can be used to illustrate the scope and diversity of multiunit bargaining.

1. In the automobile and steel industries, one employer such as General Motors or United States Steel owns a number of plants and bargains with a single union—the United Automobile Workers or the United Steel Workers.

2. In the construction and retailing industries, two or more employers in an industry may bargain with one or more national unions; the bargaining will usually be subdivided geographically into national, regional, and local areas.

3. In the bituminous coal industry, all employers bargain with one industrial union on a national basis, whereas in the railroad industry employers bargain with several groups and must consider the demands of all groups in arriving at a settlement.

4. In various Western cities, where labor has been aggressive and relatively scarce since the "Gold Rush" days of the mid-nineteenth century, bargaining has developed on an area-wide basis between employer associations and unions that cut across industry lines.

5. In the 1960s, a new movement was started by the AFL–CIO called *coalition bargaining*. The AFL–CIO tries to coordinate and establish common termination dates for contracts with firms that deal with a number of unions at their plants throughout the United States and Canada, so that it can strengthen its bargaining position by threatening to close down all plants simultaneously.

Multiunit bargaining in the United States is thus a widespread and complex process that varies by industry, geography, and even by the nature of the issues involved. This explains why the expression "industry-wide bargaining" is usually not completely accurate. The chief advantages of multiunit bargaining are that it: (1) strengthens the union wage structure within markets and industries by making union-management contracts easier to negotiate and enforce; and (2) increases labor stability by making it more difficult for a rival union to enter an

industry. But because of its large-scale and often national nature, multiunit bargaining poses several important problems:

First, it gives unions a strong degree of monopoly power which, coupled with the employer's fear of a widespread strike, often enables them to extract highly inflationary wage settlements.

Second, it tends to focus on the national settlement of basic economic issues involving wages and working conditions, while leaving important "noneconomic" issues like work standards and working rules for settlement at the local plant level—often at disproportionately higher costs to employers because they lack the funds for counteroffers after national issues have been settled.

Third, it frequently allows matters of local concern to become subjects of national negotiations which might lead to strikes, even though the issues may eventually be referred back and settled at the local level.

SETTLING LABOR-MANAGEMENT DISPUTES

The collective bargaining process can be likened to a game of strategy between opposing players, with each side threatening to employ its own unique weapons in order to defeat the other.

The employer's major weapons include injunctions and lockouts. An *injunction* is a court order forbidding an individual or group of individuals (such as a union) from taking a specified action. Employers' use of this device has been severely restricted since the Norris-LaGuardia Act of 1932. A *lockout* is the closing down of a plant by an employer in order to keep workers out of their jobs.

The union's major weapons include boycotts and strikes. A *boycott* (sometimes called a *primary boycott*) is a campaign by workers to discourage people from dealing with an employer or buying his products. A *strike* is a mutual agreement among workers to stop working, without resigning from their jobs, until their demands are met.

Experience indicates that it is rarely necessary for either side to use its maximum economic strength. Thus:

Although the power to strike is labor's "ultimate"

The Wrath of Grapes

In the 1930s, John Steinbeck awakened the American conscience to the hapless life of the migrant farmworkers—mostly "Okies"—in his famous book, The Grapes of Wrath.

In the late 1960s, many college students tried to awaken the American conscience for the hapless grape pickers—mostly Chicanos or Mexican-Americans—through the use of boycotts.

The purpose of these aggressive activities was to bring agriculture under NLRB regulation, because farm workers were excluded from coverage under the federal labor-relations law. In this photograph, the public is being urged to boycott stores and supermarkets handling California grapes.

By 1970, most major grape growers had signed labor contracts with the union.

Wide World Photos

weapon, it is a major and costly one which unions do not use lightly. An analysis of data since 1935 indicates that on an annual basis, the number of man-days lost due to strikes has never been as high as 1½ percent of total labor-days worked, and has averaged less than ½ percent of that amount. This is far less than the proportion of time lost from work due to the common cold.

Arbitration and Mediation (Conciliation)

What happens if labor-management negotiations break down? In that case the unsuccessful bargainers may have to resolve their disagreements through processes known as arbitration and mediation.

Arbitration is a method of settling differences between two parties by the use of an impartial third party called an arbitrator who is acceptable to both sides and whose decision is binding and legally enforceable on the contesting parties. The arbitration procedure consists of the company and the union submitting their disagreement to the arbitrator, who, after hearing all of the evidence, issues a decision which is based not on what he thinks is wise and fair, but upon how he understands the language of the contract to apply to the case at hand. Thus, an arbitrator is like a judge: he relates the case to the contract, just as a judge relates a case to the law.

This is voluntary arbitration, for which the great majority of all collective bargaining agreements that are in effect today make provision. There is no doubt that the existence and extensive use of this type of arbitration has aided materially in reducing the number of strikes in our economy.

Another plan that has often been proposed as a key to industrial peace, especially in the case of prolonged strikes, is "compulsory arbitration." Obviously, however, this is not a substitute for free collective bargaining, and the evidence indicates that where it has been tried—e.g., Australia—it has caused more turmoil than peace, and has not stopped strikes. (See Box 2 on page 506.)

Mediation (sometimes called *conciliation*) is a process by which a third party, the mediator, attempts to reconcile the differences between contesting parties. The mediator may try to maintain constructive discussions, search for common areas

Viewpoint

Should Civil Servants Be Allowed to Strike?

The cop on the corner, the fireman in his firehouse, the tax collector in his office—few people love them. For many, those and other employees of government are objects of scorn, derision, and even violence. "We have to travel in armor-plating," says a New York fireman who steers the rear end of a fire appliance. "We used to be heroes; now we are shot at, or pelted with garbage. Nobody looks up to us any more."

Perhaps. But to the recruiting officers of organized labor public employees are a tempting prize. State and local governments alone employ more than 9 million workers, triple the number in 1945. By 1975, according to some estimates, another 3 million will be on state and local government payrolls. By that time, the unions hope, virtually all will be dues-paying members.

Old Issue, New Prominence

If the unions succeed in their objective—and there are signs that they will—an old issue will come into new prominence. It is this: should public employees have the right to strike? At every level of government—federal, state, and local—civil service strikes are usually illegal. Yet many of the civil servants who join unions proclaim with words and with actions their belief that they should be able to wield the ultimate weapon of organized labor—the right to withold their services.

The no-strike principle may seem unfair, and is certainly spotty in its application: for example, why should the employees of a privately owned school bus company be allowed to strike, but not the employees of a publicly owned system? Nevertheless, the no-strike rule has justice on its side.

The various levels of government are not organized for profit; thus, the conventional notion that a strike is a test of strength in the marketplace does not apply. Government is—or should be—the embodiment of all the people. It cannot be forced out of business by market pressures.

Rising Defiance

A. H. Raskin, of the *New York Times*, declares that a strike by public employees is "an effort by one segment of the people to misuse its control over a specific service as a weapon with which to bludgeon the entire community into submission."

Disturbingly, the number and seriousness of public-sector strikes has been rising. In 1960 there were only 36 work stoppages; in 1967, the latest year for which figures are available, there were 181. The number of man-days lost rose in that period from 58,400 to 1.2 million. Even more significantly, those figures do not include federal employees, who until 1970 had a strike-free record. Then, in a strike unprecedented in nature and scope, Post Office workers across the nation defied law and custom by walking off the job. In 1971 they were followed by the police in New York and other cities.

Rising militance by public employees underlines the urgent need for a solution. In fact, there is not one solution but many to conflict between civil servants' right to bargain collectively and the public's right to demand that the strike weapon should not be used. Probably the most vital part of that multipart solution is the necessity for government at all levels to realize that it must be a model employer: it cannot afford to abuse its legal power to break

strikes. Additionally, there should be at every level of government an efficient, respected mechanism for arbitrating the differences between employer and employed. Next, the present high emotional temperature could be cooled if representatives of government and the unions sat down regularly to discuss issues, instead of waiting for the crunch period of contract negotiations. That strategy may be valid when employers lose by allowing a strike to occur during a period of high demand for their products, but is totally inappropriate in the public sector, which is not "selling" anything.

Mitigating Militance

In the last analysis, however, it is the public that can mitigate the militance of public employees. It can do this by demonstrating, in its daily attitudes and its ballot-box decisions, that public-sector employees are valued, not scorned. Streets do have to be cleaned, criminals do have to be apprehended, and buses do have to be driven. The world with government may be dismaying; the world without it would be even worse. And even those who regard government as, at best, a necessary evil are making a wild, unjustified leap of the imagination by identifying the garbage collector with the establishment—and thus as a person to be treated meanly.

R. B.

How can we determine what constitutes fair wages and working conditions for public employees? And given the nature of our political institutions, how can we be sure that we will be able to get the money to maintain these standards?

Box 2

Taking the Grief out of Grievances

Say "arbitration" to most people and they will think of compulsory arbitration, where the government steps into a labor-management contract dispute and names an arbitrator who dictates a settlement. It is a technique generally abhorred by labor and management, and rarely employed in the United States.

But say "arbitration" to an industrial relations director, or to a union official, and he will think of something quite different: voluntary—or grievance—arbitration. It's one of the handiest tools in his professional kit—and one of the most effective systems yet developed in the United States for stabilizing labor relations.

This kind of arbitration deals only with the interpretation of an existing contract. Union and management negotiate the provisions; the arbitrator clarifies their meaning when differences of opinion cannot be settled on the lower reaches of the grievance procedure. Meanwhile, work continues on the production line or at the office. That's what a grievance procedure culminating in arbitration is all about—in contrast to the British system, which gives the worker no institutional alternative but a wildcat strike if management shrugs off his grievance.

SOURCE: Adapted from *Business Week*, March 8, 1969.

---

of agreement, or suggest compromises, but his decisions are not binding, and need not be accepted by the contesting parties. The United States government provides most mediation services through an independent agency called the Federal Mediation and Conciliation Service, while most states and some large municipalities provide similar services.

The Economics of Unions

Labor unions have a measurable—though debatable—influence on the economy. Their influence is particularly relevant in the spheres of resource allocation, economic stability, and growth.

HOW UNIONS MAY RAISE WAGES

Chief among the unions' many objectives is the raising of wages. Several interesting theories and models

of wage determination can be developed to illustrate different kinds of competitive and monopolistic market situations. Some of these have been formulated in previous chapters that dealt with marginal productivity, income distribution, and the determination of factor prices. In this chapter, we shall focus on some simple competitive models that employ familiar supply and demand diagrams. Three types of situations are illustrated in Exhibit 2, where the supply and demand curves in each diagram relate the price of labor, expressed in wages, and the quantity of labor supplied and demanded.

"Featherbedding" Model

In Exhibit 2a, the union seeks to increase the demand for labor—that is, shift the demand curve to the right—through the use of *featherbedding* techniques. These are "make-work" rules or practices designed by unions to restrict output by increasing artificially the amount of labor or labor time employed on a particular job. For example, the Painters Union has limited the width of brushes and the sizes of rollers; the Meat Cutters Union has required prewrapped meat to be rewrapped on the job; the Trainmen's Union has demanded that railroads eliminate the use of radio telephones by crewmen and revert back to hand signals and lanterns; the Railroad Brotherhood was able for years to maintain a "fireman" on diesel locomotives that have no fire; and bus drivers in New York and other large cities have sometimes effected slowdowns by observing all safety regulations to the letter, with the result that buses have been put an average of 30 minutes behind schedule on moderately long runs.

Most featherbedding practices are imposed under the guise of promoting health or safety, but in reality they are often self-protective devices which often reflect the insecurity of workers in a declining industry. There is a fundamental need, therefore, for adequate retraining programs to permit the shifting of workers to new jobs. Otherwise, featherbedding practices, like other restrictive devices whether they are employed by unions or by business firms, must ultimately result in higher prices to consumers as well as a misallocation of society's resources.

Exhibit 2

How Unions May Raise Wages in Competitive Markets

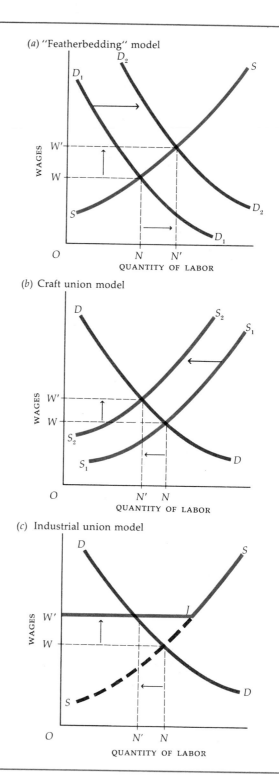

(a) "Featherbedding" model

Increase the Demand for Labor

Through "featherbedding" or other restrictive and make-work practices, unions may succeed in shifting the demand for labor to the right from D_1D_1 to D_2D_2. This will increase the equilibrium quantity of labor from ON to ON', and the equilibrium wage from OW to OW'.

(b) Craft union model

Decrease the Supply of Labor

If a craft union can restrict the supply of labor by shifting the supply curve from S_1S_1 to S_2S_2, it will reduce the equilibrium quantity of labor from ON to ON' and raise the equilibrium wage from OW to OW'.

(c) Industrial union model

Organize all Workers in an Industry

An industrial union covering an entire industry would seek a wage level such as OW' which is above the equilibrium wage of OW. The supply curve of labor would thus change from SS to W'JS, and the equilibrium quantity would therefore change from ON to ON'.

Craft Union Model

In chart (b), a craft union composed of workers in a particular trade, such as carpenters or electricians, seeks to restrict the supply of labor in order to raise wages. The union may do this by imposing high obstacles to entry for those seeking membership—such as long apprenticeship requirements, high initiation fees, closed membership periods, and so forth. In the more general sense, unions have often sought to restrict the overall supply of labor in the economy by supporting legislation to: (1) curb immigration, (2) shorten the workweek, (3) reduce child labor, and (4) assure compulsory retirement.

Industrial Union Model

In chart (c), the union seeks to organize all workers in an industry and to impose a wage which is above the equilibrium wage. This changes the supply curve as explained in the exhibit. Thus at the union-imposed wage of OW', employers can hire as many as $W'J$ units of labor, and they can hire no labor at less than this wage. The new supply curve $W'JS$ is thus perfectly elastic over the segment $W'J$, signifying that the industry can buy this much labor at the union wage. If it wants more than $W'J$ units of labor, it will have to pay a higher wage. According to the diagram, of course, the industry will demand only ON' units of labor at the wage rate imposed by the union.

ARE UNIONS TOO BIG?

These three models of how unions may seek to raise wages illustrate the following basic criticism often leveled against them:

Unions are monopolies; as such they engage in restrictive practices in order to achieve benefits (wages) above the free market equilibrium levels that would exist in a competitive system, and thereby cause resource misallocation, unemployment, and inflation.

Keep in mind, however, that the same restrictive charges can equally well be leveled against any organization that has a substantial degree of monopoly power—whether it be General Motors, U.S. Steel, or the American Medical Association.

Exhibit 3 examines this criticism from both sides of the fence by comparing the charges often made against unions and their responses to these charges—both based on various pamphlets and leaflets that have been published and widely circulated by the AFL–CIO.

Exhibit 3

Are Unions Too Big?

The Charges Against Unions

1. Unions fix the price of labor through the exertion of their monopoly power and thereby extract excessively high wages.

2. Unions monopolize job opportunities through the use of the union shop.

3. Unions have the power to shut down whole industries as a result of multiunit bargaining.

4. Unions have become financial giants because of their tax-exempt status and the use of the dues checkoff system.

5. Unions, because of their great monopolistic power, can determine the life or death of thousands of individual businesses.

How the Unions Reply

1. Despite the alleged monopoly power of unions, the average worker's take-home pay is still inadequate.

2. The union shop is simply an application of the democratic principle of majority rule.

3. Multiunit bargaining is necessary in order to stabilize wage rates among competing employers.

4. The assets of unions have made possible many significant advances in social welfare, and these assets are minute compared to the assets of giant corporations.

5. Unions seek countervailing power against the firms with which they bargain; they try to benefit their workers, not drive firms out of business.

These and other criticisms of unions have led to suggestions that their monopolistic power should be restricted or controlled. At least four common remedies, along with an equal number of responses by unions, have been proposed:

Subject Unions to the Antitrust Laws

LABOR'S REPLY. The antitrust laws were designed for profit-motivated corporations, not welfare-motivated unions. These laws involve complex issues which are not directly applicable to union practices and objectives, and it would be logically wrong as well as socially and economically unjust to subject unions to them.

Prohibit Multiunit Bargaining

LABOR'S REPLY. Multiunit bargaining enables small businesses to present a united front against union demands. Otherwise, small businesses would be overpowered by unions.

Break Large Unions up into Local Bodies

LABOR'S REPLY. Breaking up large unions into smaller ones would make them even more monopolistic in setting the price of labor. There would be several unions in each major industry, with each union monopolizing its own labor supply and seeking the highest possible wage from its employer. The union in General Motors, for example, would press for its own demands without concern with whether Ford, Chrysler, or American Motors could match those demands.

Outlaw the Union Shop

LABOR'S REPLY. Since workers elect the union that will represent them, the existence of union shops is democracy in action. Besides, eliminating the union shop would not necessarily reduce a union's ability to employ weapons such as boycotts and strikes.

The problem of union monopoly is thus a complex one. Although there is no doubt that unions possess varying degrees of monopoly power, there is no simple solution to the question of what should be done about it. Most economists would probably agree, however, that an attack against specific abuses rather than a sweeping attack against unions in general provides the most realistic and desirable approach.

SUMMARY OF IMPORTANT IDEAS

1. The chief overall objective of unions is to improve the wages and working conditions of their members by bargaining with employers. Much of the history of the union movement in America can be viewed as an attempt to achieve this goal.

2. The period from the Revolution to the Civil War witnessed the beginnings of the American labor movement. Some craft unions were started despite the opposition of employers. The courts, whose judges came mostly from upper-middle-class backgrounds, were largely unsympathetic to labor's cause. Strikes and boycotts, the drive for the closed shop, and the federating of unions at the local and national level were begun during this period.

3. From the end of the Civil War to the Depression was the formative period of unionism. For a short time the Knights of Labor dominated the labor movement, but it began to be replaced by the American Federation of Labor in the late 1880s. Under the leadership of Samuel Gompers, and in the face of great hostility toward unions that often resulted in violence and bloodshed, the AFL's philosophy of business unionism, federalism, and voluntarism emerged as the expressed views of the majority of organized workers.

4. From the depression years of the thirties until the end of World War II, the labor movement expanded rapidly. Under the Norris-LaGuardia Act (1932), the yellow-dog contract was outlawed and the use of injunctions against unions was greatly restricted. Under the National Labor Relations Act (Wagner Act) of 1935, labor's right to organize and bargain collectively with employers was guaranteed, and unfair labor practices by employers were prohibited. The Congress of Industrial Organizations emerged in this period and was extremely successful in organizing industrial unions.

5. After World War II, unions entered an age of maturity. The following have been among the chief events since then:

a. Congress sought to curb some of the power of labor unions by passing the National Labor Relations Act (Taft-Hartley Act) of 1947. This law prohibited the closed shop, outlawed "unfair labor practices" of unions, and imposed other regulations on union practices.

b. The AFL and CIO merged in 1955 to form one huge labor organization for the purpose of strengthening the bargaining position of workers.

c. The Labor-Management Reporting and Disclosure Act (Landrum-Griffin Act) of 1959 constrained further the power of unions by requiring unions and union officers to submit periodic financial reports, and by imposing other restrictions on various union practices.

d. In 1968, the United Automobile Workers under Walter Reuther disaffiliated from the AFL–CIO and joined with the International Brotherhood of Teamsters to form a new labor organization—the Alliance For Labor Action.

6. Unions try to improve the status of workers by bargaining collectively with management. Although there is no "typical" collective bargaining agreement, the major issues usually involve matters pertaining to wages, industrial relations, multiunit bargaining, and the settlement of labor-management disputes.

7. The chief issues of collective bargaining may often consist of the following: wages, dealing with questions concerning time versus incentive payments, profit sharing, wage structures, job classifications, and supplementary or fringe benefits; industrial relations, involving the rules and regulations pertaining to union-management relationships; multiunit bargaining, dealing with the nature of the collective bargaining arrangement; settlement of labor-management disputes, such as the use of arbitration or mediation.

8. Various supply and demand models may be constructed to illustrate how unions seek to raise the wages of their members. Thus in a featherbedding model, the union tries to shift the demand curve for labor to the right; in a craft union model, the union tries to shift the supply curve of labor to the left; in an industrial union model, the union seeks to impose a wage "floor" above the market equilibrium level.

9. The basic criticism of unions is that they are monopolies which engage in restrictive practices in order to raise wages above free market equilibrium levels, and hence cause resource misallocation, unemployment, and inflation. Unions reply that they exert countervailing power against the firms with which they bargain and that they thereby benefit not only workers but also society as a whole.

FOR HOMEWORK AND DISCUSSION

1. *Terms and concepts to review:*

union
craft union
Commonwealth (Mass.) vs. Hunt (1842)
yellow-dog contract
National Labor Relations (Wagner) Act (1935)
National Labor Relations Board
company union
industrial union
Labor-Management Relations (Taft-Hartley) Act (1947)
jurisdictional strike
secondary boycott
featherbedding
union shop
right-to-work laws
independent union
American Federation of Labor–Congress of Industrial Organizations
Norris LaGuardia Act (1932)

closed shop
Knights of Labor
Labor-Management Reporting and Disclosure (Landrum-Griffin) Act (1959)
Alliance for Labor Action
collective bargaining
collective agreement
basic wages
supplementary (fringe) benefits
job classification
industrial relations
open shop
checkoff
multiunit bargaining
coalition bargaining
injunction
lockout
boycott
strike
arbitration
mediation (conciliation)

2. Outline briefly the highlights of the labor movement from the time of the Revolution to the present.

3. Pro-labor factions have argued that the Taft-Hartley Act was a major setback to the labor movement and unfair to organized labor. If you were a *defender* of the Act, how would you criticize this viewpoint? Give some examples.

4. If you were a union leader bargaining for better wages and working conditions, what criteria would you use to support your arguments? What kinds of issues might you want to negotiate?

5. What would be the probable effects of a law that required all labor-management disputes to be settled by government arbitration?

6. Which has a greater degree of monopoly power—a union's monopoly of a labor market, or a firm's monopoly of a product market? Why?

7. Do unions really raise wages? That is, do wages in unionized industries rise faster than they would if those industries were nonunionized? What are some of the basic considerations to take into account in answering these questions?

REFERENCES AND READING SUGGESTIONS

BEAL, EDWIN F., and EDWARD D. WICKERSHAM, *The Practice of Collective Bargaining,* 3d ed., Irwin, Homewood, Illinois, 1967.

BERNSTEIN, IRVING, *The Turbulent Years,* Houghton-Mifflin, Boston, 1970. A history of the American worker during the gut era of the labor movement, 1933–1941. The same author's *The Lean Years* covers the period 1920–1933. Both books are part of a two-volume series.

BLOOM, GORDON F., and HERBERT R. NORTHRUP, *Economics of Labor Relations,* 5th ed., Irwin, Homewood, Illinois, 1965.

CARTTER, ALLAN M., and F. RAY MARSHALL, *Labor Economics,* Irwin, Homewood, Illinois, 1967.

ROWAN, RICHARD L., and HERBERT R. NORTHRUP (eds.), *Readings In Labor Economics and Labor Relations,* Irwin, Homewood, Illinois, 1968.

CHAPTER 30

Social Welfare: Can We Overcome Insecurity and Poverty?

CHAPTER PREVIEW

What chief social measures exist today to provide protection against the insecurity of old age, unemployment, disability, ill health, and death?

How can we explain the fact that in the richest country on earth, at least 15 percent of American families are poor?

What can be done about the problems of poverty and deprivation that confront more than 25 million Americans? In general, what are the economic effects of proposed programs for social reform?

Security or insecurity? Welfare or illfare?

These are the alternatives that are sometimes posed in discussions of America's social problems—the problems of insecurity and poverty. For there are those who contend that a concern for social welfare makes men dependent on their government and is therefore contrary to the American tradition—a tradition based on the Puritan ethic of self-reliance, industry, and thrift.

But anyone who is familiar with the history of social reform in America knows that these contentions are nothing new. From the nineteenth century to the present, we have seen the abolition of slavery, the introduction of free public education, the passage of protective legislation for labor, the provision of public charity for the needy, and the enactment of social security legislation providing some protection against the losses that may result from old age, disability, ill health, and unemployment. And always there were those who cried that such measures of protection were alien to the American tradition. In view of our history, it seems evident that our tradition is not as simple and Puritanical as these stalwart defenders make it out to be.

Thus, we shall find in this chapter that the social welfare measures which are proposed today are no different in their underlying philosophy than those which were introduced a century or more ago. The differences that do exist are to be found in the scope of their objectives and in the details that compose them.

Insecurity and Social Security

A family is insecure if it stands a chance of suffering economically from a loss of income. Such losses may occur as a result of unemployment, illness, injury, retirement, or death of the breadwinner. Because of such contingencies, and the consequent hardships, our present program of social security was instituted during the Great Depression.

The *Social Security Act of 1935* is the basic comprehensive social security law of the United States. It provides for: (1) social insurance programs for old age, survivors, disability, and health insurance (OASDHI), and for unemployment, both of which yield payments to insured persons or their survivors;

and (2) a public charity program in the form of welfare services, institutional care, food, housing, and other forms of assistance. Some of the provisions of the Act (with its many subsequent amendments) are administered and financed by the federal government, some by state and local governments, and some by all three levels of government. See Exhibit 1.

By sketching some of the Act's main features, we can gain a better understanding of the underlying logic and philosophy of our social security system.

SOCIAL INSURANCE PROGRAMS

The several insurance programs that are contained in the Act are diverse in their coverage, benefits,

Exhibit 1

Social Welfare Expenditures Under Selected Public Programs: 1960 to 1970*

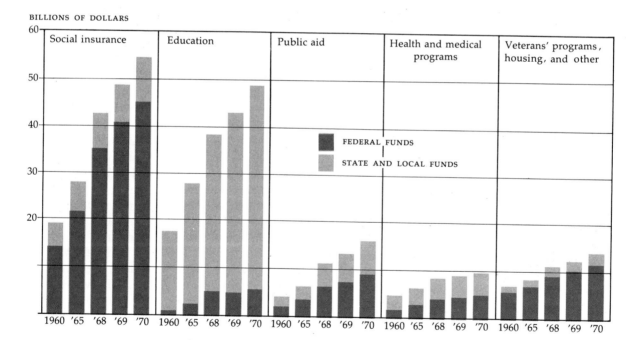

* Fiscal year data.

SOURCE: U.S. Department of Commerce, Bureau of the Census. Data from Department of Health, Education and Welfare, Social Security Administration.

financing, and administration. They can be classified, however, into two categories providing protection against: (1) old age, disability, ill health, and death; and (2) unemployment.

Old Age, Survivors, Disability, and Health Insurance (OASDHI)

The OASDHI program embraces what most people commonly refer to as "social security." It is actually an annuity scheme—that is, a special type of compulsory saving program—which provides cash benefits when earnings are cut off by old age, total disability, or death. The benefits vary according to the amount of social security taxes collected from the employer and the employee. These rates increase over the years, presumably to compensate for inflation. More than 90 percent of all employed persons are eligible for benefits, including retirement benefits at age 65, and a similar proportion of mothers and children are eligible to receive survivors' payments if the head of the family dies. Since 1966, medical and hospital insurance for the aged (over 65), commonly known as Medicare, provides for the health needs of elderly people with modest incomes.

Unemployment Insurance

The unemployment insurance program is administered by the individual states within a general framework established by the federal government. It provides for *unemployment benefits*—that is, weekly payments to "covered" workers who are involuntarily unemployed for a specified number of weeks. The specific figures, of course, vary from state to state; but in the late 1960s about 50 million workers, or two-thirds of the civilian labor force, were eligible for unemployment benefits. The average payment made was $41 per week, and the average period of payment was 11 weeks.

CHARITABLE PROGRAMS—WELFARE

The noninsurance part of the social security system consists of charitable or welfare programs administered by federal, state, and local governments, to which the federal government contributes substan-

tially. They are often referred to as special assistance programs because they are intended to help special categories of needy persons. The more important programs are:

1. Aid to the aged, the blind, and the totally and permanently disabled

2. Medical assistance to the needy

3. Food distribution through relief programs, food stamp plans, and government subsidization of school lunches

4. Housing subsidies to provide public housing projects and cash rent supplements for low-income groups

5. Welfare services in the form of institutional care for needy adults and children (such as free hospitals and orphanages), health, rehabilitation, and counseling services, and financial assistance to needy families

In addition to these, there are general assistance programs administered and financed exclusively by various state and local governments.

EVALUATING SOCIAL SECURITY: IS IT ADEQUATE?

The social security system—including both federal and state programs—provides a measure or protection against most major forms of insecurity. Nevertheless, it has been the subject of severe criticisms.

First, social insurance benefits paid by the federal government to the aged, survivors, and permanently disabled are too low, and payments made by state insurance programs to the temporarily unemployed and disabled are woefully inadequate. Although benefits from both sources have increased over the years, they still lag behind the increase in living standards and costs, and are generally below the poverty line. As for coverage, the federal insurance program against old age, survivorship, and total disability covers virtually the entire civilian labor force, but state insurance coverage against occupational injury, illness, and unemployment is far less complete.

Second, the charitable or welfare programs have been the most controversial part of the system. Since the federal government pays most of the bill, but the administration of the programs is left largely up to the states, coverage has been nonuniform and eligibility has been restricted by arbitrary residence requirements and embarrassing means tests. In most places the amounts provided have been pitifully low and far short of need. Various estimates have indicated that less than a third of the people living in poverty have been helped.

WELFARE—"RESENTED," "DERIDED," "HATED"

During the 1960s, criticisms began to mount both in and out of Washington against the welfare programs, particularly a part called Aid to Families With Dependent Children (AFDC)—a program providing assistance to families with young or otherwise dependent children in which there was either no breadwinner present or one whose earning ability was greatly impaired. As shown in Exhibit 2, this group rose from less than one-third of the nation's 3.1 million welfare receivers in the mid-forties to over two-thirds of its 9.3 million recipients in the late sixties.

Aside from this alarming increase, welfare in general and AFDC in particular were attacked as inefficient, costly, grossly unfair and nonuniform among the states, and contributing to family disunion by encouraging the father to leave home so that the mother and children could become eligible for payments. These grim social and economic consequences were epitomized by Mayor Lindsay of New York when he stated in his budget request for 1969: "Welfare is resented by those who pay for it, derided by those who administer it, and hated by those who receive it."

THE NIXON FAS PROPOSAL

The situation finally came to a head in late 1969. On August 8 of that year, in a television address to the nation, President Nixon denounced the welfare system as "a colossal failure." In its place, he proposed a revised system with the following fundamental features.

1. The federal government would set uniform minimum benefit levels for welfare recipients, thereby

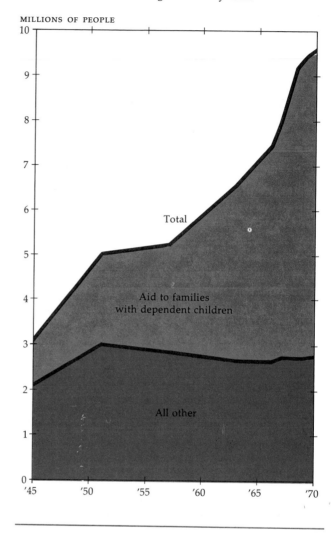

Exhibit 2

Number of Persons Receiving Welfare Payments

MILLIONS OF PEOPLE

replacing state standards. The states and cities, however, could still add to the federal base if they choose to do so.

2. Family units—regardless of whether or not there was a father in the home—would be eligible for benefits according to their income. The benefits would decrease as the family's income increased, thus providing more of a financial incentive to work.

3. An able-bodied but unemployed father must register with a local employment service and be willing to accept "suitable" work or job training if available, in order to be eligible for a portion of federal benefits. Failure to do so would make the balance of the federal benefits payable to the mother and children through a trustee or welfare agency.

4. To encourage vocational education, new federal job-training programs would be made available, accompanied by a monthly stipend for those who enroll.

5. New and expanded child day-care centers would be available so that poor mothers of dependent children would be encouraged to work.

6. Families of the working poor, who previously received no help, would be subsidized so that they ended up with more income than a family entirely on welfare.

President Nixon referred to his program as a Family Assistance System (FAS). He emphasized that it would do away with the widely criticized AFDC plan, that it would encourage the Puritan work ethic by getting able-bodied parents off the dole as soon as possible, and that it would raise the benefits in low-paying welfare states like Mississippi, thereby stemming or even reversing the flow of poor people into high-paying welfare states like New York. See Box 1.

Many economists and political leaders agree with these arguments. It now remains to be seen how the plan (or some modification of it) works out if it is approved by Congress.

Affluence and Poverty: A Nation Within a Nation

America's aggregate wealth and opportunity are unmatched by any nation in history. Its fields and factories generate a superabundance of foods, goods, and gadgets; its people possess over 60 million automobiles, and 70 million television sets (10 million with color); more than two-thirds of its families own their homes.

The signs of affluence are everywhere—except for 25 to 30 million Americans who live in poverty and deprivation. This group is three times the population of Belgium. It is composed of all races of men, women, and children who live near or below the bare subsistence level.

WHAT IS POVERTY?

What constitutes "bare subsistence"? Ever since 1962, economists and statisticians have grappled with the problem of defining and measuring poverty. Central to the concept is the so-called *"poverty line"* —a sliding income scale which varies between rural and urban locations according to family size. The level for an urban family of four—which is regarded as fairly typical—was somewhat under $4,000 in 1970.

Of course, many of the people who fall below the line, such as a married medical school student or an elderly couple on social security who own their home and car, are poor only by definition. Nor does the poverty line distinguish between costs of living in different areas of the country: $4,000 goes a lot farther in Meridian, Mississippi, than in San Francisco or New York City. Nevertheless, in view of the following facts, the definition of poverty seems to understate the real dimensions of the situation.

1. A poverty-line income of $4,000 for a family of four allows for no dental care and practically no medical care; it also permits no movies, newspapers, or books, and very little clothing, meat, fruits, or vegetables.

2. Approximately 13 percent of the total population is classified as poor. However, contrary to widespread public opinion, Negroes are not the largest proportion of the group: two out of every three poor Americans are white; among the 11 million rural poor, almost 9 million are white.

3. About 70 percent of the total population live in cities and towns, and so it is not surprising that over 60 percent of the poor are urban dwellers. About half the poor are under 21 years old, and a third—about 5½ million of them—are over 65.

Box 1

Nixon's Proposed Welfare Plans, 1969 and 1972

Nixon's 1969 proposal introduced a federal welfare minimum of $1,600 a year for a family of four, with an extra $300 for each additional member. The basic allowance would be reduced as private income increased. When the family reached an income of $3,920, all federal assistance would end. Benefits paid by local or state authorities, however, could be added to the total.

Up to $720 in earned income would be allowed without suffering any reduction in the maximum federal subsidy of $1,600. (The $720 constituted what the government considered the cost of working, such as transportation, clothes, and lunches, for a year.) The descending scale of federal subsidy—apart from any state payment—would work this way for a family of four:

Earnings	Benefit	Total
$ 720	$1,600	$2,300
1,000	1,460	2,460
2,000	960	2,960
3,000	460	3,460
3,920	0	3,920

In 1972, Nixon urged Congress to enact his revised Family Assistance System, which included a guaranteed annual income of $2,400 for a family of four.

How Welfare Varies Among the States

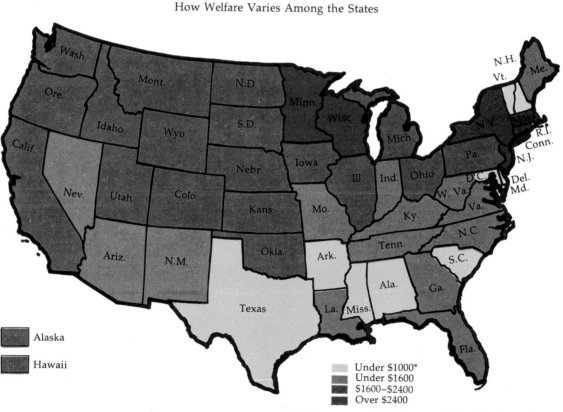

Alaska

Hawaii

Under $1000*
Under $1600
$1600–$2400
Over $2400

* Average annual ADC payments for a family of four.

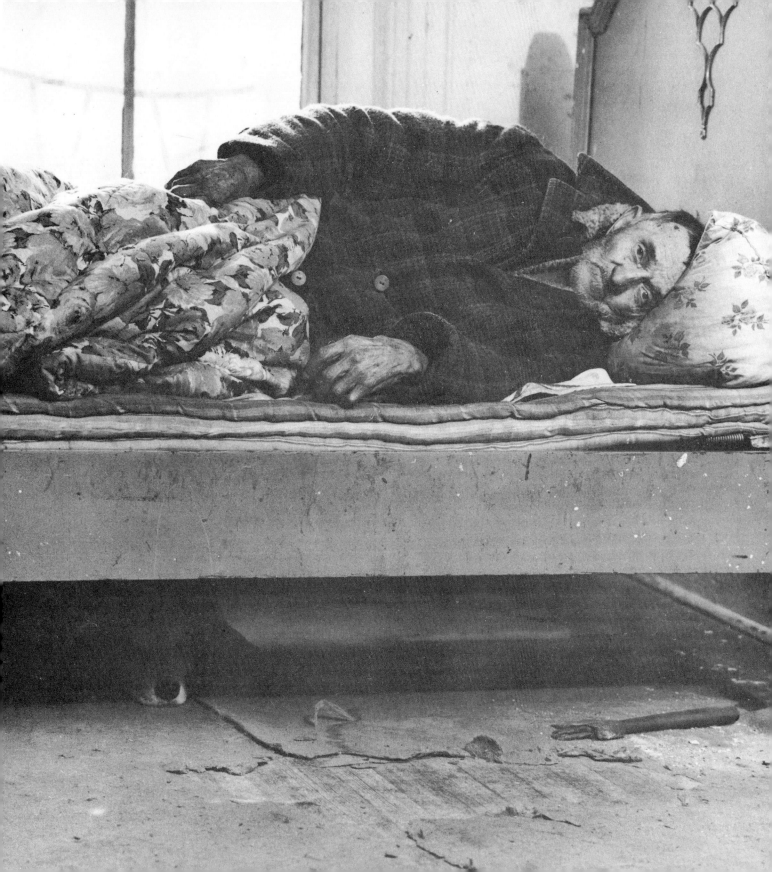

Poverty

Who are the nation's poor? For many Americans the image of a typical family living in poverty is something like this: lazy and irresponsible, probably black, recently arrived from the Deep South to get higher welfare benefits, and carelessly breeding children; with little effort, they cheat their way onto the relief rolls and live better than they could if they worked.

Although there may be some who fit this picture, the vast majority of America's poor do not. Of the 25.4 million Americans living below the poverty level, half live outside the cities. 17.4 million are white, and more than half are under 25 years old. 2.1 million heads of poverty families did not work at all in 1968, but 2.3 million worked full time—and still could not raise their families out of poverty.

Charles Harbutt

Statistically, these families are not large; the 2.3 million families receiving federal aid to dependent children in 1970 had an average of less than three children.

Although most of America's poor are white, a much greater percentage of blacks are living below the poverty level; 34.7 percent live in poverty com-

pared with 10 percent of whites—an indication of the dislocation and discrimination in American society.

Life at the bottom is a difficult and humiliating ordeal. It means poor diet, overcrowded rooms, broken plumbing, decaying housing, and inadequate facilities for education and recreation—not to mention the shocking health conditions that prevail in most poverty areas. And it means a constant struggle against despair.

Many suggestions have been advanced for lifting the burden of poverty, and a great deal of money is being spent. State and local welfare expenditures totaled more than $11.2 billion in 1968, and the federal Office of Economic Opportunity committed $7.6 billion to VISTA, the Job Corps, rural loans, and other anti-poverty programs. But no comprehensive national plan has yet been adopted. Such a plan would have to include a reform of the entire welfare system and might also involve an incentive program such as the negative income tax. Legislation will not eliminate the causes of poverty. Yet some type of sweeping policy must eventually be adopted if America is to measure up to its ideals.

As suggested by Exhibit 3, there is no simple and unique definition of poverty. It is an economic and psychological state of being that varies for different people from time to time and from place to place.

WHAT ARE THE CAUSES AND COSTS OF POVERTY?

We may distinguish among three different "types" of poverty, according to the economic, social, and personal factors that cause them. These also give rise to economic and social costs.

Cyclical Poverty. A fall in aggregate demand may cause a depression or a deep recession; the result is mass unemployment and widespread poverty. This situation occurred in the depression of the 1930s. However, with the growth of modern macroeconomic theory and policy, political leaders have learned how to avoid such severe setbacks in the economy, and hence this cause of poverty is no longer considered a serious problem.

Exhibit 3

The Paradox of Poverty

What constitutes poverty? In some of the poorest counties of the nation, the great majority of homes lack baths and inside toilets, and a large minority have no running water. By present-day American standards they would be classified as poverty-stricken.

But let us examine the situation more closely:

In Tunica County, Mississippi, where 80 percent of the families live below the poverty line, 40 percent or more of the households own washing machines and over 50 percent own cars and television sets (some of them in color).

In Harlan County, Kentucky, one of the poorest in the country:

    88 percent have washing machines
    67 percent have TV
    42 percent have a telephone
    59 percent have a car

The poor in America thus have many of the accoutrements of an affluent society. This is the paradox of poverty. *The American poor are not the same as the starving poor of India or China, but they are poor nevertheless.*

Community Poverty. A region may lose its economic base or its major source of income and employment, thereby leaving an entire populance in a state of economic deprivation. Among the classic examples of this are the Appalachian coal regions, which have suffered drastically from declining demands for coal and from the introduction of labor-saving technology in coal mining. This type of poverty can be remedied only through regional economic development programs or outward migration.

Personal Poverty. Poverty has always existed among some individuals and families, in prosperity as well as in depression, in high-income regions and in low-income ones. It is due to personal and social factors, some of which are beyond the individual's control. For example, aside from that small proportion of the poor whom sociologists refer to as the "disreputable poor" (i.e., the tramps, beggars, derelicts, etc.) there are those families that are poverty-stricken because they are victims of racial prejudice, inadequate training and job opportunities, physical or mental handicaps, desertion of the breadwinner, and other causes.

Poverty levies serious economic and social costs. Sociological studies have concluded that it causes ill health and emotional disturbance and helps to spread disease. It also causes delinquency, vice, and crime. All these impose heavy costs on the community, which must maintain police and fire protection, courts and jails, public health and sanitation facilities, and welfare programs.

Further, there is evidence that poverty breeds poverty—that the children of the poor grow up and marry others who are similarly deprived both physically and culturally. They tend to have more children than they can provide with a proper start in life. These children are likewise raised in a poverty environment, and so the cycle perpetuates itself from one generation to the next.

The War on Poverty

Considering the high cost of poverty, what can be done about America's nation of the poor? In order to launch an attack on the problem, Congress passed the *Economic Opportunity Act of 1964,* declaring that a national policy goal will be:

> . . . to eliminate the paradox of poverty in the midst of plenty in this Nation by opening to everyone the opportunity for education and training, the opportunity to work, and the opportunity to live in decency and dignity.

The Economic Opportunity Act opened one of many doors to waging a war on poverty. In addition, a number of specific proposals have been advanced —beyond those involving improvements in the welfare system itself—which fall loosely into two groups: (1) family allowances or guaranteed annual incomes; and (2) negative income taxes.

FAMILY ALLOWANCES OR GUARANTEED ANNUAL INCOMES

Many sociologists and social workers have suggested the adoption of a *family allowance* system. Under this plan, every family in the country, rich or poor, would receive a certain amount of money based exclusively on the number and age of its children. Those families that are above certain designated income levels would return all or part of the money with their income taxes; those below specified income levels would keep it. More than 60 nations, including Canada and all the European countries, give family allowances.

A modified version of the family allowance plan is the *guaranteed annual income.* This would award all families under the "poverty line" a straight allowance for each parent plus specified amounts for each child according to the size of the family. As the family's income rose, the payment would be reduced until a break-even level a little higher than the poverty line was reached.

Under both the family allowance and guaranteed annual income plans, families would not be as well or better off by not working. Nevertheless, there is substantial opposition to these proposals in Congress, partly because of the fear that they would be too costly, and partly because many legislators believe that they place more emphasis on governmental "big brother" paternalism than on providing jobs.

A NEGATIVE INCOME TAX

A scheme which has received widespread interest and support from economists, businessmen, and political leaders—regardless of their liberal or conservative leanings—has been the *negative income tax.* This would guarantee the poor a certain minimum income through a type of reverse income tax: a poor family, depending on its size and private income level, would be paid by the government enough either to reduce or close the gap between what it earned and some explicit minimum level of income which might be equal to or modestly above the government's designated poverty line. The size of payments, of course, would depend on the specific formula adopted. A hypothetical illustration appears in Exhibit 4.

Several major advantages are claimed for this proposal.

Administrative Efficiency. The present governmental administrative machinery—namely the Internal Revenue Service and the Treasury—would handle records and disburse payments, so that a new government agency would not be needed.

Income Criterion. Income deficiency would be the sole criterion for establishing eligibility for subsidy, instead of the plethora of criteria that have existed in the past. Many more millions of poor families would thus be eligible. With the resulting expanded coverage, many poor families would have an income "floor" under them and would begin to break the cycle of poverty that has kept some of them on welfare for several generations.

Incentive Maintenance. As the family's income increased, payments from the government would decrease. Thus the incentive to work in order to gain more income would not be reduced.

But despite these advantages, there are also difficulties to be recognized.

High Cost. The negative income tax could not be administered, as many of its proponents claim, with only a small addition to the staff of the Internal Revenue Service. Checks would have to be sent out

Exhibit 4

How the Negative Income Tax Might Someday Work

This is how the negative income tax plan might work for a family of six, consisting of two adults and four children:

1. As the family's income increases, the government payments that it receives decrease according to the formula:

$$\text{Government payments} = \$2,600 - \tfrac{1}{2} (\text{earned income})$$

Thus you can verify with the formula or from the chart that if earned income is zero, the family receives a government payment of $2,600 a year. If earned income rises to $1,000, the family receives a government payment of $2,100, giving it a spendable income of $3,100. Similarly, at an earned income of $2,000, the government payment is $1,600, thus making spendable income $3,600.

2. The break-even point occurs at an earned income of $5,200. At this point government payments are zero, and at higher income levels the family begins to pay income taxes.

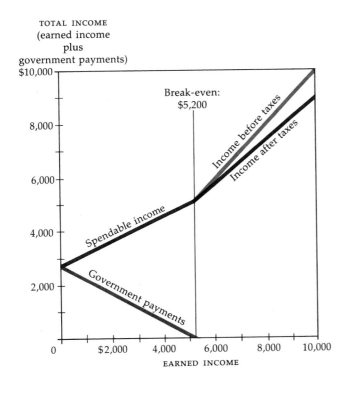

monthly or weekly, and effective controls established. This large task would require substantial changes in the IRS administrative structure.

Opposition by Middle-Income Classes. Workers in the middle-income groups would receive no benefits from the negative income tax, as they would from a family allowance plan. In addition, they would undoubtedly resent paying taxes to subsidize families whose annual incomes were only a few hundred dollars less than their own.

CONCLUSION

Virtually all income plans that are now in existence or being talked about have at least three variables in common:

1. An income "floor"—that is, a minimum level of income to be received by everyone

2. A positive "tax" rate which decreases government allowances as income increases

3. A break-even level of income at which the government allowance is zero

The problem in setting up an income plan, of course, involves the correct selection of these variables while maintaining proper work incentives. The minimum income and break-even levels should not be set so high as to subsidize those who do not need assistance.

In general, all income plans aim at the same goal—to put money into the hands of the poor. At best, therefore, they can only relieve the symptoms of poverty—not its cause. To cure the disease itself, an income plan must be combined with proper work incentive and job training programs.

SUMMARY OF IMPORTANT IDEAS

1. The United States social security system is based primarily on the Social Security Act of 1935 and its many subsequent amendments. Through social insurance, the system provides a measure of protection against old age, unemployment, disability, ill health, and death; through charity, it provides welfare services for the needy. For the most part, the benefits provided are below living standards and costs.

America's Own Underdeveloped Nation

In its constant search for new markets and influence, United States business would be delighted to discover a nation the size of Spain that desperately needs more goods and services, raises no tariff barriers, welcomes American investment, and adheres to the American political and economic system.

Such a nation exists—here in America. It is the country of the American poor. Despite its eagerness to invest in nations that promise profit and stability, United States business has done little about that opportunity on its own doorstep. In that neglect it has resembled government. Until they gave themselves visibility and clout by rioting, the poor were virtually ignored by most affluent Americans.

Even today, the size, nature, and seriousness of the problem are still indistinct, and the commitment to its cure is still lukewarm. Government agencies disagree on the number of poor people because they differ over definitions of poverty. Indeed, government estimates range all the way from 15 million to 34 million poor people. Whatever the precise figure, two facts stand out. First, there are more poor whites than poor blacks—though a higher percentage of black people than white are poor. Second, rural people are worse off in every measurable way than their urban counterparts.

No Real Help For People

Rural problems are at the roots of today's urban poverty. In the past thirty years, new technology has raised farm productivity to levels that are the envy of other nations. Government policy aided that "green revolution." But it did little to help the millions of people displaced by ma-

chines. They were given the choice of starving where they were, or moving to the cities, where there is at least the hope of a job—or welfare payments large enough to sustain them.

Most farmworkers are poorly educated and lack skills marketable in the cities. Many who migrated to the cities were black, and were forced to challenge the barriers of race as well as ignorance. Like all great migratory movements, the flight from farm to city also broke up families. To compound the problem, the great influx of migrants coincided with a rush of middle-class whites to the suburbs. Some left to avoid poor neighbors—usually because they were black as well as poor. Other whites left for more honorable reasons: business and jobs were moving out of the cities—partly to avoid taxes, partly because modern production techniques require large, single-story factories that simply are not available in densely populated places.

Needed: Restoratives, not Placebos

All the programs launched since President Kennedy's time have merely alleviated poverty. The poor have had a dose of soothing syrup, not a restorative. To cure what ails the poor, government and business must understand the nature of poverty—and disabuse themselves of the idea that the poor can follow the legendary route of self-help. The overwhelming majority of poor people lack the knowledge, confidence, and opportunity to remedy their own condition. They are victims of the poverty cycle, which saps a man's health with poor diet, his ambition with failure, and his chances with miserable education.

The poor need education more than

the affluent do; yet they go to the worst schools. What should education in the slums be for? Clearly, it should not be designed—as it is presently—to fit its graduates for a middle-class life. Most of them will never reach that level. Instead, education should offer them confidence, as well as marketable skills. Those who can benefit from a college education should get one; but the main objective should be to raise the *general* level of education, not to create an elite within the underprivileged.

Tasks for a Partnership

Jobs are in the wrong place. Business must take jobs to the people—and people to the jobs. More plants should be encouraged to locate in the slums; others, in rural areas, as alternatives to the vanishing agricultural economic base. If no existing bus services can take workers to the plant, then businessmen must be given the incentive to provide buses—a system common in Europe, but virtually unknown here.

Through its hiring and plant location policies business has helped to create poverty. But it cannot bear alone the burden of curing it. What is needed is a partnership between business and government. So far, that partnership is more of a hope than a reality, despite pioneering efforts in some cities.

R. B.

1. *If you were to design a total program to fight poverty, what individual programs would you include?*

2. *What arguments would you make to convince the government, business, and the people in general that such a program would make sense from an economic standpoint?*

2. Poverty is one of today's most fundamental issues, affecting more than 25 million Americans. Among the basic causes or "types" are cyclical poverty, community poverty, and personal poverty. The great social and economic costs of poverty have resulted in many proposals for reform.

3. Various income schemes and assistance plans have been proposed to revise and improve our welfare program. Among the most popular are family allowances, the guaranteed annual income, and the negative income tax. No matter which approach is adopted, it must be combined with a work incentive and job training program if it is to remove people from a lifetime on the dole and make them productive, useful members of society.

FOR HOMEWORK AND DISCUSSION

1. *Terms and concepts to review:*

Social Security Act (1935)	family allowance plan
unemployment benefits	guaranteed annual income
"poverty line"	negative income tax

2. What are the main features of our social security system? Is the system adequate? Explain.

3. Why not solve the problem of poverty by simply redistributing income equally to everyone?

4. It has been suggested that there is a remarkable inverse relationship between fecundity and "hot baths"—i.e., the reasonable creature comforts of life, such as a basic but adequate amount of food, clothing, housing, sanitation facilities, etc. Therefore, it might be better to break the poverty cycle by providing poor people with these goods. What do you think of this argument? (NOTE: Do you think the same argument could apply to underdeveloped, overpopulated regions like India, China, etc.?)

5. In contrast to Question 4, suppose that providing income allowances to poor families increased their birth rates. What might this imply about the elasticity relationship between the supply of children and family income? Explain the various implications of this.

6. Evaluate the various income plans that have been proposed for attacking the problem of poverty.

REFERENCES AND READING SUGGESTIONS

BUDD, EDWARD C. (ed.), *Inequality and Poverty,* Norton, New York, 1967.

CHAMBERLAIN, NEIL W. (ed.), *Contemporary Economic Issues,* Irwin, Homewood, Illinois, 1969. Chapter 2 deals with poverty; Chapter 3 with health services.

FISHMAN, LEO (ed.), *Poverty and Affluence,* Yale University Press, New Haven, 1966.

THEOBALD, ROBERT (ed.), *The Guaranteed Income,* Doubleday, New York, 1966.

WILCOX, CLAIR, *Toward Social Welfare,* Irwin, Homewood, Illinois, 1969.

CHAPTER 31

Agricultural Decline in a Growing Economy

CHAPTER PREVIEW

How does the economics of agriculture cause the farm problem?

How effective are federal farm policies?

What would happen if different policies were adopted?

What reforms are needed?

American agriculture has been staggering from crisis to crisis for more than a century. Innumerable congressional committees, official commissions, and groups of experts have studied the farm problem. Government has spent billions of dollars to alleviate it. But a set of stubborn economic facts has so far defied solution:

1. Crops are too abundant. Abundance guarantees that most Americans will never starve—but it also keeps the price of farm products low.

2. Because Americans do have enough to eat, they will not buy much more food when their incomes rise. In other words, the demand for agricultural products is relatively income-inelastic.

3. Too much capital and too many people are employed in agriculture; *total* farm income is not enough to provide a fair return on capital, or a living wage for all farm people.

4. Government policies tend to encourage the continued employment of those unnecessarily large financial and human resources.

Somebody once said that politics is concerned with who gets what, when, and how. That epigram is particularly true of agricultural policies, which involve the spending of huge sums of government money and their distribution among various claimants. As a result, politics is inextricably intertwined with agriculture, and federal farm policies frequently contradict the prescriptions dictated by economic logic.

Economics of Agriculture: Causes of the Farm Problem

America's economic growth has created most of the problems that farmers face. Four characteristics of United States agriculture provide a useful framework for analysis:

1. Price and income inelasticities
2. Highly competitive structure
3. Rapid technological change
4. Resource immobility

These features are not unique to American agriculture. They dominate the industry in other advanced market economies, and cause similar problems.

PRICE AND INCOME INELASTICITIES

Most of the demand for agricultural products is a *derived demand*. This means that food and fiber produced on the farm are usually bought to satisfy the demand for some other commodity. For example, most people buy specific cuts of meat, not live animals; and they demand suits or dresses, not raw cotton which they would have to process themselves.

One result of the derived nature of demand for farm products is that people do not buy many more of them when prices fall, or fewer when they rise—i.e., the demand is relatively inelastic. (Remember that *price elasticity of demand* measures the percentage change in the quantity demanded of a good resulting from a 1 percent change in its price). Although the elasticities differ among various agricultural products, they are considerably less than unity for most. Studies show, for example, price elasticities ranging from 0.1 to 0.3 for wheat, cotton, tobacco, milk, sugar, and potatoes; between 0.4 and 0.6 for feed grains; and from 0.6 to 0.9 for various meats, including beef, pork, and veal.

The *price elasticity of supply*—especially within a given year—is also less than unity because production cannot be increased greatly in a single season. If prices are high, additional feed and fertilizer can be applied, and land farmed more intensively; but the industry's "plant"—the land itself—cannot be expanded very much.

Agricultural products tend also to be income-inelastic in demand. The *income elasticity of demand* is the percentage change in the quantity purchased of a good resulting from a 1 percent change in income. For most farm products this elasticity is less than 1.0 —somewhere between 0.1 and 0.2. We may therefore expect a 10 percent rise in real per capita disposable income to cause only a 1 to 2 percent rise in the purchase of most agricultural commodities.

Some Implications

Three important implications of these inelasticities should be noted.

1. Price inelasticities of demand and supply mean that small fluctuations in the output of farm products lead to large fluctuations in their prices.

2. Income inelasticity of demand means that total demand for farm products is limited largely by the rate of growth of total population. This characteristic holds in all wealthy nations: the proportion of any increase in income spent for food is always smaller in well-fed countries than in poorly fed ones.

3. As a result of both price and income inelasticities, increases in the rate of growth of farm production that exceed increases in the rate of growth of consumption will cause a downward trend in farm prices and in farmers' incomes. This has been the long-run trend in the United States. The effects are illustrated in Exhibit 1, which consists of three series: (1) an index of prices received by farmers for the products they sell; (2) an index of prices paid by farmers for the products they buy; and (3) a *parity ratio*, which is simply the index of the prices farmers receive divided by the index of the prices they pay. The parity ratio provides a measure of agriculture's economic well-being.

HIGHLY COMPETITIVE STRUCTURE

Competition is a second major characteristic of American agriculture. By competition we mean three things:

First, there are many farms in the United States—

Exhibit 1

How Well Off Are Farmers?

The long-run trend of the parity ratio has been downward since the index of prices received by farmers started dropping rapidly in 1952.

PERCENT OF 1910–1914

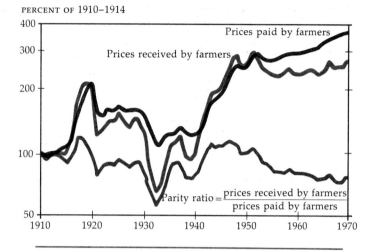

over 3 million in 1970. As a result, virtually no single farm can influence the market price by deciding to sell or not to sell. (NOTE: We say "virtually" because today there are a few large farms that can exert an influence on the market price of some commodities. This has been so only since the 1960s.)

Second, agricultural products are homogeneous—at least within broad categories. Grains, for example, are not branded products, and hence cannot be identified by the farm they came from. Milk, meat, and produce may carry the name of a store or processor, but not usually the name of the producer. Agricultural products within each class are therefore highly substitutable, and each farmer finds himself faced with a perfectly elastic demand curve at the market price for the goods he sells.

Third, there are few barriers to entering the agricultural industry. No licenses, union membership, or formal education are required. Anyone who wants to farm, and has the capital, can grow what he wants. The only exceptions are a few crops like cotton, tobacco, and rice, for which the government sets quotas. These exceptions will be examined later.

RAPID TECHNOLOGICAL CHANGE

American agriculture has made striking gains in productivity since 1930—greater gains, indeed, than were made in the previous two centuries.

What has been the nature of these advances? They have consisted of the introduction of new seeds, fertilizers, and pesticides; of improved breeds and feeds for livestock and poultry; and of the mechanization and electrification of farming. These advances have gone hand-in-hand with the development of improved capital and credit facilities, and the emergence of more technically trained and educated farmers—many of them graduates of land-grant colleges.

Government has fostered many of these advances. Much research has been sponsored by the U.S. Department of Agriculture; most of the findings have been disseminated through federal-state agricultural extension services; and government has encouraged the growth of private and public institutions to serve agriculture with new ideas and techniques.

These changes have wrought profound social and economic effects, as illustrated in Exhibit 2. The farm population and the number of farms have dropped steadily, while the average size of farms, their total output, and their output per man-hour have steadily risen. However, improvements in agriculture have not been uniform. Many farmers are still poor because they lack the capital and knowledge to become efficient producers. This, as we shall see, is the crux of the farm problem.

RESOURCE IMMOBILITY

Although the number of farms and farmworkers has been declining, there are still too many farmers on too many farms. Why should this be? Why has agriculture, which has experienced a long-run trend of declining prices and incomes relative to the rest of the economy, failed to reduce sufficiently its stock of human and nonhuman resources? Is not this failure contrary to what the "laws" of supply and demand would lead us to expect?

The fundamental difficulty is that agricultural resources are immobile. Farmers and farmworkers, for example, cannot use many of their skills in other

Exhibit 2

Farms and Farm Output

The long-run trends of the farm population, number of farms, and labor input on farms have been decreasing while those of the average size of farms, their total output, and their output per man-hour have been increasing.

Farm population, farms, and farm sizes

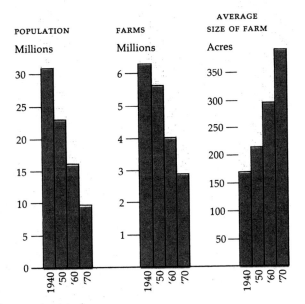

Farm output indexes

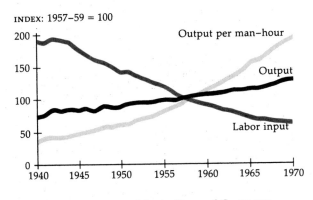

SOURCE: U.S. Departments of Agriculture and Commerce.

activities; hence they tend to remain in farming because it is the only type of work they know. Further, many of them prefer to eke out an existence in rural areas rather than seek employment in the cities.

CONCLUSION: AGRICULTURE— A DECLINING INDUSTRY

The four major economic characteristics of agriculture—namely, price and income inelasticities, a highly competitive structure, rapid technological change, and resource immobility—create a special problem in a progressive society.

As an economy grows in wealth, it devotes less of its total resources to agriculture, and more to manufacturing and services.

The cause is simple. In technologically advanced societies, the farmer can produce enough not only for himself and his family, but also for many other people. In underdeveloped countries, on the other hand, nearly everyone is forced to farm: productivity is so low that the farmer has little left to sell after growing food and fibers to feed and clothe himself and his family. The *relative* magnitude of the agricultural resource base is thus smaller in rich societies than in poor ones, and this base is being constantly "squeezed" as the society grows. Agriculture then becomes a declining industry in a growing economy, with the *proportion* of total resources employed in agriculture continuously contracting.

Many economic characteristics of agriculture can be illustrated with supply and demand curves. You will be asked to demonstrate some of the principles in problems posed at the end of this chapter.

Government Policies Toward Agriculture: Parity and Price Supports

The American farm problem can be traced back to the last third of the nineteenth century. Times were grindingly hard for farmers then; as shown in Exhibit 3, farm incomes rose very little, while farm prices fell, because the production of agricultural products rose faster than their consumption. Among the major reasons for this were:

1. The number of farms almost trebled, largely as a result of westward migration. At the same time, mechanization and scientific discoveries were raising the productivity of land and labor.

2. The rise in consumption was falling off, primarily because the *rate* of population growth had fallen significantly—from 25 percent per decade in the 1870s and 1880s to about 20 percent per decade in the 1890s. Concurrently, the proportion of per capita income spent on farm products declined from roughly a third to a fifth.

3. Although agricultural exports rose steadily, thereby helping to reduce surpluses, they did not rise fast enough, partly because competition from Canada, Australia, New Zealand, and Argentina challenged America's position in world markets.

THE GOLDEN AGE: 1896 TO WORLD WAR I

There was a dramatic change in the fortunes of American farmers as the nineteenth century drew to a close. Indeed, the years from 1896 to the end of World War I have been called by some historians "The Golden Age" of American agriculture. As Exhibit 3 shows, farm income and prices rose steadily during this period; furthermore, the agricultural population remained stable at about 32 million because the natural increase in population of about 650,000 a year went to work in the factories of America's growing cities. As a result, per capita incomes in agriculture rose relative to those in industry. Meanwhile, the value of farmers' assets—their land, buildings, livestock, and capital improvements—also appreciated in value. By World War I, although many farm people were still abysmally poor, the relative economic position of agriculture as a whole —and especially the position of major producers— had greatly improved.

Further improvement came with the outbreak of war. Foreign demand for American food and fiber increased as other nations diverted their resources to the production of war goods. As a look at Exhibit 3 shows, farm prices and incomes soared during the war and immediate postwar period.

Exhibit 3

Farm Income, Prices, and Production, 1870–1920

Farm income rose relatively little during most of the late nineteenth century, but increased sharply from 1896 until the post-World War I period.

DOLLARS (in billions)

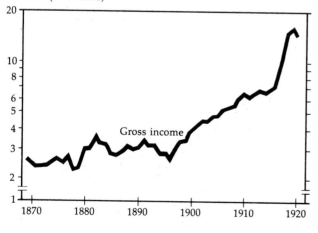

After almost a third of a century of downward prices reflecting unfavorable supply and demand conditions, prices rebounded after 1896. Production, meanwhile, rose steadily due to larger numbers of farms and advancing technology.

1909–1913 = 100

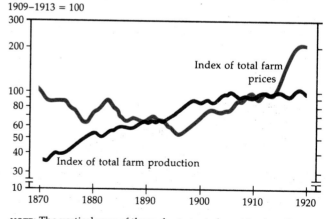

NOTE: The vertical axes of these charts are in logarithmic or "ratio" terms, thus permitting comparisons of rates of change to be made.

Agriculture: A Changing Technology

The amazing growth of agricultural output and productivity has been stimulated by improvements in technology. These pictures illustrate some of the changes that have taken place from early forms of horsepower to modern forms of machine power.

In the nineteenth century, the transition was from manpower to horsepower. The need for high horsepower posed serious logistical problems before the invention of steam- and gasoline-powered tractors. The combine was the farmer's most valuable and proud possession, as suggested by this picture of a family in the Pacific Northwest.

In the twentieth century, horsepower gave way to the tractor and to other forms of mechanical power, thereby greatly enhancing the productivity of agriculture.

Oregon Historical Society.

J. C. Allen and Co.

EARLY FORMS OF ASSISTANCE

A sharp deflation in 1920 and 1921 hurt farmers more than it did most people. Prices of agricultural commodities dropped sharply, some by more than 50 percent in less than 18 months. They never really recovered. By late 1921, to be sure, the economy had turned around; but agriculture did not share proportionately in the fruits of the prosperous 1920s. At home, the demand for farm products was dampened by a slowing in the rate of population growth; abroad, American farmers faced fiercer competition. But American agricultural output did not drop appreciably, and the result was a fall in farm prices and incomes. Many farm families lost their homes and their livelihoods through sales for delinquent taxes and mortgage foreclosures.

Agriculture's forced adjustment to new conditions was largely complete by the mid-1920s. There were fewer farmers, but as a group they were almost as prosperous as they had been before and during the War. However, they were still painfully vulnerable to swings in the economy and to the inexorable forces of supply and demand. The federal government tried during this period to cushion farmers against harsh economic realities; but the attempts were mostly failures. Under President Hoover, for example, the Agricultural Marketing Act of 1929 created a Federal

Farm Board, which tried to promote the orderly marketing of farm products. It bought products when they were in surplus, and resold them when they were scarce. But the plan collapsed in 1931, when a bumper crop drove farm prices down to their lowest levels of the century, and the Board exhausted its funds by trying to support the market. The mistake was that the Act focused entirely on the marketing of farm products and did not attempt to control their production.

NEW LEGISLATION INTRODUCED

When President Roosevelt took office in 1933, he inherited from previous administrations a concept known as "equality for agriculture." This meant that farm prices should be raised to levels that bore the same relation to the prices of other goods as existed before World War I. Under the name of "parity," this concept became the chief goal of Roosevelt's New Deal policy for agriculture.

Agricultural Adjustment Act of 1933

The new Administration's first farm legislation was the Agricultural Adjustment Act (AAA) of 1933. It contained three key provisions:

1. Production was to be controlled. This lesson was learned from the failure of previous farm programs that had concentrated solely on marketing. The Secretary of Agriculture was empowered to enter into contracts with farmers who would agree voluntarily to restrict their planting of wheat, corn, cotton, and tobacco; and their production of hogs and milk. In return they would receive cash payments and other benefits.

2. Parity was defined as the establishment of "prices to farmers at a level that will give agricultural commodities a purchasing power with respect to articles farmers buy equivalent to the purchasing power of agricultural commodities in the base period . . . August, 1909–July, 1914." Later, base-period dates were applied for tobacco and some other commodities.

3. Parity was to be achieved through loans, purchases, and storage of surplus commodities. A Commodity Credit Corporation was to support prices and make "nonrecourse" loans to farmers on agricultural commodities—that is, loans which did not have to be repaid if prices fell below certain specified levels.

The AAA of 1933 thus sought to improve farm incomes in two ways: by subsidizing farmers to keep them from producing, and by curtailing farm output so as to raise prices. Farmers were paid to plow under some of their crops; the government also bought surplus livestock, some of which it distributed to the poor and some of which it simply destroyed. On the whole, the program was successful in reducing farm output and raising prices. Part of this success was due to control over acreage; a larger part was probably due to a lack of rain.

The Soil Conservation Act of 1936

The AAA of 1933 provided that payments to farmers were to be derived from a tax on the processors of basic commodities—wheat, cotton, meat, and so on. In 1936, the Supreme Court declared the Act unconstitutional on the grounds that the tax was discriminatory.

The administration, having alleviated the difficulties of farmers, was anxious to continue its program without violating the Court's ruling. Accordingly, the Soil Conservation and Domestic Allotment Act of 1936 was passed as a temporary measure. The stated objective was "to promote the conservation and profitable use of agricultural land." The new law defined parity in a similar manner as before, and continued to control production by paying farmers to grow "soil-building" crops instead of "soil-depleting" crops. The former, by a remarkable coincidence, turned out to be unmarketable grasses and legumes; the latter, on the other hand, were the same basic crops whose output the government had previously sought to curtail.

Agricultural Adjustment Act of 1938

Since the Soil Conservation Act was admittedly a stopgap measure, Congress passed a more comprehensive law two years later—the Agricultural Adjustment Act of 1938. This is usually referred to as the second AAA. It retained the same basic philosophy as the first AAA—namely, to protect the economic well-being of farmers by raising agricultural prices and incomes through the continuance of production controls.

The *Agricultural Adjustment Act of 1938* (with subsequent amendments) is the basic farm law of the United States. It provides for:

1. Price supports of selected farm products at specified levels, to be implemented by purchases and nonrecourse loans by the Commodity Credit Corporation

2. Production control through acreage allotments of certain crops

3. Marketing agreements and quotas between the Department of Agriculture and producers in order to control the distribution of selected commodities

4. Payments to farmers and others who follow approved soil conservation practices

5. Parity payments to farmers for selected agricultural staples

These provisions are purposely stated in general terms because, as described below, they have often been amended and revised since the Act was passed.

WORLD WAR II AND SUBSEQUENT TRENDS

The ink was barely dry on the new law when World War II broke out in 1939. As a look back at Exhibit 1 indicates, prices received by farmers turned upward. Surpluses were replaced by shortages, deflation by inflation, and in 1942 the ratio of prices received to prices paid—i.e., the parity index—reached its goal of 100. The index continued to rise until the late 1940s, as American agriculture supplied not only domestic needs but also a rising proportion of foreign demand as well.

Following a general recession and price setback in 1949, the Commodity Credit Corporation managed to sell some of its accumulating stocks of farm commodities in 1950 as a result of the demand created by the Korean War. Then, in 1952, the downslide began (see Exhibit 1). With rapidly rising agricultural productivity and no wars or crop failures to absorb the growing supply, the CCC found it in-

creasingly difficult to sell its accumulating surpluses without further depressing farm prices. Despite extraordinary efforts by the government to halt the mounting surplus—through marketing quotas, special export provisions, domestic and foreign donations, and the institution of a "soil bank" to retire millions of acres of cropland—farm commodity stocks continued to rise until the Vietnam conflict increased demand.

Commodities cost money to acquire, to store, and to handle. In the early 1960s, stocks of corn, wheat, and cotton ranged from one-half to more than twice our domestic annual consumption, and support of farm prices and incomes cost more than $4 billion annually. Despite the government's efforts, per capita farm income was low; it averaged slightly better than one-half the nonfarm average, while total returns to agricultural resources in general were considerably below those received by resources employed elsewhere in the economy.

Government Policies in Operation

Since the late 1920s, government support for agriculture has taken on different forms. In general, it has been marked by four major policy approaches:

1. Parity prices
2. Storage programs
3. Surplus disposal practices
4. Production controls

All four policies have been used in combination, but it is convenient for us to examine the highlights of each of them separately.

PARITY PRICES

There is a story of a farmer who, during a television interview, was asked the meaning of parity. He replied: "If a man could take a bushel of wheat to the market in 1912, sell it, and use the money to buy a shirt, then he ought to be able to do the same today. That's parity."

The dictionary will tell you that parity means the same thing as "equivalence." When applied to agriculture, therefore, a *parity price* is one that gives a commodity the same purchasing power, in terms of the goods that farmers buy, that it had in a previous base period.

Calculating Parity

The base period is therefore of critical importance. As pointed out by the Department of Agriculture, the proper calculation of parity requires that "the base period be fairly representative of the kind of agriculture that is likely to prevail for some years ahead. Otherwise the parity measurement has little meaning in appraising the agricultural situation as it develops in the future."

Thus since the 1930s, the parity prices of agricultural products have been related in one way or another to a 1910–1914 base period. Until the decade of the fifties, for example, the parity price of a specific commodity was calculated by a formula similar to the following:

Parity price of a commodity in a given year =

$$\begin{pmatrix} \text{average price of the} \\ \text{commodity in the} \\ \text{base period 1910–14} \end{pmatrix} \times \begin{pmatrix} \dfrac{\text{index of prices paid by}}{\text{farmers in the given year}} \\ \overline{100 \; (= \text{index of prices paid by}} \\ \text{farmers in the base period 1910–14}) \end{pmatrix}$$

To illustrate: What was the parity price of wheat for the year 1950, according to this formula? In order to answer this question, we may note that the average price of wheat in the years 1910–1914 was 86.8 cents per bushel. In 1950, the index of prices paid by farmers stood at 256. This means that the prices paid by farmers were 2.56 times higher in 1950 than they were in the base period, for which the average is taken to be 100. Substituting in the formula:

Parity price of wheat in 1950 = 86.8 cents $\times \frac{256}{100}$ = \$2.22

Hence in 1950, the farmer was held to be justly entitled to receive a price of \$2.22 per bushel of wheat. The government's support price, however, was often set at less than parity. In 1950 it was 90 percent. The average price received by farmers in that year, therefore, was \$2 per bushel.

Over the years, the term "parity" has also come to be used in a different sense to mean *parity ratio*. As we have already seen in Exhibit 1, this is the ratio of prices received to prices paid by farmers; hence it serves as an economic indicator of agricultural well-being. This ratio is often quoted in the news media. A parity ratio of 80, for example, might be interpreted by some people to mean that the prices of farm products are 20 percent too low. Various farm programs have been proposed with the objective of raising farm commodity prices to 100 percent of parity, on the grounds that this would restore the fair economic status of agriculture.

"Modernizing" the Formula

By the late 1940s, it was recognized by economists and political leaders that the above formula for calculating the parity prices of specific farm commodities, based on 1910–1914, was outdated. In fact, there was widespread agreement that our farm policy was impeding the adjustment of agricultural production to changes in demand. The demand for wheat and other price-supported field crops had decreased, while the demand had increased for perishables like fruits, vegetables, meats, and dairy products, which were largely unsupported because of the difficulty of storing them. Agricultural resources, therefore, should have been transferred out of the declining activities and into the expanding ones. But our farm policy in general and the parity formula in particular largely prevented this from happening because it kept the relative prices of supported products too high and those of unsupported products too low.

In 1948, therefore, Congress provided for a gradual modernization of the parity formula. In general, it retained the 1910–1914 parity ratio of farm to nonfarm prices as a goal for agricultural commodities as a whole. But in calculating parity for individual commodities, it permitted an index of the average prices received by farmers during the most recent 10 years to be incorporated in the formula as part of an "adjustment factor."

The revised formula thus enables the calculated specific parity prices to reflect more recent developments, but the index of average prices—i.e., the adjustment factor in the formula—is still tied to a 1910–

Box 2

The Granger Movement

The late nineteenth century saw the growth of big business and monopoly, and the exaltation of commerce and the machine. In the industrial sector, labor responded to this grievous loss of status by forming unions, the best known ones being the Knights of Labor and the American Federation of Labor. In the agricultural sector, farmers responded through the formation of the National Grange and the Farmers' Alliance, both of which worked to improve the economic position of farmers.

In several Western states, the Grangers were successful in: (1) getting laws passed which set upper limits on railroad,

warehouse, and elevator charges; and (2) persuading Congress as well as state legislatures to create regulatory commissions. Our federal Interstate Commerce Commission, established in 1887, was partly the result of the Granger movement.

The print on the left shows a Granger meeting at Scott County, Illinois to protest monopolies, tariffs, and low prices for farm products.

The print below, "Gift For The Grangers," was published in Cincinnati in 1873. It exalts the virtues of the farmer and emphasizes his role as the "source" of society's wealth.

Library of Congress.

Library of Congress.

1914 base period. Hence the revised formula only "updates" the relations between the prices themselves; it does not affect the level of parity prices as a whole, since this is determined by the structure of the formula. For example:

Parity can be raised by: (1) shifting the base from the years 1910–1914 to another period when prices were more favorable; (2) expanding the index of prices paid to include wages, interest, taxes, freight rates, etc.; (3) changing the "weights" or relative importance of the items in the index and the components of the formula.

All three of these methods have been employed by the government since the 1930s to increase parity prices for selected individual and groups of commodities. Since the parity formula depends on human judgment, the desirable thing for Congress to do if it wishes to retain the formula is to "modernize" it every decade or so and to update the base period. But this of course, would require new legislation.

STORAGE PROGRAMS

It has often been suggested that storage operations could reduce the fluctuations of prices. If this were the goal, the government could estimate periodically the prices needed to establish long-run equilibrium between supply and demand of agricultural products. It would then set price limits above and below the equilibrium level. If the market price fell below the lower limit, the government could pull it up by purchasing commodities and storing them; if the price rose above the upper limit, the government could push it down by selling commodities that it had previously stored. In this way, farmers would receive a more stable price, consumers a more stable supply, and the government would break even on its storage operations over the long run.

Under our price support program, however, the government has engaged in lending, purchasing, and storing operations—not to stabilize prices, but to raise them. Prices have been set above the equilibrium level with the result that excessive production has been encouraged and enormous volumes of

inventories have been accumulated at costs to American taxpayers of literally millions of dollars a day.

Where does the government store the billions of bushels of wheat, millions of tons of feed grain, and huge surpluses of other commodities that it accumulates? This is a question that people often ask, and part of the answer usually comes as a surprise. As might be expected, the Commodity Credit Corporation has its own storage bins, it rents commercial warehouse space, and it permits farmers themselves to store commodities in their own bins and cribs which are then sealed by government inspectors. But what is not expected is that the CCC also stores millions of tons of grain in rented airplane hangars, public garages, movie theaters, and merchant ships anchored in rivers and ports. The costs of these operations—including the costs of acquisition, transportation, storage, selling, losses on sales, and interest on investment—have risen from several hundred million dollars a year in the 1940s to many billions of dollars a year since the 1950s.

SURPLUS DISPOSAL PRACTICES

Ways must be found to reduce accumulated surpluses. The most common methods have been:

Foreign Dumping. Foods and fibers, while sold at higher prices at home, have been sold (dumped) at very low prices abroad. This is resented by foreign producers who are unable to compete at the lower prices. It also amounts to American subsidy of foreign consumers.

Domestic Dumping. Foods have been distributed to needy families and to welfare and charitable institutions. These plans, however, have done little to boost consumption or absorb surpluses because the markets for domestic dumping are either not large enough or not sufficiently elastic.

Foreign Aid. Large volumes of surplus food and fiber have been donated to countries suffering from natural disasters, or have been "sold" to underdeveloped countries—not for dollars which are scarce and which they must conserve, but for their own currencies which they create themselves. Aid to underdeveloped countries, of course, is socially desirable, as are the domestic dumping plans. But they should be adopted on their own merits instead of being merely incidental to the disposal of surpluses that result from our nation's agricultural policy.

Destruction and Spoilage. The government has sometimes destroyed large quantities of food. In 1943–1950, for example, when it was required to support the price of potatoes, millions of bushels were burned; millions more were dyed blue to keep them out of commercial markets, and then resold to farmers at a fraction of their original price for use as feed and fertilizer. Deterioration and spoilage have also reduced surpluses.

Industrial Uses. Government and industry have spent a great deal of time and money to find new industrial uses for food and fibers. The results have been relatively insignificant. Nor is there any cause for optimism, for there is no apparent reason why other materials cannot be substituted for agricultural commodities in meeting the needs of industry. Hence the greater use of farm products in manufacturing may well require considerable subsidies.

PRODUCTION CONTROLS

With surpluses accumulating, the government has sought to limit its losses by imposing production controls. Two approaches are used: (1) the curtailment of acreage that may be planted to particular crops; and (2) the establishment of voluntary marketing quotas. The latter, however, are not set in physical units such as bushels or pounds. Instead they are formulated for a farmer on the basis of his average yield per acre in previous years, and he is permitted to market as much as he produces on his alloted acres. In effect, therefore, the basic method of reducing output is by *restriction of acreage.* However, as a result of political pressures from farm groups, Congress has set lower limits on acreage curtailment—limits below which allotments cannot be cut—for such commodities as wheat, cotton, rice, and peanuts.

Have reductions in acreage brought about reductions in output? The answer is surprising:

Acreage reductions have tended to result in less than proportionate decreases in production—and sometimes they have resulted in increases. In other words, a given percentage cut in acres planted has resulted in either: (1) a smaller percentage decrease in output; (2) no percentage change in output; or (3) a substantial percentage increase in output.

The reasons for this are not hard to find. Land is only one of the factors of production used in farming. When this is reduced, the farmer substitutes more labor and capital. He retires his poorest land and retains his best, and with the stimulus of higher prices he cultivates the land more intensively by planting the rows closer together, using more fertilizer, insecticides, and manpower. In this way he increases his yields per acre and often maintains if not expands his total output.

Are Marketing Quotas a Solution?

Because of this, it has been suggested that marketing quotas based on *physical units* would control production better. Each farmer would be given certificates permitting him to sell a certain number of units of a commodity at the support price. Any production in excess of these legal quotas would be subject to punitive taxes.

Such marketing quotas existed for tobacco, cotton, and potatoes under the first AAA before that law was declared unconstitutional. A general plan of this type, applicable to all price-supported commodities, was proposed by President Kennedy in 1961. Congress rejected it under the pressure of middle- and upper-income farm groups who would have been made worse off under such a scheme.

The introduction of marketing quotas based on physical units would have both advantages and disadvantages. On the positive side it would: (1) reduce the costs of buying, storing, and selling surplus commodities; (2) lessen the opposition of foreign producers and governments who resent our practice of dumping surpluses in their countries at low prices; and (3) reduce the burden of price supports on American taxpayers. On the negative side the plan would: (1) provide a windfall for owners of farmland when the quotas are introduced, because the quotas would make existing farms more valuable; (2) impede adjustments in production to changes in demand, and hence maintain rigidity in the allocation of agricultural resources; and (3) not lessen the burden on consumers, since they would still have to pay support prices for the food they buy.

CONCLUSION

On balance, it is evident that our agricultural policy has been price-oriented, focusing on the parity concept as a goal. This has been unsatisfactory for two reasons: First, it has had little effect on the fundamental problem of *poverty* in agriculture; and second, it has resulted in wasteful administrative measures which have often been self-defeating and even disastrous.

Thus, despite the long-run decline in the farm population, a substantial proportion of the people living on farms may still be classified as "poor." They are concentrated mostly in the South—particularly in the Appalachians and in the Mississippi Valley. For these families, a policy of raising farm prices has practically no effect because they consume most or all of what they produce. At best, only the middle- and upper-income farmers—the ones who sell most of what they produce—can benefit from the raising of farm prices. Yet our agricultural policy has been promoted as a way of helping all farmers on the grounds that they are all poor. In reality only *some* farmers are poor, while others are actually quite rich.

As the chart in Exhibit 4 shows, about 50 percent of the recipients receive 90 percent of the payments, while the remaining 50 percent of the recipients receive only 10 percent of the payments. What the chart does not reveal is that the upper half of payment recipients consists mostly of middle-class and wealthy farmers who dominate agricultural organizations and political pressure groups, whereas the lower half is composed of those for whom our agricultural support program was originally intended. Little has been done to correct the situation, largely because the big farmers' influence in Congress is still strong.

Exhibit 4

Cumulative Percentage Distribution of Government Payments in the United States in 1970

This Lorenz curve, comparing the actual distribution of payments received by farmers to the diagonal line of equal distribution, emphasizes the inequities of our support program. Among those that receive payments, the chart shows that about 50 percent of the producers receive 90 percent of the payments, while the remaining 50 percent of producers receive about 10 percent of the payments.

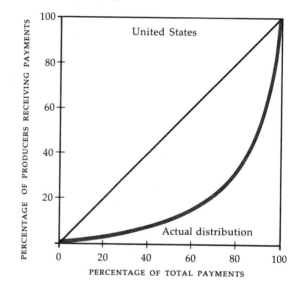

SOURCE: U.S. Department of Agriculture.

Alternatives to Our Farm Policy

The obvious shortcomings of our existing farm policy, and its tremendous drain on the federal budget, have led to various suggestions for reform. Four alternative proposals may be considered:

1. Return to free markets
2. Direct payments
3. Multiple-price systems
4. Land retirement

All four of these have existed in one form or another in American agricultural history.

Some people have argued that our farm policy has intensified rather than alleviated the problem of agricultural adjustment and that a return to free markets without government intervention would bring about the needed adjustment more smoothly. Let us evaluate this argument more closely.

In general, it is likely that a return to free markets for farm products would not encourage agricultural progress and the readjustment of resources that is needed. There are several reasons for this:

First, even without price supports, technical and economic advancement would continue to increase farm productivity and output. However, the income elasticity of demand for farm products will continue to decline as the nation's income rises, while the price elasticity of demand will at most remain constant but will probably also decline. The result of this is lower farm incomes, lower returns to resources in agriculture, and hence a slowing down of the rate of agricultural economic progress—regardless of whether we return to free markets or not.

Second, the flow of resources between the farm and nonfarm sectors of the economy is determined by relative economic returns. Without price supports or government programs, therefore, agriculture would become relatively less profitable compared to industry, thereby reducing the flow of fixed resources (such as land, buildings, and machines) as well as human resources (especially younger people) into farming. On the other hand, the outflow of fixed resources would be retarded because of their highly specialized nature, while the outflow of human resources would be limited for the most part to younger men for whom better incomes were available elsewhere.

Various technical studies have concluded that a return to free markets would result in a prolonged period of low incomes in agriculture without solving the basic problem of resource adjustment. Besides, since the political entrenchment of agricultural interests in Washington has succeeded in maintaining the existing system of price supports since the 1930s, this alternative appears to be as unrealistic as it is unpalatable.

In 1949, Secretary of Agriculture Charles F. Brannan (under President Truman) proposed a system of direct payments to farmers, commonly referred to as the *Brannan Plan*. This plan would eliminate parity payments to farmers and allow the prices of agricultural products to be determined in a free market by supply and demand; government would compensate farmers for the difference between the market price they receive and some higher target price established according to a selected base period in the past.

Direct payments are not a new idea. They were initiated under the first AAA and have been introduced for a few commodities since the 1950s. There is clear evidence that they provide high prices to producers and low prices to consumers. But despite this strong political appeal, the Brannan Plan was flatly rejected by major farm organizations and by their supporters in Congress. The reasons for this became readily apparent at an early stage in various hearings and debates: The agricultural interests feared that the subsidy, if brought out into the open instead of remaining hidden, might be reduced, and the increase in production might lead to stricter controls.

Direct Payments: Good or Bad?

Under a direct-payments plan, market prices would adjust freely to whatever levels were necessary to move the whole supply into consumption. As a result, the plan would have the following favorable and unfavorable features.

On the positive side, the principal advantages are that it would: do away with the cost of storage, and the wastes of destruction and spoilage; bring lower prices to consumers on the domestic market; eliminate the pressure for export dumping at low prices and the resulting resentment of foreign governments; and make the farm subsidy visible, requiring it to be debated and voted each year.

The principal disadvantages, on the other hand, are largely matters of costs. Direct payments would be more costly to the government, and hence to the taxpayer, than price supports because they would cover more commodities. These costs would grow as production increased. Therefore, direct payments would be more likely than price supports to lead to stricter production controls.

MULTIPLE-PRICE SYSTEMS

Farm incomes could be increased through a system of multiple prices. This is technically known as *price discrimination* (or *differential pricing*)—the charging of different prices to the same or to different buyers for the same good.

Through a system of price discrimination, a commodity like wheat, for example, could be sold at multiple prices in three different markets: (1) in a relatively high-priced market to millers for domestic consumer use; (2) in a somewhat lower-priced market to exporters for shipment overseas; and (3) in a still lower-priced or "basic" market for use as animal feed.

Here, in essence, is how the system might work. The price in the basic market could be established by supply and demand or by government support. Exporters and millers, however, would have to purchase special certificates from the government which they would be required to use, along with money, to buy wheat at higher prices in their respective markets. When the farmer received the certificates, he would be permitted to cash them (like savings bonds) in his local bank at specified rates. The certificates would thus serve merely as devices to *segment* the total market for wheat into several distinct submarkets, thereby assuring a different price structure in each market.

This type of system, called a "domestic allotment plan," was widely discussed in the 1920s, authorized in a modified version under the first AAA of 1933, and adopted for wheat in 1962. Like all proposals, however, it has both advantages and disadvantages.

On the one hand, the multiple-price system is designed to minimize stocks, thereby reducing storage costs to the government and to the taxpayer. On the other hand, the farmer's average return declines because the proportion of output going into higher-priced human consumption decreases while the pro-portion going into lower-priced exports and animal feeds increases.

LAND RETIREMENT

Government has repeatedly tried, with little success, to reduce output by removing land from agricultural use. Many millions of acres of farm land have been retired as a result of the government's purchasing and renting not only portions of farms but also entire farms since the 1930s. In addition, acreage reserve programs and conservation reserve programs have been instituted.

Land retirement is convenient; it is cheaper than price supports and is easier to administer than production controls. But as we have seen, it has had limited effects—and sometimes even inverse effects—on output, because farmers usually sell or rent their poorest lands and increase their production on the superior land they retain. When the government retires land, therefore, it must do so on a scale large enough to avoid engaging in what would otherwise be a costly and largely self-defeating activity. For as long as farmers can make profits by producing at supported prices, the government must offer higher and higher purchase prices or rental fees in order to acquire the more productive land. The people who benefit from this are landowners, who are not usually farmers.

Exhibit 5 provides a useful conclusion to this discussion. It illustrates and explains the effects of the three major types of agricultural aid programs that constitute the core of our farm policy.

Evaluation and Proposals

We may conclude this chapter by evaluating the achievements and failures of our agricultural policy and by suggesting approaches to agricultural reform.

ACCOMPLISHMENTS AND SHORTCOMINGS

Our farm policy has had both good and bad features. Perhaps the best way to evaluate it is in terms of three broad questions: Is parity justifiable? What are

Exhibit 5

Three Major Types of Agricultural-Aid Programs

In all three cases, the supply curve at harvest time is perfectly inelastic. Each plan thus has the following effects:

1. A price-support plan [chart (a)] establishes a price floor at some level above the equilibrium price. Consumers pay and producers receive the higher price, and the resulting surplus is purchased and stored by the government.

2. A crop-restriction plan [chart (b)] imposes production controls which shift the supply curve to the left from S_1 to S_2.

At the new equilibrium point after crop restriction, consumers pay and producers receive a higher price, and total consumption and production are less than before.

3. A direct-payments (Brannan) plan [chart (c)] permits consumers to pay the lower free market equilibrium price and producers to receive the higher support price, with the government simply making up the price difference to farmers. The total amount of government payments is shown by the area of the rectangle.

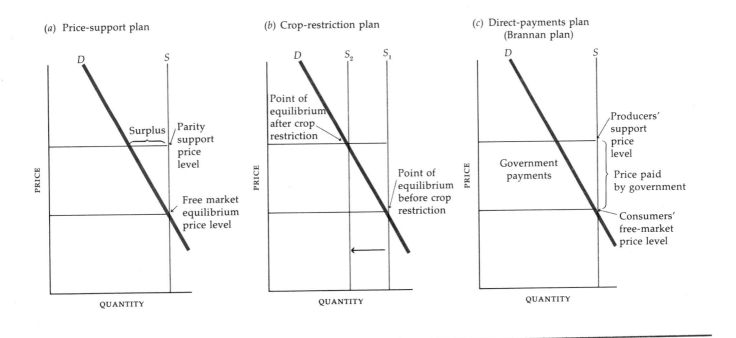

(a) Price-support plan (b) Crop-restriction plan (c) Direct-payments plan (Brannan plan)

the burdens and benefits? How is resource allocation affected?

Is Parity Justifiable?

Those who defend parity argue that farmers should get the same share of national income, and stand in the same relationship to nonfarmers, as they did in a previous base period. Is this position justifiable? It is not, for several reasons.

1. If an occupational group's relative worth to society is declining, there is no reason why its relative income should be maintained. This applies to any group—whether it be farmers, blacksmiths, glass-blowers, or horse-and-buggy manufacturers.

2. Parity, according to the farmer, means that if a bushel of wheat could once buy a shirt, it should continue to do so. But this argument is no more valid than one which says that a typewriter should always be equivalent in value to a suit. In other words,

as the demands for and production costs of products change, their relative values should change; otherwise the pricing mechanism is distorted and some groups are helped while others are hurt.

3. The entire operation of parity is inequitable. The prices of some crops are supported while others are not; the parity formula favors certain crops over others; and the benefits are distributed disproportionately, going mostly to middle- and upper-income farmers while largely by-passing poor farmers.

What Are the Burdens and Benefits?

The annual cost to the taxpayer of our agricultural programs has mounted from hundreds of millions of dollars in the 1930s to billions of dollars since the 1950s. The costs to consumers, on the other hand, are more difficult to establish because price increases have undoubtedly been due not only to support operations, but also to the exercise of some monopolistic market power at the wholesale and retail level. However, our farm policy has also yielded certain important benefits. These have included remarkable advances in productivity (although some gains would have occurred anyway) and extraordinary education and research programs.

How Is Resource Allocation Affected?

In an advancing economy, the proportion of resources devoted to agriculture must decline. Although this has been the trend in agriculture, it has not occurred fast enough; hence agricultural incomes are low relative to the nonfarm sector, and surpluses are chronic. Agricultural policy has distorted and misallocated society's resources by retarding shifts in production that would have occurred if the price system had been permitted to reflect the unrestrained interaction of supply and demand.

PROPOSALS FOR REFORM

Does this mean that we should return to free competition? We have already seen that such an alternative is neither socially desirable nor politically realistic. However, it seems clear that the concepts of base-period price parity and price supports should

be abandoned, and government should turn instead to solving the really fundamental problems of agriculture. These include: (1) the elimination of rural poverty; (2) the establishment of forward prices or price guarantees; (3) the greater stabilization of farm incomes; and (4) the avoidance of overproduction.

Eliminating Rural Poverty

The need to move people out of farming is part of a larger problem of rural poverty—a phenomenon which exists on farms that are too small and whose operators lack the knowledge and capital to produce efficiently. In order to solve this problem, two things must be done.

First, as many of the less-productive farmers as possible should be encouraged to move to other jobs. Some steps can be taken in this direction by (1) providing information to farmers about employment opportunities, (2) subsidizing the retraining and moving costs of farmers, and (3) promoting the industrialization of underdeveloped areas as was done in the Tennessee Valley.

Second, those poor farmers who remain should be helped to increase their productivity. This can be done by providing (1) instruction in farm management, (2) loans to finance the purchase of larger farms and improved equipment, and (3) grants-in-aid to the states for better educational and medical facilities.

The government has already followed these approaches in its Rural Development program and through its Farm Home Administration, at costs that are a small fraction of the amount spent on price supports. This is the sort of path that should be followed in attacking the causes of rural poverty at its roots.

Establishing Forward Prices

How do farmers decide what and how much to produce? To a large extent their decisions are based on prices that they think will prevail in the future. There is thus a good deal of uncertainty in farming that arises from speculative fluctuations in prices.

In order to reduce this uncertainty so that prices can serve as a more reliable guide for farmers to follow in making their production decisions, some economists have suggested the adoption of *forward prices* in agriculture. This is a plan whereby a government-appointed board of experts predicts periodically in advance of seeding or breeding time the equilibrium prices of commodities, based on expected supply and demand. The government then guarantees these forward prices in two ways: by storage programs and direct payments to farmers if actual prices fall below forward prices, and by a direct tax on farmers if actual prices rise above forward prices.

Forward prices, therefore, are prices that are expected to clear the market, whereas support prices are prices that are above market-clearing levels. This helps to explain why Congress has not replaced the present policy of support prices with a system of forward prices. They are not related to any base period, and they do not seek to raise farm incomes. Their only purposes are to reduce price uncertainty and to encourage greater agricultural stability without eliminating the essential function of price as an automatic adjustor of supply and demand.

Improving Stability of Farm Incomes

Specific practices which seek to reduce fluctuations in supply and demand and bring about greater stability of farm incomes should be adopted. In the case of supply, for example, commodities should be purchased for storage when crops are large, and sold when crops are small, in order to stabilize outputs rather than raise prices. Such operations would lessen fluctuations in prices and in farm incomes. In the case of demand, a type of "unemployment compensation" for farmers might be introduced. This plan would put a floor, not under prices, but under farm incomes at a level somewhat below their long-run average, to be financed by taxes on farmers during periods of prosperity and by government subsidies to make up the difference when necessary.

Avoiding Overproduction

The immediate challenge is surplus production. Therefore, we must formulate policies that tend to reduce it. Two things that can be done are: (1) adopt a systematic plan which reduces price supports for selected commodities, thereby encouraging farmers to shift into the production of other products; and (2) retire more farms and more farmland, including good acres as well as poor ones, and convert them into timber and grazing lands.

CONCLUSION

It is clear that policies such as these are needed to correct the imbalances that exist in American agriculture. As a result of the steady rise that has taken place in agricultural productivity over the years, our nation simply has too large a proportion of its resources on farms. The remedy is not to provide the owners of these resources with price and income supports that keep them where they are, but to subsidize them to get out. It would be cheaper and healthier for agriculture and for the economy as a whole to spend money for this than to continue the expense of accumulating costly surpluses.

SUMMARY OF IMPORTANT IDEAS

1. Agriculture in the United States is characterized by: (*a*) products which are price-inelastic and income-inelastic in demand; (*b*) a highly competitive structure; (*c*) rapid technological change; and (*d*) resource immobility. These characteristics mean that small fluctuations in output lead to large fluctuations in prices; further, as the economy grows, the proportion of its total resources that it devotes to agriculture declines and the proportion that it devotes to manufacturing and services increases.

2. Most of the late nineteenth century was a depressed period for farmers. On the other hand, the years from 1891 to World War I were relatively prosperous ones, and have been termed the "Golden Age" of American agriculture.

3. Some relatively insignificant attempts at government aid to agriculture were made during the 1920s, but the most important laws were passed in the following decade. Of these, the Agricultural Adjustment Act of 1938 (with subsequent amendments) is the nation's basic farm law. Among other things, this

act provides for agricultural price supports, production controls, marketing agreements, soil-conservation practices, and parity payments.

4. Government assistance for agriculture has consisted mainly of parity prices, storage programs, surplus disposal practices, and production controls. In general, our agricultural policy has done little to solve the fundamental problem of poverty in agriculture, and has resulted in wasteful practices which have often been self-defeating and even disastrous.

5. Among the major alternatives to our present farm policy are: (a) a return to free markets; (b) direct payments; (c) multiple-price systems; and (d) land retirement. All four have existed in varying degrees at one time or another. Each one, as would be expected, has its advantages and shortcomings.

6. Parity has been unethical and inequitable, the burden on taxpayers has been high, and it has resulted in a misallocation of society's resources. An appropriate policy, therefore, should seek to solve the really fundamental problems of agriculture. These include measures to: (a) eliminate rural poverty; (b) establish forward prices or price guarantees; (c) provide for greater stabilization of farm incomes; and (d) avoid overproduction.

FOR HOMEWORK AND DISCUSSION

1. *Terms and concepts to review:*

income elasticity of demand	parity price
parity ratio	Brannan Plan
Agricultural Adjustment Act of 1938	price discrimination
	forward prices

2. "The aggregate demand for agricultural products is relatively inelastic. Over the long run, aggregate demand has not increased as fast as aggregate supply. Hence the pressure on prices has generally been downward." Illustrate graphically.

3. "Agricultural products are relatively inelastic in demand, whereas many manufactured goods are relatively elastic in demand. Therefore, a technological improvement in agriculture which results in a price reduction will bring about a decrease in the total revenue received by farmers; on the other hand, a technological improvement in manufacturing which results in a price reduction will often bring about an increase in the total revenue received by producers. This helps to explain why agriculture must decline in a technologically advancing society." Illustrate with the use of demand curves.

4. "The demand for agricultural products is such that small increases in output resulting from improved technology result in relatively large decreases in price and income (i.e., total revenue)." What type of elasticity is indicated here? Illustrate with a demand curve.

5. Which is likely to have the most favorable effect on agriculture as a whole: a 10 percent decrease in farm prices; a 10 percent increase in real disposable personal income; or a 10 percent increase in population? Explain.

6. "It is only humanitarian to help the poor. Therefore, we should help farmers because they are poor." Do you agree? Explain.

7. It has been said that parity prices cause resource misallocation and that the Employment Act of 1946 provides a better farm policy for society than all of our farm legislation put together. True or false? Explain.

8. In general, what do you see as the central problem of American agriculture? Discuss.

REFERENCES AND READING SUGGESTIONS

HATHAWAY, DALE E., *Problems of Progress in the Agricultural Economy,* Scott-Foresman, Glenview, Ill., 1964.

HEADY, EARL O., *A Primer on Food, Agriculture, and Public Policy,* Random House, New York, 1967.

HOUTHAKER, HENDRIK S., *Economic Policy for the Farm Sector,* American Enterprise Institute, Washington, D.C., 1967.

THE PRESIDENT'S NATIONAL ADVISORY COMMISSION ON RURAL POVERTY, *The People Left Behind,* Government Printing Office, 1967.

WILCOX, CLAIR, *Public Policies Toward Business,* 3d ed., Irwin, Homewood, Illinois, 1966, chap. 31.

CHAPTER 32

Urban Crises

CHAPTER PREVIEW

Education, housing, and transportation are among the critical problems of our cities. What are some of the important principles and concepts that economics can offer as a guide for coping with these problems?

Since the late 1960s there have been government-supported efforts to establish black ownership and control of business in the ghettos. Are such efforts desirable, or are there better ways of helping the nation's largest minority group?

Many of our cities today are faced with a serious fiscal dilemma. What is the nature of this dilemma? How did it arise? What measures can be taken to resolve it in order to improve our urban environment?

The eminent philosopher Alfred North Whitehead once remarked: "The major advances in civilization are processes which all but wreck the societies in which they occur."

According to some observers, American society is already close to being wrecked. Since World War I, the everyday life of Western man has undergone greater changes than it has since the dawn of the Christian era, as a revolution in agricultural technology has shifted a high proportion of the population from the farms to the cities.

In 1918, fifty percent of the nation's population was rural, as shown in Exhibit 1. In 1970, about 67 percent of the population was urban, and living on only 1 percent of the land; by the year 2000, more than 80 percent of the population will be living in urban areas and much of the remaining 20 percent will be at least "semiurbanized."

This trend toward urbanization has created social and economic problems of enormous significance—problems of mass transit, suburban sprawl, medical care, education, crime control, housing, urban renewal, and ghetto unemployment, to mention only a few. As a result, the problems of American cities are among the most seriously debated issues of our time.

The social problems of urbanization are inseparable from the economic ones. We shall focus most of our attention on the economic issues, with the objective of highlighting and analyzing some of the more important aspects of this extremely complex subject.

Exhibit 1

Ruralization and Urbanization

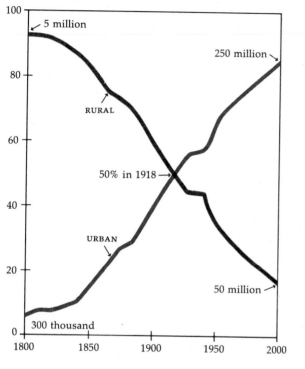

PERCENT OF U.S. POPULATION

An Overview of Urban Problems

The problems of American cities result from a unique set of pressures. Some of them are deeply rooted in the nation's history; others go back only a few decades. Taken together, they have posed issues and initiated controversies that will be with us for many years to come. Since it is impossible to analyze all the problem areas, we may begin by sketching a few that are of major concern.

Education. One of the most technologically *unprogressive* segments of the economy is education. It has had to expand its resources to meet the needs of a growing population and to transmit the results of a knowledge explosion. However, it has not expanded efficiently—especially in urban areas where the demands upon it have been relatively greatest. Society has borne the cost in the form of higher taxes and inferior results. New ways must be sought to improve the efficiency and quality of the education industry. The most promising possibility is to move the public schools out of the public sector, where they have been dominated by rigid bureaucratic controls, and into the private sector, where they can compete freely for consumers' dollars. Some city governments have already taken steps in this direction, and others are giving it serious thought.

Housing. American cities have long had to face the task of assuring an adequate number of decent homes for everyone. Considerable government aid has been given to the middle-income groups, but not enough to the poor. As a result, the cities are still confronted with a mounting demand for low-cost dwellings. Added to this are the problems of discrimination which blacks and other minority groups encounter in the housing market. These are among the more important difficulties that make "the housing problem" a multidimensional issue of great social as well as economic significance.

Transportation. The ability to move goods and people is basic to the life of a city. Motor vehicles have come to play a dominant role, but cannot alone carry the burden. Hence the cities must now create properly balanced transportation systems. Such systems, consisting of highways, buses, monorails, subways, parking spaces, etc., seek to optimize the use of transportation facilities with minimum congestion and maximum efficiency. At the present time many urban transportation ills are apparent: frequent overcrowding, poor service, inequitable sharing of burdens, and inadequate planning for future needs and costs. With the growth of population and industry, these problems will become progressively worse unless new transportation policies are formulated.

Black Business. Federal funding of black entrepreneurship has been one of the ways in which government has sought to improve the economic and social conditions of Negroes living in the inner cities. It is hoped that such programs will give Negroes a greater share in America by promoting black employment and black ownership of business assets. But some people doubt that this approach will achieve the desired goals. Black enterprises are frequently small, and lack the money and managerial talent to compete with well-established firms. Therefore, the funds for these entrepreneurship programs might better be used to set up education and training courses which would prepare Negroes to compete in the labor market at large.

Urban Finance. The most fundamental economic challenge facing the cities is to find ways of raising the money needed to pay for urban improvements. The problems are manifold. Increases in low-income urban populations have brought greater demands for community services such as education, public health, and public safety. Middle- and upper-income groups, as well as businesses, have been moving out of urban areas and into the suburbs, thus depleting the "tax base" of the cities. Local governments have become fragmented and increasingly inefficient in their efforts to meet new and expanding area-wide needs. What steps can be taken to reduce these difficulties? There are several, but they require the will to do so at all levels of government.

A Free Market in Education

One major problem of all large cities is the public educational system. Critics have accused the public schools of being rigid bureaucracies. Conservatives, liberals, and radicals, regardless of race, have complained that the political mechanisms which are supposed to make public schools accountable to their communities have either failed to work or have worked very clumsily. As a result, only the rich now have a choice—they can either move to other school districts or they can enroll their children in expensive private schools. The average parent, on the other hand, has no alternative but to remain with his local public school. The parent who belongs to one of several religious faiths may be able to send his child to a low-cost church school—but such schools are relatively few.

What can be done to correct the situation? One controversial suggestion is to weaken the monopoly powers of public schools by making them more competitive. The argument can be reduced to three basic propositions:

1. The public schools are monopolies, and monopolies do not offer sufficient quality or diversity of product.

2. If American public schools are to provide variety and excellence, they must be subjected to the competitive pressures of a free market—a market in which parents and children exercise consumer sovereignty by paying their money and taking their choice.

3. If consumers are given this opportunity, they will usually choose the better schools and, in so doing, will force the quality of all schools to improve.

This argument has been advanced by numerous critics from the right and from the left. Like all panaceas, it suffers from oversimplification. Nevertheless, it has considerable merit when viewed as part of a larger, comprehensive effort at school reform. Although there are various means, political and fiscal, of encouraging a free market in education, four proposals in particular have received the greatest attention:

1. Decentralization of school systems
2. Creation of publicly financed private schools
3. Education by contract (Performance Contracting)
4. The voucher system

An analysis of each of these approaches will provide an understanding of the role which competition can play in a sorely needed program for school reform.

DECENTRALIZATION OF SCHOOL SYSTEMS

A proposal that is frequently suggested to encourage competition is for school systems to be decentralized so as to make them more responsive to the particular needs of their own communities—whether white or black, rich or poor. Most of the people who favor this approach do not base their beliefs on the benefits of competition per se, but on the conviction that the interests of minority groups in large cities have been totally disregarded by the monopolistic system. The issue came to a head during the late 1960s in New York City's Ocean Hill–Brownsville district, whose residents are mostly blacks and Puerto Ricans. Community leaders demanded control over the schools on the grounds that children were not only receiving an inferior education, but also one which was dominated by white middle-class values.

Would total decentralization of large school systems create the beneficial effects of competition that the advocates of this approach seek? Probably not—for several reasons:

1. Each relatively homogeneous community—whether white or black, rich or poor—would be given monopolistic control over its schools. This would fragment the school systems, reduce their efficiency, and return them to the situation that existed in the 1890s. At that time school administrators cried for consolidation rather than decentralization in the hope of bringing about greater economies of scale.

2. The biases and bigotries of each community would be given a disproportionate influence over the education of its children, most of whom are not likely to remain in the same district after their schooling is completed. Further, since teachers are professionals who seek to apply professional standards, they will resent working under local pressures and will find it extremely difficult to introduce pedagogical reform.

3. Parents who are dissatisfied with the decentralized school system in one district may in principle be able to move to another, but whether they can do so *in fact* is doubtful. In New York, Chicago, and other major cities, the better schools would be unable to absorb the large numbers who would want to enroll. And in the suburbs, lower- and middle-income blacks would continue to be effectively restricted from the better schools located in middle-income white communities.

Despite these educational drawbacks, total decentralization may nevertheless be inevitable—for political rather than economic reasons. The black community, too long frustrated, wants to control what its children learn and what its teachers teach. Hence it is not likely to give much weight to the disadvantages of decentralization as a method of achieving its goal.

PUBLICLY FINANCED PRIVATE SCHOOLS

A second proposal for providing free consumer choice in education is the use of public money to create both public schools and private schools—the latter designed to meet the needs of particular minority groups. This means that in a typical large city with a population composed of diverse religions and races, there would be not only public schools run by the city, but also private schools run by different denominations and racial groups for their own constituents. The private schools might receive public financial support based on enrollment, community income levels, or other criteria—somewhat as certain private American universities receive partial financial aid from the federal government.

This proposal is actually another form of decentralization. The difference is that it bases decentralization on religion and race instead of geographic location. Hence it would create competition among schools—but only in terms of ideology rather than educational quality. Even though such schools would be open to all, they would in effect be segregated by race and by religion. Admittedly, segregation has long existed in many school districts, but such a system would tend to perpetuate and perhaps even to encourage it—certainly not reduce it.

EDUCATION BY CONTRACT (Performance Contracting)

A third competitive scheme proposes that each school district specify the exact educational program it wants and then invite private firms to bid for the opportunity of supplying the desired "package." The firm which offered to deliver the package at the lowest price would be awarded the contract. This scheme would stimulate competition and growth in the educational systems industry, thereby encouraging the development of better teaching machines, learning materials, and other pedagogical aids. Parents, children, and taxpayers would all benefit because they would be getting the program they want at the lowest possible cost, and school districts would be making the most efficient use of the limited funds available to them.

This plan, known as "performance contracting," has had wide appeal. Its chief difficulty is that it requires a measurable product. Although certain parts of education are well-defined and involve the acquisition of basic skills which are measurable, many other parts are ill-defined and consist of learning how to relate, interpret, and appreciate. These latter parts are not ordinarily susceptible to the type of measurement that would be needed for contractual purposes. As a result, this proposal would have only limited applicability. Its greatest usefulness lies in the role that it might play as part of a more general plan.

THE VOUCHER SYSTEM

A fourth proposal for increasing competition is to give money, or more specifically "vouchers," to families with children and let them choose the school they want—public, parochial, or private. The vouchers would be equivalent in value to the community's expenditures per public school pupil, and the city would reimburse the school to the amount of the voucher. This scheme has long been advocated by various leading educators and economists, among them Professor Milton Friedman of the University of Chicago. In fact, economists have sometimes referred to the proposal as the "Friedman Plan."

According to its supporters, the plan would promote competition in several ways. First, schools would be pressured into stating clearly their objectives and programs—and in living up to them at the risk of being squeezed out of the market. Second, assuming an "open enrollment" policy, parents would be free to choose the type of school that seemed best to them—traditional or progressive, private or public. Third, if "bonus" vouchers for poor or disadvantaged youngsters were provided, as some supporters of the plan have suggested, schools which have significant numbers of such pupils could better afford to develop programs of wide appeal to *all* students. And fourth, some of the better suburban schools, faced with mounting educational expenditures, might be bribed into admitting many poor students from the inner city, thus bringing about a greater degree of class as well as racial integration.

The voucher system, therefore, would provide lower-income families with a range of choice in education that is roughly comparable to that enjoyed by the middle class. This by itself may make it worthy of adoption. Nevertheless, those who support the plan are well aware of its controversial nature and shortcomings. According to them:

1. It might encourage the creation of racially segregated schools—a trend that would run counter to the stated objectives of the government.

2. It would result in the public schools' becoming a "last choice" for students not wanted by other schools.

3. It would lead to public support of parochial schools, thereby violating the Constitutional principle of separation of church and state.

4. It would encourage the establishment of weak schools and "diploma mills" by sharp operators seeking to exploit the public's lack of knowledge of educational programs and curricula.

Several suggestions have been made to overcome these objections. For example, racial segregation could be prevented by requiring each school to fill at least half of its openings by lottery among its applicants; administrative controls could be introduced to minimize public subsidization of religious instruction; and last but not least, state-supervised educational and accreditation standards could be vigorously enforced to prevent the establishment of fly-by-night schools.

NEED FOR COMPREHENSIVE REFORM

These, in brief, are the chief devices that have been proposed for extending competition among schools. There is substantial agreement that increased competition is needed to weaken the monopolistic power of public education. The crisis that exists in public school systems today is due in large measure to their rigid, dull conformity and their failure to respond to new demands. By turning itself into an educational marketplace in which children and their parents could afford to choose the type of school they want, the school system would become more sensitive to the real needs of children and parents.

Competition, however, is not a complete solution. Educational quality should not be decided exclusively in the marketplace, because most parents and children are not capable of evaluating the "product" they are buying. Nevertheless, they should have some significant influence over it. Therefore, what is needed is a comprehensive program of reform in which some competitive elements represented by all four of the above proposals can play a part. The challenge of developing such a scheme is posed as a problem at the end of this chapter.

Housing in the Inner Cities

The desperate shortage of adequate living space for the poor is one of the major failures of American cities. Large-scale and costly efforts by government to solve the problem have met with only limited success. Nor has entrepreneurial initiative succeeded where government has failed. The provision of low-income housing in the inner cities is one activity in which exclusive reliance on private enterprise has proved to be inadequate.

What are the reasons for this? There are many, including problems of taxation, financing, technology, racial discrimination, law, and politics—to mention only a few. Because of these complexities, it is doubtful that private enterprise can ever solve the problems of low-income urban housing, or the closely related problems of urban renewal, without the help of a comprehensive policy by government. Such a policy has been developing since the 1930s, but it has been painfully slow in its evolution and frequently muddled in its administration.

GOVERNMENT HOUSING POLICIES

Although government has failed to develop an effective housing policy, it has not been unconcerned with resolving important issues. Over the years it has: (1) regulated private housing through zoning laws, building codes, and rent controls; (2) promoted private housing construction by making available needed supplies of credit; (3) engaged in the ownership and operation of public housing; and (4) subsidized urban renewal programs by private builders.

Regulation of Private Housing. Government has been directly involved in the regulation of private housing in two major ways: by specifying the conditions under which dwellings can be built, and by limiting the rents that tenants must pay.

All local governments have zoning laws which control the allocation of land for commercial and industrial buildings, and for residential dwellings of the single- and multiple-family type. They also have building and housing codes which specify standards of ventilation, sanitation, and structural safety. Unfortunately, many of these laws are unduly restrictive, and their enforcement has been weakened by political influences. As a result, their economic effect has been to limit the quantity and types of housing that are most needed for large cities, and hence to contribute—along with rising population and income—to the upward pressure on rents in these areas.

To curb such pressures, particularly during war periods, government has sometimes imposed rent controls to keep rents from soaring. Rent "ceilings" may be necessary during emergencies, but as a permanent policy can be more harmful than beneficial—for several reasons:

1. They cause a malallocation of dwelling space, since families who can afford higher-rent apartments are encouraged to remain where they are instead of moving to make room for lower-income newcomers.

2. They limit the returns to landlords as compared with returns on invested funds in other fields, thereby encouraging them to neglect the maintenance of their buildings and even to abandon them.

3. They curb the supply of rental housing and may even cause it to decline.

All three of these consequences, therefore, tend to injure tenants over the long run rather than help them.

The experiences of various cities with rent controls, both in the United States and abroad, strongly confirm these conclusions. New York City, for example, has retained rent controls since World War II, largely because of political pressures, and has suffered drastically from all these effects. A number of its apartment buildings in slum areas are without adequate heat or sanitation, and many have literally been abandoned by their owners in favor of a tax loss.

Promotion of Private Housing. Since the 1930s, the federal government has encouraged the construction of private housing and promoted homeownership through various agencies such as the Federal Housing Administration and the Veterans Administration. It has sought to achieve these goals by expanding the supply of housing credit—through federally chartered savings and loan associations, provisions for mortgage insurance, creation of a secondary market for mortgages, and other devices. This program has succeeded in promoting family home ownership, but it has done little to increase the supply of housing for the poor. Its benefits have gone primarily to middle-income rather than to lower-income groups.

Public Housing. Government has been involved in public housing—that is, housing which is privately designed and built, but is then owned and operated on a rental basis by public authorities—since the thirties. Under the Housing Act of 1937 and its subsequent amendments, the federal government is authorized to extend financial aid to state and local governments in order to help them provide low-rent housing to low-income families. Municipal governments, through the sale of bonds, contribute 10 percent of the total capital investment for each project, and the federal government pays the remaining 90 percent. The municipal public housing authorities collect the rents and operate the projects—with the objective of breaking even on operating costs. In effect, however, the federal government subsidizes virtually all these projects because interest received by municipal bondholders is exempt from federal income taxes and the projects themselves are exempt from local property taxes. On the whole, the federal government has succeeded through its public housing policies in expanding the supply of low-rent

housing, but congressional appropriations have usually been insufficient to meet the huge need that exists.

Urban Renewal. During the fifties, there began a pronounced shift in emphasis from the construction of housing for the poor to the rehabilitation of the cities. Sponsored jointly by federal and municipal governments, and financed primarily by the former, the objective of urban renewal has been to rebuild old or decayed neighborhoods in order to attract industry, stimulate commercial activity, encourage the upper economic classes to return from the suburbs to the cities, and in general to restore property values and tax yields. Although urban renewal programs in the downtown centers of many cities have been impressive, they have also failed on a number of fronts. Reconstruction has been confined to limited areas without relation to an overall plan. Projects have usually been selected for their commercial value and "show appeal" instead of their usefulness to the community as a whole. Tremendous hardships have been imposed on many of the people evicted from renewal areas—most of them blacks who have few if any alternative areas to which they can move, and small-scale neighborhood businessmen whose livelihoods are destroyed because they are unable to relocate at rents they can afford.

PROBLEMS OF HOUSING

The enormous need for city housing poses staggering problems of a multidimensional nature. The first and most fundamental problem is the gap between housing costs and what low-income families can pay. With the shortage of land in large cities, the kind of housing that is needed is apartment buildings, either new or rehabilitated. Even if such buildings could be made available in the quantity and density desired, government estimates show that the rental rates (ranging from about $150 to $200 monthly for a one- or two-bedroom apartment) would be beyond the means of most low-income families. In fact, more than two-thirds of such families could not afford to pay even *half* these rents.

A second problem is that government programs to

correct this difficulty have been inadequate. Congress has created one program after another since the 1930s, but many have been insufficiently funded and very poorly conceived. As a result, they have often overlapped and even conflicted with earlier programs, creating chaos, together with fantastic amounts of red tape, while exerting relatively little impact on urban problems. Nor has urban renewal been of much help because most localities have been concerned with broadening their tax base and have used renewal programs to construct new commercial development or upper-middle-income housing rather than provide low-income housing.

A third problem is that rehabilitation of slum housing is an alternative to the construction of new housing, but not an overall solution. There are several reasons. Rehabilitation does not increase the total supply of housing units. It displaces people without successfully relocating them. It is not cheaper than new housing—especially when planning and the costs of rehabilitation are considered. And, it does not reduce the social and cultural barriers which separate the poor from the rest of society.

APPROACHES TO A SOLUTION

There is widespread agreement that ways must be found to broaden the choices available to consumers in the urban housing market. Three general approaches that would lower the price of dwellings are especially noteworthy.

1. Uniform National Building Code

Local building codes vary widely in the several thousand jurisdictions in the United States. Most set standards far above what is needed for safety and durability, and specify the materials and production methods that must be used. They are thus designed to protect special-interest groups such as building-components manufacturers and trade unions, rather than provide the largest possible supply of housing at the lowest possible prices.

To correct this situation, builders' associations, construction engineers, and governmental advisory groups have long advocated a uniform national building code. Ideally, such a code should specify performance standards rather than materials and methods, thereby encouraging components manufacturers as well as builders to develop new, cost-saving substitutes. Until such a uniform national code is established, there is little hope of improving production efficiency in the home-building industry —an industry which consists mainly of small firms catering to a highly fragmented housing market.

2. Rent Supplements

A direct approach to widening the housing market for the poor is for the government to supplement a portion of the rental payments of low-income families. This might be done by the government's making up the difference in rents for those families below a specified income level who cannot obtain decent housing at rental rates not exceeding one-fourth of their incomes. (The figure of one-fourth is typically used as a national average by budget counselling services and welfare agencies, but higher or lower figures might be more appropriate in different regions.) Thus the tenant pays one-fourth of his income toward rent, and the government pays the balance up to the "fair market value." As the tenant's income rises, the government's supplement falls until the tenant is paying the full rent himself and the government is paying nothing.

The chief disadvantage of this plan is in its administration: tenants and landlords must be audited periodically to see that the government is not being overcharged. But the plan has several factors in its favor: (1) It gives tenants a wider choice in seeking apartments instead of confining them to public housing projects; (2) it avoids the stigma attached to public housing; and (3) it does not reduce the tenant's incentive to work.

A system of rent supplements somewhat similar to this was established by the government in 1965. Despite its advantages—including the fact that it is less costly to administer than public housing—it has been politically unpopular and has been supported on a limited scale with relatively small budgets.

3. Interest Subsidies

To encourage home ownership by low-income families, the government could subsidize interest payments on housing—that is, contribute a proportion of the monthly interest which a family must pay on its home mortgage. To help poorer families who would rather rent than buy, an equivalent arrangement could be made in which the government paid the landlord a proportion of his contractual interest and the landlord in turn reduced the tenant's rent. In both instances, the government's interest subsidy varies inversely with the family's income. As the latter rises toward some specified level, the former declines toward zero.

This type of plan was adopted in the Housing and Urban Development Act of 1968. However, it was geared toward helping families whose incomes are just above the poverty line instead of below it. On the whole, the Act made a substantial start toward expanding the supply of new dwellings for low- and moderate-income families; but it was only a start. Extensions are needed if decent housing is to be provided for the poorest segments of the population.

CONCLUSION

Any solution to city housing problems must involve some sort of government subsidy. There is a gap between what low-income families can pay for housing and what private enterprise can supply at a reasonable profit. Subsidies are a realistic means of closing this gap.

The most common types of subsidy, in the form of below-market interest rates, rent supplements, and long-term mortgages, can continue, but more extensive plans are also needed. An effective and far-reaching program would be one in which the federal government acquires the land it needs, provides for the construction of dwelling units by private enterprise, and pays no property taxes as long as the buildings are occupied by low-income families. However, since the cities cannot afford to lose the taxes on these properties, the federal government could relieve them of all health, education, and welfare costs, since these services are a national concern. Such a plan would permit business and government to work together in meeting the housing needs of all low-income groups.

Transportation Systems

Any discussion of urban crises must include transportation. The central task is to correct the imbalance that exists between automobiles and other forms of transportation, such as subways and monorails. Why this imbalance? A significant cause is the Federal Highway Act itself; this law allows 90 percent federal funding for expressways, thereby providing cities with virtually free highways which they have found too tempting to resist. The result has been mounting traffic congestion, a tearing apart of the cities as well as the countryside, and the creation of distorted transportation systems which tend to increase the economic and social costs of movement.

A city's transportation system consists of all the vehicles and "fixed plant" necessary to move people and goods from one place to another. It may thus include not only automobiles, taxis, buses, and subway trains, but also streets, freeways, stations, parking spaces, and similar facilities. There is no doubt that continued investment in all of these will occur in many large cities during the coming years. Since it is desirable that the growth of urban transportation systems be economically sensible, two classes of policy proposals should be considered: (1) transportation pricing; and (2) technological improvements and innovations in transportation systems.

TRANSPORTATION PRICING

We know from the study of supply and demand that a price system rations the use of existing goods among buyers who are willing to pay the market price, and guides the distribution of resources to their most rewarding alternatives. Can a price system be used to help correct urban transportation problems?

There is excessive traffic congestion in our cities because of an imbalance between automobiles and other forms of transportation. Most cities have created this imbalance themselves by subsidizing the use of automobiles and discouraging the use of mass transit. They have done this by constructing and maintaining streets and freeways without charging users sufficiently high fees to allow a proper allocation of this resource. Therefore, if the situation is to be corrected, a fundamental principle must be recognized:

At any given time the supply of streets, bridges, and other traffic facilities is fixed. If during some period there is congestion on the roads or shortages of parking spaces, this means that the quantity demanded of the facility at that moment exceeds the quantity supplied, and hence a higher price is needed to bring the two quantities into balance, i.e., to "clear" the market.

At the present time the use of most roads is allocated to users on the basis of time delays that they are willing to tolerate. Thus everyone who uses a road at any given moment enjoys the same service; but during rush hours, a person whose time is more valuable pays a higher price in terms of delays than the person whose time is less valuable. This means that the former individual, in effect, "subsidizes" the latter.

Variable Tolls

A *variable toll system* that charged a direct toll to users of certain roads according to mileage and direction traveled on the basis of time of day and day of week—and increased the toll when demand was high and decreased it when demand was low—would greatly reduce if not eliminate the overall problem of "congestion" and "shortage." For example, if higher tolls were charged during morning and evening rush hours on major freeways connecting the suburbs with the cities, users whose time was relatively more valuable to society would still travel regularly at those hours, while others would shift their travel to alternate roads or to off-peak times, or else seek different forms of transportation, such as rapid transit.

Of course, there may be some technical problems in implementing such a proposal, but the solution is well within the grasp of modern technology. In some cases it would be feasible to introduce existing toll systems of the types currently found on various turnpikes and highways, but these could be gradually replaced with modern roadway devices such as magnetic car identifiers and automated computer systems, thus permitting motorists to be billed monthly for the benefits they derive from the use of roads. A considerable amount of research on this has already been done in the United States and other countries, and some of the world's largest cities are considering introducing differential pricing systems in which fares or tolls are based on time, distance, and direction of travel.

Economic analysis thus suggests that with the development of diverse transportation facilities in the cities, the adoption of a variable toll system would correct much of the imbalance that exists between private automobile and public transportation. It would continue to give motorists a free choice as to the alternative streets and the amount of street space they wish to utilize, thereby allocating scarce public streets according to the *benefit principle,* i.e., a principle which holds that people should be "taxed" for a service in proportion to the benefit they receive from it.

Public Transit Systems

Variable tolls, as opposed to flat fares, are equally desirable for public transit systems including subways, buses, etc. Such systems are used at full capacity during the morning and evening peak periods, and usually underutilized the rest of the time. Low or even free off-peak fares would relieve much of the rush-hour congestion. Further, this pricing scheme could be adopted at little or no additional cost to the transit system (other than the expense of installing new turnstiles or fare boxes), since the cost of operating the vehicles is substantially the same whether they are full or empty.

It is sometimes contended that differential transit fares would burden the poor, since they rely heavily on public transportation. There are three major weaknesses in this argument. First, the poor tend to live closer to the inner cities and to travel shorter distances; hence a fare based on mileage would actually benefit them. Second, many of the poor who

Urban Transportation

The major transportation problem facing large cities is to get hundreds of thousands—and in some cases millions—of people to and from work in the central business districts with minimum congestion, maximum efficiency, and reasonable comfort.

New York City exemplifies the complex problems of urban mass transit. Each working day, nine square miles of Manhattan ingest and disgorge over two million people—more than the combined populations of Baltimore, Boston, and Cincinnati. Subways, buses, railroads, automobiles, taxis, and ferries all share the load; but whether they accomplish their task with efficiency or comfort is another question.

In economic terms, the difficulties include problems of costs, revenues, pricing, and financing. Costs are a problem because mass transit systems such as commuter trains and subways suffer from a limited ability to adjust variable costs to fluctuations in passenger volume, and they require large amounts of capital investment to provide for modernization and expansion. In order to handle peak rush-hour loads, for instance, the New York subway system employs 39,000 people to run 7,000 cars on 240 miles of track. During many hours each day, the cars are nearly empty. A planned expansion of the system will cost at least $1.5 billion.

Charles Harbutt

Charles Harbutt

Revenues are inadequate because political pressures have forced regulatory agencies to keep tolls and fares low—too low to meet operating costs, let alone replace obsolete equipment. Pricing policies create other difficulties; distorted fare structures have caused some facilities to be overused while others are relatively idle. Financing is hard to obtain because efforts to support mass transit operations out of general funds have met with considerable resistance. Many people feel that mass transit bene-

Burk Uzzle

fits only commuters, rather than the public as a whole; and most cities and states are financially hard-pressed.

Clearly, some guidelines for policy are needed. Three in particular may be mentioned:

☐ Fast, efficient mass transit is vital to the economic health of our big cities.

☐ Public funds must subsidize both capital investment and operating costs of mass transit. At-tempts to cover constantly rising operating expenses by increasing fares have diverted commuters to highways.

☐ Tolls for the use of highways, bridges, and tunnels should more closely reflect the economic and social costs of commuting by private car. The excess revenues should be allocated to mass transit. Such action would help to offset current highway-biased subsidy arrangements.

Viewpoint

Cars Versus Mass Transit

For millions of Americans both travel and arrival have become daily penances. They embark hopefully in their cars or on trains; but on the highways and streets of urban America they are delayed by traffic jams, and on the rails are frequently afflicted by breakdowns of the heating in winter and of the air-conditioning in summer.

To be sure, the federal government has pumped over $50 billion into the 43,000-mile interstate highway system since World War II. States and cities have spent additional billions. Government has also spent billions of dollars to build and improve airports. But federal, state, and city governments have spent relatively little to strengthen urban mass transportation. On the contrary, it has decayed, and some 235 urban mass transit systems have gone out of business in the past few years.

Chaotic Patchwork

The magnitude and allocation of government expenditures suggest that the United States has a coordinated national transportation policy. It does not. Instead, it has what President Kennedy called "a chaotic patchwork of inconsistent and often obsolete legislation . . . evolved from a history of specific actions addressed to specific problems of specific industries at specific times."

Only in the past few years has there been a real attempt to impose order on that chaos. Under President Johnson, the Department of Urban Transportation was founded. It will have its work cut out: transportation is an industry of impressive size, in which powerful special interests have strong voices. It accounts for about 20 percent of the gross national product; provides some 18 percent of total federal taxes; consumes 75 percent of the rubber, 56

percent of the petroleum, 29 percent of the steel, and 20 percent of the aluminum produced; and employs directly or in related activities about 13 percent of the total work-force. Of the total transportation bill, which is approaching $200 billion, close to two-thirds is paid by passengers. Predictably, the bulk of their money goes into the buying and running of private cars.

New technology, including monorails, will play a part in the solution of transportation problems. For many years to come, however, the main burdens will be carried by cars and trains. In the country and small cities, the car remains the most convenient form of transport; in some places it is the only form. But in the big cities the car is far from ideal.

Some experts estimate that 20 highways of four lanes are needed to carry the people who can be carried on just two railroad tracks. To be fair to the car, such estimates are based on the twin assumptions that cars will be carrying an average of about 1.5 persons, while trains will be full.

Case against Cars

There are further indictments against the car. It must be parked at its destination, which means that huge amounts of land and money have to be invested in parking spaces. And the car is much more dangerous than mass transit vehicles. In 1967, rail passengers died at the rate of 0.09 per 100 million miles, bus passengers at 0.20, and passengers in cars at the rate of 2.40 (all figures exclude deaths of nonpassengers). Finally, the car is a major polluter of the atmosphere.

Despite overwhelming evidence in its favor, the commuter rail system continues to ail. Unlike highways and

airports, all commuter railroads have until recently been privately owned and operated. Only with marked reluctance do public authorities take over commuter routes when the private owners are forced to abandon them—usually by a mixture of mismanagement, rising costs, and declining revenues.

Task: to Discover True Costs

For economists a task of fascinating complexity lies ahead. It is to devise an analytical framework that will enable them to discover the true costs, social as well as financial, of different modes of transport. The old criteria of economic efficiency will not satisfy a society increasingly concerned with social and environmental costs.

Is there a case for saying that mass transit fares should be low enough to wean commuters from cars even though that policy would require massive subsidies? And what would the true cost of those subsidies be, after deducting such measurable savings as avoided highway deaths?

At present economists are asking more questions of that kind than they are answering. But the discussion is lively, and it is urgent. Out of it should come a more realistic way of setting objectives—and, hopefully, a national transportation system to replace the "chaotic patchwork" excoriated by President Kennedy.   R. B.

1. *Can you see any ways in which a good mass transit program could have a beneficial effect on the problem of poverty?*

2. *What factors would you consider if you were asked to calculate the economic cost per mile of operating an automobile?*

travel to get to work, such as those who perform domestic service in the suburbs or work as cleaning women in office buildings, travel against the major flow of traffic or at off-peak times; therefore, they too would benefit from a differential fare system. Third, some studies have shown that the poor tend to rely as much or more on public transportation for nonwork trips, so that a lower fare during off-peak hours would be to their advantage.

In general, therefore, although some lower-income families would undoubtedly be hurt by a differential fare structure, it appears that many more would benefit.

TECHNOLOGICAL IMPROVEMENTS AND INNOVATIONS

In addition to establishing an appropriate pricing system for rationing the use of transportation facilities, various technological improvements and supplemental policies are possible. Three independent classes of proposals, none of which would require a massive investment in new facilities, may be considered.

1. Electronic control systems, which regulate access to urban freeways through strategically placed sensors and traffic signals, can be introduced. Such controls have been employed successfully in a number of cities in the United States and Europe. They are likely to gain large-scale adoption in the coming years.

2. Subsidies can be used to reorient bus services in the inner cities. Various studies indicate that present bus systems often do not provide adequate connection and transfer points to meet the needs of the working poor—especially those who must commute by bus to work in the suburbs.

3. Taxicab and jitney services can be expanded. Merely by relaxing somewhat the restrictions which almost all cities exercise on the supply of taxis, their number could be increased and the rates reduced. And by permitting the use of jitneys—that is, cars or station wagons which carry passengers at nominal rates (a very common form of public transportation in many foreign and in some American cities)—much of the problem of automobile congestion in the cities would be eliminated.

These proposals suggest that there is much the cities can do at relatively little cost to relieve the transportation pressures they now face. Experimentation with new and flexible approaches is needed in order to find the "transport mix" that is best suited to the requirements of each city. The money that can be saved from optimum use of a well-designed transportation system might better be spent on education, housing, pollution abatement, and other measures that will make the city a more desirable place to live.

Black Capitalism

When Richard Nixon was running for President in 1968, he made a big play for fostering the growth of black enterprise throughout urban America. This approach to improving the economic conditions of the ghetto has come to be known as *black capitalism*— a term which has broad appeal because it means different things to different people. For purposes of economics, however, it may be defined as an effort to increase Negro ownership and control of business —especially the latter; it thus differs from the traditional meaning of capitalism, since there are ways of bringing about effective black control whether business is owned by private individuals, by community groups, or even partly by government.

Since the 1968 Presidential election, black capitalism has received little support from Washington. Nevertheless it is still advocated by many white and Negro groups. Since it may eventually become more than a political slogan, we will examine it briefly here.

Several schemes have been proposed, each with a different structure of ownership and control. Until now, most of the outside help which black businessmen have received has been in the form of loans granted by various federal, state, and local agencies, and free accounting, legal, and management advice provided by local professional associations of accountants, lawyers, and businessmen. It seems clear that if black capitalism is to succeed, it will need the support of government—through tax incentives, subsidies, liberal credit policies, or other schemes. In the opinion of some economists and political leaders, however, there is reason to believe that such plans may do more harm than good—for reasons that are explained below.

OBJECTIVES OF BLACK CAPITALISM

Advocates of black capitalism hope it will bring about economic improvements in three different areas—the job market, the ghetto economy, and the black community. Each of these raises different sets of problems.

First, studies done by the U.S. Department of Labor, as well as other public and private groups, have led to certain important findings about the job market:

1. Black workers tend to be concentrated in the low-wage, least-skilled occupational groups; these categories include domestic service workers, unskilled farm and nonfarm laborers, and operatives.

2. There is a growing trend toward increasing rates of employment for blacks in the higher-paid occupations—such as craftsmen and foremen, sales workers, managers, and professional and technical workers.

3. Despite this rate of growth, blacks will continue to be heavily concentrated in the low-wage occupations for many years to come.

This Negro employment picture is the result of several factors—discrimination in the job market, lack of training and education, inadequate employment opportunities near major Negro ghetto areas, and the inability of Negroes, due to housing discrimination, financial immobility, etc., to move to suburban locations where employment is expanding most rapidly. By providing jobs in black-controlled businesses, black capitalism hopes to avoid if not overcome many of these obstacles. But there is no doubt that substantial infusions of government aid are necessary to provide the financing and training needed for making the program a success.

Second, advocates of black capitalism believe that their plan will lead to more than just jobs; it will transform the ghetto economy into a more efficient structure. This is particularly true of retailing, where lower prices are needed to make the black consumer's dollar worth more.

Studies done in a number of major cities support the contention that prices, especially for durable goods, are higher in the ghetto than elsewhere—sometimes nearly twice as high as in stores located in white neighborhoods. These higher prices, however, do not always translate into higher profits. Some studies have shown that the expenses of doing business in the ghetto are larger due to greater salary and commission expenses (perhaps resulting from door-to-door selling), higher insurance costs, and a greater percentage of bad-debt losses.

Changing the ownership from white to black will not of course, in itself end higher retail prices in the ghetto. This can be accomplished only if either: (1) Washington provides subsidies for ghetto stores, or (2) the efficiency of ghetto stores is improved—perhaps by changing from small stores to large ones. Many supporters of black capitalism have suggested both these approaches. Subsidies, they feel, may be needed to get started, but the ultimate goal is to transform the retail structure of the ghetto into large-store complexes. By shifting business ownership from white to black, there may be a greater interest in keeping profits within the ghetto. In the final analysis, however, investment money—whether it comes from white or black sources—is likely to move where the returns are greatest, so profitability is the fundamental test.

Third, a more general objective of black capitalism is to strengthen political and civic leadership, as well as the economic influence, of the black community. As integration of Negroes into management positions of white-run corporations proceeds, the development of black capitalism might help put these business decision makers into positions of civic and political responsibility where they will have the power to sponsor and improve ghetto programs.

IS BLACK CAPITALISM A MISTAKE?
A BRIDGE TO NOWHERE?

Black capitalism has both strengths and weaknesses. It will undoubtedly offset some of the effects of discrimination in the job market; it may solve some of the economic problems of the ghetto; and it may indeed strengthen the voice of the Negro community.

On the negative side, the fundamental improvements needed in the retail structure of the ghetto will not readily follow from a change of ownership from white to black. There are major obstacles to overcome in training workers and in acquiring managerial talent. The creation of successful new firms requires a high level of entrepreneurial ability, and the supply of skilled Negro managers is as yet relatively small.

In addition to these general considerations, the entire concept of black capitalism has come under strong attack from various quarters. One of the most articulate critics has been Dr. Andrew Brimmer, an economist member of the Federal Reserve's Board of Governors and one of the highest-ranking black men in the government. In Dr. Brimmer's view, black capitalism is doomed to failure because at best it does not promise a big enough payoff to be of value to most Negroes, and at worst may retard the Negro's advancement by discouraging him from full participation in the national economy. There are several reasons for this, according to Brimmer:

☐ The typical urban Negro, characterized by low income, high unemployment, and large debts, is not a promising source of business talent.

☐ Negroes, as self-employed businessmen, would be part of a risky, low-paid, and rapidly declining segment of our modern economy; the rewards of employment in salaried positions are substantially greater.

☐ The black businessman, already handicapped, is not likely to be able to swim against the tide, and stands an even greater chance of failure than the high mortality rates of small business indicate.

What Negroes need, Brimmer has said, is to be brought into the mainstream of the economy as salaried employees or craftsmen for major companies; here they will find a much broader range of challenges and opportunities.

Financing Local Government: Our Urban Fiscal Dilemma

Any discussion of urban policies must eventually deal with the difficult problem of balancing local government revenues and expenditures. Why is the problem difficult? Mr. Micawber in *David Copperfield* described a situation that epitomizes the financial squeeze which many of our cities are experiencing today:

> Annual income twenty pounds, annual expenditure nineteen six: result, happiness.
>
> Annual income twenty pounds, annual expenditure twenty pounds ought and six: result, misery.

This is indeed the essence of our urban fiscal dilemma. It is a dilemma which has arisen because of the rapidly changing socioeconomic structures of our cities—their spiraling welfare costs and record budgets in the midst of an affluent and expanding population that leaves many unfortunate people in its wake.

Stated briefly, the fundamental economic problem facing an increasing number of American cities—and cities in many other countries as well—is a growing inability to finance public services. The reasons for this can be summarized briefly:

1. As our population expands and our economy grows richer, we not only purchase more goods and services from the private sector, but we also increase our demands from the public sector as well.

2. To meet these demands, urban governments have to increase their expenditures on virtually all types of public services such as sanitation, police and fire protection, education, health, welfare, transportation, recreation, and cultural facilities.

3. While cities have been left to grapple with soaring municipal costs, the groups which pay the heaviest share of taxes—namely business firms and middle-income families—have for decades been moving to the suburbs, and have been replaced by an ever-expanding population of the poor who need but cannot afford the more expensive education, welfare, health services, and other public benefits. (See Box 1.)

These conditions have led most cities to face a growing fiscal problem: To raise the revenue needed to pay for public services, they must increase taxes; however, taxes in the cities are already burdensome, and further increases may only hasten the exodus of people and businesses to nearby suburbs where taxes are relatively lower.

The Unheavenly City?

Is the American city really headed toward decay and disaster as many urbanologists believe? Or are most problems of the city largely imaginary? The answer to the first question is no, and to the second yes—according to Edward Banfield, a professor of urban government at Harvard University.

In his highly controversial book, The Unheavenly City *(Little, Brown, 1970), Banfield argues that all things considered, the cities are better than ever. Traffic congestion and smog are admittedly annoying, but such discomforts can be tolerated. Indeed, he says, they are the price to be paid for living where the action is. Much more important, in his opinion, is the inexorable progress of the cities and their success in turning out a more humane and wealthier citizenry.*

Banfield makes a number of points—some of them highly argumentative. Examples:

1. It has always been the function of the cities to attract the rural poor from the United States and abroad and to provide them with opportunities for a better life. As the poor crowd into the low-cost housing sections of the inner cities, others—including blacks—move up the scale just as rapidly as immigrant groups have done in the past.

2. Most people in the lowest income groups, including both blacks and whites, can never escape from poverty. This is not the fault of the city, but of their class outlook: They refuse to make present sacrifices for future gains. Behavioral patterns which are common in these groups, such as erratic work habits, unstable families, and tendencies toward violence, all appear to confirm this view.

3. Government programs have done little good for the urban poor, and some harm. Urban renewal has thrown them out of their homes; antipoverty funds have been wasted; large-scale employment programs have been self-defeating because they have attracted the rural poor to the cities and hence have not reduced urban unemployment.

4. In most states the minimum age for dropping out of school is too high. This keeps those lower-class students who are unresponsive to formal education in the classroom, and builds up their frustrations which they then vent on society. Some corrective steps that should be taken include: lowering the school quitting age; preventing unions from discriminating; and repealing minimum wage and occupational licensing laws. Such measures would enable bored students to leave school in order to pursue more exciting and responsible lives as construction workers, lumberjacks, and longshoremen.

5. The government is permissive toward crime. This is a subtle form of white racism because blacks are by far the main victims of urban crime. It is necessary that blacks who are capable of making progress—those in the working and middle classes—be separated from the ghettos so that they can be spared from violence and allowed to develop their full potentials. And for those individuals who show tendencies toward violent crime, various repressive measures are needed—including preventive detention.

What does the future hold? Banfield puts his faith in the functioning of the system. Economic growth, he believes, will eliminate urban poverty by the end of this century, and hence the need for many costly services which the cities now provide. In fact, the natural working of the economy (i.e., laissez faire) will ultimately do more, in Banfield's view, than even the most massive federal aid programs.

There is no doubt that Banfield has leveled a probing attack against a number of critical problems. But he has also offended many liberals, and has touched off some heated debates among urbanologists. Even if his prognosis is correct, he still leaves a disquieting question unanswered: What should society be doing about urban problems like crime control, low-cost housing, and ghetto unemployment while it waits for the millennium to arrive?

Most cities have often run deficits amounting to many millions of dollars—deficits which they covered by dipping into reserves, by borrowing against future budgets, and by selling long-term notes. Not since the days of the Depression, however, has the plight of many city treasuries been as bleak as in the years since the late sixties.

How should the various levels of government direct their limited resources to combat poverty, crime, pollution, eyesores, and ghetto unemployment, while improving education, housing, mass transit, and the other amenities of a better urban America? The solution rests on finding more effective ways of raising revenues while improving the efficiency of local government. Several proposals for achieving these objectives may be considered:

1. Minimize fiscal disparities
2. Introduce revenue sharing
3. Impose user charges
4. Restructure the property tax
5. Establish metropolitan government

A broad approach to financing urban government should draw on all these proposals.

MINIMIZE FISCAL DISPARITIES

Cities provide many goods and services whose benefits and costs are not appropriately apportioned. People benefit in varying degrees from the expenditures of local governments, and they pay in varying degrees for the values they receive. But the disparities between costs and benefits may be wide because the people who work in the city and the people who visit the city are not always the same people as the taxpayers who own property or live in the city. As a result of these misalignments, there tend to be wide differences not only in the taxable bases and expenditure requirements of the more than 80,000 local governmental units in the United States, but also in the quantity and quality of services provided by these units.

The divergencies of costs and benefits have created extensive "spillover" effects among a wide array of urban government expenditures ranging from health, education, and welfare services to environmental control. Two examples are indicative:

1. The mounting education and welfare budgets of New York, Chicago, Philadelphia, Detroit, and other major cities have been due in large part to our national agricultural policy which, since World War II, has promoted the subsidization and mechanization of the South's cotton and tobacco fields, driving out millions of displaced workers who have streamed into the cities looking for jobs. Since most of these people are poor, unskilled, and usually illiterate, they have either become public charges or at best have been able to find menial employment at the minimum wage. Meanwhile, many of the "expatriots"—the former residents of the cities—continue to work in the cities and hold the higher-paying jobs while turning over the bulk of their tax bills to the suburban municipalities in which they reside.

2. In the area of environmental control, it was once thought that air and water pollution were strictly local problems peculiar to a few cities. But now it is recognized that geographic boundaries in such matters are largely irrelevant and that the issues are of national or even international concern. Canadian residents, for example, have entered suits in United States federal courts against American firms for contaminating the air over Canada.

In these and many other classes of local government expenditures, the disparities between costs and benefits should be minimized. The most effective way to accomplish this is for the federal government to absorb a much larger share of the financial burden. At the present time state and local governments pay almost all the costs of public safety, transportation (except highways), elementary and secondary education, water supply and treatment, parks and recreation, and garbage collection, plus a substantial part of the cost of health, welfare, and social security programs. If a larger portion of the costs of these local activities could be transferred to Washington, many of the spillover effects would be greatly reduced or eliminated and the city governments would be relieved of enormous tax responsibilities.

INTRODUCE REVENUE SHARING

A promising approach for relieving the mounting fiscal pressures facing states and cities is for the federal government to engage in *revenue sharing*. Such a plan requires that the federal government turn over *automatically* a portion of its tax revenues to state and local governments each year. In 1969 and again in 1971 President Nixon proposed plans for revenue sharing, but the details and formulas must be worked out before Congress can pass on it. This may be forthcoming some time in the 1970s.

The concept of revenue sharing makes a great deal of practical sense—not just to many economists but to a large number of businessmen and political leaders as well. They base their justification for it on certain fundamental facts and relationships involving both revenues and expenditures.

First, the federal government collects most of the taxes levied; state and local governments collect a relatively minor proportion. The federal government's chief source of revenue is the income tax, which, because of its progressive rate structure, yields approximately a 1.5 percent increase in revenues for every 1 percent increase in GNP. The state and local governments, on the other hand, receive the great bulk of their revenues from property, sales, and other taxes, and these tend to increase by about 1 percent for every 1 percent increase in GNP.

Second, state and local spending has been increasing at rates of about 7 percent to 10 percent a year—roughly twice as fast as the growth in GNP. At the same time, state and local governments have met growing public resistance to increases in taxes, the imposition of new taxes, and the sale of bonds—these being the only methods available to finance their rising expenditures. Federal government spending, on the other hand (except for extraordinary military needs), tends to rise less than federal revenues when the economy is at full employment, thereby leaving a *fiscal dividend.*

According to the revenue-sharing advocates, *the salvation of states and cities lies in sharing the fiscal dividend.* Of course, the federal government has long poured out money to states and localities, but this has been largely in the form of grants-in-aid for specific programs to which Washington attaches many bureaucratic strings and controls. What the governors and mayors want is a kind of philosophical Jeffersonianism—an arrangement whereby the federal government gives out "blocks" of grants for broad general purposes while allowing all or most of the spending decisions to be made at state and local levels. In this way, by sharing a percentage of its revenues on a fixed basis with hard-pressed states and cities, Washington can encourage much greater local initiative.

IMPOSE USER CHARGES

Local governments obtain their revenues from various sources—taxation, license fees, interest earnings, special assessments, sale of property, charges for municipal services, etc. The last item, often called "user charges," offers promising opportunities for additional revenues. At present, people who receive the benefits of city hospitals, public housing, treated water, mass transit, refuse collection, and public schools help support part of the costs of these locally provided services through special payments, rents, and fees, as well as through taxation. The issue is whether the cities should revise their systems of user charges for these services, and whether they should charge for services which are presently financed out of tax revenues.

The answer to both questions is yes—for several reasons. First, a revision of user charges is based on the recognition that if certain types of services are available too cheaply or at flat rates, their limited supply will be rationed by congestion whenever the quantity demanded exceeds the quantity supplied at the existing price. Mass transit facilities during rush hours serve as striking illustrations. In such cases a differential pricing structure rather than a single price would not only provide a better rationing mechanism, but a larger total revenue as well.

Second, by imposing charges on certain services which are currently financed entirely from tax revenues, and by varying the charges according to their use, a more efficient utilization of resources and a greater volume of total revenue can be realized. Public libraries and marinas provide typical examples. The services of these facilities are usually offered free or at little cost to residents of the suburbs as well as the cities. Since the poor make relatively less use of these amenities, the overall effect is for middle-income households to be subsidized in large measure from taxes paid by low-income groups.

User charges have a number of advantages. Among the more important: (1) they enable the municipal government to know the value of its services to its users; (2) they reduce benefit spillovers resulting from geographic differences; and (3) they permit greater efficiency of production, less oversupply of services, and larger total revenues than would occur with tax financing. But user charges also have at least two closely related limitations. First, they are inappropriate for financing "pure public goods"—that is, goods whose benefits are available to everyone—such as clean streets, traffic lights, and public safety. Second, they are difficult to apply where specific benefits to users are hard to identify and measure.

RESTRUCTURE THE PROPERTY TAX

A fourth approach to improving the finances of local governments is to revise the existing structure of the property tax. This tax, with its diverse rates and bases, is imposed only at the state and local levels, not at the federal level. The importance of the property tax to local governments, including cities, counties, townships, and special districts, is evidenced by two significant sets of facts. First, it is levied by the great majority of local governmental units (about 71,000 out of some 81,000) in the United States. Second, it produces over 85 percent of the tax receipts of all local governments, and between 70 and 75 percent of the tax revenues of all city governments. In general, although local governments have other sources of revenue such as sales and excise taxes, income taxes, utility revenue, and liquor store revenue, the property tax is nevertheless their largest single source of funds. This tax helps pay most of the local share of school costs as well as a large part of the expenses incurred for public safety, sanitation, street lighting, and the bulk of other community services.

Despite its widespread use, the property tax suffers from a number of shortcomings. Three are particularly important:

1. It requires tax assessors to "guess" the market value of taxable property, since the true market value cannot be known unless the property is sold. As a result, wide differentials and inequities of assessment exist both within and between districts.

2. The tax is extremely regressive. It bears down much harder on poorer families than richer ones because housing is such a large part of consumer spending for lower-income groups.

3. It causes "fiscal zoning"—that is, the control of land use in order to maximize the tax base. For example, it encourages laws requiring large minimum lot sizes, thereby raising land costs and discouraging the construction of smaller homes for moderate-income families.

These and other factors make the property tax one of the most controversial in the entire tax structure. Nevertheless, it continues to exist, partly because it raises so much revenue and partly because it is the major tax which local governments can levy. Other forms of taxes such as income and payroll taxes are used primarily by the federal government, and sales taxes are used mainly by the states. Although some cities also levy income and sales taxes, local governments have always felt freer to impose property taxes and have tended to do so as their needs have grown.

The Land Value Tax

The many bad economic effects of the property tax have resulted in various proposals for its revision. The most desirable and feasible way to correct its deficiencies would be to restructure it in favor of a land value tax—a tax on bare sites exclusive of buildings that stand on them. This idea was first proposed by the American economist Henry George in his *Progress and Poverty* (1879). But unlike George, who advocated a tax on land as a "single tax" to replace all others, it is suggested here as a partial but substantial substitute for the property tax.

The fundamental idea is to tax the annual unearned gains from land—the so-called economic rent or surplus which accrues to the owners of land not because of improvements they have made upon it but because of community development and population growth which have caused the market value of land to rise. Among the chief arguments advanced in favor of such a tax are that it discourages land from being held out of productive use, it encourages building on property, and it returns to society the increases in the value of land resulting from economic growth. The major criticism of the tax is that it is difficult to administer because it cannot distinguish between increases in the value of land resulting from economic growth and increases due to improvements made on the land.

Even though this criticism is valid, its adverse effects can certainly be mitigated through appropriate tax laws. Experience in other countries which make use of land value taxation, including market-oriented economies such as Canada, Australia, and New Zealand, indicate that such laws are feasible and workable.

At present, the property tax in the United States is relatively light on land and heavy on buildings.

Hence the tax favors landowners, who tend to be in the higher-income groups, and speculators who find it more profitable to hold land for future resale than to build upon it. By restructuring the property tax so that it bears down relatively heavier on land than on buildings, these undesirable effects would be greatly reduced without causing revenue losses to local governments. In fact, various studies have concluded that a land value tax which averages less than 5 percent nationally would yield the same total revenue that is now produced by property taxes on land and buildings.

ESTABLISH METROPOLITAN GOVERNMENT

A fifth means of coping with the challenges facing local governments is one which realizes the need for regional attacks on pressing urban problems. This approach is as much political as economic. It is based on the recognition that local government authority in most metropolitan areas is too fragmented to provide for overall balanced systems of land use, transportation, public health, and the like. In metropolitan Chicago, for example, there are over 1,100 local government units; many other large urban areas like New York, Philadelphia, Pittsburgh, etc., have considerably more than 500 local units each. The effects of such proliferation are fiscal duplication, administrative inefficiency, and suburban separatism which hurts minority groups.

To help correct these deficiencies, some form of consolidation is needed. One of the more feasible possibilities is to set up a "two-tier" system of metropolitan government in urban regions. Such a system could consist of an area government and local governments, with functions assigned to each. At the area level, the functions assigned could be those which have broad overlapping interests or which offer advantages of economies of scale, for example, planning, zoning, water supply, sewage disposal, transportation, and public health. At the local levels, community governments could administer their own police departments, fire services, and education. Some functions, of course, could also be shared at both levels where it is advantageous to do so.

There are three major advantages to such a plan: (1) efficiency would be increased by consolidating some of the functions of smaller governmental units; (2) governmental units at all levels would become more responsive to human needs and preferences as a result of decentralizing some of the functions of the larger cities; and (3) the relationship of local governmental units to the states and federal government would be strengthened by a more rational allocation of functions among the various levels.

Metropolitan government has been adopted in varying degrees by some cities in the United States and Canada. But most local officials oppose the idea because they fear the loss of power. Consequently, the majority of states have been reluctant to pass the necessary enabling legislation. Hopefully, if Washington would expand the program of grants which it already provides for some regional activities, it could offer additional incentives to the states and local governments by rewarding them financially if they initiate plans for the establishment of some form of metropolitan government.

SUMMARY OF IMPORTANT IDEAS

1. Critics have accused the public schools—especially those in large cities—of being rigidly controlled educational monopolies. This makes them insensitive to community desires and unresponsive to the need for change. By subjecting them to competition in a free market, it is argued, the quality of all schools will improve. Four proposals that have been advanced for increasing competition are: decentralization of school systems; creation of publicly financed private schools; education by contract; and the voucher system.

2. The inner cities have long been faced with the problem of providing adequate housing for the poor. Government has tried to help but sometimes has done more harm than good. The ultimate solution rests on developing a proper system of federal subsidies to help support low-income housing. The federal government should also absorb the health, education, and welfare costs of the cities so that the latter can afford to exempt all low-income housing from property taxes.

3. The transportation crisis of the cities is due primarily to an imbalance between private automobile and public transportation. This results in congestion, time delays, and a general malallocation of transportation facilities. Two broad steps that can be taken toward developing a balanced transportation system are: (a) the introduction of an appropriate pricing system, in the form of variable tolls, to ration the use of scarce transportation facilities; and (b) technological improvements and innovations such as electronic control systems, mass-transit subsidy schemes, and relaxed restrictions on the use of taxicab and jitney services.

4. The development of black capitalism may have many desirable effects—political and social as well as economic. But the funds to encourage black entrepreneurship, and the supply of trained talent among Negroes, are limited. Some critics believe, therefore, that the money might better be used to train Negroes for more responsible jobs in today's economy.

5. The most fundamental problem of the cities is to finance needed urban improvements. This requires that they resolve their present fiscal dilemma. The recommended measures are: minimize fiscal disparities; introduce revenue sharing; impose user charges; restructure the property tax; and establish metropolitan government.

FOR HOMEWORK AND DISCUSSION

1. *Terms and concepts to review:*

black capitalism	revenue sharing
benefit principle	fiscal dividend

2. Can you propose some guidelines for improving public education in the United States, by suggesting the kinds of decisions that should be centralized and decentralized at different levels of state and local government?

3. "If the government would stop interfering in the housing market, the price of housing would adjust to the free interaction of supply and demand and there would be no problem." Do you agree? Explain.

4. Various public transit systems have considered raising their fares during morning and evening rush hours and lowering them at other times. Despite the advantages of such schemes, they have rarely been adopted. Why?

5. "If Negroes are to be encouraged to break away from the ghettos, black capitalism is not the way to do it." Why or why not?

6. If the cities need more money to finance urban improvements, why do they not simply raise taxes or borrow?

7. It may be argued that when a city makes available "free" museums, "free" golf courses, "free" tennis courts, "free" marinas, etc., it is redistributing income *from the poor to the rich!* How might this happen? What can be done about it?

REFERENCES AND READING SUGGESTIONS

CHAMBERLIN, NEIL W. (ed.), *Business and the Cities*, Basic Books, New York, 1970.

CROSS, THEODORE, *Black Capitalism*, Atheneum, New York, 1969.

Education In the Ghetto, A Search For Solutions, *Saturday Review*, January 11, 1969. Contains several articles on educational problems, but see especially the one by Theodore R. Sizer, Dean of the Graduate School of Education at Harvard University.

FRIEDMAN, MILTON, *Capitalism and Freedom*, University of Chicago Press, Chicago, 1962, chap. 6.

HECHINGER, FRED M., "School Vouchers: Can the Plan Work," *The New York Times*, June 7, 1970, Sec. E–11.

NETZER, DICK, *Economics and Urban Problems*, Basic Books, New York, 1970.

NEVITT, ADELA ADAM (ed.), *The Economic Problems of Urban Housing*, St. Martin's Press, New York, 1967.

WILCOX, CLAIR, *Toward Social Welfare*, Irwin, Chicago, 1969, chap. 16.

PART 8

International Economics. The World's Economies

CHAPTER 33

International Trade:
The Commerce of Nations

CHAPTER PREVIEW

What are the chief highlights of world trade? Are there significant regional patterns of trade for the United States?

Why do nations trade? What benefits do they receive? What costs do they incur?

Why do countries impose obstacles to trade? Are their reasons valid?

How does international trade affect income and employment? Is there a relationship between a country's imports, exports, and national income?

In this chapter you will embark on the study of international economics. The subject is timely, because the countries of the world are increasingly interdependent economically. Many of the issues that can either tie nations closer together or drive them apart have their roots in economics.

In general, international economics is concerned with the same fundamental questions as "domestic" economics. Thus the problems of *what* to produce, *how much,* and *for whom,* are still foremost; the difference is that they are studied for several economies or nations rather than for one.

On the microeconomic side, for example, international economics may study how the price systems of different countries interact to affect resource allocation and income distribution. On the macroeconomic side it may be concerned with the ways in which imports, exports, and investment expenditures among nations affect income, employment, and economic growth. Both micro and macro principles are often employed simultaneously in the study of international economics.

In this chapter we will concentrate on one broad segment of international economics—trade among nations. The principles of international finance and the results of various commercial and financial policies will be considered in later chapters.

Major Features of United States and World Trade

It is appropriate to begin the study of international trade by asking two questions: (1) Of what relative significance is world trade to the United States and other leading nations? (2) What are the distributional patterns of trade between the United States and the major regions of the world?

THE IMPORTANCE OF WORLD TRADE

American students are not as familiar with the importance of international trade as are students in most other countries. The reason for this is brought out in Exhibit 1. In many nations the volume of exports or imports ranges from 10 percent of GNP to more than a third. But only about 4 or 5 percent of the GNP of the United States is sold abroad, and approximately the same percentage or slightly less is purchased abroad.

However, neither the dollar volume of trade nor the products involved are trivial. Even the 4 percent

of GNP that was exported by the United States in the late 1960s amounted to more than $30 billion annually, while imports were only a few billion dollars less. In total dollar volume, this is far larger than the trade carried on by other countries. (See also Box 1.)

American exports and imports consist of the goods shown in Exhibit 2. In terms of value, agricultural goods represent less than 20 percent of what we import and export, whereas nonagricultural goods represent more than 80 percent of these totals.

Exhibit 1

Merchandise Exports as a Percent of GNP for Selected Countries

Country	Average 1965–70
Belgium	38%
Netherlands	34
Denmark	22
Switzerland	21
Norway	21
Sweden	20
Canada	19
West Germany	18
United Kingdom	14
Italy	13
France	11
United States	4

SOURCE: *International Financial Statistics*, various issues.

Exhibit 2

Exports and Imports of the United States, 1969

Item	Merchandise exports	Merchandise imports
	Billions of dollars	
Agricultural products	$ 5.9	$ 5.0
Nonagricultural products	31.5	31.1
Total	37.4	36.1
Food and live animals: Meats, grains, cereals	3.7	4.5
Beverages and tobacco	0.7	0.8
Crude materials: Cotton, soybeans, metal ores	3.6	3.5
Mineral fuels, lubricants: Coal and petroleum products	1.1	2.8
Animal and vegetable oils, fats, waxes	0.3	0.1
Chemicals	3.4	1.2
Manufactured goods: Textiles, iron and steel, nonferrous metals	4.6	7.9
Machinery and transport equipment: Agricultural, metalworking, construction, excavation, electrical; motor vehicles, parts, and products	16.4	9.8
All other	3.6	5.4

SOURCE: U.S. Department of Commerce.

Box 1

World Trade Continues to Grow

The rapid growth of world trade . . .

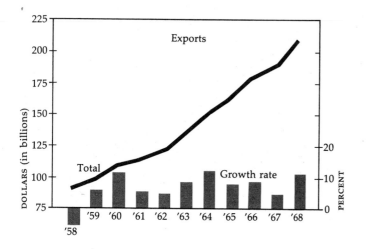

. . . does not reflect the diverse fortunes of the leading traders.

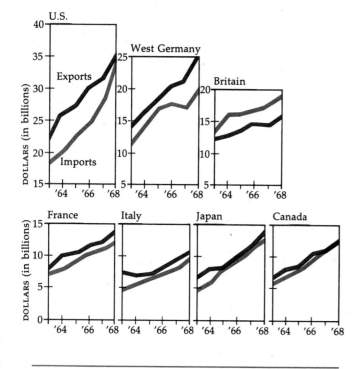

Since World War II, the major industrial nations' share of world trade has been rising and the underdeveloped nations' has been falling. As a result there is growing concern over how the poor countries can develop their own manufacturing industries, thereby competing more effectively in world markets. We shall find that this problem is of major interest in international economics.

REGIONAL PATTERNS OF UNITED STATES TRADE

Where do our imports come from? Where do our exports go? Exhibit 3 shows clearly that the least-industrialized areas of the world are neither America's biggest suppliers nor its biggest customers. Europe, which includes most of the leading industrial countries of the world, is America's largest market for purchases and sales of goods. Canada and Asia, notably Japan, are the next largest markets.

Of course, changes in the world's economies since the early part of this century have brought changes in our patterns of trade. For example, trade with Asia has grown in relative importance, while trade with Europe, though still large in absolute terms, has declined to roughly one-third of the total.

Exhibit 3

United States Merchandise Exports and Imports, 1970

Region	Merchandise exports	Merchandise imports
	Billions of dollars	
Africa	$ 1.6	$ 1.1
Asia	10.0	9.6
Australia and Oceania	1.2	0.9
Europe	14.8	11.4
Canada	9.1	11.1
Mexico and Central America	3.3	2.9
South America	3.2	3.0

SOURCE: U.S. Department of Commerce.

Why Do Countries Trade?

Imagine what would happen if you tried to be completely self-sufficient. You would have to grow your own food, make your own clothing, build your own means of transportation, construct your own shelter, make your own furniture, treat your own illnesses, and provide for all your needs and desires. There are obviously many things you would not be able to do because you lack the necessary material resources, time, and skills. Hence your level of living would be much lower than it is now.

How could you correct the situation? You could *specialize*—that is, concentrate on the things you do best. In that way, you could produce more than enough for yourself, and sell or trade your surpluses for the other things you want. That is essentially what we all do. A carpenter, a salesman, a doctor, a teacher, a bricklayer—each "specializes" in the activity that he does best and thereby earns enough to buy the goods and services that he does not produce for himself.

This tendency among individuals also exists among nations:

Human and nonhuman resources are distributed unevenly throughout the world. Some countries have more or better land, or labor, or capital than others, so it may pay for them to *specialize*. In this way, a larger quantity and greater variety of goods are produced, which nations can exchange with one another. The quantity would be smaller and the variety less if each nation tried to be "self-sufficient."

These ideas can be understood more clearly by examining the principles and consequences that underlie the exchange of goods between nations and regions.

LAW OF ABSOLUTE ADVANTAGE

The simplest and most obvious reason for trade is provided by what is known as the *law of absolute advantage*. This principle states that a basis for trade exists between regions when each, due to natural or acquired endowments, can provide the other with a good or service for less than it would pay to produce the product at home. Thus, the United States buys coffee from Brazil, and Brazil buys steel from the United States; Libya buys lumber from Sweden, and Sweden buys oil from Libya; Florida buys cars made in Michigan, and Michigan buys oranges grown in Florida. In general, this kind of trading helps both parties. Imagine how costly it would be, for example, if some Florida businessmen tried to acquire the factories and skilled workers needed to make automobiles, or if some Michigan businessmen tried to build the huge hothouses that would be needed for growing orange trees.

NOTE. For convenience, we ordinarily speak of "countries" or "regions" as buyers and sellers of products. But the governments of those areas are not doing all the buying and selling. Most international trade is carried on by corporations and private firms; only in communist or command economies do governments engage significantly in trade.

THE CONCEPT OF COMPARATIVE ADVANTAGE

The reasons for trade are not always as obvious as in the above examples. Trade between individuals or nations can be profitable even if one of the parties can produce *both* products more efficiently than the other. This involves a concept known as "comparative advantage."

For example, a doctor may also be a fast typist. Yet he hires a typist, even though she may not type as well as he does, because the time he spends at his medical practice is more profitable than the time he spends at the typewriter. Thus, suppose the doctor can do all the typing he needs in one hour, whereas the typist he hires takes three hours to do the same amount of typing. If the doctor earns $30 an hour by practicing medicine, and pays the typist $3 an hour, he gains $21 a day by sticking to his profession. Or, to put the example in a different but equivalent way, he can earn enough money in eighteen minutes by practicing medicine to pay for three hours of the typist's time.

An Application to Nations

Applying the same principle to nations, let us take the case of England and Portugal, both producing two products—cloth and wine. (This was the kind of example used in 1817 by the great English classical economist David Ricardo, when he first explained the mutual advantages of trade between nations in terms of what we now call the law of comparative advantage.)

An illustration based on hypothetical data appears in Exhibit 4. It is clear from the table that Portugal is equally as efficient as England in the production of cloth, but three times as efficient as England in the production of wine. Hence we say that Portugal has a comparative (or relative) advantage in wine production.

These data are presented in the accompanying charts in the form of production-possibilities curves. The "curves," however, are shown here as straight lines, whereas in earlier chapters they appeared as curved lines that were bowed outward. This is because we are assuming for simplicity that production takes place under conditions of constant rather than increasing costs.

Thus in England, the intersection of the production-possibilities curve *DE* with the two axes of the chart tells us that one day's labor can produce either 30 yards of cloth or 10 gallons of wine, or any particular combination in between as determined by

---

Exhibit 4

The Law of Comparative Advantage

The curves DE and D'E' are production-possibilities curves for each country. Without trade between the two nations, England may choose to be "self-sufficient" in both cloth and wine by producing a combination represented by point K; similarly, Portugal may choose to be "self-sufficient" by producing a combination represented by point K'.

Production from one day's labor at full employment.

	Cloth output (yards per day)	Wine output (gallons per day)	Cost ratio (cloth/wine)
England	30	10	3/1
Portugal	30	30	1/1

England

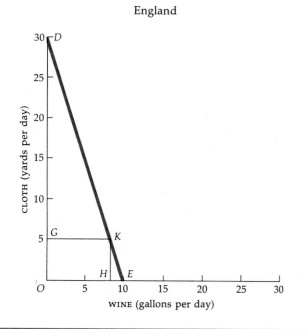

Portugal

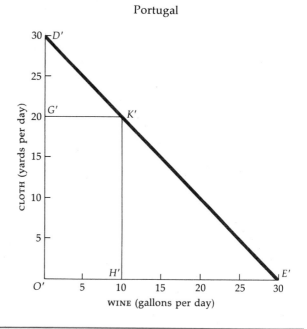

any given point along the line. Hence the steepness (slope) of *DE* measures the relative cost of the two products in England and is constant at the ratio 3:1. Similarly in Portugal, the intersection of *D'E'* with the two axes signifies that one day's labor can produce either 30 yards of cloth or 30 gallons of wine, or any specific combination in between as determined by any given point along the line. Therefore, the steepness (slope) of *D'E'* measures the relative cost of the two products in Portugal and is constant at the ratio 1:1.

How much will each country produce? It is impossible to answer this question without knowing the demands for each product in the two countries. However, if we assume that there is no trade between them, it may be inferred that each will try to be self-sufficient by producing some cloth and some wine as denoted by any given point on each nation's production-possibilities curve. Thus England might choose the point *K* representing *OG* yards of cloth and *OH* gallons of wine; Portugal might choose the point *K'* representing *O'G'* yards of cloth and *O'H'* gallons of wine.

Introducing Trade

What will happen if the two countries decide to engage in free and unrestricted trade? Let us assume for simplicity that for both countries: (1) there are no transportation costs between them, (2) competitive conditions prevail, and (3) labor is the only scarce factor of production and hence prices of the products are equal to their relative labor costs. This means that since the costs, and therefore prices, in both countries are

Price in England: 3 yards cloth = 1 gallon wine
Price in Portugal: 1 yard cloth = 1 gallon wine

it is obvious that *cloth is cheaper in England and wine is cheaper in Portugal.* Therefore, England will import wine from Portugal and Portugal will import cloth from England. As exports of Portuguese wine enter England, the supply of wine in England will increase and its price will fall; likewise, as exports of English cloth enter Portugal, the supply of cloth in Portugal will increase and its price will fall.

THE GAINS FROM TRADE

The price ratios in England and Portugal will thus become equal to one another because, as we have assumed above, there is competition in both nations and there are no trade restrictions or transportation costs between them; hence the two countries will comprise in effect a *single market* with a *single price ratio.* At this new price ratio, it will pay for England to specialize in the production of cloth and for Portugal to specialize in the production of wine, and for both nations to trade a portion of these outputs with one another. In that way the citizens of the two countries can end up with more wine and more cloth than if each country tried to produce both products by itself.

The point is illustrated graphically in Exhibit 5. Chart (*a*) is constructed by combining the two previous charts from Exhibit 4. Thus the chart for England is in the same relative position as before, but the chart for Portugal is "flipped over" so that its origin is in the upper right-hand corner at *O'*. The construction procedure is shown in chart (*b*).

By studying chart (*a*), we can observe several interesting features:

1. The dashed line *DL* defines the trading possibilities for both countries. Since it is a straight line, it has a constant price ratio (or slope) which is somewhere between the price ratios represented by the old production-possibilities curves *DE* and *D'E'*.

2. An "exchange point" will tend to be established in the vicinity of *P* because at a point such as this both England and Portugal can have more cloth and more wine by specializing and trading than by trying to be "self-sufficient." For example, suppose England specializes entirely in cloth and produces *OD* yards of it. If it consumes *OM* yards of cloth, it can export the remaining *MD* yards and acquire *ON* (= *MP*) gallons of wine in return. It thus ends up at the point *P* where it has *more* cloth than when it was self-sufficient at the point *K*.

3. Similarly, if Portugal specializes completely in wine, it can produce *O'E'* gallons. If it consumes *O'N'* of this, it has left over *N'E'* which it can export to England in return for *O'M'* yards of cloth. In this way Portugal also ends up at the point *P*, where it

Exhibit 5

The Terms of Trade and the Gains from Trade

Chart (a) is constructed by combining the two separate charts of England and Portugal from the previous exhibit, as illustrated in chart (b). The dashed arrows show that the chart for England is transferred directly, whereas the chart for Portugal is rotated or "flipped over."

The lines DE and D'E' are the production-possibilities curves from the previous exhibit. Before trade begins, England is producing at point K and Portugal at point K'. As a result of trade, both countries may extend their production frontiers to the point P, where each country receives more of both goods

than before. These increased benefits of trade are called the gains from trade.

The dashed line DL is the new price line representing the trading possibilities of both nations. Its steepness (slope) measures the terms of trade, which is the amount of goods that each nation must give up (or export) for one unit of goods that it receives (or imports). The line must fall somewhere between the two old price lines DE and D'E' in order for trade to occur. If it falls to the left of DE (or to the right of D'E'), it will be cheaper for England (or for Portugal) to produce both products and not trade.

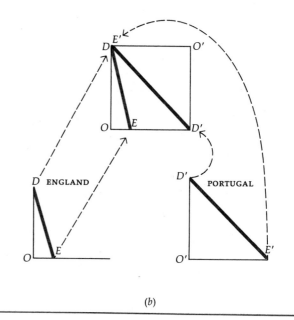

(a)

(b)

consumes *more* of both cloth and wine than when it was self-sufficient at the point K'.

4. Both countries thus benefit from international specialization and exchange. The amount by which a country benefits from trade is called the *gains from trade*. This concept plays an important role in the trading policies of nations.

It is interesting to note from the chart that only in the vicinity of point P along the line DL will both

countries gain by having more of both wine and cloth. At exchange points which are much higher or lower, one country may gain while the other loses, as compared to when each was self-sufficient without trade. Thus at point S, for example, England will gain by having more cloth and more wine than it had at point K, but Portugal will lose by having more wine and less cloth than it had at point K'. At point T, on the other hand, England will have comparatively less cloth and more wine, while Portugal has more of both. Only in the vicinity of point P can *both* countries experience the mutual benefits of having more of *both* products. Hence under conditions of competition and unrestricted trade, the exchange point will tend to settle at or near P.

THE TERMS OF TRADE

Each country thus gains by specializing in what it can produce with the greatest comparative or relative advantage. The gains will then be divided between them according to the new price ratio which, as we have seen, is simply the slope of the trading-possibilities line DL in the chart.

Thus the closer that the line DL is to DE, the higher will be the price of wine relative to cloth, and hence the greater the gain to Portugal as compared to England. If DL should coincide with DE, which is unlikely, Portugal will receive all the gains from trade and England will receive none. The converse of these principles, of course, are equally applicable if the line DL shifts in the opposite direction toward $D'E'$.

In general, the new price line DL must always be somewhere between the old price lines DE and $D'E'$ in order for trade to occur. For if DL is, say, to the left of (or steeper than) DE, the trading price of wine will be *greater* than the old price ratio in England. England will then find it cheaper to produce its own wine than to import it from Portugal. Similarly, if the line DL is to the right of $D'E'$, it will pay for Portugal to produce its own cloth instead of trading with England.

These ideas involve what is known as the *terms of trade*. It is defined as the number of units of goods that must be given up for one unit of goods received by each party to a transaction. (Graphically, the terms of trade are measured by the slope of the line DL in the chart.) In any transaction, the terms of trade are determined by the relative demands of the trading parties. In general, the terms of trade are said to move *in favor* of the party which gives up less units of goods for one unit of goods received, and *against* the party which gives up more units of goods for one unit of goods received. As we shall see, the terms of trade play a vital and intensely practical role in evaluating exchange relationships between nations.

CONCLUSION: AN IMPORTANT LAW

The foregoing ideas permit us to formulate a principle of fundamental significance in economics, especially in international economics. It is based on the concept of comparative advantage which was developed earlier, but the concept may now be expressed more formally as a law.

The *law of comparative advantage* states that if one nation can produce each of two products more efficiently than another nation, and it can produce one of these commodities with comparatively greater efficiency than the other commodity, it should specialize in the production of the product in which it is most efficient and leave the production of the alternative product to the other country. The two nations will then have more of both goods by engaging in trade. This principle is also applicable to individuals and regions as well as to nations.

The law of comparative advantage thus leads to an important conclusion:

Free and unrestricted trade among nations encourages international specialization according to comparative advantage. It thereby *tends* to bring about: (1) the most efficient allocation of world resources as well as a maximization of world production; (2) a redistribution of relative product demands, resulting in greater equality of product prices among trading nations; and (3) a redistribution of relative resource demands to correspond with relative product demands, resulting in greater equality of resource prices among trading nations.

It is important to emphasize that these outcomes are *tendencies* rather than certainties, because they are based on such idealistic assumptions as the existence of competition and the absence of trade restrictions (including transportation costs) among trading nations. Since these assumptions are not entirely realized in practice, the consequences of free trade will deviate from the above-mentioned tendencies.

Instruments of Protection

Despite the fundamental advantages of free trade—namely, encouragement of the most efficient allocation of world resources and the maximization of world production—nations have not been quick to adopt it. They have often chosen instead to institute various methods of protecting their home industries by imposing barriers to free trade. The reasons usually advanced for such actions will be explained subsequently. But first, the chief forms of protection may be noted briefly.

TARIFFS

Tariffs have played a very significant role in various political and sectional disputes in the United States. What is a *tariff*? It may be defined as a customs duty or tax imposed by a government on the importation (or exportation) of a good. Tariffs may be: (1) specific, based on a tax per unit of the commodity, or (2) ad valorem, based on the value of the commodity. There are a number of reasons, some of them rather complex, why a government might impose a tariff. For present purposes, however, it will be simplest for us to think of a tariff as a tax on imports exclusively, and to assume that it is imposed for the primary purpose of protecting domestic industry from foreign competition, or for providing the government with more revenue.

Exhibit 6 presents a history of tariff levels in the United States since 1820. Since a tariff is a law which must be approved by Congress, it is often named after the Congressman who sponsored it. As the chart shows, the highest tariffs existed in 1830 and in 1930, at rates of about 60 percent. The trend since 1930 has been sharply downward, with average rates of about 12 percent during the 1950s and 1960s. But the decade of the seventies may see a sharp reversal in the trend, due to renewed protectionist efforts in Congress.

QUOTAS AND OTHER NONTARIFF DEVICES

Tariffs are not the only means that nations employ to protect their home industries. Another common instrument of protection is the *import quota*, which places a precise legal limit on the number of units of a commodity that may be imported during a given period. In addition, countries may impose customs procedures and laws involving import financing, foreign exchange requirements, and regulations involving labeling, health, safety, and shipping, some of which are expressly designed as protectionist devices. (See Box 2.) Quotas and other nontariff devices have become relatively more significant than tariffs as protective instruments in many countries including the United States.

Box 2

A Salami May Sometimes Be Just a Lot of Bologna

When is a sausage not a sausage?

The not-so-simple answer is: When it is exported and bumps into another country's definition of a sausage.

Many countries, mostly European, have their own idea of what a sausage should be—defined by its size, shape, casing, color, the mix of ingredients, and, in some instances, the number per link. Anything that doesn't conform to a particular country's definition of a sausage is ruled a nonsausage and may not be imported.

The restrictions are what are known as nontariff barriers. *Broadly, these are any obstacles to international trade other than import duties or tariffs. Studies of the extent of nontariff barriers are only in the early stages, but the findings so far indicate that their varieties are almost endless. They include import quotas, import licensing and foreign exchange controls, state trading monopolies and preferential, nationalistic buying by Government agencies. Other, less subtle restrictions range through labeling and packaging requirements, health and industrial standards, and discriminatory taxes and fees.*

But the classic nontariff barrier most often cited by foreign traders is the provision of a German tariff law of 1902, now obsolete, affecting the import of cows. This granddaddy of nontariff barriers was designed to exclude Dutch and Russian cattle competitive with German types, but allow entry of Swiss cattle. It did so with a definition that gave an extra low duty rate to "large dappled mountain cattle or brown cattle reared at a spot 300 meters above sea level and which have at least one month's grazing at a spot at least 800 meters above sea level."

The old German law, while not mentioning any country, achieved its aim with what amounted to a description of Swiss cattle-raising practices. Modern nontariff barriers, however, are not so diplomatic. The catalogue of such barriers seems infinite, and as research develops, almost every country, including the United States, is seen to be a prime offender.

What are the economic consequences of protection? In general, all forms of protection tend to impede the full advantages of international specialization that are to be gained from free or unrestricted trade. When a nation adopts protective devices such as tariffs, quotas, etc., it causes (1) a shift of resources from more efficient to less efficient uses, and (2) a restriction of consumers' freedom of choice.

Arguments for Protection

Despite the fact that the law of comparative advantage and the economic benefits of free trade have never been successfully refuted—although there have been many heroic attempts to do so—efforts by special-interest groups to obtain protection are common. American history, for example, is replete

---

Exhibit 6

Average Tariff Rates in the United States

Tariffs have often been a political football in American history. Their average rates have fluctuated widely, but the trend has been sharply downward since the early thirties. Since the post- *World War II years, America has been a leading low-tariff nation. But the trend may be reversed in the seventies, due to renewed protectionist efforts in Congress.*

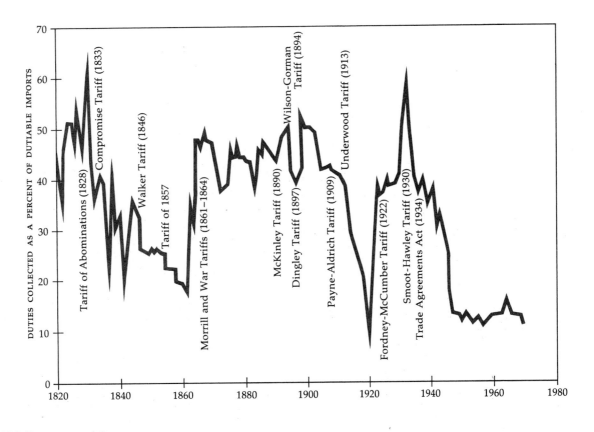

SOURCE: U.S. Department of Commerce.

with long and eloquent pleas by businessmen, union representatives, and political leaders contending that theirs is a "different" situation requiring special consideration. Most of these arguments for protection can be grouped into one of the following categories:

1. Infant-industry argument
2. National-security argument
3. Diversified-economy argument
4. Wage-protection argument
5. Employment-protection argument

We shall see below that there are fallacies in all these arguments. But before we do, the following fundamental point should be understood:

We can sell abroad only if we buy abroad. When the United States imports from foreign countries, those countries earn most of the dollars they need to purchase American exports. In general, *exports are the cost of trade, imports the return from trade,* not the other way around. Over the long run a nation must export in order to import.

As you will see in the following paragraphs, this basic principle is essential for understanding the fallacies that underlie almost all arguments for protection—*including both tariffs and quotas.*

THE INFANT-INDUSTRY ARGUMENT

When George Washington was inaugurated in 1789, he appointed Alexander Hamilton as the first Secretary of the Treasury. In 1791, Hamilton issued his famous *Report on Industry and Commerce* wherein he articulated with remarkable depth and clarity the economic problems of the time, and proposed the nation's first protective tariff system. A fundamental justification for this system was the new nation's need to protect its growing infant industries.

An *infant industry* is an underdeveloped industry which may not be able to survive competition from abroad. The "infant-industry argument" for protection says that such industries should be shielded temporarily with high tariffs or quotas until they develop technological efficiency and economies of scale which will enable them to compete with foreign industries.

This type of plea was the basis on which tariffs were established for a number of industries during the nineteenth and twentieth centuries. But economists have come to recognize three major shortcomings of this argument:

1. Tariffs or other protective devices become the vested interests of particular business and political groups and are extremely difficult to eliminate.

2. Some protected industries never grow out of the "infant" stage—that is, they never become able to compete effectively with more mature industries in other countries.

3. An increase in tariffs or quotas results in higher prices to domestic consumers; therefore, if an industry must be shielded from foreign competition, a subsidy would be more desirable because it tends to increase output as well as reduce costs and prices, and above all is visible and must be voted periodically by Congress.

NATIONAL-SECURITY ARGUMENT

Since the 1960s, the American steel industry has made every effort, in the halls of Congress and through the news media, to gain protection from the competitive onslaught of Japanese and European steel. In one of his many pleas for increased protection, Roger Blough, chairman of the board of the U.S. Steel Corporation, asked a Congressional committee in the late sixties: "Can we, for example, be assured of the strong industrial base in steel we need for modern defense if one-quarter or more of the steel we require were imported from countries lying uncomfortably close to the Soviet Union or China?"

This quotation provides a superb illustration of the "national-security argument"—an argument which contends that a nation should be as self-sufficient as possible in the production of goods that it needs for war and defense. On the face of it, this plea for protection seems persuasive, but on closer examination the following criticisms become apparent:

1. It is a political and military argument rather than an economic one, and hence should be decided by the proper authorities in a calm and rational manner without the distortions of parties that have a direct business interest in the outcome. The economist can

help by pointing out the costs of protection in terms of resource misallocation and a reduced level of living.

2. Many industries are important for defense or national security, and hence could qualify equally well for increased protection.

3. As in the infant-industry argument, if some form of shielding is necessary, a subsidy is preferable to a tariff or quota.

DIVERSIFIED-ECONOMY ARGUMENT

"Don't put all your eggs in one basket." This maxim is as true for nations as it is for individuals—according to the "diversified-economy" theorists, who contend that increased protection is desirable because it enables a nation to build up a variety of industries for greater economic stability. In that way, they say, a highly specialized economy—like Bolivia's tin economy or Chile's copper economy—will be less susceptible to adverse swings in the world's demand for its exports. This argument contains some elements of truth. A single-crop or single-product economy is highly vulnerable to swings in demand —which may be permanent. Thus, the introduction of manmade fibers has impoverished or severely damaged economies that concentrated on production of natural fibers. Further, specialized economies are frequently dependent on relatively few purchasers of their goods: the oil-producing nations of the Middle East, for example, sell to a relatively small number of oil companies—the giants in the field. When oil is in short supply, the producing countries can drive hard bargains; when oil is ample, the oil companies have the last word in any bargaining session.

But the diversified-economy argument also contains some shortcomings:

1. It is of little significance to economies that are already diversified and advanced, such as the United States.

2. It assumes that the government is more clairvoyant than private investors, and thus more able to envision the future economic benefits flowing from new and diversified industries.

3. It overlooks the inefficiencies that may result from forced, "unnatural" diversification, and the consequent increase in cost which may more than offest any economic gains.

WAGE-PROTECTION ARGUMENT

Because wages in the United States are higher than they are in other industrialized nations, some economists and business leaders argue that tariffs or quotas are needed to protect American workers from the products of cheap labor abroad.

In essence, advocates of this argument are contending that a high-wage nation cannot compete with a low-wage nation. In reality, however, the contention is false. The products of high-wage United States labor compete daily in world markets with the products of low-wage labor. The fact is that for many products high wages do not of themselves prevent or even hinder trade among nations.

Three criticisms and qualifications of the wage-protection argument are particularly important:

1. It assumes that labor is the only resource entering into production, when in fact it is a resource that is combined in each nation with varying inputs of capital and labor; as a result, the products of countries may often be characterized as *labor-intensive, capital-intensive,* or *land-intensive,* depending on the relative proportions of resources that are employed in production.

2. Low-wage countries will have an advantage over high-wage countries *only* with products that are labor-intensive—that is, products for which wages are a large proportion of total costs. High-wage countries may be better off not to compete with low-wage countries in these products.

3. Even where labor-intensive products are concerned, however, high-wage countries may be able to compete effectively with low-wage countries if labor productivity in the former is high enough to compensate for lower wage levels in the latter. (See Box 3.)

EMPLOYMENT-PROTECTION ARGUMENT

Supporters of tariff protection often argue that tariffs are desirable because they reduce imports relative to exports and thus encourage a favorable balance of trade—that is, a surplus of exports over imports. This in turn stimulates the export industries and helps to bring about a higher level of domestic income, employment, and production.

Is this a valid plea for protection? Like the previous arguments it may seem persuasive, but the following considerations should be kept in mind:

1. Any benefits in the form of higher income and employment, if they occur, are not likely to last long. The history of tariffs and quotas shows that in the long run nations tend to retaliate with their own protective measures, leaving all nations worse off than before.

2. Tariffs and quotas tend to result in higher prices, thus penalizing domestic consumers while benefiting domestic, inefficient producers; in the long run

---

Box 3

Should the Steel Industry Be Protected?

Yes	No
THE PAUPER LABOR ARGUMENT. *"Many things should and must be protected. For example, millions of our people—and a number of government agencies—are laudably striving to protect certain vanishing forms of wildlife that are threatened with extinction; and one may reasonably wonder, I suppose, how far down the road to oblivion some of our major industries must go before they are deemed to merit similar concern. . . .*	THE PAUPER LABOR FALLACY. *One of the oldest arguments for trade protection is that it guards America's high-wage standards. U.S. industries are eager to compete, the reasoning runs, but they're confounded by the foreign producers' lower labor costs.*

THE PAUPER LABOR ARGUMENT. *"Many things should and must be protected. For example, millions of our people—and a number of government agencies—are laudably striving to protect certain vanishing forms of wildlife that are threatened with extinction; and one may reasonably wonder, I suppose, how far down the road to oblivion some of our major industries must go before they are deemed to merit similar concern. . . .*

"Whenever the subject of steel quotas arises, the importers—who are understandably opposed to any restrictions—send forth one or two spokesmen of scholarly repute who seek to show that the American steel industry has been backward in its research and delinquent in adopting the new steelmaking processes which have been developed abroad. They charge that inefficiency is responsible for our inability to undersell foreign steel here in the American market, and that we have no one to blame but ourselves. And they persist tenaciously in this belief, like the wife who said: Look, George, I already know what I think, so don't try to confuse me with a lot of facts.

"But studies show that the average output per manhour in the American steel industry is higher than in any other steel-producing nation in the free world; so there must be some other explanation of the advantage which imported steel enjoys in the market place. Could it lie in the fact that the wages and benefits paid by foreign producers are from 25 to about 40 dollars a ton lower than those paid in the United States? And have our detractors stopped to figure out that to overcome a 40-dollar disadvantage in employment costs, we would have to cut the manhours required to make a ton of steel from the present low level of 13 down to a miraculous 4? That's quite a trick if we could do it!"

SOURCE: "In Steel . . . Progress Is Not Our Most *Imported* Product." From an address by Roger Blough, Chairman of the Board, United States Steel Corporation, 1969.

THE PAUPER LABOR FALLACY. *One of the oldest arguments for trade protection is that it guards America's high-wage standards. U.S. industries are eager to compete, the reasoning runs, but they're confounded by the foreign producers' lower labor costs.*

Though the pauper labor theory is demolished by economics textbooks, it still persists. In one guise or another it is even now advanced by the steel, textile, shoe and other industries as justification for import quotas.

One current refinement of the "pauper labor" argument contends that the problem is only temporary. Steel executives are wont to argue that foreign firms not only have lower labor costs but have in some cases caught up with American technology. Import quotas, it is contended, are needed to give the domestic industry time to modernize its plants and otherwise upgrade its productivity.

Where countries are beginning to catch up with the U.S. in technology, however, they also are narrowing the gap in wages. Thus average wages in Japan have risen much faster than average American pay. High and rising wages in any country testify to high and rising productivity.

If the U.S. or any other country imposes quotas to benefit a domestic industry, it cannot help but reduce the industry's incentive to keep boosting its productivity. With a protected market the companies could go on using old plants and old methods and still make a profit, so why gamble millions on anything new? Anything that stifles competition, domestic or foreign, also works to stifle efficiency.

In international trade just about the only element that's constant is change, and change often demands difficult adjustments. A nation that uses the old pauper labor argument to restrict trade runs a real risk of eventually impoverishing itself.

SOURCE: *The Wall Street Journal*, October 22, 1969.

this encourages a movement of resources out of more efficient industries into less efficient (protected) ones, thereby raising costs and reducing comparative advantage.

3. In international trade goods pay for goods, and hence in the long run a nation which exports must also import; protective measures tend to impede the operation of this principle and therefore in the long run limit rather than encourage higher real income and employment.

A fitting conclusion to these arguments for and against protection is presented in Box 4.

The Foreign-Trade Multiplier

How does foreign trade affect a nation's income and employment? In order to answer this question, we must think of imports and exports in a special way.

Imports should be regarded as withdrawals from a nation's circular flow of income because they represent money earned at home but not put back into the income stream through consumption expenditures. Thus if students in the United States decide to buy more Hondas and fewer American-made motorcycles, the American motorcycle industry will sell less. As a result, it will reduce its investment expenditures and lay off workers. These unemployed workers will then buy fewer television sets, vacation trips, automobiles, etc. Their reduced demands for these products and services will in turn result in a further decline in investment and employment. The initial increase in imports, therefore, will eventually bring about a *multiplied* decrease in national income and output.

Exports should be regarded as injections into a nation's circular flow of income because they represent money received from foreigners who have bought American goods. For example, if Germans decide to buy fewer Volkswagens and more American cars, the American automobile industry will find the demand for its products increasing. It will then expand its investment in plant and equipment and hire more workers, who in turn will buy more of other products and thereby encourage the expansion of other industries. The initial increase in exports,

Box 4

In Defense of Free Trade

Adam Smith defended free trade and condemned protection as long ago as 1776, in this famous passage from the Wealth of Nations:

... It is the highest impertinence of kings and ministers, to pretend to watch over the economy of private people and to restrain their expense, either by sumptuary laws, or by prohibiting the importation of foreign luxuries. They are themselves always, and without any exception, the greatest spend-thrifts in the society. Let them look well after their own expense, and they may safely trust, private people with theirs. If their own extravagence does not ruin the state, that of their subjects never will. ...

To give the monopoly of the home market to the produce of domestic industry ... must in almost all cases be either a useless or a hurtful regulation. If the produce of domestic industry can be bought there as cheap as that of foreign industry, the regulation is evidently useless. If it cannot, it must generally be hurtful.

It is the maxim of every prudent master of a family, never to attempt to make at home what it will cost him more to make than to buy. The tailor does not attempt to make his own shoes, but buys them of a shoemaker. The shoemaker does not attempt to make his own clothes, but employs a tailor; the farmer attempts to make neither the one nor the other, but employs those different artificers. All of them find it in their interests to employ their whole industry in a way in which they will have some advantage over their neighbors, and to purchase with a part of its produce, or what is the same thing, with the price of a part of it, whatever else they have occasion for. What is prudence in the conduct of every private family, can scarce be folly in that of a great kingdom. ...

That it was the spirit of monopoly which originally both invented and propagated this protectionist doctrine cannot be doubted; and they who first taught it were by no means such fools as they who believed it. In every country it always is and must be the interest of the great body of the people to buy whatever they want of those who sell it cheapest. The proposition is so very manifest, that it seems ridiculous to take any pains to prove it; nor could it ever have been called in question had not the interested sophistry of merchants and manufacturers confounded the common sense of mankind.

therefore, eventually brings about a *multiplied* increase in national income and output.

These ideas suggest the existence of a "foreign-trade multiplier"—one of several multiplier concepts in economics. It may be described in the following way:

The *foreign-trade multiplier* is a principle which states that fluctuations in exports or imports may generate magnified variations in national income. It is based on the idea that a change in exports relative to imports has the same multiplier effect on national income as a change in autonomous expenditures; similarly, a change in imports relative to exports has the same multiplier effect on national income as a change in withdrawals from the income stream.

In general, an increase in exports tends to raise domestic income, but the increased income also induces some imports which act as "leakages" tending to reduce the full multiplier effect that would exist if imports remained constant.

SUMMARY OF IMPORTANT IDEAS

1. World trade is important to the United States and to most other countries. In quantitative terms, merchandise imports or exports range anywhere from about 4 to 40 percent of GNP for many major countries; in qualitative terms, many goods that the United States and other nations import are virtually impossible to produce domestically.

2. Nations can raise their material standards of living by specializing and trading instead of trying to be self-sufficient. Two basic principles of specialization are the law of absolute advantage and the law of comparative advantage. The latter is more general because it demonstrates that nations can mutually benefit from specialization and trade even if each has only a relative rather than complete advantage over the other in the production of commodities. The *gains* from trade are the benefits that nations receive, whereas the *terms* of trade are the real sacrifices they must make in terms of the goods they give up in return for the goods they receive.

3. Despite the mutual benefits of free and unrestricted trade, nations have instituted various forms of protection. These common instruments of protection consist of tariffs, import quotas, and other protective devices such as unusual types of customs procedures and laws pertaining to import financing, foreign exchange requirements, and regulations involving labeling, health, safety, and shipping.

4. Many pleas may be advanced in favor of protection. Most can be classified into one of five categories: the infant-industry argument, the national-security argument, the diversified-economy argument, the wage-protection argument, and the employment-protection argument. Each needs qualification and most involve logical fallacies.

5. The foreign-trade multiplier is one of several multiplier concepts in economics. It is a principle which states that fluctuations in a nation's exports or imports may cause magnified changes in its national income.

FOR HOMEWORK AND DISCUSSION

1. *Terms and concepts to review:*

law of absolute advantage	tariff
gains from trade	import quota
terms of trade	infant industry
law of comparative advantage	foreign-trade multiplier

2. Consider the following production-possibilities table based on hypothetical data.

Country	Labor input (days)	Output of shoes (pairs)	beef (pounds)
Italy	3	100	75
Argentina	3	50	60

   a. Which country, if any, has an absolute advantage in production? A comparative advantage? Explain.

   b. What is the *range* of possible barter terms—that is, the range within which the two countries may exchange goods? (HINT: What are the *domestic terms of trade* in each country?)

   c. What will determine the actual terms of exchange? Explain carefully.

3. The Constitution of the United States (Article 1, Sec. 10) states: "No State shall, without the consent of the Congress, lay any imposts or duties on imports or exports, except what may be absolutely necessary for executing its inspection laws." Do you think the Founding Fathers were wise to pass this law? What would happen to the American standard of living if each state was allowed to impose protective barriers to trade?

4. "If you believe in the free movement of goods between nations, you should logically believe in the free movement of people, too. This means that cheap foreign labor should be admitted to the United States, even if it results in the displacement of American labor." Do you agree? Explain your answer.

5. An editorial in the *Washington Inquirer* stated that:

The United States should develop a large shipbuilding industry. Such an industry would provide more jobs and higher income for workers. Moreover, the ships could be used for passenger and cargo service in peacetime, and could be quickly converted for military purposes in case of war. In view of these advantages, it would be wise for the U.S. government to protect the domestic shipbuilding industry from foreign competition until it can grow to a stronger competitive position.

Do you agree with this editorial? Explain.

6. Abraham Lincoln is reputed to have remarked: "I don't know much about the tariff. But I do know that when I buy a coat from England, I have the coat and England has the money. But when I buy a coat in America, I have the coat and America has the money." Can you show that Lincoln was correct only in the first sentence of his remark?

7. The foreign-trade multiplier is ordinarily smaller than the domestic-investment multiplier. Why?

REFERENCES AND READING SUGGESTIONS

ELLSWORTH, PAUL T., *The International Economy*, 4th ed., Macmillan, New York, 1969, chaps. 4–9, 12, 14–15.

KENEN, PETER B., *International Economics*, 2d ed., Prentice-Hall, New York, 1967, chaps. 1, 2, 4.

KINDLEBERGER, CHARLES P., *International Economics*, 4th ed., Irwin, Homewood, Illinois, 1968, chaps. 1–4.

PEN, JAN, *A Primer on International Trade*, Random House, New York, 1967.

CHAPTER 34

International Finance:
The Payments of Nations

CHAPTER PREVIEW

What is the foreign exchange market, and what important economic functions does it perform?

How are money flows into and out of a country recorded? Can we analyze the nature and sources of such flows?

What are the economic implications of an "imbalance" or disequilibrium in a nation's money inflows and outflows?

What are the methods and effects of correcting a disequilibrium in a nation's international money flows?

There was a time when the study of international economics dealt primarily with the theory and problems of trade between nations. But this has long since ceased to be true. The economic relationships of countries depend as much on financial considerations as on trade. Hence an understanding of international finance is essential in gaining a general familiarity with world economic problems.

What do we mean by international finance? In the most general sense it deals with the monetary side of international trade. It is therefore concerned with the nature of international transactions—their forms of payment, the ways in which they are recorded for purposes of analysis and interpretation, their economic effects on the nations that are involved, and the methods by which their undesirable consequences can be minimized. Since these statements may seem somewhat vague at this point, the questions in the chapter preview will help focus your attention on the more specific issues involved.

International Payments
and Foreign Exchange

We live in a world in which each nation has its own unit of currency. This means that one currency must be converted into another when transactions are conducted across national borders.

For example, if a French importer buys machinery from the United States, the American exporter eventually receives payment in dollars, not French francs.

Similarly, if an American tourist visits England, he pays for his hotel room, restaurant meals, and other goods and services in British pounds, not dollars. The instruments used to make international payments are called *foreign exchange*. They consist not only of currency, but also to a much larger extent of checks, drafts, or bills of exchange which are simply orders to pay currency.

FUNCTION OF THE FOREIGN EXCHANGE MARKETS

International transactions go on all the time. As a result, some people have dollars which they want to exchange for pounds, and others have pounds which they want to exchange for dollars. How do these people acquire the foreign exchange they desire?

The answer is that foreign exchange is bought and sold in organized markets through dealers, just as stocks, bonds, wheat, and many other commodities are bought and sold. In the United States, the foreign exchange dealers are the large commercial banks located in New York, San Francisco, and other major cities. Overseas, the major foreign exchange centers include London, Zurich, Paris, Brussels, Tokyo, and Hong Kong. If an individual wants to acquire or dispose of foreign exchange, he can easily do so by communicating directly with a dealer or by going through his local commercial bank which will arrange the transaction through one of the large banks dealing in foreign exchange.

The most fundamental function performed by the foreign exchange markets is that they provide a means for transferring purchasing power from one country to another and from one currency to another. Without them, international trade would be virtually limited to barter.

EFFECTS OF INTERNATIONAL TRANSACTIONS

Suppose an American exporter sells a machine to a British importer. The importer might pay for it by purchasing a draft from his bank—that is, an order to pay a specified number of pounds sterling to the American exporter. The exporter then converts the draft into dollars so that he can meet his expenses and have something left over for profit. He does this by selling the draft to a foreign exchange dealer. The number of dollars the dealer pays for the draft depends on the rate of exchange between dollars and pounds. (The dealer, like a broker in any other type of business, will also impose a commission charge.)

The American exporter now has his dollars, and the dealer has a draft payable in British pounds. What will each of them do? Since they are businessmen, they are likely to deposit the funds in their own commercial bank accounts so that they can continue to write the checks they need to carry on their businesses. Thus the American exporter will deposit the dollars in his American bank, and the American foreign exchange dealer will send the draft to England for deposit in his British bank. The dealer, by having such an account, can write a draft or "check" against it, and sell it to an American importer who needs pounds to pay for goods purchased from a British exporter.

What are the results of these activities? In general, international transactions have two economic effects:

1. An export transaction increases the supply of money in the exporting country and reduces it in the importing country. The converse of this, resulting from an import transaction, is also true. (Can you explain why?)

2. By exporting, a nation obtains the foreign monies it needs to acquire imports. In other words, a nation which sells abroad can also buy abroad. (Japan, for example, sells motorcycles, television sets, etc., to the United States, and is thereby able to obtain the dollars it needs to buy American machines, agricultural goods, and other products.)

The Balance of Payments

So far, we have assumed that economic relationships among nations are based solely on international trade. In reality, this is not the whole story. Foreign exchange is demanded and supplied as a result of various other important types of transactions besides importing and exporting. It is necessary, therefore, that we examine the nature of these transactions.

You already know that corporations prepare periodic reports such as balance sheets and income (or profit and loss) statements, summarizing in money terms the results of their business activities. These reports are used by bankers, businessmen, stockholders, creditors, or any other interested parties—even by the government—to evaluate a company's financial position.

What you may not know, however, is that each nation prepares a somewhat similar periodic report called a "balance of payments." The report summarizes in money terms the results of its international economic activities by showing how some transactions cause an outflow of funds and others an inflow. It should be apparent, therefore, that a nation's balance of payments is of concern not only to economists, but also to businessmen, bankers, government leaders, and anyone interested in world affairs.

AN ILLUSTRATIVE MODEL OF THE BALANCE OF PAYMENTS

What does a balance of payments statement actually look like? How is it interpreted? We can best answer these questions by first analyzing the structure of an idealized balance of payments form like the one shown in Exhibit 1. This illustration is a generalized model; that is, it clearly emphasizes the major categories and subcategories that should be understood. You will find yourself referring back to this model quite often because, as will be seen later on, most countries do not publish their balance of payments statements in such a convenient form.

As was pointed out above, a nation's balance of payments is a financial summary of its international transactions. The first thing to notice, however, is that these money flows are represented in the last two columns of the statement by so-called "debits" and "credits"—two terms that are widely used in discussions involving the balance of payments:

A *debit* is any transaction which results in a money outflow or payment to a foreign country; it may be represented on a balance of payments statement by a negative sign. A *credit* is any transaction which results in a money inflow or receipt from a foreign

Exhibit 1

A General Model of the Balance of Payments

	Debit (money outflows or payments) (−)	Credit (money inflows or receipts) (+)
I. Current account:		
A. Merchandise trade:		
1. Merchandise imports	X	
2. Merchandise exports		X
B. Service transactions:		
1. Transportation:		
a. Rendered by foreign vessels, airlines, etc.	X	
b. Rendered by domestic vessels, airlines, etc.		X
2. Travel expenditures:		
a. In foreign countries	X	
b. By foreigners in home country		X
3. Interest and dividends:		
a. Paid to foreigners	X	
b. Received from abroad		X
4. Banking and insurance services:		
a. Rendered by foreign institutions	X	
b. Rendered to foreigners by domestic institutions		X
5. Government expenditures:		
a. By home government abroad	X	
b. By foreign government in home country		X
II. Capital account:		
A. Long-term:		
1. Purchase of securities from foreigners	X	
2. Sale of securities to foreigners		X
B. Short-term.*		
1. Increase of bank and brokerage balances abroad	X	
2. Decrease of foreign-held bank and brokerage balances in home country	X	
3. Increase of foreign-held bank and brokerage balances in home country		X
4. Decrease of bank and brokerage balances abroad		X
III. Unilateral transfer account:		
A. Private:		
1. Personal and institutional remittances to nonresidents	X	
2. Remittances received from abroad		X
B. Governmental:		
1. Grants, indemnities, gifts, and reparations made to other countries	X	
2. Grants, indemnities, gifts, and reparations received from other countries		X
IV. Gold account:		
A. Import of gold and increase of earmarked gold abroad†	X	
B. Export of gold and increase of earmarked gold for foreign account†		X
Errors and omissions		

* Also includes currency holdings, acceptances, and other short-term claims not listed.

† "Earmarked" gold is gold physically held in one country for the account of another.

SOURCE: Adapted with some changes from Delbert Snider, *Introduction to International Economics*, 4th edition. Richard D. Irwin, Inc., Homewood, Illinois, 1967.

country; it may be represented on a balance of payments statement by a positive sign. (NOTE: These definitions are applicable only in international economics; if you take a course in accounting, you will find that the terms "debit" and "credit" are defined in a different way.)

The balance of payments model shown in the exhibit is actually self-explanatory. All you have to do is go down the list and verify for yourself that each item would logically result in either an outflow or inflow of money, and hence would be recorded as either a debit or credit.

The balance of payments is divided into four major categories; these are ranked in what is for most countries the following (decreasing) order of importance: (1) current account; (2) capital account; (3) unilateral transfer account; and (4) gold account. Within these categories, the subclassification at the top denoting merchandise trade usually involves the largest debits and credits in balance of payments statements. Thus a merchandise import is a debit item because it results in a money outflow or payment to the exporting country; conversely, a merchandise export is a credit item because it results in a money inflow or receipt to the importing country.

The remaining items can be interpreted in a similar way. In the last category, confusion will be avoided by thinking of gold like any other commodity (rather than as money) as far as debits and credits are concerned. Thus, imports of gold are debits; exports of gold are credits.

THE BALANCE OF PAYMENTS ALWAYS BALANCES (IN ACCOUNTING)

If you ever take a basic course in accounting, you will learn to apply a principle known as *double-entry bookkeeping*. This principle holds that every transaction is of a twofold nature and must be expressed for accounting purposes in the form of *both* debits and credits. In more general terms, for any given debit there must be one or more credits whose total will precisely equal the debit; conversely, for any given credit there must be one or more debits whose total will precisely equal the credit.

This idea can be illustrated with reference to the balance of payments model in Exhibit 1. Suppose, for example, that an American firm exports equipment worth $1 million to a foreign country. This part of the transaction is a merchandise export and appears as a credit item on the United States balance of payments. The importing country may pay for the goods in any one or combination of several ways, all of which are recorded as debit items on the United States balance of payments. For instance, it may pay in dollars by decreasing its foreign-held bank balances in the United States, or it may pay in its own currency, which has the effect of increasing United States bank balances held abroad, or it may receive the equipment as a gift under the United States foreign aid program, in which case it is a unilateral transfer similar to a grant.

Double-entry bookkeeping assures in principle that *total debits equal total credits*—or, in other words, that the *balance of payments always balances* in an accounting sense. In practice, however, since a country's balance of payments summarizes millions of individual international transactions, it is rarely accurate down to the last dollar. Hence, total debits will either be less than or greater than total credits. To correct this situation, a balance of payments statement will often show an item called "errors and omissions." This equals the difference between actual total debits and actual total credits, and is added to the smaller of these two totals to bring the total payments into balance.

In a more fundamental sense, however, there is an obvious realistic reason why the balance of payments always balances:

A country, like a household, cannot spend more than its current income unless it draws on its cash reserves, sells some of its assets, borrows, or receives gifts—all of which are credit items; conversely, it cannot spend less than its current income unless it accumulates cash reserves, acquires some assets, lends, or gives gifts—all of which are debit items. Therefore, total debits must always equal total credits.

THE FOUR MAJOR ACCOUNTS

The balance of payments model, as we have seen, contains four major accounts. Let us survey briefly the contents of each.

Current Account. This includes all imports and exports of goods and services and is the most basic in the balance of payments. It is the "stuff" of which international economic relations are composed. The other three accounts, as we shall see, fulfill what are largely auxiliary functions by facilitating the flow of goods and services.

Capital Account. This is composed entirely of paper claims and obligations. The long-term component consists of loans and investments maturing in more than one year. The short-term component consists of claims maturing in less than one year and of foreign exchange and bank balances; these short-term capital movements may flow into or out of a country in order to make up for differences in payments and receipts resulting from a gap between imports and exports or from other transactions.

Unilateral Transfer Account. This account is somewhat like the capital account, except that it involves capital movements and gifts for which there are no return commitments or claims. Thus, a personal remittance to a resident of a foreign country involves no commitment for repayment and is classified as a unilateral transfer.

Gold Account. This reflects gold flows and the claims to gold among governments. Gold movements are like short-term capital movements; they serve primarily to make up the differences in payments and receipts resulting from other international transactions.

Against this background, let us summarize what is meant by "balance of payments":

The *balance of payments* is a statement of the money value of all transactions that take place between a nation and the rest of the world during a given period. These transactions may consist of imports and exports of goods and services, and movements of short-term and long-term investments, gifts, currency, and gold; they may be classified for convenience into several categories: current account, capital account, unilateral transfer account, and gold account.

THE UNITED STATES BALANCE OF PAYMENTS

A chart of the United States balance of payments is shown in Exhibit 2. Note that the balance of trade is not the same thing as the balance of payments, although many people confuse the two. The *balance of trade* is that part of a nation's balance of payments dealing with merchandise imports and exports. A "favorable" balance of trade exists when the value of a nation's exports exceeds the value of its imports; conversely, an "unfavorable" balance of trade exists when the value of its imports exceeds the value of its exports. The United States long had a favorable balance of trade, but the gap began to narrow in the late 1960s because the rising pressure of inflation made American goods too expensive for foreigners to purchase.

What about the United States' balance of payments? The long-run trends have varied. For many years prior to the late 1940s the United States had a surplus or favorable balance of payments because of its strong trade position and its receipt of long-term capital from abroad. As a result, its money inflows exceeded its money outflows. Since 1950, however, the United States has run an almost consistent deficit or unfavorable balance for various reasons: military spending overseas; free-spending American tourists going abroad; surging private foreign investments; and government grants-in-aid to foreign nations. Thus its money outflows have exceeded its money inflows.

Of what significance is this deficit? The theory of balance of payments surpluses and deficits is a topic of major importance in international finance; it cannot be overemphasized. Hence, the remainder of this chapter will be devoted to an analysis of its causes, nature, and methods of correction.

OFFICIAL SETTLEMENTS BASIS OR LIQUIDITY BASIS?

In a strict accounting sense, of course, the balance of payments always balances because total debits always equal total credits. But a simple accounting balance must not be confused with a meaningful economic balance because the economic behavior underlying some of the transactions may not be sus-

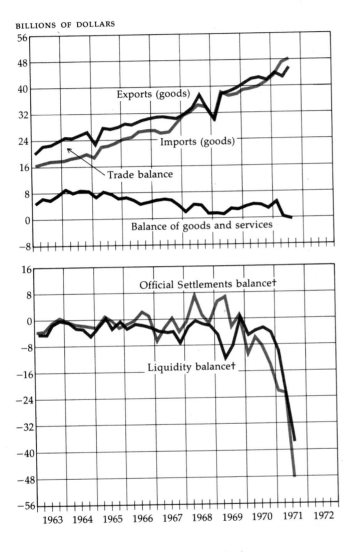

Exhibit 2

United States Balance of Payments and Components

[(+) Surplus; (−) Deficit]

BILLIONS OF DOLLARS

1963 1964 1965 1966 1967 1968 1969 1970 1971 1972

Seasonally adjusted annual rates: quarterly data
† Official Settlement deficit measured by net decline in United
States monetary reserve assets plus net increase in liquid and
certain nonliquid United States liabilities to foreign official
agencies. Liquidity deficit measured by net decline in United
States monetary reserve assets plus net increase in United States
liabilities to all foreigners.
SOURCE: U.S. Department of Commerce and Federal Reserve Bank
of St. Louis.

tainable. For this reason, economists and government officials use two different bases for measuring the "balance" in the balance of payments—that is, two different measures of surpluses and deficits: the *official settlements balance* and the *liquidity balance*. Both are shown in Exhibit 2.

Two measures are used because of a disagreement in defining which international transactions *cause* a deficit in the balance of payments and which *finance* a deficit. Most of the disagreement hinges on the way in which short-term dollar liabilities of American banks and the U.S. Treasury are treated for balance of payments purposes, since some of those liabilities are held by official foreign government agencies and some by private foreign individuals and organizations. Thus:

☐ Those who favor the official settlements basis as the best measure of the United States payments position assume that the only direct claims on the United States government's reserve assets, such as its gold and convertible foreign currencies, are the short-term dollar liabilities held by official foreign agencies. Why? Because the United States government will sell gold only to such agencies, not to private individuals or firms. Therefore, a deficit in the balance of payments is financed by drawing on the government's official reserve assets or by borrowing from foreign government agencies.

☐ Those who favor the liquidity basis argue that foreign private holders of short-term dollar liabilities can easily turn them over to an official foreign agency, such as their central bank, so that these, too, represent a significant potential claim on gold. Therefore, a deficit in the balance of payments is financed not only by borrowing from official agencies, but also by short-term borrowing from private foreign individuals and organizations as well.

Which of these two bases is correct? The question is significant because the two measures may occasionally give conflicting results—one of them showing a surplus and the other a deficit—at the same time. In practice, the liquidity balance is more commonly used, but from a theoretical view the true position is probably somewhere between the official settlements balance and the liquidity balance.

Economic Balance
and Imbalance

Although a nation's balance of payments always balances in the accounting sense—that is, in the sense that total debits always equal total credits—it need not balance in an economic sense. Among the reasons for economic imbalance are the lack of appropriate relationships between exchange rates, prices, income, and capital movements. In order to comprehend the underlying economic forces that are at work, we must understand two important sets of concepts associated with balance of payments analysis: (1) autonomous and compensatory transactions, and (2) equilibrium and disequilibrium.

AUTONOMOUS AND COMPENSATORY TRANSACTIONS

It is useful to think of a nation's balance of payments as a record which reports two distinctly different types of transactions—autonomous and compensatory.

Autonomous transactions are undertaken for reasons that are independent of the balance of payments. Referring back to the general model in Exhibit 1, we see that the main classes of autonomous transactions are merchandise trade and services, long-term capital movements, and unilateral transfers. The reasons for calling these autonomous are not hard to see. Merchandise trade and services are a response to relative differences in prices at home and abroad; long-term capital movements are a response to relative differences in expected rates of return on financial investments at home and abroad; and unilateral transfers are a response to private and governmental decisions based on personal, military, or political considerations. These autonomous transactions are thus unrelated to the balance of payments as such, and may result in total money receipts being greater or less than total money payments.

Compensatory transactions, in contrast, are undertaken as a direct response to balance of payments considerations. They may be thought of as balancing items which arise in order to accommodate differences in money inflows and outflows resulting from autonomous transactions. Looking back at the general model in Exhibit 1, we see there are two main classes of compensatory transactions: short-term capital movements and shifts in gold holdings. Since these involve primarily changes in bank balances and gold claims at home and abroad, it seems clear that they serve largely as adjustment items to correct for imbalances in autonomous transactions. Thus, in a sense, a man who borrows to pay a debt is financing a deficit in his personal "balance of payments" by means of a compensatory transaction—the money he borrows.

EQUILIBRIUM AND DISEQUILIBRIUM

How do autonomous and compensatory transactions affect the economic position of a nation in relation to other nations? The answer to this question involves the notion of equilibrium and disequilibrium. As we know from earlier chapters in this book, an economic "object" (such as a market price or quantity) is in equilibrium when it is in a state of balance among opposing forces; conversely, it is in disequilibrium when there is an absence of such a state of balance. The same ideas of equilibrium or disequilibrium can be applied to a nation's international economic position as reflected by its balance of payments:

Balance of payments disequilibrium exists when, over a given period (usually several years), the sum of autonomous receipts (credits) does not equal the sum of autonomous payments (debits). A *deficit* disequilibrium occurs when total autonomous payments exceed total autonomous receipts; conversely, a *surplus* disequilibrium occurs when total autonomous receipts exceed total autonomous payments.

The existence of compensatory transactions is evidence of a nation's balance of payments disequilibrium. In practice, of course, we do not actually expect the sum of autonomous receipts and payments to match each other exactly—any more than we expect total supply and demand in a competitive market to be precisely equal—because of the numerous decision-making organisms that are involved. But we do expect periodic deficits and surpluses to balance out approximately over a period of

THOMAS MUN

1571–1641

Mercantilist

At the end of the fifteenth century, a new philosophy of statism emerged in Western Europe. Absolute monarchy had replaced the decentralized structure of feudalism; the oceans had been conquered and were no longer considered barriers to trade; and the expansion of world commerce had occurred simultaneously with the development of banking and credit institutions. These factors encouraged dramatic struggles for power by kings and princes, resulting in ultranationalistic policies that tended to make all states enemies, as each sought to achieve world military and economic leadership.

These developments gave rise to what is known as mercantilism—a set of doctrines and practices aimed at promoting national prosperity and the power of the state by: (1) seeking the accumulation of precious metals (mainly gold and silver) through the maintenance of favorable trade balances or excesses of exports over imports; (2) achieving economic self-sufficiency through imperialism; and (3) exploiting colonies for the benefit of the mother country by monopolizing their raw materials and precious metals while reserving them as exclusive markets for exports. Mercantilism reached its peak in the seventeenth century, serving as a political and economic ideology in England, France, Spain, and Germany.

The majority of those who wrote on mercantilist theory were businessmen. The most notable example was Thomas Mun, a leading English merchant and for many years a director of the famous British East India Company. His book, England's Treasure by Forraign Trade, *was published posthumously by his son in 1664. This treatise is regarded as the outstanding exposition of mercantilist doctrine. It stressed the importance to England of maintaining a favorable balance of trade—a doctrine of fundamental significance in mercantilism since it was a key means of accumulating bullion—and was the first work to show that it was not the specific balance of trade with any particular nation that was the important consideration, but the total balance with all nations. The former could be unfavorable, according to Mun, as long as the latter was favorable.*

In Germany, the chief goal of mercantilism was to increase the revenue of the state; hence it became known as cameralism *(after Kammer, the name of the royal treasury), and its principles were extensively implemented as government policy during the eighteenth century.*

a few years. When such a tendency is not apparent there is reason to suspect trouble.

The most common situation is one in which a country suffers from a persistent deficit disequilibrium for a number of years. This means that the nation is spending more than it is earning, and hence must be either drawing on its cash reserves, selling its assets, borrowing, or receiving gifts from other countries.

Adjusting to Equilibrium

How can a nation correct a disequilibrium in its balance of payments? The answer is straightforward: Since disequilibrium is the result of a gap between a country's total autonomous payments and receipts, the factors that determine these autonomous transactions must undergo a change so that the nation's total money outflows and inflows can be brought into equality. We can best approach the problem by analyzing the adjustment process in terms of four sets of circumstances:

1. Freely fluctuating exchange rates
2. Price and income changes
3. The gold standard
4. Government controls

Let us see how adjustments in the balance of payments are brought about under each of these conditions.

ADJUSTMENT THROUGH FREELY FLUCTUATING EXCHANGE RATES

The *foreign exchange rate* is the price of one currency in terms of another. If in the wheat market the price of wheat were $1 a bushel, this would mean that anyone could take $1 to the market and exchange it for a bushel of wheat and anyone could take a bushel of wheat to the market and exchange it for $1. Similarly, if in the foreign exchange market the price of British pounds in terms of dollars were $2 = £1, it would mean that anyone could take $1 to the market and exchange it for the equivalent of £$\frac{1}{2}$, or anyone could take £1 to the market and exchange it for $2.

The foreign exchange market is a competitive market which behaves according to the laws of supply and demand. This means that fluctuations in the price of foreign exchange are the result of changes in the demand and supply curves of buyers and sellers. The basic idea is illustrated in Exhibit 3. In this simple model, the "commodity" being bought and sold is British pounds and the price is expressed in terms of dollars. (A similar situation could be depicted in which the commodity is dollars and the price is expressed in terms of British pounds.) For simplicity, we are assuming that there are only two countries, the United States and Britain. The interaction of the demand curve for pounds with the supply curve of pounds thus determines the equilibrium price OP and the equilibrium quantity ON.

In the foreign exchange market Americans (such as importers, tourists, etc.) are always looking to buy pounds; and Britons are always looking to buy dollars. Hence at any given time there are "dollars looking for pounds" and there are "pounds looking for dollars." This makes an active market in foreign exchange.

Exhibit 3

Supply of and Demand for British Pounds

An increase in demand for British pounds will raise the equilibrium price from OP to OP' and the equilibrium quantity from ON to ON'.

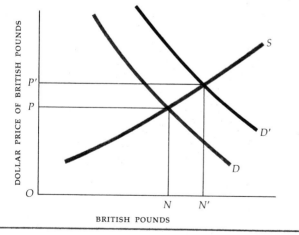

The Adjustment Process

In order to understand how international adjustments take place under freely fluctuating exchange rates, let us begin by assuming a state of equilibrium in which the exchange rate is at OP and there is neither a deficit nor a surplus in the American balance of payments. If American imports of British goods should now rise, and if this increase is not offset by long-term capital movements or unilateral transfers from Britain to the United States, the American demand for pounds will also increase; i.e., the demand curve in Exhibit 3 will shift to the right from D to D'. As the price rises toward the new equilibrium level OP', British pounds will become more expensive for Americans to buy, thereby causing the United States to cut down its purchases of British goods. Conversely, American dollars will become cheaper for Britons, thereby causing Britain to expand its purchases of American goods. This reduction of American imports from Britain, and expansion of American exports to Britain, will continue until a new equilibrium in the United States balance of payments is reached which accords with the equilibrium price in the foreign exchange market.

Freely fluctuating exchange rates perform at least three important functions: (1) they automatically correct a disequilibrium in the balance of payments through the free play of international market forces; (2) they may make imports cheaper and exports dearer, or vice versa, by altering the price of foreign exchange without *necessarily* affecting domestic or foreign price levels; and (3) to the extent that they operate independently of domestic price and income levels, they bear the burden of balance of payments adjustments without imposing constraints on the domestic economy (as will be explained shortly).

Despite these desirable features, freely fluctuating exchange rates involve some disadvantages:

First, they make it difficult and risky for traders to commit themselves for weeks or months in advance to international transactions, since the exchange rate may change between the time that goods are ordered and the time that they are received. This uncertainty may reduce trade between nations.

Second, they turn the terms of trade against a nation whose currency is depreciated in the foreign exchange market. For example, we saw that an increase in the demand for pounds resulted in a price increase or appreciation in the dollar price of pounds and a price decrease or depreciation in the pound price of dollars. This means that the United States must export more goods to Britain to earn the same total revenue as it earned before.

Third, they *may* stimulate or depress a nation's export industries by making its currency either cheaper or dearer in international markets. This could tend to encourage fluctuations in income and employment, i.e., business cycles.

ADJUSTMENT THROUGH PRICE AND INCOME CHANGES

A moment's reflection will make it evident that if exchange rate adjustments can conceivably bring about an equilibrium in the balance of payments while domestic price and income levels remain stable, the converse principle is also true: Changes in domestic price and income levels can restore equilibrium in a nation's balance of payments while exchange rates remain stable. Let us see why.

Price Changes

In terms of our previous example, if there is a deficit in the United States balance of payments due to an excess of imports over exports, a deflation of American prices can have the same effect as a depreciation of the dollar in the foreign exchange market. For if prices in the United States are reduced, it becomes cheaper for Britons to buy American goods. American exports to Britain will therefore increase, and this will tend to eliminate the United States balance of payments deficit. (Equivalently, an inflation in Britain can have the same effect as an appreciation of the pound in the foreign exchange market. Can you explain why?)

How might a deflation be brought about? There are three possibilities:

1. Some deflationary pressures will be induced automatically through market forces because the excess of American imports over exports will cause a reduction in the United States money supply.

2. Contractionary monetary and fiscal policies may have to be invoked in order to exert a downward push on prices.

3. United States manufacturers may try to reduce or stabilize prices so as to compete with foreigners.

We have already learned in earlier chapters that there is likely to be a "tradeoff" between price changes and the level of employment in that reductions in prices will probably increase unemployment and thereby bring about a recession. The question, therefore, is whether we should incur such a high cost in order to achieve balance of payments equilibrium. Most economists believe that we should not, and that some other solution should be sought.

Income Changes

A country's balance of payments is also related to its national income. Thus if the domestic level of income increases while exchange rates and domestic prices remain stable, people will tend to import more goods from abroad and to take more trips abroad. (For balance of payments purposes, an American tourist visiting a foreign country is equivalent to the United States importing "scenery" from that country.) A deficit in the United States balance of payments, therefore, can be corrected through a decrease in the domestic level of income. (Equivalently, it can also be corrected through an increase in other nations' level of income, since American exports will increase if foreign income rises.) The disadvantages of adjustment through domestic income reduction, however, are essentially the same as those of price deflation: Contractionary monetary and fiscal policies would have to be invoked in order to cause a downward pressure on national income; this in turn would probably induce a recession and unemployment—a price which most economists would regard as too high to pay for the purpose of achieving balance of payments equilibrium.

Before proceeding with further aspects of this important problem, it will be helpful to conclude our discussion thus far with an important principle:

The influence of adjustments in exchange rates, price levels, and income levels on a balance of payments disequilibrium will depend on the relevant elasticities involved.

For example: A general 10 percent reduction in domestic prices, with foreign prices remaining the same, would have the same effect as a 10 percent depreciation in the exchange rate as far as corrections in a deficit are concerned, although it would have quite different effects in other respects. Likewise, the influence of income changes on a country's trade depends, among other things, on its income elasticity of demand for imports. What happens if its income elasticity of demand is less than unity? Greater than unity? Factors such as these are of considerable practical significance. Indeed, they have played extremely important roles in the international financial policies of nations, as we shall see later on.

ADJUSTMENT UNDER THE GOLD STANDARD: THE CLASSICAL MODEL

A very interesting process of adjustment takes place when the trading nations' monetary systems are on a gold standard. This situation existed for several dozen countries during the half century before World War I, and for a short time thereafter until the onset of the depression. From a theoretical standpoint, it can be considered a part of the classical model of income and employment which was studied in earlier chapters. To understand how this adjustment method works, it is necessary to explain both (1) the operation of the gold standard mechanism, and (2) the adjustment process.

The Gold Standard

When a nation is on a gold standard, it is obliged to: (1) buy and sell gold to the public in exchange for paper money at a *fixed legal rate;* and (2) permit gold to be imported and exported without restrictions. Under these circumstances, the exchange rate will tend to be stable and will never fluctuate beyond very narrow limits.

In 1930, for example, when the United States and England were both on a gold standard, the U.S. Treasury was required by law to buy and sell gold to the public at a price of $20.67 per fine ounce; similarly, the Bank of England was required by law to buy and sell gold at a price of £4.25 per fine ounce.

It follows that since an ounce (which is equal to 480 grains) of gold could be exchanged for $20.67 in the United States or for £4.25 in England,

$$\$20.67 = £4.25 \quad (= 1 \text{ ounce gold or } 480 \text{ grains})$$

and hence the par rate of exchange between the two countries was determined by the ratio $\$20.67 \div £4.25$, or

$$\$4.86 = £1 \quad (= 0.24 \text{ ounce gold or } 113 \text{ grains})$$

In 1930, the cost (including insurance and freight) of shipping 0.24 ounces or 113 grains of gold between New York and London was about $0.02. As a result, the exchange rate or dollar price of pounds remained within the range of $4.84 and $4.88 for the following reasons:

☐ If the price of pounds in the foreign exchange market rose, say, to $4.89, it would be cheaper for an American importer to acquire 113 grains of gold for his $4.86 and then ship the gold to London at a cost of 2 cents in order to pay the British exporter. The importer would *in effect* by paying $4.88 for a pound instead of $4.89.

☐ If the price in the foreign exchange market fell, say, to $4.83, a British importer would be better off to acquire gold for his £1 (= $4.86) and then ship the gold to New York at a cost of 2 cents in order to pay the American exporter. The importer would *in effect* be getting $4.84 for his pound instead of $4.83.

The upper and lower limits of foreign exchange were thus $4.88 and $4.84, respectively. These were known as the *gold points*—a technical expression which represents the range within which the foreign exchange rates of gold standard currencies will fluctuate. Thus the gold points are equal to the par rate of exchange plus and minus the cost (including insurance) of shipping gold. The upper and lower gold points for a nation are called its *gold export point* and *gold import point* respectively, because gold will be exported when the foreign exchange rate rises above the upper level, and imported when the rate falls below the lower level. One nation's gold export point is thus another nation's gold import point, and vice versa.

We may conclude, therefore, that since a gold standard provides free convertibility between paper money and gold, as well as the unrestricted shipment of gold into and out of the country, the exchange rate under such circumstances tends to remain stable within the limits set by the gold points.

The Adjustment Process

How does the existence of a gold standard affect the restoration of equilibrium due to a trade deficit in a nation's balance of payments? This in effect was a question which the classical economists asked—and their answer was that the adjustment is brought about automatically through changes in the price level. Why? Because they assumed that the price level is directly related to the quantity of money in circulation, which in turn is tied to the volume of gold holdings.

Thus if a country experiences a disequilibrium in its balance of payments as a result of a trade deficit, its demand for foreign exchange will rise at least to the gold export point. As gold leaves the country, the quantity of money will decrease, which in turn will reduce prices. With lower prices, the country's exports will rise and its imports fall, thereby correcting the disequilibrium.

What happens if a country experiences a disequilibrium in its balance of payments due to a trade surplus? The process is exactly the opposite: Its demand for foreign exchange will fall, gold will be imported, prices will increase, and exports will fall while imports rise until equilibrium is again restored.

This explanation of the adjustment process, it should be emphasized, was the classical solution. Logically, it was an integral part of the classical theory of income and employment because it assumed that: (1) there was full employment, and hence an increase in the quantity of money would assure an increase in the general price level; and (2) prices and costs were flexible rather than "sticky," and hence would readily respond to changes in total spending. We have already learned in earlier chapters, of course, that with the development and extensions of Keynesian economics since the 1930s, the first assumption of full employment has been recognized as a special rather than general case, and the second assumption of flexible prices and costs—especially on the downward side—is incorrect in our modern economy, where big businesses and big unions exert monopolistic influences in the marketplace.

We can conclude, therefore, that the gold standard has both desirable and undesirable features: (1) on the one hand it provides for stable exchange rates which tend to reduce risks and encourage international trade, while automatically correcting international disequilibrium; (2) on the other hand it requires that each nation submit to painful processes of deflation (or inflation) by subordinating its domestic economy to the dictates of external economic relations in order to achieve international equilibrium.

ADJUSTMENT THROUGH GOVERNMENT CONTROLS

The previous methods of adjustment relied on market forces to correct a disequilibrium in the balance of payments. Now we turn our attention to a final and radically different method of adjustment—one which suppresses market forces by imposing direct government controls on international transactions. The list of specific controls is almost endless, but they can be grouped for analysis into two categories: (1) exchange controls, and (2) trade controls.

Exchange Controls

One way in which a nation might seek to correct a deficit in its balance of payments is to limit the freedom of its residents to import goods and services and to export capital. To accomplish this objective, the government would impose direct controls over those types of international transactions that are to be curbed, while leaving others relatively uncontrolled or even "free."

Under such a system, all foreign exchange earnings must be sold to the government and all foreign exchange needed to pay for international transactions must be bought from the government. The rates at which the government buys and sells foreign exchange are officially established and need not be equal. The typical method of doing this is by the adoption of a "multiple exchange system." Thus the government may set a relatively high price or rate of exchange on the foreign exchange needed to import unessential luxury goods, and a relatively low rate on the importation of vitally needed raw materials and capital goods. It may also designate some types of transactions as unrestricted and sell portions of its foreign exchange to the highest bidders.

In general, exchange controls require that the government, rather than the free market, decide the order of priority for the importation of goods and services. This decision may then be implemented by allocating the limited supply of foreign exchange among competing uses.

Nations have instituted exchange controls for various reasons and in diverse circumstances: to provide better centralized control over the economy; to reduce wide economic fluctuations; to eliminate persistent deficits in the balance of payments; and to assure essential imports for hastening economic growth and development. The chief advantage of controls is that *some* method of adjustment must be employed to correct a significant balance of payments deficit disequilibrium. Exchange controls are usually the least undesirable and least painful of the various choices that have been discussed.

On the other hand, exchange controls also have several disadvantages:

1. By preventing or even limiting the importation of certain goods, controls may shift the demand for these goods to domestic producers, thereby stimulating inflation at home as well as an exodus of resources out of export industries. This will encourage a drop in exports and aggravate rather than cure the deficit disequilibrium.

2. Since exchange controls prevent the free expression of market forces, they encourage the creation of an illegal black market in foreign exchange.

3. By curbing imports, controls help bring on deflation in those countries whose export industries are adversely affected; this may encourage retaliatory measures by the injured nations, thereby reducing trade.

Trade Controls

A government may use another general class of measures, called trade controls, to adjust a balance of payments deficit disequilibrium. These may take such forms as tariffs and quotas to curb imports, special taxes on outflows of capital and on tourists going abroad, and subsidies to encourage the export industries. Measures such as these, as we have already learned, prevent the operation of the law of comparative advantage, misallocate world resources, and discourage the flow of trade. As with exchange controls, they may also invite retaliation by other nations.

SUMMARY OF IMPORTANT IDEAS

1. Since nations carry on their business in different currencies, foreign exchange markets exist where currencies and related instruments can be bought and sold, or "converted." The existence of such markets enables nations to engage in international transactions.

2. The international transactions of nations are summarized periodically in a financial statement known as the balance of payments. This records money inflows and outflows, classified in categories of accounts.

3. In accounting terms a nation's balance of payments always balances because the sum of its money inflows must equal the sum of its money outflows—by virtue of the principle of double-entry bookkeeping. But in an economic sense, the balance of payments may not balance because certain transactions may not be sustainable.

4. Balance of payments disequilibrium may be corrected by: (1) movements in exchange rates; (2) adjustments in price and income levels; (3) gold flows, with consequent price and income adjustments if nations are on a gold standard; and (4) government controls over foreign exchange and foreign trade. The first three of these rely on market forces to bring about the needed adjustment; the fourth suppresses market forces by substituting the hand of government.

FOR HOMEWORK AND DISCUSSION

1. *Terms and concepts to review:*

foreign exchange autonomous transactions

debit   compensatory transactions

credit   balance of payments

balance of payments   disequilibrium

balance of trade   foreign exchange rate

mercantilism   gold points

cameralism

2. In a free market, if the dollar rate of exchange on French francs rises, what happens to the French rate of exchange on dollars? Explain.

3. How does each of the following transactions affect the supply of money in the United States:

a. The United States sells Chevrolets to England.

b. France sells perfume to the United States.

c. An American tourist visits Japan.

d. A Japanese tourist visits the United States.

4. Which of the following transactions results in a debit, and which in a credit, on the United States balance of payments:

a. An American student buys a new Honda motorcycle.

b. An American tourist flies Air France to Paris.

c. General Motors pays a dividend to a British stockholder.

d. The U.S. Army builds a new military base in southeast Asia.

e. An American resident buys shares of stock in a British corporation.

f. An American resident sends money to his relatives in another country.

5. Can there be a net positive or net negative balance in the balance of payments?

6. Why are autonomous debits and credits not likely to be equal?

7. Compare the processes of adjustment to disequilibrium under (a) freely fluctuating exchange rates, (b) price and income changes, (c) the gold standard, and (d) government controls. (SUGGESTION: Think in terms of what these systems have in common, and develop your answer accordingly.)

REFERENCES AND READING SUGGESTIONS

ELLSWORTH, PAUL T., *The International Economy*, 4th ed., Macmillan, New York, 1969, chaps. 16–19.

KENEN, PETER B., *International Economics*, 2d ed., Prentice-Hall, New York, 1967, chap. 4.

SNIDER, DELBERT A., *International Monetary Relations*, Random House, New York, 1966, chaps. 1–4.

SNIDER, DELBERT A., *Introduction to International Economics*, 4th ed., Irwin, Homewood, Illinois, 1967, chaps. 15–17.

WASSERMAN, MAX J., CHARLES W. HULTMAN, and LASZLO ZSOLDOS, *International Finance*, Heath, Boston, 1966, chaps. 1, 3–7.

CHAPTER 35

International Commercial and Financial Policies

CHAPTER PREVIEW

What economic changes that took place during World Wars I and II led to a weakening and disintegration of the world economy?

How did nations respond to these changes after World War II?

What problems of international economic adjustment have nations come to face, and what can be done to solve those problems?

The late Lord Rothschild, a world-famous financier, was once asked by a friend to explain the international financial system. He replied, "My dear chap, there are only two men in the world who understand the international financial system—a young economist in the Treasury and a rather junior man in the Bank of England. Unfortunately, they disagree."

There is no doubt that most people are unfamiliar with the international monetary system, despite the fact that in recent history the dollar was under attack by foreigners, the Daughters of the American Revolution found the loss of gold a national scandal, and American tourists visiting London, Rome, and various other places were astounded to be told (for several days in March, 1968) that they could not convert their dollar travelers' checks into foreign currencies.

These are only a few of the events that have occurred in the esoteric world of international finance. But important happenings have also taken place in the area of international trade. In this chapter we shall review the background and consequences of these developments and make recommendations for improving the community of sovereign nations held together by economic interdependence.

The Interwar Period: Weakening and Disintegration of the World Economy

In the century before World War I, most major countries were closely integrated through a well-developed network of trade and finance. The essential features of this complex system may be characterized briefly:

☐ Nations and regions tended to specialize on the basis of their factor endowments, thus making multilateral trade necessary.

☐ Tariffs for the most part only moderately affected the international flow of goods according to the principle of comparative advantage.

☐ London was the center of finance and trade, with its supporting facilities of banks, brokerage houses, insurance companies, shipping firms, and communication lines extending throughout the world.

☐ Almost all major nations and many minor ones—several dozen in all—were on the gold standard, thus permitting the easy convertibility of currencies that is needed for carrying on international transactions smoothly and efficiently.

This was also an era of rapid advances in technology and large migrations of labor and capital. These fundamental changes were assimilated, though not, to be sure, without some major political and economic upheavals. Most trading nations were on a gold standard, and their balances of payments tended to adjust fairly smoothly to gold movements, while exchange rates remained stable.

This, briefly, was the nature of the relatively harmonious international economic setting that prevailed until the eve of World War I. In the next three decades, however, the world economy experienced a series of deep disturbances:

1. Structural weakening during the 1920s

2. Disintegration during the 1930s

3. Disruption during World War II

The highlights of these developments are sketched below.

STRUCTURAL WEAKENING DURING THE 1920s

World War I destroyed the economic relations between nations that had developed through almost five decades of peace in Europe. International commercial and financial links were broken, markets were disorganized, and the marketing system was shattered. All belligerent nations except the United States abandoned the gold standard; the American government officially discouraged gold withdrawals from banks; and gold exports were subjected to strict legal controls. These steps were necessary to prevent the hoarding of gold and its flight to safer havens in neutral nations—common phenomena in periods of crisis.

After the war there were violent inflations in Continental Europe, and the restoration of the gold standard became a major objective of international policy. Between 1925 and 1929, more than forty countries returned to gold; only a few continued to operate on the basis of inconvertible paper. But the new gold standard established during this period was based on economic conditions and philosophies different from those that existed before 1914. Some of the more important changes that took place may be noted briefly.

Changes in National Objectives

Governments began to place less emphasis on the automatic operation of an international monetary system provided by the gold standard, and more on *domestic* economic stability. The war and postwar years brought severe monetary disturbances, inflation, and then depression. With the establishment of the Federal Reserve System in the United States just before the war, and the creation of similar institutions in many other countries during the 1920s, the possibility of stabilizing prices and economic activity through central bank policy increasingly interested government officials.

With each nation determining its supply of money independently in order to gain greater *internal* economic control, monetary reserves became a matter of secondary concern. From 1920 to 1924, for example, the United States experienced a substantial net inflow of gold. But the Federal Reserve authorities, in order to maintain stable credit conditions, offset the monetary effects of these accumulating gold balances by selling securities in the market. Similarly, in the late 1920s the Bank of England neutralized the effects of gold movements by selling securities when gold flowed into the country and buying securities when gold flowed out. Although these actions may have been justified in terms of *domestic* economic conditions in both countries, they were clearly contrary to traditional (pre-1914) gold standard policies which dictated that a nation's supply of money vary directly with the supply of gold.

Increased Government Intervention

In the United States, the decade after the war was marked by the beginnings of a retreat from laissez-faire as farmers, labor unions, consumers, and other special-interest groups pressed for greater government protection and reforms. This gave rise to growing nationalism. The Underwood Tariff of 1913, passed by a Democratic Congress, represented important steps toward freer international trade, but in 1922 the Republicans restored the rates to new protective levels in the Fordney-McCumber Tariff. The United States was not alone in this regard. Many other nations, including Australia, England, India, and Japan, enacted new protective legislation during the 1920s.

Conclusion

These developments weakened the international monetary mechanism by making it more rigid. At the same time, the United States gained increasing dominance in the international economy. By 1929, it had become the world's largest exporter, the second largest importer (after Great Britain), and chief creditor. This meant that with other nations heavily dependent on it, the United States would have to maintain a stable, high level of income and employment, and a steady flow of lending to other nations if the well-being of the world economy was to be preserved. Any sudden changes in American economic stability, tariff rates, or credit flows could

affect access to markets and produce severe international repercussions. This, as we shall see, is precisely what happened.

DISINTEGRATION DURING THE 1930s

In the United States, the prosperous twenties began in 1922 and reached a peak in the first half of 1929. During this period American investment, income, and employment climbed to unprecedented heights. But then the overall decline in economic activity set in—first with a drop in industrial production in July, 1929, and then with a collapse of the stock market three months later.

With this bursting of the bubble of optimism, the economy turned sharply downward, producing severe effects in other countries. In the brief span of only three years—from 1929 to 1932—the total dollars spent or invested abroad by Americans (in the form of imports, service transactions, long-term loans, etc.) fell from $7.4 billion to a mere $2.4 billion—a drop of 68 percent. As would be expected, the foreign-trade multiplier exerted its influence: The export industries of other nations that were closely tied to American markets were adversely affected, thereby pulling down the levels of income and employment.

How did the major trading nations respond to these depressing effects on world commerce? There were several types of reaction, which we shall now examine. As will be seen later, they significantly affected the international economic policies of nations after World War II.

Higher Tariffs

In the United States, Germany, Italy, Russia, Great Britain, and other countries there was a marked tendency to subordinate international trade to national interests. The United States made access to its domestic market difficult by passing the Smoot-Hawley Tariff of 1930. This new law broadened the range of protected commodities to over 25,000, and provided for increases in some 800 rates covering a wide variety of both agricultural and industrial goods. Great Britain, which had been the citadel of free trade for

80 years, abandoned its policy and adopted a protective tariff in 1932. Similarly, other countries attempted to control their foreign trade by establishing tariffs, quotas, special exchange allocations, bilateral trade agreements for the trading of specific products, and monopolistic state-controlled trading systems.

In democratic countries such as the United States and Great Britain, the motivation for increased protection stemmed from the depressed economic conditions of the time; but among the new totalitarian governments in Germany, Italy, and Russia, both economic and military considerations were involved. Whatever the motives, however, the actions undertaken during this period more than offset years of effort by the League of Nations to establish freer international trade.

Financial Crises and the Abandonment of Gold

A second major development of international significance occurred in the spring of 1931. The Credit Anstalt, Austria's largest commercial bank, announced it was technically insolvent—i.e., its liabilities exceeded its assets. This produced a run on the bank as domestic and foreign creditors rushed to claim their funds. The Austrian government had barely brought the panic under control (through a "freeze" on all obligations to creditors) when the Reichsbank, a major commercial bank in Germany, failed. The fear of further bank failures spread, and the German government instituted a system of exchange controls to prevent a run on the country's gold and foreign exchange reserves.

This action placed Britain in a tenuous position. Germany, as well as other central European countries, had borrowed heavily from British banks; they now found their credits frozen. Britain, in turn, was in debt to foreigners to the tune of more than half a billion pounds; the British budget was rapidly sliding into a heavy deficit; and Britain's balance of payments was steadily worsening. As foreign confidence in Britain's financial system declined, foreign withdrawals mounted. The situation reached crisis proportions, and both the Bank of France and the U.S. Federal Reserve System extended over $130 million to the Bank of England. But this was not enough to halt the drain of gold and foreign exchange from

Britain. Finally, on September 21, 1931, Parliament announced that the Bank of England would no longer be required by law to sell gold. This meant, of course, that Britain had officially gone off the gold standard.

In the months that followed, the international depression deepened and financial panics were repeated in various nations. Waves of domestic and foreign drains on gold reserves were experienced by banking systems throughout the world. By the end of 1932, twenty-four countries had abandoned gold. In the meantime, world trade had disintegrated still further.

Devaluation of the Dollar

The United States, of course, was not immune to the effects of the Depression. The period 1929–1932 was one of severe deflation; wholesale prices fell 32 percent and national income dropped by 50 percent. Banks were especially hard hit as the security behind their loans disappeared with the decline in property values. During these three years more than 5,000 banks—about one-third of the nation's total—were declared insolvent.

Early in 1933, the weakness of the banks became widely recognized, and a wave of currency and gold hoarding ensued. This forced President Roosevelt to declare a bank "holiday," to place an embargo on the export of gold, and to prevent banks and the Treasury from paying out the precious metal. These steps placed the United States on a *gold bullion standard* in which gold was nationalized by the Treasury, taken out of domestic circulation as money, and made available in the form of gold bullion only for industrial uses and international transactions in return for other money.

Meanwhile, despite the fact that the United States was in a strong balance of payments position compared to other countries, advisors to President Roosevelt increasingly felt that American exports should be stimulated relative to imports. Hence, the government's attempt at currency stabilization was finalized early in the following year with the devaluation of the dollar.

What is *devaluation*? It may be defined as an official act which makes a domestic currency cheaper in terms of gold or foreign currencies, and is typically undertaken for the purpose of increasing a nation's exports while reducing its imports. Thus on January 31, 1934, the United States devalued the dollar relative to gold by approximately 41 percent, by raising the Treasury's buying and selling price of gold from $20.67 an ounce to $35 an ounce. This act made it cheaper for foreigners to buy dollars, and more expensive for Americans to buy foreign currencies.

Consequences of Devaluation

Other countries responded to the devaluation by imposing higher tariffs and other trade restrictions.

But the devalued dollar, which was now stabilized in relation to other depreciated currencies, exerted mounting balance of payments pressures on the remaining gold standard countries with their overvalued currencies. This, in combination with the growing fear of war in Europe, resulted in a heavy net inflow of capital and gold to the United States for safekeeping during the mid-thirties. Between 1934 and 1938, the remaining gold standard nations —Belgium, Switzerland, France, and the Netherlands—unable to sustain any further drain, abandoned gold and devalued their currencies. Thus came the end of an era. (See Box 1.)

Box 1

How Did the Gold Standard Come About?

Since the gold standard is always a topic for interesting conversation, it might be worthwhile to see how England came to adopt the gold standard in the first place.

The great historian Macaulay wrote: "In the autumn of 1695, it could hardly be said that the country possessed, for practical purposes, any measure of value of commodities. It was a mere chance [because of "underweighting" of coins] whether what was called a shilling, was really tenpence, sixpence, or a groat."

William and Mary appointed a committee to make recommendations for solving the problems. The membership was quite extraordinary: Sir Isaac Newton, Master of the Mint, John Locke, the great philosopher, and Lord Somers.

Sir Isaac recommended that the Government call in the old coin at face value and issue new full weight coins and that the ratio of silver to gold be established at 16 silver to 1 gold (shades of Bryan!). In major countries on the Continent the ration was $15\frac{1}{2}$ to 1. Sir Thomas Gresham could have predicted the results a century before! Relatively, England overvalued gold and the Continent overvalued silver. Gold was taken to England for exchange into silver, which was taken to the Continent for exchange into gold, which. . . . Newton later recognized his error and recommended that it be corrected, but this latter advice was not followed.[1]

A century passes and England is once again involved in war with her old enemy, France; this time under Napoleon. She abandons redemption of the currency but decides to resume

convertibility after the war. The mint, of course, had very little silver to coin and Lord Liverpool decided to close it to the free coinage of silver because England was "naturally a gold country" and that "gold was the natural currency of England." And, indeed, it was if one admits, as he should, that it is only "natural" for even a Sir Isaac to make a mistake and for this mistake to have "natural" consequences.

It is irrelevant but tempting to speculate what might have happened if Sir Isaac had made a mistake in the other direction, say by adopting a ratio of 15 to 1. England might well have become "naturally a silver country." With the role that sterling acquired on the basis of English leadership in industry and commerce throughout the world, who knows, the world might naturally have been on the silver standard.

Thus it appears that England arrived on the gold standard because of a mistake by Sir Isaac Newton in 1696. The gold standard survived the nineteenth century only because of the miracles of new gold discoveries in the 1840s and 1890s. Finally, when one sees the incredibly small amount of gold frequently held by the Bank of England, he is forced to conclude it was not a self-regulating system but was in fact maintained through management by the Bank of England. Thus, a mistake, miracles, and management describe the system more accurately than does a mystical natural providence.

[1] This is the story as told by George F. Warren and Frank A. Pearson in their *Prices*, New York, 1933, p. 159.
SOURCE: Adapted from an address by Karl R. Bopp, President, Federal Reserve Bank of Philadelphia.

Conclusion

By the eve of World War II, the leading trading countries of the Western world had learned at least two important lessons:

By releasing their currencies from gold, nations could be free to manage their economies by fiscal and monetary means without the fear of losing reserves and without the need to be regulated by international gold movements. Devaluation, however, is not ordinarily a one-way street; it usually causes opposing reactions by other nations in the form of trade restrictions or retaliatory devaluation.

The remaining highlights of the immediate pre-World War II years may be summarized briefly.

1. The United States and most Western European countries entered an agreement which, for international purposes, represented a compromise between the rigidities of the gold standard and domestic currency management. Thus:

a. Each country established its own government stabilization fund to buy and sell foreign exchange in the open market in quantities necessary to maintain reasonable stability of its own currency in relation to foreign currencies.

b. Competitive devaluation for the purpose of expanding exports was renounced.

c. The central banks of the participating countries were authorized to buy gold without limit, but gold served largely as an equilibrating device for balance of payments purposes.

On the whole, exchange rate equilibrium was restored among the democratic trading nations, while totalitarian countries like Germany and Russia maintained tightly controlled systems for allocating foreign exchange.

2. In the area of international trade, the United States established a *Reciprocal Trade Agreements program*—a plan for expanding American exports through legislation which authorized the President to negotiate United States tariff reductions with other nations in return for parallel concessions. The program consists of the Trade Agreements Act of 1934, with subsequent amendments, and related legislation.

An interesting feature of the Reciprocal Trade Agreements program has been the widespread use of what is known as a *most favored nation clause*. Its inclusion in a trade treaty means that each of the signatories agrees to extend to the other the same preferential tariff and trade concessions that each may in the future extend to nonsignatories, i.e., the same treatment that each gives to its "most favored nation." The great majority of trading countries have adhered to this principle since 1948.

DISRUPTION DURING WORLD WAR II

The war disrupted world trade. The belligerents as well as the leading neutral nations were largely prevented from engaging in exchange transactions with the United States and the Allies. In order to help the allied nations to buy the goods they needed but could not pay for, the United States instituted a system of Lend Lease in 1941. It provided advances in goods and supplies in return for "reverse" Lend Lease by the recipient countries in the form of care and housing for American troops. In money terms, the value of the grants given by the United States far exceeded the value of the services that it received in return. But as Prime Minister Winston Churchill remarked to Parliament, Lend Lease was not intended to provide for an equal *quid pro quo;* indeed, it was "the most unsordid act in the history of any nation."

Postwar Reconstruction and Its Aftermath

In the summer of 1944, few people were concerned about the problems of international trade and finance. Allied troops were engaged in the great battle of the Normandy beachhead; a group of German army officers had tried unsuccessfully to assassinate Adolf Hitler; and a politically obscure man named Harry S. Truman was emerging as the potential running mate of President Roosevelt in the latter's bid for a fourth term.

At the same time, an event of less colorful but highly durable significance was taking place in the lovely bucolic setting of Bretton Woods, New Hampshire. There, in the Mount Washington Hotel, at the foot of New England's highest mountain, the United Nations Monetary and Financial Conference was holding an international meeting destined to affect the world's economic structure for decades to come. Present at the meeting were representatives from 16 governments, including Lord Keynes in his capacity as advisor to the British treasury.

The primary result of this historic gathering was the formation of a plan to establish a new and remarkable international financial system. The original agreement was developed largely by the British and American delegations, and signed by 35 nations, but the membership has since increased to more than three times that amount. We shall examine the nature and operation of this system, and related aspects of world trade, in the remaining portions of this chapter.

EUROPEAN ECONOMIC RECOVERY

When the war ended, the European economy was devastated. For five years after the war, Europe's balance of payments on current account suffered from a substantial trade deficit. Among the factors that were responsible for this deficit were (1) the pressure of inflation, (2) the reduction of productive capacity due to the war, and (3) the loss of overseas export markets.

The immediate task, of course, was to rebuild the European economy while, at the same time, financing its deficit. Most of the responsibility fell on the United States, which extended approximately $17 billion in foreign aid between 1945 and 1948, about half of which was in the form of outright gifts and half in the form of loans. But it was recognized that these were merely stopgap measures, and that more consistent and far-reaching policies were necessary. The result was the formulation of two important types of American aid programs that have had a substantial influence on the economic development of other nations.

1. European Recovery Program (Marshall Plan)

On June 5, 1947, Secretary of State George C. Marshall delivered a commencement address at Harvard University in which he proposed what came to be known as the *European Recovery Program* (ERP) or *Marshall Plan*. The plan was a comprehensive blueprint for the economic recovery of European countries. Financed by the United States, its purposes were to (1) increase their productive capacity, (2) stabilize their financial systems, (3) promote their mutual economic cooperation, and (4) reduce their dependence on United States assistance. Out of this came the Organization for European Economic Cooperation, an association consisting initially of 17 European countries which sought to cooperate in assuring their own economic recovery.

The Marshall Plan ended in 1951, after providing over $10 billion in aid. About 90 percent of this was in outright grants, and the rest in loans. There is widespread agreement that the program was a success. It contributed substantially to raising the average level of industrial production among participating nations by more than half their 1947 level, and to suppressing a decade of rapid inflation.

2. Mutual Security Administration

By late 1951, the American emphasis had shifted from direct economic aid to defense against Communist aggression. The immediate cause of this change in attitude was the outbreak of the Korean War in June, 1950. As a result, the ERP was absorbed by the Mutual Security Administration, which provided both military and economic assistance to various nations throughout the world. Since the early fifties, a substantial part of American economic aid has been directed at the underdeveloped countries in Africa, Asia, and Latin America. Much of it has gone to countries which are regarded as bulwarks against communism. The results have not always been favorable. America has been criticized for propping up repressive regimes, and is often regarded by the peoples of such countries as a supporter of dictatorship and even of political terrorism.

TRADE LIBERALIZATION AND REGIONAL INTEGRATION

Even during World War II, it was evident to many political leaders that a new multilateral trading system would be needed after the war—one which provided for liberalization and economic integration of world trade. A significant step in this direction, as we have seen, was the Reciprocal Trade Agreements program adopted by the United States. This program empowered the President to agree on mutual tariff reductions with other countries and to incorporate most favored nation clauses in such agreements. After the war, various trading nations endorsed and adopted additional measures designed to strengthen world commerce. We may examine the more important ones briefly.

General Agreement on Tariffs and Trade (GATT)

The first major postwar step toward liberalization of world trade was the *General Agreement on Tariffs and Trade* (GATT), an international agreement signed in 1947 by 23 countries including the United States, dedicated to four basic principles: (1) nondiscrimination in trade through adherence to unconditional most favored nation treatment; (2) reduction of tariffs by negotiation; (3) elimination of import quotas (with some exceptions permitted); and (4) resolution of differences through consultation. The number of nations participating in GATT has since increased by several dozen, and there is general agreement that it has been an important and successful force for the liberalization of world trade.

Regional Integration

Despite the fact that nations have erected trade barriers to shield themselves from one another, the underlying desire for free trade has nevertheless been persistent. Although worldwide free trade may never become a reality, regional free-trade agreements among two or more nations are commonplace. Such agreements have typically taken three forms: free-trade areas, customs unions, and common markets.

1. A *free-trade area* is an association of trading nations whose participants agree to impose no restrictive devices such as tariffs or quotas on one another, although each is free to impose whatever restrictions it wishes on nonparticipants. The best-known example is the European Free Trade Association (EFTA), or so-called "outer seven," established in 1960. It consists of Austria, Great Britain, Sweden, Norway, Denmark, Switzerland, and Portugal. Similar organizations have been established or proposed among Latin American, Asian, and African countries.

2. A *customs union* is an agreement among two or more trading nations to abolish trade barriers such as tariffs and quotas among themselves, and to adopt a common external policy of trade (such as a common external tariff) with all nonmember nations. The most familiar example is Benelux—consisting of Belgium, the Netherlands, and Luxembourg. Similar plans have been adopted or proposed in other geographic areas.

3. A *common market* is an association of trading nations which agrees to (*a*) impose no trade restrictions such as tariffs or quotas among participants, (*b*) establish common external barriers (such as a common external tariff) to nonparticipants, and (*c*) impose no national restrictions on the movement of labor and capital among participants. The most significant example has been the European Economic Community (EEC), or so-called "inner six," established in 1958, which consists of Belgium, France, West Germany, Italy, Luxembourg, and the Netherlands—an organization commonly referred to as the European Common Market.

A free-trade area, a customs union, and a common market (in that order) represent increasing degrees of economic integration. Of these, the common market is the most significant. What can be said about its economic effects?

On the favorable side, a common market (1) encourages a more efficient allocation of member nations' resources in accordance with the laws of comparative advantage, and (2) expands the size of the market for member nations, thereby enabling their industries to gain the economies (lower unit costs) of large-scale prodution. On the unfavorable side, a common market places a trade barrier—typically a tariff wall—between the member countries as a whole and all nonmember nations; the result may be a diversion of trade between the two groups, thereby causing an economic loss for all parties concerned.

The Kennedy Round

The United States has long desired to foster greater economic and political unification in Europe and to avoid the diversion of trade that could result from the European Common Market. Therefore, in order to encourage a low common tariff wall against American exports and those of other nonmember nations, the United States passed the Trade Expansion Act of 1962 as part of its Reciprocal Trade Agreements program. This new law greatly broadened the powers of the President; it gave him authority to:

1. Negotiate tariff reductions on broad categories of goods instead of on specific commodities, as had previously been the case

2. Lower or eliminate tariffs on those goods for which the Common Market and the United States together account for at least 80 percent of total world exports

3. Lower tariffs by as much as 50 percent on the basis of reciprocal trade agreements, provided that such agreements include most favored nation clauses so that the benefits of reduced tariffs are extended to other countries

4. Grant vocational, technical, and financial assistance to American employees and businessmen whose industries are adversely affected by tariff reduction.

This act enabled the United States to embark on the so-called Kennedy Round of tariff negotiations (named after President Kennedy), the purpose of which was to reduce tariffs gradually over a period of five years. In all, 37 nations became involved in duty reductions. On the whole, most progress was made in lowering the duties on manufactured goods, whereas agricultural products were less affected. Some nations whose industries were injured by tariff reductions have found themselves faced with increased protectionist pressures, and have either adopted or are considering adopting various forms of nontariff barriers to trade such as quotas, license requirements, border taxes, and the like.

INTERNATIONAL MONETARY FUND

These postwar developments in international trade were paralleled by equally momentous changes in international finance. As we have already learned, representatives of the Allied nations met in Bretton Woods in 1944 to construct an orderly system of international monetary cooperation that would be conducive to global trade. The experiences of the 1930s were still fresh in everyone's mind, and it was clear that neither a system of freely fluctuating exchange rates nor one of fixed rates which permitted easy devaluations was the way to strengthen the financial relationships of nations in the postwar world.

One of the most important products of the Bretton Woods conference was the formation of the *International Monetary Fund* (IMF), an organization established by the United Nations in 1944 for the purposes of: (1) eliminating exchange restrictions and providing for worldwide convertibility of currencies so as to encourage multilateral trade based on international specialization; (2) stabilizing exchange rates to reduce or eliminate short-term international fluctuations in a nation's economy due to changes in its imports, exports, or speculative capital movements; and (3) assuring that changes in a country's exchange rate would occur only with the Fund's approval, and only after the country had experienced a prolonged deficit in its balance of payments for a number of years. Today well over 100 nations are members of the Fund.

How does the Fund achieve its objectives? On the basis of three major operating policies:

1. Member countries are required to contribute a "quota" consisting of gold and their own national currencies to the Fund. The size of each country's quota is based on its relative economic strength as determined by its national income, population, and volume of world trade.

2. Each member country agrees to maintain a par value or fixed exchange rate between its currency and all other national currencies. It may do this by withdrawing from the Fund the currencies of the countries with which it has a deficit and using them to reduce its deficits. However, the member country must meet three important conditions: the amount that it can withdraw is determined by the size of its quota; it can only make such withdrawals for up to five years; and it must agree to follow economic policies that are expected to eliminate the deficit.

3. A member nation whose deficit is not corrected by this method and continues to suffer a serious and enduring "fundamental disequilibrium" in its balance of payments will be permitted by the Fund to devalue its currency by as much as 10 percent. If the member country wishes to devalue by more than this amount, it must negotiate the change with the Fund's chief officials.

The IMF has helped many countries to overcome temporary balance of payments deficits that might otherwise have resulted in competitive currency devaluations. It has also been a powerful force in helping to maintain stable exchange rates, even though there have been times when some member countries altered their exchange rates without the Fund's approval. These and other occurrences have raised debate over the desirability of exchange rates' being stable. We shall take up the matter in further detail later in the chapter.

FROM DOLLAR SHORTAGE TO DOLLAR SURPLUS

The United States emerged from the war as a large creditor to the Allied countries. After the war, American lending continued to mount into the billions of dollars as the United States shifted its emphasis from the provision of military goods to the provision of civilian goods to the war-torn nations. The latter, of course, had little if anything to export in return; nor did they have the gold or dollar reserves with which to pay for the American goods that they received. Hence a "dollar shortage" became one of the most talked-about problems of the postwar decade

as the United States continued to show a rather persistent deficit in its balance of payments after 1950.

Further, since gold and dollars were the major source of international monetary reserves, the dollar (and to a lesser extent the pound sterling) became known as a *key currency*—in effect, a substitute for gold in meeting international obligations. This meant that during the 1950s, while the United States was accumulating a huge deficit in its balance of payments, other countries—mainly the European nations—were adding to their reserves, primarily in the form of dollar deposits in United States banks or of short-term government securities.

By the mid-1950s, the European and Japanese economies were not only rehabilitated, but also thriving. The United States, however, was still maintaining heavy troop commitments overseas, providing economic aid to underdeveloped countries, and experiencing a mounting outflow of American tourists going abroad. All this added up to continued deficits, and by the late 1950s it was recognized throughout the world that the dollar shortage had now been transformed into a serious and dangerous dollar surplus.

"DEFENDING THE DOLLAR"

How might the deficit be corrected? There were three plausible choices: (1) domestic deflation, (2) devaluation of the dollar, and (3) reductions in foreign outlays. The first two would increase international earnings by expanding United States exports relative to imports, whereas the third would simply decrease United States expenses.

The first choice was ruled out because deflation would lead to an increase in the unemployment rate, which was already averaging close to 5 percent. The second choice was also ruled out because devaluation by a major trading country such as the United States would undoubtedly have brought on a chain of competitive devaluations by most other countries. This left the third choice—reduction of foreign outlays as a means of "defending the dollar."

The measures adopted in the early 1960s took several major forms: Families of servicemen stationed overseas were sent back to the United States;

the limits on duty-free goods owned by returning American tourists were cut; European countries were exhorted to carry a larger share of the mutual defense burden and of foreign aid; an "interest equalization tax" and "voluntary restraints" were imposed on the outflow of American capital; nations in debt to the United States were asked to speed up their payments; trading nations were urged to end their remaining restrictions against American imports; and so on.

What were the consequences? At worst, they did not succeed in eliminating the deficit; at best, they may have merely helped to keep the deficit from becoming still larger. But in any case they were more than straws in the wind, for they portended a series of international monetary crises that shook the financial world.

INTERNATIONAL MONETARY CRISES

In terms of what it set out to do, the 1944 conference at Bretton Woods was a smashing success. It stabilized exchange rates and created an international monetary system that was highly productive of world trade and investment. This was accomplished by establishing a modified type of gold exchange standard with two distinctive features:

1. The dollar was tied to gold, and the U.S. Treasury agreed to make gold and dollars mutually convertible to foreign central banks at the rate of $35 an ounce of gold.

2. Each nation fixed an exchange rate or par value for its currency in relation to the dollar and agreed to maintain that rate within a 1 percent range by buying and selling when others are selling and buying.

This meant that businessmen anywhere in the world could trade with Britain, for example, and be certain that the value of the pound would not vary by more than a few pennies above or below its established rate. As before, however, nations still needed monetary reserves to settle their international monetary deficits. Under the pure gold standard, such reserves consisted of gold; under the postwar modified gold exchange standard, however, reserves

consisted primarily of gold and dollars, and to a lesser extent of British pounds. The dollars, as we have seen, were derived largely from United States deficits and held mainly in the form of bank deposits and short-term government securities. Because of this, the United States became known as the "world's banker," with the dollar serving as the key or reserve currency.

As American and British deficits continued to mount, and as inflationary forces pushed up prices not only in the United States but also in England and various other major trading nations, the accumulation of pressures erupted in large speculative flows of funds that endangered the international payments system. For example, speculative fevers struck the German mark in 1961 and 1968, the Italian lira in 1963, the British pound in 1961, 1964, 1967, and 1968, and the French franc and United States dollar in 1968. Both psychological and economic factors were responsible for these crises, but one of the chief causes was a wavering confidence in the dollar—that is, recurring doubts as to whether the United States would be willing and able to maintain convertibility of the dollar into gold at the fixed price of $35 for an ounce of gold. As shown in Exhibit 1, increasing proportions of dollars were converted into gold during the 1960s by foreign speculators and others who thought it would be safer or more profitable to hold the yellow metal instead of the green paper.

Finally, in the late 1960s, three sets of events capped a decade of international monetary crises.

1. Special Drawing Rights ("Paper Gold")

After 1958, the European countries began to press the United States to reduce its balance of payments deficit. The United States, in return, urged throughout the sixties that a plan be developed for increasing international liquidity in the absence of dollar outflows. After almost five years of discussion and four years of negotiation, *Special Drawing Rights* (SDRs) —popularly known as "paper gold"—were approved by the International Monetary Fund in 1969. The SDRs are supplementary reserves in the form of account entries on the books of the IMF, and are allocated among participating countries in accordance

Exhibit 1

United States Gold Stocks and Short-Term Liabilities in the 1960s

As American gold stocks continued to decline, the potential demand for them—in the form of short-term liabilities held by foreigners, including dollars spent by American tourists and American corporate purchases abroad—rose sharply.

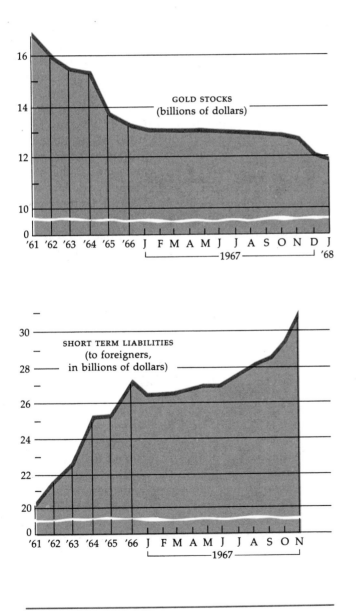

with their quotas. They can be drawn upon by governments to help finance balance-of-payments deficits, and it is hoped they will provide an orderly growth of reserves to meet the expanding needs of world trade. In the opinion of some economists, however, SDRs are a device for postponing what is more fundamentally needed, namely a better mechanism for international adjustment. The implications of this will be considered later in the chapter. Meanwhile, see Exhibit 2.

2. Devaluation

On November 19, 1967, the twenty-sixth Sunday after Trinity, churchgoers in England heard a somber and particularly apt text from Anglican pulpits. The lesson, from *St. James*, Chapter 5, Verses 1 to 3, was:

> Go to now, ye rich men, weep and howl for your miseries that shall come upon you.
>
> Your riches are corrupted, and your garments are moth-eaten.
>
> Your gold and silver is cankered; and the rust of them shall be a witness against you, and shall eat your flesh as it were fire. Ye have heaped treasure together for the last days.

Why this curious reading from scripture? The answer is that while the creation of SDRs was being discussed among governments, Britain was indulging herself with an easy-money policy that was contributing to inflation, trade deficits, and financial strains. On November 18, 1967, she succumbed to international economic pressures and devalued the pound from $2.80 to $2.40, a decrease of 14.3 percent. This was the third devaluation for Britain in 36 years, and was intended to give the country a sharper competitive edge in world markets as well as the breathing time needed to repair its foundering economy and deficit-ridden balance of payments.

Whether or not a devaluation succeeds in eliminating a deficit depends on the various policy measures taken at home to curb inflation. Such measures, which Britain adopted belatedly, included heavy new taxes, broad wage controls, and a tight national budget. In the long run, if an austerity policy is sufficiently harsh and if it is combined with an appropriate restrictive monetary policy, it can succeed in curbing an inflation and thereby make a devalua-

Exhibit 2

The Implications of Special Drawing Rights

WHAT DO SDRs MEAN FOR THE UNITED STATES? *SDRs are of special significance for the United States because of the role of the dollar in international monetary arrangements. Both the practical usage of SDRs and their long run implications are somewhat different for the United States than for any other country.*

The usage of SDRs by the United States derives from the unique way this country finances its balance of payments deficits or surpluses. Unlike other countries, the United States monetary authorities do not buy and sell foreign exchange to maintain the exchange rate of the dollar within the prescribed limits. The operations undertaken by individual countries on behalf of the dollar rate are sufficient to achieve stability. Instead, the United States undertakes to convert into gold or convertible currencies extra dollars accumulated by other central banks and to sell dollars to them for gold.

Historically, the United States used its gold stock or its "credit line" with the IMF to absorb unwanted dollars that accrued to foreign central banks as the result of the U.S. deficit. With the introduction of SDRs, the United States has, within the rules governing the use of the SDRs by any one country, the additional option of affecting the absorption by exchanging the unwanted dollars for SDRs. This aids conservation of the U.S. gold stock and thus contributes to the viability of the existing international payments mechanism.

In the long run, the introduction of SDRs may be expected to modify the role of the dollar as a reserve currency. The view that the dollar cannot and should not be expected to meet the world's future needs for growth of reserves was the underlying rationale for the introduction of the SDRs. Thus, the relative importance of the dollar as a source of international liquidity

The changing mix in world reserves

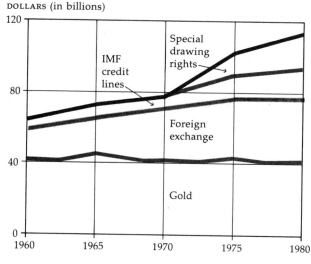

DOLLARS (in billions)

DATA: International Monetary Fund.

should diminish gradually as more SDRs are introduced over time.

At the same time, however, the vital function the dollar has performed as the "international transactions currency" will, most likely, remain unaffected; indeed this role may be strengthened by the introduction of arrangements that hold a promise of a better functioning international payments system.

SOURCE: Adapted from Federal Reserve Bank of Chicago.

---

tion yield lasting economic benefits.

3. A Two-Tier System for Gold

Following the devaluation of the pound in 1967, confidence in the dollar was further weakened by inflation in the United States and the expectation that the dollar would have to be devalued. Consequently, a rush to buy gold developed late in the year. Most of the buyers were speculators who ex-

pected to make a quick profit by reselling the gold at the higher price.

In the meantime, seven countries known as the Gold Pool nations—the United States, Britain, West Germany, Belgium, Italy, the Netherlands, and Switzerland—had, since 1961, been holding the free market price of gold in London, Brussels, Zurich, and certain other cities at the American price of $35 an ounce by pooling their gold and standing ready to buy or sell as the need arose. With the onset of the new "gold rush," there was a danger that the gold holdings of these nations would be depleted, thus endangering the entire international monetary system. The speculative fever reached a dramatic climax in March, 1968, with the announcement of a two-tier (or two-price) system for gold by the Gold Pool nations. Henceforth, they said, their central banks would (1) exchange existing gold stocks among themselves at the historic official price of $35 per ounce, and (2) no longer buy or sell gold in private markets, thus leaving the free price of gold to rise or fall like any other commodity. (See Box 2.)

This action further demonetized gold—that is, reduced its influence in the monetary system and thereby removed its threat to the dollar. Thus by the end of the sixties, the dollar seemed victorious over gold for several reasons: The West German mark had been revalued upward, and the French franc had been devalued, both to more realistic levels; Britain's trade balance had improved; and South Africa, the world's largest producer of gold, was mining the metal faster than the free market could absorb it,

thus creating a huge "overhang" of potential supply. These factors contributed to bringing the free price of gold down to the near $35 level as shown in Exhibit 3.

Problems of International Adjustment

Looking back over these historical developments, it is appropriate for us to ask why international monetary crises have occurred. The reasons can be summarized in four steps.

1. Under the Bretton Woods agreement, central banks keep their foreign exchange rates within 1 percent of par value by buying or selling their currencies in the market as the need arises.

2. The international supply of a nation's currency will tend to exceed the demand for it when that country runs a *deficit* in its balance of payments. This

---

Box 2

Who Are the Gold Speculators?

In the United States and Britain, it is illegal for private citizens to buy or sell gold. But in many other countries everyone is free to trade in it. Who are the chief purchasers in those countries? By visiting any of the major gold markets of the world—in London, Paris, Brussels, Zurich, or Hong Kong—and conversing with dealers, one can conjecture that there is a mixed bag of gold-buying types: oil-rich sheiks from the Middle East, millionaires from Europe and the Far East, foreign commercial banks, corporations, and businessmen. But the names of these buyers are virtually impossible to obtain, for secrecy is a fetish in gold transactions.

During the week of the mad gold rush in mid-March of 1968, the famous Bourse in Paris was the center of activity. There, according to Newsweek *magazine, "a shoving, sweating mob of dealers transacted their business amid shouts of 'Stop pushing, dammit!' and 'Give me room!' The action got so feverish at one point that the gendarmes were called in to make sure that the gold crisis did not claim its first life."*

Exhibit 3

Price of Gold on the Free Market*

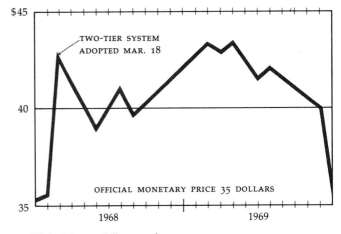

*United States dollars per fine ounce

---

occurs when the nation pays out more money than it takes in, by spending, investing, or giving it away. In order to buy its currency back, the monetary authority must spend its reserves of dollars or gold (by selling the gold to foreign central banks) or borrow from the International Monetary Fund.

3. Conversely, the international demand for a nation's currency will tend to exceed the supply of it when the country runs a *surplus* in its balance of payments. In that case the nation is taking in more money than it is paying out, and to meet foreign demand the central bank must sell its currency in return for foreign exchange. This results in an accumulation of reserves, mostly dollars, which the central bank in the surplus country can then present to the United States for payment in gold at the official rate of $35 an ounce.

4. The problem, therefore, is for each of the leading trading countries to maintain a tendency toward balance between its money inflows and outflows; otherwise, the international monetary system will be threatened whenever major nations continue to run large deficits or surpluses for prolonged periods of time. See Exhibit 4.

What difficulties do nations encounter in achieving international monetary balance? It is to this problem that we now turn our attention.

THE RELUCTANCE TO ADJUST

The heart of any international monetary system is its adjustment mechanism—the process by which nations achieve payments balance.

Under the old gold standard, the adjustment was automatic; a nation with a deficit in its balance of payments tended to lose gold, and the loss of gold brought about a domestic deflation which resulted in increased exports and decreased imports. This meant, however, that the domestic economic goal of full employment through appropriate fiscal and monetary policies had to take second place to international economic adjustment—a situation that all nations found untenable.

Under the Bretton Woods system, exchange rates remain fixed, and so the process of adjustment is left to nations themselves. This means that countries

Exhibit 4

Why International Monetary Crises Are Inescapable

Though the present international system is sometimes called a fixed-rate arrangement, it was originally intended to be a system of "managed flexibility." The men who met at Bretton Woods near the end of World War II realized that fixed rates work well only under very special circumstances. Either the price levels of trading nations must remain stable, or, if they change, it must be in unison. If, however, the price levels of nations move in opposite directions or change at different speeds—as is usually the case in real life—a fixed-rate system makes balance of payments maladjustments inevitable.

Such imbalances can be corrected if countries with below-average rates of inflation allow their prices to rise more rapidly, while those with too much inflation trim down. While these adjustments are taking place, payments imbalances can be financed by the transfer of gold and foreign exchange reserves. But if nations resist the appropriate changes in their price levels, the burden of adjustment falls on exchange rates as long as currencies are freely convertible. When rates remain immovable, imbalances pile up beyond the capacity of nations to finance them, and exchange controls or international crises are inescapable.

Even if nations somehow managed to maintain identical rates of growth and inflation, their currencies might still tend to change in relative value over time. As world income grows, nations both sell and buy more abroad. For any given increase in world income, however, some countries' exports grow at a faster rate than their imports. This may be because the kinds of goods they sell are simply more "income elastic" than the kinds of goods they buy. Or it may be because productivity in their export- and import-competing industries rises much faster than it does in other nations. For example, if every nation's economy grew at the same rate, each 1 percent increase in Japan's GNP would tend to increase its imports by approximately 1.2 percent, and an equal rate of growth in world income would increase its exports by over 3 percent. On the other hand, every 1 percent rise in GNP would push up Britain's exports by only 0.9 percent but would raise imports by 1.7 percent. Thus Japan's economy can grow about three times as fast as that of the rest of the world without causing that country balance of payments headaches; Britain's can grow only half as fast as the rest of the world if it wishes to maintain the external value of the pound—unless, of course, it keeps on getting fresh capital infusions from abroad.

SOURCE: Adapted from *Fortune*, August 15, 1969.

must be willing to adopt deflationary policies to correct persistent balance of payments deficits, or "reflationary" policies to reduce balance of payments surpluses. Of course, the pressure on deficit nations to change their domestic policies depends for the most part on how long their reserves hold out or how long they can continue to borrow; surplus nations, on the other hand, tend to gain reserves, and hence may be able to avoid adjustment almost indefinitely. See Exhibit 5.

In general, nations that are committed to the maintenance of full employment do not find it easy to adopt a policy of domestic deflation. The United States and Britain have been prime examples. Both have gone through long periods of deficits, but both were able to delay adjustments because the dollar and the pound are reserve currencies. Eventually, when the United States was forced to adjust because it was losing gold, it took the easier and less effective route of employing indirect forms of exchange controls—such as interest equalization taxes and the imposition of limits on capital exports, corporate overseas investing, and bank lending abroad.

In terms of historical experience, it appears that the most positive approach a government can take to correct an imbalance is to change the par value of its

---

Exhibit 5

World Liquidity During the Years of International Monetary Crises, 1960–1968

World monetary reserves expanded as a result of a sharp rise in foreign exchange holdings, . . .

but the growth in official reserves fell below the growth in world trade. . .

while the share of the industrialized countries in the world total did not expand.

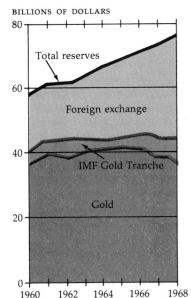

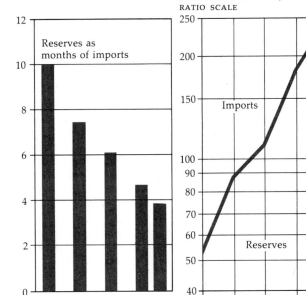

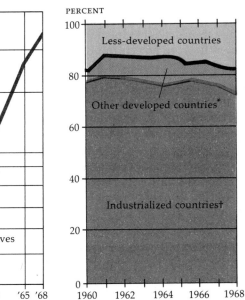

† Industrial Europe, United States, Canada, Japan.

* Other Europe, Australia, New Zealand, South Africa.

currency. But this is considered to be the most drastic of measures. Thus if a country has been suffering from deficits, a depreciation of its currency in order to restore balance involves a sacrifice of international prestige, for its political leaders are thereby admitting to the world that they have been unable to manage domestic economic affairs properly. On the other hand, if a country has been experiencing surpluses in its balance of payments, an appreciation or upward revaluation of its currency may cause some domestic unemployment, especially in its export industries, and hence is a step which elected political leaders are not easily persuaded to take.

These tendencies are readily apparent. Britain waited more than a year before devaluing in 1967, and did so only after it could no longer borrow money to support the pound. France suffered a $3 billion reserve loss in 1968, but deemed it a point of national honor not to devalue the franc, and hence imposed a strict domestic austerity program instead. Finally, however, it had to succumb to the reality of devaluation in August, 1969. And West Germany, after experiencing years of domestic prosperity and surpluses in its balance of payments, finally yielded to persistent pressure from other deficit nations; in September, 1969, *after* a close election, the mark was permitted to float freely, and its price in the market promptly rose.

THE INEVITABILITY OF ADJUSTMENT

Ultimately, of course, nations do adjust, because the forces that create international imbalances—inflation or deflation—also cause domestic economic difficulties which require correction. But the adjustment may take a long time in coming, and in the meantime nations can bump along from one crisis to another.

Was this the world that the men at Bretton Woods

Exhibit 5 (continued)

These countries experienced the best reserve gains from 1960 to 1968 . . .

while these countries showed largest reserve losses.

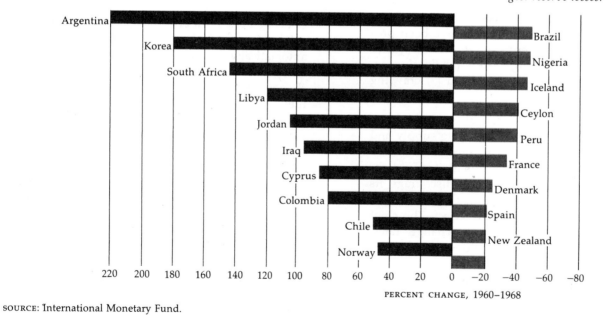

PERCENT CHANGE, 1960–1968

SOURCE: International Monetary Fund.

envisaged? The answer is no. They never thought that the dollar would remain the world's key currency for several decades after the war, nor that it would be a currency whose supply might someday exceed the quantity that central banks wish to hold. Likewise, they never foresaw the possibility that there would someday be a huge market for *Eurodollars*, which are dollar deposits in banks outside the United States, mostly in Europe. Eurodollars are held by American or foreign banks, corporations, and individuals, and represent dollar obligations which are constantly crossing national frontiers in search of the highest return; hence they may affect balances of payments and may even turn pressure on a currency into an international monetary crisis.

The basic problem, therefore, is for nations to find a suitable method of adjustment; otherwise, the system will continue to stumble along.

Fixed, Floating, Adjustable, or Crawling Rates?

What can be done to improve the world's monetary system? Central bankers and economists are interested in three types of reform that have been proposed to replace the present Bretton Woods system of prolonged fixed exchange rates: (1) floating exchange rates; (2) adjustable pegs; and (3) crawling pegs.

Floating Exchange Rates. Such rates would leave currencies free to fluctuate according to supply and demand. Thus a decrease in the price of a nation's currency in the foreign exchange market would encourage that country's exports and discourage its imports; conversely, an increase in the price of its currency would have the opposite effect. The chief advantages of freely fluctuating exchange rates, therefore, are that: (1) they provide for automatic adjustment in the balance of payments without the intervention of a central authority; and (2) they eliminate the need for stabilization funds and international reserves such as those held by the IMF. The chief disadvantages are that: (1) they may restrict

the expansion of world trade by leaving importers, exporters, creditors, etc., in a greater state of uncertainty about future exchange rates; and (2) they may encourage speculation in foreign exchange which could accentuate price swings and cause a destabilization of world trade. These undesirable consequences might eventually lead to more rather than fewer trade controls. See, however, Exhibit 6.

Adjustable Pegs. An *adjustable peg* system permits changes in the par rate of exchange after a long-run disequilibrium in the balance of payments; in addition, it allows for short-run variations in the exchange rate within a few specified percentage points around the par value. (This is somewhat like the present Bretton Woods system. However, the present system usually permits years of long-run disequilibrium before an adjustment is effected through the IMF.) The most desirable feature of such a system is that it would operate efficiently only if the par rate were consistent with the nation's long-run equilibrium in its balance of payments, so that the adjustment problem is then entirely of a short-term nature. The most undesirable feature is that the threat of speculation and disruption of foreign exchange markets would exist when a change in the basic par rate became necessary.

Crawling Pegs. Under a *crawling peg* system the par value of a nation's exchange rate would change automatically by small increments, downward or upward, if in actual daily trading on the foreign exchange markets the price of its currency persisted on the "floor" or "ceiling" of the established range for a specified period of time. The changes in the par value would be small and gradual (probably about 3 percent annually) so as to discourage speculation, yet sufficient to correct for fundamental imbalances in the balance of payments. The crawling peg system thus represents a compromise between floating exchange rates and the adjustable peg. Although the crawling peg would not eliminate the need for international reserves, it would permit fewer reserves to be needed than with fixed rates. And, since everyone would know how far and in what direction exchange rates were moving, speculation would tend to be minimal while world trade and investment continued to expand. See Exhibit 7.

Exhibit 6

Currency Protection in the Forward Exchange Market

Forward exchange is bought (or sold) at a given time and at a stipulated current or "spot" price, but is payable at some future date. By buying or selling forward exchange, importers and exporters can protect themselves against the risks of fluctuations in the current exchange market.

The spread between spot and future prices can vary considerably, as the chart shows. Currencies that are in strong demand tend to sell at a premium, while those that are in a weaker position sell at a discount. In 1969, for example, French importers from Germany paid heavily by buying forward marks at a premium, thus restricting their purchases of Volkswagens. But German importers found forward francs so cheap they could afford to buy a lot more French wine.

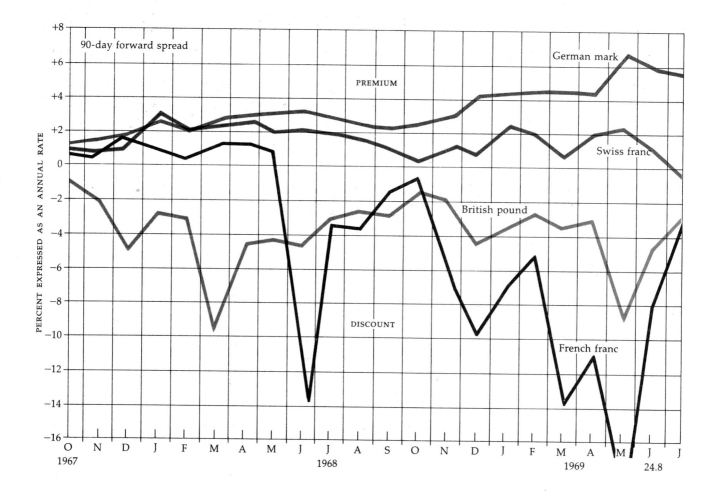

Exhibit 7

How the Crawling Peg Would Work

Under the crawling peg system a deficit nation would find that its exchange rate stayed at the lower level of the allowable band of fluctuation. So its exchange rate would move downward in predictable fashion until the impact of a lower exchange rate brought its balance of payments back into equilibrium. On the other side, the exchange rate of a surplus nation would increase in a manner which would gradually reduce its surplus. In effect, other currencies would move around the dollar, which would remain pegged to gold at $35 per ounce. The merit of the crawling peg is that its movements would be predictable and it would facilitate the adjustment process on the part of both deficit and surplus nations.

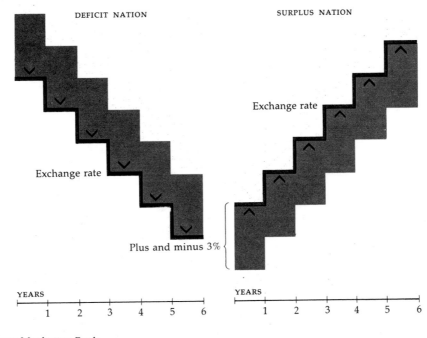

SOURCE: Adapted from Chase Manhattan Bank.

CONCLUSION

The choice between the Bretton Woods system of prolonged fixed exchange rates and one that permits either floating, more frequently adjustable, or crawling rates has been discussed by bankers, economists, and political leaders for years. Governments tend to believe that the prolonged fixed exchange rate system must stay. Economists, on the other hand, especially those in the academic world, have come increasingly to favor the more flexible systems such as the three described above. Nothing much is likely to happen, however, unless monetary crises occur with sufficient magnitude and frequency to force a change in the present system. In the words of one European central banker: "It is unrealistic to assume that any government would go along with a policy of flexible exchange rates based on some agreed-upon mechanism that could easily be discarded in a period of adversity."

Nixon's "International" N.E.P.: Wrong War, Wrong Weapons?*

Throughout the 1960s foreign governments looked with dismay and disapproval at the spectacle of the U.S. regularly spending more overseas than it earned—and refusing to take measures that would enable it to pay its way in the world.

By the turn of the decade the chronic deficit had ballooned to the point of crisis. U.S. imports were rising far faster than exports; banks and corporations were putting billions of dollars annually into investments abroad; and defense spending, swollen by the Vietnam war, was a hemorrhage through which other billions leaked out.

Moreover, foreigners were holding billions of dollars they did not want. In the summer of 1971 certain countries, headed by France and Switzerland, rushed to convert their dollar holdings into gold. By July only $10 billion was left in Fort Knox. The crunch came on August 15. Then, as part of his package of economic policies, President Nixon announced:

The U.S. would no longer exchange dollars for gold;

Imports would be subject to a 10 percent surcharge on existing tariffs;

American-made capital goods would earn a special tax credit denied to foreign-made rival products.

All those measures were described as temporary; but the president made it clear that none would be ended until other countries had agreed to a combination of monetary revaluations and tariff concessions intended to propel the U.S. towards a balance of payments surplus.

Reluctant Realignment

The U.S. and its leading trading partners reached a settlement of sorts in December, 1971: the U.S. agreed to devalue the dollar against gold by 8.6 percent, and other nations promised to revalue their currencies upwards by varying amounts. Europe, Canada, and Japan also agreed to talk about reducing tariffs and other trade barriers.

The U.S. had won a victory. Yet many experts believe that the Administration had fought the wrong battle in the wrong war with the wrong weapons.

The August 15 announcement and its aftermath concentrated on a single aspect of the payments problem: visible trade. To be sure, the U.S. surplus on trade had dwindled during the sixties and early seventies, to become a $1.5 billion deficit in 1971. But the *total* 1971 deficit was almost $30 billion. Much of that huge sum was accounted for by U.S. exports of capital. Part of that capital was invested in plant and equipment, and will eventually produce profits for repatriation to the U.S.—an income that will show up in the balance of payments under "invisible earnings." But another large part of the flow is highly volatile. It floods into the U.S. when prospects for profits are high, and rushes out again when prospects are better elsewhere.

Some of those ebbs and flows of capital are used to speculate in currencies. For example, banks and businesses will switch out of dollars into German marks if they think the dollar is likely to fall in market value. Thus the Administration was correct in believing that specula-

tive money flows would be reduced if confidence in the dollar were restored. But it is clear that no conceivable increase in U.S. visible trade can pay for both imported goods *and* capital exports: the total deficit is of such a magnitude that the rest of the world simply could not absorb enough additional U.S. goods to turn it into a surplus.

Restricted Rights?

What else could the U.S. have done to strengthen the dollar? In the view of many European experts it should have restricted the right of U.S. banks, corporations, and citizens to send dollars abroad. It should also have required U.S. businesses abroad to remit more of their profits to the U.S., thereby strengthening invisible earnings.

In fact, the Administration set its face against any such restrictions. That refusal made many foreign observers suspect that its strategy was to force other countries into buying more American goods while exporting less to the U.S., and thereby to enable U.S. firms to continue their expansion abroad. As one European banker put it: "The U.S. wants us to buy more of its goods so that it can buy more of our industry. That is dollar imperialism."

R. B.

The U.S. has supported the free trade principle since World War II. Does the size of the payments deficit now make that principle a luxury the U.S. cannot afford?

America's huge capital exports could be financed in part by bigger foreign investment in the U.S. What are the arguments for and against that investment?

* Domestic aspects of Nixon's N.E.P. are discussed on page 223.

SUMMARY OF IMPORTANT IDEAS

1. For several decades before World War I, most national economies were closely integrated through a well-developed network of trade and finance. Despite rapid advances in technology and heavy migrations of labor and capital, the international economic setting remained relatively harmonious until the outbreak of the War.

2. World War I disrupted national trading and financial relationships. Although efforts were made at postwar reconstruction, there was a structural weakening of the international economy during the decade of the twenties as nations shifted their economic goals toward greater internal stability and control at the expense of automatic external adjustment.

3. The world economy, and particularly the interdependence of nations, underwent major deterioration during the Depression of the thirties. Governments sought to protect themselves from economic crises by imposing higher tariffs, by going off the gold standard, and by devaluing their currencies. Although some significant steps toward international economic reform were made during the late 1930s, the outbreak of World War II prevented further progress.

4. After the War, most of the war-torn nations of the world became beneficiaries of American economic aid. Major steps were taken toward trade liberalization through GATT, and toward economic integration through the development of common markets. In the area of international finance, the Bretton Woods conference of 1944 established the IMF and a world monetary arrangement that was enormously successful in encouraging international trade.

5. By the 1960s, however, it was apparent that economic conditions had changed so much that the world's monetary system was out of date. The volume of world trade increased faster than reserves, causing international monetary crises that resulted in exchange controls and devaluations. Among the measures taken to alleviate the pressures were the introduction of SDRs and a two-tier (or two-price) system for gold.

6. The most positive step a nation can take to correct a fundamental imbalance is to change the par value of its currency by devaluation or revaluation. But this involves deep political as well as economic considerations which are often too serious for nations to overlook. Hence, they often adopt alternative short-term or stopgap measures such as controls, taxes, or other devices to regulate imports and exports.

7. Three methods that have been suggested to replace the present Bretton Woods system of fixed exchange rates have been (1) floating or freely fluctuating exchange rates, (2) an adjustable peg system, and (3) a crawling peg system. Political considerations being what they are, however, it is unlikely that the system of fixed exchange rates will be modified unless international monetary crises repeat themselves with sufficient intensity and frequency to force a change.

FOR HOMEWORK AND DISCUSSION

1. *Terms and concepts to review:*

gold bullion standard	common market
devaluation	Trade Expansion Act (1962)
Reciprocal Trade Agreements program	International Monetary Fund (IMF)
most favored nation clause	Special Drawing Rights (SDRs or "paper gold")
European Recovery Program (ERP)	
General Agreements on Tariffs and Trade (GATT)	floating exchange rates
	adjustable peg
free-trade area	crawling peg
customs union	forward exchange

2. What major features would you stress if you were to write a research paper on the history of international commercial and financial policies?

3. If a country's balance of payments is in equilibrium and the nation experiences a decline in exports, does its balance of payments go into disequilibrium? What happens if floating exchange rates prevail?

4. Devaluation stimulates a nation's exports while curbing its imports; upward revaluation has the

opposite effects. In view of this, would you recommend the use of devaluation and revaluation as useful countercyclical policies to combat recessions and inflations, similar to the way we currently use fiscal and monetary policies for such purposes? Explain.

5. From the experiences of the 1960s, would you say that the dollar was overvalued or undervalued in world markets? What could have been done to correct the situation?

6. Why do you suppose that many "anti-Keynesians" often propose that the United States go on a gold standard?

7. The economic regions of the United States, i.e., Northeast, Southwest, etc., are somewhat like countries, each with their own different types of economies. However, unlike countries, they all use the same currency, namely dollars, which puts them in effect on a fixed exchange rate with respect to one another. What happens when some of these regions experience deficits and others surpluses? How do they adjust? How does the regional adjustment process compare with that of nations?

8. Deficits in the United States balance of payments were welcomed in the early 1950s but viewed with great concern a decade later. Why?

9. It is often said that the Bretton Woods arrangement resulted in a compromise between fixed and floating exchange rates. Is this true? Explain. What would have been a better compromise?

REFERENCES AND READING SUGGESTIONS

ELSWORTH, PAUL T., *The International Economy*, 4th ed., Macmillan, New York, 1969, chaps. 25, 26.

EVANS, JOHN W., *U.S. Trade Policy*, Harper & Row, New York, 1967.

FRIEDMAN, MILTON, and ROBERT V. ROOSA, *The Balance of Payments: Free Versus Fixed Exchange Rates*, American Enterprise Association, Washington, D.C., 1967.

KENEN, PETER B., *International Economics*, 2d ed., Prentice-Hall, New York, 1967, chaps. 3, 5.

SNIDER, DELBERT, *Introduction to International Economics*, 4th ed., Irwin, Homewood, Illinois, 1967, chaps. 9, 21.

CHAPTER 36

The Less Developed Countries: Nations in Poverty

CHAPTER PREVIEW

What are the chief economic characteristics of less developed countries? How do these countries compare with the more advanced nations?

What major forms of assistance have been provided to the less developed countries? Has this assistance been effective? What problems should be understood if foreign aid is to achieve its desired objectives?

Can a set of principles and policies be developed to provide a framework for analyzing the process of development?

In his 1968 Message to Congress, President Johnson said:

> Peace will never be secure as long as:
>
> Seven out of ten people on earth cannot read or write
>
> Tens of millions of people each day—most of them children—are maimed and stunted by malnutrition
>
> Diseases long conquered by science still ravage cities and villages around the world

Conditions have not changed significantly since President Johnson issued his warning.

At home, as we have learned already, a considerable minority of Americans do not share either the opportunity or the affluence of our time. Abroad, as we shall see in this chapter, the poor countries contain three-fourths of the world's population. Hence it is the affluent who are in the minority in today's world.

Nations in poverty are part of the larger study of economic growth and development, but with some applications of international economics as well. Although there is no explicit or unified theory of economic development, some of today's most significant insights stem from Adam Smith's *Wealth of Nations* (1776), which was written before the main thrust of the industrial revolutions, but after many important agricultural revolutions.

Some Characteristics of Less Developed Countries

The poor nations are commonly referred to as *less developed countries* (LDCs), or underdeveloped countries, or low-income countries. They are usually characterized by:

☐ Poverty levels of income (typically defined as less than $500 per capita annually), and hence little or no saving

☐ High rates of population growth

☐ Substantial majorities of the labor force employed in agriculture

☐ Low proportions of adult literacy

☐ Extensive *disguised unemployment*—a situation in which employed resources are not being used in their most efficient ways (also commonly called *underemployment*)

☐ Heavy reliance on one or a few items for export

☐ Government control by a wealthy elite, which opposes any changes that would harm its economic interests

These characteristics are tendencies rather than certainties among underdeveloped nations; exceptions can be found to all of them.

A question that naturally arises is: How many countries of the world are considered to be "less developed," and which ones are they? From time to time the United Nations has designated dozens of countries as LDCs, with the number ranging between 75 and 100 since the 1960s. These nations are located primarily in Asia, Latin America, and Africa. Among them are Indonesia, Burma, India, Kenya, Pakistan, Nigeria, Syria, Morocco, Brazil, Taiwan, Paraguay, Ecuador, Honduras, Turkey, and Colombia.

A STUDY IN CONTRASTS

It is necessary to compare the gap, at different points in time, between per capita incomes in the less developed and the advanced countries to see whether the gulf has widened, narrowed, or remained the same. For example, in 1955, average per capita annual income in the half-dozen poorest countries of the world was $97, while in the half-dozen richest countries it was $1,228—more than twelve times higher. Ten years later, in 1965, some of the countries in each group had changed, but average income per capita was still about the same in the six poorest countries, while it had risen to over $2,200 in the six richest. This indicates that the per capita income gap between the richest and the poorest nations has been widening, thus portending serious consequences for the world community.

It is not enough, of course, simply to measure differences in the economic progress of nations; we must see clearly why these differences occur. This requires us to understand the factors determining a nation's economic development—its quantity and quality of human and natural resources, its rate of capital accumulation, its degree of specialization and scale of production, its rate of technological progress, and its environmental factors, including the political, social, cultural, and economic framework within which growth and development take place. Once we comprehend the significance of these factors, it becomes easy to appreciate why the rich nations are getting richer while the poor ones are getting relatively poorer.

This point can be illustrated by comparing the United States with most underdeveloped countries. The United States has a large labor force with a relatively high proportion of skilled labor, and its business leaders are numerous and disciplined. It has a substantial and diversified quantity of natural resources, an extensive system of transportation and power, an efficient and productive technology financed by an adequate supply of savings, a stable and comparatively uncorrupt government, and a culture in which the drive for profit and material gain is generally accepted. These factors in combination have stimulated America's economic development.

In the less developed countries, on the other hand, most of these conditions are absent. Labor is largely unskilled and inefficient, and is often chronically ill and undernourished. Savings are small or even negative, resulting in low rates of investment and capital accumulation. The cultural environment favors the clergy, the military, or government adminstration, while frowning upon commerce and finance, thus creating a dearth of entrepreneurial talent; and government is often unstable or, if stable, dictatorial, corrupt, and inefficient. Paradoxically, many poor countries are rich in natural resources; but because these are usually controlled by foreigners for their own profit, relatively little of the revenue goes into the local economy. A combination of these factors retards economic development.

WHAT IS ECONOMIC DEVELOPMENT?

The fundamental challenge facing the poor countries is to transform their economies from underdeveloped to developed status. This is what the expression "economic development" means. It is a process that has continued at an accelerating pace in the advanced countries since the birth of capitalism in the late Middle Ages. Today's less developed countries cannot hope, however, to start a similar process without help from the rich nations. Some help has been offered: loans, grants, and technical assistance have enabled certain poor countries to acquire greater quantities of capital and achieve faster rates of economic growth than would otherwise have been possible.

As we shall see later in this chapter, many of the less developed countries are trapped in a vicious circle of poverty from which escape is extremely difficult. Hence the problems which cause this vicious circle must be solved if economic development is to occur. Among those problems are bad government. As many critics point out, the world's largest source of aid, the United States, offers help mainly to governments it wants to keep in power. Foreign aid has thus been a tool of foreign policy; and governments considered desirable by the U.S. State Department are not always those best able to foster economic growth.

Milestones in Foreign Aid

As World War II drew to a close, it became apparent that the richer nations would have to provide substantial aid to countries devastated by war. Accordingly, various agencies were established under the auspices of the United Nations. Among the most important was the United Nations Educational, Scientific and Cultural Organization (UNESCO), which today is an association of more than 100 countries that channels a wide range of services to the underdeveloped regions of the world.

The major forms and features of foreign aid since World War II may be sketched within the following framework:

1. The International Bank for Reconstruction and Development ("The World Bank")

2. Technical cooperation and assistance programs

3. Problems and dilemmas of foreign aid

Let us see what each involves.

INTERNATIONAL BANK FOR RECONSTRUCTION AND DEVELOPMENT

While the Bretton Woods conference was setting up the International Monetary Fund in 1944, plans were also being formulated for a special type of bank that would promote the well-being of member nations. The result was the *International Bank For Reconstruction And Development*. Popularly known as the World Bank, it was established by the United Nations in 1945 to provide loans and credit for postwar reconstruction and to promote development of poorer countries. The Bank's chief function today is to finance basic development projects such as dams, communication and transportation facilities, health programs, etc., by insuring or otherwise guaranteeing private loans or, when private capital is not available, by providing loans itself. In 1956 and 1960, the Bank established two affiliated agencies, the International Finance Corporation (IFC) and the International Development Association (IDA). These help to finance higher-risk investment projects for both private and public enterprises in underdeveloped countries.

There is widespread agreement that the Bank has been deficient in several respects: (1) It has failed to stimulate sufficient private investment in underdeveloped countries; (2) it has not always made full use of its lending ability; (3) it has often been too restrictive in its lending policies; and (4) it has not always allocated its loans to the neediest nations.

Because of these shortcomings, the Bank has been only moderately successful in fostering successful development. It seems that fundamental changes in policy will be needed if the Bank is to overcome these deficiencies.

TECHNICAL COOPERATION AND ASSISTANCE PROGRAMS

By the late 1940s it became clear that the United Nations' agencies would be insufficient to meet Europe's postwar reconstruction needs. Accordingly a plan known as the Point Four Program was launched by President Truman in his inaugural address of January 20, 1949. He declared: "Fourth, we must embark on a bold new program for making the benefits of our scientific advances and industrial progress available for improvement and growth of underdeveloped areas."

The *Point Four Program* was enacted into law as part of the Foreign Economic Assistance Act of 1950. It seeks to raise living standards in underdeveloped countries by making available to them United States technical and financial assistance, largely in the areas of agriculture, public health, and education. Today, this work is carried out partly by specialized agencies of the United Nations.

In subsequent years the United States initiated other forms of technical, financial, and developmental assistance. These have included: (1) the Peace Corps, a group of mostly young people whose objective is to aid in training the masses of the underdeveloped countries; (2) the Alliance for Progress, which helps to finance economic development in Latin American countries that adopt tax and land reform; and (3) several banks that specialize in financing those functions and activities that are beyond the scope of the International Bank For Reconstruction and Development. Perhaps the most important organization established by the United States is the *Agency for International Development* (with the appropriate initials AID), a semiautonomous unit of the U.S. State Department. AID's function is to administer funds voted annually by Congress for the purpose of providing economic, technical, and defense assistance to nations that are identified with the free world.

It should not be assumed that the United States is the only source of assistance to underdeveloped countries. Since the early 1950s, the Soviet Union and other nations have played an increasingly important role. Unlike the United States, which has tended to focus on basic capital projects such as irrigation and transportation systems because they appear to be economically "sound," the Soviets have been relatively more willing to finance riskier programs, such as the construction of steel mills and cement plants, in order to encourage a faster rate of industrialization. Although there is no concrete evidence to show which of these approaches best stimulates development, certain theoretical considerations outlined later in the chapter provide some useful guides for judgment.

SOME PROBLEMS AND DILEMMAS OF FOREIGN AID

So far we have done little more than sketch the chief forms of economic assistance. It remains for us to identify some of the problems and dilemmas that arise in the provision of such assistance. The basic questions involve the classes, amounts, conditions, and forms of aid that should be given.

1. Should the United States confine its aid to specific capital projects, or should it provide aid for general programs? The International Bank, the U.S. Congress, and AID have tended to follow the project approach, because it appears more concrete and less wasteful. Economists, however (including those at AID), tend to prefer the program approach, because it permits greater flexibility, a more general use of the underdeveloped country's resources, and a recognition of the fact that capital projects which are really needed will probably be undertaken sooner or later anyhow. This latter view seems to make more sense, since in the long run a nation's economic development is not so much dependent on single projects as on a total program whose effectiveness is determined by the way in which it manages its own general resources.

2. How much aid should the United States give? Various criteria have been proposed. For example: (*a*) aid should be provided until income per capita

in the recipient country has been raised by a certain percentage; or (b) sufficient aid should be given to make up a deficit in the recipient country's balance of payments; or (c) aid should be provided in proportion to a recipient country's needs as measured by its income per capita. No matter how rational these and other criteria may seem, they ignore the fact that foreign aid is more a tool of foreign policy than an application of economic logic. Demonstrations outside an American embassy, the burning of a U.S. Information Agency library, or the thwarting of a Communist coup can influence congressional appropriations for assistance more than the rational dictates of economic experts. (See also Box 1.)

3. Should conditions be imposed on foreign aid? Many political leaders feel that assistance should be provided to any poor country that is trying to improve its economic position. But problems and dilemmas of a political and quasi-political nature tend to obfuscate this simple criterion. For instance, should aid be given to some Communist countries

---

Box 1

Sharing the Aid

Government aid accounts for only 2 percent of the under-developed world's income, but its influence is often decisive. Aid finances from 10 to 50 percent of the total investment in various third-world countries.

Most of the advanced nations conduct foreign-aid programs.

Their share of the world aid costs has been steadily increasing, while the United States share has correspondingly declined. In 1962, the United States provided about 59 percent of total official aid from the advanced nations; in 1968, 52 percent. In 1969, the United States share was down to less than 47 percent.

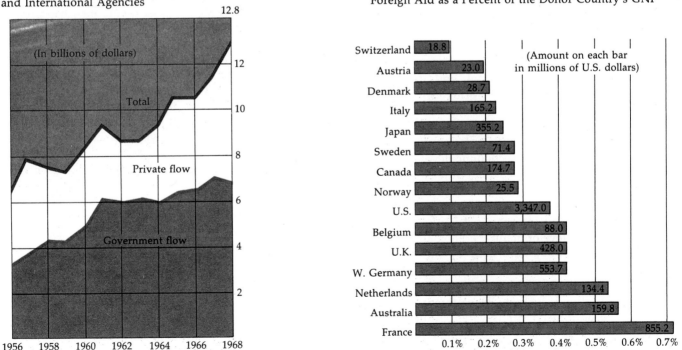

Foreign Aid to Less-Developed Countries and International Agencies

Foreign Aid as a Percent of the Donor Country's GNP

SOURCE: OECD.

like Poland or Yugoslavia, but not to others like China or Cuba? Should we confine aid only to the non-Communist countries? Should we see to it that the benefits of aid are spread throughout a country rather than being concentrated in a single class? Should aid be given only to countries that accomplish reforms (such as tax, budget, and land reforms), or should it be given without restrictions? These are typical of the problems that face the United States in its foreign-assistance programs. Some people have proposed that aid be given with no strings attached, but this would ordinarily be a foolish course for the United States to follow. With few exceptions, it should at least approve of the goals for which the aid is to be used, and impose conditions that will assure reasonable efficiency in the attainment of these goals.

4. Should foreign assistance take the form of loans or grants? The answer to this question involves not only economic, but also moral, ethical, and social considerations. In the Muslim world, for instance, interest on loans carries an unfavorable religious connotation because it implies that the lender is taking unfair advantage of the distress of the borrower. Nevertheless, some guide for policy decisions is needed. Perhaps the most feasible guide is an "international welfare criterion"—one which provides grants to countries whose per capita incomes are below a specified level, and loans to countries above that level. There seems to be no logic in giving grants to advanced Western nations for the purpose of raising their relatively high per capita consumption levels, while providing loans to underdeveloped nations for the purpose of raising their per capita incomes.

Economic Growth in the Less Developed Countries

What has been the less developed countries' record of growth? The United Nations designated as a target for them in the 1960s an average annual growth of 5 percent in real GNP. At the time this goal was thought too high. Before the end of the decade, however, it was clear that the target would be realized. As shown in Exhibit 1, the growth of GNP in real terms for the less developed countries averaged 5.2

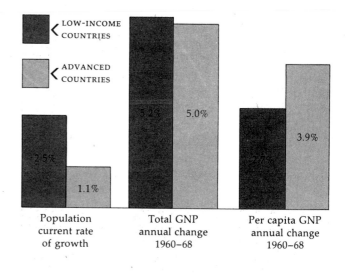

Exhibit 1

Average Annual Growth Rates, 1960–1968: Low-Income Countries Versus Advanced Countries

SOURCE: Committee for Economic Development. Data: Agency for International Development, April 25, 1969.

percent during the period 1960–1968, or approximately 2.7 percent per capita.

This is indeed an extraordinary achievement when it is considered that (1) long-run growth rates for most of Asia and Africa have been close to zero on a per capita basis, and (2) for the period 1870–1964, no country in the Western world attained overall growth rates exceeding 3.8 percent, or per capita growth rates higher than 2.0 percent. It is possible, therefore, that the less developed world after centuries of stagnation may be in the early stages of a vast transformation or developmental process.

DISPARITY IN GROWTH RATES

We must be careful of averages. Although the average growth rate is impressive, there is a wide disparity among the underdeveloped nations and regions of the world. Since 1960, for instance, the most rapid growth has taken place in certain countries of the Middle East and East Asia, while the poorest growth rates have been registered in parts of Africa, Latin America, and South Asia. Thus, countries like Israel, Taiwan, Korea, and Pakistan have shown better than average per capita growth rates, while Burma, India, and the Philippines have been below average.

Does this mean that the lagging countries are doomed to remain within the vicious circle of poverty and stagnation? Not necessarily. As will be seen later, certain policies can lead to higher rates of economic growth. Nations such as Pakistan and Guatemala, for example, were regarded in 1958 as among the poorest prospects for successful economic development, but within 10 years they made a dramatic turnaround.

ECONOMIC ASSISTANCE AND THE STAGES OF DEVELOPMENT

Countries differ in size, resource endowments, state of technology, extent of specialization, social and political environment—in short, in most of the factors that determine economic development. Since each country is unique, no single course of development is best for all. However, there appears to be a relationship between the stage of development already achieved and the form of assistance that is needed:

1. In the earliest stage there is a lack of basic skills; hence, technical assistance is needed to establish a political, social, and economic framework for development.

2. The next stage requires development of an essential infrastructure in the form of roads, harbors, communication and transportation facilities, power plants, etc. Since domestic saving is insufficient to pay for these requirements, external financing is needed.

3. The third stage is one of industrialization and agricultural modernization. At this point the nation is short of the foreign exchange it needs for raw materials and intermediate products that are part of its expanding industrial and changing agricultural sector.

4. In the final stage the nation's exports increase rapidly. The need for foreign assistance tends to diminish, and the country is able to finance an increasing proportion of its capital imports on normal commercial terms.

These four stages are only an approximate pattern of the development process; in any given country two or more of the stages may overlap. Nevertheless, the pattern tends to be typical, and it emphasizes the role of foreign assistance in conjunction with private investment as the means of helping less developed countries make the most effective use of their human and material resources.

Some Principles, Policies, and Problems of Development

Although there is no single or unified theory of development, various principles and policies would undoubtedly serve as ingredients if such a theory should ever evolve. Moreover, a modern theory would have to embrace *several* social sciences rather than economics alone. This will become evident as we discuss some of the more important concepts and issues of development theory within the framework of these critical areas:

1. Needed: an agricultural revolution
2. Escaping from the "population trap"
3. Investing in physical capital
4. Investing in human capital
5. Labor-intensive versus capital-intensive projects
6. Small versus large projects
7. Private versus community profitability

NEEDED: AN AGRICULTURAL REVOLUTION

One of the most important propositions of economic development is that in an underdeveloped economy, the growth of the industrial sector is directly dependent on technical progress in the agricultural sector. The reason is not hard to see. Underdeveloped countries have the great bulk of their human resources devoted to agriculture, and because these resources are inefficiently employed, there is a great deal of disguised unemployment or so-called underemployment. Since agriculture for the most part produces the nation's "means of subsistence," it follows that there must be improvements in agricultural efficiency so as to produce a "surplus" of food over and above what the agricultural sector itself consumes. When this happens, human resources can be spared from the farms to work in factories, where they can build an expanding industrial sector while consuming the surplus of the agricultural sector.

The operation of this important principle has been amply demonstrated in economic history. For example, the development of towns during the Middle Ages was accompanied by, and to a larger extent preceded by, improved methods of agricultural production—in particular, by the adoption of the three-field system. And the industrial revolution of the eighteenth and nineteenth centuries in Europe and the United States was the result of an agricultural revolution. This was marked by a number of major innovations, including the introduction of root crops, horse-hoeing husbandry, four-course rotation, and scientific animal breeding. The implications of developments such as these are brilliantly described in the quotation in Exhibit 2. (See also Box 2.)

Exhibit 2

The Necessity of an Agricultural Revolution

It is an instructive exercise in the interpretation of economic history to consider how far the discovery of root crops (e.g., the turnip) is responsible for the development of the past three centuries.

Root crops did two main things: they eliminated the "fallow field" and made possible scientific animal breeding. The fallow field was necessary to eliminate weeds, and the practice of planting roots in rows between which horses could hoe the ground made the fallow field unnecessary. Also the roots enabled the farmer to feed his stock through the winter and thereby prevented the monstrous slaughter at Christmas. This made selective breeding possible, with astounding results. The increased production of food probably was the principal cause of the amazing fall in mortality, and especially in infant mortality, in the middle years of the eighteenth century, to which most of the rise in population of the western world is due. The extra food enabled more babies to live and thus provided the inhabitants for the industrial cities. The new techniques enabled agriculture to produce a large surplus and thus made it possible to feed the hungry mouths of the new towns. Even if there had been no startling changes in industrial techniques, therefore, it is probable that the agricultural revolution itself would have produced many of the phenomena which we usually associate with the industrial revolution. It is possible that the vast developments in agricultural techniques which are now proceeding may foreshadow a new revolution in economic life as great as that of the last century.

SOURCE: Kenneth E. Boulding, *Economic Analysis*, 3d ed., Harper & Row, New York, 1955, p. 719n.

Box 2

India Organizes for a 'Green Revolution'

FOURTH FIVE YEAR PLAN STRESSES AGRICULTURAL DEVELOPMENT. *The "green revolution" is the great surge in agricultural production brought about in the less developed world through high-yielding seeds, greater use of fertilizer, and improved farm practices. Agriculture is increasingly the pivotal sector of development, and upon the success or failure of the green revolution hangs the fate—food or famine—of millions upon millions of our fellow human beings.*

As agriculture goes, so goes the Indian economy

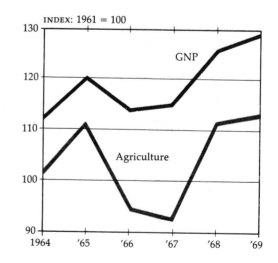

DATA: Government of India.

An agricultural revolution seldom occurs without land reform. In many underdeveloped countries, agricultural land is owned by a small number of rich people but is farmed by large numbers of poor families. Proponents of land reform have almost always advocated the division of the land among the families working it, on the grounds that the broadening of land ownership would yield important psychological and political values as well as possible economic benefits. But various studies of land reform have found that: (1) The economic effects of fragmenting land ownership have often been to reduce farm productivity rather than raise it; (2) in order to achieve increases in productivity, it is likely that land reform must be accompanied (as in Taiwan and Mexico, for example) by agricultural reform such as improvements in plant strains, irrigation systems, and fertilization programs; and (3) nominal ownership of land is less of a determinant of agricultural productivity than the availability of financial resources and skills.

ESCAPING FROM THE "POPULATION TRAP"

To solve their economic problems the less developed countries must either avoid or extricate themselves from the "population trap"—that is, they must enter a growth path along which real GNP continues to increase faster than population.

Although not all underdeveloped countries are "overpopulated," most of them are, and they tend to be concentrated in Asia, parts of Latin America, and Africa. In poor regions such as these, where population presses heavily on physical resources, accumulation or saving is difficult because the level of production is low and resources are committed primarily to agriculture in order to produce the bare necessities of consumption. As long as the pressure on food supplies continues, large numbers of people must subsist at the barest survival level, making it extremely difficult if not impossible for a nation to extricate itself from the population trap. One solution to the problem, of course, would be for people to emigrate from overpopulated to underpopulated regions, but legal, social, and economic obstacles prevent this adjustment from taking place.

The most practical solution is to meet the population problem head-on. Various studies have demonstrated quite conclusively that (1) it is cheaper to increase real incomes per capita by slowing population growth than by investing in new factories,

---

Box 3

Family Planning

The hope which the agricultural revolution promises of averting catastrophic famine can be fulfilled only if the growth of the earth's population can be brought under control. When the excess of births over deaths reaches 2 percent, a country's population doubles in 36 years. In the less developed countries, population growth rates range between 2.5 and 3.8 percent. Overpopulation and underdevelopment go hand in hand; where a country's production increase is matched by its population increase, the people of that country gain nothing.

There is more than one key to lower population growth rates. General economic development is probably the long-range solution. Parents with a reasonable expectation that their children will survive to adulthood are less likely to have large families. Parents who do not expect to be dependent in their old age on their children will probably have fewer children.

Family planning programs, however, are more immediate in their effect. Thus:

1. In India government family planning efforts are aimed at reducing a birth rate of 41 per thousand to 22 per thousand by 1978. Twenty-eight thousand planning centers have been established, and the government is committing increasing resources to this effort.

2. Korea has an effective family planning program which began in 1962. In seven years, the rate of population growth dropped from 2.9 to 2.4 percent, and the goal is a rate below 2 percent.

3. Pakistan's family planning program, in operation since 1965, has strong support from the highest levels of government down to the 90,000 village-level workers. Monetary incentives are given to doctors, rural organizations, and individuals to participate in the program.

irrigation, infrastructure, etc.; and (2) it is not so much the absolute *size* of the population as the population growth *rate* that lessens improvements in real income per capita. Because of this, a number of countries, including Japan, Korea, Taiwan, India, and Pakistan, have instituted family planning programs. These have ranged from simple counseling services to large-scale voluntary sterilization schemes (usually vasectomies). A chief difficulty is that any population control scheme may interfere with local religious traditions, thereby impeding if not preventing the development of effective programs. (See Box 3.)

An interesting *economic* approach to the problem is proposed in Exhibit 3. Although it is not likely that such a plan would ever be adopted, it provides a thought-provoking exercise for discussion.

INVESTING IN PHYSICAL CAPITAL

Until around 1960, many economists and government officials believed that massive infusions of "capital" were alone sufficient to induce economic development. "Capital is (virtually) everything" was the motto until that time; increases in real output, it was contended, were attributable almost entirely to expansions in the stock of capital rather than to increases in labor employment or improvements in technology.

Why this unusual assumption? The answer is based on the economic concept of *marginal productivity*—that is, the increase in output resulting from a unit change in a variable input while all other inputs are held fixed. This concept, it will be recalled, is associated with the familiar "law of diminishing

---

Exhibit 3

Can Population Be Controlled Through the Price System?

Can the price system be used to help plan the size of a nation's population?

Population control might be exercised through the sale of "birth rights." The government, for example, might decide that each married couple should be entitled to two "free births." Beyond that, a couple would have to pay a price if they wanted to have more children. How much would they have to pay? The answer depends on the current market price of "birth rights" or certificates, each certificate permitting a woman to have one complete pregnancy.

The government would issue a fixed amount of these certificates for a period of time. Hence the supply curve S_1 would be a vertical line, but the demand curve D_1 would be normal or downward-sloping. Through the free interaction of supply and demand, the equilibrium price would settle at OP_1 and the corresponding equilibrium quantity at OQ_1.

Over a period of time income (and perhaps population) would grow, and hence the demand curve would shift rightward to D_2. The government might then decide to issue additional certificates as shown by the new supply curve S_2. This would result in a different equilibrium price OP_2 and equilibrium quantity OQ_2. The additional certificates the government decided to issue would depend on the degree of control it wished to exercise over the market price and the size of the population.

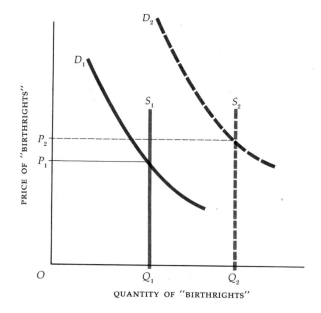

Supply of, and demand for, "birth rights"

QUESTION. *What are some of the social or economic difficulties in implementing such a system?*

returns." Thus, since most underdeveloped countries have a shortage of capital and a surplus of labor, the marginal productivity of capital in such countries is high while the marginal productivity of labor is low or close to zero (or perhaps even negative). Therefore, the infusion of large doses of capital appears to be the most effective means of raising real GNP per capita.

This conclusion, though largely correct, has been greatly modified since about 1960. Research studies and experiences in less developed countries have revealed several interesting findings:

1. There are limits to the amount of new capital that LDCs can "absorb" or utilize effectively in any given period. These limits depend on such factors as the availability of related skilled labor and the level of effective demand for the output of the new capital. It does little good, for example, to build a railroad if there is not enough skilled labor to operate and maintain it, and enough demand to support it.

2. It is necessary to have both extra capital as well as extra but related labor in order to obtain extra output. The notion that in the LDCs the marginal productivity of capital is high while that of labor is low is undoubtedly correct, but only in a general sense. When used in proper combinations, the marginal productivities of *related* classes of labor and capital may be quite high.

3. The marginal productivity of farm labor may be low because it is being employed in densely populated areas where arable land is relatively scarce. Yet in most LDCs there are large sections of fairly fertile lands which are underpopulated for cultural, political, or locational reasons. Injections of capital may help; but increases in output would be greater if the infusions of capital were accompanied by shifts in farm labor from overpopulated to underpopulated areas.

INVESTING IN HUMAN CAPITAL

Investments in physical capital must be accompanied by investments in human capital if increased productivity is to accelerate economic development. The "quality" of a people, as measured by its skills, education, and health, is more important than its quantity in influencing a nation's cultural and economic progress. It is no accident that the populations of advanced countries have higher average levels of education and greater longevity than those of underdeveloped countries.

Three main areas call for particular attention:

1. *Emphasize Basic Technical Training.* Underdeveloped countries usually suffer from a glut of unskilled and shortage of skilled workers. These nations should place more emphasis on vocational instruction and less on academic. For example, primary and secondary school curricula should be oriented toward technical education and on-the-job training in such fields as agriculture, commerce, industry, and construction rather than concentrating on preparing students for passing entrance examinations at universities in London and Paris.

2. *Develop Middle-Level Skills.* Similarly, most LDCs suffer from a relative shortage of people with middle-level as compared to high-level skills—for example, draftsmen rather than engineers, technicians rather than scientists. Universities and educational institutes should therefore focus on the development of these middle-level skills in order to enhance productivity.

3. *Utilize Foreign Experts.* The LDCs have long suffered from a serious "brain drain" that results from their most talented younger people going to universities in the advanced nations, and then remaining there instead of returning to their home countries where they are desperately needed. Although underdeveloped nations may not always be able to eliminate this form of emigration, they can minimize it by making greater use of foreign experts in domestic education and training programs.

In addition to education, there is the need for investment in health. For the most part this takes the form of public health programs to reduce mortality rates. But reductions in mortality rates result in greater population growth, thereby adding to the burden of people pressing against limited resources. The solution is not to reduce public health, but to supplement it with voluntary birth control programs. Only when men and women gain some degree of control over their lives does investment in human capital become a force for cultural as well as economic change.

LABOR-INTENSIVE VERSUS CAPITAL-INTENSIVE PROJECTS

Should an underdeveloped country that is trying to industrialize concentrate on labor-using or capital-using investment projects? Consulting economists have often had to face this issue when advising their own as well as recipient governments on the problems of administering foreign assistance.

The fundamental issue can be expressed in terms of what may conveniently be called a "labor-intensity" versus a "capital-intensity" criterion. The labor-intensity criterion states that where labor is excessive relative to capital, emphasis should be placed on projects that make maximum use of the redundant factor of production, i.e., labor, and minimum use of the scarce factor, i.e., capital. Such an approach will tend to reduce the degree of disguised unemployment while increasing industrial output.

The capital-intensity criterion, which has received much less attention than the labor-intensity argument, holds that capital-using projects should be favored even if labor is excessive, because the potential gains in productivity which are achieved by maximizing the amount of capital per worker will more than offset the loss of output resulting from unemployment. This is particularly true, it is argued, when the developing country must face competition for its manufactured products from more advanced industrial economies. Thus, in viewing the economic history of Europe during the nineteenth century, the impression is very strong that only when industrial development and modern technology took root on a large scale did a rapid "takeoff" phase of economic development really commence.

To a considerable extent, the controversy over labor-intensive versus capital-intensive investments is academic, and shows a lack of understanding of the real nature of manufacturing processes. In most industries there is little room for substitution between capital and labor because production processes within plants are *predetermined* by technology.

Combinations of labor and capital are established by engineering rather than economic requirements on the basis of previous experiences and known efficiencies. A given plant is designed with a predetermined capacity, to be operated by a certain number of workers. Although some variations in output may be made within a single-shift operation, multiple shifts are the only way in which large changes in output can be realized.

It is a fact of life, and one which often comes as a great shock to American economists serving as first-time consultants to LDCs, that the governments of these countries usually want the most modern factories and equipment—regardless of how well these investments mesh with their total economic needs and resources. Hence, the labor-intensity versus capital-intensity criterion is usually of little practical value in implementing investment decisions *within* a particular industry. On the other hand, it assumes greater realism when it is used to compare *interindustry* investments for the purpose of noting which projects will tend to be more labor-using (or capital-saving) and which more capital-using (or labor-saving). Such comparisons can help in deciding the types of industries that should be promoted by a developing country.

SMALL VERSUS LARGE PROJECTS

Should LDCs try to develop large and complex production operations, or should they concentrate first on small-scale industries?

Practical considerations favor the latter approach. In most underdeveloped countries it is highly probable that one or more of the necessary ingredients of industrialization, such as adequate capital, transportation facilities, suitable marketing channels, modern technical knowledge, and effective managerial skills, will be lacking. Small projects are therefore advantageous because they demand fewer of the scarce ingredients; at the same time they develop needed entrepreneurship, can be instituted more rapidly, and can begin to impart their beneficial economic effects to the community more quickly. Large industrial projects, on the other hand, have a smaller chance of succeeding under these conditions, and their payoffs in terms of economic benefits to the nation are likely to be a very long time in coming.

The limitations of this conclusion must be recognized, however. The distinction between "small" and "large" projects is not always clear-cut. Moreover, such projects are often complementary rather than competitive; a large manufacturing plant, for instance, will frequently stimulate the development of many small plants to provide parts and services. Hence, it cannot be stated as a firm rule that one size or scale of manufacturing is always preferable to another. The alternatives must be identified and measured in each case. For certain types of manufacturing, a large, integrated production process may be necessary in order to gain economies that will permit internationally competitive pricing. For other types of manufacturing, differences in scale may hinge on other factors besides productive efficiency: size of market, availability of the right type of labor supply, etc. In many LDCs, modern manufacturing plants and paved roads have been provided by foreign aid, while ox-drawn wagons are used to transport the goods. Hence there are more than cost factors to consider when deciding on the size of plant to be constructed.

PRIVATE VERSUS COMMUNITY PROFITABILITY

Every real investment gives rise to two kinds of returns: One may be called the "private" rate of return; the other can be referred to as the "community" or "social" rate of return. Both types may be identical under certain theoretical conditions. In reality, however, they will usually differ, sometimes by a wide margin. Therefore an explanation of the nature of these rates of return and their role as guides for promoting the best type of real investment for a particular nation or community is warranted.

The *private rate of return* on an investment is the financial rate—the rate which businessmen try to anticipate prior to investing their funds—and is the expected net profit after taxes and all costs, including depreciation. It may typically be expressed as a percentage annual return upon either the total cost of the project or upon the net worth of the stockholder-owners. From the viewpoint of investors, this rate is the most important criterion, since it measures the profitability of the investment.

The *community* or *social rate of return* (the term "community" may refer to a town, city, state, or country) is the net value of the project to the economy. It is estimated on the basis of the net increase in output which a project such as a new industry may be expected to bring, directly or indirectly, to the area being developed. The industry's contribution is measured by subtracting from the value of what it produces the cost of the resources it uses. Therefore the concept of a community rate of return is that of a net return.

A divergence usually exists between the private and community rates of return because: (1) the costs of various inputs to the private owner may be different from the cost to the economy; and (2) the value of the sales receipts to the private owner may be different from the value to the economy of having the goods produced.

For example, consider the case of a factory in a certain area. This investment may yield a high private rate of return to its owners. If the factory employs a significant segment of the area's labor force, it may also seem to be yielding a high community rate of return. However, before the latter can be ascertained, it would be necessary to consider such offsetting factors as the pattern of resource utilization by the factory, the alternative uses of those resources, the social "disproduct" created in the area, and so on.

After these considerations are taken into account, the difference between the private and community rates may be quite substantial. Indeed, a project may have a high private rate of return and a low—possibly even negative—community rate, as in the case of an industry that pollutes its environment. Alternatively, a high community rate and a low private rate may also be encountered, as might happen with certain types of public works projects. In between these extremes is a range of projects which is suitable for a particular community in accordance with its stock of human and material resources. This is the range which must be sought out, identified, and developed by the government agencies and organizations that are encouraging industrialization.

The Great Bahamian Dilemma

The seven hundred islands, islets, and cays that make up the Commonwealth of the Bahamas are everyone's ideal of a semitropical paradise. Yet within this tranquil setting a drama of the post-colonial era is being played out; and nobody can predict with certainty whether the last act will provide a tragic or a happy ending.

For most of their recorded history, the Bahamas were a British colony, populated by white settlers and the black slaves they brought over from Africa. Today, the descendants of those settlers and their slaves live in a politically free but economically dependent condition. The whites, who own or control most of the islands' wealth, constitute about one-fifth of the population; the blacks control the government, but not the economy. And both blacks and whites depend heavily on a single industry for their livelihood: the tourist trade.

Dangers of an Ebb Tide

To be sure, the tourists have brought prosperity to the Bahamas. With an income per capita of $1,260 in 1968 (the latest year for which figures are available), the people of the Bahamas are statistically better off than the inhabitants of any Latin American country, and second only to the Virgin Islanders in the Caribbean. But if the tide of tourists should ever ebb—as it did slightly in 1970—the Bahamians would have little else to fall back on. Furthermore, the Bahamas has been able to achieve its standard of living only by importing foreigners with skills that are scarce or nonexistent locally.

Until the first black government was elected in 1967, the white community ran the country for its own advantage: education was scanty and economic

development was unplanned. Admittedly, the speed of development in the past two decades provided more jobs than there were Bahamians to fill them; but in general black Bahamians did the menial work, and white Bahamians or foreigners took the better-paid, more prestigious jobs.

Painful Tradeoff

With the rise of black pride and Black Power, that situation was increasingly challenged. But the government of Lynden O. Pindling, a lawyer from the island of Andros, was faced with a painful tradeoff. On the one hand, the government had to satisfy the legitimate demands of black people for better jobs and more status; on the other, it had to recognize that the Bahamas' relatively high level of living depended in part on the continued importation of foreign workers.

In the long run, the government would like to diversify the economy. The reason for that desire is clear. About 71 percent of the GNP is accounted for by tourism; but because the islands lack industry, tourism does not bring the benefits it might otherwise do. In a report prepared for the government by a consulting firm (Checchi and Company of Washington, D.C.) the following estimates of tourist income are given for 1968. Total tourist expenditures were about $1,000 per capita of population. However, from those expenditures $61 million had to be deducted for foreign purchases, leaving a net first-round income of only $119 million, or $333 per head of population. Using the familiar multiplier technique, Checchi and Company concluded that the second and subsequent rounds of income brought the total income attrib-

utable to tourism to $161 million, or $894 per capita.

Obviously, the benefits of tourism would be increased if part of that $61 million in foreign expenditures were spent in the Bahamas. But that could happen only if more local industries were developed—and they can be developed only if the Bahamians are willing to open the doors of immigration.

In the real world, however, governments cannot always follow the dictates of economic sense. In the Bahamas, there is an upsurge of xenophobia and a split between the moderates, who believe in recruiting foreign workers for the benefit of the economy, and the militants, who believe in the Bahamas for the Bahamians.

Benefits from Chauvinism?

What we are witnessing in the Bahamas, in fact, is a conflict between aspirations and history, ambitions and reality, and economics and nationalism. An economist might well conclude that more foreign workers are a small price for the Bahamian to pay for a rising standard of living. But many Bahamians have decided that the price is too high: they prefer to sacrifice the measurable benefits of a rising GNP for the less tangible but equally real benefits of increased national identity.

Who is to say which view is correct? The Bahamian conflict, played on a small stage to a sparse audience, is likely to be repeated wherever an emergent nation is trying to rid itself of historical handicaps so that it may determine its own future.

R. B.

Can you think of any programs that could be implemented to permit the black Bahamians to qualify for the jobs that imported labor would otherwise hold?

1. The per capita income gap between the richest nations and the poorest nations appears to be widening over the long run. This is due to differences in the factors that account for economic development—for example, the quantity and quality of human and natural resources, the rate of capital accumulation, the degree of specialization and scale of production, the rate of technological progress, and the environmental (political, social, cultural, and economic) framework.

2. The International Bank for Reconstruction and Development, with its affiliates, helps to finance loans for investment projects in underdeveloped countries. The United States, through its technical cooperation and assistance programs, has also been a major source of foreign aid, along with several other countries including the Soviet Union.

3. A number of problems and dilemmas of foreign aid are of continuous concern to government officials. They involve such questions as (a) the purposes for which aid should be given, (b) the amount of aid to be provided, (c) the conditions under which aid may be extended, and (d) the forms which aid may take. Since political and foreign-policy considerations play a significant role in foreign aid, it is probably impossible to establish a firm set of guidelines that will be applicable in all situations.

4. Average growth rates of many underdeveloped countries have been extremely impressive for the years since 1960. But averages can be deceptive; actually, there is still a wide disparity in performance among the underdeveloped nations and regions of the world. A study of the development process indicates that foreign assistance in conjunction with private investment is necessary if the LDCs are to make the most effective use of their human and material resources.

5. The economic process of development can be analyzed within a framework of certain fundamental ideas. Some of the more important are: (a) the need for an agricultural revolution to release underemployed resources for industrialization; (b) the need to reduce birth rates so as to relieve the pressure of population against resources; (c) the recognition that investment in physical capital alone is not the most effective way of stimulating development; (d) the realization that investment in human capital, as well as physical capital, is important; (e) the distinction between labor-intensive and capital-intensive projects; (f) the difference between small-scale and large-scale projects, which is often more relevant for interindustry than for intraindustry investment planning; and (g) the distinction between private and community profitability, which is a useful guide for judging the desirability of an investment project.

FOR HOMEWORK AND DISCUSSION

1. *Terms and concepts to review:*
   less developed (underdeveloped) country
   disguised unemployment (underemployment)
   International Bank for Reconstruction and Development (World Bank)
   Point Four Program
   Agency for International Development
   marginal productivity
   private rate of return
   community or social rate of return

2. It is sometimes suggested that underdeveloped nations which are seeking to industrialize should simply follow the historical paths taken by the more advanced nations. After all, why not benefit from the experiences of others? Evaluate this argument.

3. In the early years of the Point Four Program, it was argued by many critics that the provision of health and sanitation facilities to LDCs would worsen their situation rather than better it because it would *reduce* their death rate. Can you explain the logic of this argument?

4. It is an interesting fact that among the first investments usually undertaken by LDCs are (1) an international airline, and (2) a steel mill. Does this make sense? Explain.

5. Rapid economic development requires that a nation save and invest a substantial proportion of its income. What would you advise for the many

LDCs whose savings rates are low or virtually zero because the great majority of their population is close to starvation?

6. "Rapid population growth is by far the single most serious obstacle to overcome as far as most LDCs are concerned." Can you suggest some *economic* approaches to the solution of this problem?

7. Evaluate the proposals made in Box 4.

Box 4

A Gloomy Dissent on South Asia

To Gunnar Myrdal, the 69-year-old Swedish economist who wrote the classic study of race relations in the U.S., An American Dilemma, *prospects for real growth in at least one part of the underdeveloped world—South Asia—are gloomy indeed. That is the clear implication of* Asian Drama, *a three-volume, 2221-page inquiry into development in eight countries, released [in 1968] by the Twentieth Century Fund. Reporting on 10 years of study and observation, Myrdal concluded that growth in South Asia is hamstrung by hostile social, cultural, and political institutions. Thus, development plans that seek to manipulate strictly economic factors are doomed to failure.*

Instead, says Myrdal, countries have to massively reform their institutions before any real growth will take place. Among his proposals:

□ *Governments must be strengthened—for better policy-making and greater immunity from ethnic, social, and geographic divisions.*

□ *Patterns of land ownership must be changed—to give the men who work the land an incentive to improve it.*

□ *Population growth must be slowed—because, says Myrdal, it "holds the threat of economic stagnation or deterioration."*

□ *Education must be modernized—to make it an instrument of development policy.*

Up to now, says Myrdal, governments have always depended on aid from the West—partly because that is what economic theories dictated, partly because the reforms needed to produce economic growth would have antagonized the ruling classes. "The population explosion has been the only major economic and social change in these countries," says Myrdal. He hopes that his book will redirect the Western point of view on development, which he says is "corrupt and biased."

SOURCE: *Business Week,* March 16, 1968.

REFERENCES AND READING SUGGESTIONS

BRYCE, MURRAY, *Industrial Development,* McGraw-Hill, New York, 1960.

COMMITTEE FOR ECONOMIC DEVELOPMENT, *How Low Income Countries Can Advance Their Own Growth,* 1966.

COMMITTEE FOR ECONOMIC DEVELOPMENT, *Assisting Development in Low Income Countries,* 1969.

ELLSWORTH, PAUL T., *The International Economy,* 4th ed., Macmillan, New York, 1969, chap. 30.

ENKE, STEPHEN, "Economists And Development: Rediscovering Old Truths," *Journal of Economic Literature,* December, 1969, pp. 1125–1139.

KINDLEBERGER, CHARLES P., *International Economics,* 4th ed., Irwin, Homewood, Illinois, 1968, chap. 22.

CHAPTER 37

Understanding Socialism and Communism

CHAPTER PREVIEW

What major types of radical philosophy have grown up as reactions to capitalism?

Who was Karl Marx, and what radical theories did he propose that virtually shook the world?

What are the shortcomings of Marx's theories, and what can we gain from an understanding of them?

How do socialism and communism today differ from the concepts of socialism and communism that were developed by Marx in the third quarter of the nineteenth century?

The history of socialism is a history of social protest. Protest against what? All the economic, social, political, and cultural ailments of capitalism.

Social protest is by no means new, of course. It can be found in writings dating back at least as far as the Old Testament. But two characteristics distinguish socialism from most earlier rebellions against established orders.

First, it is avowedly economic in nature. Second, it is international in scope and appeal. Socialism as we know it today has roots less than two centuries old. But in that time—brief as history goes—the movement has split into two streams. The first, and older, seeks to right wrongs primarily through democratic procedures. The second, communism, regards parliamentary democracy as a tool of capitalism.

Each of these broad streams has, in turn, split into further rivulets of theory and practice. But despite the many different types of socialist theory that flourish in various parts of the world, all have this much in common: *They seek to change the structure of capitalist institutions and to establish new institutions for the purpose of building a better world.*

Reactions to Capitalism: Four Radical Philosophies

Modern socialism, like capitalism, grew out of the industrial revolution. While such early British classical economists as Adam Smith, Thomas Malthus, and David Ricardo were seeking to explain and justify the economic transformation that was taking place in England during the late eighteenth and early nineteenth centuries, and were advocating policies of economic liberalism such as laissez-faire and free or unrestricted international trade, other scholars both in Britain and on the Continent were challenging the classicists with ideas of their own.

In England, for example, the factory system had already taken hold. Critics of the new order saw frightful working conditions (including cases of horrible cruelty toward very young children in the factories and mines), crowded and filthy cities, and mobs of angry workers displaced by the introduction of new machines. In France, years of wars and waste had brought crushing taxes for the support of a corrupt government, resulting in the Revolution of 1789, one of the greatest social upheavals in world history. And in Germany manufacturers were seeking to build up industrial establishments that could compete with the British.

Against this setting arose several major reactions to capitalism. They took the form of four great radical philosophies:

1. Utopian socialism
2. Marxian socialism and communism
3. Syndicalism
4. Christian socialism

We can sketch briefly the historical backgrounds of these movements before proceeding to a closer examination of the second and most important one, Marxian socialism and communism.

UTOPIAN SOCIALISM

There have always been men who have dreamed of a better world—Moses, Buddha, Plato, Jesus, Mohammed, Aquinas, and Maimonedes, to mention only a few. It is correct, therefore, to refer to such people as "socialists"—that is, as social reformers.

In this sense, the first and perhaps the best book in socialist literature was written by Sir Thomas More (1478–1535), the famous English statesman under Henry VIII, as well as saint and martyr in the Roman Catholic Church. More's great satirical classic, *Utopia* (which is often required reading in

English literature courses), was an attack on the evils of poverty, waste, idleness, and the institution of private property—the last, of course, being a pillar of capitalism. More was critical of conditions in England and certain other European states during the early sixteenth century. As a solution, he proposed the creation of a "utopia"—an ideal city-state (somewhat similar to Plato's *Republic*) in which everyone was happily employed, there was ample opportunity for cultural enrichment, and democracy prevailed with all citizens working for the good of society.

More's book stimulated a flood of publications advocating social reform—a flood which has lasted until the present day. First among these reformist writers were the so-called *utopian socialists*—a group of English and French theorists of the early nineteenth century who proposed the creation of model communities, largely self-contained, where the instruments of production were collectively owned, and government was primarily on a voluntary and wholly democratic basis. The chief propagators of such plans were, in England, Robert Owen (1771–1858) and, in France, Charles Fourier (1772–1837).

Robert Owen was by far the best known of the utopian socialists. In the gloomy squalor of factory life in Britain, this young Horatio Alger rose from an apprentice to co-proprietor and manager, in his twenties, of a huge cotton mill at New Lanark in Scotland.

Here, in the first quarter of the nineteenth century, he built a model community of neat houses and free schools for his workers and their families—a community which attracted many thousand of visitors, including political dignitaries, social reformers, writers, and businessmen from around the world. He shortened the workday, improved working conditions, and rewarded each employee in proportion to his actual hours of labor. Later he constructed similar model communities—one of them in the United States, in New Harmony, Indiana—but they turned out to be financial failures.

Owen's place as a social reformer is significant. He played a key role in giving England its first effective factory laws for the protection of workers—the Factory Act of 1844. In retrospect, of course, it is now evident that he was a prophet of improvements he never lived to see, for his ideas profoundly influenced the betterment of industrial life both in Britain and the United States.

In 1884, a movement known as *Fabian socialism* was founded in England. An outgrowth of utopian socialism, it advocated gradual or evolutionary reform within a democratic framework. The movement has attracted many prominent people over the years. Some of its most active supporters were the economists Beatrice and Sydney Webb, who helped to build the British Labour Party; the distinguished British dramatist George Bernard Shaw; and the noted economist and historian G. D. H. Cole.

MARXIAN SOCIALISM AND COMMUNISM

Toward the middle of the nineteenth century, a series of events began to unfold in Europe that strongly influenced the future course of the world.

In December, 1847, on one of London's typically damp and cold winter days, a small but clamorous group of labor leaders met at a convention of the newly formed Communist League. There were strong currents of anxiety and trepidation in the air, for although England was relatively calm at the time, the Continent was on the verge of an upheaval. Through an almost continuous belt stretching from France to Russia, there was seething discontent over the long prevailing miseries of poverty, injustice, and political and social intolerance. No one doubted that a series of revolutions would sweep Europe in the coming months.

Among those who attended this historic meeting were two relatively young and unknown intellectual radicals: one was Karl Marx, aged twenty-nine; the other was his close friend and associate, Friedrich Engels, aged twenty-seven. They had been commissioned by the League to prepare a statement of principles and a program for action that would help incite the masses and foment revolt against the existing order of society. Their tract opened with the following inflammatory, dramatic, and ominous words:

> A spectre is haunting Europe—the spectre of Communism. All the powers of old Europe have entered into a Holy Alliance to exorcise this spectre; Pope and Czar, Metternich and Guizot, French radicals and German police-spies.

After pages of historical analyses and predictions, their treatise ended with the following exhortation:

> The Communists disdain to conceal their views and aims. They openly declare that their ends can be attained only by the forcible overthrow of all existing social conditions. Let the ruling classes tremble at a Communist revolution. The proletarians have nothing to lose but their chains. They have a world to win.
> Working men of all countries, unite!

In the following month, January, 1848, this statement of principles and objectives was published as a pamphlet under the title of the *Communist Manifesto*. It is significant, not for its economic content, for it had practically none. Its importance lies in the manner in which it presented Marx as a brilliant and forceful revolutionary.

But there is another side of Marx—that of a ponderous scholar and deep philosophical economist—which is of much greater significance. In most of the three decades that followed publication of the *Manifesto*, Marx devoted almost all his working time to developing an extensive and extraordinary "scientific" theory, which was eventually published as a mammoth treatise entitled *Das Kapital* (1867). This was the so-called "Doomsday Book of Capitalism"—a powerfully written work in which Marx predicted the revolutionary overthrow of the capitalistic system and its ultimate replacement by a *classless* society composed only of workers, or proletariats, who owned and operated the means of production for the benefit of all.

Marx called this ultimate state "communism" in order to distinguish it from various "unscientific" forms of socialism, such as utopian socialism, which existed during his time. Much of the spirit of his ideas was incorporated in the Russian and Chinese revolutionary systems of communism that were established in the twentieth century. In contrast, there were also founded in some Western nations various evolutionary or moderate Marxian systems represented largely by social-democratic types of political parties. These groups have preferred to retain the title of socialism in order to help bridge the gap between certain features of Marxian theory and the rest of the socialist movement. In general,

Marxism is by far the most significant of the radical philosophies to have emerged as a reaction to capitalism.

SYNDICALISM

The third great radical philosophy spawned by the industrial revolution was "syndicalism." This movement, which was both a strategy of revolution and a plan for social reorganization, was influenced by the wave of anarchism that spread through parts of Europe during the late nineteenth and early twentieth centuries.

The advocates of *syndicalism* demanded the abolition of both capitalism and the state, which they viewed as instruments of oppression, and the reorganization of society into industry-wide associations or syndicates of workers. Thus there would be a syndicate of all the steel mills, which would be owned and operated by the workers in the steel industry; a syndicate of all the coal mines made up of workers in the coal industry; and so on. In this way, the syndicates, which were fundamentally trade unions, would replace the state, each one governing its own members in their activities as producers, but leaving them free from interference in all other matters. The chief exponent of syndicalism was the French social philosopher Georges Sorel (1847–1922); ironically, his views later influenced the growth of fascism.

In the United States the syndicalists organized a revolutionary industrial union in 1905 called the Industrial Workers of the World (IWW). The union was founded in Chicago by Eugene V. Debs, William D. Haywood, and Daniel De Leon—all of them well-known names in the history of radicalism. It was the group's avowed aim to overthrow capitalism and to establish socialism by calling a general strike throughout industry, locking out employers, and seizing the nation's factories. Despite the organization's success in gathering a peak membership of 100,000 before World War I and in leading over 150 strikes, it suffered from growing internal dissension and almost fell apart after the war. However, it continued to survive. Today, with its distinctly moderate philosophy, it is a small but vigorous union.

CHRISTIAN SOCIALISM

The late nineteenth century also saw the rise of the Christian socialists, whose ideas were the most moderate of the four great radical philosophies. The movement was started in France by a Catholic priest; it then spread to England, where it caught on among a number of Protestant intellectuals and clerics, and subsequently reached the United States. Variations of it still exist in these and other countries.

In general, *Christian socialism* is a movement of various church groups to preach the "social gospel" —a type of social legislation and reform that is grounded in theology. It seeks to improve the well-being of industrial workers by advocating the formation of labor unions, the passage of legislation, and above all by appealing to employers to respect the dignity of workers as men and as Christians, rather than as so much muscle or physical power. It also repudiates the Marxian doctrine of the class war or revolution. Among the leading forces in this movement have been Pope Leo XIII, the "workingman's Pope," whose famous encyclical *Rerum Novarum* (1891) enunciated these principles; Pope Pius XI, whose encyclical *Quadragesimo Anno* (1931) reaffirmed them; and Protestant theologians like Reinhold Niebuhr and Paul Tillich.

The Economic Theories of Karl Marx

Among the various radical philosophies that emerged as reactions to capitalism during the nineteenth century, none has had deeper or more widespread effects than that of Karl Marx. Indeed, his views, in one form or another, are the basic beliefs of more than a third of the inhabited globe.

Marx was a "philosophical economist." He was deeply influenced by the writings of the eminent early-nineteenth-century German philosopher Georg Hegel, and in particular by the latter's *dialectic*. This technical term denotes a method of logic or reasoning in Hegelian philosophy. It holds that any concept, which may be called a *thesis,* can have meaning only when it is related to its opposite or contradictory concept called an *antithesis;* the interaction of the two then forms a new concept of understanding called a *synthesis*. Thus the concept of "high" (thesis) evokes the opposite concept of "low" (antithesis), and the two then interact to form the new concept of "height" (synthesis). Similarly, contradictory concepts like "light" and "dark," "truth" and "falsity," "being" and "not being," interact to form new concepts, each of which brings us a step closer to understanding the ever-changing nature of the real world.

In Hegelian philosophy, the dialectic process, through its reconciliation of opposites, becomes a method of interpreting history. Thus in the evolution of cultures, we observe a process in which the higher form of culture triumphs over the lower form; in the development of art, one "period" is succeeded by another; in the history of religion, primitive and simplistic types of worship give way to more sophisticated forms and concepts. In general, history is a record of progress from lower to higher manifestations of the dialectic principle.

How did these Hegelian ideas influence Marx's thinking? We can seek to answer this question by sketching briefly the fundamental doctrines that appear in his enormous work *Das Kapital* (translated *Capital*) published in 1867:

1. Economic interpretation of history
2. Theory of value and wages
3. Theory of surplus value and capital accumulation
4. The class struggle
5. Theory of socialist and communist evolution

These doctrines constitute the framework of Marxian theory. Although they are attributed to Marx, they were formulated during his many years of association with his close friend and intellectual collaborator, Friedrich Engels. Each man had a profound influence on the other.

ECONOMIC INTERPRETATION OF HISTORY

Marx sought to discover the basic principles of history. His method was to construct what he regarded as a completely logical system in which he presented in scientific fashion the laws of historical development, the sources of economic and social power, and a prediction of the inevitable future.

In order to predict the future course of events, Marx had to understand the causal forces that were at work. This, he believed, could only be done by studying the past. Hence he looked for the fundamental causes of historical events, and he found them in the economic environments in which societies develop.

According to Marx, all great political, social, intellectual, and ethical movements of history are determined by the ways in which societies organize their social institutions to carry on the basic economic activities of production, exchange, distribution, and consumption of goods. Although economic motives may not always be the sole cause of human behavior, every fundamental historical development is basically the result of changes in the way in which one or more of these economic activities is carried out. This, in essence, is the *economic interpretation of history*.

Thus in the Marxian system, economic forces are the prime cause of change—the alpha and omega of history—which operate with the inevitability of natural laws to determine the development of a society. Even the Protestant Reformation of the sixteenth century, which for all intents and purposes was a major religious movement in world history, was cloaked in ideological veils according to Marx, thereby serving to conceal its true causes, which were fundamentally economic.

Dialectical Materialism

This philosophy became known as *dialectical materialism*—a logical method of historical analysis used by Marx which employed the philosopher Hegel's idea that historical change is the result of conflicting forces and that these forces are basically economic or materialistic. In the Marxian view of history, every economic system, based on a set of established production, exchange, distribution, and consumption relationships, grows to a state of maximum efficiency and then develops internal contradictions or weaknesses which cause it to decay. By this time the roots of an opposing system have already begun to take hold; eventually this new system displaces the old while absorbing its most useful features. This dynamic process continues, with society being propelled from one historical stage to another as each new system triumphs over the old.

THEORY OF VALUE AND WAGES

The second major doctrine in Marxian economics is the theory of value and wages. This, of course, was also a fundamental area of concern to the classical economists who preceded Marx—including Smith, Ricardo, and others. But Marx, unlike the other classical economists, used these concepts to a different end in explaining the historical development and future course of capitalism.

To Marx, the term "value" had the same meaning as it had to other orthodox economists both before and after: *value* is the power of a commodity to command other commodities in exchange for itself; this power is measured by the proportional quantities in which a commodity exchanges with all other commodities. Likewise, to Marx and other economists, the *price* of a commodity is its power to command money in exchange for itself; price is simply the "money name" of the value of a commodity.

But what determines the value of a commodity? The answer, according to Marx, is labor. In his words:

That which determines the magnitude of the value of any article is the amount of . . . labor time socially necessary for its production. . . . Commodities, therefore, in which equal quantities of labor are embodied, or which can be produced in the same time, have the same value. The value of one commodity is to the value of another, as the labor-time necessary for the production of one is to that necessary for the production of the other. As values, all commodities are only definite masses of congealed labor time.

In general terms, therefore, if it takes twice as much labor-time to produce coats as hats, the price of coats will be twice the price of hats. Note from the last sentence of this quotation that Marx did not restrict his concept of labor-time to direct labor spent on the production of commodities; he included indirect labor as well, such as the labor-time necessary to construct the factories and machines which are then used to produce other goods. Therefore:

Since capital and all other commodities are congealed labor, they are all reducible to the common denominator of labor-time, and will exchange for one another at prices that are proportional to the amount of labor-time they contain.

From this theory of value, it was a short step for Marx to develop his theory of wages. In his view, a mature capitalistic society consists of only two classes—a capitalist class which owns and controls the means of production, and a working class which owns and controls nothing and is subservient to the capitalist class. (The landowning class, at this relatively advanced stage of capitalism's development, has declined to a position of minor importance.) This leads to the following theory of wages:

The capitalist class finds, in its competitive struggle to earn profits, that it must pay the lowest possible level of wages to the working class. The wages it will pay, therefore, will be at a subsistence level— a wage level which is just high enough for the working population to maintain itself, based primarily on its physical or biological needs and to a lesser extent on its social and customary needs.

This theory of wages, it may be noted, did not originate with Marx. It was the familiar *subsistence theory of wages* which Marx adopted from the classical economists who preceded him.

THEORY OF SURPLUS VALUE AND CAPITAL ACCUMULATION

When Marx combined his theories of value and wages, the logical outcome was the third feature of his theoretical system: the doctrine of surplus value. From this, there emerged the natural process of capital accumulation.

In Marx's model, surplus value arises in the following way: When a worker is employed in the production of a commodity, it is the capitalist who sets the length of the working day. Thus on the one hand, the value of what the worker produces is determined by the labor time embodied in the commodity; on the other hand, the wage that the worker receives is determined by the "subsistence level" of living. The worker does not stop producing when the value of what he creates is equal to his subsistence wage;

instead, he continues to produce, and the value that he creates over and above his subsistence wage represents "surplus value," which goes to the capitalist. In numerical terms, the capitalist may set the working day at 12 hours, but the worker may produce a value equal to his subsistence wage in 7 hours; the remaining 5 hours of his labor time is, therefore, surplus value which is literally appropriated or stolen by the capitalist.

To Marx, surplus value is the driving force of the capitalistic system—the key incentive that prompts capitalists to carry on production. Efforts on the part of capitalists to increase surplus value may take the form of (1) increasing the length of the working day, (2) intensifying or speeding up the worker's production (by offering "piece rates" or other incentives), and (3) introducing labor-saving machinery, thereby permitting some workers to be released while those who remain are made to work longer hours or more intensively.

Capital Accumulation

What does the capitalist do with the surplus value which, according to Marx, has been literally stolen from the labor of workers? Marx's answer is that the capitalist uses part of the surplus for his personal consumption, and part to acquire more labor and machines. He acquires these, of course, because he expects to get back more money than he lays out. His inflow of surpluses, over and above his money outlays, continues in an unending series from one production operation to the next, thereby generating a sequence of capital accumulations. Thus, whereas other economists contended that capitalists were engaging in "abstinence" or "saving" when they acquired funds to hire more labor for production, Marx argued that the funds which capitalists "saved" were stolen from workers in the form of surplus value.

These ideas, which lie at the heart of the Marxian model of capitalism, may be summarized briefly:

Surplus value is the difference between the value that a worker creates as determined by the labor time embodied in a commodity that he produces, and the value that he receives as determined by the subsistence level of wages. Surplus value is not created by the capitalist, but is appropriated by him through his exploitation of the worker; hence the capitalist is a robber who steals the fruits of the laborer's toil. The accumulation of capital comes from surplus value, and is the key to, as well as the incentive for, the development of a capitalistic system.

It is interesting to note that Marx harbored no particular animosity toward the capitalist as such, even though he characterized him as a greedy robber baron. In Marx's view it was the competitive capitalistic system itself that was evil. The capitalist was merely a participant in the great race; he had to exploit and accumulate or else he would be exploited and accumulated.

THE CLASS STRUGGLE

What are the consequences of capitalist production? In order to answer this question, Marx turned to an examination of the past, and again used the method of dialectical analysis—thesis and antithesis—to interpret the historical process.

All history, he said, is composed of struggles between classes. In ancient Rome it was a struggle between patricians and plebeians and between masters and slaves; in the Middle Ages it was a conflict between guildmasters and journeymen and between lords and serfs; and in the modern society that has sprouted from the ruins of feudal society, class antagonisms have narrowed down to a struggle between two opposing groups—the oppressing capitalist or bourgeois class and the oppressed proletariat or working class. The former derive their income from *owning* the means of production and from exploiting the labor of workers; the latter own nothing but their labor power and, since they are dependent for a living upon the receipt of a wage, must sell their labor power in order to exist.

What is the role of the state in this two-class society? Marx's answer was precise: "The state," he said, "is nothing but the organized collective power of the possessing classes." It is an agency controlled by the bourgeoisie to advance its own interests, and its power "grows stronger in proportion as the class antagonisms within the state grow sharper." The state, in short, is an agency of oppression.

The Consequences of Capitalist Production

The class struggle might go on indefinitely, according to Marx, were it not for certain "contradictions" that automatically and inevitably develop within the capitalistic system. Among the more important ones are these:

Increasing Unemployment. The capitalists' drive to increase their surplus value and to accumulate capital results in the displacement of labor (i.e., in modern terminology, technological unemployment), and in ever-increasing misery as a "reserve army of the unemployed" builds up.

Declining Rate of Profits. As capital accumulates, a growing proportion of it goes into physical capital such as labor-saving machinery, which yields no surplus value, while a declining proportion of it goes into human capital or labor, which is the sole producer of surplus value. Hence the capitalist's rate of profit—or the surplus value that he appropriates from labor—tends to be a declining percentage of the total capital that is accumulated.

Business Cycles. With increasing unemployment, a declining rate of profit, and the tendency for wages to remain at the subsistence level, uncertainty and instability are inevitable; depressions recur "each time more threateningly" as capitalists find themselves under continual competitive pressure to acquire more physical capital and to displace workers.

Concentration and Monopolization of Capital. Competition among capitalists thus becomes increasingly intense. A dog-eat-dog situation develops as small capitalists are either fatally weakened or absorbed by a few larger ones. In this way capital becomes concentrated in large-scale industrial units or monopolies. As Marx put it, "hand in hand with this centralization" of capital goes the "expropriation of many capitalists by the few."

Finance Capitalism and Imperialism. Marx implied that a fifth "contradiction" would emerge from the monopoly stage of capitalist development. The nature of this contradiction was amplified in the early twentieth century by V. I. Lenin, the founder of Soviet Russia. Lenin argued that the growing tendency toward concentration and monopolization of capital would produce an economy dominated by "finance capital"—a situation in which huge business trusts or monopolies, in conjunction with a handful of large banks, control and manipulate the masses. Those who manage finance capital would then reach out beyond their own national boundaries, forming cartels and international combines to dominate and control the markets and resources of other nations. When this happens, the economy has reached the state of "capitalistic imperialism"—the highest stage of capitalism.

Summary

Marx concluded that these conditions, especially the first, imposed miseries and hardships on workers which they would not tolerate indefinitely. The working class, he said, would eventually revolt against the capitalist class and bring about a system in which economic justice prevails. Before we examine the nature of this change, let us summarize the foregoing Marxian ideas briefly.

The *class struggle* represents an irreconcilable clash of interests between the bourgeoisie or capitalist class and the proletariat or working class. The source of this clash is the surplus value which capitalists steal from workers, resulting over the long run in increasing unemployment, a declining rate of profit, business cycles, concentration of capital, and finance capitalism and imperialism.

According to Marx, the class struggle will eventually be resolved when the proletariat overthrows the bourgeoisie and establishes a new and equitable economic order.

THEORY OF SOCIALIST AND COMMUNIST EVOLUTION

Thus Marx held that capitalism must someday receive its death blow at the hands of the workers. When this happens, capitalism will be succeeded by socialism which Marx regarded as a *transitory stage* on the road to communism. This stage will have two major characteristics:

1. *"Dictatorship of the proletariat"*—a state of affairs in Marxian socialism in which the bourgeoisie have been toppled from power and are subject to the

control of the working class; in other words, the "expropriators have been expropriated," and capitalists' properties are under the management of the proletariat who are also in control of the state.

2. *Payment in accordance with work performed*—that is, laborers will earn wages, each worker receiving "for an equal quantity of labor an equal quantity of products," and "he who does not work, shall not eat".

Socialism, in Marxian ideology, may thus be defined as a transitory stage between capitalism and full communism—a stage in which the means of production are owned by the State, the State in turn is controlled by the workers (i.e., "dictatorship of the proletariat"), and the economy's social output is distributed by the formula: from each according to his ability, to each according to his labor.

Communism, in Marxian ideology, is the final, perfect goal of historical development. It means: (1) a classless society in which all men live by earning and no man lives by owning; (2) the state is nonexistent, having been relegated to the museum of antiquities "along with the bronze ax and the spinning wheel"; and (3) the wage system is completely abolished and all citizens live and work according to the motto: *"from each according to his ability, to each according to his needs."*

This last quotation, it may be noted, represents the essence of pure communism, and is one of the most famous phrases in all of literature.

Evaluation of Marxian Theory

Now that we have sketched the main features of Marxian theory, it is appropriate for us to discuss its achievements and failures. It is evident that Marx sought to reach three major objectives:

1. To develop a *theory of history* which would explain the fundamental causes of capitalist development.

2. To formulate *theories of value, wages, and surplus value* which would describe the basic processes at work in the capitalist economy.

3. To establish a foundation for *revolutionary socialism and communism.*

We may evaluate Marx's theories in terms of these objectives.

THEORY OF HISTORY

As you recall, Marx's interpretation of history was based on *economic* thesis and antithesis. Although he recognized that political, social, and other factors influenced historical development, he regarded them as distinctly subordinate. To him, the basic or causal forces were fundamentally economic, centering around the activities and institutions relating to production, exchange, distribution, and consumption of goods.

Critics have pointed out that this is a one-sided, oversimplified interpretation because it leaves out or fails to give sufficient weight to the many noneconomic forces and institutions in history. Despite this criticism, many distinguished historians have long believed that Marx's interpretation of history provided the first deep awareness of the importance of economic forces in the historical process.

In the past several decades modern historians have increasingly incorporated economic causation in their historical studies. Although it cannot be said that Marx was solely responsible for this trend, there is general agreement that his approach to the study of history played a significant role.

THEORIES OF VALUE, WAGES, AND SURPLUS VALUE

Marx's theory of value, we have seen, was a *labor* theory of value. In essence, his argument can be stated in the form of a syllogism—i.e., a type of reasoning in logic consisting of two premises or assumptions, and a logical conclusion which follows directly from the premises. Thus, according to Marx:

> Labor creates all value
>
> Labor does not receive all of the value it has created
>
> Therefore, labor is being cheated

It should be remembered, of course, that according to Marx: the first premise is true because capital and all other commodities are nothing more than congealed labor; the second premise is true because labor receives a subsistence wage which is less than the value it creates; and the conclusion is true because capitalists literally appropriate or steal the surplus value of labor for themselves.

Was Marx correct? We can answer this question by offering the following criticisms of his ideas, based on economic principles and concepts learned in previous chapters.

Neglect of Entrepreneurial Functions

By attributing all value to labor alone, Marx neglected the functions performed by the entrepreneur as a risk taker and organizer of the factors of production. Without him, labor would be an amorphous mass. It is the entrepreneur who gives "shape and form" to labor by bringing workers together, providing them with capital, and giving them a purpose for working. In a socialistic or communistic society, these functions might be performed by the government or by a committee of workers, but in any case they are functions that must be performed by somebody.

Failure to Recognize Demand

Marx's theory of value, based as it was on the labor-time embodied in a commodity, failed to recognize that the normal value of a good is as much a result of demand as of supply. As we know already, in a competitive capitalistic system the concept of long-run normal value is that of an equilibrium value which reflects diverse consumer demands bidding for the services and products of scarce factors of production. This means that consumers must be willing and able to buy and to express their preferences through the price system if prices are to serve the function of inducing both human and nonhuman resources into production. Marx did not fully understand this role of the price system, and hence his theory of value provided an inaccurate and unrealistic measure of the real values at which commodities are exchanged.

Inadequate Theoretical Support of Surplus Value

Surplus value, according to Marx, arises because workers are paid a subsistence wage which is less than the value of the commodities that they create. The question we must now ask is whether this theory of surplus value is plausible. The answer appears to be no, for the following reasons:

Definition of Subsistence is Vague. Marx did not use the concept of subsistence in a consistent manner, nor did he define it as a determinate quantity. At certain times he employed the term in a biological sense to refer to the goods needed for physical well-being, and at other times he used it to mean the "conventional" goods to which people become "socially accustomed."

Competition Among Capitalists Will Eliminate the Surplus. Marx placed strong emphasis on the competitive forces that exist in a capitalistic society—and in particular the highly competitive relationships among capitalists themselves. This means that if wages are sufficiently flexible to adjust to the "socially accustomed" level of living, there is every reason to believe that the surplus itself will be eliminated as capitalist employers bid higher and higher wages for the services of employees. For if an employee yields a surplus to *his* capitalist employer, it will pay for *some other* capitalist employer to hire him away at a higher wage. Competition among capitalists will thus bid wages up to a level at which the surplus no longer exists.

These are among the chief reasons to conclude that Marx's theory of surplus value lacks theoretical support. Further, there is no evidence to indicate that there exists in the capitalistic system a fund of value of the type that Marx conceived in his concept of surplus value.

REVOLUTIONARY SOCIALISM AND COMMUNISM

Marx predicted that the increasing misery of workers would prompt the proletariat class to overthrow capitalism and to replace it first by socialism and then by communism. This, he said, would be the inevitable result of the "internal contradictions" that were inherent in capitalism and that would eventually destroy it.

Was Marx's prediction correct? For the most part no—at least not in the sense that he meant. For de-

KARL HEINRICH MARX

1818–1883

If it is true that a man is ultimately judged by the influence of his ideas, then Karl Marx surely ranks as one of the most important individuals who ever lived. For his thoughts have shaped the policies of nations and have affected the lives of millions of people.

Who was Karl Marx? He was born in Treves, Germany, the son of a successful lawyer with liberal philosophical leanings. The young Marx was educated at the Universities of Bonn and Berlin, and received his doctorate in philosophy from the University of Jena in 1841 at the age of 23.

In Marx's undergraduate years his radical ideas began to flourish when he fell in with an extremist student group called the Young Hegelians—disciples of the German philosopher Georg Hegel. During the 1840s while Marx was still in his twenties, he spent short periods in Germany, France, and Britain, always one step ahead of the police who continually sought to expel him because of his incendiary articles in newspapers and other periodicals extolling communism and revolution, and his attacks against religion and utopian socialism. "Religion," he once wrote in a quotation that has since become famous, ". . . is the sigh of the oppressed creature, . . . the opium of the people." As for utopian socialism, it was "unscientific" because it lacked an understanding of the role of history and of the certainty of the class struggle.

It was also during this period of the 1840s that Marx became involved with the two most important people of his life: one of them was named Jenny von Westphalen, daughter of an aristocrat who was a privy councilor of Treves; the other was

Culver Pictures

spite the mistakes that exist in the Marxian model, the views of its author have long been accepted by hundreds of millions of people in many nations. In some totalitarian countries his theory was adopted intact; in many nontotalitarian nations a brand of "modified" or "revised" Marxism developed. We may refer to the latter as *post-Marxism*—a type of socialism which is not necessarily antagonistic to capitalism, but which seeks to achieve its goals through a much greater degree of government regulation and control than exists in market-oriented capitalistic systems. More will be said about this later.

CONCLUSIONS

We may conclude this evaluation of Marxian theory by answering briefly three fundamental questions that are often asked.

a gallant named Friedrich Engels, son of a wealthy industrialist.

Marx married Jenny whom he had known since childhood; she was literally "the girl next door." The match itself was a study in opposites: she was slender, beautiful, and genteel; he was short, stocky, and caustic. But they loved each other deeply, and she gave up her refined and prestigious life in Treves in return for his unstinting devotion to her and to their children. Their life together was one of great hardship and extreme poverty as they moved from one slum to another while Marx struggled to earn a living—a task which, as a writer, he never mastered.

Marx met Engels during a brief stay in Paris in 1843. The two men struck up an immediate intellectual rapport—a fact which was especially surprising because Engels' father was a rich businessman who owned factories in Germany and England, and the young Engels never exhibited any aversion to the social and pecuniary advantages which this background afforded him. Engels became Marx's lifelong friend, collaborator, and alter ego, as well as his benefactor. Indeed, there is no evidence that Marx ever had any other close friends.

In 1849, after being hounded by police and expelled from three countries, Marx moved to London, where he lived, except for brief intervals, until the time of his death. Here he existed in the depths of poverty, depending for bare survival on small and irregular remunerations of $5 to $10 that he received for articles submitted to the New York Tribune, and on the benevolence of Engels who, for some unexplained reason, led a double life: he was fully in accord with Marx's anticapitalistic views, yet he also managed his father's factory in Manchester and even held a seat on the Manchester Stock Exchange.

Marx sacrificed everything for his research, an activity which engaged his full time and effort from morning until night in the great library of the British Museum. The result, after many years of painstaking work, was the publication of his enormous treatise, Das Kapital (vol. I, 1867). But his health was never too good; in 1881, after the death of two of his five children, his devoted and tired wife Jenny also passed away, and Marx followed her two years later. His eulogy was delivered by Engels and the funeral was attended by eight persons.

Engels labored on Marx's notes for the next several years, thereby making possible the publication of volumes II and III of Das Kapital (1885, 1894). Four additional volumes titled Theorien über den Mehrwert (Theories of Surplus Value) were published from still other notes in the period 1905–1910. On the basis of these and many other writings, Marx has come to be regarded as an economist of major significance. But note this important point: It was Lenin, not Marx, who fashioned the content of communism; Marx predicted its eventual occurrence, while it remained for Lenin to design the final structure. This he did in his writings and speeches during the first two decades of the present century, and in his founding of Soviet Russia after the Revolution of 1917.

1. Have Marx's Deductions Been Borne Out?

Some of Marx's deductions of the so-called "economic consequences of capitalist production" have evidently not been realized. Thus: (a) The proletariat, far from experiencing increasing misery, has in fact experienced a long-run growth of real wages and a rising standard of living. (b) The rate of profits has not declined, nor have business cycles been entirely an overproduction phenomenon as Marx claimed. (c) The proletariat and the capitalists, at least in the United States, have not congealed into two distinct and opposing classes; indeed, they often overlap to the extent that the great majority of corporation stockholders are also workers.

There is thus no question that some of Marx's most important theoretical deductions have turned out to be fallacious.

2. Are There Elements of Truth in Marx's Predictions?

However, despite his incorrect predictions of economic events, we cannot conclude that Marx was totally wrong. Some of his prophecies contained important grains of truth. For example: (a) It would be foolish to deny that technological, cyclical, and structural unemployment have continued to plague the capitalistic system. (b) There has certainly been a growth in the concentration of capital and monopoly power since the time of Marx's writings during the third quarter of the nineteenth century (although there is considerable disagreement among economists as to the direction of monopoly trends during most of the present century). (c) Although capitalism has not ended in final collapse, it was certainly dealt a serious blow in 1930 with the emergence of a prolonged and desperate depression that eventually ushered in many new measures of social reform.

On this score, therefore, some of Marx's prophesies were disturbingly meaningful.

3. What is the Value of Marxian Theory?

We are thus led to conclude that Marx put his finger on some of the most important economic problems of our society—problems of unemployment, business cycles, and industrial concentration and monopoly, to mention a few. Most of our efforts in previous chapters were devoted to the development of methods for curing these ills within a framework of democratic capitalism. It is appropriate, therefore, that in the remainder of this book we focus our attention on the ways in which Marxian theory has been adapted and modified by socialist nations in their efforts to solve some of these and other basic economic problems that confront them.

The Meaning of Socialism and Communism

When the nineteenth century drew to a close, Marxism had already become an international movement of considerable significance. But it was a movement whose members had divergent viewpoints. As a result, the followers of Marx began to divide into two factions: One of these consisted of a large and heterogeneous majority called "revisionists"; the other was composed of a smaller but more homogeneous minority known as "strict Marxists."

The basic philosophies of these two groups is implied by their names. The revisionists believed that the theories of Marx must be *revised* in order to accord with conditions of the times and that socialism should be achieved by peaceful and gradual means through a process of evolution rather than revolution. The strict Marxists, on the other hand, adhered to a literal interpretation of their master's teachings, contending that the workers of the world formed one great brotherhood which must revolt in order to overthrow the capitalistic system and establish a dictatorship of the proletariat.

Since the early part of this century, the revisionists have been in control of most of the socialist parties of Western nations—the Unified Socialist Party in France, the Social Democratic Party in Germany, and the Socialist Party in the United States—to mention only a few. In Britain, mass support for socialism has come from the Labour Party, whose leaders are primarily Fabian socialists, and in Scandinavia from large-scale consumer cooperative movements. Christian Socialist parties have also exercised influence in some countries.

By the end of World War I, all ties between the moderate revisionists and the strict Marxists were severed. The latter group withdrew completely from the socialist parties and became known as Communists. As we shall see below, although modern socialism and communism have evolved as branches of the same Marxian trunk, they are vastly different both politically and economically. In general, since the first third of this century, socialist governments have been in power at one time or another in a number of democratic countries, including England, France, Sweden, Norway, Denmark, Australia, and New Zealand. In these and various other nations, socialist leaders were placed in office through free elections. This suggests that when we talk about socialism we are referring to *democratic* socialism of the liberal reformist type, as distinguished from authoritarian socialism or communism such as exists in the Soviet Union and China.

SOCIALISM BETWEEN WORLD WARS I AND II

In order to appreciate the meaning of modern democratic socialism, it is desirable that we sketch briefly the historical development of socialist thought and practice in the period between the two World Wars.

During the 1920s and 1930s, socialists of peaceful Marxian persuasion both in Europe and America launched a renewed and vigorous attack against the shortcomings of capitalism. Expressions like "economic inequality," "chronic unemployment," "private wealth and public poverty," and "degeneration of social and cultural values" become familiar shibboleths. In Europe, social democratic parties were strongly committed to revisionist Marxism, the solidarity of the working class, and the ultimate establishment of socialism by democratic means as a way of correcting the deficiencies of the capitalistic system. This was an era of great ferment in socialist activity.

The Theoretical Model

At the same time, some economists at European and American universities began to grapple with a question that eventually evolved into one of the most interesting controversies in the history of economics. The essence of the problem may be summarized by noting that in the theoretical or pure model of capitalism there are at least three important features: (1) the means of production are privately owned; (2) product and resource prices are freely determined in competitive markets; and (3) resources are allocated efficiently in accordance with consumer and occupational choice. Now, if we adopt the classical definition of socialism as an economy in which the means of production are owned by society, the question we ask is this:

Can a socialistic economic system, seeking to be democratic rather than authoritarian, and lacking the prices that are freely established in competitive markets, achieve the same degree of efficiency in resource allocation as the pure model of capitalism, without destroying the basic economic freedoms of consumer and occupational choice?

This question, it may be noted, is the fundamental theoretical problem of democratic socialism.

Notice that the issue is complicated by the fact that the system must remain democratic. It might be easier to achieve greater efficiencies in resource use by *telling* consumers what they can have and by *ordering* workers to their jobs, but such actions would be completely contrary to the basic philosophy of democratic socialism.

This problem became the subject of widespread discussion in the 1930s, and was finally resolved in 1938 with the publication of a remarkable theoretical model of a socialist economy. The chief architect of the model was a well-known Polish economist, Professor Oskar Lange.

According to this theoretical model, a democratic socialist economy could be administered by a Central Planning Board which would set prices *"as if"* the competitive market had set them. The Board would, for example, manipulate prices in the product and resource markets with the objective of equating supplies and demands, thereby assuring that equilibrium was maintained without surpluses or shortages. In this way the Board, through *trial-and-error*, would guide the factors of production into their most efficient uses in accordance with the wishes expressed by households—*all through the operation of a price system which permits freedom of consumer and occupational choice.*

This type of economy, the socialist theorists contended, would yield a double benefit; it would achieve efficient resource utilization as in the theoretical competitive model of capitalism, while at the same time overcoming the major disadvantages of real-world capitalism by bringing about: (1) a more equitable distribution of income resulting from the elimination of private ownership; (2) an adjustment of production according to consumer demands; and (3) a continuous high level of employment assured by stable investment policies by government.

DEVELOPMENTS SINCE WORLD WAR II: A NEW CONCEPT OF SOCIALISM

The outbreak of World War II prevented these ideas from being put into action. Nor were they implemented after the war, because of three major developments which reduced much of the enthusiasm for "traditional" socialism:

1. Mixed capitalist-socialist economies like Austria, Belgium, England, France, Italy, the Scandinavian nations, and West Germany went through a rapid post-war recovery in the late forties and then experienced moderate to high rates of economic growth during the fifties. This alone was sufficient to prove that capitalism was not an anachronistic economic system, as many socialists had contended.

2. Various conservative governments in Western Europe adopted far-reaching social welfare measures which even transcended the New Deal policies instituted by President Roosevelt during the 1930s. So significant were these new changes that by 1960, socialist leaders throughout the Western world were pointing proudly to policies which their parties had long advocated that were now laws.

3. A number of nationalization policies (involving government ownership of the means of production) that had been adopted in varying degrees by some West European nations turned out to yield disappointing results. Many socialist leaders agreed that such nationalization policies created problems of excessive bureaucratization and inefficiency which were even greater than the problems they were originally designed to solve. Further, among the more sophisticated socialists there was a growing realization during the fifties that by carefully constructed legislation, tax policies, and other devices, a government could control its important industries without necessarily owning them.

These events led to a substantial change in the mainstream of socialist thinking. By the early 1960s, many of the European social democratic parties severed completely whatever remaining ideological ties they had with Marx, abandoned their traditional opposition to private property and their goal of total social ownership, and turned their attention instead toward "improving the mix" in already mixed economies. As a result, the distinction between socialism and the modern "welfare state" has now come to be recognized as only a difference in degree. In general terms, the following definition of modern socialism sums up the present position of most social democratic parties in the Western world:

Socialism of the modern democratic form is a movement which seeks to improve society's well-being by: (1) permitting predominately private ownership of the means of production; (2) instituting public ownership only where it appears necessary in the interests of society; and (3) placing maximum reliance on the market economy while supplementing it with government direction and planning in order to achieve desired social and economic objectives.

NOTE. This definition represents a fundamental change in socialist thought since about 1960. Prior to that time it was the primary objective of socialism to replace private property with public ownership of the means of production and distribution.

As C. A. R. Crosland, a distinguished socialist and British Labor Party leader, stated in the late 1950s, there is now considerable doubt about the compatibility of State monopoly and the freedoms that socialists cherish; further, we are ". . . less concerned about who owns a factory, and more concerned about who manages it and how, and whether it is working according to socialist plans."

These views, it may be noted, have subsequently been echoed by many other democratic socialist leaders throughout the Western world.

WHAT IS COMMUNISM?

This modern concept of socialism, of course, does not even remotely resemble the type which Marxists envision as the stage through which society must pass in its evolution from capitalism to full communism. How does Marxian ideology differ from this view? We can perhaps best answer this question by expressing three operating principles of modern communism.

1. Social Ownership of Property

Communist countries have developed the Marxian theory that private property is not only the means by which capitalists can exploit workers in order to gain an unearned share of the social product; it is also the basis for dividing society into two great classes. Accordingly, state ownership of the means of production is fostered in communist nations, with some concession to small-scale private ownership in the production or distribution of consumer goods. These concessions, however, are only temporary; they exist during the transitional stage of Marxian socialism and are expected to disappear when full communism is achieved and all property is in the generalized possession of everyone.

2. Government Planning and Control

A second keynote of communism today is extensive government planning and control of the economic system. The method of *command* largely replaces the method of the free market. Capital investment, innovation, technological change, income distribution, resource allocation—all these strategic economic activities and functions are part of a centralized decision-making process rather than the result of free market interactions between buyers and sellers. Although market mechanisms may be used—such as price increases or decreases to balance supplies and demands—they are used to fulfill the objectives of the plan or to regulate certain segments of the economy which the leaders do not wish to regulate themselves.

3. System of Rewards and Punishments

In accordance with Marxian ideology, communist nations today do not claim to have arrived at the stage of full communism where the State is non-existent and workers live by the motto: "From each according to his ability, to each according to his *needs.*" Instead, they claim to be in the preparatory or transitory stage of socialism where income is distributed by the formula: "From each according to his ability, to each according to his *labor.*" Payments to workers in communist countries today, therefore, are based on skill, rate of output, and type of work performed—or in other words on the kinds of incentives that are used in capitalistic and in democratic socialistic countries. This system of rewards has been supplemented by a system of punishments, including various types of penalties and even forced labor for those found guilty of excessive absenteeism, tardiness, and other poor work habits.

But rewards and punishments are expected to vanish when full communism is achieved, since people will then work cheerfully and efficiently for the common good.

Finally, from a noneconomic standpoint, communism as we know it today is also a political system involving one-party rule and the indoctrination of the population to full participation in the communist movement.

We can summarize the foregoing ideas with the following definition:

Communism today, as an economic system, is based on: (1) social ownership of property including most of the means of production and distribution; (2) government planning and control of the economy; and (3) a scheme of rewards and punishments to achieve maximum productive effort. According to communist leaders, the system that exists in communist nations today is not true communism; instead, it is socialism of the type which Marxian ideology holds as being preparatory for the attainment of full communism.

SUMMARY OF IMPORTANT IDEAS

1. The major reactions to capitalism have been utopian socialism, Marxian socialism and communism, syndicalism, and Christian socialism. Of these, the Marxian reaction has had the most significant impact on the political and economic relationships of nations.

2. Karl Marx was strongly influenced by the early-nineteenth-century German philosopher Georg Hegel, and particularly by the latter's use of the dialectic—the reconciliation of opposites—as a method of interpreting history. This approach provided much of the basis for Marx's (and Engel's) theories. The Marxian system can be represented by five major features which are the pillars of his model:

a. Economic interpretation of history

b. Theory of value and wages

c. Theory of surplus value and capital accumulation

d. The class struggle

e. Theory of socialist and communist evolution

3. Critics of Marx have pointed out that: (a) his economic interpretation of history is oversimplified and one-sided, although there has indeed been a growing emphasis on economic causation in modern historical studies; and (b) his theories of value, wages, and surplus value neglected the entrepreneurial functions, failed to recognize the role of demand in the determination of value, and rested on inadequate theoretical foundations. Despite these criticisms, there are elements of truth in Marx's predictions, and much is to be gained from a knowledge of Marxian theory in understanding some of the pronouncements and policies of communist nations today.

4. Socialism in the Western world is conceived as a democratic process. Since about 1960, the mainstream of socialist thinking has been disassociated completely from Marxism, and has come increasingly closer to matching the concept of a "welfare state."

5. Communism today is not the pure communism that Marx envisioned; instead, according to communist leaders, it is the transitory stage of socialism which Marx predicted, and merely a preparatory state for the eventual attainment of full communism. The future date of this millenium is not known, however, and its prediction is not ventured by the leaders of the communist movement.

FOR HOMEWORK AND DISCUSSION

1. *Terms and concepts to review:*

utopian socialism	subsistence theory of wages
Fabian socialism	
syndicalism	surplus value
Christian socialism	class struggle
dialectical materialism	socialism
economic interpretation of history	"dictatorship of the proletariat"
value	communism
price	

2. Why should a student of today be familiar with the nature and origins of radical ideas, some of which are well over a century old?

3. What is meant by an "interpretation of history"? Can you suggest several different types of interpretations? In your previous history courses in high school or college, which interpretations were stressed?

4. Marx was aware of the fact that direct labor is only one of several inputs used in production, and that raw materials, machines, and other resources were also necessary. How, then, could he argue that labor alone was the basis of value?

5. According to Marx, would there be such a thing as surplus value if capitalists paid workers "what they were worth"? Explain.

6. Do you believe that there is such a thing as a "class struggle" in the Marxian sense? Why or why not? (HINT: Can we really divide a complex social structure into dichotomous or opposed subclasses?)

7. If we prove that Marx's theory of surplus value is logically incorrect, does this mean that workers *in fact* are not exploited in our capitalistic system? Explain by defining what you mean by "exploitation." (NOTE: If you were a profit-maximizing employer, would you hire someone to work for you if the added value he created were less than the wages you paid him?)

8. What major shortcoming do you find in the Marxian model of capitalism?

9. Marxism, it has been said, is like religion: "For those who believe, no explanation is necessary; for those who do not believe, no explanation is possible. Logical arguments, therefore, are not the grounds for acceptance or rejection. It is emotion, not logic, that is the influencing factor. This is why Marxism remains as the basic ideology of several nations and many millions of people throughout the world." Do you agree? Can you add anything to the proposition?

10. How did socialist ideology compare with communist ideology prior to about 1960? What have been the major changes in these ideologies since 1960?

11. Is it possible to have political and social freedom in a command economy? Is it possible to have a market economy without political and social freedom? Explain.

REFERENCES AND READING SUGGESTIONS

BELL, JOHN FRED, *A History of Economic Thought,* 2d ed., Ronald, New York, 1967, chap. 15.

LOUCKS, WILLIAM N., and WILLIAM G. WHITNEY, *Comparative Economic Systems,* 8th ed., Harper & Row, New York, 1969, chaps. 5–13.

NEWMAN, CHARLES P., ARTHUR D. GAYER, and MILTON H. SPENCER, *Source Readings in Economic Thought,* Norton, New York, 1954, pp. 240–86.

PRESTON, NATHANIEL STONE, *Politics, Economics, and Power,* Macmillan, New York, 1967, chaps. 3, 4.

CHAPTER 38

The Command Economies of Russia and China

CHAPTER PREVIEW

What is the nature of the Soviet economy—its methods of operation, its accomplishments, and its failures?

How has the economy of Mainland China progressed since the Communist takeover in 1949, and what would be an optimum economic policy for that country today?

Is a gradual convergence taking place between communism and capitalism—an eventual meeting of East and West?

Russia and China remain mysterious to most Americans. Though they are constantly in the news, their economic policies and performance are widely misunderstood. Indeed public opinion surveys made in the United States have found that of those people who believe they know something about the Soviet Union and China a surprisingly large proportion think they have puny economies, simply because their levels of living have not caught up with that of America. Such beliefs can lead to serious misconceptions.

Why should we study the Soviet Union and China? The answer is that they are the major examples of what are known as *planned economies*— that is, economic systems in which the government directs resources for the purpose of deciding what to produce, how much, and possibly for whom. These are fundamental problems in every economy—capitalist, socialist, and communist. What distinguishes communist economies from all others is their virtually total reliance on government mandate rather than market forces for solutions to these problems.

The Soviet Economy

In November, 1917, the revolutionary Bolshevik (later known as Communist) party of Russia, under the leadership of V. I. Lenin, overthrew the government and, five years later, established the Union of Soviet Socialist Republics. The ultimate objective of the party, which identified itself with the "dictator-ship of the proletariat," was to establish Marxian socialism and eventually full communism in Russia and throughout the world, thereby ending what it referred to as the "want, misery, and injustice of capitalist society."

When the Communists took over, Russia was poor, predominantly agricultural, but with the fifth largest industrial complex in the world (after the United States, England, Germany, and France). To revive the war-ravaged economy, Lenin inaugurated the moderately capitalistic New Economic Policy of 1921 which restored temporarily a limited system of private enterprise. Lenin died in 1924 and was succeeded by the general secretary of the Communist party, Joseph Stalin, who ruled the country as an absolute dictator until his death in 1953.

Under Stalin, the Soviet system became a command economy with the primary objective of raising itself to the status of a major industrial and military power. It eventually attained these goals with little outside help, largely through a series of so-called Five-Year Plans—the first in 1928—which aimed at rapid industrialization and centralization of the economy's resources. By the time World War II broke out, Russia had achieved among other things: (1) a planned economy which could operate without unemployment; (2) a major expansion of industrialization with all factories, mines, railroads, and public utilities owned by the state; (3) a virtual elimination of private manufacturing and private trade; and (4) a practically complete socialization of all stores and farms, either by outright government ownership or by collective ownership on a cooperative basis. Social and cultural achievements included the opening of educational opportunities to the common people, a substantial reduction in the illiteracy rate, government assistance for working mothers and their children, and free medical and hospital care for most citizens.

But these accomplishments were not realized without heavy costs. Industrialization and defense were pushed at maximum speed with almost no concern for the severe privations imposed on the public, and a ruthless reign of police terror liquidated dozens of Stalin's political opponents while sending more than 9 million other persons to prison or Siberia.

This brief historical sketch is useful only as a background, for the Soviet economic system has undergone many significant changes since World War II. We can best understand the Soviet economy of today by surveying it in terms of the following distinguishing features:

1. Soviet economic institutions and organization
2. Soviet economic planning
3. The challenge of economic growth
4. Reorganization and changes in the Soviet economy

In discussing these aspects of the Soviet system, we shall often find it meaningful to provide comparisons with the United States.

SOVIET ECONOMIC INSTITUTIONS AND ORGANIZATION

Every society is characterized by certain institutions —that is, established ways of doing things based on customs, practices, laws, etc., which in combination affect its organizational structure. We may examine the more important ones in the Soviet economy.

Social Ownership of Industry

The Soviet Union defines its economic system as socialist, not communist. The former, according to Marxian doctrine, is a preparatory stage in the attainment of full communism. Unlike the United States, therefore, all means of industrial production in the U.S.S.R. which require the use of hired labor are owned by "society," represented by the government. Although individuals such as professionals and handicraftsmen can work for themselves, they must do so without the help of hired labor; except for a few special cases (e.g., domestic servants), no individual may employ another for a wage or for private gain. In general, the publicly owned enterprises in the U.S.S.R. are not significantly different in form from similar types of publicly owned firms in the United States such as the TVA, the U.S. Post Office, and municipally owned public utilities.

Public ownership, however, does not apply to

consumer goods. In the Soviet Union, virtually all consumer goods are privately owned. And, as in the United States, people may own their own automobiles, houses, furniture, clothing, government bonds, savings deposits, and so on.

Social Ownership of Agriculture

Agriculture in the U.S.S.R. is organized along somewhat more complex lines. Two types of farms are in operation, both socially owned:

1. *State farms* are agricultural lands owned and operated as state enterprises under government-appointed managing directors. Workers and administrators are hired to run the farms, and are usually paid set wages as well as bonuses if their work exceeds basic norms of output.

2. *Collective farms* are agricultural cooperatives, consisting of communities of farmers who pool their resources, lease land from the government on a long-term basis, and divide the profits among the members according to the amount and kind of work done by each. Collective farms, which are subject to detailed government regulation, are the dominant form of agriculture in the Soviet Union.

Collective farms were introduced in the late twenties as a compromise between socialist principles and political expediency. They were meant to reduce the hostile resistance of the agrarian class (at that time about 80 percent of the Russian population) to total centralization and control of agriculture. Under the collectivization laws, the farms must sell the bulk of their output to the government at low preset prices, and can dispose of the rest as they wish—usually through "farmers' markets" or bazaars. These are free markets where prices and quality are invariably higher than in government stores.

The agricultural sector has lagged far behind the industrial sector in terms of efficiency. There are several reasons for this: (1) much of the fertile land is located too far north, where growing seasons are short and dry; (2) economic incentives have usually been inadequate to stimulate sufficient productivity; (3) continued heavy emphasis on industrialization and defense has drained able-bodied men from the rural areas, leaving a disproportionate number of women, older men, and children in the agricultural labor force; and (4) government investment programs have typically given greater weight to capital expansion in industry than in agriculture, leaving the farms with inadequate power and mechanical facilities. Despite the government's efforts to correct these shortcomings through various agricultural reform measures, it is evident that the Soviets have not yet solved the problem of farm inefficiency.

Economic Incentives

A fundamental feature of the Soviet economy is its widespread use of monetary rewards to induce people to exert the efforts needed for accomplishing specific tasks. Two major forms of economic incentive exist:

First, differential rewards are paid to persons in occupations requiring different skills. For example, within the high-income groups are academic research scientists, ballet and opera stars, and university professors of science; in the middle-income groups are engineers, physicians, teachers, and skilled workers; in the lower-income groups are technicians, semiskilled workers, and unskilled workers.

Second, productivity incentives are provided for workers and managers. Thus basic pay rates for workers in industry and on state farms are usually calculated not in relation to hours of work, but in terms of units produced, with special graduated rates paid to those who exceed the norm. (It is interesting to note that piecework payments of this type have long been bitterly criticized by labor unions in the United States and other noncommunist countries as exploitative.) Managerial incentives, on the other hand, consist of bonuses and various types of "fringe benefits" including housing, free meals at the plant, and so forth.

Are economic incentives of this type contrary to Marxian thinking? The Soviets contend they are not. In a *socialist* society, they say, people have not yet been prepared for full communism, and therefore incentives may be needed to persuade individuals to produce at their full potential.

Freedom of Consumer and Occupational Choice

In the competitive model of capitalism, there is both consumer sovereignty and freedom of consumer choice. That is, consumers register their demands for goods through the price system, and producers compete with one another to fulfill those demands. In such a system the consumer is theoretically king; he not only decides *what* is produced, but also is free to choose *how much* he wants from the supplies that are available.

In the Soviet economy the State decides which and how many consumer goods will be produced (except for the free market portion of goods produced by collective farms). It then places these goods in government stores—under normal conditions without rationing—and at equilibrium prices that it believes will clear the market in a given period. Consumers are then free to purchase the products or not, as they see fit, at the established prices. Hence it is correct to say that generally speaking there is freedom of consumer choice in the Soviet Union, but there is not consumer sovereignty.

In a similar vein, under normal conditions there is also freedom of occupational choice. As was suggested above, the State sets differential wage and salary structures according to types of occupation, skill, geographic location, etc., and workers are largely free to choose the kinds of jobs for which they can qualify.

Broadly speaking, therefore, Soviet households have much the same freedoms of consumer and occupational choice as do households in the United States and most other countries. Although there are exceptions to this tendency, the Soviet leaders have found through hard experience that the preservation of such freedoms provides for more orderly markets and much greater administrative efficiency.

Money and Taxes

The monetary unit in the Soviet Union is the ruble, but in effect two kinds of money circulate: (1) currency, which is used for transactions within the household sector and between households and the state; and (2) bank money, which is used in the government sector among state enterprises. These currencies are convertible into one another for business purposes (e.g., to pay wages), but such conversion is under strict government control. The dual monetary system is designed to prevent the excessive issue of currency in the household sector and to facilitate budgetary control over state enterprises.

Taxes in the Soviet Union, as a percentage of national income, are much higher than in the United States, and probably higher than in most other countries. The reason is the Soviet government's greater proportion of total expenditures: its military outlays; its welfare spending on socialized medicine, free education, and numerous other benefits; its complete operation of state enterprises; and its financing of most new investment in industry, trade, communication, and transport. What are the chief sources of the revenue that pays for these expenditures? In the United States it would be primarily a graduated personal income tax and to a lesser extent a corporation income tax—the latter averaging roughly 50 percent of corporate profits. But in the Soviet Union the bulk of the government's revenue comes from a profits tax on state enterprises and a sales tax—called a "turnover" tax—on goods sold to the public. Although the rates vary, the profits tax has tended to bring in about 40 percent of the State's annual revenue, and the sales tax about 30 percent.

SOVIET ECONOMIC PLANNING

The Soviet Union has been a planned economy since the twenties, but its economic plans have varied from time to time. What do we mean by an *economic plan?* It may be defined as a detailed method, formulated beforehand, for achieving specific objectives by governing the activities and interrelationships of those economic organisms (e.g., firms and households) that have an influence on the desired outcome.

In the Soviet Union, economic plans have taken the form of enormous comprehensive blueprints for coordinating the parts of most or all of the economy. Beginning in 1928, the State embarked on a series of Five-Year Plans (with occasional shorter or longer ones at different times), each with the purpose of achieving certain objectives. Since there is no need for us to explore the details of each of these plans, it will be more useful instead to examine their general features.

The Problems of Balance and Flexibility

Some of the difficulties that arise very early in the planning process involve the problems of achieving appropriate balance and flexibility among the interrelated parts of the economy.

In formulating a five-year plan, for example, production targets are established not only for enterprises and industries but also for geographic regions of the economy. If the plan is to be ideal, it must make full utilization of all resources in the most efficient way. Therefore, the quantities of inputs to be produced, such as iron, steel, and glass, must be balanced by the quantities of outputs such as houses, automobiles, and other products to be produced which utilize these inputs. Otherwise, there will be excess production of some of these commodities relative to others with the result that certain resources will be used inefficiently.

These difficulties are further complicated by the fact that the planned balances must be dynamic rather than static—that is, they must allow for growth in the quantities of outputs and inputs to be produced over a period of time. This requires that the plan be sufficiently flexible to permit readjustment of any of its parts at any point during the life of the plan in the event that the desired targets are not being met as originally intended.

How is this needed flexibility achieved in Soviet planning? One major device is the formulation of plans which sketch the intended goals of the economy for the coming year—its volume of consumption, its level and distribution of investment, its national product, and so forth. Thus a five-year plan (or any other plan of several years duration) may be regarded as a series of consecutive one-year plans, each of which picks up where the various segments of the economy left off at the end of the preceding year's plan.

The Formulation of Objectives

The various five-year plans that have guided the Soviet Union since 1928 have emphasized different objectives based on economic, social, political, and military considerations. For the most part, the biggest problem has been deciding on the proportion of the nation's limited resources to be devoted to the production of consumer goods, capital goods, and military goods. In general, the major objectives of the plans, stated in qualitative rather than quantitative terms, have been to:

☐ Attain the highest standard of living in the world by overtaking the advanced capitalistic countries in output per capita as rapidly as possible.

☐ Build a major military complex with the most modern nuclear capabilities

☐ Provide for universal health and education so as to further the nation's growth and scientific progress

☐ Achieve a substantial degree of economic independence from the outside world

On the whole, the effort to attain these goals has made it necessary for the Soviet planners to follow a threefold strategy: (1) place major reliance on agriculture to supply the food and raw materials needed for rapid industrialization; (2) give high priority to the use of the country's limited resources for the development of heavy industry such as steel, machine-building, fuel, and power; and (3) give low priority to the production of consumer goods. The consequences of these policies on the Soviet Union have been painful. Standards of living have remained low compared to the United States, and agriculture has experienced repeated failures and setbacks which have been the cause of serious concern to government leaders.

The Details of Planning

A comprehensive economic plan of the type prepared in the Soviet Union is extraordinarily detailed. It includes a number of "subplans," such as an output plan, a capital budget or expenditures plan, a financial plan, a labor utilization plan, and various regional plans. A few words may be said about the problems of preparing the first two of these plans: the output plan and the capital budget.

Output Plan. In the preparation of the output plan, the government leaders must be concerned both with (1) consumer preferences, and (2) sacrifices in production.

The Soviets recognize that, on the one hand, it would be irrational to produce goods that consumers desire if the production of such goods interfered with the overall objectives of the plan. On the other hand, it would be equally irrational to produce goods that consumers do not desire—that is, would not purchase in sufficient quantities at specified prices. This helps to explain why advertising exists in the Soviet Union, although on a much smaller scale than in the United States: it not only seeks to influence the marketing of new products, but also helps to clear the market of unsold goods.

Soviet planners must take relative production costs into account when they set output targets. Labor costs are relatively easy to measure because they are reflected by wage rates which serve as an indication of the "real costs" of labor, i.e., the sacrifices in production that must be made in order to attract labor out of alternative employments. But the means by which the Soviet leaders measure nonlabor costs of production are not always so clear. For example, some experts in the field believe that the Soviet authorities do not attempt to include in their estimates of money costs all the real sacrifices in production resulting from the use of natural resources, capital funds, and land. Nor do they include the value of distributing goods (e.g., warehousing, transportation, etc.) in their calculation of national income, because they regard distribution activities as unproductive.

These Soviet attitudes are due partly to the difficulties of measurement, partly to the influence of Marxist ideology, and partly to the belief that certain types of price and cost calculations are "capitalistic economics." As a result, there is no doubt that the Soviet planners must often sacrifice economic efficiency in order to attain desired objectives.

Capital Budget. How do the Soviet authorities determine the output of specific types of producers' goods—for example, a bulldozer versus a power shovel or a truck versus a railroad flat car? Such decisions are governed by the capital budget. This is a list of specific investment projects arranged in decreasing order of priority according to each project's *coefficient of relative effectiveness* (CRE)—a technical term used in the Soviet Union to mean the expected payoff or percent rate of return on a capital investment; it is akin to the concept of "marginal efficiency of investment" encountered in Western economics. A particular investment project is thus either accepted or rejected by the planning authorities according to whether its CRE is above or below the prescribed minimum. In this sense, the CRE is seen to be a device for rationing the scarce supply of capital among alternative uses, and its method of calculation is quite similar to procedures used by business economists and financial managers in the United States. The factors that enter into its calculation include economic costs, interest rates, and the returns and expenses expected on the project over its estimated life.

Adoption and Supervision of the Plan

When the Soviet planners complete their plan, it is reviewed by the government, by the representatives of labor and management, and by the Communist Party. The advice and suggestions of these groups may then be incorporated by the planners before they submit it to the Politbureau or the highest organ of the Communist Party for the resolution of disputes and final approval. Supervision of the plan is then entrusted to various agencies whose responsibility is to see it through to fulfillment. In the process of supervision, however, the plan is revised periodically to correct for unforeseen developments and errors. As stated earlier, therefore, the "plan" is actually a series of plans rather than a rigid once-and-for-all arrangement.

THE CHALLENGE OF ECONOMIC GROWTH

The major challenge to the Soviet Union, of course, is to achieve rapid economic growth. All its other goals can be subsumed under this.

How successful have the Soviets been in attaining a high rate of economic growth? The answer is difficult because various problems of definition and measurement are encountered in dealing with Soviet data, and this makes comparisons with the United States that much harder. Nevertheless the available data suggest the following growth patterns:

1. During the 1950s and 1960s, the growth of real GNP in the Soviet Union averaged approximately 6 percent a year, compared with about 4 percent for the United States.

2. Within the two decades of the 1950s and 1960s, the growth of the Soviet economy slowed down, but its annual percentage increases in output nevertheless exceeded those of the United States. Hence, real GNP in the Soviet Union continued to increase relative to the United States, but at a slower rate in the sixties than in the fifties.

3. In 1950, real GNP in the Soviet Union was about one-third that of the United States; in 1970 it was approximately one-half. However, almost the entire gain was made during the 1950s; the ratio of Soviet to United States GNP was fairly constant at almost 50 percent during the 1960s.

How can we explain this substantial growth record? Is Soviet success based on some magic formula? The answer is no. It is simply due to a consistent economic policy which has stressed several underlying factors: (1) the maintenance of a high proportion (between 1/4 and 1/3) of gross investment to GNP; (2) the granting of major priority to the development of heavy industries such as steel, machine-building, power, etc., all of which have high multiplier effects on income and output; (3) the construction and importation of vast quantities of modern equipment; and (4) the training of hundreds of thousands of technicians to operate and maintain the physical plant. These factors have been combined with a rapid increase in the nonagricultural labor force, thereby helping to provide the supply of labor needed in the industrial sector.

REORGANIZATION AND CHANGES IN THE SOVIET ECONOMY

In the early 1960s, the Soviet economy experienced an alarming slowdown in growth rates. At the same time, several studies published in the United States and abroad came up with a number of interesting conclusions. Some of the more important ones were

that: Soviet labor productivity is lower than United States labor productivity, but Soviet capital productivity is at least equal to if not greater than that of the United States; Soviet labor-and-capital productivity combined is substantially lower than the level prevailing in the United States; the concentration on output goals by Soviet planners has resulted in a neglect of cost, efficiency, and quality considerations; and Soviet ideology has brought about unrealistic policies which tend to prevent the development of adequate measures of economic efficiency. (For example, Soviet planners long refused to follow the "capitalistic" practice of calculating interest on capital investment.)

To repeat: These were among the typical criticisms that were hurled at the Soviet economy prior to the mid-sixties—and some of them, of course, are still heard from reliable sources today. Moreover, they were criticisms leveled not only by outsiders, but also by some economists inside the Soviet Union as well.

"Libermanism"

Among the insiders was Professor Yevsei Liberman, a spokesman for the reformers who led the way to certain significant reorganizational changes that began taking place in the Soviet economy during the years 1965–1966. Western observers have dubbed these changes "Libermanism." Fundamentally, they took three major forms:

1. Production targets and delivery dates should still be established by a central authority, but enterprise managers should be free to make decisions on all other matters, including hiring workers, setting wages, varying product mixes, contracting with suppliers, and making small investments in new equipment. This would enable managers to exercise greater control over their production efficiency and the salability of their products.

2. A system of incentives should be introduced in which workers receive bonuses, welfare benefits, etc., according to the efficiency of the enterprise. Efficiency should be measured by the ratio of the firm's profit to its total capital investment (i.e., by its "return on assets," primarily fixed assets). In

order to encourage improvements in quality and the production of commodities that consumers want, the profits of enterprises should be linked to goods *sold* rather than to goods *produced*.

3. Pricing methods should be revised so as to reflect production costs more accurately, and interest should be charged (in the form of a tax) on all fixed and working capital made available to enterprises.

Liberman's proposals thus placed greater reliance on economic indicators and incentives and less on administrative fiat as a basis for Soviet economic planning. Do these changes sound too "capitalistic" for Western observers? Liberman anticipated that they would, and hence was prompted to express himself on the matter in a Russian publication (*Literaturnaya Gazeta,* March 5, 1966) in the following way:

> These methods fit in well within the framework of a centralized planned economy. There is no need for us engaging in economic hypocrisy and claiming that we can solve, by methods of direct administration, tasks which can best be solved by methods of economic stimulation. Scientific prognostication and optimal planning, effective stimulation of production through profitability—such is our economic weapon, and we are confident that it will bring us victory.
>
> Make no mistake, you Western observers, this will not be a step back to capitalism, but a step forward, to the consolidation and development of socialism. There is not even a hint here of distribution by capital [i.e. profit-making in the capitalist sense], it is only a more efficient distribution by labor, i.e., compensation of each enterprise for genuine services to its only boss—society.

Various reform measures adopted by the Soviets since the mid-sixties have adhered closely to Liberman's proposals, and other reforms are still underway. In the opinion of most economists, these measures, as Liberman suggested above, are not a closer step toward capitalism. For it is the disposition of the surplus over cost in Soviet enterprises that is the critical consideration. The economic process under socialism may generate a profit or surplus, but as long as this profit is not distributed to private owners, it does not play the overriding role in re-source allocation that it does in a capitalistic economy. (See, however, Box 1.)

The Economic Policies of Communist China

In 1949, the Communist People's Liberation Army swept victoriously into Peking, the ancient capital of China. Under the leadership of Mao Tse-tung, it took control of a largely underdeveloped economy containing one-quarter of the world's population in an area one-third larger than the continental United States.

What was the nature of the Chinese economy when the Communists came into power? First of all, the country had been devastated by many years of war with Japan. Foreign trade was negligible, labor productivity was extremely low, currency was wildly inflated, there was virtually no saving or capital formation, and farming was primitive. The Chinese people were in the deepest conceivable state of poverty, and the economy was battered and disordered.

This, in bare essence, was the economic heritage of the Chinese Communists. Consequently, one of the chief tasks facing the administration in 1949 was to restore some order to the disintegrated economy and to embark on as rapid a rate of economic growth as possible. Accordingly, it launched the first Five-Year Plan of 1952–57 in which the following key features were stressed:

1. Emphasis on a high rate of investment in heavy industry such as iron and steel manufacturing, mining, and machinery construction.

2. Retention and moderate expansion of the handicraft and small-scale industries.

3. Reorganization of agriculture through (*a*) redistribution of land from wealthy to poor peasants, and (*b*) collective ownership of farms by groups of households with payment to each on the basis of labor days worked.

This plan took the form of a concentrated drive toward industrialization which was perhaps the

Recent Failures in Russia's Economy

In 1965, the Soviet party unveiled a massive program of higher prices for farm products and huge investments in agriculture, both designed to step up food production sharply. The Premier also announced a major reform of Soviet economic organization designed to provide incentives for better work and to give factory managers more independence so they could increase efficiency. For a time these programs worked. In retrospect, the years 1966 to 1968 look like the golden age of the Soviet economy, years in which industrial output and farm production sprinted ahead.

Superficially, 1969's slowdown of industrial growth and the actual decline of farm production can be explained by temporary factors, notably bad weather which cut factory output and the grain harvest. But recent Moscow comment makes plain that Soviet leaders fear much more than bad weather is involved, that long-run retarding forces are at work. Certainly one such long-term force is the frequent tendency of Soviet planners to over-commit the economy, to try to do more than they have resources to accomplish.

But a behind-the-scenes battle rages as to where responsibility for slowdowns should be assigned. A conservative group argues that the fault lies with economic reform. By giving factory managers and other local officials excessive power, these conservatives hold, the reform has permitted squandering of resources, wage inflation, and successful efforts to evade government plans. How-ever, the reformers counter attack with the charge that the real problem is conservative sabotage of the scheme.

For the moment, the Soviet economy has by no means lost all forward momentum. But continuation of the economic slowdown and the food shortages into the early 1970s could produce dramatic results—including the possibility of a political shake-up at the highest levels.

Recent Soviet failures to fulfill planned production are exemplified by the performance of the Soviet automobile industry.

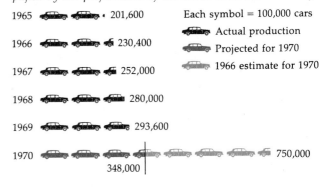

Year		Production
1965		201,600
1966		230,400
1967		252,000
1968		280,000
1969		293,600
1970	348,000	750,000

Each symbol = 100,000 cars
Actual production
Projected for 1970
1966 estimate for 1970

SOURCE: Adapted from *The New York Times*, February 8, 1970

greatest of its type in world history—considering the large numbers of people involved, the quantities of material used, the number of industrial plants erected, and the resulting increases in output that were achieved. Flushed with success at the remarkable economic transformation they had brought about, the Chinese Communist leaders embarked in 1958 on a second phase of development. However, this new policy for economic growth failed almost completely and left the economy near collapse. We may outline the main features of this and other aspects of Chinese economic development within a framework of four major areas:

1. The Great Leap Forward
2. Consequences of the Great Leap
3. Shift in priority from industry to agriculture
4. Conclusion: an optimum economic policy

THE GREAT LEAP FORWARD

The plan launched in 1958 was called the Great Leap Forward, and was a topic of discussion throughout the world. Its objective was to accelerate enormously the rate of China's economic growth. There were three essentials of the plan:

First, individual output was to be increased by at least 25 percent per annum. This represented a substantial increase over the extraordinary gains that had already been made in the First Five-Year Plan of 1952–57.

Second, a dual economy consisting of producer goods and consumer goods was to be encouraged. The producer goods sector was to place an even heavier emphasis on rapid development of heavy industry than before, but with greater use of labor-intensive rather than capital-intensive processes in order to reduce the unemployment that resulted from a rapid rate of modernization. The consumer goods sector was to be dominated by small-scale enterprises using a very high proportion of labor-intensive techniques in order to provide new employment opportunities.

Third, the supervision of all enterprises, except for the large heavy industrial plants, was to be transferred from central government to local appointees. The purpose of this decentralization was to encourage greater initiative at the local level.

What was the economic rationale behind this strategy? China was faced at the time with a fundamental problem of *underemployment*—a situation in which employed resources are not being used in their most efficient ways. In such circumstances there is a tendency, especially among the self-employed, to spread the work thinly by sharing it among members of the family or group. It was plausible for the Chinese planners to assume, therefore, that if jobs could be found for the underemployed—even jobs involving the lowliest tasks—the result would be a gain in the nation's net product. Further, since the underemployed were already living at a subsistence level, the additional costs of putting them to work would consist primarily of the extra food that would be required for sustenance plus the minimum equipment needed for performing the simplest tasks.

CONSEQUENCES OF THE GREAT LEAP

How successful was the plan? One way of answering this question is to compare China's economic development with that of Russia's during the first 10 years of each nation's Communist regime. On this score, as shown in Exhibit 1, the Chinese appear to have advanced much more than the Russians. But such a chart may also be deceiving because it says nothing about the *means* that were used, the differences in the timing of plans, or the *real costs* of China's advances.

In order to accelerate industrialization, the Chinese authorities should have relied more on better machines and technology, and on the training of personnel and the granting of material rewards, than on propaganda-inspired speeches and slogans. For as subsequent events indicated, to say that the Great Leap Forward was a failure is a gross understatement; it was a disaster which brought a near-collapse of the Chinese economy.

The fundamental difficulty was that the program was unrealistic. Many millions of workers were engaged in producing products that were of little or no value. Females of all ages were employed to replace the men on the farms, who in turn were assigned to the construction of large-scale and frequently misplanned irrigation projects. Tens of millions of men, women, and children were ordered to make steel, using primitive, unsafe, backyard furnaces which produced iron of inferior and often unusable quality. Farm and city workers alike put in 12- to 14-hour days which for the most part turned out to be wasted and even destructive because of poor planning and inefficiencies. And, in order to hasten industrialization, there was an excessive transfer of labor from the agricultural to the industrial sector which resulted in a serious food shortage.

By 1960, the consequences of the Great Leap Forward were a bitter reality. Urban unemployment was high, morale had largely collapsed, and the nation was in a major economic crisis. Most of what had been gained from a decade of hard work and deprivation had been wiped out. It was clear to the Chinese authorities that a new and different type of economic policy was needed.

SHIFT IN PRIORITY FROM INDUSTRY TO AGRICULTURE

In 1961, the Chinese Communist Party announced a fundamental change in development planning. A new national policy was instituted which, paraphrased briefly, consisted of three major features:

1. Agriculture was to become the foundation of the national economy, with assistance provided to it by all other sectors.

2. The light industries were to overcome the problem of raw material shortages by exploring new sources of raw material while doing their best to increase production and to guarantee the supply of necessities of living.

Exhibit 1

China's and Russia's Economic Development

These charts compare China's and Russia's economic development in the pre-Communist peak production years (bars at left in each chart) and during the first 10 years of each country's Communist regime.

The more rapid growth of China compared to the Soviet Union can be attributed to such factors as (1) help from other Communist countries, (2) a tighter degree of discipline, (3) a larger work force, and (4) opportunities to take advantage of more advanced technology. It should be remembered, too, that economic planning in Russia did not start until 1928, whereas it began in China in 1952. This makes a true comparison more difficult.

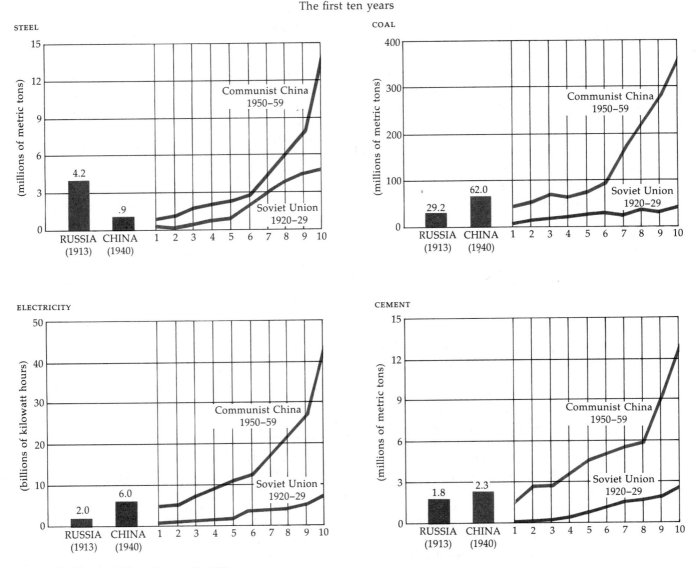

The first ten years

SOURCE: *The New York Times*, January 31, 1960.

3. The heavy industries were to undergo a readjustment in their rate of development, with greater emphasis to be placed on improvements in efficiency, cost reduction, labor productivity, and product quality.

The Chinese planners thus shifted the nation's priority from industry to agriculture. The test of whether new industrial investment should be undertaken became a question of what the effects would be on agriculture. A new investment project such as a chemical fertilizer plant or a farm machinery factory, for example, would directly benefit agriculture, and hence would receive priority over investment projects that were aimed at producing capital goods for nonagricultural purposes. Emphasis also came to be placed on the modernization of existing plants rather than on the construction of new ones. And in the consumer goods industries, priorities were given over heavy industries to those firms that produced goods for peasant consumption.

One might expect that with the greater priority that was given to agriculture, this sector of the economy would experience a rapid recovery. But such was not the case. Agriculture had been too long neglected, and had suffered too much damage during the Great Leap period, to undergo rapid growth. Although there were some significant improvements such as the greater used of chemical fertilizers and the development of new irrigation systems, the gains in farm output were relatively moderate. Indeed, by the mid-1960s the cultivated area and the level of crop production per capita were considerably less than they had been 10 years earlier.

On the whole, however, Chinese economic development during these early years of planning was not unimpressive. For the 15-year period 1950–65, the average annual rate of growth was about 4 percent. But the pattern of growth was distorted rather than "balanced." By the end of the 1960s, China had developed an industrial base that was economically capable of producing a variety of important manufactured goods as well as supporting a thermonuclear capability. However, its agriculture was still inefficient, underemployment was still prevalent, and there was no indication that the Malthusian specter of an expanding population pressing on a limited food supply was any less serious than it had been when the Communists took over in 1949.

CONCLUSION: AN OPTIMUM ECONOMIC POLICY

The Communist regime has had a profound influence on the shaping of Chinese society and culture. Never before in the country's long history had so many people been changed in such a short time. Legal equality was established between the sexes; medical and sanitation facilities were greatly expanded in the cities and villages; education was revised and extended by establishing full-time day schools, part-time evening and correspondence schools, and combined work-study programs; and language reform was undertaken to promote unification and simplification—with the eventual goal of replacing the characters with more easily learned phonetic symbols. On the whole, while China is still poor in comparison with Western nations, there is no doubt that most of her people have acquired more material necessities under communism than they ever had in previous centuries.

Against this background, what steps should the Chinese leadership take to assure a steady and self-sustaining rate of growth for the economy as a whole? Three proposals may be regarded as essential ingredients of an optimum economic policy.

Population

China's rate of population growth should be reduced. In 1970 the country had a population of close to 750 million which was increasing at an annual rate of 2 percent, thus portending a rise to 1 billion in little more than a decade. Although the Chinese leadership at first derided Malthusian theories and hailed the growth in population as an indication of a new-found robustness brought about by socialism, it has since had second thoughts about the matter and has played an increasing role in encouraging the practice of birth control.

Agriculture

China's agricultural productivity should be increased. The nation needs a dramatic expansion in farm output so that a significant portion of its human resources can be moved out of agriculture into nonagricultural pursuits. The required gain in farm production cannot be achieved merely by intensifying the use of labor or by cultivating additional land. These traditional methods have already been employed to their limit. What is needed instead is the adoption of new technology and new practices through the use of improved seeds, fertilizers, pesticides, and farm equipment.

Foreign Trade

China should expand its foreign trade so that it may become an integral part of the world economy. In this way it could specialize in the production of labor-intensive commodities embracing a wide array of agricultural and handicraft products, along the lines dictated by the law of comparative advantage. In view of China's factor endowments, the development of large capital-using plants producing automobiles, steel, ships, and heavy machinery should be deemphasized in favor of small labor-using plants producing clothing, textiles, toys, electronics, and optical goods. The latter types of products have played an important part in Japan's economic growth, and could be increasingly absorbed by China in her path toward further development.

The Convergence Hypothesis: A Meeting of East and West?

The only choice is either bourgeois or socialist ideology. There is no middle course.

—V. I. Lenin

Is this view of Lenin's really true? Some scholars in both the East and West think not. They believe in a so-called *convergence hypothesis*—a theory which proposes that capitalism and communism, driven by the process of industrialization, will eventually merge to form a new kind of society in which the personal freedoms and profit motive of Western capitalistic democracies blend with the government

controls that exist in a communistic (especially in the Soviet) economy.

Perhaps the most dramatic statement of this rapprochement between East and West was made by the distinguished Soviet physicist Andrei Sakharov. In a 10,000-word essay that was smuggled to the West in 1968, he wrote (according to a translation appearing in *The New York Times,* July 22, 1968):

> The continuing economic progress being achieved under capitalism should be a fact of great theoretical significance for any dogmatic Marxist. It is precisely this fact that lies at the basis of peaceful coexistence and it suggests, in principle, that if capitalism ever runs into an economic blind alley it will not necessarily have to leap into a desperate military adventure. Both capitalism and socialism are capable of long-term development, borrowing positive elements from each other and actually coming closer to each other in a number of essential aspects.

The only hope for world peace, Sakharov concluded, was a coalescence of socialistic and capitalistic systems. Otherwise we stand on the brink of disaster.

THREE BASIC ASSUMPTIONS

The convergence hypothesis, of course, is an adaptation of the familiar Marxian doctrine that economic forces determine a nation's political and social development. But it departs from orthodox Marxism by challenging the conviction that communism is the only route to attaining the highest form of social evolution. Thus in the simplest sense, the key factor is the ongoing process of industrialization. As Harvard economist John Kenneth Galbraith put it in his *New Industrial State,* advancing technology has different implications for the United States and for the Soviet Union. In the United States it must lead to increased intellectual curiosity and freedom; in the Soviet Union, to much greater government planning and control.

The convergence hypothesis rests on three basic assumptions:

1. Industrialization leads to urbanization and to many common challenges of effective resource orga-

nization and management. The skills, training, and desires of a steel worker in Pittsburgh are not significantly different from one in Magnitogorsk. Hence they tend to evolve toward a similar way of life.

2. Industrialization inevitably produces a more complex society with problems of specialization and exchange that are common to all advanced economies.

3. Industrialization raises living standards and improves economic well-being. This in turn leads to intellectual independence and probably to ideological nonconformity.

CONCLUSION

On the basis of these assumptions, there appear to be more surface similarities today between the United States and the Soviet Union than there were several decades ago. Thus in order to make its economy work better, the United States has accepted a degree of "socialism" and welfare statism which in the more distant past would have been unthinkable; the Soviet Union, on the other hand, has followed a policy of greater freedom and decentralization since the mid-sixties.

Are we to conclude from this that the convergence hypothesis is becoming a reality? The answer is no. For even if communism is capable of achieving its economic goals, the evidence does not show that the political and social objectives of the United States are anywhere present in communist countries. Indeed, there is at least as much evidence to suggest that social and political inequalities are widening, thus bringing into question some of the underlying implications of the above assumptions. We are led to the conclusion, therefore, that even if the Soviet Union and the United States actually do come closer in the economic sphere, there are still major if not unbridgeable gaps over the traditions, value systems, and goals of the two societies.

FOR HOMEWORK AND DISCUSSION

1. *Terms and concepts to review:*

   planned economy

   state farms

   collective farms

   economic plan

   coefficient of relative effectiveness (CRE)

   Great Leap Forward

   underemployment (disguised unemployment)

   convergence hypothesis

2. Since the Soviet Union is a centrally directed and collectivist economy, there is no competition as in American capitalism. True or false? Explain.

3. Why would a socialist economy such as the Soviet Union's want to employ the capitalistic device of providing economic incentives? What types of incentives do they use?

4. Is there freedom of consumer choice in the Soviet Union? Is there consumer sovereignty? Explain.

5. Which would you suggest as a better guide for judging the efficiency of firms in the United States and in the Soviet Union: profits or sales? What are some of the assumptions underlying your answer?

6. What criteria would you use in judging whether one nation's economy is better than another? Are there noneconomic criteria too?

7. Why do the Soviet authorities want to engage in the complex and difficult task of planning? Why do they not simply let a free market system allocate the resources and distribute the income for them?

8. What are some of the "capitalistic" practices that the Soviet Union has adopted over the years? Do the Soviets view these as a step toward capitalism? Explain.

9. Was China's Great Leap Forward a success or a failure? Explain.

10. What steps should China take to improve its rate of economic development and to achieve balanced growth?

REFERENCES AND READING SUGGESTIONS

CAMPBELL, ROBERT W., *Soviet Economic Power,* 2d ed., Houghton-Mifflin, Boston, 1966.

GALENSON, WALTER, and NAI-RUENN CHEN, *The Chinese Economy Under Communism,* Aldine, Chicago, 1969.

GROSSMAN, GREGORY, *Economic Systems,* Prentice-Hall, New York, chap. 6.

LOUCKS, WILLIAM N., and WILLIAM G. WHITNEY, *Comparative Economic Systems,* 8th ed., Harper & Row, New York, 1969, chaps. 24, 30.

OXENFELDT, ALFRED, *Economic Systems in Action,* rev. ed., Holt, New York, 1958, chap. 3.

SHERMAN, HOWARD J., *The Soviet Economy,* Little, Brown, Boston, 1969, chaps. 1, 6, 7.

E. Rent Control in New York City

New York is the only city in the United States that still retains rent control—i.e., ceilings on rents—as a holdover from World War II. During the War, rent controls prevailed throughout the country because materials and labor were insufficient to meet the demand for housing. However, whereas other cities abandoned rent controls within a few years after the War, New York retained the system primarily because of political pressures from labor unions and other groups. The following case, adapted from a study done in July, 1969, by the First National City Bank of New York, provides an interesting account of the consequences of rent control.

NEW YORK CITY'S HOUSING SHORTAGE

New York City suffers from an acute shortage of reasonably priced housing, and current trends point to a worsening of this situation. One official count indicates that during the sixties, growth in the number of households has exceeded that of housing units by 27 percent. The rental vacancy rate, low at 1.2 percent in April 1968, now is estimated to be dropping out of sight. Long lists of families (131,000 by the latest count) await public housing, and musty, old-law tenements, obsolete 50 or more years ago, continue to be rented and occupied. Although unsatisfied demand bears most heavily on low- and moderate-income families, lately—because of substantial increases in costs—even middle-income groups have been priced out of the market for conventionally financed new housing.

Reflecting sharply rising costs of building and maintaining housing and the growing imbalance between supply and demand, apartment rents climbed steeply in 1968. Apartments account for about 75 percent of the City's total housing stock. These boosts were particularly marked in the previously uncontrolled part of the City's rental inventory. In their wake, allegations of "gouging" led to enactment of a new City law limiting rent rises on most "uncontrolled" apartments to 10 percent on two-year leases and 15 percent on leases of three years. Meanwhile, even New York City's Housing Authority has had to announce increases in monthly rents for welfare families living in public housing projects—added costs which fall on the Welfare budget, not on the families themselves.

POLITICAL AND SOCIAL OBSTACLES

It is only too easy to attribute New York City's rental housing problems to the venality of landlords. It is important, however, to examine carefully the impact of the rent control system. This was legislated during World War II when, despite shortages in housing, materials and labor limitations prevented expansion in supply. When controls restrict yields to below those of alternative investment opportunities, they force property owners to subsidize not only low-income families who cannot sustain rents sufficient to maintain buildings properly, but also families who can afford the necessary rents.

The New York City rent control law permits landlords to increase rents by 15 percent when apartments are vacated and rerented. However yield limitations under rent controls induce landlords to cut corners in building maintenance, thus contributing to relatively rapid housing deterioration. Furthermore, because attractive returns are possible on investments in commercial development and in housing elsewhere in the nation, responsible property owners and financial institutions tend to withdraw their connection with properties subject to public price administration. Then less skilled or unscrupulous operators take over. The inevitable results are excessive code violations, suspension of rent payments, and abandonment, to the detriment of all parties concerned.

By exempting from its wartime-imposed rent controls private housing built after 1947, while maintaining controls on most pre-1947 inventory, New York City has sought, in effect, to eat its cake and have it too. This effort was largely successful until the middle of the 1960s. For example, over 150,000 privately sponsored new dwelling units were built between 1960 and 1966. The result of this political accommodation, however, has been to institutionalize an anti-free market condition and make disengagement extremely difficult.

Experience with rent control meant, moreover, that when, in 1967–68, builders began to fear that it might be extended to post-1947 housing, new construction was curtailed sharply. Rapidly rising operating costs and expectations that they would keep on rising made the impact of the threat of expanded rent controls all the more disastrous. Concurrently, public and publicly assisted housing completions took a downturn as sharply rising costs reduced the marketability as well as the numbers of units that could be produced under available programs and funds.

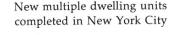

New multiple dwelling units completed in New York City

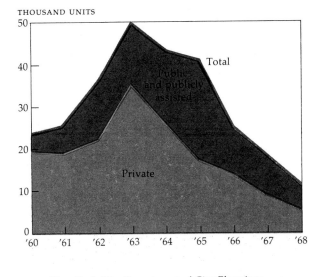

SOURCE: New York City Department of City Planning.

An additional reason for the decline in private apartment construction was the 1962 change in the zoning laws. The new zoning ordinance made it far more difficult, costly and time consuming for builders to assemble sites of sufficient size for an economic scale of construction. Furthermore, competition for space by industrial and commercial users pushed up land and construction costs faster than they would have increased if only housing demand had been growing. It is considerably easier to pass on these higher costs to commercial tenants than to residential tenants.

BUILDING ABANDONMENT

The drastic curtailment of new supply has accompanied a far more ominous development—widespread building abandonment. Squeezed between accelerating operating costs and rent control ceilings, confronted with vigorous code enforcement, and faced with numerous vacancies as tenants fled crime-ridden areas, many owners chose to shut down or walk away from their properties. Evidence strongly suggests that during the sixties, New York City suffered an unrecorded housing inventory loss of well over 100,000 units. This massive removal is a basic cause of the shortage of reasonably priced housing in the City. Thus New York confronts an economically pathological condition of wasted moderate-rent housing in the face of a dwelling unit shortage.

The streets of Brooklyn, the Bronx, and upper Manhattan abound with boarded-up, broken-windowed, burned-out, empty eyesores. The contrasts between well-maintained streets containing excellent middle-class housing and other areas with exactly the same basic structures that bear the scars of neglect, abuse, and vandalism present convincing evidence of social malaise. In one neighborhood, real estate shops gaudily exhort local residents to "Sell your house and buy in Queens or Long Island."

NEW DIRECTIONS TO MORE AND BETTER HOUSING?

The battery of obstacles facing New York's free housing market has all but eliminated the conventional entrepreneur-developer of multiple housing who selects the site, acquires capital, arranges construction contracts, operates and manages the property. Since 1963, when a peak of 35,000 privately financed apartment units were completed, the trend has been steadily downward to a low of 5,000 units in 1968. In contrast, national multifamily housing starts, which rose steeply in the late fifties and early sixties but fell off in the mid-sixties, rebounded to new highs in the late 1960s.

Under the present conditions in New York City, which are likely to persist into the foreseeable future, prospects are poor for the strictly private developer except in the case of high-rent luxury apartments, many of which are marketed under cooperative arrangements, and all of which are occupied as soon as they are produced. The record of the past few years demonstrates, moreover, that public efforts alone are increasingly less able to resolve the housing problem. Meeting the needs of the nation's largest metropolis will require a combination of public assistance and private enterprise, with profit conditions attractive enough to induce sufficient private capital and entrepreneurial talent into the housing industry.

QUESTIONS

1. Using supply and demand curves, illustrate in general terms the nature of the housing shortage in New York City over a period of years. Make sure you include the influence of rent control in your diagram.

2. Can housing deterioration take place in the absence of rent controls? Explain.

3. Is rent control "fair?" (HINT: It is often said that the New York rent control system subsidizes middle- and upper-income families while discriminating against lower-income families and new arrivals to the city. How can this happen? Explain.)

F. The Case for a Volunteer Army

Following is a portion of the report of the President's Commission on an All-Volunteer Army, released by the White House on February 22, 1970.

VOLUNTEER FORCE URGED

We unanimously believe that the nation's interest will be better served by an all-volunteer force, supported by an effective stand-by draft, than by a mixed force of volunteers and conscripts; that steps should be taken promptly to move in this direction, and that the first indispensable step is to remove the present inequity in the pay of men serving their first term in the armed forces.

The United States has relied throughout history on a voluntary armed force except during major wars and since 1948. A return to an all-volunteer force will strengthen our freedoms, remove an inequity now imposed on the expression of the patriotism that has never been lacking among our youth, promote the efficiency of the armed forces and enhance their dignity. It is the system for maintaining standing forces that minimizes Government interference with the freedom of the individual to determine his own life in accord with his values.

A voluntary force of 3 million men would require 400,000 enlistments each year, or 150,000 additional volunteers from the 1.5 million eligible 19-year olds. Smaller forces would require fewer than 75,000 additional volunteers annually. Reasonable improvements in pay and benefits in the early years of service should increase the number of volunteers by these amounts.

EQUALITY IN PAY SOUGHT

In any event, such improvements are called for on the ground of equality alone. Because conscription has been used to provide raw recruits, the pay of men entering the services has been kept at a very low level.

It has not risen nearly as rapidly as the pay of experienced military personnel, and it is now about 60 percent of comparable civilian pay. Similarly, the pay of first-term officers has not been kept in line with the pay of more experienced officers, or with comparable civilians.

Correcting this inequity for first-term enlisted men and first-term officers will add about $2.7-billion to the defense budget. Regardless of the fate of the draft, the commission strongly recommends elimination of this discrimination against first-termers.

If the commission's recommendations are put into effect, they will entail a budget increase of an estimated $3.3

billion for the following expenditures:

Basic pay increase (billions)	$2.68
Proficiency pay	.21
Reserve pay increase	.15
Additional Medical Corps expense	.12
Recruiting R.O.T.C. and miscellaneous	.08
	$3.24

The additional proficiency pay is required to attract individuals in the first term with special skills and talents.

QUESTIONS

1. Some people who oppose a volunteer Army have argued that it would likely evolve into a dangerously alienated military clique. Do you agree? Explain.

2. Instead of having a costly volunteer army composed of Americans, wouldn't it be cheaper to hire lower-priced foreign mercenaries instead? For example, the United States could undoubtedly attract Orientals and African Blacks for less money than Americans. Discuss.

3. If the army relies entirely on Americans, wouldn't the cost of attracting enough volunteers be prohibitively high? After all, a draftee is much cheaper than a volunteer. Discuss. (HINT: Think in terms of *economic* costs.)

G. The Automobile Industry: Demand Elasticity and Price Reduction

Union leaders, government economists, and various other people have contended from time to time that since the overall demand for automobiles is relatively elastic, an across-the-board price cut of, say, 10 percent, would increase the sale of automobiles and therefore the profits of the companies. These arguments are particularly prominent during periods of recession, since an increase in the sale of a product like automobiles would have significant beneficial effects on other industries, e.g., steel, rubber, etc., and would thereby help boost the level of employment, national income, and economic activity in general.

On the face of it, this argument may seem plausible. Upon further analysis, however, it becomes apparent that there are actually two sets of elasticities to be considered:

1. *Demand elasticity,* since there is a question of the effect which the price reduction will have on demand and thus on revenues.

2. *Cost elasticity,* since there is a question of the effect which the increased sales volume will have on production and thus on costs.

Obviously, both questions would have to be considered by automobile manufacturers if they were contemplating a general price reduction. However, those who have suggested such price reductions have usually considered only the former and have completely neglected the latter.

Economists who have conducted demand analyses for new automobiles have estimated price elasticities of demand ranging from 0.5 to 1.5. Obviously, the higher the coefficient of elasticity, the greater the percentage increase in quantity demanded which will result from a given percentage decrease in price. Thus, if we assume an elasticity as high as 1.5, this means that a 1 percent decrease in price would produce a 1.5 percent increase in quantity demanded, and hence a larger total revenue for the seller than he would obtain with a lower elasticity coefficient. Therefore, let us agree on this liberal elasticity measure of 1.5, and proceed to explore the question of whether it pays, even with such a high elasticity, for an automobile manufacturer to reduce the list price of a line of cars by, say, $100.

We must assume, of course, that a price reduction by one producer will be met by his competitors. (Why?) Therefore, we are not considering a relative price advantage but rather the effect of a general price change by all sellers. In addition, the following conditions may also be specified:

Average price of the line of cars	$2,500 per car
Expected sales volume @ $2,500 per car	1,000,000 cars
Average total cost of the line of cars	$2,300 per car
Total variable cost	$1,840,000,000

QUESTIONS

1. What is the change in total revenue, if any, resulting from a price reduction of $100?

2. What will profit be before the price reduction?

3. Find total fixed cost, average fixed cost, and average variable cost before the price reduction.

4. What will profit be after the price reduction?

5. The price reduction of $100 has reduced revenues per car by $100. How much did it change the cost per car? What will average total cost be at the new sales volume?

6. What do you conclude from your calculations?

7. What is the proportion of total variable cost to total cost? Total fixed cost to total cost? Are these proportions realistic?

8. "In general, the higher the level of total fixed cost relative to total cost (or the lower the level of total variable cost relative to total cost), the lower the price elasticity of demand must be in order to justify a price reduction, and *vice versa.*" True or false? Why?

9. The following *special formula* (based on certain assumed straight-line relationships) may be used to determine the price elasticity of demand that is needed for a given price reduction, leaving profits unimpaired, when the respective ratios of fixed and variable cost to total cost within the expected volume range are known.

Q = Percentage increase of output quantity required.

P = Price decrease in dollars

$\overline{N}$ = Net profit per unit at the old price (read: "N-bar")

$\overline{C}$ = Cost per unit (i.e., average total cost) at the old price (read: "C-bar")

V/C = Ratio of total variable cost to total cost

$$Q = \frac{P}{\overline{N} - P + [1 - (V/C)]\overline{C}}$$

The elasticity coefficient is then

$$\text{Elasticity} = \frac{Q(\overline{N} + \overline{C})}{P}$$

How much would the elasticity have to be in order to justify a price reduction? How does your answer compare with measures of demand elasticity for automobiles that have been estimated by various scholars? Interpret your result.

10. What conclusion do you draw as to the advisability of a price reduction in order to increase the sale of automobiles?

H. Should We End Restrictive Licensing?

Would you like to operate a radio or TV station? All you have to do is persuade the Federal Communications Commission to grant you a license. The cost of the license would be nominal—if you could get it. And, if you waited a reasonable time, you could sell the license to a "reputable" buyer at an extraordinary profit—without the FCC so much as raising an eyebrow.

You don't want to operate a radio or TV station? Then how about a commercial airline instead? In that case you would have to persuade the Civil Aeronautics Board to grant you the necessary license. This too would be extremely difficult.

Perhaps you want to go into the oil business. If so, you can purchase foreign oil for about $1.25 a barrel cheaper than domestic oil—provided you can first convince the Department of Interior to grant you a permit.

If you want to open a liquor store, set up a bank, own a taxi, run a barber shop or in some places even a bootblack stand, you must first acquire a license. In most cases the number of licenses granted is strictly limited, and for many activities they are simply unobtainable. Hence the licensing mechanism, instead of being a legitimate device which government can use to raise revenue and to protect the general welfare, has too often become a restrictive measure for controlling competition within an industry.

WHAT SHOULD BE DONE?

This view has long been held by many economists. But none has expressed it more forcefully than the University of Chicago's eminent Professor Milton Friedman. In various books and articles, he has argued that most restrictive licensing should be abolished completely. (He even believes that medical doctors should not be licensed —i.e., that anyone who wants to practice medicine should be free to do so.) For example: TV and radio should not be controlled by government. Oil import quotas should be eliminated, and we should buy the oil where we can get it at the lowest price, not subsidize high-cost domestic producers. Free competition should be permitted on the airlines, subject only to objective safety standards. Since 1938, when CAB control was introduced, not a single new line has been granted permission by the CAB to operate— and not for lack of applicants. Similarly, anyone who wants to set up a liquor store, or a commercial bank, or drive a cab should be free to do so, provided he can satisfy objective minimum standards of responsibility or competence. His freedom to sell a product or service should not, as now, depend also on a bureaucrat's judgment whether additional units are "necessary" to serve the public. Let the market decide.

AUCTIONING RIGHTS

Suppose, however, that the government decides to limit the number who may engage in any activity to a smaller number than wish to do so. The least it can do is to avoid giveaways. It can determine how many people it is going to permit in an activity, specify the terms and conditions, announce these publicly, and hold an open auction to decide which particular persons will engage in the activity.

This is a simple and direct way to end giveaways. TV licenses can be auctioned off. So can rights to import oil. Rights to particular air routes, to establish one of a limited number of liquor stores, to operate one of a limited number of cabs—each and every one of these can be auctioned off. The public will still suffer from governmentally created monopoly, but at least it will recover some of its loss in the form of revenue.

The general principle works both ways. The argument for selling limited rights to the highest bidder and not giving them away is precisely the same as the argument for buying resources that government needs rather than commandeering them—whether those resources be land for public buildings, or the services of policemen, or the services of soldiers.

QUESTIONS

1. In his argument for free TV, how do you suppose Professor Friedman would reply to the question: "But the number of TV channels is limited to a fairly small number. Shouldn't the government, in all fairness, decide who is to use them?" Explain your answer.

2. If you were to ask Professor Friedman to describe the type of TV system that would emerge in a free and unrestricted market, what do you suppose would be his answer? (HINTS: Think of the different kinds of newspapers, magazines, books, and various other publications we have today, some supported all or in part by advertising, fees, subscriptions, etc. Would a similar situation develop with free TV? Would TV programs be better or worse?)

I. Protectionism for Steel?

The following statement by R. Heath Larry, executive vice president of U.S. Steel Corporation, is adapted from an article in *The Wall Street Journal,* January 8, 1969.

If steel is an important basis of our growing economy, and if its availability is essential to our national defense—which it certainly is—then the question which all of us must face is: How much of the vitality of the domestic industry are we willing to see dissipated by imports? And the next question is whether we are willing to face up to the fact that steel's problems are not of its own making, and therefore not soluble solely by its own efforts. The world of trade which steel must confront is anything but a world of free trade.

RISING IMPORTS

By this time there must be a general public awareness of steel import trends. In 1957 only a little over a million tons of steel were imported. Their impact was limited in terms of product and geography. Since then world steel capacity has grown by leaps and bounds—much more than have world markets for steel. Thus the pressure is on to sell the surplus; and this country offers the greatest market and the easiest entry.

Why do steel users in the United States buy foreign steel? By and large, the answer is quite simple; it is a matter of price, most often a price of $25 to $45 a ton lower than domestic prices. Why then don't we just cut the price and solve the problem? Price difference is basically cost difference because most of price is cost. Profits in the domestic steel industry have steadily declined, and cuts in prices of such proportions as $25 to $45 per ton on all products would invite financial disaster to the industry, its employes, and stockholders.

The critics of the domestic steel industry often argue, and I am sure they would like to believe, that the problem is caused by a lack of research on the part of the domestic steel industry, and by its alleged backwardness in terms of technology and managerial skill. But the fact is that the domestic steel industry is not backward in technology. Its companies undoubtedly spend far more on research than those of any other steel-producing nation in the world.

Unfortunately, however, steel labor costs are not the same everywhere. They are, in fact, greatly different. In the Japanese steel industry, for example, employment cost per hour is only about one-quarter of that in the United States. To equalize this kind of cost advantage on the basis of an improvement in efficiency would require that United States steelmakers discover a technological forward leap which could reduce their 13 man-hours a ton down to approximately 4 man-hours a ton.

Such an accomplishment is today unforeseeable on the basis of technology now known or even dreamed of, anywhere. Further, this labor cost differential seems to be growing despite higher percentage increases in employment costs abroad, because our base costs were so much higher to start with.

THREE IMPORTANT DIFFERENCES

Here then are the problems:

First, relative parity of technology has been reached in the principal steel-producing nations of the world, considerably ahead of relative parity in labor standards. Fur-

ther, governmental monetary and fiscal policies in recent years have been all-important influences in producing and tolerating inflationary trends in this country of such order as continually to aggravate this problem. And, the fact is that there will be no satisfactory solution to the import problems of the steel industry or of other industries until there is a constructive and a continuing reversal of these past Governmental policies toward inflation.

A second part of the steel import problem grows out of the assortment of subsidies, nontariff barriers (including the impact of border taxes and value-added tax schemes) by which other governments effectively give protection to the steel industries within their own markets, and at the same time provide assistance to their steel industries when they move into external markets, the most important of which is ours.

United States Foreign Trade in Steel Mill Products

MILLIONS
OF NET TONS

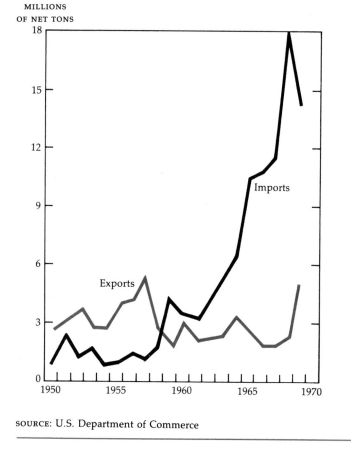

SOURCE: U.S. Department of Commerce

Hourly Employment Costs of Steel Industry Wage Employers

DOLLARS
PER HOUR

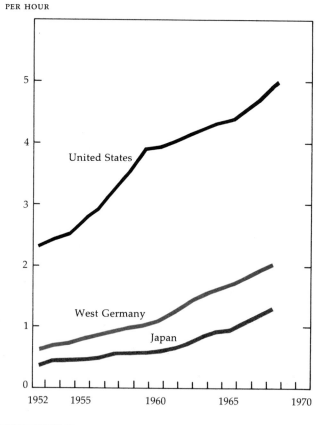

The fact of the matter is that while Japan and members of the Common Market talk glowingly of free trade, their own economies are loaded with devices which tend to give their own producers a strong advantage. And they continue to show every intention of pursuing their foreign policies and their trade policies with the single purpose of giving first support to their own respective economies. They are first and foremost pragmatists. Thereafter, they are very vocal free trade theorists, mainly when it seems to their advantage to be so. Some "retaliation" against their protective devices could very well serve as leverage to move reality closer to theory.

A third point is that just as in the case of their agriculture, most other nations take a very paternalistic view toward their own steel industries. A great part of the steel industry in the rest of the world is either government-owned or under various forms of government direction or control. The result is steel industries whose export marketing and pricing policies are more often keyed to reacting to government pressures, be they those directed in support of full employment programs or in support of acquisition of foreign exchange, than to the forces of competition in a free market.

CONCLUSION

What then is to happen meanwhile?

Unless the domestic steel industry can participate proportionately in the growth of the domestic steel market, it is unlikely that our domestic steel producers will have either the ability or the desire to continue to invest record-breaking sums in new facilities and in steel research in the United States. And, by placing an ever greater reliance upon foreign sources for its most vital metal, the United States is risking both its national security and the basis for a sound and continuing growth of its total economy. An adequate, continuing and immediately available source of domestic steel is something the United States cannot afford to be without.

We know of no other effective and prompt means of achieving the needed help other than some reasonable and effective form of limitation upon the access of foreign steel producers to the domestic steel market—the most effective form of which would be quota legislation.

We know of no other major steel-producing nation in the world whose policies toward trade in steel are sufficiently free that they could have any justifiable objection to practical steps which might be taken by the United States to assist its steel industry in this fashion.

In short, as long as we do not yet have a world of free trade in steel, we must face the world as it is rather than as we wish it were. Thus we should and we must move in tactical and practical ways wherever, as in the case of steel, there is a critical problem—even if so doing may offend long-term theory in which all of us, including those of us in steel, still believe.

QUESTION

1. What arguments do you see here for trade protection? What do you think of the proposed solution to this problem? Explain. Can you suggest some alternative proposals?

J. The Rockefeller Proposal For Latin America: An Historic Flop

WHAT'S CAUSING THE UNREST IN LATIN AMERICA?

When Governor Rockefeller was asked at a Congressional hearing in 1969 what would happen in Latin America if the Nixon Administration failed in implementing its new policies based on his far-ranging economic recommendations, he had a simple and succinct reply. "Utter chaos," he said.

In contrast, it took the Governor nearly 50,000 words in his exhaustive report on the "Quality of Life in the Americas" to justify and present the 83 recommendations that, he believes, should form the foundations of new United States attitudes toward Latin America at a time of new crisis and when the hemisphere stands at a "crossroads."

The thrust of the report was that unless the United States turns to drastic measures to alleviate the economic and social situation in the southern republics—a situation that has deteriorated despite nearly a decade of aid programs under the Alliance for Progress—then new revolutionary and anti-American waves will sweep Latin America, and this country will find itself hopelessly isolated in the hemisphere.

The most far-reaching recommendation offered by Governor Rockefeller—and formally accepted by President Nixon—called for granting Latin America preferential trade treatment in the United States.

Governor Rockefeller's proposal is perhaps the most important innovation in United States trade policies since the completion of the Kennedy Round negotiations, which cut down world tariffs across the board. It would open

United States markets to Latin American industrialized goods and, for the first time, bring the region out of its traditional and frustrating role of being a supplier of raw materials and commodities.

The only advantage now granted Latin American trade in the United States—which has no generalized system of preferences—is the duty-free entry of green coffee, sugar, crude oil, and raw metals. But oil and sugar are governed by volume import quotas, and, in general, the world prices of commodities are so low that, with few exceptions, the Latin American nations suffer from an appalling and ever-rising gap between their export earnings and their import costs.

This gap is so wide that in many cases the repayment of debts that the hemisphere republics had to contract to be able to go on importing essential equipment exceeds the dollar aid they receive from the United States and world financial institutions. As an urgent relief step, Mr. Rockefeller has recommended that the United States refinance the debts due to this country, and President Nixon has so instructed the Treasury.

SOURCE: Adapted from an article in *The New York Times Student Weekly*, December 8, 1969.

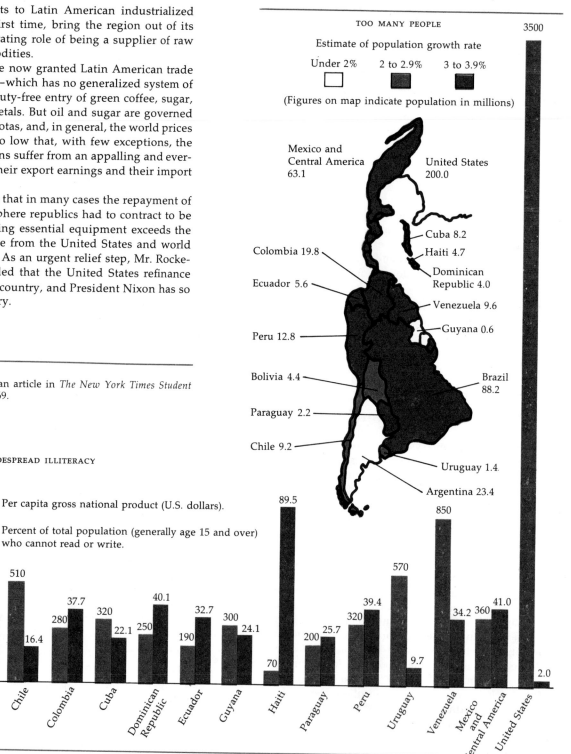

TOO MANY PEOPLE

Estimate of population growth rate

Under 2%   2 to 2.9%   3 to 3.9%

(Figures on map indicate population in millions)

3500

Mexico and Central America 63.1

United States 200.0

Cuba 8.2
Haiti 4.7
Dominican Republic 4.0
Venezuela 9.6
Guyana 0.6

Colombia 19.8
Ecuador 5.6
Peru 12.8
Bolivia 4.4
Paraguay 2.2
Chile 9.2

Brazil 88.2

Uruguay 1.4
Argentina 23.4

EXTREME POVERTY . . . WIDESPREAD ILLITERACY

Per capita gross national product (U.S. dollars).

Percent of total population (generally age 15 and over) who cannot read or write.

Country	Per capita GNP	Illiteracy %
Argentina	780	8.6
Bolivia	160	67.9
Brazil	240	39.3
Chile	510	16.4
Colombia	280	37.7
Cuba	320	22.1
Dominican Republic	250	40.1
Ecuador	190	32.7
Guyana	300	24.1
Haiti	70	89.5
Paraguay	200	25.7
Peru	320	39.4
Uruguay	570	9.7
Venezuela	850	34.2
Mexico and Central America	360	41.0
United States	3500	2.0

But, in the long run, the key issue is Latin America's ability to earn its own way through profitable exports as its industry develops and acquires a sense of sophistication.

It is widely acknowledged that the Rockefeller proposal was an intelligent and imaginative response to the needs of Latin America. But like the Alliance for Progress, it never really got off the ground. Nevertheless it provides a valuable exercise in international economics and economic development.

QUESTIONS

1. The lack of foreign exchange to pay for needed imports of machinery and other equipment is one of the chief obstacles faced by the LDCs in their efforts to achieve higher growth rates. Can you suggest and evaluate at least three methods of increasing the flow of foreign exchange to these countries?

2. What are some of the difficulties that are raised by the Rockefeller proposal for trade preferences to Latin American countries?

K. Galbraith's "New Industrial State": Fact or Fiction?

The American economic system has frequently been criticized by particular groups—workers, farmers, consumers, small businessmen, etc.—and these criticisms have often resulted in successful measures of reform. But not since John Maynard Keynes's book, *The General Theory of Employment, Interest, and Money* (1936), did any economist write a treatise that sought to challenge conventional economic thinking.

That is to say, no such treatise appeared until the publication of John Kenneth Galbraith's *The New Industrial State* (Houghton Mifflin, 1969). Galbraith is a professor of economics at Harvard, a former Ambassador to India (1961–63), and a man whose intellectual ideas have attracted a substantial following among college students. A provocative teacher, the 6 ft. 8 in. professor is also the author of a number of other books, some of which have been quite controversial.

The New Industrial State is no exception. Here Professor Galbraith sets forth what he believes are not only the failures of the American economic system, but the failures of economics as well. His argument can be summarized with disturbing simplicity:

The modern industrial state is not an economy of free enterprise or of consumer sovereignty. It is an economy dominated by a relatively small number of large corporations—in the United States, about 500, most if not all of them directly or indirectly dependent on Pentagon contracts. These corporations have long since experienced a separation of ownership and control so that they are governed today, not by capitalists or stockholders, but by a highly bureaucratic "technostructure" composed of the managerial and technological elite who comprise the corporate sector's "organized intelligence."

The goal of the technostructure is not to maximize profits, since these would not accrue to it anyway, but to seek its own security and to produce the "minimum levels of earnings" necessary to assure corporate growth. In its quest for these goals, the technostructure *plans* the organization's future in two ways: (1) It finances corporate growth with retained earnings rather than with new security issues, thereby freeing the firm from reliance on the capital market; and (2) it engages in the "management of demand" through advertising, thereby insulating the firm from the free market and from the whims of consumer sovereignty. In seeking security and corporate growth, the technostructure is not entirely on its own; it is aided by a government which establishes fiscal, monetary, and welfare policies to assure an adequate level of aggregate demand while subsidizing technological research and development.

The cooperation between the technostructure and the state depends, of course, on the consent of the people, who are taught to believe through "systematic public bamboozlement" that sustained economic growth and steadily rising incomes are *the* national goals. But this process is self-defeating, for as people become more educated they begin to realize that the costs of their material gains are the sacrifices they must make of truth, beauty, leisure, fellowship, etc.—in short, those ingredients that determine the quality of life. The result can only be mounting dissatisfaction with the prevailing system, as evidenced by large segments of today's college-age youth.

What is the solution for improving the quality of life? The answer is that there must be a vast expansion of the public sector—both economically and politically—in order to lessen the interest in economic growth for its own sake and permit greater emphasis on The Higher Things in Life. Otherwise, political forces must sooner or later arise that will seek to wrest the privilege of economic decision making away from the "corporate technostructure."

QUESTIONS

1. Do you agree with Galbraith's contention that the 500 largest corporations dominate the American economy? Can you suggest any qualifying remarks?

2. Is it true that firms engage in the "management of demand"? Does this mean that they thereby insulate themselves from a free market?

3. Comment on the following statements made by Galbraith:

a. Corporations are "free of the financial market because they can finance their own needs through retained earnings."

b. "Like other prices in the industrial system interest rates tend to be firmly stable."

c. "The industrial system is profoundly dependent on commercial television and could not exist without it."

d. "In areas of most exacting and advanced technology the market is most completely replaced and planning is therefore most secure."

e. "Scientific truth in economics is not always what exists; often it is what can be handled by seemingly scientific methods."

f. "Economics, as it is conventionally taught, is in part a system of belief designed less to reveal truth than to reassure its communicants about established social arrangements."

Dictionary of Economic Terms and Concepts

This dictionary catalogues the definitions of every technical word, phrase and concept given in the text. It also presents brief examples and cross references that explain the significance of important terms. Hence it will be a convenient and permanent source of reference—not only for this course, but for future courses you may take in economics, business administration, and other social sciences.

ability-to-pay principle: Theory of taxation which holds that the fairest tax is based on the financial ability of the taxpayer—regardless of any benefit he may receive from the tax. Financial ability may be determined by wealth or income. The U.S. personal income tax is founded on this principle.

absolute advantage, law of: Principle which states that a basis for trade exists between nations or regions when each of them, due to natural or acquired advantages, can provide a good or service that the other wants at a lower cost than if each were to provide it for itself. This law accounts for much of the world's trade.

accelerator principle: Proposition that small changes in the demand for consumer goods can generate magnified changes in the demand for investment goods (including inventory holdings) needed for their production. The accelerator coefficient is measured by the formula:

$$\text{Accelerator} = \frac{\text{Change in net investment}}{\text{Change in consumption from preceding period}}$$

The principle can also be used to show that a mere slowing down of the percentage rate of growth in consumption is capable of producing an actual decline in net investment, and hence an adverse effect on income.

accounts payable: A company's debts to suppliers of goods or services.

accounts receivable: Amounts due to a firm from customers.

accrued expenses payable: Obligations such as wages and salaries, interest on borrowed funds, pensions, etc.

adjustable peg: System which permits changes in the par rate of foreign exchange after a nation has had long-run disequilibrium in its balance of payments. It allows also for short-run variations within a narrow range of a few percent around the par value.

ad valorem subsidy: Fixed percentage subsidy based on the price or value of a commodity.

ad valorem tax: Fixed percentage tax on the price or value of a commodity. *Examples:* sales taxes, property taxes, and most import duties.

Agency for International Development: Semiautonomous unit of the State Department. It administers funds voted by Congress for economic, technical, and defense assistance to nations identified with the "free world."

aggregate demand: Total value of output that all sectors of the economy are willing to purchase at any given time.

aggregate supply: Total value of output produced or available for purchase by the economy at any given time.

Agricultural Adjustment Act (1938): Basic farm law (with subsequent amendments) of the United States. It provides for: (1) price supports of selected farm products at specified levels, to be implemented by purchases and nonrecourse loans by the Commodity Credit Corporation; (2) production control through acreage allotments of certain crops; (3) marketing agreements and quotas between the Department of Agriculture and producers in order to control the distribution of selected commodities; (4) payments to farmers and others who follow approved soil conservation practices; and (5) parity payments to farmers for selected agricultural staples.

Alliance for Labor Action (ALA): Federation of unions started in 1968 by the United Automobile Workers (which disaffiliated itself from the AFL-CIO) and the International Brotherhood of Teamsters.

American Federation of Labor-Congress of Industrial Organizations (AFL-CIO): Federation of labor unions formed in 1955 by a merger of the AFL and CIO. Its purposes are to improve the wages, hours, and conditions of workers, and to realize the benefits of free collective bargaining. It exercises no authority or control over member unions other than requiring them to abide by its constitution and code of ethical practices.

annually balanced budget: Philosophy which holds that total revenues and expenditures in the government's budget should be balanced or brought into equality every year.

antitrust laws: Acts passed by Congress since 1890 to prevent monopoly and to maintain competition. The chief ones are: (1) the Sherman Antitrust Act (1890); (2) the Clayton Antitrust Act (1914); (3) the Federal Trade Commission Act (1914); (4) the Robinson-Patman Act (1936); (5) the Wheeler-Lea Act (1938); and (6) the Celler Antimerger Act (1950).

arbitrage: Act of buying a commodity in one market and simultaneously selling it in a dearer market at a higher price. Arbitrage tends to equalize prices of a commodity in different markets, except for differences in the costs of transportation, risk, etc.

arbitration: Settlement of differences between parties (such as a union and management) by the use of an impartial third party called an arbitrator who is acceptable to both sides and whose decision is binding and legally enforceable on the contesting parties. The arbitrator issues a decision based not on what he

thinks is wise and fair, but on how he thinks the language of the contract applies to the case.

assets: Resources or things of value owned by a firm or individual. *Examples:* cash, property, and the rights to property.

automatic fiscal stabilizers: Nondiscretionary or "built-in" features that automatically cushion recession by helping to create a budget deficit, and curb inflation by helping to create a budget surplus. *Examples:* (1) income tax receipts; (2) unemployment taxes and benefits; (3) agricultural price supports; and (4) corporate dividend policies.

autonomous investment: Investment independent of income, output, and general economic activity.

autonomous transactions: Transactions among nations that arise from factors unrelated to the balance of payments as such. The main classes are merchandise trade and services, long-term capital movements, and unilateral transfers.

average cost pricing: *See* **full cost pricing.**

average fixed cost: Ratio of a firm's total fixed cost to the quantity it produces. Also, the difference between average total cost and average variable cost. Thus:

$$\text{Average fixed cost} = \frac{\text{Total fixed cost}}{\text{Quantity of output}}$$

Also:

$$\text{Average fixed cost} = \text{Average total cost} - \text{Average variable cost}$$

average-marginal relationship: Relationship between all corresponding average and marginal curves such that: when an average curve is rising, its corresponding marginal curve is above it; when an average curve is falling, its corresponding marginal curve is below it; and when an average curve is neither rising nor falling, i.e., it is either at a maximum or at a minimum, its corresponding marginal curve intersects (is equal to) it.

average product: Ratio of total product to the amount of variable input needed to produce that product. Thus:

$$\text{Average product} = \frac{\text{Total product}}{\text{Variable input}}$$

average propensity to consume: Ratio of consumption to income:

$$\text{Average propensity to consume} = \frac{\text{Consumption}}{\text{Income}}$$

It thus reveals the proportion of income that is spent on consumption.

average propensity to save: Ratio of saving to income:

$$\text{Average propensity to save} = \frac{\text{Saving}}{\text{Income}}$$

It thus reveals the proportion of income that is saved (i.e., not spent on consumption).

average revenue: Ratio of a firm's total revenue to its quantity of output sold—or equivalently, its price per unit of quantity sold. Thus:

$$\text{Average revenue} = \frac{\text{Total revenue}}{\text{Quantity}} = \frac{\text{(Price)(Quantity)}}{\text{Quantity}} = \text{Price}$$

average revenue product: Ratio of total revenue to the quantity of an input employed. Thus:

$$\text{Average revenue product} = \frac{\text{Total revenue}}{\text{Quantity of input employed}}$$

average tax rate: Ratio or percentage of a total tax to the base on which it is imposed. *Example:*

$$\text{Average personal income tax rate} = \frac{\text{Total personal income tax}}{\text{Total taxable income}}$$

average total cost: Ratio of a firm's total cost to the quantity it produces. Also, the sum of average fixed cost and average variable cost. Thus:

$$\text{Average total cost} = \frac{\text{Total cost}}{\text{Quantity of output}}$$

Also:

$$\text{Average total cost} = \text{Average fixed cost} + \text{Average variable cost}$$

average variable cost: Ratio of a firm's total variable cost to the quantity it produces. Also, the difference between a firm's average total cost and average fixed cost. Thus:

$$\text{Average variable cost} = \frac{\text{Total variable cost}}{\text{Quantity of output}}$$

Also:

$$\text{Average variable cost} = \text{Average total cost} - \text{Average fixed cost}$$

balanced budget: Budget with total revenues and total expenditures that are equal.

balanced-budget multiplier: Principle which asserts that if government spending and taxes are increased or decreased simultaneously by a balanced or equal amount, national income will be increased or decreased by the same amount. *Example:* A balanced increase in government spending and taxes of $1 will raise national income by $1, and a balanced decrease of $1 will lower national income by $1. The reason for this is that the effects of balanced increases in government spending and taxes are equal but opposite, and hence the two multiplier processes cancel each other out—except on the first round when the full amount of government spending is added to national income.

balance of payments: Statement of the money value of all transactions between a nation and the rest of the world during a given period. These transactions may consist of imports and exports of goods and services, and movements of short-term and long-term investments, gifts, currency, and gold; they may be classified as: current account, capital account, unilateral transfer account, and gold account.

balance of payments disequilibrium: Circumstance which exists when, over an unspecified period lasting several years, a nation's autonomous receipts (credits) do not equal its autonomous payments (debits). A deficit disequilibrium exists when total auton-

omous payments exceed total autonomous receipts; a surplus disequilibrium occurs when total autonomous receipts exceed total autonomous payments.

balance of trade: That part of a nation's balance of payments dealing with merchandise imports and exports. A "favorable" balance of trade exists when the value of exports exceeds the value of imports; an "unfavorable" balance exists when the value of imports exceeds the value of exports.

balance sheet: Statement of a firm's financial position on a given date. It shows what the firm owns (its assets), what it owes (its liabilities), and the residual or equity of the owners (the net worth).

banker's acceptance: Bill of exchange drawn on or accepted by a bank instead of an individual or firm. It is a promise by a bank to pay specific bills for one of its customers when the bills become due. (*See* **bill of exchange; draft.**)

barter: Simple exchange of one good for another without the use of money.

basic wages: Payments received by workers for work performed, based on time or output.

benefit-cost analysis: Technique of evaluating alternative programs by comparing for each the (discounted) present value of all expected benefits with all expected costs. The discount factor is a percentage representing the "opportunity cost" of capital—that is, what the funds would have earned in their best alternative use at equal risk. The chief weakness of benefit-cost analysis is that some benefits and costs cannot always be defined and measured. Hence the use of relative benefits and costs for setting priorities among different programs may result in conflicting choices.

benefit principle: Theory of taxation which holds that a fair tax is one which is levied on people according to the benefits they receive from government. The chief difficulties are that: (1) for many goods, benefits cannot be readily determined (e.g., national defense, public education, police and fire protection, etc.); and (2) those who receive the benefits are not always able to pay for them (e.g., recipients of welfare or unemployment compensation).

bilateral monopoly: Market structure in which a monopsonist buyer faces a monopolist seller. The equilibrium quantity may be determinate. However, the price level for that quantity is logically indeterminate. That is, the price will end up somewhere between the minimum price preferred by the monopsonist and the maximum price preferred by the monopolist.

bill of exchange: Draft (or type of "check") used between countries. (*See* **draft.**)

bimetallic standard: Monetary standard which defines the national unit of currency (such as the dollar) in terms of a fixed weight of two metals, usually gold and silver. The U.S. was on this standard during the 19th century, but it usually worked unsatisfactorily due to the operation of Gresham's Law. (*See* **Gresham's Law; mint ratio.**)

black capitalism: Effort begun in the late 1960s to increase Negro ownership and control of business—especially the latter. Its objectives are to improve the job market, the ghetto economy, and the condition of the black community.

black market: Illegal market in which a good is sold for more than the legal ceiling price.

Board of Governors: Group of seven people that supervises the Federal Reserve System. Members are appointed by the President and confirmed by the Senate for terms of 14 years each, one term expiring every two years.

bond: Agreement to pay a specified sum (called the "principal") either at a future date or periodically over the course of a loan, during which time a fixed rate of interest may be paid on certain dates. Bonds are issued by corporations, and by the federal, state and local governments. They are typically used for long-term financing.

boycott: Campaign to discourage people from dealing with a particular firm. (Sometimes called a "primary boycott.")

Brannan Plan: Proposal made by Secretary of Agriculture Charles F. Brannan in 1949. It would eliminate parity payments to farmers and give them direct payments instead. Under the plan, agricultural prices would be determined in a free market by supply and demand; farmers would then be compensated by a subsidy from the government for the difference between the market price they receive and some higher target price established according to a selected base period in the past.

breakeven point: Level of output at which a firm's total revenue equals its total cost (or its average revenue equals its average total cost) so that its net revenue is zero. At a breakeven point as defined in economics, a firm is normally profitable since total cost in economics includes normal profit.

budget: Itemized estimate of expected revenues and expenditures for a given period in the future.

budget deficit: Budget in which total expenditures exceed total revenues.

budget surplus: Budget in which total revenues exceed total expenditures.

business cycles: Recurrent but nonperiodic fluctuations in general business and economic activity that take place over a period of years. They occur in aggregate variables like income, output, employment, and prices, most of which may move at approximately the same time in the same direction, but at different rates.

cameralism: Form of mercantilism extensively implemented by German governments during the 18th century. Its chief objective was to increase the revenue of the state. (The word comes from *Kammer,* the name of the royal treasury.)

capital: 1. As a factor of production, capital is a produced means of further production (such as capital goods or investment goods in the form of raw materials, machines, equipment, etc.) for the ultimate purpose of manufacturing consumer goods. Hence human resources are also part of an economy's capital. **2.** As money, capital represents the funds which businessmen use to purchase capital goods. **3.** In accounting, capital may sometimes represent net worth or the stockholders' equity in a business.

capital consumption allowance: Expression used in national income accounting to represent the difference between "gross" and "net" private domestic investment. It consists almost entirely of depreciation and is often used synonomously with it.

capital deepening: Increase in capital relative to other resources, especially labor. Usually applied to a nation, but can equally apply to a region, or even to a firm.

capitalism: Economic organization characterized by private ownership of the means of production and distribution (such as land, factories, railroads, etc.) and their operation for profit under predominantly competitive conditions.

capital market: Center where long-term credit instruments such as bonds, stocks, and mortgages are bought and sold.

capital/output ratio: Concept sometimes used in a "total" sense, and sometimes in a "marginal" sense. Thus: **1.** The "total" capital/output ratio is the ratio of an economy's total stock of real capital to the level of its income or output. **2.** The "marginal" capital/output ratio is the change in an economy's income or output resulting from a unit change in its stock of real capital. Thus a ratio of 3/1 means that three units of additional capital produces one unit of additional output.

capital stock: Unit of ownership in a corporation. It represents the stockholder's proprietary interest. Two major classes are common stock and preferred stock.

cartel: International association of firms in the same industry, established to allocate world markets among its members and to regulate prices. Sometimes called an "international monopoly."

Celler Antimerger Act (1950): Major antitrust law. An extension of Section 7 of the Clayton Antitrust Act, it prohibits a corporation from acquiring the stock *or assets* of another corporation if the effect would be a substantial lessening of competition or tendency toward monopoly. *Note:* prior to this law, only the acquisition of *stock* by competing corporations was illegal under the Clayton Act.

certificate of deposit (CD): Special type of time deposit which a purchaser agrees to keep in a bank for a specified period, usually three months or more. Many CDs are negotiable, and hence can be sold in a secondary market because they offer both liquidity and a yield. Banks began to offer CDs in the early 1960s at rates competitive with other money market instruments, in order to discourage corporations from withdrawing money for the purpose of investing in securities.

change in amount consumed: Increase or decrease in the amount of consumption expenditure due to a change in income. It may be represented by a movement along a consumption-function curve.

change in consumption: Increase or decrease in consumption, represented by a shift of the consumption-function curve to a new position. The shift results from a change in any of the factors that were assumed to remain constant when the curve was drawn. These may include (1) the volume of liquid assets owned by households, (2) expectations of future prices and incomes, (3) anticipations of product shortages, and (4) credit conditions.

change in demand: Increase or decrease in demand, represented by a shift of the demand curve to a new position. The shift results from a change in any of the factors that were assumed to remain constant when the curve was drawn. These may include (1) buyers' money incomes, (2) the prices of related goods, (3) buyers' tastes or preferences, (4) the number of buyers in the market, and (5) buyers' expectations about future prices and incomes.

change in quantity demanded: Increase or decrease in the quantity demanded of a good due to a change in its price. It may be represented by a movement along a demand curve.

change in quantity supplied: Increase or decrease in the quantity supplied of a good due to a change in its price. It may be represented by a movement along a supply curve.

change in supply: Increase or decrease in supply, represented by a shift of the supply curve to a new position. The shift results from a change in any of the factors that were assumed to remain constant when the curve was drawn. These may include (1) the state of technology, (2) resource prices or the costs of the factors of production, (3) the prices of other goods, (4) the number of sellers in the market, and (5) sellers' expectations regarding future prices.

checkoff: Procedure by which an employer, with the written permission of the worker, withholds union dues and other assessments from paychecks and then transfers the funds to the union. This provides an efficient means by which the union can collect dues from its members.

Christian socialism: Movement, since the late 19th century, by various church groups to preach the "social gospel"—a type of social legislation and reform that seeks to improve the well-being of the working classes by appealing to Christian ethical and humanitarian principles.

circular flow of economic activity: Model demonstrating the movement of goods, resources, payments, and expenditures among sectors of the economy. A simple model may include the household and business sectors, and the product and resource markets—but other models may be constructed which are more complex.

classical economics: Body of economic thought dominant in the western world from the late 18th century until the 1930s. Among its chief proponents were Adam Smith (1723–1790), Jean Baptiste Say (1767–1832), Jeremy Bentham (1748–1832), Thomas Robert Malthus (1766–1834), David Ricardo (1772–1823), and John Stuart Mill (1806–1873). They emphasized man's self-interest, and the operation of universal economic laws which tend automatically to guide the economy toward full employment equilibrium if the government adheres to a policy of laissez-faire or noninterventionism.

class struggle: In the theories of Karl Marx, an irreconcilable clash between the bourgeoisie or capitalist class and the proletariat or working class, arising out of the surplus value which capitalists appropriate from workers. The class struggle will eventually be resolved when the proletariat overthrows the bourgeoisie and establishes a new and equitable economic order.

Clayton Antitrust Act (1914): A major antitrust law aimed at preventing unfair, deceptive, dishonest, or injurious methods of competition. It declares as illegal, where the effect is a substantial lessening of competition or tendency toward monopoly: (1) price

discrimination, except where there are differences in grade, quality, or quantity sold, or where the lower prices make due allowances for cost differences in selling or transportation, or where the lower prices are offered in good faith to meet competition; (2) tying contracts between sellers and purchasers; and (3) intercorporate stockholdings among competing corporations. It also makes illegal, regardless of the effect on competition: (4) interlocking directorates if the corporations involved are competitive and if any one of them has capital, surplus, and undivided profits in excess of $1 million.

closed shop: A firm which agrees that an employee must be a union member before he is employed, and must remain a union member after he is employed. Outlawed by the Labor-Management Relations (Taft-Hartley) Act of 1947.

coalition bargaining: Method of bargaining by which a federation of unions (such as the AFL-CIO) tries to coordinate and establish common termination dates for contracts with firms that deal with a number of unions at their plants throughout the economy. Its purpose is to enable the federation to strengthen union bargaining positions by threatening to close down all plants simultaneously.

cobweb theorem: Generic name for a theory of cyclical fluctuations in the prices and quantities of various agricultural commodities—fluctuations which arise because for certain agricultural products: (1) the quantity demanded of the commodity at any given time depends on its price at that time, whereas (2) the quantity supplied at any given time depends on its price at a previous time when production plans were initially formulated. Hogs and beefcattle have been notable examples.

coefficient of relative effectiveness (CRE): Term used in the Soviet Union to mean the expected payoff or percent rate of return on a capital investment; akin to the concept of marginal efficiency of investment in Western economics.

coincident indicators: Time series that tend to move approximately "in phase" with the aggregate economy, and hence are measures of current economic activity.

collective agreement: A collective bargaining contract worked out between union and management, describing wages, working conditions, and related matters.

collective bargaining: Negotiation between a company's management and a union for the purpose of agreeing on mutually acceptable wages and working conditions for employees.

collective farms: Agricultural cooperatives in the Soviet Union, consisting of communities of farmers who pool their resources, lease land from the government, and divide the profits among the members according to the amount and kind of work done by each. This type of farming, which is subject to detailed government regulation, dominates agriculture in the Soviet Union.

command economy: Economic system in which an authoritarian government exercises primary control over decisions concerning what and how much to produce; it may also, but does not necessarily, decide for whom to produce. (Contrast with **planned economy.**)

commercial bank: Financial institution, chartered by federal or state governments, primarily engaged in making short-term industrial and commercial loans by creating demand or checking deposits, and retiring loans by canceling demand deposits. It may also perform other financial functions such as holding time or savings deposits and making long-term mortgage loans.

common market: Association of trading nations which agrees to: (1) impose no trade restrictions such as tariffs or quotas among participants; (2) establish common external barriers (such as a common external tariff) to nonparticipants; and (3) impose no national restrictions on the movement of labor and capital among participants. *Example:* European Economic Community (EEC).

common stock: Shares that have no fixed rate of dividends, and hence may receive higher dividends than the fixed rate on preferred stock if the corporation's earnings are sufficiently high.

Commonwealth (Mass.) vs. Hunt (1842): The first case in which a (Massachusetts) court held a trade union to be a lawful organization. It declared that workers could form a union to bargain collectively with employers.

communism: 1. In the theories of Karl Marx, the final and perfect goal of historical development, characterized by: (1) a classless society in which all men live by earning and no man lives by owning; (2) a nonexistent state; and (3) a wage system which is completely abolished and all citizens live and work according to the motto: "from each according to his ability, to each according to his needs." **2.** In most communist countries today, an economic system based on: (1) social ownership of property including most of the means of production and distribution; (2) government planning and control of the economy; and (3) a scheme of rewards and penalties to achieve maximum productive effort. *Note:* Communist leaders claim that the system which exists in communist countries today is socialism of the type which Marxian ideology holds as being preparatory to the attainment of full communism.

community (social) rate of return: Net value of a project to an economy (i.e., a town, city, state, or country). It is estimated on the basis of the net increase in output which a project such as a new industry may be expected to bring, directly or indirectly, to the area being developed. The industry's contribution is determined by subtracting from the value of what it produces the cost of the resources it uses. Hence the measure is intended to reflect all economic and social benefits as well as costs. (Contrast with **private rate of return.**)

company union: A labor union limited to a particular firm. It is usually unaffiliated with any other union.

comparative advantage, law of: Principle which states that if one nation can produce each of two products more efficiently than another nation, and can produce one of these commodities more efficiently than the other, it should specialize in the product in which it is most efficient and leave production of the alternative product to the other country. The two nations will then have more of both goods by engaging in trade. This principle is applicable to individuals and regions as well as to nations.

compensatory transactions: Transactions among nations that are a direct response to balance-of-payments considerations. They may be thought of as balancing items which arise to accommodate differences in money inflows and outflows resulting from so-called autonomous transactions. The two main classes are short-term capital movements, and shifts in gold holdings.

complementary goods: Two or more commodities that are related because a change in the quantity demanded of one results in a *direct* change in the quantity demanded of the other, within a consumer's given budget. For example, if a fall in the price of bread causes a consumer to increase his quantity demanded of bread, and this in turn raises his quantity demanded of butter, then bread and butter are complements within his given budget. (Contrast with **substitute goods.**)

competition: Rivalry among buyers and sellers of goods or resources. Competition tends to be directly related to the degree of diffusion (as opposed to the concentration) of market power, and the freedom with which buyers and sellers can enter or leave particular markets. It is sometimes used to mean perfect (pure) competition, depending on whether it is employed in that context.

compound interest: Interest computed on a principal sum and also on all the interest earned by that principal sum as of a given date.

concentration ratio: Percentage of an industry's output accounted for by its four leading firms.

conglomerate merger: Amalgamation under one ownership of unlike plants producing unrelated products. It reflects a desire by the acquiring company to spread risks, find outlets for idle capital funds, add products which can be sold with the firm's merchandising knowledge and skills, or simply gain economic power on a broader front.

conscious parallel action: Identical price behavior among competing firms. It may or may not be the result of collusion or prior agreement, but has nevertheless been held illegal by the courts in various antitrust cases.

consent decree: A means of settling cases in equity among the parties involved (such as a defendant firm and the Department of Justice). The defendant does not declare himself guilty, but agrees nevertheless to cease and desist from certain practices and abide by the rules of behavior set down in the decree. This is the chief instrument employed by the Justice Department and by the Federal Trade Commission in the enforcement of the Sherman and Clayton Acts. The majority of antitrust violations are settled in this manner.

"conspicuous consumption": Expression originated by Thorstein Veblen (1857–1929) to mean that those above the subsistence level, i.e., the so-called "leisure class," are mainly concerned with impressing others through their standard of living, taste, and dress—that is, through what he called "pecuniary emulation." ("Keeping up with the Joneses" is a popular expression of this concept).

constant-cost industry: Industry which experiences no increases in resource prices or in costs of production as it expands, despite new firms entering it. This will happen only when the industry's demand for the resources it employs is an insignificant proportion of the total demand for those resources.

constant dollars: Expression reflecting the actual prices of a previous year or the average of actual prices of a previous period of years. Hence economic data are often quoted in constant dollars. (Contrast with **current dollars.**)

consumer sovereignty: Concept of the consumer as "king"—in the sense that the consumer registers his preferences for goods by his "dollar votes" in the marketplace. In a highly competitive economy competition among producers will cause them to adjust their production to the changing patterns of consumer demands. In less competitive economies, where monopolistic forces and other imperfections exist, resources will not be allocated entirely in accordance with consumer wishes.

consumer's surplus: Value or utility that accrues to a buyer for paying less than the maximum amount he would have been willing to pay for the quantity of the commodity he purchases.

consumption: Expenditures on consumer goods and services.

consumption function: Relationship between consumption expenditures and income such that as income increases, consumption increases, but not as fast as income. The expression **propensity to consume** is often used synonymously. (*Note:* Since the word "function" is employed here in its mathematical sense to mean a variable whose value depends on the value of another variable, the expression "consumption function" can also be used to designate *any* type of relationship between consumption and income—not necessarily the type defined above. However, the above type is the most common one.)

convergence hypothesis: Conjecture that capitalism and communism, driven by the process of industrialization, will eventually merge to form a new kind of society in which the personal freedoms and profit motive of Western capitalistic democracies blend with the government controls that exist in a communistic (especially Soviet) economy.

corporation: Association of stockholders created under law, but regarded by the courts as an artificial person existing only in the contemplation of the law. The chief characteristics of a corporation are: (1) limited liability of its stockholders; (2) stability and permanence; and (3) ability to accumulate large sums of capital for expansion through the sale of stocks and bonds.

countervailing power: Proposition that in the U.S. the growth of market power by one group may tend to stimulate the growth of a counterreaction and somewhat offsetting influence by another group. *Examples:* big labor unions face big corporations at the bargaining table; chain stores deal with large processing and manufacturing firms; and big government faces big business and big unions.

cost: Sacrifice that must be made to do or to acquire something. What is sacrificed may be money, goods, leisure time, security, prestige, power or pleasure.

cost-effectiveness analysis: Technique of selecting from alternative programs the one that attains a given objective at the lowest cost. It is a type of analysis most useful when benefits cannot be measured in money.

cost-push inflation: Condition of generally rising prices caused by production costs that increase faster than productivity or efficiency.

craft union: Labor union composed of workers in a particular trade such as bakers, carpenters, and teamsters. It is thus a "horizontally" organized union.

crawling peg: System of foreign exchange rates which permits the par value of a nation's currency to change automatically by small increments, downward or upward, if in actual daily trading on the foreign exchange markets the price in terms of other currencies persists on the "floor" or "ceiling" of the established range for a specified period.

credit: In international economics, any transaction which results in a money inflow or receipt from a foreign country. It may be represented on a balance-of-payments statement by a plus sign.

credit instrument: Written or printed financial document serving as either a promise or order to transfer funds from one person to another.

creeping inflation: Slow but persistent upward movement in the general level of prices over a long period of years, typically at an average annual rate of up to 3 percent.

currency: Coins and paper money.

current assets: Cash and other assets that can be turned quickly into cash.

current dollars: An expression reflecting actual prices of each year. Hence economic data are often quoted in current dollars. (Contrast with **constant dollars.**)

current liabilities: Debts that fall due within a year.

customs union: Agreement among two or more trading nations to abolish trade barriers such as tariffs and quotas among themselves, and to adopt a common external policy of trade (such as a common external tariff with all nonmember nations). *Example:* Benelux (i.e., Belgium, Luxembourg, and the Netherlands).

cyclically balanced budget: Philosophy which holds that total revenues and expenditures in the government's budget should be balanced or brought into equality over the course of a business cycle.

cyclical unemployment: Unemployment which results from business recessions or depressions because aggregate demand falls too far below the full employment level of aggregate output and income.

death taxes: Taxes on estates and inheritances. They are imposed by federal and state governments at progressive rates.

debit: In international economics, any transaction which results in a money outflow or payment to a foreign country. It may be represented on a balance-of-payments statement by a minus sign.

decreasing-cost industry: Industry which experiences decreases in resource prices or in its costs of production as it expands because of new firms entering it. This situation might arise for a while as a result of substantial external economies of scale.

deduction: In logical thinking, a process of reasoning from premises to conclusions. The premises are more general than the conclusions, so deduction is often defined as reasoning from the general to the particular. (Opposite of **induction**.)

deflation: 1. Statistical adjustment of data by which an economic time series expressed in current dollars is converted into a series expressed in constant dollars of a previous period. The purpose of the adjustment is to compensate for the distorting effects of inflation—i.e., the long-run upward trend of prices—through a reverse process of "deflation." **2.** Decline in the general price level of all goods and services—or equivalently, a rise in the purchasing power of money. (Contrast with **inflation**.)

deflationary gap: Amount by which aggregate demand falls short of full-employment aggregate supply, thereby pulling down the real value of a nation's output.

demand: Relation expressing the various amounts of a commodity that buyers would be willing and able to purchase at possible alternative prices during a given period of time, all other things remaining the same. This relation may be expressed as a table (called a **demand schedule**), as a graph (called a **demand curve**), or as a mathematical equation.

demand curve: Graph of a demand schedule, showing the number of units of a commodity that buyers would be able and willing to purchase at various possible prices during a given period of time, all other things remaining the same.

demand deposit: Promise by a bank to pay immediately an amount of money specified by the customer who owns the deposit. It is thus "checkbook money" because it permits transactions to be paid for by check rather than with currency.

demand, law of: Principle which states that the quantity demanded of a commodity varies inversely with its price, assuming that all other things which may affect demand remain the same. These "all other" things include: (1) buyers' money incomes; (2) the prices of related goods; (3) buyers' tastes or preferences; (4) the number of buyers in the market; and (5) buyers' expectations regarding future prices and incomes.

demand price: Highest price a buyer is willing to pay for a given quantity of a commodity.

demand-pull inflation: Condition of generally rising prices caused by increases in aggregate demand at a time when available supplies of goods are becoming more limited. Goods may go into short supply because resources are fully utilized or because production cannot be increased rapidly enough to meet growing demand.

demand schedule: Table showing the number of units of a commodity that buyers would be able and willing to purchase at various possible prices during a given period of time, all other things remaining the same.

deposit expansion multiplier: Proposition that an increase in a bank's deposits may, because of an increase in its excess reserves, cause a larger or magnified increase in the deposits of the banking system as a whole. The converse of this in the case of a deposit decrease is also true. The total cumulative expansion (or contraction) will at most be some multiple of the initial deposit. The deposit expansion multiplier can be given by the formula:

$$\text{Deposit expansion multiplier} = \frac{1}{\text{Legal reserve ratio}}$$

There are "leakages," however, which prevent this multiplier from exerting its full impact. They include: (1) the leakage of cash into circulation, since some deposits will be withdrawn in cash and some checks will be "cashed" instead of deposited; (2) a margin of excess reserves which banks for one reason or another may not lend out; and (3) the failure of businessmen to borrow all that the banks want to lend.

depreciation: Decline in the useful value of a fixed asset, such as plant or equipment, due to wear and tear, destruction, or obsolescence resulting from the development of new and better techniques.

depression: Lower phase of a business cycle in which the economy is operating with substantial unemployment of its resources, and a sluggish rate of capital investment and consumption resulting from little business and consumer optimism.

derived demand: Demand for a product or resource based on its contribution to the product for which it is used. *Examples:* the separate demands for bricks, lumber, etc., are derived partly from the demand for construction; the demand for steel is derived partly from the demand for automobiles.

devaluation: Official act which makes a domestic currency cheaper in terms of gold or foreign currencies. It is typically designed to increase a nation's exports while reducing its imports. *Example:* The U.S. devalued the dollar relative to gold in 1934 by raising the Treasury's buying and selling price of gold from $20.67 an ounce to $35 an ounce. This made it cheaper for foreigners to buy dollars, and more expensive for Americans to buy foreign currencies.

dialectical materialism: Logical method of historical analysis. In particular, it was used by Karl Marx, who employed the philosopher Hegel's idea that historical change is the result of inherently conflicting or opposing forces in society, and that the forces are basically economic or materialistic.

"dictatorship of the proletariat": Expression used by Karl Marx to describe a stage of Marxian socialism in which the bourgeoisie or capitalist class has been toppled from power and, along with its properties, is under the management of the proletariat or working class, which is also in control of the state.

diminishing marginal utility, law of: In a given period of time, the consumption of a product while tastes remain constant may at first result in increasing marginal utilities per unit of the product consumed, but a point will be reached beyond which further units of consumption of the product will result in decreasing marginal utilities per unit of the product consumed. This is the point of diminishing marginal utility. *Note:* Even though marginal utility may rise at first, it *must eventually fall*. It is the diminishing phase of marginal utility that is relevant, and serves as the basis for the law.

diminishing returns (variable proportions), law of: In a given state of technology, the addition of a variable factor of production to other fixed factors of production may at first yield increasing marginal returns per unit of the variable factor added, but a point will be reached beyond which further additions of the variable factor will yield diminishing marginal returns per unit of the variable factor added. This is the point of diminishing marginal returns. *Note:* Even though marginal returns may rise at first, they *must eventually fall.* It is the diminishing phase of marginal returns that is relevant, and serves as the basis for the law.

direct tax: Tax that is not shifted—that is, its burden is borne by the persons or firms originally taxed. *Examples:* personal income taxes, social security taxes paid by employees, and death taxes.

discount rate: Interest rate charged to member banks on their loans from the Federal Reserve Banks. It is called a "discount rate" because the interest on the loans is discounted when the loan is made, rather than collected when the loan is repaid.

disequilibrium: State of nonequilibrium. *Example:* a situation in which the quantities supplied and demanded of a commodity at a given price are unequal, so that there is a tendency for market prices and/or quantities to change. Any economic organism or system such as a household, a firm, a market, or an economy which is not in equilibrium is said to be in disequilibrium.

disguised unemployment (underemployment): Situation in which employed resources are not being used in their most efficient ways.

disinvestment: Reduction in the total stock of capital goods caused by failure to replace it as it wears out. *Example:* the consumption or using up of factories, machines, etc., at a faster rate than they are being replaced so that the productive base is diminishing.

disposable personal income: Income remaining after payment of personal taxes.

dissaving: Expenditure on consumption in excess of income. This may be accomplished by drawing on past savings, borrowing, or receiving help from others.

dividend: Earnings which a corporation pays to its stockholders. Payments are usually in cash, but may also be in property, securities, or other forms.

division of labor: Specialization in productive activities among workers, resulting in increased production because it: (1) permits development and refinement of skills; (2) avoids the time that is wasted in going from one job to another; and (3) allows the employment of persons best suited to particular types of work.

double coincidence of wants: Situation which is necessary in a barter exchange, because each party must have what the other wants, and must be willing to trade at the exact quantities and terms suitable to both.

double taxation: Taxation of the same base in two different forms. A typical example is the corporate income tax: the corporation pays an income tax on its profits, and the stockholder pays an income tax on the dividends he receives from those profits.

draft: Unconditional written order by one party (the creditor or drawer) on a second party (the debtor or drawee) directing him to pay a third party (the bearer or payee) a specified sum of money. An ordinary check, therefore, is an example of a draft.

dumping: Sale of the same product in different markets at different prices. *Example:* A monopolist might restrict his output in the domestic market and charge a higher price because demand is relatively inelastic, and "dump" the rest of his output in a foreign market at a lower price because demand there is relatively elastic. He thereby gains the benefit of lower average total costs on his entire output (domestic plus foreign), and earns a larger net profit than if he sold the entire output in the domestic market—which he could do only by charging a lower price per unit on all units sold.

duopoly: Oligopoly consisting of two sellers. Hence it may be either a perfect duopoly or an imperfect one, depending on whether the product is standardized or differentiated.

economic man: The notion that each individual in a capitalistic society, whether he be a worker, businessman, consumer, investor, etc., is motivated by economic forces, and hence will always act to obtain the greatest satisfaction for the least sacrifice or cost. Satisfaction may take the form of profits to a businessman, leisure hours to a worker, pleasure to a consumer from the goods that he purchases, and so on.

economic plan: Detailed method, formulated beforehand, for achieving specific economic objectives by governing the activities and interrelationships of those economic organisms, namely firms, households, and governments, that have an influence on the desired outcome.

economic (pure) profit: Payment to a firm in excess of its economic costs, including normal profit. It is the same as **net revenue.**

economic rent: Payment to an owner of a factor of production, in an industry in equilibrium, in excess of the factor's supply price or opportunity cost—that is, in excess of the minimum amount necessary to keep that factor in its present occupation. It is thus a surplus to the recipient.

economics: Social science concerned chiefly with the way society chooses to employ its limited resources, which have alternative uses, to produce goods and services for present and future consumption.

economic system: Relationships between the organisms or components of an economy (such as its households, firms, and government) and the institutional framework of laws and customs within which these organisms operate.

economies (diseconomies) of scale: The decreases (increases) in a firm's long-run average costs as the size of its plant is increased. Those factors that give rise to economies of scale or decreasing long-run average costs of production as the plant size increases are: (1) greater specialization of resources; (2) more efficient utilization of equipment; (3) reduced unit costs of inputs; (4) opportunities for economical utilization of by-products; and (5) growth of auxiliary facilities. Diseconomies of scale may eventually set in, however, due to: (1) limitations of (or "diminishing returns" to) management in its decision-making function; and (2) competition among firms in bidding up the prices of limited resources.

econometrics: Integration of economic theory, mathematics, and statistics. It consists of expressing economic relationships in the form of mathematical equations, and verifying the resulting models by statistical methods.

economic costs: Payments made to the owners of the factors of production to persuade them to supply their resources in a particular activity.

economic good: Scarce good—that is, any good for which the market price is greater than zero at a particular time and place. (Opposite of **free good**.)

economic growth: Rate of increase in an economy's real output or income over time—that is, the rise in its full employment output in constant prices. Economic growth may be expressed in terms of either real GNP or real NNP, on either a total or per capita basis over a period of time. The "total" measure is employed to describe the expansion of a nation's economic output or potential, whereas the "per capita" measure is used to express its material standard of living and to compare it with other countries.

economic indicators: Time series of economic data, classified as either leading, lagging, or coincident indicators. They are used in business cycle analysis and forecasting.

economic interpretation of history: Proposition advanced by Karl Marx (and others) that the great political, social, intellectual, and ethical movements of history are determined by the ways in which societies organize their social institutions to carry on the basic economic activities of production, exchange, distribution, and consumption of goods. Thus, economic forces are the prime cause of fundamental historical change.

elasticity: Percentage change in quantity demanded or supplied resulting from a 1% change in price. Mathematically, it is the ratio of the percentage change in quantity (demanded or supplied) to the percentage change in price:

$$\text{Elasticity, } E = \frac{\text{Percentage change in quantity}}{\text{Percentage change in price}}$$

$$= \frac{(Q_2 - Q_1)/(Q_2 + Q_1)}{(P_2 - P_1)/(P_2 + P_1)}$$

where Q_1 and Q_2, and P_1 and P_2, denote the corresponding quantities and prices before and after the change. This coefficient of elasticity is usually stated numerically without regard to algebraic sign, and may range from zero to infinity. It may take any of five forms:

perfectly elastic ($E = \infty$)
relatively elastic ($E > 1$)
unit elastic ($E = 1$)
relatively inelastic ($E < 1$)
perfectly inelastic ($E = 0$)

The above definition refers to what is known as *price elasticity* of demand or supply. It is one of several types of elasticities that exist in economics, and is the one that is commonly understood unless otherwise specified. In general, elasticity may be thought of as the responsiveness of changes in one variable to changes in another, where responsiveness is measured in terms of percentage changes.

Employment Act of 1946: Act of Congress which requires the government to maintain high levels of employment, production, and purchasing power. To assist the President in this task, the Act authorizes him to appoint a panel of experts known as the Council of Economic Advisors.

Engel's Laws: Set of relationships between consumer expenditures and income, derived by a 19th century German statistician, Ernst Engel, based on research into workingmen's purchases in Western Europe during the 1850s. The relationships state that as a family's income increases: (1) the percentage it spends on food decreases; (2) the percentage it spends on housing and household operations remains about constant (except for fuel, light, and refrigeration, which increases); and (3) the percentage it spends on all other categories and the amount it saves increases (except for medical care and personal care items, which remain fairly constant). In general, the *total* amount spent increases as a family's income increases. *Note:* Strictly speaking, only the first relationship above is attributed to Engel; the other two are modernized versions of his early findings, based on more recent research.

entrepreneurship: Factor of production which designates the function performed by those who assemble the other factors of production, raise the necessary money, organize the management, make the basic business policy decisions, and reap the gains of success or the losses of failure. The entrepreneur is the innovator and the catalyst in a capitalistic system. He need not be exclusively an owner or a manager; the entrepreneurial function may be performed by both, depending on the size and complexity of the firm.

equation of exchange: Expression of the relation between the quantity of money (M), its velocity of circulation (V), the average price (P) of final goods and services, and the physical quantity (Q) of those goods and services, thus:

$$MV = PQ$$

The equation is actually an identity which states that the total amount of money spent on goods and services (MV) is equal to the total amount of money received for goods and services (PQ). (See **quantity theory of money**.)

equilibrium: State of balance between opposing forces. An object in equilibrium is in a state of rest and has no tendency to change.

equilibrium conditions: Set of relationships that defines the equilibrium properties of an economic organism such as a household, a firm, or an entire economy.

equilibrium price: 1. Price of a commodity determined in the market by the intersection of a supply and demand curve. (Also called **normal price**.) 2. Price (and corresponding equilibrium quantity) that maximizes a firm's profit.

equilibrium quantity: 1. Quantity of a commodity determined in the market by the intersection of a supply and demand curve. 2. Quantity (and corresponding equilibrium price) that maximizes a firm's profit.

European Recovery Program (ERP): Commonly known as the "Marshall Plan" (after Secretary of State George C. Marshall who proposed it in 1947), this was a comprehensive recovery blueprint for European countries, financed by the United States, for the purposes of: (1) increasing their productive capacity; (2) stabilizing their financial systems; (3) promoting their mutual economic cooperation; and (4) reducing their dependence on U.S. assistance. The ERP was terminated in 1951 after considerable success, and its functions were absorbed by other government agencies and programs.

excess reserve: Surplus of vault cash or deposits with other banks which a bank has available for loans and investments. It is the amount over and above its legal reserve.

excise tax: Tax imposed on the manufacture, sale, or consumption of various commodities such as liquor, tobacco, gasoline, etc.

explicit costs: Money outlays of a firm recorded in its books of account. (Contrast with **implicit costs.**)

external economies and diseconomies of scale: Conditions that bring about decreases or increases in a firm's long-run average costs or scale of operations as a result of factors that are entirely outside of the firm as a producing unit. They depend on adjustments of the industry and are related to the firm only to the extent that the firm is a part of the industry. *Example:* external economies may result from improvements in public transportation and marketing facilities as an industry develops in a particular geographic area; however, diseconomies may eventually set in as firms bid up the prices of limited resources in the area.

Fabian socialism: Form of socialism founded in England in 1884. It emerged as an outgrowth of utopian socialism by advocating gradual and evolutionary reform within a democratic framework.

factors of production: Human and nonhuman productive resources of an economy, usually classified into four groups: land, labor, capital, and entrepreneurship.

family allowance plan: Plan that provides every family, rich or poor, with a certain amount of money based exclusively on the number and age of its children. Families above certain designated income levels return all or a portion of the money with their income taxes, but those below specified income levels keep it. More than 60 countries have family allowance plans.

featherbedding: Labor-union "make work" rules designed to increase the labor or labor time on a particular job. Outlawed by the Labor-Management Relations (Taft-Hartley) Act of 1947.

Federal Advisory Council: Committee within the Federal Reserve System that advises the Board of Governors on important current developments.

Federal Open Market Committee: The most important policy-making body of the Federal Reserve System. Its chief function is to establish policy for the System's purchase and sale of Government and other securities in the open market.

Federal Reserve Bank: One of the twelve banks (and branches) which make up the Federal Reserve System. Each serves as a "banker's bank" for the member banks in its district by acting as a source of credit and a depository of resources, and by performing other useful functions.

Federal Reserve System: Central banking system created by Congress in 1913. It consists of: (1) twelve Federal Reserve Banks—one located in each of twelve districts in the country; (2) a Board of Governors; (3) a Federal Open Market Committee and various other committees; and (4) several thousand member banks which hold the great majority of all commercial bank deposits in the nation.

Federal Trade Commission: Government agency created in 1914. It is charged with preventing unfair business practices by enforcing the Federal Trade Commission Act, and exercising concurrently with the Justice Department the enforcement of prohibited provisions of the Clayton Antitrust Act as amended by the Robinson-Patman Act.

Federal Trade Commission Act (1914): A major antitrust law of the U.S. Its chief purpose is to prevent unfair (i.e., deceptive, dishonest, or injurious) methods of competition and, as amended by the Wheeler-Lea Act (1938), to safeguard the public by preventing the dissemination of false and misleading advertising of food, drugs, cosmetics, and therapeutic devices.

financial intermediaries: Nonbank saving and lending institutions such as savings and loan associations, insurance companies, personal finance companies, and credit unions. These organizations do not create demand deposits, but have large volumes of savings that they invest or lend to the public. Hence they may sometimes help to offset restrictive monetary policies which the Federal Reserve authorities are pursuing.

firm: Business organization which owns and directs the activities of one or more of its plants or offices.

fiscal dividend: Disbursement of accumulated budgetary surpluses by the federal government to society, thereby offsetting the effect of fiscal drag. The fiscal dividend may consist of: (1) increased federal spending on public goods; (2) reduced taxes on the private sector; and (3) larger grants-in-aid to state and local governments. Any of these would help stimulate further consumption and investment expenditures.

fiscal drag: Tendency of a high-employment economy to be held back from its full growth potential because it is incurring budgetary surpluses. Such surpluses may arise because, other things being equal, a progressive tax system tends to generate increases in revenues relative to expenditures during periods of high employment.

fiscal policy: Deliberate exercise of the government's power to tax and spend in order to help dampen the swings of business cycles and bring the nation's output and employment to desired levels.

fixed assets: Durable assets of an enterprise used to carry on its business, such as land, buildings, machinery, equipment, office furniture, automobiles, and trucks.

fixed costs: Costs that do not vary with a firm's output. *Examples:* rental payments, interest on debt, property taxes.

floating exchange rates: Foreign exchange rates determined in a free market by supply and demand.

"forced" saving: Situation in which consumers are prevented from spending part of their income on consumption. Some examples include: (1) prices rising faster than money wages, causing a decrease in real consumption and hence an increase in real (forced) saving; (2) a corporation which plows back some of its profit instead of distributing it as dividend income to stockholders; and (3) a government which taxes its citizens and uses the funds for investment, thereby preventing the public from utilizing a portion of its income for the purchase of consumer goods.

foreign exchange: Instruments used for international payments: they consist not only of currency, but also of checks, drafts, and bills of exchange (which are orders to pay currency).

foreign exchange rate: Price of one currency in terms of another.

foreign-trade multiplier: Principle which states that fluctuations in exports or imports may generate magnified variations in national income. It is based on the idea that a change in exports relative to imports has the same multiplier effect on national income as a change in autonomous expenditures; similarly, a change in imports relative to exports has the same multiplier effect on national income as a change in withdrawals from the income stream. In general, an increase in exports tends to raise domestic income, but the increased income also induces some imports which act as "leakages" tending to reduce the full multiplier effect that would exist if imports remained constant.

forward exchange: Foreign exchange bought (or sold) at a given time and at a stipulated current or "spot" price, but payable at some future date. By buying or selling forward exchange, importers and exporters can protect themselves against the risks of fluctuations in the current exchange market.

forward prices: Proposed plan for reducing price uncertainty and encouraging greater stability in agriculture through the use of the price system as an adjustment mechanism. Under the plan, a government-appointed board would predict in advance of breeding or seeding time the equilibrium prices of commodities, based on expected supply and demand. The government would then guarantee those predicted or forward prices in two ways: by storage programs and direct payments to farmers if actual prices should fall below forward prices, and by a direct tax on farmers if actual prices should rise above forward prices.

free good: Good for which the market price is zero at a particular time and place.

free-trade area: Association of trading nations whose participants agree to impose no restrictive devices such as tariffs or quotas on one another, but are free to impose whatever restrictive devices they wish on nonparticipants. *Example:* The European Free Trade Association (EFTA).

frictional unemployment: Unemployment of a short-run nature due to "frictions" in the economic system resulting from imperfect labor mobility, imperfect knowledge of job opportunities, and a general inability of the economy to match people with jobs instantly and smoothly. A common form of frictional unemployment

consists of people who are temporarily out of work because they are between jobs.

full cost (average cost) pricing: Setting of a price for a given volume of output so that it is at least high enough to cover all of a firm's costs of production—that is, its average total cost for that volume of output. If demand is great enough to enable the firm to sell its entire output at that price, then the firm will earn a normal profit. If it can sell its output at a still higher price, it will earn an economic or pure profit.

full employment: Situation in which everyone who wants a job can find one without unreasonable difficulty and at prevailing rates of pay. Full employment does not include those who are temporarily out of work or who are changing jobs. A figure of about 3 percent of the labor force unemployed is considered to be full employment.

full-employment budget: Estimate of annual government expenditures and revenues that would occur if the economy were operating at full employment—that is, at an unemployment rate of about 3 percent. Any resulting surplus (or deficit) is called a full employment surplus (or deficit).

"functional finance": Philosophy which holds that the government should pursue whatever fiscal measures are needed to achieve noninflationary full employment and economic growth—without regard to budget balancing per se. The federal budget is thus viewed functionally as a flexible fiscal tool for achieving economic objectives, rather than as an accounting statement to be balanced periodically.

functional income distribution: Payments in the form of wages, rents, interest, and profits made to the owners of the factors of production in return for supplying their labor, land, capital, and entrepreneurial ability.

gains from trade: Net benefits or increases in goods which a country receives as a result of trade.

General Agreements on Tariffs and Trade (GATT): International commercial agreement signed in 1947 by the U.S. and many other countries for the purpose of achieving four basic long-run objectives: (1) nondiscrimination in trade through adherence to unconditional most-favored-nation treatment; (2) reduction of tariffs by negotiation; (3) elimination of import quotas (with some exceptions); and (4) resolution of differences through consultation.

general equilibrium theory: Approach which explores interrelations between prices and outputs of goods and resources in different markets, and the possibility of simultaneous equilibrium among all of them. It is primarily of theoretical interest, but focuses attention on the fact that in the real world markets are often interdependent.

general price level: Expression representing the "average" level of prices in the economy. It is often represented by the Consumer Price Index, although no index can accurately reflect all prices.

gift tax: Tax on the transfer of ownership of an asset when the value of the asset exceeds a specified amount.

gold bullion standard: Monetary standard under which: (1) the national unit of currency (such as the dollar, pound, mark, etc.) is defined in terms of a fixed weight of gold; (2) gold is held by the government in the form of bars rather than coin; (3) there is no circulation of gold in any form within the economy; and (4) gold is available solely to meet the needs of industry (e.g., jewelry, dentistry) and settle international transactions among central banks or treasuries. This is the standard that the U.S. and most advanced nations adopted when they went off the gold coin standard in the early 1930s.

gold (coin) standard: Monetary standard under which: (1) the national unit of currency (such as the dollar, pound, franc, etc.) is defined by law in terms of a fixed weight of gold; (2) there is a free and unrestricted flow of the metal in any form into and out of the country; (3) gold coins are full legal tender for all debts; (4) there is free convertibility between the national currency and gold coins at the defined rate; and (5) there are no restrictions on the coinage of gold. Nearly fifty countries of the world were on this standard in the late 19th and early 20th centuries.

gold exchange standard: Monetary standard under which a nation that is not itself on a gold standard will redeem its money on demand in the form of drafts (such as checks) written against banks in a gold-standard country in which it has deposits. In this way, the non gold-standard country can keep its money on a par with gold without having to maintain gold reserves. This standard was particularly popular among nations which lacked gold or were politically dependent on other nations after World War I (e.g., British Commonwealth countries). However, it ceased to exist with the worldwide abandonment of gold in the 1930s.

gold points: Range within which the foreign exchange rates of gold standard countries will fluctuate. Thus, the gold points are equal to the par rate of exchange plus and minus the cost (including insurance) of shipping gold. The upper and lower gold points for a nation are called its "gold export point" and "gold import point" respectively, because gold will be exported when the foreign exchange rate rises above the upper level, and will be imported when the rate falls below the lower level. One nation's gold export point is thus another nation's gold import point, and vice versa.

goodwill: One of the "intangible" assets of a firm (like patents and trademarks), the value of which is arbitrarily established on a company's balance sheet.

government monopoly: Monopoly both owned and operated by either a federal or local government. *Examples:* the U.S. Post Office, many water and sewer systems, and the central banks of most countries.

grants-in-aid: Financial aid at the intergovernmental level which consists of: (1) revenues received by local governments from their states and from the federal government; and (2) revenues received by state governments from the federal government. These revenues are used mainly to help pay for public welfare assistance, highways, and education.

Great Leap Forward: Ambitious economic plan undertaken by Mainland China during 1958–60 to accelerate enormously its rate of economic growth. The plan was unrealistic and forced the country into a major economic crisis.

Gresham's Law: Principle which asserts that cheap money tends to drive dear money out of circulation. Thus, if two kinds of metals such as gold and silver circulate with equal legal tender powers (as happened in the U.S. under the bimetallic standard during the 19th century), the cheaper metal will become the chief circulating medium while the dearer metal will be hoarded, melted down, or exported, thereby disappearing from circulation. The Law is named after Sir Thomas Gresham, Master of the Mint under Queen Elizabeth I during the 16th century. (*See* **bimetallic standard; mint ratio.**)

gross national disproduct: Sum of all social costs or reductions in benefits to society that result from producing the gross national product. *Example:* Pollution of air and water is part of gross national disproduct, to the extent that it is caused by production of the gross national product.

gross national expenditure: Total amount spent by the four sector accounts of the economy (i.e., household, government, business, and international) on the nation's output of goods and services. It is equal, by definition, to gross national product.

gross national income: The equivalent of gross national product from the "income" viewpoint. It consists of national income at factor cost (i.e., the sum of wages, rent, interest, and profit) plus two non-income or business expense items: indirect business taxes and capital consumption allowance.

gross national product: Total market value of all final goods and services produced by an economy during a year.

guaranteed annual income: Plan that awards all families under a certain "poverty line" level a straight allowance for each parent plus specified amounts for each child according to the size of the family. No family receives less than a designated amount, and as a family's income rises the payment from the government is reduced until a break-even level, which is a little higher than the poverty line, is reached.

hard-core unemployed: People who are unemployed because they lack the education and skills for today's complex economy. (Discrimination may also be a contributing factor.) They consist mainly of certain minority groups such as Negroes, Mexicans, the "too-old," the "too-young," the high-school dropouts, and the permanently displaced who are victims of technological change.

high-employment budget: Estimate of annual government expenditures and revenues that would occur if the economy were operating at a high level of employment—that is, at an unemployment rate of about 4 percent. Any resulting surplus (or deficit) in this budget is called a high employment surplus (or deficit). (Contrast with **full-employment budget.**)

hog-corn price ratio: Number of bushels of corn required to buy 100 pounds of live pork, thus:

$$\text{Hog-corn price ratio} = \frac{\text{Price of live hogs per 100 pounds}}{\text{Price of corn per bushel}}$$

When the ratio is relatively low, hog production decreases because farmers find it more profitable to sell their corn in the market than to use it for feeding hogs; conversely, when the ratio is relatively high, hog production increases because farmers use the corn to feed more hogs, and to market them at heavier weights.

horizontal merger: Amalgamation under one ownership of like plants engaged in like products. The products might be close or moderate substitutes (e.g., cement plants; tin cans and jars). The objective is to round out a product line which is sold through the same distribution channels, thereby offering joint economies in selling and distribution efforts.

human resources: Productive physical and mental talents of the people who comprise an economy.

hyperinflation: Situation in which prices are rising with little or no increases in output; hence it is also sometimes called "runaway" or "galloping" inflation.

hypothesis: A working guess about the behavior of things, or an expression about the relationship between variables in the real world. In economics, the "things" may include consumers, workers, business firms, investors, etc., and the variables may include prices, wages, consumption, production, or other economic quantities.

imperfect competition: A classification of market structures that falls between the two extremes of perfect competition and monopoly. It consists of monopolistic competition and oligopoly.

implicit costs: Costs of self-owned or self-employed resources that are not entered in a company's book of account. *Example:* The alternative interest return, rental receipts, and wages that a self-employed proprietor foregoes by owning and operating his own business.

import quota: Law that limits the number of units of a commodity that may be imported during a given period.

incidence: Range of occurrence or influence of an economic act. It is a term used primarily in the study of taxation, and refers to the economic organism such as a household or a firm that bears the ultimate burden of a tax.

income: Gain derived from the use of human or material resources. A flow of dollars per unit of time. (Contrast with **wealth.**)

income-consumption curve: In indifference-curve analysis, a line showing the amounts of two commodities that a consumer will purchase when his income changes while the prices of the commodities remain the same. Geometrically, it is a line connecting the tangency points of price lines and indifference curves as income changes while prices remain constant.

income effect: Increase or decrease in a buyer's real income—that is, in goods purchased—resulting from a change in the price of a commodity while his money income, tastes, and the prices of all other goods remain the same.

income elasticity of demand: Percentage change in the quantity purchased of a good resulting from a one percent change in income. Thus:

Income elasticity of demand

$$= \frac{\text{Percentage change in quantity purchased}}{\text{Percentage change in income}}$$

$$= \frac{(Q_2 - Q_1)/(Q_2 + Q_1)}{(Y_2 - Y_1)/(Y_2 + Y_1)}$$

where Q_1 and Q_2 represent the quantities purchased before and after the change in income, and Y_1 and Y_2 represent the corresponding levels of income before and after the change. Thus it denotes the responsiveness of changes in purchases to changes in income, where responsiveness is measured in terms of percentage changes.

income statement: Financial statement of a firm showing its revenues, costs, and profit during a period. Also known as a profit-and-loss statement.

income tax: Tax on the net income or residual that remains after certain items are subtracted from gross income. The two major types of income taxes are the personal income tax and the corporation income tax.

income velocity of money: Average number of times per year that a dollar is spent on purchasing the economy's annual flow of final goods and services—its GNP. It equals the ratio of GNP to the quantity of money. (See **equation of exchange.**)

inconvertible paper standard: Monetary standard under which the nation's unit of currency may or may not be defined in terms of any metal or other precious substance; however, there is no free convertibility into these other forms. Historically, this standard has existed on a domestic basis in all countries since the worldwide abandonment of gold in the 1930s.

increasing-cost industry: Industry which experiences increases in resource prices or in its costs of production as it expands because of new firms entering it. This will happen when the industry's demand for the resources it employs is a significant proportion of the total demand for those resources.

increasing costs, law of: Principle which states that on an economy's production possibilities curve relating two kinds of goods, the real cost of acquiring either good is not the money that must be spent for it, but the increasing amount of the alternative good that the society must sacrifice or "give up" because it cannot have all it wants of both goods.

independent union: Labor union not affiliated with any federation of labor organizations. It may be national or international, and is not limited to workers in any one firm.

index numbers: Figures which disclose the relative changes in a series of numbers, such as prices or production, from a base period. The base period is usually defined as being equal to an index number of 100%, and all other numbers in the series both before or after that period are expressed as percentages of that period. Index numbers are widely used in reporting business and economic data.

indifference curve: Graph of an indifference schedule. Every point along the curve represents a different combination of two commodities, and each combination is equally satisfactory to a recipient because each one yields the same total utility.

indifference schedule: Table showing the various combinations of two commodities that would be equally satisfactory or yield the same total utility to a recipient at a given time.

indirect tax: Tax that can be shifted either partially or entirely to someone other than the individual or firm originally taxed. *Examples:* sales taxes, excise taxes, taxes on business and rental properties.

induced investment: Tendency of rising income, output, and economic activity to stimulate higher levels of investment. (Contrast with **autonomous investment.**)

induction: Process of reasoning from particular observations or cases to general laws or principles. Most human knowledge is inductive or empirical since it is based on the experiences of our senses. (Opposite of **deduction.**)

industrial relations: Rules and regulations governing the relationship between union and management. It often deals with such matters as union security (e.g., the type of recognition that the union is accorded, its financial arrangement for collecting dues, etc.) and methods of controlling the quantity and kind of union membership through apprenticeship requirements, licensing provisions, initiation fees, and seniority rules.

industrial union: Labor union consisting of all members from a particular industry, such as a union of coal miners or a union of steel workers. It is thus a "vertically" organized union.

industry: Group of firms producing similar or identical products.

infant industry: Underdeveloped industry which, in the face of competition from abroad, may not be able to survive the early years of struggle before reaching maturity.

inferior good: Good whose purchases are decreased relative to other goods as the consumer's income rises. *Examples:* potatoes, used clothing, and other so-called "poor man's goods."

inflation: Rise in the general price level (or average level of prices) of all goods and services—or equivalently, a decline in the purchasing power of money. The general price level thus varies inversely with the purchasing power of money. For example: if prices double, purchasing power decreases by one-half; if prices halve, purchasing power doubles.

inflationary gap: Amount by which aggregate demand exceeds aggregate supply at full employment, thereby causing inflationary pressures.

injunction: Court order requiring that a defendant refrain from certain practices, or that he take a particular action.

innovation: Adoption of a new or different product, or of a new or different method of production, marketing, financing, etc. It thus establishes a new relation between the output and the various kinds of inputs (capital, land, labor, etc.) in a production process. In a more formal sense, it is the setting up of a new production function.

innovation theory: Theory originated by Joseph Schumpeter (1883–1950) which attributes business cycles and economic de-

velopment to innovations that forward-looking businessmen adopt in order to reduce costs and increase profits. Once an innovation proves successful, other businessmen follow with the same or with similar techniques, and these innovations cause fluctuations in investment which result in business cycles. The innovation theory has also been used as a partial explanation of how profits arise in a competitive capitalistic system.

interest: 1. Return to those who supply the factor of production known as "capital," i.e., the payment for supplying the funds with which businessmen buy capital goods. **2.** Price paid for the use of money or loanable funds over a period. It is stated as a rate—that is, as a percentage of the amount of money borrowed. Thus an interest rate of 5% means that the borrower pays 5¢ per $1 borrowed per year, or $5 per $100 borrowed per year, and so on.

interlocking directorate: Situation in which an individual serves on two or more boards of directors of competing corporations.

internal economies and diseconomies of scale: Conditions that bring about decreases or increases in a firm's long-run average costs or scale of operations as a result of size adjustments within the firm as a producing unit; they occur irrespective of adjustments within the industry and are due mainly to physical economies or diseconomies. *Example:* internal economies may result from greater specialization and more efficient utilization of the firm's resources as its scale of operations increases, but internal diseconomies may eventually set in because of the limited decision making abilities of the top management group.

International Bank For Reconstruction And Development (World Bank): Established by the United Nations in 1945 to provide loans for postwar reconstruction, and to promote development of less developed countries. The Bank's chief function is to aid the financing of basic development projects such as dams, communication and transportation facilities, health programs, etc., by insuring or otherwise guaranteeing private loans or, when private capital is not available, by providing loans from its own resources and credit. Affiliated agencies also exist to help finance higher-risk investment projects in underdeveloped countries.

International Monetary Fund (IMF): Established by the United Nations in 1944 for the purpose of: (1) eliminating exchange restrictions and providing for worldwide convertibility of currencies so as to encourage multilateral trade based on international specialization; (2) stabilizing exchange rates to reduce or eliminate short-term fluctuations in a nation's economy due to changes in its imports, exports, or speculative capital movements; and (3) assuring that changes in a country's exchange rate occur only with the Fund's approval, and only after the country has experienced a prolonged deficit or surplus in its balance of payments. Over 100 nations are in the Fund.

inventory: Stocks of goods which business firms have on hand, including raw materials, supplies, and finished goods.

investment: Spending by business firms on new job-creating and income-producing goods. It consists of replacements of or additions to the nation's stock of capital including its plant, equipment, and inventories, i.e., its nonhuman productive assets.

"invisible hand": Expression coined by Adam Smith in his *Wealth of Nations* to convey the idea that each individual, if left to pursue his self-interest without interference by government, would be led as if by an invisible hand to achieve the best good for society.

involuntary unemployment: Situation in which people who want work are unable to find jobs at going wage rates for the related skills and experiences they have to offer.

job classification: Process of describing the duties, responsibilities, and characteristics of jobs, point-rating them (perhaps by established formulas based on engineering time-studies of workers in such jobs), and then grouping the jobs into graduated classifications with corresponding wage rates and wage ranges.

jurisdictional strike: Strike caused by a dispute between two or more craft unions over which shall perform a particular job. Outlawed by the Taft-Hartley Act, 1947.

kinked demand curve: A "bent" demand curve, and a corresponding discontinuous marginal revenue curve, facing an oligopolistic seller. It signifies that if the seller raises his price above the kink, his sales will fall off rapidly because other sellers are not likely to follow his price upward; if he drops his price below the kink, he will expand his sales relatively little because other sellers are likely to follow his price downward. The market price, therefore, tends to stabilize at the kink.

Knights of Labor: National labor organization founded in 1869. It rejected the traditional organizing of workers by crafts, preferring instead the mass unionization of both unskilled and skilled workers. The Knights championed the cause of workers and achieved many liberal improvements and reforms, but began to decline in the late 1880s due to several factors: (1) opposition by craft leaders who preferred organization along craft lines; (2) internal dissension among leading members and groups; and (3) suspicion—unproved—of its involvement in Chicago's Haymarket riot and bombing of 1886. By 1917 it ceased to exist.

labor: 1. Factor of production which represents those hired workers whose human efforts or activities are directed toward production. **2.** All personal services including the activities of wageworkers, professional people, and independent businessmen. "Laborers" may thus receive compensation not only in the form of wages, but also as salaries, bonuses, commissions, etc.

labor force: All people sixteen years of age or older who are employed, plus all those who are unemployed, but actively seeking work.

Labor-Management Relations (Taft-Hartley) Act (1947): An amendment to the National Labor Relations (Wagner) Act of 1935. It retains the rights given to labor by the 1935 Act, but also: (1) outlaws "unfair labor practices" of unions, such as coercion of workers to join unions, failure to bargain in good faith, jurisdictional strikes, secondary boycotts, and featherbedding; (2) outlaws the closed shop but permits the union shop; (3) requires unions to file financial reports with the NLRB, and union officials to sign non-Communist affidavits; (4) prohibits strikes called before the end of a 60-day notice period prior to the expiration of a collective bargaining agreement; and (5) enables the President to obtain an 80-day court injunction against strikes which endanger national health or safety.

Labor-Management Reporting and Disclosure (Landrum-Griffin) Act (1959): Act which amended the National Labor Relations Act of 1935 by: (1) requiring detailed financial reports of all unions and union officers; (2) severely tightening restrictions on secondary boycotting and picketing; (3) requiring periodic secret-ballot elections of union officers; and (4) imposing restrictions on ex-convicts and Communists in holding positions as union officers.

lagging indicators: Time series that tend to follow or trail aggregate economic activity.

laissez faire: "Leave us alone"—an expression coined in France during the late 17th century, but which today is interpreted to mean freedom from government intervention in all economic affairs.

land: Factor of production which includes land itself in the form of real estate as well as mineral deposits, timber, water, and other nonhuman or "natural" resources.

law: Expression of a relationship between variables, based on a high degree of unvarying uniformity under the same conditions. (Often used synonomously with **principle**.)

leading indicators: Time series that tend to move ahead of aggregate economic activity, thus reaching peaks and troughs before the economy as a whole.

legal reserve: Minimum proportion of its demand deposits that a bank is required by law to keep in the form of vault cash or as a deposit at the central bank (i.e., the Federal Reserve Bank). A decrease in the legal reserve requirement is expansionary because it enables banks to increase their loans; an increase in the legal reserve requirement is contractionary because it forces banks to reduce their loans.

less developed (underdeveloped) country: A nation which, in comparison with the more advanced countries, tends to exhibit such characteristics as: (1) poverty level of income and hence little or no saving; (2) high rate of population growth; (3) substantial majority of its labor force employed in agriculture; (4) low proportion of adult literacy; (5) extensive disguised unemployment; and (6) heavy reliance on a few items for export.

liabilities: Monetary debts that a business firm or individual owes to creditors.

limited liability: Restriction of the liability of an investor, such as a stockholder in a corporation, to the amount of his investment.

liquidity preference (theory of interest): Theory formulated by J. M. Keynes (1883–1946) contending that households or businesses would rather hold their assets in the most liquid form, namely cash or checking accounts, in order to satisfy three motives: (1) the "transactions motive" to carry out everyday purchasing needs; (2) the "precautionary motive" to meet possible unforeseen emergencies; and (3) the "speculative motive" to engage in financial investment or to take advantage of a rise in interest rates. Therefore, interest is the price or reward that must be paid to overcome liquidity preference.

loanable funds theory of interest: Theory which holds that the interest rate is determined by the demand for, and supply of, loanable funds only, as distinguished from *all* money. The sources of demand for loanable funds are businesses that want to invest, households that want to finance consumer purchases, and government agencies that want to finance deficits. The sources of supply of loanable funds are the central banking system which influences the supply of money (and hence loanable funds) in the economy, and households and businesses that make loanable funds available out of their past or present savings.

lockout: Closing down of a plant by an employer in order to keep workers out of their jobs.

long run: Period that is long enough for a firm to enter or leave an industry, and to vary its output by varying all of its factors of production including its plant scale.

long-run average cost curve (planning curve): Curve that is tangent to, or envelops, the various short-run average total cost curves of a firm over a range of output representing different scales or sizes of plant. Thus it shows what the level of average costs would be for alternative outputs of different-sized plants.

long-run industry supply curve: Locus or "path" of a competitive industry's long-run equilibrium points. That is, the long-run industry supply curve connects the stable equilibrium points of the industry's supply and demand curves over a period of time, both before and after these curves have adjusted completely to changed market conditions. The long-run industry supply curve may be either upward sloping, horizontal, or downward sloping, depending on whether the industry is an increasing-, constant-, or decreasing-cost industry.

Lorenz curve: Graphic device for comparing cumulative percentage relationships between two variables. It is often used to compare a society's actual distribution of income with an equal distribution. For example, each axis of the chart is scaled from 0 to 100%, and the cumulative percentage relationships between two variables such as "percent of income" and "percent of families" are plotted against each other. The resulting curve of actual income distribution is then compared to a 45° diagonal line representing equal income distribution. The degree of departure between the two curves indicates the extent of income inequality. Similar curves may be constructed to show other types of distributions (e.g., distribution of wealth, distribution of wages in a factory, etc.).

macroeconomics: That part of economics which studies and theorizes about the economy as a whole, or about large subdivisions of it. It analyzes the economic "forest" as distinct from its "trees."

Malthusian theory of population: First published by Thomas Malthus in 1798 and then revised in 1803, this theory states that population tends to increase as a geometric progression (1, 2, 4, 8, 16, 32, etc.) while the means of subsistence increase at most only as an arithmetic progression (1, 2, 3, 4, 5, 6, etc.). This is because a growing population applied to a fixed amount of land results in eventually diminishing returns to workers. Human beings are therefore destined to misery and poverty unless the rate of pop-

ulation growth is retarded. This may be accomplished either by: (1) preventive checks such as moral restraint, late marriages, and celibacy, or if these fail then by (2) positive checks such as wars, famines, and disease.

marginal cost: Change in total cost resulting from a unit change in quantity. It is measured by the ratio:

$$\text{Marginal cost} = \frac{\text{Change in total cost}}{\text{Change in quantity}}$$

Marginal cost is also the change in total variable cost resulting from a unit change in quantity, since total cost changes because total variable cost changes, whereas total fixed cost remains constant. In general, marginal cost measures the gain in total cost from an additional unit of quantity produced.

marginal cost pricing: Production and pricing of output as determined by the point at which a firm's marginal cost equals its average revenue. This is an optimum price for society, because the value of the last unit to the marginal user (measured by the price he pays for the last unit, which is equal to the price he pays for all units) is equivalent to the value of the resources used to produce that unit. However, this so-called marginal cost price will leave the firm suffering a loss if it results in a price below the firm's average total cost.

marginal efficiency of investment: Expected rate of return on an addition to investment. It is determined by such factors as: (1) the demand for the product which the investment will produce; (2) the level of production costs in the economy; (3) technology and innovation; and (4) the stock of capital available to meet existing and future market demands.

marginal product: Change in total product resulting from a unit change in the quantity of a variable input employed. It is measured by the ratio.

$$\text{Marginal product} = \frac{\text{Change in total product}}{\text{Change in a variable input}}$$

Marginal product thus measures the gain (or loss) in total product from adding an additional unit of a variable factor of production.

marginal productivity theory of income distribution: Principle that when there is perfect competition for inputs, a firm will purchase factors of production up to the point where the price or marginal cost of the factor is equal to its marginal revenue productivity. Therefore, in real terms, each factor of production will be paid a value equal to what it contributes to total output—that is, it will be paid what it is "worth."

marginal propensity to consume: Change in total consumption resulting from a unit change in income. It is measured by the ratio:

$$\text{Marginal propensity to consume} = \frac{\text{Change in total consumption}}{\text{Change in income}}$$

It thus reveals the fraction of each extra dollar of income that is spent on consumption.

marginal propensity to save: Change in total saving resulting from a unit change in income. It is measured by the ratio:

$$\text{Marginal propensity to save} = \frac{\text{Change in total saving}}{\text{Change in income}}$$

It thus reveals the fraction of each extra dollar of income that is saved.

marginal rate of substitution: In demand theory, the rate at which a consumer is willing to substitute one commodity for another along an indifference curve. It is the amount of change in the holdings of one commodity that will just offset a unit change in the holdings of another commodity, so that the consumer's total utility remains the same. Thus, along an indifference curve:

$$\text{Marginal rate of substitution} = -\frac{\text{Change in commodity Y}}{\text{Change in commodity X}}$$

The marginal rate of substitution is always negative because one commodity must be decreased when the other is increased in order to keep total utility the same, i.e., to remain on a given indifference curve. (A parallel concept involving factor substitution exists in production theory.)

marginal revenue: Change in total revenue resulting from a unit change in quantity. It is measured by the ratio:

$$\text{Marginal revenue} = \frac{\text{Change in total revenue}}{\text{Change in quantity}}$$

Marginal revenue thus measures the gain (or loss) in total revenue that results from producing and selling an additional unit.

marginal revenue product: Change in total revenue resulting from a unit change in the quantity of a variable input employed. It is measured by the ratio:

$$\text{Marginal revenue product} = \frac{\text{Change in total revenue}}{\text{Change in a variable input}}$$

Marginal revenue product thus measures the gain (or loss) in total revenue from adding an additional unit of a variable factor of production.

marginal tax rate: Ratio, expressed as a percentage, of the change in a total tax resulting from a unit change in the base on which it is imposed. *Example:*

Marginal personal income tax rate
$$= \frac{\text{Change in total personal income tax}}{\text{Change in total taxable income}}$$

marginal utility: Change in total utility resulting from a unit change in the quantity of a commodity consumed. It is given by the ratio:

$$\text{Marginal utility} = \frac{\text{Change in total utility}}{\text{Change in quantity consumed}}$$

Marginal utility thus measures the gain (or loss) in satisfaction from an additional unit of a good.

margin regulations: Percentage downpayment required of a borrower to finance purchase of stock. This rate is set by the Federal Reserve System's Board of Governors. An increase in margin requirements is designed to dampen security purchases; a decrease to encourage it.

market economy: Economic system in which the questions of what to produce, how much to produce, and for whom to produce are decided in an open market through the free operation of supply and demand. There are no "pure" market economies, but several specialized markets (such as the organized commodity exchanges) closely approximate some of the properties of a pure market system.

market price: Actual price that prevails in a market at any particular moment.

median: Special type of average that divides a distribution of numbers into two equal parts—one-half of all cases being equal to or greater than the median value, and one-half being equal to or less.

mediation: Method of settling differences between two parties (such as a union and management) by the use of an impartial third party, called a mediator, who is acceptable to both sides but makes no binding decisions. The mediator tries to maintain constructive discussions, search for common areas of agreement, and suggest compromises. Federal, state, and most large local governments provide mediation services for labor-management disputes. Mediation is also sometimes called "conciliation."

member bank: Bank which belongs to the Federal Reserve System. All national banks (chartered by the federal government) must be members. State banks may join if they meet certain requirements.

mercantilism: Set of doctrines and practices aimed at promoting national prosperity and the power of the state by: (1) accumulating precious metals (mainly gold and silver) through the maintenance of favorable trade balances; (2) achieving economic self-sufficiency through imperialism; and (3) exploiting colonies by monopolizing their raw materials and precious metals while reserving them as exclusive markets for exports. Mercantilism reached its peak in the 17th century, serving as a political and economic ideology in England, France, Spain, and Germany.

merger: Amalgamation of two or more firms under one ownership. The three common forms are: (1) *horizontal,* uniting similar plants and products; (2) *vertical,* uniting dissimilar plants in various stages of production; and (3) *conglomerate,* uniting dissimilar plants and products.

microeconomics: That part of economics which studies and theorizes about the specific economic units or parts of an economic system, such as its firms, industries, and households, and the relationships between these parts. It analyzes the "trees" of the economy as distinct from the "forest."

mint ratio: Under a bimetallic standard, the ratio of the weight of one metal to the other, and their equivalent in terms of the national unit of currency (such as the dollar) as defined by the government. For example, during the 19th century when the U.S. was on a bimetallic standard, the government defined the mint ratio for many years as:

$$15 \text{ grains silver} = 1 \text{ grain gold} = \$1$$

The mint ratio was therefore 15 to 1. Since it remained fixed by law, it resulted in either gold or silver being driven out of circulation, depending on the relative market values of the two metals. (*See* **Gresham's Law; bimetallic standard.**)

mixed economy: Economic system in which the questions of what to produce, how much to produce, and for whom to produce, are decided partially by the free market and partially by a central governmental authority. There are varying forms and degrees of mixed economies.

model: Representation of the essential features of a theory or of a real-world situation, expressed in the form of words, diagrams, graphs, mathematical equations, or combinations of these.

monetary standard: Laws and practices which determine the quantity and quality of a nation's money, and establish the conditions, if any, under which its currency is ultimately redeemable.

monetary theory of business cycles: Theory which attributes business cycles to monetary factors, such as changes in the quantity of money and credit, or to changes in interest rates. Upswings occur when credit and borrowing conditions become favorable enough for businessmen to borrow; downswings occur when the banking system begins to restrict its expansion of money and credit.

money: Anything which has at least these four functions: (1) a medium of exchange for conducting transactions; (2) a measure of value for expressing the prices of current and future transactions; (3) a standard of deferred payments which permits borrowing or lending for future repayment with interest; and (4) a store of value which permits saving for future as well as current spending.

money income: Amount of money received for work done. (Contrast with **real income.**)

money market: Center where short-term credit instruments are bought and sold.

"Money Supply Rule": Guide for economic expansion advanced by the "Monetarist" school of thought, especially by Professor Milton Friedman. The "Rule" states that the Federal Reserve should expand the nation's money supply at a steady rate in accordance with the economy's growth and capacity to produce, such as 3 to 5 percent a year for the U.S. More than this would lead to strong inflationary pressures; less would tend to be stagnating if not deflationary.

money wages: Wages received in cash. (Contrast with **real wages.**)

monopolistic competition: Industry or market structure characterized by a large number of firms of different sizes producing heterogeneous (similar but not identical) products, with relatively easy entry into the industry.

monopoly: Industry or market structure characterized by a single firm producing a product for which there are no close substitutes. The firm thus constitutes the entire industry and is a "pure" monopoly.

monopoly pricing: Production and pricing of output as determined by where a firm's marginal cost equals its marginal revenue. At the corresponding price and output the firm will maximize its profit. It is called "monopoly pricing" because in the field of wel-

fare economics, where concern is focused mainly on principles of social optimization, this type of pricing is contrasted with other forms such as **full cost pricing** and **marginal cost pricing.**

monopsony: Market structure consisting of a single buyer of a good or service. It may be thought of as a "buyer's monopoly."

moral suasion: Oral or written appeals by the Federal Reserve Board to member banks, urging them to expand or restrict credit but without requiring them to comply.

most-favored-nation clause: Clause in a trade treaty by which each signatory nation agrees to extend to the other the same preferential tariff and trade concessions that it may in the future extend to non-signatories, i.e., the same treatment that each gives to its "most favored nation." Most trading countries have adhered to this principle since 1948.

multiple expansion of bank deposits: Process by which a loan made by one bank is used to finance business transactions, and ends up as a deposit in another bank. Part of this may be used by the second bank as a reserve, and the rest lent out for business use so that it is eventually deposited in a third bank, etc. The total amount of credit granted by the banking system as a whole will thus be a multiple of the initial deposit. (*See* **deposit expansion multiplier.**)

multiplier: Principle which states that changes in investment bring about magnified changes in income, as expressed by the equation: multiplier × change in investment = change in income. The multiplier coefficient is given by the formula:

$$\text{Multiplier} = \frac{\text{Change in income}}{\text{Change in investment}} = \frac{1}{MPS} = \frac{1}{1 - MPC}$$

where *MPS* stands for the marginal propensity to save, and *MPC* the marginal propensity to consume. (*Note:* This multiplier is sometimes called the "investment multiplier" in order to distinguish it from other types of multipliers in economics.)

multiunit bargaining: Collective bargaining arrangement covering more than one plant. It may occur between one or more firms in an industry and one or more unions, and it may take place on a national, regional, or local level. It is sometimes inaccurately called "industry-wide bargaining," although it is rarely completely industrywide.

national income (at factor cost): 1. Total of all net incomes earned by or ascribed to the factors of production—that is, the sum of wages, rent, interest, and profit which accrues to the suppliers of labor, land, capital, and entrepreneurship. (*Note:* It should not be confused with the total income received by people from all sources, i.e., personal income. The difference between the two is based on various accounting considerations.) **2.** In general terms and in theoretical discussions, the expression "national income" is often used in a simple generic sense to represent the income or output of an economy.

National Labor Relations (Wagner) Act (1935): Basic labor relations law of the United States. It: (1) guarantees the right of workers to organize and bargain collectively through representatives of their own choosing; (2) forbids employers to engage in "unfair labor practices" such as discrimination or interference; and (3) authorizes the National Labor Relations Board to enforce the Act and supervise free elections among a company's employees.

National Labor Relations Board: Government agency established under the National Labor Relations Act of 1935 to enforce that Act; investigate violations of it; and supervise free elections among a company's employees so as to determine which union, if any, is to represent them in collective bargaining.

natural monopoly: "Legal" monopoly established by a state or federal government, usually because: (1) there are increasing economies of scale over a wide range of output, so that one firm can supply the market more efficiently than several; or (2) unrestricted competition among firms in the industry is deemed socially undesirable. *Examples:* public utilities or other "business affected with a public interest" as stated in numerous judicial opinions. Natural monopolies are also called "legal monopolies" or "virtual monopolies."

near-monies: Assets which are almost, but not quite, money. They can easily be converted into money because their monetary values are known. *Examples:* time or savings deposits, U.S. government bonds, and cash values of insurance policies.

negative income tax: Plan for guaranteeing the poor a minimum income through a type of reverse income tax. A poor family, depending on its size and other income, would be paid by the government enough either to reduce or close the gap between what it earns and some explicit minimum level of income. That level might be equal to or above the government's designated "poverty line." As the family's income increases, the government's payment declines to zero.

neoclassical economics: Approach to economics which flourished in Europe and the United States between 1870 and World War I. Among its leaders were William Stanley Jevons in England; Carl Menger in Austria; Leon Walras in France; Vilfredo Pareto in Switzerland; Alfred Marshall in England; and John Bates Clark and Irving Fisher in the United States. The neoclassicists were primarily concerned with refining the principles of price and allocation theory, "marginalism," the theory of capital, and related aspects of economics. They made early and extensive use of mathematics, especially differential and integral calculus, in the development of their analyses and models. Much of the structure of modern economic science is built on their pioneering work.

net national product: Total sales value of goods and services available for society's consumption and for adding to its stock of capital equipment. It represents society's net output for the year, and may be obtained by deducting a capital consumption allowance from gross national product.

net profit ratio: Ratio of a firm's net profit after taxes to its net sales. It is one of several general measures of a company's performance.

net revenue: A firm's "pure" or net profit—equal to its total revenue minus its total cost.

net worth: Difference between the total assets or things of value owned by a firm or individual, and the liabilities or monetary debts that are owed.

New Economics: Body of economic thought which originated with the British economist John Maynard Keynes (1883–1946) in the 1930s. It has since been extended and modified to the point where its basic analytical tools and methods are now used by practically all economists. In contrast to classical economics, which emphasized the automatic tendency of the economy to achieve full employment equilibrium under a government policy of laissez faire, the New Economics demonstrates that an economy may be in equilibrium at any level of employment. It therefore concludes that appropriate government fiscal and monetary policies are needed in order to maintain full employment and steady economic growth with a minimum of inflation.

nonprice competition: Methods of competition that do not involve changes in selling price. *Examples:* advertising, product differentiation, customer service, etc.

normal goods: Goods whose purchases are increased as buyers' incomes rise, and decreased as buyers' incomes fall. Most consumer goods are normal goods.

normal price: The dynamic equilibrium price toward which the market price is always tending but may never reach.

normal profit: Least payment that the owner of an enterprise will accept as compensation for his entrepreneurial function, including risk-taking, management, etc. Normal profit is part of a firm's total economic costs, since it is a payment which the owner must receive in order to keep him from withdrawing his capital and managerial effort and putting them into some other alternative.

normative economics: Approach to economics which deals with what "ought to be" as compared to what "is." It involves statements which are value judgments, and hence much of it cannot be empirically verified. (Contrast with **positive economics.**)

Norris La Guardia Act (1932): Act of Congress which outlawed the yellow-dog contract and greatly restricted the conditions under which court injunctions against labor unions could be issued.

notes payable: Promises to pay the holder, such as a bank, a sum of money within the year at a stated rate of interest.

oligopoly: Industry or market structure composed of a few firms selling either: (1) a homogeneous or undifferentiated product, which is then called a "perfect" or "pure" oligopoly; or (2) heterogeneous or differentiated products, which is then called an "imperfect" oligopoly. Some examples of perfect oligopoly are the copper, steel, and cement industries; some examples of imperfect oligopoly are the automobile, soap, detergent and household appliance industries.

open market operations: Purchases and sales of government securities by the Federal Reserve System. Purchases of securities are expansionary because they add to commercial banks' reserves; sales of securities are contractionary because they reduce commercial banks' reserves.

open shop: Business firm in which the employer is free to hire either union or nonunion members.

operating profit ratio: Ratio of a firm's operating profit to its net sales.

opportunity cost: Value of the benefit that is foregone by choosing one alternative rather than another. Also called "alternative cost" since it represents the implicit cost of the foregone alternative to the individual, household, firm, or other decision-making organism. Opportunity costs are not entered in a firm's public accounting records. (Contrast with **outlay costs.**)

outlay costs: Money expended to carry on a particular activity. They are the explicit costs which are entered in a firm's public accounting records, such as its income statement, to arrive at a measure of profit. *Examples:* wages and salaries, rent, and other money expenditures of a firm.

overinvestment theory: Theory of business cycles which holds that economic fluctuations are caused by too much investment in the economy as businessmen try to anticipate rising demands during an upswing, and from sharp cutbacks in investment during a downswing when businessmen realize they expanded too much in the previous prosperity.

paradox of thrift: Proposition which demonstrates that an increase in saving may be desirable for an individual or family, but for an entire economy will lead to a reduction in income, employment, and output if it is not offset by an increase in investment. The concept was first introduced by Bernard Mandeville in *The Fable of the Bees* (1714) and was later recognized in the writings of the classical economists.

parity price: Price which yields an equivalence to some defined standard. *Examples:* **1.** In agriculture, a price of an agricultural commodity which gives the commodity a purchasing power, in terms of the goods that farmers buy, equivalent to that which it had in a previous base period. **2.** In international economics, the price or exchange rate between the currencies of two countries that makes the purchasing power of one currency substantially equivalent to the purchasing power of the other.

parity ratio: In agriculture, an index of the prices farmers receive divided by an index of the prices they pay. It is used to measure the economic well-being of agriculture.

partial equilibrium theory: Theory or model of a particular market that assumes other markets are in balance. It thus ignores the interrelationships of prices and quantities that may exist between markets. *Example:* Ordinary supply and demand analysis is normally of a partial equilibrium nature since it usually focuses on a single market while neglecting others.

partnership: Association of two or more individuals to carry on, as co-owners, a business for profit. The partners are solely responsible for the activities and liabilities of the business.

patent: Exclusive right conferred by government on an inventor, for a limited time. It authorizes the inventor to make, use, transfer, or withhold his invention, which he might do even without a patent, but it also gives him the right to exclude others or to admit them on his own terms, which he can only do with a patent. Patents are thus a method of promoting invention by granting temporary monopolies to inventors.

patent monopoly: Firm which exercises a monopoly because the government has conferred upon it the exclusive right—through issuance of a patent—to make, use, or vend its own invention or discovery.

perfect competition: Name given to an industry or market structure characterized by a large number of buyers and sellers all engaged in the purchase and sale of a homogeneous commodity, with perfect knowledge of market prices and quantities, no discrimination in buying or selling, and perfect mobility of resources. *Note:* The term is usually employed synonymously with *pure competition,* although there is a technical distinction: pure competition does not require perfect knowledge or perfect resource mobility, and hence does not produce as smooth or rapid an adjustment to equilibrium as does perfect competition. However, both types of competition lead to essentially the same results in economic theory.

personal income: In national income accounting, the total income received by persons from all sources.

personal income distribution: The way in which income is distributed within the economy—often expressed in terms of percentages of aggregate income received by each fifth of all families, or in terms of the percentage of families falling within specific income classes.

Phillips curve: Curve which represents a tradeoff between unemployment and inflation. Every point along the curve denotes a different combination of unemployment and inflation, and a movement along the curve measures the reduction in one of these at the expense of a gain in the other.

planned economy: Economic system in which the government, according to a preconceived plan, plays a primary role in directing economic resources for the purpose of deciding what to produce, how much, and possibly for whom. A planned economy may or may not be a command economy, depending on whether the government operates within a substantially authoritarian or democratic framework. (*See* **command economy.**)

plant: Establishment or unit that produces or distributes goods and services. In economics, a "plant" is usually thought of as a firm, but it may also be one of several plants owned by a firm.

Point Four Program: Part of the Foreign Economic Assistance Act of 1950. The Program seeks to raise living standards in the underdeveloped countries by making available to them U.S. technical and financial assistance, largely in the areas of agriculture, public health, and education. Much of this work is now carried out by agencies of the United Nations and by the U.S. Agency for International Development.

positive economics: An approach to economics which deals with what "is" as compared with what "ought to be." Much of positive economics involves the use of statements that can be verified by empirical research, i.e., by an appeal to the facts. (Contrast with **normative economics.**)

"poverty line": Measure of poverty among families, defined in terms of a sliding income scale which varies between rural and urban locations according to family size.

precautionary motive: Desire on the part of households and businesses to hold part of their assets in liquid form so that they can be prepared for adverse contingencies. This motive is influenced primarily by income levels rather than by changes in the interest rate, and is one of the chief sources of demand for loanable funds in the modern theory of interest.

preferred stock: Shares of stock that receive preference over common stock at a fixed rate in the distribution of dividends, or in the distribution of assets if the company is liquidated.

prepayments: Business expenditures made in advance for items that will yield portions of their benefits in the present and in future years. *Examples:* Advance premiums on a fire insurance policy; expenses incurred in marketing a new product.

price: Power of a commodity to command money in exchange for itself; hence, price is the "money name" of the value of a commodity.

price-consumption curve: In indifference curve analysis, a line which connects the tangency points of price lines and indifference curves by showing the amounts of two commodities that a consumer will purchase when his income and the price of one commodity remain constant while the price of the other commodity varies.

price discrimination: Practice by a seller of charging different prices to the same or to different buyers for the same good.

price leadership: Adherence by firms in an oligopolistic industry, often tacitly and without formal agreement, to the pricing policies of one of its members. Frequently but not always, the price leader will be the largest firm in the industry, and other firms will simply go along with the leader, charging the same price as he charges.

price line (budget line): In indifference curve analysis, a line representing all of the possible combinations of two commodities that a consumer can purchase at a particular time, given the market prices of the commodities and the consumer's money budget or income.

price system: Mechanism that allocates scarce goods or resources by rationing them among those buyers and sellers in the marketplace who are willing and able to deal at the going prices. The term is often used to express the way prices are established through the free play of supply and demand in competitive markets composed of many buyers and sellers. In reality, of course, there may be "noncompetitive" price systems in markets where buyers or sellers are relatively few in number.

prime rate: Interest rate charged by banks on loans to their most credit-worthy customers.

principle: Fundamental law or general truth. It is often stated as an expression of a relationship between two or more variables. (*See* **law**.)

private benefit: Reward that accrues to an individual, household, or firm as a result of a particular act. (Contrast with **social benefit**.)

private cost: Economic cost that accrues to an individual, household, or firm as a result of a particular act. (Contrast with **social cost**.)

private property: Basic institution of capitalism which gives each individual the right to: (1) own goods or economic resources; (2) exercise control over their use; and (3) dispose of them or bequeath them to others as he wishes. These rights may be modified by society to the extent that they affect its health, safety, or welfare.

private rate of return: The business or financial rate of return on an investment—that is, the rate which businessmen try to anticipate before investing their funds. In financial terms, it is the expected net profit after taxes and all costs, including depreciation, and may typically be expressed as a percentage annual return upon either the total cost of a project, or upon the net worth of the stockholder owners. (Contrast with **community rate of return**.)

private sector: That segment of the total economy consisting of households and businesses, but excluding government.

"process of creative destruction": An expression coined by the economist Joseph Schumpeter (1883–1950) to describe the growth of a capitalistic economy as a process of replacing the old with the new—that is, old methods of production, old sources of supply, and old skills and resources with new ones.

production function: Relationship between the number of units of output that a firm produces and the number of units of various types of inputs that it employs.

production possibilities curve: Curve which depicts all possible combinations of total output for an economy, assuming that there is: (1) a choice between producing either one or both of two kinds of goods; (2) full and efficient employment of all resources (i.e., no underemployment); and (3) a fixed supply of resources and a given state of technological knowledge.

product markets: Markets in which businesses sell the outputs that they produce (in contrast with resource markets in which they buy the inputs they need in order to produce).

profit: 1. Return to those who perform the entrepreneurial function. The residual (if any) after the payment of wages, rent, and interest to the owners of labor, land, and capital. **2.** Difference between total revenue and total cost. It is the same as net revenue, a residual or surplus over and above normal profit that accrues to the entrepreneur-owner after all economic costs including explicit (outlay) costs and implicit (opportunity) costs have been deducted from total revenue.

profit-push inflation: Situation in which prices and business profits begin to rise before any increase in wages or other production costs takes place. This process stimulates labor unions to seek wage increases, thereby prompting further price increases by sellers.

promissory note: Promise by one person to pay another a specified sum of money by a given date, usually within a year.

progressive tax: Tax whose percentage rate increases as the tax base increases. The U.S. personal income tax is an example. The tax is graduated so that, other things being equal and assuming no loopholes, a man with a higher income pays a greater percentage of his income and a larger amount of tax than a man with a lower income.

propensity to consume: Relationship between consumption expenditures and income such that as income increases, consumption increases, but not as fast as income. The expression **consumption function** is often used synonomously.

propensity to save: Relationship between saving and income such that as income increases, saving increases, but faster than income.

property resources: Nonhuman productive resources of an economy, such as its natural resources, raw materials, machinery and equipment, transportation and communication facilities, etc.

property tax: Tax on any kind of property, such as real property in the form of land and buildings, or personal property like stocks, bonds, and home furnishings.

proportional tax: Tax whose percentage rate remains constant as the tax base increases; hence the amount of the tax paid is proportional to the tax base. The property tax is an example. Thus if the tax rate remains constant at 10%, a taxpayer who owns $10,000 worth of property pays $1,000 in taxes; a taxpayer who owns $100,000 worth of property pays $10,000 in taxes.

proprietorship: Simplest form of business organization in which the owner or proprietor is solely responsible for the activities and liabilities of the business.

prosperity: Upper phase of a business cycle in which the economy is operating at or near full employment, and a high degree of business and consumer optimism is reflected by a vigorous rate of capital investment and consumption.

psychological theory (of business cycles): Theory which holds that business cycles arise from people's responses to political, social, and economic events. These responses become cumulative waves of optimism and pessimism, setting off cycles in economic activity.

public works: Government-sponsored construction, defense, or development projects which usually (but not always) entail public investment expenditures that would not ordinarily be undertaken by the private sector of the economy.

pure competition: *See* **perfect competition** for similarities and differences.

pure interest rate: Theoretical interest rate on a long-term, riskless loan, where the interest payments are made solely for the use of someone else's money. In practice, this rate is often approximated by the interest rate on long-term U.S. government bonds.

pure market economy: Competitive economic system composed of many buyers and sellers, so that prices are determined by the free interaction of supply and demand.

quantity theory of money: Classical theory of the relationship between the price level and the money supply. It holds that the level of prices in the economy is directly proportional to the quantity of money in circulation, such that a given percentage change in the stock of money will cause an equal percentage change in the price level. The theory assumes that the income velocity of circulation of money remains fairly stable, and that the quantity of

goods and services is constant because the economy always tends toward full employment. (*See* **equation of exchange.**)

ratio (logarithmic) scale: Scale on a chart such that equal distances are represented by equal percentage changes. (It is equivalent to plotting the *logarithms* of the same data on an ordinary arithmetic scale.)

rationing: Any method of restricting the purchases or usage of a good when the quantity demanded of the good exceeds the quantity supplied at a given price.

real income: Purchasing power of money income or the quantity of goods and services that can be bought with money income. (Contrast with **money income.**)

real output: Value of physical output unaffected by price changes.

real wages: Quantity of goods that can be bought with money wages. Real wages thus depend on the prices of the goods bought with money wages.

recession: Downward phase of a business cycle in which the economy's income, output, and employment are decreasing, and a falling off of business and consumer optimism is reflected by a declining rate of capital investment and consumption.

Reciprocal Trade Agreements program: Plan for expanding American exports through legislation which authorizes the President to negotiate U.S. tariff reductions with other nations in return for parallel concessions. The program consists of the Trade Agreements Act of 1934, with subsequent amendments, and related legislation.

recovery: Upward phase of a business cycle in which the economy's income, output, and employment are rising, and a growing degree of business and consumer optimism is reflected by an expanding rate of capital investment and consumption.

refunding: Replacement or repayment of outstanding bonds by the issue of new bonds. It is thus a method of prolonging a debt by paying off old obligations with new obligations.

regressive tax: Tax whose percentage rate decreases as the tax base increases. In this strict sense there is no regressive tax in the U.S. However, if we compare the rate structure of the tax with the taxpayer's net income rather than with its actual base, the term regressive applies to any tax which takes a larger share of income from low-income taxpayers than from high-income taxpayers. Most proportional taxes are thus seen to have regressive effects. A sales tax, for instance, is the same for rich people as for poor people, but the latter spend a larger percentage of their incomes on consumer goods and hence the sales taxes they pay—assuming that there are few if any exemptions—are a greater proportion of their incomes.

rent: Return to those who supply the factor of production known as "land."

resale price maintenance: Practice whereby a manufacturer or distributor of a branded product sets the minimum retail price at which that product can be sold, thereby eliminating price competition at the retail level.

resource markets: Markets in which businesses buy the inputs or factors of production they need to carry on their operations.

restrictive agreement: Conspiracy of firms that restrains trade among separate companies. It may involve a direct or indirect form of price fixing, output control, market sharing, coercion, exclusion of competitors, etc., and is illegal under the antitrust laws.

restrictive license: Agreement whereby a patentee permits a licensee to sell a patented product under restricted conditions. The restrictions may include the patentee's fixing the geographic area of the licensee, his level of output, or the price he may charge in selling the patented good.

return on net worth: Ratio of a firm's net profit after taxes to its net worth. It provides a measure of the rate of return on stockholders' investment.

return on total assets: Ratio of a firm's net profit after taxes to its total assets. It measures the rate of return on, or productivity of, total assets.

revenue sharing: Plan by which the federal government turns over a portion of its tax revenues to state and local governments each year.

right-to-work laws: State laws which make it illegal to require membership in a union as a condition of employment. These laws exist mostly in southern and midwestern states; their main effect is to outlaw the union shop, but in practice they have been relatively ineffective.

risk: Quantitative measurement of an outcome, such as a gain or a loss, in a manner such that the mathematical probability (or "odds") of the outcome can be predicted. Since risk is predictable, losses that arise from risk can be estimated in advance and can be "insured" against—either by the firm itself or by an insurance company. *Examples:* the losses resulting from rejects on an assembly line can be "self insured" by being built into the firm's cost structure; the possibility of fire damage can be externally insured by an insurance company.

Robinson-Patman Act (1936): A major antitrust law of the United States, and an amendment to Section 2 of the Clayton Antitrust Act dealing with price discrimination. Commonly referred to as the "Chain Store Act," it was passed to protect independent retailers and wholesalers from "unfair discriminations" by large sellers who enjoy "tremendous purchasing power." The Act declared the following illegal: (1) payment of brokerage fees where no independent broker is employed; (2) granting of discounts and other concessions by sellers such as manufacturers to buyers such as wholesalers and retailers, unless such concessions are made to all buyers on proportionately equal terms; (3) price discrimination, except where the price differences make "due allowances" for differences in cost or are offered "in good faith to meet an equally low price of a competitor"; and (4) charging lower prices in one locality than in another, or selling at "unreasonably low prices," where either of these practices is aimed at "destroying competition or eliminating a competitor."

"rule of reason": Interpretation of the courts (first announced in the Standard Oil case of 1911) that the mere size of a corporation, no matter how impressive, is no offense, and that it requires "unreasonable" behavior in the form of actual exertion of monop-

oly power, as shown by unfair practices, for a firm to be held in violation of the antitrust laws. This interpretation, also known as the "good-trust-versus-bad-trust" criterion, was largely reversed in the Aluminum Company of America case in 1945, as well as in subsequent cases.

"rule of 72": Approximate formula for expressing the relationship between the number of years Y required for a quantity to double if it grows at an annual rate of compound interest R. Thus:

$$YR = 72$$

therefore:

$$Y = \frac{72}{R}, \text{ and } R = \frac{72}{Y}$$

Example: At 6% interest compounded annually, a quantity will double in $Y = \frac{72}{6} = 12$ years. Conversely, if a quantity doubles in 12 years, the compounded annual rate of growth is $R = \frac{72}{12} = 6\%$.

sales tax: A flat percentage levy imposed on retail prices of items.

"satisfice": A concept to convey the idea that in reality firms do not seek to maximize profit, but rather to achieve certain levels of satiation. For example, they try to attain a particular target level or rate of profit, and they try to achieve a specific share of the market or a certain level of sales.

saving: That part of income not spent on the consumption of goods and services.

Say's Law: An assertion that "supply creates its own demand." That is, the total supply of goods produced must always equal the total demand for them, since goods fundamentally exchange for goods while money serves only as a convenient medium of exchange. Therefore, any general overproduction is impossible. This assertion, named after the French economist Jean Baptiste Say (1767–1832), was fundamental in classical economic thought, for it led to the conclusion that the economy would automatically tend toward full-employment equilibrium if the government followed a policy of laissez faire.

scarcity, law of: Principle which states that at any given time and place economic goods, including resources and finished goods, are scarce in the sense that there are not enough to provide all that people want at a given price; these scarce goods can be increased, if at all, only through sacrifice.

scientific method: A disciplined mode of inquiry represented by the processes of induction, deduction, and verification. The essential steps of the scientific method consist of: (1) recognition and definition of a problem; (2) observation and collection of relevant data; (3) organization and classification of data; (4) formulation of hypotheses; (5) deductions from the hypotheses; and (6) testing and verification of the hypotheses. All scientific laws may be modified or challenged by alternative theoretical formulations, and hence the entire cycle consisting of these six steps is a self-corrective process.

seasonal fluctuations: Short-term fluctuations in business and economic activity within the year, due to weather and custom.

Examples: upswings in retail sales during holiday periods such as Christmas and Easter; changes between winter and summer buying patterns.

secondary boycott: Attempts by a union through strikes, picketing, or other methods to stop one employer from doing business with another employer. Outlawed by the Labor-Management Relations (Taft-Hartley) Act of 1947.

selling costs: Marketing expenditures aimed at adapting the buyer to the product. *Examples:* advertising, sales promotion, merchandising, etc.

separation of ownership and control: The notion that in a modern large corporation there is a distinction between those who own the business (the stockholders) and those who control it (the hired managers). If stock ownership is widely dispersed, the managers may be able to keep themselves in power for their own benefit rather than for the primary benefit of the corporation and its stockholders.

Sherman Antitrust Act (1890): A major antitrust law of the United States. It prohibits contracts, combinations, and conspiracies in restraint of trade, as well as monopolization or attempts to monopolize in interstate trade or foreign commerce. Violations are punishable by fines and/or imprisonment.

shortage: Any type of deficiency. For example: the amount by which the quantity demanded of a commodity exceeds the quantity supplied at a given price, as when the given price is below the free-market equilibrium price. (Contrast with **surplus.**)

short run: Period in which a firm can vary its output through a more or less intensive use of its resources, but cannot vary production capacity because it has a fixed plant scale.

single tax: Proposal advanced by the American economist Henry George (1839–1897) that the only tax a society should impose is a tax on land, because all rent on land is unearned surplus which increases as a result of natural progress and economic growth. Three major shortcomings leveled against this thesis are that the single tax would: (1) not yield enough revenues to meet government's spending needs; (2) be unjust, because surpluses may accrue to other resource owners besides landlords if the owners can gain some monopolistic control over the sale of their resources in the marketplace; and (3) be difficult to administer because it does not distinguish between land and capital—that is, between the proportion of rent that represents a surplus and the proportion that results from improvements made on the land.

slope: Rate of change or steepness of a line as measured by the change (increase or decrease) in its vertical distance per unit of change in its horizontal distance. It may be measured by the ratio:

$$\text{Slope} = \frac{\text{Change in vertical distance}}{\text{Change in horizontal distance}}$$

Hence a horizontal line has a zero slope; a vertical line has an "infinite" slope. All straight lines which are upward or positively inclined have a slope greater than zero. (Analogously, all straight lines which are downward or negatively inclined have a slope less than zero.) Parallel lines have equal slopes. The slope of a straight line is the same at every point, but the slope of a curved line differs at every point. Geometrically, the slope of a curve at a particular point can be found by drawing a straight-line tangent to the curve at that point. The slope of the tangent will then be equal to the slope of the curve at the point of tangency. In economics, all "marginals" are slopes or rates of change of their corresponding "totals." *Examples:* the marginal propensity to consume represents the rate of change or slope of its corresponding total propensity to consume; a marginal cost curve is the slope of its corresponding total cost curve; a marginal revenue curve is the slope of its corresponding total revenue curve; and so on. The concept of slope or rate of change (i.e., "marginal") is unquestionably the most powerful and important analytical tool of economics.

social benefit: Reward that accrues to society as a result of a particular act. (Contrast with **private benefit.**)

social cost: Cost to society of a particular act. It includes real costs, the costs of sacrificed alternatives, and reductions in incomes or benefits caused by the act. In a broad sense it may include noneconomic as well as economic costs. (Contrast with **private cost.**)

socialism: 1. In the theories of Karl Marx, a transitory stage between capitalism and full communism, in which the means of production are owned by the state, the state in turn is controlled by the workers (i.e., "dictatorship or the proletariat"), and the economy's social output is distributed by the formula: from each according to his ability, to each according to his labor. 2. In its non-Marxist form, a movement which seeks to improve society's well-being by: (1) permitting predominantly private ownership of the means of production; (2) instituting public ownership only where it appears necessary in the interests of society; and (3) placing maximum reliance on the market economy while supplementing it with government direction and planning in order to achieve desired social and economic objectives. (*Note:* This definition represents a fundamental change in socialist thought since about 1960. Before then, western socialism emphasized the replacement of private property with public ownership of the means of production and distribution. Today it is more of a "welfare state" concept.)

Social Security Act (1935): A basic comprehensive social security law of the United States. It provides for two types of social security: (1) social insurance programs for old age, survivors, disability, and health insurance (OASDHI), and for unemployment, both of which yield payments to insured persons or their survivors; and (2) a public charity program in the form of welfare services, institutional care, food, housing, and other forms of assistance. Some of the provisions of the Act (with its many subsequent amendments) are administered and financed by the federal government, some by state and local governments, and some by all three levels of government.

social security tax: Payroll tax which finances the U.S. compulsory social insurance program covering old-age and unemployment benefits. The taxes are paid by both employees and employers, based on the incomes of the former.

Special Drawing Rights (SDRs or "paper gold"): Supplementary reserves (established in 1969) in the form of account entries on the books of the International Monetary Fund. They are allocated among participating countries in accordance with their quotas, and can be drawn upon by governments to help finance balance-of-payments deficits. They are meant to promote an orderly growth of reserves that will help the long-run expanding needs of world trade.

specialization: Division of productive activities among individuals and regions so that no one person or area is self-sufficient. Total production is increased by specialization, thus permitting all participants to share in a greater volume of output through the process of exchange or trade.

specific subsidy: Per-unit subsidy of a commodity. (*See* **subsidy.**)

specific tax: Per-unit tax on a commodity. (*See* **tax.**)

speculation: Act of buying or selling goods or securities in the hope of making a profit on price movements.

speculative motive: Desire on the part of households and businesses to hold part of their assets in liquid form so that they can undertake financial investments at higher returns when the interest rate rises. This motive is influenced directly by the interest rate and is one of the chief sources of demand for loanable funds in the modern theory of interest.

state farms: Lands in the Soviet Union that are owned and operated as state enterprises under elected or governmentally appointed managing directors. Workers and technicians are hired to run the farms, and are usually paid set wages as well as bonuses if their work exceeds basic norms of output.

stock: Units of ownership interest in a corporation. The kinds of stock include common stock, preferred stock, and capital stock.

strategic-resource monopoly: Firm which has a monopoly because it controls an essential input to a production process. *Example:* DeBeers of South Africa owns most of the world's diamond mines.

strike: Agreement among workers to stop working, without resigning from their jobs, until their demands are met.

structural inflation: Condition of generally rising prices caused by uneven upward demand or cost pressures in some key industries such as automobiles, construction, or steel, even if aggregate demand is in balance with aggregate supply for the economy as a whole.

structural unemployment: Type of long-run unemployment which results from "structural" or fundamental economic and social changes within the economy that prevent people from getting jobs because of their race, age, lack of education or training, or geographic location. These people constitute the so-called hard-core unemployed.

subsidy: Payment (usually by a government) to individuals or businesses that enables them to continue to produce a product in larger quantities or at lower prices than they could otherwise.

subsistence theory of wages: Theory developed by some classical economists of the late 18th and early 19th centuries. It held that wages per worker tend to equal what the workers needs to "subsist"—that is, to maintain himself and to rear children. If wages per worker rose above the subsistence level, people would tend

to have more children and the population would increase, thereby lowering per capita real incomes; conversely, if wages per worker fell below the subsistence level, people would tend to have fewer children and the population would decline, thereby increasing per capita real incomes. Wages per worker would thus tend to remain at the subsistence level over the long run. This theory is also known as the "brazen" or "iron law of wages."

substitute goods: Two or more commodities such that a change in the quantity demanded of one results in an inverse change in the quantity demanded of the other, within a consumer's given budget. For example, if a fall in the price of coffee causes a consumer to increase his quantity demanded of coffee, and this in turn reduces his quantity demanded of tea, then coffee and tea are substitutes within his given budget. (Contrast with **complementary goods.**)

substitution effect: Extent to which a buyer substitutes a cheaper commodity for other relatively more expensive goods as its price falls while his income, tastes, and other prices remain the same.

sunspot theory: Theory of business cycles proposed in England during the late 19th century. It held that sunspot cycles (disturbances on the surface of the sun) exhibited an extremely high correlation with agricultural cycles for a number of years; therefore, sunspots must affect the weather, the weather influences agricultural crops, and the crops affect business conditions. This theory received worldwide popularity when it was first introduced, but then fell into disrepute because the high correlation between sunspots and agricultural cycles did not endure; it was the result of accidental rather than causal factors.

superior good: A good whose purchases are increased relative to other goods as the consumer's income rises. *Examples:* dairy products and beef relative to bread and potatoes.

supplementary (fringe) benefits: Forms of compensation to workers other than basic wages, such as bonuses, pension benefits, and holiday and vacation pay.

supply: A relation expressing the various amounts of a commodity that sellers would be willing and able to make available for sale at possible alternative prices during a given period of time, all other things remaining the same. This relation may be expressed as a table (called a supply schedule), as a graph (called a supply curve), or as a mathematical equation.

supply curve: Graph of a supply schedule, showing the number of units of a commodity that sellers would be able and willing to sell at various possible prices during a given period of time, all other things remaining the same.

supply, law of: A principle which states that the quantity supplied of a commodity varies directly with its price, assuming that all other things which may affect supply remain the same. These "all other" things include: (1) the state of technology; (2) resource prices; (3) the prices of other goods; (4) the number of sellers in the market; and (5) sellers' expectations regarding future prices.

supply price: Least price necessary to bring forth a given output. Hence it is the lowest price a seller is willing to accept in order to persuade him to supply a given quantity of a commodity.

supply schedule: Table showing the number of units of a commodity that sellers would be able and willing to sell at various possible prices during a given period of time, all other things remaining the same.

surplus: Any type of excess. For example: the amount by which the quantity supplied of a commodity exceeds the quantity demanded at a given price, as when the given price is above the free-market equilibrium price. (Contrast with **shortage.**)

surplus value: In the theories of Karl Marx, the difference between the value that a worker creates as determined by the labor time embodied in the commodity that he produces, and the value that he receives as determined by the subsistence level of wages. This surplus, according to Marx, is appropriated by the capitalist, and is the incentive for the development of a capitalistic system.

surtax: Tax imposed on a tax base in addition to a so-called normal tax. *Example:* a surtax on income in addition to the normal income tax. Note that a surtax is imposed on an existing tax base; it is not a "tax on a tax" as is popularly believed.

syndicalism: Economic system which demands the abolition of both capitalism and the state as instruments of oppression, and in its place the reorganization of society into industry-wide associations or syndicates of workers. The syndicates, fundamentally trade unions, would replace the state. Each syndicate would then govern its own members in their activities as producers, but leave them free from interference in all other matters. The chief exponent of syndicalism was the French social philosopher Georges Sorel (1847–1922), some of whose views later influenced the growth of fascism.

tariff: Customs duty or tax imposed by a government on the importation (or exportation) of a good. Tariffs may be: (1) specific, based on a tax per unit of the commodity; or (2) ad valorem, based on the value of the commodity.

tax: Compulsory payment to the government (federal, state, or local) to help meet its costs.

tax avoidance: Legal methods or "loopholes" used by taxpayers to reduce their taxes. (Contrast with **tax evasion.**)

tax base: An object that is being taxed, such as income in the case of an income tax, or the value of property in the case of a property tax, or the value of goods sold in the case of a sales tax.

tax evasion: Illegal methods of escaping taxes, such as lying or cheating about income or expenses. (Contrast with **tax avoidance.**)

tax incidence: Burden of a tax—that is, the economic organisms such as households, consumers, sellers, etc. that ultimately bear the tax.

tax shifting: Changing of the burden or incidence of a tax from the economic organism upon which it is initially imposed to some other economic organism. *Example:* Sales and excise taxes are imposed on the products of sellers, but these taxes are shifted in whole or in part through higher prices to buyers of the goods.

terms of trade: Number of units of goods that must be given up for one unit of goods received, by each party (e.g., nation) to a transaction. In general, the terms of trade are said to move in favor of the party that gives up fewer units of goods for one unit of goods

received, and against the party that gives up more units of goods for one unit of goods received. In international economics, the concept of "terms of trade" plays an important role in evaluating exchange relationships between nations.

theory: Set of definitions, assumptions, and hypotheses put together in a manner that expresses apparent relationships or underlying principles of certain observed phenomena in a meaningful way.

time deposit: Money held in a bank account of an individual or firm for which the bank can require advance notice of withdrawal.

time series: A set of data ordered chronologically. Most of the published data of business and economics are expressed in the form of time series.

token money: Any object (usually coins) whose value as money is greater than the market value of the materials of which it is composed. *Example:* pennies, nickels, etc.

total cost: Sum of a firm's total fixed costs and total variable costs.

total fixed costs: Costs that do not vary with a firm's output. *Examples:* rental payments, interest on debt, property taxes.

total-marginal relationship: Relationship between all corresponding total and marginal curves such that: when a total curve is increasing at an increasing rate, its corresponding marginal curve is rising; when a total curve is increasing at a decreasing rate, its corresponding marginal curve is falling; and when a total curve is increasing at a zero rate as occurs when it is at a maximum, its corresponding marginal curve is zero. (*Note:* The case of decreasing total curves gives rise to negative marginal curves, but these situations need not be included in the definition because they are not ordinarily relevant or realistic in an economic sense.)

total revenue: A firm's total receipts; equal to price per unit times the number of units sold.

total variable costs: Costs that vary directly with a firm's output, rising as output increases over the full range of production. *Examples:* costs of raw materials, fuel, labor, etc.

Trade Expansion Act (1962): Part of the U.S. Reciprocal Trade Agreements program, this Act broadened the powers of the President to: (1) negotiate further tariff reductions on broad categories of goods; (2) lower or eliminate tariffs on those goods for which the European Common Market and the United States together account for at least 80 percent of total world exports; (3) lower tariffs by as much as 50 percent on the basis of reciprocal trade agreements, provided that such agreements include most-favored-nation clauses so that the benefits of reduced tariffs are extended to other countries; and (4) grant vocational, technical, and financial assistance to American employees and businessmen whose industries are adversely affected by tariff reduction.

transactions motive: Desire on the part of households and businesses to hold some of their assets in liquid form so that they can engage in day-to-day spending activities. This motive is influenced primarily by the level of income rather than by changes in the interest rate, and is one of the chief sources of demand for loanable funds in the modern theory of interest.

transfer payments: Shifts in funds from the government sector to the private sector with no corresponding contribution to current production. *Examples:* social security payments; interest paid on government bonds issued in previous years; veterans' bonuses, etc.

trend: Long-run growth or decline of an economic time series over a long period of years.

tying contract (tie-in sale): Practice whereby a seller requires the buyer to purchase one or more additional or "tied" products as a condition for purchasing the desired or "tying" product. *Examples:* block bookings of motion pictures in which movie theaters are required to take Grade B films as a condition for obtaining Grade A films; the United Shoe Machinery Co., which once required shoemakers to purchase other materials as a condition for purchasing shoe machinery.

uncertainty: State of knowledge in which the probabilities of outcomes resulting from specific actions are not known and cannot be predicted because they are subjective rather than objective phenomena. Uncertainties, therefore, are not insurable, and cannot be integrated into the firm's cost structure.

underconsumption theory: Theory of business cycles which holds that recessions result from consumer expenditures lagging behind output because too large a proportion of society's income is not spent on consumption. According to the theory, society distributes income too inequitably to enable people to purchase all the goods produced.

underemployment (disguised unemployment): State of affairs in which employed resources are not being used in their most efficient ways.

unemployment: Situation which exists whenever resources are out of work or are not being used efficiently. There are various types of unemployment such as technological, frictional, structural, disguised, involuntary, and cyclical.

unemployment benefits: Weekly payments to "covered" workers who are involuntarily unemployed.

unfair competition: Competition that involves deceptive, dishonest, or injurious methods. Such practices are illegal under the antitrust laws.

union: Organization of workers which seeks to gain a degree of monopoly power in the sale of its services so that it may be able to secure higher wages, better working conditions, and other economic improvements for its members.

union shop: Business firm whose employer allows a nonunion member to be hired on condition that he join the union after he is employed.

utility: Ability or power of a good to satisfy a want as determined by the satisfaction that one receives from consuming something.

utopian socialism: Philosophy advanced by a group of English and French writers in the early 19th century which advocated the creation of model communities, largely self-contained, where the instruments of production were collectively owned and government was primarily on a voluntary and wholly democratic basis.

The leading propagators were Robert Owen in England (1771–1858) and Charles Fourier (1772–1837) in France.

value: Power of a commodity to command other commodities in exchange for itself, as measured by the proportional quantities in which a commodity exchanges with all other commodities.

value added: Increment in value at each stage in the production of a good. The sum of the increments for all stages of production gives the total income—the aggregate of wages, rent, interest, and profit—derived from the production of the good.

variable costs: Costs that vary directly with a firm's output, rising as output increases over the full range of production. *Examples:* costs of raw materials, fuel, labor, etc.

variable proportions, law of: *See* **diminishing returns, law of.**

verification: Testing of alternative hypotheses or conclusions by means of actual observation or experimentation—that is, by reference to the facts.

vertical merger: Amalgamation under one ownership of unlike plants engaged in various stages of production from raw materials to finished products. It may take the form of forward integration into buyer markets or backward integration into supplier markets. The chief objective is to achieve greater economies by combining different production stages and by regularizing supplies, thereby increasing profit margins.

wage-push inflation: Condition of generally rising prices caused by labor unions managing to gain wage increases that exceed advances in labor productivity.

wages: 1. Payment to those owners of resources who supply the factor of production known as "labor." This payment includes wages, salaries, commissions, etc. **2.** The price paid for the use of labor. It is usually expressed as time rates such as so much per hour, day, or week, or less frequently as rates of so much per unit of work performed.

wages-fund theory: Classical theory of wages best articulated by John Stuart Mill in 1848. It held that producers set aside a portion of their capital funds for the purpose of hiring workers needed for production. The amount of the fund depends on the stock of capital relative to the number of workers. In the long run, however, the accumulation of capital is itself limited or determined by the tendency toward a minimum "subsistence rate" of profits; hence the only effective way to raise real wages is to reduce the number of workers or size of the population. (*Note:* This theory was a reformulation of the **subsistence theory of wages.**)

"wastes" of monopolistic competition: Expression used to denote overcrowded "sick" industries of monopolistic competition, characterized by chronic excess capacity and inefficient operations. *Examples:* retail trades; textile manufacturing.

wealth: Anything which has value because it is capable of producing income. A "stock" of value as compared to a "flow" of income. (Contrast with **income.**)

Wheeler-Lea Act (1938): Amendment to the Federal Trade Commission Act. It was passed primarily to protect consumers, rather than just business competitors, from unfair (deceptive, dishonest, or injurious) methods of competition. Thus injured consumers are given equal protection before the law with injured merchants. The Act also prohibits false or misleading advertisements for food, drugs, cosmetics, and therapeutic devices.

yellow-dog contract: Contract which requires an employee to promise as a condition of employment that he will not belong to a labor union. Declared illegal in the Norris-La Guardia Act of 1932.

yield: Effective or going market rate of interest on a debt security such as a bond. In a broader sense, it is the effective rate of return on any type of investment.

Index

ability-to-pay principle, 93
absolute advantage, law of, 568
accelerator-multiplier interaction, 170–171
accelerator principle, 167–170
  qualifications, 169–170
adjustable pegs, 612
ad valorem subsidy; tax, 324
advertising, evaluation of, 420–421
Agency for International Development, 621
Agricultural Adjustment Act of 1933, 529
  of 1938, 529–530
agricultural reform, 537 ff.
agricultural revolution, 624, 625
agriculture, history, 526 ff.
Alliance for Labor Action, 495
alternative costs, 361
American Federation of Labor, 490
  -Congress of Industrial Organizations, 495
annually balanced budget, 181
antitrust laws, 462 ff.
  summarized, 468
Aquinas, St. Thomas, Leader in Economics, 35
arbitrage, 333
arbitration, 504
Aristotle, Leader in Economics, 4
assets, 76
automatic fiscal stabilizers, 177
autonomous investment, 161
autonomous transactions, 587
average-marginal relationship, 368
average product, 364

average propensity, to consume, 147
  to save, 147
average revenue, 382
average revenue product, 434

balanced-budget multiplier principle, 176
"balanced" growth, 273
balance of payments, 582 ff.
  adjusting to equilibrium, 588 ff.
  equilibrium and disequilibrium, 587
  and full employment, conflicts, 221–222
balance of trade, 585
balance sheet, 76–78
banker's acceptance, 198
barter, 38–39
basic wages, 499
"bathtub theorem", 158
benefit-cost analysis, 287
benefit principle, of taxation, 93
bilateral monopoly, 445–446
bill of exchange, 198
bimetallic standard, 194
black capitalism, 553
black market model, 332
Board of Governors, 210
bond, 198
  prices and yields, 213
boycott, 503
Brannan Plan, 536, 538
break-even point, 382
Bretton Woods, 601 ff.
Brown Shoe case, 473
budget line, 351

budget policies, 181–184
budgets, government, 83 ff.
business cycles, 118 ff.
  forecasting, 125–127
  historical chart, 120–121
  idealized curves, 121
  known and not known, 122
  theories of, 124–125

cameralism, 588
capital, as a factor of production, 18
capital consumption allowance, 109–110
capital-intensive investment, 629
capital market, 199
capital-output ratio, 256
capital stock, 77
capitalism, meaning of, 31 ff.
  pillars of, 31–34
cartel, 478
Celler Antimerger Act, 466
Chamberlin, Edward Hastings, Leader in Economics, 428
checkoff, 502
China, problems and policies, 659 ff.
Christian socialism, 637
circular flow of economic activity, 40
Clark, John Bates, Leader in Economics, 440
classical economics, 139
classical theory, 139–142
class struggle, 640
Clayton Antitrust Act, 463
closed shop, 489, 501
coalition bargaining, 503
cobweb theorem, 335 ff.

General Business and Economic Indicators

POPULATION, EMPLOYMENT, WAGES, AND PRODUCTIVITY

Year	Population	Civilian labor force	Unemployment	Unemployment as percent of civilian labor force	Average weekly hours of work — Total non-agricultural private sector	Average gross hourly earnings — Total non-agricultural private sector	Index of output per man-hour — Total private sector
	Millions of persons	Millions of persons	Millions of persons	Percent	Hours	Dollars	1967 = 100
1929	121.9	49.2	1.6	3.2	—	—	—
1930	123.2	49.8	4.3	8.7	—	—	—
1931	124.1	50.4	8.0	15.9	—	—	—
1932	124.9	51.0	12.1	23.6	—	—	—
1933	125.7	51.6	12.8	24.9	—	—	—
1934	126.5	52.2	11.3	21.7	—	—	—
1935	127.4	52.9	10.6	20.1	—	—	—
1936	128.2	53.4	9.0	16.9	—	—	—
1937	129.0	54.0	7.7	14.3	—	—	—
1938	130.0	54.6	10.4	19.0	—	—	—
1939	131.0	55.2	9.5	17.2	—	—	—
1940	132.1	55.6	8.1	14.6	—	—	—
1941	133.4	55.9	5.6	9.9	—	—	—
1942	134.9	56.4	2.7	4.7	—	—	—
1943	136.7	55.5	1.1	1.9	—	—	—
1944	138.4	54.6	0.7	1.2	—	—	—
1945	140.0	53.9	1.0	1.9	—	—	—
1946	141.4	57.5	2.3	3.9	40.3	1.131	45.6
1947	144.1	59.4	2.3	3.9	40.0	1.225	47.8
1948	146.6	60.6	2.3	3.8	39.4	1.275	47.6
1949	149.2	61.3	3.6	5.9	39.8	1.335	52.5
1950	151.7	62.2	3.3	5.3	39.9	1.45	55.8
1951	154.3	62.0	2.1	3.3	39.9	1.52	57.2
1952	157.0	62.1	1.9	3.0	39.6	1.61	60.1
1953	159.6	63.0	1.8	2.9	39.1	1.65	59.3
1954	162.4	63.6	3.5	5.5	39.6	1.71	64.3
1955	165.3	65.0	2.9	4.4	39.3	1.80	65.6
1956	168.2	66.6	2.8	4.1	38.8	1.89	66.5
1957	171.3	66.9	2.9	4.3	38.5	1.95	65.6
1958	174.1	67.6	4.6	6.8	39.0	2.02	70.2
1959	177.1	68.4	3.7	5.5	38.6	2.09	71.9
1960	180.7	69.6	3.9	5.5	38.6	2.14	73.2
1961	183.8	70.5	4.7	6.7	38.7	2.22	78.2
1962	186.7	70.6	3.9	5.5	38.8	2.28	81.5
1963	189.4	71.8	4.1	5.7	38.7	2.36	86.2
1964	192.1	73.1	3.8	5.2	38.8	2.45	91.8
1965	194.6	74.5	3.4	4.5	38.6	2.56	97.7
1966	197.0	75.8	2.9	3.8	38.0	2.68	100.0
1967	199.1	77.3	3.0	3.8	37.8	2.85	104.8
1968	201.2	78.7	2.8	3.6	37.7	3.04	107.5
1969	203.2	80.7	2.8	3.5	37.1	3.22	106.8
1970	204.8	82.7	4.1	4.9	37.0	3.42	109.9
1971	207.0	84.1	4.9	5.9			

PRODUCTION AND BUSINESS ACTIVITY

Year	Index of industrial production	Business expenditures for new plant and equipment	New construction activity — Value put in place	New housing starts — Total farm and non-farm	Manufacturers' new orders
	1967 = 100	Billions of dollars	Millions of dollars	Thousands of units	Millions of dollars
1929	21.6	—	10,793	—	—
1930	18.0	—	8,741	—	—
1931	14.9	—	6,427	—	—
1932	11.6	—	3,538	—	—
1933	13.7	—	2,879	—	—
1934	15.0	—	3,720	—	—
1935	17.3	—	4,232	—	—
1936	20.4	—	6,497	—	—
1937	22.3	—	6,999	—	—
1938	17.6	—	6,980	—	—
1939	21.7	—	8,198	—	—
1940	25.4	—	8,682	—	—
1941	31.6	—	11,957	—	—
1942	36.3	—	14,075	—	—
1943	44.0	—	8,301	—	—
1944	47.4	—	5,259	—	—
1945	40.6	—	5,809	—	—
1946	35.0	—	14,308	—	—
1947	39.4	19.33	20,041	—	15,256
1948	41.0	21.30	26,078	—	17,692
1949	38.8	18.98	26,722	—	15,614
1950	44.9	20.21	33,575	—	20,110
1951	48.7	25.46	35,435	—	23,907
1952	50.6	26.43	36,828	—	23,203
1953	54.8	28.20	39,136	—	23,533
1954	51.9	27.19	41,380	—	22,313
1955	58.5	29.53	46,519	—	27,423
1956	61.1	35.73	47,601	—	28,383
1957	61.9	37.94	49,139	—	27,514
1958	57.9	31.89	50,153	—	26,901
1959	64.8	33.55	55,305	1,553.5	30,679
1960	66.2	36.75	54,632	1,296.0	30,115
1961	66.7	35.91	56,292	1,365.0	31,085
1962	72.2	38.39	59,965	1,492.4	33,005
1963	76.5	40.77	64,563	1,642.0	35,322
1964	81.7	46.97	67,413	1,561.6	37,952
1965	89.2	54.42	73,412	1,509.6	41,803
1966	97.9	63.51	76,002	1,196.2	45,912
1967	100.0	65.47	77,503	1,321.9	46,707
1968	105.7	67.76	86,626	1,545.5	50,505
1969	110.7	75.56	93,347	1,499.6	53,768
1970	106.7	79.71	94,265	1,469.0	53,866
1971	106.5	81.47	108,440	2,080.5	57,589